Visual Basic .NET

How to Program, 2/e

Deitel™ Books, Cyber Classrooms, Complete Tra published by

HOW TO PROGRAM Series

Advanced Java™ 2 Platform How to Program
C How to Program, 3/E
C++ How to Program, 3/E
C# How to Program
e-Business and e-Commerce How to Program
Internet and World Wide Web How to Program, 2/E
Java™ How to Program, 4/E
Perl How to Program
Python How to Program
Visual Basic® 6 How to Program
Visual Basic® .NET How to Program, 2/E
Wireless Internet & Mobile Business How to Program
XML How to Program

DEITEL™ Developer's Series

C#: A Programmer's Introduction
C# for Experienced Programmers
Java™ Web Services for Experienced Programmers
Visual Basic® .NET for Experienced Programmers
Visual C++® .NET: A Managed Code Approach For Experienced Programmers
Web Services: A Technical Introduction
Java 2 Micro Edition for Experienced Programmers (Spring 2003)
ASP .NET and Web Services with Visual Basic® .NET for Experienced Programmers (Fall 2002)
ASP .NET and Web Services with C# for Experienced Programmers (Spring 2003)

.NET How to Program Series

C# How to Program
Visual Basic® .NET How to Program, 2/E

Visual Studio® Series

C# How to Program
Visual Basic® .NET How to Program, 2/E
Getting Started with Microsoft® Visual C++™ 6 with an Introduction to MFC
Visual Basic® 6 How to Program

For Managers Series

e-Business and e-Commerce for Managers

Coming Soon

e-books and e-whitepapers
Premium CourseCompass, WebCT and Blackboard Multimedia Cyber Classroom versions

ining Courses and Web-Based Training Courses
Prentice Hall

Multimedia Cyber Classroom and *Web-Based Training* Series

(For information regarding Deitel™ Web-based training visit **www.ptgtraining.com**)

C++ Multimedia Cyber Classroom, 3/E

C# Multimedia Cyber Classroom

e-Business and e-Commerce Multimedia Cyber Classroom

Internet and World Wide Web Multimedia Cyber Classroom, 2/E

Java™ 2 Multimedia Cyber Classroom, 4/E

Perl Multimedia Cyber Classroom

Python Multimedia Cyber Classroom

Visual Basic® 6 Multimedia Cyber Classroom

Visual Basic® .NET Multimedia Cyber Classroom, 2/E

Wireless Internet & Mobile Business Programming Multimedia Cyber Classroom

XML Multimedia Cyber Classroom

The Complete Training Course Series

The Complete C++ Training Course, 3/E

The Complete C# Training Course

The Complete e-Business and e-Commerce Programming Training Course

The Complete Internet and World Wide Web Programming Training Course, 2/E

The Complete Java™ 2 Training Course, 4/E

The Complete Perl Training Course

The Complete Python Training Course

The Complete Visual Basic® 6 Training Course

The Complete Visual Basic® .NET Training Course, 2/E

The Complete Wireless Internet & Mobile Business Programming Training Course

The Complete XML Programming Training Course

To communicate with the authors, send e-mail to:

deitel@deitel.com

For information on corporate on-site seminars and public seminars offered by Deitel & Associates, Inc. worldwide, visit:

www.deitel.com

For continuing updates on Prentice Hall and Deitel publications visit:

www.deitel.com,
www.prenhall.com/deitel or
www.InformIT.com/deitel

To follow the Deitel publishing program, please register at

www.deitel.com/newsletter/subscribe.html

for the *Deitel™ Buzz Online* e-mail newsletter.

In loving memory of our Grandmother and
Great Grandmother Pauline Deitel:

> *Your courage, strength, tenderness and love
> will never be forgotten.*
>
> *Harvey and Paul Deitel*

To John Hageman

> *A mentor and a friend.*
>
> *Tem R. Nieto*

VISUAL BASIC .NET
HOW TO PROGRAM, 2/E

H. M. Deitel
Deitel & Associates, Inc.

P. J. Deitel
Deitel & Associates, Inc.

T. R. Nieto
Deitel & Associates, Inc.

Prentice Hall

PRENTICE HALL, Upper Saddle River, New Jersey 07458

Library of Congress Cataloging-in-Publication Data

On file

Vice President and Editorial Director: *Marcia Horton*
Acquisitions Editor: *Petra J. Recter*
Assistant Editor: *Sarah Burrows*
Project Manager: *Crissy Statuto*
Vice President and Director of Production and Manufacturing, ESM: *David W. Riccardi*
Director of Creative Services: *Paul Belfanti*
Creative Director: *Heather Scott*
Chapter Opener and Cover Designer: *Tamara Newnam*
Manufacturing Manager: *Trudy Pisciotti*
Manufacturing Buyer: *Lisa McDowell*
Marketing Manager: *Pamela Shaffer*

 © 2002, 1999, 1997, 1995 by Prentice-Hall, Inc.
Upper Saddle River, New Jersey 07458

The authors and publisher of this book have used their best efforts in preparing this book. These efforts include the development, research, and testing of the theories and programs to determine their effectiveness. The authors and publisher make no warranty of any kind, expressed or implied, with regard to these programs or to the documentation contained in this book. The authors and publisher shall not be liable in any event for incidental or consequential damages in connection with, or arising out of, the furnishing, performance, or use of these programs.

Many of the designations used by manufacturers and sellers to distinguish their products are claimed as trademarks and registered trademarks. Where those designations appear in this book, and Prentice Hall and the authors were aware of a trademark claim, the designations have been printed in initial caps or all caps. All product names mentioned remain trademarks or registered trademarks of their respective owners.

All rights reserved. No part of this book may be
reproduced, in any form or by any means,
without permission in writing from the publisher.

Printed in the United States of America

10 9 8 7 6 5 4 3 2

ISBN 0-13-029363-6

Pearson Education Ltd., *London*
Pearson Education Australia Pty. Ltd., *Sydney*
Pearson Education Singapore, Pte. Ltd.
Pearson Education North Asia Ltd., *Hong Kong*
Pearson Education Canada, Inc., *Toronto*
Pearson Educacion de Mexico, S.A. de C.V.
Pearson Education–Japan, *Tokyo*
Pearson Education Malaysia, Pte. Ltd.
Pearson Education, Inc., *Upper Saddle River, New Jersey*

Trademarks

Adobe® Photoshop® Elements are either registered trademarks or trademarks of Adobe Systems Incorporated in the United States and/or other countries.

Compaq, the Compaq Logo, iPAQ, and the iPAQ Pocket PC product design are trademarks of Compaq Information Technologies Group, L.P. in the United States and other countries.

Java and all Java-based marks are trademarks or registered trademarks of Sun Microsystems, Inc. in the United States and other countries. Prentice Hall is independent of Sun Microsystems, Inc.

Microsoft® Visual Studio® .NET are either registered trademarks or trademarks of Microsoft Corporation in the United States and/or other countries.

Contents

Contents		vii
Illustrations		xxviii
Preface		xxxvii

1 Introduction to Computers, Internet and Visual Basic .NET — 1

1.1	Introduction	2
1.2	What Is a Computer?	3
1.3	Computer Organization	4
1.4	Evolution of Operating Systems	5
1.5	Personal Computing, Distributed Computing and Client/Server Computing	5
1.6	Machine Languages, Assembly Languages and High-Level Languages	6
1.7	Visual Basic .NET	7
1.8	C, C++, Java™ and C#	9
1.9	Other High-Level Languages	10
1.10	Structured Programming	10
1.11	Key Software Trend: Object Technology	11
1.12	Hardware Trends	13
1.13	History of the Internet and World Wide Web	14
1.14	World Wide Web Consortium (W3C)	15
1.15	Extensible Markup Language (XML)	16
1.16	Introduction to Microsoft .NET	17
1.17	.NET Framework and the Common Language Runtime	18
1.18	Tour of the Book	20
1.19	Internet and World Wide Web Resources	29

Contents

2 Introduction to the Visual Studio .NET IDE — 33
2.1 Introduction — 34
2.2 Overview of the Visual Studio .NET IDE — 34
2.3 Menu Bar and Toolbar — 37
2.4 Visual Studio .NET IDE Windows — 39
   2.4.1 **Solution Explorer** — 40
   2.4.2 **Toolbox** — 41
   2.4.3 **Properties** Window — 41
2.5 Using Help — 44
2.6 Simple Program: Displaying Text and an Image — 45
2.7 Internet and World Wide Web Resources — 55

3 Introduction to Visual Basic Programming — 61
3.1 Introduction — 62
3.2 Simple Program: Printing a Line of Text — 62
3.3 Another Simple Program: Adding Integers — 70
3.4 Memory Concepts — 73
3.5 Arithmetic — 74
3.6 Decision Making: Equality and Relational Operators — 78
3.7 Using a Dialog to Display a Message — 82
3.8 Internet and World Wide Web Resources — 88

4 Control Structures: Part 1 — 96
4.1 Introduction — 97
4.2 Algorithms — 97
4.3 Pseudocode — 98
4.4 Control Structures — 98
4.5 **If/Then** Selection Structure — 102
4.6 **If/Then/Else** Selection Structure — 104
4.7 **While** Repetition Structure — 106
4.8 **Do While/Loop** Repetition Structure — 108
4.9 **Do Until/Loop** Repetition Structure — 109
4.10 Assignment Operators — 110
4.11 Formulating Algorithms: Case Study 1 (Counter-Controlled Repetition) — 112
4.12 Formulating Algorithms with Top-Down, Stepwise Refinement: Case Study 2 (Sentinel-Controlled Repetition) — 114
4.13 Formulating Algorithms with Top-Down, Stepwise Refinement: Case Study 3 (Nested Control Structures) — 119
4.14 Formulating Algorithms with Top-Down, Stepwise Refinement: Case Study 4 (Nested Repetition Structures) — 123
4.15 Introduction to Windows Application Programming — 127

5 Control Structures: Part 2 — 144
5.1 Introduction — 145
5.2 Essentials of Counter-Controlled Repetition — 145
5.3 **For/Next** Repetition Structure — 146
5.4 Examples Using the **For/Next** Structure — 149

5.5		**Select Case** Multiple-Selection Structure	155
5.6		**Do/Loop While** Repetition Structure	159
5.7		**Do/Loop Until** Repetition Structure	160
5.8		Using the **Exit** Keyword in a Repetition Structure	162
5.9		Logical Operators	164
5.10		Structured Programming Summary	170

6 Procedures — 182

6.1		Introduction	183
6.2		Modules, Classes and Procedures	183
6.3		**Sub** Procedures	185
6.4		**Function** Procedures	188
6.5		Methods	190
6.6		Argument Promotion	195
6.7		Option Strict and Data-Type Conversions	196
6.8		Value Types and Reference Types	198
6.9		Passing Arguments: Pass-by-Value vs. Pass-by-Reference	200
6.10		Duration of Identifiers	202
6.11		Scope Rules	203
6.12		Random-Number Generation	206
6.13		Example: Game of Chance	213
6.14		Recursion	218
6.15		Example Using Recursion: Fibonacci Series	221
6.16		Recursion vs. Iteration	225
6.17		Procedure Overloading and Optional Arguments	226
	6.17.1	Procedure Overloading	226
	6.17.2	Optional Arguments	228
6.18		Modules	231

7 Arrays — 245

7.1		Introduction	246
7.2		Arrays	246
7.3		Declaring and Allocating Arrays	248
7.4		Examples Using Arrays	249
	7.4.1	Allocating an Array	250
	7.4.2	Initializing the Values in an Array	251
	7.4.3	Summing the Elements of an Array	252
	7.4.4	Using Arrays to Analyze Survey Results	253
	7.4.5	Using Histograms to Display Array Data Graphically	256
7.5		Passing Arrays to Procedures	260
7.6		Passing Arrays: **ByVal** vs. **ByRef**	264
7.7		Sorting Arrays	268
7.8		Searching Arrays: Linear Search and Binary Search	272
	7.8.1	Searching an Array with Linear Search	272
	7.8.2	Searching a Sorted Array with Binary Search	275
7.9		Multidimensional Rectangular and Jagged Arrays	279

Contents   XI

7.10	Variable-Length Parameter Lists	287
7.11	**For Each/Next** Repetition Structure	288

8   Object-Based Programming   296

8.1	Introduction	297
8.2	Implementing a Time Abstract Data Type with a Class	298
8.3	Class Scope	306
8.4	Controlling Access to Members	306
8.5	Initializing Class Objects: Constructors	308
8.6	Using Overloaded Constructors	308
8.7	Properties	314
8.8	Composition: Objects as Instance Variables of Other Classes	321
8.9	Using the **Me** Reference	324
8.10	Garbage Collection	326
8.11	**Shared** Class Members	327
8.12	**Const** and **ReadOnly** Members	331
8.13	Data Abstraction and Information Hiding	334
8.14	Software Reusability	335
8.15	Namespaces and Assemblies	336
8.16	**Class View** and **Object Browser**	340

9   Object-Oriented Programming: Inheritance   349

9.1	Introduction	350
9.2	Base Classes and Derived Classes	351
9.3	**Protected** and **Friend** Members	354
9.4	Relationship between Base Classes and Derived Classes	354
9.5	Case Study: Three-Level Inheritance Hierarchy	372
9.6	Constructors and Finalizers in Derived Classes	376
9.7	Software Engineering with Inheritance	382

10   Object-Oriented Programming: Polymorphism   388

10.1	Introduction	389
10.2	Derived-Class-Object to Base-Class-Object Conversion	389
10.3	Type Fields and **Select Case** Statements	396
10.4	Polymorphism Examples	397
10.5	Abstract Classes and Methods	398
10.6	Case Study: Inheriting Interface and Implementation	400
10.7	**NotInheritable** Classes and **NotOverridable** Methods	408
10.8	Case Study: Payroll System Using Polymorphism	409
10.9	Case Study: Creating and Using Interfaces	419
10.10	Delegates	432

11   Exception Handling   441

11.1	Introduction	442
11.2	Exception Handling Overview	443
11.3	Example: **DivideByZeroException**	446
11.4	.NET **Exception** Hierarchy	450

11.5	**Finally** Block	452
11.6	**Exception** Properties	459
11.7	Programmer-Defined Exception Classes	464
11.8	Handling Overflows	468

12 Graphical User Interface Concepts: Part 1   475

12.1	Introduction	476
12.2	Windows Forms	478
12.3	Event-Handling Model	480
12.4	Control Properties and Layout	487
12.5	**Label**s, **TextBox**es and **Button**s	491
12.6	**GroupBox**es and **Panel**s	494
12.7	**CheckBox**es and **RadioButton**s	497
12.8	**PictureBox**es	508
12.9	Mouse-Event Handling	510
12.10	Keyboard-Event Handling	513

13 Graphical User Interface Concepts: Part 2   523

13.1	Introduction	524
13.2	Menus	524
13.3	**LinkLabel**s	534
13.4	**ListBox**es and **CheckedListBox**es	538
	13.4.1 **ListBox**es	540
	13.4.2 **CheckedListBox**es	542
13.5	**ComboBox**es	545
13.6	**TreeView**s	550
13.7	**ListView**s	555
13.8	Tab Control	562
13.9	Multiple-Document-Interface (MDI) Windows	567
13.10	Visual Inheritance	576
13.11	User-Defined Controls	580

14 Multithreading   592

14.1	Introduction	593
14.2	Thread States: Life Cycle of a Thread	595
14.3	Thread Priorities and Thread Scheduling	596
14.4	Thread Synchronization and Class **Monitor**	601
14.5	Producer/Consumer Relationship without Thread Synchronization	603
14.6	Producer/Consumer Relationship with Thread Synchronization	609
14.7	Producer/Consumer Relationship: Circular Buffer	618

15 Strings, Characters and Regular Expressions   633

15.1	Introduction	634
15.2	Fundamentals of Characters and Strings	634
15.3	**String** Constructors	635
15.4	**String Length** and **Chars** Properties, and **CopyTo** Method	637
15.5	Comparing **String**s	639

15.6	**String** Method **GetHashCode**	643
15.7	Locating Characters and Substrings in **String**s	644
15.8	Extracting Substrings from **String**s	647
15.9	Concatenating **String**s	648
15.10	Miscellaneous **String** Methods	649
15.11	Class **StringBuilder**	651
15.12	**StringBuilder** Indexer, **Length** and **Capacity** Properties, and **EnsureCapacity** Method	652
15.13	**StringBuilder Append** and **AppendFormat** Methods	654
15.14	**StringBuilder Insert**, **Remove** and **Replace** Methods	657
15.15	**Char** Methods	660
15.16	Card Shuffling and Dealing Simulation	663
15.17	Regular Expressions and Class **Regex**	667

16 Graphics and Multimedia 683

16.1	Introduction	684
16.2	Graphics Contexts and Graphics Objects	686
16.3	Color Control	687
16.4	Font Control	694
16.5	Drawing Lines, Rectangles and Ovals	699
16.6	Drawing Arcs	702
16.7	Drawing Polygons and Polylines	705
16.8	Advanced Graphics Capabilities	709
16.9	Introduction to Multimedia	714
16.10	Loading, Displaying and Scaling Images	714
16.11	Animating a Series of Images	716
16.12	Windows Media Player	729
16.13	Microsoft Agent	731

17 Files and Streams 752

17.1	Introduction	753
17.2	Data Hierarchy	753
17.3	Files and Streams	755
17.4	Classes **File** and **Directory**	757
17.5	Creating a Sequential-Access File	767
17.6	Reading Data from a Sequential-Access File	778
17.7	Random-Access Files	789
17.8	Creating a Random-Access File	794
17.9	Writing Data Randomly to a Random-Access File	797
17.10	Reading Data Sequentially from a Random-Access File	802
17.11	Case Study: A Transaction-Processing Program	807

18 Extensible Markup Language (XML) 833

18.1	Introduction	834
18.2	XML Documents	834
18.3	XML Namespaces	839
18.4	Document Object Model (DOM)	842

18.5		Document Type Definitions (DTDs), Schemas and Validation	860
	18.5.1	Document Type Definitions	861
	18.5.2	Microsoft XML Schemas	865
18.6		Extensible Stylesheet Language and **XslTransform**	870
18.7		Microsoft BizTalk™	877
18.8		Internet and World Wide Web Resources	880

19 Database, SQL and ADO .NET   887

19.1		Introduction	888
19.2		Relational Database Model	889
19.3		Relational Database Overview: **Books** Database	890
19.4		Structured Query Language (SQL)	896
	19.4.1	Basic **SELECT** Query	897
	19.4.2	**WHERE** Clause	898
	19.4.3	**ORDER BY** Clause	901
	19.4.4	Merging Data from Multiple Tables: **INNER JOIN**	903
	19.4.5	Joining Data from Tables **Authors**, **AuthorISBN**, **Titles** and **Publishers**	906
	19.4.6	**INSERT** Statement	909
	19.4.7	**UPDATE** Statement	910
	19.4.8	**DELETE** Statement	911
19.5		ADO .NET Object Model	912
19.6		Programming with ADO .NET: Extracting Information from a Database	913
	19.6.1	Connecting to and Querying an Access Data Source	913
	19.6.2	Querying the **Books** Database	921
19.7		Programming with ADO .NET: Modifying a Database	923
19.8		Reading and Writing XML Files	932

20 ASP .NET, Web Forms and Web Controls   941

20.1		Introduction	942
20.2		Simple HTTP Transaction	943
20.3		System Architecture	945
20.4		Creating and Running a Simple Web-Form Example	946
20.5		Web Controls	958
	20.5.1	Text and Graphics Controls	958
	20.5.2	**AdRotator** Control	964
	20.5.3	Validation Controls	969
20.6		Session Tracking	979
	20.6.1	Cookies	980
	20.6.2	Session Tracking with **HttpSessionState**	989
20.7		Case Study: Online Guest book	998
20.8		Case Study: Connecting to a Database in ASP .NET	1004
20.9		Tracing	1019
20.10		Internet and World Wide Web Resources	1021

21 ASP .NET and Web Services   1030

21.1	Introduction	1031

21.2	Web Services	1032
21.3	Simple Object Access Protocol (SOAP) and Web Services	1036
21.4	Publishing and Consuming Web Services	1037
21.5	Session Tracking in Web Services	1053
21.6	Using Web Forms and Web Services	1066
21.7	Case Study: Temperature Information Application	1072
21.8	User-Defined Types in Web Services	1081
21.9	Internet and World Wide Web Resources	1091

22 Networking: Streams-Based Sockets and Datagrams — 1096

22.1	Introduction	1097
22.2	Establishing a Simple Server (Using Stream Sockets)	1098
22.3	Establishing a Simple Client (Using Stream Sockets)	1100
22.4	Client/Server Interaction via Stream-Socket Connections	1101
22.5	Connectionless Client/Server Interaction via Datagrams	1110
22.6	Client/Server Tic-Tac-Toe Using a Multithreaded Server	1116

23 Data Structures and Collections — 1136

23.1	Introduction	1137
23.2	Self-Referential Classes	1137
23.3	Linked Lists	1139
23.4	Stacks	1152
23.5	Queues	1156
23.6	Trees	1160
	23.6.1 Binary Search Tree of Integer Values	1161
	23.6.2 Binary Search Tree of **IComparable** Objects	1168
23.7	Collection Classes	1175
	23.7.1 Class **Array**	1176
	23.7.2 Class **ArrayList**	1179
	23.7.3 Class **Stack**	1185
	23.7.4 Class **Hashtable**	1189

24 Accessibility — 1203

24.1	Introduction	1204
24.2	Regulations and Resources	1205
24.3	Web Accessibility Initiative	1207
24.4	Providing Alternatives for Images	1208
24.5	Maximizing Readability by Focusing on Structure	1209
24.6	Accessibility in Visual Studio .NET	1209
	24.6.1 Enlarging Toolbar Icons	1210
	24.6.2 Enlarging the Text	1211
	24.6.3 Modifying the Toolbox	1212
	24.6.4 Modifying the Keyboard	1213
	24.6.5 Rearranging Windows	1214
24.7	Accessibility in Visual Basic	1215
24.8	Accessibility in XHTML Tables	1221

24.9	Accessibility in XHTML Frames	1225
24.10	Accessibility in XML	1226
24.11	Using Voice Synthesis and Recognition with VoiceXML™	1226
24.12	CallXML™	1233
24.13	JAWS® for Windows	1240
24.14	Other Accessibility Tools	1240
24.15	Accessibility in Microsoft® Windows® 2000	1241
	24.15.1 Tools for People with Visual Impairments	1243
	24.15.2 Tools for People with Hearing Impairments	1246
	24.15.3 Tools for Users Who Have Difficulty Using the Keyboard	1247
	24.15.4 Microsoft Narrator	1251
	24.15.5 Microsoft On-Screen Keyboard	1252
	24.15.6 Accessibility Features in Microsoft Internet Explorer 5.5	1253
24.16	Internet and World Wide Web Resources	1255

A Operator Precedence Chart — 1264

B Number Systems (on CD) — 1266

B.1	Introduction	1267
B.2	Abbreviating Binary Numbers as Octal Numbers and Hexadecimal Numbers	1270
B.3	Converting Octal Numbers and Hexadecimal Numbers to Binary Numbers	1272
B.4	Converting from Binary, Octal or Hexadecimal to Decimal	1272
B.5	Converting from Decimal to Binary, Octal or Hexadecimal	1273
B.6	Negative Binary Numbers: Two's Complement Notation	1274

C Career Opportunities (on CD) — 1280

C.1	Introduction	1281
C.2	Resources for the Job Seeker	1282
C.3	Online Opportunities for Employers	1283
	C.3.1 Posting Jobs Online	1285
	C.3.2 Problems with Recruiting on the Web	1287
	C.3.3 Diversity in the Workplace	1287
C.4	Recruiting Services	1288
C.5	Career Sites	1289
	C.5.1 Comprehensive Career Sites	1289
	C.5.2 Technical Positions	1290
	C.5.3 Wireless Positions	1290
	C.5.4 Contracting Online	1291
	C.5.5 Executive Positions	1292
	C.5.6 Students and Young Professionals	1293
	C.5.7 Other Online Career Services	1293
C.6	Internet and World Wide Web Resources	1294

D Visual Studio .NET Debugger — 1302

D.1	Introduction	1303
D.2	Breakpoints	1304
D.3	Examining Data	1306

D.4	Program Control	1308
D.5	Additional Procedure Debugging Capabilities	1312
D.6	Additional Class Debugging Capabilities	1314

E ASCII Character Set — 1319

F Unicode® (on CD) — 1320

F.1	Introduction	1321
F.2	Unicode Transformation Formats	1322
F.3	Characters and Glyphs	1323
F.4	Advantages/Disadvantages of Unicode	1324
F.5	Unicode Consortium's Web Site	1324
F.6	Using Unicode	1325
F.7	Character Ranges	1327

G COM Integration (on CD) — 1332

G.1	Introduction	1332
G.2	ActiveX Integration	1333
G.3	DLL Integration	1337
G.4	Internet and World Wide Web Resources	1341

H Introduction to HyperText Markup Language 4: Part 1 (on CD) — 1344

H.1	Introduction	1345
H.2	Markup Languages	1345
H.3	Editing HTML	1346
H.4	Common Elements	1346
H.5	Headers	1349
H.6	Linking	1350
H.7	Images	1352
H.8	Special Characters and More Line Breaks	1356
H.9	Unordered Lists	1358
H.10	Nested and Ordered Lists	1359
H.11	Internet and World Wide Web Resources	1362

I Introduction to HyperText Markup Language 4: Part 2 (on CD) — 1367

I.1	Introduction	1368
I.2	Basic HTML Tables	1368
I.3	Intermediate HTML Tables and Formatting	1370
I.4	Basic HTML Forms	1373
I.5	More Complex HTML Forms	1376
I.6	Internal Linking	1383
I.7	Creating and Using Image Maps	1386
I.8	`<meta>` Tags	1388
I.9	**frameset** Element	1390

I.10	Nested **frameset**s	1392
I.11	Internet and World Wide Web Resources	1394

J   Introduction to XHTML: Part 1 (on CD)   1400

J.1	Introduction	1401
J.2	Editing XHTML	1401
J.3	First XHTML Example	1402
J.4	W3C XHTML Validation Service	1405
J.5	Headers	1406
J.6	Linking	1408
J.7	Images	1411
J.8	Special Characters and More Line Breaks	1415
J.9	Unordered Lists	1417
J.10	Nested and Ordered Lists	1418
J.11	Internet and World Wide Web Resources	1421

K   Introduction to XHTML: Part 2 (on CD)   1426

K.1	Introduction	1427
K.2	Basic XHTML Tables	1427
K.3	Intermediate XHTML Tables and Formatting	1430
K.4	Basic XHTML Forms	1432
K.5	More Complex XHTML Forms	1435
K.6	Internal Linking	1443
K.7	Creating and Using Image Maps	1446
K.8	**meta** Elements	1448
K.9	**frameset** Element	1449
K.10	Nested **frameset**s	1454
K.11	Internet and World Wide Web Resources	1456

L   HTML/XHTML Special Characters   1462

M   HTML/XHTML Colors   1463

N   Crystal Reports® for Visual Studio .NET   1466

N.1	Introduction	1466
N.2	Crystal Reports Web Site Resources	1466
N.3	Crystal Reports and Visual Studio .NET	1467
	N.3.1 Crystal Reports in Web Applications	1469
	N.3.2 Crystal Reports and Web Services	1469

Bibliography   1471

Index   1475

Illustrations

1 Introduction to Computers, Internet and Visual Basic .NET
1.1	.NET Languages.	19

2 Introduction to the Visual Studio .NET IDE
2.1	**Start Page** in Visual Studio .NET.	35
2.2	**New Project** dialog.	36
2.3	**Design** view of Visual Studio .NET IDE.	37
2.4	Visual Studio .NET IDE menu bar.	38
2.5	Summary of Visual Studio .NET IDE menus.	38
2.6	IDE Toolbar.	38
2.7	Tool tip demonstration.	39
2.8	Toolbar icons for three Visual Studio .NET IDE windows.	39
2.9	Auto-hide feature demonstration.	40
2.10	**Solution Explorer** with an open solution.	41
2.11	**Toolbox** window.	42
2.12	**Properties** window.	43
2.13	**Help** menu commands.	44
2.14	**Dynamic Help** window.	44
2.15	Simple program executing.	45
2.16	Creating a new **Windows Application**.	46
2.17	Setting the project location in the **Project Location** dialog.	47
2.18	Setting the form's `Text` property.	47
2.19	Form with sizing handles.	48
2.20	Changing the form's `BackColor` property.	48
2.21	Adding a label to the form.	49
2.22	GUI after the form and label have been customized.	50
2.23	**Properties** window displaying the label's properties.	50
2.24	**Font** dialog for selecting fonts, styles and sizes.	51

2.25	Centering the label's text.	51
2.26	Inserting and aligning the picture box.	52
2.27	**Image** property of the picture box.	52
2.28	Selecting an image for the picture box.	53
2.29	Picture box displaying an image.	53
2.30	IDE in run mode, with the running application in the foreground.	54

3 Introduction to Visual Basic Programming

3.1	Simple Visual Basic program.	63
3.2	Creating a **Console Application** with the **New Project** dialog.	65
3.3	IDE with an open console application.	66
3.4	Renaming the program file in the **Properties** window.	66
3.5	IntelliSense feature of the Visual Studio .NET IDE.	68
3.6	Parameter Info and Parameter List windows.	68
3.7	Executing the program shown in Fig. 3.1.	68
3.8	IDE indicating a syntax error.	69
3.9	Using multiple statements to print a line of text.	69
3.10	Addition program that adds two numbers entered by the user.	70
3.11	Dialog displaying a run-time error.	72
3.12	Memory location showing name and value of variable `number1`.	74
3.13	Memory locations after values for variables `number1` and `number2` have been input.	74
3.14	Memory locations after an addition operation.	74
3.15	Arithmetic operators.	75
3.16	Precedence of arithmetic operators.	76
3.17	Order in which a second-degree polynomial is evaluated.	79
3.18	Equality and relational operators.	79
3.19	Performing comparisons with equality and relational operators.	80
3.20	Precedence and associativity of operators introduced in this chapter.	82
3.21	Displaying text in a dialog.	83
3.22	Dialog displayed by calling `MessageBox.Show`.	85
3.23	Obtaining documentation for a class by using the **Index** dialog.	85
3.24	Documentation for the `MessageBox` class.	85
3.25	Adding a reference to an assembly in the Visual Studio .NET IDE.	86
3.26	Internet Explorer window with GUI components.	87

4 Control Structures: Part 1

4.1	Sequence structure flowchart.	100
4.2	Keywords in Visual Basic.	101
4.3	`If/Then` single-selection structure flowchart.	103
4.4	`If/Then/Else` double-selection structure flowchart.	105
4.5	`While` repetition structure used to print powers of two.	107
4.6	`While` repetition structure flowchart.	107
4.7	`Do While/Loop` repetition structure demonstration.	108
4.8	`Do While/Loop` repetition structure flowchart.	109
4.9	`Do Until/Loop` repetition structure demonstration.	109

4.10	**Do Until/Loop** repetition structure flowchart.	110
4.11	Assignment operators.	111
4.12	Exponentiation using an assignment operator.	111
4.13	Pseudocode algorithm that uses counter-controlled repetition to solve the class-average problem.	112
4.14	Class-average program with counter-controlled repetition.	112
4.15	Pseudocode algorithm that uses sentinel-controlled repetition to solve the class-average problem.	116
4.16	Class-average program with sentinel-controlled repetition.	117
4.17	Pseudocode for examination-results problem.	122
4.18	Nested control structures used to calculate examination results.	122
4.19	Second refinement of the pseudocode.	126
4.20	Nested repetition structures used to print a square of *****s.	126
4.21	IDE showing program code for Fig. 2.15.	129
4.22	Windows Form Designer generated code when expanded.	130
4.23	Code generated by the IDE for **lblWelcome**.	130
4.24	**Properties** window used to set a property value.	131
4.25	Windows Form Designer generated code reflecting new property values.	132
4.26	Changing a property in the code view editor.	132
4.27	New **Text** property value reflected in design mode.	132
4.28	Adding program code to **FrmASimpleProgram_Load**.	133
4.29	Method **FrmASimpleProgram_Load** containing program code.	134
4.30	Changing a property value at runtime.	134

5   Control Structures: Part 2

5.1	Counter-controlled repetition with the **While** structure.	146
5.2	Counter-controlled repetition with the **For/Next** structure.	146
5.3	**For/Next** header components.	148
5.4	**For/Next** repetition structure flowchart.	149
5.5	**For/Next** structure used for summation.	150
5.6	Message dialog icon constants.	151
5.7	Message dialog button constants.	151
5.8	**For/Next** structure used to calculate compound interest.	152
5.9	Formatting codes for **String**s.	154
5.10	**Select Case** structure used to count grades.	155
5.11	**Select Case** multiple-selection structure flowchart.	158
5.12	**Do/Loop While** repetition structure.	159
5.13	**Do/Loop While** repetition structure flowchart.	160
5.14	**Do/Loop Until** repetition structure.	160
5.15	**Do/Loop Until** repetition structure flowchart.	161
5.16	**Exit** keyword in repetition structures.	162
5.17	Truth table for the **AndAlso** operator.	165
5.18	Truth table for the **OrElse** operator.	166
5.19	Truth table for the logical exclusive OR (**Xor**) operator.	167
5.20	Truth table for operator **Not** (logical NOT).	167
5.21	Logical operator truth tables.	168

5.22	Precedence and associativity of the operators discussed so far.	169
5.23	Visual Basic's single-entry/single-exit sequence and selection structures.	170
5.24	Visual Basic's single-entry/single-exit repetition structures.	171
5.25	Structured programming rules.	172
5.26	Simplest flowchart.	173
5.27	Repeatedly applying rule 2 of Fig. 5.25 to the simplest flowchart.	173
5.28	Applying rule 3 of Fig. 5.25 to the simplest flowchart.	174
5.29	Stacked, nested and overlapped building blocks.	175
5.30	Unstructured flowchart.	175

6 Procedures

6.1	Hierarchical boss-procedure/worker-procedure relationship.	185
6.2	**Sub** procedure for printing payment information.	185
6.3	**Function** procedure for squaring an integer.	188
6.4	Method that determines the largest of three numbers.	190
6.5	*Parameter Info* feature of the Visual Studio .NET IDE.	193
6.6	*IntelliSense* feature of the Visual Studio .NET IDE.	193
6.7	**Math** class methods.	194
6.8	Widening conversions.	196
6.9	**Property Pages** dialog with **Option Strict** set to **On**.	197
6.10	Visual Basic primitive data types.	198
6.11	Literals with type characters.	199
6.12	**ByVal** and **ByRef** used to pass value-type arguments.	201
6.13	Scoping rules in a class.	204
6.14	Random integers created by calling method **Next** of class **Random**.	208
6.15	Demonstrates 4 die rolls.	209
6.16	**Random** class used to simulate rolling 12 six-sided dice.	211
6.17	Craps game using class **Random**.	214
6.18	Recursive evaluation of 5!.	*219*
6.19	Recursive factorial program.	220
6.20	Recursively generating Fibonacci numbers.	222
6.21	Recursive calls to method **Fibonacci**.	224
6.22	Overloaded methods.	226
6.23	Syntax error generated from overloaded procedures with identical parameter lists and different return types.	228
6.24	**Optional** argument demonstration with method **Power**.	229
6.25	Module used to define a group of related procedures.	231
6.26	Testing the **modDice** procedures.	232
6.27	Printing the results of cubing 10 numbers.	238
6.28	Towers of Hanoi for the case with four disks.	244

7 Arrays

7.1	Array consisting of 12 elements.	247
7.2	Creating an array.	250
7.3	Initializing array elements two different ways.	251
7.4	Computing the sum of the elements in an array.	252
7.5	Simple student-poll analysis program.	254

7.6	Program that prints histograms.	256
7.7	Using arrays to eliminate a **Select Case** structure.	257
7.8	Passing arrays and individual array elements to procedures.	261
7.9	Passing an array reference with **ByVal** and **ByRef**.	265
7.10	**BubbleSort** procedure in **modBubbleSort**.	268
7.11	Sorting an array with bubble sort.	269
7.12	Procedures for performing a linear search.	272
7.13	Linear search of an array.	273
7.14	Binary search of a sorted array.	276
7.15	Two-dimensional array with three rows and four columns.	280
7.16	Initializing multidimensional arrays.	281
7.17	Using jagged two-dimensional arrays.	283
7.18	Creating variable-length parameter lists.	287
7.19	Using **For Each/Next** with an array.	288

8 Object-Based Programming

8.1	Abstract data type representing time in 24-hour format.	299
8.2	Using an abstract data type.	303
8.3	Attempting to access restricted class members results in a syntax error.	307
8.4	Overloading constructors.	309
8.5	Overloaded-constructor demonstration.	312
8.6	Properties in a class.	314
8.7	Graphical user interface for class **CTime3**.	318
8.8	**CDay** class encapsulates day, month and year information.	321
8.9	**CEmployee** class encapsulates employee name, birthday and hire date.	323
8.10	Composition demonstration.	324
8.11	Class using **Me** reference.	325
8.12	**Me** reference demonstration.	326
8.13	**CEmployee2** class objects share **Shared** variable.	328
8.14	**Shared** class member demonstration.	330
8.15	Constants used in class **CCircleConstants**.	332
8.16	**Const** and **ReadOnly** class member demonstration.	333
8.17	**CEmployee3** class to store in class library.	336
8.18	Simple class library project.	338
8.19	Module **modAssemblyTest** references **EmployeeLibrary.dll**.	339
8.20	**Class View** of Fig. 8.1 and Fig. 8.2.	341
8.21	Invoking the **Object Browser** from the development environment.	342
8.22	**Object Browser** when user selects **Object** from development environment.	343

9 Object-Oriented Programming: Inheritance

9.1	Inheritance examples.	352
9.2	Inheritance hierarchy for university **CCommunityMember**s.	353
9.3	Portion of a **CShape** class hierarchy.	354
9.4	**CPoint** class represents an *x-y* coordinate pair.	355
9.5	**modPointTest** demonstrates class **CPoint** functionality.	357

9.6	**CCircle** class contains an *x-y* coordinate and a radius.	358
9.7	**modCircleTest** demonstrates class **CCircle** functionality.	360
9.8	**CCircle2** class that inherits from class **CPoint**.	362
9.9	**CPoint2** class represents an *x-y* coordinate pair as **Protected** data.	364
9.10	**CCircle3** class that inherits from class **CPoint2**.	365
9.11	**modCircleTest3** demonstrates class **CCircle3** functionality.	367
9.12	**CCircle4** class that inherits from class **CPoint**, which does not provide **Protected** data.	369
9.13	**modCircleTest4** demonstrates class **CCircle4** functionality.	371
9.14	**CCylinder** class inherits from class **CCircle4** and **Overrides** method **Area**.	373
9.15	Testing class **CCylinder**.	375
9.16	**CPoint3** base class contains constructors and finalizer.	378
9.17	**CCircle5** class inherits from class **CPoint3** and overrides a finalizer method.	379
9.18	Demonstrating order in which constructors and finalizers are called.	381

10 Object-Oriented Programming: Polymorphism

10.1	**CPoint** class represents an *x-y* coordinate pair.	390
10.2	**CCircle** class that inherits from class **CPoint**.	391
10.3	Assigning derived-class references to base-class references.	393
10.4	Abstract **CShape** base class.	400
10.5	**CPoint2** class inherits from **MustInherit** class **CShape**.	401
10.6	**CCircle2** class that inherits from class **CPoint2**.	403
10.7	**CCylinder2** class inherits from class **CCircle2**.	404
10.8	**CTest2** demonstrates polymorphism in Point-Circle-Cylinder hierarchy.	406
10.9	**MustInherit** class **CEmployee** definition.	410
10.10	**CBoss** class inherits from class **CEmployee**.	411
10.11	**CCommissionWorker** class inherits from class **CEmployee**.	412
10.12	**CPieceWorker** class inherits from class **CEmployee**.	414
10.13	**CHourlyWorker** class inherits from class **CEmployee**.	416
10.14	**CTest** class tests the **CEmployee** class hierarchy.	417
10.15	**Interface** for returning age of objects of disparate classes.	420
10.16	**CPerson** class implements **IAge** interface.	421
10.17	**CTree** class implements **IAge** interface.	422
10.18	Demonstrate polymorphism on objects of disparate classes.	423
10.19	**IShape** interface provides methods **Area** and **Volume** and property **Name**.	426
10.20	**CPoint3** class implements interface **IShape**.	426
10.21	**CCircle3** class inherits from class **CPoint3**.	427
10.22	**CCylinder3** class inherits from class **CCircle3**.	429
10.23	**CTest3** uses interfaces to demonstrate polymorphism in Point-Circle-Cylinder hierarchy.	431
10.24	Bubble sort using delegates.	433
10.25	Bubble-sort **Form** application.	435

Illustrations xxv

11 Exception Handling

11.1	Exception handlers for `FormatException` and `DivideByZeroException`.	447
11.2	`Finally` statements always execute, regardless of whether an exception occurs.	454
11.3	`Exception` properties and stack unwinding.	462
11.4	`ApplicationException` derived class thrown when a program performs an illegal operation on a negative number.	465
11.5	`FrmSquareRoot` class throws an exception if an error occurs when calculating the square root.	466
11.6	`OverflowException` cannot occur if user disables integer-overflow checking.	468

12 Graphical User Interface Concepts: Part 1

12.1	GUI components in a sample Internet Explorer window.	477
12.2	Some basic GUI components.	477
12.3	Components and controls for Windows Forms.	478
12.4	Common `Form` properties, methods and events.	479
12.5	Event-handling model using delegates.	480
12.6	Events section in the Method Name drop-down menu.	482
12.7	Simple event-handling example using visual programming.	482
12.8	List of `Form` events.	486
12.9	`Click` event details.	486
12.10	Class `Control` properties and methods.	487
12.11	Anchoring demonstration.	489
12.12	Manipulating the **Anchor** property of a control.	489
12.13	Docking demonstration.	490
12.14	`Control` layout properties.	490
12.15	Common `Label` properties.	491
12.16	`TextBox` properties and events.	492
12.17	`Button` properties and events.	493
12.18	Program to display hidden text in a password box.	493
12.19	`GroupBox` properties.	495
12.20	`Panel` properties.	495
12.21	Creating a `Panel` with scrollbars.	495
12.22	Using `GroupBox`es and `Panel`s to arrange `Button`s.	496
12.23	`CheckBox` properties and events.	498
12.24	Using `CheckBox`es to change font styles.	498
12.25	`RadioButton` properties and events.	501
12.26	Using `RadioButton`s to set message-window options.	502
12.27	`PictureBox` properties and events.	508
12.28	Using a `PictureBox` to display images.	508
12.29	Mouse events, delegates and event arguments.	510
12.30	Using the mouse to draw on a form.	511
12.31	Keyboard events, delegates and event arguments.	513

12.32	Demonstrating keyboard events.	514
12.33	Abbreviations for controls introduced in chapter.	517

13 Graphical User Interface Concepts: Part 2

13.1	Expanded and checked menus.	525
13.2	Visual Studio .NET Menu Designer	526
13.3	Adding **MenuItem**s to **MainMenu**.	527
13.4	**MainMenu** and **MenuItem** properties and events.	527
13.5	Menus for changing text font and color.	528
13.6	**LinkLabel** control in running program.	534
13.7	**LinkLabel** properties and events.	534
13.8	**LinkLabel**s used to link to a drive, a Web page and an application.	536
13.9	**ListBox** and **CheckedListBox** on a form.	538
13.10	**ListBox** properties, methods and events.	538
13.11	**String Collection Editor**.	540
13.12	Program that adds, removes and clears **ListBox** items.	540
13.13	**CheckedListBox** properties, methods and events.	543
13.14	**CheckedListBox** and **ListBox** used in a program to display a user selection.	544
13.15	**ComboBox** demonstration.	546
13.16	**ComboBox** properties and events.	546
13.17	**ComboBox** used to draw a selected shape.	547
13.18	**TreeView** displaying a sample tree.	550
13.19	**TreeView** properties and events.	550
13.20	**TreeNode** properties and methods.	551
13.21	**TreeNode Editor**.	552
13.22	**TreeView** used to display directories.	553
13.23	**ListView** properties and events.	556
13.24	**Image Collection Editor** window for an **ImageList** component.	556
13.25	**ListView** displaying files and folders.	557
13.26	Tabbed windows in Visual Studio .NET.	562
13.27	**TabControl** with **TabPage**s example.	563
13.28	**TabPage**s added to a **TabControl**.	563
13.29	**TabControl** properties and events.	564
13.30	**TabControl** used to display various font settings.	564
13.31	MDI parent window and MDI child windows.	568
13.32	SDI and MDI forms.	568
13.33	MDI parent and MDI child events and properties.	569
13.34	Minimized and maximized child windows.	570
13.35	**MenuItem** property **MdiList** example.	571
13.36	**LayoutMdi** enumeration values.	572
13.37	MDI parent-window class.	572
13.38	MDI child **FrmChild.**	575
13.39	Class **FrmInheritance**, which inherits from class **Form**, contains a button (**Learn More**).	577
13.40	Visual Inheritance through the Form Designer.	578

13.41	Class **FrmVisualTest**, which inherits from class **VisualForm.FrmInheritance**, contains an additional button.	579
13.42	Custom control creation.	581
13.43	**UserControl**-defined clock.	581
13.44	Custom-control creation.	583
13.45	Project properties dialog.	583
13.46	Custom control added to the **ToolBox**.	584
13.47	Custom control added to a **Form**.	584
13.48	Prefixes for controls used in chapter.	585

14 Multithreading

14.1	Thread life cycle.	595
14.2	Thread-priority scheduling.	597
14.3	**ThreadStart** delegate **Print** displays message and sleeps for arbitrary duration of time.	598
14.4	Threads sleeping and printing.	600
14.5	Unsynchronized shared **Integer** buffer.	604
14.6	Producer places **Integer**s in unsynchronized shared buffer.	605
14.7	Consumer reads **Integer**s from unsynchronized shared buffer.	606
14.8	Producer and consumer threads accessing a shared object without synchronization.	608
14.9	Synchronized shared **Integer** buffer.	610
14.10	Producer places **Integer**s in synchronized shared buffer.	612
14.11	Consumer reads **Integer**s from synchronized shared buffer.	612
14.12	Producer and consumer threads accessing a shared object with synchronization.	613
14.13	Synchronized shared circular buffer.	620
14.14	Producer places **Integer**s in synchronized circular buffer.	623
14.15	Consumer reads **Integer**s from synchronized circular buffer.	624
14.16	Producer and consumer threads accessing a circular buffer.	625

15 Strings, Characters and Regular Expressions

15.1	**String** constructors.	635
15.2	**String Length** and **Chars** properties, and **CopyTo** method.	637
15.3	**String** test to determine equality.	639
15.4	**StartsWith** and **EndsWith** methods.	642
15.5	**GetHashCode** method demonstration.	643
15.6	Searching for characters and substrings in **String**s.	644
15.7	Substrings generated from **String**s.	647
15.8	**Concat Shared** method.	648
15.9	**String** methods **Replace**, **ToLower**, **ToUpper**, **Trim** and **ToString**.	649
15.10	**StringBuilder** class constructors.	651
15.11	**StringBuilder** size manipulation.	653
15.12	Append methods of **StringBuilder**.	655
15.13	**StringBuilder**'s **AppendFormat** method.	656
15.14	**StringBuilder** text insertion and removal.	658

15.15	**StringBuilder** text replacement.	659
15.16	**Char**'s **Shared** character-testing methods and case-conversion methods.	661
15.17	**CCard** class.	663
15.18	Card dealing and shuffling simulation.	664
15.19	Character classes.	668
15.20	Regular expressions checking birthdays.	668
15.21	Quantifiers used regular expressions.	670
15.22	Validating user information using regular expressions.	670
15.23	**Regex** methods **Replace** and **Split**.	675

16 Graphics and Multimedia

16.1	**System.Drawing** namespace's Classes and Structures.	685
16.2	GDI+ coordinate system. Units are measured in pixels.	686
16.3	**Color** structure **Shared** constants and their RGB values.	688
16.4	**Color** structure members.	688
16.5	Classes that derive from class **Brush**.	689
16.6	Color value and alpha demonstration.	689
16.7	**ColorDialog** used to change background and text color.	692
16.8	**Font** class read-only properties.	694
16.9	**Font**s and **FontStyle**s.	695
16.10	An illustration of font metrics.	697
16.11	**FontFamily** methods that return font-metric information.	697
16.12	**FontFamily** class used to obtain font-metric information.	697
16.13	**Graphics** methods that draw lines, rectangles and ovals.	699
16.14	Drawing lines, rectangles and ellipses.	700
16.15	Ellipse bounded by a rectangle.	702
16.16	Positive and negative arc angles.	702
16.17	**Graphics** methods for drawing arcs.	703
16.18	Arc method demonstration.	703
16.19	**Graphics** methods for drawing polygons.	705
16.20	Polygon drawing demonstration.	705
16.21	Shapes drawn on a form.	709
16.22	Paths used to draw stars on a form.	712
16.23	Image resizing.	714
16.24	Animation of a series of images.	717
16.25	Container class for chess pieces.	718
16.26	Chess-game code (part 1 of 9).	720
16.27	Windows Media Player demonstration.	729
16.28	Peedy introducing himself when the window opens.	732
16.29	Peedy's *Pleased* animation.	733
16.30	Peedy's reaction when he is clicked.	734
16.31	Peedy flying animation	734
16.32	Peedy waiting for speech input.	735
16.33	Peedy repeating the user's request for Seattle style pizza.	736
16.34	Peedy repeating the user's request for anchovies as an additional topping.	736
16.35	Peedy recounting the order.	737

16.36	Peedy calculating the total.	737
16.37	Microsoft Agent demonstration.	738
16.38	GUI for eight queens exercise.	751

17 Files and Streams

17.1	Data hierarchy.	755
17.2	Visual Basic's view of an *n-byte* file.	756
17.3	**File** class methods (partial list).	757
17.4	**Directory** class methods (partial list).	758
17.5	**FrmFileTest** class tests classes **File** and **Directory**.	759
17.6	**FrmFileSearch** class uses regular expressions to determine file types.	762
17.7	**FrmBankUI** class is the base class for GUIs in our file-processing applications.	767
17.8	**CRecord** class represents a record for sequential-access file-processing applications.	770
17.9	**FrmCreateSequentialAccessFile** class creates and writes to sequential-access files.	772
17.10	Sample data for the program of Fig. 17.9.	779
17.11	**FrmReadSequentialAccessFile** class reads sequential-access files.	779
17.12	**FrmCreditInquiry** class is a program that displays credit inquiries.	783
17.13	Random-access file with fixed-length records.	790
17.14	**CRandomAccessRecord** class represents a record for random-access file-processing applications.	791
17.15	**FrmCreateRandomAccessFile** class creates files for random-access file-processing applications.	794
17.16	**FrmWriteRandomAccessFile** class writes records to random-access files.	798
17.17	**FrmReadRandomAccessFile** class reads records from random-access files sequentially.	802
17.18	**CTransaction** class handles record transactions for the transaction-processor case study.	808
17.19	**FrmTransactionProcessor** class runs the transaction-processor application.	812
17.20	**FrmStartDialog** class enables users to access dialog boxes associated with various transactions.	813
17.21	**FrmNewDialog** class enables users to create records in transaction-processor case study.	816
17.22	**FrmUpdateDialog** class enables users to update records in transaction-processor case study.	819
17.23	**FrmDeleteDialog** class enables users to remove records from files in transaction-processor case study.	825
17.24	Inventory of a hardware store.	832

18 Extensible Markup Language (XML)

18.1	XML used to mark up an article.	834
18.2	**article.xml** displayed by Internet Explorer.	837
18.3	XML to mark up a business letter.	837

18.4	XML namespaces demonstration.	839
18.5	Default namespaces demonstration.	841
18.6	Tree structure for Fig. 18.1.	842
18.7	**XmlNodeReader** iterates through an XML document.	843
18.8	DOM structure of an XML document.	846
18.9	**XPathNavigator** class navigates selected nodes.	852
18.10	XML document that describes various sports.	859
18.11	XPath expressions and descriptions.	860
18.12	Document Type Definition (DTD) for a business letter.	861
18.13	XML document referencing its associated DTD.	863
18.14	XML Validator validates an XML document against a DTD.	864
18.15	XML Validator displaying an error message.	865
18.16	XML document that conforms to a Microsoft Schema document.	865
18.17	Schema file that contains structure to which **book.xml** conforms.	866
18.18	Schema-validation example.	867
18.19	XML file that does not conform to the Schema in Fig. 18.17.	869
18.20	XML document containing book information.	871
18.21	XSL document that transforms **sorting.xml** into XHTML.	872
18.22	XSL style sheet applied to an XML document.	875
18.23	BizTalk terminology.	877
18.24	BizTalk markup using an offer Schema.	878

19 Database, SQL and ADO .NET

19.1	Relational-database structure of an **Employee** table.	889
19.2	Result set formed by selecting **Department** and **Location** data from the **Employee** table.	890
19.3	**Authors** table from **Books**.	890
19.4	Data from the **Authors** table of **Books**.	890
19.5	**Publishers** table from **Books**.	891
19.6	Data from the **Publishers** table of **Books**.	891
19.7	**AuthorISBN** table from **Books**.	892
19.8	Data from **AuthorISBN** table in **Books**.	892
19.9	**Titles** table from **Books**.	893
19.10	Data from the **Titles** table of **Books**.	893
19.11	Table relationships in **Books**.	896
19.12	SQL query keywords.	897
19.13	**authorID** and **lastName** from the **Authors** table.	898
19.14	Titles with copyrights after 1999 from table **Titles**.	899
19.15	Authors from the **Authors** table whose last names start with **D**.	900
19.16	Authors from table **Authors** whose last names contain **i** as their second letter.	901
19.17	Authors from table **Authors** in ascending order by **lastName**.	901
19.18	Authors from table **Authors** in descending order by **lastName**.	902
19.19	Authors from table **Authors** in ascending order by **lastName** and by **firstName**.	903
19.20	Books from table **Titles** whose titles end with **How to Program** in ascending order by **title**.	904

19.21	Authors from table **Authors** and ISBN numbers of the authors' books, sorted in ascending order by **lastName** and **firstName**.	905
19.22	Joining tables to produce a result set in which each record contains an author, title, ISBN number, copyright and publisher name.	906
19.23	Portion of the result set produced by the query in Fig. 19.22.	907
19.24	Table **Authors** after an **INSERT** operation to add a record.	909
19.25	Table **Authors** after an **UPDATE** operation to change a record.	910
19.26	Table **Authors** after a **DELETE** operation to remove a record.	911
19.27	Database access and information display.	913
19.28	SQL statements executed on a database.	921
19.29	Database modification demonstration.	923
19.30	XML representation of a **DataSet** written to a file.	932
19.31	XML document generated from **WriteXML**.	934

20 ASP .NET, Web Forms and Web Controls

20.1	Client interacting with Web server. Step 1: The **GET** request, **GET /books/downloads.htm HTTP/1.1**.	944
20.2	Client interacting with Web server. Step 2: The HTTP response, **HTTP/1.1 200 OK**.	944
20.3	Three-tier architecture.	945
20.4	ASPX page that displays the Web server's time.	946
20.5	Code-behind file for a page that displays the Web server's time.	948
20.6	HTML response when the browser requests **WebTime.aspx**.	951
20.7	Creating an **ASP.NET Web Application** in Visual Studio.	953
20.8	Visual Studio creating and linking a virtual directory for the **WebTime** project folder.	953
20.9	**Solution Explorer** window for project **WebTime**.	953
20.10	**Web Forms** menu in the **Toolbox**.	954
20.11	**Design** mode of Web Form designer.	954
20.12	**HTML** mode of Web-Form designer.	955
20.13	Code-behind file for **WebForm1.aspx** generated by Visual Studio .NET.	956
20.14	**FlowLayout** and **GridLayout** illustration.	956
20.15	**WebForm.aspx** after adding two **Label**s and setting their properties.	957
20.16	Commonly used Web controls.	958
20.17	Web-controls demonstration.	959
20.18	**AdRotator** class demonstrated on a Web form.	964
20.19	Code-behind file for page demonstrating the **AdRotator** class.	965
20.20	**AdvertisementFile** used in **AdRotator** example.	967
20.21	Validators used in a Web Form that generates possible letter combinations from a phone number.	970
20.22	Code-behind file for the word-generator page.	972
20.23	HTML and JavaScript sent to the client browser.	976
20.24	ASPX file that presents a list of programming languages.	981
20.25	Code-behind file that writes cookies to the client.	983
20.26	ASPX page that displays book information.	986
20.27	Cookies being read from a client in an ASP .NET application.	987

20.28	**HttpCookie** properties.	989
20.29	Options supplied on an ASPX page.	989
20.30	Sessions are created for each user in an ASP .NET Web application.	991
20.31	**HttpSessionState** properties.	995
20.32	Session information displayed in a **ListBox**.	995
20.33	Session data read by an ASP .NET Web application to provide recommendations for the user.	996
20.34	Guest-book application GUI.	998
20.35	ASPX file for the guest-book application.	999
20.36	Code-behind file for the guest-book application.	1001
20.37	Login Web Form.	1005
20.38	ASCX code for the header.	1007
20.39	Code-behind file for the login page for authors application.	1007
20.40	ASPX file that allows a user to select an author from a drop-down list.	1013
20.41	Database information being inputted into a **DataGrid**.	1014
20.42	ASPX page with tracing turned off.	1020
20.43	Tracing enabled on a page.	1020
20.44	Tracing information for a project.	1021

21 ASP .NET and Web Services

21.1	ASMX file rendered in Internet Explorer.	1033
21.2	Service description for a Web service.	1034
21.3	Invoking a method of a Web service from a Web browser.	1035
21.4	Results of invoking a Web-service method from a Web browser.	1035
21.5	SOAP request message for the **HugeInteger** Web service.	1036
21.6	**HugeInteger** Web service.	1038
21.7	Design view of a Web service.	1044
21.8	Adding a Web service reference to a project.	1045
21.9	**Add Web Reference** dialog.	1046
21.10	Web services located on **localhost**.	1046
21.11	Web reference selection and description.	1047
21.12	**Solution Explorer** after adding a Web reference to a project.	1047
21.13	Using the **HugeInteger** Web service.	1049
21.14	**Blackjack** Web service.	1054
21.15	Blackjack game that uses the **Blackjack** Web service.	1057
21.16	Airline reservation Web service.	1066
21.17	Airline Web Service in design view.	1069
21.18	ASPX file that takes reservation information.	1069
21.19	Code-behind file for the reservation page.	1070
21.20	**TemperatureServer** Web service.	1073
21.21	Class that stores weather information about a city.	1076
21.22	Receiving temperature and weather data from a Web service.	1077
21.23	Class that stores equation information.	1082
21.24	Web service that generates random equations.	1085
21.25	Returning an object from a Web-service method.	1086
21.26	Math-tutor application.	1087

22 Networking: Streams-Based Sockets and Datagrams

22.1	Server portion of a client/server stream-socket connection.	1101
22.2	Client portion of a client/server stream-socket connection.	1104
22.3	Server-side portion of connectionless client/server computing.	1110
22.4	Client-side portion of connectionless client/server computing.	1112
22.5	Server side of client/server Tic-Tac-Toe program.	1116
22.6	**CPlayer** class represents a Tic-Tac-Toe player.	1119
22.7	Client side of client/server Tic-Tac-Toe program.	1122
22.8	**CSquare** class represents a square on the Tic-Tac-Toe board.	1128
22.9	English letters of the alphabet and decimal digits as expressed in international Morse code.	1135

23 Data Structures and Collections

23.1	Self-referential **CNode** class definition.	1138
23.2	Self-referential class objects linked together.	1139
23.3	Linked-list graphical representation.	1141
23.4	Self-referential class **CListNode.**	1141
23.5	Linked-list **CList** class.	1142
23.6	Exception thrown when removing node from empty linked list.	1145
23.7	Linked-list demonstration.	1146
23.8	**InsertAtFront** graphical representation.	1148
23.9	**InsertAtBack** graphical representation.	1149
23.10	**RemoveFromFront** graphical representation.	1150
23.11	**RemoveFromBack** graphical representation.	1151
23.12	Stack implementation by inheritance from class **CList**.	1153
23.13	Stack-by-inheritance test.	1154
23.14	Stack-by-composition test.	1155
23.15	Queue implemented by inheritance from class **CList**.	1157
23.16	Queue-by-inheritance test.	1158
23.17	Binary tree graphical representation.	1160
23.18	Binary search tree containing 12 values.	1160
23.19	Tree-node data structure.	1162
23.20	Tree data structure.	1163
23.21	Tree-traversal demonstration.	1166
23.22	A binary search tree.	1167
23.23	Tree node contains **IComparable**s as data.	1169
23.24	Binary tree stores nodes with **IComparable** data.	1171
23.25	**IComparable** binary-tree demonstration.	1173
23.26	**Array** class demonstration.	1176
23.27	**ArrayList** methods (partial list).	1180
23.28	**ArrayList** class demonstration.	1180
23.29	**Stack** class demonstration.	1185
23.30	**Hashtable** class demonstration.	1190
23.31	**CEmployee** class.	1194

24 Accessibility

24.1	Acts designed to ensure Internet access for people with disabilities.	1205
24.2	We Media's home page. Wemedia.com home page (Courtesy of We Media Inc.)	1206
24.3	Enlarging icons using the **Customize** feature.	1210
24.4	Enlarged icons in the development window.	1210
24.5	Text Editor before modifying the font size.	1211
24.6	Enlarging text in the **Options** window.	1211
24.7	Text Editor after the font size is modified.	1212
24.8	Adding tabs to the **Toolbox**.	1213
24.9	Shortcut key creation.	1214
24.10	Removing tabs from the Visual Studio environment.	1214
24.11	Console windows with tabs and without tabs.	1215
24.12	Properties of class `Control` related to accessibility.	1216
24.13	Application with accessibility features.	1217
24.14	XHTML table without accessibility modifications.	1222
24.15	Table optimized for screen reading using attribute `headers`.	1223
24.16	Home page written in VoiceXML.	1227
24.17	Publication page of Deitel and Associates' VoiceXML page.	1229
24.18	VoiceXML tags.	1233
24.19	**Hello World** CallXML example. (Courtesy of Voxeo, © Voxeo Corporation 2000–2001).	1234
24.20	CallXML example that reads three ISBN values. (Courtesy of Voxeo, © Voxeo Corporation 2000–2001.)	1235
24.21	CallXML elements.	1238
24.22	**Text Size** dialog.	1242
24.23	**Display Settings** dialog.	1243
24.24	**Accessibility Wizard** initialization options.	1243
24.25	Scroll Bar and Window Border Size dialog.	1244
24.26	Adjusting up window element sizes.	1244
24.27	**Display Color Settings** options.	1245
24.28	**Accessibility Wizard** mouse cursor adjustment tool.	1245
24.29	**SoundSentry** dialog.	1246
24.30	**ShowSounds** dialog.	1246
24.31	**StickyKeys** window.	1247
24.32	**BounceKeys** dialog.	1247
24.33	**ToggleKeys** window.	1248
24.34	**Extra Keyboard Help** dialog.	1248
24.35	**MouseKeys** window.	1249
24.36	**Mouse Button Settings** window.	1249
24.37	**Mouse Speed** dialog.	1250
24.38	**Set Automatic Timeouts** dialog.	1250
24.39	Saving new accessibility settings.	1251
24.40	**Narrator** window.	1252
24.41	**Voice Settings** window.	1252
24.42	**Narrator** reading **Notepad** text.	1253

24.43	Microsoft **On-Screen Keyboard**.	1253
24.44	Microsoft Internet Explorer 5.5's accessibility options.	1254
24.45	Advanced accessibility settings in Microsoft Internet Explorer 5.5.	1255

A   Operator Precedence Chart

A.1	Operator precedence chart.	1264

B   Number Systems (on CD)

B.1	Digits of the binary, octal, decimal and hexadecimal number systems.	1268
B.2	Comparison of the binary, octal, decimal and hexadecimal number systems.	1269
B.3	Positional values in the decimal number system.	1269
B.4	Positional values in the binary number system.	1269
B.5	Positional values in the octal number system.	1270
B.6	Positional values in the hexadecimal number system.	1270
B.7	Decimal, binary, octal, and hexadecimal equivalents.	1270
B.8	Converting a binary number to decimal.	1272
B.9	Converting an octal number to decimal.	1272
B.10	Converting a hexadecimal number to decimal.	1273

C   Career Opportunities (on CD)

C.1	`Monster.com` home page. (Courtesy of `Monster.com`.]	1283
C.2	`FlipDog.com` job search. (Courtesy of `Flipdog.com`.)	1284
C.3	List of a job seeker's criteria.	1286
C.4	Advantage Hiring, Inc.'s Net-Interview™ service. (Courtesy of Advantage Hiring, Inc.)	1289
C.5	`eLance.com` request for proposal (RFP) example. (Courtesy of eLance, Inc.]	1292

D   Visual Studio .NET Debugger

D.1	Syntax error.	1303
D.2	Debug sample program.	1304
D.3	Debug configuration setting.	1305
D.4	Setting a breakpoint.	1305
D.5	Console application suspended for debugging.	1305
D.6	Execution suspended at a breakpoint.	1306
D.7	**Watch** window.	1307
D.8	**Autos** and **Locals** windows.	1308
D.9	**Immediate** window.	1308
D.10	**Debug** toolbar icons.	1309
D.11	**Breakpoints** window.	1310
D.12	Disabled breakpoint.	1310
D.13	**New Breakpoint** dialog.	1311
D.14	**Breakpoint Hit Count** dialog.	1311
D.15	**Breakpoint Condition** dialog.	1311
D.16	Demonstrates procedure debugging.	1312
D.17	**Call Stack** window.	1312

D.18	IDE displaying a procedures calling point.	1313
D.19	Debug program control features.	1313
D.20	Using the **Immediate** window to debug procedures.	1314
D.21	Debugging a class.	1314
D.22	Breakpoint location for class debugging.	1315
D.23	Expanded class in **Watch** window.	1316
D.24	Expanded array in **Watch** window.	1316

E ASCII Character Set

E.1	ASCII character set.	1319

F Unicode® (on CD)

F.1	Correlation between the three encoding forms.	1323
F.2	Various glyphs of the character A.	1323
F.3	Windows application demonstrating Unicode encoding.	1326
F.4	Some character ranges.	1328

G COM Integration (on CD) 1332

G.1	ActiveX control registration.	1333
G.2	**Customize Toolbox** dialog with an ActiveX control selected.	1334
G.3	IDE's toolbox and `LabelScrollbar` properties.	1335
G.4	ActiveX COM control integration in Visual Basic .NET.	1335
G.5	**Add Reference** dialog DLL Selection.	1338
G.6	COM DLL component in Visual Basic.NET.	1339

H Introduction to HyperText Markup Language 4: Part 1 (on CD)

H.1	Basic HTML file.	1347
H.2	Header elements `h1` through `h6`.	1349
H.3	Linking to other Web pages.	1350
H.4	Linking to an email address.	1351
H.5	Placing images in HTML files.	1352
H.6	Using images as link anchors.	1354
H.7	Inserting special characters into HTML.	1356
H.8	Unordered lists in HTML.	1358
H.9	Nested and ordered lists in HTML.	1359

I Introduction to HyperText Markup Language 4: Part 2 (on CD)

I.1	HTML table.	1368
I.2	Complex HTML table.	1371
I.3	Simple form with hidden fields and a text box.	1373
I.4	Form including textareas, password boxes and checkboxes.	1376
I.5	Form including radio buttons and pulldown lists.	1379
I.6	Using internal hyperlinks to make your pages more navigable.	1383
I.7	Picture with links anchored to an image map.	1386
I.8	Using `meta` to provide keywords and a description.	1388

I.9	Web site using two frames—navigation and content.	1390
I.10	Framed Web site with a nested frameset.	1393

J Introduction to XHTML: Part 1 (on CD)

J.1	First XHTML example.	1402
J.2	Validating an XHTML document. (Courtesy of World Wide Web Consortium (W3C).)	1405
J.3	XHTML validation results. (Courtesy of World Wide Web Consortium (W3C).)	1406
J.4	Header elements **h1** through **h6**.	1407
J.5	Linking to other Web pages.	1408
J.6	Linking to an e-mail address.	1410
J.7	Placing images in XHTML files.	1411
J.8	Using images as link anchors.	1413
J.9	Inserting special characters into XHTML.	1415
J.10	Unordered lists in XHTML	1417
J.11	Nested and ordered lists in XHTML.	1418

K Introduction to XHTML: Part 2 (on CD)

K.1	XHTML table.	1427
K.2	Complex XHTML table.	1430
K.3	Simple form with hidden fields and a textbox.	1433
K.4	Form with textareas, password boxes and checkboxes.	1436
K.5	Form including radio buttons and drop-down lists.	1439
K.6	Using internal hyperlinks to make pages more easily navigable.	1443
K.7	Image with links anchored to an image map.	1446
K.8	Using **meta** to provide keywords and a description.	1448
K.9	Web document containing two frames—navigation and content.	1450
K.10	XHTML document displayed in the left frame of Fig. K.9.	1453
K.11	Framed Web site with a nested frameset.	1455
K.12	XHTML table for Exercise K.7.	1460
K.13	XHTML table for Exercise K.8.	1461

L HTML/XHTML Special Characters

L.1	XHTML special characters.	1462

M HTML/XHTML Colors

M.1	HTML/XHTML standard colors and hexadecimal RGB values.	1463
M.2	XHTML extended colors and hexadecimal RGB values.	1464

N Crystal Reports® for Visual Studio .NET

N.1	Report expert choices. (Courtesy Crystal Decisions)	1467
N.2	Expert formatting menu choices. (Courtesy of Crystal Decisions)	1468
N.3	Crystal Reports designer interface. (Courtesy of Crystal Decisions)	1469

Preface

Live in fragments no longer. Only connect.
Edward Morgan Forster

We wove a web in childhood,
A web of sunny air.
Charlotte Brontë

Welcome to Visual Basic .NET and the exciting world of Windows, Internet and World-Wide-Web programming with Visual Studio and the .NET platform! This book is the first in our new *.NET How to Program* series, which presents various leading-edge computing technologies in the context of the .NET platform.

Visual Basic .NET provides the features that are most important to programmers, such as object-oriented programming, strings, graphics, graphical-user-interface (GUI) components, exception handling, multithreading, multimedia (audio, images, animation and video), file processing, prepackaged data structures, database processing, Internet and World-Wide-Web-based client/server networking and distributed computing. The language is appropriate for implementing Internet-based and World-Wide-Web-based applications that seamlessly integrate with PC-based applications. Visual Basic .NET is the next phase in the evolution of Visual Basic, the world's most popular programming language.

The .NET platform offers powerful capabilities for software development and deployment, including independence from a specific language or platform. Rather than requiring developers to learn a new programming language, programmers can contribute to the same software project, but write code using any (or several) of the .NET languages (such as Visual Basic .NET, Visual C++ .NET, C# and others) with which they are most competent. In addition to providing language independence, .NET extends program portability by enabling .NET applications to reside on, and communicate across, multiple platforms—thus facilitating the delivery of Web services over the Internet. .NET enables Web-based applications to be distributed to consumer-electronic devices, such as cell phones and personal digital assistants, as well as to desktop computers. The capabilities that Microsoft has incorporated into the .NET platform create a new software-development paradigm that will increase programmer productivity and decrease development time.

New Features in *Visual Basic .NET How to Program: Second Edition*

This edition contains many new features and enhancements, including:

- *Full-Color Presentation.* This book is now in full color. In the book's previous edition, the programs were displayed in black and the screen captures appeared in a second color. Full color enables readers to see sample outputs as they would appear on a color monitor. Also, we now syntax color the Visual Basic .NET code, similar to the way Visual Studio .NET colors the code in its editor window. Our syntax-coloring conventions are as follows:

    ```
    comments appear in green
    keywords appear in dark blue
    literal values appear in light blue
    text, class, method and variable names appear in black
    errors and ASP delimiters appear in red
    ```

- *"Code Washing."* This is our term for the process we use to format the programs in the book so that they have a carefully commented, open layout. The code appears in full color and grouped into small, well-documented pieces. This greatly improves code readability—an especially important goal for us, considering that this book contains about 21,000 lines of code.

- *Web Services and ASP .NET.* Microsoft's .NET strategy embraces the Internet and Web as integral to the software development and deployment processes. Web services, a key technology in this strategy, enables information sharing, commerce and other interactions using standard Internet protocols and technologies, such as Hypertext Transfer Protocol (HTTP), Simple Object Access Protocol (SOAP) and Extensible Markup Language (XML). Web services enable programmers to package application functionality in a form that turns the Web into a library of reusable software components. In Chapter 21, ASP .NET and Web Services, we present a Web service that allows users to make airline seat reservations. In this example, a user accesses a Web page, chooses a seating option and submits the page to the Web server. The page then calls a Web service that checks seat availability. We also present information relating to Web services in Appendix N, Crystal Reports for Visual Studio .NET, which discusses popular reporting software for database-intensive Visual Basic .NET applications. Crystal Reports, which is integrated into Visual Studio .NET, provides the ability to expose a report as a Web service. The appendix provides introductory information and then directs readers to a walkthrough of this process on the Crystal Decisions Web site (**www.crystaldecisions.com/net**).

- *Web Forms, Web Controls and ASP .NET.* Applications developers must be able to create robust, scalable Web-based applications. The .NET platform architecture supports such applications. Microsoft's .NET server-side technology, Active Server Pages (ASP) .NET, allows programmers to build Web documents that respond to client requests. To enable interactive Web pages, server-side programs process information users input into HTML forms. ASP .NET is a significant departure from previous versions of ASP, allowing developers to program Web-based applications using the powerful object-oriented languages of .NET. ASP .NET also provides enhanced visual programming capabilities, similar to those used in building Windows forms for desktop programs. Programmers can create Web pages visually, by dragging and dropping Web controls onto a Web form. Chapter 20, ASP .NET, Web Forms and Web Controls, introduces these powerful technologies.

- *Object-Oriented Programming.* Object-oriented programming is the most widely employed technique for developing robust, reusable software, and Visual Basic .NET offers enhanced object-oriented programming features. This text offers a rich presentation of object-oriented programming. Chapter 8, Object-Based Programming, introduces how to create classes and objects. These concepts are extended in Chapter 9, Object-Oriented Programming: Inheritance—which discusses how programmers can create new classes that "absorb" the capabilities of existing classes. Chapter 10, Object-Oriented Programming: Polymorphism—familiarizes the reader with the crucial concepts of polymorphism, abstract classes, concrete classes and interfaces, which facilitate powerful manipulations among objects belonging to an inheritance hierarchy.

- *XML.* Use of Extensible Markup Language (XML) is exploding in the software-development industry, the e-business and e-commerce communities, and is pervasive throughout the .NET platform. Because XML is a platform-independent technology for describing data and for creating markup languages, XML's data portability integrates well with Visual Basic .NET's portable applications and services. Chapter 18, Extensible Markup Language (XML) introduces XML. In this chapter, we introduce basic XML markup and discuss the technologies such as DTDs and Schema, which are used to validate XML documents' contents. We also explain how to programmatically manipulate XML documents using the Document Object Model (DOM™) and how to transform XML documents into other types of documents via Extensible Stylesheet Language Transformations (XSLT).

- *Multithreading.* Computers enable us to perform many tasks in parallel (or concurrently), such as printing documents, downloading files from a network and surfing the Web. Multithreading is the technology through which programmers can develop applications that perform concurrent tasks. Historically, a computer has contained a single, expensive processor, which its operating system would share among all applications. Today, processors are becoming so inexpensive that it is possible to build affordable computers containing many processors that work in parallel—such computers are called multiprocessors. Multithreading is effective on both single-processor and multiprocessor systems. Visual Basic .NET's multithreading capabilities make the platform and its related technologies better prepared to deal with today's sophisticated multimedia-intensive, database-intensive, network-based, multiprocessor-based, distributed applications. Chapter 14, Multithreading provides a detailed discussion of multithreading.

- *Visual Studio .NET Debugger.* Debuggers are programs that help programmers find and correct logic errors in program code. Visual Studio .NET contains a powerful debugging tool that allows programmers to analyze their program line-by-line as the program executes. In Appendix D, Visual Studio .NET Debugger, we

Preface   XLI

- *Appendix C, Career Opportunities.* This appendix introduces career services available on the Internet. We explore online career services from both the employer's and employee's perspectives. We list many Web sites at which you can submit applications, search for jobs and review applicants (if you are interested in hiring someone). We also review services that build recruiting pages directly into e-businesses. One of our reviewers told us that he had used the Internet as a primary tool in a recent job search, and that this appendix would have helped him expand his search dramatically.

- *Appendix F, Unicode.* As computer systems evolved worldwide, computer vendors developed numeric representations of character sets and special symbols for the local languages spoken in different countries. In some cases, different representations were developed for the same languages. Such disparate character sets hindered communication among computer systems. Visual Basic .NET supports the *Unicode Standard* (maintained by a non-profit organization called the *Unicode Consortium*), which maintains a single character set that specifies unique numeric values for characters and special symbols in most of the world's languages. This appendix discusses the standard, overviews the Unicode Consortium Web site (**www.unicode.org**) and presents a Visual Basic .NET application that displays "Welcome to Unicode!" in several languages.

- *COM (Component Object Model) Integration.* Prior to the introduction of .NET, many organizations spent tremendous amounts of time and money creating reusable software components called COM components, which include ActiveX® controls and ActiveX DLLs (dynamic link libraries) for Windows applications. Visual Basic programmers traditionally have been the largest group of COM component users. In the appendix, COM Integration, we discuss some of the tools available in Visual Studio .NET for integrating these legacy components into .NET applications. This integration allows programmers to use existing sets of COM-based controls with .NET components.

- *XHTML.* The World Wide Web Consortium (W3C) has declared HTML to be a legacy technology that will undergo no further development. HTML is being replaced by the Extensible Hypertext Markup Language (XHTML)—an XML-based technology that is rapidly becoming the standard for describing Web content. We use XHTML in Chapter 18, Extensible Markup Language (XML), and offer an introduction to the technology in Appendix J, Introduction to XHTML: Part 1, and Appendix K, Introduction to XHTML: Part 2. These appendices overview headers, images, lists, image maps and other features of this emerging markup language. (We also present a treatment of HTML in Appendices H and I, because ASP .NET, used in Chapters 20 and 21, generates HTML content).

- *Accessibility.* Currently, although the World Wide Web has become an important part of many people's lives, the medium presents many challenges to people with disabilities. Individuals with hearing and visual impairments, in particular, have difficulty accessing multimedia-rich Web sites. In an attempt to improve this situation, the World Wide Web Consortium (W3C) launched the Web Accessibility

Initiative (WAI), which provides guidelines for making Web sites accessible to people with disabilities. Chapter 24, Accessibility, describes these guidelines and highlights various products and services designed to improve the Web-browsing experiences of individuals with disabilities. For example, the chapter introduces VoiceXML and CallXML, two XML-based technologies for increasing the accessibility of Web-based content for people with visual impairments.

Some Notes to Instructors

Students Enjoy Learning a Leading-Edge Language
Dr. Harvey M. Deitel taught introductory programming courses in universities for 20 years with an emphasis on developing clearly written, well-designed programs. Much of what is taught in these courses represents the basic principles of programming, concentrating on the effective use of data types, control structures, arrays and functions. Our experience has been that students handle the material in this book in about the same way that they handle other introductory and intermediate programming courses. There is one noticeable difference, though: Students are highly motivated by the fact that they are learning a leading-edge language, Visual Basic .NET, and a leading-edge programming paradigm (object-oriented programming) that will be immediately useful to them as they enter a business world in which the Internet and the World Wide Web have a massive prominence. This increases their enthusiasm for the material—which is essential when you consider that there is much more to learn in a Visual Basic .NET course now that students must master both the base language and substantial class libraries as well. Although Visual Basic .NET is a significant departure from Visual Basic 6.0, forcing programmers to revamp their skills, programmers will be motivated to do so because of the powerful range of capabilities that Microsoft is offering in its .NET initiative.

A World of Object Orientation
When we wrote the first edition of *Visual Basic 6 How to Program*, universities were still emphasizing procedural programming. The leading-edge courses were using object-oriented C++, but these courses generally mixed a substantial amount of procedural programming with object-oriented programming—something that C++ lets programmers do. Many instructors now are emphasizing a pure object-oriented programming approach. This book—the second edition of *Visual Basic .NET How to Program* and the first text in our .NET series—takes a predominantly object-oriented approach because of the enhanced object orientation provided in Visual Basic .NET.

Focus of the Book
Our goal was clear: Produce a Visual Basic .NET textbook for introductory university-level courses in computer programming aimed at students with little or no programming experience, yet offer the depth and the rigorous treatment of theory and practice demanded by both professionals and students in traditional, upper-level programming courses. To meet these objectives, we produced a comprehensive book that patiently teaches the principles of computer programming and of the Visual Basic .NET language, including control structures, object-oriented programming, Visual Basic .NET class libraries, graphical-user-interface concepts, event-driven programming and more. After mastering the material in this book, students will be well-prepared to program in Visual Basic .NET and to employ the capabilities of the .NET platform.

Multimedia-Intensive Communications

People want to communicate. Sure, they have been communicating since the dawn of civilization, but the potential for information exchange has increased dramatically with the evolution of various technologies. Until recently, even computer communications were limited mostly to digits, alphabetic characters and special characters. The current wave of communication technology involves the distribution of multimedia—people enjoy using applications that transmit color pictures, animations, voices, audio clips and even full-motion color video over the Internet. At some point, we will insist on three-dimensional, moving-image transmission.

There have been predictions that the Internet will eventually replace radio and television as we know them today. Similarly, it is not hard to imagine newspapers, magazines and books delivered to "the palm of your hand" (or even to special eyeglasses) via wireless communications. Many newspapers and magazines already offer Web-based versions, and some of these services have spread to the wireless world. When cellular phones were first introduced, they were large and cumbersome. Today, they are small devices that fit in our pockets, and many are Internet-enabled. Given the current rate of advancement, wireless technology soon could offer enhanced streaming-video and graphics-packed services, such as video conference calls, and high-power, multi-player video games.

Teaching Approach

Visual Basic .NET How to Program, Second Edition contains a rich collection of examples, exercises and projects drawn from many fields and designed to provide students with a chance to solve interesting, real-world problems. The book concentrates on the principles of good software engineering, and stressing program clarity. We are educators who teach edge-of-the-practice topics in industry classrooms worldwide. We avoid arcane terminology and syntax specifications in favor of teaching by example. Our code examples have been tested on Windows 2000 and Windows XP. The text emphasizes good pedagogy.[1]

LIVE-CODE™ Teaching Approach

Visual Basic .NET How to Program, Second Edition is loaded with numerous LIVE-CODE™ examples. This style exemplifies the way we teach and write about programming, as well as being the focus of our multimedia *Cyber Classrooms* and Web-based training courses. Each new concept is presented in the context of a complete, working example that is immediately followed by one or more windows showing the program's input/output dialog. We call this method of teaching and writing the **LIVE-CODE™ Approach**. *We use programming languages to teach programming languages.* Reading the examples in the text is much like entering and running them on a computer.

World Wide Web Access

All of the examples for *Visual Basic .NET How to Program, Second Edition* (and our other publications) are available on the Internet as downloads from the following Web sites:

    `www.deitel.com`
    `www.prenhall.com/deitel`

---

1. We use fonts to distinguish between IDE features (such as menu names and menu items) and other elements that appear in the IDE. Our convention is to emphasize IDE features in a sans-serif bold Helvetica font (e.g., **Project** menu) and to emphasize program text in a serif bold Courier font (e.g., `Dim x As Boolean`).

Registration is quick and easy and these downloads are free. We suggest downloading all the examples, then running each program as you read the corresponding text. Making changes to the examples and immediately see the effects of those changes—a great way to learn programming. Each set of instructions assumes that the user is running Windows 2000 or Windows XP and is using Microsoft's Internet Information Services (IIS). Additional setup instructions for Web servers and other software can be found at our Web sites along with the examples. [*Note:* This is copyrighted material. Feel free to use it as you study, but you may not republish any portion of it in any form without explicit permission from Prentice Hall and the authors.]

Additionally, Visual Studio .NET, which includes Visual Basic .NET, can be purchased and downloaded from Microsoft. Three different version of Visual Studio .NET are available—Enterprise, Professional and Academic. Visit `developerstore.com/devstore/` for more details and to order. If you are a member of the Microsoft Developer Network, visit `msdn.microsoft.com/default.asp`.

Objectives

Each chapter begins with objectives that inform students of what to expect and give them an opportunity, after reading the chapter, to determine whether they have met the intended goals. The objectives serve as confidence builders and as a source of positive reinforcement.

Quotations

The chapter objectives are followed by sets of quotations. Some are humorous, some are philosophical and some offer interesting insights. We have found that students enjoy relating the quotations to the chapter material. Many of the quotations are worth a "second look" *after* you read each chapter.

Outline

The chapter outline enables students to approach the material in top-down fashion. Along with the chapter objectives, the outline helps students anticipate future topics and set a comfortable and effective learning pace.

21,300 Lines of Code in 193 Example Programs (with Program Outputs)

We present Visual Basic .NET features in the context of complete, working Visual Basic .NET programs. The programs range in size from just a few lines of code to substantial examples containing several hundred lines of code. All examples are available on the CD that accompanies the book or as downloads from our Web site, `www.deitel.com`.

689 Illustrations/Figures

An abundance of charts, line drawings and program outputs is included. The discussion of control structures, for example, features carefully drawn flowcharts. [*Note:* We do not teach flowcharting as a program-development tool, but we do use a brief, flowchart-oriented presentation to explain the precise operation of each Visual Basic .NET control structure.]

458 Programming Tips

We have included programming tips to help students focus on important aspects of program development. We highlight hundreds of these tips in the form of *Good Programming Practices, Common Programming Errors, Testing and Debugging Tips, Performance Tips, Portability Tips, Software Engineering Observations* and *Look-and-Feel Observations*.

These tips and practices represent the best the authors have gleaned from a combined seven decades of programming and teaching experience. One of our students—a mathematics major—told us that she feels this approach is like the highlighting of axioms, theorems and corollaries in mathematics books; it provides a foundation on which to build good software.

83 Good Programming Practices

Good Programming Practices *are tips that call attention to techniques that will help students produce better programs. When we teach introductory courses to nonprogrammers, we state that the "buzzword" for each course is "clarity," and we tell the students that we will highlight (in these Good Programming Practices) techniques for writing programs that are clearer, more understandable and more maintainable.*

136 Common Programming Errors

Students learning a language—especially in their first programming course—tend to make certain kinds of errors frequently. Pointing out these Common Programming Errors *reduces the likelihood that students will make the same mistakes. It also shortens long lines outside instructors' offices during office hours!*

49 Testing and Debugging Tips

When we first designed this "tip type," we thought the tips would contain suggestions strictly for exposing bugs and removing them from programs. In fact, many of the tips describe aspects of Visual Basic .NET that prevent "bugs" from getting into programs in the first place, thus simplifying the testing and debugging process.

49 Performance Tips

In our experience, teaching students to write clear and understandable programs is by far the most important goal for a first programming course. But students want to write programs that run the fastest, use the least memory, require the smallest number of keystrokes or dazzle in other ways. Students really care about performance and they want to know what they can do to "turbo charge" their programs. We have included 49 Performance Tips *that highlight opportunities for improving program performance—making programs run faster or minimizing the amount of memory that they occupy.*

14 Portability Tips

We include Portability Tips *to help students wrie portable code and to provide insights on how Visual Basic .NET achieves its high degree of portability.*

102 Software Engineering Observations

The object-oriented programming paradigm necessitates a complete rethinking of the way we build software systems. Visual Basic .NET is an effective language for achieving good software engineering. The Software Engineering Observations *highlight architectural and design issues that affect the construction of software systems, especially large-scale systems. Much of what the student learns here will be useful in upper-level courses and in industry as the student begins to work with large, complex real-world systems.*

25 Look-and-Feel Observations

We provide Look-and-Feel Observations *to highlight graphical-user-interface conventions. These observations help students design attractive, user-friendly graphical user interfaces that conform to industry norms.*

Summary (1313 Summary bullets)
Each chapter ends with additional pedagogical devices. We present a thorough, bullet-list-style summary of the chapter. On average, there are 41 summary bullets per chapter. This helps the students review and reinforce key concepts.

Terminology (2980 Terms)
We include in a *Terminology* section an alphabetized list of the important terms defined in the chapter. Again, this serves as further reinforcement. On average, there are 93 terms per chapter. Each term also appears in the index, so the student can locate terms and definitions quickly.

654 Self-Review Exercises and Answers (Count Includes Separate Parts)
Extensive self-review exercises and answers are included for self-study. These questions and answers give the student a chance to build confidence with the material and prepare for the regular exercises. Students should be encouraged to attempt all the self-review exercises and check their answers.

364 Exercises (Solutions in Instructor's Manual; Count Includes Separate Parts)
Each chapter concludes with a substantial set of exercises that involve simple recall of important terminology and concepts; writing individual Visual Basic .NET statements; writing small portions of Visual Basic .NET methods and classes; writing complete Visual Basic .NET methods, classes and applications; and writing major projects. These exercises cover a wide variety of topics, enabling instructors to tailor their courses to the unique needs of their audiences and to vary course assignments each semester. Instructors can use the exercises to form homework assignments, short quizzes and major examinations. The solutions for the exercises are included in the *Instructor's Manual* and on the disks *available only to instructors* through their Prentice-Hall representatives. [**NOTE: Please do not write to us requesting the instructor's manual. Distribution of this publication is strictly limited to college professors teaching from the book. Instructors may obtain the solutions manual from their regular Prentice Hall representatives. We regret that we cannot provide the solutions to professionals.**] Solutions to approximately half the exercises are included on the *Visual Basic .NET Multimedia Cyber Classroom, Second Edition* CD-ROM (available in April 2002 at **www.InformIT.com/cyberclassrooms**; also see the last few pages of this book or visit **www.deitel.com** for ordering instructions). Also available in April 2002 is the boxed product, *The Complete Visual Basic .NET Training Course, Second Edition*, which includes both our textbook, *Visual Basic .NET How to Program, Second Edition* and the *Visual Basic .NET Multimedia Cyber Classroom, Second Edition*. All of our *Complete Training Course* products are available at bookstores and online booksellers, including **www.InformIT.com**.

Approximately 5,400 Index Entries (with approximately 6,750 Page References)
We have included an extensive Index at the back of the book. Using this resource, students can search for any term or concept by keyword. The Index is especially useful to practicing programmers who use the book as a reference. Each of the 2,980 terms in the Terminology sections appears in the Index (along with many more index items from each chapter). Students can use the index in conjunction with the Terminology sections to ensure that they have covered the key material in each chapter.

"Double Indexing" of All Visual Basic .NET LIVE-CODE™ Examples

Visual Basic .NET How to Program, Second Edition has 193 LIVE-CODE™ examples and 364 exercises (including parts). Many of the exercises are challenging problems or projects requiring substantial effort. We have "double indexed" each of the LIVE-CODE™ examples and most of the more challenging exercises. For every Visual Basic .NET source-code program in the book, we took the file name with the `.vb` extension, such as `ChessGame.vb`, and indexed it both alphabetically (in this case, under "C") and as a subindex item under "Examples." This makes it easier to find examples using particular features.

Visual Basic .NET Multimedia Cyber Classroom, Second Edition and *The Complete Visual Basic .NET Training Course, Second Edition*

We have prepared an interactive, CD-ROM-based, software version of *Visual Basic .NET How to Program, Second Edition* called the *Visual Basic .NET Multimedia Cyber Classroom, Second Edition*. This resource is loaded with e-Learning features that are ideal for both learning and reference. The *Cyber Classroom* is packaged with the textbook at a discount in *The Complete Visual Basic .NET Training Course, Second Edition*. If you already have the book and would like to purchase the *Visual Basic .NET Multimedia Cyber Classroom, Second Edition* separately, please visit `www.InformIT.com/cyberclassrooms`. The ISBN number for the *Visual Basic .NET Multimedia Cyber Classroom, Second Edition*, is 0-13-065193-1. All Deitel™ *Cyber Classrooms* are available in CD-ROM and Web-based training formats.

The CD provides an introduction in which the authors overview the *Cyber Classroom*'s features. The textbook's 193 LIVE-CODE™ example Visual Basic .NET programs truly "come alive" in the *Cyber Classroom*. If you are viewing a program and want to execute it, you simply click the lightning-bolt icon, and the program will run. You immediately will see—and hear, when working with audio-based multimedia programs—the program's outputs. If you want to modify a program and see the effects of your changes, simply click the floppy-disk icon that causes the source code to be "lifted off" the CD and "dropped into" one of your own directories so you can edit the text, recompile the program and try out your new version. Click the audio icon, and one of the authors will discuss the program and "walk you through" the code.

The *Cyber Classroom* also provides navigational aids, including extensive hyperlinking. The *Cyber Classroom* is browser based, so it remembers sections that you have visited recently and allows you to move forward or backward among these sections. The thousands of index entries are hyperlinked to their text occurrences. Furthermore, when you key in a term using the "find" feature, the *Cyber Classroom* will locate occurrences of that term throughout the text. The Table of Contents entries are "hot," so clicking a chapter name takes you immediately to that chapter.

Students like the fact that solutions to approximately half the exercises in the book are included with the *Cyber Classroom*. Studying and running these extra programs is a great way for students to enhance their learning experience.

Students and professional users of our *Cyber Classrooms* tell us that they like the interactivity and that the *Cyber Classroom* is an effective reference due to its extensive hyperlinking and other navigational features. We received an e-mail from a person who said that he lives "in the boonies" and cannot take a live course at a university, so the *Cyber Classroom* provided an ideal solution to his educational needs.

Professors tell us that their students enjoy using the *Cyber Classroom* and spend more time on the courses and master more of the material than in textbook-only courses. For a complete list of the available and forthcoming *Cyber Classrooms* and *Complete Training Courses*, see the *Deitel™ Series* page at the beginning of this book, the product listing and ordering information at the end of this book or visit **www.deitel.com**, **www.prenhall.com/deitel** and **www.InformIT.com/deitel**.

Deitel e-Learning Initiatives

e-Books and Support for Wireless Devices
Wireless devices will play an enormous role in the future of the Internet. Given recent bandwidth enhancements and the emergence of 2.5 and 3G technologies, it is projected that, within two years, more people will access the Internet through wireless devices than through desktop computers. Deitel & Associates, Inc., is committed to wireless accessibility and has recently published *Wireless Internet & Mobile Business How to Program*. To fulfill the needs of a wide range of customers, we currently are developing our content both in traditional print formats and in newly developed electronic formats, such as e-books so that students and professors can access content virtually anytime, anywhere. Visit **www.deitel.com** for periodic updates on this initiative.

e-Matter
Deitel & Associates, Inc., is partnering with Prentice Hall's parent company, Pearson PLC, and its information technology Web site, **InformIT.com**, to launch the Deitel e-Matter series at **www.InformIT.com/deitel**. This series will provide professors, students and professionals with an additional source of information on specific programming topics. e-Matter consists of stand-alone sections taken from published texts, forthcoming texts or pieces written during the Deitel research-and-development process. Developing e-Matter based on pre-publication books allows us to offer significant amounts of the material to early adopters for use in courses. Some possible Visual Basic .NET e-Matter titles we are considering include *Object-Based Programming and Object-Oriented Programming in Visual Basic .NET*; *Graphical User Interface Programming in Visual Basic .NET*; *Multithreading in Visual Basic .NET*; *ASP .NET and Web Forms: A Visual Basic .NET View;* and *ASP .NET and Web Services: A Visual Basic .NET View*.

Course Management Systems: WebCT, Blackboard, and CourseCompass
We are working with Prentice Hall to integrate our *How to Program Series* courseware into three Course Management Systems: WebCT, Blackboard and CourseCompass. These Course Management Systems enable instructors to create, manage and use sophisticated Web-based educational programs. Course Management System features include course customization (such as posting contact information, policies, syllabi, announcements, assignments, grades, performance evaluations and progress tracking), class and student management tools, a gradebook, reporting tools, communication tools (such as chat rooms), a whiteboard, document sharing, bulletin boards and more. Instructors can use these products to communicate with their students, create online quizzes and tests from questions directly linked to the text and automatically grade and track test results. For more information about these upcoming products, visit **www.deitel.com/whatsnew.html**. For demonstrations of existing WebCT, Blackboard and CourseCompass courses, visit **cms.pren_hall.com/WebCT**,

cms.prenhall.com/Blackboard and cms.prenhall.com/CourseCompass, respectively.

Deitel and InformIT Newsletters

Deitel Column in the InformIT Newsletters
Deitel & Associates, Inc., contributes a weekly column to the popular *InformIT* newsletter, currently subscribed to by more than 800,000 IT professionals worldwide. For opt-in registration, visit www.InformIT.com.

Deitel Newsletter
Our own free, opt-in newsletter includes commentary on industry trends and developments, links to articles and resources from our published books and upcoming publications, information on future publications, product-release schedules and more. For opt-in registration, visit www.deitel.com.

The Deitel .NET Series

Deitel & Associates, Inc., is making a major commitment to .NET programming through the launch of our .NET Series. *Visual Basic .NET How to Program, Second Edition* and *C# .NET How to Program* are the first books in this new series. We intend to follow these books with *Advanced Visual Basic .NET How to Program* and *Advanced C# .NET How to Program*, which will be published in December 2002. We also plan to publish *Visual C++ .NET How to Program* in July 2002, followed by *Advanced Visual C++ .NET How to Program* in July 2003.

Advanced Visual Basic .NET How to Program

Visual Basic .NET How to Program, Second Edition covers introductory through intermediate-level Visual Basic .NET programming topics, as well as core programming fundamentals. By contrast, our upcoming textbook *Advanced Visual Basic .NET How to Program* will be geared toward experienced Visual Basic .NET developers. This new book will cover enterprise-level programming topics, including: Creating multi-tier, database intensive ASP .NET applications using ADO .NET and XML; constructing custom Windows controls; developing custom Web controls; and building Windows services. The book also will include more in-depth explanations of object-oriented programming (with the UML), ADO .NET, XML Web services, wireless programming and security. *Advanced Visual Basic .NET How to Program* will be published in December 2002.

Acknowledgments

One of the great pleasures of writing a textbook is acknowledging the efforts of many people whose names may not appear on the cover, but whose hard work, cooperation, friendship and understanding were crucial to the production of the book.

Many other people at Deitel & Associates, Inc., devoted long hours to this project.

- Matthew R. Kowalewski, a graduate of Bentley College with a degree in Accounting Informations Systems, is the Director of Wireless Development at Deitel & Associates, Inc., and served as the project manager. He assisted in the development and certification of Chapters 2–7, 13, 15 and 18–21 and Appendices D, F and H–M. He also edited the Index and managed the review process for the book.

- Jonathan Gadzik, a graduate of the Columbia University School of Engineering and Applied Science with a degree in Computer Science, co-authored Chapters 8–10, 17 and 22. He also reviewed Chapters 10–11, 18 and 23.

- Kyle Lomelí, a graduate of Oberlin College with a degree in Computer Science and a minor in East Asian Studies, co-authored Chapters 10–15, 19 and 24 and contributed to Chapter 23. He also reviewed Chapters 3–9.

- Lauren Trees, a graduate of Brown University with a degree in English, edited the entire manuscript for smoothness, clarity and effectiveness of presentation; she also co-authored the Preface, Chapter 1 and Appendix N.

- Rashmi Jayaprakash, a graduate of Boston University with a degree in Computer Science, co-authored Chapter 24 and Appendix F.

- Laura Treibick, a graduate of the University of Colorado at Boulder with a degree in Photography and Multimedia, is Director of Multimedia at Deitel & Associates, Inc. She contributed to Chapter 16 and enhanced many of the text's graphics.

- Betsy DuWaldt, a graduate of Metropolitan State College of Denver with a degree in Technical Communications and a minor in Computer Information Systems, is Editorial Director at Deitel & Associates, Inc. She co-authored the Preface, Chapter 1 and Appendix N and managed the permissions process for the book.

- Barbara Deitel applied the copy edits to the manuscript. She did this in parallel with handling her extensive financial and administrative responsibilities at Deitel & Associates, Inc., which include serving as Chief Financial Officer. [Everyone at the company works on book content.]

- Abbey Deitel, a graduate of Carnegie Mellon University's Industrial Management Program and President of Deitel & Associates, Inc., recruited 40 additional full-time employees and interns during 2001. She also leased, equipped, and furnished our second building to create the work environment from which *Visual Basic .NET How to Program, Second Edition* and our other year 2001 publications were produced. She suggested the title for the *How to Program* series, and edited this preface and several of the book's chapters.

We would also like to thank the participants in the Deitel & Associates, Inc., College Internship Program.[2]

- Andrew C. Jones, a senior in Computer Science at Harvard University, co-authored Chapters 2–7, 15, Appendix A and Appendix D and reviewed Chapters 8–

---

2. The *Deitel & Associates, Inc. College Internship Program* offers a limited number of salaried positions to Boston-area college students majoring in Computer Science, Information Technology, Marketing, Management and English. Students work at our corporate headquarters in Sudbury, Massachusetts full-time in the summers and (for those attending college in the Boston area) part-time during the academic year. We also offer full-time internship positions for students interested in taking a semester off from school to gain industry experience. Regular full-time positions are available to college graduates. For more information about this competitive program, please contact Abbey Deitel at **deitel@deitel.com** and visit our Web site, **www.deitel.com**.

13. He certified the technical integrity of Chapters 16, 19, 23, Appendices F and H–K. Andrew took the semester off to work full-time at Deitel & Associates, Inc., to gain industry experience.

- Jeffrey Hamm, a sophomore at Northeastern University in Computer Science, co-authored Chapters 16, 18, 20–21 and Appendices D and G. He also coded examples for Chapter 6.

- Su Kim, a senior at Carnegie Mellon University with a double major in Information Systems and Economics, contributed to Chapter 1 and the Preface, coded solutions for Chapters 3–14 and contributed to code examples in Chapters 3–22. Su was the project manager during the early stages of the book.

- Jeng Lee, a junior in Information Systems at Carnegie Mellon University, coded Chapters 3–13 in Visual Basic .NET Beta 1 and converted Chapter 19 from Visual Basic .NET Beta 1 to Beta 2. He researched new features in Visual Basic .NET and coded examples in Chapters 5–12 and Chapters 17–24, using Visual Basic .NET, Beta 2.

- Thiago Lucas da Silva, a sophomore at Northeastern University in Computer Science, He contributed to Chapter 18 and Appendix D. He coded examples and solutions for Chapters 4–5, 17–18, 20–22 and Appendix G and tested all the programming examples through the various beta releases and release candidates of Visual Studio .NET. He also created ancillary materials for Chapters 2–7 and 18.

- Mike Preshman, a sophomore at Northeastern University with a major in Computer Science and minors in Electrical Engineering and Math, produced code examples for Chapters 9, 21 and 22 and solutions for Chapters 9, 16 and 17. He researched URLs for the Internet and World Wide Web Resource sections, helped with the Bibliography and produced PowerPoint-slide ancillaries for Chapters 2–7, 20, 21 and 24.

- Wilson Wu, a junior in Information Systems at Carnegie Mellon University, coded chapter examples, took screen captures in Visual Studio .NET Beta 1 for Chapters 3–16 and converted code sections of Chapters 20–21 from Beta 1 to Beta 2.

- Christina Carney, a senior in Psychology and Business at Framingham State College, researched URLs for the Internet and World Wide Web Resource sections and helped with the Preface.

- Brian Foster, a sophomore at Northeastern University in Computer Science, created ancillaries for Chapters 1–19 and 22–23 and helped with the Preface and Bibliography.

- Adam Sparrow, a senior at Bentley College with a major in Computer Information Systems, created ancillaries for Chapters 1–5, 7–8, 11 and 15–16.

- Zach Bouchard, a junior at Boston College in Economics and Philosophy, contributed to the Instructor's Manual and tested code solutions for Chapter 11.

- Carlo Garcia, a graduate of Metropolitan College of Boston University in Computer Science, managed the early stages of the project. He created some of the book's initial examples using the Visual Studio .NET Technology Preview Edition and mentored other interns learning Visual Basic .NET.

We are fortunate to have been able to work on this project with the talented and dedicated team of publishing professionals at Prentice Hall. We especially appreciate the extraordinary efforts of our Computer Science editor, Petra Recter and her boss—our mentor in publishing—Marcia Horton, Editorial Director of Prentice-Hall's Engineering and Computer Science Division. Vince O'Brien did a marvelous job managing the production of the book. Sarah Burrows handled editorial responsibilities on the book's extensive ancillary package.

The *Visual Basic .NET Multimedia Cyber Classroom, Second Edition* was developed in parallel with *Visual Basic .NET How to Program, Second Edition*. We sincerely appreciate the "new media" insight, savvy and technical expertise of our electronic-media editors, Mark Taub and Karen McLean. They and project manager Mike Ruel did a wonderful job bringing the *Visual Basic .NET Multimedia Cyber Classroom, Second Edition* and *The Complete Visual Basic .NET Training Course, Second Edition* to publication.

We owe special thanks to the creativity of Tamara Newnam (`smart_art@earthlink.net`), who produced the art work for our programming-tip icons and for the cover. She created the delightful creature who shares with you the book's programming tips. Barbara Deitel, Tem Nieto and Michelle Gopen contributed the bugs' names for the front cover.

We wish to acknowledge the efforts of our reviewers and to thank Crissy Statuto of Prentice Hall, who recruited the reviewers and managed the review process. Adhering to a tight time schedule, these reviewers scrutinized the text and the programs, providing countless suggestions for improving the accuracy and completeness of the presentation. It is a privilege to have the guidance of such talented and busy professionals.

Visual Basic .NET How to Program, Second Edition reviewers:
Lars Bergstrom (Microsoft)
Christopher Brumme (Microsoft)
Alan Carter (Microsoft)
Greg Lowney (Microsoft)
Cameron McColl (Microsoft)
Tania Means (Microsoft)
Dale Michalk (Microsoft)
Eric Olson (Microsoft)
Paul Vick (Microsoft)
Jeff Welton (Microsoft)
Joan Aliprand (Unicode Consortium)
Paul Bohman (Technology Coordinator, WebAIM)
Harlan Brewer (Utah State University)
Carl Burnham (Southpoint)
Clinton Chadwick (Valtech)
Mario Chavez-Rivas (Trane Corp.)
Ram Choppa (Baker Hughes)
Douglas Bass (University of St. Thomas)
Ken Cox (Sympatico)
Anthony Fadale (State of Kansas, Accessibility Committee)
J. Mel Harris (OnLineLiveTraining.com)
Terry Hull (CEO, Enterprise Component Technologies, Inc.)
Balaji Janamanchi (Texas Tech)

Preface

Amit Kalani (MobiCast, co-author of *Inside ASP.NET* and *.NET Mobile Web Developer's Guide*)
Stan Kurkovsky (Columbus State University)
Stephen Longo (LaSalle University)
Rick McGowan (Unicode Consortium)
Michael Paciello (Founder, WebABLE)
Chris Panell (Heald College)
Kevin Parker (Idaho State College)
Bryan Plaster (Valtech)
Andre Pool (Florida Community College-Jacksonville)
T. J. Racoosin (rSolutions)
Nancy Reyes (Heald College)
Chris Ridpath (A-Prompt Project, University of Toronto)
Wally Roth (Taylor University)
Craig Shofding (CAS Training)
Bill Stutzman (Consultant)
Jutta Treviranus (A-Prompt Project, University of Toronto)
Tim Thomas (Xtreme Computing)
Mark Thomas (University of Cincinnati)
Bill Tinker (Aries Software)
Joel Weinstein (Northeastern University)

We also would like to thank our first edition reviewers:
Sean Alexander (Microsoft Corporation)
Dave Glowacki (Microsoft Corporation)
Phil Lee (Microsoft Corporation)
William Vaughn (Microsoft Corporation)
Scott Wiltamuth (Microsoft Corporation)
Mehdi Abedinejad (Softbank Marketing Services, Inc.)
David Bongiovanni (Bongiovanni Research & Technology, Inc.)
Rockford Lhotka

We would sincerely appreciate your comments, criticisms, corrections and suggestions for improving the text. Please address all correspondence to:

> `deitel@deitel.com`

We will respond promptly.

Well, that's it for now. Welcome to the exciting world of Visual Basic .NET programming. We hope you enjoy this look at leading-edge computer applications. Good luck!

Dr. Harvey M. Deitel
Paul J. Deitel
Tem R. Nieto

About the Authors

Dr. Harvey M. Deitel, CEO and Chairman of Deitel & Associates, Inc., has 40 years experience in the computing field, including extensive industry and academic experience. Dr.

Deitel earned B.S. and M.S. degrees from the Massachusetts Institute of Technology and a Ph.D. from Boston University. He worked on the pioneering virtual-memory operating-systems projects at IBM and MIT that developed techniques now widely implemented in systems such as UNIX, Linux and Windows NT. He has 20 years of college teaching experience, including earning tenure and serving as the Chairman of the Computer Science Department at Boston College before founding Deitel & Associates, Inc., with his son, Paul J. Deitel. He is the author or co-author of several dozen books and multimedia packages and is writing many more. With translations published in Japanese, Russian, Spanish, Traditional Chinese, Simplified Chinese, Korean, French, Polish, Italian and Portuguese, Dr. Deitel's texts have earned international recognition. Dr. Deitel has delivered professional seminars to major corporations and to government organizations and various branches of the military.

Paul J. Deitel, Executive Vice President and Chief Technical Officer of Deitel & Associates, Inc., is a graduate of the Massachusetts Institute of Technology's Sloan School of Management, where he studied Information Technology. Through Deitel & Associates, Inc., he has delivered Java, C, C++, Internet and World Wide Web courses to industry clients including Compaq, Sun Microsystems, White Sands Missile Range, Rogue Wave Software, Boeing, Dell, Stratus, Fidelity, Cambridge Technology Partners, Open Environment Corporation, One Wave, Hyperion Software, Lucent Technologies, Adra Systems, Entergy, CableData Systems, NASA at the Kennedy Space Center, the National Severe Storm Laboratory, IBM and many other organizations. He has lectured on C++ and Java for the Boston Chapter of the Association for Computing Machinery and has taught satellite-based Java courses through a cooperative venture of Deitel & Associates, Inc., Prentice Hall and the Technology Education Network. He and his father, Dr. Harvey M. Deitel, are the world's best-selling Computer Science textbook authors.

Tem R. Nieto, Director of Product Development of Deitel & Associates, Inc., is a graduate of the Massachusetts Institute of Technology, where he studied engineering and computing. Through Deitel & Associates, Inc., he has delivered courses for industry clients including Sun Microsystems, Compaq, EMC, Stratus, Fidelity, NASDAQ, Art Technology, Progress Software, Toys "R" Us, Operational Support Facility of the National Oceanographic and Atmospheric Administration, Jet Propulsion Laboratory, Nynex, Motorola, Federal Reserve Bank of Chicago, Banyan, Schlumberger, University of Notre Dame, NASA, various military installations and many others. He has co-authored numerous books and multimedia packages with the Deitels and has contributed to virtually every Deitel & Associates, Inc., publication.

For a complete listing of Deitel & Associates, Inc., textbooks, *Cyber Classrooms* and *Complete Training Courses*, see either the series page at the front of the book, the advertorial pages at the back of the book or our Web sites:

```
www.deitel.com
www.prenhall.com/deitel
www.InformIT.com/deitel
```

About Deitel & Associates, Inc.

Deitel & Associates, Inc., is an internationally recognized corporate training and content-creation organization specializing in Internet/World Wide Web software technology, e-business/e-commerce software technology, object technology and computer programming languages education. The company provides courses on Internet and World Wide Web/

programming, wireless Internet programming, object technology, and major programming languages and platforms, such as Visual Basic .NET, C#, Java, advanced Java, C, C++, XML, Perl, Python and more. The founders of Deitel & Associates, Inc., are Dr. Harvey M. Deitel and Paul J. Deitel. The company's clients include many of the world's largest computer companies, government agencies, branches of the military and business organizations. Through its 25-year publishing partnership with Prentice Hall, Deitel & Associates, Inc., publishes leading-edge programming textbooks, professional books, interactive CD-ROM-based multimedia *Cyber Classrooms*, *Complete Training Courses*, e-books, e-whitepapers, Web-based training courses and course management systems e-content. Deitel & Associates, Inc., and the authors can be reached via e-mail at:

`deitel@deitel.com`

To learn more about Deitel & Associates, Inc., its publications and its worldwide corporate on-site curriculum, see the last few pages of this book or visit:

`www.deitel.com`

Individuals wishing to purchase Deitel books, *Cyber Classrooms*, *Complete Training Courses* and Web-based training courses can do so through bookstores, online booksellers and through:

`www.deitel.com`
`www.prenhall.com/deitel`
`www.InformIT.com/deitel`

Bulk orders by corporations and academic institutions should be placed directly with Prentice Hall. See the last few pages of this book for worldwide ordering details.

The World Wide Web Consortium (W3C)

Deitel & Associates, Inc., is a member of the *World Wide Web Consortium (W3C)*. The W3C was founded in 1994 "to develop common protocols for the evolution of the World Wide Web." As a W3C member, Deitel & Associates, Inc., holds a seat on the W3C Advisory Committee (the company's representative is our Chief Technology Officer, Paul Deitel). Advisory Committee members help provide "strategic direction" to the W3C through meetings held around the world. Member organizations also help develop standards recommendations for Web technologies (such as XHTML, XML and many others) through participation in W3C activities and groups. Membership in the W3C is intended for companies and large organizations. To obtain information on becoming a member of the W3C visit `www.w3.org/Consortium/Prospectus/Joining`.

1

Introduction to Computers, Internet and Visual Basic .NET

Objectives

- To understand basic computer concepts.
- To learn about various programming languages.
- To appreciate the importance of object technology.
- To become familiar with the history of the Visual Basic .NET programming language.
- To learn about the evolution of the Internet and World Wide Web.
- To understand the Microsoft® .NET initiative.
- To preview the remaining chapters of the book.

Things are always at their best in their beginning.
Blaise Pascal

High thoughts must have high language.
Aristophanes

Our life is frittered away by detail…Simplify, simplify.
Henry David Thoreau

Before beginning, plan carefully….
Marcus Tullius Cicero

Look with favor upon a bold beginning.
Virgil

I think I'm beginning to learn something about it.
Auguste Renoir

Outline

1.1 Introduction
1.2 What Is a Computer?
1.3 Computer Organization
1.4 Evolution of Operating Systems
1.5 Personal Computing, Distributed Computing and Client/Server Computing
1.6 Machine Languages, Assembly Languages and High-Level Languages
1.7 Visual Basic .NET
1.8 C, C++, Java™ and C#
1.9 Other High-Level Languages
1.10 Structured Programming
1.11 Key Software Trend: Object Technology
1.12 Hardware Trends
1.13 History of the Internet and World Wide Web
1.14 World Wide Web Consortium (W3C)
1.15 Extensible Markup Language (XML)
1.16 Introduction to Microsoft .NET
1.17 .NET Framework and the Common Language Runtime
1.18 Tour of the Book
1.19 Internet and World Wide Web Resources

Summary • Terminology • Self-Review Exercises • Answers to Self-Review Exercises • Exercises

1.1 Introduction

Welcome to Visual Basic .NET! In creating this book, we have worked hard to provide students with the most accurate and complete information regarding the Visual Basic .NET language and its applications. The book is designed to be appropriate for readers at all levels, from practicing programmers to individuals with little or no programming experience. We hope that working with this text will be an informative, entertaining and challenging learning experience for you.

How can one book appeal to both novices and skilled programmers? The core of this book emphasizes the achievement of program clarity through proven techniques of *structured programming*, *object-based programming*, *object-oriented programming (OOP)* and *event-driven programming*. Nonprogrammers learn basic skills that underlie good programming; experienced developers receive a rigorous explanation of the language and may improve their programming styles. Perhaps most importantly, the book presents hundreds of complete, working Visual Basic .NET programs and depicts their outputs. We call this the *LIVE-CODE*™ *approach*. All of the book's examples are available on the CD-ROM that accompanies this book and on our Web site, **www.deitel.com**.

Computer use is increasing in almost every field of endeavor. In an era of steadily rising costs, computing costs have decreased dramatically because of rapid developments in both hardware and software technology. Computers that filled large rooms and cost millions of dollars just two decades ago now can be inscribed on the surfaces of silicon chips smaller than a fingernail, costing perhaps a few dollars each. Silicon is one of the most abundant materials on earth—it is an ingredient in common sand. Silicon-chip technology has made computing so economical that hundreds of millions of general-purpose computers are in use worldwide, helping people in business, industry, government and their personal lives. Given the current rate of technological development, this number could easily double over the next few years.

In beginning to study this text, you are starting on a challenging and rewarding educational path. As you proceed, if you would like to communicate with us, please send an e-mail to **deitel@deitel.com** or browse our World Wide Web sites at **www.deitel.com**, **www.prenhall.com/deitel** and **www.InformIT.com/deitel**. We hope that you enjoy learning Visual Basic .NET through reading *Visual Basic .NET How to Program, Second Edition*.

1.2 What Is a Computer?

A *computer* is a device capable of performing computations and making logical decisions at speeds millions and even billions of times faster than those of human beings. For example, many of today's personal computers can perform hundreds of millions—even billions—of additions per second. A person operating a desk calculator might require decades to complete the same number of calculations that a powerful personal computer can perform in one second. (*Points to ponder*: How would you know whether the person had added the numbers correctly? How would you know whether the computer had added the numbers correctly?) Today's fastest *supercomputers* can perform hundreds of billions of additions per second—about as many calculations as hundreds of thousands of people could perform in one year! Trillion-instruction-per-second computers are already functioning in research laboratories!

Computers process *data* under the control of sets of instructions called *computer programs*. These programs guide computers through orderly sets of actions that are specified by individuals known as *computer programmers*.

A computer is composed of various devices (such as the keyboard, screen, mouse, disks, memory, CD-ROM and processing units) known as *hardware*. The programs that run on a computer are referred to as *software*. Hardware costs have been declining dramatically in recent years, to the point that personal computers have become a commodity. Conversely, software-development costs have been rising steadily, as programmers develop ever more powerful and complex applications without being able to improve significantly the technology of software development. In this book, you will learn proven software-development methods that can reduce software-development costs—top-down stepwise refinement, functionalization and object-oriented programming. Object-oriented programming is widely believed to be the significant breakthrough that can greatly enhance programmer productivity.

1.3 Computer Organization

Virtually every computer, regardless of differences in physical appearance, can be envisioned as being divided into six *logical units*, or sections:

1. *Input unit.* This "receiving" section of the computer obtains information (data and computer programs) from various *input devices*. The input unit then places this information at the disposal of the other units to facilitate the processing of the information. Today, most users enter information into computers via keyboards and mouse devices. Other input devices include microphones (for speaking to the computer), scanners (for scanning images) and digital cameras (for taking photographs and making videos).

2. *Output unit.* This "shipping" section of the computer takes information that the computer has processed and places it on various *output devices,* making the information available for use outside the computer. Computers can output information in various ways, including displaying the output on screens, playing it on audio/video devices, printing it on paper or using the output to control other devices.

3. *Memory unit.* This is the rapid-access, relatively low-capacity "warehouse" section of the computer, which facilitates the temporary storage of data. The memory unit retains information that has been entered through the input unit, enabling that information to be immediately available for processing. In addition, the unit retains processed information until that information can be transmitted to output devices. Often, the memory unit is called either *memory* or *primary memory—random access memory* (*RAM*) is an example of primary memory. Primary memory is usually volatile, which means that it is erased when the machine is powered off.

4. *Arithmetic and logic unit (ALU).* The ALU is the "manufacturing" section of the computer. It is responsible for the performance of calculations such as addition, subtraction, multiplication and division. It also contains decision mechanisms, allowing the computer to perform such tasks as determining whether two items stored in memory are equal.

5. *Central processing unit (CPU).* The CPU serves as the "administrative" section of the computer. This is the computer's coordinator, responsible for supervising the operation of the other sections. The CPU alerts the input unit when information should be read into the memory unit, instructs the ALU about when to use information from the memory unit in calculations and tells the output unit when to send information from the memory unit to certain output devices.

6. *Secondary storage unit.* This unit is the long-term, high-capacity "warehousing" section of the computer. Secondary storage devices, such as hard drives and disks, normally hold programs or data that other units are not actively using; the computer then can retrieve this information when it is needed—hours, days, months or even years later. Information in secondary storage takes much longer to access than does information in primary memory. However, the price per unit of secondary storage is much less than the price per unit of primary memory. Secondary storage is usually nonvolatile—it retains information even when the computer is off.

1.4 Evolution of Operating Systems

Early computers were capable of performing only one *job* or *task* at a time. In this mode of computer operation, often called single-user *batch processing,* the computer runs one program at a time and processes data in groups called *batches.* Users of these early systems typically submitted their jobs to a computer center on decks of punched cards. Often, hours or even days elapsed before printouts were returned to the users' desks.

To make computer use more convenient, software systems called *operating systems* were developed. Early operating systems oversaw and managed computers' transitions between jobs. By minimizing the time it took for a computer operator to switch from one job to another, the operating system increased the total amount of work, or *throughput,* computers could process in a given time period.

As computers became more powerful, single-user batch processing became inefficient, because computers spent a great deal of time waiting for slow input/output devices to complete their tasks. Developers then looked to multiprogramming techniques, which enabled many tasks to *share* the resources of the computer to achieve better utilization. *Multiprogramming* involves the "simultaneous" operation of many jobs on a computer that splits its resources among those jobs. However, users of early multiprogramming operating systems still submitted jobs on decks of punched cards and waited hours or days for results.

In the 1960s, several industry and university groups pioneered *timesharing* operating systems. Timesharing is a special type of multiprogramming that allows users to access a computer through *terminals*, or devices with keyboards and screens. Dozens or even hundreds of people can use a timesharing computer system at once. It is important to note that the computer does not actually run all the users' requests simultaneously. Rather, it performs a small portion of one user's job and moves on to service the next user. However, because the computer does this so quickly, it can provide service to each user several times per second. This gives users' programs the appearance of running simultaneously. Timesharing offers major advantages over previous computing systems in that users receive prompt responses to requests, instead of waiting long periods to obtain results.

The UNIX operating system, which is now widely used for advanced computing, originated as an experimental timesharing operating system. Dennis Ritchie and Ken Thompson developed UNIX at Bell Laboratories beginning in the late 1960s and developed C as the language in which they wrote it. They created UNIX as *open-source* software, freely distributing the source code to other programmers who wanted to use, modify and extend it. A large community of UNIX users quickly developed. The operating system grew as UNIX users contributed their own programs and tools. Through a collaborative effort among numerous researchers and developers, UNIX became a powerful and flexible operating system able to handle almost any type of task that a user required. Many versions of UNIX have evolved, including today's phenomenally popular Linux operating system.

1.5 Personal Computing, Distributed Computing and Client/Server Computing

In 1977, Apple Computer popularized the phenomenon of *personal computing*. Initially, it was a hobbyist's dream. However, the price of computers soon dropped so far that large numbers of people could buy them for personal or business use. In 1981, IBM, the world's largest computer vendor, introduced the IBM Personal Computer. Personal computing rapidly became legitimate in business, industry and government organizations.

The computers first pioneered by Apple and IBM were "stand-alone" units—people did their work on their own machines and transported disks back and forth to share information. (This process was often called "sneakernet.") Although early personal computers were not powerful enough to timeshare several users, the machines could be linked together into computer networks, either over telephone lines or via *local area networks* (*LANs*) within an organization. These networks led to the phenomenon of *distributed computing*, in which an organization's computing is distributed over networks to the sites at which the work of the organization is performed, instead of the computing being performed only at a central computer installation. Personal computers were powerful enough to handle both the computing requirements of individual users, and the basic tasks involved in the electronic transfer of information between computers. *N-tier applications* split up an application over numerous computers. For example, a three-tier application might have a user interface on one computer, business-logic processing on a second and a database on a third; all three interact as the application runs.

Today's most advanced personal computers are as powerful as the million-dollar machines of just two decades ago. High-powered desktop machines—called *workstations*—provide individual users with enormous capabilities. Information is easily shared across computer networks, in which computers called *servers* store programs and data that can be used by *client* computers distributed throughout the network. This type of configuration gave rise to the term *client/server computing*. Today's popular operating systems, such as UNIX, Linux, Solaris, MacOS, Windows 2000 and Windows XP, provide the kinds of capabilities discussed in this section.

1.6 Machine Languages, Assembly Languages and High-Level Languages

Programmers write instructions in various programming languages, some of which are directly understandable by computers and others of which require intermediate *translation* steps. Although hundreds of computer languages are in use today, the diverse offerings can be divided into three general types:

1. Machine languages

2. Assembly languages

3. High-level languages

Any computer can understand only its own *machine language* directly. As the "natural language" of a particular computer, machine language is defined by the computer's hardware design. Machine languages generally consist of streams of numbers (ultimately reduced to 1s and 0s) that instruct computers how to perform their most elementary operations. Machine languages are *machine-dependent*, which means that a particular machine language can be used on only one type of computer. The following section of a machine-language program, which adds *overtime* pay to *base pay* and stores the result in *gross pay*, demonstrates the incomprehensibility of machine language to the human reader.

```
    +1300042774
    +1400593419
    +1200274027
```

As the popularity of computers increased, machine-language programming proved to be excessively slow, tedious and error prone. Instead of using the strings of numbers that computers could directly understand, programmers began using English-like abbreviations to represent the elementary operations of the computer. These abbreviations formed the basis of *assembly languages*. *Translator programs* called *assemblers* convert assembly language programs to machine language at computer speeds. The following section of an assembly-language program also adds *overtime pay* to *base pay* and stores the result in *gross pay*, but presents the steps more clearly to human readers than does its machine-language equivalent:

```
    LOAD    BASEPAY
    ADD     OVERPAY
    STORE   GROSSPAY
```

Although such code is clearer to humans, it is incomprehensible to computers until translated into machine language.

Although computer use increased rapidly with the advent of assembly languages, these languages still required many instructions to accomplish even the simplest tasks. To speed up the programming process, *high-level languages*, in which single statements accomplish substantial tasks, were developed. Translation programs called *compilers* convert high-level-language programs into machine language. High-level languages enable programmers to write instructions that look almost like everyday English and contain common mathematical notations. A payroll program written in a high-level language might contain a statement such as

```
    grossPay = basePay + overTimePay
```

Obviously, programmers prefer high-level languages to either machine languages or assembly languages. Visual Basic .NET is one of the most popular high-level programming languages in the world.

The compilation of a high-level language program into machine language can require a considerable amount of time. This problem was solved by the development of *interpreter* programs that can execute high-level language programs directly, bypassing the compilation step. Although programs already compiled execute faster than interpreted programs, interpreters are popular in program-development environments. In these environments, developers change programs frequently as they add new features and correct errors. Once a program is fully developed, a compiled version can be produced so that the program runs at maximum efficiency.

1.7 Visual Basic .NET

Visual Basic .NET evolved from BASIC (Beginner's All-Purpose Symbolic Instruction Code), developed in the mid-1960s by Professors John Kemeny and Thomas Kurtz of Dartmouth College as a language for writing simple programs. BASIC's primary purpose was to familiarize novices with programming techniques.

The widespread use of BASIC on various types of computers (sometimes called *hardware platforms*) had led to many enhancements to the language. When Bill Gates founded Microsoft Corporation, he implemented BASIC on several early personal computers. With the development of the Microsoft Windows graphical user interface (GUI) in the late 1980s and the early 1990s, the natural evolution of BASIC was Visual Basic, introduced by Microsoft in 1991.

Until Visual Basic appeared in 1991, developing Microsoft Windows-based applications was a difficult and cumbersome process. Although Visual Basic is derived from the BASIC programming language, it is a distinctly different language that offers such powerful features as graphical user interfaces, event handling, access to the *Windows 32-bit Application Programming Interface* (*Win32 API*), object-oriented programming and exception handling. Visual Basic .NET is an event-driven, visual programming language in which programs are created using an *Integrated Development Environment* (*IDE*). With the IDE, a programmer can write, run, test and debug Visual Basic programs conveniently, thereby reducing the time it takes to produce a working program to a fraction of the time it would have taken without using the IDE. The process of rapidly creating an application is typically referred to as *Rapid Application Development (RAD)*. Visual Basic is the world's most widely used RAD language.

The advancement of programming tools and consumer-electronic devices created many challenges. Integrating software components from diverse languages proved difficult, and installation problems were common because new versions of shared components were incompatible with old software. Developers also discovered they needed Web-based applications that could be accessed and used via the Internet. As programmable devices, such as *personal digital assistants* (*PDA*s) and cell phones, grew in popularity in the late 1990s, the need for these components to interact with others via the Internet rose dramatically. As a result of the popularity of mobile electronic devices, software developers realized that their clients were no longer restricted to desktop users. Developers recognized the need for software accessible to anyone from almost any type of device.

To address these needs, Microsoft announced the introduction of the Microsoft *.NET* (pronounced "dot-net") strategy in 2000. The .NET platform is one over which Web-based applications can be distributed to a variety of devices (such as cell phones) and to desktop computers. The .NET platform offers a new programming model that allows programs created in disparate programming languages to communicate with each other.

Microsoft has designed a version of Visual Basic for .NET. Earlier versions of Visual Basic did offer object-oriented capabilities, but Visual Basic .NET offers enhanced object orientation, including a powerful library of components, allowing programmers to develop applications even more quickly. Visual Basic .NET also enables enhanced language interoperability: Software components from different languages can interact as never before. Developers can package even old software to work with new Visual Basic .NET programs. Also, Visual Basic .NET applications can interact via the Internet, using industry standards such as the Simple Object Access Protocol (SOAP) and XML, which we discuss in Chapter 18, Extensible Markup Language (XML). Visual Basic .NET is crucial to Microsoft's .NET strategy, enabling existing Visual Basic developers to migrate to .NET easily. The advances embodied in .NET and Visual Basic .NET will lead to a new programming style, in which applications are created from components called *Web Services* available over the Internet.

1.8 C, C++, Java™ and C#

As high-level languages develop, new offerings build on aspects of their predecessors. C++ evolved from C, which in turn evolved from two previous languages, BCPL and B. Martin Richards developed BCPL in 1967 as a language for writing operating systems, software and compilers. Ken Thompson modeled his language, B, after BCPL. In 1970, Thompson used B to create early versions of the UNIX operating system. Both BCPL and B were "typeless" languages, meaning that every data item occupied one "word" in memory. Using these languages, programmers assumed responsibility for treating each data item as a whole number or real number.

The C language, which Dennis Ritchie evolved from B at Bell Laboratories, was originally implemented in 1973. Although C employs many of BCPL and B's important concepts, it also offers data typing and other features. C first gained widespread recognition as a development language of the UNIX operating system. However, C is now available for most computers, and many of today's major operating systems are written in C or C++. C is a hardware-independent language, and, with careful design, it is possible to write C programs that are portable to most computers.

C++, an extension of C using elements from Simula 67 (a simulation programming language) was developed by Bjarne Stroustrup in the early 1980s at Bell Laboratories. C++ provides a number of features that "spruce up" the C language, but, more importantly, it provides capabilities for *object-oriented programming (OOP)*.

At a time when demand for new and more powerful software is soaring, the ability to build software quickly, correctly and economically remains an elusive goal. However, this problem can be addressed in part through the use of *objects,* or reusable software *components* that model items in the real world (see Section 1.11). Software developers are discovering that a modular, object-oriented approach to design and implementation can make software development groups much more productive than is possible using only previous popular programming techniques, such as structured programming. Furthermore, object-oriented programs are often easier to understand, correct and modify.

In addition to C++, many other object-oriented languages have been developed. These include Smalltalk, which was created at Xerox's Palo Alto Research Center (PARC). Smalltalk is a pure object-oriented language, which means that literally everything is an object. C++ is a hybrid language—it is possible to program in a C-like style, an object-oriented style or both. Although some perceive this range of options as a benefit, most programmers today believe that it is best to program in a purely object-oriented manner.

In the early 1990s, many individuals projected that intelligent consumer-electronic devices would be the next major market in which microprocessors would have a profound impact. Recognizing this, Sun Microsystems in 1991 funded an internal corporate research project code-named Green. The project resulted in the development of a language based on C and C++. Although the language's creator, James Gosling, called it Oak (after an oak tree outside his window at Sun), it was later discovered that a computer language called Oak already existed. When a group of Sun employees visited a local coffee place, the name Java was suggested, and it stuck.

But the Green project ran into some difficulties. The marketplace for intelligent consumer-electronic devices was not developing as quickly as Sun had anticipated. Worse yet, a major contract for which Sun competed was awarded to another company. The project was, at this point, in danger of being canceled. By sheer good fortune, the World Wide Web exploded in popularity in 1993, and Sun saw immediate potential for using Java to create *dynamic content* (i.e., animated and interactive content) for Web pages.

Sun formally announced Java at a conference in May 1995. Ordinarily, an event like this would not generate much publicity. However, Java grabbed the immediate attention of the business community because of the new, widespread interest in the World Wide Web. Developers now use Java to create Web pages with dynamic content, to build large-scale enterprise applications, to enhance the functionality of World Wide Web servers (the computers that provide the content distributed to our Web browsers when we browse Web sites), to provide applications for consumer devices (e.g., cell phones, pagers and PDAs) and for many other purposes.

In 2000, Microsoft announced *C#* (pronounced "C-Sharp") and its *.NET* (pronounced "dot-net") strategy. The .NET strategy incorporates the Internet with a new programming model to create Web-based applications that users can access from various devices—including desktop computers, laptop computers and wireless devices.

The C# programming language, developed at Microsoft by Anders Hejlsberg and Scott Wiltamuth, was designed specifically for the .NET platform. It has roots in C, C++ and Java, adapting the best features of each. Like Visual Basic .NET, C#[1] is object-oriented and contains a powerful class library of prebuilt components, enabling programmers to develop applications quickly.

1.9 Other High-Level Languages

Although hundreds of high-level languages have been developed, only a few have achieved broad acceptance. This section overviews several languages that, like BASIC, are long-standing and popular high-level languages. IBM Corporation developed Fortran (FORmula TRANslator) between 1954 and 1957 to create scientific and engineering applications that require complex mathematical computations. Fortran is still widely used.

COBOL (COmmon Business Oriented Language) was developed in 1959 by a group of computer manufacturers in conjunction with government and industrial computer users. COBOL is used primarily for commercial applications that require the precise and efficient manipulation of large amounts of data. A considerable portion of today's business software is still programmed in COBOL. Approximately one million programmers are actively writing in COBOL.

Pascal was designed in the late 1960s by Professor Nicklaus Wirth and was intended for academic use. We explore Pascal in the next section.

1.10 Structured Programming

During the 1960s, many large software-development efforts encountered severe difficulties. Development typically ran behind schedule, costs greatly exceeded budgets and the finished products were unreliable. People began to realize that software development was a far more complex activity than they had imagined. Research activity, intended to address these issues, resulted in the evolution of *structured programming*—a disciplined approach to the creation of programs that are clear, demonstrably correct and easy to modify.

---

1. The reader interested in learning C# may want to consider our book, *C# How to Program.*

One of the more tangible results of this research was the development of the *Pascal* programming language in 1971. Pascal, named after the seventeenth-century mathematician and philosopher Blaise Pascal, was designed for teaching structured programming in academic environments and rapidly became the preferred introductory programming language in most universities. Unfortunately, because the language lacked many features needed to make it useful in commercial, industrial and government applications, it was not widely accepted in these environments. By contrast, C, which also arose from research on structured programming, did not have the limitations of Pascal, and programmers quickly adopted it.

The *Ada* programming language was developed under the sponsorship of the United States Department of Defense (DOD) during the 1970s and early 1980s. Hundreds of programming languages were being used to produce DOD's massive command-and-control software systems. DOD wanted a single language that would meet its needs. Pascal was chosen as a base, but the final Ada language is quite different from Pascal. The language was named after Lady Ada Lovelace, daughter of the poet Lord Byron. Lady Lovelace is generally credited with writing the world's first computer program, in the early 1800s (for the Analytical Engine mechanical computing device designed by Charles Babbage). One important capability of Ada is *multitasking*, which allows programmers to specify that many activities are to occur in parallel. As we will see in Chapter 14, Visual Basic .NET offers a similar capability, called *multithreading*.

1.11 Key Software Trend: Object Technology

One of the authors, HMD, remembers the great frustration felt in the 1960s by software-development organizations, especially those developing large-scale projects. During the summers of his undergraduate years, HMD had the privilege of working at a leading computer vendor on the teams developing time-sharing, virtual-memory operating systems. It was a great experience for a college student, but, in the summer of 1967, reality set in. The company "decommitted" from producing as a commercial product the particular system that hundreds of people had been working on for several years. It was difficult to get this software right. Software is "complex stuff."

As the benefits of structured programming (and the related disciplines of *structured systems analysis and design*) were realized in the 1970s, improved software technology did begin to appear. However, it was not until the technology of object-oriented programming became widely used in the 1980s and 1990s that software developers finally felt they had the necessary tools to improve the software-development process dramatically.

Actually, object technology dates back to at least the mid-1960s, but no broad-based programming language incorporated the technology until C++. Although not strictly an object-oriented language, C++ absorbed the capabilities of C and incorporated Simula's ability to create and manipulate objects. C++ was never intended for widespread use beyond the research laboratories at AT&T, but grass-roots support rapidly developed for the hybrid language.

What are objects, and why are they special? Object technology is a packaging scheme for creating meaningful software units. These units are large and focused on particular applications areas. There are date objects, time objects, paycheck objects, invoice objects, audio objects, video objects, file objects, record objects and so on. In fact, almost any noun can be reasonably represented as a software object. Objects have *properties* (i.e., *attributes*, such as color, size and weight) and perform *actions* (i.e., *behaviors*, such as moving, sleeping or drawing). Classes are groups of related objects. For example, all cars belong to the "car" class, even though individual cars vary in make, model, color and options packages. A class specifies the general format of its objects, and the properties and actions available to an object depend on its class.

We live in a world of objects. Just look around you—there are cars, planes, people, animals, buildings, traffic lights, elevators and so on. Before object-oriented languages appeared, *procedural programming languages* (such as Fortran, Pascal, BASIC and C) focused on actions (verbs) rather than things or objects (nouns). We live in a world of objects, but earlier programming languages forced individuals to program primarily with verbs. This paradigm shift made program writing a bit awkward. However, with the advent of popular object-oriented languages, such as C++, C# and Visual Basic .NET, programmers can program in an object-oriented manner that reflects the way in which they perceive the world. This process, which seems more natural than procedural programming, has resulted in significant productivity gains.

One of the key problems with procedural programming is that the program units created do not mirror real-world entities effectively and therefore are not particularly reusable. Programmers often write and rewrite similar software for various projects. This wastes precious time and money as people repeatedly "reinvent the wheel." With object technology, properly designed software entities (called classes) can be reused on future projects. Using libraries of reusable componentry, such as *MFC* (*Microsoft Foundation Classes*), can greatly reduce the amount of effort required to implement certain kinds of systems (as compared to the effort that would be required to reinvent these capabilities in new projects).

Some organizations report that software reusability is not, in fact, the key benefit that they garner from object-oriented programming. Rather, they indicate that object-oriented programming tends to produce software that is more understandable because it is better organized and has fewer maintenance requirements. As much as 80 percent of software costs are not associated with the original efforts to develop the software, but instead are related to the continued evolution and maintenance of that software throughout its lifetime. Object orientation allows programmers to abstract the details of software and focus on the "big picture." Rather than worrying about minutiae, the programmer can focus on the behaviors and interactions of objects. A roadmap that showed every tree, house and driveway would be difficult, if not impossible, to read—when such details are removed and only the essential information (roads) remains, the map becomes easier to understand. In the same way, a program that is divided into objects is easy to understand, modify and update because it hides much of the detail. It is clear that object-oriented programming will be the key programming methodology for at least the next decade.

Software Engineering Observation 1.1

Use a building-block approach to creating programs. By reusing existing pieces, programmers avoid reinventing the wheel. This is called software reuse, *and it is central to object-oriented programming.*

[*Note*: We will include many of these *Software Engineering Observations* throughout the text to explain concepts that affect and improve the overall architecture and quality of a software system and, particularly, of large software systems. We will also highlight *Good Programming Practices* (practices that can help you write programs that are clearer, more understandable, more maintainable and easier to test and debug), *Common Programming Errors* (problems to watch for to ensure that you do not make these same errors in your programs), *Performance Tips* (techniques that will help you write programs that run faster and use less memory), *Portability Tips* (techniques that will help you write programs that can run, with little or no modification, on a variety of computers), *Testing and Debugging Tips* (techniques that will help you remove bugs from your programs and, more importantly, write bug-free programs in the first place) and *Look-and-Feel Observations* (techniques that will help you design the "look and feel" of your graphical user interfaces for appearance and ease of use). Many of these techniques and practices are only guidelines; you will, no doubt, develop your own preferred programming style.]

The advantage of creating your own code is that you will know exactly how it works. The code will be yours to examine, modify and improve. The disadvantage is the time and effort that goes into designing, developing and testing new code.

Performance Tip 1.1

Reusing proven code components instead of writing your own versions can improve program performance, because these components normally are written to perform efficiently.

Software Engineering Observation 1.2

Extensive class libraries of reusable software components are available over the Internet and the World Wide Web; many are offered free of charge.

1.12 Hardware Trends

Every year, people generally expect to pay at least a little more for most products and services. The opposite has been the case in the computer and communications fields, especially with regard to the costs of hardware supporting these technologies. For many decades, and continuing into the foreseeable future, hardware costs have fallen rapidly, if not precipitously. Every year or two, the capacities of computers approximately double.[2] This is especially true in relation to the amount of memory that computers have for programs, the amount of secondary storage (such as disk storage) they have to hold programs and data over longer periods of time and their processor speeds—the speeds at which computers execute their programs (i.e., do their work). The same growth has occurred in the communications field, in which costs have plummeted as enormous demand for communications bandwidth has attracted tremendous competition. We know of no other fields in which technology moves so quickly and costs fall so rapidly. Such phenomenal improvement in the computing and communications fields is truly fostering the so-called "Information Revolution."

When computer use exploded in the 1960s and 1970s, many people discussed the dramatic improvements in human productivity that computing and communications would cause. However, these improvements did not materialize. Organizations were spending vast sums of capital on computers and employing them effectively, but without realizing the expected productivity gains. The invention of microprocessor chip technology and its wide deployment in the late 1970s and 1980s laid the groundwork for the productivity improvements that individuals and businesses have achieved in recent years.

---

2. This often is called *Moore's Law*.

1.13 History of the Internet and World Wide Web

In the late 1960s, one of the authors (HMD) was a graduate student at MIT. His research at MIT's Project Mac (now the Laboratory for Computer Science—the home of the World Wide Web Consortium) was funded by ARPA—the Advanced Research Projects Agency of the Department of Defense. ARPA sponsored a conference at which several dozen ARPA-funded graduate students were brought together at the University of Illinois at Urbana-Champaign to meet and share ideas. During this conference, ARPA rolled out the blueprints for networking the main computer systems of approximately a dozen ARPA-funded universities and research institutions. The computers were to be connected with communications lines operating at a then-stunning 56 Kbps (1 Kbps is equal to 1,024 bits per second), at a time when most people (of the few who had networking access) were connecting over telephone lines to computers at a rate of 110 bits per second. HMD vividly recalls the excitement at that conference. Researchers at Harvard talked about communicating with the Univac 1108 "supercomputer," which was located at the University of Utah, to handle calculations related to their computer graphics research. Many other intriguing possibilities were discussed. Academic research was about to take a giant leap forward. Shortly after this conference, ARPA proceeded to implement what quickly became called the *ARPAnet*, the grandparent of today's *Internet*.

Things worked out differently from the original plan. Although the ARPAnet did enable researchers to network their computers, its chief benefit proved to be the capability for quick and easy communication via what came to be known as *electronic mail* (*e-mail*). This is true even on today's Internet, with e-mail, instant messaging and file transfer facilitating communications among hundreds of millions of people worldwide.

The network was designed to operate without centralized control. This meant that, if a portion of the network should fail, the remaining working portions would still be able to route data packets from senders to receivers over alternative paths.

The protocol (i.e., set of rules) for communicating over the ARPAnet became known as the *Transmission Control Protocol (TCP)*. TCP ensured that messages were properly routed from sender to receiver and that those messages arrived intact.

In parallel with the early evolution of the Internet, organizations worldwide were implementing their own networks for both intra-organization (i.e., within the organization) and inter-organization (i.e., between organizations) communication. A huge variety of networking hardware and software appeared. One challenge was to enable these diverse products to communicate with each other. ARPA accomplished this by developing the *Internet Protocol* (*IP*), which created a true "network of networks," the current architecture of the Internet. The combined set of protocols is now commonly called *TCP/IP*.

Initially, use of the Internet was limited to universities and research institutions; later, the military adopted the technology. Eventually, the government decided to allow access to the Internet for commercial purposes. When this decision was made, there was resentment among the research and military communities—it was felt that response times would become poor as "the Net" became saturated with so many users.

In fact, the opposite has occurred. Businesses rapidly realized that, by making effective use of the Internet, they could refine their operations and offer new and better services to their clients. Companies started spending vast amounts of money to develop and enhance their Internet presence. This generated fierce competition among communications carriers and hardware and software suppliers to meet the increased infrastructure demand. The result is that *bandwidth* (i.e., the information-carrying capacity of communications lines) on the Internet has increased tremendously, while hardware costs have plummeted. It is widely believed that the Internet played a significant role in the economic growth that the United States and many other industrialized nations experienced over the last decade.

The *World Wide Web* allows computer users to locate and view multimedia-based documents (i.e., documents with text, graphics, animations, audios and/or videos) on almost any subject. Even though the Internet was developed more than three decades ago, the introduction of the World Wide Web (WWW) was a relatively recent event. In 1989, Tim Berners-Lee of CERN (the European Organization for Nuclear Research) began to develop a technology for sharing information via hyperlinked text documents. Basing the new language on the well-established *Standard Generalized Markup Language* (*SGML*)—a standard for business data interchange—Berners-Lee called his invention the *HyperText Markup Language* (*HTML*). He also wrote communication protocols to form the backbone of his new hypertext information system, which he referred to as the *World Wide Web*.

The Internet and the World Wide Web will surely be listed among the most important and profound creations of humankind. In the past, most computer applications ran on "stand-alone" computers (computers that were not connected to one another). Today's applications can be written to communicate among the world's hundreds of millions of computers (this is, as we will see, the thrust of Microsoft's .NET strategy). The Internet and World Wide Web merge computing and communications technologies, expediting and simplifying our work. They make information instantly and conveniently accessible to large numbers of people. They enable individuals and small businesses to achieve worldwide exposure. They are profoundly changing the way we do business and conduct our personal lives.

1.14 World Wide Web Consortium (W3C)

In October 1994, Tim Berners-Lee founded an organization, called the *World Wide Web Consortium* (*W3C*), that is devoted to developing nonproprietary, interoperable technologies for the World Wide Web. One of the W3C's primary goals is to make the Web universally accessible—regardless of disabilities, language or culture.

The W3C (`www.w3.org`) is also a standardization organization and is comprised of three *hosts*—the Massachusetts Institute of Technology (MIT), France's INRIA (Institut National de Recherche en Informatique et Automatique) and Keio University of Japan—and over 400 *members*, including Deitel & Associates, Inc. Members provide the primary financing for the W3C and help provide the strategic direction of the Consortium.

Web technologies standardized by the W3C are called *Recommendations*. Current W3C Recommendations include *Extensible HyperText Markup Language (XHTML™)*, *Cascading Style Sheets (CSS™)* and the *Extensible Markup Language (XML)*. Recommendations are not actual software products, but documents that specify the role, syntax and rules of a technology. Before becoming a W3C Recommendation, a document passes through three major phases: *Working Draft*—which, as its name implies, specifies an evolving draft; *Candidate Recommendation*—a stable version of the document that industry can begin to implement; and *Proposed Recommendation*—a Candidate Recommendation that is considered mature (i.e., has been implemented and tested over a period of time) and is ready to be considered for W3C Recommendation status. For detailed information about the W3C Recommendation track, see "6.2 The W3C Recommendation track" at

```
www.w3.org/Consortium/Process/Process-19991111/
process.html#RecsCR
```

1.15 Extensible Markup Language (XML)

As the popularity of the Web exploded, HTML's limitations became apparent. HTML's lack of *extensibility* (the ability to change or add features) frustrated developers, and its ambiguous definition allowed erroneous HTML to proliferate. In response to these problems, the W3C added limited extensibility to HTML and created a new technology for formatting HTML documents, called Cascading Style Sheets (CSS). These were, however, only temporary solutions—the need for a standardized, fully extensible and structurally strict language was apparent. As a result, XML was developed by the W3C. XML combines the power and extensibility of its parent language, Standard Generalized Markup Language (SGML), with the simplicity that the Web community demands. At the same time, the W3C began developing XML-based standards for style sheets and advanced hyperlinking. *Extensible Stylesheet Language* (*XSL*) incorporates elements of both CSS and *Document Style and Semantics Specification Language* (*DSSSL*), which is used to format SGML documents. Similarly, the *Extensible Linking Language* (*XLink*) combines ideas from *HyTime* and the *Text Encoding Initiative* (*TEI*), to provide extensible linking of resources.

Data independence, the separation of content from its presentation, is the essential characteristic of XML. Because XML documents describes data, any application conceivably can process XML documents. Recognizing this, software developers are integrating XML into their applications to improve Web functionality and interoperability. XML's flexibility and power make it perfect for the middle tier of client/server systems, which must interact with a wide variety of clients. Much of the processing that was once limited to server computers now can be performed by client computers, because XML's semantic and structural information enables it to be manipulated by any application that can process text.

This reduces server loads and network traffic, resulting in a faster, more efficient Web. XML is not limited to Web applications. Increasingly, XML is being employed in databases—the structure of an XML document enables it to be integrated easily with database applications. As applications become more Web enabled, it seems likely that XML will become the universal technology for data representation. All applications employing XML would be able to communicate, provided that they could understand each others' XML markup, or *vocabulary*.

Simple Object Access Protocol (SOAP) is a technology for the distribution of objects (marked up as XML) over the Internet. Developed primarily by Microsoft and DevelopMentor, SOAP provides a framework for expressing application semantics, encoding that data and packaging it in modules. SOAP has three parts: The *envelope*, which describes the content and intended recipient of a SOAP message; the SOAP *encoding rules*, which are XML-based; and the SOAP *Remote Procedure Call* (*RPC*) *representation* for commanding other computers to perform a task. Microsoft .NET (discussed in the next two sections) uses XML and SOAP to mark up and transfer data over the Internet. XML and SOAP are at the core of .NET—they allow software components to interoperate (i.e., communicate easily with one another). SOAP is supported by many platforms, because of its foundations in XML and *HTTP* (*HyperText Transfer Protocol*—the key communication protocol of the World Wide Web). We discuss XML in Chapter 18, Extensible Markup Language (XML) and SOAP in Chapter 21, ASP .NET and Web Services.

1.16 Introduction to Microsoft .NET

In June 2000, Microsoft announced its *.NET initiative*, a broad new vision for embracing the Internet and the Web in the development, engineering and use of software. One key aspect of the .NET strategy is its independence from a specific language or platform. Rather than forcing developers to use a single programming language, developers can create a .NET application in any .NET-compatible language. Programmers can contribute to the same software project, writing code in the .NET languages (such as Visual Basic .NET, Visual C++ .NET, C# and others) in which they are most competent. Part of the initiative includes Microsoft's *Active Server Pages (ASP) .NET* technology, which allows programmers to create applications for the Web.

The .NET architecture can exist on multiple platforms, further extending the portability of .NET programs. In addition, the .NET strategy involves a new program-development process that could change the way programs are written and executed, leading to increased productivity.

A key component of the .NET architecture is *Web services*, which are applications that can be used over the Internet. Clients and other applications can use these Web services as reusable building blocks. One example of a Web service is Dollar Rent a Car's reservation system.[3] An airline partner wanted to enable customers to make rental-car reservations from the airline's Web site. To do so, the airline needed to access Dollar's reservation system. In response, Dollar created a Web service that allowed the airline to access Dollar's database and make reservations. Web services enable the two companies to communicate over the Web, even though the airline uses UNIX systems and Dollar uses Microsoft Windows. Dollar could have created a one-time solution for that particular airline, but the company would not have been able to reuse such a customized system. By creating a Web service, Dollar can allow other airlines or hotels to use its reservation system without creating a custom program for each relationship.

The .NET strategy extends the concept of software reuse to the Internet, allowing programmers to concentrate on their specialties without having to implement every component of every application. Instead, companies can buy Web services and devote their time and energy to developing their products. The .NET strategy further extends the concept of software reuse to the Internet by allowing programmers to concentrate on their specialties without having to implement every component. Visual programming (discussed in Chapter 2) has become popular, because it enables programmers to create applications easily, using such prepackaged components as buttons, textboxes and scrollbars. Similarly, programmers can create applications using Web services for databases, security, authentication, data storage and language translation without having to know the details of those components. The Web services programming model is discussed in Chapter 21.

The .NET strategy incorporates the idea of software reuse. When companies link their products in this way, a new user experience emerges. For example, a single application could manage bill payments, tax refunds, loans and investments, using Web services from various companies. An online merchant could buy Web services for online credit-card payments, user authentication, network security and inventory databases to create an e-commerce Web site.

---

3. Microsoft Corporation, "Dollar Rent A Car E-Commerce Case Study on Microsoft Business," 1 July 2001 <www.microsoft.com/BUSINESS/casestudies/b2c/dollarrentacar.asp>.

The keys to this interaction are XML and SOAP, which enable Web services to communicate. XML gives meaning to data, and SOAP is the protocol that allows Web services to communicate easily with one another. XML and SOAP act as the "glue" that combines various Web services to form applications.

Universal data access is another essential concept in the .NET strategy. If two copies of a file exist (such as on a personal computer and a company computer), the less recent version must constantly be updated—this is called file *synchronization*. If the separate versions of the file are different, they are *unsynchronized*, a situation that could lead to serious errors. Under .NET, data could reside in one central location rather than on separate systems. Any Internet-connected device could access the data (under tight control, of course), which would then be formatted appropriately for use or display on the accessing device. Thus, the same document could be seen and edited on a desktop PC, a PDA, a cell phone or other device. Users would not need to synchronize the information, because it would be fully up-to-date in a central area.

Microsoft's *HailStorm Web services* facilitate such data organization.[4] HailStorm allows users to store data so that it is accessible from any HailStorm-compatible device (such as a PDA, desktop computer or cell phone). HailStorm offers a suite of services, such as an address book, e-mail, document storage, calendars and a digital wallet. Third-party Web services also can interact with HailStorm—users can be notified when they win online auctions or have their calendars updated if their planes arrive late. Information can be accessed from anywhere and cannot become unsynchronized. Privacy concerns, however, increase, because all of a user's data resides in one location. Microsoft has addressed this issue by giving users control over their data. Users must authorize access to their data and specify the duration of that access.

Microsoft plans to create Internet-based client applications. For example, software could be distributed over the Internet on a *subscription basis*, enabling immediate corrections, updates and communication with other applications over the Internet. HailStorm provides basic services at no charge and users can pay via subscription for more advanced features.

The .NET strategy is an immense undertaking. We discuss various aspects of .NET throughout this book. Additional information is available on Microsoft's Web site (**www.microsoft.com/net**).

1.17 .NET Framework and the Common Language Runtime

The Microsoft *.NET Framework* is at the heart of the .NET strategy. This framework manages and executes applications and Web services, contains a class library (called the *Framework class library* or *FCL*), enforces security and provides many other programming capabilities. The details of the .NET Framework are found in the *Common Language Specification* (*CLS*), which contains information about the storage of data types, objects and so on. The CLS has been submitted for standardization to ECMA (the European Computer Manufacturers Association), making it easier to create the .NET Framework for other platforms. This is like publishing the blueprints of the framework—anyone can build it, following the specifications. Currently, the .NET Framework exists only for the Microsoft Windows platform, although a version is under development for the FreeBSD operating

---

4. Microsoft Corporation, "Building User-Centric Experiences: An Introduction to Microsoft Hail-Storm," 30 July 2001 <**http://www.microsoft.com/net/hailstorm.asp**>.

system.[5] The FreeBSD project provides a freely available and open-source UNIX-like operating system that is based on that UC Berkeley's *Berkeley System Distribution* (BSD).

The *Common Language Runtime (CLR)* is another central part of the .NET Framework—it executes Visual Basic .NET programs. Programs are compiled into machine-specific instructions in two steps. First, the program is compiled into *Microsoft Intermediate Language (MSIL)*, which defines instructions for the CLR. Code converted into MSIL from other languages and sources can be woven together by the CLR. Then, another compiler in the CLR translates the MSIL into machine code (for a particular platform), creating a single application.

Why bother having the extra step of converting from Visual Basic .NET to MSIL, instead of compiling directly into machine language? The key reasons are portability between operating systems, interoperability between languages and execution-management features such as memory management and security.

If the .NET Framework exists (and is installed) for a platform, that platform can run any .NET program. The ability of a program to run (without modification) across multiple platforms is known as *platform independence*. Code written once can be used on another machine without modification, saving both time and money. In addition, software can target a wider audience—previously, companies had to decide whether converting their programs to different platforms (sometimes called *porting*) was worth the cost. With .NET, porting is no longer an issue.

The .NET Framework also provides a high level of *language interoperability*. Programs written in different languages are all compiled into MSIL—the different parts can be combined to create a single, unified program. MSIL allows the .NET Framework to be *language independent*, because .NET programs are not tied to a particular programming language. Any language that can be compiled into MSIL is called a *.NET-compliant language*. Figure 1.1 lists many of the current languages that support the .NET platform.[6]

Programming Languages	
APL	Oberon
C#	Oz
COBOL	Pascal
Component Pascal	Perl
Curriculum	Python
Eiffel	RPG
Fortran	Scheme
Haskell	Smalltalk
J#	Standard ML

Fig. 1.1 .NET Languages (part 1 of 2).

---

5. Microsoft Corporation, "The Microsoft Shared Source C# and CLI Specifications," 30 July 2001 `<http://www.microsoft.com/net/sharedsourcewp.asp>`.
6. Table information from Microsoft Web site, **www.microsoft.com**.

Programming Languages (Cont.)	
JScript	Visual Basic .NET
Mercury	Visual C++ .NET

Fig. 1.1   .NET Languages (part 2 of 2).

Language interoperability offers many benefits to software companies. Visual Basic .NET, C# and Visual C++ .NET developers can work side-by-side on the same project without having to learn another programming language—all their code compiles into MSIL and links together to form one program. In addition, the .NET Framework can package old and new components to work together. This allows companies to reuse the code that they have spent years developing and integrate it with the new .NET code that they write. Integration is crucial, because companies cannot migrate easily to .NET unless they can stay productive, using their existing developers and software.

Another benefit of the .NET Framework is the CLR's execution-management features. The CLR manages memory, security and other features, relieving the programmer of these responsibilities. With languages like C++, programmers must take memory management into their own hands. This leads to problems if programmers request memory and never return it—programs could consume all available memory, which would prevent applications from running. By managing the program's memory, the .NET Framework allows programmers to concentrate on program logic.

The .NET Framework also provides programmers with a huge library of classes. This library, called the *Framework Class Library (FCL)*, can be used by any .NET language. The FCL contains a variety of reusable components, saving programmers the trouble of creating new components. This book explains how to develop .NET software with Visual Basic .NET. Steve Ballmer, Microsoft's CEO, stated in May 2001 that Microsoft was "betting the company" on .NET. Such a dramatic commitment surely indicates a bright future for Visual Basic .NET and its community of developers.

1.18 Tour of the Book

In this section, we tour the chapters of *Visual Basic .NET How to Program, Second Edition*. In addition to the topics presented in each chapter, several of the chapters contain an Internet and World Wide Web Resources section that lists additional sources from which readers can enhance their knowledge of Visual Basic .NET programming.

Chapter 1—Introduction to Computers, Internet and Visual Basic .NET
The first chapter familiarizes the reader with what computers are, how they work and how they are programmed. We explain the evolution of programming languages, from their origins in machine languages to the development of high-level, object-oriented languages. We overview the history of the Internet, World Wide Web and various technologies (such as HTTP, SOAP and XML) that have led to advances in how computers are used. We then discuss the development of the Visual Basic .NET programming language and the Microsoft .NET initiative, including Web services. We explore the impact of .NET on software development and conclude by touring the remainder of the book.

Chapter 2—Introduction to the Visual Studio® .NET IDE

Chapter 2 introduces Microsoft Visual Studio .NET, an *integrated development environment* (*IDE*) for creating Visual Basic .NET programs. Visual Studio .NET enables *visual programming*, in which *controls* (such as buttons or text boxes) are "dragged" and "dropped" into place, rather than added by typing code. Visual programming has led to greatly increased productivity of software developers because it eliminates many of the tedious tasks that programmers face. For example, object properties (information such as height and color) can be modified through Visual Studio .NET windows, allowing changes to be made quickly and causing the results to appear immediately on the screen. Rather than having to guess how the GUI will appear while writing a program, programmers view the GUI exactly as it will appear when the finished program runs. Visual Studio .NET also contains advanced tools for debugging, documenting and writing code. The chapter presents features of Visual Studio .NET, including its key windows, toolbox and help features and overviews the process of running programs. We provide an example of the capabilities of Visual Studio .NET by using it to create a simple Windows application without typing a single line of code.

Chapter 3—Introduction to Visual Basic Programming

This chapter introduces readers to our LIVE-CODE™ approach. We try to present every concept in the context of a complete working Visual Basic .NET program and follow each program with one or more screenshots depicting the program's execution. In our first example, we print a line of text and carefully discuss each line of code. We then discuss fundamental tasks, such as how a program inputs data from its users and how to write arithmetic expressions. The chapter's last example demonstrates how to print a variety of character strings in a window called a message box.

Chapter 4—Control Structures: Part 1

This chapter formally introduces the principles of structured programming, a technique that will help the reader develop clear, understandable, maintainable programs throughout the text. The first part of this chapter presents program-development and problem-solving techniques. The chapter demonstrates how to transform a written specification into a program by using such techniques as *pseudocode* and *top-down, stepwise refinement*. We then progress through the entire process, from developing a problem statement into a working Visual Basic .NET program. The notion of algorithms is also discussed. We build on information presented in the previous chapter to create interactive programs (i.e., programs that receive inputs from, and display outputs to, the program users). The chapter then introduces the use of control structures that affect the sequence in which statements are executed. Proper use of control structures helps produce programs that are easily understood, debugged and maintained. We discuss the three forms of program control—sequence, selection and repetition—focusing on the `If/Then` and `While` control structures. Flowcharts (i.e., graphical representations of algorithms) appear throughout the chapter, reinforcing and augmenting the explanations.

Chapter 5—Control Structures: Part 2

Chapter 5 introduces additional control structures and the logical operators. It uses flowcharts to illustrate the flow of control through each control structure, including the `For/Next`, `Do/Loop While` and `Select Case` structures. We explain the `Exit` keyword and the logical operators. Examples include calculating compound interest and printing the distribution of grades on an exam (with some simple error checking). The chapter concludes with a structured programming summary, including each of Visual Basic .NET's control structures. The techniques discussed in Chapters 4 and 5 constitute a large part of what has been taught traditionally under the topic of structured programming.

Chapter 6—Procedures
A *procedure* allows the programmer to create a block of code that can be called from various points in a program. A program can be formed by aggregating groups of related procedures into units called classes and modules. Programs are divided into simple components that interact in straightforward ways. We discuss how to create our own procedures that can take inputs, perform calculations and return outputs. We examine the .NET library's **Math** class, which contains methods (i.e., procedures in a class) for performing complex calculations (e.g., trigonometric and logarithmic calculations). *Recursive* procedures (procedures that call themselves) and procedure overloading, which allows multiple procedures to have the same name, are introduced. We demonstrate overloading by creating two **Square** procedures that take an integer (i.e., whole number) and a floating-point number (i.e., a number with a decimal point), respectively. To conclude the chapter, we create a graphical simulation of the dice game "craps," using the random-number generation techniques presented in the chapter.

Chapter 7—Arrays
Chapter 7 discusses our first data structures, arrays. (Chapter 24 discusses the topic of data structures in depth.) Data structures are crucial to storing, sorting, searching and manipulating large amounts of information. *Arrays* are groups of related data items that allow the programmer to access any element directly. Rather than creating 100 separate variables that are all related in some way, the programmer instead can create an array of 100 elements and access these elements by their location in the array. We discuss how to declare and allocate arrays, and we build on the techniques of the previous chapter by passing arrays to procedures. In addition, we discuss how to pass a variable number of arguments to procedures. Chapters 4 and 5 provide essential background for the discussion of arrays, because repetition structures are used to iterate through elements in the array. The combination of these concepts helps the reader create highly-structured and well-organized programs. We then demonstrate how to sort and search arrays. We discuss multidimensional and jagged arrays, which can be used to store tables of data.

Chapter 8—Object-Based Programming
Chapter 8 serves as our introduction into the powerful concepts of objects and *classes* (classes are programmer-defined types). As mentioned in Chapter 1, object technology has led to considerable improvements in software development, allowing programmers to create reusable components. In addition, objects allow programs to be organized in natural and intuitive ways. In this chapter, we present the fundamentals of object-based programming, such as encapsulation, data abstraction and abstract data types (ADTs). These techniques hide the details of components so that the programmer can concentrate on the "big picture." To demonstrate these concepts, we create a time class, which displays the time in standard and military formats. Other topics examined include abstraction, composition, reusability and inheritance. We overview how to create reusable software components with assemblies, modules and Dynamic Link Library (DLL) files. We show how to create classes like

those in the Framework Class Library. Other Visual Basic .NET features discussed include properties and the **ReadOnly** and **Const** keywords. This chapter lays the groundwork for the next two chapters, which introduce object-oriented programming.

Chapter 9—Object-Oriented Programming: Inheritance
In this chapter, we discuss inheritance—a form of software reusability in which classes (called *derived classes*) are created by absorbing attributes and methods of existing classes (called *base classes*). The inherited class (i.e., the derived class) can contain additional attributes and methods. We show how finding the commonality between classes of objects can reduce the amount of work it takes to build large software systems. These proven techniques help programmers create and maintain software systems. A detailed case study demonstrates software reuse and good programming techniques by finding the commonality among a three-level inheritance hierarchy: the point, circle and cylinder classes. We discuss the software engineering benefits of object-oriented programming. We present important object-oriented programming fundamentals, such as creating and extending customized classes and separating a program into discrete components.

Chapter 10—Object-Oriented Programming: Polymorphism
Chapter 10 continues our formal introduction of object-oriented programming. We discuss polymorphic programming and its advantages. *Polymorphism* permits classes to be treated in a general manner, allowing the same method call to act differently depending on context (e.g., "move" messages sent to a bird and a fish result in dramatically different types of action—a bird flies and a fish swims). In addition to treating existing classes in a general manner, polymorphism allows new classes to be added to a system easily. We identify situations in which polymorphism is useful. A payroll system case study demonstrates polymorphism—the system determines the wages for each employee differently to suit the type of employee (bosses who are paid fixed salaries, hourly workers paid by the hour, commission workers who receive a base salary plus commission and piece workers who are paid per item produced). These programming techniques and those of the previous chapter allow the programmer to create extensible and reusable software components.

Chapter 11—Exception Handling
Exception handling is one of the most important topics in Visual Basic .NET from the standpoint of building mission-critical and business-critical applications. People can enter incorrect data, data can be corrupted and clients can try to access records that do not exist or are restricted. A simple division-by-zero error may cause a calculator program to crash, but what if such an error occurs in the navigation system of a flying airplane? Programmers must deal with these situations—in some cases, the results of program failure could be disastrous. Programmers need to know how to recognize the errors (*exceptions*) that could occur in software components and handle those exceptions effectively, allowing programs to deal with problems and continue executing instead of "crashing." This chapter overviews the proper use of exception handling and various exception-handling techniques. We cover the details of Visual Basic .NET exception handling, the termination model of exception handling, throwing and catching exceptions, and the library class **Exception**. Programmers who construct software systems from reusable components built by other programmers must deal with the exceptions that those components may throw.

Chapter 12—Graphical User Interface Concepts: Part 1

Chapter 12 explains how to add graphical user interfaces (GUIs) to programs, providing a professional look and feel. By using the techniques of rapid application development (RAD), we can create a GUI from reusable components, rather than explicitly programming every detail. The Visual Studio .NET IDE makes developing GUIs even easier by allowing the programmer to position components in a window through so-called visual programming. We discuss how to construct user interfaces with *Windows Forms* GUI components such as labels, buttons, textboxes, scroll bars and picture boxes. We also introduce *events*, which are messages sent by a program to signal to an object or a set of objects that an action has occurred. Events are most commonly used to signal user interactions with GUI components, but also can signal internal actions in a program. We overview event handling and discuss how to handle events specific to controls, the keyboard and the mouse. Tips are included throughout the chapter to help the programmer create visually appealing, well-organized and consistent GUIs.

Chapter 13—Graphical User Interface Concepts: Part 2

Chapter 13 introduces more complex GUI components, including menus, link labels, panels, list boxes, combo boxes and tab controls. In a challenging exercise, readers create an application that displays a drive's directory structure in a tree—similar to how Windows Explorer does this. The *Multiple Document Interface (MDI)* is presented, which allows multiple documents (i.e., forms) to be open simultaneously in a single GUI. We conclude with a discussion of how to create custom controls by combining existing controls. The techniques presented in this chapter allow readers to create sophisticated and well-organized GUIs, adding style and usability to their applications.

Chapter 14—Multithreading

We have come to expect much from our applications. We want to download files from the Internet, listen to music, print documents and browse the Web—all at the same time! To do this, we need a technique called *multithreading*, which allows applications to perform multiple activities concurrently. Visual Basic .NET includes built-in capabilities to enable multithreaded applications, while shielding programmers from complex details. Visual Basic .NET is better equipped to deal with more sophisticated multimedia, network-based and multiprocessor-based applications than other languages that do not have multithreading features. This chapter overviews the built-in threading classes of Visual Basic .NET and covers threads, thread life-cycles, time-slicing, scheduling and priorities. We analyze the producer-consumer relationship, thread synchronization and circular buffers. This chapter lays the foundation for creating the impressive multithreaded programs that clients demand.

Chapter 15—Strings, Characters and Regular Expressions

In this chapter, we discuss the processing of words, sentences, characters and groups of characters. In Visual Basic .NET, `String`s (groups of characters) are objects. This is yet another benefit of Visual Basic .NET's emphasis on object-oriented programming. `String` objects contain methods that can copy, create hash codes, search, extract sub-`String`s and concatenate `String`s with one another. As an interesting example of `String`s, we create a card shuffling-and-dealing simulation. We discuss regular expressions, a powerful tool for searching and manipulating text.

Chapter 16—Graphics and Multimedia

In this chapter, we discuss *GDI+* (an extension of the *Graphics Device Interface—GDI*), the Windows service that provides the graphical features used by .NET. The extensive graphical capabilities of GDI+ can make programs more visual and fun to create and use. We discuss Visual Basic .NET's treatment of graphics objects and color control, and we discuss how to draw arcs, polygons and other shapes. We use various pens and brushes to create color effects and include an example demonstrating gradient fills and textures. This chapter introduces techniques for turning text-only applications into exciting, aesthetically pleasing programs that even novice programmers can write with ease. The second half of the chapter focuses on audio, video and speech technology. We discuss adding sound, video and animated characters to programs (primarily using existing audio and video clips). You will see how easy it is to incorporate multimedia into Visual Basic .NET applications. This chapter introduces an exciting technology called *Microsoft Agent* for adding *interactive animated characters* to a program. Each character allows users to interact with the application, using natural human communication techniques, such as speech. The agent characters accept mouse and keyboard interaction, speak and hear (i.e., they support speech synthesis and speech recognition). With these capabilities, your applications can speak to users and can even respond to their voice commands!

Chapter 17—Files and Streams

Imagine a program that could not save data to a file. Once the program is closed, all the work performed in the program is lost forever. For this reason, this chapter is one of the most important for programmers who will be developing commercial applications. We explain how to input and output streams of data from and to files, respectively. We present how programs read and write data from and to secondary storage devices (such as disks). A detailed example demonstrates these concepts by allowing the user to read and write bank account information to and from files. We introduce those classes and methods in Visual Basic .NET that help perform file input and output conveniently—they demonstrate the power of object-oriented programming and reusable classes. We discuss benefits of sequential files, random-access files and buffering. This chapter is crucial for developing Visual Basic .NET file-processing applications and networking applications, which also use the techniques in this chapter to send and receive data.

Chapter 18—Extensible Markup Language (XML)[7]

The Extensible Markup Language (XML) derives from SGML (Standardized General Markup Language), which became an industry standard in 1986. Although SGML is employed in publishing applications worldwide, it has not been incorporated into mainstream computing and information technology curricula because of its sheer size and complexity. XML is an effort to make SGML-like technology available to a much broader community. It was created by the World Wide Web Consortium (W3C) for describing data in a portable format, is one of most important technologies in industry today and is being integrated into almost every field. XML differs in concept from markup languages such as the HyperText Markup Language (HTML). HTML is a markup language for describing how information is rendered in a browser. XML is a language for creating markup languages for virtually any

---

7. The reader interested in a deeper treatment of XML may want to consider our book, *XML How to Program.*

type of information. Document authors use XML to create entirely new markup languages to describe specific types of data, including mathematical formulas, chemical molecular structures, music and recipes. Markup languages created with XML include WML (Wireless Markup Language), XHTML (Extensible HyperText Markup Language, for Web content), MathML (for mathematics), VoiceXML™ (for speech), SMIL™ (Synchronized Multimedia Integration Language, for multimedia presentations), CML (Chemical Markup Language, for chemistry) and XBRL (Extensible Business Reporting Language, for financial data exchange). Companies and individuals constantly are finding new and exciting uses for XML. In this chapter, we present examples that illustrate the basics of marking up data with XML. We demonstrate several XML-derived markup languages, such as *XML Schema* (for checking an XML document's grammar), *XSLT (Extensible Stylesheet Language Transformations*, for transforming an XML document's data into an XHTML document) and Microsoft's *BizTalk*™ (for marking up business transactions). (For readers who are unfamiliar with XHTML, we provide Appendices J and K, which carefully introduce XHTML.)

Chapter 19—Database, SQL and ADO .NET

Access and storage of data are integral to creating powerful software applications. This chapter discusses .NET support for database manipulation. Today's most popular database systems are relational databases. In this chapter, we introduce the Structured Query Language (SQL) for performing queries on relational databases. We introduce ADO .NET—an extension of Microsoft's ActiveX Data Objects that enables .NET applications to access and manipulate databases. ADO .NET allows data to be "exported" as XML, which enables applications that use ADO .NET to communicate with a variety of programs that understand XML. The reader will learn how to create database connections, using tools provided in Visual Studio .NET, and will learn how to use the classes in the `System.Data` namespace.

Chapter 20—ASP .NET, Web Forms and Web Controls

Previous chapters demonstrated how to create applications that execute locally on the user's computer. In this chapter and the next, we discuss how to create Web-based applications using *Active Server Pages (ASP) .NET*. This is a crucial aspect of .NET and Microsoft's vision of how software should be deployed on the Internet. ASP .NET is an integral technology for creating dynamic Web content marked up as HTML. (For readers who are unfamiliar with HTML, we provide Appendices H and I, which carefully introduce HTML). *Web Forms* provide GUIs for ASP .NET pages and can contain *Web controls*, such as labels, buttons and text boxes with which users interact. Like Windows Forms, Web Forms are designed using visual programming. This chapter presents many interesting examples, which include an online guest book application and a multi-tier, database intensive application that allows users to query a database for a list of publications by a specific author. Debugging Web Forms using the `Trace` property is also discussed.

Chapter 21—ASP .NET and Web Services

Chapter 21 continues our discussion of ASP .NET. In this chapter, we introduce *Web services*, which are programs that "expose" services (i.e., methods) to clients. Using Web Services, programmers can create methods that are accessible over the Internet. This functionality allows applications residing on a local computer to invoke methods that reside on other servers. Web services offer increased software reusability, making the Internet, in essence, a programming library available to programmers worldwide. Web services use XML and SOAP to mark up and send information, respectively. This chapter presents several examples that include Web services for manipulating huge numbers (up to 100 digits), simulating the card game of blackjack and implementing a simple airline reservation system. One particularly interesting example is our temperature server, a Web service that gathers weather information for dozens of cities in the United States.

Chapter 22—Networking: Streams-Based Sockets and Datagrams
Chapter 22 introduces the fundamental techniques of Visual Basic .NET-based networking—streams and datagrams. We demonstrate how using *sockets* allows us to hide many networking details—we can program as if we were reading from and writing to a file. One example in this chapter demonstrates using streams-based sockets to communicate between two Visual Basic .NET programs. In another example (an interactive tic-tac-toe game), a server is created that exchanges packets of data with multiple clients. Several of these networking programs use multithreading (discussed in Chapter 14).

Chapter 23—Data Structures and Collections
This chapter discusses arranging data into aggregations—called collections—such as linked lists, stacks, queues and trees. Each data structure has important properties that are useful in a wide variety of applications, from sorting elements to keeping track of method calls. We discuss how to build each of these data structures. The examples provide particularly valuable experiences in crafting useful classes. In addition, we cover prebuilt collection classes in the .NET Framework Class Library. These data structures have many useful methods for sorting, inserting, and deleting items, plus methods to enable data structures to resize themselves dynamically. When possible, Visual Basic .NET programmers should search the Framework Class Library to reuse existing data structures, rather than implementing these data structures themselves. This chapter reinforces much of the object technology discussed in Chapters 8, 9 and 10, including classes, inheritance and composition.

Chapter 24—Accessibility
The World Wide Web presents a challenge to individuals with disabilities. Multimedia-rich Web sites are difficult for text readers and other programs to interpret; thus, users with hearing and visual impairments have difficulty browsing such sites. To rectify this situation, the World Wide Web Consortium (W3C) launched the *Web Accessibility Initiative (WAI)*, which provides guidelines for making Web sites accessible to people with disabilities. This chapter provides a description of these guidelines, such as the use of the **`<headers>`** tag to make tables more accessible to page readers, the **`alt`** attribute of the **`<img>`** tag to describe images, and XHTML and CSS to ensure that a page can be viewed on almost any type of display or reader. We illustrate key accessibility features of Visual Studio .NET and of Windows 2000. We also introduce *VoiceXML* and *CallXML*, two technologies for increasing the accessibility of Web content. VoiceXML helps people with visual impairments to access Web content via speech synthesis and speech recognition. CallXML allows users with visual impairments to access Web-based content through a telephone. In the chapter exercises, readers create their own voice mail applications, using CallXML.

Appendix A—Operator Precedence Chart
This appendix lists Visual Basic .NET operators and their precedence.

Appendix B—Number Systems
This appendix explains the binary, octal, decimal and hexadecimal number systems. It also reviews the conversion of numbers among these bases and illustrates mathematical operations in each base.

Appendix C—Career Opportunities
This appendix provides career resources for Visual Basic .NET programmers.

Appendix D—Visual Studio .NET Debugger
This appendix introduces the Visual Studio .NET debugger for locating logic errors in programs. Key features of this appendix include setting breakpoints, stepping through programs line-by-line and "watching" variable values.

Appendix E—ASCII Character Set
This appendix contains a table of the 128 alphanumeric symbols and their corresponding ASCII (American Standard Code for Information Interchange) numbers.

Appendix F—Unicode®
This appendix introduces the Unicode Standard, an encoding scheme that assigns unique numeric values to the characters of most of the world's languages. We include a Windows application that uses Unicode encoding to print welcome messages in several different languages.

Appendix G—COM Integration
Prior to .NET, COM (Component Object Model) was critical for specifying how different Windows programming languages communicate at the binary level. For example, COM components such as ActiveX controls and ActiveX DLLs often were written in Microsoft Visual C++, but used in Visual Basic programs. The .NET platform does not directly support COM components, but Microsoft provides tools for the integration of COM components with .NET applications. In this appendix, we explore some of these tools by integrating an ActiveX control and an ActiveX DLL into Visual Basic .NET applications.

Appendices H and I—Introduction to HyperText Markup Language 4: 1 & 2 (on CD)
These appendices provide an introduction to *HTML*—the *Hypertext Markup Language*. HTML is a *markup language* for describing the elements of an HTML document (Web page) so that a browser, such as Microsoft's Internet Explorer, can render (i.e., display) that page. These appendices are included for our readers who do not know HTML or who would like a review of HTML before studying Chapter 20, ASP .NET, Web Forms and Web Controls. We do not present any Visual Basic .NET programming in these appendices. Some key topics covered in Appendix H include: incorporating text and images in an HTML document, linking to other HTML documents on the Web, incorporating special characters (such as copyright and trademark symbols) into an HTML document and separating parts of an HTML document with horizontal lines (called *horizontal rules*). In Appendix I, we discuss more substantial HTML elements and features. We demonstrate how to present information in *lists* and *tables*. We discuss how to collect information from people browsing a site. We explain how to use *internal linking* and *image maps* to make Web pages easier to navigate. We also discuss how to use *frames* to display multiple documents in the browser window.

Appendices J and K—Introduction to XHTML: Parts 1 & 2 (on CD)
In these appendices, we introduce the Extensible Hypertext Markup Language (XHTML). XHTML is a W3C technology designed to replace HTML as the primary means of describing Web content. As an XML-based language, XHTML is more robust and extensible than HTML. XHTML incorporates most of HTML 4's elements and attributes—the focus of these appendices. Appendices J and K are included for our readers who do not know XHTML or who would like a review of XHTML before studying Chapter 18, Extensible Markup Language (XML) and Chapter 24, Accessibility.

Appendix L—HTML/XHTML Special Characters (on CD)
This appendix provides many commonly used HTML/XHTML special characters, called *character entity references*.

Appendix M—HTML/XHTML Colors (on CD)
This appendix lists commonly used HTML/XHTML color names and their corresponding hexadecimal values.

1.19 Internet and World Wide Web Resources

www.deitel.com
This site offers updates, corrections and additional resources for Deitel & Associates, Inc., publications. We suggest that readers visit our site regularly to obtain any new information.

www.prenhall.com/deitel
This is the Deitel & Associates, Inc. page on the Prentice Hall Web site, which contains information about our products and publications, downloads, Deitel curriculum and author information.

www.w3.org
The World Wide Web Consortium (W3C) is an organization that develops technologies for the Internet and World Wide Web. This Web page includes links to W3C technologies, news, mission statements and frequently asked questions (FAQs).

www.softlord.com/comp
This site outlines the history of computers, from the early days of computing to the evolution of present-day machines.

www.elsop.com/wrc/h_comput.htm
This site presents the history of computing. It features content about famous innovators, the evolution of languages and the development of operating systems.

www.w3.org/History.html
This site overviews the history of the Internet. After briefly covering developments from 1945–1988, the site details technological advances on a year-by-year basis, from 1989 to the present day.

www.netvalley.com/intval.html
This site provides a short history of the Internet. In particular, it describes the history of the World Wide Web. Illustrations and abundant links are provided for many of the topics discussed.

www.microsoft.com
This is Microsoft's Web site. It contains extensive resources on topics including .NET, enterprise software, Windows and Visual Basic .NET.

SUMMARY

[This chapter is primarily a summary of the rest of the book, so we have not provided a summary section. The remaining chapters include detailed summaries of their contents.]

TERMINOLOGY

action
"administrative" section of the computer
Advanced Research Projects Agency (ARPA)
algorithm
Apple Computer
arithmetic and logic unit (ALU)
assembler
assembly language
bandwidth
batch
batch processing
building-block approach
C programming language
C# programming language
C++ programming language
calculation
Cascading Style Sheets (CSS)
central processing unit (CPU)
clarity
class
class libraries
Common Language Runtime (CLR)
Common Language Specification (CLS)
compiler
component
computation
computer
computer program
computer programmer
data
data independence
decision
disk
distributed computing
ECMA (European Computer Manufacturer's Association)
e-mail (electronic mail)
Framework Class Library (FCL)
HailStorm Web service
hardware
hardware platform
high-level language
HTML (HyperText Markup Language)
HTTP (HyperText Transfer Protocol)
IBM (International Business Machines)
Information Revolution
input device
input unit
integrated development environment (IDE)
Internet
interpreter
intranet
IP (Internet Protocol)
Java programming language
job
keyboard
language independence
language interoperability
live-code™ approach
logical decision
logical unit
machine dependent
machine language
maintenance of software
"manufacturing" section of the computer
memory
memory unit
Microsoft .NET
Microsoft Intermediate Language (MSIL)
module
mouse
multiprogramming
multitasking
n-tier application
.NET Framework
.NET initiative
.NET language
object
object-based programming
object-oriented language
object-oriented programming (OOP)
operating system
output device
output unit
Pascal programming language
personal computer
platform independence
portability
porting
primary memory
processing unit
program
programmer
property of an object
"receiving" section of the computer
reusable software component
screen
share the resources of a computer

"shipping" section of the computer
silicon chip
SOAP (Simple Object Access Protocol)
software
software component
software reuse
structured programming
subscription-based software
task
TCP (Transmission Control Protocol)
TCP/IP (Transmission Control
    Protocol/Internet Protocol)
terminal
throughput
timesharing
translator program

UNIX
universal data access
virtual-memory operating system
Visual Basic .NET programming language
visual programming
"warehouse" section of the computer
W3C (World Wide Web Consortium)
W3C Recommendation
Web Form
Web service
Web site
Win32 API (Windows 32-bit Application
    Programming Interface)
World Wide Web (WWW)
XML (Extensible Markup Language)

SELF-REVIEW EXERCISES

1.1 Fill in the blanks in each of the following statements:
   a) Computers can directly understand only their native _____ language, which is composed only of 1s and 0s.
   b) Computers process data under the control of sets of instructions called computer _____.
   c) SOAP is an acronym for _____.
   d) _____ is a technology derived from SGML that is used to create mark up languages.
   e) The three types of languages discussed in the chapter are machine languages, _____ and _____.
   f) Programs that translate high-level language programs into machine language are called _____.
   g) Visual Studio .NET is a/an _____ (IDE) in which Visual Basic .NET programs are developed.
   h) C is widely known as the development language of the _____ operating system.
   i) Microsoft's _____ provides a large programming library for .NET languages.
   j) The Department of Defense developed the Ada language with a capability called _____, which allows programmers to specify activities that can proceed in parallel. Visual Basic .NET offers a similar capability called multithreading.
   k) Web services use _____ and _____ to mark up and send information over the Internet, respectively.

1.2 State whether each of the following is *true* or *false*. If *false*, explain why.
   a) Universal data access is an essential part of .NET.
   b) W3C standards are called recommendations.
   c) Visual Basic .NET is an object-oriented language.
   d) The Common Language Runtime (CLR) requires that programmers manage their own memory.
   e) Visual Basic .NET is the only language available for programming .NET applications.
   f) Procedural programming models the world better than object-oriented programming.
   g) Computers can directly understand high-level languages.

h) MSIL is the common intermediate format to which all .NET programs compile, regardless of their original .NET language.
i) The .NET Framework is portable to non-Windows platforms.
j) Compiled programs run faster than their corresponding interpreted programs.
k) Throughput is the amount of work a computer can process in a given time period.

ANSWERS TO SELF-REVIEW EXERCISES

1.1 a) machine. b) programs. c) Simple Object Access Protocol. d) XML. e) assembly languages, high-level languages. f) compilers. g) integrated development environment (IDE). h) UNIX. i) Framework Class Library (FCL). j) multitasking. k) XML, SOAP.

1.2 a) True. b) True. c) True. d) False. The CLR handles memory management. e) False. Visual Basic .NET is one of many .NET languages (others include C# and Visual C++). f) False. Object-oriented programming is a more natural way to model the world than is procedural programming. g) False. Computers can directly understand only their own machine languages. h) True. i) True. j) True. k) True.

EXERCISES

1.3 Categorize each of the following items as either hardware or software:
  a) CPU.
  b) Compiler.
  c) Input unit.
  d) A word-processor program.
  e) A Visual Basic .NET program.

1.4 Distinguish between the terms HTML, XML and XHTML.

1.5 Translator programs, such as assemblers and compilers, convert programs from one language (referred to as the source language) to another language (referred to as the object language or target language). Determine which of the following statements are *true* and which are *false*:
  a) A compiler translates high-level language programs into object language.
  b) An assembler translates source language programs into machine language programs.
  c) A compiler converts source-language programs into object-language programs.
  d) High-level languages are generally machine dependent.
  e) A machine-language program requires translation before it can be run on a computer.
  f) The Visual Basic .NET compiler translates a high-level language into SMIL.

1.6 What are the basic requirements of a .NET language? What is needed to run a .NET program on a new type of computer (machine)?

1.7 Expand each of the following acronyms:
  a) W3C.
  b) XML.
  c) SOAP.
  d) TCP/IP.
  e) OOP.
  f) CLR.
  g) CLS.
  h) FCL.
  i) MSIL.

1.8 What are the key benefits of the .NET Framework and the CLR? What are the drawbacks?

Introduction to the Visual Studio .NET IDE

Objectives

- To be introduced to the Visual Studio .NET Integrated Development Environment (IDE).
- To become familiar with the types of commands contained in the IDE's menus and toolbars.
- To understand the use of various kinds of windows in the Visual Studio .NET IDE.
- To understand Visual Studio .NET's help features.
- To be able to create, compile and execute a simple Visual Basic program.

Seeing is believing.
Proverb

Form ever follows function.
Louis Henri Sullivan

Intelligence… is the faculty of making artificial objects, especially tools to make tools.
Henri-Louis Bergson

Introduction to the Visual Studio .NET IDE

Outline

2.1 Introduction
2.2 Overview of the Visual Studio .NET IDE
2.3 Menu Bar and Toolbar
2.4 Visual Studio .NET IDE Windows
    2.4.1 Solution Explorer
    2.4.2 Toolbox
    2.4.3 Properties Window
2.5 Using Help
2.6 Simple Program: Displaying Text and an Image
2.7 Internet and World Wide Web Resources

Summary • Terminology • Self-Review Exercises • Answers to Self-Review Exercises • Exercises

2.1 Introduction

Visual Studio .NET is Microsoft's Integrated Development Environment (IDE) for creating, running and debugging programs (also called *applications*) written in a variety of .NET programming languages. This IDE is a powerful and sophisticated tool for creating business-critical and mission-critical applications. In this chapter, we provide an overview of the Visual Studio .NET IDE and demonstrate how to create a simple Visual Basic program by dragging and dropping predefined building blocks into place—this technique is called *visual programming*.

2.2 Overview of the Visual Studio .NET IDE

When Visual Studio .NET begins execution, the **Start Page**[1] displays (Fig. 2.1). The left-hand side of the **Start Page** contains a list of helpful links, such as **Get Started**. Clicking a link displays its contents. We refer to single-clicking with the left mouse button as *selecting*, or *clicking*, whereas we refer to double-clicking with the left mouse button as *double-clicking*.

When clicked, **Get Started** loads a page that contains a table listing the names of recent *projects* (such as **ASimpleProgram** in Fig. 2.1), along with the dates on which these projects were last modified. A project is a group of related files, such as the Visual Basic code and images that make up a program. When you load Visual Studio .NET for the first time, the list of recent projects is empty. There are two *buttons* on the page—**Open Project** and **New Project**, which are used to open an existing project (such as the ones in the table of recent projects) and to create a new project, respectively. We discuss the process of creating new projects momentarily.

Other links on the **Start Page** offer information and resources related to Visual Studio .NET. Clicking **What's New** displays a page that lists new features and updates for Visual Studio .NET, including downloads for code samples and programming tools. **Online Community** links to online resources for contacting other software developers through *newsgroups* (organized message boards on the Internet) and Web sites.

---

1. Depending on your version of Visual Studio .NET, the **Start Page** may be different.

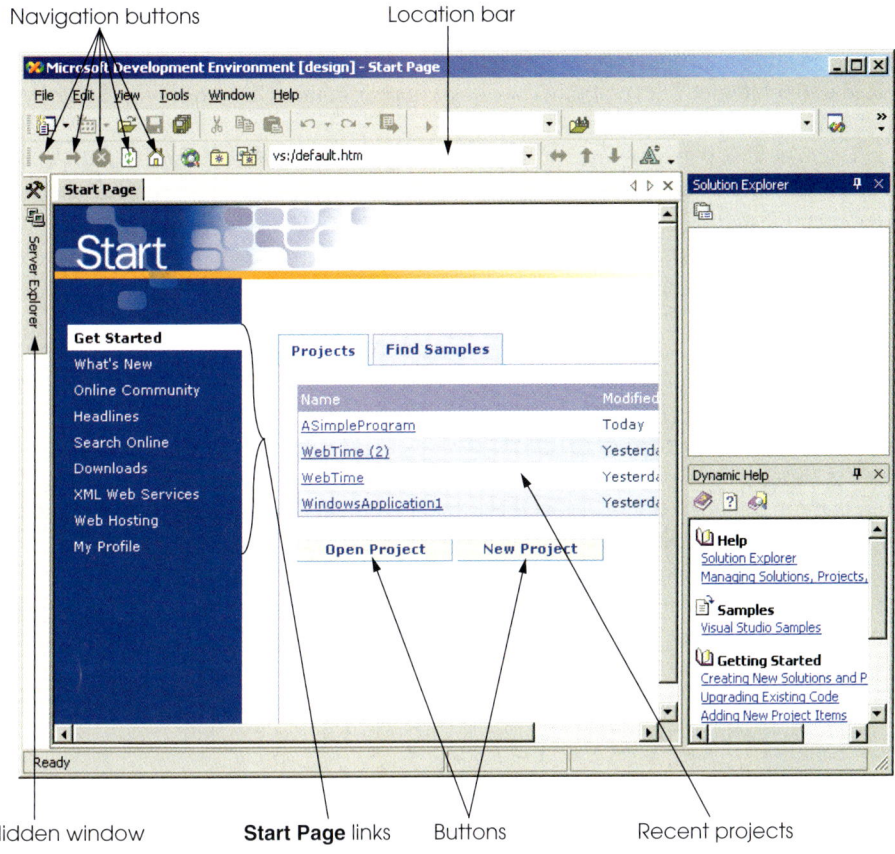

Fig. 2.1 **Start Page** in Visual Studio .NET.

Headlines provides a page for browsing news, articles and how-to guides. To access more extensive information, users can select **Search Online** and begin browsing through the *MSDN* (*Microsoft Developer Network*) online library, which contains numerous articles, downloads and tutorials on various technologies of interest to Visual Studio .NET developers. When clicked, **Downloads** displays a page that provides programmers access to product updates, code samples and reference materials. The **XML Web Services** page provides programmers with information about *Web services*, which are reusable pieces of software available on the Internet. We discuss this technology in Chapter 21, ASP.NET and Web Services. The **Web Hosting** page allows programmers to post their software (such as Web services) online for public use. The **My Profile** link loads a page where users can adjust and customize various Visual Studio .NET settings, such as keyboard schemes and window layout preferences. The programmer also can customize the Visual Studio .NET IDE by selecting the **Tools** menu's **Options...** command and the **Tools** menu's **Customize...** command. [*Note*: From this point onward, we use the **>** character to indicate the selection of a menu command. For example, we use the notation **Tools > Options...** and **Tools > Customize...** to indicate the selection of the **Options...** and **Customize...** commands, respectively.]

Programmers can browse the Web from the IDE using Internet Explorer (also called the *internal Web browser* in Visual Studio .NET). To request a Web page, type its address into the location bar (Fig. 2.1) and press the *Enter* key. [*Note*: The computer must be connected to the Internet.] Several other windows appear in the IDE besides the **Start Page**; we discuss them in subsequent sections.

To create a new Visual Basic program, click the **New Project** button (Fig. 2.1), which displays the **New Project** *dialog* (Fig. 2.2). Dialogs are windows that facilitate user-computer communication.

The Visual Studio .NET IDE organizes programs into projects and *solutions*, which contain one or more projects. Multiple-project solutions are used to create large-scale applications in which each project performs a single, well-defined task.

The Visual Studio .NET IDE provides project types for a variety of programming languages. This book focuses on Visual Basic, so we select the **Visual Basic Projects** folder from the **Project Types** *window* (Fig. 2.2). We use some of the other project types in later chapters. A **Windows Application** is a program that executes inside the Windows OS (e.g., Windows 2000 or Windows XP). Windows applications include customized software that programmers create, as well as software products like Microsoft Word, Internet Explorer and Visual Studio .NET.

By default, the Visual Studio .NET IDE assigns the name **WindowsApplication1** to the new project and solution (Fig. 2.2). The **Visual Studio Projects** folder in the **My Documents** folder is the default folder referenced when Visual Studio .NET is executed for the first time. Programmers can change both the name of the project and the location where it is created. After selecting a project's name and location, click **OK** to display the IDE in *design view* (Fig. 2.3), which contains all the features necessary to begin creating programs.

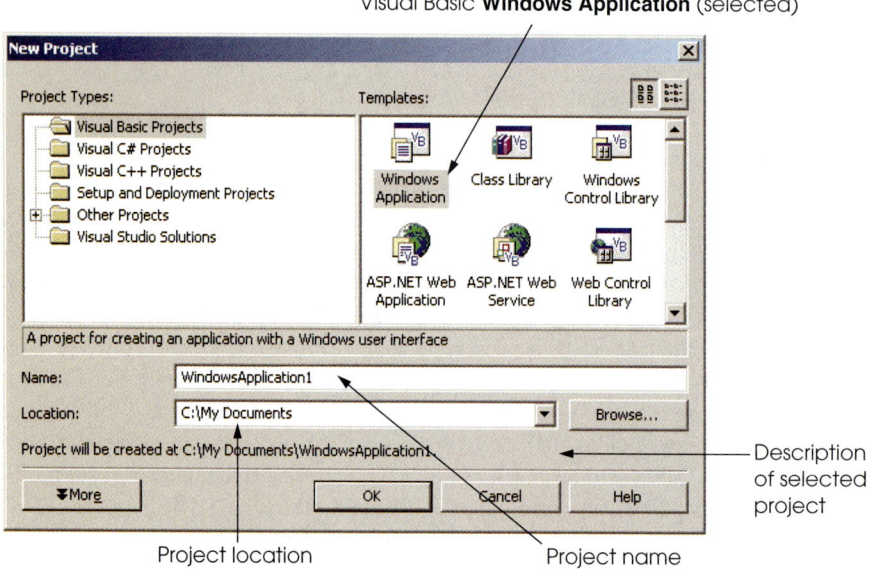

Fig. 2.2 **New Project** dialog.

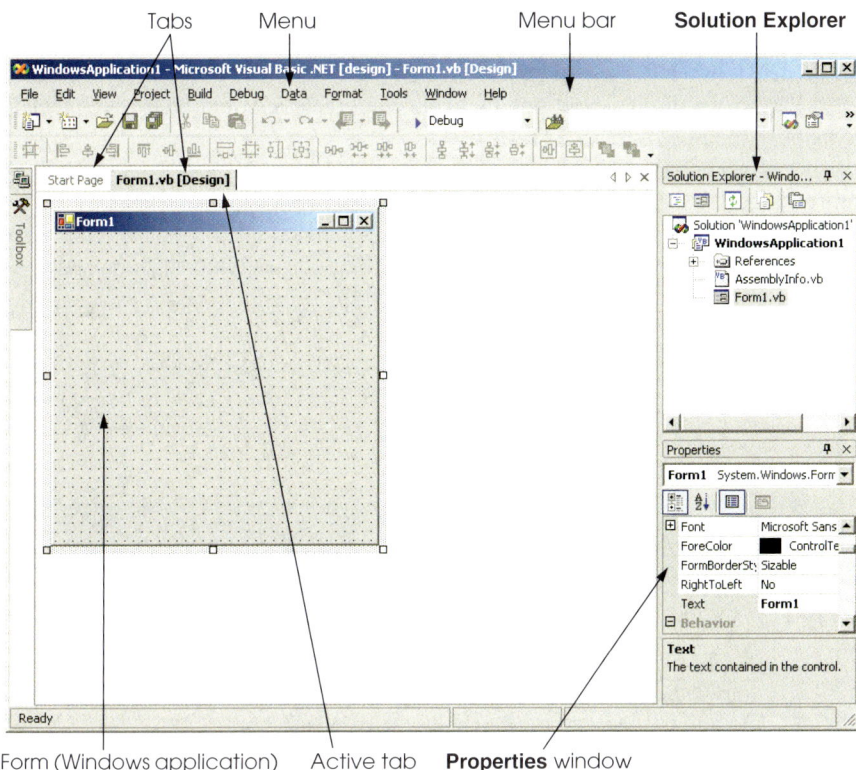

Fig. 2.3 Design view of Visual Studio .NET IDE.

The gray rectangle (called a *form*) titled **Form1** represents the Windows application that the programmer is creating. Later in this chapter, we discuss how to customize this form by adding *controls* (i.e., reusable components, such as buttons). Collectively, the form and controls constitute the program's *Graphical User Interface* (*GUI*), which is the visual part of the program with which the user interacts. Users enter data (*inputs*) into the program by typing at the keyboard, by clicking the mouse buttons and in a variety of other ways. Programs display instructions and other information (*outputs*) for users to read in the GUI. For example, the **New Project** dialog in Fig. 2.2 presents a GUI where the user clicks with the mouse button to select a project type and then inputs a project name and location from the keyboard.

The name of each open document is listed on a *tab*. In our case, the documents are the **Start Page** and **Form1.vb [Design]** (Fig. 2.3). To view a document, click its tab. Tabs save space and facilitate easy access to multiple documents. The *active tab* (the tab of the document currently displayed in the IDE) is displayed in bold text (e.g., **Form1.vb [Design]**) and is positioned in front of all the other tabs.

2.3 Menu Bar and Toolbar

Commands for managing the IDE and for developing, maintaining and executing programs are contained in the menus, which are located on the menu bar (Fig. 2.4). Menus contain groups of related commands (also called *menu items*) that, when selected, cause the IDE to perform specific actions (e.g., open a window, save a file, print a file and execute a program). For example, new projects are created by selecting **File > New > Project...**. The menus depicted in Fig. 2.4 are summarized in Fig. 2.5. In Chapter 13, Graphical User Interfaces: Part 2, we discuss how programmers can create and add their own menus and menu items to their programs.

Rather than having to navigate the menus for certain commonly used commands, the programmer can access them from the *toolbar* (Fig. 2.6), which contains pictures, called *icons*, that graphically represent commands. To execute a command via the toolbar, click its icon. Some icons contain a down arrow that, when clicked, displays additional commands.

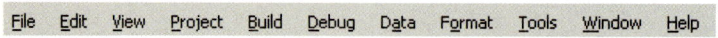

Fig. 2.4 Visual Studio .NET IDE menu bar.

Menu	Description
File	Contains commands for opening projects, closing projects, printing project data, etc.
Edit	Contains commands such as cut, paste, find, undo, etc.
View	Contains commands for displaying IDE windows and toolbars.
Project	Contains commands for managing a project and its files.
Build	Contains commands for compiling a program.
Debug	Contains commands for *debugging* (i.e., identifying and correcting problems in a program) and running a program.
Data	Contains commands for interacting with *databases* (i.e., files that store data, which we discuss in Chapter 19, Databases, SQL and ADO .NET).
Format	Contains commands for arranging a form's controls.
Tools	Contains commands for accessing additional IDE tools and options that enable customization of the IDE.
Windows	Contains commands for arranging and displaying windows.
Help	Contains commands for accessing the IDE's help features.

Fig. 2.5 Summary of Visual Studio .NET IDE menus.

Fig. 2.6 IDE Toolbar.

Positioning the mouse pointer over an icon highlights the icon and, after a few seconds, displays a description called a *tool tip* (Fig. 2.7). Tool tips help novice programmers become familiar with the IDE's features.

2.4 Visual Studio .NET IDE Windows

The IDE provides windows for accessing project files and customizing controls. In this section, we introduce several windows that are essential in the development of Visual Basic applications. These windows can be accessed via the toolbar icons (Fig. 2.8) or by selecting the name of the desired window in the **View** menu.

Visual Studio .NET provides a space-saving feature called *auto-hide* (Fig. 2.9). When auto-hide is enabled, a toolbar appears along one of the edges of the IDE. This toolbar contains one or more icons, each of which identifies a hidden window. Placing the mouse pointer over one of these icons displays that window, but the window is hidden once the mouse pointer is moved outside the window's area. To "pin down" a window (i.e., to disable auto-hide and keep the window open), click the pin icon. Notice that, when a window is "pinned down," the pin icon has a vertical orientation, whereas, when auto-hide is enabled, the pin icon has a horizontal orientation (Fig. 2.9).

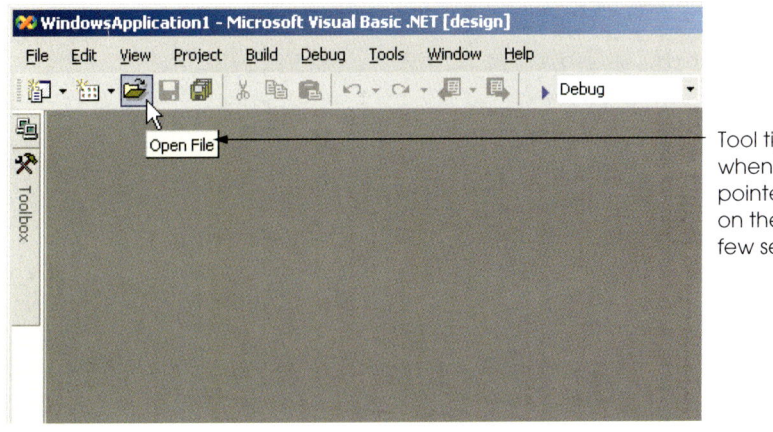

Fig. 2.7 Tool tip demonstration.

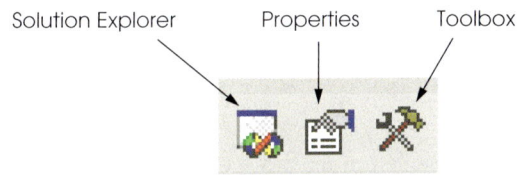

Fig. 2.8 Toolbar icons for three Visual Studio .NET IDE windows.

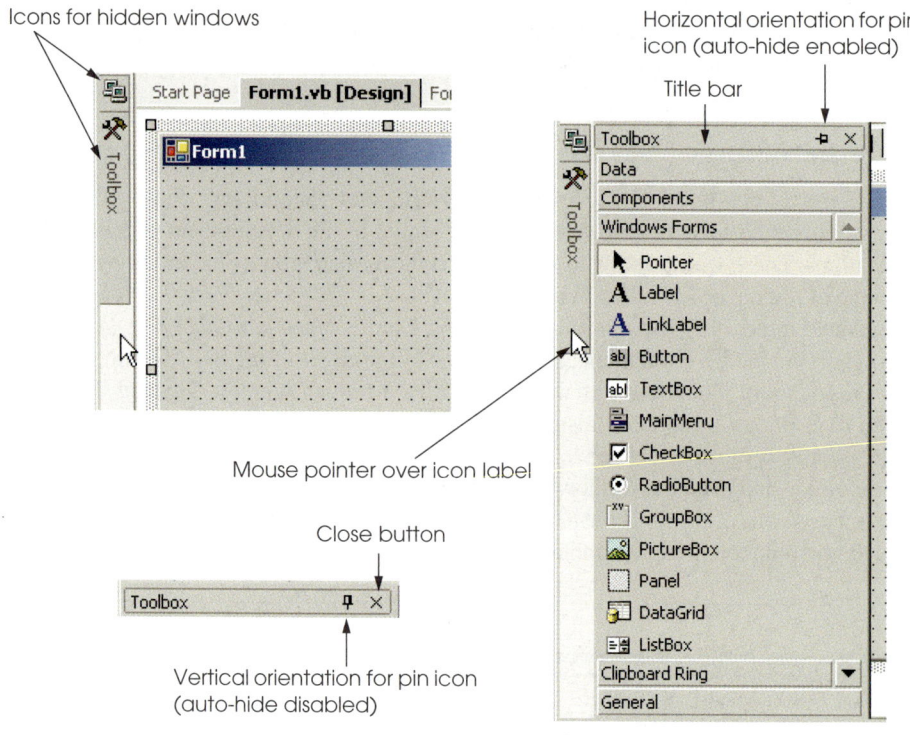

Fig. 2.9 Auto-hide feature demonstration.

2.4.1 Solution Explorer

The **Solution Explorer** window (Fig. 2.10) provides access to all the files in the solution. When the Visual Studio .NET IDE is first loaded, the **Solution Explorer** is empty; there are no files to display. Once a solution is open, the **Solution Explorer** displays that solution's contents.

The solution's *startup project* is the project that runs when the program executes and appears in bold text in the **Solution Explorer**. For our single-project solution, the startup project is the only project (**WindowsApplication1**). The Visual Basic file, which corresponds to the form shown in Fig. 2.3, is named `Form1.vb`. (Visual Basic files use the `.vb` filename extension, which is short for "Visual Basic.") The other files and folders are discussed later in the book.

[*Note*: We use fonts to distinguish between IDE features (such as menu names and menu items) and other elements that appear in the IDE. Our convention is to emphasize IDE features in a **sans-serif bold helvetica** font and to emphasize other elements, such as file names (e.g., `Form1.vb`) and property names (discussed in Section 2.4.3), in a `serif bold courier` font.]

The plus and minus boxes to the left of the project name and the **References** folder expand and collapse the tree, respectively. Click a plus box to display items grouped under the heading to the right of the plus box; click the minus box to collapse a tree already in its expanded state. Other Visual Studio windows also use this plus-box/minus-box convention.

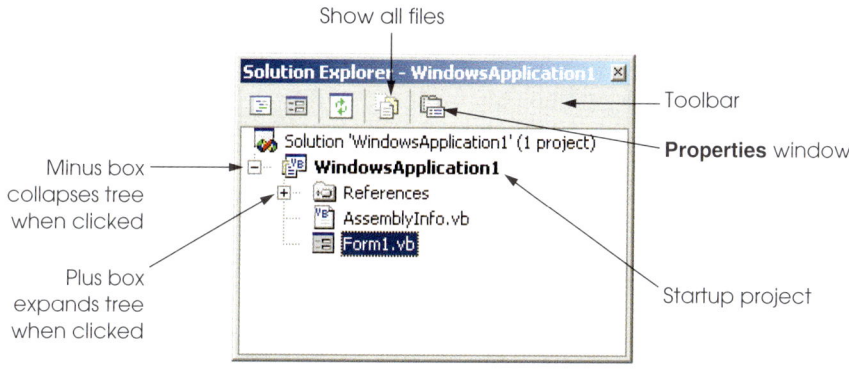

Fig. 2.10 Solution Explorer with an open solution.

The **Solution Explorer** window includes a toolbar that contains several icons. When clicked, the *show all files icon* displays all the files in the solution. The number of icons present in the toolbar is dependent on the type of file selected. We discuss additional toolbar icons later in the book.

2.4.2 Toolbox

The **Toolbox** (Fig. 2.11) contains controls used to customize forms. Using *visual programming*, programmers can "drag and drop" controls onto the form instead of building them by writing code. Just as people do not need to know how to build an engine to drive a car, programmers do not need to know how to build a control to use the control. The use of preexisting controls enables developers to concentrate on the "big picture," rather than on the minute and complex details of every control. The wide variety of controls that are contained in the **Toolbox** is a powerful feature of the Visual Studio .NET IDE. We will use the **Toolbox** when we create our own program later in the chapter.

The **Toolbox** contains groups of related controls (e.g., **Data**, **Components** in Fig. 2.11). When the name of a group is clicked, the list expands to display the various controls contained in the group. Users can scroll through the individual items by using the black *scroll arrows* to the right of the group name. When there are no more members to reveal, the scroll arrow appears gray, meaning that it is *disabled* (i.e., it will not perform its normal function if clicked). The first item in the group is not a control—it is the *mouse pointer*. The mouse pointer is used to navigate the IDE and to manipulate a form and its controls. In later chapters, we discuss many of the **Toolbox**'s controls.

2.4.3 Properties Window

The **Properties** window (Fig. 2.12) displays the *properties* for a form or control. Properties specify information such as size, color and position. Each form or control has its own set of properties; a property's description is displayed at the bottom of the **Properties** window whenever that property is selected. If the **Properties** window is not visible, selecting **View > Properties Window**, displays the **Properties** window.

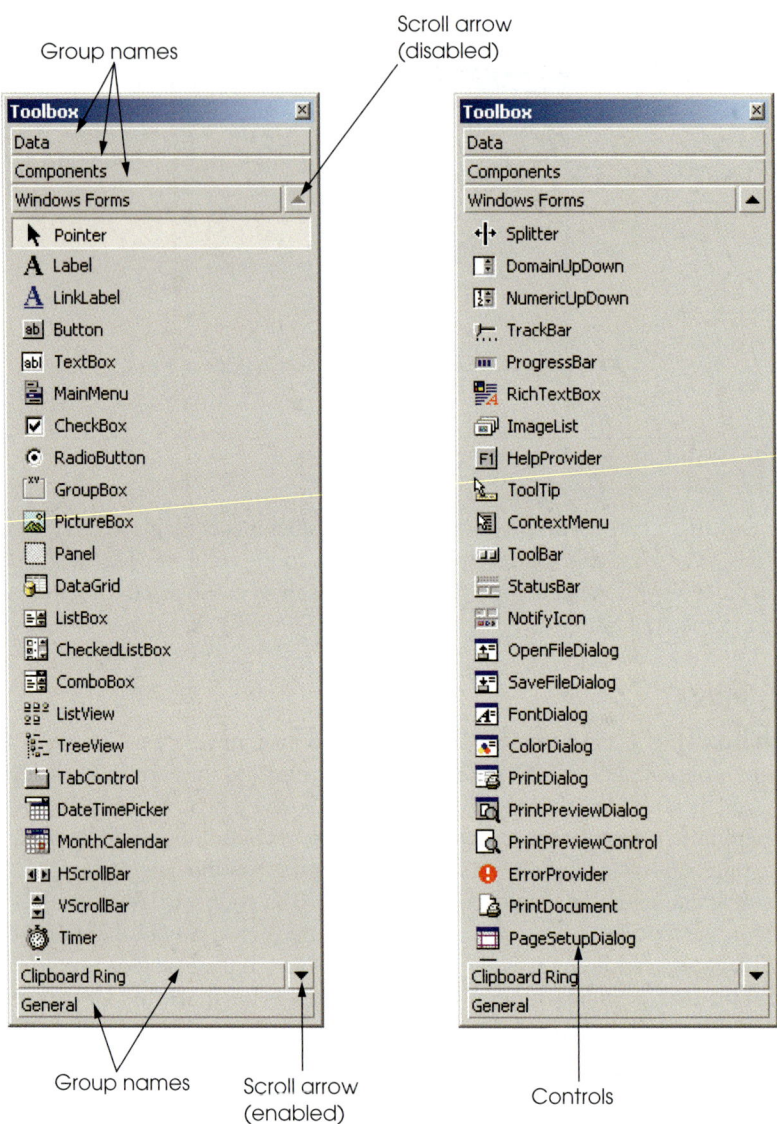

Fig. 2.11 **Toolbox** window.

In Fig. 2.12, the form's **Properties** window is shown. The left column of the **Properties** window lists the form's properties; the right column displays the current value of each property. Icons on the toolbar sort the properties either alphabetically (by clicking the *alphabetic icon*) or categorically (by clicking the *categorized icon*). Users can scroll through the list of properties by *dragging* the scrollbar's scrollbox up or down. We show how to set individual properties later in this chapter and throughout the book.

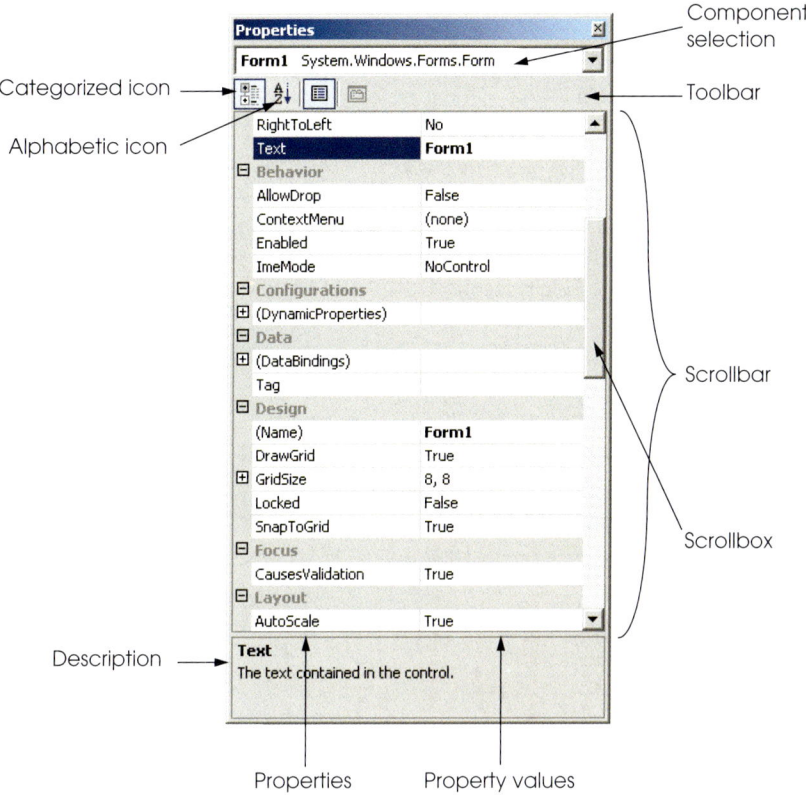

Fig. 2.12 Properties window.

The **Properties** window is crucial to visual programming; it allows programmers to modify controls visually, without writing code. This capability provides a number of benefits. First, programmers can see which properties are available for modification and, in many cases, can learn the range of acceptable values for a given property. Second, the programmer does not have to remember or search the Visual Studio .NET documentation for the possible settings of a particular property. Third, this window also displays a brief description of the selected property, helping programmers understand the property's purpose. Fourth, a property can be set quickly using this window—usually, only a single click is required, and no code needs to be written. All these features are designed to help programmers avoid repetitive tasks while ensuring that settings are correct and consistent throughout the project.

At the top of the **Properties** window is the *component selection* drop-down list, which allows programmers to select the form or control whose properties are displayed in the **Properties** window. When a form or control in the list is selected, the properties of that form or control appear in the **Properties** window.

2.5 Using Help

The Visual Studio .NET IDE provides extensive help features. The **Help** *menu* contains a variety of commands, which are summarized in Fig. 2.13.

Dynamic help (Fig. 2.14) is an excellent way to get information about the IDE and its features, as it provides a list of articles pertaining to the current content (i.e., the items around the location of the mouse cursor). To open the **Dynamic Help** window (if it is not already open), select **Help > Dynamic Help**. Then, when you click a word or component (such as a form or a control), links to relevant help articles appear in the **Dynamic Help** window. The window lists help topics, samples and "Getting Started" information. There is also a toolbar that provides access to the **Contents**, **Index** and **Search** help features.

Command	Description
Contents...	Displays a categorized table of contents in which help articles are organized by topic.
Index...	Displays an alphabetized list of topics through which the programmer can browse.
Search...	Allows programmers to find help articles based on search keywords.

Fig. 2.13 **Help** menu commands.

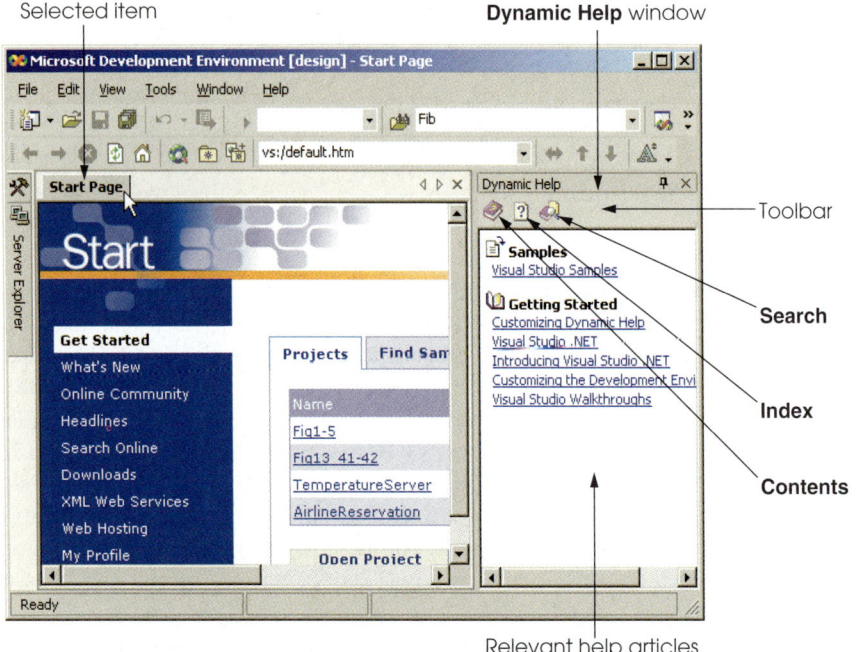

Fig. 2.14 **Dynamic Help** window.

Visual Studio .NET also provides *context-sensitive help*, which is similar to dynamic help, except that it immediately displays a relevant help article, rather than presenting a list of articles. To use context-sensitive help, click an item and press *F1*. Help can appear either *internally* or *externally*. When external help is selected, a relevant article immediately pops up in a separate window outside the IDE. When internal help is selected, a help article appears as a tabbed window inside the IDE. The help options can be set in the **Start Page**'s **My Profile** section by selecting **Internal Help** (the default) or **External Help**.

2.6 Simple Program: Displaying Text and an Image

In this section, we create a program that displays the text "**Welcome to Visual Basic!**" and an image of the Deitel & Associates bug mascot. The program consists of a single form that uses a *label control* (i.e., a control that displays text which the user cannot modify) and a picture box to display the image. Figure 2.15 shows the results of the program as it executes. The program and the image are available on the CD-ROM that accompanies this book, as well as on our Web site (**www.deitel.com**) under the **Downloads/Resources** link.

To create the program whose output is shown in Fig. 2.15, we did not write a single line of program code. Instead, we use the techniques of visual programming. Visual Studio .NET processes programmer actions (such as mouse clicking, dragging and dropping) to generate program code. In the next chapter, we begin our discussion of how to write program code. Throughout the book, we produce increasingly substantial and powerful programs. Visual Basic programs usually include a combination of code written by the programmer and code generated by Visual Studio .NET.

Visual programming is useful for building GUI-intensive programs that require a significant amount of user interaction. Some programs are not designed to interact with users and therefore do not have GUIs. Programmers must write the code for the latter type of program directly.

Fig. 2.15 Simple program executing.

To create, run and terminate this first program, perform the following steps:

1. *Create the new project.* If a project is already open, close it by selecting **File > Close Solution**. A dialog asking whether to save the current solution might appear. Click **Yes** to save any changes. To create a new Windows application for our program, select **File > New > Project...** to display the **New Project** dialog (Fig. 2.16). Click the **Visual Basic Projects** folder to display a list of project types. From this list, select **Windows Application**. Name the project **ASimpleProgram**, and select the directory in which the project will be saved. To select a directory, click the **Browse...** button, which opens the **Project Location** dialog (Fig. 2.17). Navigate through the directories, find one in which to place the project and click **OK** to close the dialog. The selected folder now appears in the **Location** text box. Click **OK** to close the **New Project** dialog. The IDE then loads the new single-project solution, which contains a form named **Form1**.

2. *Set the text in the form's title bar.* The text in the form's title bar is determined by the form's `Text` property (Fig. 2.18). If the **Properties** window is not open, click the properties icon in the toolbar or select **View > Properties Window**. Click the form to display the form's properties in the **Properties** window. Click in the textbox to the right of the `Text` property's box and type **A Simple Program**, as in Fig. 2.18. Press the *Enter* key (*Return* key) when finished; the form's title bar is updated immediately.

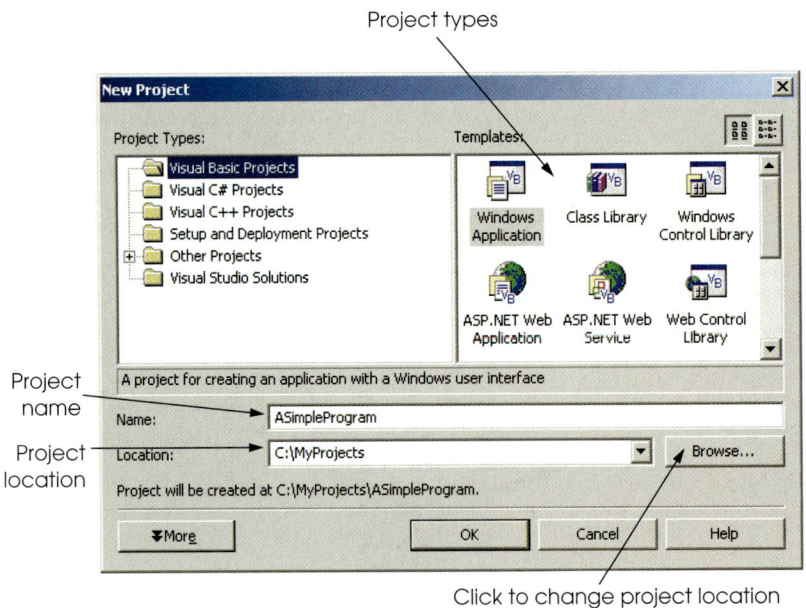

Fig. 2.16 Creating a new **Windows Application**.

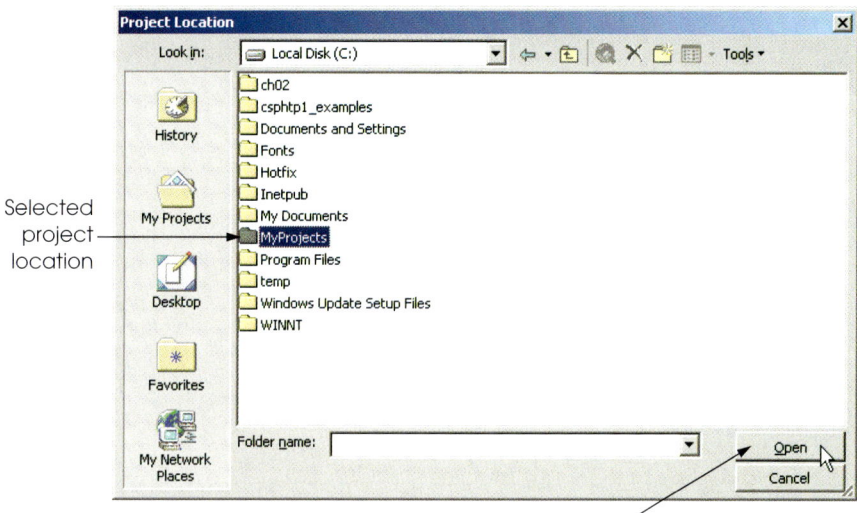

Fig. 2.17 Setting the project location in the **Project Location** dialog.

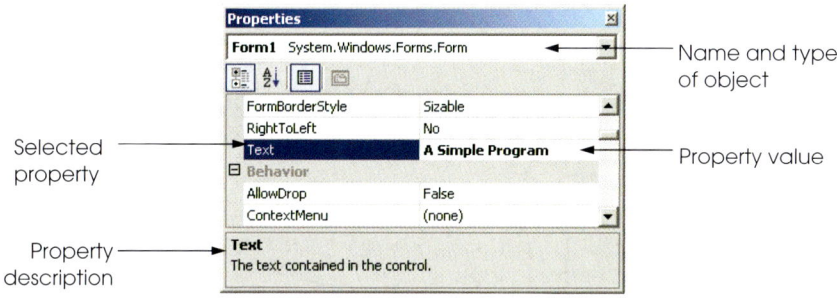

Fig. 2.18 Setting the form's **Text** property.

3. *Resize the form.* Click and drag one of the form's *enabled sizing handles* (the small white squares that appear around the form shown in Fig. 2.19). The appearance of the mouse pointer changes (i.e., it becomes a pointer with one or more arrows) when it is over an enabled sizing handle. The new pointer indicates the direction(s) in which resizing is permitted. *Disabled sizing handles* appear in gray and cannot be used to resize the form. The *grid* on the background of the form is used by programmers to align controls and is not present when the program is running.

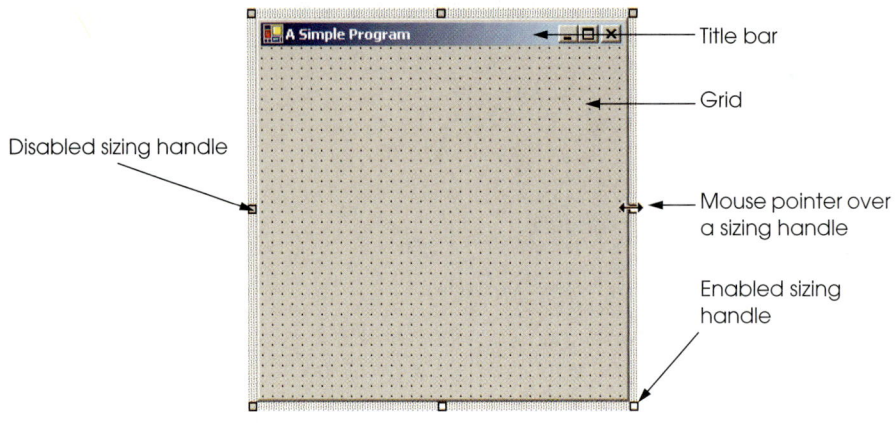

Fig. 2.19 Form with sizing handles.

4. *Change the form's background color.* The **BackColor** property specifies a form's or control's background color. Clicking **BackColor** in the **Properties** window causes a down-arrow button to appear next to the value of the property (Fig. 2.20). When clicked, the down-arrow button displays a set of other options, which varies depending on the property. In this case, the arrow displays tabs for **System** (the default), **Web** and **Custom**. Click the **Custom** tab to display the *palette* (a series of colors). Select the box that represents light blue. Once you select the color, the palette closes, and the form's background color changes to light blue (Fig. 2.21).

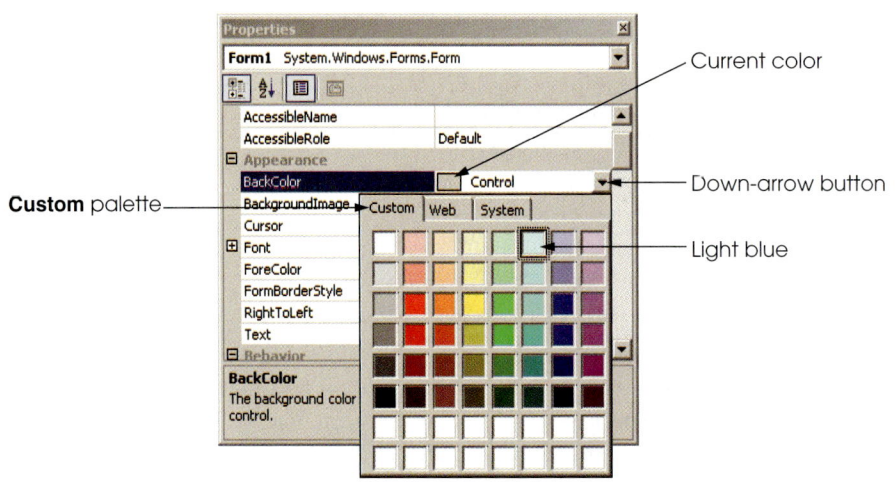

Fig. 2.20 Changing the form's **BackColor** property.

5. *Add a label control to the form.* Click the **Windows Forms** button in the **Toolbox**. Next, double-click the **Label** control in the **Toolbox**. This action causes a label to appear in the upper-left corner of the form (Fig. 2.21). Although double-clicking any **Toolbox** control places the control on the form, programmers also can "drag" controls from the **Toolbox** to the form. Labels display text; our label displays the text **Label1** by default. Notice that our label's background color is the same as the form's background color. When a control is added to the form, its `BackColor` property is set to the form's `BackColor`.

6. *Customize the label's appearance.* Select the label by clicking it. Its properties now appear in the **Properties** window. The label's `Text` property determines the text (if any) that the label displays. The form and label each have their own `Text` property. Forms and controls can have the same types of properties (such as `BackColor`, `Text`, etc.) without conflict. Set the label's `Text` property to **Welcome to Visual Basic!**. Resize the label (using the sizing handles) if the text does not fit. Move the label to the top center of the form by dragging it or by using the keyboard's left and right arrow keys to adjust its position. Alternatively, you can center the label control horizontally by selecting **Format > Center In Form > Horizontally**. The form should appear as shown in Fig. 2.22.

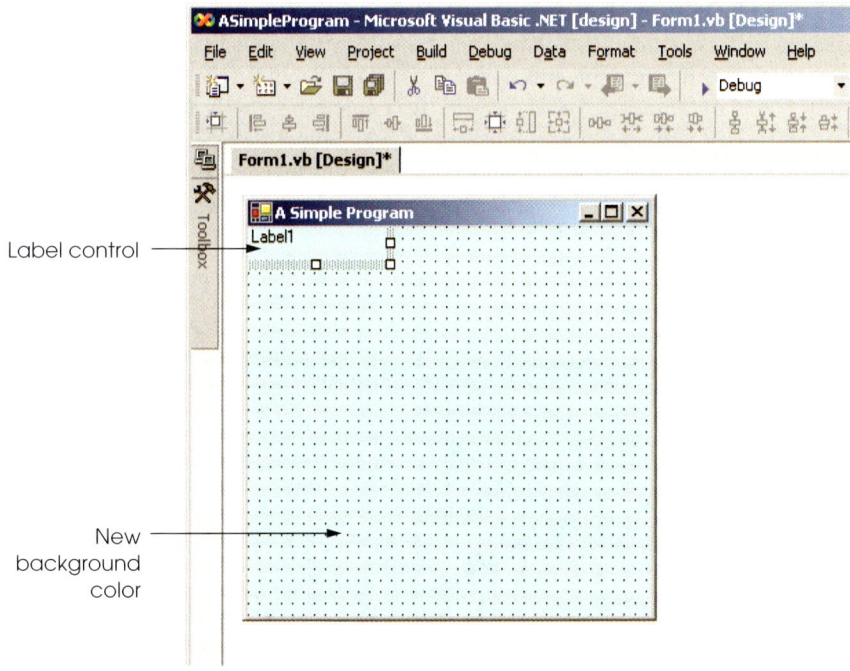

Fig. 2.21 Adding a label to the form.

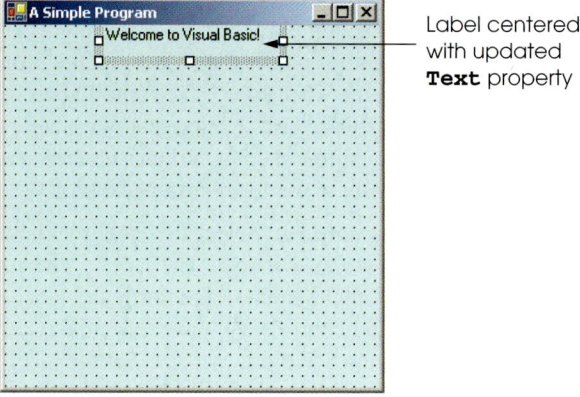

Fig. 2.22 GUI after the form and label have been customized.

7. *Set the label's font size and align its text.* Clicking the value of the **Font** property causes an *ellipsis button* (**...**) to appear next to the value, as shown in Fig. 2.23. When the ellipsis button is clicked, a dialog that provides additional values—in this case, the **Font** dialog (Fig. 2.24)—is displayed. Programmers can select the font name (**MS Sans Serif**, **Mistral**, etc.), font style (**Regular**, **Bold**, etc.) and font size (**12**, **14**, etc.) in this dialog. The text in the **Sample** area displays the selected font. Under the **Size** category, select **24** points and click **OK**. If the label's text does not fit on a single line, it wraps to the next line. Resize the label vertically if it is not large enough to hold the text. Next, select the label's **TextAlign** property, which determines how the text is aligned within the label. A three-by-three grid of buttons representing alignment choices is displayed (Fig. 2.25). The position of each button corresponds to where the text appears in the label. Click the top-center button in the three-by-three grid; this selection causes the text to appear at the top-center position in the label.

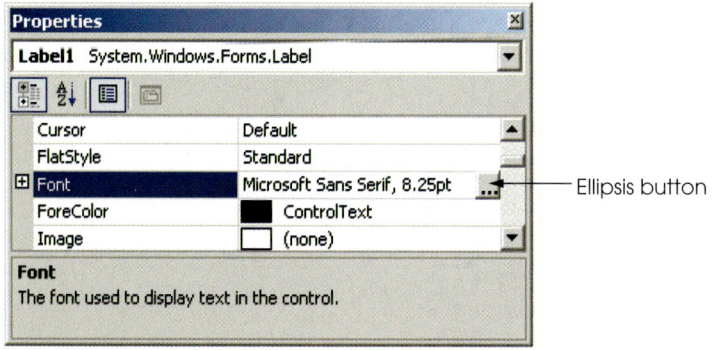

Fig. 2.23 **Properties** window displaying the label's properties.

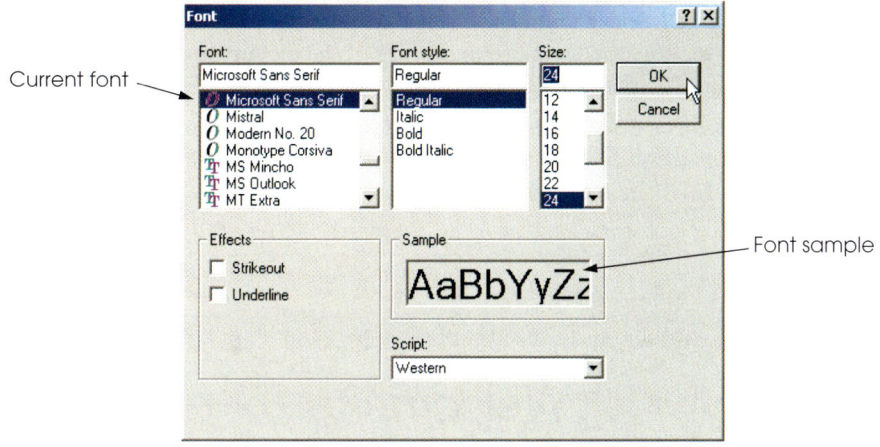

Fig. 2.24 **Font** dialog for selecting fonts, styles and sizes.

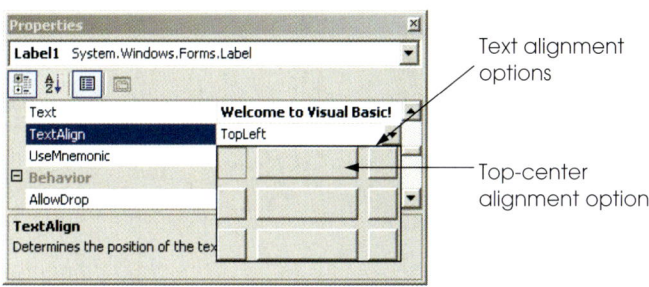

Fig. 2.25 Centering the label's text.

8. *Add a picture box to the form.* The picture-box control displays images. The process involved in this step is similar to that of Step 5, in which we added a label to the form. Locate the picture box in the **Toolbox** and then double click it to add it to the form. When the picture box appears, move it underneath the label, either by dragging it or using the arrow keys (Fig. 2.26).

9. *Insert an image.* Click the picture box to display its properties in the **Properties** window. Locate the **Image** *property*, which displays a preview of the image (if one exists). No picture has been assigned (Fig. 2.27), so the value of the *Image* property displays **(none)**. Click the ellipsis button to display the **Open** dialog (Fig. 2.28). Browse for an image to insert, select it with the mouse and press the *Enter* key. Supported image formats include *PNG* (*Portable Networks Graphic*), *GIF* (*Graphic Interchange Format*), *JPEG* (*Joint Photographic Experts Group*) and *BMP* (*Windows bitmap*). The creation of a new image requires image-editing software, such as Jasc® Paint Shop Pro™ (**www.jasc.com**), Adobe® Photoshop™ Elements (**www.adobe.com**) or Microsoft Paint (provided with Windows). In our case, the picture is **bug.png**. Once the image is selected, the

picture box displays the image, and the **Image** property displays a preview. To size the image to the picture box, change the ***SizeMode*** *property* to ***Stretch-Image***, which scales the image to the size of the picture box. Resize the picture box, making it larger (Fig. 2.29).

10. *Save the project*. Select **File > Save All** to save the entire solution. The solution file contains the name(s) and location(s) of its project(s), and the project file contains the names and locations of all the files in the project.

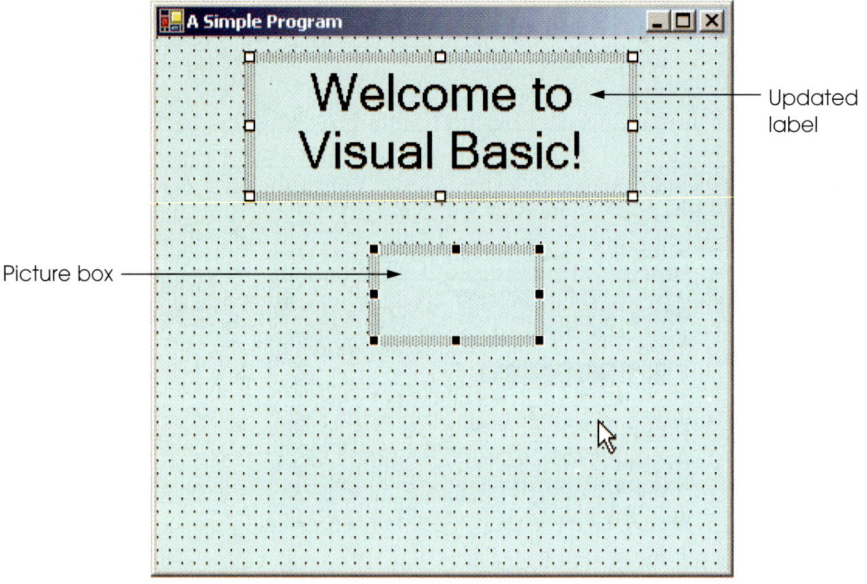

Fig. 2.26 Inserting and aligning the picture box.

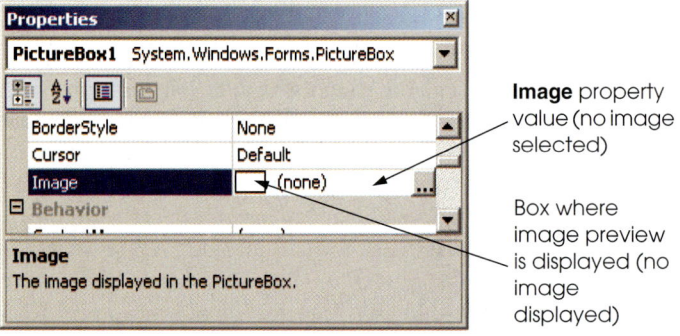

Fig. 2.27 **Image** property of the picture box.

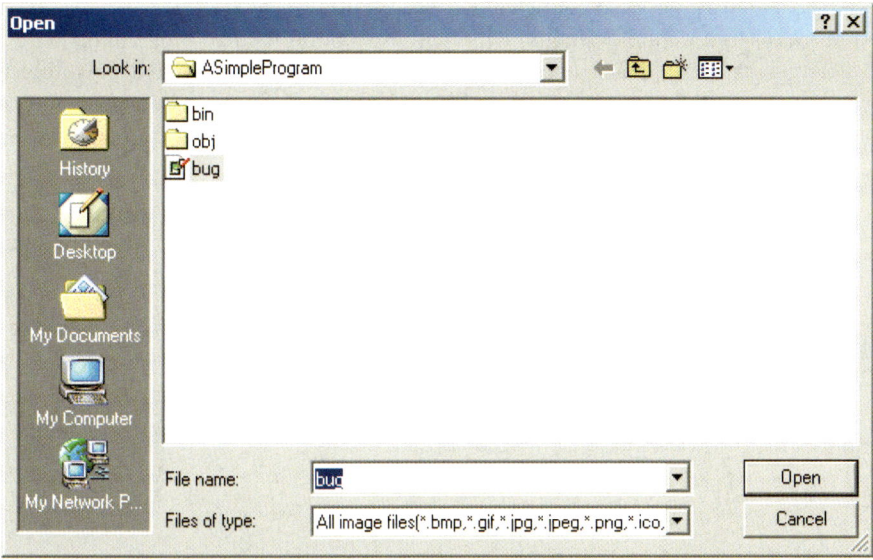

Fig. 2.28 Selecting an image for the picture box.

Newly inserted image

Fig. 2.29 Picture box displaying an image.

11. *Run the project.* Up to this point, we have been working in the IDE *design mode* (i.e., the program being created is not executing). This mode is indicated by the text **Microsoft Visual Basic.NET [design]** in the title bar. While in design mode, programmers have access to all the environment windows (e.g., **Toolbox**, **Properties**, etc.), menus and toolbars. In *run mode*, the program is executing, and programmers can interact with only a few IDE features. Features that are not

available are disabled or grayed out. The text **Form1.vb [Design]** in the title bar means that we are designing the form visually, rather than programmatically. If we had been writing code, the title bar would have contained only the text **Form1.vb**. Selecting **Debug > Start Without Debugging** executes the program. Figure 2.30 shows the IDE in run mode. Note that many toolbar icons and menus are disabled.

12. *Terminate execution.* To terminate the program, click the running application's *close* button (the **x** in the top-right corner). This action stops program execution and returns the IDE to design mode.

Software Engineering Observation 2.1

Visual programming can be simpler and faster than writing code when developing GUI-based applications.

Fig. 2.30 IDE in run mode, with the running application in the foreground.

> **Software Engineering Observation 2.2**
>
> *Most programs require more than visual programming. For these programs, at least some, and often all, code must be written by the programmer. Examples of such programs include programs that use event handlers (used to respond to the user's actions), as well as database, security, networking, text-editing, graphics, multimedia and other types of applications.*

In this chapter, we introduced key features of the Visual Studio .NET Integrated Development Environment (IDE). We then used the technique of visual programming to create a working Visual Basic .NET program without writing a single line of code! In the next chapter, we discuss "nonvisual," or "conventional," programming—we create programs that contain code. Visual Basic programming is a mixture of the two styles: Visual programming allows us to develop GUIs easily and avoid tedious GUI programming; conventional programming is employed to specify the behavior of our program.

2.7 Internet and World Wide Web Resources

www.msdn.microsoft.com/vstudio
This site is the home page for Microsoft Visual Studio .NET and provides a variety of information, including news, documentation, downloads and other resources.

www.worldofdotnet.net
This site offers a wide variety of information on .NET. It contains articles, news and links to newsgroups and other resources.

www.vbi.org
This site contains articles, reviews of books and software, documentation, downloads, links and searchable information on Visual Basic listed by subject.

SUMMARY

- Visual Studio .NET is Microsoft's Integrated Development Environment (IDE) used by Visual Basic and other languages to create, run and debug programs.
- When Visual Studio .NET is executed, the **Start Page** is displayed. This page contains helpful links, such as recent projects, online newsgroups and downloads.
- Programs in the Visual Studio .NET IDE are organized into projects and solutions. A project is a group of related files that form a program, and a solution is a group of projects.
- The **Get Started** page contains links to recent projects.
- The **My Profile** page allows programmers to customize the Visual Studio .NET IDE.
- In the Visual Studio .NET IDE, programmers can browse the Web using the internal Web browser.
- Dialogs are windows used to communicate with users.
- Windows applications are programs that execute inside the Windows OS; these include Microsoft Word, Internet Explorer and Visual Studio .NET. They contain reusable, graphical components, such as buttons and labels, with which the user interacts.
- The form and its controls constitute the graphical user interface (GUI) of the program and are what users interact with when the program is run. Controls are the graphical components with which the user interacts. Users enter data (inputs) into the program by entering information from the keyboard and by clicking mouse buttons. The program displays instructions and other information (outputs) for users to read in the GUI.

- The IDE's title bar displays the name of the project, the programming language, the mode of the IDE, the name of the file being viewed and the mode of the file being viewed.
- To view a tabbed document, click the tab displaying the document's name.
- Menus contain groups of related commands that, when selected, cause the IDE to perform some action. They are located on the menu bar.
- The toolbar contains icons that represent menu commands. To execute a command, click its corresponding icon. Click the down-arrow button beside an icon to display additional commands.
- Moving the mouse pointer over an icon highlights the icon and displays a description called a tool tip.
- The **Solution Explorer** window lists all the files in the solution.
- The solution's startup project is the project that runs when the program is executed.
- The **Toolbox** contains controls for customizing forms.
- By using visual programming, programmers can place predefined controls onto the form instead of writing the code themselves.
- Moving the mouse pointer over a hidden window's icon opens that window. When the mouse pointer leaves the area of the window, the window is hidden. This feature is known as auto-hide. To "pin down" a window (i.e., to disable auto-hide), click the pin icon in the upper-right corner.
- The **Properties** window displays the properties for a form or control. Properties are information about a form or control, such as size, color and position. The **Properties** window allows programmers to modify controls visually, without writing code.
- Each control has its own set of properties. The left column of the **Properties** window shows the properties of the control, whereas the right column displays property values. This window's toolbar contains options for organizing properties either alphabetically (when the alphabetic icon is clicked) or categorically (when the categorized icon is clicked).
- The **Help** menu contains a variety of options: The **Contents** menu item displays a categorized table of contents; the **Index** menu item displays an alphabetical index that the programmer can browse; the **Search** feature allows programmers to find particular help articles, by entering search keywords.
- **Dynamic Help** provides a list of articles based on the current content (i.e., the items around the location of the mouse pointer).
- Context-sensitive help is similar to dynamic help, except that it immediately brings up a relevant help article instead of a list of articles. To use context-sensitive help, click an item, and press the *F1* key.
- Visual Basic programming usually involves a combination of writing a portion of the program code and having the Visual Studio .NET IDE generate the remaining code.
- The text that appears at the top of the form (the title bar) is specified in the form's `Text` property.
- To resize the form, click and drag one of the form's enabled sizing handles (the small squares around the form). Enabled sizing handles are white; disabled sizing handles are gray.
- The grid on the background of the form is used to align controls and is not displayed at run time.
- The `BackColor` property specifies a form's or control's background color. The form's background color is the default background color for any controls added to the form.
- Double-clicking any **Toolbox** control icon places a control of that type on the form. Alternatively, programmers can "drag and drop" controls from the **Toolbox** to the form.
- The label's `Text` property determines the text (if any) that the label displays. The form and label each have their own `Text` property.
- A property's ellipsis button, when clicked, displays a dialog containing additional options.

- In the **Font** dialog, programmers can select the font for a form's or label's text.
- The `TextAlign` property determines how the text is aligned within the label's boundaries.
- The picture-box control displays images. The `Image` property specifies the image that is displayed.
- Select **File > Save All** to save the entire solution.
- IDE design mode is indicated by the text **Microsoft Visual Basic .NET [Design]** in the title bar. When in design mode, the program is not executing.
- While in run mode, the program is executing, and programmers can interact with only a few IDE features.
- When designing a program visually, the name of the Visual Basic file appears in the title bar, followed by **[Design]**.
- Terminate execution by clicking the close button.

TERMINOLOGY

active tab
`Alignment` property
Alphabetic icon
Appearance category in the
    Properties window
application
auto-hide
`BackColor` property
background color
Build menu
button
Categorized icon
clicking
close a project
close button
collapse a tree
compile a program
component selection
context-sensitive help
control
control a form's layout
customize a form
customize Visual Studio .NET
Data menu
debug a program
Debug menu
design mode
dialog
double-clicking
down arrow
dynamic help
Dynamic Help window
Edit menu
expand a tree

external help
F1 help key
File menu
find
Font property
font size
font style
Font window
form
Format menu
form's background color
form's title bar
GUI (graphical user interface)
Help menu
icon
IDE (integrated development environment)
input
internal help
internal Web browser
Internet Explorer
label
menu
menu item
menu bar in Visual Studio .NET
mouse pointer
new project in Visual Studio .NET
opening a project
output
palette
paste
picture box
pin a window
print a project
project

Project menu
Properties window
property for a form or control
recent project
run mode
selecting
single-clicking with left the mouse button
sizing handle
solution
Solution Explorer in Visual Studio .NET
Start Page
startup project
StretchImage property
tabbed window
Text property
title bar
tool tip
toolbar
toolbar icon
Toolbox
Tools menu
.vb file extension
View menu
visual programming
Visual Studio .NET
window layout
Windows application
Windows menu

SELF-REVIEW EXERCISES

2.1 Fill in the blanks in each of the following statements:
   a) The technique of _____ allows programmers to create GUIs without writing any code.
   b) A _____ is a group of one or more projects that collectively form a Visual Basic program.
   c) The _____ feature hides a window when the mouse pointer is moved outside the window's area.
   d) A _____ appears when the mouse pointer hovers over an icon.
   e) The _____ window allows programmers to browse solution files.
   f) A plus box indicates that the tree in the **Solution Explorer** can _____.
   g) The **Properties** window's properties can be sorted _____ or _____.
   h) A form's _____ property specifies the text displayed in the form's title bar.
   i) The _____ allows programmers to add controls to the form in a visual manner.
   j) _____ displays relevant help articles, based on the current context.
   k) Property _____ specifies how text is aligned within a label's boundaries.

2.2 State whether each of the following is *true* or *false*. If *false*, explain why.
   a) The title bar displays the IDE's mode.
   b) The option for customizing the IDE on the **Start Page** is **Get Started**.
   c) The **x** button toggles auto hide.
   d) The toolbar icons represent various menu commands.
   e) The toolbar contains icons that represent controls.
   f) A form's sizing handles are always enabled.
   g) Both forms and labels have a title bar.
   h) Control properties can be modified only by writing code.
   i) Buttons typically perform actions when clicked.
   j) A form's grid is visible only in design mode.
   k) Visual Basic files use the file extension **.basic**.
   l) A form's background color is set using the **BackColor** property.

ANSWERS TO SELF-REVIEW EXERCISES

2.1 a) visual programming. b) solution. c) auto-hide. d) tool tip. e) **Solution Explorer**. f) expand. g) alphabetically, categorically. h) **Text**. i) **Toolbox**. j) **Dynamic Help**. k) **TextAlign**.

2.2 a) True. b) False. The programmer can customize the IDE by clicking the **My Profile** link on the **Start Page**. c) False. The pin icon toggles auto-hide. The **x** button closes a window. d) True. e) False. The **Toolbox** contains icons that represent controls. f) False. Some of a form's sizing handles are disabled. g) False. Forms have a title bar, but labels do not. h) False. Control properties can be modified using the **Properties** window. i) True. j) True. k) False. Visual Basic files use the file extension **.vb**. l) True.

EXERCISES

2.3 Fill in the blanks in each of the following statements:
   a) When an ellipses button is clicked, a _____ is displayed.
   b) To save every file in a solution, select _____.
   c) _____ help immediately displays a relevant help article. It can be accessed using the _____ key.
   d) "GUI" is an acronym for _____.

2.4 State whether each of the following is *true* or *false*. If *false*, explain why.
   a) A control can be added to a form by double-clicking its control icon in the **Toolbox**.
   b) The form, label and picture box have identical properties.
   c) If their machines are connected to the Internet, programmers can browse the Internet from the Visual Studio .NET IDE.
   d) Visual Basic programmers often create complex applications without writing any code.
   e) Sizing handles are visible during execution.

2.5 Some features that appear throughout Visual Studio perform similar actions in different contexts. Explain and give examples of how the plus and minus boxes, ellipsis buttons, down-arrow buttons and tool tips act in this manner. Why do you think the Visual Studio .NET IDE was designed this way?

2.6 Build the GUIs given in each part of this exercise. (You need not provide any functionality.) Execute each program, and determine what happens when a control is clicked with the mouse. Drag controls from the **Toolbox** onto the form and resize them as necessary.
   a) This GUI consists of a **MainMenu** and a **RichTextBox**. After inserting the **MainMenu**, add items by clicking the **Type Here** section, typing a menu name and pressing *Enter*. Resize the **RichTextBox** to fill the form.

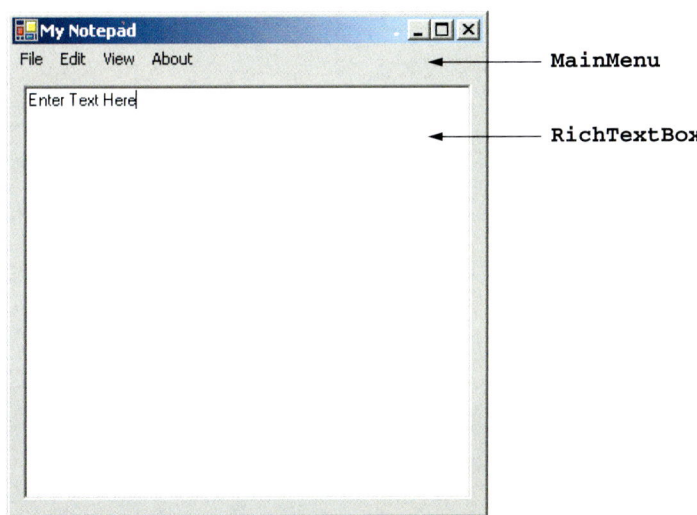

b) This GUI consists of two **Label**s (12-point font size, yellow background), a **MonthCalendar** and a **RichTextBox**. The calendar is displayed when the **MonthCalendar** is dragged onto the form. [*Hint*: Use the **BackColor** property to change the background color of the labels.]

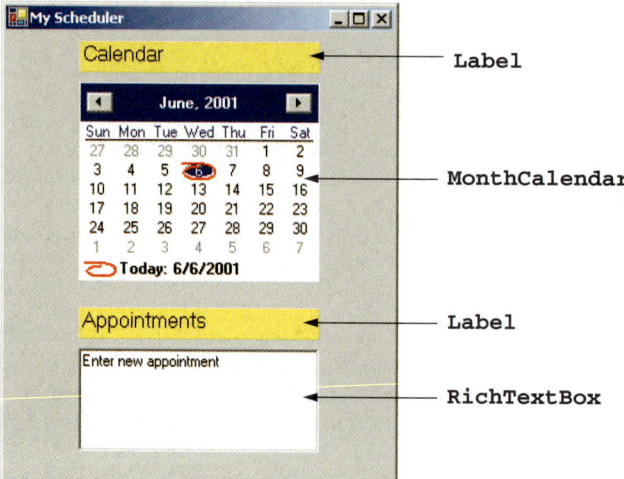

2.7 Fill in the blanks in each of the following statements:
    a) The _____ property specifies which image a picture box displays.
    b) The _____ has an icon in the **Toolbox**, but is not a control.
    c) The _____ menu contains commands for arranging and displaying windows.
    d) Property _____ determines a form's or control's background color.

2.8 Briefly describe each of the following terms:
    a) toolbar
    b) menu bar
    c) Toolbox
    d) control
    e) form
    f) project
    g) title bar
    h) solution

Introduction to Visual Basic Programming

Objectives

- To be able to write simple Visual Basic programs.
- To be able to use input and output statements.
- To become familiar with data types.
- To understand basic memory concepts.
- To be able to use arithmetic operators.
- To understand the precedence of arithmetic operators.
- To be able to write decision-making statements.
- To be able to use equality and relational operators.
- To be able to use dialogs to display messages.

Comment is free, but facts are sacred.
C. P. Scott

The creditor hath a better memory than the debtor.
James Howell

When faced with a decision, I always ask, "What would be the most fun?"
Peggy Walker

Equality, in a social sense, may be divided into that of condition and that of rights.
James Fenimor Cooper

Outline

3.1 Introduction
3.2 Simple Program: Printing a Line of Text
3.3 Another Simple Program: Adding Integers
3.4 Memory Concepts
3.5 Arithmetic
3.6 Decision Making: Equality and Relational Operators
3.7 Using a Dialog to Display a Message
3.8 Internet and World Wide Web Resources

Summary • Terminology • Self-Review Exercises • Answers to Self-Review Exercises • Exercises

3.1 Introduction

Visual Basic .NET enables a disciplined approach to computer-program design. In this chapter, we introduce Visual Basic programming and present examples that illustrate several important features of the language. To help readers better understand the examples in this and other chapters, program code is analyzed one line at a time. In this chapter, we introduce *console applications*—applications that contain only text output. There are several types of Visual Basic projects; the console application is one of the simplest types. Text output in a console application is displayed in a *command window* (also called a *console window*). On Microsoft Windows 95/98, the command window is called the *MS-DOS prompt*; on Microsoft Windows NT/2000/XP, the command window is called the *command prompt*. With a sophisticated language like Visual Basic, programmers can create programs that input and output information in a variety of ways, which we discuss throughout the book. For instance, in Chapter 2, we created a simple graphical user interface (GUI) for a Windows application, using visual programming techniques. Windows applications are discussed in greater detail in Chapters 4 and 5, Control Structures: Part 1 and Control Structures: Part 2, respectively. These chapters provide a more detailed introduction to *program development* in Visual Basic.

3.2 Simple Program: Printing a Line of Text

Visual Basic .NET uses some notations that might appear strange to nonprogrammers. To explain these notations, we begin by considering a simple program (Fig. 3.1) that displays a line of text. When this program is run, the output appears in a command window.

This program illustrates several important Visual Basic features. For the reader's convenience, all program listings in this text include line numbers—these line numbers are not part of Visual Basic programs. In addition, each program is followed by one or more windows showing the program's output.

Line 1 begins with a *single-quote character* (`'`) which indicates that the remainder of the line is a *comment*. Programmers insert comments in a *program*, or code listing, to improve the readability of their code. Comments can be placed either on their own line (we call these "full-line comments") or at the end of a line of Visual Basic code (we call these

```
1    ' Fig. 3.1: Welcome1.vb
2    ' Simple Visual Basic program.
3
4    Module modFirstWelcome
5
6       Sub Main()
7          Console.WriteLine("Welcome to Visual Basic!")
8       End Sub ' Main
9
10   End Module ' modFirstWelcome
```

```
Welcome to Visual Basic!
```

Fig. 3.1 Simple Visual Basic program .

"end-of-line comments"). The Visual Basic compiler ignores comments, which means that comments do not cause the computer to perform any actions when the program is run. The comment in line 1 simply indicates the figure number and file name for this program. Line 2 provides a brief description of the program. By convention, every program in this book begins in this manner—you can write anything you want in a comment. In this case, the file is named **Welcome1.vb**. Recall that **.vb** is the file extension for Visual Basic files.

Good Programming Practice 3.1
Every program should begin with one or more comments describing the program's purpose.

Good Programming Practice 3.2
Comments written at the end of a line should be preceded by one or more spaces to enhance program readability.

Lines 4–10 define our first *module* (these lines collectively are called a *module definition*). Visual Basic console applications consist of pieces called modules, which are logical groupings of *procedures* that simplify program organization. Procedures perform tasks and can return information when the tasks are completed. Every console application in Visual Basic consists of at least one module definition and one procedure. In Chapter 6, Procedures, we discuss modules and procedures in detail.

The word **Module** is an example of a *keyword* (or *reserved word*). Keywords are reserved for use by Visual Basic (a complete list of Visual Basic keywords is presented in the next chapter). The name of the **Module** (i.e., **modFirstWelcome**) is known as an *identifier*, which is a series of characters consisting of letters, digits, and underscores (_). Identifiers cannot begin with a digit and cannot contain spaces. Examples of valid identifiers are **value1**, **xy_coordinate**, **_total** and **cmdExit**. The name **7Welcome** is not a valid identifier because it begins with a digit, and the name **input field** is not a valid identifier because it contains a space.

Good Programming Practice 3.3
*Begin each module identifier with **mod** to make modules easier to identify.*

Visual Basic keywords and identifiers are not *case sensitive*. This means that uppercase and lowercase letters are considered to be identical, which causes **modfirstwelcome** and **modFirstWelcome** to be interpreted as the same identifier. Although keywords appear to be case sensitive, they are not. Visual Studio applies the "proper" case to each letter of a keyword, so, when **module** is typed, it is changed to **Module** when the *Enter* key is pressed.

Lines 3 and 5 are blank lines. Often, blank lines and space characters are used throughout a program to make the program easier to read. Collectively, blank lines, space characters and tab characters are known as *whitespace* (space characters and tabs are known specifically as *whitespace characters*). Several conventions for using whitespace characters are discussed in this and subsequent chapters.

Good Programming Practice 3.4

Use blank lines, space characters and tab characters in a program to enhance program readability.

Line 6 is present in all Visual Basic console applications. These applications begin executing at **Main**, which is known as the *entry point of the program*. The parentheses that appear after **Main** indicate that **Main** is a procedure.

Notice that lines 6–8 are indented relative to lines 4 and 10. This is one of the spacing conventions mentioned earlier. Indentation improves program readability. We refer to each spacing convention as a *Good Programming Practice*.

Keyword **Sub** (line 7) begins the *body of the procedure definition* (the code that will be executed as part of our program). Keywords **End Sub** (line 8) close the procedure definition's body. Notice that the line of code (line 7) in the procedure body is indented several additional spaces to the right relative to lines 6 and 8.

Good Programming Practice 3.5

Indent the entire body of each procedure definition one "level" of indentation. This emphasizes the structure of the procedure, improving the procedure definition's readability.

Line 7 in Fig. 3.1 does the "real work" of the program, displaying the phrase **Welcome to Visual Basic!** on the screen. Line 7 instructs the computer to perform an *action*—namely, to print the series of characters contained between the double quotation marks. Characters delimited in this manner are called *strings*, which also are called *character strings* or *string literals*.

The entire line, including **Console.WriteLine** and its *argument* in the parentheses (the string), is called a *statement*. When this statement executes, it *displays* (or *prints*) the message **Welcome to Visual Basic!** in the command window (Fig. 3.1).

Notice that **Console.WriteLine** contains two distinct identifiers (i.e., **Console** and **WriteLine**) separated by the *dot operator* (**.**). The identifier to the right of the dot operator is the *method* name, and the identifier to the left of the dot operator is the *class* name to which the method belongs. Classes organize groups of related methods and data, whereas methods perform tasks and can return information when the tasks are completed. For instance, the **Console** class contains methods, such as **WriteLine**, that communicate with users via the command window. We discuss classes and methods in detail in Chapter 8, Object-Based Programming. Chapter 6 introduces methods.

When method **WriteLine** completes its task, it positions the *output cursor* (the location where the next character will be displayed) at the beginning of the next line in the command window. This behavior produces a result similar to that of pressing the *Enter* key when typing in a text editor window—the cursor is repositioned at the beginning of the next line in the file. Program execution terminates when the program encounters the **End Sub** in line 8.

Now that we have presented our first console application, we provide a step-by-step explanation of how to create and run it using the features of the Visual Studio .NET IDE.

1. *Create the console application.* Select **File > New > Project...** to display the **New Project** dialog (Fig. 3.2). In the left pane, select ***Visual Basic Projects***, and, in the right pane, select ***Console Application***. In the dialog's **Name** field, type **Welcome1**. The location in which project files will be created is specified in the **Location** field. By default, projects are saved in the folder **Visual Studio Projects** inside the **My Documents** folder (on the Windows desktop). Click **OK** to create the project. The IDE now contains the open console application, as shown in Fig. 3.3. Notice that the editor window contains four lines of code provided by the IDE. The coloring scheme used by the IDE is called *syntax-color highlighting* and helps programmers visually differentiate programming elements. Keywords appear in blue, whereas text is black. When present, comments are colored green. In Step 4, we discuss how to use the editor window to write code.

2. *Change the name of the program file.* For programs in this book, we change the name of the program file (i.e., **Module1.vb**) to a more descriptive name. To rename the file, click **Module1.vb** in the **Solution Explorer** window, this step will display the program file's properties in the **Properties** window (Fig. 3.4). Change the *File Name* property to **Welcome1.vb**.

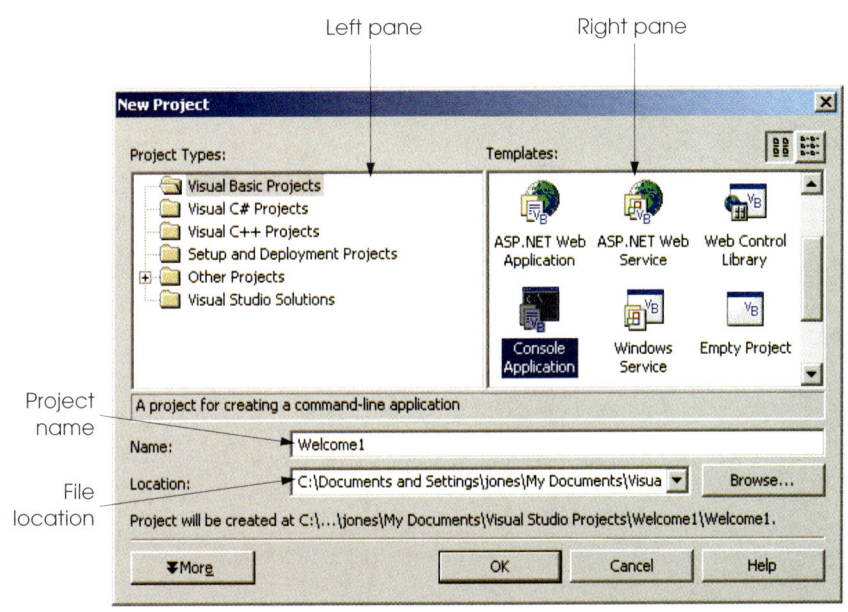

Fig. 3.2 Creating a **Console Application** with the **New Project** dialog.

66 Introduction to Visual Basic Programming Chapter 3

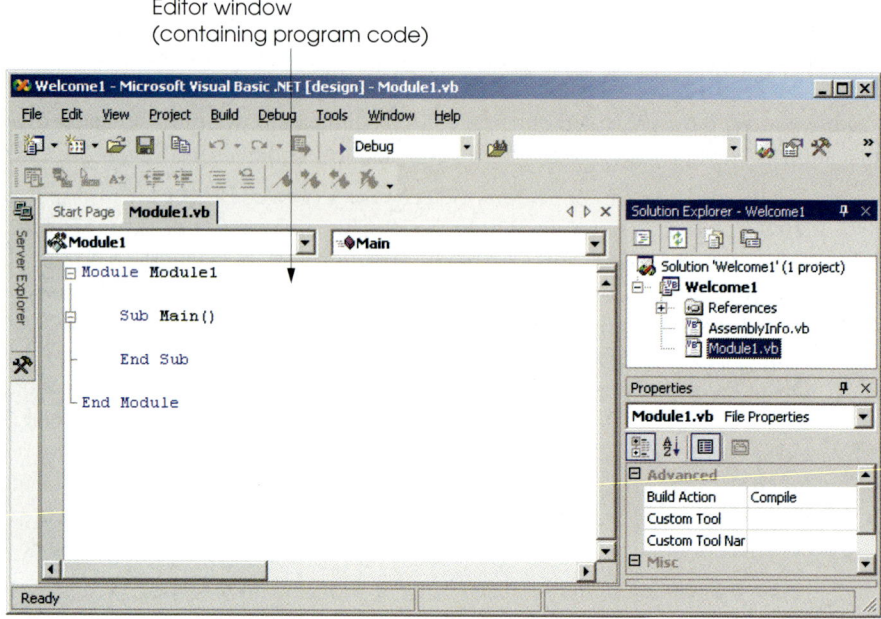

Fig. 3.3 IDE with an open console application.

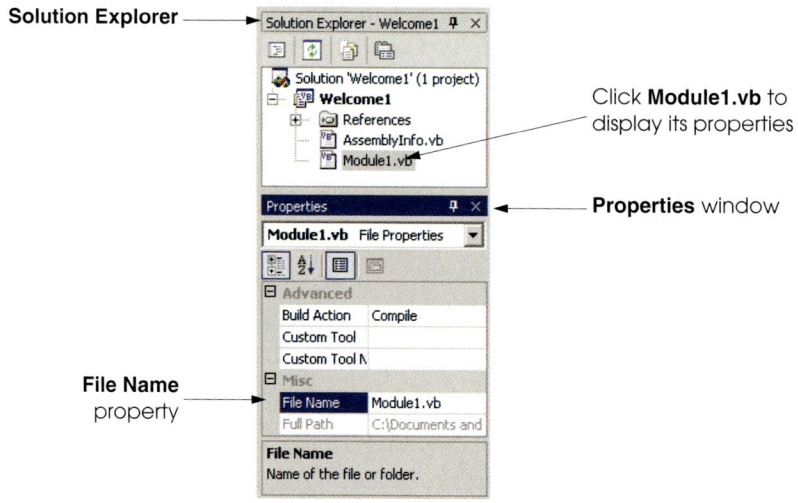

Fig. 3.4 Renaming the program file in the **Properties** window.

Testing and Debugging Tip 3.1

Syntax-color highlighting helps programmers avoid accidentally misusing keywords.

3. *Change the name of the module.* Notice that changing the name of the program file does not affect the module name in the program code. Module names must be modified in the editor window. To do so, replace the identifier **Module1** with **modFirstWelcome** by deleting the old name and typing the new name after the keyword **Module**.

4. *Writing code.* In the editor window, type the code contained in line 7 of Fig. 3.1 between **Sub Main()** and **End Sub**. After the programmer types the class name and the dot operator (i.e., **Console.**), a window containing a scrollbar is displayed (Fig. 3.5). This Visual Studio .NET IDE feature, called *IntelliSense,* lists a class's *members*, which include method names. As the programmer types characters, the first member that matches all the characters typed is highlighted, and a tool tip containing a description of that member is displayed. The programmer can either type the complete member name (e.g., **WriteLine**), double-click the member name in the list or press the *Tab* key to complete the name. Once the complete name is provided, the IntelliSense window closes. When the programmer types the open parenthesis character, **(**, after **Console.WriteLine**, two additional windows are displayed (Fig. 3.6). These are the *Parameter Info* and *Parameter List* windows. The Parameter Info window displays information about a method's arguments. This window indicates how many versions of the selected method are available and provides *up and down arrows* for scrolling through the different versions. For example, there are 18 versions of the **WriteLine** method used in our example. The Parameter List window lists possible arguments for the method shown in the Parameter Info window. These windows are part of the many features provided by the IDE to aid program development. You will learn more about information displayed in these windows over the next several chapters. In this case, because we know that we want to use the version of **WriteLine** that takes a string argument, we can close these windows by pressing the *Escape* key twice (i.e., once for each of the windows).

Testing and Debugging Tip 3.2

Visual Basic provides a large number of classes and methods. The Parameter Info and Parameter List windows help ensure that a method is being used correctly.

5. *Run the program.* We are now ready to compile and execute our program. To do this, we simply follow steps similar to those provided in Chapter 2. To compile the program, select **Build > Build Solution**. This creates a new file, named **Welcome1.exe**, in the project's directory that contains the Microsoft Intermediate Language (MSIL) code for our program. The **.exe** file extension denotes that the file is executable (i.e., contains instructions that can be executed by another program, such as the Common Language Runtime). To run this console application (i.e., **Welcome1.exe**), select **Debug > Start Without Debugging**.[1]

---

1. Selecting **Debug Start Without Debugging** causes the command window to prompt the user to press a key after the program terminates, allowing the user to observe the program's output. In contrast, if we run this program using **Debug > Start**, as we did for the Windows application in Chapter 2, a command window opens, the program displays the message **Welcome to Visual Basic!**, then the command window closes immediately.

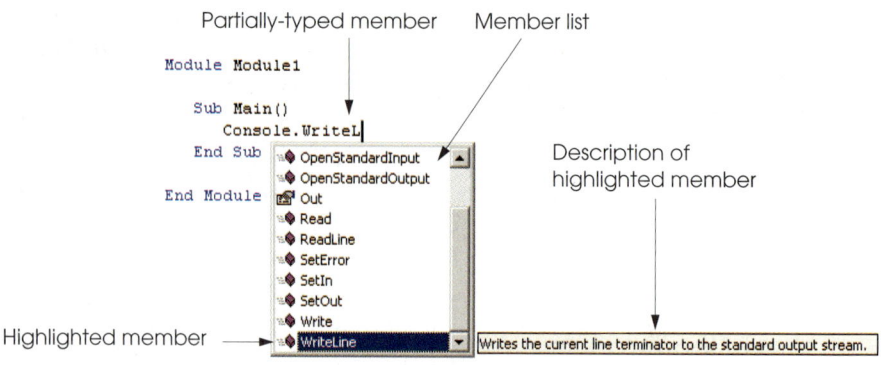

Fig. 3.5 IntelliSense feature of the Visual Studio .NET IDE.

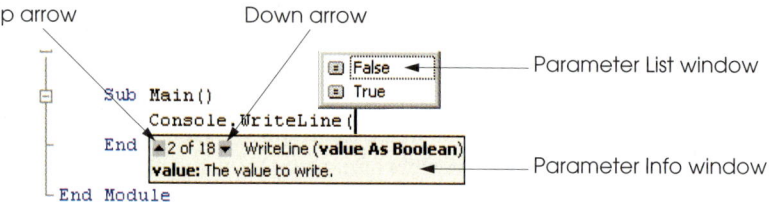

Fig. 3.6 Parameter Info and Parameter List windows.

When the program runs, procedure **Main** is invoked, which is considered the entry point to the program. Next, the statement on line 7 of **Main** displays **Welcome to Visual Basic!**. Figure 3.7 shows the result of program execution.

When the programmer types a line of code and presses the *Enter* key, the Visual Studio .NET IDE responds either by applying syntax-color highlighting or by generating a *syntax error* (also called a *compile-time error*), which indicates a violation of the language syntax (i.e., one or more statements are not written correctly). Syntax errors occur for various reasons, such as when keywords are misspelled. When a syntax error occurs, the Visual Studio .NET IDE underlines the error in blue, and provides a description of the error in the **Task List** window (Fig. 3.8). If the **Task List** window is not visible in the IDE, select **View > Other Windows > Task List** to display it. [*Note*: One syntax error can lead to multiple entries in the **Task List** window.]

Fig. 3.7 Executing the program shown in Fig. 3.1.

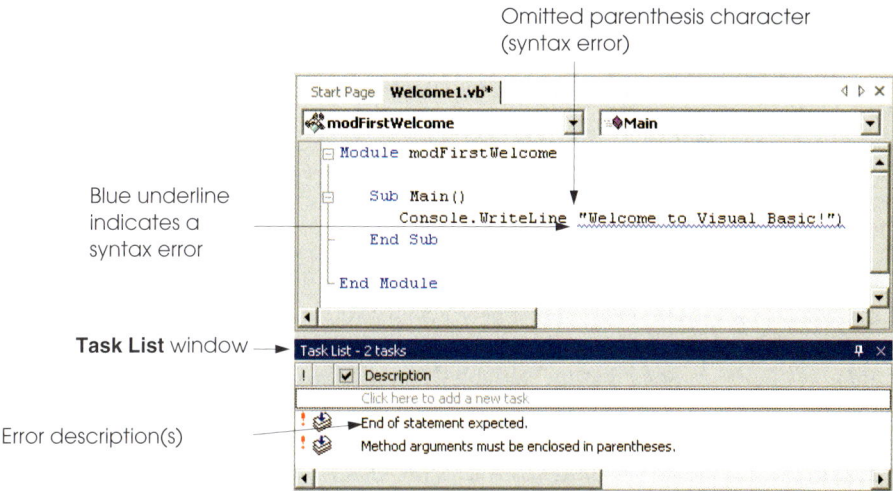

Fig. 3.8 IDE indicating a syntax error.

The message **Welcome to Visual Basic!** can be displayed using multiple method calls. The program in Fig. 3.9 uses two statements to produce the same output as that of the program in Fig. 3.1.

Lines 7–8 of Fig. 3.9 display one line of text in the command window. The first statement calls **Console** method *Write* to display a string. Unlike **WriteLine**, **Write** does not position the output cursor at the beginning of the next line in the command window after displaying its string. Instead, the next character displayed in the command window appears immediately after the last character displayed with **Write**. Thus, when line 8 executes, the first character displayed, "**V**," appears immediately after the last character displayed with **Write** (i.e., the space character after the word **"to"** in line 7). Each **Write** or **WriteLine** outputs its characters at the exact location where the previous **Write**'s or **WriteLine**'s output ended.

```
1    ' Fig. 3.9: Welcome2.vb
2    ' Writing line of text with multiple statements.
3
4    Module modSecondWelcome
5
6       Sub Main()
7          Console.Write("Welcome to ")
8          Console.WriteLine("Visual Basic!")
9       End Sub ' Main
10
11   End Module ' modSecondWelcome
```

```
Welcome to Visual Basic!
```

Fig. 3.9 Using multiple statements to print a line of text.

3.3 Another Simple Program: Adding Integers

Our next program (Fig. 3.10) inputs two integers (whole numbers) provided by a user, computes the sum of these integers and displays the result. As the user inputs each integer and presses the *Enter* key, the integer is read into the program and added to the total.

Good Programming Practice 3.6

Precede every full-line comment or group of full-line comments with a blank line. The blank line makes the comments stand out and improves program readability.

Lines 9 and 12 are *declarations,* which begin with keyword **Dim** The words **firstNumber**, **secondNumber**, **number1**, **number2** and **sumOfNumbers** are the names of *variables,* or locations in the computer's memory where values can be stored for use by a program. All variables must be declared before they can be used in a program. The declaration in line 9 specifies that the variables **firstNumber** and **secondNumber** are data of type **String**, which indicates that these variables store strings of characters. Line 12 declares that variables **number1**, **number2** and **sumOfNumbers** are data of type **Integer**, which means that these variables store *integer* values (i.e., whole numbers such as 919, –11, 0 and 138624). Data types already defined in Visual Basic, such as **String** and **Integer**, are known as *built-in data types* or *primitive data types*. Primitive data type names are keywords. The 11 primitive data types are summarized in Chapter 6.

```
1    ' Fig. 3.10: Addition.vb
2    ' Addition program.
3
4    Module modAddition
5
6       Sub Main()
7
8          ' variables for storing user input
9          Dim firstNumber, secondNumber As String
10
11         ' variables used in addition calculation
12         Dim number1, number2, sumOfNumbers As Integer
13
14         ' read first number from user
15         Console.Write("Please enter the first integer: ")
16         firstNumber = Console.ReadLine()
17
18         ' read second number from user
19         Console.Write("Please enter the second integer: ")
20         secondNumber = Console.ReadLine()
21
22         ' convert input values to Integers
23         number1 = firstNumber
24         number2 = secondNumber
25
26         sumOfNumbers = number1 + number2 ' add numbers
27
28         ' display results
29         Console.WriteLine("The sum is {0}", sumOfNumbers)
```

Fig. 3.10 Addition program that adds two numbers entered by the user (part 1 of 2).

Chapter 3   Introduction to Visual Basic Programming   71

```
30
31      End Sub ' Main
32
33   End Module ' modAddition
```

```
Please enter the first integer: 45
Please enter the second integer: 72
The sum is 117
```

Fig. 3.10   Addition program that adds two numbers entered by the user (part 2 of 2).

A variable name can be any valid identifier. Variables of the same type can be declared in separate statements or they can be declared in one statement with each variable in the declaration separated by a comma. The latter format uses a *comma-separated list* of variable names.

Good Programming Practice 3.7
Choosing meaningful variable names helps a program to be "self-documenting" (i.e., the program can be understood by others without the use of manuals or excessive comments).

Good Programming Practice 3.8
By convention, variable-name identifiers begin with a lowercase letter. As with module names, every word in the name after the first word should begin with a capital letter. For example, identifier **firstNumber** *has a capital* **N** *beginning its second word,* **Number**.

Good Programming Practice 3.9
Some programmers prefer to declare each variable on a separate line. This format allows for easy insertion of a comment next to each declaration.

Line 15 prompts the user to enter the first of two integers that will be added together. Line 16 obtains the value entered by the user and assigns it to variable **firstNumber**. The argument passed to **Write** (line 15) is called a *prompt*, because it directs the user to take a specific action. The method **ReadLine** (line 16) causes the program to pause and wait for user input. After entering the integer via the keyboard, the user presses the *Enter* key to send the integer to the program.

Technically, the user can send any character to the program as input. For this program, if the user types a non-integer value, such as "**hello**," a *run-time error* (an error that has its effect at execution time) occurs (Fig. 3.11). Chapter 11, Exception Handling, discusses how to handle such an error to make programs more robust.

Once the user has entered a number and pressed *Enter*, this number is assigned to variable **firstNumber** (line 16) with the *assignment operator*, **=**. The statement is read as, "**firstNumber** *gets* the value returned by method **ReadLine** of the **Console** class." The assignment operator is called a *binary operator*, because it has two *operands—* **firstNumber** and the value returned by **Console.ReadLine**. The entire statement is called an *assignment statement* because it assigns a value to a variable.

Good Programming Practice 3.10
Place spaces on either side of a binary operator. The spaces make the operator stand out and improve the readability of the statement.

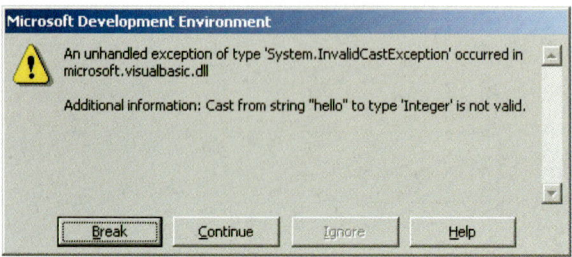

Fig. 3.11 Dialog displaying a run-time error.

Lines 19–20 prompt the user to enter a second integer and assign the input value to **secondNumber**. User input from the command window is sent to a console application as a **String**. For example, if the user types the characters **7** and **2** and then presses *Enter*, the value returned by **ReadLine** is **"72"**. To perform arithmetic operations using the input values, the **String**s first must be converted to **Integer**s.

Lines 23–24 *implicitly convert* the two **String**s typed by the user to **Integer** values. Visual Basic performs data-type conversions whenever necessary. In this case, the assignment of a **String** value to an **Integer** variable (i.e., **number1**) invokes the conversion, because **Integer** variables can accept only **Integer** values. The value obtained by converting the **String** value in line 23 is assigned to **Integer** variable **number1**. In this program, any subsequent references to the value of **number1** indicate this **Integer** value. Likewise, the **Integer** value obtained by converting the **String** in line 24 is assigned to variable **number2**. The value of **number2** refers to this **Integer** value in the ensuing discussion. The values stored in **firstNumber** and **secondNumber** remain **String**s.

Alternatively, this implicit conversion, can be performed so as to eliminate the need for the **String** variables. For example,

```
Dim number1 As Integer
number1 = Console.ReadLine()
```

does not use a **String** variable (i.e., **firstNumber**). In this case, Visual Basic knows that **Console.ReadLine** returns a **String**, and the program performs the necessary conversion. When the **String** is both read and converted in a single line of code, the **String** variable (i.e., **firstNumber**) becomes unnecessary.

The assignment statement on line 26 calculates the sum of the **Integer** variables **number1** and **number2** and assigns the result to variable **sumOfNumbers**, using the assignment operator, **=**. The statement is read as, "**sumOfNumbers** *gets* the value of **number1 + number2**." Most calculations are performed in assignment statements.

After the calculation is completed, line 29 displays the result of the addition. The *comma-separated* argument list given to **WriteLine**

```
"The sum is {0}.", sumOfNumbers
```

use **{0}** to indicate that we are printing out the contents of a variable. If we assume that **sumOfNumbers** contains the value **117**, the expression evaluates as follows: Visual Basic encounters a number in curly braces, (**{0}**), known as a *format*. A format indicates that the argument after the string (in this case, **sumOfNumbers**) will be evaluated and incorporated into the string, in place of the format. The resulting string is "**The sum is 117**." Additional formats (**{1}**, **{2}**, **{3}**, etc.) can be inserted into the string. Each additional format requires a corresponding variable name or value. For example, if the arguments to **WriteLine** are

    "The values are {0}, {1} and {2}", **number1, number2, 7**

the value of **number1** replaces **{0}** (because it is the first variable), the value of **number2** replaces **{1}** (because it is the second variable) and the value **7** replaces **{2}** (because it is the third value). Assuming **number1** is **45** and **number2** is **72**, the string contains **"The values are 45, 72 and 7"**.

Good Programming Practice 3.11
Place a space after each comma in a method's argument list to make method calls more readable.

When reading or writing a program, some programmers find it difficult to match **End Sub** statements with their procedure definitions. For this reason, programmers sometimes include an end-of-line comment after **End Sub**, as we do in line 31. This practice is especially helpful when modules contain multiple procedures. Although, for now, our modules contain only one procedure, we place the comment after **End Sub** as a good programming practice. We discuss how to create procedures in Chapter 6, Procedures.

Good Programming Practice 3.12
*Follow a procedure's **End Sub** with a end-of-line comment. This comment should contain the procedure name that the **End Sub** terminates.*

3.4 Memory Concepts

Variable names, such as **number1**, **number2** and **sumOfNumbers**, correspond to actual *locations* in the computer's memory. Every variable has a *name, type, size* and *value*. In the addition program in Fig. 3.10, when the statement (line 23)

    number1 = firstNumber

executes, the **String** previously input by the user in the command window and stored in **firstNumber** is converted to an **Integer**. This **Integer** is placed into a memory location to which the name **number1** has been assigned by the compiler. Suppose the user enters the characters **45** and presses *Enter*. This input is returned by **ReadLine** as a **String** and assigned to **firstNumber**. The program then converts the **String "45"** to an **Integer**, and the computer places the **Integer** value **45** into location **number1**, as shown in Fig. 3.12.

Whenever a value is placed in a memory location, this value replaces the value previously stored in that location. The previous value is destroyed (lost).

Suppose that the user then enters the characters **72** and presses *Enter*. Line 20

    secondNumber = Console.ReadLine()

converts **secondNumber** to an **Integer**, placing the **Integer** value **72** into location **number2**, and memory appears as shown in Fig. 3.13.

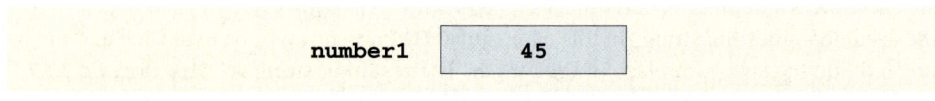

Fig. 3.12 Memory location showing name and value of variable **number1**.

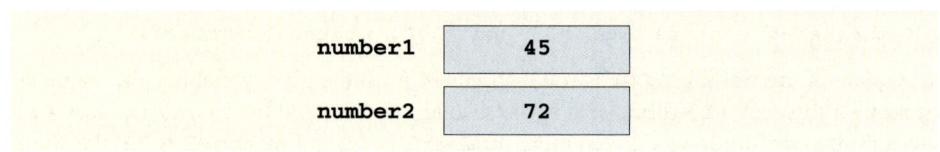

Fig. 3.13 Memory locations after values for variables **number1** and **number2** have been input.

Once the program has obtained values for **number1** and **number2**, it adds these values and places their total into variable **sumOfNumbers**. The statement

```
sumOfNumbers = number1 + number2
```

performs the addition and replaces (i.e., destroys) **sumOfNumbers**'s previous value. After **sumOfNumbers** is calculated, memory appears as shown in Fig. 3.14. Note that the values of **number1** and **number2** appear exactly as they did before they were used in the calculation of **sumOfNumbers**. Although these values were used when the computer performed the calculation, they were not destroyed. This illustrates that, when a value is read from a memory location, the process is *nondestructive*.

3.5 Arithmetic

Most programs perform arithmetic calculations. The *arithmetic operators* are summarized in Fig. 3.15. Note the use of various special symbols not used in algebra. For example, the *asterisk* (*****) indicates multiplication, and the keyword **Mod** represents the *modulus operator*, which is discussed shortly. The majority of arithmetic operators in Fig. 3.15 are binary operators, because each operates using two operands. For example, the expression **sum + value** contains the binary operator **+** and the two operands **sum** and **value**. Visual Basic also provides *unary operators*, i.e., operators that take only one operand. For example, unary versions of plus (**+**) and minus (**–**) are provided, so that programmers can write expressions such as **+9** and **–19**.

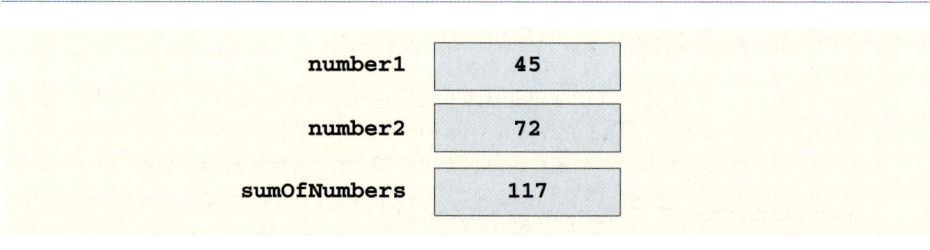

Fig. 3.14 Memory locations after an addition operation.

Visual Basic operation	Arithmetic operator	Algebraic expression	Visual Basic expression
Addition	+	$f + 7$	`f + 7`
Subtraction	-	$p - c$	`p - c`
Multiplication	*	bm	`b * m`
Division (float)	/	x/y or $\frac{x}{y}$ or $x \div y$	`x / y`
Division (integer)	\	none	`v \ u`
Modulus	Mod	r modulo s	`r Mod s`
Exponentiation	^	q^p	`q ^ p`
Unary Negative	-	$-e$	`-e`
Unary Positive	+	$+g$	`+g`

Fig. 3.15 Arithmetic operators.

Visual Basic has separate operators for integer division (the backslash, ****) and floating-point division (the forward slash, **/**). **Integer** division takes two **Integer** operands and yields an **Integer** result; for example, the expression **7 \ 4** evaluates to **1**, and the expression **17 \ 5** evaluates to **3**. Note that any fractional part in the **Integer** division result simply is discarded (i.e., truncated)—no rounding occurs. When floating-point numbers are used with the integer division operator, the numbers are first rounded to the nearest whole number, then divided. This means that, although **7.1 \ 4** evaluates to **1** as expected, the statement **7.7 \ 4** evaluates to **2**, because **7.7** is rounded to **8** before the division occurs.

The modulus operator, **Mod**, yields the remainder after **Integer** division in Visual Basic programs. The expression **x Mod y** yields the remainder after **x** is divided by **y**. Thus, **7 Mod 4** yields **3** and **17 Mod 5** yields **2**. This operator is used most commonly with **Integer** operands, but also can be used with other types. In later chapters, we consider interesting applications of the modulus operator, such the determination of whether one number is a multiple of another.

Arithmetic expressions in Visual Basic must be written in *straight-line form* so that programs can be entered into a computer. Thus, expressions such as "**a** divided by **b**" must be written as **a / b** so that all *constants* (such as **45** and **72** in the previous example), variables and operators appear in a straight line. The following algebraic notation generally is not acceptable to compilers:

$$\frac{a}{b}$$

Parentheses are used in Visual Basic expressions in the same manner as in algebraic expressions. For example, to multiply **a** times the quantity **b + c**, we write

`a * ( b + c )`

Visual Basic applies the operators in arithmetic expressions in a precise sequence, determined by the following *rules of operator precedence*, which are generally the same as those followed in algebra:

1. Operators in expressions contained within a pair of parentheses are evaluated first. Thus, *parentheses can be used to force the order of evaluation to occur in any sequence desired by the programmer.* Parentheses are at the highest level of precedence. With *nested* (or *embedded*) parentheses, the operators contained in the innermost pair of parentheses are applied first.

2. Exponentiation is applied next. If an expression contains several exponentiation operations, operators are applied from left to right.

3. Unary positive and negative, **+** and **-**, are applied next. If an expression contains several sign operations, operators are applied from left to right. Sign operations **+** and **-** are said to have the same level of precedence.

4. Multiplication and floating-point division operations are applied next. If an expression contains several multiplication and floating-point division operations, operators are applied from left to right. Multiplication and floating-point division have the same level of precedence.

5. **Integer** division is applied next. If an expression contains several **Integer** division operations, operators are applied from left to right.

6. Modulus operations are applied next. If an expression contains several modulus operations, operators are applied from left to right.

7. Addition and subtraction operations are applied last. If an expression contains several addition and subtraction operations, operators are applied from left to right. Addition and subtraction have the same level of precedence.

The rules of operator precedence enable Visual Basic to apply operators in the correct order. When we say operators are applied from "left to right," we are referring to the *associativity* of the operators. If there are multiple operators, each with the same precedence, the order in which the operators are applied is determined by the operators' associativity. Figure 3.16 summarizes the rules of operator precedence. This table will be expanded as we introduce additional Visual Basic operators in subsequent chapters. A complete operator-precedence chart is available in Appendix A.

Operator(s)	Operation	Order of evaluation (precedence)
( )	Parentheses	Evaluated first. If the parentheses are nested, the expression in the innermost pair is evaluated first. If there are several pairs of parentheses "on the same level" (i.e., not nested), they are evaluated from left to right.
^	Exponentiation	Evaluated second. If there are several such operators, they are evaluated from left to right.

Fig. 3.16 Precedence of arithmetic operators (part 1 of 2).

Operator(s)	Operation	Order of evaluation (precedence)
+, −	Sign operations	Evaluated third. If there are several such operators, they are evaluated from left to right.
*, /	Multiplication and Division	Evaluated fourth. If there are several such operators, they are evaluated from left to right.
\	**Integer** division	Evaluated fifth. If there are several such operators, they are evaluated from left to right.
Mod	Modulus	Evaluated sixth. If there are several such operators, they are evaluated from left to right.
+, −	Addition and Subtraction	Evaluated last. If there are several such operators, they are evaluated from left to right.

Fig. 3.16 Precedence of arithmetic operators (part 2 of 2).

Notice, in the table, that we make note of nested parentheses. Not all expressions with several pairs of parentheses contain nested parentheses. For example, although the expression

```
a * ( b + c ) + c * ( d + e )
```

contains multiple sets of parentheses, none of the parentheses are nested. Rather, these sets are referred to as being "on the same level."

Let us consider several expressions in light of the rules of operator precedence. Each example lists an algebraic expression and its Visual Basic equivalent.

The following is an example of an arithmetic mean (average) of five terms:

Algebra: $m = \dfrac{a + b + c + d + e}{5}$

Visual Basic: `m = ( a + b + c + d + e ) / 5`

The parentheses are required, because floating-point division has higher precedence than addition. The entire quantity **(a + b + c + d + e)** is to be divided by **5**. If the parentheses are omitted, erroneously, we obtain **a + b + c + d + e / 5**, which evaluates as

$$a + b + c + d + \dfrac{e}{5}$$

The following is the equation of a straight line:

Algebra: $y = mx + b$

Visual Basic: `y = m * x + b`

No parentheses are required. The multiplication is applied first, because multiplication has a higher precedence than addition. The assignment occurs last because it has a lower precedence than multiplication and addition.

The following example contains modulus (**Mod**), multiplication, division, addition and subtraction operations (we use % to represent the modulus in algebra):

Algebra: $z = pr\%q + w/x - y$

Visual Basic: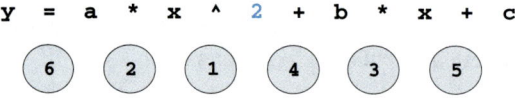

The circled numbers under the statement indicate the order in which Visual Basic applies the operators. The multiplication and division operators are evaluated first in left-to-right order (i.e., they associate from left to right). The modulus operator is evaluated next. The addition and subtraction operators are applied next, from left to right. The assignment operator is evaluated last.

To develop a better understanding of the rules of operator precedence, consider how a second-degree polynomial ($y = ax^2 + bx + c$) is evaluated:

```
y = a * x ^ 2 + b * x + c
    6   2   1   4   3   5
```

The circled numbers under the statement indicate the order in which Visual Basic applies the operators. In Visual Basic, x^2 is represented as **x ^ 2**.

Now, suppose that **a**, **b**, **c** and **x** are initialized as follows: **a = 2**, **b = 3**, **c = 7** and **x = 5**. Figure 3.17 illustrates the order in which the operators are applied.

As in algebra, it is acceptable to place unnecessary parentheses in an expression to make the expression easier to read—these parentheses are called *redundant parentheses*. For example, the preceding assignment statement might be parenthesized as

```
y = ( a * x ^ 2 ) + ( b * x ) + c
```

Good Programming Practice 3.13

The use of redundant parentheses in more complex arithmetic expressions can make the expressions easier to read.

3.6 Decision Making: Equality and Relational Operators

This section introduces Visual Basic's **If/Then** structure, which allows a program to make a decision based on the truth or falsity of some expression. The expression in an **If/Then** structure is called the *condition*. If the condition is met (i.e., the condition is *true*), the statement in the body of the **If/Then** structure executes. If the condition is not met (i.e., the condition is *false*), the body statement is not executed. Conditions in **If/Then** structures can be formed by using the *equality operators* and *relational operators* (also called *comparison operators*), which are summarized in Fig. 3.18. The relational and equality operators all have the same level of precedence and associate from left to right.

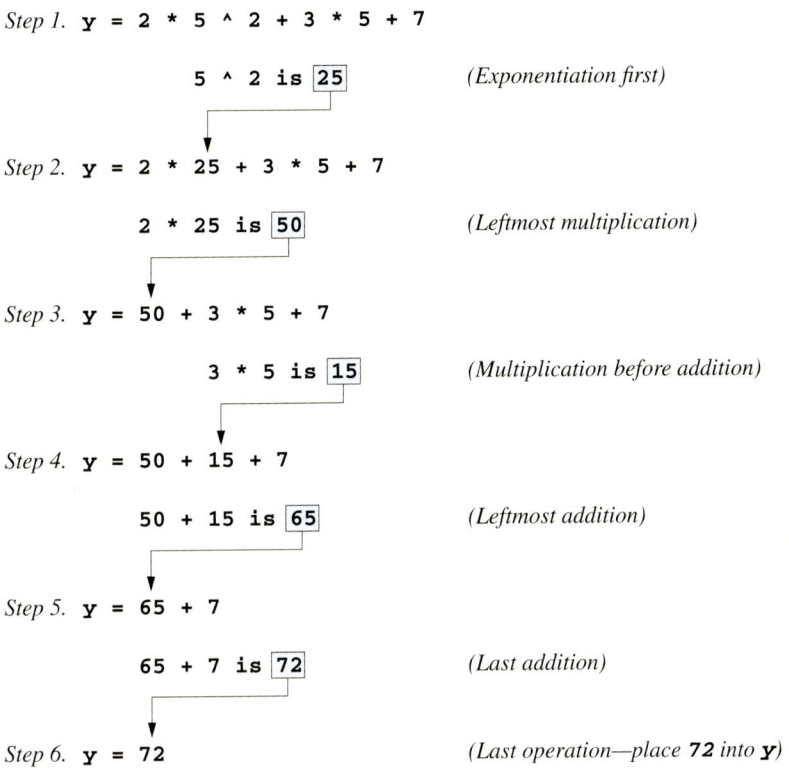

Fig. 3.17 Order in which a second-degree polynomial is evaluated.

Standard algebraic equality operator or relational operator	Visual Basic equality or relational operator	Example of Visual Basic condition	Meaning of Visual Basic condition
Equality operators			
=	=	x = y	**x** is equal to **y**
≠	<>	x <> y	**x** is not equal to **y**
Relational operators			
>	>	x > y	**x** is greater than **y**
<	<	x < y	**x** is less than **y**
≥	>=	x >= y	**x** is greater than or equal to **y**
≤	<=	x <= y	**x** is less than or equal to **y**

Fig. 3.18 Equality and relational operators.

Common Programming Error 3.1

It is a syntax error to add spaces between the symbols in the operators `<>`, `>=` and `<=` (as in `< >`, `> =`, `< =`).

Common Programming Error 3.2

Reversal of the operators `<>`, `>=` and `<=` (as in `><`, `=>`, `=<`) is a syntax error.

The next example uses six **If/Then** statements to compare two numbers entered into a program by the user. If the condition in any of these **If/Then** statements is true, the output statement associated with that **If/Then** executes. The user inputs these values, which are converted to **Integer**s and stored in variables **number1** and **number2**, respectively. The comparisons are performed, and the results of the comparison are displayed in the command window. The program and outputs are shown in Fig. 3.19.

```vb
1   ' Fig. 3.19: Comparison.vb
2   ' Using equality and relational operators.
3
4   Module modComparison
5
6      Sub Main()
7
8         ' declare Integer variables for user input
9         Dim number1, number2 As Integer
10
11        ' read first number from user
12        Console.Write("Please enter first integer: ")
13        number1 = Console.ReadLine()
14
15        ' read second number from user
16        Console.Write("Please enter second integer: ")
17        number2 = Console.ReadLine()
18
19        If number1 = number2 Then
20           Console.WriteLine("{0} = {1}", number1, number2)
21        End If
22
23        If number1 <> number2 Then
24           Console.WriteLine("{0} <> {1}", number1, number2)
25        End If
26
27        If number1 < number2 Then
28           Console.WriteLine("{0} < {1}", number1, number2)
29        End If
30
31        If number1 > number2 Then
32           Console.WriteLine("{0} > {1}", number1, number2)
33        End If
34
35        If number1 <= number2 Then
36           Console.WriteLine("{0} <= {1}", number1, number2)
37        End If
```

Fig. 3.19 Performing comparisons with equality and relational operators (part 1 of 2).

```
38
39          If number1 >= number2 Then
40              Console.WriteLine("{0} >= {1}", number1, number2)
41          End If
42
43      End Sub ' Main
44
45  End Module ' modComparison
```

```
Please enter first integer: 1000
Please enter second integer: 2000
1000 <> 2000
1000 < 2000
1000 <= 2000
```

```
Please enter first integer: 515
Please enter second integer: 49
515 <> 49
515 > 49
515 >= 49
```

```
Please enter first integer: 333
Please enter second integer: 333
333 = 333
333 <= 333
333 >= 333
```

Fig. 3.19 Performing comparisons with equality and relational operators (part 2 of 2).

Line 9 declares the variables that are used in procedure **Main**. In this line, two variables of type **Integer** are declared. Remember that variables of the same type may be declared either in one declaration or in multiple declarations. Also recall that, when more than one variable is placed in a declaration, those variables must be separated by commas (**,**). The comment that precedes the declaration indicates the purpose of the variables in the program.

Lines 13 and 17 both retrieve inputs from the user, convert the inputs to type **Integer** and assign the values to the appropriate variables (i.e., **number1** or **number2**) in one step.

The **If/Then** structure in lines 19–21 compares the values of the variables **number1** and **number2** for equality. If the values are equal, the program outputs the **String** generated by the arguments that are given to **WriteLine** in line 20.

If **number1** contains the value **1000** and **number2** contains the value **1000**, the expression evaluates as follows: **number1** and **number2** are converted to **String**s, which are placed in the string **"{0} = {1}"** in place of the **{0}** and **{1}** formats. At this point, the **String**, namely **"1000 = 1000"**, is sent to **WriteLine** to be printed. As the program proceeds through the **If/Then** structures, additional **String**s are output by these **Console.WriteLine** statements. For example, when given the value **1000** for **number1** and **number2**, the **If/Then** conditions in lines 35 (**<=**) and 39 (**>=**) also are true. Thus, the output displayed is

```
1000 =  1000
1000 <= 1000
1000 >= 1000
```

Notice the indentation in the **If/Then** statements throughout the program. Such indentation enhances program readability.

Good Programming Practice 3.14
*Indent the statement in the body of an **If/Then** structure to emphasize the body of the structure and to enhance program readability.*

Common Programming Error 3.3
*Omission of the **Then** keyword in an **If/Then** structure is a syntax error.*

The table in Fig. 3.20 shows the precedence of the operators introduced in this chapter. The operators are displayed from top to bottom in decreasing order of precedence. All operators in Visual Basic .NET associate from left to right.

Testing and Debugging Tip 3.3
When uncertain about the order of evaluation in a complex expression, use parentheses to force the order, as you would do in an algebraic expression. Doing so can help avoid subtle bugs.

3.7 Using a Dialog to Display a Message

Although the programs discussed thus far display output in the command window, most Visual Basic programs use *dialogs* to display output. Dialogs are windows that typically display messages to the user. Visual Basic provides class **MessageBox** for creating dialogs. The program in Fig. 3.21 uses a dialog to display the square root of 2.

In this example, we present a program that contains a simple GUI (i.e., the dialog). The .NET Framework Class Library (FCL) contains a rich collection of classes that can be used to construct GUIs. FCL classes are grouped by functionality into *namespaces*. Line 4 is an **Imports** statement that indicates we are using the features provided by the **System.Windows.Forms** namespace. For example, **System.Windows.Forms** contains windows-related classes (i.e., forms and dialogs). We discuss this namespace in detail after we discuss the code in this example.

Operators	Type
( )	parentheses
^	exponentiation
* /	multiplicative
\	**Integer** division
Mod	modulus

Fig. 3.20 Precedence and associativity of operators introduced in this chapter (part 1 of 2).

Operators	Type
+ -	additive
= <> < <= > >=	equality and relational

Fig. 3.20 Precedence and associativity of operators introduced in this chapter (part 2 of 2).

```
1   ' Fig. 3.21: SquareRoot.vb
2   ' Displaying the square root of 2 in dialog.
3
4   Imports System.Windows.Forms ' namespace containing MessageBox
5
6   Module modSquareRoot
7
8      Sub Main()
9
10        ' calculate square root of 2
11        Dim root As Double = Math.Sqrt(2)
12
13        ' display results in dialog
14        MessageBox.Show("The square root of 2 is " & root, _
15           "The Square Root of 2")
16
17     End Sub ' Main
18
19  End Module ' modSquareRoot
```

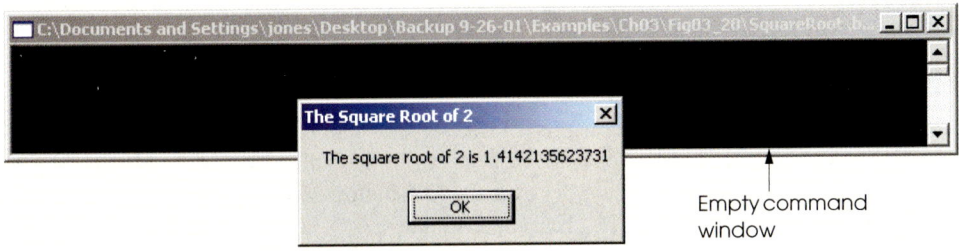

Fig. 3.21 Displaying text in a dialog.

Line 11 calls the **Sqrt** method of the **Math** class to compute the square root of 2. The value returned is a floating-point number, so we declare the variable **root** as type **Double**. The **Double** data type stores floating-point numbers (i.e., numbers such as 2.3456 and –845.7840). Notice that we declare and initialize **root** on a single line.

Notice the use of spacing in lines 14–15 of Fig. 3.21. To improve readability, long statements may be split over several lines using the *line-continuation character*, _ . Line 14 uses the line-continuation character to indicate that line 15 is a continuation of the previous line. A single statement can contain as many line-continuation characters as necessary. However, at least one whitespace character must precede each line-continuation character.

Common Programming Error 3.4
Splitting a statement over several lines without including the line-continuation character is a syntax error.

Common Programming Error 3.5
Failure to precede the line-continuation character with at least one whitespace character is a syntax error.

Common Programming Error 3.6
Placing anything, including comments, after a line-continuation character is a syntax error.

Common Programming Error 3.7
Splitting a statement in the middle of an identifier or string is a syntax error.

Good Programming Practice 3.15
A lengthy statement may be spread over several lines. If a single statement must be split across lines, choose breaking points that make sense, such as after a comma in a comma-separated list or after an operator in a lengthy expression. If a statement is split across two or more lines, indent all subsequent lines with one level of indentation.

Lines 14–15 (Fig. 3.21) call method **Show** of class **MessageBox**. This method takes two arguments. The first argument is the **String** that is displayed in the dialog. The second argument is the **String** that is displayed in the dialog's title bar.

In this case, the first argument to method **Show** is the expression

```
"The square root of 2 is " & root
```

which uses the *string concatenation operator*, **&**, to combine a **String** (the literal **"The square root of 2 is "**) and the value of the variable **root** (the **Double** variable containing the square root of **2**). The string concatenation operator is a binary operator used to combine two **String**s. This operation results in a new, longer **String**. If an argument given to the string concatenation operator is not of type **String**, the program creates a **String** representation of the argument.

When executed, lines 14–15 display the dialog shown in Fig. 3.22. The dialog includes an **OK** button that allows the user to *dismiss* (or *close*) the dialog by positioning the *mouse pointer* (also called the *mouse cursor*) over the **OK** button and clicking the mouse. Once the dialog has been dismissed, the program terminates.

Many classes provided by Visual Basic .NET (such as **MessageBox**) must be added to the project before they can be used in a program. These *compiled classes* are located in a file, called an assembly, that has a **.dll** (or *dynamic link library*) extension.

Information about the assembly that we need can be found in the Visual Studio .NET documentation (also called the *MSDN Documentation*). The easiest way to locate this information is by selecting **Help > Index...** to display the **Index** dialog (Fig. 3.23).

Type the class name in the **Look for:** box, and select the appropriate *filter*, which narrows the search to a subset of the documentation. Visual Basic programmers should select **Visual Basic and Related**. Next, click the **MessageBox class** link to display documentation for the **MessageBox** class (Fig. 3.24). The **Requirements** section of the documentation lists the assembly that contains the class. Class **MessageBox** is located in assembly **System.Windows.Forms.dll**.

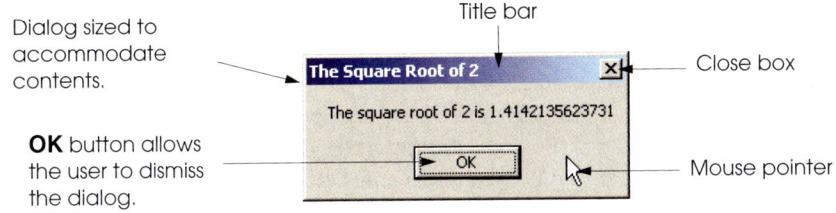

Fig. 3.22 Dialog displayed by calling `MessageBox.Show`.

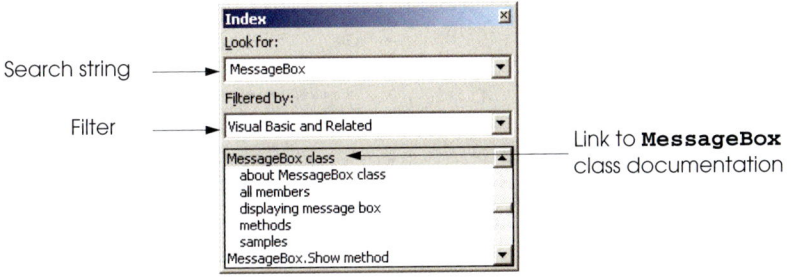

Fig. 3.23 Obtaining documentation for a class by using the **Index** dialog.

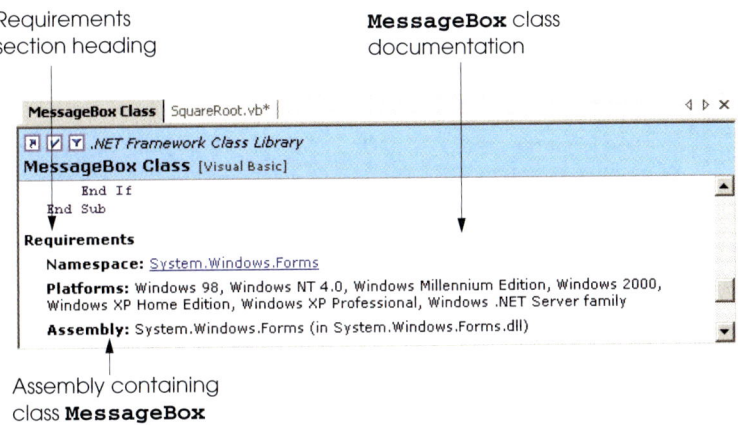

Fig. 3.24 Documentation for the `MessageBox` class.

It is necessary to *add a reference* to this assembly (i.e., to place an assembly in the **Solution Explorer**'s **References** folder) if we wish to use class `MessageBox` in our program. Visual Studio provides a simple process by which to add a reference. Let us discuss the process of adding a reference to `System.Windows.Forms`.

Common Programming Error 3.8

Including a namespace with the `Imports` *statement without adding a reference to the proper assembly is a syntax error.*

To add a reference to an existing project, select **Project > Add Reference...** to display the **Add Reference** dialog (Fig. 3.25). Locate and double click `System.Windows.Forms.dll` to add this file to the **References** folder, and then click **OK**. Notice that `System.Windows.Forms` is now listed in the **References** folder of the **Solution Explorer** (Fig. 3.25).

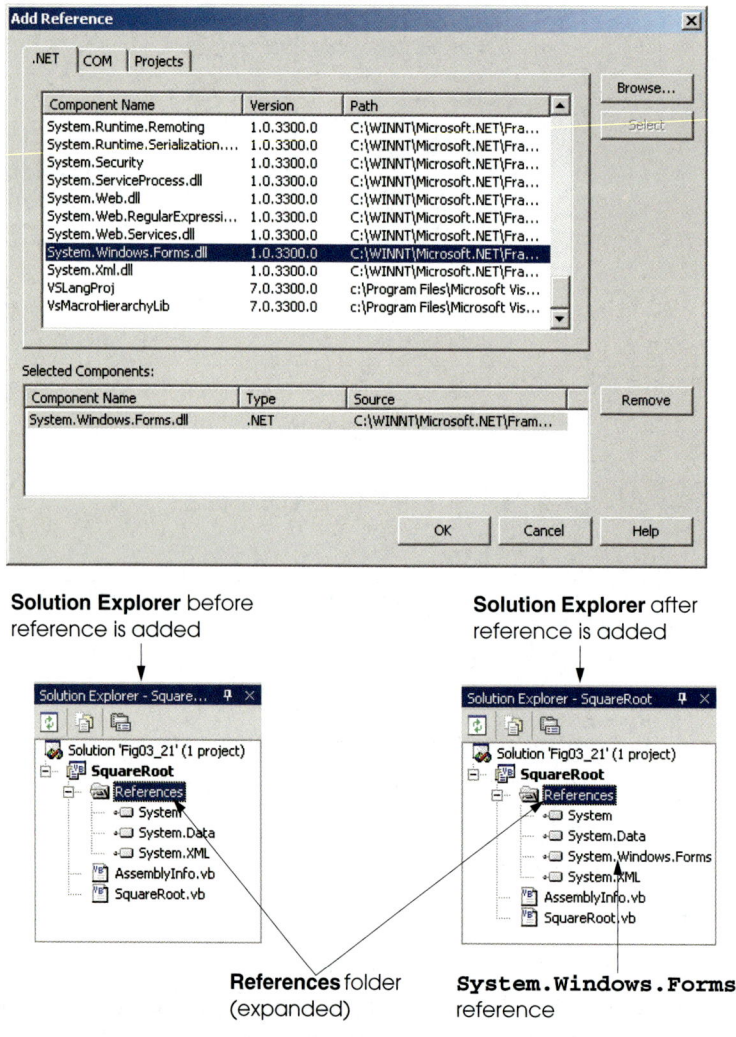

Fig. 3.25 Adding a reference to an assembly in the Visual Studio .NET IDE.

Now that the assembly **System.Windows.Forms.dll** is referenced, we can use the classes that are a part of the assembly. The namespace that includes class **MessageBox**, **System.Windows.Forms**, also is specified with the **Imports** statement in line 4 of our code (Fig. 3.21). [*Note*: The **Imports** statement is not added to the program by Visual Studio; programmers must add this line to their code.]

Common Programming Error 3.9

*Forgetting to add an **Import**s statement for a referenced assembly is a syntax error.*

We did not have to add references to any of our previous programs, because Visual Studio .NET adds some references to assemblies when the project is created. The references added depend on the project type that is selected in the **New Project** dialog. Some assemblies do not need to be referenced. Class **Console**, for instance, is located in the assembly **mscorlib.dll**, but we did not need to reference this assembly explicitly to use it.

The **System.Windows.Forms** namespace contains many classes that help Visual Basic programmers define graphical user interfaces (GUIs) for their applications. *GUI components* (such as buttons) facilitate both data entry by the user and the formatting or presenting of data outputs to the user. For example, Fig. 3.26 is an Internet Explorer window with a menu bar containing various menus, such as **File**, **Edit**, and **View**. Below the menu bar is a tool bar that consists of buttons. Each button, when clicked, executes a task. Beneath the tool bar is a *text box* in which the user can type the location of a World Wide Web site to visit. To the left of the text box is a *label* that indicates the purpose of the text box. The menus, buttons, text boxes and labels are part of Internet Explorer's GUI, they enable users to interact with the Internet Explorer program. Visual Basic provides classes for creating the GUI components shown here. Other classes that create GUI components will be described in Chapters 12 and 13, Graphical User Interface Concepts: Part 1 and Graphical User Interface Concepts: Part 2.

In this chapter, we have introduced important features of Visual Basic, including displaying data on the screen, inputting data from the keyboard, performing calculations and making decisions. Many similar techniques are demonstrated in the next chapter as we reintroduce Visual Basic Windows applications (applications that provide a graphical user interface). The next chapter also begins our discussion of *structured programming* and familiarizes the reader further with indentation techniques. We study how to specify and vary the order in which statements are executed—this order is called *flow of control*.

3.8 Internet and World Wide Web Resources

www.vb-world.net
VB-World provides a variety of information on Visual Basic, including offering users the opportunity to query an expert in the .NET platform. This site also hosts an active discussion list.

www.devx.com/dotnet
This Web site contains information about the .NET platform, with topics ranging from Visual Basic .NET to Active Server Pages .NET. The site includes links to articles, books and current news.

www.vbcity.com
The vbCity Web site lists numerous links to articles, books and tutorials on Visual Basic .NET. The site allows programmers to submit code and have it rated by other developers. This site also polls visitors on a variety of Visual Basic topics and provides access to archives, which include code listings and news.

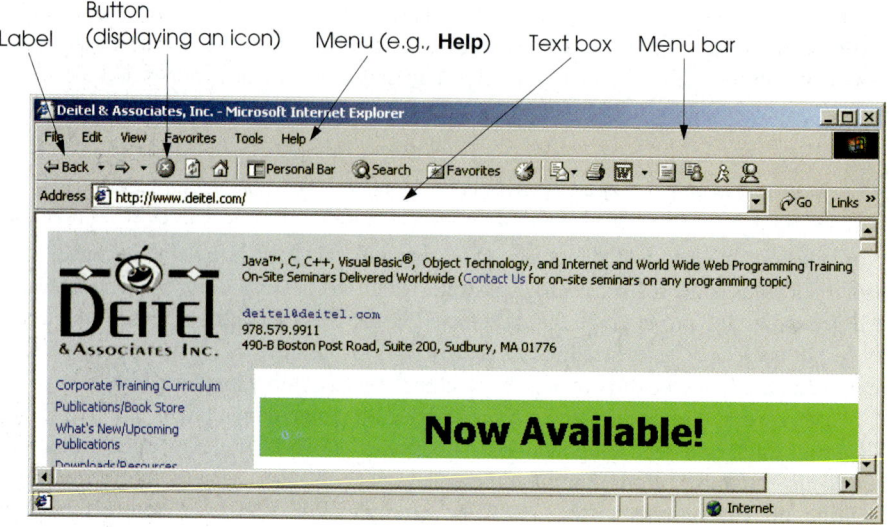

Fig. 3.26 Internet Explorer window with GUI components.

www.cyber-matrix.com/vb.htm
This site links to Visual Basic tutorials, books, tips and tricks, controls, programming tools, magazines, news groups and more.

searchvb.techtarget.com
This site offers a search engine designed specifically to discover Visual Basic Web sites.

www.aewnet.com/root/dotnet/vbnet
The site links to demos, articles, tutorials, and to other Visual Basic .NET sites in various languages (e.g., German).

SUMMARY

- A console application is an application that primarily displays text output in a command window. In Microsoft Windows 95/98, the command window is called the MS-DOS prompt. In Microsoft Windows NT/2000/XP, the command window is called the command prompt.

- The single quote character, ', indicates that the remainder of a line is a comment.

- Programmers insert comments in a program to improve the readability of their code. Comments are ignored by the Visual Basic compiler; they do not cause the computer to perform any actions when the program is run.

- Visual Basic console applications consist of pieces called modules, which are logical groupings of procedures that simplify program organization.

- Procedures perform tasks and can return information when the tasks are completed. Every console application in Visual Basic consists of at least one module definition and one procedure.

- Keywords are words that are reserved for use by Visual Basic; programmers must choose other names as identifiers.

- The name of a module is an example of an identifier. An identifier is a series of characters, consisting of letters, digits and underscores (_), that does not begin with a digit and does not contain spaces.

- Visual Basic keywords and identifiers are case insensitive—uppercase and lowercase letters are considered to be identical. Thus, **modfirstwelcome** and **modFirstWelcome** are the same identifier.
- Blank lines, tabs and space characters are often used throughout a program to make the program easier to read. Collectively, blank lines, tabs and space characters are known as whitespace.
- Console applications begin executing at procedure **Main**, which is known as the entry point of the program.
- Keyword **Sub** begins the body of a procedure definition. Keywords **End Sub** close the procedure definition's body.
- Characters delimited by double quotation marks are called strings, character strings or string literals.
- Methods perform tasks and return data when the tasks are completed. Groups of related methods are organized into classes.
- The dot operator, **.**, denotes a member of a particular class. The identifier to the right of the dot operator is the member name, and the identifier to the left of the dot operator indicates the name of the class name to which the member belongs.
- The **Console** class contains methods, such as **WriteLine**, that communicate with users via the command window.
- Syntax-color highlighting helps programmers visually differentiate programming elements. Keywords appear in blue, whereas text is black. When present, comments are colored green.
- The IntelliSense feature lists a class's members, which include method names.
- The Parameter Info window displays information about a method's arguments. The Parameter List window lists possible arguments for the method highlighted in the Parameter Info window. These windows are part of the many features provided by the IDE to aid program development.
- The **ReadLine** method causes the program to pause and wait for user input. Once the user presses the *Enter* key, the input is returned to the program, and execution resumes.
- A syntax error (also called a compile error) is a violation of the language syntax.
- Unlike **WriteLine**, **Write** does not position the output cursor at the beginning of the next line in the command window after displaying its string.
- Declarations begin with keyword **Dim** and allow the programmer to specify the name, type, size and value of a variable.
- Variables are locations in the computer's memory where values can be stored for use by a program. Every variable has a name, type, size and value.
- All variables must be declared before they can be used in a program.
- Data types already defined in Visual Basic, such as **String** and **Integer**, are known as built-in data types or primitive data types.
- Primitive type names are keywords.
- Variables of type **Integer** store integer values (i.e., whole numbers such as 919, –11 and 0).
- A run-time error is an error that affects the program during execution (unlike a syntax error, which affects the program when it is compiled).
- The assignment operator, **=**, assigns a value to a variable.
- Visual Basic performs an implicit conversion between data types whenever necessary. For example, a **String** is converted to an **Integer** to perform an arithmetic operation.

- A format, such as **{0}**, in a **String** indicates that the argument after the **String** will be evaluated and incorporated into the **String** in place of the format.
- Whenever a value is placed in a memory location, this value replaces the value previously stored in that location. The previous value is destroyed.
- When a value is read from a memory location, the process is nondestructive, meaning the value is not changed.
- Binary operators operate on two operands; unary operators operate on one operand.
- Visual Basic has separate operators for **Integer** division (the backslash, ****) and floating-point division (the forward slash, **/**). **Integer** division yields an **Integer** result. Any fractional part in **Integer** division is discarded (i.e., truncated).
- The modulus operator, **Mod**, yields the remainder after **Integer** division.
- Arithmetic expressions in Visual Basic must be written in straight-line form to facilitate entering programs into a computer.
- Parentheses are used in Visual Basic expressions in the same manner as in algebraic expressions.
- Visual Basic applies the operators in arithmetic expressions in a precise sequence, which is determined by the rules of operator precedence.
- If an expression contains multiple operators with the same precedence, the order in which the operators are applied is determined by the associativity of the operators.
- As in algebra, it is acceptable to place unnecessary parentheses in an expression to make the expression easier to read.
- Visual Basic's **If/Then** structure allows a program to make a decision based on the truth or falsity of some condition. If the condition is met (i.e., the condition is true), the statement in the body of the **If/Then** structure executes. If the condition is not met (i.e., the condition is false), the body statement is not executed.
- Conditions in **If/Then** structures can be formed by using the equality operators and relational operators. (Equality operators and relational operators also are called comparison operators.)
- All relational and equality operators have the same level of precedence and associate from left to right.
- Dialogs are windows that typically display messages to the user. Visual Basic provides class **MessageBox** for the creation of dialogs.
- The .NET Framework Class Library organizes groups of related classes into namespaces.
- The **System.Windows.Forms** namespace contains windows-related classes (i.e., forms and dialogs) that help Visual Basic programmers define graphical user interfaces (GUIs) for their applications.
- GUI components facilitate data entry by the user and the formatting or presenting of data outputs to the user.
- An **Imports** statement indicates that a program uses the features provided by a specific namespace, such as **System.Windows.Forms**.
- To improve readability, long statements may be split over several lines with the line-continuation character, **_**. Although a single statement can contain as many line-continuation characters as necessary, at least one whitespace character must precede each line-continuation character.
- Compiled classes, called assemblies, are located in a file with a **.dll** (or dynamic link library) extension.

TERMINOLOGY

' comment
" (double quotation)
_ (underscore) line-continuation character
, (comma)
< (less-than operator)
<= (less-than-or-equal-to operator)
<> (inequality operator)
= assignment operator
= equality operator
> (greater-than operator)
>= (greater-than-or-equal-to operator)
Add Reference dialog
algebraic notation
application
argument
arithmetic calculation
arithmetic operator
assembly
assignment statement
associativity of operators
asterisk (*) indicating multiplication
average
binary operator
blank line
body of a procedure definition
built-in data type
button
carriage return
case sensitive
character set
character string
class
class name
command prompt
command window
comma-separated list
comment
comparison operator
compiler
compile-time error
concatenation of **String**s
condition
console application
Console class
console window
Console.Write method
Console.WriteLine method
data type
decision

declaration
dialog
Dim keyword
display output
documentation
dot (.) operator
embedded parentheses
empty string ("")
End Sub keywords
Enter (or *Return*) key
entry point of a program
error handling
escape sequence
exponentiation
falsity
flow of control
format
formatting strings
GUI component
identifier
If/Then structure
Imports keyword
indentation in **If/Then** structure
indentation techniques
Index dialog
innermost pair of parentheses
inputting data from the keyboard
integer division
keyword
left-to-right evaluation
location in the computer's memory
logic error
Main procedure
making decisions
MessageBox class
method
Mod (modulus operator)
MS-DOS prompt
name of a variable
namespace
nested parentheses
nondestructive
OK button on a dialog
operand
operator precedence
output
parentheses ()
parentheses "on the same level"
performing a calculation

pop-up menu
precedence
primitive data type
programmer-defined class
prompt
readability
ReadLine method
real number
redundant parentheses
reserved word
reuse
robust
rounding
run-time logic error
self-documenting
single-line comment
space character
spacing convention
special character
split a statement
standard output
statement
straight-line form
string
String concatenation

string formatting
string literal
string of characters
String type
structured programming
Sub keyword
syntax error
System namespace
System.dll assembly
System.Windows.Forms assembly
System.Windows.Forms namespace
Task List window
Then keyword
truncate
truth
type of a variable
unary operator
unnecessary parentheses
valid identifier
value of a variable
variable
Visual Basic compiler
whitespace character
Windows application

SELF-REVIEW EXERCISES

3.1 Fill in the blanks in each of the following statements:
  a) Keyword _____ begins the body of a module, and keyword(s) _____ end(s) the body of a module.
  b) _____ begins a comment.
  c) _____, _____ and _____ collectively are known as whitespace.
  d) Class _____ contains methods for displaying dialogs.
  e) _____ are reserved for use by Visual Basic.
  f) Visual Basic console applications begin execution at procedure _____.
  g) Methods _____ and _____ display information in the command window.
  h) Keyword _____ begins the procedure body and keyword(s) _____ end(s) the procedure body.
  i) A Visual Basic program uses a/an _____ statement to indicate that a namespace is being used.
  j) When a value is placed in a memory location, this value _____ the previous value in that location.
  k) The indication that operators are applied from left to right refers to the _____ of the operators.
  l) Visual Basic's **If/Then** structure allows a program to make a decision based on the _____ or _____ of a condition.
  m) Types such as **Integer** and **String** are often called _____ data types.
  n) A variable is a location in the computer's _____ where a value can be stored for use by a program.

Chapter 3 Introduction to Visual Basic Programming

o) The expression to the _____ of the assignment operator (=) is always evaluated first before the assignment occurs.
p) Arithmetic expressions in Visual Basic .NET must be written in _____ form to facilitate entering programs into the computer.

3.2 State whether each of the following is *true* or *false*. If *false*, explain why.
a) Comments cause the computer to print the text after the ' on the screen when the program executes.
b) All variables must be declared before they can be used in a Visual Basic .NET program.
c) Visual Basic considers the variables **number** and **NuMbEr** to be different.
d) The arithmetic operators *****, **/**, **+** and **-** all have the same level of precedence.
e) A string of characters contained between double quotation marks is called a phrase or phrase literal.
f) Visual Basic console applications begin executing in procedure **Main**.
g) **Integer** division yields an **Integer** result.

ANSWERS TO SELF-REVIEW EXERCISES

3.1 a) **Module, End Module**. b) Single quotation mark, '. c) Blank lines, space characters, tab characters. d) **MessageBox**. e) Keywords. f) **Main**. g) **Write, WriteLine**. h) **Sub, End Sub**. i) **Imports**. j) replaces. k) associativity. l) truth, falsity. m) primitive (or built-in). n) memory. o) right. p) straight-line.

3.2 a) False. Comments do not cause any action to be performed when the program executes. They are used to document programs and improve their readability. b) True. c) False. Visual Basic identifiers are not case sensitive, so these variables are identical. d) False. The operators ***** and **/** are on the same level of precedence, and the operators **+** and **-** are on a lower level of precedence. e) False. A string of characters is called a string or string literal. f) True. g) True.

EXERCISES

3.3 Write Visual Basic statements that accomplish each of the following tasks:
a) Display the message **"Hello"** using class **MessageBox**.
b) Assign the product of variables **number** and **userData** to variable **result**.
c) State that a program performs a sample payroll calculation (i.e., use text that helps to document a program).

3.4 What displays in the dialog when each of the following statements is performed? Assume the value of **x** is **2** and the value of **y** is **3**.
a) `MessageBox.Show("x", x)`
b) `MessageBox.Show((x + x), _`
    `"(x + x)")`
c) `MessageBox.Show("x + y")`
d) `MessageBox.Show( _`
    `(x + y), (y + y))`

3.5 Given $z = 8e^5 - n$, which of the following are correct statements for this equation?
a) `z = 8 * e ^ 5 - n`
b) `z = ( 8 * e ) ^ 5 - n`
c) `z = 8 * ( e ^ 5 ) - n`
d) `z = 8 * e ^ ( 5 - n )`
e) `z = ( 8 * e ) ^ ( ( 5 ) - n )`
f) `z = 8 * e * e ^ 4 - n`

3.6 Indicate the order of evaluation of the operators in each of the following Visual Basic statements, and show the value of **x** after each statement is performed.
    a) `x = 7 + 3 * 3 \ 2 - 1`
    b) `x = 2 Mod 2 + 2 * 2 - 2 / 2`
    c) `x = ( 3 * 9 * ( 3 + ( 9 * 3 / ( 3 ) ) ) )`

3.7 Write a program that displays the numbers **1** to **4** on the same line, with each pair of adjacent numbers separated by one space. Write the program using the following:
    a) Use one **Write** statement.
    b) Use four **Write** statements.

3.8 Write a program that asks the user to enter two numbers, obtains the two numbers from the user and prints the sum, product, difference and quotient of the two numbers. Use the command window for input and output.

3.9 Write a program that inputs from the user the radius of a circle and prints the circle's diameter, circumference and area in the command window. Use the following formulas (*r* is the radius): *diameter = 2r, circumference = 2πr, area = πr²*. Use *3.14159* for *π*.

3.10 Write a program that displays a box, an oval, an arrow and a diamond using asterisks (*****) as follows:

```
*********        ***            *               *
*       *       *   *          ***             * *
*       *      *     *        *****           *   *
*       *      *     *          *            *     *
*       *      *     *          *           *       *
*       *      *     *          *            *     *
*       *      *     *          *             *   *
*       *       *   *           *              * *
*********        ***            *               *
```

Use the command window for output.

3.11 What does the following code print?

```
Console.Write("*")
Console.Write("***")
Console.WriteLine("*****")
Console.Write("****")
Console.WriteLine("**")
```

3.12 What do the following statements print?

```
Console.WriteLine("   {0}", "  *  ")
Console.WriteLine("   {0}", "  * **")
Console.WriteLine("   {0}*{1}", " * ", " *")
Console.WriteLine("   * *{0}* *", "  ")
Console.WriteLine("{1}*{0} *", " * *", "* ")
```

3.13 Write a program that reads in two integers and determines and prints whether the first is a multiple of the second. For example, if the user inputs **15** and **3**, the first number is a multiple of the second. If the user inputs **2** and **4**, the first number is not a multiple of the second. Use the command window for input and output. [*Hint*: Use the modulus operator.]

3.14 Write a program that inputs one number consisting of five digits from the user, separates the number into its individual digits and prints the digits separated from one another by three spaces each. For example, if the user types in the number **42339**, the program should print

```
4   2   3   3   9
```

Use the command window for input and output. [*Hint*: This exercise is possible with the techniques discussed in this chapter. You will need to use both division and modulus operations to "pick off" each digit.]

For the purpose of this exercise, assume that the user enters the correct number of digits. What happens when you execute the program and type a number with more than five digits? What happens when you execute the program and type a number with fewer than five digits?

3.15 Using only the programming techniques discussed in this chapter, write a program that calculates the squares and cubes of the numbers from **0** to **5** and prints the resulting values in table format as follows:

```
number   square   cube
0        0        0
1        1        1
2        4        8
3        9        27
4        16       64
5        25       125
```

Use the command window for input and output. [*Note*: This program does not require any input from the user.]

Control Structures: Part 1

Objectives

- To understand basic problem-solving techniques.
- To develop algorithms through the process of top-down, stepwise refinement.
- To use the **If/Then** and **If/Then/Else** selection structures to choose among alternative actions.
- To use the **While**, **Do While/Loop** and **Do Until/Loop** repetition structures to execute statements in a program repeatedly.
- To understand counter-controlled repetition and sentinel-controlled repetition.
- To use the assignment operators.
- To create basic Windows applications.

Let's all move one place on.
Lewis Carroll

The wheel is come full circle.
William Shakespeare, *King Lear*

How many apples fell on Newton's head before he took the hint?
Robert Frost, comment

Outline

4.1 Introduction
4.2 Algorithms
4.3 Pseudocode
4.4 Control Structures
4.5 `If/Then` Selection Structure
4.6 `If/Then/Else` Selection Structure
4.7 `While` Repetition Structure
4.8 `Do While/Loop` Repetition Structure
4.9 `Do Until/Loop` Repetition Structure
4.10 Assignment Operators
4.11 Formulating Algorithms: Case Study 1 (Counter-Controlled Repetition)
4.12 Formulating Algorithms with Top-Down, Stepwise Refinement: Case Study 2 (Sentinel-Controlled Repetition)
4.13 Formulating Algorithms with Top-Down, Stepwise Refinement: Case Study 3 (Nested Control Structures)
4.14 Formulating Algorithms with Top-Down, Stepwise Refinement: Case Study 4 (Nested Repetition Structures)
4.15 Introduction to Windows Application Programming

Summary • Terminology • Self-Review Exercises • Answers to Self-Review Exercises • Exercises

4.1 Introduction

Before writing a program to solve a problem, it is essential to have a thorough understanding of the problem and a carefully planned approach. When writing a program, it is equally important to recognize the types of building blocks that are available and to employ proven program-construction principles. In this chapter and the next, we present the theory and principles of structured programming. The techniques presented are applicable to most high-level languages, including Visual Basic .NET. When we study object-based programming in greater depth in Chapter 8, we will see that control structures are helpful in building and manipulating objects. The control structures discussed in this chapter enable such objects to be built quickly and easily. In this chapter, we continue our study of console applications and our discussion of Windows applications that we began in Chapter 2.

4.2 Algorithms

Any computing problem can be solved by executing a series of actions in a specific order. A *procedure* for solving a problem, in terms of

1. the *actions* to be executed and
2. the *order* in which these actions are to be executed,

is called an *algorithm*. The following example demonstrates the importance of correctly specifying the order in which the actions are to be executed.

Consider the "rise-and-shine algorithm" followed by one junior executive for getting out of bed and going to work: (1) get out of bed, (2) take off pajamas, (3) take a shower, (4) get dressed, (5) eat breakfast and (6) carpool to work. This routine prepares the executive for a productive day at the office.

However, suppose that the same steps are performed in a slightly different order: (1) get out of bed, (2) take off pajamas, (3) get dressed, (4) take a shower, (5) eat breakfast, (6) carpool to work. In this case, our junior executive shows up for work soaking wet.

Indicating the appropriate sequence in which to execute actions is equally crucial in computer programs. *Program control* refers to the task of ordering a program's statements correctly. In this chapter, we begin to investigate the program-control capabilities of Visual Basic.

4.3 Pseudocode

Pseudocode is an informal language that helps programmers develop algorithms. The pseudocode we present is particularly useful in the development of algorithms that will be converted to structured portions of Visual Basic programs. Pseudocode is similar to everyday English; it is convenient and user-friendly, but it is not an actual computer programming language.

Pseudocode programs are not executed on computers. Rather, they help the programmer "think out" a program before attempting to write it in a programming language, such as Visual Basic. In this chapter, we provide several examples of pseudocode programs.

Software Engineering Observation 4.1

Pseudocode helps the programmer conceptualize a program during the program-design process. The pseudocode program can be converted to Visual Basic at a later point.

The style of pseudocode that we present consists solely of characters, so that programmers can create, share and modify pseudocode programs using editor programs. A carefully prepared pseudocode program can be converted easily by a programmer to a corresponding Visual Basic program. Much of this conversion is as simple as replacing pseudocode statements with their Visual Basic equivalents.

Pseudocode normally describes only executable statements—the actions that are performed when the corresponding Visual Basic program is run. Declarations are not executable statements. For example, the declaration

```
Dim number As Integer
```

informs the compiler of **number**'s type and instructs the compiler to reserve space in memory for this variable. The declaration does not cause any action, such as input, output or a calculation, to occur when the program executes. Some programmers choose to list variables and their purposes at the beginning of a pseudocode program.

4.4 Control Structures

Normally, statements in a program are executed one after another in the order in which they are written. This is called *sequential execution*. However, various Visual Basic statements enable the programmer to specify that the next statement to be executed might not be the next one in sequence. A *transfer of control* occurs when an executed statement does not directly follow the previously executed statement in the written program.

During the 1960s, it became clear that the indiscriminate use of transfers of control was causing difficulty for software development groups. The problem was the **GoTo** *statement*, which allows the programmer to specify a transfer of control to one of a wide range of possible destinations in a program. The excessive use of **GoTo** statements caused programs to become quite unstructured and hard to follow. Since that point in time, the notion of *structured programming* became almost synonymous with "**GoTo** elimination."

The research of Bohm and Jacopini[1] demonstrated that all programs containing **GoTo** statements could be written without them. Programmers' challenge during the era was to shift their styles to "**GoTo**-less programming." It was not until the 1970s that programmers started taking structured programming seriously. The results have been impressive, as software development groups have reported reduced development times, more frequent on-time delivery of systems and more frequent within-budget completion of software projects. The key to these successes is that structured programs are clearer, easier to debug and modify and more likely to be bug-free in the first place.

Bohm and Jacopini's work demonstrated that all programs could be written in terms of only three *control structures*: Namely, the *sequence structure*, the *selection structure* and the *repetition structure*. The sequence structure is built into Visual Basic. Unless directed to act otherwise, the computer executes Visual Basic statements sequentially. The *flowchart* segment of Fig. 4.1 illustrates a typical sequence structure in which two calculations are performed in order.

A flowchart is a graphical representation of an algorithm or of a portion of an algorithm. Flowcharts are drawn using certain special-purpose symbols, such as rectangles, diamonds, ovals and small circles. These symbols are connected by arrows called *flowlines*, which indicate the order in which the actions of the algorithm execute. The order of execution is known as the *flow of control*.

Like pseudocode, flowcharts often are useful for developing and representing algorithms, although many programmers prefer pseudocode. Flowcharts show clearly how control structures operate; that is their instructive purpose in this text. The reader should compare carefully the pseudocode and flowchart representations of each control structure.

Consider the flowchart segment for the sequence structure in Fig. 4.1. We use the *rectangle symbol*, also called the *action symbol,* to indicate any type of action, including a calculation or an input/output operation. The flowlines in the figure indicate the order in which the actions are to be performed—first, **grade** is to be added to **total**, then **1** is to be added to **counter**. We can have as many actions as we want in a sequence structure. Anywhere in a sequence that a single action may be placed, several actions may also be placed.

When drawing a flowchart that represents a complete algorithm, an *oval symbol* containing the word "Begin" (by convention) is the first symbol used; an oval symbol containing the word "End" (by convention) indicates the termination of the algorithm. When drawing only a portion of an algorithm, as in Fig. 4.1, the oval symbols are omitted in favor of using *small circle symbols,* also called *connector symbols.*

---

1. Bohm, C., and G. Jacopini, "Flow Diagrams, Turing Machines, and Languages with Only Two Formation Rules," *Communications of the ACM*, Vol. 9, No. 5, May 1966, pp. 336–371.

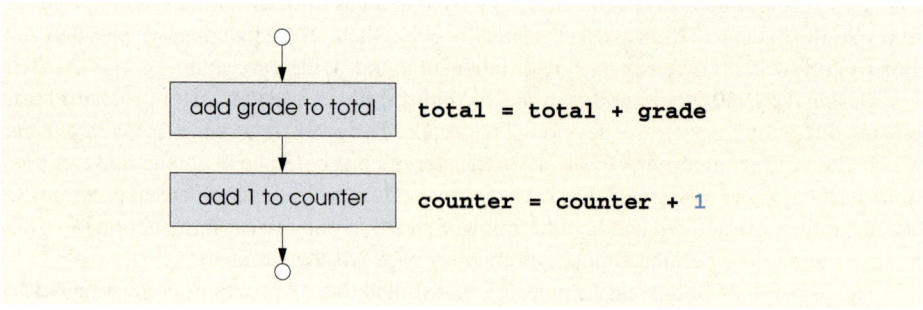

Fig. 4.1 Sequence structure flowchart.

Perhaps the most important flowcharting symbol is the *diamond symbol*, alternatively referred to as the *decision symbol,* which indicates that a decision is to be made. We discuss the diamond symbol in Section 4.5.

Visual Basic provides three types of selection structures, which we discuss in this chapter and the next. The **If/Then** selection structure performs (selects) an action (or sequence of actions) if a condition is true or skips the action (or sequence of actions) if the condition is false. The **If/Then/Else** selection structure performs an action (or sequence of actions) if a condition is true and performs a different action (or sequence of actions) if the condition is false. The **Select Case** structure, discussed in Chapter 5, Control Structures: Part 2, performs one of many actions (or sequences of actions), depending on the value of an expression.

The **If/Then** structure is called a *single-selection structure* because it selects or ignores a single action (or a sequence of actions). The **If/Then/Else** structure is called a *double-selection structure* because it selects between two different actions (or sequences of actions). The **Select Case** structure is called a *multiple-selection structure* because it selects among many different actions or sequences of actions.

Visual Basic provides seven types of repetition structures—**While, Do While/Loop, Do/Loop While, Do Until/Loop, Do/Loop Until, For/Next** and **For Each/Next**. (Repetition structures **While, Do While/Loop** and **Do Until/Loop** are covered in this chapter; **Do/Loop While, Do/Loop Until,** and **For/Next** are covered in Chapter 5, Control Structures: Part 2; and **For Each/Next** is covered in Chapter 7, Arrays.) The words **If, Then, Else, End, Select, Case, While, Do, Until, Loop, For, Next** and **Each** are all Visual Basic keywords (Fig. 4.2). We discuss many of Visual Basic's keywords and their respective purposes throughout this book. Visual Basic has a much larger set of keywords than most other popular programming languages.

Visual Basic has 11 control structures—sequence, three types of selection and seven types of repetition. Each program is formed by combining as many of each type of control structure as is necessary. As with the sequence structure in Fig. 4.1, each control structure is flowcharted with two small circle symbols—one at the entry point to the control structure and one at the exit point.

Single-entry/single-exit control structures (i.e., control structures that each have one entry point and one exit point) make it easy to build programs—the control structures are attached to one another by connecting the exit point of one control structure to the entry point of the next. This is similar to stacking building blocks, so, we call it *control-structure stacking*. There is only one other method of connecting control structures, and that is through *control-structure nesting*, where one control structure can be placed inside another. Thus, algorithms in Visual Basic programs are constructed from only 11 different types of control structures combined in only two ways—the essence of simplicity.

Visual Basic Keywords			
AddHandler	AddressOf	Alias	And
AndAlso	Ansi	As	Assembly
Auto	Boolean	ByRef	Byte
ByVal	Call	Case	Catch
CBool	CByte	CChar	CDate
CDec	CDbl	Char	CInt
Class	CLng	CObj	Const
CShort	CSng	CStr	CType
Date	Decimal	Declare	Default
Delegate	Dim	DirectCast	Do
Double	Each	Else	ElseIf
End	Enum	Erase	Error
Event	Exit	False	Finally
For	Friend	Function	Get
GetType	GoTo	Handles	If
Implements	Imports	In	Inherits
Integer	Interface	Is	Lib
Like	Long	Loop	Me
Mod	Module	MustInherit	MustOverride
MyBase	MyClass	Namespace	New
Next	Not	Nothing	NotInheritable
NotOverridable	Object	On	Option
Optional	Or	OrElse	Overloads
Overridable	Overrides	ParamArray	Preserve
Private	Property	Protected	Public
RaiseEvent	ReadOnly	ReDim	REM
RemoveHandler	Resume	Return	Select
Set	Shadows	Shared	Short
Single	Static	Step	Stop
String	Structure	Sub	SyncLock
Then	Throw	To	True

Fig. 4.2 Keywords in Visual Basic (part 1 of 2).

Visual Basic Keywords			
`Try`	`TypeOf`	`Unicode`	`Until`
`When`	`While`	`With`	`WithEvents`
`WriteOnly`	`Xor`		
The following are retained as keywords, although they are no longer supported in Visual Basic.NET			
`Let`	`Variant`	`Wend`	

Fig. 4.2 Keywords in Visual Basic (part 2 of 2).

4.5 If/Then Selection Structure

In a program, a selection structure chooses among alternative courses of action. For example, suppose that the passing grade on an examination is 60 (out of 100). Then the pseudocode statement

> *If student's grade is greater than or equal to 60*
> *Print "Passed"*

determines whether the condition "student's grade is greater than or equal to 60" is true or false. If the condition is true, then "Passed" is printed, and the next pseudocode statement in order is "performed" (remember that pseudocode is not a real programming language). If the condition is false, the print statement is ignored, and the next pseudocode statement in order is performed.

The preceding pseudocode *If* statement may be written in Visual Basic as

```
If studentGrade >= 60 Then
    Console.WriteLine("Passed")
End If
```

Notice that the Visual Basic code corresponds closely to the pseudocode, demonstrating the usefulness of pseudocode as a program-development tool. The statement in the body of the **If/Then** structure outputs the string **"Passed"**. Note also that the output statement in this selection structure is indented. Such indentation is optional, but it is highly recommended because it emphasizes the inherent organization of structured programs.

The Visual Basic compiler ignores white-space characters, such as spaces, tabs and newlines used for indentation and vertical spacing, unless the whitespace characters are contained in **String**s. Some whitespace characters are required, however, such as the newline at the end of a statement and the space between variable names and keywords. Programmers insert extra white-space characters to enhance program readability.

Good Programming Practice 4.1

*Consistent application of indentation conventions throughout programs improves program readability. We suggest a fixed-size tab of about 1/4 inch, or three spaces per indent. In Visual Studio, tab sizes can be set by selecting **Tools > Options**, navigating to **Text Editor > Basic > Tabs** in the directory tree at left side of the **Options** dialog and changing the numbers in the **Tab size** and **Indent size** text fields.*

The preceding **If/Then** selection structure also could be written on a single line as

```
If studentGrade >= 60 Then Console.WriteLine("Passed")
```

In the multiple-line format, all statements in the body of the **If/Then** are executed if the condition is true. In the single-line format, only the statement immediately after the **Then** keyword is executed if the condition is true. Although writing the **If/Then** selection structure in the latter format saves space, we believe that the organization of the structure is clearer when the multiple-line format is used.

Good Programming Practice 4.2

*Although **If/Then** single-selection structures can be written on one line, using the multiple-line format improves program readability and adaptability, as it is easier to insert statements into the body of a structure that is not confined to a single line.*

Common Programming Error 4.1

*Writing the closing **End If** keywords after a single-line **If/Then** structure is a syntax error.*

Whereas syntax errors are caught by the compiler, *logic errors*, such as the error caused when the wrong comparison operator is used in the condition of a selection structure, affect the program only at execution time. A *fatal logic error* causes a program to fail and terminate prematurely. A *nonfatal logic error* does not terminate a program's execution but causes the program to produce incorrect results.

The flowchart in Fig. 4.3 illustrates the single-selection **If/Then** structure. This flowchart contains the most important flowcharting symbol—the diamond (or decision) symbol—which indicates that a decision is to be made. The decision symbol contains a condition, that is either true or false. The decision symbol has two flowlines emerging from it. One indicates the direction to be taken when the condition in the symbol is true; the other indicates the direction to be taken when the condition is false.

Note that the **If/Then** structure, is a single-entry/single-exit structure. The flowcharts for the remaining control structures also contain (aside from small circle symbols and flowlines) only rectangle symbols, indicating actions to be performed, and diamond symbols, indicating decisions to be made. Representing control structures in this way emphasizes the *action/decision model of programming*.

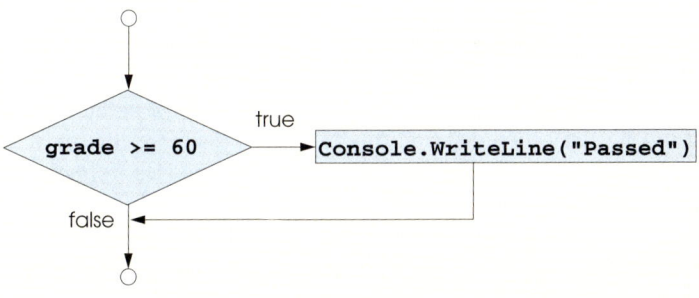

Fig. 4.3 **If/Then** single-selection structure flowchart.

To understand the process of structured programming better, we can envision 11 bins, each containing a different type of the 11 possible control structures. The control structures in each bin are empty, meaning that nothing is written in the rectangles or diamonds. The programmer's task is to assemble a program using as many control structures as the algorithm demands, combining those control structures in only two possible ways (stacking or nesting) and filling in the actions and decisions in a manner appropriate to the algorithm.

4.6 If/Then/Else Selection Structure

As we explained, the **If/Then** selection structure performs an indicated action (or sequence of actions) only when the condition evaluates to true; otherwise, the action (or sequence of actions) is skipped. The **If/Then/Else** selection structure allows the programmer to specify that a different action (or sequence of actions) be performed when the condition is true than when the condition is false. For example, the pseudocode statement

> *If student's grade is greater than or equal to 60*
>   *Print "Passed"*
> *Else*
>   *Print "Failed"*

prints "*Passed*" if the student's grade is greater than or equal to 60, and prints "Failed" if the student's grade is less than 60. In either case, after printing occurs, the next pseudocode statement in sequence is "performed."

The preceding pseudocode *If/Else* structure may be written in Visual Basic as

```
If studentGrade >= 60 Then
    Console.WriteLine("Passed")
Else
    Console.WriteLine("Failed")
End If
```

Note that the body of the **Else** clause is indented so that it lines up with the body of the **If** clause.

Good Programming Practice 4.3
*Indent both body statements of an **If/Then/Else** structure to improve readability.*

A standard indentation convention should be applied consistently throughout your programs. It is difficult to read programs that do not use uniform spacing conventions.

The flowchart in Fig. 4.4 illustrates the flow of control in the **If/Then/Else** structure. Following the action/decision model of programming, the only symbols (besides small circles and arrows) used in the flowchart are rectangles (for actions) and a diamond (for a decision).

*Nested **If/Then/Else** structures* test for multiple conditions by placing **If/Then/Else** structures inside other **If/Then/Else** structures. For example, the following pseudocode statement will print "A" for exam grades greater than or equal to 90, "B" for grades in the range 80–89, "C" for grades in the range 70–79, "D" for grades in the range 60–69 and "F" for all other grades.

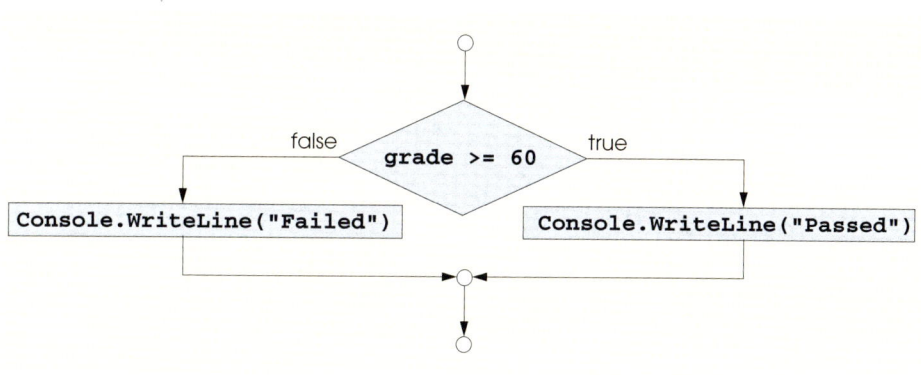

Fig. 4.4 If/Then/Else double-selection structure flowchart.

If student's grade is greater than or equal to 90
    Print "A"
Else
    If student's grade is greater than or equal to 80
        Print "B"
    Else
        If student's grade is greater than or equal to 70
            Print "C"
        Else
            If student's grade is greater than or equal to 60
                Print "D"
            Else
                Print "F"

The pseudocode above may be written in Visual Basic as

```
If studentGrade >= 90 Then
   Console.WriteLine("A")
Else
   If studentGrade >= 80 Then
      Console.WriteLine("B")
   Else
      If studentGrade >= 70 Then
         Console.WriteLine("C")
      Else
         If studentGrade >= 60 Then
            Console.WriteLine("D")
         Else
            Console.WriteLine("F")
         End If
      End If
   End If
End If
```

If **studentGrade** is greater than or equal to 90, the first four conditions are true, but only the **Console.WriteLine** statement in the body of the first test is executed. After that particular `Console.WriteLine` executes, the `Else` part of the "outer" `If/Then/Else` statement is skipped.

Good Programming Practice 4.4

If there are several levels of indentation, each level should be indented additionally by the same amount of space.

Most Visual Basic programmers prefer to write the preceding `If/Then/Else` structure using the `ElseIf` keyword as

```
If grade >= 90 Then
   Console.WriteLine("A")
ElseIf grade >= 80 Then
   Console.WriteLine("B")
ElseIf grade >= 70 Then
   Console.WriteLine("C")
ElseIf grade >= 60 Then
   Console.WriteLine("D")
Else
   Console.WriteLine("F")
End If
```

Both forms are equivalent, but the latter form is popular because it avoids the deep indentation of the code. Such deep indentation often leaves little room on a line, forcing lines to be split and decreasing program readability.

4.7 `While` Repetition Structure

A *repetition structure* allows the programmer to specify that an action should be repeated, depending on the value of a condition. The pseudocode statements

> *While there are more items on my shopping list*
>   *Purchase next item*
>   *Cross it off my list*

describe the repetitive actions that occur during a shopping trip. The condition, "there are more items on my shopping list" can be true or false. If it is true, then the actions, "Purchase next item" and "Cross it off my list" are performed in sequence. These actions execute repeatedly while the condition remains true. The statement(s) contained in the *While* repetition structure constitute the body of the *While*. Eventually, the condition becomes false (when the last item on the shopping list has been purchased and crossed off the list). At this point, the repetition terminates, and the first statement after the repetition structure executes.

As an example of a `While` structure, consider a program designed to find the first power of two larger than 1000 (Fig. 4.5). In line 7, we take advantage of a Visual Basic feature that allows variable initialization to be incorporated into a declaration. When the `While` structure is entered (line 11), `product` is `2`. Variable `product` is repeatedly multiplied by `2` (line 13), taking on the values `4`, `8`, `16`, `32`, `64`, `128`, `256`, `512` and `1024`, successively. When `product` becomes `1024`, the condition `product <= 1000` in the `While` structure becomes false. This terminates the repetition with `1024` as `product`'s final value. Execution continues with the next statement after the keywords `End While`. [*Note*: If a `While` structure's condition is initially false, the body statement(s) are not performed.]

The flowchart in Fig. 4.6 illustrates the flow of control of the **While** repetition structure shown in Fig. 4.5. Note that (besides small circles and arrows) the flowchart contains only a rectangle symbol and a diamond symbol.

The flowchart clearly shows the repetition. The flowline emerging from the rectangle wraps back to the decision, creating a *loop*. The decision is tested each time the loop iterates until the condition in the decision eventually becomes false. At this point, the **While** structure is exited, and control passes to the next statement in the program following the loop.

```vb
1   ' Fig. 4.5: While.vb
2   ' Demonstration of While structure.
3
4   Module modWhile
5
6      Sub Main()
7         Dim product As Integer = 2
8
9         ' structure multiplies and displays product
10        ' while product is less than or equal to 1000
11        While product <= 1000
12           Console.Write("{0}   ", product)
13           product = product * 2
14        End While
15
16        Console.WriteLine() ' write blank line
17
18        ' print result
19        Console.WriteLine("Smallest power of 2 " & _
20           "greater than 1000 is {0}", product)
21     End Sub ' Main
22
23  End Module ' modWhile
```

```
2  4  8  16  32  64  128  256  512
Smallest power of 2 greater than 1000 is 1024
```

Fig. 4.5 **While** repetition structure used to print powers of two.

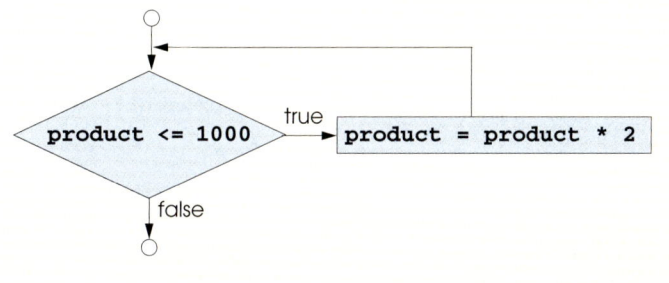

Fig. 4.6 **While** repetition structure flowchart.

> **Common Programming Error 4.2**
>
> *Failure to provide the body of a **While** structure with an action that eventually causes the condition to become false is a logic error. Normally, such a repetition structure never terminates, resulting in an error called an "infinite loop."*

4.8 Do While/Loop Repetition Structure

The **Do While/Loop** repetition structure behaves like the **While** repetition structure. As an example of a **Do While/Loop** structure, consider another version of the program designed to find the first power of two larger than 1000 (Fig. 4.7).

When the **Do While/Loop** structure is entered, the value of **product** is **2**. The variable **product** is repeatedly multiplied by **2**, taking on the values **4**, **8**, **16**, **32**, **64**, **128**, **256**, **512** and **1024**, successively. When **product** becomes **1024**, the condition in the **Do While/Loop** structure, **product <= 1000**, becomes false. This terminates the repetition, with the final value of **product** being **1024**. Program execution continues with the next statement after the **Do While/Loop** structure. The flowchart in Fig. 4.8 illustrates the flow of control of the **Do While/Loop** repetition structure, which is identical to the flow of control in the flowchart of the **While** repetition structure Fig. 4.6.

> **Common Programming Error 4.3**
>
> *Failure to provide the body of a **Do While/Loop** structure with an action that eventually causes the condition in the **Do While/Loop** to become false creates an infinite loop.*

```
1   ' Fig. 4.7: DoWhile.vb
2   ' Demonstration of the Do While/Loop structure.
3
4   Module modDoWhile
5
6      Sub Main()
7         Dim product As Integer = 2
8
9         ' structure multiplies and displays
10        ' product while product is less than or equal to 1000
11        Do While product <= 1000
12           Console.Write("{0}  ", product)
13           product = product * 2
14        Loop
15
16        Console.WriteLine() ' write blank line
17
18        ' print result
19        Console.WriteLine("Smallest power of 2 " & _
20           "greater than 1000 is {0}", product)
21     End Sub ' Main
22
23  End Module ' modDoWhile
```

```
2  4  8  16  32  64  128  256  512
Smallest power of 2 greater than 1000 is 1024
```

Fig. 4.7 Do While/Loop repetition structure demonstration.

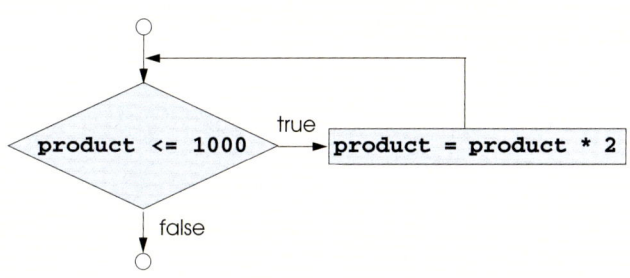

Fig. 4.8 Do While/Loop repetition structure flowchart.

4.9 Do Until/Loop Repetition Structure

Unlike the **While** and **Do While/Loop** repetition structures, the **Do Until/Loop** repetition structure tests a condition for falsity for repetition to continue. Statements in the body of a **Do Until/Loop** are executed repeatedly as long as the loop-continuation test evaluates to false. As an example of a **Do Until/Loop** repetition structure, once again consider a program (Fig. 4.9) designed to find the first power of two larger than 1000.

```
1   ' Fig. 4.9: DoUntil.vb
2   ' Demonstration of the Do Until/Loop structure.
3
4   Module modDoUntil
5
6      Sub Main()
7         Dim product As Integer = 2
8
9         ' find first power of 2 greater than 1000
10        Do Until product > 1000
11           Console.Write("{0}  ", product)
12           product = product * 2
13        Loop
14
15        Console.WriteLine() ' write blank line
16
17        ' print result
18        Console.WriteLine("Smallest power of 2 " & _
19           "greater than 1000 is {0}", product)
20     End Sub ' Main
21
22  End Module ' modDoUntil
```

```
2    4    8    16    32    64    128    256    512
Smallest power of 2 greater than 1000 is 1024
```

Fig. 4.9 Do Until/Loop repetition structure demonstration.

The flowchart in Fig. 4.10 illustrates the flow of control in the **Do Until/Loop** repetition structure shown in Fig. 4.9.

Common Programming Error 4.4

*Failure to provide the body of a **Do Until/Loop** structure with an action that eventually causes the condition in the **Do Until/Loop** to become true creates an infinite loop.*

4.10 Assignment Operators

Visual Basic .NET provides several assignment operators for abbreviating assignment statements. For example, the statement

```
value = value + 3
```

can be abbreviated with the *addition assignment operator* **+=** as

```
value += 3
```

The **+=** operator adds the value of the right operand to the value of the left operand and stores the result in the left operand's variable. Any statement of the form

variable = *variable operator expression*

can be written in the form

variable operator= *expression*

where *operator* is one of the binary operators **+**, **-**, *****, **^**, **&**, **/** or ****, and *variable* is an <*lvalue*> ("left value"). An *lvalue* is a variable that can appear on the left side of an assignment statement. Figure 4.11 includes the arithmetic assignment operators, sample expressions using these operators and explanations.

Although the symbols **=**, **+=**, **-=**, ***=**, **/=**, **\=**, **^=** and **&=** are operators, we do not include them in operator-precedence tables. When an assignment statement is evaluated, the expression to the right of the operator is always evaluated first, then assigned to the *lvalue* on the left. Unlike Visual Basic's other operators, the assignment operators can only occur once in a statement. Figure 4.12 calculates a power of two using the exponentiation assignment operator.

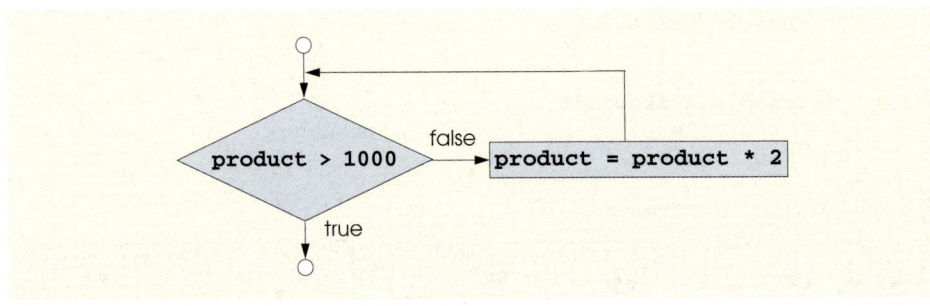

Fig. 4.10 Do Until/Loop repetition structure flowchart.

Assignment operator	Sample expression	Explanation	Assigns
Assume: c = 4, d = "He"			
+=	c += 7	c = c + 7	11 to c
-=	c -= 3	c = c - 3	1 to c
*=	c *= 4	c = c * 4	16 to c
/=	c /= 2	c = c / 2	2 to c
\=	c \= 3	c = c \ 3	1 to c
^=	c ^= 2	c = c ^ 2	16 to c
&=	d &= "llo"	d = d & "llo"	"Hello" to d

Fig. 4.11 Assignment operators.

```
1   ' Fig. 4.12: Assignment.vb
2   ' Using an assignment operator to calculate a power of 2.
3
4   Module modAssignment
5
6      Sub Main()
7         Dim exponent As Integer ' power input by user
8         Dim result As Integer = 2 ' number to raise to a power
9
10        ' prompt user for exponent
11        Console.Write("Enter an integer exponent: ")
12        exponent = Console.ReadLine()
13
14        result ^= exponent ' same as result = result ^ exponent
15        Console.WriteLine("result ^= exponent: {0}", result)
16
17        result = 2 ' reset result to 2
18        result = result ^ exponent
19        Console.WriteLine("result = result ^ exponent: {0}", result)
20
21     End Sub ' Main
22
23  End Module ' modAssignment
```

```
Enter an integer exponent: 8
result ^= exponent: 256
result = result ^ exponent: 256
```

Fig. 4.12 Exponentiation using an assignment operator.

Lines 14 and 18 have the same effect on the variable **result**. Both statements raise **result** to the value of variable **exponent**. Notice that the results of these two calculations are identical.

4.11 Formulating Algorithms: Case Study 1 (Counter-Controlled Repetition)

To illustrate how algorithms are developed, we solve two variations of a class-averaging problem. Consider the following problem statement:

> *A class of ten students took a quiz. The grades (integers in the range from 0 to 100) for this quiz are available to you. Determine the class average on the quiz.*

The class average is equal to the sum of the grades divided by the number of students. The algorithm for solving this problem on a computer must input each of the grades, perform the averaging calculation and print the result.

Let us use pseudocode to list the actions to be executed and to specify the order of execution. We use *counter-controlled repetition* to input the grades one at a time. This technique uses a variable called a *counter* to specify the number of times that a set of statements will execute. Counter-controlled repetition also is called *definite repetition* because the number of repetitions is known before the loop begins executing. In this example, repetition terminates when the counter exceeds 10. This section presents a pseudocode algorithm (Fig. 4.13) and the corresponding program (Fig. 4.14). In Sections 4.12, 4.13 and 4.14, we show how pseudocode algorithms are developed.

Set total to zero
Set grade counter to one

While grade counter is less than or equal to 10
    Input the next grade
    Add the grade to the total
    Add one to the grade counter

Set the class average to the total divided by 10
Print the class average

Fig. 4.13 Pseudocode algorithm that uses counter-controlled repetition to solve the class-average problem.

```
1    ' Fig. 4.14: Average1.vb
2    ' Using counter-controlled repetition.
3
4    Module modAverage
5
6       Sub Main()
7          Dim total As Integer          ' sum of grades
8          Dim gradeCounter As Integer   ' number of grades input
9          Dim grade As Integer          ' grade input by user
10         Dim average As Double         ' class average
11
```

Fig. 4.14 Class-average program with counter-controlled repetition (part 1 of 2).

```
12          ' initialization phase
13          total = 0                       ' set total to zero
14          gradeCounter = 1                ' prepare to loop
15
16          ' processing phase
17          While gradeCounter <= 10
18
19              ' prompt for input and read grade from user
20              Console.Write("Enter integer grade: ")
21              grade = Console.ReadLine()
22
23              total += grade      ' add grade to total
24
25              gradeCounter += 1 ' add 1 to gradeCounter
26          End While
27
28          ' termination phase
29          average = total / 10
30
31          ' write blank line and display class average
32          Console.WriteLine()
33          Console.WriteLine("Class average is {0}", average)
34
35      End Sub ' Main
36
37  End Module ' modAverage
```

```
Enter integer grade: 89
Enter integer grade: 70
Enter integer grade: 73
Enter integer grade: 85
Enter integer grade: 64
Enter integer grade: 92
Enter integer grade: 55
Enter integer grade: 57
Enter integer grade: 93
Enter integer grade: 67

Class average is 74.5
```

Fig. 4.14 Class-average program with counter-controlled repetition (part 2 of 2).

Note the references in the algorithm (Fig. 4.13) to a total and a counter. A *total* is a variable used to calculate the sum of a series of values. A counter is a variable that counts—in this case, the counter records the number of grades input by the user. It is important that variables used as totals and counters have appropriate initial values before they are used. Counters usually are initialized to one. Totals generally are initialized to zero. If a numerical variable is not initialized before its first use, Visual Basic initializes it to a default value of **0**.

Good Programming Practice 4.5

*Although Visual Basic initializes numerical variables to **0**, it is a good practice to initialize variables explicitly to avoid confusion and improve program readability.*

Lines 7–10 declare variables **total**, **gradeCounter**, and **grade** to be of type **Integer** and **average** to be of type **Double**. In this example, **total** accumulates the sum of the grades entered, and **gradeCounter** counts the number of grades entered. Variable **grade** stores the value entered (line 21).

Good Programming Practice 4.6

Always place a blank line between declarations and executable statements. This makes the declarations stand out in a program and contributes to program readability.

Notice from the output that although each grade entered is an integer, the averaging calculation is likely to produce a number with a decimal point (i.e., a floating-point number). The type **Integer** cannot represent floating-point numbers, so this program uses data type **Double**, which stores *double-precision floating-point* numbers. Visual Basic also provides data type **Single** for storing *single-precision floating-point* numbers. Data type **Double** requires more memory to store a floating-point value, but is more accurate than type **Single**. Type **Single** is useful in applications that need to conserve memory and do not require the accuracy provided by type **Double**.

Lines 13–14 initialize **total** to **0** and **gradeCounter** to **1**. Line 17 indicates that the **While** structure should iterate while the value of **gradeCounter** is less than or equal to **10**. Lines 20–21 correspond to the pseudocode statement *"Input the next grade."* The statement on line 20 displays the prompt **Enter integer grade:** in the command window. The second statement (line 21) reads the value entered by the user, and stores that value in the variable **grade**.

Next, the program updates the **total** with the new **grade** entered by the user—line 23 adds **grade** to the previous value of **total** and assigns the result to **total**—using the **+=** assignment operator. Variable **gradeCounter** is incremented (line 25) to indicate that a grade has been processed. Line 25 adds **1** to **gradeCounter**, so the condition in the **While** structure eventually becomes false, terminating the loop. Line 29 assigns the results of the average calculation to variable **average**. Line 32 writes a blank line to enhance the appearance of the output. Line 33 displays a message containing the string **"Class average is "** followed by the value of variable **average**.

4.12 Formulating Algorithms with Top-Down, Stepwise Refinement: Case Study 2 (Sentinel-Controlled Repetition)

Let us generalize the class-average problem. Consider the following problem:

> *Develop a class-averaging program that averages an arbitrary number of grades each time the program is run.*

In the first class-average example, the number of grades (10) was known in advance. In this example, no indication is given of how many grades are to be input. The program must process an arbitrary number of grades. How can the program determine when to stop the input of grades? How will it know when to calculate and print the class average?

One way to solve this problem is to use a special value called a *sentinel value* (also called a *signal value*, a *dummy value* or a *flag value*) to indicate "end of data entry." The user inputs all grades and then types the sentinel value to indicate that the last grade has been entered. Sentinel-controlled repetition is called *indefinite repetition* because the number of repetitions is not known before the loop begins its execution.

It is crucial to employ a sentinel value that cannot be confused with an acceptable input value. Grades on a quiz are normally nonnegative integers, thus –1 is an acceptable sentinel value for this problem. A run of the class-average program might process a stream of inputs such as 95, 96, 75, 74, 89 and –1. The program would then compute and print the class average for the grades 95, 96, 75, 74 and 89. The sentinel value, –1, should not enter into the averaging calculation.

Common Programming Error 4.5

Choosing a sentinel value that is also a legitimate data value could result in a logic error that would cause a program to produce incorrect results.

When solving more complex problems, such as that contained in this example, the pseudocode representation might not appear obvious. For this reason we approach the class-average program with *top-down, stepwise refinement*, a technique for developing well-structured algorithms. We begin with a pseudocode representation of the *top:*

Determine the class average for the quiz

The top is a single statement that conveys the overall function of the program. As such, the top is a complete representation of a program. Unfortunately, the top rarely conveys a sufficient amount of detail from which to write the Visual Basic algorithm. Therefore, we conduct the refinement process. This involves dividing the top into a series of smaller tasks that are listed in the order in which they must be performed resulting in the following *first refinement*:

Initialize variables
Input, sum and count the quiz grades
Calculate and print the class average

Here, only the sequence structure has been used—the steps listed are to be executed in order, one after the other.

Software Engineering Observation 4.2

Each refinement, including the top, is a complete specification of the algorithm; only the level of detail in each refinement varies.

To proceed to the next level of refinement (i.e., the *second refinement*), we commit to specific variables. We need a running total of the numbers, a count of how many numbers have been processed, a variable to receive the value of each grade and a variable to hold the calculated average. The pseudocode statement

Initialize variables

can be refined as follows:

Initialize total to zero
Initialize counter to zero

Notice that only the variables *total* and *counter* are initialized before they are used; the variables *average* and *grade* (the program in Fig. 4.16 uses these variables for the calculated average and the user input, respectively) need not be initialized because the assignment of their values does not depend on their previous values, as is the case for *total* and *counter*.

The pseudocode statement

Input, sum and count the quiz grades

requires a repetition structure (i.e., a loop) that processes each grade. We do not know how many grades are to be processed, thus we use sentinel-controlled repetition. The user enters legitimate grades one at a time. After the last legitimate grade is typed, the user types the sentinel value. The program tests for the sentinel value after each grade is input and terminates the loop when the user enters the sentinel value. The second refinement of the preceding pseudocode statement is then

> *Input the first grade (possibly the sentinel)*
>
> *While the user has not yet entered the sentinel*
>   *Add this grade to the running total*
>   *Add one to the grade counter*
>   *Input the next grade (possibly the sentinel)*

The pseudocode statement

> *Calculate and print the class average*

may be refined as follows:

> *If the counter is not equal to zero*
>   *Set the average to the total divided by the counter*
>   *Print the average*
> *Else*
>   *Print "No grades were entered"*

We test for the possibility of division by zero—a logic error that, if undetected, causes the program to produce invalid output. The complete second refinement of the pseudocode algorithm for the class-average problem is shown in Fig. 4.15.

Initialize total to zero
Initialize counter to zero

Input the first grade (possibly the sentinel)

While the user has not as yet entered the sentinel
  Add this grade to the running total
  Add one to the grade counter
  Input the next grade (possibly the sentinel)

If the counter is not equal to zero
  Set the average to the total divided by the counter
  Print the average
Else
  Print "No grades were entered"

Fig. 4.15 Pseudocode algorithm that uses sentinel-controlled repetition to solve the class-average problem.

Testing and Debugging Tip 4.1

When performing division by an expression whose value could be zero, explicitly test for this case and handle it appropriately in your program. Such handling could be as simple as printing an error message. Sometimes more sophisticated processing is required.

Good Programming Practice 4.7

Include blank lines in pseudocode programs to improve readability. The blank lines separate pseudocode control structures and the program's phases.

Software Engineering Observation 4.3

Many algorithms can be divided logically into three phases: An initialization phase that initializes the program variables, a processing phase that inputs data values and adjusts program variables accordingly and a termination phase that calculates and prints the results.

The pseudocode algorithm in Fig. 4.15 solves the general class-averaging problem presented at the beginning of this section. This algorithm was developed after only two levels of refinement—sometimes more levels of refinement are necessary.

Software Engineering Observation 4.4

The programmer terminates the top-down, stepwise refinement process when the pseudocode algorithm is specified in sufficient detail for the pseudocode to be converted to a Visual Basic program. The implementation of the Visual Basic program then occurs in a normal, straightforward manner.

The Visual Basic program for this pseudocode is shown in Fig. 4.16. In this example, we examine how control structures can be "stacked on top of one another," in sequence. The **While** structure (lines 23–31) is followed immediately by an **If/Then** structure (lines 34–42). Much of the code in this program is identical to the code in Fig. 4.14, so we concentrate only on the new features.

```
1   ' Fig. 4.16: ClassAverage2.vb
2   ' Using sentinel-controlled repetition to
3   ' display a class average.
4
5   Module modClassAverage
6
7      Sub Main()
8         Dim total As Integer          ' sum of grades
9         Dim gradeCounter As Integer   ' number of grades input
10        Dim grade As Integer          ' grade input by user
11        Dim average As Double         ' average of all grades
12
13        ' initialization phase
14        total = 0                     ' clear total
15        gradeCounter = 0              ' prepare to loop
16
17        ' processing phase
18        ' prompt for input and read grade from user
19        Console.Write("Enter integer grade, -1 to quit: ")
20        grade = Console.ReadLine()
```

Fig. 4.16 Class-average program with sentinel-controlled repetition (part 1 of 2).

```vb
21
22          ' sentinel-controlled loop where -1 is the sentinel value
23          While grade <> -1
24             total += grade      ' add gradeValue to total
25             gradeCounter += 1 ' add 1 to grade
26
27             ' prompt for input and read grade from user
28             Console.Write("Enter integer grade, -1 to quit: ")
29             grade = Console.ReadLine()
30          End While
31
32          ' termination phase
33          If gradeCounter <> 0 Then
34             average = total / gradeCounter
35
36             ' display class average
37             Console.WriteLine()
38             Console.WriteLine("Class average is {0:F}", average)
39          Else ' no grades were entered
40             Console.WriteLine("No grades were entered")
41          End If
42
43       End Sub ' Main
44
45    End Module ' modClassAverage
```

```
Enter integer grade, -1 to quit: 97
Enter integer grade, -1 to quit: 88
Enter integer grade, -1 to quit: 72
Enter integer grade, -1 to quit: -1

Class average is 85.67
```

Fig. 4.16 Class-average program with sentinel-controlled repetition (part 2 of 2).

Line 11 declares variable **average** to be of type **Double**. This allows the result of the class-average calculation to be stored as a floating-point number. Line 15 initializes **gradeCounter** to **0** because no grades have been input yet—recall that this program uses sentinel-controlled repetition. To keep an accurate record of the number of grades entered, variable **gradeCounter** is incremented only when a valid grade value is input.

Notice the differences between sentinel-controlled repetition and the counter-controlled repetition of Fig. 4.14. In counter-controlled repetition, we read a value from the user during each iteration of the **While** structure. In sentinel-controlled repetition, we read one value (line 20) before the program reaches the **While** structure. This value determines whether the program's flow of control should enter the body of the **While** structure. If the **While** structure condition is false (i.e., the user has entered the sentinel value), the body of the **While** structure does not execute (no grades were entered). If, on the other hand, the condition is true, the body begins execution, and the value entered by the user is processed (added to the **total**). After the value is processed, the next value is input by the user before the end of the **While** structure's body. When **End While** is reached at line 30, execution continues with the next test of the **While** structure condition. The new value entered by the user indicates whether the **While** structure's body should execute again. Notice that the next value always is input from the user immediately before the **While** structure condition is evaluated (line 23). This allows the program to determine if the value is the sentinel value before processing that value (i.e., adding it to the **total**). If the value is the sentinel value, the **While** structure terminates, and the value is not added to the **total**.

Good Programming Practice 4.8

In a sentinel-controlled loop, the prompts requesting data entry should remind the user of the sentinel value.

Common Programming Error 4.6

Using floating-point numbers in a manner that assumes that they are precisely represented real numbers can lead to incorrect results. Computers represent real numbers only approximately.

Good Programming Practice 4.9

Do not compare floating-point values for equality or inequality. Rather, test that the absolute value of the difference is less than a specified small value.

Despite the fact that floating-point numbers are not always "100 percent precise," they have numerous applications. For example, when we speak of a "normal" body temperature of 98.6, we do not need to be precise to a large number of digits. When we view the temperature on a thermometer and read it as 98.6, it may actually be 98.5999473210643. Calling such a number simply 98.6 is appropriate for most applications.

Floating-point numbers also develop through division. When we divide 10 by 3, the result is 3.3333333..., with the sequence of 3s repeating infinitely. The computer allocates only a fixed amount of space to hold such a value, so the stored floating-point value can be only an approximation.

In line 38 of Fig. 4.16, method **WriteLine** uses the format **{0:F}** to print the value of **average** in the command window as a *fixed-point number*, (i.e., a number with a specified number of places after the decimal point). Visual Basic provides the *standard number formats* for controlling the way numbers are printed as **String**s. We discuss the various standard number formats in Chapter 5, Control Structures Part 2.

4.13 Formulating Algorithms with Top-Down, Stepwise Refinement: Case Study 3 (Nested Control Structures)

Let us consider another complete problem. Again we formulate the algorithm using pseudocode and top-down, stepwise refinement; we then write a corresponding Visual Basic program. We have seen in previous examples that control structures may be stacked on top of one another (in sequence) just as a child stacks building blocks. In this case study, we demonstrate the only other structured way that control structures can be combined, namely through the nesting of one control structure inside another.

Consider the following problem statement:

> *A college offers a course that prepares students for the state licensing exam for real estate brokers. Last year, 10 of the students who completed this course took the licensing examination. The college wants to know how well its students did on the exam. You have been asked to write a program to summarize the results. You have been given a list of the 10 students. Next to each name is written a "P" if the student passed the exam and an "F" if the student failed the exam.*

Your program should analyze the results of the exam as follows:

1. *Input each exam result (i.e., a "P" or an "F"). Display the message "Enter result" each time the program requests another exam result.*
2. *Count the number of passes and failures.*
3. *Display a summary of the exam results, indicating the number of students who passed and the number of students who failed the exam.*
4. *If more than 8 students passed the exam, print the message "Raise tuition."*

After reading the problem statement, we make the following observations about the problem:

1. The program must process exam results for 10 students, so a counter-controlled loop is appropriate.
2. Each exam result is a **String**—either a "P" or an "F". Each time the program reads an exam result, the program must determine if the input is a "P" or an "F." We test for a "P" in our algorithm. If the input is not a "P," we assume it is an "F." (An exercise at the end of the chapter considers the consequences of this assumption. For instance, consider what happens in this program when the user enters a lowercase "p.")
3. Two counters store the exam results—one to count the number of students who passed the exam and one to count the number of students who failed the exam.
4. After the program has processed all the exam results, it must determine if more than eight students passed the exam.

Let us proceed with top-down, stepwise refinement. We begin with a pseudocode representation of the top:

Analyze exam results and decide if tuition should be raised

Once again, it is important to emphasize that the top is a complete representation of the program, but several refinements likely are needed before the pseudocode can be evolved into a Visual Basic program. Our first refinement is

Initialize variables
Input the ten exam grades and count passes and failures
Print a summary of the exam results and decide if tuition should be raised

Even though we have a complete representation of the entire program, further refinement is necessary. We must commit to specific variables. Counters are needed to record the passes and failures. A counter controls the looping process and a variable stores the user input. The pseudocode statement

Initialize variables

may be refined as follows:

Initialize passes to zero
Initialize failures to zero
Initialize student counter to one

Only the counters for the number of passes, number of failures and number of students are initialized. The pseudocode statement

Input the ten quiz grades and count passes and failures

requires a loop that inputs the result of each exam. Here it is known in advance that there are precisely ten exam results, so counter-controlled repetition is appropriate. Inside the loop (i.e., *nested* within the loop) a double-selection structure determines whether each exam result is a pass or a failure, and the structure increments the appropriate counter accordingly. The refinement of the preceding pseudocode statement is then

> *While student counter is less than or equal to ten*
>   *Input the next exam result*
>
>   *If the student passed*
>   *Add one to passes*
>   *Else*
>   *Add one to failures*
>
>   *Add one to student counter*

Notice the use of blank lines to set off the *If/Else* control structure to improve program readability. The pseudocode statement

> *Print a summary of the exam results and decide if tuition should be raised*

may be refined as follows:

> *Print the number of passes*
> *Print the number of failures*
>
> *If more than eight students passed*
>   *Print "Raise tuition"*

The complete second refinement appears in Fig. 4.17. Notice that blank lines also offset the *While* structure (lines 13–25) for program readability.

The pseudocode now is refined sufficiently for conversion to Visual Basic. The program and sample executions are shown in Fig. 4.18.

The **While** loop (lines 13–25) inputs and processes the 10 examination results. The **If/Then/Else** structure on lines 18–22 is a nested control structure because it is enclosed inside the **While**. The condition in line 18 tests if **String** variable **result** is equal to **"P"**. If so, **passes** is incremented by **1**. Otherwise, **failures** is incremented by **1**. [*Note*: **String**s are case sensitive—uppercase and lowercase letters are different. Only **"P"** represents a passing grade. In the exercises, we ask the reader to enhance the program by processing lowercase input such as **"p"**.]

Note that line 29 contains an identifier, **vbCrLf**, that is not declared explicitly in the program code. Identifier **vbCrLf** is one of several *constants* provided by Visual Basic. Constants contain values that programmers cannot modify. In the case of **vbCrLf**, the value represented is the combination of the *carriage return* and *linefeed* characters, which cause subsequent output to print at the beginning of the next line. When printed, the effect of this constant is similar to calling **Console.WriteLine()**.

Although not demonstrated in this example, Visual Basic also provides the **vbTab** constant, which represents a *tab* character. Several of the chapter exercises ask you to use these constants. In Chapter 6, Procedures, we discuss how programmers can create their own constants.

Initialize passes to zero
Initialize failures to zero
Initialize student to one

While student counter is less than or equal to ten
    Input the next exam result

    If the student passed
        Add one to passes
    Else
        Add one to failures

    Add one to student counter

Print the number of passes
Print the number of failures

If more than eight students passed
    Print "Raise tuition"

Fig. 4.17 Pseudocode for examination-results problem.

```vb
1    ' Fig. 4.18: Analysis.vb
2    ' Using counter-controlled repetition to display exam results.
3
4    Module modAnalysis
5
6       Sub Main()
7          Dim passes As Integer = 0    ' number of passes
8          Dim failures As Integer = 0  ' number of failures
9          Dim student As Integer = 1   ' student counter
10         Dim result As String         ' one exam result
11
12         ' process 10 exam results; counter-controlled loop
13         While student <= 10
14            Console.Write("Enter result (P = pass, F = fail): ")
15            result = Console.ReadLine()
16
17            ' nested control structure
18            If result = "P" Then
19               passes += 1     ' increment number of passes
20            Else
21               failures += 1   ' increment number of failures
22            End If
23
```

Fig. 4.18 Nested control structures used to calculate examination results (part 1 of 2).

```
24              student += 1        ' increment student counter
25          End While
26
27          ' display exam results
28          Console.WriteLine("Passed: {0}{1}Failed: {2}", passes, _
29              vbCrLf, failures)
30
31          ' raise tuition if more than 8 students pass
32          If passes > 8 Then
33              Console.WriteLine("Raise Tuition")
34          End If
35
36      End Sub ' Main
37
38  End Module ' modAnalysis
```

```
Enter result (P = pass, F = fail): P
Enter result (P = pass, F = fail): F
Enter result (P = pass, F = fail): P
Enter result (P = pass, F = fail): P
Enter result (P = pass, F = fail): P
Enter result (P = pass, F = fail): P
Enter result (P = pass, F = fail): P
Enter result (P = pass, F = fail): P
Enter result (P = pass, F = fail): P
Enter result (P = pass, F = fail): P
Passed: 9
Failed: 1
Raise Tuition
```

```
Enter result (P = pass, F = fail): P
Enter result (P = pass, F = fail): F
Enter result (P = pass, F = fail): P
Enter result (P = pass, F = fail): F
Enter result (P = pass, F = fail): F
Enter result (P = pass, F = fail): P
Enter result (P = pass, F = fail): P
Enter result (P = pass, F = fail): P
Enter result (P = pass, F = fail): F
Enter result (P = pass, F = fail): P
Passed: 6
Failed: 4
```

Fig. 4.18 Nested control structures used to calculate examination results (part 2 of 2).

4.14 Formulating Algorithms with Top-Down, Stepwise Refinement: Case Study 4 (Nested Repetition Structures)

Let us present another complete example. Once again, we formulate the algorithm using pseudocode and top-down, stepwise refinement, then write the corresponding program.

Again, we use stacked and nested control structures to solve the problem. In this case study, we demonstrate nested repetition structures.

Consider the following problem statement:

> *Write a program that draws in the command window a filled square consisting solely of * characters. The side of the square (i.e., the number of * characters to be printed side by side) should be input by the user and should not exceed 20.*

Your program should draw the square as follows:

1. Input the side of the square.
2. Validate that the side is less than or equal to 20. (Note: It is possible for the user to input values less than 1. We explore in the chapter exercises how this can be prevented.)
3. Use repetition to draw the square by printing only one * at a time.

After reading the problem statement, we make the following observations (in no particular order):

1. The program must draw *n* rows, each containing *n* * characters. Counter-controlled repetition should be used.
2. A test must be employed to ensure that the value of *n* is less than or equal to 20.
3. Three variables should be used—one that represents the length of the side of the square, one that represents the row in which each * appears and one that represents the column in which each * appears.

Let us proceed with top-down, stepwise refinement. We begin with a pseudocode representation of the top:

> *Draw a square of * characters*

Once again, it is important to emphasize that the top is a complete representation of the program, but several refinements are likely to be needed before the pseudocode can be naturally evolved into a program. Our first refinement is

> *Initialize variables*
> *Prompt for the side of the square*
> *Input the side of the square, making sure that it is less than or equal to 20*
> *Draw the square*

Here, too, even though we have a complete representation of the entire program, further refinement is necessary. We now commit to specific variables. A variable is needed to store the length of the side, a variable is needed to store the row where printing is occurring and a variable is needed to store the column where printing is occurring. The pseudocode statement

> *Initialize variables*

can be refined as follows:

> *Initialize row to one*
> *Initialize side to the value input*

The pseudocode statement

> *Input the side of the square, making sure that it is less than or equal to 20*

requires that a value be obtained from the command window. The pseudocode statement

> *Validate that the side is less than or equal to 20*

can be refined as

> *If side is less than or equal to 20*

which explicitly tests whether *side is less than or equal to 20*. If the condition (i.e., *side is less than or equal to 20*) is true, the first statement in the body of the *If* is executed. If the condition is false, the body of the *If* is not executed. These two control structures are said to be *nested*—meaning that one is inside the body of the other.

The pseudocode statement

> *Draw the square*

can be implemented by using nested loops to draw the square. In this example, it is known in advance that there are precisely *n* rows of *n* * characters each, so counter-controlled repetition is appropriate. One loop controls the row in which each * is printed. Inside this loop (i.e., nested within this loop), a second loop prints each individual *. The refinement of the preceding pseudocode statement is, then,

> *Set column to one*
>
> *While column is less than or equal to side*
>   *Print ***
>   *Increment column by one*
>
> *Print a line feed/carriage return*
> *Increment row by one*

After *column* is set to one, the inner loop executes to completion (i.e., until *column* exceeds *side*). Each iteration of the inner loop prints a single *. A line feed/carriage return is then printed to move the cursor to the beginning of the next line, to prepare to print the next row of the square. Variable *row* is incremented by one. If the outer loop condition allows the body of the loop to be executed, *column* is reset to one, because we want the inner loop to execute again and print another row of * characters. If *column* is not initialized to 1 before each iteration of the inner loop, the repetition condition of the inner loop will fail for all but the first row of output. Variable *row* is incremented by one. This process is repeated until the value of *row* exceeds *side* at which point the square of *'s has been printed.

The complete second refinement appears in Fig. 4.19. Notice that blank lines are used to separate the nested control structures for program readability. Also notice that we added an *Else* clause that prints a message if the value input for *side* is too large.

Good Programming Practice 4.10

Too many levels of nesting can make a program difficult to understand. If possible, try to avoid using more than three levels of nesting.

The pseudocode now is refined sufficiently for conversion to Visual Basic. The Visual Basic program and sample executions are shown in Fig. 4.20.

Initialize side to the value input
Initialize row to 1

If side is less than or equal to 20

    While row is less than or equal to side
        Set column to one

        While column is less than or equal to side
            Print *
            Increment column by one

        Print a line feed/carriage return
        Increment row by one

Else
    Print "Side is too large"

Fig. 4.19 Second refinement of the pseudocode.

Software Engineering Observation 4.5

The most difficult part of solving a problem on a computer is developing the algorithm for the solution. Once a correct algorithm has been specified, the process of producing a working Visual Basic program from the algorithm is usually straightforward.

```vb
1   ' Fig. 4.20: PrintSquare.vb
2   ' Program draws square of *.
3
4   Module modPrintSquare
5
6      Sub Main()
7         Dim side As Integer      ' square's side
8         Dim row As Integer = 1   ' current row
9         Dim column As Integer    ' current column
10
11        ' obtain side from user
12        Console.Write("Enter side length (must be 20 or less): ")
13        side = Console.ReadLine()
14
15        If side <= 20 Then ' if true, while is tested
16
17           ' this While is nested inside the If
18           While row <= side ' controls row
19              column = 1
20
```

Fig. 4.20 Nested repetition structures used to print a square of *s (part 1 of 2).

```
21                  ' this loop prints one row of * characters
22                  ' and is nested inside While in line 18
23                  While column <= side
24                     Console.Write("* ")   ' print * character
25                     column += 1           ' increment column
26                  End While
27
28                  Console.WriteLine() ' position cursor on next line
29                  row += 1            ' increment row
30               End While
31
32            Else ' condition (side <= 20) is false
33               Console.WriteLine("Side too large")
34            End If
35
36         End Sub ' Main
37
38   End Module ' modPrintSquare
```

```
Enter side length (must be 20 or less): 8
* * * * * * * *
* * * * * * * *
* * * * * * * *
* * * * * * * *
* * * * * * * *
* * * * * * * *
* * * * * * * *
* * * * * * * *
```

Fig. 4.20 Nested repetition structures used to print a square of *s (part 2 of 2).

Software Engineering Observation 4.6

Many experienced programmers write programs without ever using program development tools like pseudocode. These programmers feel that their ultimate goal is to solve the problem on a computer and that writing pseudocode merely delays producing final outputs. Although this might work for simple and familiar problems, it can lead to serious problems on large, complex projects.

4.15 Introduction to Windows Application Programming

Today, users demand software with rich graphical user interfaces (GUIs) that allow them to click buttons, select items from menus and much more. In this chapter and the previous one, we created console applications. However, the vast majority of Visual Basic programs used in industry are Windows applications with GUIs. For this reason, we have chosen to introduce Windows applications early in the book, although doing so exposes some concepts that cannot be explained fully until later chapters.

In Chapter 2, Introduction to the Visual Studio .NET IDE, we introduced the concept of visual programming, which allows programmers to create GUIs without writing any program code. In this section, we combine visual programming with the conventional programming techniques introduced in this chapter and Chapter 3, Introduction to Visual Basic

Programming. Through this combination, we can enhance considerably the Windows application introduced in Chapter 2.

Before proceeding, load the project **ASimpleProgram** from Chapter 2 into the IDE, and change the **(Name)** properties of the form, label and picture box to **FrmASimpleProgram**, **lblWelcome** and **picBug**, respectively. The modification of these names enables us to identify easily the form and its controls in the program code. [*Note*: In this section, we changed the file name from **Form1.vb** to **ASimpleProgram.vb** to enhance clarity.]

> **Good Programming Practice 4.11**
>
> *The prefixes **Frm**, **lbl** and **pic** allow forms, labels and picture boxes to be identified easily in program code.*

With visual programming, the IDE generates the program code that creates the GUI. This code contains instructions for creating the form and every control on it. Unlike a console application, a Windows application's program code is not displayed initially in the editor window. Once the program's project (e.g., **ASimpleProgram**) is opened in the IDE, the program code can be viewed by selecting **View > Code**. Figure 4.21 shows the code editor displaying the program code.

Notice that no module is present. Instead, Windows applications use classes. We already have seen examples of classes such as **Console** and **MessageBox**, which are defined within the .NET Framework Class Library. Like modules, classes are logical groupings of procedures and data that simplify program organization. Modules are discussed in detail in Chapter 6, Procedures. In-depth coverage of classes is provided in Chapter 8, Object-Based Programming.

Every Windows application consists of at least one class that **Inherits** from class **Form** (which represents a form) in the .NET Framework Class Library's **System.Windows.Forms** namespace. The keyword **Class** begins a class definition and is followed immediately by the class name (**FrmASimpleProgram**). Recall that the form's name is set using the **(Name)** property. Keyword **Inherits** indicates that the class **FrmASimpleProgram** inherits existing pieces from another class.

The class from which **FrmASimpleProgram** inherits—here, **System.Windows.Forms.Form**—appears to the right of the **Inherits** keyword. In this inheritance relationship, **Form** is called the *superclass* or *base class*, and **FrmASimpleProgram** is called the *subclass* or *derived class*. The use of inheritance results in a **FrmASimpleProgram** class definition that has the *attributes* (data) and *behaviors* (methods) of class **Form**. We discuss the significance of the keyword **Public** in Chapter 8, Object-Based Programming.

A key benefit of inheriting from class **Form** is that someone else has previously defined "what it means to be a form." The Windows operating system expects every window (e.g., form) to have certain capabilities (attributes and behaviors). However, because class **Form** already provides those capabilities, programmers do not need to "reinvent the wheel" by defining all those capabilities themselves. In fact, class **Form** has over 400 methods! In our programs up to this point, we have used only one method (i.e., **Main**), so you can imagine how much work went into creating class **Form**. The use of **Inherits** to extend from class **Form** enables programmers to create forms quickly and easily.

Chapter 4   Control Structures: Part 1   129

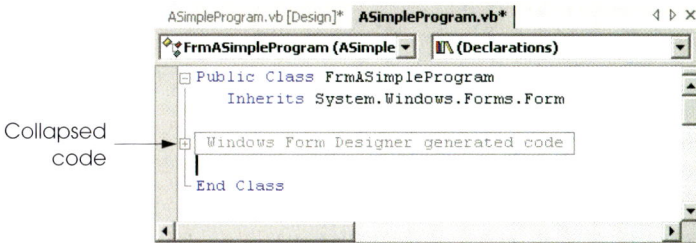

Collapsed code

Fig. 4.21 IDE showing program code for Fig. 2.15.

In the editor window (Fig. 4.21), notice the text **Windows Form Designer generated code**, which is colored gray and has a plus box next to it. The plus box indicates that this section of code is *collapsed*. Although collapsed code is not visible, it is still part of the program. Code collapsing allows programmers to hide code in the editor, so that they can focus on key code segments. Notice that the entire class definition also can be collapsed by clicking the minus box to the left of **Public**. In Fig. 4.21, the description to the right of the plus box indicates that the collapsed code was created by the *Windows Form Designer* (i.e., the part of the IDE that creates the code for the GUI). This collapsed code contains the code created by the IDE for the form and its controls, as well as code that enables the program to run. Click the plus box to view the code.

Upon initial inspection, the *expanded code* (Fig. 4.22) appears complex. This code is created by the IDE and normally is not edited by the programmer. We feel it is important for novice programmers to see the code that is generated by the IDE, even though much of the code is not explained until later in the book. This type of code is present in every Windows application. Allowing the IDE to create this code saves the programmer considerable development time. If the IDE did not provide the code, the programmer would have to write it, and this would require a considerable amount of time. The vast majority of the code shown has not been introduced yet, so you are not expected to understand how it works. However, certain programming constructs, such as comments and control structures, should be familiar. Our explanation of this code enable us to discuss visual programming in greater detail. As you continue to study Visual Basic, especially in Chapters 8–13, the purpose of this code will become clearer.

When we created this application in Chapter 2, we used the **Properties** window to set properties for the form, label and picture box. Once a property was set, the form or control was updated immediately. Forms and controls contain a set of *default properties*, which are displayed initially in the **Properties** window when a form or control is selected. These default properties provide the initial characteristics of a form or control when it is created. When a control, such as a label, is placed on the form, the IDE adds code to the class (e.g., **FrmASimpleProgram**) that creates the control and that sets some of the control's property values, such as the name of the control and its location on the form. Figure 4.23 shows a portion of the code generated by the IDE for setting the label's (i.e., **lblWelcome**'s) properties. These include the label's **Font**, **Location**, **Name**, **Text** and **TextAlign** properties. Recall from Chapter 2 that we explicitly set values for the label's **Name**, **Text** and **TextAlign** properties. Other properties, such as **Location** are set only when the label is placed on the form.

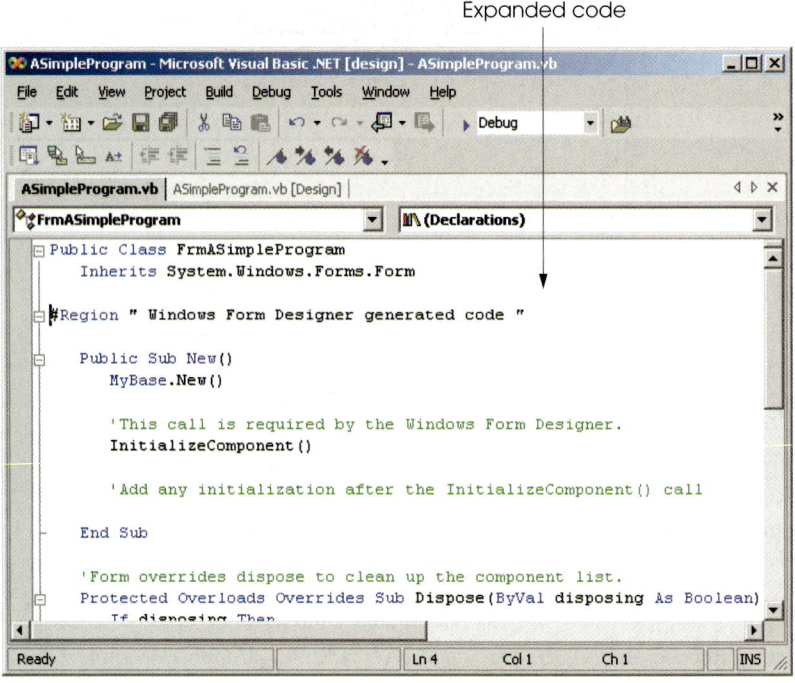

Fig. 4.22 Windows Form Designer generated code when expanded.

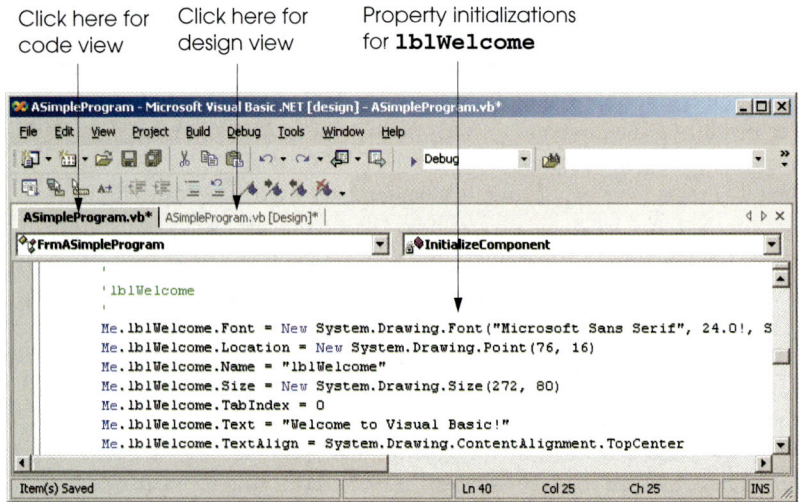

Fig. 4.23 Code generated by the IDE for `lblWelcome`.

The values assigned to the properties are based on the values in the **Properties** window. We now demonstrate how the IDE updates the Windows Form Designer generated code created when a property value in the **Properties** window changes. During this process, we must switch between code view and design view. To switch views, select the corresponding tabs—**ASimpleProgram.vb** for code view and **ASimpleProgram.vb [Design]** for design view. Alternatively, the programmer can select **View > Code** or **View > Designer**. Perform the following steps:

1. *Modify the file name.* First, change the name of the file from `Form1.vb` to `ASimpleProgram.vb` by clicking the file name in the **Solution Explorer** and changing the `File Name` property.

2. *Modify the label control's `Text` property using the **Properties** window.* Recall that properties can be changed in design view by clicking a form or control to select it, then modifying the appropriate property in the **Properties** window. Change the `Text` property of the label to "`Deitel and Associates`" (Fig. 4.24).

3. *Examine the changes in the code view.* Switch to code view and examine the code. Notice that the label's `Text` property is now assigned the text that we entered in the **Properties** window (Fig. 4.25). When a property is changed in design mode, the Windows Form Designer updates the appropriate line of code in the class to reflect the new value.

4. *Modifying a property value in code view.* In the code view editor, locate the three lines of comments indicating the initialization for `lblWelcome`, and change the `String` assigned to `Me.lblWelcome.Text` from "`Deitel and Associates`" to "`Visual Basic .NET`" (Fig. 4.26). Now, switch to design mode. The label now displays the updated text, and the **Properties** window for `lblWelcome` displays the new `Text` value (Fig. 4.27). [*Note*: Property values should not be set using the techniques presented in this step. Here, we modify the property value in the IDE generated code only as a demonstration of the relationship between program code and the Windows Form Designer.]

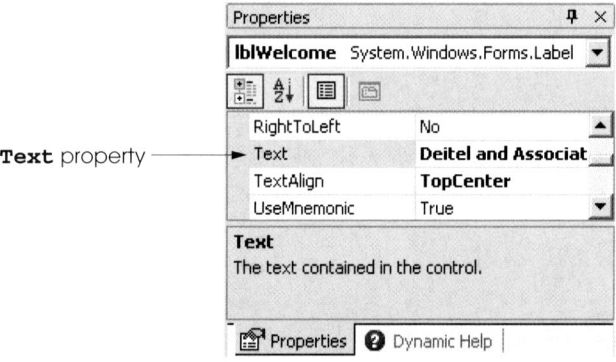

Fig. 4.24 **Properties** window used to set a property value.

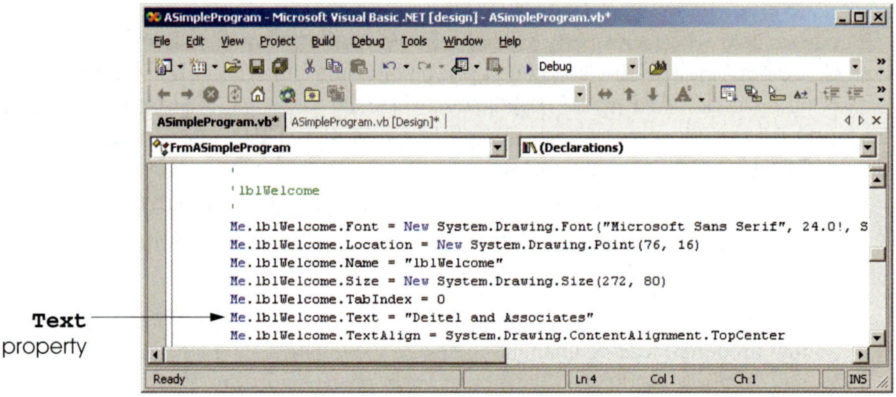

132 Control Structures: Part 1 Chapter 4

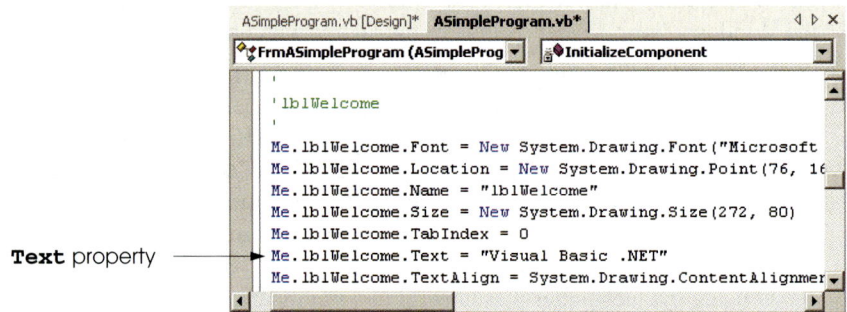

Fig. 4.25 Windows Form Designer generated code reflecting new property values.

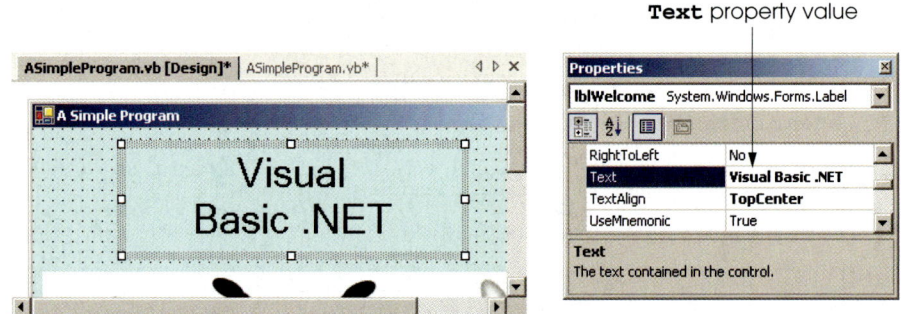

Fig. 4.26 Changing a property in the code view editor.

Fig. 4.27 New **Text** property value reflected in design mode.

5. *Change the label's **Text** property at runtime.* In the previous steps, we set properties at design time. Often, however, it is necessary to modify a property while a program is running. For example, to display the result of a calculation, a label's text can be assigned a **String** containing the result. In console applications, such code is located in **Main**. In Windows applications, we must create a method that executes when the form is loaded into memory during program execution. Like **Main**, this method is invoked when the program is run. Double-clicking the form in design view adds a method named **FrmASimpleProgram_Load** to the class (Fig. 4.28). Notice that **FrmASimpleProgram_Load** is not part of the Windows Form Designer generated code. Add the statement **lblWelcome.Text = "Visual Basic"** in the body of the method definition (Fig. 4.28). In Visual Basic, properties are accessed by placing the property name (i.e., **Text**) after the class name (i.e., **lblWelcome**), separated by the dot operator. This syntax is similar to that used when accessing class methods. Notice that the IntelliSense feature displays the **Text** property in the member list after the class name and dot operator have been typed (Fig. 4.29). In Chapter 8, Object-Based Programming, we discuss how programmers can create their own properties.

6. *Examine the results of the **FrmASimpleProgram_Load** method.* Notice that the text in the label looks the same in **Design** mode as it did in Fig. 4.27. Note also that the **Property** window still displays the value "**Visual Basic .NET**" as the label's **Text** property. The IDE-generated code has not changed either. Select **Build > Build Solution** then **Debug > Start** to run the program. Once the form is displayed, the text in the label reflects the property assignment in **FrmASimpleProgram_Load** (Fig. 4.30).

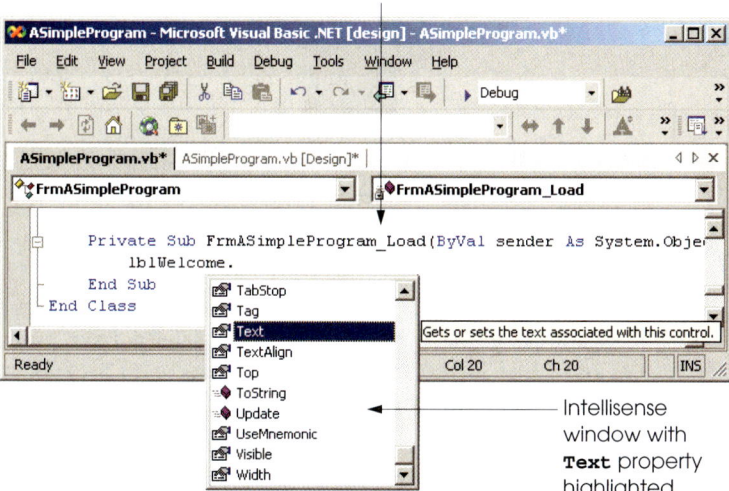

Fig. 4.28 Adding program code to **FrmASimpleProgram_Load**.

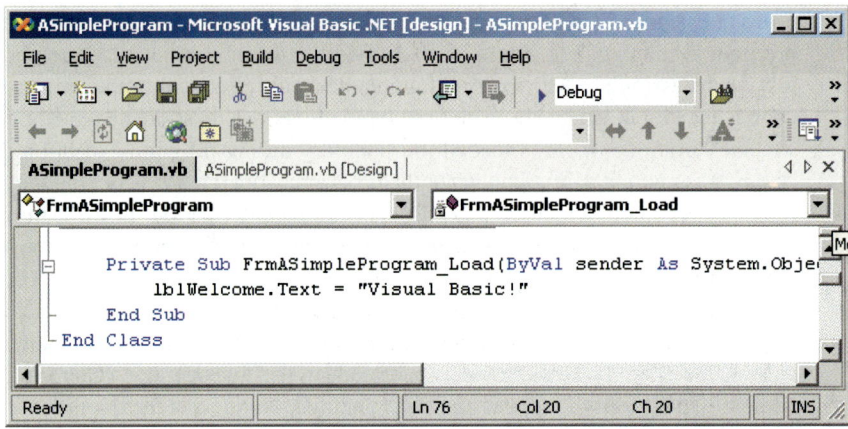

Fig. 4.29 Method `FrmASimpleProgram_Load` containing program code.

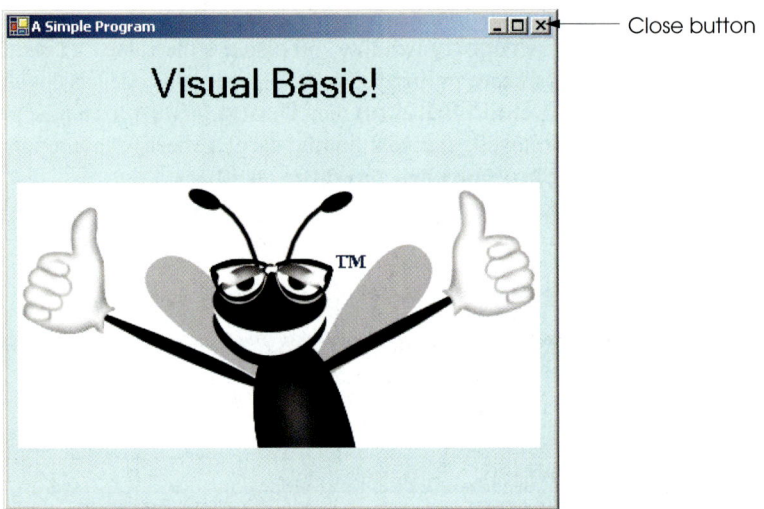

Fig. 4.30 Changing a property value at runtime.

7. *Terminate program execution.* Click the close button to terminate program execution. Once again, notice that both the label and the label's **Text** property contain the text **Visual Basic .NET**. The IDE generated code also contains the text **Visual Basic .NET**, which is assigned to the label's **Text** property.

In this chapter, we introduced program building blocks called control structures. We also discussed aspects of Windows application programming. In Chapter 5, Control Structures: Part 2, we continue our discussion of control structures by presenting additional selection and repetition structures. In addition, we also build upon the Windows application concepts presented in this chapter by creating a richer Windows application.

SUMMARY

- Any computing problem can be solved by executing a series of actions in a specific order.
- An algorithm is a procedure for solving a problem in terms of the actions to be executed and the order in which these actions are to be executed.
- Program control refers to the task of ordering a program's statements correctly.
- Pseudocode is an informal language that helps programmers develop algorithms and helps the programmer "think out" a program before attempting to write it in a programming language.
- A carefully prepared pseudocode program can be converted easily by a programmer to a corresponding Visual Basic program.
- Normally, statements in a program are executed one after another in the order in which they are written. This is called sequential execution.
- Various Visual Basic statements enable the programmer to specify that the next statement to be executed might not be the next one in sequence. This is called a transfer of control.
- Many programming complications in the 1960s were a result of the **GoTo** statement, which allows the programmer to specify a transfer of control to one of a wide range of possible destinations in a program. The notion of structured programming became almost synonymous with "**GoTo** elimination."
- Bohm and Jacopini's work demonstrated that all programs could be written in terms of only three control structures—the sequence structure, the selection structure and the repetition structure.
- The sequence structure is built into Visual Basic. Unless directed to act otherwise, the computer executes Visual Basic statements one after the other in the order in which they are written.
- A flowchart is a graphical representation of an algorithm or of a portion of an algorithm. Flowcharts are drawn using certain special-purpose symbols, such as rectangles, diamonds, ovals and small circles. These symbols are connected by arrows called *flowlines*, which indicate the order in which the actions of the algorithm execute.
- The **If/Then** single-selection structure selects or ignores a single action (or a single group of actions) based on the truth or falsity of a condition.
- The **If/Then/Else** double-selection structure selects between two different actions (or groups of actions) based on the truth or falsity of a condition.
- A multiple-selection structure selects among many different actions or groups of actions.
- Programs are formed by combining as many of each type of Visual Basic's 11 control structures as is appropriate for the algorithm the program implements.
- Single-entry/single-exit control structures make it easy to build programs.
- In control-structure stacking, the control structures are attached to one another by connecting the exit point of one control structure to the entry point of the next.
- In control-structure nesting, one control structure is placed inside another.
- Algorithms in Visual Basic programs are constructed from only 11 different types of control structures combined in only two ways.
- In the action/decision model of programming, control structure flowcharts contain (besides small circle symbols and flowlines) only rectangle symbols to indicate actions and diamond symbols to indicate decisions.
- The decision symbol has two flowlines emerging from it. One indicates the direction to be taken when the condition in the symbol is true; the other indicates the direction to be taken when the condition is false.

- Syntax errors are caught by the compiler. Logic errors affect the program only at execution time. Fatal logic errors cause a program to fail and terminate prematurely. Nonfatal logic errors do not terminate a program's execution but cause the program to produce incorrect results.
- Nested **If/Then/Else** structures test for multiple conditions by placing **If/Then/Else** structures inside other **If/Then/Else** structures.
- The **While** and **Do While/Loop** repetition structures allow the programmer to specify that an action is to be repeated while a specific condition remains true.
- Eventually, the condition in a **While** or **Do While/Loop** structure becomes false. At this point, the repetition terminates, and the first statement after the repetition structure executes.
- Failure to provide in the body of a **While** or **Do While/Loop** structure an action that eventually causes the condition to become false is a logic error. Normally, such a repetition structure never terminates, resulting in an error called an "infinite loop."
- Statements in the body of a **Do Until/Loop** are executed repeatedly as long as the loop-continuation test evaluates to false.
- Failure to provide the body of a **Do Until/Loop** structure with an action that eventually causes the condition in the **Do Until/Loop** to become true creates an infinite loop.
- Visual Basic provides the assignment operators **+=, -=, *=, /=, \=, ^=** and **&=** for abbreviating assignment statements.
- In counter-controlled repetition, a counter is used to repeat a set of statements a certain number of times. Counter-controlled repetition is also called definite repetition because the number of repetitions is known before the loop begins executing.
- A total is a variable used to calculate the sum of a series of values.
- It is important that variables used as totals and counters have appropriate initial values before they are used. Counters usually are initialized to one. Totals generally are initialized to zero.
- Data types **Double** and **Single** store floating-point numbers. Data type **Double** requires more memory to store a floating-point value, but is more accurate and generally more efficient than type **Single**.
- In sentinel-controlled repetition, the number of repetitions is not known before the loop begins its execution. Sentinel-controlled repetition uses a sentinel value (also called a signal value, dummy value or flag value) to terminate repetition.
- We approach programming problems with top-down, stepwise refinement, a technique essential to the development of well-structured algorithms.
- The top is a single statement that conveys the overall function of the program. As such, the top is a complete representation of a program.
- Through the process of refinement, we divide the top into a series of smaller tasks that are listed in the order in which they must be performed. Each refinement, including the top, is a complete specification of the algorithm; only the level of detail in each refinement varies.
- Many algorithms can be divided logically into three phases: An initialization phase that initializes the program variables, a processing phase that inputs data values and adjusts program variables accordingly, and a termination phase that calculates and prints the results.
- The programmer terminates the top-down, stepwise refinement process when the pseudocode algorithm is specified in sufficient detail for the pseudocode to be converted to a Visual Basic program. The implementation of the Visual Basic program then occurs in a normal, straightforward manner.
- The constants **vbCrLf** and **vbTab** represent the *carriage return/linefeed* character and the *tab* character, respectively.

- With visual programming, the IDE actually generates program code that creates the GUI. This code contains instructions for creating the form and every control on it.
- Windows application code is contained in a class. Like modules, classes are logical groupings of procedures and data that simplify program organization.
- Using keyword **Inherits** to extend from class **Form** enables programmers to create forms quickly, without "reinventing the wheel." Every Windows application consists of at least one class that **Inherits** from class **Form** in the **System.Windows.Forms** namespace.
- The region of collapsed code labelled **Windows Form Designer generated code** contains the code created by the IDE for the form and its controls, as well as code that enables the program to run.
- Forms and controls contain a set of default properties, which are displayed initially in the **Properties** window when a form or control is selected. These default properties provide the initial characteristics a form or control has when it is created.
- When a change is made in design mode, such as changing a property value, the Windows Form Designer creates code that implements the change.
- Often it is necessary to modify a property while a program is running. In Windows applications, such code is placed in a procedure that executes when the form is loaded, which can be created by double-clicking the form in design view.
- In Visual Basic, properties are accessed by placing the property name (e.g., **Text**) after the class name (e.g., **lblWelcome**), separated by the dot operator.

TERMINOLOGY

&= (string concatenation assignment operator)
*= (multiplication assignment operator)
+= (addition assignment operator)
/= (division assignment operator)
= (assignment operator)
-= (subtraction assignment operator)
\= (**Integer** division assignment operator)
^= (exponentiation assignment operator)
action symbol
action/decision model of programming
algorithm
attribute
behavior
body of a **While**
building block
collapsed code
complete representation of a program
conditional expression
connector symbol
constant
control structure
control-structure nesting
control-structure stacking
counter
counter-controlled repetition
decision symbol

declaration
default property
definite repetition
diamond symbol
division by zero
Do While/Loop repetition structure
Do Until/Loop repetition structure
Double primitive data type
double-selection structure
Else keyword
ElseIf keyword
end of data entry
entry point of control structure
exit point of control structure
expanded code
first refinement
flag value
floating-point division
floating-point number
flow of control
flowchart
flowline
fractional result
GoTo elimination
"**GoTo**-less programming"
graphical representation of an algorithm

If/Then selection structure
If/Then/Else selection structure
indefinite repetition
infinite loop
inheriting from
    System.Windows.Forms.Form class
initialization at the beginning of each repetition
initialization phase
initialize
input/output operation
Integer primitive data type
level of refinement
logic error
loop
looping process
multiple-selection structure
multiplicative operators: *****, **/**, **** and **Mod**
nested loop
nonfatal logic error
oval symbol
primitive (or built-in) data type
procedure for solving a problem
processing phase
program control
pseudocode
pseudocode algorithm
pseudocode statement

real number
rectangle symbol
refinement process
repetition control structure
unary operator
While repetition structure
whitespace character
Windows Form Designer
second refinement
selection control structure
sentinel-controlled repetition
sentinel value
sequence control structure
sequential execution
signal value
Single primitive data type
single-entry/single-exit control structure
single-selection structure
String data type
structured programming
syntax error
System.Windows.Forms.Form class
termination phase
top
top-down, stepwise refinement
transfer of control

SELF-REVIEW EXERCISES

4.1   Answer each of the following questions.
    a) All programs can be written in terms of three types of control structures: _____, _____ and _____.
    b) The _____ selection structure executes one action (or sequence of actions) when a condition is true and another action (or sequence of actions) when a condition is false.
    c) Repetition of a set of instructions a specific number of times is called _____ repetition.
    d) When it is not known in advance how many times a set of statements will be repeated, a _____ value can be used to terminate the repetition.
    e) Specifying the order in which statements are to be executed in a computer program is called program _____.
    f) _____ is an artificial and informal language that helps programmers develop algorithms.
    g) _____ are reserved by Visual Basic to implement various features, such as the language's control structures.
    h) The _____ selection structure is called a multiple-selection structure because it selects among many different actions (or sequence of actions).

4.2   State whether each of the following is *true* or *false*. If *false*, explain why.
    a) It is difficult to convert pseudocode into a Visual Basic program.
    b) Sequential execution refers to statements in a program that execute one after another.

c) It is recommended that Visual Basic programmers use the **GoTo** statement for program control.
d) The **If/Then** structure is called a single-selection structure.
e) Structured programs are clear, easy to debug, modify and more likely than unstructured programs to be bug-free in the first place.
f) The sequence structure is not built into Visual Basic.
g) Pseudocode closely resembles actual Visual Basic code.
h) The **While** structure is terminated with keywords **End While**.

4.3 Write two different Visual Basic statements that each add **1** to **Integer** variable **number**.

4.4 Write a statement or a set of statements to accomplish each of the following:
a) Sum the odd **Integer**s between **1** and **99** using a **While** structure. Assume that variables **sum** and **count** have been declared explicitly as **Integer**s.
b) Sum the squares of even numbers between **1** and **15** using a **Do While/Loop** repetition structure. Assume that the **Integer** variables **sum** and **count** have been declared and initialized to **0** and **2**, respectively.
c) Print the numbers from **20** to **1** in a **MessageBox** using a **Do Until/Loop** and **Integer** counter variable **counterIndex**. The **MessageBox** should display one number at a time. Assume that the variable **counterIndex** is initialized to **20**.
d) Repeat Exercise 4.4 (c) using a **Do While/Loop** structure.

4.5 Write a Visual Basic statement to accomplish each of the following tasks:
a) Declare variables **sum** and **number** to be of type **Integer**.
b) Assign **1** to variable **number**.
c) Assign **0** to variable **sum**.
d) Total variables **number** and **sum**, and assign the result to variable **sum**.
e) Print **"The sum is: "** followed by the value of variable **sum**.

4.6 Combine the statements that you wrote in Exercise 4.5 into a program that calculates and prints the sum of the **Integer**s from **1** to **10**. Use the **While** structure to loop through the calculation and increment statements. The loop should terminate when the value of control variable **number** becomes **11**.

4.7 Identify and correct the error(s) in each of the following (you may need to add code):
a) Assume that **value** has been initialized to **50**. The values from **0** to **50** should be summed.

```
While value >= 0
    sum += value
End While
```

b) This segment should read an unspecified number of values from the user and sum them. Assume that **number** and **total** are declared as **Integer**s.

```
total = 0

Do Until number = -1
    Console.Write("Enter a value ")
    number = Console.ReadLine()
    total += number
Loop

Console.WriteLine(total)
```

c) The following code should print the squares of **1** to **10** in a **MessageBox**.

```
Dim number As Integer = 1

Do While number < 10
   MessageBox.Show(number ^ 2)
While End
```

d) This segment should print the values from **888** to **1000**. Assume **value** to be declared as an **Integer**.

```
value = 888

While value <= 1000
   value -= 1
End While
```

4.8 State whether each of the following are *true* or *false*. If the answer is *false*, explain why.
a) Pseudocode is a structured programming language.
b) The body of a **Do While/Loop** is executed only if the loop continuation test is false.
c) The body of a **While** is executed only if the loop continuation test is false.
d) The body of a **Do Until/Loop** is executed only if the loop continuation test is false.

ANSWERS TO SELF-REVIEW EXERCISES

4.1 a) sequence, selection, repetition. b) **If/Then/Else**. c) counter-controlled or definite. d) sentinel, signal, flag or dummy. e) control. f) pseudocode. g) keywords. h) **Select Case**.

4.2 a) False. Pseudocode should convert easily into Visual Basic code. b) True. c) False. Some programmers argue that **GoTo** statements violate structured programming and cause considerable problems. d) True. e) True. f) False. The sequence structure is built into Visual Basic; lines of code execute in the order in which they are written, unless explicitly directed to do otherwise. g) True. h) True.

4.3
```
number = number + 1
number += 1
```

4.4
```
a) count = 1
   sum = 0

   While count <= 99
      sum += count
      count += 2
   End While

b) Do While count <= 15
      sum += count ^ 2
      count += 2
   Loop
```

c) ```
Do Until counterIndex < 1
    MessageBox.Show(counterIndex)
    counterIndex -= 1
Loop
```
d) ```
Do While counterIndex >= 1
    MessageBox.Show(counterIndex)
    counterIndex -= 1
Loop
```

4.5
a) `Dim sum, number As Integer`
b) `number = 1`
c) `sum = 0`
d) `sum += number` or `sum = sum + number`
e) `Console.WriteLine("The sum is: " & sum)` or
   `Console.WriteLine("The sum is: {0}", sum)`

4.6

```
1   ' Ex. 4.6: Calculate.vb
2   ' Calculates the sum of the integers from 1 to 10.
3
4   Module modCalculate
5
6      Sub Main()
7         Dim sum = 0, number As Integer = 1
8
9         While number <= 10
10           sum += number
11           number += 1
12        End While
13
14        Console.WriteLine("The sum is: " & sum)
15     End Sub ' Main
16
17  End Module ' modCalculate
```

4.7 a) Error: Repetition condition may never become false, resulting in an infinite loop.
```
While value >= 0
    sum += value
    value -= 1
End While
```
b) Error: The sentinel value (-1) is added to **total** producing an incorrect sum.
```
total = 0
Console.Write("Enter a value")
number = Console.ReadLine()

Do Until number = -1
    total += number
    Console.WriteLine("Enter a value")
    number = Console.ReadLine()
Loop

Console.WriteLine(total)
```

c) Errors: The counter is never incremented, resulting in an infinite loop. The repetition condition uses the wrong comparison operator. Keywords **While End** are used instead of keyword **Loop**.

```
Dim number As Integer = 1

Do While number <= 10
   MessageBox.Show(number ^ 2)
   number += 1
Loop
```

d) Error: The values are never printed and are decremented instead of incremented.

```
value = 888

While value <= 1000
   Console.WriteLine(value)
   value += 1
End While
```

4.8   a) False. Pseudocode is not a programming language.
b) False. The loop condition must evaluate to true for the body to be executed.
c) False. The loop condition must evaluate to true for the body to be executed.
d) True.

EXERCISES

4.9 Drivers are concerned with the mileage obtained by their automobiles. One driver has kept track of several tankfuls of gasoline by recording miles driven and gallons used for each tankful. Develop a program that inputs the miles driven and gallons used (both as **Double**s) for each tankful. The program should calculate and display the miles per gallon obtained for each tankful and print the combined miles per gallon obtained for all tankfuls. All average calculations should produce floating-point results.

4.10 Develop a program that determines if a department store customer has exceeded the credit limit on a charge account. For each customer, the following facts are available:
   a) Account number
   b) Balance at the beginning of the month
   c) Total of all items charged by this customer this month
   d) Total of all credits applied to this customer's account this month
   e) Allowed credit limit

The program should input as **Integer**s each of these facts, calculate the new balance (= *beginning balance + charges – credits*), display the new balance and determine if the new balance exceeds the customer's credit limit. For those customers whose credit limit is exceeded, the program should display the message, "Credit limit exceeded."

4.11 A palindrome is a number or a text phrase that reads the same backwards as forwards. For example, each of the following five-digit **Integer**s are palindromes: 12321, 55555, 45554 and 11611. Write an application that reads in a five-digit **Integer** and determines whether it is a palindrome. [*Hint*: Check if 1st digit equals 5th, 2nd digit equals 4th.]

4.12 A company wants to transmit data over the telephone, but they are concerned that their phones may be tapped. All their data is transmitted as four-digit **Integer**s. They have asked you to write a program that encrypts their data so that it may be transmitted more securely. Your program should read a four-digit **Integer** entered by the user and encrypt it as follows: Replace each digit by *(the sum of that digit plus 7) modulo 10*. Then swap the first digit with the third, and swap the second digit with the fourth. Print the encrypted **Integer**. Write a separate program that inputs an encrypted four-digit **Integer** and decrypts it to form the original number.

4.13 The factorial of a nonnegative **Integer** *n* is written *n*! (pronounced "*n* factorial") and is defined as follows:

$$n! = n \cdot (n-1) \cdot (n-2) \cdot \ldots \cdot 1 \quad \text{(for values of } n \text{ greater than or equal to 1)}$$

and

$$n! = 1 \quad \text{(for } n = 0\text{)}.$$

For example, 5! = 5 · 4 · 3 · 2 · 1, which is 120.

    a) Write an application that reads a nonnegative **Integer** from an input dialog and computes and prints its factorial.

    b) Write an application that estimates the value of the mathematical constant *e* by using the formula

$$e = 1 + \frac{1}{1!} + \frac{1}{2!} + \frac{1}{3!} + \ldots$$

    c) Write an application that computes the value of e^x by using the formula:

$$e^x = 1 + \frac{x}{1!} + \frac{x^2}{2!} + \frac{x^3}{3!} + \ldots$$

4.14 Modify the program in Fig. 4.18 to process the four **String**s: **"P"**, **"p"**, **"F"** and **"f"**. If any other **String** input is encountered, a message should be displayed informing the user of invalid input. Only increment the loop's counter if one of the four previously mentioned **String**s is input.

4.15 Modify the program in Fig. 4.20 to test if the value input for the side is less than **1**. [Hint: This requires that another **If/Then** structure be added to the code.]

4.16 Write a program that uses looping to print the following table of values:

N	10*N	100*N	1000*N
1	10	100	1000
2	20	200	2000
3	30	300	3000
4	40	400	4000
5	50	500	5000

*[Hint: Use **vbTab** to separate the columns of output.]*

Control Structures: Part 2

Objectives

- To be able to use the `For/Next`, `Do/Loop While` and `Do/Loop Until` repetition structures to execute statements in a program repeatedly.
- To understand multiple selection using the `Select Case` selection structure.
- To be able to use the `Exit Do` and `Exit For` program control statements.
- To be able to use logical operators.
- To be able to form more complex conditions.

Who can control his fate?
William Shakespeare, *Othello*

The used key is always bright.
Benjamin Franklin

Man is a tool-making animal.
Benjamin Franklin

Intelligence... is the faculty of making artificial objects, especially tools to make tools.
Henri Bergson

Chapter 5

Outline

5.1	Introduction
5.2	Essentials of Counter-Controlled Repetition
5.3	`For/Next` Repetition Structure
5.4	Examples Using the `For/Next` Structure
5.5	`Select Case` Multiple-Selection Structure
5.6	`Do/Loop While` Repetition Structure
5.7	`Do/Loop Until` Repetition Structure
5.8	Using the `Exit` Keyword in a Repetition Structure
5.9	Logical Operators
5.10	Structured Programming Summary

Summary • Terminology • Self-Review Exercises • Answers to Self-Review Exercises • Exercises

5.1 Introduction

Before writing a program to solve a particular problem, it is essential to have a thorough understanding of the problem and a carefully planned approach to solving it. It is equally essential to understand the types of building blocks available and to employ proven program-construction principles. In this chapter, we discuss these issues in conjunction with our presentation of the theory and principles of structured programming. The techniques we explore are applicable to most high-level languages, including Visual Basic. In Chapter 8, Object-Based Programming, we show how the control structures we present in this chapter are useful in the construction and manipulation of objects.

5.2 Essentials of Counter-Controlled Repetition

In the last chapter, we introduced the concept of counter-controlled repetition. In this section, we formalize the elements needed in counter-controlled repetition, namely:

1. The *name* of a *control variable* (or loop counter) that is used to determine whether the loop continues to iterate.
2. The *initial value* of the control variable.
3. The *increment* (or *decrement*) by which the control variable is modified during each iteration of the loop, or each time the loop is performed).
4. The condition that tests for the *final value* of the control variable (i.e., whether looping should continue).

The example in Fig. 5.1 uses the four elements of counter-controlled repetition to display the even digits from 2–10.

The declaration in line 8 *names* the control variable (**counter**), indicates that it is of data type **Integer**, reserves space for it in memory and sets it to an *initial value* of **2**. This

```
1    ' Fig. 5.1: WhileCounter.vb
2    ' Using the While structure to demonstrate counter-controlled
3    ' repetition.
4
5    Module modWhileCounter
6
7       Sub Main()
8          Dim counter As Integer = 2 ' initialization
9
10         While counter <= 10 ' repetition condition
11            Console.Write(counter & " ")
12            counter += 2 ' increment counter
13         End While
14
15      End Sub ' Main
16
17   End Module ' modWhileCounter
```

```
2 4 6 8 10
```

Fig. 5.1 Counter-controlled repetition with the **While** structure.

declaration includes an initialization. The initialization portion of this statement is executable, and, therefore, the statement itself also is executable.

Consider the **While** structure (lines 10–13). Line 11 displays the current value of **counter**, and line 12 *increments* the control variable by **2** upon each iteration of the loop. The loop-continuation condition in the **While** structure (line 10) tests whether the value of the control variable is less than or equal to **10**, meaning that **10** is the *final value* for which the condition is true. The body of this **While** is performed even when the control variable is **10**. The loop terminates when the control variable exceeds **10** (i.e., when **counter** becomes **12** because the loop is incrementing each time by **2**).

5.3 For/Next Repetition Structure

The **For/Next** repetition structure handles the details of counter-controlled repetition. To illustrate the power of **For/Next**, we now rewrite the program in Fig. 5.1. The result is displayed in Fig. 5.2.

```
1    ' Fig. 5.2: ForCounter.vb
2    ' Using the For/Next structure to demonstrate counter-controlled
3    ' repetition.
4
5    Module modForCounter
6
7       Sub Main()
8          Dim counter As Integer
9
```

Fig. 5.2 Counter-controlled repetition with the **For/Next** structure (part 1 of 2).

```
10          ' initialization, repetition condition and
11          ' incrementing are all included in For structure
12          For counter = 2 To 10 Step 2
13              Console.Write(counter & " ")
14          Next
15
16      End Sub ' Main
17
18  End Module ' modForCounter
```

```
2 4 6 8 10
```

Fig. 5.2 Counter-controlled repetition with the **For/Next** structure (part 2 of 2).

Good Programming Practice 5.1

Place a blank line before and after each control structure to make it stand out in the program.

Good Programming Practice 5.2

Vertical spacing above and below control structures, as well as indentation of the bodies of control structures, gives programs a two-dimensional appearance that enhances readability.

The **Main** procedure of the program operates as follows: When the **For/Next** structure (lines 12–14) begins its execution, the control variable **counter** is initialized to **2**, thus addressing the first two elements of counter-controlled repetition—control variable *name* and *initial value*. Next, the implied loop-continuation condition **counter <= 10** is tested. The **To** keyword is required in the **For/Next** structure. The optional **Step** keyword specifies the increment (i.e., the amount that is added to **counter** each time the **For/Next** body is executed). The increment of a **For/Next** structure could be negative, in which case it is a decrement, and the loop actually counts downwards. If **Step** and the value following it are omitted, the increment defaults to **1**. Programmers typically omit the **Step** portion for increments of **1**.

Because, the initial value of **counter** is **2**, the implied condition is satisfied (i.e., **True**), and the **counter**'s value **2** is output in line 13. The required **Next** keyword marks the end of the **For/Next** repetition structure. When the **Next** keyword is reached, variable **counter** is incremented by the specified value of **2**, and the loop begins again with the loop-continuation test.

At this point, the control variable is equal to **4**. This value does not exceed the final value, so the program performs the body statement again. This process continues until the **counter** value of **10** has been printed and the control variable **counter** is incremented to **12**, causing the loop-continuation test to fail and repetition to terminate. The program continues by performing the first statement after the **For/Next** structure. (In this case, procedure **Main** terminates, because the program reaches the **End Sub** statement on line 16.)

Testing and Debugging Tip 5.1

*Use a **For/Next** loop for counter-controlled repetition. Off-by-one errors (which occur when a loop is executed for one more or one less iteration than is necessary) tend to disappear, because the terminating value is not ambiguous.*

Figure 5.3 takes a closer look at the **For/Next** structure from Fig. 5.2. The first line of the **For/Next** structure sometimes is called the **For/Next** *header*. Notice that the **For/Next** header specifies each of the items needed to conduct counter-controlled repetition with a control variable.

Common Programming Error 5.1

Counter-controlled loops should not be controlled with floating-point variables. Floating-point values are represented only approximately in the computer's memory, often resulting in imprecise counter values and inaccurate tests for termination.

In many cases, the **For/Next** structure can be represented with another repetition structure. For example, an equivalent **While** structure would be of the form

    variable **=** *start*
    While *variable* **<=** *end*
      statement
      variable **+=** *increment*
    End While

For example, lines 8–13 of Fig. 5.1 are equivalent to lines 8–14 of Fig. 5.2.

The starting value, ending value and increment portions of a **For/Next** structure can contain arithmetic expressions. The expressions are evaluated once (when the **For/Next** structure begins executing) and used as the starting value, ending value and increment of the **For/Next** header. For example, assume that **value1** = 2 and **value2** = 10. The header

    For j = value1 To 4 * value1 * value2 Step value2 \ value1

is equivalent to the header

    For j = 2 To 80 Step 5

If the loop-continuation condition is initially false (e.g., if the starting value is greater than the ending value and the increment is positive), the **For/Next**'s body is not performed. Instead, execution proceeds with the statement after the **For/Next** structure.

The control variable frequently is printed or used in calculations in the **For/Next** body, but it does not have to be. It is common to use the control variable exclusively to control repetition and never mention it in the **For/Next** body.

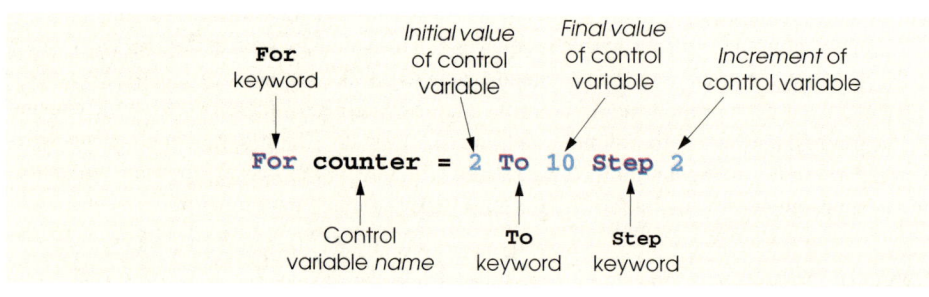

Fig. 5.3 **For/Next** header components.

Testing and Debugging Tip 5.2

*Although the value of the control variable can be changed in the body of a **For/Next** loop, avoid doing so, because this practice can lead to subtle errors.*

Common Programming Error 5.2

*In nested **For/Next** loops, the use of the same control-variable name in more than one loop is a syntax error.*

The flowchart for the **For/Next** structure is similar to that of the **While** structure. For example, the flowchart of the **For/Next** structure

```
For counter = 1 To 10
    Console.WriteLine(counter * 10)
Next
```

is shown in Fig. 5.4. This flowchart clarifies that the initialization occurs only once and that incrementing occurs *after* each execution of the body statement. Note that, besides small circles and flowlines, the flowchart contains only rectangle symbols and a diamond symbol. The rectangle symbols and diamond symbol are filled with actions and decisions that are appropriate to the algorithm the programmer is implementing.

5.4 Examples Using the `For/Next` Structure

The following examples demonstrate different ways of varying the control variable in a **For/Next** structure. In each case, we write the appropriate **For/Next** header.

a) Vary the control variable from **1** to **100** in increments of **1**.

```
For i = 1 To 100    or    For i = 1 To 100 Step 1
```

b) Vary the control variable from **100** to **1** in increments of **-1** (decrements of **1**).

```
For i = 100 To 1 Step -1
```

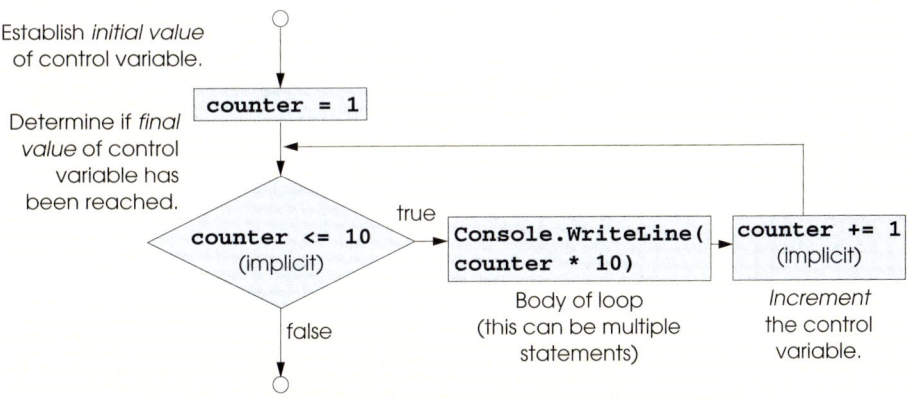

Fig. 5.4 `For/Next` repetition structure flowchart.

c) Vary the control variable from **7** to **77** in increments of **7**.

```
For i = 7 To 77 Step 7
```

d) Vary the control variable from **20** to **2** in increments of **-2** (decrements of **2**).

```
For i = 20 To 2 Step -2
```

e) Vary the control variable over the sequence of the following values: **2**, **5**, **8**, **11**, **14**, **17**, **20**.

```
For i = 2 To 20 Step 3
```

f) Vary the control variable over the sequence of the following values: **99**, **88**, **77**, **66**, **55**, **44**, **33**, **22**, **11**, **0**.

```
For i = 99 To 0 Step -11
```

The next two examples demonstrate simple applications of the **For/Next** repetition structure. The program in Fig. 5.5 uses the **For/Next** structure to sum the even integers from **2** to **100**. Remember that the use of the **MessageBox** class requires the addition of a reference to **System.Windows.Forms.dll**, as explained in Section 3.7.

```
1   ' Fig. 5.5: Sum.vb
2   ' Using For/Next structure to demonstrate summation.
3
4   Imports System.Windows.Forms
5
6   Module modSum
7
8      Sub Main()
9         Dim sum = 0, number As Integer
10
11         ' add even numbers from 2 to 100
12         For number = 2 To 100 Step 2
13            sum += number
14         Next
15
16         MessageBox.Show("The sum is " & sum, _
17            "Sum even integers from 2 to 100", _
18            MessageBoxButtons.OK, MessageBoxIcon.Information)
19
20      End Sub ' Main
21
22   End Module ' modSum
```

MessageBoxIcon.Information — Title bar text

Sum even integers from 2 to 100

The sum is 2550 — Message text

MessageBoxButton.OK — OK

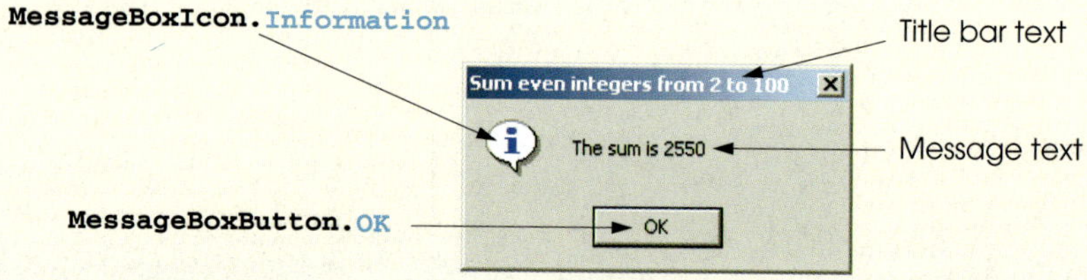

Fig. 5.5 **For/Next** structure used for summation.

Chapter 5   Control Structures: Part 2   151

The version of method **MessageBox.Show** called in Fig. 5.5 (lines 16–18) is different from the version discussed in earlier examples in that it takes four arguments instead of two. The dialog shown at the bottom of Fig. 5.5 is labelled to emphasize the four arguments. The first two arguments are **String**s displayed in the dialog and the dialog's title bar, respectively. The third and fourth arguments are constants representing buttons and icons. The third argument indicates which button(s) to display, and the fourth argument indicates an icon that appears to the left of the message. The MSDN documentation provided with Visual Studio includes the complete listing of **MessageBoxButtons** and **MessageBoxIcon** constants. Message dialog icons are described in Fig. 5.6; message dialog buttons are described in Fig. 5.7, including how to display multiple buttons.

MessageBoxIcon Constants	Icon	Description
MessageBoxIcon. Exclamation		Icon containing an exclamation point. Typically used to caution the user against potential problems.
MessageBoxIcon. Information		Icon containing the letter "i." Typically used to display information about the state of the application.
MessageBoxIcon. Question		Icon containing a question mark. Typically used to ask the user a question.
MessageBoxIcon. Error		Icon containing an **x** in a red circle. Typically used to alert the user of errors or critical situations.

Fig. 5.6   Message dialog icon constants.

MessageBoxButton constants	Description
MessageBoxButtons.OK	**OK** button. Allows the user to acknowledge a message. Included by default.
MessageBoxButtons.OKCancel	**OK** and **Cancel** buttons. Allow the user to either continue or cancel an operation.
MessageBoxButtons. YesNo	**Yes** and **No** buttons. Allow the user to respond to a question.
MessageBoxButtons. YesNoCancel	**Yes**, **No** and **Cancel** buttons. Allow the user to respond to a question or cancel an operation.
MessageBoxButtons. RetryCancel	**Retry** and **Cancel** buttons. Typically used to allow the user to either retry or cancel an operation that has failed.

Fig. 5.7   Message dialog button constants (part 1 of 2).

MessageBoxButton constants	Description
MessageBoxButtons.AbortRetryIgnore	**Abort**, **Retry** and **Ignore** buttons. When one of a series of operations has failed, these buttons allow the user to abort the entire sequence, retry the failed operation or ignore the failed operation and continue.

Fig. 5.7 Message dialog button constants (part 2 of 2).

The next example computes compound interest using the **For/Next** structure. Consider the following problem statement:

> A person invests $1000.00 in a savings account that yields 5% interest. Assuming that all interest is left on deposit, calculate and print the amount of money in the account at the end of each year over a period of 10 years. To determine these amounts, use the following formula:
>
> $$a = p(1 + r)^n$$
>
> where
>
> > p is the original amount invested (i.e., the principal)
> > r is the annual interest rate (e.g., .05 stands for 5%)
> > n is the number of years
> > a is the amount on deposit at the end of the nth year.

This problem involves a loop that performs the indicated calculation for each of the 10 years that the money remains on deposit. The solution is shown in Fig. 5.8.

Line 9 declares two **Decimal** variables. Type **Decimal** is used for monetary calculations. Line 10 declares **rate** as type **Double** and lines 14–15 initialize **principal** to **1000.00** and **rate** to **0.05**, (i.e., 5%).

```
1   ' Fig. 5.8: Interest.vb
2   ' Calculating compound interest.
3
4   Imports System.Windows.Forms
5
6   Module modInterest
7
8      Sub Main()
9         Dim amount, principal As Decimal  ' dollar amounts
10        Dim rate As Double                ' interest rate
11        Dim year As Integer               ' year counter
12        Dim output As String              ' amount after each year
13
14        principal = 1000.00
15        rate = 0.05
16
17        output = "Year" & vbTab & "Amount on deposit" & vbCrLf
18
```

Fig. 5.8 **For/Next** structure used to calculate compound interest (part 1 of 2).

```
19          ' calculate amount after each year
20          For year = 1 To 10
21             amount = principal * (1 + rate) ^ year
22             output &= year & vbTab & _
23                String.Format("{0:C}", amount) & vbCrLf
24          Next
25
26          ' display output
27          MessageBox.Show(output, "Compound Interest", _
28             MessageBoxButtons.OK, MessageBoxIcon.Information)
29
30       End Sub ' Main
31
32    End Module ' modInterest
```

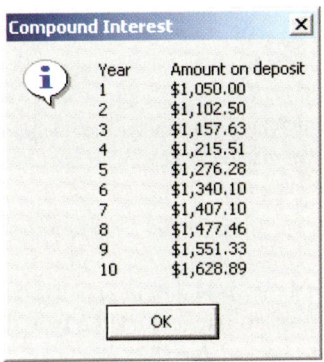

Fig. 5.8 For/Next structure used to calculate compound interest (part 2 of 2).

The **For/Next** structure executes its body 10 times, varying control variable **year** from **1** to **10** in increments of **1**. Line 21 performs the calculation from the problem statement

$$a = p(1 + r)^n$$

where a is **amount**, p is **principal**, r is **rate** and n is **year**.

Lines 22–23 append additional text to the end of **String output**. The text includes the current **year** value, a tab character (**vbTab**) to position to the second column, the result of the method call **String.Format("{0:C}", amount)** and, finally, a newline character (**vbCrLf**) to start the next output on the next line. The first argument passed to **Format** is the format string. We have seen **String**s containing **{0}**, **{1}** and so on, where the digit within the braces indicates the argument being displayed. In Chapter 4, we used a more complicated format string to print a floating-point number with two digits after the decimal. In these more complicated format strings, such as **"{0:C}"**, the first digit (**0**) serves the same purpose. The information specified after the colon (**:**) is called the *formatting code*. The **C** (for "currency") *formatting code* indicates that its corresponding argument (**amount**) should be displayed in monetary format. Figure 5.9 shows several formatting codes; a complete list can be found in the MSDN documentation "Standard Numeric Format Strings." All formatting codes are case insensitive. Note that format codes **D** and **X** can be used only with integer values.

Format Code	Description
C	Currency. Precedes the number with **$**, separates every three digits with commas and sets the number of decimal places to two.
E	Scientific notation. Displays one digit to the left of the decimal and six digits to the right of the decimal, followed by the character **E** and a three-digit integer representing the exponent of a power of 10. For example, **956.2** is formatted as **9.562000E+002**.
F	Fixed point. Sets the number of decimal places to two.
G	General. Visual Basic chooses either **E** or **F** for you, depending on which representation generates a shorter string.
D	Decimal integer. Displays an integer as a whole number in standard base-10 format.
N	Number. Separates every three digits with a comma and sets the number of decimal places to two.
X	Hexadecimal integer. Displays the integer in hexadecimal (base-16) notation. We discuss hexadecimal notation in Appendix B.

Fig. 5.9 Formatting codes for **String**s.

Variables **amount** and **principal** are of type **Decimal**. We do this because we are dealing with fractional parts of dollars and need a type that allows precise calculations with monetary amounts—**Single** and **Double** do not. Using floating-point data types, such as **Single** or **Double**, to represent dollar amounts (assuming that dollar amounts are displayed with two digits to the right of the decimal point) can cause errors. For example, two **Double** dollar amounts stored in the machine could be 14.234 (normally rounded to 14.23) and 18.673 (normally rounded to 18.67). When these amounts are added together, they produce the internal sum 32.907, which normally rounds to 32.91. Thus, the printout could appear as

```
    14.23
  + 18.67
  -------
    32.91
```

but a person adding the individual numbers as printed would expect the sum 32.90. Therefore, it is inappropriate to use **Single** or **Double** for dollar amounts.

Good Programming Practice 5.3

*Do not use variables of type **Single** or **Double** to perform precise monetary calculations. The imprecision of floating-point numbers can cause errors that result in incorrect monetary values. Use the data type **Decimal** for monetary calculations.*

Variable **rate** is of type **Double** because it is used in the calculation **1.0 + rate**, which appears as the right operand of the exponentiation operator. In fact, this calculation produces the same result each time through the loop, so performing the calculation in the body of the **For/Next** loop is wasteful.

Performance Tip 5.1

Avoid placing inside a loop the calculation of an expression whose value does not change each time through the loop. Such an expression should be evaluated only once and prior to the loop.

5.5 Select Case Multiple-Selection Structure

In the last chapter, we discussed the **If/Then** single-selection structure and the **If/Then/Else** double-selection structure. Occasionally, an algorithm contains a series of decisions in which the algorithm tests a variable or expression separately for each value that the variable or expression might assume. The algorithm then takes different actions based on those values. Visual Basic provides the **Select Case** multiple-selection structure to handle such decision making. The program in Fig. 5.10 uses a **Select Case** to count the number of different letter grades on an exam. Assume the exam is graded as follows: 90 and above is an A, 80–89 is a B, 70–79 is a C, 60–69 is a D and 0–59 is an F. This "generous" instructor gives a minimum grade of 10 for students who were present for the exam. Students not present for the exam receive a 0.

Line 7 in Fig. 5.10 declares variable **grade** as type **Integer**. This variable stores each grade that is input. Lines 8–12 declare variables that store the total number grades of each type. Lines 18–57 use a **While** loop for sentinel-controlled repetition.

Line 20

```
Select Case grade
```

begins the **Select Case** structure. The expression following the keywords **Select Case** is called the *controlling expression*. The controlling expression (i.e., the value of **grade**) is compared sequentially with each **Case**. If a matching **Case** is found, the code in the **Case** executes, then program control proceeds to the first statement after the **Select Case** structure (line 55).

Common Programming Error 5.3

*Duplicate **Case** statements are logic errors. At run time, the first matching **Case** is executed.*

```
1    ' Fig. 5.10: SelectTest.vb
2    ' Using the Select Case structure.
3
4    Module modEnterGrades
5
6       Sub Main()
7          Dim grade As Integer = 0   ' one grade
8          Dim aCount As Integer = 0  ' number of As
9          Dim bCount As Integer = 0  ' number of Bs
10         Dim cCount As Integer = 0  ' number of Cs
11         Dim dCount As Integer = 0  ' number of Ds
12         Dim fCount As Integer = 0  ' number of Fs
13
14         Console.Write("Enter a grade, -1 to quit: ")
15         grade = Console.ReadLine()
```

Fig. 5.10 **Select Case** structure used to count grades (part 1 of 3).

```vbnet
16
17         ' input and process grades
18         While grade <> -1
19
20            Select Case grade      ' check which grade was input
21
22               Case 100             ' student scored 100
23                  Console.WriteLine("Perfect Score!" & vbCrLf & _
24                     "Letter grade: A" & vbCrLf)
25                  aCount += 1
26
27               Case 90 To 99        ' student scored 90-99
28                  Console.WriteLine("Letter Grade: A" & vbCrLf)
29                  aCount += 1
30
31               Case 80 To 89        ' student scored 80-89
32                  Console.WriteLine("Letter Grade: B" & vbCrLf)
33                  bCount += 1
34
35               Case 70 To 79        ' student scored 70-79
36                  Console.WriteLine("Letter Grade: C" & vbCrLf)
37                  cCount += 1
38
39               Case 60 To 69        ' student scored 60-69
40                  Console.WriteLine("Letter Grade: D" & vbCrLf)
41                  dCount += 1
42
43               ' student scored 0 or 10-59 (10 points for attendance)
44               Case 0, 10 To 59
45                  Console.WriteLine("Letter Grade: F" & vbCrLf)
46                  fCount += 1
47
48               Case Else
49
50                  ' alert user that invalid grade was entered
51                  Console.WriteLine("Invalid Input. " & _
52                     "Please enter a valid grade." & vbCrLf)
53            End Select
54
55            Console.Write("Enter a grade, -1 to quit: ")
56            grade = Console.ReadLine()
57         End While
58
59         ' display count of each letter grade
60         Console.WriteLine(vbCrLf & _
61            "Totals for each letter grade are: " & vbCrLf & _
62            "A: " & aCount & vbCrLf & "B: " & bCount _
63            & vbCrLf & "C: " & cCount & vbCrLf & "D: " & _
64            dCount & vbCrLf & "F: " & fCount)
65
66      End Sub ' Main
67
68 End Module ' modEnterGrades
```

Fig. 5.10 Select Case structure used to count grades (part 2 of 3).

```
Enter a grade, -1 to quit: 84
Letter Grade: B

Enter a grade, -1 to quit: 100
Perfect Score!
Letter grade: A

Enter a grade, -1 to quit: 3000
Invalid Input. Please enter a valid grade.

Enter a grade, -1 to quit: 95
Letter Grade: A

Enter a grade, -1 to quit: 78
Letter Grade: C

Enter a grade, -1 to quit: 64
Letter Grade: D

Enter a grade, -1 to quit: 10
Letter Grade: F

Enter a grade, -1 to quit: -1

Totals for each letter grade are:
A: 2
B: 1
C: 1
D: 1
F: 1
```

Fig. 5.10 **Select Case** structure used to count grades (part 3 of 3).

The first **Case** statement (line 22) determines if the value of **grade** is exactly equal to **100**. The next **Case** statement (line 27) determines if **grade** is between **90** and **99** inclusive. Keyword **To** specifies the range. Lines 31–44 use this keyword to present a series of similar **Case**s.

Common Programming Error 5.4

*If the value on the left side of the **To** keyword in a **Case** statement is larger than the value on the right side, the **Case** is ignored during program execution, potentially causing a logic error.*

When multiple values are tested in a **Case** statement, they are separated by commas (line 44). Either **0** or any value in the range **10** to **59**, inclusive matches this **Case**. Line 48 contains the optional **Case Else**, which is executed when input does not match any of the previous **Case**s. **Case Else** commonly is used to check for invalid input. When employed, the **Case Else** must be the last **Case**.

The required **End Select** keywords terminate the **Select Case** structure. Note that the body of the **Select Case** structure is indented to emphasize structure and improve program readability.

Common Programming Error 5.5

*When using the optional **Case Else** statement in a **Select Case** structure, failure to place the **Case Else** as the last **Case** is a syntax error.*

Testing and Debugging Tip 5.3

*Provide a **Case Else** in **Select Case** structures. **Case**s not handled in a **Select Case** structure are ignored unless a **Case Else** is provided. The inclusion of a **Case Else** statement facilitates the processing of exceptional conditions. In some situations, no **Case Else** processing is needed.*

Case statements also can use relational operators to determine whether the controlling expression satisfies a condition. For example

```
Case Is < 0
```

uses keyword **Is** along with the relational operator, **<**, to test for values less than 0. Figure 5.11 flowcharts the **Select Case** structure.

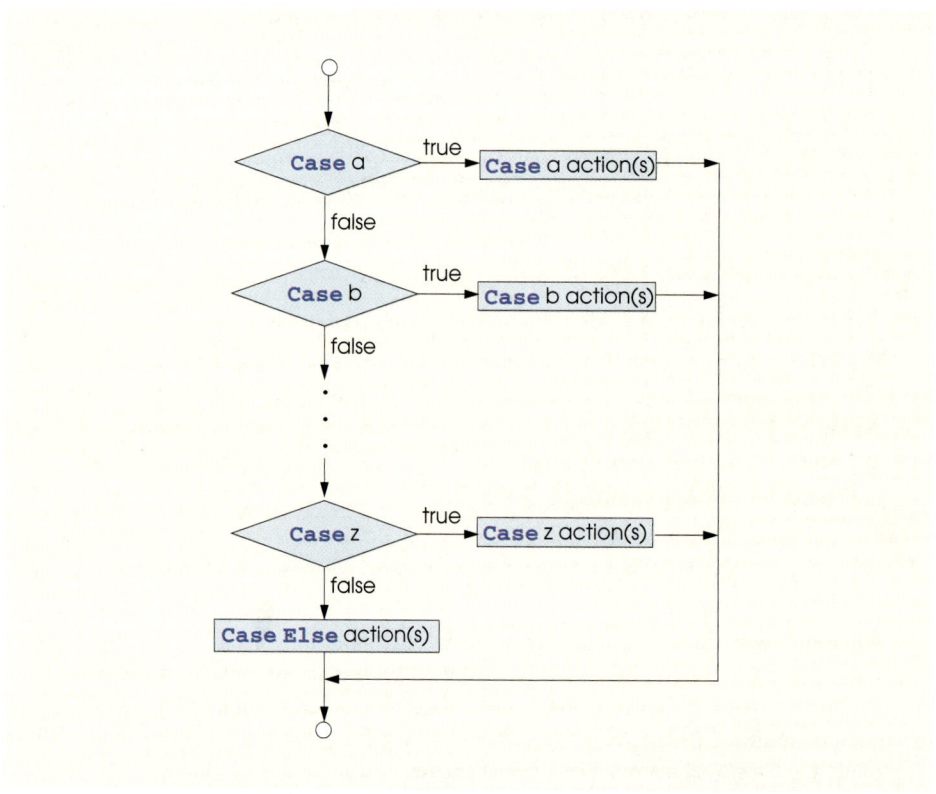

Fig. 5.11 **Select Case** multiple-selection structure flowchart.

Again, note that (besides small circles and flowlines) the flowchart contains only rectangle and diamond symbols. Imagine, as we did in the previous chapter, that the programmer has access to a deep bin of empty structures. This time, the bin contains **Select Case** structures, and the programmer can stack and nest as many as are necessary with other control structures to form a structured implementation of an algorithm's flow of control. The programmer fills the rectangles and diamonds with actions and decisions appropriate to the algorithm. Although nested control structures are common, it is rare to find nested **Select Case** structures in a program.

In Chapter 10, Object-Oriented Programming: Part 2, we present a more elegant method of implementing multiple selection logic. We use a technique called polymorphism to create programs that are often clearer, more manageable, and easier to extend than programs that use **Select Case** logic.

5.6 Do/Loop While Repetition Structure

The **Do/Loop While** repetition structure is similar to the **While** structure and **Do While/Loop** structure. In the **While** and **Do While/Loop** structures, the loop-continuation condition is tested at the beginning of the loop, before the body of the loop is performed. The **Do/Loop While** structure tests the loop-continuation condition *after* the loop body is performed. Therefore, in a **Do/Loop While** structure, the loop body is always executed at least once. When a **Do/Loop While** structure terminates, execution continues with the statement after the **Loop While** clause. The program in Fig. 5.12 uses a **Do/Loop While** structure to output the values 1–5.

Testing and Debugging Tip 5.4

*Infinite loops occur when the loop-continuation condition in a **While**, **Do While/Loop** or **Do/Loop While** structure never becomes false.*

```
1   ' Fig. 5.12: DoWhile.vb
2   ' Demonstrating the Do/Loop While repetition structure.
3
4   Module modDoWhile
5
6      Sub Main()
7         Dim counter As Integer = 1
8
9         ' print values 1 to 5
10        Do
11           Console.Write(counter & " ")
12           counter += 1
13        Loop While counter <= 5
14
15     End Sub ' Main
16
17  End Module ' modDoWhile
```

```
1 2 3 4 5
```

Fig. 5.12 Do/Loop While repetition structure.

Lines 10–13 demonstrate the **Do/Loop While** structure. The first time that the structure is encountered, lines 11–12 are executed, displaying the value of **counter** (at this point, **1**) then incrementing **counter** by **1**. Then, the condition in line 13 is evaluated. Variable **counter** is **2**, which is less than or equal to **5**; because the condition is met, the **Do/Loop While** structure executes again. The fifth time that the structure executes, line 11 outputs the value **5**, and, in line 12, **counter** is incremented to **6**. At this point, the condition on line 13 evaluates to false, and the program exits the **Do/Loop While** structure.

The **Do/Loop While** flowchart (Fig. 5.13) illustrates the fact that the loop-continuation condition is not evaluated until the structure body is executed at least once. The flowchart contains only a rectangle and a diamond. Imagine, once again, that the programmer has access to a bin of empty **Do/Loop While** structures—as many as the programmer might need to stack and nest with other control structures to form a structured implementation of an algorithm. The programmer fills the rectangles and diamonds with actions and decisions appropriate to the algorithm.

5.7 Do/Loop Until Repetition Structure

The **Do/Loop Until** structure is similar to the **Do Until/Loop** structure, except that the loop-continuation condition is tested after the loop body is performed; therefore, the loop body executes at least once. When a **Do/Loop Until** terminates, execution continues with the statement after the **Loop Until** clause. Figure 5.14 uses a **Do/Loop Until** structure to print the numbers from 1–5.

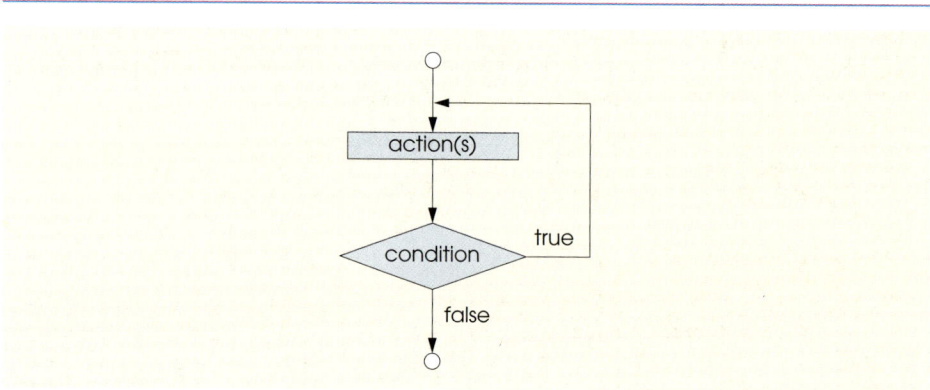

Fig. 5.13 Do/Loop While repetition structure flowchart.

```
1   ' Fig. 5.14: LoopUntil.vb
2   ' Using Do/Loop Until repetition structure.
3
4   Module modLoopUntil
5
6      Sub Main()
7         Dim counter As Integer = 1
```

Fig. 5.14 Do/Loop Until repetition structure (part 1 of 2).

```
 8
 9          ' print values 1 to 5
10          Do
11             Console.Write(counter & " ")
12             counter += 1
13          Loop Until counter > 5
14
15       End Sub ' Main
16
17    End Module ' modLoopUntil
```

```
1 2 3 4 5
```

Fig. 5.14 Do/Loop Until repetition structure (part 2 of 2).

The **Do/Loop Until** structure is flowcharted in Fig. 5.15. This flowchart makes it clear that the loop-continuation condition is not evaluated until after the body is executed at least once. Again, note that (besides small circles and flowlines) the flowchart contains only a rectangle symbol and a diamond symbol.

Imagine, again, that the programmer has access to a deep bin of empty **Do/Loop Until** structures—as many as the programmer might need to stack and nest with other control structures to form a structured implementation of an algorithm's flow of control. And again, the rectangles and diamonds are then filled with actions and decisions appropriate to the algorithm.

Common Programming Error 5.6
Including an incorrect relational operator or an incorrect final value for a loop counter in the condition of any repetition structure can cause off-by-one errors.

Testing and Debugging Tip 5.5
*Infinite loops occur when the loop-continuation condition in a **Do Until/Loop** or **Do/Loop Until** structure never becomes true.*

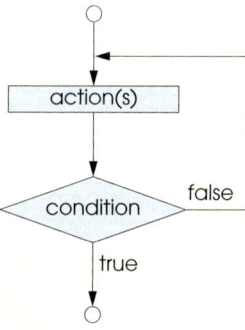

Fig. 5.15 Do/Loop Until repetition structure flowchart.

Testing and Debugging Tip 5.6

In a counter-controlled loop, make sure the control variable is incremented (or decremented) appropriately in the body of the loop.

Testing and Debugging Tip 5.7

In a sentinel-controlled loop, make sure the sentinel value is eventually input.

Testing and Debugging Tip 5.8

*Including a final value in the condition of a repetition structure (and choosing the appropriate relational operator) can reduce the risk of off-by-one errors. For example, in a **While** loop used to print the values 1–10, the loop-continuation condition should be **counter <= 10**, rather than **counter < 10** (which is an off-by-one error) or **counter < 11** (which is nevertheless correct).*

5.8 Using the `Exit` Keyword in a Repetition Structure

The **Exit Do**, **Exit While** and **Exit For** statements alter the flow of control by causing immediate exit from a repetition structure. The **Exit Do** statement can be executed in a **Do While/Loop**, **Do/Loop While**, **Do Until/Loop** or **Do/Loop Until** structure, to cause the program to exit immediately from that repetition structure. Similarly, the **Exit For** and **Exit While** statements cause immediate exit from **For/Next** and **While** loops, respectively. Execution continues with the first statement that follows the repetition structure.

Figure 5.16 demonstrates the **Exit For**, **Exit Do** and **Exit While** statements in various repetition structures.

```
1    ' Fig. 5.16: ExitTest.vb
2    ' Using the Exit keyword in repetition structures.
3
4    Imports System.Windows.Forms
5
6    Module modExitTest
7
8       Sub Main()
9          Dim output As String
10         Dim counter As Integer
11
12         For counter = 1 To 10
13
14            ' skip remaining code in loop only if counter = 3
15            If counter = 3 Then
16               Exit For
17            End If
18
19         Next
20
21         output = "counter = " & counter & _
22            " after exiting For/Next structure" & vbCrLf
```

Fig. 5.16 **Exit** keyword in repetition structures (part 1 of 2).

```
23
24          Do Until counter > 10
25
26              ' skip remaining code in loop only if counter = 5
27              If counter = 5 Then
28                  Exit Do
29              End If
30
31              counter += 1
32          Loop
33
34          output &= "counter = " & counter & _
35              " after exiting Do Until/Loop structure" & vbCrLf
36
37          While counter <= 10
38
39              ' skip remaining code in loop only if counter = 7
40              If counter = 7 Then
41                  Exit While
42              End If
43
44              counter += 1
45          End While
46
47          output &= "counter = " & counter & _
48              " after exiting While structure"
49
50          MessageBox.Show(output, "Exit Test", _
51              MessageBoxButtons.OK, MessageBoxIcon.Information)
52      End Sub ' Main
53
54  End Module ' modExitTest
```

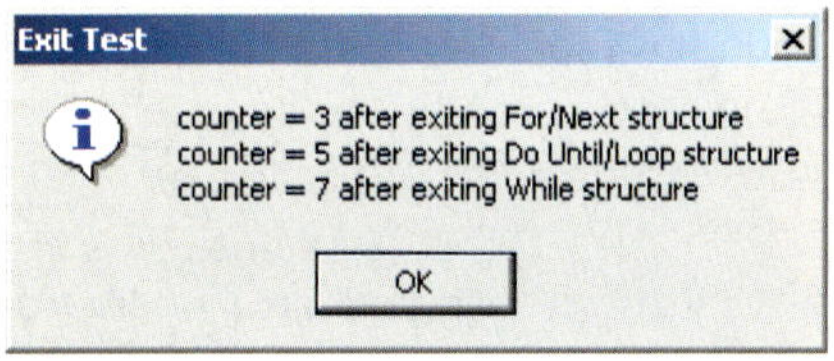

Exit Test

counter = 3 after exiting For/Next structure
counter = 5 after exiting Do Until/Loop structure
counter = 7 after exiting While structure

OK

Fig. 5.16 **Exit** keyword in repetition structures (part 2 of 2).

The header of the **For/Next** structure (line 12) indicates that the body of the loop should execute ten times. During each execution, the **If/Then** structure (lines 15–17) checks if the control variable, **counter**, is equal to **3**. If so, the **Exit For** statement (line 16) executes. Thus, as the body of the **For/Next** structure executes for the third time (i.e, **counter** is **3**), the **Exit For** statement terminates execution of the loop. Program control then proceeds to the assignment statement (lines 21–22) which appends the current value of **counter** to **String** variable **output**.

The header of the **Do Until/Loop** structure (line 24) indicates that the loop should continue executing until **counter** is greater than **10**. (Note that **counter** is **3** when the **Do Until/Loop** structure begins executing.) When **counter** has the values **3** and **4**, the body of the **If/Then** structure (lines 27–29) does not execute, and **counter** is incremented (line 31). However, when **counter** is **5**, the **Exit Do** statement (line 28) executes, terminating the loop. The assignment statement (lines 34–35) appends the value of **counter** to **output**. Note that the program does not increment **counter** (line 31) after the **Exit Do** statement executes.

The **While** structure (lines 37–45) behaves similarly to the **Do While/Loop**. In this case, the value of **counter** is **5** when the loop begins executing. When **counter** is **7**, the **Exit While** statement (line 41) executes, terminating execution of the **While** structure. Lines 47–48 append the final value of **counter** to **String** variable **output**, which is displayed in a message dialog (lines 50–51).

Software Engineering Observation 5.1

*Some programmers feel that **Exit Do**, **Exit While** and **Exit For** violate the principles of structured programming. The effects of these statements can be achieved by structured programming techniques that we discuss soon.*

Software Engineering Observation 5.2

Debates abound regarding the relative importance of quality software engineering and program performance. Often, one of these goals is accomplished at the expense of the other. For all but the most performance-intensive situations, apply the following guidelines: First, make your code simple and correct; then make it fast and small, but only if necessary.

5.9 Logical Operators

So far, we have studied only *simple conditions,* such as **count <= 10**, **total > 1000** and **number <> sentinelValue**. Each selection and repetition structure evaluated only one condition with one of the operators **>**, **<**, **>=**, **<=**, **=** and **<>**. To make a decision that relied on the evaluation of multiple conditions, we performed these tests in separate statements or in nested **If/Then** or **If/Then/Else** structures.

To handle multiple conditions more efficiently, Visual Basic provides *logical operators* that can be used to form complex conditions by combining simple ones. The logical operators are **AndAlso**, **And**, **OrElse**, **Or**, **Xor** and **Not**. We consider examples that use each of these operators.

Suppose we wish to ensure that two conditions are *both* true in a program before a certain path of execution is chosen. In such case, we can use the logical **AndAlso** operator as follows:

```
If gender = "F" AndAlso age >= 65 Then
    seniorFemales += 1
End If
```

This **If/Then** statement contains two simple conditions. The condition **gender = "F"** determines whether a person is female and the condition **age >= 65** determines whether a person is a senior citizen. The two simple conditions are evaluated first, because the precedences of **=** and **>=** are both higher than the precedence of **AndAlso**. The **If/Then** statement then considers the combined condition

```
gender = "F" AndAlso age >= 65
```

This condition evaluates to true *if and only if* both of the simple conditions are true. When this combined condition is true, the count of **seniorFemales** is incremented by **1**. However, if either or both of the simple conditions are false, the program skips the increment and proceeds to the statement following the **If/Then** structure. The readability of the preceding combined condition can be improved by adding redundant (i.e., unnecessary) parentheses:

```
(gender = "F") AndAlso (age >= 65)
```

Figure 5.17 illustrates the effect of using the **AndAlso** operator with two expressions. The table lists all four possible combinations of true and false values for *expression1* and *expression2*. Such tables often are called *truth tables*. Visual Basic evaluates to true or false expressions that include relational operators, equality operators and logical operators.

Now let us consider the **OrElse** operator. Suppose we wish to ensure that either *or* both of two conditions are true before we choose a certain path of execution. We use the **OrElse** operator in the following program segment:

```
If (semesterAverage >= 90 OrElse finalExam >= 90) Then
    Console.WriteLine("Student grade is A")
End If
```

This statement also contains two simple conditions. The condition **semesterAverage >= 90** is evaluated to determine whether the student deserves an "A" in the course because of an outstanding performance throughout the semester. The condition **finalExam >= 90** is evaluated to determine if the student deserves an "A" in the course because of an outstanding performance on the final exam. The **If/Then** statement then considers the combined condition

```
(semesterAverage >= 90 OrElse finalExam >= 90)
```

and awards the student an "A" if either or both of the conditions are true. Note that the text "**Student grade is A**" is *always* printed, unless both of the conditions are false. Figure 5.18 provides a truth table for the **OrElse** operator.

The **AndAlso** operator has a higher precedence than the **OrElse** operator. An expression containing **AndAlso** or **OrElse** operators is evaluated only until truth or falsity is known. For example, evaluation of the expression

```
(gender = "F" AndAlso age >= 65)
```

expression1	expression2	expression1 AndAlso expression2
False	False	False
False	True	False
True	False	False
True	True	True

Fig. 5.17 Truth table for the **AndAlso** operator.

expression1	expression2	expression1 `OrElse` expression2
`False`	`False`	`False`
`False`	`True`	`True`
`True`	`False`	`True`
`True`	`True`	`True`

Fig. 5.18 Truth table for the `OrElse` operator.

stops immediately if **gender** is not equal to **"F"** (i.e., the entire expression is false); the evaluation of the second expression is irrelevant because the first condition is false. Evaluation of the second condition occurs if and only if **gender** is equal to **"F"** (i.e., the entire expression could still be true if the condition **age >= 65** is true). This performance feature for the evaluation of **AndAlso** and **OrElse** expressions is called *short-circuit evaluation*.

Performance Tip 5.2

*In expressions using operator **AndAlso**, if the separate conditions are independent of one another, place the condition most likely to be false as the leftmost condition. In expressions using operator **OrElse**, make the condition most likely to be true the leftmost condition. Each of these suggestions can reduce a program's execution time.*

The *logical AND operator without short-circuit evaluation* (**And**) and the *logical inclusive OR operator without short-circuit evaluation* (**Or**) are similar to the **AndAlso** and **OrElse** operators, with one exception—the **And** and **Or** logical operators always evaluate both of their operands. No short-circuit evaluation occurs when **And** and **Or** are employed. For example, the expression

```
(gender = "F" And age >= 65)
```

evaluates **age >= 65**, even if **gender** is not equal to **"F"**.

Normally, there is no compelling reason to use the **And** and **Or** operators instead of **AndAlso** and **OrElse**. However, some programmers make use of them when the right operand of a condition produces a *side effect* (such as a modification of a variable's value) or if the right operand includes a required method call, as in the following program segment:

```
Console.WriteLine("How old are you?")
If (gender = "F" And Console.ReadLine() >= 65) Then
   Console.WriteLine("You are a female senior citizen.")
End If
```

Here, the **And** operator guarantees that the condition **Console.ReadLine() >= 65** is evaluated, so **ReadLine** is called regardless of whether the overall expression is true or false. It would be better to write this code as two separate statements—the first would store the result of **Console.ReadLine()** in a variable, then the second would use that variable with the **AndAlso** operator in the condition.

Testing and Debugging Tip 5.9

Avoid expressions with side effects in conditions; these side effects often cause subtle errors.

A condition containing the *logical exclusive OR* (**Xor**) operator is true *if and only if one of its operands results in a true value and the other results in a false value*. If both operands are true or both are false, the entire condition is false. Figure 5.19 presents a truth table for the logical exclusive OR operator (**Xor**). This operator always evaluates both of its operands (i.e., there is no short-circuit evaluation).

Visual Basic's **Not** (logical negation) operator enables a programmer to "reverse" the meaning of a condition. Unlike the logical operators **AndAlso**, **And**, **OrElse**, **Or** and **Xor**, that each combine two conditions (i.e., these are all binary operators), the logical negation operator is a unary operator, requiring only one operand. The logical negation operator is placed before a condition to choose a path of execution if the original condition (without the logical negation operator) is false. The logical negation operator is demonstrated by the following program segment:

```
If Not (grade = sentinelValue) Then
   Console.WriteLine("The next grade is " & grade)
End If
```

The parentheses around the condition **grade = sentinelValue** are necessary, because the logical negation operator (**Not**) has a higher precedence than the equality operator. Figure 5.20 provides a truth table for the logical negation operator.

In most cases, the programmer can avoid using logical negation by expressing the condition differently with relational or equality operators. For example, the preceding statement can be written as follows:

```
If grade <> sentinelValue Then
   Console.WriteLine("The next grade is " & grade)
End If
```

This flexibility aids programmers in expressing conditions more naturally.

expression1	expression2	expression1 Xor expression2
False	False	False
False	True	True
True	False	True
True	True	False

Fig. 5.19 Truth table for the logical exclusive OR (**Xor**) operator.

expression	Not expression
False	True
True	False

Fig. 5.20 Truth table for operator **Not** (logical NOT).

The Windows application in Fig. 5.21 demonstrates the use of the logical operators by displaying their truth tables in six labels.

```vb
1   ' Fig. 5.21: LogicalOperator.vb
2   ' Using logical operators.
3
4   Public Class FrmLogicalOperator
5      Inherits System.Windows.Forms.Form
6
7      ' Visual Studio .NET generated code
8
9      Private Sub FrmLogicalOperator_Load( _
10        ByVal sender As System.Object, _
11        ByVal e As System.EventArgs) Handles MyBase.Load
12
13        lblAndAlso.Text = "AndAlso" & vbCrLf & vbCrLf & _
14           "False AndAlso False: " & (False AndAlso False) & _
15           vbCrLf & "False AndAlso True: " & _
16           (False AndAlso True) & vbCrLf & _
17           "True AndAlso False: " & (True AndAlso False) & _
18           vbCrLf & "True AndAlso True: " & (True AndAlso True)
19
20        lblOrElse.Text = "OrElse" & vbCrLf & vbCrLf & _
21           "False OrElse False: " & (False OrElse False) & _
22           vbCrLf & "False OrElse True: " & (False OrElse True) & _
23           vbCrLf & "True OrElse False: " & (True OrElse False) & _
24           vbCrLf & "True OrElse True: " & (True OrElse True)
25
26        lblAnd.Text = "And" & vbCrLf & vbCrLf & _
27           "False And False: " & (False And False) & vbCrLf & _
28           "False And True: " & (False And True) & vbCrLf & _
29           "True And False: " & (True And False) & vbCrLf & _
30           "True And True: " & (True And True)
31
32        lblOr.Text = "Or" & vbCrLf & _
33           vbCrLf & "False Or False: " & (False Or False) & _
34           vbCrLf & "False Or True: " & (False Or True) & _
35           vbCrLf & "True Or False: " & (True Or False) & _
36           vbCrLf & "True Or True: " & (True Or True)
37
38        lblXor.Text = "Xor" & vbCrLf & _
39           vbCrLf & "False Xor False: " & (False Xor False) & _
40           vbCrLf & "False Xor True: " & (False Xor True) & _
41           vbCrLf & "True Xor False: " & (True Xor False) & _
42           vbCrLf & "True Xor True: " & (True Xor True)
43
44        lblNot.Text = "Not" & vbCrLf & vbCrLf & _
45           "Not False: " & (Not False) & vbCrLf & "Not True: " & _
46           (Not True)
47
48     End Sub ' FrmLogicalOperator_Load
49
50   End Class ' FrmLogicalOperator
```

Fig. 5.21 Logical operator truth tables (part 1 of 2).

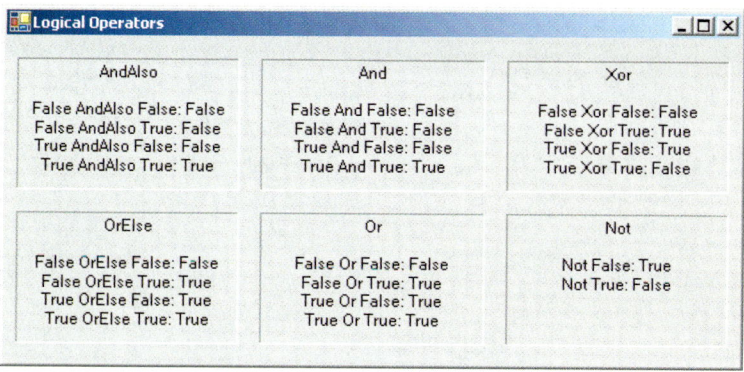

Fig. 5.21 Logical operator truth tables (part 2 of 2).

Line 4 begins class **FrmLogicalOperator**. Recall from our discussion in Chapter 4 that Visual Studio creates the initial code for a Windows application. Programmers then enhance this code to create their own applications. Because the code created by Visual Studio uses many concepts that have not been presented yet, we replace the Visual Studio generated code with the comment in line 7. In Chapter 12, we carefully explain the Visual Studio generated code line-by-line. Line 9 begins the definition of procedure **FrmLogicalOperator_Load**. An empty procedure definition for a Windows application can be obtained by double-clicking the form in the **Design** view. Procedures created this way are executed when the program loads. In this case, the procedure creates **String**s representing the truth tables of the logical operators and displays them on six labels using the **Text** property. Lines 13–18 demonstrate operator **AndAlso**; lines 20–24 demonstrate operator **OrElse**. The remainder of procedure **FrmLogicalOperator_Load** demonstrates the **And**, **Or**, **Xor** and **Not** operators. We use keywords *True* and *False* in the program to specify values of the **Boolean** data type. Notice that when a **Boolean** value is concatenated to a **String**, Visual Basic concatenates the string **"False"** or **"True"** on the basis of the **Boolean**'s value.

The chart in Fig. 5.22 displays the precedence of the Visual Basic operators introduced so far. The operators are shown from top to bottom in decreasing order of precedence.

Operators	Type
( )	parentheses
^	exponentiation
+ -	unary plus and minus
* /	multiplicative
\	integer division
Mod	modulus

Fig. 5.22 Precedence of the operators discussed so far (part 1 of 2).

Operators	Type
`+ -`	additive
`&`	concatenation
`< <= > >= = <>`	relational and equality
`Not`	logical NOT
`And AndAlso`	logical AND
`Or OrElse`	logical inclusive OR
`Xor`	logical exclusive OR

Fig. 5.22 Precedence and associativity of the operators discussed so far (part 2 of 2).

5.10 Structured Programming Summary

Just as architects design buildings by employing the collective wisdom of their profession, so should programmers design programs. Our field is younger than architecture is, and our collective wisdom is considerably sparser. We have learned that structured programming produces programs that are easier to understand, test, debug, modify and prove correct in a mathematical sense than unstructured programs. Visual Basic's control structures are summarized in Fig. 5.23 and Fig. 5.24.

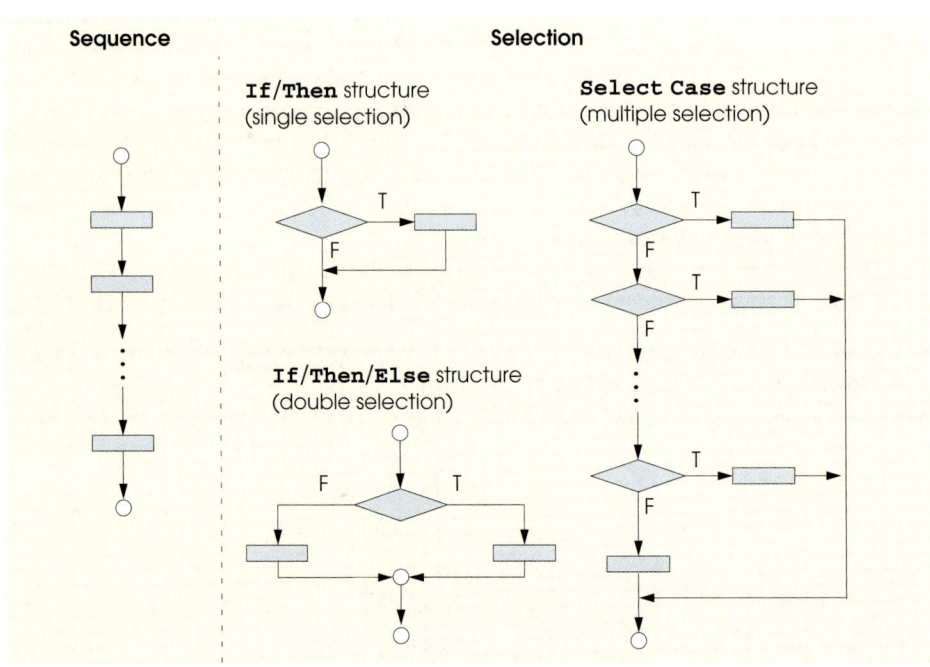

Fig. 5.23 Visual Basic's single-entry/single-exit sequence and selection structures.

Small circles in the figures indicate the single entry point and the single exit point of each structure. Connecting individual flowchart symbols arbitrarily can lead to unstructured programs. Therefore, the programming profession has chosen to employ only a limited set of control structures and to build structured programs by combining control structures in only two simple ways.

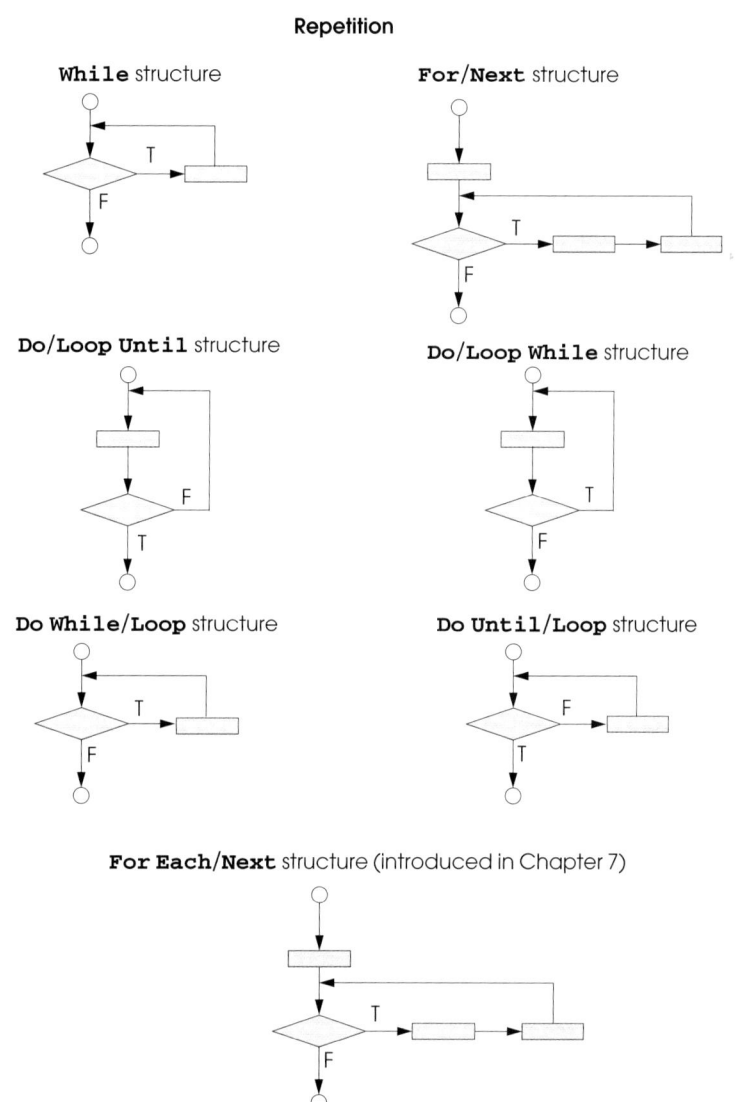

Fig. 5.24 Visual Basic's single-entry/single-exit repetition structures.

For the sake of simplicity, only single-entry/single-exit control structures are used—there is only one way to enter and only one way to exit each control structure. To connect control structures in sequence to form structured programs, the exit point of one control structure is connected to the entry point of the next control structure (i.e., the control structures simply are placed one after another in a program). We call this process *control structure stacking*. The rules for the formation of structured programs also allow control structures to be nested, i.e., placed one inside the other. Figure 5.25 contains the rules for the formation of properly structured programs. The rules assume that the rectangle flowchart symbol can indicate any action, including input/output.

Applying the rules of Fig. 5.25 always results in a structured flowchart with a neat, building-block appearance. For example, repeatedly applying rule 2 to the simplest flowchart (Fig. 5.26) results in a structured flowchart that contains many rectangles in sequence (Fig. 5.27). Notice that rule 2 generates a stack of control structures; therefore, we call rule 2 the *stacking rule*.

Rule 3 is the *nesting rule*. Repeatedly applying rule 3 to the simplest flowchart results in a flowchart with neatly nested control structures. For example, in Fig. 5.28, the rectangle in the simplest flowchart (in the top-left portion of the figure) is first replaced with a double-selection (**If/Then/Else**) structure. Then, rule 3 is applied again to both rectangles in the double-selection structure, replacing each of these rectangles with a double-selection structure. The dashed boxes around each of the double-selection structures represent the rectangles that were replaced with these structures.

Good Programming Practice 5.4

Excessive levels of nesting can make a program difficult to understand. As a general rule, try to avoid using more than three levels of nesting.

Rule 4 generates larger, more involved and deeply-nested structures. The flowcharts that emerge from applying the rules in Fig. 5.25 constitute the set of all possible structured flowcharts and the set of all possible structured programs. The structured approach has the advantage of using only eleven simple single-entry/single-exit pieces and allowing us to combine them in only two simple ways. Figure 5.29 depicts the kinds of correctly stacked building blocks that emerge from applying rule 2 and the kinds of correctly nested building blocks that emerge from applying rule 3. The figure also shows the kind of overlapped building blocks that cannot appear in structured flowcharts.

Rules for Forming Structured Programs

1) Begin with the "simplest flowchart" (Fig. 5.26).

2) Any rectangle (action) can be replaced by two rectangles (actions) in sequence.

3) Any rectangle (action) can be replaced by any control structure (sequence, **If/Then**, **If/Then/Else**, **Select Case**, **While**, **Do/Loop While**, **Do While/Loop**, **Do Until/Loop**, **Do/Loop Until**, **For/Next** or the **For Each/Next** structure introduced in Chapter 7, Arrays).

4) Rules 2 and 3 may be applied as often as you like and in any order.

Fig. 5.25 Structured programming rules.

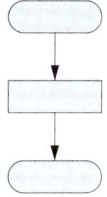

Fig. 5.26 Simplest flowchart.

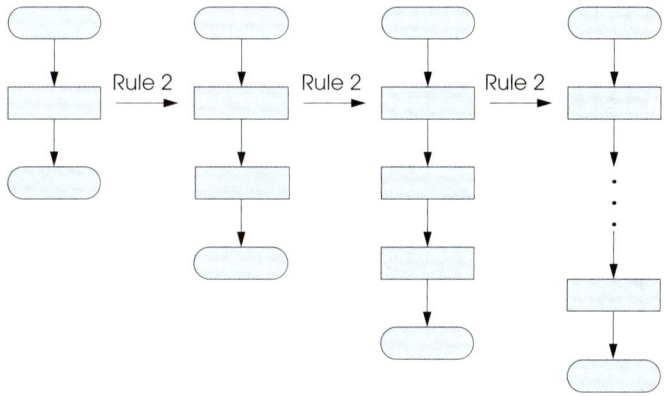

Fig. 5.27 Repeatedly applying rule 2 of Fig. 5.25 to the simplest flowchart.

If the rules in Fig. 5.25 are followed, an unstructured flowchart (such as that in Fig. 5.30) cannot be created. If you are uncertain about whether a particular flowchart is structured, apply the rules in Fig. 5.25 in reverse to try to reduce the flowchart to the simplest flowchart. If the flowchart can be reduced to the simplest flowchart, the original flowchart is structured; otherwise, it is not.

Structured programming promotes simplicity. Bohm and Jacopini have demonstrated that only three forms of control are necessary:

- sequence
- selection
- repetition

Sequence is trivial. Selection is implemented in one of three ways:

- **If/Then** structure (single selection)
- **If/Then/Else** structure (double selection)
- **Select Case** structure (multiple selection)

It can be proven straightforwardly that the **If/Then** structure is sufficient to provide any form of selection. Everything done with the **If/Then/Else** structure and the **Select Case** structure can be implemented by combining multiple **If/Then** structures (although perhaps not as elegantly).

Repetition is implemented in one of seven ways:
- **While** structure
- **Do While/Loop** structure
- **Do/Loop While** structure
- **Do Until/Loop** structure
- **Do/Loop Until** structure
- **For/Next** structure
- **For Each/Next** structure (introduced in Chapter 7)

It can be proven straightforwardly that the **While** structure is sufficient to provide any form of repetition. Everything that can be done with the **Do While/Loop**, **Do/Loop While**, **Do Until/Loop**, **Do/Loop Until**, **For/Next** and **For Each/Next** structures can be done with the **While** structure (although perhaps not as elegantly).

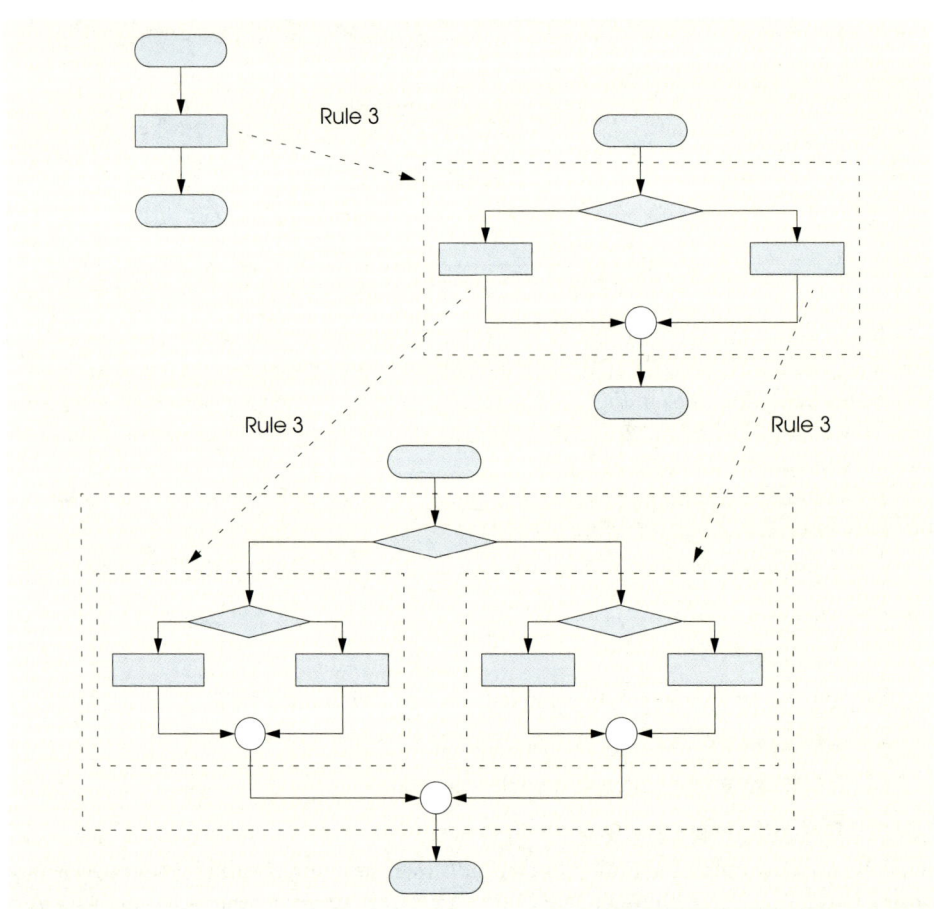

Fig. 5.28 Applying rule 3 of Fig. 5.25 to the simplest flowchart.

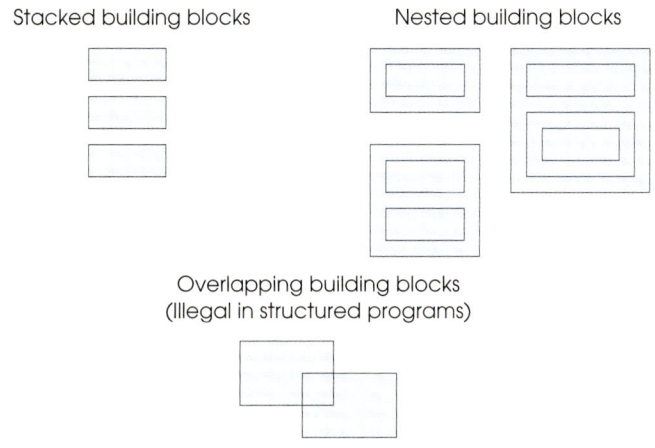

Fig. 5.29 Stacked, nested and overlapped building blocks.

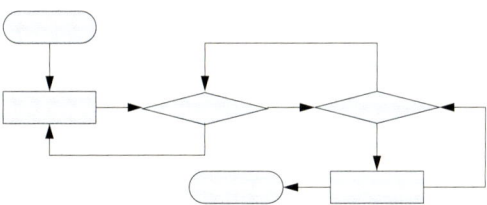

Fig. 5.30 Unstructured flowchart.

The combination of these results illustrates that any form of control ever needed in a Visual Basic program can be expressed in terms of:

- sequence
- **If/Then** structure (selection)
- **While** structure (repetition)

These control structures can be combined in only two ways—stacking and nesting. Indeed, structured programming promotes simplicity.

In this chapter, we discussed the composition of programs from control structures that contain actions and decisions. In Chapter 6, Procedures, we introduce another program structuring unit called the *procedure*. We show how to construct large programs by combining procedures that are composed of control structures. We also discuss the ways in which procedures promote software reusability. In Chapter 8, Object-Based Programming, we offer a detailed introduction to another Visual Basic program structuring unit, called the *class*. We then create objects from classes (that are composed of procedures) and proceed with our treatment of object-oriented programming—the key focus of this book.

SUMMARY

- Counter-controlled repetition requires the name of a control variable (or loop counter), the initial value of the control variable, the increment (or decrement) by which the control variable is modified during each iteration of the loop and the condition that tests for the final value of the control variable (i.e., whether looping should continue).
- Declarations that include initialization are executable statements.
- The **For/Next** repetition structure handles the details of counter-controlled repetition. The required **To** keyword specifies the initial value and the final value of the control variable. The optional **Step** keyword specifies the increment.
- Counting loops should not be controlled with floating-point variables. Floating-point values are represented only approximately in the computer's memory, often resulting in imprecise counter values and inaccurate tests for termination.
- When supplying four arguments to method **MessageBox.Show**, the first two arguments are strings displayed in the dialog and the dialog's title bar. The third and fourth arguments are constants representing buttons and icons, respectively.
- Method **String.Format** inserts values into a **String** using Visual Basic's format codes.
- Visual Basic provides the **Decimal** data type, which is designed specifically for monetary calculations. It is inappropriate to use **Single** or **Double** for dollar amounts.
- Visual Basic provides the **Select Case** multiple-selection structure to test a variable or expression separately for each value that the variable or expression might assume. The **Select Case** structure consists of a series of **Case** labels and an optional **Case Else**. Each **Case** contains statements to be executed if that **Case** is selected.
- Each **Case** in a **Select Case** structure can test for a specific value, a range of values (using keyword **To**) or a condition (using keyword **Is** and a relational operator). The comma can be used to specify a list of values, ranges and conditions that satisfy a **Case** statement.
- The **Do/Loop While** and **Do/Loop Until** structures test the loop-continuation condition after the loop body is performed; therefore, the loop body is always executed at least once.
- The **Exit Do**, **Exit While** and **Exit For** statements alter the flow of control by causing immediate exit from a repetition structure.
- The logical operators are **AndAlso** (logical AND with short-circuit evaluation), **And** (logical AND without short-circuit evaluation), **OrElse** (logical inclusive OR with short-circuit evaluation), **Or** (logical inclusive OR without short-circuit evaluation), **Xor** (logical exclusive OR) and **Not** (logical NOT, also called logical negation).
- The **AndAlso** operator can be used to ensure that two conditions are both true.
- The **OrElse** operator can be used to ensure that at least one of two conditions is true.
- The **And** and **Or** operators are similar to the **AndAlso** and **OrElse** operators, except that they always evaluate both of their operands.
- A condition containing the logical exclusive OR (**Xor**) operator is true if and only if exactly one of its operands is true.
- A condition that begins with the logical NOT (**Not**) operator is true if and only if the condition to the right of the logical NOT operator is false.
- In flowcharts, small circles indicate the single entry point and exit point of each structure.
- Connecting individual flowchart symbols arbitrarily can lead to unstructured programs. Therefore, the programming profession has chosen to employ only a limited set of control structures and to build structured programs by combining control structures in only two simple ways.

- To connect control structures in sequence to form structured programs, the exit point of one control structure is connected to the entry point of the next control structure (i.e., the control structures simply are placed one after another in a program). We call this process "control structure stacking."
- The rules for forming structured programs also allow control structures to be nested.
- Structured programming promotes simplicity.
- Bohm and Jacopini have demonstrated that only three forms of control are necessary—sequence, selection and repetition.
- Selection is implemented with one of three structures—**If/Then**, **If/Then/Else** and **Select Case**.
- Repetition is implemented with one of seven structures—**While**, **Do While/Loop**, **Do/Loop While**, **Do Until/Loop**, **Do/Loop Until**, **For/Next**, and **For Each/Next** (introduced in Chapter 7, Arrays).
- The **If/Then** structure is sufficient to provide any form of selection.
- The **While** structure is sufficient to provide any form of repetition.
- Control structures can be combined in only two ways—stacking and nesting.

TERMINOLOGY

AbortRetryIgnore constant
body of a loop
Boolean values
buttons for a message dialog
Case keyword
Case Else statement
control structure
control-structure nesting
control-structure stacking
controlling expression
counter-controlled repetition
Decimal data type
decrement of loop
diamond symbol
Do/Loop Until structure
Do/Loop While structure
double-selection structure
End Select statement
entry point of a control structure
Exit Do statement
Exit For statement
Exit While statement
For Each/Next structure
For/Next header
For/Next structure
hexadecimal (base 16) number system
icon for a message dialog
If/Then structure
If/Then/Else structure
increment of control variable
Is keyword

iteration of a loop
levels of nesting
logical AND with short-circuit evaluation (**AndAlso**)
logical AND without short-circuit valuation (**And**)
logical exclusive OR (**Xor**)
logical inclusive OR with short-circuit evaluation (**OrElse**)
logical inclusive OR without short-circuit evaluation (**Or**)
logical NOT (**Not**)
logical operator
loop body
loop counter
loop-continuation condition
message dialog button
message dialog icon
MessageBoxButtons. AbortRetryIgnore constant
MessageBoxButtons.OK constant
MessageBoxButtons.OKCancel constant
MessageBoxButtons.RetryCancel constant
MessageBoxButtons.YesNo constant
MessageBoxButtons.YesNoCancel constant
MessageBoxButtons class
MessageBoxIcon class
MessageBoxIcon.Error constant
MessageBoxIcon.Exclamation constant

`MessageBoxIcon.Information` constant
`MessageBoxIcon.Question` constant
multiple-selection structure
nested building block
nested control structure
nesting
nesting rule
`Next` keyword
overlapped building block
program construction principle
rectangle symbol
repetition
`Select Case` structure
selection
sequence
short-circuit evaluation
`Show` method of class `MessageBox`
simplest flowchart
single selection
single-entry/single-exit sequence, selection and repetition structures
stacking rule
`Step` keyword in a `For/Next` structure
`String` formatting code
structured programming
`To` keyword in a `For/Next` structure
unary operator
unstructured flowchart

SELF-REVIEW EXERCISES

5.1 State whether each of the following is *true* or *false*. If *false*, explain why.
  a) The `Case Else` is required in the `Select Case` selection structure.
  b) The expression `x > y AndAlso a < b` is true if either `x > y` is true or `a < b` is true.
  c) An expression containing the `OrElse` operator is true if either or both of its operands is true.
  d) The expression `x <= y And y > 4` is true if `x` is less than or equal to `y` and `y` is greater than `4`.
  e) Logical operator `Or` performs short-circuit evaluation.
  f) A `While` structure with the header

   `While (x > 10 AndAlso x < 100)`

   iterates while $10 < x < 100$.
  g) The `Exit Do`, `Exit For` and `Exit While` statements, when executed in a repetition structure, cause immediate exit from the repetition structure.
  h) History has shown that good software engineering always allows programmers to achieve the highest levels of performance.
  i) The `OrElse` operator has a higher precedence than the `AndAlso` operator.

5.2 Fill in the blanks in each of the following statements:
  a) Keyword _____ is optional in a `For/Next` header when the control variable's increment is one.
  b) Monetary values should be stored in variables of type _____.
  c) A `Case` that handles all values larger than a specified value must precede the `>` operator with the _____ keyword.
  d) In a `For/Next` structure, incrementing occurs _____ the body of the structure is performed.
  e) Placing expressions whose values do not change inside _____ structures can lead to poor performance.
  f) The four types of `MessageBox` icons are exclamation, information, error and _____.
  g) The expression following the keywords `Select Case` is called the _____.

5.3 Write a Visual Basic statement or a set of Visual Basic statements to accomplish each of the following:

a) Sum the odd integers between **1** and **99** using a **For/Next** structure. Assume that the integer variables **sum** and **count** have been declared.
b) Write a statement that exits a **While** loop.
c) Print the integers from **1** to **20**, using a **Do/Loop While** loop and the counter variable **x**. Assume that the variable **x** has been declared, but not initialized. Print only five integers per line. [*Hint*: Use the calculation **x Mod 5**. When the value of this is **0**, print a newline character; otherwise, print a tab character. Call **Console.WriteLine** to output the newline character and call **Console.Write(vbTab)** to output the tab character.]
d) Repeat part c, using a **For/Next** structure.

ANSWERS TO SELF-REVIEW EXERCISES

5.1 a) False. The **Case Else** is optional. b) False. Both of the relational expressions must be true for the entire expression to be true. c) True. d) True. **4**. e) False. Logical operator **Or** always evaluates both of its operands. f) True. g) True. h) False. There is often a trade-off between good software engineering and high performance. i) False. The **AndAlso** operator has higher precedence than the **OrElse** operator.

5.2 a) **Step**. b) **Decimal**. c) **Is**. d) after. e) repetition. f) question mark. g) controlling expression.

5.3 a)
```
sum = 0

For count = 1 To 99 Step 2
    sum += count
Next
```
b) `Exit While`
c)
```
x = 1

Do
    Console.Write(x)

    If x Mod 5 = 0 Then
        Console.WriteLine()
    Else
        Console.Write(vbTab)
    End If

    x += 1
Loop While x <= 20
```

or

```
x = 1

Do
    If x Mod 5 = 0 Then
        Console.WriteLine(x)
    Else
        Console.Write(x & vbTab)
    End If
```

```
        x += 1
    Loop While x <= 20
d)  For x = 1 To 20
        Console.Write(x)

        If x Mod 5 = 0 Then
            Console.WriteLine()
        Else
            Console.Write(vbTab)
        End If

    Next

    or

    For x = 1 To 20

        If x Mod 5 = 0 Then
            Console.WriteLine(x)
        Else
            Console.Write(x & vbTab)
        End If

    Next
```

EXERCISES

5.4 The *factorial* method is used frequently in probability problems. The factorial of a positive integer *n* (written *n!* and pronounced "n factorial") is equal to the product of the positive integers from 1 to *n*. Even for relatively small values of *n*, the factorial method yields extremely large numbers. For instance, when *n* is 13, *n!* is 6227020800—a number too large to be represented with data type **Integer** (a 32-bit integer value). To calculate the factorials of large values of *n*, data type **Long** (a 64-bit integer value) must be used. Write a program that evaluates the factorials of the integers from 1 to 20 using data type **Long**. Display the results in a two column output table. [*Hint*: create a Windows application, use **Label**s as the columns and the **vbCrLf** constant to line up the rows.] The first column should display the *n* values (1–20). The second column should display *n!*.

5.5 Write two programs that each print a table of the binary, octal, and hexadecimal equivalents of the decimal numbers in the range 1–256. If you are not familiar with these number systems, read Appendix B, Number Systems, first.
    a) For the first program, print the results to the console without using any **String** formats.
    b) For the second program, print the results to the console using both the decimal and hexadecimal **String** formats (there are no formats for binary and octal in Visual Basic).

5.6 (*Pythagorean Triples*) Some right triangles have sides that are all integers. A set of three integer values for the sides of a right triangle is called a Pythagorean triple. These three sides must satisfy the relationship that the sum of the squares of the two sides is equal to the square of the hypotenuse. Write a program to find all Pythagorean triples for **side1**, **side2** and **hypotenuse**, none larger than 30. Use a triple-nested **For/Next** loop that tries all possibilities. This is an example of "brute force" computing. You will learn in more advanced computer science courses that there are some problems for which there is no known algorithmic approach other than using sheer brute force.

5.7 Write a program that displays the following patterns separately, one below the other. Use **For/Next** loops to generate the patterns. All asterisks (*****) should be printed by a single statement of the form **Console.Write("*")** (this causes the asterisks to print side by side). A statement of the form **Console.WriteLine()** can be used to position to the next line and a statement of the form **Console.WriteLine(" ")** can be used to display spaces for the last two patterns. There should be no other output statements in the program. [*Hint*: The last two patterns require that each line begin with an appropriate number of blanks.] Maximize your use of repetition (with nested **For/Next** structures) and minimize the number of output statements.

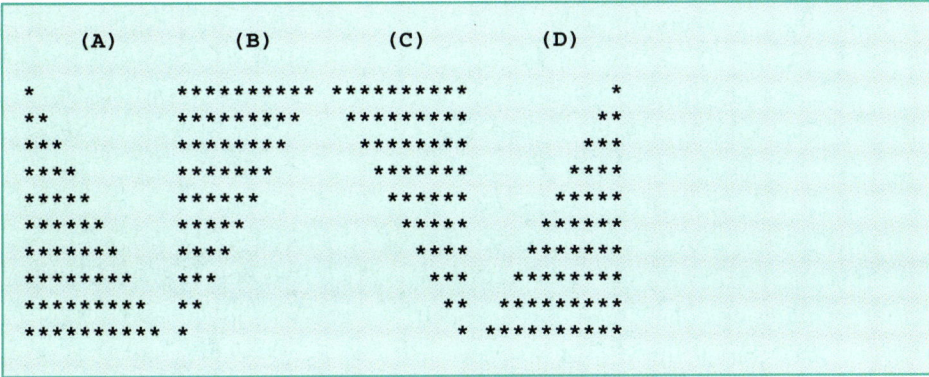

5.8 Modify Exercise 5.7 to combine your code from the four separate triangles of asterisks into a single program that prints all four patterns side by side, making clever use of nested **For/Next** loops.

5.9 Write a program that prints the following diamond shape. You may use output statements that print a single asterisk (*****), a single space or a single newline character. Maximize your use of repetition (with nested **For/Next** structures) and minimize the number of output statements.

5.10 Modify the program you wrote in Exercise 5.9 to read an odd number in the range from 1 to 19 to specify the number of rows in the diamond. Your program should then display a diamond of the appropriate size. Use a **Do/Loop Until** to validate user input.

6

Procedures

Objectives

- To construct programs modularly from pieces called procedures.
- To introduce the common **Math** methods available in the Framework Class Library.
- To create new procedures.
- To understand the mechanisms used to pass information between procedures.
- To introduce simulation techniques that employ random-number generation.
- To understand how the visibility of identifiers is limited to specific regions of programs.
- To understand how to write and use recursive procedures (procedures that call themselves).

Form ever follows function.
Louis Henri Sullivan

E pluribus unum.
(One composed of many.)
Virgil

O! call back yesterday, bid time return.
William Shakespeare, *Richard II*

Call me Ishmael.
Herman Melville, *Moby Dick*

When you call me that, smile.
Owen Wister

Outline

6.1	Introduction
6.2	Modules, Classes and Procedures
6.3	Sub Procedures
6.4	`Function` Procedures
6.5	Methods
6.6	Argument Promotion
6.7	Option Strict and Data-Type Conversions
6.8	Value Types and Reference Types
6.9	Passing Arguments: Pass-by-Value vs. Pass-by-Reference
6.10	Duration of Identifiers
6.11	Scope Rules
6.12	Random-Number Generation
6.13	Example: Game of Chance
6.14	Recursion
6.15	Example Using Recursion: Fibonacci Series
6.16	Recursion vs. Iteration
6.17	Procedure Overloading and Optional Arguments
	6.17.1 Procedure Overloading
	6.17.2 Optional Arguments
6.18	Modules

Summary • Terminology • Self-Review Exercises • Answers to Self-Review Exercises • Exercises

6.1 Introduction

Most computer programs that solve real-world problems are much larger than the programs presented in the first few chapters of this text. Experience has shown that the best way to develop and maintain a large program is to construct it from small, manageable pieces. This technique is known as *divide and conquer*. In this chapter, we describe many key features of the Visual Basic language that facilitate the design, implementation, operation and maintenance of large programs.

6.2 Modules, Classes and Procedures

Visual Basic programs consist of many pieces, including modules and classes. The programmer combines new modules and classes with "prepackaged" classes available in the .*NET Framework Class Library (FCL)*. These modules and classes are composed of smaller pieces called *procedures*. When procedures are contained in a class, we refer to them as *methods*.

The FCL provides a rich collection of classes and methods for performing common mathematical calculations, string manipulations, character manipulations, input/output operations, error checking and many other useful operations. This framework makes the programmer's job easier, because the methods provide many of the capabilities programmers need. In earlier chapters, we introduced some FCL classes, such as **Console**, which provides methods for inputting and outputting data.

Software Engineering Observation 6.1
Familiarize yourself with the rich collection of classes and methods in the Framework Class Library.

Software Engineering Observation 6.2
When possible, use .NET Framework classes and methods instead of writing new classes and methods. This reduces program development time and avoids introducing new errors.

Performance Tip 6.1
.NET Framework Class Library methods are written to perform efficiently.

Although the FCL provides methods that perform many common tasks, it cannot provide every conceivable feature that a programmer could want, so Visual Basic allows programmers to create their own *programmer-defined procedures* to meet the unique requirements of a particular problem. Three types of procedures exist: **Sub** *procedures*, **Function** *procedures* and *event procedures*. Throughout this chapter, the term "procedure" refers to both **Sub** procedures and **Function** procedures unless otherwise noted.

Programmers write procedures to define specific tasks that a program may use many times during its execution. Although the same programmer-defined procedure can be executed at multiple points in a program, the actual statements that define the procedure are written only once.

A procedure is *invoked* (i.e., made to perform its designated task) by a *procedure call*. The procedure call specifies the procedure name and provides information (as *arguments*) that the *callee* (i.e, the procedure being called) requires to do its job. When the procedure completes its task, it returns control to the *caller* (i.e., the *calling procedure*). In some cases, the procedure also returns a result to the caller. A common analogy for this is the hierarchical form of management. A boss (the caller) asks a worker (the callee) to perform a task and *return* (i.e., report on) the results when the task is done. The boss does not need to know how the worker performs the designated task. For example, the worker might call other workers—the boss would be unaware of this. Soon, we show how this *hiding of implementation details* promotes good software engineering. Figure 6.1 depicts a **Boss** procedure communicating with worker procedures **Worker1**, **Worker2** and **Worker3** in a hierarchical manner. Note that **Worker1** acts as a "boss" procedure to **Worker4** and **Worker5** in this particular example.

There are several motivations for the division of code into procedures. First, the divide-and-conquer approach makes program development more manageable. Another motivation is software reusability—the ability to use existing procedures as building blocks for new programs. When proper naming and definition conventions are applied, programs can be created from standardized pieces that accomplish specific tasks, to minimize the need for customized code. A third motivation involves avoiding the repetition of code in a program. When code is packaged as a procedure, the code can be executed from several locations in a program simply by calling, or invoking, the procedure.

Chapter 6   Procedures

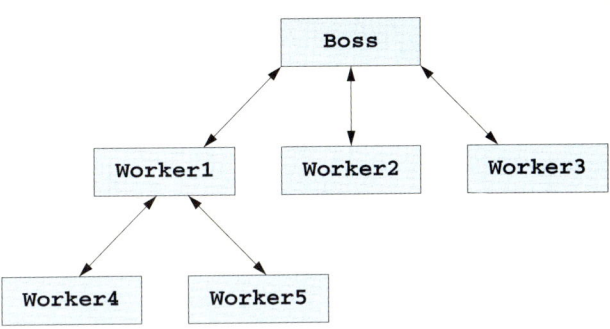

Fig. 6.1   Hierarchical boss-procedure/worker-procedure relationship.

Good Programming Practice 6.1
Use modularity to increase the clarity and organization of a program. This not only helps others understand the program, but also aids in program development, testing and debugging.

Software Engineering Observation 6.3
To promote reusability, the capabilities of each procedure should be limited to the performance of a single, well-defined task, and the name of the procedure should express that task effectively.

Software Engineering Observation 6.4
If you cannot choose a concise name that expresses the task performed by a procedure, the procedure could be attempting to perform too many diverse tasks. It is usually best to divide such a procedure into several smaller procedures.

6.3 Sub Procedures

The programs presented earlier in the book each contained at least one procedure definition (e.g., **Main**) that called FCL methods (such as **Console.WriteLine**) to accomplish the program's tasks. We now consider how to write customized procedures.

Consider the console application in Fig. 6.2, which uses a **Sub** procedure (invoked from the application's **Main** procedure) to print a worker's payment information.

```
1   ' Fig. 6.2: Payment.vb
2   ' Sub procedure that prints payment information.
3
4   Module modPayment
5
6      Sub Main()
7
8         ' call Sub procedure PrintPay 4 times
9         PrintPay(40, 10.5)
10        PrintPay(38, 21.75)
```

Fig. 6.2   **Sub** procedure for printing payment information (part 1 of 2).

```
11              PrintPay(20, 13)
12              PrintPay(50, 14)
13
14          End Sub ' Main
15
16          ' print dollar amount earned in command window
17          Sub PrintPay(ByVal hours As Double, ByVal wage As Decimal)
18
19              ' pay = hours * wage
20              Console.WriteLine("The payment is {0:C}", hours * wage)
21          End Sub ' PrintPay
22
23      End Module ' modPayment
```

```
The payment is $420.00
The payment is $826.50
The payment is $260.00
The payment is $700.00
```

Fig. 6.2 Sub procedure for printing payment information (part 2 of 2).

The program contains two *procedure definitions*. Lines 6–14 define **Sub** procedure **Main**, which executes when the console application is loaded. Lines 17–21 define **Sub** procedure **PrintPay**, which executes when it is *invoked*, or *called*, from another procedure, in this case **Main**.

Main makes four calls (lines 9–12) to **Sub** procedure **PrintPay**, causing **PrintPay** to execute four times. Although the procedure arguments in this example are constants, arguments can also be variables or expressions. For example, the statement

```
PrintPay(employeeOneExtraHours, employeeOneWage * 1.5)
```

could be used to display payment information for an employee who is being paid time-and-a-half for working overtime.

When **Main** calls **PrintPay**, the program makes a copy of the value of each argument (e.g., **40** and **10.5** on line 9), and program control transfers to the first line of procedure **PrintPay**. Procedure **PrintPay** receives the copied values and stores them in the *parameter variables* **hours** and **wage**. Then, **PrintPay** calculates **hours * wage** and displays the result, using the currency format (line 20). When the **End Sub** statement on line 21 is encountered, control is returned to the calling procedure, **Main**.

The first line of procedure **PrintPay** (line 17) shows (inside the parentheses) that **PrintPay** declares a **Double** variable **hours** and a **Decimal** variable **wage**. These parameters hold the values passed to **PrintPay** within the definition of this procedure. Notice that the entire procedure definition of **PrintPay** appears within the body of module **modPayment**. All procedures must be defined inside a module or a class.

The format of a procedure definition is

```
Sub procedure-name(parameter-list)
    declarations and statements
End Sub
```

Good Programming Practice 6.2

Place a blank line between procedure definitions to separate the procedures and enhance program readability.

Common Programming Error 6.1

Defining a procedure outside of a class or module definition is a syntax error.

The first line is sometimes known as the *procedure header*. The *procedure-name*, which directly follows the **Sub** keyword in the procedure header, can be any valid identifier and is used to call this **Sub** procedure within the program.

The *parameter-list* is a comma-separated list in which the **Sub** procedure declares each parameter variable's type and name. There must be one argument in the procedure call for each parameter in the procedure header (we will see an exception to this rule in Section 6.17). The arguments also must be compatible with the parameter's type (i.e., Visual Basic must be able to assign the value of the argument to the parameter). For example, a parameter of type **Double** could receive the value of 7.35, 22 or −.03546, but not **"hello"**, because a **Double** value cannot contain a **String**. In Section 6.6 we discuss this issue in detail. If a procedure does not receive any values, the parameter list is empty (i.e., the procedure name is followed by an empty set of parentheses).

Notice that the parameter declarations in the procedure header for **PrintPay** (line 17) look similar to variable declarations, but use keyword **ByVal** instead of **Dim**. **ByVal** specifies that the calling program should pass a copy of the value of the argument in the procedure call to the parameter, which can be used in the **Sub** procedure body. Section 6.9 discusses argument passing in detail.

Common Programming Error 6.2

Declaring a variable in the procedure's body with the same name as a parameter variable in the procedure header is a syntax error.

Testing and Debugging Tip 6.1

Although it is allowable, an argument passed to a procedure should not have the same name as the corresponding parameter in the procedure definition. This distinction prevents ambiguity that could lead to logic errors.

The declarations and statements in the procedure definition form the *procedure body*. The procedure body contains Visual Basic code that performs actions, generally by manipulating or interacting with the parameters. The procedure body must be terminated with keywords **End Sub**, which define the end of the procedure. The procedure body is also referred to as a *block*. A block is a sequence of statements and declarations grouped together as the body of some structure and terminated with an **End**, **Next**, **Else** or **Loop** statement, depending on the type of structure. Variables can be declared in any block, and blocks can be nested.

Common Programming Error 6.3

Defining a procedure inside another procedure is a syntax error—procedures cannot be nested.

Control returns to the caller when execution reaches the **End Sub** statement (i.e., the end of the procedure body). Alternatively, keywords **Return** and **Exit Sub** can be used anywhere in a procedure to return control to the point at which a **Sub** procedure was invoked. We discuss **Return** and **Exit Sub** in detail, momentarily.

Good Programming Practice 6.3
The selection of meaningful procedure names and parameter names makes programs more readable and reduces the need for excessive comments.

Software Engineering Observation 6.5
*Procedure names tend to be verbs because procedures typically perform operations on data. By convention, programmer-defined procedure names begin with an uppercase first letter. For example, a procedure that sends an e-mail message might be named **SendMail**.*

Software Engineering Observation 6.6
A procedure that requires a large number of parameters might be performing too many tasks. Consider dividing the procedure into smaller procedures that perform separate tasks. As a "rule of thumb," the procedure header should fit on one line (if possible).

Software Engineering Observation 6.7
As a "rule of thumb," a procedure should be limited to one printed page. Better yet, a procedure should be no longer than half a printed page. Regardless of how long a procedure is, it should perform one task well.

Testing and Debugging Tip 6.2
Small procedures are easier to test, debug and understand than large procedures.

Performance Tip 6.2
When a programmer divides a procedure into several procedures that communicate with one another, this communication takes time and sometimes leads to poor execution performance.

Software Engineering Observation 6.8
The procedure header and procedure calls all must agree with regard to the number, type and order of parameters. We discuss exceptions to this in Section 6.17.

6.4 Function Procedures

Function procedures are similar to **Sub** procedures, with one important difference: **Function** procedures *return a value* (i.e., send a value) to the caller, whereas **Sub** procedures do not. The console application in Fig. 6.3 uses **Function** procedure **Square** to calculate the squares of the **Integer**s from 1–10.

```
1   ' Fig. 6.3: SquareInteger.vb
2   ' Function procedure to square a number.
3
4   Module modSquareInteger
5
6      Sub Main()
7         Dim i As Integer  ' counter
8
```

Fig. 6.3 **Function** procedure for squaring an integer (part 1 of 2).

```
 9          Console.WriteLine("Number" & vbTab & "Square" & vbCrLf)
10
11          ' square numbers from 1 to 10
12          For i = 1 To 10
13              Console.WriteLine(i & vbTab & Square(i))
14          Next
15
16      End Sub ' Main
17
18      ' Function Square is executed
19      ' only when the function is explicitly called.
20      Function Square(ByVal y As Integer) As Integer
21          Return y ^ 2
22      End Function ' Square
23
24  End Module ' modSquareInteger
```

Number	Square
1	1
2	4
3	9
4	16
5	25
6	36
7	49
8	64
9	81
10	100

Fig. 6.3 **Function** procedure for squaring an integer (part 2 of 2).

The **For** structure (lines 12–14) displays the results of squaring the **Integer**s from 1–10. Each iteration of the loop calculates the square of control variable **i** and displays it in the command window.

Function procedure **Square** is invoked (line 13) with the expression **Square(i)**. When program control reaches this expression, the program calls **Function Square** (lines 20–22). At this point, the program makes a copy of the value of **i** (the argument), and program control transfers to the first line of **Function Square**. **Square** receives the copy of **i**'s value and stores it in the parameter **y**. Line 21 is a **Return** statement, which terminates execution of the procedure and returns the result of **y ^ 2** to the calling program. The result is returned to the point on line 13 where **Square** was invoked. Line 13 displays the value of **i** and the value returned by **Square** in the command window. This process is repeated 10 times.

The format of a **Function** procedure definition is

```
Function procedure-name (parameter-list) As return-type
    declarations and statements
End Function
```

The *procedure-name*, *parameter-list*, and the *declarations and statements* in a **Function** procedure definition behave like the corresponding elements in a **Sub** procedure definition.

In the **Function** header, the *return-type* indicates the data type of the result returned from the **Function** to its caller. The statement

`Return` *expression*

can occur anywhere in a **Function** procedure body and returns the value of *expression* to the caller. If necessary, Visual Basic attempts to convert the *expression* to the **Function** procedure's *return-type*. **Function**s **Return** exactly one value. When a **Return** statement is executed, control returns immediately to the point at which that procedure was invoked.

Common Programming Error 6.4
*If the expression in a **Return** statement cannot be converted to the **Function** procedure's return-type, a runtime error is generated.*

Common Programming Error 6.5
*Failure to return a value from a **Function** procedure (e.g., by forgetting to provide a **Return** statement) causes the procedure to return the default value for the return-type, often producing incorrect output.*

6.5 Methods

A method is any procedure that is contained within a class. We have already presented several FCL methods (i.e., methods contained in classes that are part of the FCL). Programmers also can define custom methods in programmer-defined classes, such as a class used to define a Windows application. The Windows application in Fig. 6.4 uses two methods to calculate the largest of three **Double**s.

```vb
1   ' Fig. 6.4: Maximum.vb
2   ' Program finds the maximum of three numbers input.
3
4   Public Class FrmMaximum
5       Inherits System.Windows.Forms.Form
6
7       ' prompts for three inputs
8       Friend WithEvents lblOne As System.Windows.Forms.Label
9       Friend WithEvents lblTwo As System.Windows.Forms.Label
10      Friend WithEvents lblThree As System.Windows.Forms.Label
11
12      ' displays result
13      Friend WithEvents lblMaximum As System.Windows.Forms.Label
14
15      ' read three numbers
16      Friend WithEvents txtFirst As System.Windows.Forms.TextBox
17      Friend WithEvents txtSecond As System.Windows.Forms.TextBox
18      Friend WithEvents txtThird As System.Windows.Forms.TextBox
19
20      ' reads inputs and calculate results
21      Friend WithEvents cmdMaximum As System.Windows.Forms.Button
22
```

Fig. 6.4 Method that determines the largest of three numbers (part 1 of 2).

```
23          ' Visual Studio .NET generated code
24
25          ' obtain values in each text box, call procedure Maximum
26          Private Sub cmdMaximum_Click(ByVal sender As System.Object, _
27             ByVal e As System.EventArgs) Handles cmdMaximum.Click
28
29             Dim value1, value2, value3 As Double
30
31             value1 = txtFirst.Text
32             value2 = txtSecond.Text
33             value3 = txtThird.Text
34
35             lblMaximum.Text = Maximum(value1, value2, value3)
36          End Sub ' cmdMaximum_Click
37
38          ' find maximum of three parameter values
39          Function Maximum(ByVal valueOne As Double, _
40             ByVal valueTwo As Double, ByVal valueThree As Double) _
41             As Double
42             Return Math.Max(Math.Max(valueOne, valueTwo), valueThree)
43          End Function ' Maximum
44
45       End Class ' FrmMaximum
```

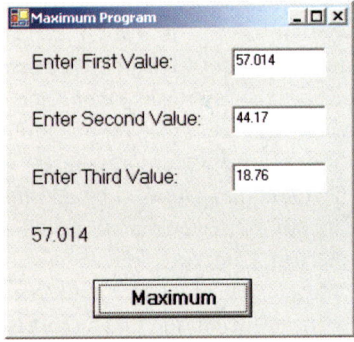

Fig. 6.4 Method that determines the largest of three numbers (part 2 of 2).

Until now, many of our applications have facilitated user interaction via either the command window (in which the user can type an input value into the program) or a message dialog (which displays a message to the user and allows the user to click **OK** to dismiss the dialog). In Chapter 4, Control Structures: Part 1, we introduced Windows applications by creating a program that displays information in a label on a form.

Although the command window and message dialogs are valid ways to receive input from a user and display output, they are limited in their capabilities—the command window can obtain only one line of input at a time from the user, and a message dialog can display only one message. It is common to receive multiple inputs at the same time (such as the three values in this example), or to display many pieces of data at once. To introduce more sophisticated user interface programming, the program in Fig. 6.4 uses GUI *event handling* (i.e., the ability to respond to a state change in the GUI, such as when the user clicks a button).

Class **FrmMaximum** uses a GUI consisting of three **TextBox**es (**txtFirst**, **txtSecond** and **txtThird**) for user input, a **Button** (**cmdMaximum**) to invoke the calculation and four **Label**s, including **lblMaximum**, which displays the results. We create these components visually, using the **Toolbox**, and change their properties in the **Properties** window. Lines 7–21 are declarations indicating the name of each component. Although these lines of code are actually part of the Visual Studio .NET generated code, we display them to indicate the objects that are part of the form (as always, the complete code for this program is on the CD-ROM that accompanies this book and at **www.deitel.com**).

Line 5 indicates that class **FrmMaximum Inherits** from **System.Windows.Forms.Form**. Remember that all forms inherit from class **System.Windows.Forms.Form**. A class can inherit attributes and behaviors (data and methods) from another class if that class is specified to the right of the **Inherits** keyword. We discuss inheritance in detail in Chapter 9, Object-Oriented Programming: Inheritance.

FrmMaximum contains two programmer-defined methods. Method **Maximum** (lines 39–43) takes three **Double** parameters and returns the value of the largest parameter. Note that this method definition looks just like the definition of a **Function** procedure in a module. The program also includes method **cmdMaximum_Click** (lines 26–36). When the user double-clicks a component, such as a **Button**, in **Design** mode, the IDE generates a method that **Handles** an event (i.e., an *event handler*). An event represents a user action, such as clicking a **Button** or altering a value. An event handler is a method that is executed (called) when a certain event is *raised* (occurs). In this case, method **cmdMaximum_Click** handles the event in which **Button cmdMaximum** is clicked. Programmers write code to perform certain tasks when such events occur. By employing both events and objects, programmers can create applications that enable more sophisticated user interactions than those we have seen previously. Event-handler names created by the IDE begin with the object's name, followed by an underscore and the name of the event. We explain how to create our own event handlers, which can be given any name, in Chapter 12, Graphical User Interface Concepts: Part 1.

When the user clicks **cmdMaximum**, procedure **cmdMaximum_Click** (lines 26–36) executes. Lines 31–33 retrieve the values in the three **TextBox**es, using the **Text** property. The values are converted implicitly to type **Double** and stored in variables **value1**, **value2** and **value3**.

Line 35 calls method **Maximum** (lines 39–43) with the arguments **value1**, **value2** and **value3**. The values of these arguments are then stored in parameters **valueOne**, **valueTwo** and **valueThree** in method **Maximum**. **Maximum** returns the result of the expression on line 42, which makes two calls to *method **Max*** of the **Math** class. Method **Max** returns the largest of its two **Double** arguments, meaning the computation in line 42 first compares **valueOne** and **valueTwo**, then compares the value returned by the first method call to **valueThree**. Calls to methods, such as **Math.Max**, that are defined in a class in the FCL must include the class name and the dot (**.**) operator (also called the *member access operator*). However, calls to methods defined in the class that contains the method call need only specify the method name.

When control returns to method **cmdMaximum_Click**, line 35 assigns the value returned by method **Maximum** to **lblMaximum**'s **Text** property, causing it to be displayed for the user.

The reader may notice that typing the opening parenthesis after a method or procedure name causes Visual Studio to display a window containing the procedure's argument names and types. This is the *Parameter Info* feature (Fig. 6.5) of the IDE. *Parameter Info* greatly simplifies coding by identifying accessible procedures and their arguments. The *Parameter Info* feature displays information for programmer-defined procedures and all methods contained in the FCL.

Good Programming Practice 6.4

Selecting descriptive parameter names makes the information provided by the Parameter Info *feature more meaningful.*

Visual Basic also provides the *IntelliSense* feature, which displays all the members in a class. For instance, when the programmer types the dot (**.**) operator (also called the *member access operator*) after the class name, **Math**, in Fig. 6.6, *IntelliSense* provides a list of all the available methods in class **Math**. The **Math** class contains numerous methods that allow the programmer to perform a variety of common mathematical calculations.

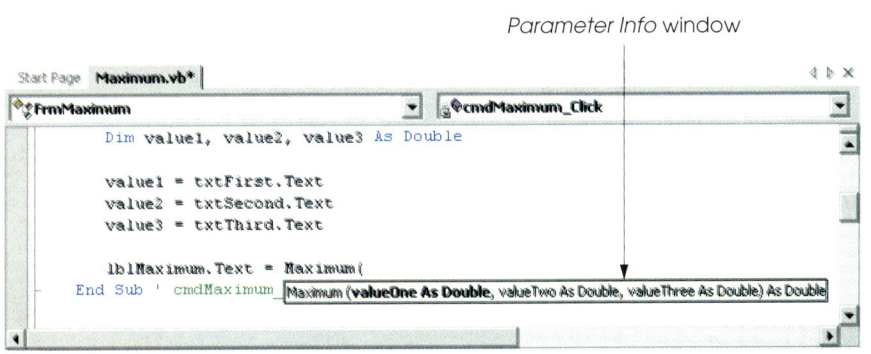

Fig. 6.5   *Parameter Info* feature of the Visual Studio .NET IDE.

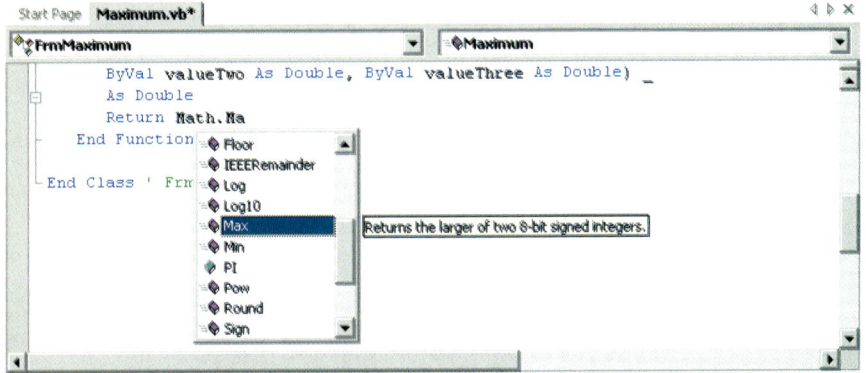

Fig. 6.6   *IntelliSense* feature of the Visual Studio .NET IDE.

As an example of the variety of FCL methods, some **Math** class methods are summarized in Fig. 6.7. Throughout the table, the variables **x** and **y** are of type **Double**; however, many of the methods also provide versions that take values of other data types as arguments. In addition, the **Math** class also defines two mathematical constants: **Math.PI** and **Math.E**. The constant **Math.PI** (**3.14159265358979323846**) of class **Math** is the ratio of a circle's circumference to its diameter (i.e., twice the radius). The constant **Math.E** (**2.7182818284590452354**) is the base value for natural logarithms (calculated with the **Math.Log** method).

Common Programming Error 6.6

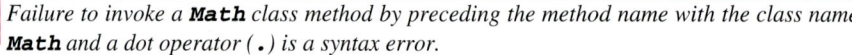

*Failure to invoke a **Math** class method by preceding the method name with the class name **Math** and a dot operator (.) is a syntax error.*

Method	Description	Example
Abs(x)	returns the absolute value of *x*	**Abs(23.7)** is **23.7** **Abs(0)** is **0** **Abs(-23.7)** is **23.7**
Ceiling(x)	rounds *x* to the smallest integer not less than *x*	**Ceiling(9.2)** is **10.0** **Ceiling(-9.8)** is **-9.0**
Cos(x)	returns the trigonometric cosine of *x* (*x* in radians)	**Cos(0.0)** is **1.0**
Exp(x)	returns the exponential e^x	**Exp(1.0)** is approximately **2.71828182845905** **Exp(2.0)** is approximately **7.38905609893065**
Floor(x)	rounds *x* to the largest integer not greater than *x*	**Floor(9.2)** is **9.0** **Floor(-9.8)** is **-10.0**
Log(x)	returns the natural logarithm of *x* (base *e*)	**Log(2.7182818284590451)** is approximately **1.0** **Log(7.3890560989306504)** is approximately **2.0**
Max(x, y)	returns the larger value of *x* and *y* (also has versions for **Single**, **Integer** and **Long** values)	**Max(2.3, 12.7)** is **12.7** **Max(-2.3, -12.7)** is **-2.3**
Min(x, y)	returns the smaller value of *x* and *y* (also has versions for **Single**, **Integer** and **Long** values)	**Min(2.3, 12.7)** is **2.3** **Min(-2.3, -12.7)** is **-12.7**
Pow(x, y)	calculates *x* raised to power *y* (x^y)	**Pow(2.0, 7.0)** is **128.0** **Pow(9.0, .5)** is **3.0**
Sin(x)	returns the trigonometric sine of *x* (*x* in radians)	**Sin(0.0)** is **0.0**

Fig. 6.7 **Math** class methods (part 1 of 2).

Method	Description	Example
`Sqrt(x)`	returns the square root of *x*	`Sqrt(9.0)` is `3.0` `Sqrt(2.0)` is `1.4142135623731`
`Tan(x)`	returns the trigonometric tangent of *x* (*x* in radians)	`Tan(0.0)` is `0.0`

Fig. 6.7   `Math` class methods (part 2 of 2).

*It is not necessary to add an assembly reference to use the **Math** class methods in a program, because class **Math** is located in namespace **System**, which is implicitly added to all console applications.*

6.6 Argument Promotion

An important feature of procedure definitions is the *coercion of arguments* (i.e., the forcing of arguments to the appropriate data type so that they can be passed to a procedure). Visual Basic supports both widening and narrowing conversions. *Widening conversion* occurs when a type is converted to another type (usually one that can hold more data) without losing data, whereas a *narrowing conversion* occurs when there is potential for data loss during the conversion (usually to a type that holds a smaller amount of data). Figure 6.8 lists the widening conversions supported by Visual Basic.

For example, the `Math` class method `Sqrt` can be called with an `Integer` argument, even though the method is defined in the `Math` class to receive a `Double` argument. The statement

```
Console.Write(Math.Sqrt(4))
```

correctly evaluates `Math.Sqrt(4)` and prints the value **2**. Visual Basic promotes (i.e., converts) the `Integer` value **4** to the `Double` value **4.0** before the value is passed to `Math.Sqrt`. In this case, the argument value does not correspond precisely to the parameter type in the method definition, so an implicit widening conversion changes the value to the proper type before the method is called. Visual Basic also performs narrowing conversions on arguments passed to procedures. For example, if `String` variable `number` contains the value `"4"`, the method call `Math.Sqrt(number)` correctly evaluates to **2**. However, some implicit narrowing conversions can fail, resulting in runtime errors and logic errors. For example, if `number` contains the value `"hello"`, passing it as an argument to method `Math.Sqrt` causes a runtime error. In the next section, we discuss some measures the programmer can take to help avoid such issues.

Common Programming Error 6.7

*When performing a narrowing conversion (e.g., **Double** to **Integer**), conversion of a primitive-data-type value to another primitive data type might change the value. Also, the conversion of any integral value to a floating-point value and back to an integral value could introduce rounding errors into the result.*

Type	Conversion Types
`Boolean`	`Object`
`Byte`	`Short`, `Integer`, `Long`, `Decimal`, `Single`, `Double` or `Object`
`Char`	`String` or `Object`
`Date`	`Object`
`Decimal`	`Single`, `Double` or `Object`
`Double`	`Object`
`Integer`	`Long`, `Decimal`, `Single`, `Double` or `Object`
`Long`	`Decimal`, `Single`, `Double` or `Object`
`Object`	none
`Short`	`Integer`, `Long`, `Decimal`, `Single`, `Double` or `Object`
`Single`	`Double` or `Object`
`String`	`Object`

Fig. 6.8 Widening conversions.

Argument promotion applies not only to primitive data-type values passed as arguments to methods, but also to expressions containing values of two or more data types. Such expressions are referred to as *mixed-type expressions*. In a mixed-type expression, each value is promoted to the "highest" data type in the expression (i.e., widening conversions are made until the values are of the same type). For example, if `singleNumber` is of type `Single` and `integerNumber` is of type `Integer`, when Visual Basic evaluates the expression

```
singleNumber + integerNumber
```

the value of `integerNumber` is converted to type `Single`, then added to `singleNumber`, producing a `Single` result. Although the values' original data types are maintained, a temporary version of each value is created for use in the expression, and the data types of the temporary versions are modified appropriately.

6.7 Option Strict and Data-Type Conversions

Visual Basic provides several options for controlling the way the compiler handles data types. These options can help programmers eliminate such errors as those caused by narrowing conversions, making code more reliable and secure. The first option is `Option Explicit`, which is set to **On** by default, meaning it was enabled in the Visual Basic programs created in Chapters 2–5. `Option Explicit` forces the programmer to declare explicitly all variables before they are used in a program. Forcing explicit declarations eliminates spelling errors and other subtle errors that may occur if `Option Explicit` is turned off. For example, when `Option Explicit` is set to **Off**, the compiler interprets misspelled variable names as new variable declarations, which create subtle errors that can be difficult to debug.

A second option, which is by default set to **Off**, is `Option Strict`. Visual Basic provides `Option Strict` as a means to increase program clarity and reduce debugging time.

When set to **On**, `Option Strict` causes the compiler to check all conversions and requires the programmer to perform an *explicit conversion* for all narrowing conversions that could cause data loss (e.g., conversion from `Double` to `Integer`) or program termination (e.g., conversion of a `String`, such as `"hello"`, to type `Integer`).

The methods in class `Convert` change data types explicitly. The name of each conversion method is the word `To`, followed by the name of the data type to which the method converts its argument. For instance, to store a `String` input by the user in variable `number` of type `Integer` (represented in Visual Basic .NET as type `Int32`, a 32-bit integer) with `Option Strict` set to **On**, we use the statement

```
number = Convert.ToInt32(Console.ReadLine())
```

When `Option Strict` is set to **Off**, Visual Basic performs such type conversions implicitly, meaning the programmer might not realize that a narrowing conversion is being performed. If the data being converted is incompatible with the new data type, a runtime error occurs. `Option Strict` draws the programmer's attention to narrowing conversions so that they can be eliminated or handled properly. In Chapter 11, Exception Handling, we discuss how to handle the errors caused by failed narrowing conversions.

Software Engineering Observation 6.10

Performing explicit conversions allows programs to execute more efficiently by eliminating the need to determine the data type of the value being changed before the conversion executes.

From this point forward, all code examples have `Option Strict` set to **On**. `Option Strict` can be activated through the IDE by right-clicking the project name in the **Solution Explorer**. From the resulting menu, select **Properties** to open the **Property Pages** dialog Fig. 6.9. From the directory tree on the left side of the dialog, select **Build** from the **Common Properties** list. In the middle of the dialog is a drop-down box labeled **Option Strict:**. By default, the option is set to **Off**. Choose **On** from the drop-down box and press **Apply**.

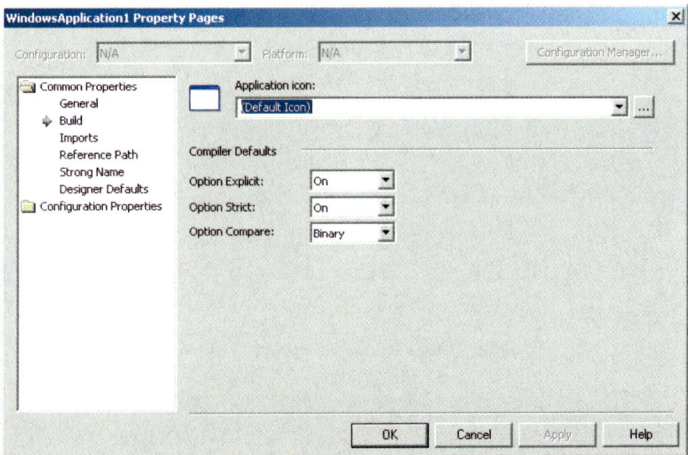

Fig. 6.9 **Property Pages** dialog with `Option Strict` set to **On**.

Setting **Option Strict** to **On** in the **Property Pages** applies the change globally, to the entire project. The programmer also can enable **Option Strict** within an individual code file by typing **Option Strict On** at the start of the file above any declarations or **Imports** statements.

6.8 Value Types and Reference Types

In the next section, we discuss passing arguments to procedures by value and by reference. To understand this, we first need to make a distinction between data types in Visual Basic. All Visual Basic data types can be categorized as either *value types* or *reference types*. A variable of a value type contains data of that type. Normally, value types are used for a single piece of data, such as an **Integer** or a **Double** value. By contrast, a variable of a reference type (sometimes called a *reference*) contains a location in memory where data is stored. The location in memory can contain many individual pieces of data. Collectively, reference types are known as objects and are discussed in detail in Chapters 8, 9 and 10, Object-Based Programming, Object-Oriented Programming: Inheritance, and Object-Oriented Programming: Polymorphism.

Both value types and reference types include built-in types and types that the programmer can create. The built-in value types include the *integral types* (**Byte**, **Short**, **Integer** and **Long**), the *floating-point types* (**Single** and **Double**) and types **Boolean**, **Date**, **Decimal** and **Char**. The built-in reference types include **Object** and **String** (although type **String** often behaves more like a value type, as we discuss in the next section). The value types that can be constructed by the programmer include **Structure**s and **Enum**erations. The reference types that can be created by the programmer include classes, interfaces and delegates. Programmer-defined types are discussed in greater detail in Chapter 8, Object-Based Programming, Chapter 9, Object-Oriented Programming: Inheritance and Chapter 15, Strings, Characters and Regular Expressions.

The table in Fig. 6.10 lists the primitive data types, which form the building blocks for more complicated types, such as classes. If **Option Explicit** is set to **On**, all variables must have a type before they can be used in a program. This requirement is referred to as *strong typing*.

Type	Size in bits	Values	Standard
Boolean	16	**True** or **False**	
Char	16	One Unicode character	(Unicode character set)
Byte	8	0 to 255	
Date	64	1 January 0001 to 31 December 9999 0:00:00 to 23:59:59	
Decimal	128	1.0E-28 to 7.9E+28	
Short	16	-32,768 to 32,767	

Fig. 6.10 Visual Basic primitive data types (part 1 of 2).

Type	Size in bits	Values	Standard
Integer	32	-2,147,483,648 to 2,147,483,647	
Long	64	-9,223,372,036,854,775,808 to 9,223,372,036,854,775,807	
Single	32	±1.5E-45 to ±3.4E+38	(IEEE 754 floating point)
Double	64	±5.0E-324 to ±1.7E+308	(IEEE 754 floating point)
Object	32	Data of any type	
String		0 to ~2000000000 Unicode characters	(Unicode character set)

Fig. 6.10 Visual Basic primitive data types (part 2 of 2).

Each value type in the table is accompanied by its size in bits (there are 8 bits to a byte) and its range of values. To promote portability, Microsoft chose to use internationally recognized standards for both character formats (Unicode) and floating-point numbers (IEEE 754). We discuss the Unicode character formats in Appendix F, Unicode.

Values typed directly in program code are called *literals*. Each literal corresponds to one of the primitive data types. We already have seen literals for commonly-used types, such as **String**, **Integer** and **Double**. However, some of Visual Basic's data types use special notations for creating literals. For instance, to create a literal of type **Char**, follow a single-character **String** with the *type character* **c**. The statement

```
Dim character As Char = "Z"c
```

declares **Char** variable **character** and initializes it to the **"Z"** character.

Similarly, literals of specific integral data types can be created by following an integer with the type character **S** (for **Short**), **I** (for **Integer**) or **L** (for **Long**). To create floating-point literals, follow a floating-point number with type character **F** (for **Single**) or **R** (for **Double**). Type character **D** can be used to create **Decimal** literals.

Visual Basic also allows programmers to type floating-point literals in scientific notation, by following a floating-point number by the character **E** and a positive or negative exponent of 10. For example, **1.909E-5** corresponds to the value **0.00001909**. This notation is useful for specifying floating-point values that are too large or too small to be written in fixed-point notation.

Figure 6.11 displays Visual Basic's type characters and examples of literals for each data type. All literals must be within the range for the literal's type, as specified in Fig. 6.10.

Type	Type character	Example
Char	c	"u"c
Single	F	9.802E+31F

Fig. 6.11 Literals with type characters (part 1 of 2).

Type	Type character	Example
Double	R	6.04E-187R
Decimal	D	128309.76D
Short	S	3420S
Integer	I	-867I
Long	L	19235827493259374L

Fig. 6.11 Literals with type characters (part 2 of 2).

6.9 Passing Arguments: Pass-by-Value vs. Pass-by-Reference

Arguments are passed in one of two ways: *Pass-by-value* and *pass-by-reference* (also called *call-by-value* and *call-by-reference*). When an argument is passed by value, the program makes a *copy* of the argument's value and passes that copy to the called procedure. With pass-by-value, changes to the called procedure's copy do not affect the original variable's value. In contrast, when an argument is passed by reference, the caller gives the called procedure the ability to access and modify the caller's original data directly. Figure 6.12 demonstrates passing value-type arguments by value and by reference.[1]

The program passes three value-type variables, **number1**, **number2** and **number3**, in different ways to procedures **SquareByValue** (lines 39–45) and **SquareByReference** (lines 48–54). Keyword **ByVal** in the procedure header of **SquareByValue** (line 39) indicates that value-type arguments should be passed by value. When **number1** is passed to **SquareByValue** (line 13), a copy of the value stored in **number1** (i.e., **2**) is passed to the procedure. Therefore, the value of **number1** in the calling procedure, **Main**, is not modified when parameter **number** is squared in procedure **SquareByValue** (line 42).

Procedure **SquareByReference** uses *keyword* **ByRef** (line 48) to receive its value-type parameter by reference. When **Main** calls **SquareByReference** (line 23), a reference to the value stored in **number2** is passed, which gives **SquareByReference** direct access to the value stored in the original variable. Thus, the value stored in **number2** after **SquareByReference** finishes executing is the same as the final value of parameter **number**.

When arguments are enclosed in parentheses, **()**, a copy of the value of the argument is passed to the procedure, even if the procedure header includes keyword **ByRef**. Thus, the value of **number3** does not change after it is passed to **SquareByReference** (line 33) via parentheses.

Passing value-type arguments with keyword **ByRef** is useful when procedures need to alter argument values directly. However, passing by reference can weaken security, because the called procedure can modify the caller's data.

Reference-type variables passed with keyword **ByVal** are effectively passed by reference, as the value that is copied is the reference for the object. Although Visual Basic allows programmers to use keyword **ByRef** with reference-type parameters, it is usually

---

1. In Chapter 7 we discuss passing reference-type arguments by value and by reference.

not necessary to do so except with type **String**. Although they technically are reference types, **String** arguments cannot be modified directly when passed with keyword **ByVal**, due to some subtle details of the **String** data type, which we discuss in Chapter 15, Strings, Characters and Regular Expressions.

```vb
1   ' Fig. 6.12: ByRefTest.vb
2   ' Demonstrates passing by reference.
3
4   Module modByRefTest
5
6      ' squares three values ByVal and ByRef, displays results
7      Sub Main()
8         Dim number1 As Integer = 2
9
10        Console.WriteLine("Passing a value-type argument by value:")
11        Console.WriteLine("Before calling SquareByValue, " & _
12           "number1 is {0}", number1)
13        SquareByValue(number1)   ' passes number1 by value
14        Console.WriteLine("After returning from SquareByValue, " & _
15           "number1 is {0}" & vbCrLf, number1)
16
17        Dim number2 As Integer = 2
18
19        Console.WriteLine("Passing a value-type argument" & _
20           " by reference:")
21        Console.WriteLine("Before calling SquareByReference, " & _
22           "number2 is {0}", number2)
23        SquareByReference(number2)   ' passes number2 by reference
24        Console.WriteLine("After returning from " & _
25           "SquareByReference, number2 is {0}" & vbCrLf, number2)
26
27        Dim number3 As Integer = 2
28
29        Console.WriteLine("Passing a value-type argument" & _
30           " by reference, but in parentheses:")
31        Console.WriteLine("Before calling SquareByReference " & _
32           "using parentheses, number3 is {0}", number3)
33        SquareByReference((number3))   ' passes number3 by value
34        Console.WriteLine("After returning from " & _
35           "SquareByReference, number3 is {0}", number3)
36
37     End Sub ' Main
38
39     ' squares number by value (note ByVal keyword)
40     Sub SquareByValue(ByVal number As Integer)
41        Console.WriteLine("After entering SquareByValue, " & _
42           "number is {0}", number)
43        number *= number
44        Console.WriteLine("Before exiting SquareByValue, " & _
45           "number is {0}", number)
46     End Sub ' SquareByValue
47
```

Fig. 6.12 **ByVal** and **ByRef** used to pass value-type arguments (part 1 of 2).

```
48      ' squares number by reference (note ByRef keyword)
49      Sub SquareByReference(ByRef number As Integer)
50         Console.WriteLine("After entering SquareByReference" & _
51            ", number is {0}", number)
52         number *= number
53         Console.WriteLine("Before exiting SquareByReference" & _
54            ", number is {0}", number)
55      End Sub ' SquareByReference
56
57   End Module ' modByRefTest
```

```
Passing a value-type argument by value:
Before calling SquareByValue, number1 is 2
After entering SquareByValue, number is 2
Before exiting SquareByValue, number is 4
After returning from SquareByValue, number1 is 2

Passing a value-type argument by reference:
Before calling SquareByReference, number2 is 2
After entering SquareByReference, number is 2
Before exiting SquareByReference, number is 4
After returning from SquareByReference, number2 is 4

Passing a value-type argument by reference, but in parentheses:
Before calling SquareByReference using parentheses, number3 is 2
After entering SquareByReference, number is 2
Before exiting SquareByReference, number is 4
After returning from SquareByReference, number3 is 2
```

Fig. 6.12 `ByVal` and `ByRef` used to pass value-type arguments (part 2 of 2).

Testing and Debugging Tip 6.3

When passing arguments by value, changes to the called procedure's copy do not affect the original variable's value. This prevents possible side effects that could hinder the development of correct and reliable software systems. Always pass value-type arguments by value unless you explicitly intend for the called procedure to modify the caller's data.

Software Engineering Observation 6.11

*Although keywords **ByVal** and **ByRef** may be used to pass reference-type variables by value or by reference, the called procedure can manipulate the caller's reference-type variable directly in both cases. Therefore, it is rarely appropriate to use **ByRef** with reference-type variables. We discuss this subtle issue in detail in Chapter 7, Arrays.*

6.10 Duration of Identifiers

Throughout the earlier chapters of this book, we have used identifiers for various purposes, including as variable names and as the names of user-defined procedures, modules and classes. Every identifier has certain attributes, including *duration* and *scope*.

An identifier's *duration* (also called its *lifetime*) is the period during which the identifier exists in memory. Some identifiers exist briefly, some are created and destroyed repeatedly, yet others are maintained through the entire execution of a program.

> **Software Engineering Observation 6.12**
>
> *When returning information from a* **Function** *procedure via a* **Return** *statement, value-type variables always are returned by value (i.e., a copy is returned), whereas reference-type variables always are returned by reference (i.e., a reference to an object is returned).*

The *scope* of an identifier is the portion of a program in which the variable's identifier can be referenced. Some identifiers can be referenced throughout a program; others can be referenced only from limited portions of a program (such as within a single procedure). This section discusses the duration of identifiers. Section 6.11 discusses the scope of identifiers.

Identifiers that represent local variables in a procedure (i.e., parameters and variables declared in the procedure body) have *automatic duration*. Automatic-duration variables are created when program control enters the procedure in which they are declared, exist while the procedure is active and are destroyed when the procedure is exited.[2] For the remainder of the text, we refer to variables of automatic duration simply as *automatic variables*, or *local variables*.

Variables declared inside a module or class, but outside any procedure definition, exist as long as their containing class or module is loaded in memory. Variables declared in a module exist throughout a program's execution. By default, a variable declared in a class, such as a **Form** class for a Windows application, is an *instance variable*. In the case of a **Form**, this means that the variable is created when the **Form** loads and exists until the **Form** is closed. We discuss instance variables in detail in Chapter 8, Object-Based Programming.

> **Software Engineering Observation 6.13**
>
> *Automatic duration is an example of the* principle of least privilege. *This principle states that each component of a system should have only the rights and privileges it needs to accomplish its designated task. This helps prevent accidental and/or malicious errors from occurring in systems. Why have variables stored in memory and accessible when they are not needed?*

6.11 Scope Rules

The *scope* (sometimes called *declaration space*) of a variable, reference or procedure identifier is the portion of the program in which the identifier can be accessed. The possible scopes for an identifier are *class scope, module scope, namespace scope* and *block scope*.

Members of a class have class scope, which means that they are visible in what is known as the *declaration space of a class*. Class scope begins at the class identifier after keyword **Class** and terminates at the **End Class** statement. This scope enables a method of that class to invoke directly all members defined in that class and to access members inherited into that class.[3] In a sense, members of a class are global to the methods of the class in which they are defined. This means that the methods can modify instance variables of the class (i.e., variables declared in the class definition, but outside any method definition) directly and invoke other methods of the class.

---

2. Variables in a procedure can also be declared using keyword **Static**, in which case the variable is created and initialized during the first execution of the procedure then maintains its value between subsequent calls to the procedure.
3. In Chapter 8, Object-Based Programming, we see that **Shared** members are an exception to this rule.

In Visual Basic .NET, identifiers declared inside a block, such as the body of a procedure definition or the body of an **If/Then** selection structure, have block scope (*local-variable declaration space*). Block scope begins at the identifier's declaration and ends at the block's **End** statement (or equivalent, e.g., **Next**). Local variables of a procedure have block scope. Procedure parameters also have block scope, because they are considered local variables of the procedure. Any block can contain variable declarations. When blocks are nested in a body of a procedure, an error is generated if an identifier declared in an outer block has the same name as an identifier declared in an inner block. However, if a local variable in a called procedure shares its name with a variable with class scope, such as an instance variable, the class-scope variable is "hidden" until the called procedure terminates execution.

Variables declared in a module have module scope, which is similar to class scope. Variables declared in a module are accessible to all procedures defined in the module. Module scope and class scope are sometimes referred to collectively as module scope. Like class-scope variables, module-scope variables are hidden when they have the same identifier as a local variable.

By default, procedures defined in a module have namespace scope, which generally means that they may be accessed throughout a project. Namespace scope is useful in projects that contain multiple pieces (i.e., modules and classes). If a project contains a module and a class, methods in the class can access the procedures of the module. Although variables declared in a module have module scope, they can be given namespace scope by replacing keyword **Dim** with keyword **Public** in the declaration. We discuss how to add modules to projects in Section 6.18.

Good Programming Practice 6.5

Avoid local-variable names that hide class-variable or module-variable names.

The program in Fig. 6.13 demonstrates scoping issues with instance variables and local variables. Instance variable **value** is declared and initialized to **1** in line 12. As explained previously, this variable is hidden in any procedure that declares a variable named **value**. The **FrmScoping_Load** method declares a local variable **value** (line 19) and initializes it to **5**. This variable is displayed on **lblOutput** (note the declaration on line 7, which is actually part of the Visual Studio .NET generated code) to illustrate that the instance variable **value** is hidden in **FrmScoping_Load**.

```
1    ' Fig. 6.13: Scoping.vb
2    ' Demonstrates scope rules and instance variables.
3
4    Public Class FrmScoping
5       Inherits System.Windows.Forms.Form
6
7       Friend WithEvents lblOutput As System.Windows.Forms.Label
8
9       ' Visual Studio .NET generated code
10
11      ' instance variable can be used anywhere in class
12      Dim value As Integer = 1
13
```

Fig. 6.13 Scoping rules in a class (part 1 of 2).

```vbnet
14     ' demonstrates class scope and block scope
15     Private Sub FrmScoping_Load(ByVal sender As System.Object, _
16        ByVal e As System.EventArgs) Handles MyBase.Load
17
18        ' variable local to FrmScoping_Load hides instance variable
19        Dim value As Integer = 5
20
21        lblOutput.Text = "local variable value in" & _
22           " FrmScoping_Load is " & value
23
24        MethodA() ' MethodA has automatic local value
25        MethodB() ' MethodB uses instance variable value
26        MethodA() ' MethodA creates new automatic local value
27        MethodB() ' instance variable value retains its value
28
29        lblOutput.Text &= vbCrLf & vbCrLf & "local variable " & _
30           "value in FrmScoping_Load is " & value
31     End Sub ' FrmScoping_Load
32
33     ' automatic local variable value hides instance variable
34     Sub MethodA()
35        Dim value As Integer = 25 ' initialized after each call
36
37        lblOutput.Text &= vbCrLf & vbCrLf & "local variable " & _
38           "value in MethodA is " & value & " after entering MethodA"
39        value += 1
40        lblOutput.Text &= vbCrLf & "local variable " & _
41           "value in MethodA is " & value & " before exiting MethodA"
42     End Sub ' MethodA
43
44     ' uses instance variable value
45     Sub MethodB()
46        lblOutput.Text &= vbCrLf & vbCrLf & "instance variable" & _
47           " value is " & value & " after entering MethodB"
48        value *= 10
49        lblOutput.Text &= vbCrLf & "instance variable " & _
50           "value is " & value & " before exiting MethodB"
51     End Sub ' MethodB
52
53  End Class ' FrmScoping
```

```
Scoping Demonstration

local variable value in FrmScoping_Load is 5

local variable value in MethodA is 25 after entering MethodA
local variable value in MethodA is 26 before exiting MethodA

instance variable value is 1 after entering MethodB
instance variable value is 10 before exiting MethodB

local variable value in MethodA is 25 after entering MethodA
local variable value in MethodA is 26 before exiting MethodA

instance variable value is 10 after entering MethodB
instance variable value is 100 before exiting MethodB

local variable value in FrmScoping_Load is 5
```

Fig. 6.13 Scoping rules in a class (part 2 of 2).

The program defines two other methods—**MethodA** and **MethodB**—which take no arguments and return nothing. Each method is called twice from **FrmScoping_Load**. **MethodA** defines local variable **value** (line 35) and initializes it to **25**. When **MethodA** is called, the variable is displayed in the label **lblOutput**, incremented and displayed again before exiting the method. Automatic variable **value** is destroyed when **MethodA** terminates. Thus, each time this method is called, **value** must be recreated and reinitialized to **25**.

MethodB does not declare any variables. Therefore, when this procedure refers to variable **value**, the instance variable **value** (line 12) is used. When **MethodB** is called, the instance variable is displayed, multiplied by **10** and displayed again before exiting the method. The next time method **MethodB** is called, the instance variable retains its modified value, **10** and line 48 causes **value** (line 12) to become **100**. Finally, the program again displays the local variable **value** in method **FrmScoping_Load** to show that none of the method calls modified this variable **value**—both methods refer to variables in other scopes.

6.12 Random-Number Generation

We now take a brief and hopefully entertaining diversion into a popular programming application—simulation and game playing. In this section and the next, we develop a structured game-playing program that includes multiple methods. The program employs many of the control structures that we have studied to this point, in addition to introducing several new concepts.

There is something in the air of a gambling casino that invigorates a wide variety of people, ranging from the high rollers at the plush mahogany-and-felt craps tables to the quarter-poppers at the one-armed bandits. Many of these individuals are drawn by the *element of chance*—the possibility that luck will convert a pocketful of money into a mountain of wealth. The element of chance can be introduced into computer applications through class **Random** (located in namespace **System**).

Consider the following statements:

```
Dim randomObject As Random = New Random()
Dim randomNumber As Integer = randomObject.Next()
```

The first statement declares **randomObject** as a reference to an object of type **Random**. The value of **randomObject** is initialized using keyword *New*, which creates a new instance of class **Random** (i.e., a **Random** object). In Visual Basic, keyword **New** creates an object of a specified type and returns the object's location in memory.

The second statement declares **Integer** variable **randomNumber** and assigns it the value returned by calling **Random** method *Next*. We access method **Next** by following the reference name, **randomObject**, by the dot (**.**) operator and the method name. Method **Next** generates a positive **Integer** value between zero and the constant **Int32.MaxValue** (2,147,483,647). If **Next** produces values at random, every value in this range has an equal *chance* (or *probability*) of being chosen when **Next** is called. The values returned by **Next** are actually *pseudo-random numbers*, or a sequence of values produced by a complex mathematical calculation. This mathematical calculation requires a *seed value*, which, if different each time the program is run, causes the series of mathematical calculations to be different as well (so that the numbers generated are indeed random). When we create a **Random** object, the current time of day becomes the seed value for the calculation. Alternatively, we can pass a seed value as an argument in the parentheses after

New Random. Passing in the same seed twice results in the same series of random numbers. Using the current time of day as the seed value is effective, because the time is likely to change for each **Random** object we create.

The generation of random numbers often is necessary in a program. However, the range of values produced by **Next** (i.e., values between 0–2,147,483,647) often is different from that needed in a particular application. For example, a program that simulates coin-tossing might require only 0 for "heads" and 1 for "tails." A program that simulates the rolling of a six-sided die would require random **Integer**s from 1–6. Similarly, a program that randomly predicts the next type of spaceship (out of four possibilities) that flies across the horizon in a video game might require random **Integer**s from 1–4.

By passing an argument to method **Next** as follows

```
value = 1 + randomObject.Next(6)
```

we can produce integers in the range 1–6. When a single argument is passed to **Next**, the values returned by **Next** will be in the range from 0 to (but not including) the value of that argument. This is called *scaling*. The number **6** is the *scaling factor*. We *shift* the range of numbers produced by adding **1** to our previous result, so that the return values are between 1 and 6, rather than 0 and 5. The values produced by **Next** are always in the range

```
x ≤ x + randomObject.Next(y) < y
```

Visual Basic simplifies this process by allowing the programmer to pass two arguments to **Next**. For example, the above statement also could be written as

```
value = randomObject.Next(1, 7)
```

Note that we must use **7** as the second argument to method **Next** to produce integers in the range from 1–6. The first argument indicates the minimum value in our desired range, whereas the second is equal to *1 + the maximum value desired*. Thus, the values produced by this version of **Next** will always be in the range

```
x ≤ randomObject.Next(x, y) < y
```

In this case, **x** is the shifting value, and **y-x** is the scaling factor. Figure 6.14 demonstrates the use of class **Random** and method **Next** by simulating 20 rolls of a six-sided die and showing the value of each roll in a **MessageBox**. Note that all the values are in the range from 1–6, inclusive.

The program in Fig. 6.15 uses class **Random** to simulate rolling four six-sided dice. We then use some of the functionality from this program in another example (Fig. 6.16) to demonstrate that the numbers generated by **Next** occur with approximately equal likelihood.

In Fig. 6.15, we use event-handling method **cmdRoll_Click**, which executes whenever the user clicks **cmdRoll**, resulting in method **DisplayDie** being called four times, once for each **Label** on the **Form**. Calling **DisplayDie** (lines 35–44) causes four dice to appear as if they are being rolled each time **cmdRoll** is clicked. Note that, when this program runs, the dice images do not appear until the user clicks **cmdRoll** for the first time.

Method **DisplayDie** specifies the correct image for the face value calculated by method **Next** (line 38). Notice that we declare **randomObject** as an instance variable of **FrmRollDice** (line 21). This allows the same **Random** object to be used each time **Dis-**

playDie executes. We use the ***Image*** *property* (line 41) to display an image on a label. We set the property's value with an assignment statement (lines 41–43). Notice that we specify the image to display through procedure ***FromFile*** in class ***Image*** (contained in the **System.Drawing** namespace). Method **Directory.GetCurrentDirectory** (contained in the **System.IO** namespace) returns the location of the folder in which the current project is located, including **bin**, the directory containing the compiled project files. The die images must be placed in this folder for the solutions in Fig. 6.15 and Fig. 6.16 to operate properly. The graphics used in this example and several other examples in this chapter were created with Adobe® Photoshop™ Elements and are located in the project directory available on the CD-ROM that accompanies this book and at **www.deitel.com**.

Notice that we must include an **Imports** directive (line 4) to use classes in **System.IO**, but not to use classes in **System.Drawing**. By default, Windows applications import several namespaces, including **Microsoft.VisualBasic**, **System**, **System.Drawing**, **System.Windows.Forms** and **System.Collections**. These namespaces are imported for the entire project, eliminating the need for **Imports** directives in individual project files. Other namespaces can be imported into a project via the **Property Pages** dialog (opened by selecting **Project > Properties** from the menu bar) in the **Imports** listing under **Common Properties**. Some of the namespaces imported by default are not used in this example. For instance, we do not yet use namespace **System.Collections**, which allows programmers to create collections of objects (see Chapter 24, Data Structures and Collections).

The Windows application in Fig. 6.16 rolls 12 dice to show that the numbers generated by class **Random** occur with approximately equal frequencies. The program displays the cumulative frequencies of each face in a **TextBox**.

```
1   ' Fig. 6.14: RandomInteger.vb
2   ' Generating random integers.
3
4   Imports System.Windows.Forms
5
6   Module modRandomInteger
7
8      Sub Main()
9         Dim randomObject As Random = New Random()
10        Dim randomNumber As Integer
11        Dim output As String = ""
12        Dim i As Integer
13
14        For i = 1 To 20
15           randomNumber = randomObject.Next(1, 7)
16           output &= randomNumber & " "
17
18           If i Mod 5 = 0 Then   ' is i a multiple of 5?
19              output &= vbCrLf
20           End If
21
22        Next
```

Fig. 6.14 Random integers created by calling method **Next** of class **Random** (part 1 of 2).

```
23
24              MessageBox.Show(output, "20 Random Numbers from 1 to 6", _
25                 MessageBoxButtons.OK, MessageBoxIcon.Information)
26         End Sub ' Main
27
28    End Module ' modRandomInteger
```

Fig. 6.14 Random integers created by calling method **Next** of class **Random** (part 2 of 2).

```
1     ' Fig. 6.15: RollDice.vb
2     ' Rolling four dice.
3
4     Imports System.IO
5
6     Public Class FrmRollDice
7        Inherits System.Windows.Forms.Form
8
9        ' button for rolling dice
10       Friend WithEvents cmdRoll As System.Windows.Forms.Button
11
12       ' labels to display die images
13       Friend WithEvents lblDie1 As System.Windows.Forms.Label
14       Friend WithEvents lblDie2 As System.Windows.Forms.Label
15       Friend WithEvents lblDie3 As System.Windows.Forms.Label
16       Friend WithEvents lblDie4 As System.Windows.Forms.Label
17
18       ' Visual Studio .NET generated code
19
20       ' declare Random object reference
21       Dim randomNumber As Random = New Random()
22
23       ' display results of four rolls
24       Private Sub cmdRoll_Click(ByVal sender As System.Object, _
25          ByVal e As System.EventArgs) Handles cmdRoll.Click
26
27          ' method randomly assigns a face to each die
28          DisplayDie(lblDie1)
29          DisplayDie(lblDie2)
30          DisplayDie(lblDie3)
31          DisplayDie(lblDie4)
32       End Sub ' cmdRoll_Click
33
```

Fig. 6.15 Demonstrates 4 die rolls (part 1 of 2).

```
34          ' get a random die image
35          Sub DisplayDie(ByVal dieLabel As Label)
36
37             ' generate random integer in range 1 to 6
38             Dim face As Integer = randomNumber.Next(1, 7)
39
40             ' load corresponding image
41             dieLabel.Image = Image.FromFile( _
42                Directory.GetCurrentDirectory & "\Images\die" & _
43                face & ".png")
44          End Sub ' DisplayDie
45
46       End Class ' FrmRollDice
```

Fig. 6.15 Demonstrates 4 die rolls (part 2 of 2).

Figure 6.16 contains two screenshots: One on the left that shows the program when the program initially executes and one on the right that shows the program after the user has clicked **Roll** over 200 times. If the values produced by method **Next** are indeed random, the frequencies of the face values (1–6) should be approximately the same (as the left screenshot illustrates).

To show that the die rolls occur with approximately equal likelihood, the program in Fig. 6.16 has been modified to keep some simple statistics. We declare counters for each of the possible rolls in line 31. Notice that the counters are instance variables, i.e., variables with class scope. Lines 60–76 display the frequency of each roll as percentages using the **"P"** format code.

As the program output demonstrates, we have utilized function **Next** to simulate the rolling of a six-sided die. Over the course of many die rolls, each of the possible faces from 1–6 appears with equal likelihood, or approximately one-sixth of the time. Note that *no* **Case Else** is provided in the **Select** structure (lines 91–111), because we know that the values generated are in the range 1–6. In Chapter 7, Arrays, we explain how to replace the entire **Select** structure in this program with a single-line statement.

Run the program several times and observe the results. Notice that a different sequence of random numbers is obtained each time the program is executed, causing the resulting frequencies to vary.

```vb
1   ' Fig. 6.16: RollTwelveDice.vb
2   ' Rolling 12 dice with frequency chart.
3
4   Imports System.IO
5
6   Public Class FrmRollTwelveDice
7      Inherits System.Windows.Forms.Form
8
9      ' labels to display die images
10     Friend WithEvents lblDie1 As System.Windows.Forms.Label
11     Friend WithEvents lblDie2 As System.Windows.Forms.Label
12     Friend WithEvents lblDie3 As System.Windows.Forms.Label
13     Friend WithEvents lblDie4 As System.Windows.Forms.Label
14     Friend WithEvents lblDie5 As System.Windows.Forms.Label
15     Friend WithEvents lblDie6 As System.Windows.Forms.Label
16     Friend WithEvents lblDie7 As System.Windows.Forms.Label
17     Friend WithEvents lblDie8 As System.Windows.Forms.Label
18     Friend WithEvents lblDie9 As System.Windows.Forms.Label
19     Friend WithEvents lblDie10 As System.Windows.Forms.Label
20     Friend WithEvents lblDie11 As System.Windows.Forms.Label
21     Friend WithEvents lblDie12 As System.Windows.Forms.Label
22
23     ' displays roll frequencies
24     Friend WithEvents displayTextBox As _
25        System.Windows.Forms.TextBox
26
27     ' Visual Studio .NET generated code
28
29     ' declarations
30     Dim randomObject As Random = New Random()
31     Dim ones, twos, threes, fours, fives, sixes As Integer
32
33     Private Sub cmdRoll_Click _
34        (ByVal sender As System.Object, _
35        ByVal e As System.EventArgs) Handles cmdRoll.Click
36
37        ' assign random faces to 12 dice using DisplayDie
38        DisplayDie(lblDie1)
39        DisplayDie(lblDie2)
40        DisplayDie(lblDie3)
41        DisplayDie(lblDie4)
42        DisplayDie(lblDie5)
43        DisplayDie(lblDie6)
44        DisplayDie(lblDie7)
45        DisplayDie(lblDie8)
46        DisplayDie(lblDie9)
47        DisplayDie(lblDie10)
48        DisplayDie(lblDie11)
49        DisplayDie(lblDie12)
50
51        Dim total As Integer = ones + twos + threes + fours + _
52           fives + sixes
53
```

Fig. 6.16 Random class used to simulate rolling 12 six-sided dice (part 1 of 3).

```vb
54          Dim output As String
55
56          ' display frequencies of faces
57          output = "Face" & vbTab & vbTab & _
58             "Frequency" & vbTab & "Percent"
59
60          output &= vbCrLf & "1" & vbTab & vbTab & ones & _
61             vbTab & vbTab & String.Format("{0:P}", ones / total)
62
63          output &= vbCrLf & "2" & vbTab & vbTab & twos & vbTab & _
64             vbTab & String.Format("{0:P}", twos / total)
65
66          output &= vbCrLf & "3" & vbTab & vbTab & threes & vbTab & _
67             vbTab & String.Format("{0:P}", threes / total)
68
69          output &= vbCrLf & "4" & vbTab & vbTab & fours & vbTab & _
70             vbTab & String.Format("{0:P}", fours / total)
71
72          output &= vbCrLf & "5" & vbTab & vbTab & fives & vbTab & _
73             vbTab & String.Format("{0:P}", fives / total)
74
75          output &= vbCrLf & "6" & vbTab & vbTab & sixes & vbTab & _
76             vbTab & String.Format("{0:P}", sixes / total) & vbCrLf
77
78          displayTextBox.Text = output
79       End Sub ' cmdRoll_Click
80
81       ' display a single die image
82       Sub DisplayDie(ByVal dieLabel As Label)
83
84          Dim face As Integer = randomObject.Next(1, 7)
85
86          dieLabel.Image = _
87             Image.FromFile(Directory.GetCurrentDirectory & _
88             "\Images\die" & face & ".png")
89
90          ' maintain count of die faces
91          Select Case face
92
93             Case 1
94                ones += 1
95
96             Case 2
97                twos += 1
98
99             Case 3
100               threes += 1
101
102            Case 4
103               fours += 1
104
105            Case 5
106               fives += 1
```

Fig. 6.16 `Random` class used to simulate rolling 12 six-sided dice (part 2 of 3).

```
107
108             Case 6
109                 sixes += 1
110
111         End Select
112
113     End Sub ' DisplayDie
114
```

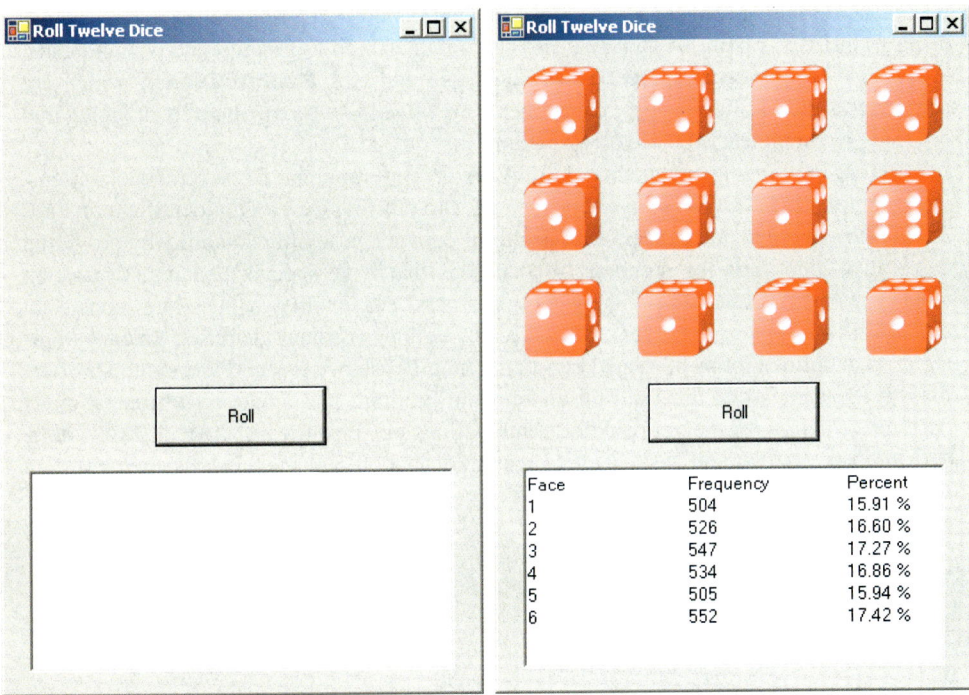

Fig. 6.16 Random class used to simulate rolling 12 six-sided dice (part 3 of 3).

6.13 Example: Game of Chance

One of the most popular games of chance is a dice game known as "craps," played in casinos and back alleys throughout the world. The rules of the game are straightforward:

> *A player rolls two dice. Each die has six faces. Each face contains 1, 2, 3, 4, 5 or 6 spots. After the dice have come to rest, the sum of the spots on the two upward faces is calculated. If the sum is 7 or 11 on the first throw, the player wins. If the sum is 2, 3 or 12 on the first throw (called "craps"), the player loses (i.e., the "house" wins). If the sum is 4, 5, 6, 8, 9 or 10 on the first throw, that sum becomes the player's "point." To win, players must continue rolling the dice until they "make their point" (i.e., roll their point value). The player loses by rolling a 7 before making the point.*

The application in Fig. 6.17 simulates the game of craps.

Notice that the player must roll two dice on the first and all subsequent rolls. When executing the application, click the **Play** button to play the game. The form displays the results of each roll. The screen captures depict the execution of two games.

Lines 9–21 indicate that this program uses classes **PictureBox**, **Label**, **Button** and **GroupBox** from namespace **System.Windows.Forms**. Although the Windows Form Designer uses the full name for these classes (e.g., **System.Windows.Forms.PictureBox**), we show only the class names for simplicity. Class names are sufficient in this case, because **System.Windows.Forms** is imported by default for Windows applications.

This program introduces several new GUI components. The first, called a **GroupBox**, displays the user's point. A **GroupBox** is a container used to group related components. Within the **GroupBox pointDiceGroup**, we add two **PictureBox**es, which are components that display images. Components are added to a **GroupBox** by dragging and dropping a component onto the **GroupBox**.

Before introducing any method definitions, the program includes several declarations, including our first **Enum**eration on lines 26–32 and our first **Const**ant identifiers on lines 35–36. **Const**ant identifiers and **Enum**erations enhance program readability by providing descriptive identifiers for numbers or **String**s that have special meaning. **Const**ant identifiers and **Enum**erations help programmers ensure that values are consistent throughout a program. Keyword **Const** creates a single constant identifier; **Enum**erations are used to define groups of related constants. In this case, we create **Const**ant identifiers for the file names that are used throughout the program and create an **Enum**eration of descriptive names for the various dice combinations in Craps (i.e., **SNAKE_EYES**, **TREY**, **CRAPS**, **YO_LEVEN** and **BOX_CARS**). **Const**ant identifiers must be assigned constant values and cannot be modified after they are declared.

```vb
1   ' Fig 6.17: CrapsGame.vb
2   ' Playing a craps game.
3
4   Imports System.IO
5
6   Public Class FrmCrapsGame
7      Inherits System.Windows.Forms.Form
8
9      Friend WithEvents cmdRoll As Button ' rolls dice
10     Friend WithEvents cmdPlay As Button ' starts new game
11
12     ' dice displayed after each roll
13     Friend WithEvents picDie1 As PictureBox
14     Friend WithEvents picDie2 As PictureBox
15
16     ' pointDiceGroup groups dice representing player's point
17     Friend WithEvents pointDiceGroup As GroupBox
18     Friend WithEvents picPointDie1 As PictureBox
19     Friend WithEvents picPointDie2 As PictureBox
20
21     Friend WithEvents lblStatus As Label
22
```

Fig. 6.17 Craps game using class **Random** (part 1 of 4).

```vb
23      ' Visual Studio .NET generated code
24
25      ' die-roll constants
26      Enum DiceNames
27         SNAKE_EYES = 2
28         TREY = 3
29         CRAPS = 7
30         YO_LEVEN = 11
31         BOX_CARS = 12
32      End Enum
33
34      ' file-name and directory constants
35      Const FILE_PREFIX As String = "/images/die"
36      Const FILE_SUFFIX As String = ".png"
37
38      Dim myPoint As Integer
39      Dim myDie1 As Integer
40      Dim myDie2 As Integer
41      Dim randomObject As Random = New Random()
42
43      ' begins new game and determines point
44      Private Sub cmdPlay_Click(ByVal sender As System.Object, _
45         ByVal e As System.EventArgs) Handles cmdPlay.Click
46
47         ' initialize variables for new game
48         myPoint = 0
49         pointDiceGroup.Text = "Point"
50         lblStatus.Text = ""
51
52         ' remove point-die images
53         picPointDie1.Image = Nothing
54         picPointDie2.Image = Nothing
55
56         Dim sum As Integer = RollDice()
57
58         ' check die roll
59         Select Case sum
60
61            Case DiceNames.CRAPS, DiceNames.YO_LEVEN
62
63               ' disable roll button
64               cmdRoll.Enabled = False
65               lblStatus.Text = "You Win!!!"
66
67            Case DiceNames.SNAKE_EYES, _
68               DiceNames.TREY, DiceNames.BOX_CARS
69
70               cmdRoll.Enabled = False
71               lblStatus.Text = "Sorry. You Lose."
72
73            Case Else
74               myPoint = sum
75               pointDiceGroup.Text = "Point is " & sum
```

Fig. 6.17 Craps game using class **Random** (part 2 of 4).

```vb
76             lblStatus.Text = "Roll Again!"
77             DisplayDie(picPointDie1, myDie1)
78             DisplayDie(picPointDie2, myDie2)
79             cmdPlay.Enabled = False
80             cmdRoll.Enabled = True
81
82         End Select
83
84     End Sub ' cmdPlay_Click
85
86     ' determines outcome of next roll
87     Private Sub cmdRoll_Click(ByVal sender As System.Object, _
88         ByVal e As System.EventArgs) Handles cmdRoll.Click
89
90         Dim sum As Integer = RollDice()
91
92         ' check outcome of roll
93         If sum = myPoint Then
94             lblStatus.Text = "You Win!!!"
95             cmdRoll.Enabled = False
96             cmdPlay.Enabled = True
97         ElseIf sum = DiceNames.CRAPS Then
98             lblStatus.Text = "Sorry. You Lose."
99             cmdRoll.Enabled = False
100            cmdPlay.Enabled = True
101        End If
102
103    End Sub ' cmdRoll_Click
104
105    ' display die image
106    Sub DisplayDie(ByVal picDie As PictureBox, _
107        ByVal face As Integer)
108
109        ' assign die image to picture box
110        picDie.Image = _
111            Image.FromFile(Directory.GetCurrentDirectory & _
112            FILE_PREFIX & face & FILE_SUFFIX)
113    End Sub ' DisplayDie
114
115    ' generate random die rolls
116    Function RollDice() As Integer
117        Dim die1, die2 As Integer
118
119        ' determine random integer
120        die1 = randomObject.Next(1, 7)
121        die2 = randomObject.Next(1, 7)
122
123        ' display rolls
124        DisplayDie(picDie1, die1)
125        DisplayDie(picDie2, die2)
126
```

Fig. 6.17 Craps game using class **Random** (part 3 of 4).

```
127            ' set values
128            myDie1 = die1
129            myDie2 = die2
130
131            Return die1 + die2
132        End Function ' RollDice
133
134 End Class ' FrmCrapsGame
```

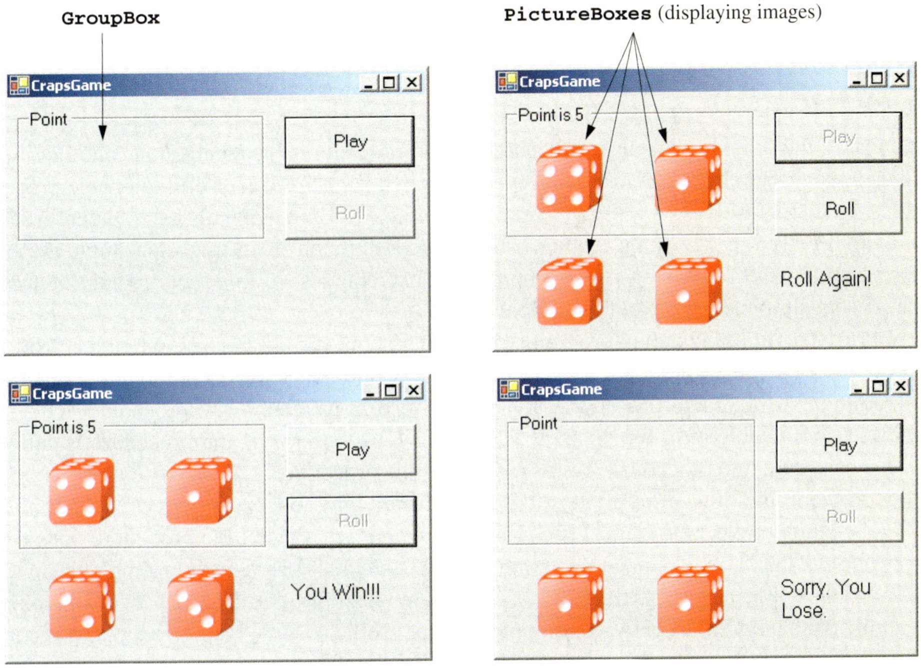

Fig. 6.17 Craps game using class **Random** (part 4 of 4).

After the constant-identifier declarations and the declarations for several instance variables (lines 38–41), method **cmdPlay_Click** is defined (lines 44–84). Method **cmdPlay_Click** is the event handler for the event **cmdPlay.Click** (created by double-clicking **cmdPlay** in **Design** mode). In this example, the method's task is to process a user's interaction with **Button cmdPlay** (which displays the text **Play** on the user interface).

When the user clicks the **Play** button, method **cmdPlay_Click** sets up a new game by initializing several values (lines 48–50). Setting the **Image** property of **picPointDie1** and **picPointDie2** to **Nothing** (lines 53–54) causes the **PictureBox**es to appear blank. Keyword **Nothing** can be used with reference-type variables to specify that no object is associated with the variable.

Method **cmdPlay_Click** executes the game's opening roll by calling **RollDice** (line 56). Internally, **RollDice** (lines 116–132) generates two random numbers and calls method **DisplayDie** (lines 106–113), which loads an appropriate die image on the **PictureBox** passed to it.

When **RollDice** returns, the **Select** structure (lines 59–82) analyzes the roll returned by **RollDice** to determine how play should continue (i.e., by terminating the game with a win or loss, or by enabling subsequent rolls). Depending on the value of the roll, the buttons **cmdRoll** and **cmdPlay** become either enabled or disabled. Disabling a **Button** causes no action to be performed when the **Button** is clicked. **Button**s can be enabled and disabled by setting the **Enabled** property to **True** or **False**.

If **Button cmdRoll** is enabled, clicking it invokes method **cmdRoll_Click** (lines 87–103), which executes an additional roll of the dice. Method **cmdRoll_Click** then analyzes the roll, letting users know whether they won or lost.

6.14 Recursion

In most of the programs we have discussed so far, procedures have called one another in a disciplined, hierarchical manner. However, in some instances, it is useful to enable procedures to call themselves. A *recursive procedure* is a procedure that calls itself either directly or indirectly (i.e., through another procedure). Recursion is an important topic that is discussed at length in upper-level computer science courses. In this section and the next, we present simple examples of recursion.

Prior to examining actual programs containing recursive procedures, we first consider recursion conceptually. Recursive problem-solving approaches have a number of elements in common. A recursive procedure is called to solve a problem. The procedure actually knows how to solve only the simplest case(s), or *base case(s)*. If the procedure is called with a base case, the procedure returns a result. If the procedure is called with a more complex problem, the procedure divides the problem into two conceptual pieces; a piece that the procedure knows how to perform (base case), and a piece that the procedure does not know how to perform. To make recursion feasible, the latter piece must resemble the original problem, but be a slightly simpler or smaller version of it. The procedure invokes (calls) a fresh copy of itself to work on the smaller problem—this is referred to as a *recursive call*, or a *recursion step*. The recursion step also normally includes the keyword **Return**, because its result will be combined with the portion of the problem that the procedure knew how to solve. Such a combination will form a result that will be passed back to the original caller.

The recursion step executes while the original call to the procedure is still "open" (i.e., has not finished executing). The recursion step can result in many more recursive calls, as the procedure divides each new subproblem into two conceptual pieces. As the procedure continues to call itself with slightly simpler versions of the original problem, the sequence of smaller and smaller problems must converge on the base case, so that the recursion can eventually terminate. At that point, the procedure recognizes the base case and returns a result to the previous copy of the procedure. A sequence of returns ensues up the line until the original procedure call returns the final result to the caller. As an example of these concepts, let us write a recursive program that performs a popular mathematical calculation.

The factorial of a nonnegative integer n, written $n!$ (and read "n factorial"), is the product

$$n \cdot (n-1) \cdot (n-2) \cdot \ldots \cdot 1$$

with $1!$ equal to 1, and $0!$ defined as 1. For example, $5!$ is the product $5 \cdot 4 \cdot 3 \cdot 2 \cdot 1$, which is equal to 120.

The factorial of an integer **number** greater than or equal to 0 can be calculated *iteratively* (nonrecursively) using a **For** repetition structure, as follows:

```
Dim counter, factorial As Integer = 1

For counter = number To 1 Step -1
    factorial *= counter
Next
```

We arrive at a recursive definition of the factorial procedure with the following relationship:

$n! = n \cdot (n-1)!$

For example, 5! is clearly equal to 5 · 4!, as is shown by the following:

$5! = 5 \cdot 4 \cdot 3 \cdot 2 \cdot 1$
$5! = 5 \cdot (4 \cdot 3 \cdot 2 \cdot 1)$
$5! = 5 \cdot (4!)$

A recursive evaluation of 5! would proceed as in Fig. 6.18. Figure 6.18a shows how the succession of recursive calls proceeds until 1! is evaluated to be 1, which terminates the recursion. Figure 6.18b depicts the values that are returned from each recursive call to its caller until the final value is calculated and returned.

The program of Fig. 6.19 recursively calculates and prints factorials. (The choice of the data type **Long** will be explained soon). The recursive method **Factorial** (lines 33–41) first tests (line 35) to determine whether its terminating condition is true (i.e., **number** is less than or equal to 1). If **number** is less than or equal to 1, **Factorial** returns **1**, no further recursion is necessary, and the method returns. If **number** is greater than **1**, line 38 expresses the problem as the product of **number** and a recursive call to **Factorial**, evaluating the factorial of **number - 1**. Note that **Factorial(number - 1)** is a slightly simpler problem than the original calculation, **Factorial(number)**.

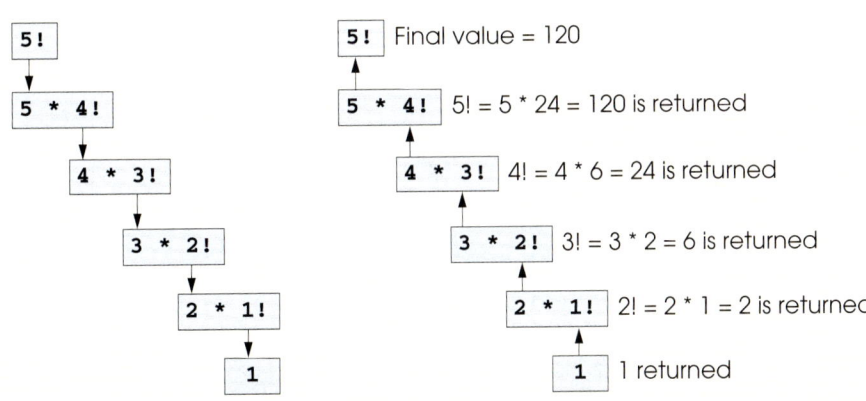

(a) Procession of recursive calls   (b) Values returned from each recursive call

Fig. 6.18 Recursive evaluation of 5!.

Function Factorial (line 33) receives a parameter of type **Long** and returns a result of type **Long**. As is seen in the output window of Fig. 6.19, factorial values escalate quickly. We choose data type **Long** to enable the program to calculate factorials greater than 12!. Unfortunately, the values produced by the **Factorial** method increase at such a rate that the range of even the **Long** type is quickly exceeded. This points to a weakness in most programming languages: They are not easily extended to handle the unique requirements of various applications, such as the evaluation of large factorials. As we will see in our treatment of object-oriented programming beginning in Chapter 8, Visual Basic is an extensible language—programmers with unique requirements can extend the language with new data types (called classes). For example, a programmer could create a **HugeInteger** class that would enable a program to calculate the factorials of arbitrarily large numbers.

```vb
1   ' Fig. 6.19: Factorial.vb
2   ' Calculating factorials using recursion.
3
4   Public Class FrmFactorial
5      Inherits System.Windows.Forms.Form
6
7      Friend WithEvents lblEnter As Label       ' prompts for Integer
8      Friend WithEvents lblFactorial As Label   ' indicates output
9
10     Friend WithEvents txtInput As TextBox     ' reads an Integer
11     Friend WithEvents txtDisplay As TextBox   ' displays output
12
13     Friend WithEvents cmdCalculate As Button  ' generates output
14
15     ' Visual Studio .NET generated code
16
17     Private Sub cmdCalculate_Click(ByVal sender As System.Object, _
18        ByVal e As System.EventArgs) Handles cmdCalculate.Click
19
20        Dim value As Integer = Convert.ToInt32(txtInput.Text)
21        Dim i As Integer
22        Dim output As String
23
24        txtDisplay.Text = ""
25
26        For i = 0 To value
27           txtDisplay.Text &= i & "! = " & Factorial(i) & vbCrLf
28        Next
29
30     End Sub ' cmdCalculate_Click
31
32     ' recursively generates factorial of number
33     Function Factorial(ByVal number As Long) As Long
34
35        If number <= 1 Then ' base case
36           Return 1
37        Else
38           Return number * Factorial(number - 1)
39        End If
```

Fig. 6.19 Recursive factorial program (part 1 of 2).

```
40
41      End Function ' Factorial
42
43  End Class ' FrmFactorial
```

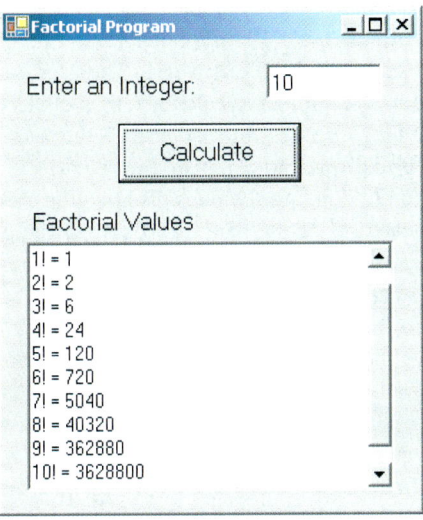

Fig. 6.19 Recursive factorial program (part 2 of 2).

Common Programming Error 6.8

Forgetting to return a value from a recursive procedure can result in logic errors.

Common Programming Error 6.9

Omitting the base case or writing the recursive step so that it does not converge on the base case will cause infinite recursion, *eventually exhausting memory. This is analogous to the problem of an infinite loop in an iterative (nonrecursive) solution.*

6.15 Example Using Recursion: Fibonacci Series

The Fibonacci series

0, 1, 1, 2, 3, 5, 8, 13, 21, ...

begins with 0 and 1 and defines each subsequent Fibonacci number as the sum of the previous two Fibonacci numbers.

The series occurs in nature and, in particular, describes a form of spiral. The ratio of successive Fibonacci numbers converges on a constant value near 1.618. This number occurs repeatedly in nature and has been called the *golden ratio* or the *golden mean*. Humans tend to find the golden mean aesthetically pleasing. Architects often design windows, rooms and buildings so that their ratios of length to width are equal to the golden mean. Similarly, postcards often are designed with a golden-mean width-to-height ratio.

The Fibonacci series can be defined recursively as follows:

fibonacci(0) = 0
fibonacci(1) = 1
fibonacci(n) = *fibonacci*(n – 1) + *fibonacci*(n – 2)

Note that there are two base cases for the Fibonacci calculation—*fibonacci(0)* is defined to be 0, and *fibonacci(1)* is defined to be 1. The application in Fig. 6.20 recursively calculates the ith Fibonacci number via method **Fibonacci**. The user enters an integer in the text box, indicating the ith Fibonacci number to calculate, then clicks **cmdCalculate**. Method **cmdCalculate_Click** executes in response to the user clicking **Calculate** and calls recursive method **Fibonacci** to calculate the specified Fibonacci number. Notice that Fibonacci numbers, like the factorial values discussed in the previous section, tend to become large quickly. Therefore, we use data type **Long** as the parameter type and the return type in method **Fibonacci**. In Fig. 6.20, the screen captures display the results of several Fibonacci-number calculations performed by the application.

The event handling in this example is similar to that of the **Maximum** application in Fig. 6.4. In this example, the user enters a value in a text box and clicks **Calculate Fibonacci**, causing method **cmdCalculate_Click** to execute.

The call to **Fibonacci** (line 23) from **cmdCalculate_Click** is not a recursive call, but all subsequent calls to **Fibonacci** (line 33) are recursive. Each time that **Fibonacci** is invoked, it immediately tests for the base case, which occurs when **number** is equal to **0** or **1** (line 30). If this condition is true, **number** is returned, because *fibonacci(0)* is **0** and *fibonacci(1)* is **1**. Interestingly, if **number** is greater than **1**, the recursion step generates *two* recursive calls, each representing a slightly simpler problem than is presented by the original call to **Fibonacci**. Figure 6.21 illustrates how method **Fibonacci** would evaluate **Fibonacci(3)**.

```
1    ' Fig. 6.20: Fibonacci.vb
2    ' Demonstrating Fibonacci sequence recursively.
3
4    Public Class FrmFibonacci
5       Inherits System.Windows.Forms.Form
6
7       Friend WithEvents lblPrompt As Label   ' prompts for input
8       Friend WithEvents lblResult As Label   ' displays result
9
10      Friend WithEvents cmdCalculate As Button  ' calculates result
11
12      Friend WithEvents txtInputBox As TextBox  ' reads an Integer
13
14      ' Visual Studio .NET generated code
15
16      ' displays Fibonacci number in txtInputBox
17      Private Sub cmdCalculate_Click(ByVal sender As System.Object, _
18         ByVal e As System.EventArgs) Handles cmdCalculate.Click
19
20         ' read input
21         Dim number As Integer = Convert.ToInt32(txtInputBox.Text)
22
```

Fig. 6.20 Recursively generating Fibonacci numbers (part 1 of 3).

```
23          lblResult.Text = "Fibonacci Value is " & Fibonacci(number)
24       End Sub ' cmdCalculate_Click
25
26       ' calculate Fibonacci value recusively
27       Function Fibonacci(ByVal number As Integer) As Long
28
29          ' check for base cases
30          If number = 1 OrElse number = 0 Then
31             Return number
32          Else
33             Return Fibonacci(number - 1) + Fibonacci(number - 2)
34          End If
35
36       End Function ' Fibonacci
37
38    End Class ' FrmFibonacci
```

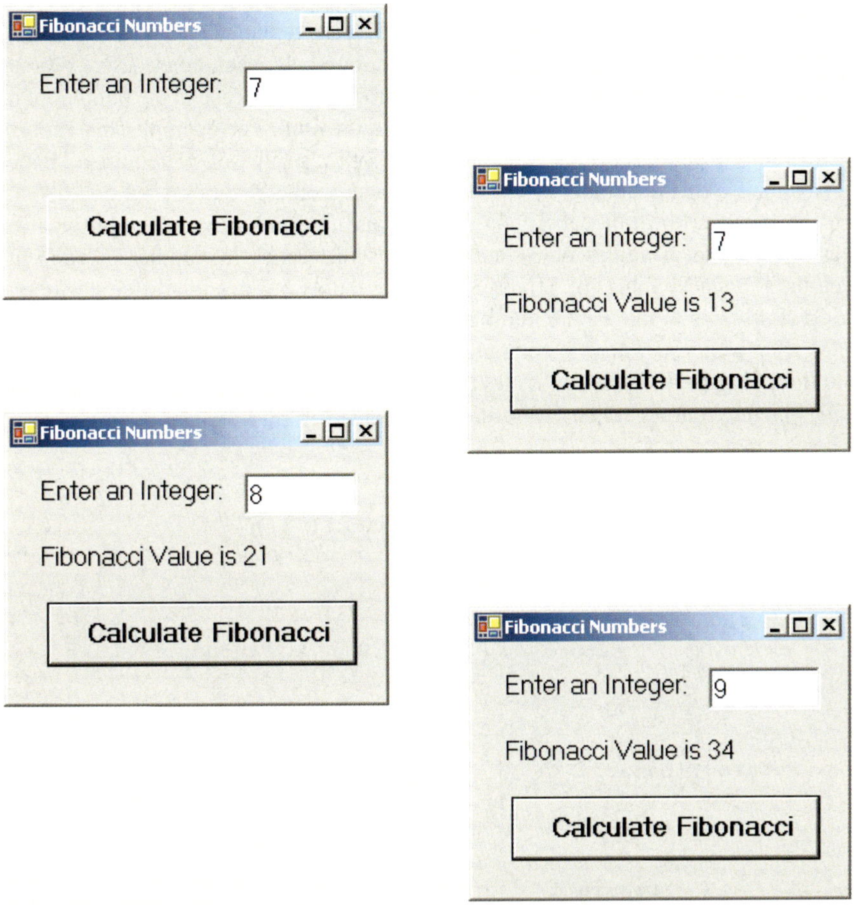

Fig. 6.20 Recursively generating Fibonacci numbers (part 2 of 3).

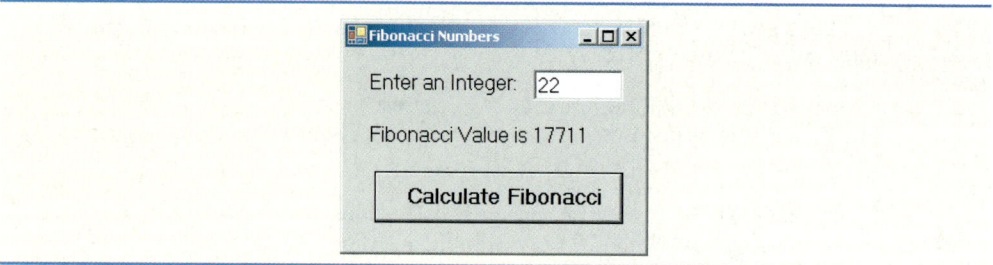

Fig. 6.20 Recursively generating Fibonacci numbers (part 3 of 3).

A word of caution about using a recursive program to generate Fibonacci numbers: Each invocation of the **Fibonacci** method that does not match one of the base cases (i.e., 0 or 1) results in two additional recursive calls to the **Fibonacci** method. This quickly results in an exponential "explosion" of calls. For example, the calculation of the Fibonacci value of 20 using the program in Fig. 6.20 requires 21,891 calls to the **Fibonacci** method; the calculation of the Fibonacci value of 30 requires 2,692,537 calls to the **Fibonacci** method.

As the programmer evaluates larger Fibonacci numbers, each consecutive Fibonacci that the program is asked to calculate results in a substantial increase in the number of calls to the **Fibonacci** method and hence in calculation time. For example, the Fibonacci value 31 requires 4,356,617 calls, whereas the Fibonacci value of 32 requires 7,049,155 calls. As you can see, the number of calls to Fibonacci increases quickly—1,664,080 additional calls between the Fibonacci values of 30 and 31, and 2,692,538 additional calls between the Fibonacci values of 31 and 32. This difference in number of calls made between the Fibonacci values of 31 and 32 is more than 1.5 times the difference between 30 and 31. Problems of this nature humble even the world's most powerful computers! In the field called *complexity theory*, computer scientists determine how hard algorithms must work to do their jobs. Complexity issues usually are discussed in detail in the upper-level computer science courses called "Algorithms."

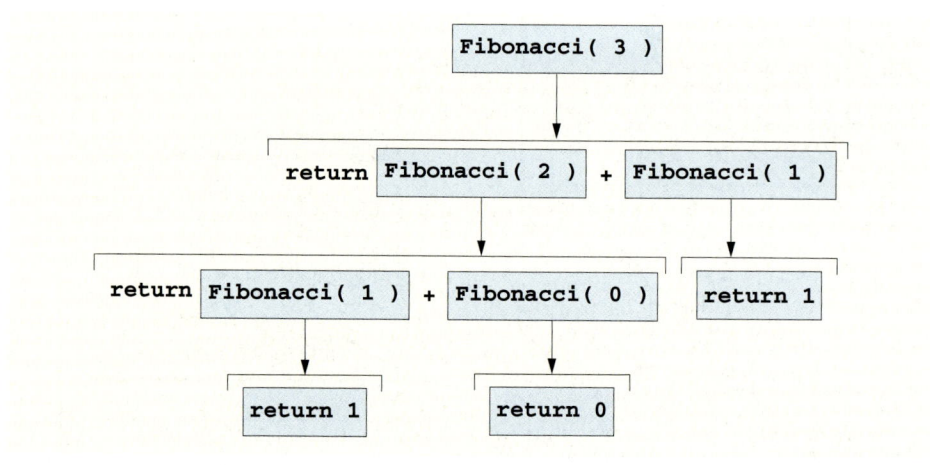

Fig. 6.21 Recursive calls to method **Fibonacci**.

Performance Tip 6.3

Avoid Fibonacci-style recursive programs, which result in an exponential "explosion" of calls.

6.16 Recursion vs. Iteration

In the previous sections, we studied two methods that can be implemented either recursively or iteratively. In this section, we compare the two approaches and discuss the reasons why the programmer might choose one approach over the other.

Iteration and recursion are based on control structures—iteration uses a repetition structure (such as **For**, **While** or **Do/Loop Until**), whereas recursion uses a selection structure (such as **If/Then**, **If/Then/Else** or **Select**). Although both processes involve repetition, iteration involves an explicit repetition structure, and recursion achieves repetition through repeated procedure calls. The termination tests employed by the two procedures are also different. Iteration with counter-controlled repetition continues to modify a counter until the counter's value satisfies the loop-continuation condition. By contrast, recursion produces simpler versions of the original problem until a base case is reached and execution stops. However, both iteration and recursion can execute infinitely: An infinite loop occurs in an iterative structure if the loop-continuation test is never satisfied; infinite recursion occurs if the recursion step does not reduce the problem so that it eventually converges on the base case.

Recursion has many disadvantages. It repeatedly invokes the mechanism, and consequently the overhead, of procedure calls, consuming both processor time and memory space. Each recursive call causes another copy of the procedure's variables to be created; when many layers of recursion are necessary, this can consume considerable amounts of memory. Iteration normally occurs within a procedure, which enables the program to avoid the overhead of repeated procedure calls and extra memory assignment. Why, then, would a programmer choose recursion?

Software Engineering Observation 6.14

Any problem that can be solved recursively also can be solved iteratively (nonrecursively). A recursive approach normally is chosen over an iterative approach when the recursive approach more naturally mirrors the problem and results in a program that is easier to understand and debug. Recursive solutions also are employed when iterative solutions are not apparent.

Performance Tip 6.4

Avoid using recursion in performance situations. Recursive calls take time and consume additional memory.

Common Programming Error 6.10

Accidentally having a nonrecursive procedure call itself through another procedure can cause infinite recursion.

Most programming textbooks introduce recursion much later than we have done in this book. However, we feel that recursion is a rich and complex topic; thus, we introduce it early and include additional examples throughout the remainder of the text.

6.17 Procedure Overloading and Optional Arguments

Visual Basic provides several ways of allowing procedures to have variable sets of parameters. *Overloading* allows the programmer to create multiple procedures with the same name, but differing numbers and types of arguments. This allows the programmer to reduce the complexity of the program and create a more flexible application. Procedures also can receive *optional arguments*. Defining an argument as optional allows the calling procedure to decide what arguments to pass. Optional arguments normally specify a default value that is assigned to the parameter if the optional argument is not passed. Overloaded procedures are generally more flexible than procedures with optional arguments. For instance, the programmer can specify varying return types for overloaded procedures. However, optional arguments present a simple way of specifying default values.

6.17.1 Procedure Overloading

By overloading, a programmer can define several procedures with the same name, as long as these procedures have different sets of parameters (number of parameters, types of parameters or order of the parameters). When an overloaded procedure is called, the compiler selects the proper procedure by examining the number, types and order of the call's arguments. Often, procedure overloading is used to create several procedures with the same name that perform similar tasks on different data types.

Good Programming Practice 6.6

The overloading of procedures that perform closely related tasks can make programs more readable and understandable.

The program in Fig. 6.22 uses overloaded method **Square** to calculate the square of both an **Integer** and a **Double**.

```
1    ' Fig. 6.22: Overload.vb
2    ' Using overloaded methods.
3
4    Public Class FrmOverload
5       Inherits System.Windows.Forms.Form
6
7       Friend WithEvents outputLabel As Label
8
9       ' Visual Studio .NET generated code
10
11      Private Sub FrmOverload_Load(ByVal sender As System.Object, _
12         ByVal e As System.EventArgs) Handles MyBase.Load
13
14         outputLabel.Text = "The square of Integer 7 is " & _
15            Square(7) & vbCrLf & "The square of Double " & _
16            "7.5 is " & Square(7.5)
17      End Sub ' FrmOverload_Load
18
19      Function Square(ByVal value As Integer) As Integer
20         Return Convert.ToInt32(value ^ 2)
21      End Function ' Square
```

Fig. 6.22 Overloaded methods (part 1 of 2).

```
22
23        Function Square(ByVal value As Double) As Double
24            Return value ^ 2
25        End Function ' Square
26
27   End Class ' FrmOverload
```

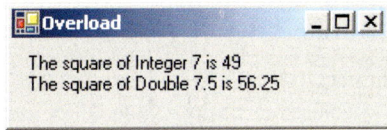

Fig. 6.22 Overloaded methods (part 2 of 2).

Overloaded procedures are distinguished by their *signatures*, which are a combination of the procedure's name and parameter types. If the compiler looked only at procedure names during compilation, the code in Fig. 6.22 would be ambiguous—the compiler would not know how to differentiate between the two **Square** methods. The compiler uses a logical process known as *overload resolution* to determine which procedure should be called. This process first searches for all procedures that *could* be used on the basis of the number and type of arguments that are present. Although it might seem that only one procedure would match, it is important to remember that Visual Basic promotes variables with implicit conversions when they are passed as arguments. Once all matching procedures are found, the compiler then selects the closest match. This match is based on a "best-fit" algorithm, which analyzes the implicit conversions that will take place.

Let us look at an example. In Fig. 6.22, the compiler might use the logical name "**Square** of **Integer**" for the **Square** method that specifies an **Integer** parameter (line 19) and "**Square** of **Double**" for the **Square** method that specifies a **Double** parameter (line 23). If a method **ExampleSub**'s definition begins as

```
Function ExampleSub(ByVal a As Integer, ByVal b As Double) _
    As Integer
```

the compiler might use the logical name "**ExampleSub** of **Integer** and **Double**." Similarly, if the parameters are specified as

```
Function ExampleSub(ByVal a As Double, ByVal b As Integer) _
    As Integer
```

the compiler might use the logical name "**ExampleSub** of **Double** and **Integer**." The order of the parameters is important to the compiler; it considers the preceding two **ExampleSub** methods to be distinct.

So far, the logical method names used by the compiler have not mentioned the methods' return types. This is because procedure calls cannot be distinguished by return type. The program in Fig. 6.23 illustrates the syntax error that is generated when two procedures have the same signature and different return types. Overloaded procedures with different parameter lists can have different return types. Overloaded procedures need not have the same number of parameters.

> **Common Programming Error 6.11**
>
> *The creation of overloaded procedures with identical parameter lists and different return types produces a syntax error.*

The output window displayed in Fig. 6.23 is the **Task List** of Visual Studio. By default, the **Task List** displays at the bottom of the IDE when a compiler error is generated.

6.17.2 Optional Arguments

Visual Basic allows programmers to create procedures that take one or more optional arguments. When a parameter is declared as optional, the caller has the *option* of passing that particular argument. Optional arguments are specified in the procedure header with keyword **Optional**. For example, the procedure header

```vb
1   ' Fig. 6.23: Overload2.vb
2   ' Using overloaded procedures with identical signatures and
3   ' different return types.
4
5   Public Class FrmOverload2
6      Inherits System.Windows.Forms.Form
7
8      Friend WithEvents outputLabel As Label
9
10     ' Visual Studio .NET generated code
11
12     Private Sub FrmOverload2_Load(ByVal sender As System.Object, _
13        ByVal e As System.EventArgs) Handles MyBase.Load
14
15        outputLabel.Text = "The square of Integer 7 is " & _
16           Square(7) & vbCrLf & "The square of Double " & _
17           "7.5 is " & Square(7.5)
18     End Sub ' FrmOverload2_Load
19
20     Function Square(ByVal value As Double) As Integer
21        Return Convert.ToInt32(value ^ 2)
22     End Function ' Square
23
24     Function Square(ByVal value As Double) As Double
25        Return value ^ 2
26     End Function ' Square
27
28  End Class ' FrmOverload2
```

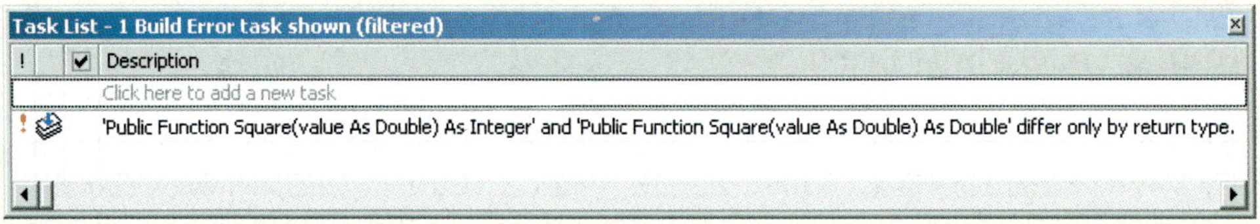

Task List - 1 Build Error task shown (filtered)

'Public Function Square(value As Double) As Integer' and 'Public Function Square(value As Double) As Double' differ only by return type.

Fig. 6.23 Syntax error generated from overloaded procedures with identical parameter lists and different return types.

```
Sub ExampleProcedure(ByVal value1 As Boolean, Optional _
    ByVal value2 As Long = 0)
```

specifies the last parameter as **Optional**. Any call to **ExampleProcedure** must pass at least one argument, or else a syntax error is generated. If the caller chooses, a second argument can be passed to **ExampleProcedure**. This is demonstrated by the following calls to **ExampleProcedure**:

```
ExampleProcedure()
ExampleProcedure(True)
ExampleProcedure(False, 10)
```

The first call to **ExampleProcedure** generates a syntax error, because a minimum of one argument is required. The second call to **ExampleProcedure** is valid because one argument is being passed. The **Optional** argument, **value2**, is not specified in the procedure call. The last call to **ExampleProcedure** also is valid: **False** is passed as the one required argument, and **10** is passed as the **Optional** argument.

In the call that passes only one argument (**True**) to **ExampleProcedure**, **value2** defaults to **0**, which is the value specified in the procedure header. **Optional** arguments must specify a *default value*, using the equals sign followed by the value. For example, the header for **ExampleProcedure** sets **0** as the default value for **value2**. Default values can be used only with parameters declared as **Optional**.

Common Programming Error 6.12

*Not specifying a default value for an **Optional** parameter is a syntax error.*

Common Programming Error 6.13

*Declaring a non-**Optional** parameter to the right of an **Optional** parameter is a syntax error.*

The example in Fig. 6.24 demonstrates the use of optional arguments. The program calculates the result of raising a base to an exponent, both of which are specified by the user. If the user does not specify an exponent, the **Optional** argument is omitted, and the default value, **2**, is used.

Line 27 determines whether **txtPower** contains a value. If true, the values in the **TextBox**es are converted to **Integer**s and passed to **Power**. Otherwise, **txtBase**'s value is converted to an **Integer** and passed as the first of two arguments to **Power** in line 31. The second argument, which has a value of **2**, is provided by the Visual Basic compiler and is not visible to the programmer in the call.

Method **Power** (lines 38–49) specifies that its second argument is **Optional**. When omitted, the second argument defaults to the value **2**.

```
1   ' Fig 6.24 Power.vb
2   ' Calculates the power of a value, defaults to square.
3
4   Public Class FrmPower
5      Inherits System.Windows.Forms.Form
6
```

Fig. 6.24 **Optional** argument demonstration with method **Power** (part 1 of 2).

```vbnet
 7      Friend WithEvents txtBase As TextBox   ' reads base
 8      Friend WithEvents txtPower As TextBox  ' reads power
 9
10      Friend WithEvents inputGroup As GroupBox
11
12      Friend WithEvents lblBase As Label    ' prompts for base
13      Friend WithEvents lblPower As Label   ' prompts for power
14      Friend WithEvents lblOutput As Label  ' displays output
15
16      Friend WithEvents cmdCalculate As Button ' generates output
17
18      ' Visual Studio .NET generated code
19
20      ' reads input and displays result
21      Private Sub cmdCalculate_Click(ByVal sender As System.Object, _
22         ByVal e As System.EventArgs) Handles cmdCalculate.Click
23
24         Dim value As Integer
25
26         ' call version of Power depending on power input
27         If Not txtPower.Text = "" Then
28            value = Power(Convert.ToInt32(txtBase.Text), _
29               Convert.ToInt32(txtPower.Text))
30         Else
31            value = Power(Convert.ToInt32(txtBase.Text))
32         End If
33
34         lblOutput.Text = Convert.ToString(value)
35      End Sub ' cmdCalculate_Click
36
37      ' use iteration to calculate power
38      Function Power(ByVal base As Integer, _
39         Optional ByVal exponent As Integer = 2) As Integer
40
41         Dim total As Integer = 1
42         Dim i As Integer
43
44         For i = 1 To exponent
45            total *= base
46         Next
47
48         Return total
49      End Function ' Power
50
51   End Class ' FrmPower
```

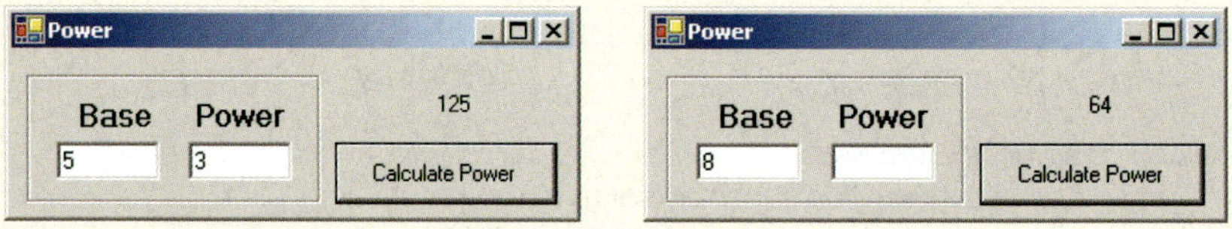

Fig. 6.24 Optional argument demonstration with method **Power** (part 2 of 2).

6.18 Modules

Programmers use modules to group related procedures so that they can be reused in other projects. Modules are similar in many ways to classes; they allow programmers to build reusable components without a full knowledge of object-oriented programming. Using modules in a project requires knowledge of scoping rules, because some procedures and variables in a module are accessible from other parts of a project. In general, modules should be self-contained, meaning that the procedures in the module should not require access to variables and procedures outside the module, except when such values are passed as arguments.

Figure 6.25 presents **modDice**, which groups several dice-related procedures into a module for reuse in other programs that use dice. Function **RollDie** (lines 11–13) simulates a single die roll and returns the result. Function **RollAndSum** (lines 17–28) uses a **For** structure (lines 22–24) to call **RollDie** the number of times indicated by **diceNumber** and totals the results. Function **GetDieImage** (lines 30–37) returns a die **Image** that corresponds to parameter **dieValue**. **Optional** parameter **baseImageName** represents the prefix of the image name to be used. If the argument is omitted, the default prefix **"die"** is used. [*Note*: New modules are added to a project by selecting **Project > Add Module**.]

FrmDiceModuleTest in Fig. 6.26 demonstrates using the **modDice** procedures to respond to button clicks. Procedure **cmdRollDie1_Click** (lines 23–27) rolls a die and obtains the default image. We call procedures contained in **modDice** by following the module name with the dot (**.**) operator and the procedure name. Using the functionality provided by **modDice**, the body of this procedure requires only one statement (line 26). Thus, we easily can create a similar **Button**, **cmdRollDie2**. In this case, procedure **cmdRollDie2_Click** (lines 29–34) uses the **Optional** argument to prefix the image name and select a different image. Procedure **cmdRollTen_Click** (lines 36–40) sets the **Text** property of **lblSum** to the result of 10 rolls.

```vb
1   ' Fig. 6.25: DiceModule.vb
2   ' A collection of common dice procedures.
3
4   Imports System.IO
5
6   Module modDice
7
8      Dim randomObject As Random = New Random()
9
10        ' rolls single die
11        Function RollDie() As Integer
12           Return randomObject.Next(1, 7)
13        End Function ' RollDie
14
15        ' die summation procedure
16        Function RollAndSum(ByVal diceNumber As Integer) _
17           As Integer
18
19           Dim i As Integer
20           Dim sum As Integer = 0
21
```

Fig. 6.25 Module used to define a group of related procedures (part 1 of 2).

```vb
22        For i = 1 To diceNumber
23           sum += RollDie()
24        Next
25
26        Return sum
27     End Function ' RollAndSum
28
29     ' returns die image
30     Function GetDieImage(ByVal dieValue As Integer, _
31        Optional ByVal baseImageName As String = "die") _
32        As System.Drawing.Image
33
34        Return Image.FromFile( _
35           Directory.GetCurrentDirectory & _
36           "\Images\" & baseImageName & dieValue & ".png")
37     End Function ' GetDieImage
38
39 End Module ' modDice
```

Fig. 6.25 Module used to define a group of related procedures (part 2 of 2).

For the program in Fig. 6.26, we add **DiceModule.vb** to the project to provide access to the procedures defined in **modDice**. To include a module in a project, select **File > Add Existing Item…**. In the dialog that is displayed, select the module file name and click **Open**. By default, a copy the file is added to the project directory unless you specify to open the module file as a linked file. Once a module has been added to a project, the procedures contained in the module have namespace scope. By default, procedures with namespace scope are accessible to all other parts of a project, such as methods in classes and procedures in other modules. Although it is not necessary, the programmer may place the file containing the module's code in the same directory as the other files for the project.

```vb
1  ' Fig. 6.26: DiceModuleTest.vb
2  ' Demonstrates modDiceModule procedures
3
4  Imports System.Drawing
5
6  Public Class FrmDiceModuleTest
7     Inherits System.Windows.Forms.Form
8
9     Friend WithEvents lblSum As Label ' displays 10-roll sum
10
11    Friend WithEvents diceGroup As GroupBox
12
13    ' dice images
14    Friend WithEvents picDie1 As PictureBox
15    Friend WithEvents picDie2 As PictureBox
16
17    Friend WithEvents cmdRollDie1 As Button ' rolls blue die
18    Friend WithEvents cmdRollTen As Button  ' simulates 10 rolls
19    Friend WithEvents cmdRollDie2 As Button ' rolls red die
```

Fig. 6.26 Testing the **modDice** procedures (part 1 of 2).

```
20
21      ' Visual Studio .NET generated code
22
23      Private Sub cmdRollDie1_Click(ByVal sender As System.Object, _
24         ByVal e As System.EventArgs) Handles cmdRollDie1.Click
25
26         picDie1.Image = modDice.GetDieImage(modDice.RollDie())
27      End Sub ' cmdRollDie1_Click
28
29      Private Sub cmdRollDie2_Click(ByVal sender As System.Object, _
30         ByVal e As System.EventArgs) Handles cmdRollDie2.Click
31
32         picDie2.Image = modDice.GetDieImage(modDice.RollDie(), _
33            "redDie")
34      End Sub ' cmdRollDie2_Click
35
36      Private Sub cmdRollTen_Click(ByVal sender As System.Object, _
37         ByVal e As System.EventArgs) Handles cmdRollTen.Click
38
39         lblSum.Text = Convert.ToString(modDice.RollAndSum(10))
40      End Sub ' cmdRollTen_Click
41
42   End Class ' FrmDiceModuleTest
```

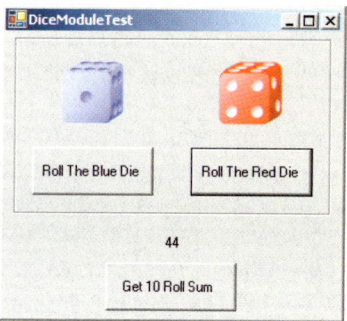

Fig. 6.26 Testing the **modDice** procedures (part 2 of 2).

SUMMARY

- Experience has shown that the best way to develop and maintain a large program is to construct it from small, manageable pieces. This technique is known as divide and conquer.
- Visual Basic programs consist of many pieces, including modules and classes.
- Modules and classes are composed of smaller pieces called procedures. When procedures are contained in a class, we refer to them as methods.
- Visual Basic provides many classes and methods in the .NET Framework Class Library (FCL). This rich collection of features allows programmers to develop robust applications quickly.
- Three types of procedures exist: **Sub** procedures, **Function** procedures and event procedures.
- Procedures promote software reusability—the ability to use existing procedures as building blocks for new programs.
- The first statement of a procedure definition is the procedure header.

- The declarations and statements in the procedure definition form the procedure body.
- The procedure header and procedure call must agree with regard to the number, type and order of arguments.
- The characteristics of **Function** procedures are similar to those of **Sub** procedures. However, **Function** procedures return a value (i.e., send back a value) to the caller.
- In a **Function** header, the return type indicates the data type of the result returned from the **Function** to its caller.
- Keyword **Return**, followed by an expression, returns a value from a **Function** procedure.
- If a **Function** procedure body does not specify a **Return** statement, program control returns to the point at which a procedure was invoked when the **End Function** keywords are encountered.
- An event represents a user action, such as the clicking of a button or the alteration of a value.
- Calls to methods, such as **Math.Max**, that are defined in a separate class must include the class name and the dot (**.**) operator (also called the member access operator). However, calls to methods defined in the class that contains the method call need only specify the method name.
- The Parameter Info feature of the IDE identifies accessible procedures and their arguments. Parameter Info greatly simplifies coding. The Parameter Info feature provides information not only about programmer-defined procedures, but about all methods contained in the FCL.
- The IntelliSense feature displays all the members in a class.
- Widening conversion occurs when a type is converted to another type (usually one that can hold more data) without losing data.
- Narrowing conversion occurs when there is potential for data loss during a conversion (usually to a type that holds a smaller amount of data). Some narrowing conversions can fail, resulting in run-time errors and logic errors.
- Visual Basic supports both widening and narrowing conversions.
- **Option Explicit**, which is set to **On** by default, forces the programmer to declare all variables explicitly before they are used in a program. Forcing explicit declarations eliminates spelling errors and other subtle errors that may occur if **Option Explicit** is turned **Off**.
- **Option Strict**, which is set to **Off** by default, increases program clarity and reduces debugging time. When set to **On**, **Option Strict** requires the programmer to perform all narrowing conversions explicitly.
- The methods in class **Convert** changes data types explicitly. The name of each conversion method is the word **To**, followed by the name of the data type to which the method converts its argument.
- All data types can be categorized as either value types or reference types. A variable of a value type contains data of that type. A variable of a reference type contains the location in memory where the data is stored.
- Both value and reference types include built-in types and types that programmers can create.
- Values typed directly in program code are called literals. Each literal corresponds to one of the primitive data types. Some of Visual Basic's data types use special notations, such as type characters, for creating literals.
- Arguments are passed in one of two ways: Pass-by-value and pass-by-reference (also called call-by-value and call-by-reference).
- When an argument is passed by value, the program makes a copy of the argument's value and passes that copy to the called procedure. Changes to the called procedure's copy do not affect the original variable's value.

- When an argument is passed by reference, the caller gives the procedure the ability to access and modify the caller's original data directly. Pass-by-reference can improve performance, because it eliminates the need to copy large data items, such as large objects; however, pass-by-reference can weaken security, because the called procedure can modify the caller's data.
- By default, the code editor includes keyword **ByVal** in parameter declarations to indicate that the parameter is passed by value. In the case of value-type variables, this means that the value stored in the variable is copied and passed to the procedure, preventing the procedure from accessing the original value in the variable.
- Value-type arguments enclosed in parentheses, **()**, are passed by value even if the procedure header declares the parameter with keyword **ByRef**.
- An identifier's duration (also called its lifetime) is the period during which the identifier exists in memory.
- Identifiers that represent local variables in a procedure (i.e., parameters and variables declared in the procedure body) have automatic duration. Automatic-duration variables are created when program control enters the procedure in which they are declared, exist while the procedure is active and are destroyed when the procedure is exited.
- Variables declared with keyword **Static** inside a procedure definition have static duration, meaning they have the same duration as the **Class** or **Module** that contains the procedure.
- The scope (sometimes called declaration space) of a variable, reference or procedure identifier is the portion of the program in which the identifier can be accessed. The possible scopes for an identifier are class scope, module scope, namespace scope and block scope.
- In Visual Basic .NET, identifiers declared inside a block, such as the body of a procedure definition or the body of an **If** selection structure, have block scope. Block scope begins at the identifier's declaration and ends at the block's **End** statement.
- Procedures in a module have namespace scope, which means that they may be accessed throughout a project.
- It is possible to create variables with namespace scope by replacing keyword **Dim** with keyword **Public** in the declaration of a variable in a module.
- **Const**ant identifiers and **Enum**erations enhance program readability by providing descriptive identifiers for numbers or **String**s that have special meaning.
- A recursive procedure is a procedure that calls itself, either indirectly (i.e., through another procedure) or directly.
- Any problem that can be solved recursively also can be solved iteratively (nonrecursively).
- The element of chance can be introduced into computer applications through class **Random** (located in namespace **System**). Method **Next** returns a random number.
- Overloading allows the programmer to define several procedures with the same name, as long as these procedures have different sets of parameters (number of parameters, types of the parameters and order of the parameters). This allows the programmer to reduce the complexity of the program and create a more flexible application.
- Overloaded procedures are distinguished by their signatures, which are a combination of the procedure's name and parameter types. The compiler uses a logical process known as overload resolution to determine which procedure should be called.
- Procedure calls cannot be distinguished by return type. A syntax error is generated when two procedures have the same signature and different return types. However, overloaded procedures with different signatures can have different return types.

- Programmers use modules to group related procedures so that they can be reused in other projects. Modules are similar in many ways to classes; they allow programmers to build reusable components without a full knowledge of object-oriented programming.
- Once a module has been added to a project, the procedures contained in the module have namespace scope. By default, procedures with namespace scope are accessible to all other parts of a project, such as methods in classes and procedures in other modules.
- Visual Basic allows programmers to create procedures that take one or more optional arguments. When a parameter is declared as optional, the caller has the option of passing that particular argument. Optional arguments are specified in the procedure header with keyword `Optional`.

TERMINOLOGY

. (dot operator)
argument to a procedure call
automatic duration
automatic initialization of a variable
base case
block scope
`Button` class
`ByRef` keyword
`ByVal` keyword
call-by-reference
call-by-value
calling procedure
class
class scope
`Click` event
coercion of arguments
comma-separated list of arguments
complexity theory
`Const` keyword
constant identifier
control structures in iteration
control structures in recursion
convergence
declaration
default argument
divide-and-conquer approach
duration of an identifier
`Enum` keyword
enumeration
event handling
exhausting memory
exponential "explosion" of calls
`Factorial` method
Fibonacci series, defined recursively
`Function` procedure
golden ratio
hierarchical structure
infinite loop

infinite recursion
inheritance
instance variables of a class
interface
invoke
iteration
lifetime of an identifier
local variable
`Math` class method
method
method body
method call
method overloading
mixed-type expression
`Module`
modularizing a program with procedures
named constant
narrowing conversion
nested block
nested control structure
`Next` method
optional argument
`Optional` keyword
overloaded procedure
parameter list
parentheses
pass-by-reference
pass-by-value
precedence
principle of least privilege
procedure
procedure body
procedure call
procedure overloading
programmer-defined procedure
promotions for primitive data types
`Public` keyword
`Random` class

recursive evaluation
recursive method
reference type
`Return` keyword
return-value type
scaling factor
scientific notation
scope of an identifier
sequence of random numbers
shifting value
side effect

signature
simulation
software reusability
`Static` duration
`Sub` procedure
termination test
type character
user-interface event
value type
widening conversion

SELF-REVIEW EXERCISES

6.1 Fill in the blanks in each of the following statements:
a) Procedures in Visual Basic can be defined in _____ and _____.
b) A procedure is invoked with a _____.
c) A variable known only within the procedure in which it is defined is called a _____.
d) The _____ statement in a called `Function` procedure can be used to pass the value of an expression back to the calling procedure.
e) A procedure defined with keyword _____ does not return a value.
f) The _____ of an identifier is the portion of the program in which the identifier can be used.
g) The three ways to return control from a called `Sub` procedure to a caller are _____, _____ and _____.
h) The _____ method in class `Random` produces random numbers.
i) Variables declared in a block or in a procedure's parameter list are of _____ duration.
j) A procedure that calls itself either directly or indirectly is a _____ procedure.
k) A recursive procedure typically has two components: One that provides a means for the recursion to terminate by testing for a _____ case, and one that expresses the problem as a recursive call for a problem slightly simpler than the original call.
l) In Visual Basic, it is possible to have various procedures with the same name that operate on different types or numbers of arguments. This is called procedure _____.
m) Local variables declared at the beginning of a procedure have _____ scope, as do procedure parameters, which are considered local variables of the procedure.
n) Iteration uses a _____ structure.
o) Recursion uses a _____ structure.
p) Recursion achieves repetition through repeated _____ calls.
q) It is possible to define procedures with the same _____, but different parameter lists.
r) Recursion terminates when the _____ is reached.
s) The _____ is a comma-separated list containing the declarations of the parameters received by the called procedure.
t) The _____ is the data type of the result returned from a called `Function` procedure.
u) An _____ is a signal that is sent when some action takes place, such as a button being clicked.

6.2 State whether each of the following is *true* or *false*. If *false*, explain why.
a) `Math` method `Abs` rounds its parameter to the smallest integer.

b) **Math** method **Exp** is the exponential method that calculates e^x.
c) A recursive procedure is one that calls itself.
d) Conversion from type **Single** to type **Double** requires a widening conversion.
e) Variable type **Char** cannot be converted to type **Integer**.
f) When a procedure recursively calls itself, it is known as the base case.
g) Forgetting to return a value from a recursive procedure when one is needed results in a logic error.
h) Infinite recursion occurs when a procedure converges on the base case.
i) Visual Basic supports **Optional** arguments.
j) Any problem that can be solved recursively also can be solved iteratively.

6.3 For the program in Fig. 6.27, state the scope (either class scope or block scope) of each of the following elements:
  a) The variable **i**.
  b) The variable **base**.
  c) The method **Cube**.
  d) The method **FrmCubeTest_Load**.
  e) The variable **output**.

6.4 Write an application that tests whether the examples of the **Math** class method calls shown in Fig. 6.7 actually produce the indicated results.

6.5 Give the procedure header for each of the following:
  a) Procedure **Hypotenuse**, which takes two double-precision, floating-point arguments, **side1** and **side2**, and returns a double-precision, floating-point result.
  b) Procedure **Smallest**, which takes three integers, **x**, **y** and **z**, and returns an integer.
  c) Procedure **Instructions**, which does not take any arguments and does not return a value.
  d) Procedure **IntegerToSingle**, which takes an integer argument, **number**, and returns a floating-point result.

6.6 Find the error in each of the following program segments and explain how the error can be corrected:

```
1   ' Fig. 6.27: CubeTest.vb
2   ' Printing the cubes of 1-10.
3
4   Public Class FrmCubeTest
5      Inherits System.Windows.Forms.Form
6
7      Friend WithEvents lblOutput As Label
8
9      ' Visual Studio .NET generated code
10
11     Dim i As Integer
12
13     Private Sub FrmCubeTest_Load(ByVal sender As System.Object, _
14        ByVal e As System.EventArgs) Handles MyBase.Load
15
16        Dim output As String = ""
17
```

Fig. 6.27 Printing the results of cubing 10 numbers (part 1 of 2).

```vbnet
18        For i = 1 To 10
19           output &= Cube(i) & vbCrLf
20        Next
21
22        lblOutput.Text = output
23     End Sub ' FrmCubeTest_Load
24
25     Function Cube(ByVal base As Integer) As Integer
26        Return Convert.ToInt32(base ^ 3)
27     End Function ' Cube
28
29  End Class ' FrmCubeTest
```

Fig. 6.27 Printing the results of cubing 10 numbers (part 2 of 2).

```vbnet
a) Sub General1()
       Console.WriteLine("Inside procedure General1")

       Sub General2()
           Console.WriteLine("Inside procedure General2")
       End Sub ' General2

   End Sub ' General1
b) Function Sum(ByVal x As Integer, ByVal y As Integer) _
       As Integer

       Dim result As Integer

       result = x + y
   End Function ' Sum
c) Sub Printer1(ByVal value As Single)
       Dim value As Single
       Console.WriteLine(value)
   End Sub ' Printer1
d) Sub Product()
       Dim a As Integer = 6
       Dim b As Integer = 5
       Dim result As Integer = a * b
       Console.WriteLine("Result is " & result)

       Return result
   End Sub ' Product
e) Function Sum(ByVal value As Integer) As Integer

       If value = 0 Then
           Return 0
       Else
           value += Sum(value - 1)
       End If

   End Function ' Sum
```

ANSWERS TO SELF-REVIEW EXERCISES

6.1 a) classes, modules. b) procedure call. c) local variable. d) **Return**. e) **Sub**. f) scope. g) **Return**, **Exit Sub**, encountering the **End Sub** statement. h) **Next**. i) automatic. j) recursive. k) base. l) overloading. m) block. n) repetition. o) selection. p) procedure. q) name. r) base case. s) parameter list. t) return-value type. u) event.

6.2 a) False. **Math** method **Abs** returns the absolute value of a number. b) True. c) True. d) True. e) False. Type **Char** can be converted to type **Integer** with a narrowing conversion. f) False. A procedure's recursively calling itself is known as the recursive call or recursion step. g) True. h) False. Infinite recursion occurs when a recursive procedure does not converge on the base case. i) True. j) True.

6.3 a) Class scope. b) Block scope. c) Class scope. d) Class scope. e) Block scope.

6.4 The following code demonstrates the use of some **Math** library method calls:

```
1   ' Ex. 6.4: MathTest.vb
2   ' Testing the Math class methods
3
4   Module modMathTest
5
6      Sub Main()
7         Console.WriteLine("Math.Abs(23.7) = " & _
8            Convert.ToString(Math.Abs(23.7)))
9         Console.WriteLine("Math.Abs(0.0) = " & _
10           Convert.ToString(Math.Abs(0)))
11        Console.WriteLine("Math.Abs(-23.7) = " & _
12           Convert.ToString(Math.Abs(-23.7)))
13        Console.WriteLine("Math.Ceiling(9.2) = " & _
14           Convert.ToString(Math.Ceiling(9.2)))
15        Console.WriteLine("Math.Ceiling(-9.8) = " & _
16           Convert.ToString(Math.Ceiling(-9.8)))
17        Console.WriteLine("Math.Cos(0.0) = " & _
18           Convert.ToString(Math.Cos(0)))
19        Console.WriteLine("Math.Exp(1.0) = " & _
20           Convert.ToString(Math.Exp(1)))
21        Console.WriteLine("Math.Exp(2.0) = " & _
22           Convert.ToString(Math.Exp(2)))
23        Console.WriteLine("Math.Floor(9.2) = " & _
24           Convert.ToString(Math.Floor(9.2))
25        Console.WriteLine("Math.Floor(-9.8) = " & _
26           Convert.ToString(Math.Floor(-9.8)))
27        Console.WriteLine("Math.Log(2.718282) = " & _
28           Convert.ToString(Math.Log(2.718282)))
29        Console.WriteLine("Math.Log(7.389056) = " & _
30           Convert.ToString(Math.Log(7.389056)))
31        Console.WriteLine("Math.Max(2.3, 12.7) = " & _
32           Convert.ToString(Math.Max(2.3, 12.7)))
33        Console.WriteLine("Math.Max(-2.3, -12.7) = " & _
34           Convert.ToString(Math.Max(-2.3, -12.7)))
35        Console.WriteLine("Math.Min(2.3, 12.7) = " & _
36           Convert.ToString(Math.Min(2.3, 12.7)))
37        Console.WriteLine("Math.Min(-2.3, -12.7) = " & _
38           Convert.ToString(Math.Min(-2.3, -12.7)))
```

```
39          Console.WriteLine("Math.Pow(2, 7) = " & _
40              Convert.ToString(Math.Pow(2, 7)))
41          Console.WriteLine("Math.Pow(9, .5) = " & _
42              Convert.ToString(Math.Pow(9, 0.5)))
43          Console.WriteLine("Math.Sin(0.0) = " & _
44              Convert.ToString(Math.Sin(0)))
45          Console.WriteLine("Math.Sqrt(9.0) = " & _
46              Convert.ToString(Math.Sqrt(9)))
47          Console.WriteLine("Math.Sqrt(2.0) = " & _
48              Convert.ToString(Math.Sqrt(2)))
49          Console.WriteLine("Math.Tan(0.0) = " & _
50              Convert.ToString(Math.Tan(0)))
51
52      End Sub ' Main
53
54  End Module ' modMathTest
```

```
Math.Abs(23.7) = 23.7
Math.Abs(0.0) = 0
Math.Abs(-23.7) = 23.7
Math.Ceiling(9.2) = 10
Math.Ceiling(-9.8) = -9
Math.Cos(0.0) = 1
Math.Exp(1.0) = 2.71828182845905
Math.Exp(2.0) = 7.38905609893065
Math.Floor(9.2) = 9
Math.Floor(-9.8) = -10
Math.Log(2.718282) = 1.00000006310639
Math.Log(7.389056) = 1.99999998661119
Math.Max(2.3, 12.7) = 12.7
Math.Max(-2.3, -12.7) = -2.3
Math.Min(2.3, 12.7) = 2.3
Math.Min(-2.3, -12.7) = -12.7
Math.Pow(2, 7) = 128
Math.Pow(9, .5) = 3
Math.Sin(0.0) = 0
Math.Sqrt(9.0) = 3
Math.Sqrt(2.0) = 1.4142135623731
Math.Tan(0.0) = 0
```

6.5 a) `Function Hypotenuse(ByVal side1 As Double, _`
         `ByVal side2 As Double) As Double`
     b) `Function Smallest(ByVal x As Integer, _`
         `ByVal y As Integer, ByVal z As Integer) As Integer`
     c) `Sub Instructions()`
     d) `Function IntegerToSingle(ByVal number As Integer) As Single`

6.6 a) Error: Procedure **General2** is defined in procedure **General1**.
        Correction: Move the definition of **General2** out of the definition of **General1**.
     b) Error: The procedure is supposed to return an **Integer**, but does not.
        Correction: Delete the statement **result = x + y** and place the following statement in the method:

```
            Return x + y
```
or add the following statement at the end of the method body:
```
            Return result
```
c) Error: Parameter `value` is redefined in the procedure definition.
   Correction: Delete the declaration `Dim value As Single`.
d) Error: The procedure returns a value, but is defined as a `Sub` procedure.
   Correction: Change the procedure to a `Function` procedure with return type `Integer`.
e) Error: The result of `value += Sum(value - 1)` is not returned by this recursive method, resulting in a logic error.
   Correction: Rewrite the statement in the `Else` clause as
```
            Return value + sum(value - 1)
```

EXERCISES

6.7 What is the value of **x** after each of the following statements is performed?
```
a) x = Math.Abs(7.5)
b) x = Math.Floor(7.5)
c) x = Math.Abs(0.0)
d) x = Math.Ceiling(0.0)
e) x = Math.Abs(-6.4)
f) x = Math.Ceiling(-6.4)
g) x = Math.Ceiling(-Math.Abs(-8 + Math.Floor(-5.5)))
```

6.8 A parking garage charges a $2.00 minimum fee to park for up to three hours. The garage charges an additional $0.50 per hour for each hour *or part thereof* in excess of three hours. The maximum charge for any given 24-hour period is $10.00. Assume that no car parks for longer than 24 hours at a time. Write a program that calculates and displays the parking charges for each customer who parked a car in this garage yesterday. You should enter in a **TextBox** the hours parked for each customer. The program should display the charge for the current customer. The program should use the method **CalculateCharges** to determine the charge for each customer. Use the techniques described in the chapter to read the **Double** value from a **TextBox**.

6.9 Write a method **IntegerPower(base, exponent)** that returns the value of

$$base^{exponent}$$

For example, **IntegerPower(3, 4)** = 3 * 3 * 3 * 3. Assume that **exponent** is a positive integer and that **base** is an integer. Method **IntegerPower** should use a **For/Next** loop or **While** loop to control the calculation. Do not use any **Math** library methods or the exponentiation operator, ^. Incorporate this method into a Windows application that reads integer values from **TextBox**es for **base** and **exponent** from the user and performs the calculation by calling method **IntegerPower**.

6.10 Define a method **Hypotenuse** that calculates the length of the hypotenuse of a right triangle when the other two sides are given. The method should take two arguments of type **Double** and return the hypotenuse as a **Double**. Incorporate this method into a Windows application that reads integer values for **side1** and **side2** from **TextBox**es and performs the calculation with the **Hypotenuse** method. Determine the length of the hypotenuse for each of the following triangles:

Triangle	Side 1	Side 2
1	3.0	4.0
2	5.0	12.0
3	8.0	15.0

6.11 Write a method **SquareOfAsterisks** that displays a solid square of asterisks whose side is specified in integer parameter **side**. For example, if **side** is **4**, the method displays

```
****
****
****
****
```

Incorporate this method into a Windows application that reads an integer value for **side** from the user and performs the drawing with the **SquareOfAsterisks** method. This method should gather data from **Textbox**es and should print to a **Label**.

6.12 Modify the method created in Exercise 6.11 to form the square out of whatever character is contained in parameter **fillCharacter**. Thus, if **side** is **5** and **fillCharacter** is "**#**", this method should print

```
#####
#####
#####
#####
#####
```

6.13 Write a Windows application that simulates coin tossing. Let the program toss the coin each time the user presses the **Toss** button. Count the number of times each side of the coin appears. Display the results. The program should call a separate method **Flip**, which takes no arguments and returns **False** for tails and **True** for heads. [*Note*: If the program simulates the coin tossing realistically, each side of the coin should appear approximately half the time.]

6.14 Computers are playing an increasing role in education. Write a program that will help an elementary school student learn multiplication. Use the **Next** method from an object of type **Random** to produce two positive one-digit integers. It should display a question, such as

```
How much is 6 times 7?
```

The student should then type the answer into a **TextBox**. Your program should check the student's answer. If it is correct, display **"Very good!"** in a **Label**, then ask another multiplication question. If the answer is incorrect, display **"No. Please try again."** in the same **Label**, then let the student try the same question again until the student finally gets it right. A separate method should be used to generate each new question. This method should be called once when the program begins execution and then each time the user answers a question correctly.

6.15 (*Towers of Hanoi*) Every budding computer scientist must grapple with certain classic problems; the Towers of Hanoi (Fig. 6.28) is one of the most famous. Legend has it that, in a temple in the Far East, priests are attempting to move a stack of disks from one peg to another. The initial stack had 64 disks threaded onto one peg and arranged from bottom to top by decreasing size. The priests are attempting to move the stack from this peg to a second peg, under the constraints that exactly one disk is moved at a time and that at no time may a larger disk be placed above a smaller disk. A third peg is available for temporarily holding disks. Supposedly, the world will end when the priests complete their task, so there is little incentive for us to facilitate their efforts.

Fig. 6.28 Towers of Hanoi for the case with four disks.

Let us assume that the priests are attempting to move the disks from peg 1 to peg 3. We wish to develop an algorithm that prints the precise sequence of peg-to-peg disk transfers.

If we were to approach this problem with conventional techniques, we would find ourselves hopelessly knotted up in managing the disks. However, if we approach the problem with recursion in mind, it becomes tractable. Moving n disks can be viewed in terms of moving only $n-1$ disks (and hence, the recursion) as follows:

a) Move $n-1$ disks from peg 1 to peg 2, using peg 3 as a temporary holding area.
b) Move the last disk (the largest) from peg 1 to peg 3.
c) Move the $n-1$ disks from peg 2 to peg 3, using peg 1 as a temporary holding area.

The process ends when the last task involves moving $n = 1$ disk (i.e., the base case). This is accomplished by moving the disk without the need for a temporary holding area.

Write a program to solve the Towers of Hanoi problem. Allow the user to enter the number of disks in a **TextBox**. Use a recursive **Tower** method with four parameters:

a) The number of disks to be moved
b) The peg on which these disks are threaded initially
c) The peg to which this stack of disks is to be moved
d) The peg to be used as a temporary holding area

Your program should display in a **TextBox** with scrolling functionality the precise instructions for moving the disks from the starting peg to the destination peg. For example, to move a stack of three disks from peg 1 to peg 3, your program should print the following series of moves:

$1 \rightarrow 3$ (This means move one disk from peg 1 to peg 3.)
$1 \rightarrow 2$
$3 \rightarrow 2$
$1 \rightarrow 3$
$2 \rightarrow 1$
$2 \rightarrow 3$
$1 \rightarrow 3$

7

Arrays

Objectives

- To introduce the array data structure.
- To understand how arrays store, sort and search lists and tables of values.
- To understand how to declare an array, initialize an array and refer to individual elements of an array.
- To be able to pass arrays to methods.
- To understand basic sorting techniques.
- To be able to declare and manipulate multidimensional arrays.

*With sobs and tears he sorted out
Those of the largest size …*
Lewis Carroll

*Attempt the end, and never stand to doubt;
Nothing's so hard, but search will find it out.*
Robert Herrick

*Now go, write it before them in a table,
and note it in a book.*
Isaiah 30:8

*'Tis in my memory lock'd,
And you yourself shall keep the key of it.*
William Shakespeare

Outline

7.1 Introduction
7.2 Arrays
7.3 Declaring and Allocating Arrays
7.4 Examples Using Arrays
    7.4.1 Allocating an Array
    7.4.2 Initializing the Values in an Array
    7.4.3 Summing the Elements of an Array
    7.4.4 Using Arrays to Analyze Survey Results
    7.4.5 Using Histograms to Display Array Data Graphically
7.5 Passing Arrays to Procedures
7.6 Passing Arrays: `ByVal` vs. `ByRef`
7.7 Sorting Arrays
7.8 Searching Arrays: Linear Search and Binary Search
    7.8.1 Searching an Array with Linear Search
    7.8.2 Searching a Sorted Array with Binary Search
7.9 Multidimensional Rectangular and Jagged Arrays
7.10 Variable-Length Parameter Lists
7.11 `For Each/Next` Repetition Structure

Summary • Terminology • Self-Review Exercises • Answers to Self-Review Exercises • Exercises • Special Section: Recursion Exercises

7.1 Introduction

This chapter introduces basic concepts and features of data structures. *Arrays* are data structures consisting of data items of the same type. Arrays are "static" entities, in that they remain the same size once they are created, although an array reference may be reassigned to a new array of a different size. We begin by discussing constructing and accessing arrays; we build on this knowledge to conduct more complex manipulations of arrays, including powerful searching and sorting techniques. We then demonstrate the creation of more sophisticated arrays that have multiple dimensions. Chapter 24, Data Structures and Collections, introduces dynamic data structures, such as lists, queues, stacks and trees, which can grow and shrink as programs execute. This later chapter also presents Visual Basic's predefined data structures that enable the programmer to use existing data structures for lists, queues, stacks and trees, rather than "reinventing the wheel."

7.2 Arrays

An array is a group of contiguous memory locations that have the same name and the same type. Array names follow the same conventions that apply to other variable names, as was discussed in Chapter 3, Introduction to Visual Basic Programming. To refer to a particular location or element in an array, we specify the name of the array and the *position number* of the element to which we refer. Position numbers are values that indicate specific locations within arrays.

Figure 7.1 depicts an integer array named **numberArray**. This array contains 12 *elements*, any one of which can be referred to by giving the name of the array followed by the position number of the element in parentheses **()**. The first element in every array is the *zeroth element*. Thus, the first element of array **numberArray** is referred to as **numberArray(0)**, the second element of array **numberArray** is referred to as **numberArray(1)**, the seventh element of array **numberArray** is referred to as **numberArray(6)** and so on. The *i*th element of array **numberArray** is referred to as **numberArray(i - 1)**.

The position number in parentheses more formally is called an *index* (or a *subscript*). An index must be an integer or an integer expression. If a program uses an expression as an index, the expression is evaluated first to determine the index. For example, if variable **value1** is equal to **5**, and variable **value2** is equal to **6**, then the statement

```
numberArray(value1 + value2) += 2
```

adds **2** to array element **numberArray(11)**. Note that an *indexed array name* (i.e., the array name followed by an index enclosed in parentheses) is an *lvalue*—it can be used on the left side of an assignment statement to place a new value into an array element.

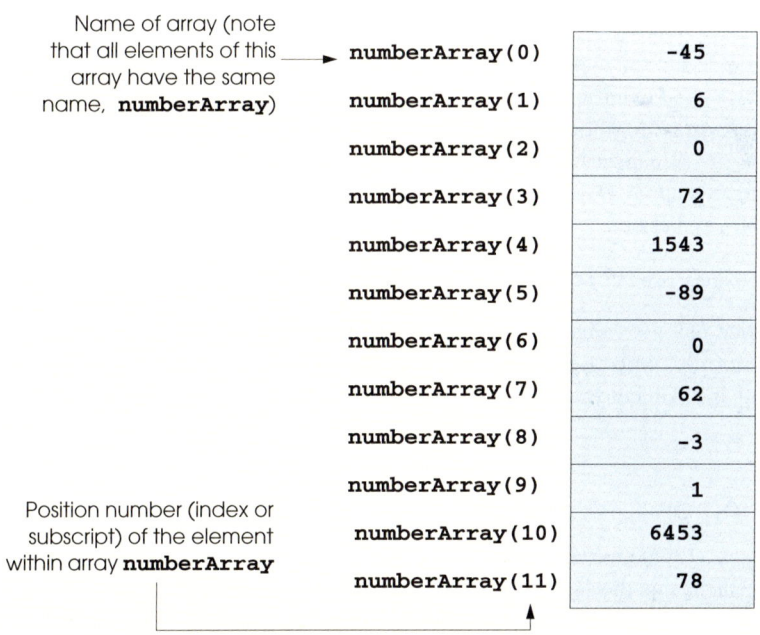

Fig. 7.1 Array consisting of 12 elements.

Let us examine array **numberArray** in Fig. 7.1 more closely. The *name* of the array is **numberArray**. The 12 elements of the array are referred to as **numberArray(0)** through **numberArray(11)**. The *value* of **numberArray(0)** is **-45**, the value of **numberArray(1)** is **6**, the value of **numberArray(2)** is **0**, the value of **numberArray(7)** is **62** and the value of **numberArray(11)** is **78**. Values stored in arrays can be employed in various calculations and applications. For example, to determine the sum of the values contained in the first three elements of array **numberArray** and then store the result in variable **sum**, we would write

```
sum = numberArray(0) + numberArray(1) + numberArray(2)
```

To divide the value of the seventh element of array **numberArray** by **2** and assign the result to the variable **result**, we would write

```
result = numberArray(6) \ 2
```

Common Programming Error 7.1

It is important to note the difference between the "seventh element of the array" and "array element seven." Array indices begin at 0, which means that the "seventh element of the array" has the index 6, whereas "array element seven" has the index 7 and is actually the eighth element of the array. This confusion is a common source of "off-by-one" errors.

Every array in Visual Basic "knows" its own length. The *length* of the array (i.e., **12** in this case) is determined by the following expression:

```
numberArray.Length
```

All arrays have access to the methods and properties of class ***System.Array***, including the ***Length*** *property*. For instance, method ***GetUpperBound*** returns the index of the last element in the array. Method **GetUpperBound** takes one argument indicating a dimension of the array. We discuss arrays with multiple dimensions in Section 7.9. For one-dimensional arrays, such as **numberArray**, the argument passed to **GetUpperBound** is **0**. For example, expression

```
numberArray.GetUpperBound(0)
```

returns **11**. Notice that the value returned by method **GetUpperBound** is one less than the value of the array's **Length** property. Classes, objects and class methods are discussed in detail in Chapter 8, Object-Based Programming.

7.3 Declaring and Allocating Arrays

Arrays occupy space in memory. The amount of memory required by an array depends on the length of the array and the size of the data type of the elements in the array. The declaration of an array creates a variable that can store a reference to an array but does not create the array in memory. To declare an array, the programmer provides the array's name and data type. The following statement declares the array in Fig. 7.1:

```
Dim numberArray As Integer()
```

The parentheses that follow the data type indicate that **numberArray** is an array. Arrays can be declared to contain any data type. In an array of primitive data types, every element of the array contains one value of the declared data type. For example, every element of an **Integer** array contains an **Integer** value.

Before the array can be used, the programmer must specify the size of the array and allocate memory for the array, using keyword **New**. Recall from Chapter 6 that keyword **New** creates an object. Arrays are represented as objects in Visual Basic, so they too, must be allocated using keyword **New**. The value stored in the array variable is actually a *reference* to the location in the computer's memory where the array object is created. All non-primitive-type variables are reference variables (normally called *references*). To allocate memory for the array **numberArray** after it has been declared, the statement

```
numberArray = New Integer(11) {}
```

is used. In our example, the number **11** defines the upper bound for the array. *Array bounds* determine what indices can be used to access an element in the array. Here, the array bounds are **0** (which is implicit in the preceding statement) and **11**, meaning that an index outside these bounds cannot be used to access elements in the array. Notice that the actual size of the array is one larger than the upper bound specified in the allocation.

The required braces (**{** and **}**) are called an *initializer list* and specify the initial values of the elements in the array. When the initializer list is empty, the elements in the array are initialized to the default value for the data type of the elements of the array. The default value is **0** for numeric primitive data-type variables, **False** for **Boolean** variables and **Nothing** for references. Keyword **Nothing** denotes an empty reference (i.e., a value indicating that a reference variable has not been assigned an address in the computer's memory). The initializer list also can contain a comma-separated list specifying the initial values of the elements in the array. For instance,

```
Dim numbers As Integer()
numbers = New Integer() {1, 2, 3, 6}
```

declares and allocates an array containing four **Integer** values. Visual Basic can determine the array bounds from the number of elements in the initializer list. Thus, it is not necessary to specify the size of the array when a non-empty initializer list is present.

The allocation of an array can be combined into the declaration, as in the statement

```
Dim numberArray As Integer() = New Integer(11) {}
```

Separating the declaration and allocation statements is useful, however, when the size of an array depends on user input or on values calculated at runtime.

Programmers can declare arrays via several alternative methods, which we discuss throughout this chapter. For example, several arrays can be declared with a single statement; the following statement declares two array variables of type **Double()**:

```
Dim array1, array2 As Double()
```

7.4 Examples Using Arrays

This section presents several examples that demonstrate the declaration, allocation and initialization of arrays, as well as various manipulations of array elements. For simplicity, the examples in this section use arrays that contain elements of type **Integer**. Please remember that a program can declare an array to have elements of any data type.

7.4.1 Allocating an Array

The program of Fig. 7.2 uses keyword **New** to allocate an array of 10 **Integer** elements, which are initially zero (the default value in an array of type **Integer**). The program displays the array elements in tabular format in a dialog.

```vb
1   ' Fig. 7.2: CreateArray.vb
2   ' Declaring and allocating an array.
3
4   Imports System.Windows.Forms
5
6   Module modCreateArray
7
8      Sub Main()
9         Dim output As String
10        Dim i As Integer
11
12        Dim array As Integer()      ' declare array variable
13        array = New Integer(9) {}   ' allocate memory for array
14
15        output = "Subscript " & vbTab & "Value" & vbCrLf
16
17        ' display values in array
18        For i = 0 To array.GetUpperBound(0)
19           output &= i & vbTab & array(i) & vbCrLf
20        Next
21
22        output &= vbCrLf & "The array contains " & _
23           array.Length & " elements."
24
25        MessageBox.Show(output, "Array of Integer Values", _
26           MessageBoxButtons.OK, MessageBoxIcon.Information)
27     End Sub ' Main
28
29  End Module ' modCreateArray
```

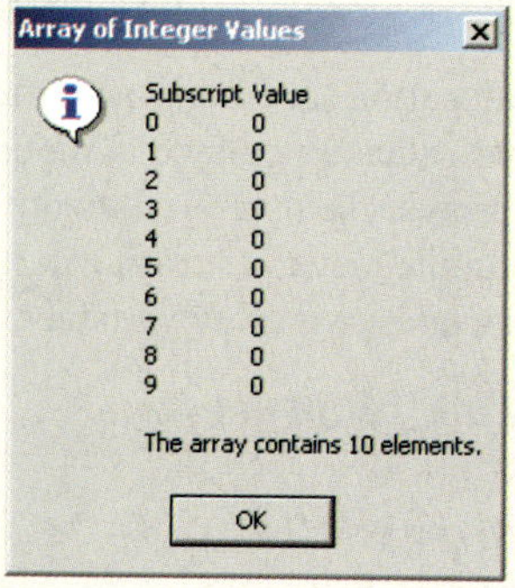

Fig. 7.2 Creating an array.

Line 12 declares **array**—a variable capable of storing a reference to an array of **Integer** elements. Line 13 allocates an array of 10 elements using **New** and assigns it to **array**. The program builds its output in **String output**. Line 15 appends to **output** the headings for the columns displayed by the program. The columns represent the index for each array element and the value of each array element, respectively.

Lines 18–20 use a **For** structure to append the index number (represented by **i**) and value of each array element (**array(i)**) to **output**. Note the use of zero-based counting (remember, indices start at 0), so that the loop accesses every array element. Also notice, in the header of the **For** structure, the expression **array.GetUpperBound(0)**, used to retrieve the upper bound of the array. The **Length** property (lines 22–23) returns the number of elements in the array.

7.4.2 Initializing the Values in an Array

The program of Fig. 7.3 creates two integer arrays of 10 elements each and sets the values of the elements, using an initializer list and a **For** structure. The arrays are displayed in tabular format in a message dialog.

Line 12 uses one statement to declare **array1** and **array2** as variables that are capable of referring to arrays of integers. Lines 16–17 allocate the 10 elements of **array1** with **New** and initialize the values in the array, using an initializer list. Line 20 allocates **array2**, whose size is determined by the expression **array1.GetUpperBound(0)**, meaning **array1** and **array2**, in this particular program, have the same upper bound.

```
1    ' Fig. 7.3: InitArray.vb
2    ' Initializing arrays.
3
4    Imports System.Windows.Forms
5
6    Module modInitArray
7
8       Sub Main()
9          Dim output As String
10         Dim i As Integer
11
12         Dim array1, array2 As Integer()   ' declare two arrays
13
14         ' initializer list specifies number of elements
15         ' and value of each element
16         array1 = New Integer() {32, 27, 64, 18, 95, _
17            14, 90, 70, 60, 37}
18
19         ' allocate array2 based on length of array1
20         array2 = New Integer(array1.GetUpperBound(0)) {}
21
22         ' set values in array2 by a calculation
23         For i = 0 To array2.GetUpperBound(0)
24            array2(i) = 2 + 2 * i
25         Next
26
```

Fig. 7.3 Initializing array elements two different ways (part 1 of 2).

```
27          output = "Subscript " & vbTab & "Array1" & vbTab & _
28             "Array2" & vbCrLf
29
30          ' display values for both arrays
31          For i = 0 To array1.GetUpperBound(0)
32             output &= i & vbTab & array1(i) & vbTab & array2(i) & _
33                vbCrLf
34          Next
35
36          MessageBox.Show(output, "Array of Integer Values", _
37             MessageBoxButtons.OK, MessageBoxIcon.Information)
38       End Sub ' Main
39
40    End Module ' modInitArray
```

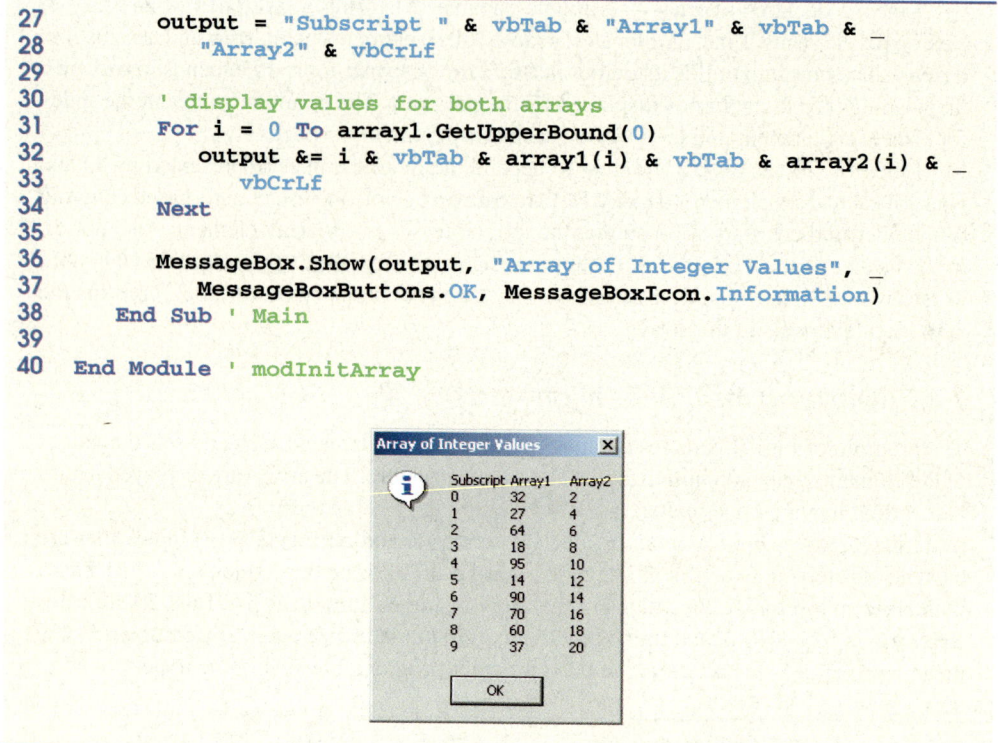

Fig. 7.3 Initializing array elements two different ways (part 2 of 2).

The **For** structure in lines 23–25 initializes each element in **array2**. The elements in **array2** are initialized (line 24) to the even integers **2**, **4**, **6**, …, **20**. These numbers are generated by multiplying each successive value of the loop counter by **2** and adding **2** to the product. The **For** structure in lines 31–34 uses the values in the arrays to build **String output**, which is displayed in a **MessageBox** (lines 36–37).

7.4.3 Summing the Elements of an Array

Often, the elements of an array represent a series of values that are employed in a calculation. For example, if the elements of an array represent a group of students' exam grades, the instructor might wish to total the elements of the array, then calculate the class average for the exam. The program in Fig. 7.4 sums the values contained in a 10-element integer array.

```
1  ' Fig. 7.4: SumArray.vb
2  ' Computing sum of elements in array.
3
4  Imports System.Windows.Forms
5
6  Module modSumArray
7
```

Fig. 7.4 Computing the sum of the elements in an array (part 1 of 2).

```
8      Sub Main()
9         Dim array As Integer() = New Integer() _
10           {1, 2, 3, 4, 5, 6, 7, 8, 9, 10}
11
12        Dim total As Integer = 0, i As Integer = 0
13
14        ' sum array element values
15        For i = 0 To array.GetUpperBound(0)
16           total += array(i)
17        Next
18
19        MessageBox.Show("Total of array elements: " & total, _
20           "Sum the elements of an Array", MessageBoxButtons.OK, _
21           MessageBoxIcon.Information)
22     End Sub ' Main
23
24  End Module ' modSumArray
```

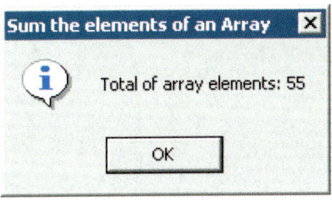

Fig. 7.4 Computing the sum of the elements in an array (part 2 of 2).

Lines 9–10 declare, allocate and initialize the 10-element array **array**. Line 16, in the body of the **For** structure, performs the addition. Alternatively, the values supplied as initializers for **array** could have been read into the program. For example, the user could enter the values through a **TextBox**, or the values could be read from a file on disk. Additional information about reading values into a program can be found in Chapter 17, Files and Streams.

7.4.4 Using Arrays to Analyze Survey Results

Our next example uses arrays to summarize data collected in a survey. Consider the following problem statement:

> Forty students were asked to rate on a scale of 1 to 10 the quality of the food in the student cafeteria, with 1 being "awful" and 10 being "excellent". Place the 40 responses in an integer array and determine the frequency of each rating.

This exercise represents a typical array-processing application (Fig. 7.5). We wish to summarize the number of responses of each type (i.e., 1–10). Array **responses** (lines 14–16) is a 40-element integer array containing the students' responses to the survey. Using an 11-element array **frequency**, we can count the number of occurrences of each response. We ignore the first element, **frequency(0)**, because it is more logical to have a survey response of **1** result in **frequency(1)** being incremented rather than incrementing **frequency(0)**. We can use each response directly as an index on the **frequency** array. Each element of the array is used as a counter for one of the possible types

254 Arrays Chapter 7

of survey responses—**frequency(1)** counts the number of students who rated the food as 1, **frequency(7)** counts the number of students who rated the food 7 and so on.

```vb
1   ' Fig. 7.5: StudentPoll.vb
2   ' Using arrays to display poll results.
3
4   Imports System.Windows.Forms
5
6   Module modStudentPoll
7
8      Sub Main()
9         Dim answer, rating As Integer
10        Dim output As String
11
12        ' student response array (typically input at run time)
13        Dim responses As Integer()
14        responses = New Integer() {1, 2, 6, 4, 8, 5, 9, 7, _
15           8, 10, 1, 6, 3, 8, 6, 10, 3, 8, 2, 7, 6, 5, 7, 6, _
16           8, 6, 7, 5, 6, 6, 5, 6, 7, 5, 6, 4, 8, 6, 8, 10}
17
18        ' response frequency array (indices 0 through 10)
19        Dim frequency As Integer() = New Integer(10) {}
20
21        ' count frequencies
22        For answer = 0 To responses.GetUpperBound(0)
23           frequency(responses(answer)) += 1
24        Next
25
26        output = "Rating " & vbTab & "Frequency " & vbCrLf
27
28        For rating = 1 To frequency.GetUpperBound(0)
29           output &= rating & vbTab & frequency(rating) & vbCrLf
30        Next
31
32        MessageBox.Show(output, "Student Poll Program", _
33           MessageBoxButtons.OK, MessageBoxIcon.Information)
34     End Sub ' Main
35
36  End Module ' modStudentPoll
```

Student Poll Program

Rating	Frequency
1	2
2	2
3	2
4	2
5	5
6	11
7	5
8	7
9	1
10	3

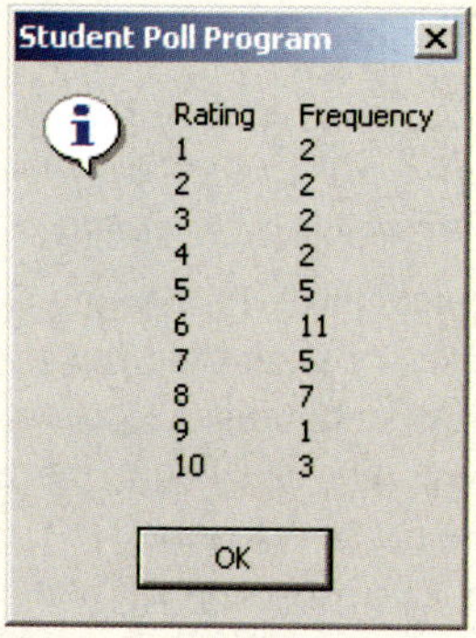

Fig. 7.5 Simple student-poll analysis program.

Good Programming Practice 7.1

Strive for program clarity. Sometimes, it is worthwhile to forgo the most efficient use of memory or processor time if the trade-off results in a clearer program.

Performance Tip 7.1

Sometimes, performance considerations outweigh clarity considerations.

The **For** structure (lines 22–24) reads the responses from the array **responses** one at a time and increments one of the 10 counters in the **frequency** array (**frequency(1)** to **frequency(10)**). The key statement in the loop appears in line 23. This statement increments the appropriate **frequency** counter as determined by the value of **responses(answer)**.

Let us consider several iterations of the **For** structure. When counter **answer** is **0**, **responses(answer)** is the value of **responses(0)** (i.e., **1**—see line 14). Therefore, **frequency(responses(answer))** actually is interpreted as **frequency(1)**, meaning the first counter in array **frequency** is incremented by one. In evaluating the expression **frequency(responses(answer))**, Visual Basic starts with the value in the innermost set of parentheses (**answer**, currently **0**). The value of **answer** is plugged into the expression, and Visual Basic evaluates the next set of parentheses (**responses(answer)**). That value is used as the index for the **frequency** array to determine which counter to increment (in this case, the **1** counter).

When **answer** is **1**, **responses(answer)** is the value of **responses(1)** (i.e., **2**—see line 14). As a result, **frequency(responses(answer))** actually is interpreted as **frequency(2)**, causing array element **2** (the third element of the array) to be incremented.

When **answer** is **2**, **responses(answer)** is the value of **responses(2)** (i.e., **6**—see line 14), so **frequency(responses(answer))** is interpreted as **frequency(6)**, causing array element **6** (the seventh element of the array) to be incremented and so on. Note that, regardless of the number of responses processed in the survey, only an 11-element array (in which we ignore element zero) is required to summarize the results, because all the response values are between 1 and 10, and the index values for an 11-element array are 0–10. Note that, in the output in Fig. 7.5, the numbers in the frequency column correctly add to 40 (the elements of the **frequency** array were initialized to zero when the array was allocated with **New**).

If the data contained out-of-range values, such as 13, the program would attempt to add **1** to **frequency(13)**. This is outside the bounds of the array. In other languages like C and C++ programming languages, such a reference would be allowed by the compiler and at execution time. The program would "walk" past the end of the array to where it thought element number 13 was located and would add 1 to whatever happened to be stored at that memory location. This could modify another variable in the program, possibly causing incorrect results or even premature program termination. Visual Basic provides mechanisms that prevent accessing elements outside the bounds of arrays.

Common Programming Error 7.2

Referencing an element outside the array bounds is a runtime error.

Testing and Debugging Tip 7.1

When a program is executed, array element indices are checked for validity (i.e., all indices must be greater than or equal to 0 and less than the length of the array). If an attempt is made to use an invalid index to access an element, Visual Basic generates an `IndexOutOfRangeException` *exception. Exceptions are discussed in greater detail in Chapter 11, Exception Handling.*

Testing and Debugging Tip 7.2

When looping through an array, the array index should remain between 0 and the upper bound of the array (i.e., the value returned by method `GetUpperBound`*). The initial and final values used in the repetition structure should prevent accessing elements outside this range.*

Testing and Debugging Tip 7.3

Programs should confirm the validity of all input values to prevent erroneous information from affecting calculations.

7.4.5 Using Histograms to Display Array Data Graphically

Many programs present data to users in a visual or graphical format. For example, numeric values are often displayed as bars in a bar chart, in which longer bars represent larger numeric values. Figure 7.6 displays numeric data graphically by creating a *histogram* that depicts each numeric value as a bar of asterisks (*****).

```vb
1   ' Fig. 7.6: Histogram.vb
2   ' Using data to create histograms.
3
4   Imports System.Windows.Forms
5
6   Module modHistogram
7
8      Sub Main()
9         Dim output As String         ' output string
10        Dim i, j As Integer          ' counters
11
12        ' create data array
13        Dim array1 As Integer() = New Integer() _
14           {19, 3, 15, 7, 11, 9, 13, 5, 17, 1}
15
16        output = "Element " & vbTab & "Value " & vbTab & _
17           "Histogram"
18
19        For i = 0 To array1.GetUpperBound(0)
20           output &= vbCrLf & i & vbTab & array1(i) & vbTab
21
22           For j = 1 To array1(i)
23              output &= "*"  ' add one asterisk
24           Next
25
26        Next
```

Fig. 7.6 Program that prints histograms (part 1 of 2).

```
27
28              MessageBox.show(output, "Histogram Printing Program", _
29                  MessageBoxButtons.OK, MessageBoxIcon.Information)
30          End Sub ' Main
31
32      End Module ' modHistogram
```

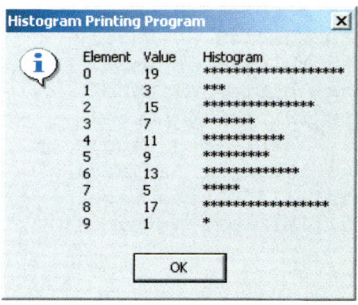

Fig. 7.6 Program that prints histograms (part 2 of 2).

The program reads numbers from an array and graphs the information in the form of a bar chart, or histogram. Each number is printed, and a bar consisting of a corresponding number of asterisks is displayed beside the number. The nested **For** loops (lines 19–26) append the bars to the **String** that is displayed in the **MessageBox**. Note the end value (**array1(i)**) of the inner **For** structure on line 22. Each time the inner **For** structure is reached (line 22), it counts from **1** to **array1(i)**, using a value in **array1** to determine the final value of the control variable **j**—the number of asterisks to display.

Sometimes programs use a series of counter variables to summarize data, such as the results of a survey. In Chapter 6, Procedures, we used a series of counters in our die-rolling program to track the number of occurrences of each side on a six-sided die as the program rolled the die 12 times. We indicated that there is a more elegant way of doing what we did in Fig. 6.11 for writing the dice-rolling program. An array version of this application is shown in Fig. 7.7.

```
1   ' Fig. 7.7: RollDie.vb
2   ' Rolling 12 dice with frequency chart.
3
4   ' Note: Directory.GetCurrentDirectory returns the directory of
5   ' the folder where the current project is plus
6   ' "bin/". This is where the images must be placed
7   ' for the example to work properly.
8
9   Imports System.IO
10  Imports System.Windows.Forms
11
12  Public Class FrmRollDie
13      Inherits System.Windows.Forms.Form
14
```

Fig. 7.7 Using arrays to eliminate a **Select Case** structure (part 1 of 4).

```vbnet
15        Dim randomNumber As Random = New Random()
16        Dim frequency As Integer() = New Integer(6) {}
17
18        ' labels
19        Friend WithEvents lblDie1 As Label
20        Friend WithEvents lblDie2 As Label
21        Friend WithEvents lblDie3 As Label
22        Friend WithEvents lblDie4 As Label
23        Friend WithEvents lblDie5 As Label
24        Friend WithEvents lblDie6 As Label
25        Friend WithEvents lblDie7 As Label
26        Friend WithEvents lblDie8 As Label
27        Friend WithEvents lblDie9 As Label
28        Friend WithEvents lblDie11 As Label
29        Friend WithEvents lblDie10 As Label
30        Friend WithEvents lblDie12 As Label
31
32        ' text box
33        Friend WithEvents txtDisplay As TextBox
34
35        ' button
36        Friend WithEvents cmdRoll As Button
37
38        ' Visual Studio .NET generated code
39
40        ' event handler for cmdRoll button
41        Private Sub cmdRoll_Click(ByVal sender As System.Object, _
42           ByVal e As System.EventArgs) Handles cmdRoll.Click
43
44           ' pass labels to a method that
45           ' randomly assigns a face to each die
46           DisplayDie(lblDie1)
47           DisplayDie(lblDie2)
48           DisplayDie(lblDie3)
49           DisplayDie(lblDie4)
50           DisplayDie(lblDie5)
51           DisplayDie(lblDie6)
52           DisplayDie(lblDie7)
53           DisplayDie(lblDie8)
54           DisplayDie(lblDie9)
55           DisplayDie(lblDie10)
56           DisplayDie(lblDie11)
57           DisplayDie(lblDie12)
58
59           Dim total As Double = 0
60           Dim i As Integer
61
62           For i = 1 To frequency.GetUpperBound(0)
63              total += frequency(i)
64           Next
65
66           txtDisplay.Text = "Face" & vbTab & vbTab & "Frequency" & _
67              vbTab & vbTab & "Percent" & vbCrLf
```

Fig. 7.7 Using arrays to eliminate a **Select Case** structure (part 2 of 4).

```
68
69          ' output frequency values
70          For i = 1 To frequency.GetUpperBound(0)
71             txtDisplay.Text &= i & vbTab & vbTab & frequency(i) & _
72                vbTab & vbTab & vbTab & String.Format("{0:N}", _
73                frequency(i) / total * 100) & "%" & vbCrLf
74          Next
75
76       End Sub ' cmdRoll_Click
77
78       ' simulate roll, display proper
79       ' image and increment frequency
80       Sub DisplayDie(ByVal lblDie As Label)
81          Dim face As Integer = 1 + randomNumber.Next(6)
82
83          lblDie.Image = _
84             Image.FromFile(Directory.GetCurrentDirectory & _
85             "\Images\die" & face & ".png")
86
87          frequency(face) += 1
88       End Sub ' DisplayDie
89
90    End Class ' FrmRollDie
```

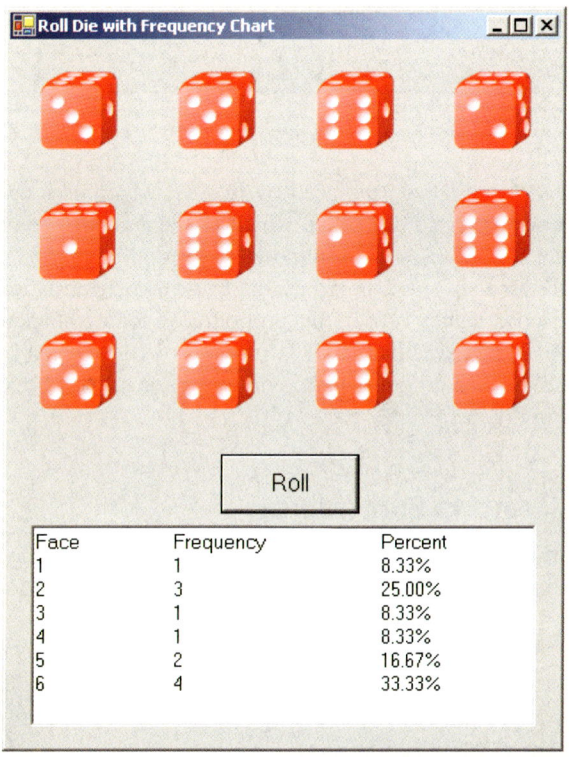

Fig. 7.7 Using arrays to eliminate a **Select Case** structure (part 3 of 4).

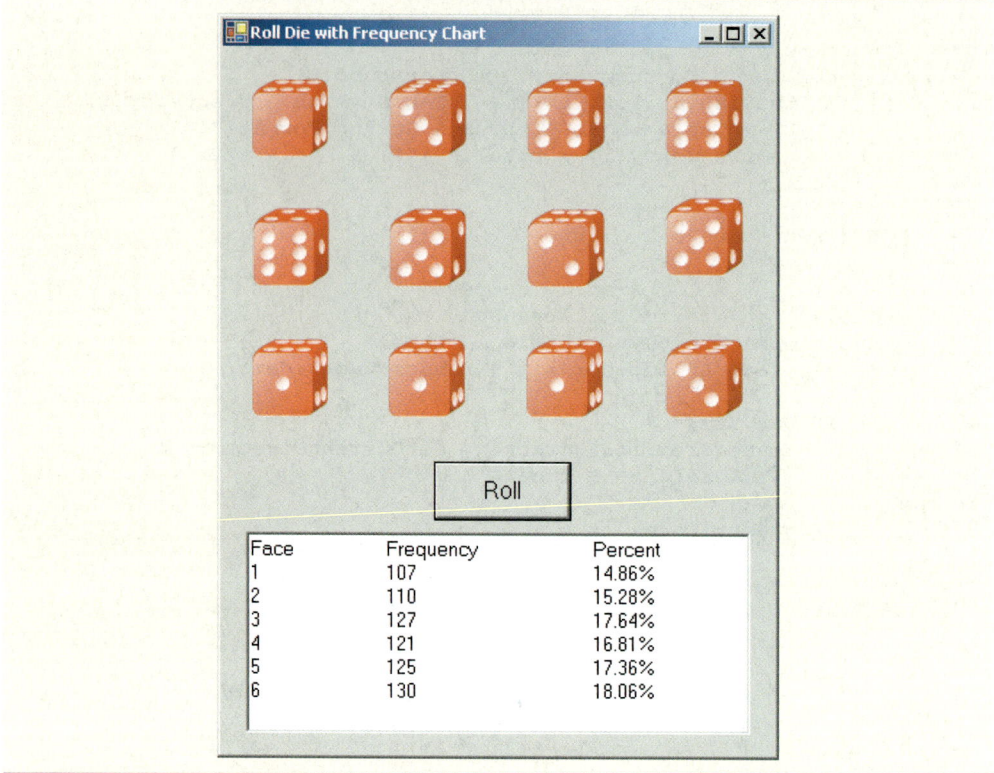

Fig. 7.7 Using arrays to eliminate a **Select Case** structure (part 4 of 4).

Lines 91–111 of Fig. 6.16 are replaced by line 87, which uses **face**'s value as the index for array **frequency** to determine which element should be incremented during each iteration of the loop. The random number calculation on line 81 produces numbers from 1–6 (the values for a six-sided die); thus, the **frequency** array must have seven elements to allow the index values 1–6. In this program, we ignore element 0 of array **frequency**. Lines 66–74 replace lines 57–78 from Fig. 6.16. We can loop through array **frequency**; therefore, we do not have to enumerate each line of text to display in the **Label**, as we did in Fig. 6.16.

7.5 Passing Arrays to Procedures

To pass an array argument to a procedure, specify the name of the array without using parentheses. For example, if array **hourlyTemperatures** has been declared as

```
Dim hourlyTemperatures As Integer() = New Integer(24) {}
```

the procedure call

```
DayData(hourlyTemperatures)
```

passes array **hourlyTemperatures** to procedure **DayData**.

Every array object "knows" its own upper bound (i.e., the value returned by the method **GetUpperBound**), so, when we pass an array object to a procedure, we do not need to pass the upper bound of the array as a separate argument.

For a procedure to receive an array through a procedure call, the procedure's parameter list must specify that an array will be received. For example, the procedure header for **DayData** might be written as

```
Sub DayData(ByVal temperatureData As Integer())
```

indicating that **DayData** expects to receive an **Integer** array in parameter **temperatureData**. In Visual Basic, arrays always are passed by reference, yet it is normally inappropriate to use keyword **ByRef** in the procedure definition header. We discuss this subtle (and somewhat complex) issue in more detail in Section 7.6.

Although entire arrays are always passed by reference, individual array elements can be passed in the same manner as simple variables of that type. For instance, array element values of primitive data types, such as **Integer**, can be passed by value or by reference, depending on the procedure definition. To pass an array element to a procedure, use the indexed name of the array element as an argument in the call to the procedure. The program in Fig. 7.8 demonstrates the difference between passing an entire array and passing an array element.

```
1   ' Fig. 7.8: PassArray.vb
2   ' Passing arrays and individual array elements to procedures.
3
4   Imports System.Windows.Forms
5
6   Module modPassArray
7      Dim output As String
8
9      Sub Main()
10         Dim array1 As Integer() = New Integer() {1, 2, 3, 4, 5}
11         Dim i As Integer
12
13         output = "EFFECTS OF PASSING ENTIRE ARRAY " & _
14            "BY REFERENCE:" & vbCrLf & vbCrLf & _
15            "The values of the original array are:" & vbCrLf
16
17         ' display original elements of array1
18         For i = 0 To array1.GetUpperBound(0)
19            output &= "   " & array1(i)
20         Next
21
22         ModifyArray(array1)  ' array is passed by reference
23
24         output &= vbCrLf & _
25            "The values of the modified array are:" & vbCrLf
26
27         ' display modified elements of array1
28         For i = 0 To array1.GetUpperBound(0)
29            output &= "   " & array1(i)
30         Next
```

Fig. 7.8 Passing arrays and individual array elements to procedures (part 1 of 3).

```
31
32         output &= vbCrLf & vbCrLf & _
33             "EFFECTS OF PASSING ARRAY ELEMENT " & _
34             "BY VALUE:" & vbCrLf & vbCrLf & "array1(3) " & _
35             "before ModifyElementByVal: " & array1(3)
36
37         ' array element passed by value
38         ModifyElementByVal(array1(3))
39
40         output &= vbCrLf & "array1(3) after " & _
41             "ModifyElementByVal: " & array1(3)
42
43         output &= vbCrLf & vbCrLf & "EFFECTS OF PASSING " & _
44             "ARRAY ELEMENT BY REFERENCE: " & vbCrLf & vbCrLf & _
45             "array1(3) before ModifyElementByRef: " & array1(3)
46
47         ' array element passed by reference
48         ModifyElementByRef(array1(3))
49
50         output &= vbCrLf & "array1(3) after " & _
51             "ModifyElementByRef: " & array1(3)
52
53         MessageBox.Show(output, "Passing Arrays", _
54             MessageBoxButtons.OK, MessageBoxIcon.Information)
55     End Sub ' Main
56
57     ' procedure modifies array it receives (note ByVal)
58     Sub ModifyArray(ByVal arrayParameter As Integer())
59         Dim j As Integer
60
61         For j = 0 To arrayParameter.GetUpperBound(0)
62             arrayParameter(j) *= 2
63         Next
64
65     End Sub ' ModifyArray
66
67     ' procedure modifies integer passed to it
68     ' original is not be modified (note ByVal)
69     Sub ModifyElementByVal(ByVal element As Integer)
70
71         output &= vbCrLf & "Value received in " & _
72             "ModifyElementByVal: " & element
73         element *= 2
74         output &= vbCrLf & "Value calculated in " & _
75             "ModifyElementByVal: " & element
76     End Sub ' ModifyElementByVal
77
78     ' procedure modifies integer passed to it
79     ' original is be modified (note ByRef)
80     Sub ModifyElementByRef(ByRef element As Integer)
81
82         output &= vbCrLf & "Value received in " & _
83             "ModifyElementByRef: " & element
```

Fig. 7.8 Passing arrays and individual array elements to procedures (part 2 of 3).

```
84          element *= 2
85          output &= vbCrLf & "Value calculated in " & _
86             "ModifyElementByRef: " & element
87       End Sub ' ModifyElementByRef
88
89   End Module ' modPassArray
```

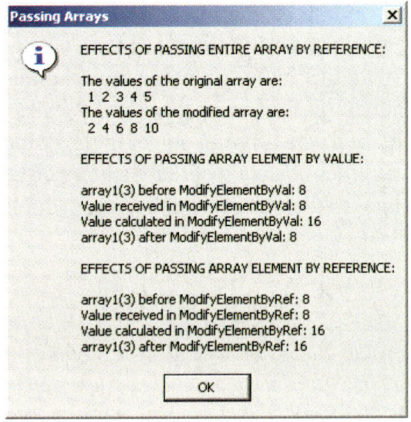

Fig. 7.8   Passing arrays and individual array elements to procedures (part 3 of 3).

The **For/Next** structure on lines 18–20 appends the five elements of integer array **array1** (line 10) to **String output**. Line 22 passes **array1** to procedure **ModifyArray** (line 58), which then multiplies each element by **2** (line 62). To illustrate that **array1**'s elements were modified in the called procedure (i.e., as enabled by passing by reference), the **For/Next** structure in lines 28–30 appends the five elements of **array1** to **output**. As the screen capture indicates, the elements of **array1** are indeed modified by **ModifyArray**.

To show the value of **array1(3)** before the call to **ModifyElementByVal**, lines 32–35 append the value of **array1(3)** to **String output**. Line 38 invokes procedure **ModifyElementByVal** and passes **array1(3)**. When **array1(3)** is passed by value, the **Integer** value in the fourth position of array **array1** (now an **8**) is copied and is passed to procedure **ModifyElementByVal**, where it becomes the value of argument **element**. Procedure **ModifyElementByVal** then multiplies **element** by **2** (line 73). The parameter of **ModifyElementByVal** is a local variable that is destroyed when the procedure terminates. Thus, when control is returned to **Main**, the unmodified value of **array1(3)** is appended to the string variable **output** (lines 40–41).

Lines 43–51 demonstrate the effects of procedure **ModifyElementByRef** (lines 80–87). This procedure performs the same calculation as **ModifyElementByVal**, multiplying **element** by **2**. In this case, **array1(3)** is passed by reference, meaning the value of **array1(3)** appended to **output** (lines 50–51) is the same as the value calculated in the procedure.

Common Programming Error 7.3

In the passing of an array to a procedure, including an empty pair of parentheses after the array name is a syntax error.

7.6 Passing Arrays: `ByVal` vs. `ByRef`

In Visual Basic .NET, a variable that "stores" an object, such as an array, does not actually store the object itself. Instead, such a variable stores a reference to the object (i.e., the location in the computer's memory where the object is already stored). The distinction between reference variables and primitive data type variables raises some subtle issues that programmers must understand to create secure, stable programs.

When used to declare a value-type parameter, keyword `ByVal` causes the value of the argument to be copied to a local variable in the procedure. Changes to the local variable are reflected in the local copy of that variable, but not in the original variable in the calling program. However, if the argument passed using keyword `ByVal` is of a reference type, the value copied is also a reference to the original object in the computer's memory. Thus, reference types (like arrays and other objects) passed via keyword `ByVal` are actually passed by reference, meaning changes to the objects in called procedures affect the original objects in the callers.

Performance Tip 7.2

Passing arrays and other objects by reference makes sense for performance reasons. If arrays were passed by value, a copy of each element would be passed. For large, frequently passed arrays, this would waste time and would consume considerable storage for the copies of the arrays—both of these problems cause poor performance.

Visual Basic also allows procedures to pass references with keyword `ByRef`. This is a subtle capability, which, if misused, can lead to problems. For instance, when a reference-type object like an array is passed with `ByRef`, the called procedure actually gains control over the passed reference itself, allowing the called procedure to replace the original reference in the caller with a different object or even with `Nothing`. Such behavior can lead to unpredictable effects, which can be disastrous in mission-critical applications. The program in Fig. 7.9 demonstrates the subtle difference between passing a reference `ByVal` vs. passing a reference `ByRef`.

Lines 11–12 declare two integer array variables, `firstArray` and `firstArray-Copy` (we make the copy so we can determine whether reference `firstArray` gets overwritten). Line 15 allocates an array containing `Integer` values **1**, **2** and **3** and stores the array reference in variable `firstArray`. The assignment statement on line 16 copies reference `firstArray` to variable `firstArrayCopy`, causing these variables to reference the same array object. The `For/Next` structure in lines 24–26 prints the contents of `firstArray` before it is passed to procedure `FirstDouble` on line 29 so we can verify that this array is passed by reference (i.e., the called method indeed changes the array's contents).

The `For/Next` structure in procedure `FirstDouble` (lines 94–96) multiplies the values of all the elements in the array by **2**. Line 99 allocates a new array containing the values **11**, **12** and **13**; the reference for this array then is assigned to parameter `array` (in an attempt to overwrite reference `firstArray` in `Main`—this, of course, will not happen, because the reference was passed `ByVal`). After procedure `FirstDouble` executes, the `For/Next` structure on lines 35–37 prints the contents of `firstArray`, demonstrating that the values of the elements have been changed by the procedure (and confirming that in Visual Basic, .NET arrays are always passed by reference). The `If` structure on lines 40–46 uses the `Is` operator to compare references `firstArray` (which we just attempted to overwrite) and `firstArrayCopy`. Visual Basic provides operator

Is for comparing references to determine whether they are referencing the same object. The expression on line 40 is true if the operands to binary operator **Is** indeed reference the same object. In this case, the object represented is the array allocated in line 15—not the array allocated in procedure **FirstDouble** (line 99).

```vbnet
1   ' Fig. 7.9: ArrayReferenceTest.vb
2   ' Testing the effects of passing array references using
3   ' ByVal and ByRef.
4
5   Module modArrayReferenceTest
6
7      Sub Main()
8         Dim i As Integer
9
10        ' declare array references
11        Dim firstArray As Integer()
12        Dim firstArrayCopy As Integer()
13
14        ' allocate firstArray and copy its reference
15        firstArray = New Integer() {1, 2, 3}
16        firstArrayCopy = firstArray
17
18        Console.WriteLine("Test passing array reference " & _
19           "using ByVal.")
20        Console.Write("Contents of firstArray before " & _
21           "calling FirstDouble: ")
22
23        ' print contents of firstArray
24        For i = 0 To firstArray.GetUpperBound(0)
25           Console.Write(firstArray(i) & " ")
26        Next
27
28        ' pass firstArray using ByVal
29        FirstDouble(firstArray)
30
31        Console.Write(vbCrLf & "Contents of firstArray after " & _
32           "calling FirstDouble: ")
33
34        ' print contents of firstArray
35        For i = 0 To firstArray.GetUpperBound(0)
36           Console.Write(firstArray(i) & " ")
37        Next
38
39        ' test whether reference was changed by FirstDouble
40        If firstArray Is firstArrayCopy Then
41           Console.WriteLine(vbCrLf & "The references are " & _
42              "equal.")
43        Else
44           Console.WriteLine(vbCrLf & "The references are " & _
45              "not equal.")
46        End If
47
```

Fig. 7.9 Passing an array reference with **ByVal** and **ByRef** (part 1 of 3).

```vbnet
48          ' declare array references
49          Dim secondArray As Integer()
50          Dim secondArrayCopy As Integer()
51
52          ' allocate secondArray and copy its reference
53          secondArray = New Integer() {1, 2, 3}
54          secondArrayCopy = secondArray
55
56          Console.WriteLine(vbCrLf & "Test passing array " & _
57             "reference using ByRef.")
58          Console.Write("Contents of secondArray before " & _
59             "calling SecondDouble: ")
60
61          ' print contents of secondArray before procedure call
62          For i = 0 To secondArray.GetUpperBound(0)
63             Console.Write(secondArray(i) & " ")
64          Next
65
66          ' pass secondArray using ByRef
67          SecondDouble(secondArray)
68
69          Console.Write(vbCrLf & "Contents of secondArray " & _
70             "after calling SecondDouble: ")
71
72          ' print contents of secondArray after procedure call
73          For i = 0 To secondArray.GetUpperBound(0)
74             Console.Write(secondArray(i) & " ")
75          Next
76
77          ' test whether the reference was changed by SecondDouble
78          If secondArray Is secondArrayCopy Then
79             Console.WriteLine(vbCrLf & "The references are " & _
80                "equal.")
81          Else
82             Console.WriteLine(vbCrLf & "The references are " & _
83                "not equal.")
84          End If
85
86       End Sub ' Main
87
88       ' procedure modifies elements of array and assigns
89       ' new reference (note ByVal)
90       Sub FirstDouble(ByVal array As Integer())
91          Dim i As Integer
92
93          ' double each element value
94          For i = 0 To array.GetUpperBound(0)
95             array(i) *= 2
96          Next
97
98          ' create new reference and assign it to array
99          array = New Integer() {11, 12, 13}
100      End Sub ' FirstDouble
```

Fig. 7.9 Passing an array reference with **ByVal** and **ByRef** (part 2 of 3).

```
101
102       ' procedure modifies elements of array and assigns
103       ' new reference (note ByRef)
104       Sub SecondDouble(ByRef array As Integer())
105          Dim i As Integer
106
107          ' double contents of array
108          For i = 0 To array.GetUpperBound(0)
109             array(i) *= 2
110          Next
111
112          ' create new reference and assign it to array
113          array = New Integer() {11, 12, 13}
114       End Sub ' SecondDouble
115
116    End Module ' modPassArray
```

```
Test passing array reference using ByVal.
Contents of firstArray before calling FirstDouble: 1 2 3
Contents of firstArray after calling FirstDouble: 2 4 6
The references are equal.

Test passing array reference using ByRef.
Contents of secondArray before calling SecondDouble: 1 2 3
Contents of secondArray after calling SecondDouble: 11 12 13
The references are not equal.
```

Fig. 7.9 Passing an array reference with **ByVal** and **ByRef** (part 3 of 3).

Lines 48–84 in procedure **Main** perform similar tests, using array variables **secondArray** and **secondArrayCopy** and procedure **SecondDouble** (lines 104–114). Procedure **SecondDouble** performs the same operations as **FirstDouble**, but receives its array argument with **ByRef**. In this case, the reference stored in **secondArray** after the procedure call is a reference to the array allocated on line 113 of **SecondDouble**, demonstrating that a reference passed with **ByRef** can be modified by the called procedure so that the reference actually points to a different object, in this case an array allocated in procedure **SecondDouble**. The **If** structure in lines 78–84 demonstrates that **secondArray** and **secondArrayCopy** no longer represent the same array.

Software Engineering Observation 7.1

*Using **ByVal** to receive a reference-type object parameter does not cause the object to pass by value—the object still passes by reference. Rather, **ByVal** causes the object's reference to pass by value. This prevents a called procedure from overwriting a reference in the caller. In the vast majority of cases, protecting the caller's reference from modification is the desired behavior. If you encounter a situation where you truly want the called procedure to modify the caller's reference, pass the reference-type object **ByRef**—but, again, such situations are rare.*

Software Engineering Observation 7.2

In Visual Basic .NET, reference-type objects (including arrays) always pass by reference. So, a called procedure receiving a reference to an object in a caller can change the caller's object.

7.7 Sorting Arrays

Sorting data (i.e., arranging the data into some particular order, such as ascending or descending order) is one of the most popular computing applications. For example, a bank sorts all checks by account number, so that it can prepare individual bank statements at the end of each month. Telephone companies sort their lists of accounts by last name and, within last-name listings, by first name, to make it easy to find phone numbers. Virtually every organization must sort some data and, often, massive amounts of it. Sorting is an intriguing problem that has attracted some of the most intense research efforts in the computer-science field. This section discusses one of the simplest sorting schemes. In the exercises at the end of this chapter, we investigate a more sophisticated sorting algorithm.

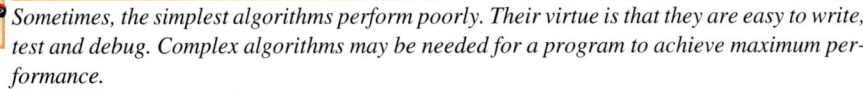

Performance Tip 7.3

Sometimes, the simplest algorithms perform poorly. Their virtue is that they are easy to write, test and debug. Complex algorithms may be needed for a program to achieve maximum performance.

The module shown in Fig. 7.10 contains procedures for sorting the values of an integer array into ascending order. The technique we use is called the *bubble sort*, or the *sinking sort*, because in an ascending sort smaller values gradually "bubble" their way to the top of the array (i.e., toward the first element) like air bubbles rising in water, while larger values sink to the bottom (i.e., toward the end) of the array. The technique uses nested loops to make several passes through the array. Each pass compares successive pairs of elements. If a pair is in increasing order (or the values are equal), the bubble sort leaves the values as they are. If a pair is in decreasing order, the bubble sort swaps their values in the array.

```vb
1   ' Fig. 7.10: BubbleSort.vb
2   ' Procedures for sorting an integer array.
3
4   Module modBubbleSort
5
6      ' sort array using bubble sort algorithm
7      Sub BubbleSort(ByVal sortArray As Integer())
8         Dim pass, i As Integer
9
10        For pass = 1 To sortArray.GetUpperBound(0)
11
12           For i = 0 To sortArray.GetUpperBound(0) - 1
13
14              If sortArray(i) > sortArray(i + 1) Then
15                 Swap(sortArray, i)
16              End If
17
18           Next
19
20        Next
21
22     End Sub ' BubbleSort
23
```

Fig. 7.10 **BubbleSort** procedure in **modBubbleSort** (part 1 of 2).

```vbnet
24        ' swap two array elements
25        Sub Swap(ByVal swapArray As Integer(), _
26           ByVal first As Integer)
27
28           Dim hold As Integer
29
30           hold = swapArray(first)
31           swapArray(first) = swapArray(first + 1)
32           swapArray(first + 1) = hold
33        End Sub ' Swap
34
35     End Module ' modBubbleSort
```

Fig. 7.10 `BubbleSort` procedure in `modBubbleSort` (part 2 of 2).

The module contains procedures **BubbleSort** and **Swap**. Procedure **BubbleSort** (lines 7–22) sorts the elements of its parameter, **sortArray**. Procedure **BubbleSort** calls procedure **Swap** (lines 25–33) as necessary to transpose two of the array elements. The Windows application in Fig. 7.11 demonstrates procedure **BubbleSort** (Fig. 7.10) by sorting an array of 10 randomly-generated elements (which may contain duplicates).

```vbnet
1   ' Fig. 7.11: BubbleSortTest.vb
2   ' Program creates random numbers and sorts them.
3
4   Imports System.Windows.Forms
5
6   Public Class FrmBubbleSort
7      Inherits System.Windows.Forms.Form
8
9      ' buttons
10     Friend WithEvents cmdCreate As Button
11     Friend WithEvents cmdSort As Button
12
13     ' labels
14     Friend WithEvents lblOriginal As Label
15     Friend WithEvents lblSorted As Label
16
17     ' textboxes
18     Friend WithEvents txtOriginal As TextBox
19     Friend WithEvents txtSorted As TextBox
20
21     ' Visual Studio .NET generated code
22
23     Dim array As Integer() = New Integer(9) {}
24
25     ' creates random generated numbers
26     Private Sub cmdCreate_Click(ByVal sender As System.Object, _
27        ByVal e As System.EventArgs) Handles cmdCreate.Click
28
```

Fig. 7.11 Sorting an array with bubble sort (part 1 of 3).

```
29         Dim output As String
30         Dim randomNumber As Random = New Random()
31         Dim i As Integer
32
33         txtSorted.Text = ""
34
35         ' create 10 random numbers and append to output
36         For i = 0 To array.GetUpperBound(0)
37            array(i) = randomNumber.Next(100)
38            output &= array(i) & vbCrLf
39         Next
40
41         txtOriginal.Text = output  ' display numbers
42         cmdSort.Enabled = True     ' enables cmdSort button
43      End Sub ' cmdCreate_Click
44
45      ' sorts randomly generated numbers
46      Private Sub cmdSort_Click(ByVal sender As System.Object, _
47         ByVal e As System.EventArgs) Handles cmdSort.Click
48
49         Dim output As String
50         Dim i As Integer
51
52         ' sort array
53         modBubbleSort.BubbleSort(array)
54
55         ' creates string with sorted numbers
56         For i = 0 To array.GetUpperBound(0)
57            output &= array(i) & vbCrLf
58         Next
59
60         txtSorted.Text = output  ' display numbers
61         cmdSort.Enabled = False
62      End Sub ' cmdSort_Click
63
64   End Class ' FrmBubbleSort
```

Fig. 7.11 Sorting an array with bubble sort (part 2 of 3).

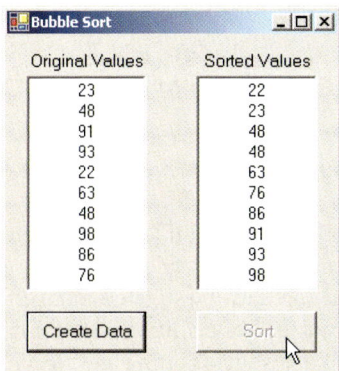

Fig. 7.11 Sorting an array with bubble sort (part 3 of 3).

The program contains methods **cmdCreate_Click** and **cmdSort_Click**. Method **cmdCreate_Click** (lines 26–43) assigns 10 random values to the elements of **array** and displays the contents of the array in **txtOriginal**. Method **cmdSort_Click** (lines 46–62) sorts **array** by calling procedure **BubbleSort** from **modBubbleSort**.

Procedure **BubbleSort** receives the array as parameter **sortArray**. The nested **For/Next** structures in lines 10–20 of Fig. 7.10 performs the sort. The outer loop controls the number of passes of the array. The inner loop (lines 12–18) controls the comparisons and swapping (if necessary) of the elements during each pass.

Procedure **BubbleSort** first compares **sortArray(0)** to **sortArray(1)**, then **sortArray(1)** to **sortArray(2)**, and so on until it completes the pass by comparing **sortArray(8)** to **sortArray(9)**. Although there are 10 elements, the comparison loop performs only nine comparisons (because the comparisons each involve a pair of numbers).

The comparisons performed in a bubble sort could cause a large value to move down the array (sink) many positions on a single pass. However, a small value cannot move up (bubble) more than one position per pass. On the first pass, the largest value is guaranteed to sink to the bottom element of the array, **sortArray(9)**. On the second pass, the second-largest value is guaranteed to sink to **sortArray(8)**. On the ninth pass, the ninth largest value sinks to **sortArray(1)**, leaving the smallest value in **sortArray(0)**. Thus, only nine passes are required to sort a 10-element array (and, in general, only *n*-1 passes are needed to sort an *n*-element array).

If a comparison reveals that the two elements are in descending order, **BubbleSort** calls procedure **Swap** to exchange the two elements, placing them in ascending order in the array. Procedure **Swap** receives the array (which it calls **swapArray**) and the index of the first element of the array to transpose (with the subsequent element). The exchange is performed by three assignments

```
hold = swapArray(first)
swapArray(first) = swapArray(first + 1)
swapArray(first + 1) = hold
```

where the extra variable **hold** temporarily stores one of the two values being swapped. The swap cannot be performed with only the two assignments

```
swapArray(first) = swapArray(first + 1)
swapArray(first + 1) = swapArray(first)
```

If **swapArray(first)** is **7** and **swapArray(first + 1)** is **5**, after the first assignment both array elements contains **5**, and the value **7** is lost—hence, the need for the extra variable **hold**.

The advantage of the bubble sort is that it is easy to program. However, the bubble sort runs slowly, as becomes apparent when sorting large arrays. In the exercises, we develop efficient versions of the bubble sort and investigate a more efficient and more complex sort, quicksort. More advanced courses (often titled "Data Structures" or "Algorithms" or "Computational Complexity") investigate sorting and searching in greater depth.

7.8 Searching Arrays: Linear Search and Binary Search

Often, programmers work with large amounts of data stored in arrays. It might be necessary in this case to determine whether an array contains a value that matches a certain *key value*. The process of locating a particular element value in an array is called *searching*. In this section, we discuss two searching techniques—the simple *linear search* technique and the more efficient (but more complex) *binary search* technique. Exercises 7.8 and 7.9 at the end of this chapter ask you to implement recursive versions of the linear and binary searches.

7.8.1 Searching an Array with Linear Search

Module **modLinearSearch** in Fig. 7.12 contains a procedure for performing a linear search. Procedure **LinearSearch** (lines 7–22) uses a **For/Next** structure containing an **If** structure (lines 15–17) to compare each element of an array with a *search key*. If the search key is found, the procedure returns the index value for the element, indicating the position of the search key in the array. If the search key is not found, the procedure returns **-1**. (The value **-1** is a good choice because it is not a valid index number.) If the elements of the array being searched are unordered, it is just as likely that the value will be found in the first element as in the last, so the procedure will have to compare the search key with half the elements of the array, on average.

```vb
1  ' Fig. 7.12: LinearSearch.vb
2  ' Linear search of an array.
3
4  Module modLinearSearch
5
6     ' iterates through array
7     Function LinearSearch(ByVal key As Integer, _
8        ByVal numbers As Integer()) As Integer
9
10       Dim n As Integer
11
```

Fig. 7.12 Procedures for performing a linear search (part 1 of 2).

```
12              ' structure iterates linearly through array
13              For n = 0 To numbers.GetUpperBound(0)
14
15                 If numbers(n) = key Then
16                    Return n
17                 End If
18
19              Next
20
21              Return -1
22           End Function ' LinearSearch
23
24     End Module ' modLinearSearch
```

Fig. 7.12 Procedures for performing a linear search (part 2 of 2).

The program in Fig. 7.13 uses module **modLinearSearch** to search a 20-element array filled with random values created when the user clicks **cmdCreate**. The user then types a search key in a **TextBox** (named *txtInput*) and clicks **cmdSearch** to start the search.

```
1    ' Fig. 7.13: LinearSearchTest.vb
2    ' Linear search of an array.
3
4    Imports System.Windows.Forms
5
6    Public Class FrmLinearSearchTest
7       Inherits System.Windows.Forms.Form
8
9       ' buttons
10      Friend WithEvents cmdSearch As Button
11      Friend WithEvents cmdCreate As Button
12
13      ' text boxes
14      Friend WithEvents txtInput As TextBox
15      Friend WithEvents txtData As TextBox
16
17      ' labels
18      Friend WithEvents lblEnter As Label
19      Friend WithEvents lblResult As Label
20
21      ' Visual Studio .NET generated code
22
23      Dim array1 As Integer() = New Integer(19) {}
24
25      ' creates random data
26      Private Sub cmdCreate_Click(ByVal sender As System.Object, _
27         ByVal e As System.EventArgs) Handles cmdCreate.Click
28
29         Dim output As String
30         Dim randomNumber As Random = New Random()
31         Dim i As Integer
```

Fig. 7.13 Linear search of an array (part 1 of 3).

```
32
33          output = "Index" & vbTab & "Value" & vbCrLf
34
35          ' creates string containing 11 random numbers
36          For i = 0 To array1.GetUpperBound(0)
37              array1(i) = randomNumber.Next(1000)
38              output &= i & vbTab & array1(i) & vbCrLf
39          Next
40
41          txtData.Text = output     ' displays numbers
42          txtInput.Text = ""        ' clear search key text box
43          cmdSearch.Enabled = True  ' enable search button
44      End Sub ' cmdCreate_Click
45
46      ' searches key of element
47      Private Sub cmdSearch_Click(ByVal sender As System.Object, _
48          ByVal e As System.EventArgs) Handles cmdSearch.Click
49
50          ' if search key text box is empty, display
51          ' message and exit procedure
52          If txtInput.Text = "" Then
53              MessageBox.Show("You must enter a search key.")
54              Exit Sub
55          End If
56
57          Dim searchKey As Integer = Convert.ToInt32(txtInput.Text)
58          Dim element As Integer = LinearSearch(searchKey, array1)
59
60          If element <> -1 Then
61              lblResult.Text = "Found Value in index " & element
62          Else
63              lblResult.Text = "Value Not Found"
64          End If
65
66      End Sub ' cmdSearch_Click
67
68  End Class ' FrmLinearSearch
```

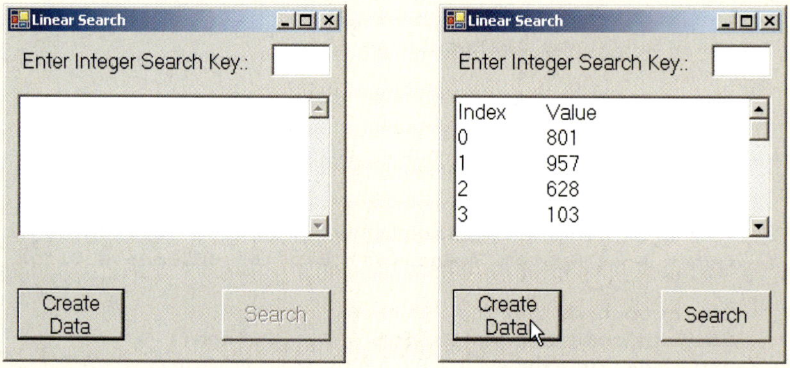

Fig. 7.13 Linear search of an array (part 2 of 3).

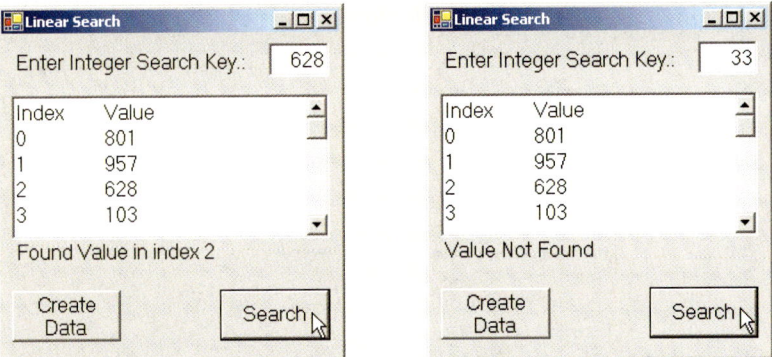

Fig. 7.13 Linear search of an array (part 3 of 3).

7.8.2 Searching a Sorted Array with Binary Search

The linear search method works well for small or unsorted arrays. However, for large arrays, linear searching is inefficient. If the array is sorted, the high-speed *binary search* technique can be used.

After each comparison, the binary search algorithm eliminates from consideration half the elements in the array that is being searched. The algorithm locates the middle array element and compares it with the search key. If they are equal, the search key has been found, and the index of that element is returned. Otherwise, the problem is reduced to searching half of the array. If the search key is less than the middle array element, the second half of the array is eliminated from consideration, and searching continues with only the first half of the array; otherwise, the second half of the array is searched. If the search key is not the middle element in the specified *subarray* (a piece of the original array), the algorithm is repeated in one quarter of the original array. The search continues until the search key is equal to the middle element of a subarray, or until the subarray consists of one element that is not equal to the search key (i.e., the search key is not found).

In a worst-case scenario, searching a sorted array of 1024 elements via binary search requires only 10 comparisons. Repeatedly dividing 1024 by 2 (after each comparison, we eliminate from consideration half the array) yields the successive values 512, 256, 128, 64, 32, 16, 8, 4, 2 and 1. The number 1024 (2^{10}) is divided by 2 only ten times to get the value 1, and division by 2 is equivalent to one comparison in the binary search algorithm. A sorted array of 1,048,576 (2^{20}) elements takes a maximum of 20 comparisons to find the key! Similarly, a key can be found in a sorted array of one billion elements in a maximum of 30 comparisons! This is a tremendous increase in performance over the linear search, which required comparing the search key with an average of half the elements in the array. For a one-billion-element array, the difference is between an average of 500 million comparisons and a maximum of 30 comparisons! The maximum number of comparisons needed to complete a binary search of any sorted array is indicated by the exponent of the first power of 2 that is greater than or equal to the number of elements in the array.

Figure 7.14 presents the iterative version of method **BinarySearch** (lines 60–86). The method receives two arguments—integer array **array1** (the array to search), and integer **searchKey** (the search key). The array is passed to **BinarySearch**, even though the array is an instance variable of the class. Once again, this is done because an array normally is passed to a procedure of another class for searching.

```vb
1   ' Fig. 7.14: BinarySearchTest.vb
2   ' Demonstrating binary search of an array.
3
4   Imports System.Windows.Forms
5
6   Public Class FrmBinarySearch
7       Inherits System.Windows.Forms.Form
8
9       ' labels
10      Friend WithEvents lblEnterKey As Label
11      Friend WithEvents lblResult As Label
12      Friend WithEvents lblResultOutput As Label
13      Friend WithEvents lblDisplay As Label
14      Friend WithEvents lblIndex As Label
15      Friend WithEvents lblIndexes As Label
16
17      ' button
18      Friend WithEvents cmdFindKey As Button
19
20      ' text box
21      Friend WithEvents txtInput As TextBox
22
23      ' Visual Studio .NET generated code
24
25      Dim array1 As Integer() = New Integer(14) {}
26
27      ' FrmBinarySearch initializes array1 to ascending values
28      ' 0, 2, 4, 6, ..., 28 when first loaded
29      Private Sub FrmBinarySearch_Load(ByVal sender As System.Object, _
30          ByVal e As System.EventArgs) Handles MyBase.Load
31
32          Dim i As Integer
33
34          For i = 0 To array1.GetUpperBound(0)
35              array1(i) = 2 * i
36          Next
37
38      End Sub ' FrmBinarySearch_Load
39
40      ' event handler for cmdFindKey button
41      Private Sub cmdFindKey_Click(ByVal sender As System.Object, _
42          ByVal e As System.EventArgs) Handles cmdFindKey.Click
43
44          Dim searchKey As Integer = Convert.ToInt32(txtInput.Text)
45
46          lblDisplay.Text = ""
47
48          ' perform binary search
49          Dim element As Integer = BinarySearch(array1, searchKey)
50
```

Fig. 7.14 Binary search of a sorted array (part 1 of 3).

```vbnet
51         If element <> -1 Then
52            lblResultOutput.Text = "Found value in element " & element
53         Else
54            lblResultOutput.Text = "Value not found"
55         End If
56
57      End Sub ' cmdFindKey_Click
58
59      ' performs binary search
60      Function BinarySearch(ByVal array As Integer(), _
61         ByVal key As Integer) As Integer
62
63         Dim low As Integer = 0                    ' low index
64         Dim high As Integer = array.GetUpperBound(0) ' high index
65         Dim middle As Integer                     ' middle index
66
67         While low <= high
68            middle = (low + high) \ 2
69
70            ' the following line displays part
71            ' of the array being manipulated during
72            ' each iteration of loop
73            BuildOutput(low, middle, high)
74
75            If key = array(middle) Then      ' match
76               Return middle
77            ElseIf key < array(middle) Then  ' search low end
78               high = middle - 1             ' of array
79            Else
80               low = middle + 1
81            End If
82
83         End While
84
85         Return -1 ' search key not found
86      End Function ' BinarySearch
87
88      Sub BuildOutput(ByVal low As Integer, _
89         ByVal middle As Integer, ByVal high As Integer)
90
91         Dim i As Integer
92
93         For i = 0 To array1.GetUpperBound(0)
94
95            If i < low OrElse i > high Then
96               lblDisplay.Text &= "    "
97            ElseIf i = middle Then  ' mark middle element in output
98               lblDisplay.Text &= String.Format("{0:D2}", _
99                  array1(i)) & "* "
100           Else
101              lblDisplay.Text &= String.Format("{0:D2}", _
102                 array1(i)) & "  "
103           End If
```

Fig. 7.14 Binary search of a sorted array (part 2 of 3).

```
104
105        Next i
106
107        lblDisplay.Text &= vbCrLf
108    End Sub ' BuildOutput
109
110 End Class ' FrmBinarySearch
```

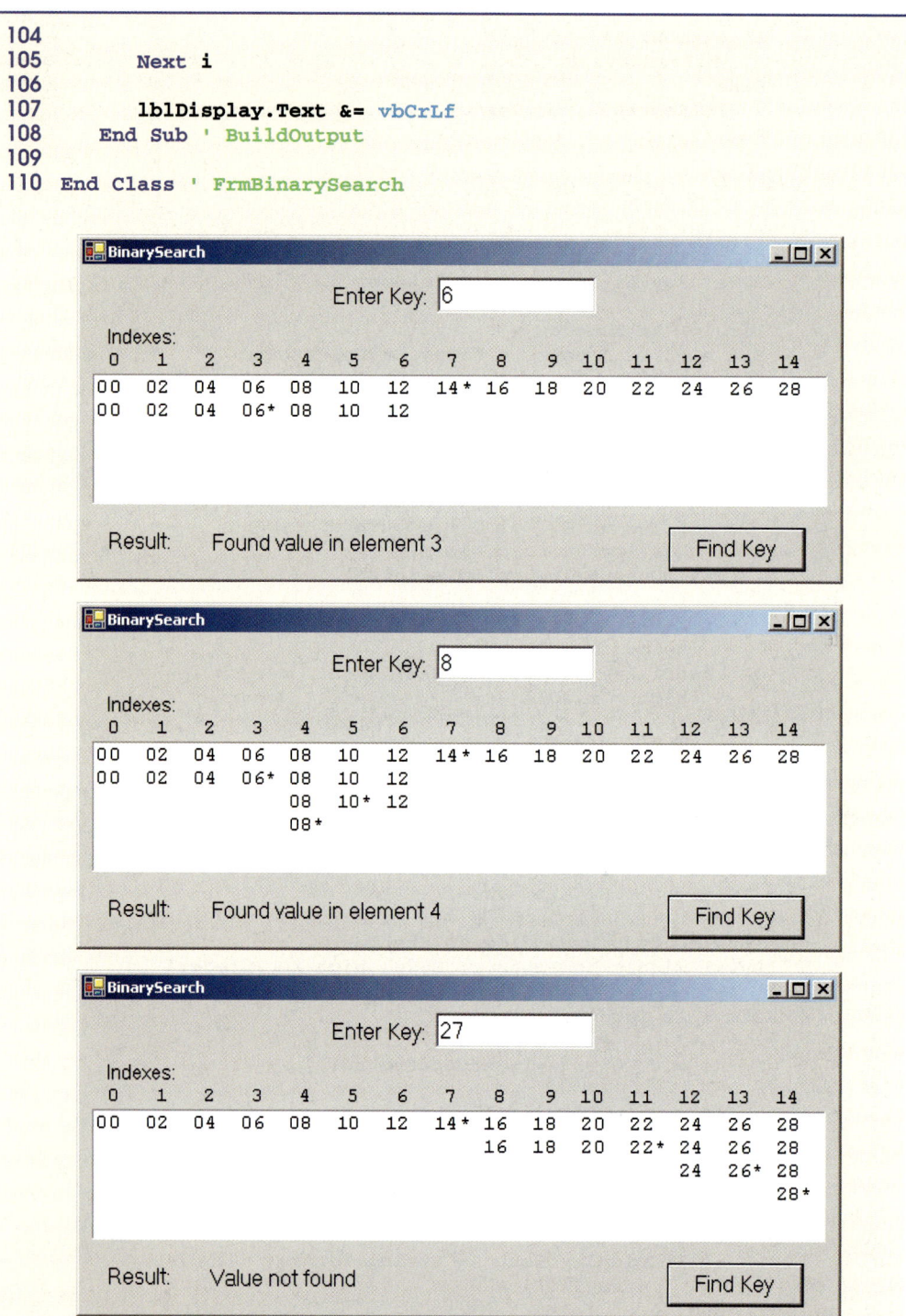

Fig. 7.14 Binary search of a sorted array (part 3 of 3).

Line 68 calculates the middle element of the array being searched by determining the number of elements in the array and then dividing this value by **2**. Recall that using the **** operator causes the remainder to be discarded. What happens, then, when there is an even number of elements in the array? In this case there is no "middle" element, and the middle of our array is actually between the two middle elements. When this occurs, the calculation on line 68 returns the smaller of the two middle values.

The **If/Else** structure on lines 75–81 compares the middle element of the array to **key**. If **key** matches the **middle** element of a subarray (line 75), **middle** (the index of the current element) is returned, indicating that the value was found and the search is complete.

If **key** does not match the **middle** element of a subarray, the **low** index or **high** index (both declared in the method) is adjusted so that a smaller subarray can be searched. If **key** is less than the middle element (line 77), the **high** index is set to **middle - 1**, and the search is continued on the elements from **low** to **middle - 1**. If **key** is greater than the middle element (line 79), the **low** index is set to **middle + 1**, and the search is continued on the elements from **middle + 1** to **high**.

The program uses a 15-element array. The first power of 2 greater than or equal to the number of array elements is 16 (2^4), so at most four comparisons are required to find the **key**. To illustrate this concept, method **BinarySearch** calls method **BuildOutput** (line 88) to output each subarray during the binary search process. The middle element in each subarray is marked with an asterisk (*****) to indicate the element with which the **key** is compared. The format string **"{0:D2}"** on lines 98 and 101 causes the values to be formatted as integers with at least two digits. Each search in this example results in a maximum of four lines of output—one per comparison.

7.9 Multidimensional Rectangular and Jagged Arrays

So far, we have studied *one-dimensional* (or *single-subscripted*) arrays—i.e., those that contain one row of values. In this section, we introduce *multidimensional* (often called *multiple-subscripted*) arrays, which require two or more indices to identify particular elements. We concentrate on *two-dimensional* (often called *double-subscripted*) arrays, or arrays that contain multiple rows of values. There are two types of multidimensional arrays—*rectangular* and *jagged*. Rectangular arrays with two indices often represent *tables* of values consisting of information arranged in *rows* and *columns*. Each row is the same size, and each column is the same size (hence, the term "rectangular"). To identify a particular table element, we must specify the two indices—by convention, the first identifies the element's row, the second the element's column. Figure 7.15 illustrates a two-dimensional rectangular array, **a**, containing three rows and four columns. A rectangular two-dimensional array with *m* rows and *n* columns is called an *m-by-n array*; the array in Fig. 7.15 is referred to as a 3-by-4 array.

Every element in array **a** is identified in Fig. 7.15 by an element name of the form **a(i, j)**, where **a** is the name of the array and **i** and **j** are the indices that uniquely identify the row and column of each element in array **a**. Notice that, because array indices are determined through zero-based counting, the names of the elements in the first row have a first index of **0**; the names of the elements in the fourth column have a second index of **3**.

Multidimensional arrays are initialized in declarations using the same process and notations employed for one-dimensional arrays. For example, a two-dimensional rectangular array **numbers** with two rows and two columns could be declared and initialized with

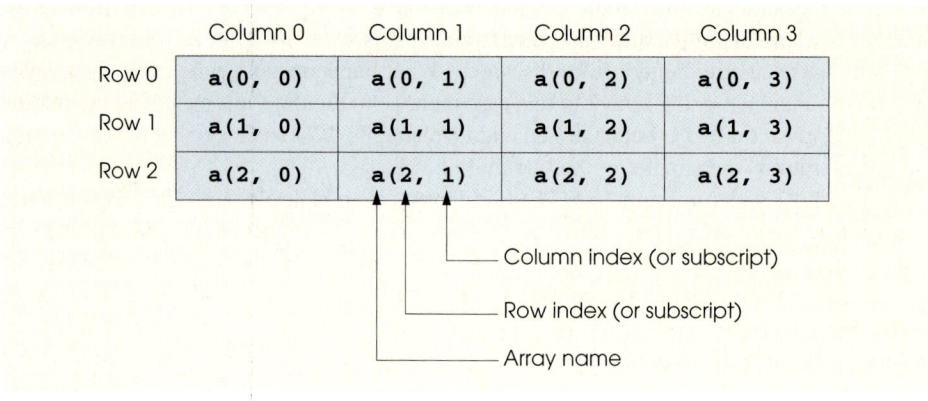

Fig. 7.15 Two-dimensional array with three rows and four columns.

```
Dim numbers As Integer(,) = New Integer(1,1) {}

numbers(0, 0) = 1
numbers(0, 1) = 2
numbers(1, 0) = 3
numbers(1, 1) = 4
```

Alternatively, the initialization can be written on one line, as shown below:

```
Dim numbers As Integer(,) = New Integer(,) {{1, 2}, {3, 4}}
```

The values are grouped by row in braces, with **1** and **2** initializing **numbers(0,0)** and **numbers(0,1)**, and **3** and **4** initializing **numbers(1,0)** and **numbers(1,1)**. The compiler determines the number of rows by counting the number of subinitializer lists (represented by sets of braces) in the main initializer list. Then, the compiler determines the number of columns in each row by counting the number of initializer values in the subinitializer list for that row. In rectangular arrays, each row has the same number of values.

Jagged arrays are maintained as arrays of arrays. Unlike rectangular arrays, rows in jagged arrays can be of different lengths. The statements

```
Dim array2 As Integer()()    ' declare jagged array

array2 = New Integer(1)() {} ' allocate two rows

' allocate columns for row 0
array2(0) = New Integer() {1, 2}

' allocate columns for 1
array2(1) = New Integer() {3, 4, 5}
```

create **Integer** array **array2** with row **0** (which is an array itself) containing two elements (**1** and **2**), and row **1** containing three elements (**3**, **4** and **5**). Notice that the array name, followed by a single index (e.g., **array2(0)**), behaves exactly like a normal one-dimensional array variable. A one-dimensional array can be created and assigned to that value.

The program in Fig. 7.16 demonstrates the initialization of a rectangular array (**array1**) and a jagged array (**array2**) in declarations and the use of nested **For/Next** loops to traverse the arrays (i.e., to manipulate every array element).

The program declares two arrays in method **Main**. The allocation of **array1** (line 14) provides six initializers in two sublists. The first sublist initializes the first row (row **0**) of the array to the values **1**, **2** and **3**; the second sublist initializes the second row (row **1**) of the array to the values **4**, **5** and **6**. The declaration and allocation of **array2** (line 17) create a jagged array of 3 arrays (specified by the **2** in the first set of parentheses after keyword **Integer**). Lines 18–20 initialize each subarray so that the first subarray contains the values **1** and **2**, the second contains the value **3** and the last contains the values **4**, **5** and **6**.

The nested **For/Next** structures in lines 24–31 append the elements of **array1** to string **output**. The nested **For/Next** structures traverse the arrays in two dimensions. The outer **For/Next** structure traverses the rows; the inner **For/Next** structure traverses the columns within a row. Each **For/Next** structure calls method **GetUpperBound** to obtain the upper bound of the dimension it traverses. Notice that the dimensions are zero-based, meaning the rows are dimension **0** and the columns are dimension **1**.

```vb
1   ' Fig. 7.16: MultidimensionalArrays.vb
2   ' Initializing multidimensional arrays.
3
4   Imports System.Windows.Forms
5
6   Module modMultidimensionalArrays
7
8      Sub Main()
9         Dim output As String
10        Dim i, j As Integer
11
12        ' create rectangular two-dimensional array
13        Dim array1 As Integer(,)
14        array1 = New Integer(,) {{1, 2, 3}, {4, 5, 6}}
15
16        ' create jagged two-dimensional array
17        Dim array2 As Integer()() = New Integer(2)() {}
18
19        array2(0) = New Integer() {1, 2}
20        array2(1) = New Integer() {3}
21        array2(2) = New Integer() {4, 5, 6}
22
23        output = "Values in array1 by row are " & vbCrLf
24
25        For i = 0 To array1.GetUpperBound(0)
26
27           For j = 0 To array1.GetUpperBound(1)
28              output &= array1(i, j) & " "
29           Next
30
31           output &= vbCrLf
32        Next
33
```

Fig. 7.16 Initializing multidimensional arrays (part 1 of 2).

```
34            output &= vbCrLf & "Values in array2 by row are " & _
35               vbCrLf
36
37            For i = 0 To array2.GetUpperBound(0)
38
39               For j = 0 To array2(i).GetUpperBound(0)
40                  output &= array2(i)(j) & " "
41               Next
42
43               output &= vbCrLf
44            Next
45
46            MessageBox.Show(output, _
47               "Initializing Multidimensional Arrays", _
48               MessageBoxButtons.OK, MessageBoxIcon.Information)
49         End Sub ' Main
50
51    End Module ' modMultidimensionalArrays
```

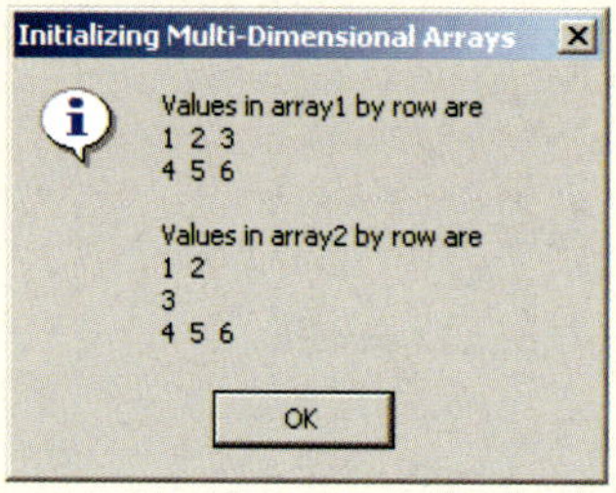

Fig. 7.16 Initializing multidimensional arrays (part 2 of 2).

The nested **For/Next** structures in lines 36–43 behave similarly for **array2**. However, in a jagged two-dimensional array, the second dimension is actually the first dimension of a separate array. In the example, the inner **For/Next** structure determines the number of columns in each row of the array by passing argument **0** to method **GetUpperBound**, called on the array returned by accessing a single row of the jagged array. Arrays of dimensions higher than two can be traversed using one nested **For/Next** structure for each dimension.

Many common array manipulations use **For/Next** repetition structures. Imagine a jagged array **jaggedArray**, which contains 3 rows, or arrays. The following **For/Next** structure sets all the elements in the third row of array **jaggedArray** to zero:

```
For column = 0 To jaggedArray(2).GetUpperBound(0)
   jaggedArray(2)(column) = 0
Next
```

We specified the *third* row; therefore, we know that the first index is always **2** (**0** is the first row and **1** is the second row). The **For/Next** loop varies only the second index (i.e., the column index). Notice the use of **jaggedArray(2).GetUpperBound(0)** as the end value of the **For/Next** structure. In this expression, we call the **GetUpperBound** method on the array contained in the third row of **jaggedArray**. This statement demonstrates that each row of **jaggedArray** is itself an array, and therefore methods called on this value behave as they would for a typical array. The preceding **For/Next** structure is equivalent to the assignment statements

```
jaggedArray(2)(0) = 0
jaggedArray(2)(1) = 0
jaggedArray(2)(2) = 0
jaggedArray(2)(3) = 0
```

The following nested **For/Next** structure determines the total of all the elements in array **jaggedArray**. We use method **GetUpperBound** in the headers of the **For/Next** structures to determine the number of rows in **jaggedArray** and the number of columns in each row.

```
Dim total, row, column As Integer

For row = 0 To jaggedArray.GetUpperBound(0)

    For column = 0 To jaggedArray(row).GetUpperBound(0)
       total += jaggedArray(row)(column)
    Next

Next
```

The nested **For/Next** structure totals the elements of the array one row at a time. The outer **For/Next** structure begins by setting the **row** index to **0**, so the elements of the first row can be totaled by the inner **For/Next** structure. The outer **For/Next** structure then increments **row** to **1**, so the second row can be totaled. The outer **For/Next** structure increments **row** to **2**, so the third row can be totaled. The result can be displayed when the outer **For/Next** structure terminates.

The program in Fig. 7.17 performs several other array manipulations on a 3-by-4 array **grades**. Each row of the array represents a student, and each column represents a grade on one of the four exams that the student took during the semester. The array manipulations are performed by four procedures: Procedure **Minimum** (line 44) determines the lowest grade of any student for the semester. Procedure **Maximum** (line 66) determines the highest grade of any student for the semester. Procedure **Average** (line 89) determines a particular student's semester average. Procedure **BuildString** (line 103) appends the two-dimensional array to string **output** in tabular format.

```
1   ' Fig 7.17: JaggedArray.vb
2   ' Jagged two-dimensional array example.
3
4   Imports System.Windows.Forms
5
6   Module modJaggedArray
7      Dim lastStudent, lastExam As Integer
8      Dim output As String
9
10     Sub Main()
11        Dim i As Integer
```

Fig. 7.17 Using jagged two-dimensional arrays (part 1 of 4).

```vbnet
12
13         ' jagged array with 3 rows of exam scores
14         Dim gradeArray As Integer()() = New Integer(2)() {}
15
16         ' allocate each row with 4 student grades
17         gradeArray(0) = New Integer() {77, 68, 86, 73}
18         gradeArray(1) = New Integer() {98, 87, 89, 81}
19         gradeArray(2) = New Integer() {70, 90, 86, 81}
20
21         ' upper bounds for array manipulations
22         lastStudent = gradeArray.GetUpperBound(0)
23         lastExam = gradeArray(0).GetUpperBound(0)
24
25         output = "Students        \        Exams" & vbCrLf
26
27         ' build output string
28         BuildString(gradeArray)
29         output &= vbCrLf & vbCrLf & "Lowest grade: " & _
30            Minimum(gradeArray) & vbCrLf & "Highest grade: " & _
31            Maximum(gradeArray) & vbCrLf
32
33         ' calculate each student's average
34         For i = 0 To lastStudent
35            output &= vbCrLf & "Average for student " & _
36               i & " is " & Average(gradeArray(i))
37         Next
38
39         MessageBox.Show(output, "Jagged two-dimensional array", _
40            MessageBoxButtons.OK, MessageBoxIcon.Information)
41      End Sub ' Main
42
43      ' find minimum grade
44      Function Minimum(ByVal grades As Integer()()) _
45         As Integer
46
47         Dim lowGrade As Integer = 100
48         Dim i, j As Integer
49
50         For i = 0 To lastStudent
51
52            For j = 0 To lastExam
53
54               If grades(i)(j) < lowGrade Then
55                  lowGrade = grades(i)(j)
56               End If
57
58            Next
59
60         Next
61
62         Return lowGrade
63      End Function ' Minimum
64
```

Fig. 7.17 Using jagged two-dimensional arrays (part 2 of 4).

```vbnet
65      ' find the maximum grade
66      Function Maximum(ByVal grades As Integer()()) _
67         As Integer
68
69         Dim highGrade As Integer = 0
70         Dim i, j As Integer
71
72         For i = 0 To lastStudent
73
74            For j = 0 To lastExam
75
76               If grades(i)(j) > highGrade Then
77                  highGrade = grades(i)(j)
78               End If
79
80            Next
81
82         Next
83
84         Return highGrade
85      End Function ' Maximum
86
87      ' determine the average grade for student
88      ' (or set of grades)
89      Function Average(ByVal setOfGrades As Integer()) _
90         As Double
91
92         Dim i As Integer, total As Integer = 0
93
94         ' find sum of student's grades
95         For i = 0 To lastExam
96            total += setOfGrades(i)
97         Next
98
99         Return total / setOfGrades.Length
100     End Function ' Average
101
102     ' creates String displaying array
103     Sub BuildString(ByVal grades As Integer()())
104        Dim i, j As Integer
105
106        ' align column heads
107        output &= "              "
108
109        For i = 0 To lastExam
110           output &= "(" & i & ")   "
111        Next
112
113        For i = 0 To lastStudent
114           output &= vbCrLf & "    (" & i & ")   "
115
```

Fig. 7.17 Using jagged two-dimensional arrays (part 3 of 4).

```
116             For j = 0 To lastExam
117                output &= grades(i)(j) & "   "
118             Next
119
120          Next
121
122       End Sub ' BuildString
123
124  End Module ' modJaggedArray
```

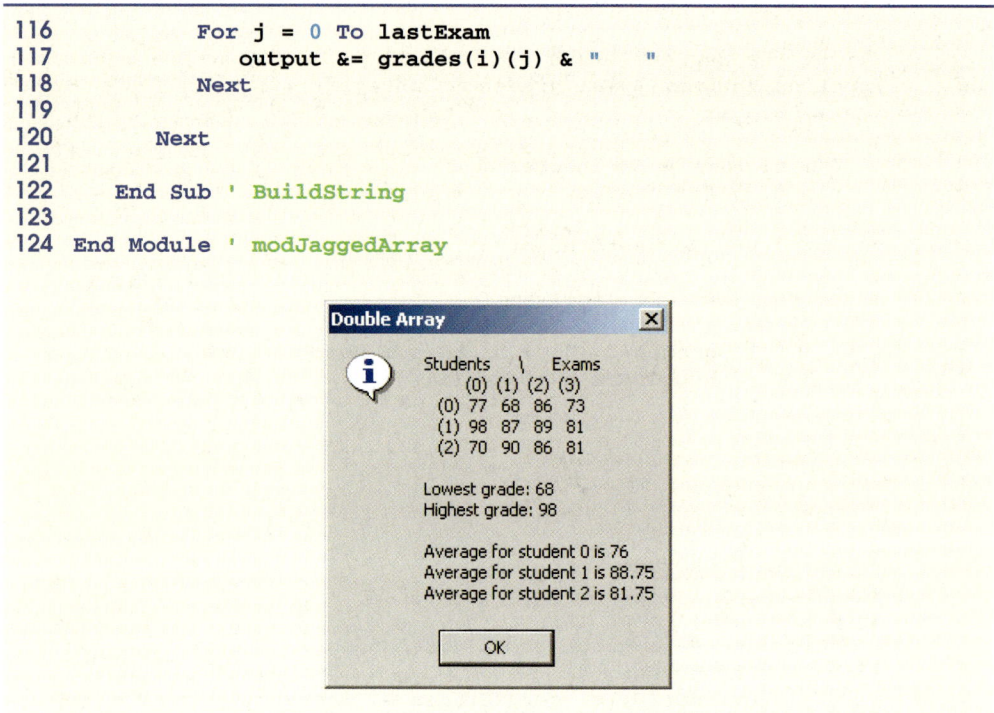

Fig. 7.17 Using jagged two-dimensional arrays (part 4 of 4).

Procedures **Minimum**, **Maximum** and **BuildString** use array **grades** and the variables **lastStudent** (upper bound for rows in the array) and **lastExam** (upper bound for columns in the array). Each procedure uses nested **For/Next** structures to iterate through array **grades**. Consider the nested **For/Next** structures in procedure **Minimum** (lines 50–60). The outer **For/Next** structure sets **i** (i.e., the row index) to **0** so the elements of the first row can be compared with variable **lowGrade** in the inner **For/Next** structure (line 54). The inner **For/Next** structure loops through the four grades of a particular row and compares each grade with **lowGrade**. If a grade is less than **lowGrade**, then **lowGrade** is assigned that grade. The outer **For/Next** structure then increments the row index by **1**. The elements of the second row are compared with variable **lowGrade**. The outer **For/Next** structure then increments the row index to **2**. The elements of the third row are compared with variable **lowGrade**. When execution of the nested structures is complete (line 62), **lowGrade** contains the smallest grade in the two-dimensional array. Procedure **Maximum** behaves similarly to procedure **Minimum**.

Procedure **Average** takes one argument—a one-dimensional array of test results for a particular student. **Average** is called (line 36) with argument **gradeArray(i)**, which is row **i** of the jagged two-dimensional array **grades**. For example, the argument **grades(1)** represents the four grades for student 1 (i.e., a one-dimensional array of grades). Remember that a jagged two-dimensional array is an array with elements that are one-dimensional arrays. Procedure **Average** calculates the sum of the array elements, divides the total by the number of test results (obtained using the **Length** property) and then returns the floating-point result as a **Double** value (line 89).

7.10 Variable-Length Parameter Lists

It is possible to create procedures that receive a variable number of arguments, using keyword **ParamArray**. The program in Fig. 7.18 calls programmer-defined procedure **AnyNumberArguments** three times, passing a different number of values each time. The values passed into procedure **AnyNumberArguments** are stored in one-dimensional **Integer** array **array1**, which is declared using **ParamArray**.

Common Programming Error 7.4

*Attempting to declare a parameter variable to the right of the **ParamArray** array variable is a syntax error.*

Common Programming Error 7.5

*Attempting to use **ParamArray** with a multidimensional array is a syntax error.*

```vb
1   ' Fig. 7.18: ParamArrayTest.vb
2   ' Using ParamArray to create variable-length parameter lists.
3
4   Module modParamArrayTest
5
6      Sub Main()
7         AnyNumberArguments()
8         AnyNumberArguments(2, 3)
9         AnyNumberArguments(7, 8, 9, 10, 11, 12)
10
11     End Sub ' Main
12
13     ' receives any number of arguments in array
14     Sub AnyNumberArguments(ByVal ParamArray array1 _
15        As Integer())
16
17        Dim i, total As Integer
18        total = 0
19
20        If array1.Length = 0 Then
21           Console.WriteLine("Procedure AnyNumberArguments" & _
22              " received 0 arguments.")
23        Else
24           Console.Write("The total of ")
25
26           For i = 0 To array1.GetUpperBound(0)
27              Console.Write(array1(i) & " ")
28              total += array1(i)
29           Next
30
31           Console.WriteLine("is {0}.", total)
32        End If
33
34     End Sub ' AnyNumberArguments
35
36  End Module ' modParamArrayTest
```

Fig. 7.18 Creating variable-length parameter lists (part 1 of 2).

```
Procedure AnyNumberArguments received 0 arguments.
The total of 2 3 is 5.
The total of 7 8 9 10 11 12 is 57.
```

Fig. 7.18 Creating variable-length parameter lists (part 2 of 2).

Common Programming Error 7.6

Using **ByRef** *with* **ParamArray** *is a syntax error.*

We call procedure **AnyNumberArguments** in lines 7–9, passing a different number of arguments each time. This procedure is defined on lines 14–34 and applies keyword **ParamArray** to **array1** in line 14. The **If** structure on lines 20–32 determines whether the number of arguments passed to the procedure is zero. If not, lines 24–31 display **array1**'s elements and their sum. All arguments passed to the **ParamArray** array must be of the same type as the array, otherwise a syntax error occurs. Though we used an **Integer** array in this example, any type of array can be used.

In the last chapter, we discussed procedure overloading. Often, programmers prefer to use procedure overloading rather than writing procedures with variable-length parameter lists.

Good Programming Practice 7.2

To increase a program's readability and performance, the programmer should use procedure overloading in favor of procedures with variable-length parameter lists.

7.11 For Each/Next Repetition Structure

Visual Basic provides the ***For Each/Next*** repetition structure for iterating through the values in a data structure, such as an array. When used with one-dimensional arrays, **For Each/Next** behaves like a **For/Next** structure that iterates through the range of indices from **0** to the value returned by **GetUpperBound(0)**. Instead of a counter, **For Each/Next** uses a variable to represent the value of each element. The program in Fig. 7.19 uses the **For Each/Next** structure to determine the minimum value in a two-dimensional array of grades.

```
1    ' Fig. 7.19: ForEach.vb
2    ' Program uses For Each/Next to find a minimum grade.
3
4    Module modForEach
5
6       Sub Main()
7          Dim gradeArray As Integer(,) = New Integer(,) _
8             {{77, 68, 86, 73}, {98, 87, 89, 81}, {70, 90, 86, 81}}
9
10         Dim grade As Integer
11         Dim lowGrade As Integer = 100
12
```

Fig. 7.19 Using **For Each/Next** with an array (part 1 of 2).

```
13        For Each grade In gradeArray
14
15            If grade < lowGrade Then
16                lowGrade = grade
17            End If
18
19        Next
20
21        Console.WriteLine("The minimum grade is: {0}", lowGrade)
22    End Sub ' Main
23
24 End Module ' modForEach
```

```
The minimum grade is: 68
```

Fig. 7.19 Using **For Each/Next** with an array (part 2 of 2).

The program behaves similarly to procedure **Minimum** of Fig. 7.17, but consolidates the nested **For** structures into one **For Each** structure. The header of the **For Each** repetition structure (line 13) specifies a variable, **grade**, and an array, **gradeArray**. The **For Each/Next** structure iterates through all the elements in **gradeArray**, sequentially assigning each value to variable **grade**. The values are compared to variable **lowGrade** (line 15), which stores the lowest grade in the array.

For rectangular arrays, the repetition of the **For Each/Next** structure begins with the element whose indices are all zero, then iterates through all possible combinations of indices, incrementing the rightmost index first. When the rightmost index reaches its upper bound, it is reset to zero, and the index to the left of it is incremented by 1. In this case, **grade** takes the values as they are ordered in the initializer list in line 8. When all the grades have been processed, **lowGrade** is displayed.

Although many array calculations are handled best with a counter, **For Each** is useful when the indices of the elements are not important. **For Each/Next** particularly is useful for looping through arrays of objects, as we discuss in Chapter 10, Object-Oriented Programming: Polymorphism

In this chapter, we showed how to program with arrays. We mentioned that Visual Basic .NET arrays are objects. In Chapter 8, Object-Based Programming, we show how to create classes, which are essentially the "blueprints" from which objects are instantiated (i.e., created).

SUMMARY

- An array is a group of contiguous memory locations that have the same name and are of the same type.
- The first element in every array is the zeroth element (i.e., element 0).
- The position number in parentheses more formally is called the index (or the subscript). An index must be an integer or an integer expression.
- All arrays have access to the methods and properties of class **System.Array**, including the **GetUpperBound** method and the **Length** property.
- To reference the ith element of an array, use $i - 1$ as the index.

- The declaration of an array creates a variable that can store a reference to an array but does not create the array in memory.
- Arrays can be declared to contain elements of any data type.
- Arrays are represented as objects in Visual Basic, so they must also be allocated with keyword **New**. The value stored in the array variable is a reference to the location in the computer's memory where the array object is created.
- Array bounds determine what indices can be used to access an element in the array.
- The initializer list enclosed in braces (**{** and **}**) specifies the initial values of the elements in the array. The initializer list can contain a comma-separated list specifying the initial values of the elements in the array. If the initializer list is empty, the elements in the array are initialized to the default value for the data type of the array.
- Keyword **Nothing** denotes an empty reference (i.e., a value indicating that a reference variable has not been assigned an address in the computer's memory).
- Unlike languages such as C and C++, Visual Basic provides mechanisms to prevent the accessing of elements that are outside the bounds of an array.
- If a program attempts to use an invalid index (i.e., an index outside the bounds of an array), Visual Basic generates an exception.
- To pass an array argument to a procedure, specify the name of the array and do not include parentheses.
- Although entire arrays are passed by reference, individual array elements of primitive data types can be passed by value.
- To pass an array element to a procedure, use the indexed name of the array element as an argument in the procedure call.
- The sorting of data (i.e., the arranging of data into some particular order, such as ascending or descending order) is one of the most important computing applications.
- A bubble sort makes several passes through the array. Each pass compares successive pairs of elements. On an ascending bubble sort, if a pair is in increasing order (or the values are equal), the bubble sort leaves the values as they are; if a pair is in decreasing order, the bubble sort swaps their values in the array.
- The advantage of the bubble sort is that it is easy to program. However, the bubble sort runs slowly, as becomes apparent during the sorting of large arrays.
- The linear search algorithm compares each element of an array against a search key. If the elements of the array being searched are not in any particular order, it is just as likely that the value will be found in the first element as in the last. Thus, the procedure compares the search key with half the elements of the array, on average. Linear search works well for small arrays and is acceptable even for large unsorted arrays.
- For sorted arrays, the binary search algorithm eliminates from consideration half the elements in the array after each comparison. The algorithm locates the middle array element and compares it with the search key. If they are equal, the search key has been found, and the index of that element is returned. Otherwise, the problem is reduced to searching half of the array. If the search key is less than the middle array element, the first half of the array is searched; otherwise, the second half of the array is searched.
- In a worst-case scenario, searching an array of 1024 elements via binary search requires only 10 comparisons. The maximum number of comparisons needed to complete a binary search of any sorted array is indicated by the exponent of the first power of two that is greater than or equal to the number of elements in the array.

- There are two types of multidimensional arrays—rectangular and jagged.
- Rectangular arrays with two indices often are used to represent tables of values consisting of information arranged in rows and columns. Each row is the same size, and each column is the same size (leading to the term "rectangular").
- A two-dimensional array with *m* rows and *n* columns is called an *m-by-n* array.
- Multidimensional arrays are initialized in declarations using the same process and notations employed for one-dimensional arrays.
- When a multidimensional array is allocated via an initializer list, the compiler determines the number of rows by counting the number of subinitializer lists (represented by sets of braces) in the main initializer list. Then, the compiler determines the number of columns in each row by counting the number of initializer values in the subinitializer list for that row.
- Jagged arrays are maintained as arrays of arrays. Unlike rectangular arrays, rows in jagged arrays can be of different lengths (so jagged arrays cannot be referred to as *m-by-n* arrays).
- Keyword **ParamArray** in a procedure definition header indicates that the procedure receives a variable number of arguments.
- Visual Basic provides the **For Each/Next** repetition structure for iterating through the values in a data structure, such as an array.

TERMINOLOGY

array allocated with **New**
array as an object
array bounds
array declaration
array elements passed by value
array initialized to zeros
array of arrays
bar chart
binary search
braces (**{** and **}**)
bubble sort
column
computational complexity
declaration and initialization of array
dice-rolling program
element
exception for invalid array indexing
For Each/Next structure
GetUpperBound method
histogram
ignoring array element zero
index
IndexOutOfRange exception
initializer list
initializing two-dimensional arrays in declarations
inner **For** structure
inner loop
innermost set of parentheses
iteration of a **For** loop

iterative binary search
jagged array
key value (in searching)
Length property
linear search
lvalue ("left value")
m-by-n array
multidimensional array
nested **For** structure
New keyword
Nothing keyword
"off-by-one" error
one-dimensional array
outer **For** structure
outer set of parentheses
ParamArray keyword
pass of a bubble sort
passing an array
passing an array element
position number
program termination
rectangular array
search key
searching
sinking sort
size of an array
sorting
sorting a large array
subarray

subinitializer list
subscript
swapping elements in an array
`System.Array` class
table
table element
tabular format

`TextBox`
two-dimensional array
variable number of arguments
"walk" past end of an array
zero-based counting
zeroth element

SELF-REVIEW EXERCISES

7.1 Fill in the blanks in each of the following statements:
a) Lists and tables of values can be stored in _____.
b) The elements of an array are related by the fact that they have the same _____ and _____.
c) The number that refers to a particular element of an array is called its _____.
d) The process of placing the elements of an array in order is called _____ the array.
e) Determining whether an array contains a certain value is called _____ the array.
f) Arrays that use two or more indices are referred to as _____ arrays.
g) Keyword _____ in a procedure definition header indicates that the procedure receives a variable number of arguments.
h) _____ arrays are maintained as arrays of arrays.
i) All arrays have access to the methods and properties of class _____.
j) When an invalid array reference is made, a/an _____ exception is thrown.

7.2 State whether each of the following is *true* or *false*. If *false*, explain why.
a) An array can store many different types of values.
b) An array index normally should be of data type `Double`.
c) Method `GetUpperBound`s returns the highest numbered index in an array.
d) The maximum number of comparisons needed for the binary search of any sorted array is the exponent of the first power of two greater than or equal to the number of elements in the array.
e) There are two types of multidimensional arrays—square and jagged.
f) After each comparison, the binary search algorithm eliminates from consideration one third of the elements in the portion of the array being searched.
g) To determine the number of elements in an array, we can use the `NumberOfElements` property.
h) The linear search works well for unsorted arrays.
i) In an *m*-by-*n* array, the *m* stands for the number of columns and the *n* stands for the number of rows.

ANSWERS TO SELF-REVIEW EXERCISES

7.1 a) arrays. b) name, type. c) index, subscript or position number. d) sorting. e) searching. f) multidimensional. g) `ParamArray`. h) Jagged. i) `System.Array`. j) `IndexOutOfRangeException`.

7.2 a) False. An array can store only values of the same type. b) False. An array index must be an integer or an integer expression. c) True. d) True. e) False. The two different types are called rectangular and jagged. f) False. After each comparison, the binary search algorithm eliminates from consideration half the elements in the portion of the array being searched. g) False. To determine the number of elements in an array, we can use the `Length` property. h) True. i) False. In an *m*-by-*n* array, the *m* stands for the number of rows and the *n* stands for the number of columns.

Chapter 7

EXERCISES

7.3 Write statements to accomplish each of the following tasks:
  a) Display the value of the seventh element of array **numbers**.
  b) Initialize each of the five elements of one-dimensional **Integer** array **values** to **8**.
  c) Total the 100 elements of floating-point array **results**.
  d) Copy 11-element array **source** into the first portion of 34-element array **sourceCopy**.
  e) Determine the smallest and largest values contained in 99-element floating-point array **data**.

7.4 Use a one-dimensional array to solve the following problem: A company pays its salespeople on a commission basis. The salespeople receive $200 per week, plus 9% of their gross sales for that week. For example, a salesperson who grosses $5000 in sales in a week receives $200 plus 9% of $5000, or a total of $650. Write a program (using an array of counters) that determines how many of the salespeople earned salaries in each of the following ranges (assume that each salesperson's salary is truncated to an integer amount):
  a) $200–$299
  b) $300–$399
  c) $400–$499
  d) $500–$599
  e) $600–$699
  f) $700–$799
  g) $800–$899
  h) $900–$999
  i) $1000 and over

7.5 Use a one-dimensional array to solve the following problem: Read in 20 numbers, each of which is between 10 and 100, inclusive. As each number is read, print it only if it is not a duplicate of a number already read. Provide for the "worst case" (in which all 20 numbers are different). Use the smallest possible array to solve this problem.

7.6 The bubble sort presented in Fig. 7.10 is inefficient for large arrays. Make the following simple modifications to improve the performance of the bubble sort:
  a) After the first pass, the largest number is guaranteed to be in the highest-numbered element of the array; after the second pass, the two highest numbers are "in place"; and so on. Instead of making nine comparisons on every pass, modify the bubble sort to make eight comparisons on the second pass, seven on the third pass and so on.
  b) The data in the array already may be in the proper order or in near-proper order, so why make nine passes if fewer will suffice? Modify the sort to check at the end of each pass on whether any swaps have been made. If none have been made, the data must already be in the proper order, so the program should terminate. If a swap has been made, at least one more pass is needed.

SPECIAL SECTION: RECURSION EXERCISES

7.7 (*Palindromes*) A palindrome is a **String** that is spelled the same forward and backward. Some examples of palindromes are: "radar," "able was i ere i saw elba" and, if blanks are ignored, "a man a plan a canal panama." Write a recursive procedure **TestPalindrome** that returns **True** if the **String** stored in the array is a palindrome, but **False** otherwise. The procedure should ignore spaces and punctuation in the **String**. [*Hint*: A **String** can be converted to a **Char** array using method **ToCharArray**. For instance, the statement

```
myArray = myString.ToCharArray()
```
stores the contents of string variable **myString** in a one-dimensional **Char** array **myArray**.]

7.8 (*Linear Search*) Modify Fig. 7.12 to use recursive **LinearSearch** procedure. This procedure should receive an integer array, a search key, the starting index and the ending index as arguments. If the search key is found, return the array index; otherwise, return **-1**.

7.9 (*Binary Search*) Modify the program in Fig. 7.14 to use a recursive **BinarySearch** procedure. This procedure should receive an integer array, a search key, the starting index and the ending index as arguments. If the search key is found, return the array index; otherwise, return **-1**.

7.10 (*Quicksort*) In this chapter, we introduced the bubble sort. We now present the recursive sorting technique called Quicksort. The basic algorithm for a one-dimensional array of values is as follows:

    a) *Partitioning Step:* Take the first element of the unsorted array and determine its final location in the sorted array (i.e., all values to the left of the element in the array are less than the element, and all values to the right of the element in the array are greater than the element). We now have one element in its proper location and two unsorted subarrays.

    b) *Recursive Step:* Perform step 1 on each unsorted subarray.

Each time step 1 is performed on a subarray, another element is placed in its final location of the sorted array, and two unsorted subarrays are created. When a subarray consists of one element, it must be sorted; therefore, that element is in its final location.

The basic algorithm seems simple, but how do we determine the final position of the first element of each subarray? Consider the following set of values (the element in bold is the partitioning element—it will be placed in its final location in the sorted array):

        37   2   6   4   89   8   10   12   68   45

    a) Starting from the rightmost element of the array, compare each element to **37** until an element less than **37** is found, then swap **37** and that element. The first element less than **37** is 12, so **37** and 12 are swapped. The new array is

        12   2   6   4   89   8   10   **37**   68   45

    Element 12 is italicized to indicate that it was just swapped with **37**.

    b) Starting from the left of the array, but beginning with the element after 12, compare each element to **37** until an element greater than **37** is found, then swap **37** and that element. The first element greater than **37** is 89, so **37** and 89 are swapped. The new array is

        12   2   6   4   **37**   8   10   *89*   68   45

    c) Starting from the right, but beginning with the element before 89, compare each element to **37** until an element less than **37** is found, then swap **37** and that element. The first element less than **37** is 10, so **37** and 10 are swapped. The new array is

        12   2   6   4   *10*   8   **37**   89   68   45

    d) Starting from the left, but beginning with the element after 10, compare each element to **37** until an element greater than **37** is found, then swap **37** and that element. There are no more elements greater than **37**, so when we compare **37** to itself, we know that **37** has been placed in its final location of the sorted array.

Once the partition has been applied to the above array, there are two unsorted subarrays. The subarray with values less than 37 contains 12, 2, 6, 4, 10 and 8. The subarray with values greater than 37 contains 89, 68 and 45. The sort continues with both subarrays being partitioned in the same manner as the original array.

Using the preceding discussion, write recursive procedure **QuickSort** to sort a one-dimensional **Integer** array. The procedure should receive as arguments an **Integer** array, a starting index and an ending index. Procedure **Partition** should be called by **QuickSort** to perform the partitioning step.

7.11 (*Maze Traversal*) The following grid of **#**s and dots (**.**) is a two-dimensional array representation of a maze.

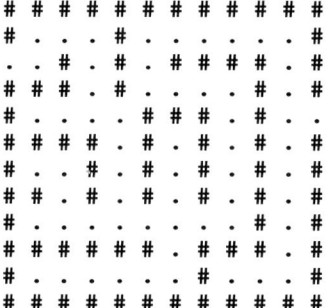

The **#**s represent the walls of the maze, and the dots represent squares in the possible paths through the maze. Moves can be made only to a location in the array that contains a dot.

There is a simple algorithm for walking through a maze that guarantees finding the exit (assuming there is an exit). If there is not an exit, you will arrive at the starting location again. Place your right hand on the wall to your right and begin walking forward. Never remove your hand from the wall. If the maze turns to the right, you follow the wall to the right. As long as you do not remove your hand from the wall, eventually you will arrive at the exit of the maze. There may be a shorter path than the one you have taken, but you are guaranteed to get out of the maze if you follow the algorithm.

Write recursive procedure **MazeTraverse** to walk through the maze. The procedure should receive as arguments a 12-by-12 **Char** array representing the maze and the starting location of the maze. As **MazeTraverse** attempts to locate the exit from the maze, it should place the character **X** in each square in the path. The procedure should display the maze after each move so, the user can watch as the maze is solved.

8

Object-Based Programming

Objectives

- To understand encapsulation and data hiding.
- To understand the concepts of data abstraction and abstract data types (ADTs).
- To be able to create, use and destroy objects.
- To be able to control access to object instance variables and methods.
- To be able to use properties to keep objects in consistent states.
- To understand the use of the **Me** reference.
- To understand namespaces and assemblies.
- To be able to use the **Class View** and **Object Browser**.

*My object all sublime
I shall achieve in time.*
W. S. Gilbert

Is it a world to hide virtues in?
William Shakespeare, *Twelfth Night*

Your public servants serve you right.
Adlai Stevenson

Classes struggle, some classes triumph, others are eliminated.
Mao Zedong

This above all: to thine own self be true.
William Shakespeare, *Hamlet*

Outline

8.1 Introduction
8.2 Implementing a Time Abstract Data Type with a Class
8.3 Class Scope
8.4 Controlling Access to Members
8.5 Initializing Class Objects: Constructors
8.6 Using Overloaded Constructors
8.7 Properties
8.8 Composition: Objects as Instance Variables of Other Classes
8.9 Using the Me Reference
8.10 Garbage Collection
8.11 `Shared` Class Members
8.12 `Const` and `ReadOnly` Members
8.13 Data Abstraction and Information Hiding
8.14 Software Reusability
8.15 Namespaces and Assemblies
8.16 Class View and Object Browser

Summary • Terminology • Self-Review Exercises • Answers to Self-Review Exercises • Exercises

8.1 Introduction

In this chapter, we investigate object orientation in Visual Basic. Some readers might ask, why did we defer this topic until now? There are several reasons. First, the objects we build in this chapter are composed partially of structured program pieces; to explain the organization of objects, we needed to establish a basis in structured programming with control structures. We also wanted to study methods in detail before introducing object orientation. Finally, we wanted to familiarize readers with arrays, which are Visual Basic objects.

In our discussions of object-oriented programs in Chapters 1–7, we introduced many basic concepts (i.e., "object think") and terminology (i.e., "object speak") that relate to Visual Basic object-oriented programming. We also discussed our program-development methodology: We analyzed many typical problems that required a program to be built and determined what classes from the .NET Framework Library were needed to implement each program. We then selected appropriate instance variables and methods for each program, as well as specifying the manner in which an object of our class collaborated with objects from the .NET Framework classes to accomplish the program's overall goals.

Let us briefly review some key concepts and terminology of object orientation. Object orientation uses classes to *encapsulate* instance variables (*data*) and methods (*behaviors*). Objects have the ability to hide their implementation from other objects (this principle is called *information hiding*). Although some objects can communicate with one another across well-defined *interfaces,* objects are unaware of how other objects are implemented.

Normally, implementation details are hidden within the objects themselves. Surely, it is possible to drive a car effectively without knowing the details of how engines, transmissions and exhaust systems operate. Later, we will see why information hiding is so crucial to good software engineering.

In C and other *procedural programming languages,* programming tends to be *action oriented.* Visual Basic programming, however, is *object oriented.* In C, the unit of programming is the *function* (called *procedures* in Visual Basic). In Visual Basic, the unit of programming is the *class* (although programs often are written with modules as well). Objects eventually are *instantiated* (i.e., created) from these classes, whereas procedures are encapsulated within the "boundaries" of classes as methods.

C programmers concentrate on writing functions. They group actions that perform some task into a function and then group functions to form a program. Data is certainly important in C, but it exists primarily to support the actions that functions perform. The *verbs* in a system-requirements document help a C programmer determine the set of functions that will work together to implement the system.

Visual Basic programmers concentrate on creating their own *user-defined types* called *classes*. We also refer to classes as *programmer-defined types*. Each class contains both data and a set of methods that manipulate the data. The data components, or *data members*, of a class are called *instance variables*, or *member variables*. Just as we call an instance of a built-in type—such as **Integer**—a *variable,* we call an *instance* of a user-defined type (i.e., a class) an *object*. In Visual Basic, attention is focused on classes, rather than methods. The *nouns* in a system-requirements document help the Visual Basic programmer determine an initial set of classes with which to begin the design process. These classes then are used to instantiate objects that work together to implement the system.

This chapter explains how to create and use classes and objects, a subject known as *object-based programming (OBP)*. Chapters 9 and 10 introduce *inheritance* and *polymorphism*—two key technologies that enable *object-oriented programming (OOP)*. Although we do not discuss inheritance in detail until Chapter 9, it is part of several Visual Basic class definitions. An example of inheritance was demonstrated when we derived a class from **System.Windows.Forms.Form** in Chapter 4.

Software Engineering Observation 8.1

All Visual Basic objects are passed by reference. Visual Basic classes are reference types.

8.2 Implementing a Time Abstract Data Type with a Class

Classes in Visual Basic facilitate the creation of special data types, called *abstract data types (ADT)*, which hide their implementation from clients. A problem in procedural programming languages, is that client code often is implementation-dependent; client code has to be written so that it uses specific data members and must be rewritten if the code with which it interfaces changes. ADTs eliminate this problem by providing implementation-independent interfaces to their clients. The creator of a class can change the implementation of that class without having to change the clients of that class.

Software Engineering Observation 8.2

It is important to write programs that are understandable and easy to maintain. Change is the rule rather than the exception. Programmers should anticipate that their code will be modified. As we will see, classes facilitate program modifiability.

Before discussing classes in detail, we review how to add classes to a project in Visual Studio. By now, you are familiar with adding a module to a project. The process of adding a class to a project is almost identical to that of adding a module to a project. To add a class to a project, select **Project > Add Class**. Enter the class name in the **Name** text field and click the **Open** button. Note that the class name (ending with the **.vb** file extension) appears in the **Solution Explorer** below the project name.

The following application consists of class `CTime` (Fig. 8.1) and module `modTimeTest` (Fig. 8.2). Class `CTime` contains the information needed to represent a specific time; module `modTimeTest` contains method `Main`, which uses an instance of class `CTime` to run the application.

In Fig. 8.1, lines 4–5 begin the `CTime` class definition, indicating that class `CTime` inherits from class `Object` (of namespace `System`). Visual Basic programmers use *inheritance* to create classes from existing classes. The `Inherits` keyword (line 5) followed by class name `Object` indicates that class `CTime` inherits existing pieces of class `Object`. If the programmer does not include line 5, the Visual Basic compiler includes it implicitly. Because this is the first chapter that exposes classes, we include these declarations for the classes in this chapter; however, we remove them in Chapter 9. A complete understanding of inheritance is not necessary to the understanding of the concepts and programs in this chapter. We explore inheritance in detail in Chapter 9.

```
1   ' Fig. 8.1: CTime.vb
2   ' Represents time in 24-hour format.
3
4   Class CTime
5      Inherits Object
6
7      ' declare Integer instance values for hour, minute and second
8      Private mHour As Integer    ' 0 - 23
9      Private mMinute As Integer  ' 0 - 59
10     Private mSecond As Integer  ' 0 - 59
11
12     ' Method New is the CTime constructor method, which initializes
13     ' instance variables to zero
14     Public Sub New()
15        SetTime(0, 0, 0)
16     End Sub ' New
17
18     ' set new time value using universal time;
19     ' perform validity checks on data;
20     ' set invalid values to zero
21     Public Sub SetTime(ByVal hourValue As Integer, _
22        ByVal minuteValue As Integer, ByVal secondValue As Integer)
23
24        ' check if hour is between 0 and 23, then set hour
25        If (hourValue >= 0 AndAlso hourValue < 24) Then
26           mHour = hourValue
27        Else
28           mHour = 0
29        End If
```

Fig. 8.1 Abstract data type representing time in 24-hour format (part 1 of 2).

```vbnet
30
31         ' check if minute is between 0 and 59, then set minute
32         If (minuteValue >= 0 AndAlso minuteValue < 60) Then
33            mMinute = minuteValue
34         Else
35            mMinute = 0
36         End If
37
38         ' check if second is between 0 and 59, then set second
39         If (secondValue >= 0 AndAlso secondValue < 60) Then
40            mSecond = secondValue
41         Else
42            mSecond = 0
43         End If
44
45      End Sub ' SetTime
46
47      ' convert String to universal-time format
48      Public Function ToUniversalString() As String
49         Return String.Format("{0}:{1:D2}:{2:D2}", _
50            mHour, mMinute, mSecond)
51      End Function ' ToUniversalString
52
53      ' convert to String in standard-time format
54      Public Function ToStandardString() As String
55         Dim suffix As String = " PM"
56         Dim format As String = "{0}:{1:D2}:{2:D2}"
57         Dim standardHour As Integer
58
59         ' determine whether time is AM or PM
60         If mHour < 12 Then
61            suffix = " AM"
62         End If
63
64         ' convert from universal-time format to standard-time format
65         If (mHour = 12 OrElse mHour = 0) Then
66            standardHour = 12
67         Else
68            standardHour = mHour Mod 12
69         End If
70
71         Return String.Format(format, standardHour, mMinute, _
72            mSecond) & suffix
73      End Function ' ToStandardString
74
75   End Class ' CTime
```

Fig. 8.1 Abstract data type representing time in 24-hour format (part 2 of 2).

Lines 4 and 75 delineate the *body* of the **CTime** class definition with keywords **Class** and **End Class**. Any information that we place in this body is contained within the class. For example, class **CTime** contains three **Integer** instance variables—**mHour**, **mMinute** and **mSecond** (lines 8–10)—that represent the time in *universal-time* format (24-

hour clock format). Note that our member-naming preference is to prefix an '**m**' to each instance variable.[1]

Good Programming Practice 8.1

*Begin class names using a capital "**C**" to distinguish those names as class names.*

Keywords **Public** and **Private** are *member access modifiers*. Instance variables or methods with member access modifier **Public** are accessible wherever the program has a reference to a **CTime** object. The declaration of instance variables or methods with member access modifier **Private** makes them accessible only to methods of that class. Member access modifiers can appear in any order in a class definition.

Good Programming Practice 8.2

For clarity, every instance variable or method definition should be preceded by a member access modifier.

Good Programming Practice 8.3

Group members in a class definition according to their member access modifiers to enhance clarity and readability.

Lines 8–10 declare each of the three **Integer** instance variables—**mHour**, **mMinute** and **mSecond**—with member access modifier **Private**, indicating that these instance variables of the class are accessible only to members of the class. When an object of the class encapsulates such instance variables, only methods of that object's class can access the variables. Normally, instance variables are declared **Private**, whereas methods are declared **Public**. However, it is possible to have **Private** methods and **Public** instance variables, as we will see later. Often, **Private** methods are called *utility methods*, or *helper methods*, because they can be called only by other methods of that class, and their purpose is to support the operation of those methods. The creation of **Public** data members in a class is an uncommon and dangerous programming practice. The provision of such access to a class's data members is unsafe; foreign code could set these members to invalid values, producing potentially disastrous results.

Software Engineering Observation 8.3

*Make a class member **Private** if there is no reason for it to be accessed outside of the class definition.*

Access methods can read or display data. Another common use for access methods is to test the truth of conditions—such methods often are called *predicate methods*. For example, we could design predicate method **IsEmpty** for a *container class*—a class capable of holding many objects, such as a linked list, a stack or a queue (these data structures are discussed in detail in Chapter 23, Data Structures and Collections). This method would return **True** if the container is empty and **False** otherwise. A program might test **IsEmpty** before attempting to read another item from the container object. Similarly, a program might call another predicate method (e.g., **IsFull**) before attempting to insert another item into a container object.

---

1. For a list of Microsoft recommended naming conventions visit **msdn.microsoft.com/library/default.asp?url=/library/en-us/vbcon98/html/vbconobject-namingconventions.asp**.

Class **CTime** contains the following **Public** methods—**New** (lines 14–16), **SetTime** (lines 21–45), **ToUniversalString** (lines 48–51) and **ToStandardString** (lines 54–73). These are the **Public** *methods* (also called the **Public** *services*, or **Public** *interfaces*) of the class. *Clients*, such as module **modTimeTest** (discussed momentarily), use these methods to manipulate the data stored in the class objects or to cause the class to perform some service.

New is a *constructor* method. (As we will see, a class can have many constructors—all share the same name (**New**), but each must have unique parameters.) A constructor is a special method that initializes an object's instance variables. The instantiation of an object of a class calls that class's constructor method. This constructor method (lines 14–16) then calls method **SetTime** (discussed shortly) with **mHour**, **mMinute** and **mSecond** values specified as **0**. Constructors can take arguments but cannot return values. An important difference between constructors and other methods is that constructors cannot specify a return data type—for this reason, Visual Basic constructors are implemented as **Sub** procedures (because **Sub** procedures cannot return values). Generally, constructors are **Public** methods of a class.

Common Programming Error 8.1

Attempting to declare a constructor as a **Function** *and/or attempting to* **Return** *a value from a constructor is a syntax error.*

Method **SetTime** (lines 21–45) is a **Public** method that uses three **Integer** arguments to set the time. A conditional expression tests each argument to determine whether the value is in a specified range. For example, the **mHour** value must be greater than or equal to 0 and less than 24, because universal-time format represents hours as integers from **0** to **23**. Similarly, both minute and second values must fall between **0** and **59**. Any values outside these ranges are invalid values and default to zero, at least ensuring that a **CTime** object always contains valid data. This is also known as *keeping the object in a consistent state*. When users supply invalid data to **SetTime**, the program might want to indicate that the entered time setting was invalid.

Good Programming Practice 8.4

Always define a class so that its instance variables maintain a consistent state.

Method **ToUniversalString** (lines 48–51) takes no arguments and returns a **String** in universal-time format, consisting of six digits—two for the hour, two for the minute and two for the second. For example, if the time were 1:30:07 PM, method **ToUniversalString** would return the **String** **"13:30:07"**. **String** method **Format** helps to configure the universal time. Line 49 passes to the method the *format control string* **"{0}:{1:D2}:{2:D2}"**, which indicates that argument **0** (the first argument after the format **String** argument) should take the default format; and that arguments **1** and **2** (the last two arguments after the format **String** argument) should take the format **D2** (base 10 decimal number format using two digits) for display purposes—thus, **8** would be converted to **08**. The two colons that separate the curly braces **}** and **{** represent the colons that separate the hour from the minute and the minute from the second, respectively.

Method **ToStandardString** (lines 54–73) takes no arguments and returns a **String** in standard-time format, consisting of the **mHour**, **mMinute** and **mSecond** values separated by colons and followed by an AM or PM indicator (e.g., **1:27:06 PM**).

Like method **ToUniversalString**, method **ToStandardString** calls method **Format** of class **String** to guarantee that the **mMinute** and **mSecond** values each appear as two digits. Lines 60–69 determine the proper formatting for the hour.

After defining the class, we can use it as a type in declarations such as

```
Dim sunset As CTime    ' reference to object of type CTime
```

The class name (**CTime**) is a type. A class can yield many objects, just as a primitive data type (e.g., **Integer**) can yield many variables. Programmers can create class types as needed; this is one reason why Visual Basic is known as an *extensible language*.

Module **modTimeTest** (Fig. 8.2) uses an instance of class **CTime**. Method **Main** (lines 8–33) declares and initializes instance **time** of class **CTime** (line 9). When the object is instantiated, *keyword **New*** allocates the memory in which the **CTime** object will be stored, then calls the **CTime** constructor (method **New** in lines 14–16 of Fig. 8.1) to initialize the instance variables of the **CTime** object. As mentioned before, this constructor invokes method **SetTime** of class **CTime** to initialize each **Private** instance variable explicitly to **0**. Method **New** then returns a reference to the newly created object; this reference is assigned to **time**.

Note that the **TimeTest.vb** file does not use keyword **Imports** to import the namespace that contains class **CTime**. If a class is in the same namespace and **.vb** file as the class that uses it, the **Imports** statement is not required. Every class in Visual Basic is part of a namespace. If a programmer does not specify a namespace for a class, the class is placed in the *default namespace*, which includes the compiled classes in the current directory (in Visual Studio, this is a project's directory). We must import classes from the .NET Framework, because their namespaces and source files are located in a different source file than those compiled with each program we write.

Line 10 declares a **String** reference **output** that will store the **String** containing the results, which later will be displayed in a **MessageBox**. Lines 12–15 assign the time to **output** in universal-time format (by invoking method **ToUniversalString** of **CTime**) and standard-time format (by invoking method **ToStandardString** of **CTime**).

```
1   ' Fig. 8.2: TimeTest.vb
2   ' Demonstrating class CTime.
3
4   Imports System.Windows.Forms
5
6   Module modTimeTest
7
8      Sub Main()
9         Dim time As New CTime()   ' call CTime constructor
10        Dim output As String
11
12        output = "The initial universal times is: " & _
13           time.ToUniversalString() & vbCrLf & _
14           "The initial standard time is: " & _
15           time.ToStandardString()
16
```

Fig. 8.2 Using an abstract data type (part 1 of 2).

```vbnet
17          time.SetTime(13, 27, 6) ' set time with valid settings
18
19          output &= vbCrLf & vbCrLf & _
20              "Universal time after setTime is: " & _
21              time.ToUniversalString() & vbCrLf & _
22              "Standard time after setTime is: " & _
23              time.ToStandardString()
24
25          time.SetTime(99, 99, 99) ' set time with invalid settings
26
27          output &= vbCrLf & vbCrLf & _
28              "After attempting invalid settings: " & vbCrLf & _
29              "Universal time: " & time.ToUniversalString() & _
30              vbCrLf & "Standard time: " & time.ToStandardString()
31
32          MessageBox.Show(output, "Testing Class CTime")
33      End Sub ' Main
34
35  End Module ' modTimeTest
```

Testing Class CTime

The initial universal times is: 00:00:00
The initial standard time is: 12:00:00 AM

Universal time after setTime is: 13:27:06
Standard time after setTime is: 1:27:06 PM

After attempting invalid settings:
Universal time: 00:00:00
Standard time: 12:00:00 AM

OK

Fig. 8.2 Using an abstract data type (part 2 of 2).

Software Engineering Observation 8.4

*When keyword **New** creates an object of a class, that class's method **New** (constructor method) is called to initialize the instance variables of that object.*

Line 17 sets the time of the **CTime** object by passing valid time arguments to **CTime**'s method **SetTime**. Lines 19–23 concatenate the time to **output** in both universal and standard formats to confirm that the time was set correctly.

To illustrate that method **SetTime** validates the values passed to it, line 25 passes invalid time arguments to method **SetTime**. Lines 27–30 concatenates the time to **output** in both formats, and line 32 displays a **MessageBox** with the results of our program. Notice in the last two lines of the output window that the time is set to midnight, which is the default value of a **CTime** object.

CTime is our first example of a *nonapplication class*, which is a class that does not define a **Main** method and therefore not executable. A module (**modTimeTest**), though technically not a class, acts like an *application class* in the sense that it defines a **Main** method, which is the starting point (referred to as the entry point) for an executable program in Visual Basic. Class **CTime** does not define **Main** and thus cannot be used as a starting point in this program.

Note that the program declares instance variables **mHour**, **mMinute** and **mSecond** as **Private**. Instance variables declared **Private** are not accessible outside the class in which they are defined. The class's clients are not concerned with the actual data representation of that class. For example, the class could represent the time internally as the number of seconds that have elapsed since the previous midnight. Suppose this representation changes. Clients still are able to use the same **Public** methods and obtain the same results (**Return** values) without becoming aware of the change in internal representation. In this sense, the implementation of a class is said to be *hidden* from its clients.

Software Engineering Observation 8.5

Information hiding promotes program modifiability and simplifies the client's perception of a class.

Software Engineering Observation 8.6

Clients of a class can (and should) use the class without knowing the internal details of how the class is implemented. If the class implementation is changed (to improve performance, for example), provided that the class's interface remains constant, the class clients' source code need not change. This makes it much easier to modify systems.

In this program, the **CTime** constructor initializes the instance variables to **0** (i.e., the universal time equivalent of 12 AM) to ensure that the object is created in a *consistent state* (i.e., all instance variable values are valid). The instance variables of a **CTime** object cannot store invalid values, because the constructor (which calls **SetTime**) is called when the **CTime** object is created. Method **SetTime** scrutinizes subsequent attempts by a client to modify the instance variables.

Normally, instance variables are initialized in a class's constructor, but they also can be initialized when they are declared in the class body. If a programmer does not initialize instance variables explicitly, the compiler initializes them. When this occurs, the compiler sets primitive numeric variables to **0**, **Boolean**s to **False** and references to **Nothing**).

Methods **ToUniversalString** and **ToStandardString** take no arguments because, by default, these methods manipulate the instance variables of the particular **CTime** object for which they are invoked. This makes method calls more concise than conventional function calls in procedural programming. It also reduces the likelihood of passing the wrong arguments, the wrong types of arguments or the wrong number of arguments.

Software Engineering Observation 8.7

The use of an object-oriented programming approach often simplifies method calls by reducing the number of parameters that must be passed. This benefit of object-oriented programming derives from the fact that encapsulation of instance variables and methods within an object gives the object's methods the right to access its instance variables.

Classes simplify programming, because the client (or user of the class object) need be concerned only with the **Public** operations encapsulated in the object. Usually, such operations are designed to be client-oriented, rather than implementation-oriented. Clients are neither aware of, nor involved in, a class's implementation. Interfaces change less frequently than do implementations. When an implementation changes, implementation-dependent code must change accordingly. By hiding the implementation, we eliminate the possibility that other program parts will become dependent on the class-implementation details.

Often, programmers do not have to create classes "from scratch." Rather, they can derive classes from other classes that provide behaviors required by the new classes. Classes also can include references to objects of other classes as members. Such *software reuse* can greatly enhance programmer productivity. Chapter 9 discusses *inheritance*—the process by which new classes are derived from existing classes. Section 8.8 discusses *composition* (*aggregation*), in which classes include as members references to objects of other classes.

8.3 Class Scope

In Section 6.11, we discussed method scope; now, we discuss class *scope*. A class's instance variables and methods belong to that class's scope. Within a class's scope, class members are accessible to all of that class's methods and can be referenced by name. Outside a class's scope, class members cannot be referenced directly by name. Those class members that are visible (such as **Public** members) can be accessed only through a "handle" (i.e., members can be referenced via the format *objectReferenceName*.*memberName*).

If a variable is defined in a method, only that method can access the variable (i.e., the variable is a local variable of that method). Such variables are said to have *block scope*. If a method defines a variable that has the same name as a variable with class scope (i.e., an instance variable), the method-scope variable hides the class-scope variable in that method's scope. A hidden instance variable can be accessed in a method by preceding its name with the keyword **Me** and the dot operator, as in **Me.mHour**. We discuss keyword **Me** later in this chapter.

8.4 Controlling Access to Members

The member access modifiers **Public** and **Private** control access to a class's instance variables and methods. (In Chapter 9, we introduce the additional access modifiers **Protected** and **Friend**.)

As we stated previously, **Public** methods serve primarily to present to the class's clients a view of the *services* that the class provides (i.e., the **Public** interface of the class). We have mentioned the merits of writing methods that perform only one task. If a method must execute other tasks to calculate its final result, these tasks should be performed by a utility method. A client does not need to call these utility methods, nor does it need to be concerned with how the class uses its utility methods. For these reasons, utility methods are declared as **Private** members of a class.

Common Programming Error 8.2

*Attempting to access a **Private** class member from outside that class is a syntax error.*

The application of Fig. 8.3 demonstrates that **Private** class members are not accessible outside the class. Line 9 attempts to access **Private** instance variable **mHour** of **CTime** object **time**. The compiler generates an error stating that the **Private** member **mHour** is not accessible. [*Note*: This program assumes that the **CTime** class from Fig. 8.1 is used.]

Good Programming Practice 8.5

We prefer to list instance variables of a class first, so that, when reading the code, programmers see the name and type of each instance variable before it is used in the methods of the class.

```
1    ' Fig. 8.3: RestrictedAccess.vb
2    ' Demonstrate error from attempt to access Private class member.
3
4    Module modRestrictedAccess
5
6       Sub Main()
7          Dim time As New CTime()
8
9          time.mHour = 7  ' error
10      End Sub ' Main
11
12   End Module ' modRestrictedAccess
```

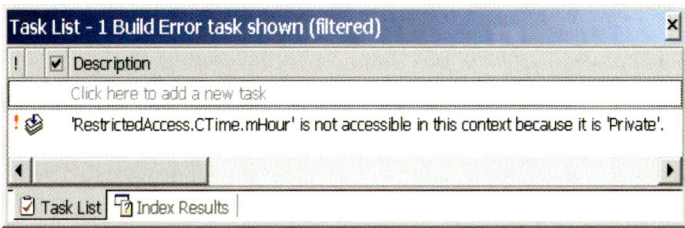

Fig. 8.3   Attempting to access restricted class members results in a syntax error.

Good Programming Practice 8.6

*Even though **Private** and **Public** members can be repeated and intermixed, list all the **Private** members of a class first in one group, then list all the **Public** members in another group.*

Software Engineering Observation 8.8

*Declare all instance variables of a class as **Private**. When necessary, provide **Public** methods to set and get the values of **Private** instance variables. This architecture hides the class's implementation from its clients, reduces bugs and improves program modifiability.*

Access to **Private** data should be controlled carefully by a class's methods. To allow clients to read the values of **Private** data, the class can provide a *property definition*, which enables users to access this **Private** data safely. Properties, which we discuss in detail in Section 8.7, contain *accessors*, or portions of code that handle the details of modifying and returning data. A property definition can contain a **Get** *accessor*, a **Set** *accessor* or both. A **Get** accessor enables a client to read a **Private** data value, whereas a **Set** accessor enables the client to modify that value. Such modification would seem to violate the notion of **Private** data. However, a **Set** accessor can provide data-validation capabilities (such as range checking) to ensure that the value is set properly. A **Set** accessor also can translate between the format of the data used in the interface and the format used in the implementation. A **Get** accessor need not expose the data in "raw" format; rather, the **Get** accessor can edit the data and limit the client's view of that data.

Testing and Debugging Tip 8.1

*Declaring the instance variables of a class as **Private** and the methods of the class as **Public** facilitates debugging, because problems with data manipulations are localized to the class's methods.*

8.5 Initializing Class Objects: Constructors

A constructor method initializes its class's members. The programmer writes code for the constructor, which is invoked each time an object of that class is instantiated. Instance variables can be initialized implicitly to their default values (**0** for primitive numeric types, **False** for **Boolean**s and **Nothing** for references). Visual Basic initializes variables to their default values when they are declared at runtime. Variables can be initialized when declared in either the class body or constructor. Regardless of whether an instance variable is initialized in a constructor, that variable is initialized (either to its default value or to the value assigned in its declaration) by the runtime before any constructors are called. Classes can contain overloaded constructors to provide multiple ways to initialize objects of that class.

Performance Tip 8.1

Because instance variables are always initialized to default values by the runtime, avoid initializing instance variables to their default values in the constructor.

It is important to note that, although references do not need to be initialized immediately by invoking a constructor, an uninitialized reference cannot be used until it refers to an actual object. If a class does not define any constructors, the compiler provides a default constructor.

Software Engineering Observation 8.9

When appropriate, provide a constructor to ensure that every object is initialized with meaningful values.

When creating an object of a class, the programmer can provide *initializers* in parentheses to the right of the class name. These initializers are the arguments to the class's constructor. In general, declarations take the form

> **Dim** *objectReference* **As New** *ClassName* **(** *arguments* **)**

where *objectReference* is a reference of the appropriate data type, **New** indicates that an object is being created, *ClassName* indicates the type of the new object and *arguments* specifies the values used by the class's constructor to initialize the object. A constructor that takes arguments often is called a *parameterized constructor*. The next example (Fig. 8.4) demonstrates the use of initializers.

If a class does not have any defined constructors, the compiler provides a default constructor. This constructor contains no code (i.e., the constructor is empty) and takes no arguments. Programmers also can provide a default constructor, as we demonstrated in class **CTime** (Fig. 8.1), and as we will see in the next example.

Common Programming Error 8.3

*If constructors are provided for a class, but none of the **Public** constructors is a default constructor, and an attempt is made to call a default constructor to initialize an object of the class, a syntax error occurs. A constructor can be called with no arguments only if there are no constructors for the class (the default constructor is called) or if the class includes a default constructor.*

8.6 Using Overloaded Constructors

Like methods, constructors of a class can be *overloaded*. This means that several constructors in a class can have the exact same method name (i.e., **New**). To overload a constructor of a class, provide a separate method definition with the same name for each version of the method. Remember that overloaded constructors must have different numbers and/or types and/or orders of parameters.

Common Programming Error 8.4
Attempting to overload a constructor of a class with another method that has the exact same signature (method name and number, types and order of parameters) is a syntax error.

The **CTime** constructor in Fig. 8.1 initialized **mHour**, **mMinute** and **mSecond** to **0** (i.e., 12 midnight in universal time) with a call to the class's **SetTime** method. Class **CTime2** (Fig. 8.4) overloads the constructor method to provide a variety of ways to initialize **CTime2** objects. Each constructor calls method **SetTime** of the **CTime2** object, which ensures that the object begins in a consistent state by setting out-of-range values to zero. The Visual Basic runtime invokes the appropriate constructor by matching the number, types and order of the arguments specified in the constructor call with the number, types and order of the parameters specified in each constructor method definition.

Because most of the code in class **CTime2** is identical to that in class **CTime**, this section concentrates only on the overloaded constructors. Line 14 defines the default constructor. Line 20 defines a **CTime2** constructor that receives a single **Integer** argument, representing the **mHour**. Line 26 defines a **CTime2** constructor that receives two **Integer** arguments, representing the **mHour** and **mMinute**. Line 33 defines a **CTime2** constructor that receives three **Integer** arguments representing the **mHour**, **mMinute** and **mSecond**. Line 40 defines a **CTime2** constructor that receives a reference to another **CTime2** object. When this last constructor is employed, the values from the **CTime2** argument are used to initialize the **mHour**, **mMinute** and **mSecond** values. Even though class **CTime2** declares these values as **Private** (lines 8–10), the **CTime2** object can access these values directly using the expressions **timeValue.mHour**, **timeValue.mMinute** and **timeValue.mSecond**.

No constructor specifies a return type; doing so is a syntax error. Also, notice that each constructor receives a different number or different types of arguments. Even though only two of the constructors receive values for the **mHour**, **mMinute** and **mSecond**, each constructor calls **SetTime** with values for **mHour**, **mMinute** and **mSecond** and substitutes zeros for the missing values to satisfy **SetTime**'s requirement of three arguments.

Software Engineering Observation 8.10
*When one object of a class has a reference to another object of the same class, the first object can access all the second object's data and methods (including those that are **Private**).*

```
1   ' Fig. 8.4: CTime2.vb
2   ' Represents time and contains overloaded constructors.
3
4   Class CTime2
5      Inherits Object
6
7      ' declare Integers for hour, minute and second
8      Private mHour As Integer      ' 0 - 23
9      Private mMinute As Integer    ' 0 - 59
10     Private mSecond As Integer    ' 0 - 59
11
```

Fig. 8.4 Overloading constructors (part 1 of 3).

```vbnet
12      ' constructor initializes each variable to zero and
13      ' ensures that each CTime2 object starts in consistent state
14      Public Sub New()
15         SetTime()
16      End Sub ' New
17
18      ' CTime2 constructor: hour supplied;
19      ' minute and second default to 0
20      Public Sub New(ByVal hourValue As Integer)
21         SetTime(hourValue)
22      End Sub ' New
23
24      ' CTime2 constructor: hour and minute supplied;
25      ' second defaulted to 0
26      Public Sub New(ByVal hourValue As Integer, _
27         ByVal minuteValue As Integer)
28
29         SetTime(hourValue, minuteValue)
30      End Sub ' New
31
32      ' CTime2 constructor: hour, minute and second supplied
33      Public Sub New(ByVal hourValue As Integer, _
34         ByVal minuteValue As Integer, ByVal secondValue As Integer)
35
36         SetTime(hourValue, minuteValue, secondValue)
37      End Sub ' New
38
39      ' CTime2 constructor: another CTime2 object supplied
40      Public Sub New(ByVal timeValue As CTime2)
41        SetTime(timeValue.mHour, timeValue.mMinute, timeValue.mSecond)
42      End Sub ' New
43
44      ' set new time value using universal time;
45      ' perform validity checks on data;
46      ' set invalid values to zero
47      Public Sub SetTime(Optional ByVal hourValue As Integer = 0, _
48         Optional ByVal minuteValue As Integer = 0, _
49         Optional ByVal secondValue As Integer = 0)
50
51         ' perform validity checks on hour, then set hour
52         If (hourValue >= 0 AndAlso hourValue < 24) Then
53            mHour = hourValue
54         Else
55            mHour = 0
56         End If
57
58         ' perform validity checks on minute, then set minute
59         If (minuteValue >= 0 AndAlso minuteValue < 60) Then
60            mMinute = minuteValue
61         Else
62            mMinute = 0
63         End If
64
```

Fig. 8.4 Overloading constructors (part 2 of 3).

```
65         ' perform validity checks on second, then set second
66         If (secondValue >= 0 AndAlso secondValue < 60) Then
67            mSecond = secondValue
68         Else
69            mSecond = 0
70         End If
71
72      End Sub ' SetTime
73
74      ' convert String to universal-time format
75      Public Function ToUniversalString() As String
76         Return String.Format("{0}:{1:D2}:{2:D2}", _
77            mHour, mMinute, mSecond)
78      End Function ' ToUniversalString
79
80      ' convert to String in standard-time format
81      Public Function ToStandardString() As String
82         Dim suffix As String = " PM"
83         Dim format As String = "{0}:{1:D2}:{2:D2}"
84         Dim standardHour As Integer
85
86         ' determine whether time is AM or PM
87         If mHour < 12 Then
88            suffix = " AM"
89         End If
90
91         ' convert from universal-time format to standard-time format
92         If (mHour = 12 OrElse mHour = 0) Then
93            standardHour = 12
94         Else
95            standardHour = mHour Mod 12
96         End If
97
98         Return String.Format(format, standardHour, mMinute, _
99            mSecond) & suffix
100     End Function ' ToStandardString
101
102 End Class ' CTime2
```

Fig. 8.4 Overloading constructors (part 3 of 3).

Common Programming Error 8.5

A constructor can call other class methods that use instance variables not yet initialized. Using instance variables before they have been initialized can lead to logic errors.

Figure 8.5 (**modTimeTest2**) demonstrates the use of overloaded constructors (Fig. 8.4). Lines 11–16 create six **CTime2** objects that invoke various constructors of the class. Line 11 specifies that it invokes the default constructor by placing an empty set of parentheses after the class name. Lines 12–16 of the program demonstrate the passing of arguments to the **CTime2** constructors. To invoke the appropriate constructor, pass the proper number, types and order of arguments (specified by the constructor's definition) to that constructor. For example, line 13 invokes the constructor that is defined in lines 26–30 of

Fig. 8.4. Lines 21–55 invoke methods **ToUniversalString** and **ToStandardString** for each **CTime2** object to demonstrate how the constructors initialize the objects.

```vb
 1    ' Fig. 8.5: TimeTest2.vb
 2    ' Demonstrates overloading constructors.
 3
 4    Imports System.Windows.Forms
 5
 6    Module modTimeTest2
 7
 8       Sub Main()
 9
10          ' use overloaded constructors
11          Dim time1 As New CTime2()
12          Dim time2 As New CTime2(2)
13          Dim time3 As New CTime2(21, 34)
14          Dim time4 As New CTime2(12, 25, 42)
15          Dim time5 As New CTime2(27, 74, 99)
16          Dim time6 As New CTime2(time4) ' use time4 as initial value
17
18          Const SPACING As Integer = 13 ' spacing between output text
19
20          ' invoke time1 methods
21          Dim output As String = "Constructed with: " & vbCrLf & _
22             " time1: all arguments defaulted" & vbCrLf & _
23             Space(SPACING) & time1.ToUniversalString() & _
24             vbCrLf & Space(SPACING) & time1.ToStandardString()
25
26          ' invoke time2 methods
27          output &= vbCrLf & _
28             " time2: hour specified; minute and second defaulted" & _
29             vbCrLf & Space(SPACING) & _
30             time2.ToUniversalString() & vbCrLf & Space(SPACING) & _
31             time2.ToStandardString()
32
33          ' invoke time3 methods
34          output &= vbCrLf & _
35             " time3: hour and minute specified; second defaulted" & _
36             vbCrLf & Space(SPACING) & time3.ToUniversalString() & _
37             vbCrLf & Space(SPACING) & time3.ToStandardString()
38
39          ' invoke time4 methods
40          output &= vbCrLf & _
41             " time4: hour, minute and second specified" & _
42             vbCrLf & Space(SPACING) & time4.ToUniversalString() & _
43             vbCrLf & Space(SPACING) & time4.ToStandardString()
44
45          ' invoke time5 methods
46          output &= vbCrLf & _
47             " time5: hour, minute and second specified" & _
48             vbCrLf & Space(SPACING) & time5.ToUniversalString() & _
49             vbCrLf & Space(SPACING) & time5.ToStandardString()
50
```

Fig. 8.5 Overloaded-constructor demonstration (part 1 of 2).

```
51              ' invoke time6 methods
52              output &= vbCrLf & _
53                 " time6: Time2 object time4 specified" & vbCrLf & _
54                 Space(SPACING) & time6.ToUniversalString() & _
55                 vbCrLf & Space(SPACING) & time6.ToStandardString()
56
57              MessageBox.Show(output, _
58                 "Demonstrating Overloaded Constructor")
59         End Sub ' Main
60
61    End Module ' modTimeTest2
```

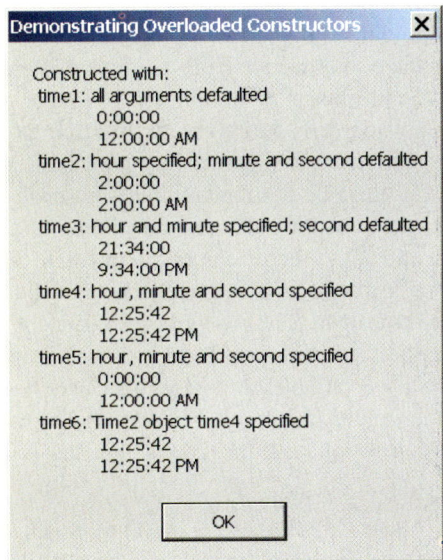

Fig. 8.5   Overloaded-constructor demonstration (part 2 of 2).

Each **CTime2** constructor can be written to include a copy of the appropriate statements from method **SetTime**. This might be slightly more efficient, because it eliminates the extra call to **SetTime**. However, consider what would happen if the programmer changes the representation of the time from three **Integer** values (requiring 12 bytes of memory) to a single **Integer** value representing the total number of seconds that have elapsed in the day (requiring 4 bytes of memory). Placing identical code in the **CTime2** constructors and method **SetTime** makes such a change in the class definition more difficult. If the implementation of method **SetTime** changes, the implementation of the **CTime2** constructors would need to change accordingly. If the **CTime2** constructors call **SetTime** directly, any changes to the implementation of **SetTime** must be made only once, thus reducing the likelihood of a programming error when altering the implementation.

Software Engineering Observation 8.11

If a method of a class provides functionality required by a constructor (or other method) of the class, call that method from the constructor (or other method). This simplifies the maintenance of the code and reduces the likelihood of introducing an error in the code.

8.7 Properties

Methods of a class can manipulate that class's **Private** instance variables. A typical manipulation might be the adjustment of a customer's bank balance—a **Private** instance variable of a class **CBankAccount**—a **ComputeInterest** method.

Classes often provide **Public** *properties* to allow clients to *set* (i.e., assign values to) or *set* (i.e., obtain the values of) **Private** instance variables. In Fig. 8.6, we show how to create three properties—**Hour**, **Minute** and **Second**. **Hour** accesses variable **mHour**, **Minute** accesses variable **mMinute** and **Second** accesses variable **mSecond**. Each property contains a *Get* accessor (to retrieve the field value) and a *Set* accessor (to modify the field value).

Although providing **Set** and **Get** accessors appears to be the same as making the instance variables **Public**, this is not the case. This is another one of Visual Basic's subtleties that makes the language so attractive from a software-engineering standpoint. If an instance variable is **Public**, the instance variable can be read or written by any method in the program. If an instance variable is **Private**, a **Public** get method seems to allow other methods to read the data at will. However, the get method can control the formatting and display of the data. A **Public** set method can scrutinize attempts to modify the instance variable's value, thus ensuring that the new value is appropriate for that data member. For example, an attempt to set the day of the month to 37 would be rejected, and an attempt to set a person's weight to a negative value would be rejected. Therefore, although set and get methods provide access to **Private** data, the implementation of these methods can restrict access to that data.

The declaration of instance variables as **Private** does not guarantee data integrity. Programmers must provide validity checking—Visual Basic provides only the framework with which programmers can design better programs.

Testing and Debugging Tip 8.2

*Methods that set the values of **Private** data should verify that the intended new values are proper; if they are not, the **Set** methods should place the **Private** instance variables into an appropriate consistent state.*

A class's **Set** accessors cannot return values indicating a failed attempt to assign invalid data to objects of the class. Such return values could be useful to a class's clients for handling errors. In this case, clients could take appropriate actions if the objects occupy invalid states. Chapter 11 presents exception handling—a mechanism that can be used to notify a class's clients of failed attempts to set objects of that class to consistent states.

Figure 8.6 enhances our **CTime** class (now called **CTime3**) to include properties for the **mHour**, **mMinute** and **mSecond Private** instance variables. The **Set** accessors of these properties strictly control the setting of the instance variables to valid values. An attempt to set any instance variable to an incorrect value causes the instance variable to be set to zero (thus leaving the instance variable in a consistent state). Each **Get** accessor returns the appropriate instance variable's value.

```
1   ' Fig. 8.6: CTime3.vb
2   ' Represents time in 24-hour format and contains properties.
3
```

Fig. 8.6 Properties in a class (part 1 of 4).

```vbnet
4    Class CTime3
5       Inherits Object
6
7       ' declare Integers for hour, minute and second
8       Private mHour As Integer
9       Private mMinute As Integer
10      Private mSecond As Integer
11
12      ' CTime3 constructor: initialize each instance variable to zero
13      ' and ensure that each CTime3 object starts in consistent state
14      Public Sub New()
15         SetTime(0, 0, 0)
16      End Sub ' New
17
18      ' CTime3 constructor:
19      ' hour supplied, minute and second defaulted to 0
20      Public Sub New(ByVal hourValue As Integer)
21         SetTime(hourValue, 0, 0)
22      End Sub ' New
23
24      ' CTime3 constructor:
25      ' hour and minute supplied; second defaulted to 0
26      Public Sub New(ByVal hourValue As Integer, _
27         ByVal minuteValue As Integer)
28
29         SetTime(hourValue, minuteValue, 0)
30      End Sub ' New
31
32      ' CTime3 constructor: hour, minute and second supplied
33      Public Sub New(ByVal hourValue As Integer, _
34         ByVal minuteValue As Integer, ByVal secondValue As Integer)
35
36         SetTime(hourValue, minuteValue, secondValue)
37      End Sub ' New
38
39      ' CTime3 constructor: another CTime3 object supplied
40      Public Sub New(ByVal timeValue As CTime3)
41         SetTime(timeValue.mHour, timeValue.mMinute, _
42            timeValue.mSecond)
43      End Sub ' New
44
45      ' set new time value using universal time;
46      ' uses properties to perform validity checks on data
47      Public Sub SetTime(ByVal hourValue As Integer, _
48         ByVal minuteValue As Integer, ByVal secondValue As Integer)
49
50         Hour = hourValue      ' looks
51         Minute = minuteValue  ' dangerous
52         Second = secondValue  ' but it is correct
53      End Sub ' SetTime
54
```

Fig. 8.6 Properties in a class (part 2 of 4).

```
55      ' property Hour
56      Public Property Hour() As Integer
57
58         ' return mHour value
59         Get
60            Return mHour
61         End Get
62
63         ' set mHour value
64         Set(ByVal value As Integer)
65
66            If (value >= 0 AndAlso value < 24) Then
67               mHour = value
68            Else
69               mHour = 0
70            End If
71
72         End Set
73
74      End Property ' Hour
75
76      ' property Minute
77      Public Property Minute() As Integer
78
79         ' return mMinute value
80         Get
81            Return mMinute
82         End Get
83
84         ' set mMinute value
85         Set(ByVal value As Integer)
86
87            If (value >= 0 AndAlso value < 60) Then
88               mMinute = value
89            Else
90               mMinute = 0
91            End If
92
93         End Set
94
95      End Property ' Minute
96
97      ' property Second
98      Public Property Second() As Integer
99
100        ' return mSecond value
101        Get
102           Return mSecond
103        End Get
104
```

Fig. 8.6 Properties in a class (part 3 of 4).

```vbnet
105            ' set mSecond value
106            Set(ByVal value As Integer)
107
108               If (value >= 0 AndAlso value < 60) Then
109                  mSecond = value
110               Else
111                  mSecond = 0
112               End If
113
114            End Set
115
116         End Property ' Second
117
118         ' convert String to universal-time format
119         Public Function ToUniversalString() As String
120            Return String.Format("{0}:{1:D2}:{2:D2}", _
121               mHour, mMinute, mSecond)
122         End Function ' ToUniversalString
123
124         ' convert to String in standard-time format
125         Public Function ToStandardString() As String
126            Dim suffix As String = " PM"
127            Dim format As String = "{0}:{1:D2}:{2:D2}"
128            Dim standardHour As Integer
129
130            ' determine whether time is AM or PM
131            If mHour < 12 Then
132               suffix = " AM"
133            End If
134
135            ' convert from universal-time format to standard-time format
136            If (mHour = 12 OrElse mHour = 0) Then
137               standardHour = 12
138            Else
139               standardHour = mHour Mod 12
140            End If
141
142            Return String.Format(format, standardHour, mMinute, _
143               mSecond) & suffix
144         End Function ' ToStandardString
145
146      End Class ' CTime3
```

Fig. 8.6 Properties in a class (part 4 of 4).

Lines 56–74, 77–95 and 98–116 define the properties **Hour**, **Minute** and **Second** of class **CTime3**, respectively. Each property begins with a declaration line, which includes an access modifier (**Public**), the property's name (**Hour**, **Minute** or **Second**) and the property's type (**Integer**).

The body of the property contains **Get** and **Set** accessors, which are declared using the keywords **Get** and **Set**. The **Get** accessor method declarations are on lines 59–61, 80–82 and 101–103. These **Get** methods return the **mHour**, **mMinute** and **mSecond** instance variable values that objects request. The **Set** accessors are declared on lines 64–72, 85–93 and 106–114. The body of each **Set** accessor performs the same conditional statement that was previously in method **SetTime** for setting the **mHour**, **mMinute** or **mSecond**.

Method **SetTime** (lines 47–53) now uses properties **Hour**, **Minute** and **Second** to ensure that instance variables **mHour**, **mMinute** and **mSecond** have valid values. After we define a property, we can use it in the same way that we use a variable. We assign values to properties using the **=** (assignment) operator. When this assignment occurs, the code in the definition of the **Set** accessor for that property is executed. Referencing the property (for instance, using it in a mathematical calculation) executes the code within the definition of the **Get** accessor for that property.

When we employ **Set** and **Get** accessor methods in class **CTime3**, we minimize the changes that we must make to the class definition, in the event that we alter the data representation from **mHour**, **mMinute** and **mSecond** to another representation (such as total elapsed seconds in the day). We must provide only new **Set** and **Get** accessor bodies. Using this technique, programmers can change the implementation of a class without affecting the clients of that class (as long as all the **Public** methods of the class are called in the same way).

Software Engineering Observation 8.12

*Accessing **Private** data through **Set** and **Get** accessors not only protects the instance variables from receiving invalid values, but also hides the internal representation of the instance variables from that class's clients. Thus, if representation of the data changes (typically, to reduce the amount of required storage or to improve performance), only the properties implementations need to change—the clients' implementations need not change as long as the service provided by the properties is preserved.*

Figure 8.7 (class **FrmTimeTest3**), which represents the GUI for class **CTime3** (line 30 represents the condensed region of code generated by the Visual Studio's *Windows Form Designer*), declares and instantiates an object of class **CTime3** (line 28). The GUI contains three text fields in which the user can input values for the **CTime3** object's **mHour**, **mMinute** and **mSecond** variables, respectively. Lines 68–92 declare three methods that use the **Hour**, **Minute** and **Second** properties of the **CTime3** object to alter their corresponding values. The GUI also contains a button that enables the user to increment the **mSecond** value by **1** without having to use the text box. Using properties, method **cmdAddSecond_Click** (lines 43–65) determines and sets the new time. For example, **23:59:59** becomes **00:00:00** when the user presses the button.

```
1   ' Fig. 8.7: TimeTest3.vb
2   ' Demonstrates Properties.
3
4   Imports System.Windows.Forms
5
6   Class FrmTimeTest3
7      Inherits Form
8
9      ' Label and TextBox for hour
10     Friend WithEvents lblSetHour As Label
11     Friend WithEvents txtSetHour As TextBox
12
```

Fig. 8.7 Graphical user interface for class **CTime3** (part 1 of 3).

```vbnet
13      ' Label and TextBox for minute
14      Friend WithEvents lblSetMinute As Label
15      Friend WithEvents txtSetMinute As TextBox
16
17      ' Label and TextBox for second
18      Friend WithEvents lblSetSecond As Label
19      Friend WithEvents txtSetSecond As TextBox
20
21      ' Labels for outputting time
22      Friend WithEvents lblOutput1 As Label
23      Friend WithEvents lblOutput2 As Label
24
25      ' Button for adding one second to time
26      Friend WithEvents cmdAddSecond As Button
27
28      Dim time As New CTime3()
29
30      ' Visual Studio .NET generated code
31
32      ' update time display
33      Private Sub UpdateDisplay()
34         lblOutput1.Text = "Hour: " & time.Hour & "; Minute: " & _
35            time.Minute & "; Second: " & time.Second
36
37         lblOutput2.Text = "Standard time is: " & _
38            time.ToStandardString & "; Universal Time is: " _
39            & time.ToUniversalString()
40      End Sub ' UpdateDisplay
41
42      ' invoked when user presses Add Second button
43      Protected Sub cmdAddSecond_Click( _
44         ByVal sender As System.Object, _
45         ByVal e As System.EventArgs) Handles cmdAddSecond.Click
46
47         ' add one second
48         time.Second = (time.Second + 1) Mod 60
49         txtSetSecond.Text = time.Second
50
51         ' add one minute if 60 seconds have passed
52         If time.Second = 0 Then
53            time.Minute = (time.Minute + 1) Mod 60
54            txtSetMinute.Text = time.Minute
55
56            ' add one hour if 60 minutes have passed
57            If time.Minute = 0 Then
58               time.Hour = (time.Hour + 1) Mod 24
59               txtSetHour.Text = time.Hour
60            End If
61
62         End If
63
64         UpdateDisplay()
65      End Sub ' cmdAddSecond_Click
```

Fig. 8.7 Graphical user interface for class **CTime3** (part 2 of 3).

```vbnet
66
67      ' handle event when txtSetHour's text changes
68      Protected Sub txtSetHour_TextChanged(ByVal sender As _
69         System.Object, ByVal e As System.EventArgs) _
70         Handles txtSetHour.TextChanged
71
72         time.Hour = Convert.ToInt32(txtSetHour.Text)
73         UpdateDisplay()
74      End Sub ' txtSetHour_TextChanged
75
76      ' handle event when txtSetMinute's text changes
77      Protected Sub txtSetMinute_TextChanged(ByVal sender As _
78         System.Object, ByVal e As System.EventArgs) _
79         Handles txtSetMinute.TextChanged
80
81         time.Minute = Convert.ToInt32(txtSetMinute.Text)
82         UpdateDisplay()
83      End Sub ' txtSetMinute_TextChanged
84
85      ' handle event when txtSetSecond's text changes
86      Protected Sub txtSetSecond_TextChanged(ByVal sender _
87         As System.Object, ByVal e As System.EventArgs) _
88         Handles txtSetSecond.TextChanged
89
90         time.Second = Convert.ToInt32(txtSetSecond.Text)
91         UpdateDisplay()
92      End Sub ' txtSetSecond_TextChanged
93
94   End Class ' FrmTimeTest3
```

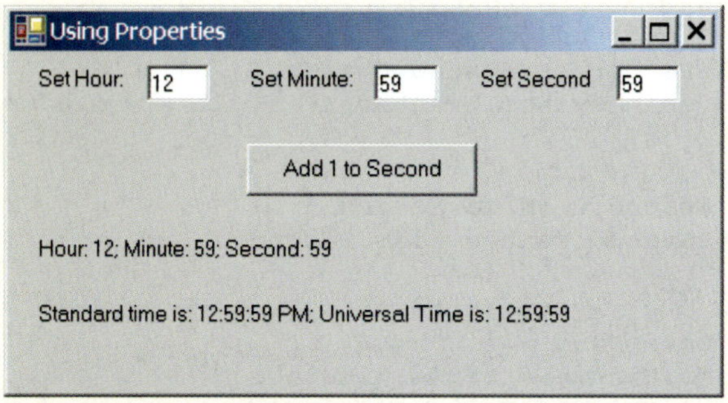

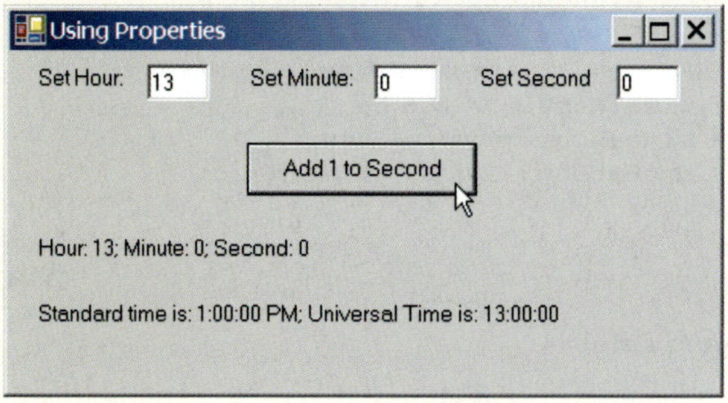

Fig. 8.7 Graphical user interface for class **CTime3** (part 3 of 3).

Not all properties need to have **Get** and **Set** accessors. A property with only a **Get** accessor is called a read-only property and must be declared using keyword **ReadOnly**. By contrast, a property with only a **Set** accessor is called a write-only property and must be declared using keyword **WriteOnly**. Generally, **WriteOnly** properties are seldom used. In Section 8.11, we use **ReadOnly** properties to prevent our programs from changing the values of instance variables.

8.8 Composition: Objects as Instance Variables of Other Classes

In many situations, referencing existing objects is more convenient than rewriting the objects' code for new classes in new projects. Suppose we were to implement an **CAlarmClock** class object that needs to know when to sound its alarm. It would be easier to reference an existing **CTime** object (like those from the previous examples in this chapter) than it would be to write a new **CTime** object. The use of references to objects of preexisting classes as members of new objects is called *composition*.

Software Engineering Observation 8.13

One form of software reuse is composition, in which a class has as members references to objects of other classes.

The application of Fig. 8.8, Fig. 8.9 and Fig. 8.10 demonstrates composition. Class **CDay** (Fig. 8.8) encapsulates information relating to a specific date. Lines 9–11 declare **Integer**s **mMonth**, **mDay** and **mYear**. Lines 15–35 define the constructor, which receives values for **mMonth**, **mDay** and **mYear** as arguments, then assigns these values to the class variables after ensuring that the variables are in a consistent state.

```
1   ' Fig. 8.8: CDay.vb
2   ' Encapsulates month, day and year.
3
4   Imports System.Windows.Forms
5
6   Class CDay
7      Inherits Object
8
9      Private mMonth As Integer   ' 1-12
10     Private mDay As Integer     ' 1-31 based on month
11     Private mYear As Integer    ' any year
12
13     ' constructor confirms proper value for month, then calls
14     ' method CheckDay to confirm proper value for day
15     Public Sub New(ByVal monthValue As Integer, _
16        ByVal dayValue As Integer, ByVal yearValue As Integer)
17
18        ' ensure month value is valid
19        If (monthValue > 0 AndAlso monthValue <= 12) Then
20           mMonth = monthValue
21        Else
22           mMonth = 1
```

Fig. 8.8 **CDay** class encapsulates day, month and year information (part 1 of 2).

```vb
23
24              ' inform user of error
25              Dim errorMessage As String = _
26                 "Month invalid. Set to month 1."
27
28              MessageBox.Show(errorMessage, "", _
29                 MessageBoxButtons.OK, MessageBoxIcon.Error)
30           End If
31
32           mYear = yearValue
33           mDay = CheckDay(dayValue) ' validate day
34
35        End Sub ' New
36
37        ' confirm proper day value based on month and year
38        Private Function CheckDay(ByVal testDayValue As Integer) _
39           As Integer
40
41           Dim daysPerMonth() As Integer = _
42              {0, 31, 28, 31, 30, 31, 30, 31, 31, 30, 31, 30, 31}
43
44           If (testDayValue > 0 AndAlso _
45              testDayValue <= daysPerMonth(mMonth)) Then
46
47              Return testDayValue
48           End If
49
50           ' check for leap year in February
51           If (mMonth = 2 AndAlso testDayValue = 29 AndAlso _
52              mYear Mod 400 = 0 OrElse mYear Mod 4 = 0 AndAlso _
53              mYear Mod 100 <> 0) Then
54
55              Return testDayValue
56           Else
57
58              ' inform user of error
59              Dim errorMessage As String = _
60                 "day " & testDayValue & "invalid. Set to day 1. "
61
62              MessageBox.Show(errorMessage, "", _
63                 MessageBoxButtons.OK, MessageBoxIcon.Error)
64
65              Return 1 ' leave object in consistent state
66           End If
67
68        End Function ' CheckDay
69
70        ' create string containing month/day/year format
71        Public Function ToStandardString() As String
72           Return mMonth & "/" & mDay & "/" & mYear
73        End Function ' ToStandardString
74
75     End Class ' CDay
```

Fig. 8.8 **CDay** class encapsulates day, month and year information (part 2 of 2).

Class **CEmployee** (Fig. 8.9) holds information relating to an employee's birthday and hire date (lines 7–10) using instance variables **mFirstName**, **mLastName**, **mBirthDate** and **mHireDate**. Members **mBirthDate** and **mHireDate** are references to **CDay** objects, each of which contains instance variables **mMonth**, **mDay** and **mYear**. In this example, class **CEmployee** is *composed of* two references of class **CDay**. The **CEmployee** constructor (lines 13–32) takes eight arguments (**firstNameValue**, **lastNameValue**, **birthMonthValue**, **birthDayValue**, **birthYearValue**, **hireMonthValue**, **hireDayValue** and **hireYearValue**). Lines 26–27 pass arguments **birthMonthValue**, **birthDayValue** and **birthYearValue** to the **CDay** constructor to create the **mBirthDate** object. Similarly, lines 30–31 pass arguments **hireMonthValue**, **hireDayValue** and **hireYearValue** to the **CDay** constructor to create the **mHireDate** object.

Module **modCompositionTest** (Fig. 8.10) runs the application with method **Main**. Lines 9–10 instantiate a **CEmployee** object (**"Bob Jones"** with birthday **7/24/1949** and hire date **3/12/1988**), and lines 12–13 display the information to the user in a **MessageBox**.

```vb
 1  ' Fig. 8.9: CEmployee.vb
 2  ' Represent employee name, birthday and hire date.
 3
 4  Class CEmployee
 5     Inherits Object
 6
 7     Private mFirstName As String
 8     Private mLastName As String
 9     Private mBirthDate As CDay ' member object reference
10     Private mHireDate As CDay ' member object reference
11
12     ' CEmployee constructor
13     Public Sub New(ByVal firstNameValue As String, _
14        ByVal lastNameValue As String, _
15        ByVal birthMonthValue As Integer, _
16        ByVal birthDayValue As Integer, _
17        ByVal birthYearValue As Integer, _
18        ByVal hireMonthValue As Integer, _
19        ByVal hireDayValue As Integer, _
20        ByVal hireYearValue As Integer)
21
22        mFirstName = firstNameValue
23        mLastName = lastNameValue
24
25        ' create CDay instance for employee birthday
26        mBirthDate = New CDay(birthMonthValue, birthDayValue, _
27           birthYearValue)
28
29        ' create CDay instance for employee hire date
30        mHireDate = New CDay(hireMonthValue, hireDayValue, _
31           hireYearValue)
32     End Sub ' New
```

Fig. 8.9 **CEmployee** class encapsulates employee name, birthday and hire date (part 1 of 2).

```
33
34         ' return employee information as standard-format String
35         Public Function ToStandardString() As String
36            Return mLastName & ", " & mFirstName & " Hired: " _
37               & mHireDate.ToStandardString() & " Birthday: " & _
38               mBirthDate.ToStandardString()
39         End Function ' ToStandardString
40
41    End Class ' CEmployee
```

Fig. 8.9 **CEmployee** class encapsulates employee name, birthday and hire date (part 2 of 2).

```
1     ' Fig. 8.10: CompositionTest.vb
2     ' Demonstrate an object with member object reference.
3
4     Imports System.Windows.Forms
5
6     Module modCompositionTest
7
8        Sub Main()
9           Dim employee As New CEmployee( _
10              "Bob", "Jones", 7, 24, 1949, 3, 12, 1988)
11
12          MessageBox.Show(employee.ToStandardString(), _
13             "Testing Class Employee")
14       End Sub ' Main
15
16    End Module ' modCompositionTest
```

Testing Class Employee
Jones, Bob Hired: 3/12/1988 Birthday: 7/24/1949
OK

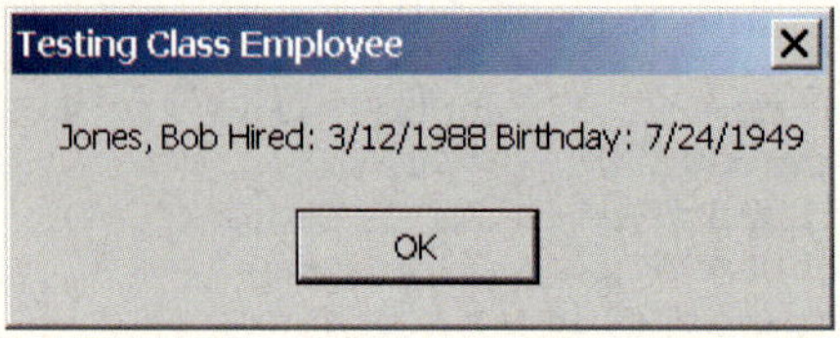

Fig. 8.10 Composition demonstration.

8.9 Using the Me Reference

Every object can access a reference to itself via the **Me** *reference*. The **Me** reference is used implicitly refer to instance variables, properties and methods of an object. We begin with an example of using reference **Me** explicitly and implicitly to display the **Private** data of an object.

Class **CTime4** (Fig. 8.11) defines three **Private** instance variables—**mHour**, **mMinute** and **mSecond** (line 5). The constructor (lines 8–14) receives three **Integer** arguments to initialize a **CTime4** object. Note that for this example, we have made the constructor's parameter names (lines 8–9) identical to the class's instance variable names (line 5). A method's local variable that has the same name as a class's instance variable hides the instance variable in that method's scope. However, the method can use reference **Me** to refer to these instance variables explicitly. Lines 11–13 of Fig. 8.11 demonstrate this feature.

```vb
1   ' Fig. 8.11: CTime4.vb
2   ' Encapsulate time using Me reference.
3
4   Class CTime4
5      Private mHour, mMinute, mSecond As Integer
6
7      ' CTime4 constructor
8      Public Sub New(ByVal mHour As Integer, _
9         ByVal mMinute As Integer, ByVal mSecond As Integer)
10
11        Me.mHour = mHour
12        Me.mMinute = mMinute
13        Me.mSecond = mSecond
14     End Sub ' New
15
16     ' create String using Me and implicit references
17     Public Function BuildString() As String
18        Return "Me.ToUniversalString(): " & Me.ToUniversalString() _
19           & vbCrLf & "ToUniversalString(): " & ToUniversalString()
20     End Function ' BuildString
21
22     ' convert to String in standard-time format
23     Public Function ToUniversalString() As String
24        Return String.Format("{0:D2}:{1:D2}:{2:D2}", _
25           mHour, mMinute, mSecond)
26     End Function ' ToUniversalString
27
28  End Class ' CTime4
```

Fig. 8.11 Class using **Me** reference.

Method **BuildString** (lines 17–20) returns a **String** created by a statement that uses the **Me** reference explicitly and implicitly. Line 18 uses the **Me** reference explicitly to call method **ToUniversalString**, whereas line 19 uses the **Me** reference implicitly to call method **ToUniversalString**. Note that both lines perform the same task (i.e., generate identical output). Because of this, programmers usually do not use the **Me** reference explicitly to reference methods.

Common Programming Error 8.6
*For a method in which a parameter has the same name as an instance variable, use reference **Me** to access the instance variable explicitly; otherwise, the method parameter is referenced.*

Testing and Debugging Tip 8.3
Avoidance of method-parameter names that conflict with instance variable names helps prevent certain subtle, hard-to-trace bugs.

Good Programming Practice 8.7
*The explicit use of the **Me** reference can increase program clarity where **Me** is optional.*

Module **modMeTest** (Fig. 8.12) runs the application that demonstrates the use of the **Me** reference. Line 9 instantiates an instance of class **CTime4**. Lines 11–12 invoke method **BuildString**, then display the results to the user in a **MessageBox**.

```vbnet
1   ' Fig. 8.12: MeTest.vb
2   ' Demonstrates Me reference.
3
4   Imports System.Windows.Forms
5
6   Module modMeTest
7
8      Sub Main()
9         Dim time As New CTime4(12, 30, 19)
10
11        MessageBox.Show(time.BuildString(), _
12           "Demonstrating the 'Me' Reference")
13     End Sub ' Main
14
15  End Module ' modMeTest
```

```
Demonstrating the 'Me' Reference
Me.ToUniversalString(): 12:30:19
ToUniversalString(): 12:30:19
                  OK
```

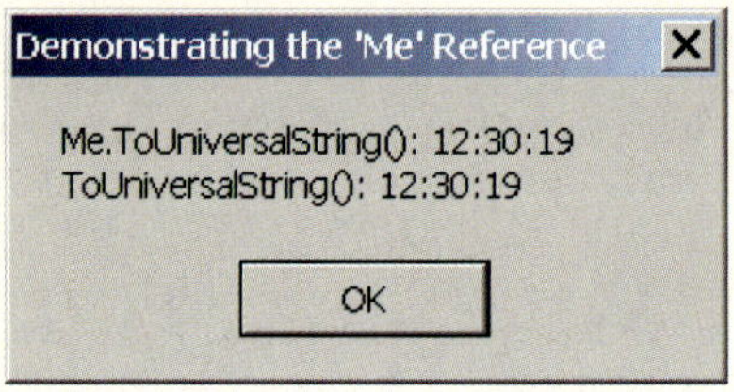

Fig. 8.12 **Me** reference demonstration.

8.10 Garbage Collection

In previous examples, we have seen how a constructor method initializes data in an object of a class after the object is created. Keyword **New** allocates memory for the object, then calls that object's constructor. The constructor might acquire other system resources, such as network connections and database connections. Objects must have a disciplined way to return memory and release resources when the program no longer uses those objects. Failure to release such resources causes *resource leaks*.

Unlike C and C++, in which programmers must manage memory explicitly, Visual Basic performs memory management internally. The .NET Framework performs *garbage collection* of memory to return memory that is no longer needed back to the system. When the *garbage collector* executes, it locates objects for which the application has no references. Such objects can be collected at that time or in a subsequent execution of the garbage collector. Therefore, the *memory leaks* that are common in such languages as C and C++, where memory is not reclaimed automatically, are rare in Visual Basic.

Dependence on Visual Basic's automatic garbage collection, however, might not be the best way to manage resources. Certain resources, such as network connections, database connections and file streams, are better handled explicitly by the programmer. One technique employed to handle these resources (in conjunction with the garbage collector) is to define a *finalizer* method that returns resources to the system. The garbage collector calls an object's finalizer method to perform *termination housekeeping* on that object just before the garbage collector reclaims the object's memory (this process is called *finalization*).

Class **Object** defines method **Finalize**, which is the finalizer method for all Visual Basic objects. Because all Visual Basic classes inherit from class **Object**, they inherit method **Finalize** and can *override* it to free resources specific to those classes. The overridden method is called before garbage collection occurs—however, we cannot determine exactly when this method is called, because we cannot determine exactly when garbage collection occurs. We discuss method **Finalize** in greater detail in Chapter 9, when we discuss inheritance.

8.11 Shared Class Members

Each object of a class has its own copy of all the instance variables of the class. However, in certain cases, all class objects should share only one copy of a particular variable. A **Shared** *class variable* is such a variable; a program contains only one copy of this variable in memory, no matter how many objects of the variable's class have been instantiated. A **Shared** class variable represents *class-wide information*—all class objects share the same piece of data. The declaration of a **Shared** member begins with the keyword **Shared**.

In Visual Basic, programmers can define what is known as a *shared constructor*, which is used only to initialize **Shared** class members. **Shared** constructors are optional and must be declared with the **Shared** keyword. Normally, **Shared** constructors are used when it is necessary to initialize a **Shared** class variable before any objects of that class are instantiated. **Shared** constructors are called before any **Shared** class members are used and before any class objects are instantiated.

We now employ a video-game example to explain the need for **Shared** class-wide data. Suppose we have a video game in which **CMartian**s attack with other space creatures. Each **CMartian** tends to be brave and willing to attack other space creatures when the **CMartian** is aware that there are at least four other **CMartian**s present. If there are fewer than a total of five **CMartian**s present, each **CMartian** becomes cowardly. For this reason, each **CMartian** must know the **martianCount**. We could endow class **CMartian** with **martianCount** as instance data. If we were to do this, then every **CMartian** would have a separate copy of the instance data, and, every time we create a **CMartian**, we would have to update the instance variable **martianCount** in every **CMartian**. The redundant copies waste space, and the updating of those copies is time-consuming. Instead, we declare **martianCount** to be **Shared** so that **martianCount** is class-wide data. Each **CMartian** can see the **martianCount** as if it were instance data of that **CMartian**, but Visual Basic maintains only one copy of the **Shared martianCount** to save space. We also save time, in that the **CMartian** constructor increments only the **Shared martianCount**. Because there is only one copy, we do not have to increment separate copies of **martianCount** for each **CMartian** object.

Performance Tip 8.2

*When a single copy of the data will suffice, use **Shared** class variables to save storage.*

Although **Shared** class variables might seem like *global variables* in C and C++ (variables that can be referenced directly by name in any C function or C++ class or method in a program), they are not the same thing. **Shared** class variables have class scope. A class's **Public Shared** members can be accessed through the class name using the dot operator (e.g., *className.sharedMemberName*). A class's **Private Shared** class members can be accessed only through methods of the class. **Shared** class members are available as soon as the class is loaded into memory at execution time; like other variables with class scope, they exist for the duration of program execution, even when no objects of that class exist. To access a **Private Shared** class member when no objects of the class exist, programmers must provide a **Public Shared** method or property.

A **Shared** method cannot access non-**Shared** class members. Unlike non-**Shared** methods, a **Shared** method has no **Me** reference, because **Shared** class variables and **Shared** class methods exist independently of any class objects and even when there are no objects of that class.

Common Programming Error 8.7
*Using the **Me** reference in a **Shared** method or **Shared** property is a syntax error.*

Class **CEmployee2** (Fig. 8.13) demonstrates the use of a **Private Shared** class variable and a **Public Shared Property**. The **Shared** class variable **mCount** is initialized to zero by default (line 11). Class variable **mCount** maintains a count of the number of objects of class **CEmployee2** that have been instantiated and currently reside in memory, including those objects that have already been marked for garbage collection but have not yet been reclaimed by the garbage collector.

When objects of class **CEmployee2** exist, **Shared** member **mCount** can be used in any method of a **CEmployee2** object—in this example, the constructor (lines 14–24) increments **mCount** (line 20) and method **Finalize** (lines 27–32) decrements **mCount** (line 28). (Note that method **Finalize** is declared using keywords **Protected** and **Overrides**—method **Finalize**'s header must contain these keywords, and we will explain them in detail in Chapter 9.) If no objects of class **CEmployee2** exist, member **mCount** can be referenced through a call to **Property Count** (lines 53–59). Because this **Property** is **Shared**, we do not have to instantiate a **CEmployee2** object to call the **Get** method inside the **Property**. Also, by declaring property **Count** as **ReadOnly**, we prevent clients from changing **mCount**'s value directly, thus ensuring that clients can change **mCount**'s value only via the class **CEmployee2** constructors and finalizer.

Module **modSharedTest** (Fig. 8.14) runs the application that demonstrates the use of **Shared** members (Fig. 8.13). Lines 11–12 use the **ReadOnly Shared Property Count** of class **CEmployee2** to obtain the current **mCount** value. Lines 14–18 then instantiate two **CEmployee2** objects, which increment the **mCount** value by two. Lines 26–29 display the names of the employees. Lines 32–33 set these objects' references to **Nothing**, so that references **employee1** and **employee2** no longer refer to the **CEmployee2** objects. This "marks" the objects for garbage collection, because there are no more references to these objects in the program.

```
1   ' Fig. 8.13: CEmployee2.vb
2   ' Class CEmployee2 uses Shared variable.
3
4   Class CEmployee2
5      Inherits Object
6
7      Private mFirstName As String
8      Private mLastName As String
9
```

Fig. 8.13 **CEmployee2** class objects share **Shared** variable (part 1 of 2).

```vbnet
10       ' number of objects in memory
11       Private Shared mCount As Integer
12
13       ' CEmployee2 constructor
14       Public Sub New(ByVal firstNameValue As String, _
15          ByVal lastNameValue As String)
16
17          mFirstName = firstNameValue
18          mLastName = lastNameValue
19
20          mCount += 1 ' increment shared count of employees
21          Console.WriteLine _
22             ("Employee object constructor: " & mFirstName & _
23             " " & mLastName)
24       End Sub ' New
25
26       ' finalizer method decrements Shared count of employees
27       Protected Overrides Sub Finalize()
28          mCount -= 1 ' decrement mCount, resulting in one fewer object
29          Console.WriteLine _
30             ("Employee object finalizer: " & mFirstName & _
31             " " & mLastName & "; count = " & mCount)
32       End Sub ' Finalize
33
34       ' return first name
35       Public ReadOnly Property FirstName() As String
36
37          Get
38             Return mFirstName
39          End Get
40
41       End Property ' FirstName
42
43       ' return last name
44       Public ReadOnly Property LastName() As String
45
46          Get
47             Return mLastName
48          End Get
49
50       End Property ' LastName
51
52       ' property Count
53       Public ReadOnly Shared Property Count() As Integer
54
55          Get
56             Return mCount
57          End Get
58
59       End Property ' Count
60
61    End Class ' CEmployee2
```

Fig. 8.13 `CEmployee2` class objects share **Shared** variable (part 2 of 2).

Performance Tip 8.3

Invocation of the garbage collector incurs a performance penalty because of such factors as the complex algorithm that determines which objects should be collected.

Common Programming Error 8.8

*A call to an instance method or an attempt to access an instance variable from a **Shared** method is a syntax error.*

Normally, the garbage collector is not invoked directly by the user. Either the garbage collector reclaims the memory for objects when it deems garbage collection is appropriate, or the operating system recovers the unneeded memory when the program terminates. Line 35 uses **Public Shared** method *Collect* from class *GC* of namespace **System** to request that the garbage collector execute. Before the garbage collector releases the memory occupied by the two **CEmployee2** objects, it invokes method **Finalize** for each **CEmployee2** object, which decrements the **mCount** value by two.

The last two lines of the console output (green window) show that the **CEmployee2** object for **Bob Jones** was finalized before the **CEmployee2** object for **Susan Baker**. However, the output of this program on your system could differ. The garbage collector is not guaranteed to collect objects in a specific order.

```vb
1    ' Fig. 8.14: SharedTest.vb
2    ' Demonstrates Shared members.
3
4    Imports System.Windows.Forms
5
6    Module modSharedTest
7
8       Sub Main()
9          Dim output As String
10
11         Console.WriteLine("Employees before instantiation: " & _
12            CEmployee2.Count)
13
14         Dim employee1 As CEmployee2 = _
15            New CEmployee2("Susan", "Baker")
16
17         Dim employee2 As CEmployee2 = _
18            New CEmployee2("Bob", "Jones")
19
20         ' output of employee2 after instantiation
21         Console.WriteLine(vbCrLf & _
22            "Employees after instantiation: " & vbCrLf & _
23            "via Employee.Count: " & CEmployee2.Count)
24
25         ' display name of first and second employee
26         Console.WriteLine(vbCrLf & "Employees 1: " & _
27            employee1.FirstName & " " & employee1.LastName & _
28            vbCrLf & "Employee 2: " & employee2.FirstName & " " & _
29            employee2.LastName)
30
```

Fig. 8.14 *Shared* class member demonstration (part 1 of 2).

```
31              ' mark employee1 and employee2 for garbage collection
32              employee1 = Nothing
33              employee2 = Nothing
34
35              System.GC.Collect()  ' request garbage collection
36          End Sub ' Main
37
38      End Module ' modShared
```

```
Employees before instantiation: 0
Employee object constructor: Susan Baker
Employee object constructor: Bob Jones

Employees after instantiation:
via Employee.Count: 2

Employees 1: Susan Baker
Employee 2: Bob Jones
Employee object finalizer: Bob Jones; count = 1
Employee object finalizer: Susan Baker; count = 0
```

Fig. 8.14 **Shared** class member demonstration (part 2 of 2).

Good Programming Practice 8.8

Although **.vb** *files import namespace* **System***, we prefer to invoke method* **GC.Collect** *by preceding* **GC** *with namespace* **System** *and a dot (* **.** *) operator to indicate explicitly that class* **GC** *belongs to namespace* **System***. This helps make programs more readable.*

8.12 Const and ReadOnly Members

Visual Basic allows programmers to create *constants*, or members whose values cannot change during program execution. To create a constant data member of a class, declare that member using either the **Const** or **ReadOnly** keyword. A data member declared as **Const** must be initialized in its declaration; a data member declared as **ReadOnly** can be initialized either in its declaration or in the class constructor. Neither a **Const** nor a **ReadOnly** value can be modified once initialized.

Testing and Debugging Tip 8.4

If a variable's value should never change, making it a constant prevents it from changing. This helps eliminate errors that might occur if the value of the variable were to change.

Common Programming Error 8.9

Declaring a class data member as **Const** *but failing to initialize it in that declaration is a syntax error.*

Common Programming Error 8.10

Assigning a value to a **Const** *data member during runtime is a syntax error.*

Members that are declared as **Const** must be assigned values at compile time. Therefore, **Const** members can be initialized only to other constant values, such as integers, string literals, characters and other **Const** members. Constant members with values that cannot be determined at compile time must be declared with the keyword **ReadOnly**. We mentioned previously that a **ReadOnly** member can be assigned a value only once, either when it is declared or within that class's constructor. When we choose to define such a member within a constructor, a **Shared** constructor must be used to initialize **Shared ReadOnly** members, and a separate non-**Shared** (instance) constructor is used to initialize non-**Shared ReadOnly** members.

Common Programming Error 8.11
*Declaring a class data member as **ReadOnly** and attempting to use it before it is initialized is a logic error.*

Common Programming Error 8.12
*A **Shared ReadOnly** data member cannot be defined in a constructor for that class, and an instance **ReadOnly** data member cannot be defined in a **Shared** constructor for that class. Attempting to define a **ReadOnly** data member in an inappropriate constructor is a syntax error.*

Common Programming Error 8.13
*The declaration of a **Const** member as **Shared** is a syntax error, because a **Const** member is **Shared** implicitly.*

Class **CCircleConstants** (Fig. 8.15) demonstrates the use of constants. Line 7 creates constant **PI** using keyword **Const** and assigns the **Double** value **3.14159**, an approximation of π. We could have used pre-defined **Const PI** of class **Math** (**Math.PI**) as the value, but we wanted to demonstrate how to create a **Const** data member explicitly. The compiler must be able to determine a **Const**'s value for that value to be assigned to the **Const** data member. The value **3.14159** is acceptable (line 7), but the expression:

```
Convert.ToDouble( "3.14159" )
```

would generate a syntax error if used in place of that value. Although this expression uses a constant value (**String** literal **"3.14159"**) as an argument, a syntax error occurs, because the compiler cannot evaluate the executable statement **Convert.ToDouble**. This restriction is lifted with **ReadOnly** members, which are assigned values at runtime. Note that line 14 (at runtime) assigns the value of constructor parameter **radiusValue** to **ReadOnly** member **mRadius**. Also, we could have used an executable statement, such as **Convert.ToDouble**, to assign a value to this **ReadOnly** member.

```
1   ' Fig. 8.15: CCircleConstants.vb
2   ' Encapsulate constants PI and radius.
3
4   Class CCircleConstants
5
6      ' PI is constant data member
7      Public Const PI As Double = 3.14159
8
9      ' radius is uninitialized constant
10     Public ReadOnly RADIUS As Integer
```

Fig. 8.15 Constants used in class **CCircleConstants** (part 1 of 2).

```
11
12         ' constructor of class CCircleConstants
13         Public Sub New(ByVal radiusValue As Integer)
14            RADIUS = radiusValue
15         End Sub ' New
16
17     End Class ' CCircleConstants
```

Fig. 8.15 Constants used in class `CCircleConstants` (part 2 of 2).

Module **modConstAndReadOnly** (Fig. 8.16) illustrates the use of **Const** and **ReadOnly** values. Lines 9–11 use class **Random** to generate a random **Integer** between **1–20** that corresponds to a circle's radius. Line 11 passes this value to the **CCircleConstant** constructor to instantiate a **CCircleConstant** object. Line 13 then accesses the **ReadOnly** variable **mRadius** through a reference to its class instance. Lines 15–17 compute the circle's circumference and assign the value to **String output**. This calculation employs the **Const** member **PI**, which we access in line 17 through its **Shared** class reference. Lines 19–20 output the radius and circumference values to a **MessageBox**.

```
1    ' Fig. 8.16: ConstAndReadOnly.vb
2    ' Demonstrates Const and ReadOnly members.
3
4    Imports System.Windows.Forms
5
6    Module modConstAndReadOnly
7
8       Sub Main()
9          Dim random As Random = New Random()
10         Dim circle As CCircleConstants = _
11            New CCircleConstants(random.Next(1, 20))
12
13         Dim radius As String = Convert.ToString(circle.RADIUS)
14
15         Dim output As String = "Radius = " & radius & vbCrLf _
16            & "Circumference = " + String.Format("{0:N3}", _
17            circle.RADIUS * 2 * CCircleConstants.PI)
18
19         MessageBox.Show(output, "Circumference", _
20            MessageBoxButtons.OK, MessageBoxIcon.Information)
21      End Sub ' Main
22
23   End Module ' modConstAndReadOnly
```

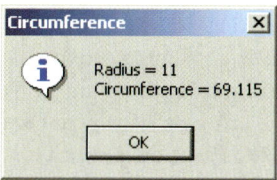

Fig. 8.16 `Const` and `ReadOnly` class member demonstration.

8.13 Data Abstraction and Information Hiding

As we pointed out at the beginning of this chapter, classes normally hide the details of their implementation from their clients. This is called *information hiding*. As an example of information hiding, let us consider a data structure called a *stack*.

Students can think of a stack as analogous to a pile of dishes. When a dish is placed on the pile, it is always placed at the top (referred to as *pushing* the dish onto the stack). Similarly, when a dish is removed from the pile, it is always removed from the top (referred to as *popping* the dish off the stack). Stacks are known as *last-in, first-out (LIFO) data structures*—the last item pushed (inserted) on the stack is the first item popped (removed) from the stack.

Stacks can be implemented with arrays and with other methods, such as linked lists (we discuss linked lists in Chapter 23, Data Structures). A client of a stack class need not be concerned with the stack's implementation. The client knows only that when data items are placed in the stack, these items will be retrieved in last-in, first-out order. The client cares about *what* functionality a stack offers, but not about *how* that functionality is implemented. This concept is referred to as *data abstraction*. Although programmers might know the details of a class's implementation, they should not write code that depends on these details. This enables a particular class (such as one that implements a stack and its operations, *push* and *pop*) to be replaced with another version without affecting the rest of the system. As long as the **Public** services of the class do not change (i.e., every method or property still has the same name, return type and parameter list in the new class definition), the rest of the system is not affected.

Most programming languages emphasize actions. In these languages, data exists to support the actions that programs must take. Data is "less interesting" than actions. Data is "crude." Only a few built-in data types exist, and it is difficult for programmers to create their own data types. Visual Basic and the object-oriented style of programming elevates the importance of data. The primary activities of object-oriented programming in Visual Basic is the creation of data types (i.e., classes) and the expression of the interactions among objects of those data types. To create languages that emphasize data, the programming-languages community needed to formalize some notions about data. The formalization we consider here is the notion of *abstract data types (ADTs)*. ADTs receive as much attention today as structured programming did decades earlier. ADTs, however, do not replace structured programming. Rather, they provide an additional formalization to improve the program-development process.

Consider built-in type **Integer**, which people would associate an **Integer** with an integer in mathematics. Unlike mathematical integers, computer **Integer**s are fixed in size. For example, **Integer** on a 32-bit machine is limited approximately to the range ±2 billion. If the result of a calculation falls outside this range, an error occurs, and the computer responds in some machine-dependent manner. It might for example, "quietly" produce an incorrect result. Mathematical integers do not have this problem. Therefore, the notion of a computer **Integer** is only an approximation of the notion of a real-world integer. The same is true of **Double** and other built-in types.

We have taken the notion of **Integer** for granted until this point, but we now consider a new perspective. Types like **Integer**, **Double**, **Char** and others are all examples of abstract data types. Representations of real-world notions to some satisfactory level of precision within a computer system.

An ADT actually captures two notions: A *data representation* and the *operations* that can be performed on that data. For example, in Visual Basic, an `Integer` contains an integer value (data) and provides addition, subtraction, multiplication, division and modulus operations; however, division by zero is undefined. In Visual Basic, programmers use classes to implement abstract data types.

Software Engineering Observation 8.14

Programmers can create types through the use of the class mechanism. These new types can be designed so that they are as convenient to use as the built-in types. This marks Visual Basic as an extensible language. Although the language is easy to extend via new types, the programmer cannot alter the base language itself.

Another abstract data type we discuss is a *queue*, which is similar to a "waiting line." Computer systems use many queues internally. We write programs that simulate queues and their behavior. A queue offers well-understood behavior to its clients: Clients place items in a queue one at a time via an *enqueue* operation, then get those items back one at a time via a *dequeue* operation. A queue returns items in *first-in, first-out (FIFO)* order, which means that the first item inserted in a queue is the first item removed. Conceptually, a queue can become infinitely long, whereas real queues are finite.

The queue hides an internal data representation that keeps track of the items currently waiting in line, and it offers a set of operations to its clients (*enqueue* and *dequeue*). The clients are not concerned about the implementation of the queue—clients depend on the queue to operate "as advertised." When a client enqueues an item, the queue should accept that item and place it in some kind of internal FIFO data structure. Similarly, when the client wants the next item from the front of the queue, the queue should remove the item from its internal representation and deliver the item in FIFO order (i.e., the item that has been in the queue the longest should be the next one returned by the next dequeue operation).

The queue ADT guarantees the integrity of its internal data structure. Clients cannot manipulate this data structure directly—only the queue ADT has access to its internal data. Clients are able to perform only allowable operations on the data representation; the ADT rejects operations that its public service does not provide.

8.14 Software Reusability

Visual Basic programmers concentrate on both crafting new classes and reusing existing classes. Many *class libraries* exist, and developers worldwide are creating others. Software is constructed from existing, well-defined, carefully tested, well-documented, portable, widely available components. Software reusability speeds the development of powerful, high-quality software. *Rapid application development (RAD)* is of great interest today in the software industry.

To realize the full potential of software reusability, we need to improve cataloging and licensing schemes, protection mechanisms that ensure master copies of classes are not corrupted, description schemes that system designers use to determine whether existing classes meet their needs and browsing mechanisms that determine whether classes are available and how closely these classes meet software developer requirements. These efforts will be worthwhile, because the value of convenient and effective software reuse is enormous.

Consider the earlier application examples of this chapter. Many of them contained a definition for some variation of a **CTime** class and a **modTimeTest** module. These definitions often contained repeated code. Programmers should not have to rewrite code. With the **CTime/modTimeTest** case, each application could have been engineered to import the functionality, thus decreasing programming overhead. We show in Section 8.15 how to import functionality.

8.15 Namespaces and Assemblies

As we have seen in almost every example in the text, classes from preexisting libraries, such as the .NET Framework, must be imported into a Visual Basic program by including a reference to those libraries (a process we demonstrated in Chapter 3). Remember that each class in the Framework Class Library belongs to a specific namespace. This preexisting code provides a mechanism that facilitates software reuse.

As we discussed in Section 8.14, when appropriate, programmers should concentrate on making the software components they create reusable. However, doing so often results in *naming collisions*, which occur when the same name is used for two classes in the same namespace, for two methods in the same class, etc.

Common Programming Error 8.14

Attempting to compile code that contains naming collisions generates a syntax error.

Namespaces help minimize this problem by providing a convention for *unique class names*. No two classes in a given namespace can have the same name, but different namespaces can contain classes with the same name. With millions of people writing Visual Basic programs, the names that one programmer chooses for classes will likely conflict with the names that other programmers choose for their classes.

Figure 8.17, which provides the code for class **CEmployee3**, demonstrates the creation of a reusable class library. Notice that this class is identical to class **CEmployee2** (Fig. 8.13), except we have declared class **CEmployee3** as a **Public** class. When other projects make use of a class library, only **Public** classes are accessible—thus, if we did not declare **CEmployee3** as **Public**, other projects could not use it. We demonstrate momentarily how to package class **CEmployee3** into **EmployeeLibrary.dll**—the *dynamic link library* that we create for reuse with other systems. As we mentioned in Chapter 3, a dynamic link library contains related classes that projects can use.

```
1    ' Fig. 8.17: CEmployee3.vb
2    ' Class CEmployee3 uses Shared variable.
3
4    Public Class CEmployee3
5       Inherits Object
6
7       Private mFirstName As String
8       Private mLastName As String
9
10      ' number of objects in memory
11      Private Shared mCount As Integer
```

Fig. 8.17 CEmployee3 class to store in class library (part 1 of 2).

```vbnet
12
13      ' CEmployee3 constructor
14      Public Sub New(ByVal firstNameValue As String, _
15         ByVal lastNameValue As String)
16
17         mFirstName = firstNameValue
18         mLastName = lastNameValue
19
20         mCount += 1 ' increment shared count of employees
21         Console.WriteLine _
22            ("Employee object constructor: " & mFirstName & _
23            " " & mLastName)
24      End Sub ' New
25
26      ' finalizer method decrements Shared count of employees
27      Protected Overrides Sub Finalize()
28         mCount -= 1 ' decrement mCount, resulting in one fewer object
29         Console.WriteLine _
30            ("Employee object finalizer: " & mFirstName & _
31            " " & mLastName & "; count = " & mCount)
32      End Sub ' Finalize
33
34      ' return first name
35      Public ReadOnly Property FirstName() As String
36
37         Get
38            Return mFirstName
39         End Get
40
41      End Property ' FirstName
42
43      ' return last name
44      Public ReadOnly Property LastName() As String
45
46         Get
47            Return mLastName
48         End Get
49
50      End Property ' LastName
51
52      ' property Count
53      Public ReadOnly Shared Property Count() As Integer
54
55         Get
56            Return mCount
57         End Get
58
59      End Property ' Count
60
61   End Class ' CEmployee3
```

Fig. 8.17 `CEmployee3` class to store in class library (part 2 of 2).

We now describe how to create a class library that includes class **CEmployee3**:

1. *Create a class library project.* Select **File > New > Project...** to display the **New Project** dialog. Select **Visual Basic Projects** from the **Project Types:** pane, then select **Class Library** from the **Templates:** pane. Name the project **EmployeeLibrary**, and choose a directory in which you would like the project to be located (you many choose any directory you wish). A class library is created, as shown in Fig. 8.18. There are two important points to note about the class library's code. The first is that there is no **Main** method. This indicates that a class library is not an executable program. Class libraries are software components that are loaded and used (and reused) by executable programs. It is not designed as a stand-alone application—rather, it is designed to be used by running programs. The second key point is that **Class1** is a **Public** class, so that it is accessible to other projects (Fig. 8.18).

2. In the **Solution Explorer**, rename **Class1.vb** to **CEmployee3.vb** (right-click **Class1.vb** and select **Rename**). Replace the following code generated by the development environment:

   ```
   Public Class Class1

   End Class
   ```

   with the entire code listing from class **CEmployee3** (Fig. 8.17).

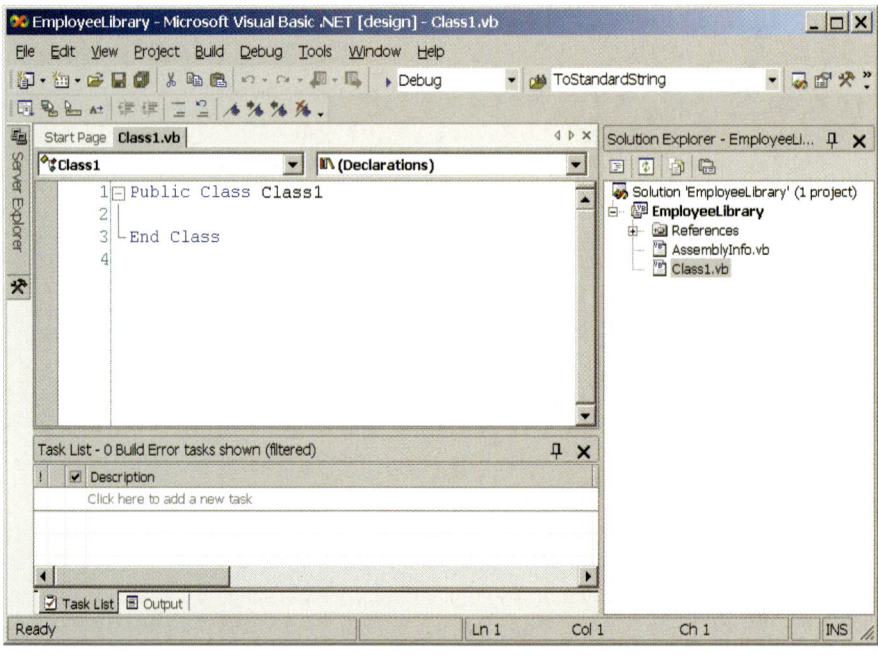

Fig. 8.18 Simple class library project.

3. Select **Build > Build Solution** to compile the code. Remember that this code is not executable. If the programmer attempts to execute the class library by selecting **Debug > Start Without Debugging**, Visual Studio displays an error message.

When the class library is compiled successfully, an assembly is created. This assembly is located in the project's `bin` directory, and by default is named `EmployeeLibrary.dll`. The assembly file contains class `CEmployee3`, which other modules, classes and systems can use. Assembly files, which have file extensions `.dll` and `.exe`, are at the core of Visual Basic application development. The Windows operating system uses executable files (`.exe`) to run applications and library files (`.dll`, or *dynamic link library*) to create code libraries.

Portability Tip 8.1

Focus on creating unique namespace names to avoid naming collisions. This is especially helpful when using someone else's code (or when someone else uses your code).

Module `modAssemblyTest` (Fig. 8.19) demonstrates the use of the assembly file in a running application. The module employs class `CEmployee3` in `EmployeeLibrary.dll` to create and mark two `CEmployee3` for garbage collection. A reference to the assembly is created by selecting **Project > Add Reference**. Using the **Browse** button, select `EmployeeLibrary.dll` (located in the `bin` directory of our `EmployeeLibrary` project), then click **OK** to add the resource to the project. Once the reference has been added, we use keyword `Imports` followed by the namespace's name (`EmployeeLibrary`) to inform the compiler that we are using classes from this namespace (line 4).

```vb
1   ' Fig. 8.19: AssemblyTest.vb
2   ' Demonstrates assembly files and namespaces.
3
4   Imports EmployeeLibrary ' contains class CEmployee3
5
6   Module modAssemblyTest
7
8      Public Sub Main()
9         Dim output As String
10
11        Console.WriteLine("Employees before instantiation: " & _
12           CEmployee3.Count)
13
14        Dim employee1 As CEmployee3 = _
15           New CEmployee3("Susan", "Baker")
16
17        Dim employee2 As CEmployee3 = _
18           New CEmployee3("Bob", "Jones")
19
20        ' output of employee after instantiation
21        Console.WriteLine(vbCrLf & "Employees after instantiation:" _
22           & vbCrLf & "via Employee.Count: " & CEmployee3.Count)
23
```

Fig. 8.19 Module `modAssemblyTest` references `EmployeeLibrary.dll` (part 1 of 2).

```
24          ' display name of first and second employee
25          Console.WriteLine(vbCrLf & "Employees 1: " & _
26             employee1.FirstName & " " & employee1.LastName & _
27             vbCrLf & "Employee 2: " & employee2.FirstName & " " & _
28             employee2.LastName)
29
30          ' mark employee1 and employee2 for garbage collection
31          employee1 = Nothing
32          employee2 = Nothing
33
34          System.GC.Collect()  ' request garbage collection
35       End Sub ' Main
36
37    End Module ' modAssemblyTest
```

```
Employees before instantiation: 0
Employee object constructor: Susan Baker
Employee object constructor: Bob Jones

Employees after instantiation:
via Employee.Count: 2

Employees 1: Susan Baker
Employee 2: Bob Jones
Employee object finalizer: Bob Jones; count = 1
Employee object finalizer: Susan Baker; count = 0
```

Fig. 8.19 Module **modAssemblyTest** references **EmployeeLibrary.dll** (part 2 of 2).

8.16 Class View and Object Browser

Now that we have introduced key concepts of object-based programming, we present two features that Visual Studio provides to facilitate the design of object-oriented applications—**Class View** and **Object Browser**.

The **Class View** displays a project's class members. To access this feature, select **View > Class View**. Figure 8.20 depicts the **Class View** for the **TimeTest** project of Fig. 8.1 and Fig. 8.2 (class **CTime** and module **modTimeTest**). **Class View** follows a hierarchical structure, with the project name (**TimeTest**) as the root. Beneath the root is a series of nodes (e.g., classes, variables, methods, etc.). If a node contains a plus box (**+**) next to it, that node is collapsed. By contrast, if a node contains a minus box (**-**) next to it, that node has been expanded (and can be collapsed). In Fig. 8.20, project **TimeTest** contains class **CTime** and module **modTimeTest** as *children*. Class **CTime** contains a constructor, methods **SetTime**, **ToStandardString** and **ToUniversalString** (indicated by purple boxes) and variables **mHour**, **mMinute** and **mSecond** (indicated by blue boxes). The lock icons, placed to the left of the blue-box icons, indicate that the variables are **Private**. Module **modTimeTest** contains method **Main**. Note that class **CTime** contains the **Bases and Interfaces** node, which contains class **Object**. This is because class **CTime** inherits from class **System.Object** (which we discuss in Chapter 9).

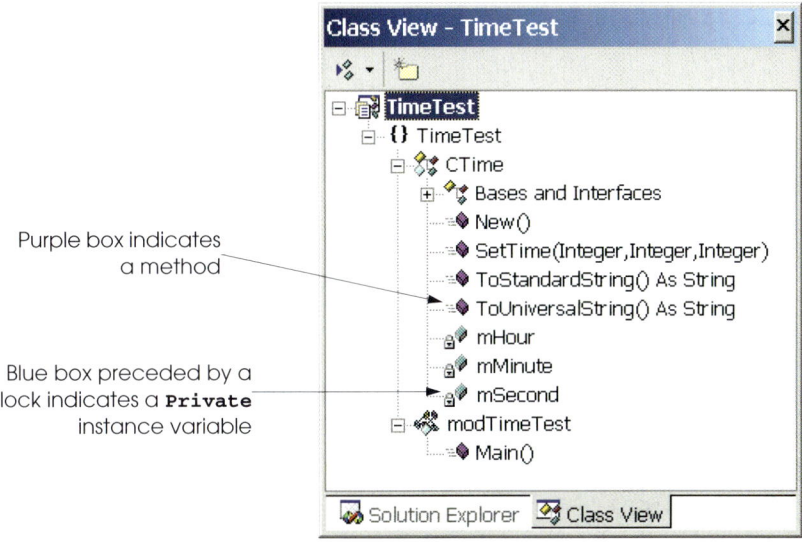

Fig. 8.20 **Class View** of Fig. 8.1 and Fig. 8.2.

The second feature that Visual Studio provides is the **Object Browser**, which lists the Framework Class Library (FCL) classes available in Visual Basic. Developers use the **Object Browser** to learn about the functionality provided by a specific object. To open the **Object Browser**, right click any Visual Basic class or method in the code editor and select **Go To Definition** (Fig. 8.21). Figure 8.22 shows the **Object Browser** when the user selects keyword **Object** in the code editor. Note that the **Object Browser** lists all non-**Private** members provided by class **Object** in the **Members of Object** window—this window offers developers "instant access" to information regarding the services of various objects. Note also that the **Object Browser** lists in the **Objects** window all objects that Visual Basic provides.

SUMMARY
- Every class in Visual Basic is a derived class of **Object**.
- Keywords **Public** and **Private** are member access modifiers.
- Instance variables, properties and methods that are declared with member access modifier **Public** are accessible wherever the program has a reference to an object of that class.
- Instance variables, properties and methods that are declared with member access modifier **Private** are accessible only to members of the class, such as other variables and methods.
- Every instance variable, property or method definition should be preceded by a member access modifier.
- **Private** methods often are called utility methods, or helper methods, because they can be called only by other methods of that class and are used to support the operation of those methods.
- The creation of **Public** data in a class is an uncommon and dangerous programming practice.

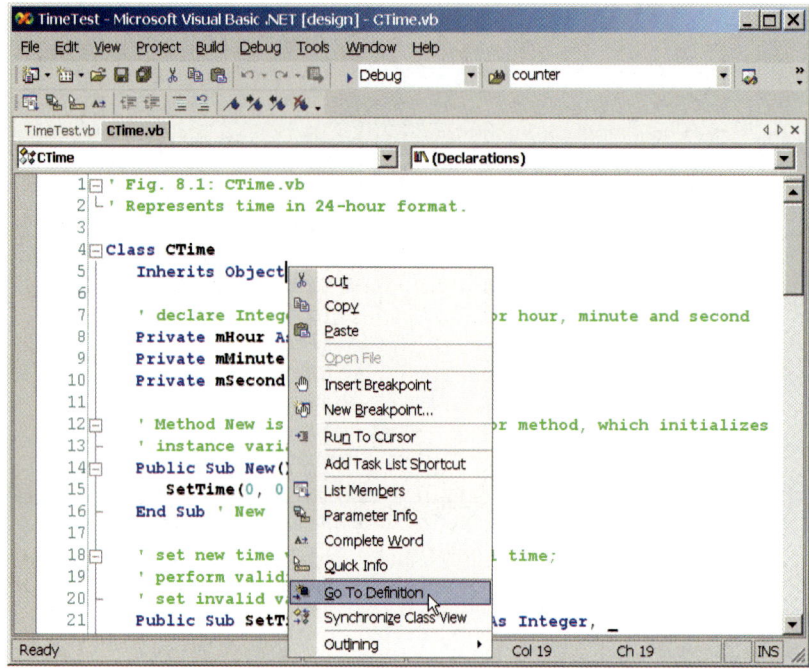

Fig. 8.21 Invoking the **Object Browser** from the development environment.

- Access methods can read or display data. Another common use for access methods is to test the truth of conditions—such methods often are called predicate methods.
- A constructor is a special method that initializes the instance variables of a class object. A class's constructor method is called when an object of that class is instantiated.
- It is common to have several constructors for a class; this is accomplished through method overloading. Normally, constructors are **Public** methods of a class.
- Every class in Visual Basic, including the classes from the .NET Framework, is part of a namespace.
- If the programmer does not specify the namespace for a class, the class is placed in the default namespace, which includes the compiled classes in the current directory.
- Instance variables can be initialized by the class's constructor, or they can be assigned values by the **Set** accessor of a property.
- Instance variables that are not explicitly initialized by the programmer are initialized by the compiler (primitive numeric variables are set to **0**, **Boolean**s are set to **False** and references are set to **Nothing**).
- Classes simplify programming, because the client (or user of the class object) need only be concerned with the **Public** operations encapsulated in the object.
- A class's instance variables, properties and methods belong to that class's scope. Within a class's scope, class members are accessible to all of that class's methods and can be referenced simply by name. Outside a class's scope, class members cannot be referenced directly by name.

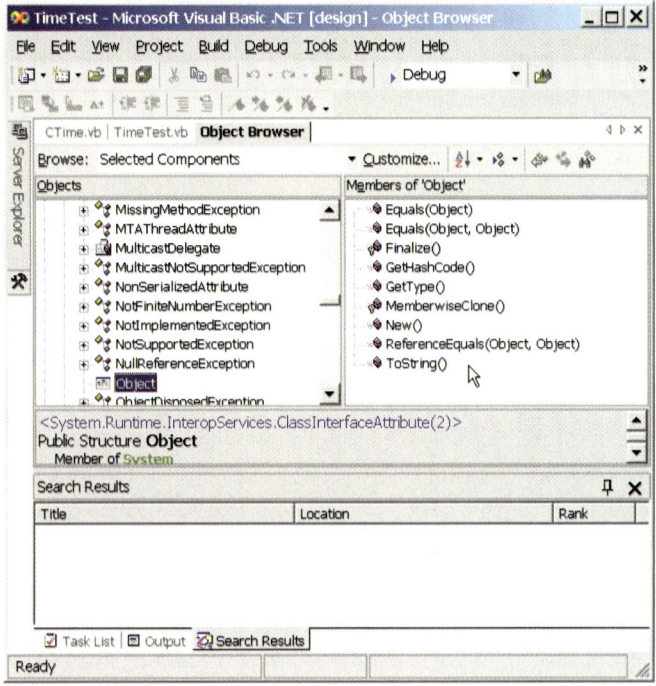

Fig. 8.22 Object Browser when user selects **Object** from development environment.

- If a method defines a variable that has the same name as a variable with class scope (i.e., an instance variable), the class-scope variable is hidden by the method-scope variable in that method scope.
- To allow clients to read the value of **Private** data, the class can provide a property definition, which enables the user to access this **Private** data in a safe way.
- A property definition contains accessors, or sections of code that handle the details of modifying and returning data.
- A property definition can contain a **Set** accessor, **Get** accessor or both. A **Get** accessor enables the client to read the field's value, and the **Set** accessor enables the client to modify the value.
- When an object is created, its members can be initialized by a constructor of that object's class.
- If no constructors are defined for a class, a default constructor is provided. This constructor contains no code (i.e., the constructor is empty) and takes no parameters.
- Methods, properties and constructors of a class can be overloaded. To overload a method of a class, simply provide a separate method definition with the same name for each version of the method. Remember that overloaded methods/properties/constructors must have different parameter lists.
- **Set** and **Get** accessors can provide access to **Private** data while ensuring that the data does not store invalid values.
- One form of software reuse is composition, in which a class contains member references to objects of other classes.

- The **Me** reference is implicitly used to refer to both the instance variables, properties and methods of an object.
- The .NET Framework performs "garbage collection," which returns memory to the system.
- When an object is no longer used in the program (i.e., there are no references to the object), the object is marked for garbage collection. The memory for such an object then is reclaimed when the garbage collector executes.
- Every class contains a finalizer that typically returns resources to the system. The finalizer for an object is guaranteed to be called to perform termination housekeeping on the object just before the garbage collector reclaims the memory for the object (called finalization).
- In certain cases, all objects of a class should share only one copy of a particular variable. Programmers use **Shared** class variables for this and other reasons.
- A **Shared** class variable represents class-wide information—all objects of the class share the same piece of data.
- The declaration of a **Shared** member begins with the keyword **Shared**.
- Although **Shared** class variables might seem like global variables, **Shared** class variables have class scope.
- **Public Shared** class members can be accessed through the class name and the dot operator (e.g., *className*.*sharedMemberName*).
- **Private Shared** class members can be accessed only through methods of the class.
- A **Shared** method cannot access non-**Shared** class members.
- Visual Basic allows programmers to create members whose values cannot change during program execution. These members are called constants.
- To create a constant member of a class, the programmer must declare that member using either the **Const** or **ReadOnly** keyword.
- Members declared **Const** must be initialized in the declaration; those declared with **ReadOnly** can be initialized in the constructor, but must be initialized before they are used.
- Neither **Const** nor **ReadOnly** values can be modified once they are initialized.
- Classes normally hide their implementation details from their clients. This is called information hiding.
- Visual Basic and the object-oriented style of programming elevate the importance of data. The primary activities of object-oriented programming in Visual Basic are the creation of data types (i.e., classes) and the expression of the interactions among objects of those data types.
- Visual Basic programmers concentrate on crafting new classes and reusing existing classes.
- Software reusability speeds the development of powerful, high-quality software. Rapid application development (RAD) is of great interest today.
- Each class in the .NET Framework belongs to a specific namespace (or library) that contains a group of related classes. Namespaces provide a mechanism for software reuse.
- It is likely that the names programmers create for classes will conflict with names that other programmers create. Namespaces help resolve this issue.
- Assembly files are either **.dll** (library code) or **.exe** (executables) files.
- The **Imports** statement informs the compiler what assembly files a **.vb** file references.
- Classes, by default, are placed in the **.exe** assembly file of an application unless they are compiled as **.dll** assembly files and imported into a program.

- If two code files are in the same assembly file, they are compiled together and can be optimized by the compiler. Assemblies, having already been compiled separately, are only linked together and are not optimized as such.
- **Class View** displays the variables, properties and methods for all classes in a project
- The **Object Browser** lists all classes in the Visual Basic library. Developers use the **Object Browser** to learn about the functionality provided by a specific object.

TERMINOLOGY

abstract data type (ADT)
access method
action
action-oriented
aggregation
assembly
assigning class objects
base class
behavior (method)
block scope
body of a class definition
built-in data type
case sensitivity
class
class definition
class library
class scope
classes to implement abstract data types
class-scope variable hidden by method-scope variable
Class View
"class-wide" information
client
client of a class
`Collect` method of `System.GC`
compile a class
composition
conditional expression
consistent state
constructor
create a code library
create classes from existing class definitions
create a namespace
create a reusable class
create a data type
data abstraction
data integrity
data member
data representation of an abstract data type
data structure
dequeue operation

derived class
`.dll` extension
dot (`.`) operator
dynamic link library
encapsulate
enqueue operation
`.exe` extension
explicit use of `Me` reference
extensible language
finalizer
first-in, first-out data structure
first-in, first-out (FIFO) order
format control string
garbage collection
garbage collector
`GC` namespace of `System`
`Get` accessor of `Property`
GUI event handling
handle
helper method
hide an instance variable
hide an internal data representation
hide implementation detail
hiding implementation
implementation
implementation detail
implementation of a class hidden from its clients
implementation-dependent code
information hiding
inheritance
initial set of classes
initialize implicitly to default values
initialize instance variables
initialized by the compiler
initializer
initializing class objects
insert an item into a container object
instance of a built-in type
instance of a user-defined type
instance variable
instance variables of a class

instantiate (or create) objects
interactions among objects
interface
internal data representation
last-in-first-out (LIFO) data structure
library
LIFO
linked list
local variable of a method
mark an object for garbage collection
member access modifier
memory leak
`Me` reference
method overloading
namespace
`New` (constructor)
`New` keyword
new type
non-`Public` method
object (or instance)
object-based programming (OBP)
Object Browser
`Object` class
object orientation
object-oriented
object-oriented programming (OOP)
object passed by reference
"object speak"
"object think"
operations of an abstract data type
overloaded constructor
overloaded method
overloading
parameterized constructor
polymorphism
popping off a stack
predicate method
`Private` keyword

`Private Shared` member
procedural programming language
process
program development process
programmer-defined type
`Public` keyword
`Public` method
`Public` operations encapsulated in an object
`Public` service
`Public Shared` member
pushing into a stack
queue
rapid application development (RAD)
reclaim memory
reference to a new object
resource leak
reusable software component
service of a class
`Set` accessor of a property
signature
software reuse
stack
standard time format
`Shared` class variable
`Shared` class variables have class scope
`Shared` class variables save storage
`Shared` keyword
`Shared` method cannot access non-`Shared` class member
structured programming
termination housekeeping
universal-time format
user-defined type
utility method
validity checking
variable
waiting line

SELF-REVIEW EXERCISES

8.1 Fill in the blanks in each of the following:
  a) Class members are accessed via the _____ operator in conjunction with a reference to an object of the class.
  b) Members of a class specified as _____ are accessible only to methods and properties of the class.
  c) A _____ is a method for initializing the instance variables of a class when the object of that class is created.
  d) A _____ accessor assigns values to instance variables of a class.
  e) Methods of a class normally are made _____ and instance variables of a class normally are made _____.

f) A _____ accessor retrieves instance-variable values.
g) Keyword _____ introduces a class definition.
h) Members and properties of a class specified as _____ are accessible anywhere that an object of the class is in scope.
i) The _____ keyword allocates memory dynamically for an object of a specified type and returns a _____ to that type.
j) A _____ variable represents class-wide information.
k) The keyword _____ specifies that an object or variable is not modifiable after it is initialized at runtime.
l) A method declared **Shared** cannot access _____ class members.

8.2 State whether each of the following is *true* or *false*. If *false* explain why.
a) All objects are passed by reference.
b) Constructors can have return values.
c) Properties must define **Get** and **Set** accessors.
d) The **Me** reference of an object is a reference to itself.
e) Calling finalizers on objects in a specific order guarantees that those objects are finalized in that order.
f) A **Shared** member can be referenced when no object of that type exists.
g) A **Shared** member can be referenced through an instance of the class.
h) **ReadOnly** variables must be initialized either in a declaration or in the class constructor.
i) Identifier names for classes, methods and properties used in one namespace cannot be repeated in another namespace.
j) **DLL** assembly files do not contain method **Main**.

ANSWERS TO SELF-REVIEW EXERCISES

8.1 a) dot (**.**). b) **Private**. c) constructor. d) **Set**. e) **Public**, **Private**. f) **Get**. g) **Class**. h) **Public**. i) **New**, reference. j) **Shared**. k) **ReadOnly**. l) non-**Shared**.

8.2 a) True. b) False. Constructors are not permitted to return values. c) False. Programmers can opt not to define either one of these accessors to restrict a property's access. d) True. e) False. The garbage collector does not guarantee that resources are reclaimed in a specific order. f) True. g) True. h) True. i) False. Different namespaces can have classes, methods and properties with the same names. j) True.

EXERCISES

8.3 Create a class named **CComplex** for performing arithmetic with complex numbers. Write a program to test your class.

Complex numbers have the form

    realPart + imaginaryPart * i

where *i* is

$$\sqrt{-1}$$

Use floating-point variables to represent the **Private** data of the class. Provide a constructor method that enables an object of this class to be initialized when it is declared. Also, provide a default constructor. The class should contain the following:

a) Addition of two **CComplex** numbers: The real parts are added together and the imaginary parts are added together.
b) Subtraction of two **CComplex** numbers: The real part of the right operand is subtracted from the real part of the left operand and the imaginary part of the right operand is subtracted from the imaginary part of the left operand.
c) Printing of **CComplex** numbers in the form **(a, b)**, where **a** is the real part and **b** is the imaginary part.

8.4 Modify the **CDay** class of Fig. 8.8 to provide a method **NextDay** to increment the day by one. The **CDay** object should always remain in a consistent state. Write a program that tests the **NextDay** method in a loop that prints the date during each iteration of the loop to illustrate that the **NextDay** method works correctly. Be sure to test the following cases:
a) Incrementing into the next month.
b) Incrementing into the next year.

8.5 Create a class **CTicTacToe** that enables you to write a complete Windows application to play the game of Tic-Tac-Toe. The class contains as **Private** data a 3-by-3 **Integer** array. The constructor should initialize the empty board to all zeros. Allow two human players. Wherever the first player moves, display an **X** in the specified **Label**; place an **O** in a **Label** wherever the second player moves. Each move must be to an empty **Label**. Players move by clicking one of nine **Label**s. After each move determine if the game has been won, or if the game is a draw via a **GameStatus** method. [*Hint*: use an enumeration constant to return the following statuses: **WIN**, **DRAW**, **CONTINUE**.] If you feel ambitious, modify your program so that the computer is the opponent. Also, allow players to specify whether they want to go first or second. If you feel exceptionally ambitious, develop a program that plays three-dimensional Tic-Tac-Toe on a 4-by-4-by-4 board [*Note*: This is a challenging project that could take many weeks of effort!]

8.6 Create a **CDateFormat** class with the following capabilities:
a) Output the date in multiple formats such as

```
MM/DD/YYYY
June 14, 2001
DDD YYYY
```

b) Use overloaded constructors to create **CDateFormat** objects initialized with dates of the formats in part a).

8.7 Create class **CSavingsAccount**. Use a **Shared** class variable to store the **mAnnualInterestRate** for all account holders. Each object of the class contains a **Private** instance variable **mSavingsBalance** indicating the amount the saver currently has on deposit. Provide method **CalculateMonthlyInterest** to calculate the monthly interest by multiplying the **mSavingsBalance** by **mAnnualInterestRate** divided by **12**; this interest should be added to **mSavingsBalance**. Provide a **Shared** method **ModifyInterestRate** that sets the **mAnnualInterestRate** to a new value. Write a program to test class **CSavingsAccount**. Instantiate two **CSavingsAccount** objects, **saver1** and **saver2**, with balances of $2000.00 and $3000.00, respectively. Set **CAnnualInterestRate** to 4%, then calculate the monthly interest and print the new balances for each of the savers. Then set the **mAnnualInterestRate** to 5% and calculate the next month's interest and print the new balances for each of the savers.

8.8 Write a console application that implements a **CSquare** shape. Class **CSquare** should contain an property **Side** for accessing **Private** data. Provide two constructors: one that takes no arguments and another that takes a **Side** length as a value.

Object-Oriented Programming: Inheritance

Objectives

- To understand inheritance and software reusability.
- To understand the concepts of base classes and derived classes.
- To understand member access modifiers **Protected** and **Friend**.
- To be able to use the **MyBase** reference to access base-class members.
- To understand the use of constructors and finalizers in base classes and derived classes.
- To present a case study that demonstrates the mechanics of inheritance.

Say not you know another entirely, till you have divided an inheritance with him.
Johann Kasper Lavater

This method is to define as the number of a class the class of all classes similar to the given class.
Bertrand Russell

Good as it is to inherit a library, it is better to collect one.
Augustine Birrell

Outline

9.1 Introduction
9.2 Base Classes and Derived Classes
9.3 `Protected` and `Friend` Members
9.4 Relationship between Base Classes and Derived Classes
9.5 Case Study: Three-Level Inheritance Hierarchy
9.6 Constructors and Finalizers in Derived Classes
9.7 Software Engineering with Inheritance

Summary • Terminology • Self-Review Exercises • Answers to Self-Review Exercises • Exercises

9.1 Introduction

In this chapter, we being our discussion of object-oriented programming (OOP) by introducing one of its main features—*inheritance*. Inheritance is a form of software reusability in which classes are created by absorbing an existing class's data and behaviors and embellishing them with new capabilities. Software reusability saves time during program development. It also encourages the reuse of proven and debugged high-quality software, which increases the likelihood that a system will be implemented effectively.

When creating a class, instead of writing completely new instance variables and methods, the programmer can designate that the new class should *inherit* the class variables, properties and methods of another class. The previously defined class is called the *base class*, and the new class is referred to as the *derived class*. (Other programming languages, such as Java, refer to the base class as the *superclass*, and the derived class as the *subclass*.) Once created, each derived class can become the base class for future derived classes. A derived class, to which unique class variables, properties and methods normally are added, is often larger than its base class. Therefore, a derived class is more specific than its base class and represents a more specialized group of objects. Typically, the derived class contains the behaviors of its base class and additional behaviors. The *direct base class* is the base class from which the derived class explicitly inherits. An *indirect base class* is inherited from two or more levels up the *class hierarchy*. In the case of *single inheritance,* a class is derived from one base class. Visual Basic does not support *multiple inheritance* (which occurs when a class is derived from more than one direct base classes), as does C++. (We explain in Chapter 10 how Visual Basic can use interfaces to realize many of the benefits of multiple inheritance while avoiding the associated problems.)

Every object of a derived class is also an object of that derived class's base class. However, base-class objects are not objects of their derived classes. For example, all cars are vehicles, but not all vehicles are cars. As we continue our study of object-oriented programming in Chapters 9 and 10, we take advantage of this relationship to perform some interesting manipulations.

Experience in building software systems indicates that significant amounts of code deal with closely related special cases. When programmers preoccupied with special cases, the details can obscure the "big picture." With object-oriented programming, programmers focus on the commonalities among objects in the system, rather than on the special cases. This process is called *abstraction*.

We distinguish between the *"is-a" relationship* and the *"has-a" relationship*. "Is-a" represents inheritance. In an "is-a" relationship, an object of a derived class also can be treated as an object of its base class. For example, a car *is a* vehicle. By contrast, "has-a" stands for composition (composition is discussed in Chapter 8). In a "has-a" relationship, a class object contains one or more object references as members. For example, a car *has a* steering wheel.

Derived class methods might require access to their base-class instance variables, properties and methods. A derived class can access the non-**Private** members of its base class. Base-class members that should not be accessible to properties or methods of a class derived from that base class via inheritance are declared **Private** in the base class. A derived class can effect state changes in **Private** base-class members, but only through non-**Private** methods and properties provided in the base class and inherited into the derived class.

Software Engineering Observation 9.1

*Properties and methods of a derived class cannot directly access **Private** members of their base class.*

Software Engineering Observation 9.2

*Hiding **Private** members helps test, debug and correctly modify systems. If a derived class could access its base class's **Private** members, classes that inherit from that derived class could access that data as well. This would propagate access to what should be **Private** data, and the benefits of information hiding would be lost.*

One problem with inheritance is that a derived class can inherit properties and methods it does not need or should not have. It is the class designer's responsibility to ensure that the capabilities provided by a class are appropriate for future derived classes. Even when a base-class property or method is appropriate for a derived class, that derived class often requires the property or method to perform its task in a manner specific to the derived class. In such cases, the base-class property or method can be *overridden* (redefined) in the derived class with an appropriate implementation.

New classes can inherit from abundant *class libraries*. Although organizations often develop their own class libraries, they also can take advantage of other libraries available worldwide. Someday, the vast majority of new software likely will be constructed from *standardized reusable components*, as most hardware is constructed today. This will facilitate the development of more powerful and abundant software.

9.2 Base Classes and Derived Classes

Often, an object of one class "is an" object of another class, as well. For example, a rectangle *is a* quadrilateral (as are squares, parallelograms and trapezoids). Thus, class **CRectangle** can be said to *inherit* from class **CQuadrilateral**. In this context, class **CQuadrilateral** is a base class, and class **CRectangle** is a derived class. A rectangle *is a* specific type of quadrilateral, but it is incorrect to claim that a quadrilateral *is a* rectangle—the quadrilateral could be a parallelogram or some other type of **CQuadrilateral**. Figure 9.1 lists several simple examples of base classes and derived classes.

Base class	Derived classes
`CStudent`	`CGraduateStudent`
	`CUndergraduateStudent`
`CShape`	`CCircle`
	`CTriangle`
	`CRectangle`
`CLoan`	`CCarLoan`
	`CHomeImprovementLoan`
	`CMortgageLoan`
`CEmployee`	`CFacultyMember`
	`CStaffMember`
`CAccount`	`CCheckingAccount`
	`CSavingsAccount`

Fig. 9.1   Inheritance examples.

Every derived-class object "is an" object of its base class, and one base class can have many derived classes; therefore, the set of objects represented by a base class typically is larger than the set of objects represented by any of its derived classes. For example, the base class **CVehicle** represents all vehicles, including cars, trucks, boats, bicycles and so on. By contrast, derived-class **CCar** represents only a small subset of all **CVehicle**s.

Inheritance relationships form tree-like hierarchical structures. A class exists in a hierarchical relationship with its derived classes. Although classes can exist independently, once they are employed in inheritance arrangements, they become affiliated with other classes. A class becomes either a base class, supplying data and behaviors to other classes, or a derived class, inheriting its data and behaviors from other classes.

Let us develop a simple inheritance hierarchy. A university community has thousands of members. These members consist of employees, students and alumni. Employees are either faculty members or staff members. Faculty members are either administrators (such as deans and department chairpersons) or teachers. This organizational structure yields the inheritance hierarchy, depicted in Fig. 9.2. Note that the inheritance hierarchy could contain many other classes. For example, students can be graduate or undergraduate students. Undergraduate students can be freshmen, sophomores, juniors and seniors. Each arrow in the hierarchy represents an "is-a" relationship. For example, as we follow the arrows in this class hierarchy, we can state, "a **CEmployee** *is a* **CCommunityMember**" or "a **CTeacher** *is a* **CFaculty** member." **CCommunityMember** is the *direct base class* of **CEmployee**, **CStudent** and **CAlumnus**. In addition, **CCommunityMember** is an *indirect base class* of all the other classes in the hierarchy diagram.

Starting from the bottom of the diagram, the reader can follow the arrows and apply the *is-a* relationship to the topmost base class. For example, a **CAdministrator** *is a* **CFaculty** member, *is a* **CEmployee** and *is a* **CCommunityMember**. In Visual Basic, a **CAdministrator** also *is an* **Object**, because all classes in Visual Basic have **Object** as either a direct or indirect base class. Thus, all classes in Visual Basic are connected via a hierarchical relationship in which they share the eight methods defined by class **Object**. We discuss some of these methods inherited from **Object** throughout the text.

Another inheritance hierarchy is the **CShape** hierarchy of Fig. 9.3. To specify that class **CTwoDimensionalShape** is derived from (or inherits from) class **CShape**, class **CTwoDimensionalShape** could be defined in Visual Basic as follows:

```
Class CTwoDimensionalShape
    Inherits CShape
```

In Chapter 8, we briefly discussed *has-a* relationships, in which classes have as members references to objects of other classes. Such relationships create classes by *composition* of existing classes. For example, given the classes **CEmployee**, **CBirthDate** and **CTelephoneNumber**, it is improper to say that a **CEmployee** *is a* **CBirthDate** or that a **CEmployee** *is a* **CTelephoneNumber**. However, it is appropriate to say that a **CEmployee** *has a* **CBirthDate** and that a **CEmployee** *has a* **CTelephoneNumber**.

With inheritance, **Private** members of a base class are not accessible directly from that class's derived classes, but these **Private** base-class members are still inherited. All other base-class members retain their original member access when they become members of the derived class (e.g., **Public** members of the base class become **Public** members of the derived class, and, as we will soon see, **Protected** members of the base class become **Protected** members of the derived class). Through these inherited base-class members, the derived class can manipulate **Private** members of the base class (if these inherited members provide such functionality in the base class).

It is possible to treat base-class objects and derived-class objects similarly; their commonalities are expressed in the member variables, properties and methods of the base class. Objects of all classes derived from a common base class can be treated as objects of that base class. In Chapter 10, we consider many examples that take advantage of this relationship.

Constructors never are inherited—they are specific to the class in which they are defined.

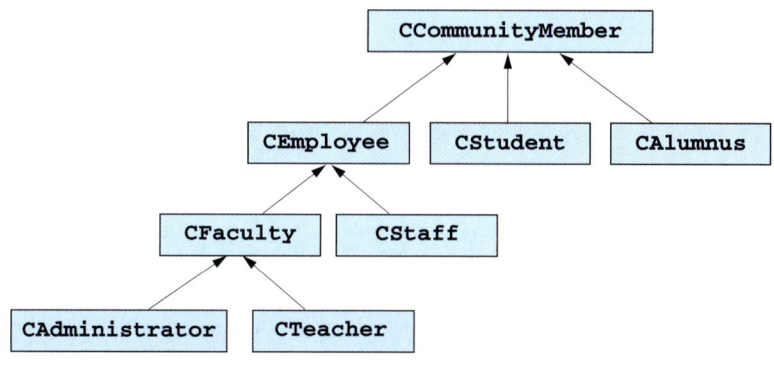

Fig. 9.2   Inheritance hierarchy for university **CCommunityMember**s.

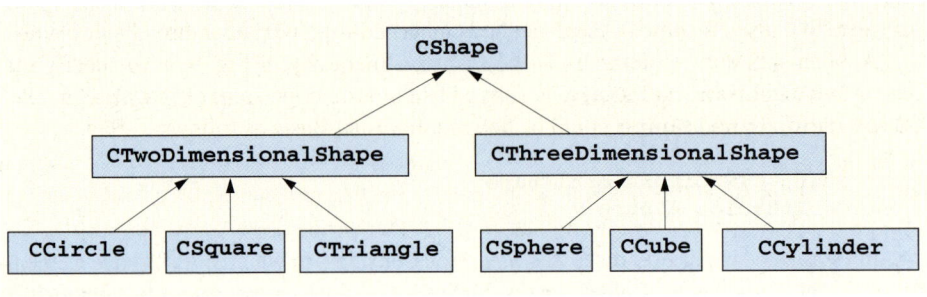

Fig. 9.3 Portion of a **CShape** class hierarchy.

9.3 Protected and Friend Members

Chapter 8 discussed **Public** and **Private** member access modifiers. A base class's **Public** members are accessible anywhere that the program has a reference to an object of that base class or one of its derived classes. A base class's **Private** members are accessible only within the body of that base class. In this section, we introduce two additional member access modifiers, *Protected* and *Friend*.

Protected access offers an intermediate level of protection between **Public** and **Private** access. A base class's **Protected** members can be accessed only in that base class or in any classes derived from that class.

Another intermediate level of access is known as **Friend** access. A base class's **Friend** members can be accessed only by objects declared in the same assembly. Note that a **Friend** member is accessible in any part of the assembly in which that **Friend** member is declared—not only in classes derived from the base class that defines the member.

Derived-class methods normally can refer to **Public**, **Protected** and **Friend** members of the base class simply by using the member names. When a derived-class method overrides a base-class member, the base-class member can be accessed from the derived class by preceding the base-class member name with keyword **MyBase**, followed by the dot operator (**.**). We discuss keyword **MyBase** in Section 9.4.

9.4 Relationship between Base Classes and Derived Classes

In this section, we use a point-circle hierarchy to discuss the relationship between a base class and a derived class. The point-circle relationship may seem slightly unnatural when we discuss it in the context of a circle "is a" point; however, this mechanical example teaches *structural inheritance*, which focuses primarily on how a base class and a derived class relate to one another. In Chapter 10, we present more "natural" inheritance examples.

We divide our discussion of the point-circle relationship into several parts. First, we create class **CPoint**, which directly inherits from class **System.Object** and contains as **Private** data an *x*-*y* coordinate pair. Then, we create class **CCircle**, which also directly inherits from class **System.Object** and contains as **Private** data an *x*-*y* coordinate pair (representing the location of the center of the circle) and a radius. We do not use inheritance to create class **CCircle**; rather, we construct the class by writing every line of code the class requires. Next, we create a separate **CCircle2** class, which directly inherits from class **CPoint** (i.e., class **CCircle2** "is a" **CPoint** but also contains a radius) and attempts to use the **CPoint Private** members—this results in compilation errors, because the derived class does not have access to the base-class's **Private** data. We then show how by declaring **CPoint**'s data as **Protected**, a separate **CCircle3** class that also inherits from class **CPoint** can access that data. Both the inherited and non-inherited **CCircle** classes contain identical functionality, but we show how the inherited **CCircle3** class is easier to create and manage. After discussing the merits of using **Protected** data, we set the **CPoint** data back to **Private**, then show how a separate **CCircle4** class (which also inherits from class **CPoint**) can use **CPoint** methods to manipulate **CPoint**'s **Private** data.

Let us first examine the **CPoint** (Fig. 9.4) class definition. The **Public** services of class **CPoint** include two **CPoint** constructors (lines 11–25), properties **X** and **Y** (lines 28–51) and method **ToString** (lines 54–56). The instance variables **mX** and **mY** of **CPoint** are specified as **Private** (line 8), so objects of other classes cannot access **mX** and **mY** directly. Technically, even if **CPoint**'s variables **mX** and **mY** were made **Public**, **CPoint** can never maintain an inconsistent state, because the *x-y* coordinate plane in infinite in both directions, so **mX** and **mY** can hold any **Integer** value. However, declaring this data as **Private**, while providing non-**Private** properties to manipulate and perform validation checking on this data, enforces good software engineering.

We mentioned in Section 9.2 that class constructors are never inherited. Therefore, class **CPoint** does not inherit class **Object**'s constructor. However, class **CPoint**'s constructors (lines 11–25) call class **Object**'s constructor implicitly. In fact, the first task undertaken by any derived-class constructor is to call its direct base class's constructor, either implicitly or explicitly. (The syntax for calling a base-class constructor is discussed later in this section.) If the code does not include an explicit call to the base-class constructor, an implicit call is made to the base class's default (no-argument) constructor. The comments in lines 13 and 22 indicate where the calls to the base-class **Object**'s default constructor occur.

```
1   ' Fig. 9.4: Point.vb
2   ' CPoint class represents an x-y coordinate pair.
3
4   Public Class CPoint
5      ' implicitly Inherits Object
6
7      ' point coordinate
8      Private mX, mY As Integer
9
10     ' default constructor
11     Public Sub New()
12
13        ' implicit call to Object constructor occurs here
14        X = 0
15        Y = 0
16     End Sub ' New
17
```

Fig. 9.4 **CPoint** class represents an *x-y* coordinate pair (part 1 of 2).

```vb
18      ' constructor
19      Public Sub New(ByVal xValue As Integer, _
20         ByVal yValue As Integer)
21
22         ' implicit call to Object constructor occurs here
23         X = xValue
24         Y = yValue
25      End Sub ' New
26
27      ' property X
28      Public Property X() As Integer
29
30         Get
31            Return mX
32         End Get
33
34         Set(ByVal xValue As Integer)
35            mX = xValue ' no need for validation
36         End Set
37
38      End Property ' X
39
40      ' property Y
41      Public Property Y() As Integer
42
43         Get
44            Return mY
45         End Get
46
47         Set(ByVal yValue As Integer)
48            mY = yValue ' no need for validation
49         End Set
50
51      End Property ' Y
52
53      ' return String representation of CPoint
54      Public Overrides Function ToString() As String
55         Return "[" & mX & ", " & mY & "]"
56      End Function ' ToString
57
58   End Class ' CPoint
```

Fig. 9.4 `CPoint` class represents an *x-y* coordinate pair (part 2 of 2).

Note that method **ToString** (lines 54–56) contains the keyword **Overrides** in its declaration. Every class in Visual Basic (such as class **CPoint**) inherits either directly or indirectly from class **System.Object**, which is the root of the class hierarchy. As we mentioned previously, this means that every class inherits the eight methods defined by class **Object**. One of these methods is **ToString**, which returns a **String** containing the object's type preceded by its namespace—this method obtains an object's **String** representation and sometimes is called implicitly by the program (such as when an object is concatenated to a **String**). Method **ToString** of class **CPoint** *overrides* the original **ToString** from class **Object**—when invoked, method **ToString** of class **CPoint** returns a **String** containing an ordered pair of the values **mX** and **mY** (line 55), instead of returning a **String** containing the object's class and namespace.

Software Engineering Observation 9.4

*The Visual Basic compiler sets the base class of a derived class to **Object** when the program does not specify a base class explicitly.*

In Visual Basic, a base-class method must be declared **Overridable** if that method is to be overridden in a derived class. Method **ToString** of class **Object** is declared **Overridable**, which enables derived class **CPoint** to override this method. To view the method header for **ToString**, select **Help > Index...**, and enter **Object.ToString method** in the search textbox. The page displayed contains a description of method **ToString**, which includes the following header:

```
Overridable Public Function ToString() As String
```

Keyword **Overridable** allows programmers to specify those methods that a derived class can override—a method that has not been declared **Overridable** cannot be overridden. We use this later in this section to enable certain methods in our base classes to be overridden.

Common Programming Error 9.1

*A derived class attempting to override (using keyword **Overrides**) a method that has not been declared **Overridable** is a syntax error.*

Module **modPointTest** (Fig. 9.5) tests class **CPoint**. Line 12 instantiates an object of class **CPoint** and assigns **72** as the *x*-coordinate value and **115** as the *y*-coordinate value. Lines 15–16 use properties **X** and **Y** to retrieve these values, then append the values to **String output**. Lines 18–19 change the values of properties **X** and **Y**, and lines 22–23 call **CPoint**'s **ToString** method to obtain the **CPoint**'s **String** representation.

```
1    ' Fig. 9.5: PointTest.vb
2    ' Testing class CPoint.
3
4    Imports System.Windows.Forms
5
6    Module modPointTest
7
8       Sub Main()
9          Dim point As CPoint
10         Dim output As String
11
12         point = New CPoint(72, 115) ' instantiate CPoint object
13
14         ' display point coordinates via X and Y properties
15         output = "X coordinate is " & point.X & _
16            vbCrLf & "Y coordinate is " & point.Y
17
18         point.X = 10 ' set x-coordinate via X property
19         point.Y = 10 ' set y-coordinate via Y property
20
```

Fig. 9.5 **modPointTest** demonstrates class **CPoint** functionality (part 1 of 2).

```
21         ' display new point value
22         output &= vbCrLf & vbCrLf & _
23            "The new location of point is " & point.ToString()
24
25         MessageBox.Show(output, "Demonstrating Class Point")
26      End Sub ' Main
27
28   End Module ' modPointTest
```

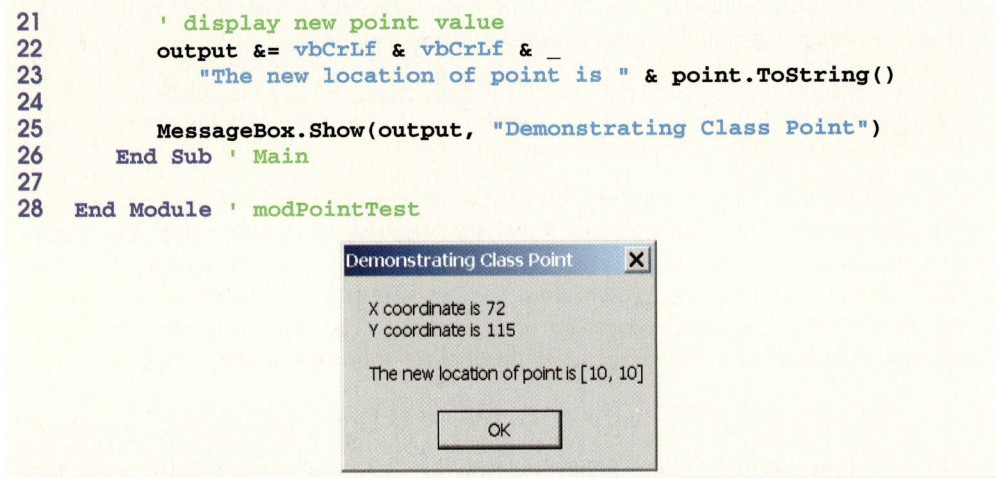

Fig. 9.5 `modPointTest` demonstrates class `CPoint` functionality (part 2 of 2).

We now discuss the second part of our introduction to inheritance by creating and testing class **CCircle** (Fig. 9.6), which directly inherits from class **System.Object** and represents an *x-y* coordinate pair (representing the center of the circle) and a radius. Lines 7–8 declare the instance variables **mX**, **mY** and **mRadius** as **Private** data. The **Public** services of class **CCircle** include two **CCircle** constructors (lines 11–27), properties **X**, **Y** and **Radius** (lines 30–70), methods **Diameter** (lines 73–75), **Circumference** (lines 78–80), **Area** (lines 83–85) and **ToString** (lines 88–91). These properties and methods encapsulate all necessary features (i.e., the "analytic geometry") of a circle; in the next section, we show how this encapsulation enables us to reuse and extend this class.

```
1    ' Fig. 9.6: Circle.vb
2    ' CCircle class contains x-y coordinate pair and radius.
3
4    Public Class CCircle
5
6       ' coordinate of center of CCircle
7       Private mX, mY As Integer
8       Private mRadius As Double ' CCircle's radius
9
10      ' default constructor
11      Public Sub New()
12
13         ' implicit call to Object constructor occurs here
14         X = 0
15         Y = 0
16         Radius = 0
17      End Sub ' New
18
```

Fig. 9.6 `CCircle` class contains an *x-y* coordinate and a radius (part 1 of 3).

```vbnet
19         ' constructor
20         Public Sub New(ByVal xValue As Integer, _
21            ByVal yValue As Integer, ByVal radiusValue As Double)
22
23            ' implicit call to Object constructor occurs here
24            X = xValue
25            Y = yValue
26            Radius = radiusValue
27         End Sub ' New
28
29         ' property X
30         Public Property X() As Integer
31
32            Get
33               Return mX
34            End Get
35
36            Set(ByVal xValue As Integer)
37               mX = xValue ' no need for validation
38            End Set
39
40         End Property ' X
41
42         ' property Y
43         Public Property Y() As Integer
44
45            Get
46               Return mY
47            End Get
48
49            Set(ByVal yValue As Integer)
50               mY = yValue ' no need for validation
51            End Set
52
53         End Property ' Y
54
55         ' property Radius
56         Public Property Radius() As Double
57
58            Get
59               Return mRadius
60            End Get
61
62            Set(ByVal radiusValue As Double)
63
64               If radiusValue > 0
65                  mRadius = radiusValue
66               End If
67
68            End Set
69
70         End Property ' Radius
71
```

Fig. 9.6 `CCircle` class contains an *x-y* coordinate and a radius (part 2 of 3).

```
72      ' calculate CCircle diameter
73      Public Function Diameter() As Double
74         Return mRadius * 2
75      End Function ' Diameter
76
77      ' calculate CCircle circumference
78      Public Function Circumference() As Double
79         Return Math.PI * Diameter()
80      End Function ' Circumference
81
82      ' calculate CCircle area
83      Public Function Area() As Double
84         Return Math.PI * mRadius ^ 2
85      End Function ' Area
86
87      ' return String representation of CCircle
88      Public Overrides Function ToString() As String
89         Return "Center = " & "[" & mX & ", " & mY & "]" & _
90            "; Radius = " & mRadius
91      End Function ' ToString
92
93   End Class ' CCircle
```

Fig. 9.6 **CCircle** class contains an *x-y* coordinate and a radius (part 3 of 3).

Module **modCircleTest** (Fig. 9.7) tests class **CCircle**. Line 12 instantiates an object of class **CCircle**, assigning **37** as the *x*-coordinate value, **43** as the *y*-coordinate value and **2.5** as the radius value. Lines 15–17 use properties **X**, **Y** and **Radius** to retrieve these values, then concatenate the values to **String output**. Lines 20–22 use **CCircle**'s **X**, **Y** and **Radius** properties to change the *x-y* coordinate pair value and radius value, respectively. Property **Radius** ensures that member variable **mRadius** cannot be assigned a negative value. Line 27 calls **CCircle**'s **ToString** method to obtain the **CCircle**'s **String** representation, and lines 31–38 call **CCircle**'s **Diameter**, **Circumference** and **Area** methods.

After writing all the code for class **CCircle** (Fig. 9.6), note that a major portion of the code in this class is similar, if not identical, to much of the code in class **CPoint**. For example, the declaration in **CCircle** of **Private** variables **mX** and **mY** and properties **X** and **Y** are identical to those of class **CPoint**. In addition, the class **CCircle** constructors and method **ToString** are almost identical to those of class **CPoint**, except that they also supply **mRadius** information. In fact, the only other additions to class **CCircle** are **Private** member variable **mRadius**, property **Radius** and methods **Diameter**, **Circumference** and **Area**.

```
1   ' Fig. 9.7: CircleTest.vb
2   ' Testing class CCircle.
3
4   Imports System.Windows.Forms
5
```

Fig. 9.7 **modCircleTest** demonstrates class **CCircle** functionality (part 1 of 2).

```vbnet
6   Module modCircleTest
7
8      Sub Main()
9         Dim circle As CCircle
10        Dim output As String
11
12        circle = New CCircle(37, 43, 2.5) ' instantiate CCircle
13
14        ' get CCircle's initial x-y coordinates and radius
15        output = "X coordinate is " & circle.X & vbCrLf & _
16           "Y coordinate is " & circle.Y & vbCrLf & "Radius is " & _
17           circle.Radius
18
19        ' set CCircle's x-y coordinates and radius to new values
20        circle.X = 2
21        circle.Y = 2
22        circle.Radius = 4.25
23
24        ' display CCircle's String representation
25        output &= vbCrLf & vbCrLf & _
26           "The new location and radius of circle are " & _
27           vbCrLf & circle.ToString() & vbCrLf
28
29        ' display CCircle's diameter
30        output &= "Diameter is " & _
31           String.Format("{0:F}", circle.Diameter()) & vbCrLf
32
33        ' display CCircle's circumference
34        output &= "Circumference is " & _
35           String.Format("{0:F}", circle.Circumference()) & vbCrLf
36
37        ' display CCircle's area
38        output &= "Area is " & String.Format("{0:F}", circle.Area())
39
40        MessageBox.Show(output, "Demonstrating Class CCircle")
41     End Sub ' Main
42
43  End Module ' modCircleTest
```

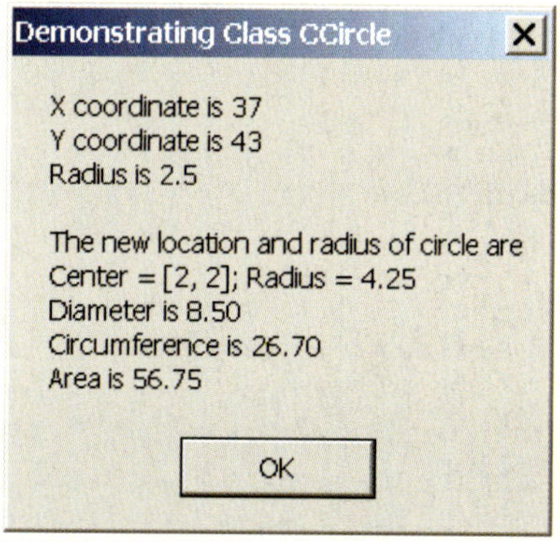

```
Demonstrating Class CCircle

X coordinate is 37
Y coordinate is 43
Radius is 2.5

The new location and radius of circle are
Center = [2, 2]; Radius = 4.25
Diameter is 8.50
Circumference is 26.70
Area is 56.75

                    OK
```

Fig. 9.7 `modCircleTest` demonstrates class `CCircle` functionality (part 2 of 2).

It appears that we literally copied code from class **CPoint**, pasted this code in the code from class **CCircle**, then modified class **CCircle** to include a radius. This "copy-and-paste" approach is often error-prone and time-consuming. Worse yet, it can result in many physical copies of the code existing throughout a system, creating a code-maintenance "nightmare."

In the next examples, we use a more elegant approach emphasizing the benefits of using inheritance. Now, we create and test a class **CCircle2** (Fig. 9.8) that inherits variables **mX** and **mY** and properties **X** and **Y** from class **CPoint** (Fig. 9.4). This class **CCircle2** "is a" **CPoint**, but also contains **mRadius** (line 7). The *Inherits* keyword in the class declaration (line 5) indicates inheritance. As a derived class, **CCircle2** inherits all the members of class **CPoint**, except for the constructors. Thus, the **Public** services to **CCircle2** include the two **CCircle2** constructors; the **Public** methods inherited from class **CPoint**; property **Radius**; and the **CCircle2** methods **Diameter**, **Circumference**, **Area** and **ToString**. We declare method **Area** as **Overridable**, so that derived class (such as class **CCylinder**, as we will see in Section 9.5) can override this method to provide a specific implementation.

```
1   ' Fig. 9.8: Circle2.vb
2   ' CCircle2 class that inherits from class CPoint.
3
4   Public Class CCircle2
5      Inherits CPoint ' CCircle2 Inherits from class CPoint
6
7      Private mRadius As Double ' CCircle2's radius
8
9      ' default constructor
10     Public Sub New()
11
12        ' implicit call to CPoint constructor occurs here
13        Radius = 0
14     End Sub ' New
15
16     ' constructor
17     Public Sub New(ByVal xValue As Integer, _
18        ByVal yValue As Integer, ByVal radiusValue As Double)
19
20        ' implicit call to CPoint constructor occurs here
21        mX = xValue
22        mY = yValue
23        Radius = radiusValue
24     End Sub ' New
25
26     ' property Radius
27     Public Property Radius() As Double
28
29        Get
30           Return mRadius
31        End Get
32
```

Fig. 9.8 **CCircle2** class that inherits from class **CPoint** (part 1 of 2).

```vbnet
33         Set(ByVal radiusValue As Double)
34
35            If radiusValue > 0
36               mRadius = radiusValue
37            End If
38
39         End Set
40
41      End Property ' Radius
42
43      ' calculate CCircle2 diameter
44      Public Function Diameter() As Double
45         Return mRadius * 2
46      End Function ' Diameter
47
48      ' calculate CCircle2 circumference
49      Public Function Circumference() As Double
50         Return Math.PI * Diameter()
51      End Function ' Circumference
52
53      ' calculate CCircle2 area
54      Public Function Area() As Double
55         Return Math.PI * mRadius ^ 2
56      End Function ' Area
57
58      ' return String representation of CCircle2
59      Public Overrides Function ToString() As String
60         Return "Center = " & "[" & mX & ", " & mY & "]" & _
61            "; Radius = " & mRadius
62      End Function ' ToString
63
64   End Class ' CCircle2
```

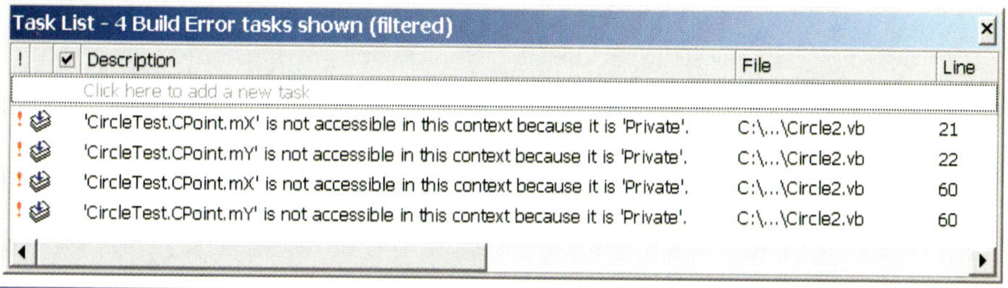

!	☑	Description	File	Line
		Click here to add a new task		
!	⚠	'CircleTest.CPoint.mX' is not accessible in this context because it is 'Private'.	C:\...\Circle2.vb	21
!	⚠	'CircleTest.CPoint.mY' is not accessible in this context because it is 'Private'.	C:\...\Circle2.vb	22
!	⚠	'CircleTest.CPoint.mX' is not accessible in this context because it is 'Private'.	C:\...\Circle2.vb	60
!	⚠	'CircleTest.CPoint.mY' is not accessible in this context because it is 'Private'.	C:\...\Circle2.vb	60

Fig. 9.8 `CCircle2` class that inherits from class `CPoint` (part 2 of 2).

Lines 12 and 20 in the **CCircle2** constructors (lines 10–24) invoke the default **CPoint2** constructor implicitly to initialize the base-class portion (variables **mX** and **mY**, inherited from class **CPoint**) of a **CCircle2** object to **0**. However, because the parameterized constructor (lines 17–24) should set the *x-y* coordinate to a specific value, lines 21–22 attempt to assign argument values to **mX** and **mY** directly. Even though lines 21–22 attempt to set **mX** and **mY** values explicitly, line 20 first calls the **CPoint** default constructor to initialize these variables to their default values. The compiler generates a syntax error for lines 21–22 (and line 60, where **CCircle2**'s method **ToString** attempts to use the values of **mX** and **mY** directly), because the derived class **CCircle2** is not allowed to access the base class **CPoint**'s **Private** members **mX** and **mY**. Visual Basic rigidly enforces restriction on accessing **Private** data members, so that even derived classes (i.e,. which are closely related to their base class) cannot access base-class **Private** data.

To enable class **CCircle2** to access **CPoint** member variables **mX** and **mY** directly, we declare those variables as **Protected**. As we discussed in Section 9.3, a base class's **Protected** members can be accessed only in that base class or in any classes derived from that class. Class **CPoint2** (Fig. 9.9) modifies class **CPoint** (Fig. 9.4) to declare variables **mX** and **mY** as **Protected** (line 8) instead of **Private**.

```vb
1   ' Fig. 9.9: Point2.vb
2   ' CPoint2 class contains an x-y coordinate pair as Protected data.
3
4   Public Class CPoint2
5       ' implicitly Inherits Object
6
7       ' point coordinate
8       Protected mX, mY As Integer
9
10      ' default constructor
11      Public Sub New()
12
13          ' implicit call to Object constructor occurs here
14          X = 0
15          Y = 0
16      End Sub ' New
17
18      ' constructor
19      Public Sub New(ByVal xValue As Integer, _
20          ByVal yValue As Integer)
21
22          ' implicit call to Object constructor occurs here
23          X = xValue
24          Y = yValue
25      End Sub ' New
26
27      ' property X
28      Public Property X() As Integer
29
30          Get
31              Return mX
32          End Get
33
34          Set(ByVal xValue As Integer)
35              mX = xValue ' no need for validation
36          End Set
37
38      End Property ' X
39
```

Fig. 9.9 **CPoint2** class represents an *x-y* coordinate pair as **Protected** data (part 1 of 2).

```
40      ' property Y
41      Public Property Y() As Integer
42
43         Get
44            Return mY
45         End Get
46
47         Set(ByVal yValue As Integer)
48            mY = yValue  ' no need for validation
49         End Set
50
51      End Property ' Y
52
53      ' return String representation of CPoint2
54      Public Overrides Function ToString() As String
55         Return "[" & mX & ", " & mY & "]"
56      End Function ' ToString
57
58   End Class ' CPoint2
```

Fig. 9.9 `CPoint2` class represents an *x-y* coordinate pair as **Protected** data (part 2 of 2).

Class **CCircle3** (Fig. 9.10) modifies class **CCircle2** (Fig. 9.4) to inherit from class **CPoint2** rather than inherit from class **CPoint**. Because class **CCircle3** is a class derived from class **CPoint2**, class **CCircle3** can access class **CPoint2**'s **Protected** member variables **mX** and **mY** directly, and the compiler does not generate errors when compiling Fig. 9.10.

Module **modCircleTest3** (Fig. 9.11) performs identical tests on class **CCircle3** as module **modCircleTest** (Fig. 9.7) performed on class **CCircle** (Fig. 9.6). Note that the outputs of the two programs are identical. We created class **CCircle** without using inheritance and created class **CCircle3** using inheritance; however, both classes provide the same functionality. However, observe that the code listing for class **CCircle3**, which is 64 lines, is considerably shorter than the code listing for class **CCircle**, which is 93 lines, because class **CCircle3** absorbs part of its functionality from **CPoint2**, whereas class **CCircle** does not.

In the previous example, we declared the base class instance variables as **Protected**, so that a derived class could modify their values directly. The use of **Protected** variables allows for a slight increase in performance, because we avoid incurring the overhead of a method call to a property's **Set** or **Get** accessor. However, in most Visual Basic application, in which user interaction comprises a large part of the execution time, the optimization offered through the use of **Protected** variables is negligible.

```
1  ' Fig. 9.10: Circle3.vb
2  ' CCircle3 class that inherits from class CPoint2.
3
4  Public Class CCircle3
5     Inherits CPoint2 ' CCircle3 Inherits from class CPoint2
```

Fig. 9.10 `CCircle3` class that inherits from class **CPoint2** (part 1 of 3).

```vbnet
 6
 7       Private mRadius As Double ' CCircle3's radius
 8
 9       ' default constructor
10       Public Sub New()
11
12          ' implicit call to CPoint2 constructor occurs here
13          Radius = 0
14       End Sub ' New
15
16       ' constructor
17       Public Sub New(ByVal xValue As Integer, _
18          ByVal yValue As Integer, ByVal radiusValue As Double)
19
20          ' implicit call to CPoint2 constructor occurs here
21          mX = xValue
22          mY = yValue
23          Radius = radiusValue
24       End Sub ' New
25
26       ' property Radius
27       Public Property Radius() As Double
28
29          Get
30             Return mRadius
31          End Get
32
33          Set(ByVal radiusValue As Double)
34
35             If radiusValue > 0
36                mRadius = radiusValue
37             End If
38
39          End Set
40
41       End Property ' Radius
42
43       ' calculate CCircle3 diameter
44       Public Function Diameter() As Double
45          Return mRadius * 2
46       End Function ' Diameter
47
48       ' calculate CCircle3 circumference
49       Public Function Circumference() As Double
50          Return Math.PI * Diameter()
51       End Function ' Circumference
52
53       ' calculate CCircle3 area
54       Public Overridable Function Area() As Double
55          Return Math.PI * mRadius ^ 2
56       End Function ' Area
57
```

Fig. 9.10 `CCircle3` class that inherits from class `CPoint2` (part 2 of 3).

```
58      ' return String representation of CCircle3
59      Public Overrides Function ToString() As String
60         Return "Center = " & "[" & mX & ", " & mY & "]" & _
61            "; Radius = " & mRadius
62      End Function ' ToString
63
64   End Class ' CCircle3
```

Fig. 9.10 `CCircle3` class that inherits from class `CPoint2` (part 3 of 3).

Unfortunately, the inclusion of **Protected** instance variables often yields two major problems. First, the derived-class object does not have to use a property to set the value of the base-class's **Protected** data. Therefore, a derived-class object can assign an illegal value to the **Protected** data, thus leaving that object in an inconsistent state. For example, if we declare **CCircle3**'s variable **mRadius** as **Protected**, a derived-class object (e.g., **CCylinder**), can assign a negative value to **mRadius**. The second problem to using **Protected** data is that derived class methods are more likely to be written to depend on base-class implementation. In practice, derived classes should depend only on the base-class services (i.e., non-**Private** methods and properties) and not depend on base-class implementation. With **Protected** data in the base class, if the base-class implementation changes, we may need to modify all derived classes of that base class. For example, if we change the names of variables **mX** and **mY** to **mXCoordinate** and **mYCoordinate**, we must do so for all occurrences in which a derived class references these variables directly. If this happens, the base class is considered *fragile*, or *brittle*. The base class should be able to change its implementation freely, while providing the same services to derived classes. (Of course, if the base class changes its services, we must reimplement our derived classes, but good object-oriented design attempts to prevent this.)

Software Engineering Observation 9.5

*The most appropriate time to use **Protected** access modifier is when a base class should provide a service only to its derived classes (i.e., should not provide the service to other clients). In this case, declare the base-class property or method as **Protected**.*

```
1    ' Fig. 9.11: CircleTest3.vb
2    ' Testing class CCircle3.
3
4    Imports System.Windows.Forms
5
6    Module modCircleTest3
7
8       Sub Main()
9          Dim circle As CCircle3
10         Dim output As String
11
12         circle = New CCircle3(37, 43, 2.5) ' instantiate CCircle3
13
```

Fig. 9.11 `modCircleTest3` demonstrates class `CCircle3` functionality (part 1 of 2).

```
14            ' get CCircle3's initial x-y coordinates and radius
15            output = "X coordinate is " & circle.X & vbCrLf & _
16               "Y coordinate is " & circle.Y & vbCrLf & "Radius is " & _
17               circle.Radius
18
19            ' set CCircle3's x-y coordinates and radius to new values
20            circle.X = 2
21            circle.Y = 2
22            circle.Radius = 4.25
23
24            ' display CCircle3's String representation
25            output &= vbCrLf & vbCrLf & _
26               "The new location and radius of circle are " & _
27               vbCrLf & circle.ToString() & vbCrLf
28
29            ' display CCircle3's diameter
30            output &= "Diameter is " & _
31               String.Format("{0:F}", circle.Diameter()) & vbCrLf
32
33            ' display CCircle3's circumference
34            output &= "Circumference is " & _
35               String.Format("{0:F}", circle.Circumference()) & vbCrLf
36
37            ' display CCircle3's area
38            output &= "Area is " & String.Format("{0:F}", circle.Area())
39
40            MessageBox.Show(output, "Demonstrating Class CCircle3")
41         End Sub ' Main
42
43      End Module ' modCircleTest3
```

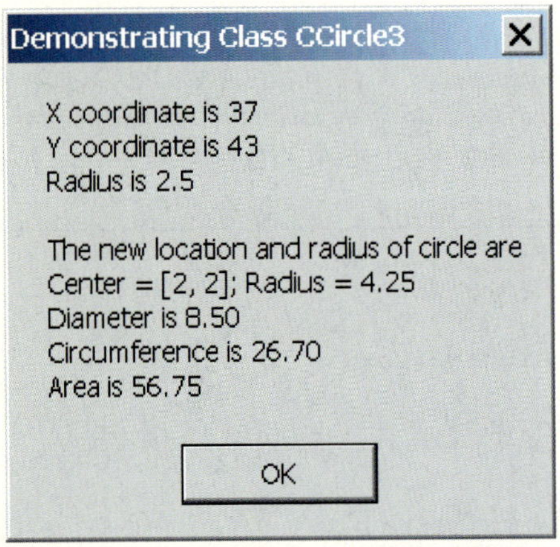

```
Demonstrating Class CCircle3

X coordinate is 37
Y coordinate is 43
Radius is 2.5

The new location and radius of circle are
Center = [2, 2]; Radius = 4.25
Diameter is 8.50
Circumference is 26.70
Area is 56.75

                    OK
```

Fig. 9.11 `modCircleTest3` demonstrates class `CCircle3` functionality (part 2 of 2).

Software Engineering Observation 9.6

Declaring base-class instance variables **Private** *(as opposed to declaring them* **Protected***) helps programmers change base-class implementation without having to change derived-class implementation.*

Testing and Debugging Tip 9.1

When possible, avoid including **Protected** *data in a base class. Rather, include non-***Private** *properties and methods that access* **Private** *data, ensuring that the object maintains a consistent state.*

We reexamine our point-circle hierarchy example once more; this time, attempting to use the best software engineering technique. We use **CPoint** (Fig. 9.4), which declares variables **mX** and **mY** as **Private**, and we show how derived class **CCircle4** (Fig. 9.12) can invoke base-class methods and properties to manipulate these variables.

```vb
1   ' Fig. 9.12: Circle4.vb
2   ' CCircle4 class that inherits from class CPoint.
3
4   Public Class CCircle4
5      Inherits CPoint ' CCircle4 Inherits from class CPoint
6
7      Private mRadius As Double
8
9      ' default constructor
10     Public Sub New()
11
12        ' implicit call to CPoint constructor occurs here
13        Radius = 0
14     End Sub ' New
15
16     ' constructor
17     Public Sub New(ByVal xValue As Integer, _
18        ByVal yValue As Integer, ByVal radiusValue As Double)
19
20        ' use MyBase reference to CPoint constructor explicitly
21        MyBase.New(xValue, yValue)
22        Radius = radiusValue
23     End Sub ' New
24
25     ' property Radius
26     Public Property Radius() As Double
27
28        Get
29           Return mRadius
30        End Get
31
32        Set(ByVal radiusValue As Double)
33
34           If radiusValue > 0
35              mRadius = radiusValue
36           End If
37
38        End Set
39
40     End Property ' Radius
```

Fig. 9.12 **CCircle4** class that inherits from class **CPoint**, which does not provide **Protected** data (part 1 of 2).

```
41
42          ' calculate CCircle4 diameter
43          Public Function Diameter() As Double
44             Return mRadius * 2
45          End Function ' Diameter
46
47          ' calculate CCircle4 circumference
48          Public Function Circumference() As Double
49             Return Math.PI * Diameter()
50          End Function ' Circumference
51
52          ' calculate CCircle4 area
53          Public Overridable Function Area() As Double
54             Return Math.PI * mRadius ^ 2
55          End Function ' Area
56
57          ' return String representation of CCircle4
58          Public Overrides Function ToString() As String
59
60             ' use MyBase reference to return CPoint String representation
61             Return "Center= " & MyBase.ToString() & _
62                "; Radius = " & mRadius
63          End Function ' ToString
64
65       End Class ' CCircle4
```

Fig. 9.12 CCircle4 class that inherits from class CPoint, which does not provide Protected data (part 2 of 2).

For the purpose of this example, to demonstrate both explicit and implicit calls to base-class constructors, we include a second constructor that calls the base-class constructor explicitly. Lines 17–23 declare the **CCircle4** constructor that invokes the second **CPoint** constructor explicitly using the *base-class constructor-call syntax* (i.e., reference **MyBase** followed by a set of parentheses containing the arguments to the base-class constructor). In this case, **xValue** and **yValue** are passed to initialize the base-class members **mX** and **mY**. The insertion of the **MyBase** reference followed by the dot operator accesses the base-class version of that method—in this constructor, **MyBase.New** invokes the **CPoint** constructor explicitly (line 21). By making this explicit call, we can initialize **mX** and **mY** to specific values, rather than to **0**. When calling the base-class constructor explicitly, the call to the base-class constructor must be the first statement in the derived-class-constructor definition.

Common Programming Error 9.2

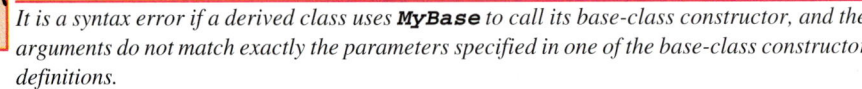

*It is a syntax error if a derived class uses **MyBase** to call its base-class constructor, and the arguments do not match exactly the parameters specified in one of the base-class constructor definitions.*

Class **CCircle4**'s **ToString** method (line 58–63) overrides class **CPoint**'s **ToString** method (lines 54–56 of Fig. 9.4). As we discussed earlier, overriding this method is possible, because method **ToString** of class **System.Object** (class **CPoint**'s base class) is declared **Overridable**. Method **ToString** of class **CCircle4** displays the **Private** instance variables **mX** and **mY** of class **CPoint** by calling the base class's **ToString** method (in this case, **CPoint**'s **ToString** method). The call is made in line 61 via the expression **MyBase.ToString** and causes the values of **mX** and **mY** to become part of the **CCircle4**'s **String** representation. Using this approach is a good software engineering practice: Recall that *Software Engineering Observation* 8.11 stated that, if an object's method performs the actions needed by another object, call that method rather than duplicating its code body. Duplicate code creates code-maintenance problems. By having **CCircle4**'s **ToString** method use the formatting provided by **CPoint**'s **ToString** method, we prevent the need to duplicate code. Also, **CPoint**'s **ToString** method performs part of the task of **CCircle4**'s **ToString** method, so we call **CPoint**'s **ToString** method from class **CCircle4** with the expression **MyBase.ToString**.

Software Engineering Observation 9.7

A redefinition in a derived class of a base-class method that uses a different signature than that of the base-class method is method overloading rather than method overriding.

Software Engineering Observation 9.8

*Although method **ToString** could be overridden to perform several actions that do not pertain to returning a **String**, the general understanding in the Visual Basic .NET community is that method **ToString** should be overridden to obtain an object's **String** representation.*

Good Programming Practice 9.1

*Each class should override method **ToString**, so that it returns useful information about objects of that class.*

Module **modCircleTest4** (Fig. 9.13) performs identical manipulations on class **CCircle4** as did modules **modCircleTest** (Fig. 9.7) and **modCircleTest3** (Fig. 9.11). Note that the outputs of all three modules are identical. Therefore, although each "circle" class appears to behave identically, class **CCircle4** is the most properly engineered. Using inheritance, we have constructed a class that has a strong commitment to **Private** data, in which a change in **CPoint**'s implementation does not affect class **CCircle4**.

```vb
1   ' Fig. 9.13: CircleTest4.vb
2   ' Testing class CCircle4.
3
4   Imports System.Windows.Forms
5
6   Module modCircleTest4
7
8      Sub Main()
9         Dim circle As CCircle4
10        Dim output As String
11
12        circle = New CCircle4(37, 43, 2.5) ' instantiate CCircle4
13
```

Fig. 9.13 **modCircleTest4** demonstrates class **CCircle4** functionality (part 1 of 2).

```vb
14         ' get CCircle4's initial x-y coordinates and radius
15         output = "X coordinate is " & circle.X & vbCrLf & _
16            "Y coordinate is " & circle.Y & vbCrLf & "Radius is " & _
17            circle.Radius
18
19         ' set CCircle4's x-y coordinates and radius to new values
20         circle.X = 2
21         circle.Y = 2
22         circle.Radius = 4.25
23
24         ' display CCircle4's String representation
25         output &= vbCrLf & vbCrLf & _
26            "The new location and radius of circle are " & _
27            vbCrLf & circle.ToString() & vbCrLf
28
29         ' display CCircle4's diameter
30         output &= "Diameter is " & _
31            String.Format("{0:F}", circle.Diameter()) & vbCrLf
32
33         ' display CCircle4's circumference
34         output &= "Circumference is " & _
35            String.Format("{0:F}", circle.Circumference()) & vbCrLf
36
37         ' display CCircle4's area
38         output &= "Area is " & String.Format("{0:F}", circle.Area())
39
40         MessageBox.Show(output, "Demonstrating Class CCircle4")
41      End Sub ' Main
42
43   End Module ' modCircleTest4
```

```
Demonstrating Class CCircle4

X coordinate is 37
Y coordinate is 43
Radius is 2.5

The new location and radius of circle are
Center = [2, 2]; Radius = 4.25
Diameter is 8.50
Circumference is 26.70
Area is 56.75

        OK
```

Fig. 9.13 modCircleTest4 demonstrates class CCircle4 functionality (part 2 of 2).

9.5 Case Study: Three-Level Inheritance Hierarchy

Let us consider a substantial inheritance example, in which we study a point-circle-cylinder hierarchy. In Section 9.4, we developed classes **CPoint** (Fig. 9.4) and **CCircle4** (Fig. 9.12). Now, we present an example in which we derive class **CCylinder** from class **CCircle4**.

The first class that we use in our case study is class **CPoint** (Fig. 9.4). We declared **CPoint**'s instance variables as **Private**. Class **CPoint** also contains properties **X** and **Y** for accessing **mX** and **mY** and method **ToString** (which **CPoint** overrides from class **Object**) for obtaining a **String** representation of the *x-y* coordinate pair.

We also created class **CCircle4** (Fig. 9.12), which inherits from class **CPoint**. Class **CCircle4** contains the **CPoint** functionality, in addition to providing property **Radius**, which ensures that the **mRadius** member variable cannot hold a negative value, and methods **Diameter**, **Circumference**, **Area** and **ToString**. Recall that method **Area** was declared **Overridable** (line 53). As we discussed in Section 9.4, this keyword enables derived classes to override a base-class method. Derived classes of class **CCircle4** (such as class **CCylinder**, which we introduce momentarily) can override these methods and provide specific implementations. A circle has an area that is calculated by the equation

$$\pi r^2$$

in which *r* represents the circle's radius. However, a cylinder has a surface area that is calculated by a different equation:

$$(2\pi r^2) + (2\pi r h)$$

in which *r* represents the cylinder's radius and *h* represents the cylinder's height. Therefore, class **CCylinder** must override method **Area** to include this calculation, so we declared class **CCircle4**'s method **Area** as **Overridable**.

Figure 9.14 presents class **CCylinder**, which inherits from class **CCircle4** (line 5). Class **CCylinder**'s **Public** services include the inherited **CCircle4** methods **Diameter**, **Circumference**, **Area** and **ToString**; the inherited **CCircle4** property **Radius**; the indirectly inherited **CPoint** properties **X** and **Y**; the **CCylinder** constructor, property **Height** and method **Volume**. Method **Area** (lines 43–45) overrides method **Area** of class **CCircle4**. Note that, if class **CCylinder** were to attempt to override **CCircle4**'s methods **Diameter** and **Circumference**, syntax errors would occur, because class **CCircle4** did not declare these methods **Overridable**. Method **ToString** (lines 53–55) overrides method **ToString** of class **CCircle4** to obtain a **String** representation for the cylinder. Class **CCylinder** also includes method **Volume** (lines 48–50) to calculate the cylinder's volume. Because we do not declare method **Volume** as **Overridable**, no derived class of class **CCylinder** can override this method.

```
1   ' Fig. 9.14: Cylinder.vb
2   ' CCylinder class inherits from class CCircle4.
3
4   Public Class CCylinder
5      Inherits CCircle4
6
7      Protected mHeight As Double
```

Fig. 9.14 **CCylinder** class inherits from class **CCircle4** and **Overrides** method **Area** (part 1 of 2).

```vb
 8
 9        ' default constructor
10        Public Sub New()
11           Height = 0
12        End Sub ' New
13
14        ' four-argument constructor
15        Public Sub New(ByVal xValue As Integer, _
16           ByVal yValue As Integer, ByVal radiusValue As Double, _
17           ByVal heightValue As Double)
18
19           ' explicit call to CCircle4 constructor
20           MyBase.New(xValue, yValue, radiusValue)
21           Height = heightValue ' set CCylinder height
22        End Sub ' New
23
24        ' property Height
25        Public Property Height() As Double
26
27           Get
28              Return mHeight
29           End Get
30
31           ' set CCylinder height if argument value is positive
32           Set(ByVal heightValue As Double)
33
34              If heightValue >= 0 Then
35                 mHeight = heightValue
36              End If
37
38           End Set
39
40        End Property ' Height
41
42        ' override method Area to calculate CCylinder area
43        Public Overrides Function Area() As Double
44           Return 2 * MyBase.Area + MyBase.Circumference * mHeight
45        End Function ' Area
46
47        ' calculate CCylinder volume
48        Public Function Volume() As Double
49           Return MyBase.Area * mHeight
50        End Function ' Volume
51
52        ' convert CCylinder to String
53        Public Overrides Function ToString() As String
54           Return MyBase.ToString() & "; Height = " & mHeight
55        End Function ' ToString
56
57     End Class ' CCylinder
```

Fig. 9.14 **CCylinder** class inherits from class **CCircle4** and **Overrides** method **Area** (part 2 of 2).

Figure 9.15 is a **modCylinderTest** application that tests the **CCylinder** class. Line 11 instantiates an object of class **CCylinder**. Lines 15–17 use properties **X**, **Y**, **Radius** and **Height** to obtain information about the **CCylinder** object, because **modCylinderTest** cannot reference the **Private** data of class **CCylinder** directly. Lines 20–23 use properties **X**, **Y**, **Height** and **Radius** to reset the **CCylinder**'s *x-y* coordinates (we assume the cylinder's *x-y* coordinates specify its position on the *x-y* plane), height and radius. Class **CCylinder** can use class **CPoint**'s **X** and **Y** properties, because class **CCylinder** inherits them indirectly from class **CPoint**—Class **CCylinder** inherits properties **X** and **Y** directly from class **CCircle4**, which inherited them directly from class **CPoint**. Line 28 invokes method **ToString** to obtain the **String** representation of the **CCylinder** object. Lines 32–36 invoke methods **Diameter** and **Circumference** of the **CCylinder** object—because class **CCylinder** inherits these methods from class **CCircle4** but cannot override them, these methods, as listed in **CCircle4**, are invoked. Lines 40–44 invoke methods **Area** and **Volume**.

Using the point-circle-cylinder example, we have shown the use and benefits of inheritance. We were able to develop classes **CCircle4** and **CCylinder** using inheritance much faster than if we had developed these classes by duplicating code. Inheritance avoids duplicating code and therefore helps avoid code-maintenance problems.

```vb
1   ' Fig. 9.15: CylinderTest.vb
2   ' Tests class CCylinder.
3
4   Imports System.Windows.Forms
5
6   Module modCylinderTest
7
8      Sub Main()
9
10        ' instantiate object of class CCylinder
11        Dim cylinder As New CCylinder(12, 23, 2.5, 5.7)
12        Dim output As String
13
14        ' properties get initial x-y coordinate, radius and height
15        output = "X coordinate is " & cylinder.X & vbCrLf & _
16           "Y coordinate is " & cylinder.Y & vbCrLf & "Radius is " & _
17           cylinder.Radius & vbCrLf & "Height is " & cylinder.Height
18
19        ' properties set new x-y coordinate, radius and height
20        cylinder.X = 2
21        cylinder.Y = 2
22        cylinder.Height = 10
23        cylinder.Radius = 4.25
24
25        ' get new x-y coordinate and radius
26        output &= vbCrLf & vbCrLf & "The new location, radius " & _
27           "and height of cylinder are" & vbCrLf & "Center = [" & _
28           cylinder.ToString() & vbCrLf & vbCrLf
29
```

Fig. 9.15 Testing class **CCylinder** (part 1 of 2).

```vbnet
30          ' display CCylinder's diameter
31          output &= "Diameter is " & _
32             String.Format("{0:F}", cylinder.Diameter()) & vbCrLf
33
34          ' display CCylinder's circumference
35          output &= "Circumference is " & _
36             String.Format("{0:F}", cylinder.Circumference()) & vbCrLf
37
38          ' display CCylinder's area
39          output &= "Area is " & _
40             String.Format("{0:F}", cylinder.Area()) & vbCrLf
41
42          ' display CCylinder's volume
43          output &= "Volume is " & _
44             String.Format("{0:F}", cylinder.Volume())
45
46          MessageBox.Show(output, "Demonstrating Class CCylinder")
47       End Sub ' Main
48
49    End Module ' modCylinderTest
```

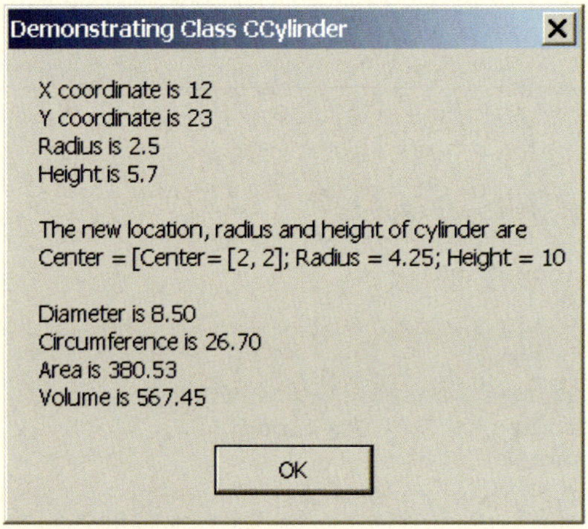

Demonstrating Class CCylinder

X coordinate is 12
Y coordinate is 23
Radius is 2.5
Height is 5.7

The new location, radius and height of cylinder are
Center = [Center= [2, 2]; Radius = 4.25; Height = 10

Diameter is 8.50
Circumference is 26.70
Area is 380.53
Volume is 567.45

OK

Fig. 9.15 Testing class **CCylinder** (part 2 of 2).

9.6 Constructors and Finalizers in Derived Classes

As we explained in the previous section, instantiating a derived-class object begins a chain of constructor calls in which the derived-class constructor, before performing its own tasks, invokes the base-class constructor either explicitly or implicitly. Similarly, if the base-class was derived from another class, the base-class constructor must invoke the constructor of the next class up in the hierarchy, and so on. The last constructor called in the chain is class **Object**'s constructor whose body actually finishes executing first—the original derived class's body finishes executing last. Each base-class constructor initializes the base-class instance variables that the derived-class object inherits. For example, consider the **CPoint/CCircle4** hierarchy from Fig. 9.4 and Fig. 9.12. When a program creates a **CCircle4** object, one of the **CCircle4** constructors is called. That

Chapter 9 Object-Oriented Programming: Inheritance 377

constructor calls class **CPoint**'s constructor, which in turn calls class **Object**'s constructor. When class **Object**'s constructor completes execution, it returns control to class **CPoint**'s constructor, which initializes the *x-y* coordinates of **CCircle4**. When class **CPoint**'s constructor completes execution, it returns control to class **CCircle4**'s constructor, which initializes the **CCircle4**'s radius.

Software Engineering Observation 9.9

When a program creates a derived-class object, the derived-class constructor calls the base-class constructor, the base-class constructor executes, then the remainder of the derived-class constructor's body executes.

When the garbage collector removes an object from memory, the garbage collector calls that object's finalizer method. This begins a chain of finalizer calls in which the derived-class finalizer and the finalizers of the direct and indirect base classes execute in the reverse order of the constructors. Executing the finalizer method should free all resources acquired by the object before the garbage collector reclaims the memory for that object. When the garbage collector calls an object's finalizer, the finalizer performs its task. Then, the programmer can use keyword **MyBase** to invoke the finalizer of the base class.

We discussed in Chapter 8 that class **Object** defines **Protected Overridable** method **Finalize**, which is the finalizer for a Visual Basic object. Because all Visual Basic classes inherit from class **Object** (either directly or indirectly), these classes inherit method **Finalize** and can *override* it to free resources specific to those objects. Although we cannot determine exactly when a **Finalize** call occurs (because we cannot determine exactly when garbage collection occurs), we still are able to specify code to execute before the garbage collector removes an object from memory.

Our next example revisits the point-circle hierarchy by defining versions of class **CPoint3** (Fig. 9.16) and class **CCircle5** (Fig. 9.17) that contain constructors *and* finalizers, each of which prints a message when it runs.

Class **CPoint3** (Fig. 9.16) contains the features as shown in Fig. 9.4, and we modified the two constructors (lines 10–16 and 19–26) to output a line of text when they are called and added method **Finalize** (lines 29–32) that also outputs a line of text when it is called. Each output statement (lines 15, 25 and 30) adds reference **Me** to the output string. This implicitly invokes the class's **ToString** method to obtain the **String** representation of **CPoint3**'s coordinates.

Because constructors are not inherited, lines 12 and 22 make implicit calls to the **Object** constructor. However, method **Finalize** is inherited and overridden from class **Object**, so line 31 uses reference **MyBase** to call the **Object** base-class method **Finalize** explicitly. If we omitted line 31, the **Object**'s **Finalize** method would not get called.

Class **CCircle5** (Fig. 9.17) contains the features in Fig. 9.8, and we modified the two constructors (lines 10–15 and 18–25) to output a line of text when they are called. We also added method **Finalize** (lines 28–31) that also outputs a line of text when it is called. Note again that line 30 uses **MyBase** to invoke **CPoint3**'s **Finalize** method explicitly—this method is not called if we omit this line. Each output statement (lines 14, 24 and 29) adds reference **Me** to the output string. This implicitly invokes the **CCircle5**'s **ToString** method to obtain the **String** representation of **CCircle5**'s coordinates and radius.

```vb
1   ' Fig. 9.16: Point3.vb
2   ' CPoint3 class represents an x-y coordinate pair.
3
4   Public Class CPoint3
5
6      ' point coordinate
7      Private mX, mY As Integer
8
9      ' default constructor
10     Public Sub New()
11
12        ' implicit call to Object constructor occurs here
13        X = 0
14        Y = 0
15        Console.Writeline("CPoint3 constructor: {0}", Me)
16     End Sub ' New
17
18     ' constructor
19     Public Sub New(ByVal xValue As Integer, _
20        ByVal yValue As Integer)
21
22        ' implicit call to Object constructor occurs here
23        X = xValue
24        Y = yValue
25        Console.Writeline("CPoint3 constructor: {0}", Me)
26     End Sub ' New
27
28     ' finalizer overrides version in class Object
29     Protected Overrides Sub Finalize()
30        Console.Writeline("CPoint3 Finalizer: {0}", Me)
31        MyBase.Finalize() ' call Object finalizer
32     End Sub ' Finalize
33
34     ' property X
35     Public Property X() As Integer
36
37        Get
38           Return mX
39        End Get
40
41        Set(ByVal xValue As Integer)
42           mX = xValue ' no need for validation
43        End Set
44
45     End Property ' X
46
47     ' property Y
48     Public Property Y() As Integer
49
50        Get
51           Return mY
52        End Get
53
```

Fig. 9.16 `CPoint3` base class contains constructors and finalizer (part 1 of 2).

```vbnet
54          Set(ByVal yValue As Integer)
55              mY = yValue ' no need for validation
56          End Set
57
58      End Property ' Y
59
60      ' return String representation of CPoint3
61      Public Overrides Function ToString() As String
62          Return "[" & mX & ", " & mY & "]"
63      End Function ' ToString
64
65  End Class ' CPoint3
```

Fig. 9.16 **CPoint3** base class contains constructors and finalizer (part 2 of 2).

Module **modConstructorAndFinalizer** (Fig. 9.18) demonstrates the order in which constructors and finalizers are called for objects of classes that are part of an inheritance class hierarchy. Method **Main** (lines 7–17) begins by instantiating an object of class **CCircle5**, then assigns it to reference **circle1** (line 10). This invokes the **CCircle5** constructor, which invokes the **CPoint3** constructor immediately. Then, the **CPoint3** constructor invokes the **Object** constructor. When the **Object** constructor (which does not print anything) returns control to the **CPoint3** constructor, the **CPoint3** constructor initializes the *x-y* coordinates, then outputs a **String** indicating that the **CPoint3** constructor was called. The output statement also calls method **ToString** implicitly (using reference **Me**) to obtain the **String** representation of the object being constructed. Then, control returns to the **CCircle5** constructor, which initializes the radius and outputs the **CCircle5**'s *x-y* coordinates and radius by calling method **ToString** implicitly.

Notice that the first two lines of the output from this program contain values for the *x-y* coordinate and the radius of the **CCircle5**. When constructing a **CCircle5** object, the **Me** reference used in the body of both the **CCircle5** and **CPoint3** constructors refers to the **CCircle5** object being constructed. When a program invokes method **ToString** on an object, the version of **ToString** that executes is always the version defined in that object's class. Because reference **Me** refers to the current **CCircle5** object being constructed, **CCircle5**'s **ToString** method executes even when **ToString** is invoked from the body of class **CPoint3**'s constructor. [*Note*: This would not be the case if the **CPoint3** constructor were called to initialize a new **CPoint3** object.] When the **CPoint3** constructor invokes method **ToString** for the **CCircle5** being constructed, the program displays **0** for the **mRadius** value, because the **CCircle5** constructor's body has not yet initialized the **mRadius**. Remember that **0** is the default value of a **Double** variable. The second line of output shows the proper **mRadius** value (**4.5**), because that line is output after the **mRadius** is initialized.

```vbnet
1   ' Fig. 9.17: Circle5.vb
2   ' CCircle5 class that inherits from class CPoint3.
3
```

Fig. 9.17 **CCircle5** class inherits from class **CPoint3** and overrides a finalizer method (part 1 of 3).

```vbnet
4   Public Class CCircle5
5      Inherits CPoint3 ' CCircle5 Inherits from class CPoint3
6
7      Private mRadius As Double
8
9      ' default constructor
10     Public Sub New()
11
12        ' implicit call to CPoint3 constructor occurs here
13        Radius = 0
14        Console.WriteLine("CCircle5 constructor: {0}", Me)
15     End Sub ' New
16
17     ' constructor
18     Public Sub New(ByVal xValue As Integer, _
19        ByVal yValue As Integer, ByVal radiusValue As Double)
20
21        ' use MyBase reference to CPoint3 constructor explicitly
22        MyBase.New(xValue, yValue)
23        Radius = radiusValue
24        Console.WriteLine("CCircle5 constructor: {0}", Me)
25     End Sub ' New
26
27     ' finalizer overrides version in class CPoint3
28     Protected Overrides Sub Finalize()
29        Console.Writeline("CCircle5 Finalizer: {0}", Me)
30        MyBase.Finalize() ' call CPoint3 finalizer
31     End Sub ' Finalize
32
33     ' property Radius
34     Public Property Radius() As Double
35
36        Get
37           Return mRadius
38        End Get
39
40        Set(ByVal radiusValue As Double)
41
42           If radiusValue > 0
43              mRadius = radiusValue
44           End If
45
46        End Set
47
48     End Property ' Radius
49
50     ' calculate CCircle5 diameter
51     Public Function Diameter() As Double
52        Return mRadius * 2
53     End Function ' Diameter
54
```

Fig. 9.17 `CCircle5` class inherits from class `CPoint3` and overrides a finalizer method (part 2 of 3).

```
55        ' calculate CCircle5 circumference
56        Public Function Circumference() As Double
57           Return Math.PI * Diameter()
58        End Function ' Circumference
59
60        ' calculate CCircle5 area
61        Public Overridable Function Area() As Double
62           Return Math.PI * mRadius ^ 2
63        End Function ' Area
64
65        ' return String representation of CCircle5
66        Public Overrides Function ToString() As String
67
68           ' use MyBase reference to return CPoint3 String
69           Return "Center = " & MyBase.ToString() & _
70              "; Radius = " & mRadius
71        End Function ' ToString
72
73     End Class ' CCircle5
```

Fig. 9.17 CCircle5 class inherits from class CPoint3 and overrides a finalizer method (part 3 of 3).

Line 11 instantiates an object of class **CCircle5**, then assigns it to reference **circle2**. Again, this begins the chain of constructor calls in which the **CCircle5** constructor, the **CCircle5** constructor and the **Object** constructor are called. In the output, notice that the body of the **CPoint3** constructor executes before the body of the **CCircle5** constructor. This demonstrates that objects are constructed "inside out" (i.e., the base-class constructor is called first).

Lines 13–14 set references **circle1** and **circle2** to **Nothing**. This removes the only references to the two **CCircle5** objects in the program. Thus, the garbage collector can release the memory that these objects occupy. Remember that we cannot guarantee when the garbage collector executes, nor can we guarantee that it collects all available objects when it does execute. To demonstrate the finalizer calls for the two **CCircle5** objects, line 16 invokes class **GC**'s method **Collect** to request the garbage collector to run. Notice that each **CCircle5** object's finalizer outputs information before calling class **CPoint3**'s **Finalize** method. Objects are finalized "outside in" (i.e., the derived-class finalizer completes its tasks before calling the base-class finalizer).

```
1  ' Fig. 9.18: ConstructorAndFinalizer.vb
2  ' Display order in which base-class and derived-class constructors
3  ' and finalizers are called.
4
5  Module modConstructorAndFinalizer
6
7     Sub Main()
8        Dim circle1, circle2 As CCircle5
9
```

Fig. 9.18 Demonstrating order in which constructors and finalizers are called (part 1 of 2).

```
10          circle1 = New CCircle5(72, 29, 4.5) ' instantiate objects
11          circle2 = New CCircle5(5, 5, 10)
12
13          circle1 = Nothing ' mark objects for garbage collection
14          circle2 = Nothing
15
16          System.GC.Collect() ' request garbage collector to execute
17       End Sub ' Main
18
19    End Module ' modConstructorAndFinalizer
```

```
CPoint3 constructor: Center = [72, 29]; Radius = 0
CCircle5 constructor: Center = [72, 29]; Radius = 4.5
CPoint3 constructor: Center = [5, 5]; Radius = 0
CCircle5 constructor: Center = [5, 5]; Radius = 10
CCircle5 Finalizer: Center = [5, 5]; Radius = 10
CPoint3 Finalizer: Center = [5, 5]; Radius = 10
CCircle5 Finalizer: Center = [72, 29]; Radius = 4.5
CPoint3 Finalizer: Center = [72, 29]; Radius = 4.5
```

Fig. 9.18 Demonstrating order in which constructors and finalizers are called (part 2 of 2).

Software Engineering Observation 9.10

*The last statement in a **Finalize** method of a derived class should invoke the base class's **Finalize** method (via keyword **MyBase**) to free any base-class resources.*

Common Programming Error 9.3

*When a base-class method is overridden in a derived class, the derived-class version often calls the base-class version to do additional work. Failure to use the **MyBase** reference when referencing the base class's method causes infinite recursion, because the derived-class method would then call itself.*

Common Programming Error 9.4

*The use of "chained" **MyBase** references to refer to a member (a method, property or variable) several levels up the hierarchy (as in **MyBase.MyBase.mX**) is a syntax error.*

9.7 Software Engineering with Inheritance

In this section, we discuss the use of inheritance to customize existing software. When we use inheritance to create a class from an existing one, the new class inherits the member variables, properties and methods of the existing class. Once the class is created, we can customize it to meet our needs both by including additional member variables, properties and methods, and by overriding base-class members.

Sometimes, it is difficult for students to appreciate the scope of problems faced by designers who work on large-scale software projects in industry. People experienced with such projects invariably say that practicing software reuse improves the software-development process. Object-oriented programming facilitates the reuse of software, thus shortening development times.

Visual Basic encourages software reuse by providing substantial class libraries, which deliver the maximum benefits of software reuse through inheritance. As interest in Visual Basic grows (it is already the world's most widely used programming language), interest in Visual Basic .NET class libraries also increases. There is a worldwide commitment to the continued evolution of Visual Basic .NET class libraries for a wide variety of applications.

Software Engineering Observation 9.11
At the design stage in an object-oriented system, the designer often determines that certain classes are closely related. The designer should "factor out" common attributes and behaviors and place these in a base class. Then, use inheritance to form derived classes, endowing them with capabilities beyond those inherited from the base class.

Software Engineering Observation 9.12
The creation of a derived class does not affect its base class' source code. Inheritance preserves the integrity of a base class.

Software Engineering Observation 9.13
Just as designers of non-object-oriented systems should avoid proliferation of functions, designers of object-oriented systems should avoid proliferation of classes. Proliferation of classes creates management problems and can hinder software reusability, because it becomes difficult for a client to locate the most appropriate class of a huge class library. The alternative is to create fewer classes, in which each provides more substantial functionality, but such classes might provide too much functionality.

Performance Tip 9.1
If classes produced through inheritance are larger than they need to be (i.e., contain too much functionality), memory and processing resources might be wasted. Inherit from the class whose functionality is "closest" to what is needed.

Reading derived-class definitions can be confusing, because inherited members are not shown physically in the derived class, but nevertheless are present in the derived classes. A similar problem exists when documenting derived class members.

In this chapter, we introduced inheritance—the ability to create classes by absorbing an existing class's data members and behaviors and embellishing these with new capabilities. In Chapter 10, we build upon our discussion of inheritance by introducing *polymorphism*—an object-oriented technique that enables us to write programs that handle, in a more general manner, a wide variety of classes related by inheritance. After studying Chapter 10, you will be familiar with encapsulation, inheritance and polymorphism—the most crucial aspects of object-oriented programming.

SUMMARY

- Software reusability reduces program-development time.
- The direct base class of a derived class is the base class from which the derived class inherits (via keyword **Inherits**). An indirect base class of a derived class is two or more levels up the class hierarchy from that derived class.
- With single inheritance, a class is derived from one base class. Visual Basic does not support multiple inheritance (i.e., deriving a class from more than one direct base class).
- Because a derived class can include its own class variables, properties and methods, a derived class is often larger than its base class.

- A derived class is more specific than its base class and represents a smaller group of objects.
- Every object of a derived class is also an object of that class's base class. However, base-class objects are not objects of that class's derived classes.
- Derived-class methods and properties can access **Protected** base-class members directly.
- An "is-a" relationship represents inheritance. In an "is-a" relationship, an object of a derived class also can be treated as an object of its base class.
- A "has-a" relationship represents composition. In a "has-a" relationship, a class object has references to one or more objects of other classes as members.
- A derived class cannot access **Private** members of its base class directly.
- A derived class can access the **Public**, **Protected** and **Friend** members of its base class if the derived class is in the same assembly as the base class.
- When a base-class member is inappropriate for a derived class, that member can be overridden (redefined) in the derived class with an appropriate implementation.
- Inheritance relationships form tree-like hierarchical structures. A class exists in a hierarchical relationship with its derived classes.
- It is possible to treat base-class objects and derived-class objects similarly; the commonality shared between the object types is expressed in the member variables, properties and methods of the base class.
- A base class's **Public** members are accessible anywhere that the program has a reference to an object of that base class or to an object of one of that base class's derived classes.
- A base class's **Private** members are accessible only within the definition of that base class.
- A base class's **Protected** members have an intermediate level of protection between **Public** and **Private** access. A base class's **Protected** members can be accessed only in that base class or in any classes derived from that base class.
- A base class's **Friend** members can be accessed only by objects in the same assembly.
- Unfortunately, the inclusion of **Protected** instance variables often yields two major problems. First, the derived-class object does not have to use a property to set the value of the base-class's **Protected** data. Second, derived class methods are more likely to be written to depend on base-class implementation.
- Visual Basic rigidly enforces restriction on accessing **Private** data members, so that even derived classes (i.e,. which are closely related to their base class) cannot access base-class **Private** data.
- When a derived-class method overrides a base-class method, the base-class method can be accessed from the derived class by preceding the base-class method name with the **MyBase** reference, followed by the dot operator (**.**).
- A derived class can redefine a base-class method using the same signature; this is called *overriding* that base-class method.
- When the method is mentioned by name in the derived class, the derived-class version is called.
- When an object of a derived class is instantiated, the base class's constructor is called immediately (either explicitly or implicitly) to do any necessary initialization of the base-class instance variables in the derived-class object (before the derived classes instance variable are initialized).
- Declaring data variables as **Private**, while providing non-**Private** properties to manipulate and perform validation checking on this data, enforces good software engineering.

- If an object's method/property performs the actions needed by another object, call that method/property rather than duplicating its code body. Duplicated code creates code-maintenance problems
- An explicit call to a base-class constructor (via the **MyBase** reference) can be provided in the derived-class constructor. Otherwise, the derived-class constructor calls the base-class default constructor (or no-argument constructor) implicitly.
- Base-class constructors are not inherited by derived classes.

TERMINOLOGY

abstraction
base class
base-class constructor
base-class default constructor
base-class finalizer
base-class object
base-class reference
behavior
class library
composition
constructor
data abstraction
default constructor
derived class
derived-class constructor
derived-class reference
direct base class
dot (`.`) operator
Friend access modifier
Friend member access
garbage collector
"has-a" relationship
hierarchy diagram
indirect base class
information hiding
inheritance
inheritance hierarchy
inherited instance variable
Inherits keyword

instance variable (of an object)
"is-a" relationship
member-access operator
member variable (of a class)
multiple inheritance
MyBase reference
Object class
object of a base class
object of a derived class
object-oriented programming (OOP)
overloaded constructor
overloading
Overridable keyword
Overrides keyword
overriding
overriding a base-class method
overriding a method
Private base-class member
Protected access
Protected base-class member
Protected member of a base class
Protected member of a derived class
Protected variable
Public member of a derived class
reusable component
single inheritance
software reusability
software reuse

SELF-REVIEW EXERCISES

9.1 Fill in the blanks in each of the following statements:
   a) _____ is a form of software reusability in which new classes absorb the data and behaviors of existing classes and embellish these classes with new capabilities.
   b) A base class's _____ members can be accessed only in the base-class definition or in derived-class definitions.
   c) In a(n) _____ relationship, an object of a derived class also can be treated as an object of its base class.
   d) In a(n) _____ relationship, a class object has one or more references to objects of other classes as members.

e) A class exists in a(n) _____ relationship with its derived classes.
f) A base class's _____ members are accessible anywhere that the program has a reference to that base class or to one of its derived classes.
g) A base class's **Protected** access members have a level of protection between those of **Public** and _____ access.
h) A base class's _____ members can be accessed only in the same assembly.
i) When an object of a derived class is instantiated, the base class's _____ is called implicitly or explicitly to do any necessary initialization of the base-class instance variables in the derived-class object.
j) Derived-class constructors can call base-class constructors via the _____ reference.

9.2 State whether each of the following is *true* or *false*. If *false*, explain why.
a) It is possible to treat base-class objects and derived-class objects similarly.
b) Base-class constructors are not inherited by derived classes.
c) The derived-class finalizer method should invoke the base-class finalizer method (as its last action) to release any resources acquired by the base-class portion of the object.
d) A "has-a" relationship is implemented via inheritance.
e) All methods, by default, can be overridden.
f) Method **ToString** of class **System.Object** is declared as **Overridable**.
g) When a derived class redefines a base-class method using the same signature, the derived class is said to overload that base-class method.
h) A **Car** class has an "is a" relationship with its **SteeringWheel** and **Brakes** objects.
i) Inheritance encourages the reuse of proven high-quality software.
j) A module can reference a base-class object's **Protected** members directly.

ANSWERS TO SELF-REVIEW EXERCISES

9.1 a) Inheritance. b) **Protected**. c) "is a." d) "has a." e) hierarchical. f) **Public**. g) **Private**. h) **Friend**. i) constructor. j) **MyBase**.

9.2 a) True. b) True. c) True. d) False. A "has-a" relationship is implemented via composition. An "is-a" relationship is implemented via inheritance. e) False. Overridable methods must be declared as **Overridable** explicitly. f) True. g) False. When a derived class redefines a base-class method using the same signature, the derived class overrides that base-class method. h) False. This is an example of a "has a" relationship. i) True. j) False. A module cannot access **Protected** members directly, and must use the class's **Public** methods and properties to access the data.

EXERCISES

9.3 Many programs written with inheritance could be written with composition instead, and vice versa. Rewrite classes **CPoint**, **CCircle4** and **CCylinder** to use composition, rather than inheritance. After you do this, assess the relative merits of the two approaches for both the **CPoint**, **CCircle4**, **CCylinder** problem, as well as for object-oriented programs in general.

9.4 Some programmers prefer not to use **Protected** access because it breaks the encapsulation of the base class. Discuss the relative merits of using **Protected** access vs. insisting on using **Private** access in base classes.

9.5 Rewrite the case study in Section 9.5 as a **CPoint**, **CSquare**, **CCube** program. Do this two ways—once via inheritance and once via composition.

9.6 Write an inheritance hierarchy for class **CQuadrilateral**, **CTrapezoid**, **CParallelogram**, **CRectangle** and **CSquare**. Use **CQuadrilateral** as the base class of the hierarchy. Make the hierarchy as deep (i.e., as many levels) as possible. The **Private** data of

CQuadrilateral should be the *x-y* coordinate pairs for the four endpoints of the **CQuadrilateral**. Write a program that instantiates objects of each of these classes; also print to the screen that each object was instantiated.

9.7 Modify classes **CPoint**, **CCircle4** and **CCylinder** to contain overridden finalizer methods. Then, modify the program of Fig. 9.18 to demonstrate the order in which constructors and finalizers are invoked in this hierarchy.

9.8 Write down all the shapes you can think of—both two-dimensional and three-dimensional—and form those shapes into a shape hierarchy. Your hierarchy should have base class **CShape** from which class **CTwoDimensionalShape** and class **CThreeDimensionalShape** are derived. Once you have developed the hierarchy, define each of the classes in the hierarchy. We will use this hierarchy in the exercises of Chapter 10 to process all shapes as objects of base-class **CShape**. (This is a technique called polymorphism.)

10

Object-Oriented Programming: Polymorphism

Objectives

- To understand the concept of polymorphism.
- To understand how polymorphism makes systems extensible and maintainable.
- To understand the distinction between abstract classes and concrete classes.
- To learn how to create abstract classes, interfaces and delegates.

*One Ring to rule them all, One Ring to find them,
One Ring to bring them all and in the darkness bind them.*
John Ronald Reuel Tolkien, *The Fellowship of the Ring*

General propositions do not decide concrete cases.
Oliver Wendell Holmes

A philosopher of imposing stature doesn't think in a vacuum. Even his most abstract ideas are, to some extent, conditioned by what is or is not known in the time when he lives.
Alfred North Whitehead

Chapter 10 — Object-Oriented Programming: Polymorphism

Outline

10.1 Introduction
10.2 Derived-Class-Object to Base-Class-Object Conversion
10.3 Type Fields and `Select Case` Statements
10.4 Polymorphism Examples
10.5 Abstract Classes and Methods
10.6 Case Study: Inheriting Interface and Implementation
10.7 `NotInheritable` Classes and `NotOverridable` Methods
10.8 Case Study: Payroll System Using Polymorphism
10.9 Case Study: Creating and Using Interfaces
10.10 Delegates

Summary • Terminology • Self-Review Exercises • Answers to Self-Review Exercises • Exercises

10.1 Introduction

The previous chapter's object-oriented programming (OOP) discussion focussed on one of its key component technologies, inheritance. In this chapter, we continue our study of OOP *polymorphism*. Both inheritance and polymorphism are crucial technologies in the development of complex software. Polymorphism enables us to write programs that handle a wide variety of related classes and facilitates adding new classes and capabilities to a system.

Using polymorphism, it is possible to design and implement systems that are easily extensible. Programs can process objects of all classes in a class hierarchy generically as objects of a common base class. Furthermore, a new class can be added with little or no modification to the generic part of the program, as long as those new classes are part of the inheritance hierarchy that the program generically processes. The only parts of a program that must be altered to accommodate new classes are those program components that require direct knowledge of the new classes that the programmer adds to the hierarchy. In this chapter, we demonstrate two substantial class hierarchies and manipulate objects from those hierarchies polymorphically.

10.2 Derived-Class-Object to Base-Class-Object Conversion

Section 9.4 created a point-circle class hierarchy, in which class **CCircle** inherited from class **CPoint**. The programs that manipulated objects of these classes always used **CPoint** references to refer to **CPoint** objects and **CCircle** references to refer to **CCircle** objects. In this section, we discuss the relationship between classes in a hierarchy that enables a program to assign derived-class objects to base-class references—a fundamental part of programs that process objects polymorphically. This section also discusses explicit casting between types in a class hierarchy.

An object of a derived class can be treated as an object of its base class. This enables various interesting manipulations. For example, a program can create an array of base-class references that refer to objects of many derived-class types. This is allowed despite the fact that the derived-class objects are of different data types. However, the reverse is not true—a base-class object is not an object of any of its derived classes. For example, a **CPoint** is not a **CCircle** based on the hierarchy defined in Chapter 9. If a base-class reference refers to a derived-class object, it is possible to convert the base-class reference to the object's actual data type and manipulate the object as that type.

Common Programming Error 10.1

Treating a base-class object as a derived-class object can cause errors.

The example in Fig. 10.1–Fig. 10.3 demonstrates assigning derived-class objects to base-class references and casting base-class references to derived-class references. Class **CPoint** (Fig. 10.1), which we discussed in Chapter 9, represents an *x-y* coordinate pair. Class **CCircle** (Fig. 10.2), which we also discussed in Chapter 9, represents a circle and inherits from class **CPoint**. Each **CCircle** object "is a" **CPoint** and also has a radius (represented via variable **mRadius**). We declare method **Area** as **Overridable**, so that a derived class (such as class **CCylinder**) can calculate its area. Class **CTest** (Fig. 10.3) demonstrates the assignment and cast operations.

```vb
1    ' Fig. 10.1: Point.vb
2    ' CPoint class represents an x-y coordinate pair.
3
4    Public Class CPoint
5
6       ' point coordinate
7       Private mX, mY As Integer
8
9       ' default constructor
10      Public Sub New()
11
12         ' implicit call to Object constructor occurs here
13         X = 0
14         Y = 0
15      End Sub ' New
16
17      ' constructor
18      Public Sub New(ByVal xValue As Integer, _
19         ByVal yValue As Integer)
20
21         ' implicit call to Object constructor occurs here
22         X = xValue
23         Y = yValue
24      End Sub ' New
25
26      ' property X
27      Public Property X() As Integer
28
29         Get
30            Return mX
31         End Get
32
```

Fig. 10.1 **CPoint** class represents an *x-y* coordinate pair (part 1 of 2).

```vbnet
33         Set(ByVal xValue As Integer)
34            mX = xValue ' no need for validation
35         End Set
36
37      End Property ' X
38
39      ' property Y
40      Public Property Y() As Integer
41
42         Get
43            Return mY
44         End Get
45
46         Set(ByVal yValue As Integer)
47            mY = yValue ' no need for validation
48         End Set
49
50      End Property ' Y
51
52      ' return String representation of CPoint
53      Public Overrides Function ToString() As String
54         Return "[" & mX & ", " & mY & "]"
55      End Function ' ToString
56
57   End Class ' CPoint
```

Fig. 10.1 `CPoint` class represents an *x-y* coordinate pair (part 2 of 2).

```vbnet
1    ' Fig. 10.2: Circle.vb
2    ' CCircle class that inherits from class CPoint.
3
4    Public Class CCircle
5       Inherits CPoint ' CCircle Inherits from class CPoint
6
7       Private mRadius As Double
8
9       ' default constructor
10      Public Sub New()
11
12         ' implicit call to CPoint constructor occurs here
13         Radius = 0
14      End Sub ' New
15
16      ' constructor
17      Public Sub New(ByVal xValue As Integer, _
18         ByVal yValue As Integer, ByVal radiusValue As Double)
19
20         ' use MyBase reference to CPoint constructor explicitly
21         MyBase.New(xValue, yValue)
22         Radius = radiusValue
23      End Sub ' New
24
```

Fig. 10.2 `CCircle` class that inherits from class `CPoint` (part 1 of 2).

```vbnet
25         ' property Radius
26         Public Property Radius() As Double
27
28            Get
29               Return mRadius
30            End Get
31
32            Set(ByVal radiusValue As Double)
33
34               If radiusValue >= 0 ' mRadius must be nonnegative
35                  mRadius = radiusValue
36               End If
37
38            End Set
39
40         End Property ' Radius
41
42         ' calculate CCircle diameter
43         Public Function Diameter() As Double
44            Return mRadius * 2
45         End Function ' Diameter
46
47         ' calculate CCircle circumference
48         Public Function Circumference() As Double
49            Return Math.PI * Diameter()
50         End Function ' Circumference
51
52         ' calculate CCircle area
53         Public Overridable Function Area() As Double
54            Return Math.PI * mRadius ^ 2
55         End Function ' Area
56
57         ' return String representation of CCircle
58         Public Overrides Function ToString() As String
59
60            ' use MyBase reference to return CCircle String representation
61            Return "Center= " & MyBase.ToString() & _
62               "; Radius = " & mRadius
63         End Function ' ToString
64
65      End Class ' CCircle
```

Fig. 10.2 `CCircle` class that inherits from class `CPoint` (part 2 of 2).

Class **CTest** (Fig. 10.3) demonstrates assigning derived-class references to base-class references and casting base-class references to derived-class references. Lines 11–12 declare two **CPoint** references (**point1** and **point2**) and two **CCircle** references (**circle1** and **circle2**). Lines 14–15 assign to **point1** a new **CPoint** object and assign to **circle1** a new **CCircle** object. Lines 17–18 invoke each object's **ToString** method, then append the **String** representations to **String output** to show the values used to initialize each object. Because **point1** is a **CPoint** object, method **ToString** of **point1** prints the object as a **CPoint**. Similarly, because **circle1** is a **CCircle** object, method **ToString** of **circle1** prints the object as a **CCircle**.

```vb
1   ' Fig. 10.3: Test.vb
2   ' Demonstrating inheritance and polymorphism.
3
4   Imports System.Windows.Forms
5
6   Class CTest
7
8      ' demonstrate "is a" relationship
9      Shared Sub Main()
10        Dim output As String
11        Dim point1, point2 As CPoint
12        Dim circle1, circle2 As CCircle
13
14        point1 = New CPoint(30, 50)
15        circle1 = New CCircle(120, 89, 2.7)
16
17        output = "CPoint point1: " & point1.ToString() & _
18           vbCrLf & "CCircle circle1: " & circle1.ToString()
19
20        ' use is-a relationship to assign CCircle to CPoint reference
21        point2 = circle1
22
23        output &= vbCrLf & vbCrLf & _
24           "CCircle circle1 (via point2): " & point2.ToString()
25
26        ' downcast (cast base-class reference to derived-class
27        ' data type) point2 to circle2
28        circle2 = CType(point2, CCircle) ' allowed only via cast
29
30        output &= vbCrLf & vbCrLf & _
31           "CCircle circle1 (via circle2): " & circle2.ToString()
32
33        output &= vbCrLf & "Area of circle1 (via circle2): " & _
34           String.Format("{0:F}", circle2.Area())
35
36        ' assign CPoint object to CCircle reference
37        If (TypeOf point1 Is CCircle) Then
38           circle2 = CType(point1, CCircle)
39           output &= vbCrLf & vbCrLf & "cast successful"
40        Else
41           output &= vbCrLf & vbCrLf & _
42              "point1 does not refer to a CCircle"
43        End If
44
45        MessageBox.Show(output, _
46           "Demonstrating the 'is a' relationship")
47     End Sub ' Main
48
49  End Class ' CTest
```

Fig. 10.3 Assigning derived-class references to base-class references (part 1 of 2).

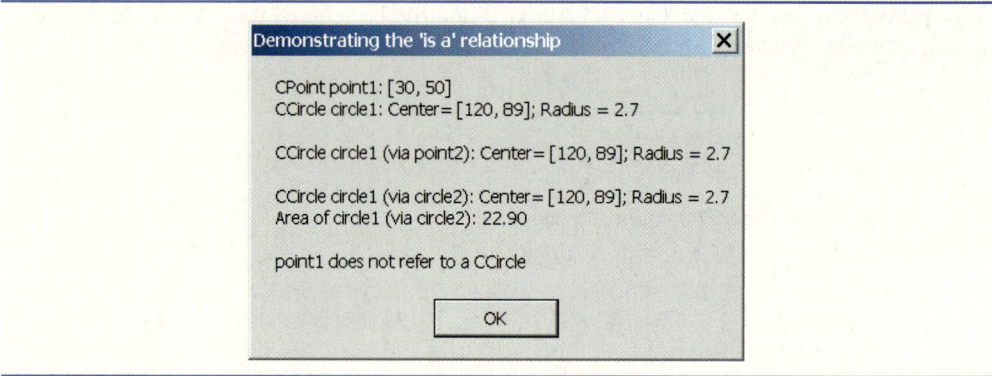

Fig. 10.3 Assigning derived-class references to base-class references (part 2 of 2).

Line 21 assigns **circle1** (a reference to a derived-class object) to **point2** (a base-class reference). In Visual Basic, it is acceptable to assign a derived-class reference to a base-class reference, because of the inheritance "is-a" relationship. A **CCircle** *is a* **CPoint** (in a structural sense, at least), because class **CCircle** inherits from class **CPoint**. However, assigning a base-class reference to a derived-class reference is potentially dangerous, as we will discuss.

Lines 23–24 invoke **point2.ToString** and append the result to **output**. When Visual Basic encounters an **Overridable** method invocation (such as method **ToString**), Visual Basic determines which version of the method to call based on the type of the object on which the method is called, not based on the type of the reference that refers to the object. In this case, **point2** refers to a **CCircle** object, so Visual Basic calls **CCircle** method **ToString** (line 24), rather than calling **CPoint** method **ToString** (as one might expect off the **point2** reference, which was declared as a **CPoint**). The decision of which method to call is an example of *polymorphism*, a concept that we discuss in detail throughout this chapter. Note that, if **point2** referenced a **CPoint** object rather than a **CCircle** object, Visual Basic would invoke **CPoint**'s **ToString** method.

Previous chapters used methods such as **Convert.ToInt32** and **Convert.ToDouble** to convert between various built-in Visual Basic types. Now, we convert between object references of user-defined types. We use method **CType** to perform this conversion, which is known as a *cast*. If the cast is valid, our program can treat a base-class reference as a derived-class reference. If the cast is invalid, Visual Basic throws an **InvalidCastException**, which indicates that the cast operation is not allowed. Exceptions are discussed in detail in Chapter 11, Exception Handling.

Common Programming Error 10.2
Assigning a base-class object (or a base-class reference) to a derived-class reference (without a cast) is a syntax error.

Software Engineering Observation 10.1
If a derived-class object has been assigned to a reference of one of its direct or indirect base classes, it is acceptable to cast that base-class reference back to a reference of the derived-class type. In fact, this must be done to send that object messages that do not appear in the base class. [Note: We sometimes use the term "messages" to represent invoking methods and properties on an object.]

Line 28 casts **point2**, which currently refers to a **CCircle** (**circle1**), to a **CCircle** and assigns the result to **circle2**. As we discuss momentarily, this cast would be dangerous if **point2** were referencing a **CPoint**. Lines 30–31 invoke method **ToString** of the **CCircle** object to which **circle2** now refers (note that the fourth line of the output demonstrates that **CCircle**'s **ToString** method is called). Lines 33–34 calculate **circle2**'s **Area** and format it with method **String.Format**. The format **"{0:F}"** (line 34) specifies the formatting for this number. By default, the number appears with two digits to the right of the decimal point.

Line 38 uses method **CType** to cast **point1** to a **CCircle**. This is a dangerous operation, because point refers to a **CPoint** object and a **CPoint** object is not a **CCircle**. Objects can be cast only to their own type or to their base-class types. If this statement were to execute, Visual Basic would determine that **point1** references a **CPoint** object, recognize the cast to **CCircle** as dangerous and indicate an improper cast with an **InvalidCastException** message. However, we prevent this statement from executing by including the **If/Else** structure (lines 37–43). The condition at line 37 uses operator **TypeOf** to determine whether the object to which **point1** refers "is a" **CCircle**. Operator **TypeOf** determines the type of the object to which **TypeOf**'s operand refers. We then compare that type to **CCircle**. In our example, **point1** does not refer to a **CCircle**, so the condition fails, and lines 41–42 append to **output** a **String** indicating the result. Note that the **Is** comparison will be **True** if the two operands are the same type or if the left operand is a derived-class of the right operand.

Common Programming Error 10.3

*Attempting to cast a base-class reference to a derived-class type causes an **InvalidCastException** if the reference refers to a base-class object rather than a derived-class object.*

If we remove the **If** test and execute the program, Visual Basic displays a **MessageBox** containing the message:

```
An unhandled exception of type 'System.InvalidCastException'
occurred in
```

followed by the name and path of the executing program. We discuss how to deal with this situation in Chapter 11.

Despite the fact that a derived-class object also "is a" base-class object, the derived-class and base-class objects are different. As we have discussed previously, derived-class objects can be treated as if they were base-class objects. This is a logical relationship, because the derived class contains members that correspond to all members in the base class. The derived class can have additional members as well. For this reason, assigning base-class objects to derived-class references is not allowed without an explicit cast (when **Option Strict** is **On**). Such an assignment would leave the additional derived-class members undefined.

There are four ways to mix base-class references and derived-class references with base-class objects and derived-class objects:

1. Referring to a base-class object with a base-class reference is straightforward.
2. Referring to a derived-class object with a derived-class reference is straightforward.

3. Referring to a derived-class object with a base-class reference is safe, because the derived-class object *is an* object of its base class. However, this reference can refer only to base-class members. If this code refers to derived-class-only members through the base-class reference, the compiler reports an error.

4. Referring to a base-class object with a derived-class reference generates a compiler error (when **Option Strict** is **On**). To avoid this error, the derived-class reference first must be cast to a base-class reference. In this cast, the derived-class reference must reference a derived-class object, or Visual Basic generates an **InvalidCastException**.

Common Programming Error 10.4
After assigning a derived-class object to a base-class reference, attempting to reference derived-class-only members with the base-class reference is a syntax error.

Common Programming Error 10.5
Treating a base-class object as a derived-class object can cause errors.

Though it is convenient to treat derived-class objects as base-class objects by manipulating derived-class objects with base-class references, doing so can cause significant problems. For example, in a payroll system we need to be able to walk through an array of employees and calculate the weekly pay for each person. Intuition suggests that using base-class references would enable the program to call only the base-class payroll calculation routine (if there is such a routine in the base class). We need a way to invoke the proper payroll calculation routine for each object, whether it is a base-class object or a derived-class object, and to do this simply by using the base-class reference. We learn how to create classes that include this behavior as we introduce polymorphism throughout this chapter.

10.3 Type Fields and **Select Case** Statements

One way to determine the type of an object that is incorporated in a larger program is to use a **Select Case** statement. This allows us to distinguish among object types, then invoke an appropriate action for a particular object. For example, in a hierarchy of shapes in which each shape object has an **mShapeType** instance variable, a **Select Case** structure could employ the object's **mShapeType** to determine which **Print** method to call.

However, using **Select**-**Case** logic exposes programs to a variety of potential problems. For example, the programmer might forget to include a type test when one is warranted or the programmer might forget to test all possible cases in a **Select Case**. When modifying a **Select**-**Case**-based system by adding new types, the programmer might forget to insert the new cases in all relevant **Select**-**Case** statements. Every addition or deletion of a class requires the modification of every **Select**-**Case** statement in the system; tracking these statements down can be time-consuming and error-prone.

Software Engineering Observation 10.2
*Polymorphic programming can eliminate the need for unnecessary **Select**-**Case** logic. By using Visual Basic's polymorphism mechanism to perform the equivalent logic, programmers can avoid the kinds of errors typically associated with **Select**-**Case** logic.*

Testing and Debugging Tip 10.1

An interesting consequence of using polymorphism is that programs take on a simplified appearance. They contain less branching logic and more simple, sequential code. This simplification facilitates testing, debugging and program maintenance.

10.4 Polymorphism Examples

In this section, we discuss several examples of polymorphism. If class **CRectangle** is derived from class **CQuadrilateral**, then a **CRectangle** object is a more specific version of a **CQuadrilateral** object. Any operation (such as calculating the perimeter or the area) that can be performed on an object of class **CQuadrilateral** also can be performed on an object of class **CRectangle**. Such operations also can be performed on other kinds of **CQuadrilateral**s, such as **CSquare**s, **CParallelogram**s and **CTrapezoid**s. When a program invokes a derived-class method through a base-class (i.e., **CQuadrilateral**) reference, Visual Basic polymorphically chooses the correct overridden method in the derived class from which the object was instantiated. We will soon investigate this behavior in LIVE-CODE™ examples.

Suppose that we design a video game that manipulates objects of many different types, including objects of classes **CMartian**, **CVenutian**, **CPlutonian**, **CSpaceShip** and **CLaserBeam**. Also imagine that each of these classes inherits from the common base class called **CSpaceObject**, which contains a method called **DrawYourself**. Each derived class implements this method. A Visual Basic screen-manager program would maintain a container (such as a **CSpaceObject** array) of references to objects of the various classes. To refresh the screen, the screen manager periodically sends each object the same message—namely, **DrawYourself**. However, each object responds in a unique way. For example, a **CMartian** object draws itself in red with the appropriate number of antennae. A **CSpaceShip** object draws itself as a bright, silver flying saucer. A **CLaserBeam** object draws itself as a bright red beam across the screen. Thus the same message sent to a variety of objects would have "many forms" of results—hence the term *polymorphism*.

A polymorphic screen manager makes it especially easy to add new types of objects to a system with minimal modifications to the system's code. Suppose we want to add class **CMercurian**s to our video game. To do so, we must build a class **CMercurian** that inherits from **CSpaceObject**, but provides its own definition of the **DrawYourself** method. Then, when objects of class **CMercurian** appear in the container, the programmer does not need to alter the screen manager. The screen manager invokes method **DrawYourself** on every object in the container, regardless of the object's type, so the new **CMercurian** objects simply "plug right in." Thus, without modifying the system (other than to build and include the classes themselves), programmers can use polymorphism to include additional types of classes that were not envisioned when the system was created.

With polymorphism, one method call can cause different actions to occur, depending on the type of the object receiving the call. This gives the programmer tremendous expressive capability. In the next several sections, we provide LIVE-CODE™ examples that demonstrate polymorphism.

Software Engineering Observation 10.3

With polymorphism, the programmer can deal in generalities and let the execution-time environment concern itself with the specifics. The programmer can command a wide variety of objects to behave in manners appropriate to those objects, even if the programmer does not know the objects' types.

Software Engineering Observation 10.4

Polymorphism promotes extensibility. Software used to invoke polymorphic behavior is written to be independent of the types of the objects to which messages (i.e., method calls) are sent. Thus, programmers can include into a system additional types of objects that respond to existing messages and can do this without modifying the base system.

10.5 Abstract Classes and Methods

When we think of a class as a type, we assume that programs will create objects of that type. However, there are cases in which it is useful to define classes for which the programmer never intends to instantiate any objects. Such classes are called *abstract classes*. Because such classes are normally used as base classes in inheritance situations, so we normally refer to them as *abstract base classes*. These classes cannot be used to instantiate objects. Abstract classes are incomplete. Derived classes must define the "missing pieces." Abstract classes normally contain one or more *abstract methods* or *abstract properties*, which are methods and properties that do not provide an implementation. Derived classes must override inherited abstract methods and properties to enable objects of those derived classes to be instantiated.

The purpose of an abstract class is to provide an appropriate base class from which other classes may inherit (we will see examples shortly). Classes from which objects can be instantiated are called *concrete classes*. Such classes provide implementations of every method and property they define. We could have an abstract base class **CTwoDimensionalObject** and derive concrete classes, such as **CSquare**, **CCircle**, **CTriangle**. We could also have an abstract base class **CThreeDimensionalObject** and derive such concrete classes as **CCube**, **CSphere** and **CCylinder**. Abstract base classes are too generic to define real objects; we need to be more specific before we can think of instantiating objects. For example, if someone tells you to "draw the shape," what shape would you draw? Concrete classes provide the specifics that make it reasonable to instantiate objects.

A class is made abstract by declaring it with keyword **MustInherit**. A hierarchy does not need to contain any **MustInherit** classes, but as we will see, many good object-oriented systems have class hierarchies headed by **MustInherit** base classes. In some cases, **MustInherit** classes constitute the top few levels of the hierarchy. A good example of this is the shape hierarchy in Fig. 9.3. The hierarchy begins with **MustInherit** (abstract) base-class **CShape**. On the next level of the hierarchy, we have two more **MustInherit** base classes, namely **CTwoDimensionalShape** and **CThreeDimensionalShape**. The next level of the hierarchy would start defining concrete classes for two-dimensional shapes such as **CCircle** and **CSquare** and such three-dimensional shapes such as **CSphere** and **CCube**.

Software Engineering Observation 10.5

*A **MustInherit** class defines a common set of **Public** methods for the various members of a class hierarchy. A **MustInherit** class typically contains one or more abstract methods or properties that derived classes will override. All classes in the hierarchy can use this common set of **Public** methods.*

MustInherit classes must specify their abstract methods or properties. Visual Basic provides keyword **MustOverride** to declare a method or property as abstract. **MustOverride** methods and properties do not provide implementations—attempting to do so is a syntax error. Every derived class must override all base-class **MustOverride** methods and properties (using keyword **Overrides**) and provide concrete implementations of those methods or properties. Any class with a **MustOverride** method in it must be declared **MustInherit**. The difference between a **MustOverride** method and an **Overridable** method is that an **Overridable** method has an implementation and provides the derived class with the option of overriding the method; by contrast, a **MustOverride** method does not provide an implementation and forces the derived class to override the method (for that derived class to be concrete).

Common Programming Error 10.6
*It is a syntax error to define a **MustOverride** method in a class that has not been declared as **MustInherit**.*

Common Programming Error 10.7
*Attempting to instantiate an object of a **MustInherit** class is an error.*

Common Programming Error 10.8
*Failure to override a **MustOverride** method in a derived class is a syntax error, unless the derived class also is a **MustInherit** class.*

Software Engineering Observation 10.6
An abstract class can have instance data and nonabstract methods (including constructors), which are subject to the normal rules of inheritance by derived classes.

Although we cannot instantiate objects of **MustInherit** base classes, we *can* use **MustInherit** base classes to declare references; these references can refer to instances of any concrete classes derived from the **MustInherit** class. Programs can use such references to manipulate instances of the derived classes polymorphically.

Let us consider another application of polymorphism. A screen manager needs to display a variety of objects, including new types of objects that the programmer will add to the system after writing the screen manager. The system might need to display various shapes, such as **CCircle**, **CTriangle** or **CRectangle**, which are derived from **MustInherit** class **CShape**. The screen manager uses base-class references of type **CShape** to manage the objects that are displayed. To draw any object (regardless of the level at which that object's class appears in the inheritance hierarchy), the screen manager uses a base-class reference to the object to invoke the object's **Draw** method. Method **Draw** is a **MustOverride** method in base-class **CShape**; therefore each derived class must override method **Draw**. Each **CShape** object in the inheritance hierarchy knows how to draw itself. The screen manager does not have to worry about the type of each object or whether the screen manager has ever encountered objects of that type.

Polymorphism is particularly effective for implementing layered software systems. In operating systems, for example, each type of physical device could operate quite differently from the others. Even so, commands to *read* or *write* data from and to devices can have a certain uniformity. The write message sent to a device-driver object needs to be interpreted specifically in the context of that device driver and how that device driver manipulates devices of a specific type. However, the write call itself is really no different from the write to any other device in the system—simply place some number of bytes from memory onto that device. An object-oriented operating system might use a **MustInherit** base class to provide an interface appropriate for all device drivers. Then, through inheritance from that **MustInherit** base class, derived classes are formed that all operate similarly. The capabilities (i.e., the **Public** interface) offered by the device drivers are provided as **MustOverride** methods in the **MustInherit** base class. The implementations of these **MustOverride** methods are provided in the derived classes that correspond to the specific types of device drivers.

It is common in object-oriented programming to define an *iterator class* that can walk through all the objects in a container (such as an array). For example, a program can print a list of objects in a linked list by creating an iterator object, then using the iterator to obtain the next element of the list each time the iterator is called. Iterators often are used in polymorphic programming to traverse an array or a linked list of objects from various levels of a hierarchy. The references in such a list are all base-class references. (See Chapter 23, Data Structures, to learn more about linked lists.) A list of objects of base class **CTwoDimensionalShape** could contain objects from classes **CSquare**, **CCircle**, **CTriangle** and so on. Using polymorphism to send a **Draw** message to each object in the list would draw each object correctly on the screen.

10.6 Case Study: Inheriting Interface and Implementation

Our next example (Fig. 10.4–Fig. 10.8) reexamines the **CPoint**, **CCircle**, **CCylinder** hierarchy that we explored in Chapter 9. In this example, the hierarchy begins with **MustInherit** base class **CShape** (Fig. 10.4). This hierarchy mechanically demonstrates the power of polymorphism. In the exercises, we explore a more substantial shape hierarchy.

```
1    ' Fig. 10.4: Shape.vb
2    ' Demonstrate a shape hierarchy using MustInherit class.
3
4    Imports System.Windows.Forms
5
6    Public MustInherit Class CShape
7
8       ' return shape area
9       Public Overridable Function Area() As Double
10         Return 0
11      End Function ' Area
12
13      ' return shape volume
14      Public Overridable Function Volume() As Double
15         Return 0
16      End Function ' Volume
17
18      ' overridable method that should return shape name
19      Public MustOverride ReadOnly Property Name() As String
20
21   End Class ' CShape
```

Fig. 10.4 Abstract **CShape** base class.

Class **CShape** defines two concrete methods and one abstract property. Because all shapes have an area and a volume, we include methods **Area** (lines 9–11) and **Volume** (lines 14–16), which return the shape's area and volume, respectively. The volume of two-dimensional shapes is always zero, whereas three-dimensional shapes have a positive, non-zero volume. In class **CShape**, methods **Area** and **Volume** return zero, by default. Programmers can override these methods in derived classes when those classes should have a different area calculation [e.g., classes **CCircle2** (Fig. 10.6) and **CCylinder2** (Fig. 10.7)] and/or a different volume calculation (e.g., **CCylinder2**). Property **Name** (line 19) is declared as **MustOverride**, so derived classes must override this property to become concrete classes.

Class **CPoint2** (Fig. 10.5) inherits from **MustInherit** class **CShape** and overrides the **MustOverride** property **Name**, which makes **CPoint2** a concrete class. A point's area and volume are zero, so class **CPoint2** does not override base-class methods **Area** and **Volume**. Lines 59–65 implement property **Name**. If we did not provide this implementation, class **CPoint2** would be an abstract class that would require **MustInherit** in the first line of the class definition.

```
1   ' Fig. 10.5: Point2.vb
2   ' CPoint2 class represents an x-y coordinate pair.
3
4   Public Class CPoint2
5      Inherits CShape ' CPoint2 inherits from MustInherit class CShape
6
7      ' point coordinate
8      Private mX, mY As Integer
9
10     ' default constructor
11     Public Sub New()
12
13        ' implicit call to Object constructor occurs here
14        X = 0
15        Y = 0
16     End Sub ' New
17
18     ' constructor
19     Public Sub New(ByVal xValue As Integer, _
20        ByVal yValue As Integer)
21
22        ' implicit call to Object constructor occurs here
23        X = xValue
24        Y = yValue
25     End Sub ' New
26
27     ' property X
28     Public Property X() As Integer
29
30        Get
31           Return mX
32        End Get
```

Fig. 10.5 **CPoint2** class inherits from **MustInherit** class **CShape** (part 1 of 2).

```vbnet
33
34         Set(ByVal xValue As Integer)
35             mX = xValue ' no need for validation
36         End Set
37
38     End Property ' X
39
40     ' property Y
41     Public Property Y() As Integer
42
43         Get
44             Return mY
45         End Get
46
47         Set(ByVal yValue As Integer)
48             mY = yValue ' no need for validation
49         End Set
50
51     End Property ' Y
52
53     ' return String representation of CPoint2
54     Public Overrides Function ToString() As String
55         Return "[" & mX & ", " & mY & "]"
56     End Function ' ToString
57
58     ' implement MustOverride property of class CShape
59     Public Overrides ReadOnly Property Name() As String
60
61         Get
62             Return "CPoint2"
63         End Get
64
65     End Property ' Name
66
67 End Class ' CPoint2
```

Fig. 10.5 `CPoint2` class inherits from `MustInherit` class `CShape` (part 2 of 2).

Figure 10.6 defines class **CCircle2** that inherits from class **CPoint2**. Class **CCircle2** contains member variable **mRadius** and provides property **Radius** (lines 26–40) to access the **mRadius**. Note that we do not declare property **Radius** as **Overridable**, so classes derived from this class cannot override this property. A circle has a volume of zero, so we do not override base-class method **Volume**. Rather, **CCircle2** inherits this method from class **CPoint2**, which inherited the method from **CShape**. However, a circle does have an area, so **CCircle2** overrides **CShape**'s method **Area** (lines 53–55). Property **Name** (lines 66–72) of class **CCircle2** overrides property **Name** of class **CPoint2**. If this class did not override property **Name**, the class would inherit the **CPoint2** version of property **Name**. In that case, **CCircle2**'s **Name** property would erroneously return "**CPoint2**."

```vbnet
1   ' Fig. 10.6: Circle2.vb
2   ' CCircle2 class inherits from CPoint2 and overrides key members.
3
4   Public Class CCircle2
5      Inherits CPoint2 ' CCircle2 Inherits from class CPoint2
6
7      Private mRadius As Double
8
9      ' default constructor
10     Public Sub New()
11
12        ' implicit call to CPoint2 constructor occurs here
13        Radius = 0
14     End Sub ' New
15
16     ' constructor
17     Public Sub New(ByVal xValue As Integer, _
18        ByVal yValue As Integer, ByVal radiusValue As Double)
19
20        ' use MyBase reference to CPoint2 constructor explicitly
21        MyBase.New(xValue, yValue)
22        Radius = radiusValue
23     End Sub ' New
24
25     ' property Radius
26     Public Property Radius() As Double
27
28        Get
29           Return mRadius
30        End Get
31
32        Set(ByVal radiusValue As Double)
33
34           If radiusValue >= 0 ' mRadius must be nonnegative
35              mRadius = radiusValue
36           End If
37
38        End Set
39
40     End Property ' Radius
41
42     ' calculate CCircle2 diameter
43     Public Function Diameter() As Double
44        Return mRadius * 2
45     End Function ' Diameter
46
47     ' calculate CCircle2 circumference
48     Public Function Circumference() As Double
49        Return Math.PI * Diameter()
50     End Function ' Circumference
51
```

Fig. 10.6 CCircle2 class that inherits from class CPoint2 (part 1 of 2).

```vbnet
52     ' calculate CCircle2 area
53     Public Overrides Function Area() As Double
54        Return Math.PI * mRadius ^ 2
55     End Function ' Area
56
57     ' return String representation of CCircle2
58     Public Overrides Function ToString() As String
59
60        ' use MyBase to return CCircle2 String representation
61        Return "Center = " & MyBase.ToString() & _
62           "; Radius = " & mRadius
63     End Function ' ToString
64
65     ' override property Name from class CPoint2
66     Public Overrides ReadOnly Property Name() As String
67
68        Get
69           Return "CCircle2"
70        End Get
71
72     End Property ' Name
73
74  End Class ' CCircle2
```

Fig. 10.6 `CCircle2` class that inherits from class `CPoint2` (part 2 of 2).

Figure 10.7 defines class **CCylinder2** that inherits from class **CCircle2**. Class **CCylinder2** contains member variable **mHeight** and property **Height** (lines 27–42) to access the **mHeight**. Note that we do not declare property **Height** as **Overridable**, so classes derived from class **CCylinder2** cannot override this property. A cylinder has different area and volume calculations than a circle, so this class overrides method **Area** (lines 45–47) to calculate the cylinder's surface area (i.e., $2\pi r^2 + 2\pi rh$) and defines method **Volume** (lines 50–52). Property **Name** (lines 60–66) overrides property **Name** of class **CCircle2**. If this class did not override property **Name**, the class would inherit property **Name** of class **CCircle2**, and this property would erroneously return "**CCircle2**."

```vbnet
1   ' Fig. 10.7: Cylinder2.vb
2   ' CCylinder2 inherits from CCircle2 and overrides key members.
3
4   Public Class CCylinder2
5      Inherits CCircle2 ' CCylinder2 inherits from class CCircle2
6
7      Protected mHeight As Double
8
9      ' default constructor
10     Public Sub New()
11
12        ' implicit call to CCircle2 constructor occurs here
13        Height = 0
14     End Sub ' New
15
```

Fig. 10.7 `CCylinder2` class inherits from class `CCircle2` (part 1 of 2).

```vbnet
16         ' four-argument constructor
17         Public Sub New(ByVal xValue As Integer, _
18            ByVal yValue As Integer, ByVal radiusValue As Double, _
19            ByVal heightValue As Double)
20
21            ' explicit call to CCircle2 constructor
22            MyBase.New(xValue, yValue, radiusValue)
23            Height = heightValue ' set CCylinder2 height
24         End Sub ' New
25
26         ' property Height
27         Public Property Height() As Double
28
29            Get
30               Return mHeight
31            End Get
32
33            ' set CCylinder2 height if argument value is positive
34            Set(ByVal heightValue As Double)
35
36               If heightValue >= 0 Then ' mHeight must be nonnegative
37                  mHeight = heightValue
38               End If
39
40            End Set
41
42         End Property ' Height
43
44         ' override method Area to calculate CCylinder2 surface area
45         Public Overrides Function Area() As Double
46            Return 2 * MyBase.Area + MyBase.Circumference * mHeight
47         End Function ' Area
48
49         ' calculate CCylinder2 volume
50         Public Overrides Function Volume() As Double
51            Return MyBase.Area * mHeight
52         End Function ' Volume
53
54         ' convert CCylinder2 to String
55         Public Overrides Function ToString() As String
56            Return MyBase.ToString() & "; Height = " & mHeight
57         End Function ' ToString
58
59         ' override property Name from class CCircle2
60         Public Overrides ReadOnly Property Name() As String
61
62            Get
63               Return "CCylinder2"
64            End Get
65
66         End Property ' Name
67
68      End Class ' CCylinder2
```

Fig. 10.7 `CCylinder2` class inherits from class `CCircle2` (part 2 of 2).

Figure 10.8 defines class **CTest2** whose method **Main** creates an object of each of the three concrete classes and manipulates the objects polymorphically using an array of **CShape** references. Lines 11–13 instantiate **CPoint2** object **point**, **CCircle2** object **circle**, and **CCylinder2** object **cylinder**, respectively. Next, line 16 instantiates array **arrayOfShapes**, which contains three **CShape** references. Line 19 assigns reference **point** to array element **arrayOfShapes(0)**, line 22 assigns reference **circle** to array element **arrayOfShapes(1)** and line 25 assigns reference **cylinder** to array element **arrayOfShapes(2)**. These assignments are possible, because a **CPoint2** is a **CShape**, a **CCircle2** is a **CShape** and a **CCylinder2** is a **CShape**. Therefore, we can assign instances of derived-classes **CPoint2**, **CCircle2** and **CCylinder2** to base-class **CShape** references.

```vb
1   ' Fig. 10.8: Test2.vb
2   ' Demonstrate polymorphism in Point-Circle-Cylinder hierarchy.
3
4   Imports System.Windows.Forms
5
6   Class CTest2
7
8      Shared Sub Main()
9
10        ' instantiate CPoint2, CCircle2 and CCylinder2 objects
11        Dim point As New CPoint2(7, 11)
12        Dim circle As New CCircle2(22, 8, 3.5)
13        Dim cylinder As New CCylinder2(10, 10, 3.3, 10)
14
15        ' instantiate array of base-class references
16        Dim arrayOfShapes As CShape() = New CShape(2){}
17
18        ' arrayOfShapes(0) refers to CPoint2 object
19        arrayOfShapes(0) = point
20
21        ' arrayOfShapes(1) refers to CCircle2 object
22        arrayOfShapes(1) = circle
23
24        ' arrayOfShapes(2) refers to CCylinder2 object
25        arrayOfShapes(2) = cylinder
26
27        Dim output As String = point.Name & ": " & _
28           point.ToString() & vbCrLf & circle.Name & ": " & _
29           circle.ToString() & vbCrLf & cylinder.Name & _
30           ": " & cylinder.ToString()
31
32        Dim shape As CShape
33
34        ' display name, area and volume for each object in
35        ' arrayOfShapes polymorphically
36        For Each shape In arrayOfShapes
37           output &= vbCrLf & vbCrLf & shape.Name & ": " & _
38              shape.ToString() & vbCrLf & "Area = " & _
```

Fig. 10.8 **CTest2** demonstrates polymorphism in Point-Circle-Cylinder hierarchy (part 1 of 2).

```
39                 String.Format("{0:F}", shape.Area) & vbCrLf & _
40                 "Volume = " & String.Format("{0:F}", shape.Volume)
41         Next
42
43         MessageBox.Show(output, "Demonstrating Polymorphism")
44      End Sub ' Main
45
46  End Class ' CTest2
```

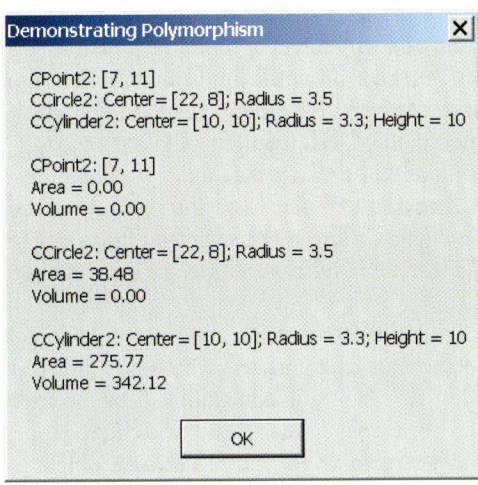

Fig. 10.8 CTest2 demonstrates polymorphism in Point-Circle-Cylinder hierarchy (part 2 of 2).

Lines 27–30 invoke property **Name** and method **ToString** for objects **point**, **circle** and **cylinder**. Property **Name** returns the object's class name and method **ToString** returns the object's **String** representation (i.e., x-y coordinate pair, radius and height, depending on each object's type). Note that lines 27–30 use derived-class references to invoke each derived-class object's methods and properties.

By contrast, the **For Each** structure (lines 36–41) uses base-class **CShape** references to invoke each derived-class object's methods and properties. The **For Each** structure calls property **Name** and methods **ToString**, **Area** and **Volume** for each **CShape** reference in **arrayOfShapes**. The property and methods are invoked on each object in **arrayOfShapes**. When the compiler looks at each method/property call, the compiler determines whether each **CShape** reference (in **arrayOfShapes**) can make these calls. This is the case for property **Name** and methods **Area** and **Volume**, because they are defined in class **CShape**. However, class **CShape** does not define method **ToString**. For this method, the compiler proceeds to **CShape**'s base class (class **Object**), and determines that **CShape** inherited a no-argument **ToString** method from class **Object**.

The screen capture of Fig. 10.8 illustrates that the "appropriate" property **Name** and methods **ToString**, **Area** and **Volume** were invoked for each type of object in **arrayOfShapes**. By "appropriate," we mean that Visual Basic maps each property and method call to the proper object. For example, in the **For Each** structure's first iteration, reference **arrayOfShapes(0)** (which is of type **CShape**) refers to the same object as **point** (which is of type **CPoint2**). Class **CPoint2** overrides property **Name** and method **ToString**, and inherits method **Area** and **Volume** from class **CShape**. At runtime, **arrayOfShapes(0)** invokes property **Name** and methods **ToString**, **Area** and **Volume** of the **CPoint** object. Visual Basic determines the correct object type, then uses that type to determine the appropriate methods to invoke. Through polymorphism, the call to property **Name** returns the string **"CPoint2:"**; the call to method **ToString** returns the **String** representation of **point**'s *x*-*y* coordinate pair; and methods **Area** and **Volume** each return **0** (as shown in the second group of outputs in Fig. 10.8).

Polymorphism occurs in the next two iterations of the **For Each** structure as well. Reference **arrayOfShapes(1)** refers to the same object as **circle** (which is of type **CCircle2**). Class **CCircle2** provides implementations for property **Name**, method **ToString** and method **Area**, and inherits method **Volume** from class **CPoint2** (which, in turn, inherited method **Volume** from class **CShape**). Visual Basic associates property **Name** and methods **ToString**, **Area** and **Volume** of the **CCircle2** object to reference **arrayOfShapes(1)**. As a result, property **Name** returns the string **"CCircle2:"**; method **ToString** returns the **String** representation of **circle**'s *x*-*y* coordinate pair and radius; method **Area** returns the area (**38.48**); and method **Volume** returns **0**.

For the final iteration of the **For Each** structure, reference **arrayOfShapes(2)** refers to the same object as **cylinder** (which is of type **CCylinder2**). Class **CCylinder2** provides its own implementations for property **Name** and methods **ToString**, **Area** and **Volume**. Visual Basic associates property **Name** and methods **ToString**, **Area** and **Volume** of the **CCylinder2** object to reference **arrayOfShapes(2)**. Property **Name** returns the string **"CCylinder2:"**; method **ToString** returns the **String** representation of **cylinder**'s *x*-*y* coordinate pair, radius and height; method **Area** returns the cylinder's surface area (**275.77**); and method **Volume** returns the cylinder's volume (**342.12**).

10.7 NotInheritable Classes and NotOverridable Methods

A class that is declared **NotInheritable** cannot be a base class. Programmers use this feature to prevent inheritance beyond the **NotInheritable** class in the hierarchy. A **NotInheritable** class is the "opposite" of a **MustInherit** class. A **NotInheritable** class is a concrete class that cannot act as a base class, whereas a **MustInherit** class is an abstract class that may act as a base class.

A method that was declared **Overridable** in a base class can be declared **NotOverridable** in a derived class. This prevents overriding the method in classes that inherit from the derived class. All classes derived from the class that contains the **NotOverridable** method use that class's method implementation. Methods that are declared **Shared** and methods that are declared **Private** implicitly are **NotOverridable**.

Software Engineering Observation 10.7

*If a method is declared **NotOverridable**, it cannot be overridden in derived classes. Calls to **NotOverridable** methods cannot be sent polymorphically to objects of those derived classes.*

> **Software Engineering Observation 10.8**
>
> *A class that is declared* **NotInheritable** *cannot be a base class (i.e., a class cannot inherit from a* **NotInheritable** *class). All methods in a* **NotInheritable** *class implicitly are* **NotOverridable***.*

10.8 Case Study: Payroll System Using Polymorphism

Let us use abstract classes (declared as **MustInherit**), abstract methods (declared as **MustOverride**) and polymorphism to perform different payroll calculations for various types of employees. We begin by creating an abstract base class **CEmployee**. The derived classes of **CEmployee** are **CBoss** (paid a fixed weekly salary, regardless of the number of hours worked), **CCommissionWorker** (paid a flat base salary plus a percentage of the worker's sales), **CPieceWorker** (paid a flat fee per item produced) and **CHourlyWorker** (paid by the hour with "time-and-a-half" for overtime). In this example, we declare all classes that inherit from class **CEmployee** as **NotInheritable**, because we do not intend to derive classes from them.

The application must determine the weekly earnings for all types of employees, so each class derived from **CEmployee** requires method **Earnings**. However, each derived class uses a different calculation to determine earnings for a specific type of employee. Therefore, we declare method **Earnings** as **MustOverride** in **CEmployee** and declare **CEmployee** to be a **MustInherit** class. Each derived class overrides this method to calculate earnings for that employee type.

To calculate any employee's earnings, the program can use a base-class reference to a derived-class object and invoke method **Earnings**. In a real payroll system, the various **CEmployee** objects might be referenced by individual elements in an array of **CEmployee** references. The program would traverse the array one element at a time, using the **CEmployee** references to invoke the appropriate **Earnings** method of each object.

> **Software Engineering Observation 10.9**
>
> *The ability to declare an abstract (***MustOverride***) method gives the class designer considerable control over how derived classes are defined in a class hierarchy. Any class that inherits directly from a base class containing an abstract method must override the abstract method. Otherwise, the new class also would be abstract, and attempts to instantiate objects of that class would fail.*

Let us consider class **CEmployee** (Fig. 10.9). The **Public** members include a constructor (lines 10–15) that takes as arguments an employee's first and last names; properties **FirstName** (lines 18–28) and **LastName** (lines 31–41); method **ToString** (lines 44–46) that returns the first name and last name separated by a space; and **MustOverride** method **Earnings** (line 50). The **MustInherit** keyword (line 4) indicates that class **CEmployee** is abstract; thus, it cannot be used to instantiate **CEmployee**. Method **Earnings** is declared as **MustOverride**, so the class does not provide a method implementation. All classes derived directly from class **CEmployee**—except for abstract derived classes—must define this method. Method **Earnings** is abstract in **CEmployee**, because we cannot calculate the earnings for a generic employee. To determine earnings, we first must know of what *kind* of employee it is. By declaring this method **MustOverride**, we indicate that we will provide an implementation in each concrete derived class, but not in the base class itself.

```vbnet
1    ' Fig. 10.9: Employee.vb
2    ' Abstract base class for employee derived classes.
3    
4    Public MustInherit Class CEmployee
5    
6       Private mFirstName As String
7       Private mLastName As String
8    
9       ' constructor
10      Public Sub New(ByVal firstNameValue As String, _
11         ByVal lastNameValue As String)
12   
13         FirstName = firstNameValue
14         LastName = lastNameValue
15      End Sub ' New
16   
17      ' property FirstName
18      Public Property FirstName() As String
19   
20         Get
21            Return mFirstName
22         End Get
23   
24         Set(ByVal firstNameValue As String)
25            mFirstName = firstNameValue
26         End Set
27   
28      End Property ' FirstName
29   
30      ' property LastName
31      Public Property LastName() As String
32   
33         Get
34            Return mLastName
35         End Get
36   
37         Set(ByVal lastNameValue As String)
38            mLastName = lastNameValue
39         End Set
40   
41      End Property ' LastName
42   
43      ' obtain String representation of employee
44      Public Overrides Function ToString() As String
45         Return mFirstName & " " & mLastName
46      End Function ' ToString
47   
48      ' abstract method that must be implemented for each derived
49      ' class of CEmployee to calculate specific earnings
50      Public MustOverride Function Earnings() As Decimal
51   
52   End Class ' CEmployee
```

Fig. 10.9 **MustInherit** class **CEmployee** definition.

Class **CBoss** (Fig. 10.10) inherits from **CEmployee**. Class **CBoss**'s constructor (lines 10–15) receives as arguments a first name, a last name and a salary. The constructor passes the first name and last name to the **CEmployee** constructor (line 13), which initializes the **FirstName** and **LastName** members of the base-class part of the derived-class object. Other **Public** methods contained in **CBoss** include method **Earnings** (lines 36–38), which defines the calculation of a boss' earnings, and method **ToString** (lines 41–43), which returns a **String** indicating the type of employee (i.e., **"CBoss: "**) and the boss's name. Class **CBoss** also includes property **WeeklySalary** (lines 18–33), which sets and gets the value for member variable **mSalary**. Note that this property ensures only that **mSalary** cannot hold a negative value—in a real payroll system, this validation would be more extensive and carefully controlled.

```vbnet
1   ' Fig. 10.10: Boss.vb
2   ' Boss class derived from CEmployee.
3
4   Public NotInheritable Class CBoss
5      Inherits CEmployee
6
7      Private mSalary As Decimal
8
9      ' constructor for class CBoss
10     Public Sub New(ByVal firstNameValue As String, _
11        ByVal lastNameValue As String, ByVal salaryValue As Decimal)
12
13        MyBase.New(firstNameValue, lastNameValue)
14        WeeklySalary = salaryValue
15     End Sub ' New
16
17     ' property WeeklySalary
18     Public Property WeeklySalary() As Decimal
19
20        Get
21           Return mSalary
22        End Get
23
24        Set(ByVal bossSalaryValue As Decimal)
25
26           ' validate mSalary
27           If bossSalaryValue > 0
28              mSalary = bossSalaryValue
29           End If
30
31        End Set
32
33     End Property ' WeeklySalary
34
35     ' override base-class method to calculate Boss earnings
36     Public Overrides Function Earnings() As Decimal
37        Return WeeklySalary
38     End Function ' Earnings
39
```

Fig. 10.10 **CBoss** class inherits from class **CEmployee** (part 1 of 2).

```
40          ' return Boss' name
41          Public Overrides Function ToString() As String
42             Return "CBoss: " & MyBase.ToString()
43          End Function ' ToString
44
45       End Class ' CBoss
```

Fig. 10.10 `CBoss` class inherits from class `CEmployee` (part 2 of 2).

Class **CCommissionWorker** (Fig. 10.11) also inherits from class **CEmployee**. The constructor for this class (lines 12–21) receives as arguments a first name, a last name, a salary, a commission and a quantity of items sold. Line 17 passes the first name and last name to the base-class **CEmployee** constructor. Class **CCommissionWorker** also provides properties **Salary** (lines 24–39), **Commission** (lines 42–57) and **Quantity** (lines 60–75); method **Earnings** (lines 78–80), which calculates the worker's wages; and method **ToString** (lines 83–85), which returns a **String** indicating the employee type (i.e., **"CCommissionWorker: "**) and the worker's name.

```
1    ' Fig. 10.11: CommissionWorker.vb
2    ' CEmployee implementation for a commission worker.
3
4    Public NotInheritable Class CCommissionWorker
5       Inherits CEmployee
6
7       Private mSalary As Decimal ' base salary per week
8       Private mCommission As Decimal ' amount per item sold
9       Private mQuantity As Integer ' total items sold
10
11      ' constructor for class CCommissionWorker
12      Public Sub New(ByVal firstNameValue As String, _
13         ByVal lastNameValue As String, ByVal salaryValue As Decimal, _
14         ByVal commissionValue As Decimal, _
15         ByVal quantityValue As Integer)
16
17         MyBase.New(firstNameValue, lastNameValue)
18         Salary = salaryValue
19         Commission = commissionValue
20         Quantity = quantityValue
21      End Sub ' New
22
23      ' property Salary
24      Public Property Salary() As Decimal
25
26         Get
27            Return mSalary
28         End Get
29
```

Fig. 10.11 `CCommissionWorker` class inherits from class `CEmployee` (part 1 of 3).

```vbnet
30          Set(ByVal salaryValue As Decimal)
31
32             ' validate mSalary
33             If salaryValue > 0 Then
34                mSalary = salaryValue
35             End If
36
37          End Set
38
39       End Property ' Salary
40
41       ' property Commission
42       Public Property Commission() As Decimal
43
44          Get
45             Return mCommission
46          End Get
47
48          Set(ByVal commissionValue As Decimal)
49
50             ' validate mCommission
51             If commissionValue > 0 Then
52                mCommission = commissionValue
53             End If
54
55          End Set
56
57       End Property ' Commission
58
59       ' property Quantity
60       Public Property Quantity() As Integer
61
62          Get
63             Return mQuantity
64          End Get
65
66          Set(ByVal QuantityValue As Integer)
67
68             ' validate mQuantity
69             If QuantityValue > 0 Then
70                mQuantity = QuantityValue
71             End If
72
73          End Set
74
75       End Property ' Quantity
76
77       ' override method to calculate CommissionWorker earnings
78       Public Overrides Function Earnings() As Decimal
79          Return Salary + Commission * Quantity
80       End Function ' Earnings
81
```

Fig. 10.11 `CCommissionWorker` class inherits from class `CEmployee` (part 2 of 3).

```vbnet
82         ' return commission worker's name
83         Public Overrides Function ToString() As String
84            Return "CCommissionWorker: " & MyBase.ToString()
85         End Function ' ToString
86
87    End Class ' CCommissionWorker
```

Fig. 10.11 `CCommissionWorker` class inherits from class `CEmployee` (part 3 of 3).

Class **CPieceWorker** (Fig. 10.12) inherits from class **CEmployee**. The constructor for this class (lines 11–19) receives as arguments a first name, a last name, a wage per piece and a quantity of items produced. Line 16 then passes the first name and last name to the base-class **CEmployee** constructor. Class **CPieceWorker** also provides properties **WagePerPiece** (lines 22–37) and **Quantity** (lines 40–55); method **Earnings** (lines 58–60), which calculates a piece worker's earnings; and method **ToString** (lines 63–65), which returns a **String** indicating the type of the employee (i.e., **"CPieceWorker: "**) and the piece worker's name.

Class **CHourlyWorker** (Fig. 10.13) inherits from class **CEmployee**. The constructor for this class (lines 11–18) receives as arguments a first name, a last name, a wage and the number of hours worked. Line 15 passes the first name and last name to the base-class **CEmployee** constructor. Class **CHourlyWorker** also provides properties **HourlyWage** (lines 21–36) and **Hours** (lines 39–54); method **Earnings** (lines 57–67), which calculates an hourly worker's earnings; and method **ToString** (lines 70–72), which returns a **String** indicating the type of the employee (i.e., **"CHourlyWorker:"**) and the hourly worker's name. Note that hourly workers are paid "time-and-a-half" for "overtimes" (i.e., hours worked in excess of 40 hours).

```vbnet
1    ' Fig. 10.12: PieceWorker.vb
2    ' CPieceWorker class derived from CEmployee.
3
4    Public NotInheritable Class CPieceWorker
5       Inherits CEmployee
6
7       Private mAmountPerPiece As Decimal ' wage per piece output
8       Private mQuantity As Integer ' output per week
9
10      ' constructor for CPieceWorker
11      Public Sub New(ByVal firstNameValue As String, _
12         ByVal lastNameValue As String, _
13         ByVal wagePerPieceValue As Decimal, _
14         ByVal quantityValue As Integer)
15
16         MyBase.New(firstNameValue, lastNameValue)
17         WagePerPiece = wagePerPieceValue
18         Quantity = quantityValue
19      End Sub ' New
20
```

Fig. 10.12 `CPieceWorker` class inherits from class `CEmployee` (part 1 of 2).

```
21      ' property WagePerPiece
22      Public Property WagePerPiece() As Decimal
23
24         Get
25            Return mAmountPerPiece
26         End Get
27
28         Set(ByVal wagePerPieceValue As Decimal)
29
30            ' validate mAmountPerPiece
31            If wagePerPieceValue > 0 Then
32               mAmountPerPiece = wagePerPieceValue
33            End If
34
35         End Set
36
37      End Property ' WagePerPiece
38
39      ' property Quantity
40      Public Property Quantity() As Integer
41
42         Get
43            Return mQuantity
44         End Get
45
46         Set(ByVal quantityValue As Integer)
47
48            ' validate mQuantity
49            If quantityValue > 0 Then
50               mQuantity = quantityValue
51            End If
52
53         End Set
54
55      End Property ' Quantity
56
57      ' override base-class method to calculate PieceWorker's earnings
58      Public Overrides Function Earnings() As Decimal
59         Return Quantity * WagePerPiece
60      End Function ' Earnings
61
62      ' return piece worker's name
63      Public Overrides Function ToString() As String
64         Return "CPieceWorker: " & MyBase.ToString()
65      End Function ' ToString
66
67   End Class ' CPieceWorker
```

Fig. 10.12 CPieceWorker class inherits from class **CEmployee** (part 2 of 2).

Method **Main** (lines 8–50) of class **CTest** (Fig. 10.14) declares **CEmployee** reference **employee** (line 9). Each employee type is handled similarly in **Main**, so we discuss only the manipulations of the **CBoss** object.

```vbnet
1   ' Fig. 10.13: HourlyWorker.vb
2   ' CEmployee implementation for an hourly worker.
3
4   Public NotInheritable Class CHourlyWorker
5      Inherits CEmployee
6
7      Private mWage As Decimal ' wage per hour
8      Private mHoursWorked As Double ' hours worked for week
9
10     ' constructor for class CHourlyWorker
11     Public Sub New(ByVal firstNameValue As String, _
12        ByVal lastNameValue As String, _
13        ByVal wageValue As Decimal, ByVal hourValue As Double)
14
15        MyBase.New(firstNameValue, lastNameValue)
16        HourlyWage = wageValue
17        Hours = hourValue
18     End Sub ' New
19
20     ' property HourlyWage
21     Public Property HourlyWage() As Decimal
22
23        Get
24           Return mWage
25        End Get
26
27        Set(ByVal hourlyWageValue As Decimal)
28
29           ' validate mWage
30           If hourlyWageValue > 0 Then
31              mWage = hourlyWageValue
32           End If
33
34        End Set
35
36     End Property ' HourlyWage
37
38     ' property Hours
39     Public Property Hours() As Double
40
41        Get
42           Return mHoursWorked
43        End Get
44
45        Set(ByVal hourValue As Double)
46
47           ' validate mHoursWorked
48           If hourValue > 0 Then
49              mHoursWorked = hourValue
50           End If
51
52        End Set
53
```

Fig. 10.13 `CHourlyWorker` class inherits from class `CEmployee` (part 1 of 2).

```vbnet
54      End Property ' Hours
55
56      ' override base-class method to calculate HourlyWorker earnings
57      Public Overrides Function Earnings() As Decimal
58
59         ' calculate for "time-and-a-half"
60         If mHoursWorked <= 40
61            Return Convert.ToDecimal(mWage * mHoursWorked)
62         Else
63            Return Convert.ToDecimal((mWage * mHoursWorked) + _
64               (mHoursWorked - 40) * 0.5 * mWage)
65         End If
66
67      End Function ' Earnings
68
69      ' return hourly worker's name
70      Public Overrides Function ToString() As String
71         Return "CHourlyWorker: " & MyBase.ToString()
72      End Function ' ToString
73
74   End Class ' CHourlyWorker
```

Fig. 10.13 **CHourlyWorker** class inherits from class **CEmployee** (part 2 of 2).

```vbnet
1    ' Fig 10.14: Test.vb
2    ' Displays the earnings for each CEmployee.
3
4    Imports System.Windows.Forms
5
6    Class CTest
7
8       Shared Sub Main()
9          Dim employee As CEmployee ' base-class reference
10         Dim output As String
11
12         Dim boss As CBoss = New CBoss("John", "Smith", 800)
13
14         Dim commissionWorker As CCommissionWorker = _
15            New CCommissionWorker("Sue", "Jones", 400, 3, 150)
16
17         Dim pieceWorker As CPieceWorker = _
18            New CPieceWorker("Bob", "Lewis", _
19               Convert.ToDecimal(2.5), 200)
20
21         Dim hourlyWorker As CHourlyWorker = _
22            New CHourlyWorker("Karen", "Price", _
23               Convert.ToDecimal(13.75), 40)
24
25         ' employee reference to a CBoss
26         employee = boss
27         output &= GetString(employee) & boss.ToString() & _
28            " earned " & boss.Earnings.ToString("C") & vbCrLf & vbCrLf
```

Fig. 10.14 **CTest** class tests the **CEmployee** class hierarchy (part 1 of 2).

```
29
30          ' employee reference to a CCommissionWorker
31          employee = commissionWorker
32          output &= GetString(employee) & _
33             commissionWorker.ToString() & " earned " & _
34             commissionWorker.Earnings.ToString("C") & vbCrLf & vbCrLf
35
36          ' employee reference to a CPieceWorker
37          employee = pieceWorker
38          output &= GetString(employee) & pieceWorker.ToString() & _
39             " earned " & pieceWorker.Earnings.ToString("C") _
40             & vbCrLf & vbCrLf
41
42          ' employee reference to a CHourlyWorker
43          employee = hourlyWorker
44          output &= GetString(employee) & _
45             hourlyWorker.ToString() & " earned " & _
46             hourlyWorker.Earnings.ToString("C") & vbCrLf & vbCrLf
47
48          MessageBox.Show(output, "Demonstrating Polymorphism", _
49             MessageBoxButtons.OK, MessageBoxIcon.Information)
50       End Sub ' Main
51
52       ' return String containing employee information
53       Shared Function GetString(ByVal worker As CEmployee) As String
54          Return worker.ToString() & " earned " & _
55             worker.Earnings.ToString("C") & vbCrLf
56       End Function ' GetString
57
58    End Class ' CTest
```

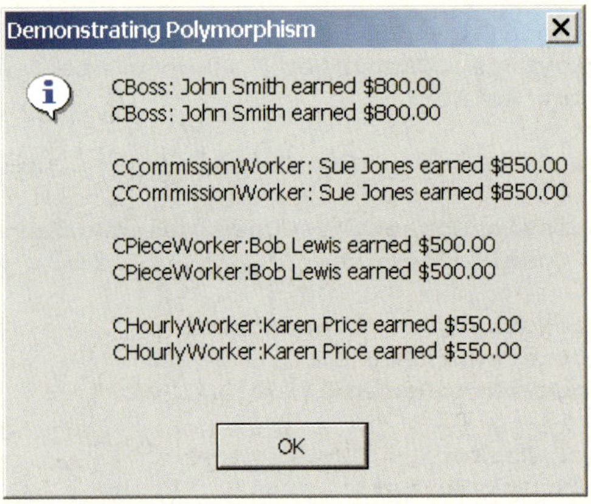

Demonstrating Polymorphism

CBoss: John Smith earned $800.00
CBoss: John Smith earned $800.00

CCommissionWorker: Sue Jones earned $850.00
CCommissionWorker: Sue Jones earned $850.00

CPieceWorker:Bob Lewis earned $500.00
CPieceWorker:Bob Lewis earned $500.00

CHourlyWorker:Karen Price earned $550.00
CHourlyWorker:Karen Price earned $550.00

Fig. 10.14 **CTest** class tests the **CEmployee** class hierarchy (part 2 of 2).

Line 12 assigns to **CBoss** reference **boss** a **CBoss** object and passes to its constructor the boss's first name ("**John**"), last name ("**Smith**") and fixed weekly salary (**800**). Line 26 assigns the derived-class reference **boss** to the base-class **CEmployee** reference **employee**, so that we can demonstrate the polymorphic determination of **boss**'s earnings. Line 27 passes reference **employee** as an argument to **Private** method **GetString** (lines 53–56), which polymorphically invokes methods **ToString** and **Earnings** on the **CEmployee** object the method receives as an argument. At this point, Visual Basic determines that the object passed to **GetString** is of type **CBoss**, so lines 54–55 invoke **CBoss** methods **ToString** and **Earnings**. These are classic examples of polymorphic behavior.

Method **Earnings** returns a **Decimal** object on which line 55 then calls method **ToString**. In this case, the string **"C"**, which is passed to an overloaded version of **Decimal** method **ToString**, stands for **Currency** and **ToString** formats the string as a currency amount.

When method **GetString** returns to **Main**, lines 27–28 explicitly invoke methods **ToString** and **Earnings** through derived-class **CBoss** reference **boss** to show the method invocations that do not use polymorphic processing. The output generated in lines 27–28 is identical to that generated by methods **ToString** and **Earnings** through base-class reference **employee** (i.e., the methods that use polymorphism), verifying that the polymorphic methods invoke the appropriate methods in derived class **CBoss**.

To prove that the base-class reference **employee** can invoke the proper derived-class versions of methods **ToString** and **Earnings** for the other types of employees, lines 31, 37 and 43 assign to base-class reference **employee** a different type of **CEmployee** object (**CCommissionWorker**, **CPieceWorker** and **CHourlyWorker**, respectively). After each assignment, the application calls method **GetString** to return the results via the base-class reference. Then, the application calls methods **ToString** and **Earnings** off each derived-class reference to show that Visual Basic correctly associates each method call to its corresponding derived-class object.

10.9 Case Study: Creating and Using Interfaces

We now present two more examples of polymorphism through the use of an *interface*, which specifies a set of **Public** services (i.e., methods and properties) that classes must implement. An interface is used when there is no default implementation to inherit (i.e., no instance variables and no default-method implementations). Whereas an abstract class is best used for providing data and services for objects in a hierarchical relationship, an interface can be used for providing services that "bring together" disparate objects that relate to one another only through that interface's services.

An interface definition begins with the keyword **Interface** and contains a list of **Public** methods and properties. To use an interface, a class must specify that it **Implements** the interface and must provide implementations for every method and property specified in the interface definition. Having a class implement an interface is like signing a contract with the compiler that states, "this class will define all the methods and properties specified by the interface."

Common Programming Error 10.9

*When a class **Implements** an **Interface**, leaving even a single **Interface** method or property undefined is an error. The class must define every method and property in the **Interface**.*

Common Programming Error 10.10

In Visual Basic, an **Interface** can be declared only as **Public** or **Friend**; the declaration of an **Interface** as **Private** or **Protected** is an error.

Interfaces provide a uniform set of methods and properties to objects of disparate classes. These methods and properties enable programs to process the objects of those disparate classes polymorphically. For example, consider disparate objects that represent a person, a tree, a car and a file. These objects have "nothing to do" with each other—a person has a first name and last name; a tree has a trunk, a set of branches and a bunch of leaves; a car has wheels, gears and several other mechanisms enabling the car to move; and a file contains data. Because of the lack in commonality among these classes, modeling them via an inheritance hierarchy with an abstract class seems illogical. However, these objects certainly have at least one common characteristic—an age. A person's age is represented by the number of years since that person was born; a tree's age is represented by the number of rings in its trunk; a car's age is represented by its manufacture date; and file's age is represented by its creation date. We can use an interface that provides a method or property that objects of these disparate classes can implement to return each object's age.

In this example, we use interface **IAge** (Fig. 10.15) to return the age information for classes **CPerson** (Fig. 10.16) and **CTree** (Fig. 10.17). The definition of interface **IAge** begins at line 4 with **Public Interface** and ends at line 10 with **End Interface**. Lines 7–8 specify properties **Age** and **Name**, for which every class that implements interface **IAge** must provide implementations. Interface **IAge** declares these properties as **ReadOnly**, but doing so is not required—an interface can also provide methods (**Sub**s and **Function**s), **WriteOnly** properties and properties with both get and set accessors. By containing these property declarations, interface **IAge** provides an opportunity for an object that implements **IAge** to return its age and name, respectively. However, the classes that implement these methods are not "required" by either interface **IAge** or Visual Basic to return an age and a name. The compiler requires only that classes implementing interface **IAge** provide implementations for the interface's properties. (Technically, interface **IAge** should not provide the opportunity for an object to return its name. However, as we will see later, clients that process interface objects polymorphically can interact with those objects only through the interface; therefore, property **Name** gives an object a chance to "identify" itself in our example.)

```
1   ' Fig. 10.15: IAge.vb
2   ' Interface IAge declares property for setting and getting age.
3
4   Public Interface IAge
5
6      ' classes that implement IAge must define these properties
7      ReadOnly Property Age() As Integer
8      ReadOnly Property Name() As String
9
10  End Interface ' IAge
```

Fig. 10.15 **Interface** for returning age of objects of disparate classes.

Line 5 of Fig. 10.16 uses keyword **Implements** to indicate that class **CPerson** implements interface **IAge**. In this example, class **CPerson** implements only one interface. A class can implement any number of interfaces in addition to inheriting from one class. To implement more than one interface, the class definition must provide a comma-separated list of interface names after keyword **Implements**. Class **CPerson** has member variables **mYearBorn**, **mFirstName** and **mLastName** (lines 7–9), for which the constructor (lines 12–29) set the values. Because class **CPerson** implements interface **IAge**, class **CPerson** must implement properties **Age** and **Name**—defined on lines 32–39 and lines 42–49, respectively. Property **Age** allows the client to obtain the person's age, and property **Name** returns a **String** containing **mFirstName** and **mLastName**. Note that property **Age** calculates the person's age by subtracting **mYearBorn** from the current year (via property **Year** of property **Date.Now**, which returns the current date). These properties satisfy the implementation requirements defined in interface **IAge**, so class **CPerson** has fulfilled its "contract" with the compiler.

```
1    ' Fig. 10.16: Person.vb
2    ' Class CPerson has a birthday.
3
4    Public Class CPerson
5       Implements IAge
6
7       Private mYearBorn As Integer
8       Private mFirstName As String
9       Private mLastName As String
10
11      ' constructor receives first name, last name and birth date
12      Public Sub New(ByVal firstNameValue As String, _
13         ByVal lastNameValue As String, _
14         ByVal yearBornValue As Integer)
15
16         ' implicit call to Object constructor
17         mFirstName = firstNameValue
18         mLastName = lastNameValue
19
20         ' validate year
21         If (yearBornValue > 0 AndAlso _
22            yearBornValue <= Date.Now.Year)
23
24            mYearBorn = yearBornValue
25         Else
26            mYearBorn = Date.Now.Year
27         End If
28
29      End Sub ' New
30
31      ' property Age implementation of interface IAge
32      ReadOnly Property Age() As Integer _
33         Implements IAge.Age
34
```

Fig. 10.16 **CPerson** class implements **IAge** interface (part 1 of 2).

```vb
35          Get
36              Return Date.Now.Year - mYearBorn
37          End Get
38
39      End Property ' Age
40
41      ' property Name implementation of interface IAge
42      ReadOnly Property Name() As String _
43          Implements IAge.Name
44
45          Get
46              Return mFirstName & " " & mLastName
47          End Get
48
49      End Property ' Name
50
51  End Class ' CPerson
```

Fig. 10.16 `CPerson` class implements `IAge` interface (part 2 of 2).

Class **CTree** (Fig. 10.17) also implements interface **IAge**. Class **CTree** has member variables **mRings** (line 7), which represents the number of rings inside the tree's trunk—this variable corresponds directly with the tree's age. The **CTree** constructor (lines 10–14) receives as an argument an **Integer** that specifies when the tree was planted. Class **CTree** includes method **AddRing** (lines 17–19), which enables a user to increment the number of rings in the tree. Because class **CTree** implements interface **IAge**, class **CTree** must implement properties **Age** and **Name**—defined on lines 22–29 and lines 32–39, respectively. Property **Age** returns the value of **mRings**, and property **Name** returns **String** "Tree."

```vb
1   ' Fig. 10.17: Tree.vb
2   ' Class CTree contains number of rings corresponding to age.
3
4   Public Class CTree
5       Implements IAge
6
7       Private mRings As Integer
8
9       ' constructor receives planting date
10      Public Sub New(ByVal yearPlanted As Integer)
11
12          ' implicit call to Object constructor
13          mRings = Date.Now.Year - yearPlanted
14      End Sub ' New
15
16      ' increment mRings
17      Public Sub AddRing()
18          mRings += 1
19      End Sub ' AddRing
20
```

Fig. 10.17 `CTree` class implements `IAge` interface (part 1 of 2).

```
21        ' property Age
22        ReadOnly Property Age() As Integer _
23           Implements IAge.Age
24
25           Get
26              Return mRings
27           End Get
28
29        End Property ' Age
30
31        ' property Name implementation of interface IAge
32        ReadOnly Property Name() As String _
33           Implements IAge.Name
34
35           Get
36              Return "Tree"
37           End Get
38
39        End Property ' Name
40
41    End Class ' CTree
```

Fig. 10.17 `CTree` class implements `IAge` interface (part 2 of 2).

Class **CTest** (Fig. 10.18) demonstrates polymorphism on the objects of disparate classes **CPerson** and **CTree**. Line 11 instantiates object tree of class **CTree**, and line 12 instantiates object **person** of class **CPerson**. Line 15 declares **iAgeArray**—an array of two references to **IAge** objects. Line 18 and 21 assign **tree** and **person** to the first and second reference in **iAgeArray**, respectively. Lines 24–26 invoke method **ToString** on **tree**, then invoke its properties **Age** and **Name** to return age and name information for object **tree**. Lines 29–31 invoke method **ToString** on **person**, then invoke its properties **Age** and **Name** to return age and name information for object **person**. Next, we manipulate these objects polymorphically through the **iAgeArray** of references to **IAge** objects. Lines 36–39 define a **For-Each** structure that uses properties **Age** and **Name** to obtain age and name information for each **IAge** object in **iAgeArray**. Note that we use **Name** so that each object in **iAgeArray** can "identify" itself in our program's output. Objects **tree** and **person** can use method **ToString** to do this, because classes **CTree** and **CPerson** both inherit from class **Object**. However, when **CTest** interacts with these objects polymorphically, **CTest** can use only properties **Age** and **Name** for each interface object. Because interface **IAge** does not provide method **ToString**, clients cannot invoke method **ToString** through interface **IAge** references.

```
1   ' Fig. 10.18: Test.vb
2   ' Demonstrate polymorphism.
3
4   Imports System.Windows.Forms
5
6   Class CTest
7
```

Fig. 10.18 Demonstrate polymorphism on objects of disparate classes (part 1 of 2).

```vb
 8      Shared Sub Main()
 9
10         ' instantiate CTree and CPerson objects
11         Dim tree As New CTree(1976)
12         Dim person As New CPerson("Bob", "Jones", 1983)
13
14         ' instantiate array of interface references
15         Dim iAgeArray As IAge() = New IAge(1){}
16
17         ' iAgeArray(0) references CTree object
18         iAgeArray(0) = tree
19
20         ' iAgeArray(1) references CPerson object
21         iAgeArray(1) = person
22
23         ' display tree information
24         Dim output As String = tree.ToString() & ": " & _
25            tree.Name & vbCrLf & "Age is " & tree.Age & vbCrLf & _
26            vbCrLf
27
28         ' display person information
29         output &= person.ToString() & ": " & _
30            person.Name & vbCrLf & "Age is " & person.Age & _
31            vbCrLf
32
33         Dim ageReference As IAge
34
35         ' display name and age for each IAge object in iAgeArray
36         For Each ageReference In iAgeArray
37            output &= vbCrLf & ageReference.Name & ": " & _
38               "Age is " & ageReference.Age
39         Next
40
41         MessageBox.Show(output, "Demonstrating Polymorphism")
42      End Sub ' Main
43
44   End Class ' CTest
```

Demonstrating Polymorphism

Interfaces.CTree: Tree
Age is 25

Interfaces.CPerson: Bob Jones
Age is 18

Tree: Age is 25
Bob Jones: Age is 18

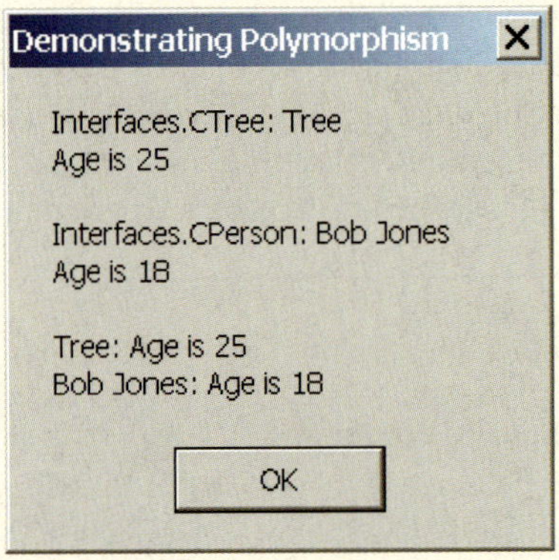

Fig. 10.18 Demonstrate polymorphism on objects of disparate classes (part 2 of 2).

Our next example reexamines the **CPoint–CCircle–CCylinder** hierarchy using an interface, rather than using an abstract class, to describe the common methods and properties of the classes in the hierarchy. We now show how a class can implement an interface, then act as a base class for derived classes to inherit the implementation. We create interface **IShape** (Fig. 10.19), which specifies methods **Area** and **Volume** and property **Name** (lines 7–9). Every class that implements interface **IShape** must provide implementations for these two methods and this property. Note that, even though the methods in this interface do not receive arguments, interface methods can receive arguments (just as regular methods can).

Good Programming Practice 10.1
*By convention, begin the name of each interface with "**I**."*

Because class **CPoint3** (Fig. 10.20) implements interface **IShape**, class **CPoint3** must implement all three **IShape** members. Lines 55–59 implement method **Area**, which returns **0**, because points have an area of zero. Lines 62–66 implement method **Volume**, which also returns **0**, because points have a volume of zero. Lines 69–76 implement **ReadOnly** property **Name**, which returns the class name as a **String** ("**CPoint3**"). Note the inclusion of keyword **Implements** followed by the interface method/property name in these method/property implementations—this keyword informs the compiler that each method/property is an implementation of its corresponding interface method/property. Also note that class **CPoint3** specifies these methods/properties as **Overridable**, enabling derived classes to override them.

Common Programming Error 10.11
*When implementing an **Interface** method, failure to include keyword **Implements** followed by that **Interface** method's name is a syntax error.*

When a class implements an interface, the class enters the same kind of *is-a* relationship that inheritance establishes. In our example, class **CPoint3** implements interface **IShape**. Therefore, a **CPoint3** object *is an* **IShape**, and objects of any class that inherits from **CPoint3** are also **IShape**s. For example, class **CCircle3** (Fig. 10.21) inherits from class **CPoint3**; thus, a **CCircle3** *is an* **IShape**. Class **CCircle3** implements interface **IShape** implicitly, because class **CCircle3** inherits the **IShape** methods that class **CPoint** implemented. Because circles do not have volume, class **CCircle3** inherits class **CPoint3**'s **Volume** method, which returns zero. However, we do not want to use the class **CPoint3** method **Area** or property **Name** for class **CCircle3**. Class **CCircle3** should provide its own implementation for these, because the area and name of a circle differ from those of a point. Lines 51–53 override method **Area** to return the circle's area, and lines 56–62 override property **Name** to return **String** "**CCircle3**".

Class **CCylinder3** (Fig. 10.22) inherits from class **CCircle3**. Class **CCylinder3** implements interface **IShape** implicitly, because class **CCylinder3** inherits method **Area** and property **Name** from class **CCircle3** and method **Volume** from class **CPoint3**. However, class **CCylinder3** overrides property **Name** and methods **Area** and **Volume** to perform **CCylinder3**-specific operations. Lines 43–45 override method **Area** to return the cylinder's surface area, lines 48–50 override method **Volume** to return the cylinder's volume and lines 58–64 override property **Name** to return **String** "**CCylinder3**".

```vbnet
1   ' Fig. 10.19: Shape.vb
2   ' Interface IShape for Point, Circle, Cylinder hierarchy.
3
4   Public Interface IShape
5
6      ' classes that implement IShape must define these methods
7      Function Area() As Double
8      Function Volume() As Double
9      ReadOnly Property Name() As String
10
11  End Interface ' IShape
```

Fig. 10.19 `IShape` interface provides methods `Area` and `Volume` and property `Name`.

```vbnet
1   ' Fig. 10.20: Point3.vb
2   ' Class CPoint3 implements IShape.
3
4   Public Class CPoint3
5      Implements IShape
6
7      ' point coordinate
8      Private mX, mY As Integer
9
10     ' default constructor
11     Public Sub New()
12        X = 0
13        Y = 0
14     End Sub ' New
15
16     ' constructor
17     Public Sub New(ByVal xValue As Integer, _
18        ByVal yValue As Integer)
19        X = xValue
20        Y = yValue
21     End Sub ' New
22
23     ' property X
24     Public Property X() As Integer
25
26        Get
27           Return mX
28        End Get
29
30        Set(ByVal xValue As Integer)
31           mX = xValue ' no need for validation
32        End Set
33
34     End Property ' X
35
```

Fig. 10.20 `CPoint3` class implements interface `IShape` (part 1 of 2).

```vbnet
36        ' property Y
37        Public Property Y() As Integer
38
39           Get
40              Return mY
41           End Get
42
43           Set(ByVal yValue As Integer)
44              mY = yValue ' no need for validation
45           End Set
46
47        End Property ' Y
48
49        ' return String representation of CPoint3
50        Public Overrides Function ToString() As String
51           Return "[" & mX & ", " & mY & "]"
52        End Function ' ToString
53
54        ' implement interface IShape method Area
55        Public Overridable Function Area() As Double _
56           Implements IShape.Area
57
58           Return 0
59        End Function ' Area
60
61        ' implement interface IShape method Volume
62        Public Overridable Function Volume() As Double _
63           Implements IShape.Volume
64
65           Return 0
66        End Function ' Volume
67
68        ' implement interface IShape property Name
69        Public Overridable ReadOnly Property Name() As String _
70           Implements IShape.Name
71
72           Get
73              Return "CPoint3"
74           End Get
75
76        End Property ' Name
77
78     End Class ' CPoint3
```

Fig. 10.20 `CPoint3` class implements interface `IShape` (part 2 of 2).

```vbnet
1     ' Fig. 10.21: Circle3.vb
2     ' CCircle3 inherits CPoint3 and overrides some of its methods.
3
4     Public Class CCircle3
5        Inherits CPoint3 ' CCircle3 Inherits from class CPoint3
6
```

Fig. 10.21 `CCircle3` class inherits from class `CPoint3` (part 1 of 3).

```vbnet
 7         Private mRadius As Double
 8
 9         ' default constructor
10         Public Sub New()
11            Radius = 0
12         End Sub ' New
13
14         ' constructor
15         Public Sub New(ByVal xValue As Integer, _
16            ByVal yValue As Integer, ByVal radiusValue As Double)
17
18            ' use MyBase reference to CPoint constructor explicitly
19            MyBase.New(xValue, yValue)
20            Radius = radiusValue
21         End Sub ' New
22
23         ' property Radius
24         Public Property Radius() As Double
25
26            Get
27               Return mRadius
28            End Get
29
30            Set(ByVal radiusValue As Double)
31
32               If radiusValue >= 0 Then
33                  mRadius = radiusValue ' mRadius cannot be negative
34               End If
35
36            End Set
37
38         End Property ' Radius
39
40         ' calculate CCircle3 diameter
41         Public Function Diameter() As Double
42            Return mRadius * 2
43         End Function ' Diameter
44
45         ' calculate CCircle3 circumference
46         Public Function Circumference() As Double
47            Return Math.PI * Diameter()
48         End Function ' Circumference
49
50         ' calculate CCircle3 area
51         Public Overrides Function Area() As Double
52            Return Math.PI * mRadius ^ 2
53         End Function ' Area
54
55         ' override interface IShape property Name from class CPoint3
56         Public ReadOnly Overrides Property Name() As String
57
```

Fig. 10.21 `CCircle3` class inherits from class `CPoint3` (part 2 of 3).

```vbnet
58          Get
59              Return "CCircle3"
60          End Get
61
62      End Property ' Name
63
64      ' return String representation of CCircle3
65      Public Overrides Function ToString() As String
66
67          ' use MyBase to return CCircle3 String representation
68          Return "Center = " & MyBase.ToString() & _
69              "; Radius = " & mRadius
70      End Function ' ToString
71
72  End Class ' CCircle3
```

Fig. 10.21 `CCircle3` class inherits from class `CPoint3` (part 3 of 3).

```vbnet
1   ' Fig. 10.22: Cylinder3.vb
2   ' CCylinder3 inherits from CCircle3 and overrides key members.
3
4   Public Class CCylinder3
5       Inherits CCircle3 ' CCylinder3 inherits from class CCircle3
6
7       Protected mHeight As Double
8
9       ' default constructor
10      Public Sub New()
11          Height = 0
12      End Sub ' New
13
14      ' four-argument constructor
15      Public Sub New(ByVal xValue As Integer, _
16          ByVal yValue As Integer, ByVal radiusValue As Double, _
17          ByVal heightValue As Double)
18
19          ' explicit call to CCircle2 constructor
20          MyBase.New(xValue, yValue, radiusValue)
21          Height = heightValue ' set CCylinder2 height
22      End Sub ' New
23
24      ' property Height
25      Public Property Height() As Double
26
27          Get
28              Return mHeight
29          End Get
30
31          ' set CCylinder3 height if argument value is positive
32          Set(ByVal heightValue As Double)
33
```

Fig. 10.22 `CCylinder3` class inherits from class `CCircle3` (part 1 of 2).

```
34             If heightValue >= 0 Then
35                 mHeight = heightValue
36             End If
37
38         End Set
39
40     End Property ' Height
41
42     ' override method Area to calculate CCylinder2 area
43     Public Overrides Function Area() As Double
44         Return 2 * MyBase.Area + MyBase.Circumference * mHeight
45     End Function ' Area
46
47     ' calculate CCylinder3 volume
48     Public Overrides Function Volume() As Double
49         Return MyBase.Area * mHeight
50     End Function ' Volume
51
52     ' convert CCylinder3 to String
53     Public Overrides Function ToString() As String
54         Return MyBase.ToString() & "; Height = " & mHeight
55     End Function ' ToString
56
57     ' override property Name from class CCircle3
58     Public Overrides ReadOnly Property Name() As String
59
60         Get
61             Return "CCylinder3"
62         End Get
63
64     End Property ' Name
65
66 End Class ' CCylinder3
```

Fig. 10.22 `CCylinder3` class inherits from class `CCircle3` (part 2 of 2).

Class **CTest3** (Fig. 10.23) demonstrates our point-circle-cylinder hierarchy that uses interfaces. Class **CTest3** has only two differences from the version in Fig. 10.8, which tested the class hierarchy created from the **MustInherit** base class **CShape**. In Fig. 10.23, line 16 declares **arrayOfShapes** as an array of **IShape** interface references, rather than **CShape** base-class references. In Fig. 10.8, calls to method **ToString** were made through **CShape** base-class references—however, because interface **IShape** does not provide method **ToString**, clients cannot invoke method **ToString** on each **IShape** object.

In Visual Basic, an interface reference may invoke only those methods and/or properties that the interface declares.

In this example, interface **IShape** declares methods **Area** and **Volume** and property **Name**, but does not declare method **ToString**. Even though every reference refers to some type of **Object**, and every **Object** has method **ToString**, if we attempt to use

IShape interface references to invoke **ToString**, the compiler will generate the following syntax error:

```
"ToString is not a member of InterfaceTest.IShape"
```

(where **InterfaceTest** is the assembly/namespace that contains interface **IShape**). Figure 10.8 was able to invoke method **ToString** through a **CShape** base-class reference, because class **CShape** inherited method **ToString** from base class **Object**. Note that the output of the program demonstrates that interface references can be used to perform polymorphic processing of objects that implement the interface.

> **Software Engineering Observation 10.11**
>
> *In Visual Basic, an interface provides only those **Public** services declared in the interface, whereas a **MustInherit** (abstract) class provides the **Public** services defined in the **MustInherit** class and those members inherited from the **MustInherit** class's base class.*

```vb
1   ' Fig. 10.23: Test3.vb
2   ' Demonstrate polymorphism in Point-Circle-Cylinder hierarchy.
3
4   Imports System.Windows.Forms
5
6   Class CTest3
7
8      Shared Sub Main()
9
10        ' instantiate CPoint3, CCircle3 and CCylinder3 objects
11        Dim point As New CPoint3(7, 11)
12        Dim circle As New CCircle3(22, 8, 3.5)
13        Dim cylinder As New CCylinder3(10, 10, 3.3, 10)
14
15        ' instantiate array of interface references
16        Dim arrayOfShapes As IShape() = New IShape(2){}
17
18        ' arrayOfShapes(0) references CPoint3 object
19        arrayOfShapes(0) = point
20
21        ' arrayOfShapes(1) references CCircle3 object
22        arrayOfShapes(1) = circle
23
24        ' arrayOfShapes(2) references CCylinder3 object
25        arrayOfShapes(2) = cylinder
26
27        Dim output As String = point.Name & ": " & _
28           point.ToString() & vbCrLf & circle.Name & ": " & _
29           circle.ToString() & vbCrLf & cylinder.Name & _
30           ": " & cylinder.ToString()
31
32        Dim shape As IShape
33
```

Fig. 10.23 **CTest3** uses interfaces to demonstrate polymorphism in Point-Circle-Cylinder hierarchy (part 1 of 2).

```
34              ' display name, area and volume for each object in
35              ' arrayOfShapes
36              For Each shape In arrayOfShapes
37                 output &= vbCrLf & vbCrLf & shape.Name & ": " & _
38                    vbCrLf & "Area = " & _
39                    String.Format("{0:F}", shape.Area) & vbCrLf & _
40                    "Volume = " & String.Format("{0:F}", shape.Volume)
41              Next
42
43              MessageBox.Show(output, "Demonstrating Polymorphism")
44           End Sub ' Main
45
46      End Class ' CTest3
```

Demonstrating Polymorphism

CPoint3: [7, 11]
CCircle3: Center = [22, 8]; Radius = 3.5
CCylinder3: Center = [10, 10]; Radius = 3.3; Height = 10

CPoint3:
Area = 0.00
Volume = 0.00

CCircle3:
Area = 38.48
Volume = 0.00

CCylinder3:
Area = 275.77
Volume = 342.12

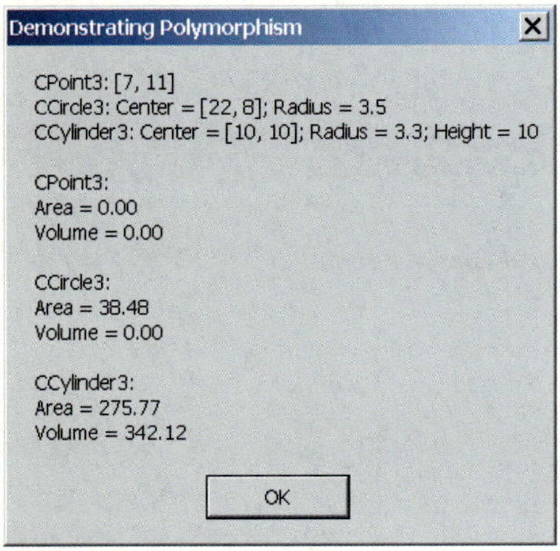

Fig. 10.23 `CTest3` uses interfaces to demonstrate polymorphism in Point-Circle-Cylinder hierarchy (part 2 of 2).

10.10 Delegates

In Chapter 6, we discussed how objects can pass member variables as arguments to methods. However, sometimes, it is beneficial for objects to pass methods as arguments to other methods. For example, suppose that you wish to sort a series of values in ascending and descending order. Rather than providing separate ascending and descending sorting methods (one for each type of comparison), we could use a single method that receives as an argument a reference to the comparison method to use. To perform an ascending sort, we could pass to the sorting method the reference to the ascending-sort-comparison method; to perform an descending sort, we could pass to the sorting method the reference to the descending-sort-comparison method. The sorting method then would use this reference to sort the list—the sorting method would not need to know whether it is performing an ascending or descending sort.

Visual Basic does not allow passing method references directly as arguments to other methods, but does provide *delegates*, which are classes that encapsulate a set of references to methods. A delegate object that contains method references can be passed to another method. Rather than send a method reference directly, an object can send the delegate instance, which contains the reference of the method that we would like to send. The method that receives the reference to the delegate then can invoke the methods the delegate contains.

Delegates containing a single method are known as *singlecast delegates* and are created or derived from class **Delegate**. Delegates containing multiple methods are *multicast delegates* and are created or derived from class **MulticastDelegate**. Both delegate classes belong to namespace **System**.

To use a delegate, we first must declare one. The delegate's declaration specifies a method signature (parameters and return value). Methods whose references will be contained within a delegate object, must have the same method signature as that defined in the delegate declaration. We then create methods that have this signature. The third step is to create a delegate instance via keyword **AddressOf**, which implicitly creates a delegate instance enclosing a reference to that method. After we create the delegate instance, we can invoke the method reference that it contains. We show this process in our next example.

Class **CDelegateBubbleSort** (Fig. 10.24), which is a modified version of the bubble-sort example in Chapter 7, uses delegates to sort an **Integer** array in ascending or descending order. Lines 7–9 provide the declaration for delegate **Comparator**. To declare a delegate (line 7), we declare a signature of a method—keyword **Delegate** after the member-access modifier (in this case, **Public**), followed by keyword **Function** (or keyword **Sub**), the delegate name, parameter list and return type. Delegate **Comparator** defines a method signature for methods that receive two **Integer** arguments and return a **Boolean**. Note that delegate **Comparator** contains no body. As we soon demonstrate, our application (Fig. 10.25) implements methods that adhere to delegate **Comparator**'s signature, then passes these methods (as arguments of type **Comparator**) to method **SortArray**. Note also that we declare delegate **Comparator** as a **Function**, because it returns a value (**Boolean**). The declaration of a delegate does not define its intended role or implementation; our application uses this particular delegate when *comparing* two **Integer**s, but other applications might use it for different purposes.

```vbnet
1   ' Fig. 10.24: DelegateBubbleSort.vb
2   ' Uses delegates to sort random numbers (ascending or descending).
3
4   Public Class CDelegateBubbleSort
5
6      ' delegate definition
7      Public Delegate Function Comparator( _
8         ByVal element1 As Integer, _
9         ByVal element2 As Integer) As Boolean
10
11     ' sort array depending on comparator
12     Public Sub SortArray(ByVal array As Integer(), _
13        ByVal Compare As Comparator)
14
15        Dim i, pass As Integer
16
```

Fig. 10.24 Bubble sort using delegates (part 1 of 2).

```
17          For pass = 0 To array.GetUpperBound(0)
18
19             ' comparison inner loop
20             For i = 0 To array.GetUpperBound(0) - 1
21
22                If Compare(array(i), array(i + 1)) Then
23                   Swap(array(i), array(i + 1))
24                End If
25
26             Next ' inner loop
27
28          Next ' outer loop
29
30       End Sub ' SortArray
31
32       ' swap two elements
33       Private Sub Swap(ByRef firstElement As Integer, _
34          ByRef secondElement As Integer)
35
36          Dim hold As Integer
37
38          hold = firstElement
39          firstElement = secondElement
40          secondElement = hold
41       End Sub ' Swap
42
43    End Class ' CDelegateBubbleSort
```

Fig. 10.24 Bubble sort using delegates (part 2 of 2).

Lines 12–30 define method **SortArray**, which takes an array and a reference to a **Comparator** delegate object as arguments. Method **SortArray** modifies the array by sorting its contents. Line 22 uses the delegate method to determine how to sort the array. Line 22 invokes the method enclosed within the delegate object by treating the delegate reference as the method that the delegate object contains. The Visual Basic invokes the enclosed method reference directly, passing it parameters **array(i)** and **array(i+1)**. The **Comparator** determines the sorting order for its two arguments. If the **Comparator** returns **True**, the two elements are out of order, so line 23 invokes method **Swap** (lines 33–41) to swap the elements. If the **Comparator** returns **False**, the two elements are in the correct order. To sort in ascending order, the **Comparator** returns **True** when the first element being compared is greater than the second element being compared. Similarly, to sort in descending order, the **Comparator** returns **True** when the first element being compared is less than the second element being compared.

Class **CFrmBubbleSort** (Fig. 10.25) displays a **Form** with two text boxes and three buttons. The first text box displays a list of unsorted numbers, and the second box displays the same list of numbers after they are sorted. The **Create Data** button creates the list of unsorted values. The **Sort Ascending** and **Sort Descending** buttons sort the array in ascending and descending order, respectively. Methods **SortAscending** (lines 31–35) and **SortDescending** (lines 38–42) each have a signature that corresponds with the signature defined by the **Comparator** delegate declaration (i.e., each receives two **Integer**s and returns a **Boolean**). As we will see, the program passes to **CDelegateBubbleSort** method **SortArray** delegates containing references to methods **SortAscending** and **SortDescending**, which will specify class **CDelegateBubbleSort**'s sorting behavior.

```vbnet
1   ' Fig. 10.25: FrmBubbleSort.vb
2   ' Create GUI that enables user to sort array.
3
4   Imports System.Windows.Forms
5
6   Public Class CFrmBubbleSort
7      Inherits Form
8
9      ' TextBox that contains original list
10     Friend WithEvents txtOriginal As TextBox
11     Friend WithEvents lblOriginal As Label
12
13     ' TextBox that contains sorted list
14     Friend WithEvents txtSorted As TextBox
15     Friend WithEvents lblSorted As Label
16
17     ' Buttons for creating and sorting lists
18     Friend WithEvents cmdCreate As Button
19     Friend WithEvents cmdSortAscending As Button
20     Friend WithEvents cmdSortDescending As Button
21
22     ' Windows Form Designer generate code
23
24     ' reference to object containing delegate
25     Dim mBubbleSort As New CDelegateBubbleSort()
26
27     ' original array with unsorted elements
28     Dim mElementArray As Integer() = New Integer(9){}
29
30     ' delegate implementation sorts in asending order
31     Private Function SortAscending(ByVal element1 As Integer, _
32        ByVal element2 As Integer) As Boolean
33
34        Return element1 > element2
35     End Function ' SortAscending
36
37     ' delegate implementation sorts in descending order
38     Private Function SortDescending(ByVal element1 As Integer, _
39        ByVal element2 As Integer) As Boolean
40
41        Return element1 < element2
42     End Function ' SortDescending
43
44     ' creates random generated numbers
45     Private Sub cmdCreate_Click(ByVal sender As System.Object, _
46        ByVal e As System.EventArgs) Handles cmdCreate.Click
47
48        txtSorted.Clear()
```

Fig. 10.25 Bubble-sort **Form** application (part 1 of 3).

```vbnet
49
50         Dim output As String
51         Dim randomNumber As Random = New Random()
52         Dim i As Integer
53
54         ' create String with 10 random numbers
55         For i = 0 To mElementArray.GetUpperBound(0)
56            mElementArray(i) = randomNumber.Next(100)
57            output &= mElementArray(i) & vbCrLf
58         Next
59
60         txtOriginal.Text = output ' display numbers
61
62         ' enable sort buttons
63         cmdSortAscending.Enabled = True
64         cmdSortDescending.Enabled = True
65      End Sub ' cmdCreate_Click
66
67      ' display array contents in specified TextBox
68      Private Sub DisplayResults()
69
70         Dim output As String
71         Dim i As Integer
72
73         ' create string with sorted numbers
74         For i = 0 To mElementArray.GetUpperBound(0)
75            output &= mElementArray(i) & vbCrLf
76         Next
77
78         txtSorted.Text = output ' display numbers
79      End Sub ' DisplayResults
80
81      ' sorts randomly generated numbers in ascending manner
82      Private Sub cmdSortAscending_Click(ByVal sender As _
83         System.Object, ByVal e As System.EventArgs) _
84         Handles cmdSortAscending.Click
85
86         ' sort array
87         mBubbleSort.SortArray(mElementArray, AddressOf SortAscending)
88
89         DisplayResults() ' display results
90
91         cmdSortAscending.Enabled = False
92         cmdSortDescending.Enabled = True
93      End Sub ' cmdSortAscending_Click
94
95      ' sorts randomly generated numbers in descending manner
96      Private Sub cmdSortDescending_Click(ByVal sender As _
97         System.Object, ByVal e As System.EventArgs) _
98         Handles cmdSortDescending.Click
99
100        ' create sort object and sort array
101        mBubbleSort.SortArray(mElementArray, AddressOf SortDescending)
```

Fig. 10.25 Bubble-sort **Form** application (part 2 of 3).

```
102
103         DisplayResults()   ' display results
104
105         cmdSortDescending.Enabled = False
106         cmdSortAscending.Enabled = True
107      End Sub ' cmdSortDescending_Click
108
109  End Class ' CFrmBubbleSort
```

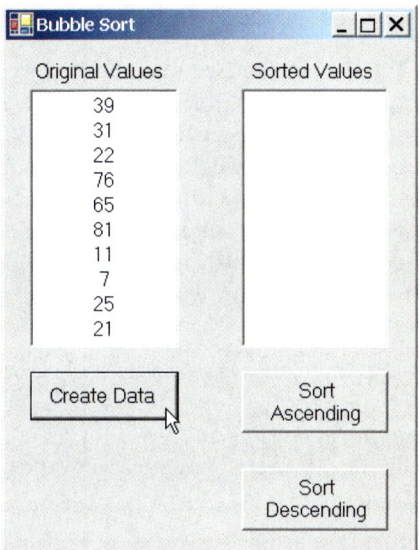
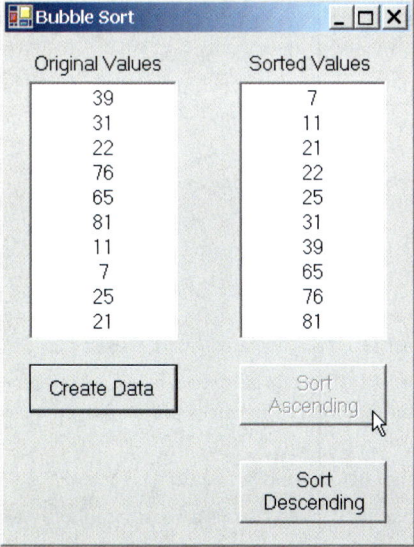
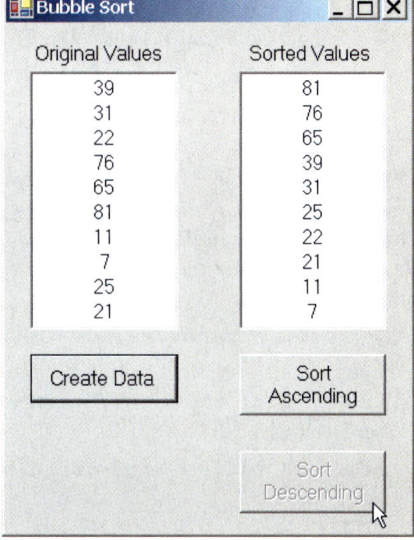

Fig. 10.25 Bubble-sort **Form** application (part 3 of 3).

Methods **cmdSortAscending_Click** (lines 82–93) and **cmdSortDescending_Click** (lines 96–107) are invoked when the user clicks the **Sort Ascending** and **Sort Descending** buttons, respectively. In method **cmdSortAscending_Click**, line 87 passes to **CDelegateBubbleSort** method **SortArray** the unsorted **mElementArray** and a reference to method **SortAscending**. Keyword **AddressOf** returns a reference to method **SortAscending**. Visual Basic implicitly converts the method reference into a delegate object that contains the method reference. The second argument of line 87 is equivalent to

```
New CDelegateBubbleSort.Comparator(AddressOf SortAscending)
```

which explicitly creates a **CDelegateBubbleSort Comparator** delegate object. In method **cmdSortDescending_Click**, line 101 passes the unsorted **mElementArray** and a reference to method **SortDescending** to method **SortArray**. We continue to use delegates in Chapters 12–14, when we discuss event handling and multithreading.

In Chapter 11, Exception Handling, we discuss how to handle problems that might occur during a program's execution. The features presented in Chapter 11 enable programmers to write more robust and fault-tolerant programs.

SUMMARY

- Polymorphism enables us to write programs in a general fashion to handle a wide variety of existing and future related classes.
- One means of processing objects of many different types is to use a **Select Case** statement to perform an appropriate action on each object based on that object's type.
- Polymorphic programming can eliminate the need for **Select Case** logic.
- When we override a base class's method in a derived class, we hide the base class's implementation of that method.
- With polymorphism, new types of objects not even envisioned when a system is created may be added without modification to the system (other than the new class itself).
- Polymorphism allows one method call to cause different actions to occur, depending on the type of the object receiving the call. The same message assumes "many forms"—hence, the term polymorphism.
- With polymorphism, the programmer can deal in generalities and let the executing program concern itself with the specifics.
- When we apply the **MustInherit** keyword to a class, we cannot create instances of that class. Instead, we create classes that inherit from the **MustInherit** class and create instances of those derived classes.
- Any class with a **MustOverride** method in it must, itself, be declared **MustInherit**.
- Although we cannot instantiate objects of **MustInherit** base classes, we can declare references to **MustInherit** base classes. Such references can manipulate instances of the derived classes polymorphically.
- A method that is declared **NotOverridable** cannot be overridden in a derived class.
- Methods that are declared **Shared** and methods that are declared **Private** are implicitly **NotOverridable**.
- A class that is declared **NotInheritable** cannot be a base class (i.e., a class cannot inherit from a **NotInheritable** class).

- A class declared **NotInheritable** cannot be inherited from, and every method in it is implicitly **NotOverridable**.
- In Visual Basic, it is impossible to pass a method reference directly as an argument to another method. To address this problem, Visual Basic allows the creation of delegates, which are classes that encapsulate a set of references to methods.
- Keyword **AddressOf** returns a reference to a delegate method. Visual Basic implicitly converts the method reference into a delegate object that contains the method reference.

TERMINOLOGY

abstract class
abstract method
AddressOf keyword
cast
class declared **NotInheritable**
class hierarchy
concrete class
delegate
information hiding
inheritance
inheritance hierarchy
interface
InvalidCastException
"is-a" relationship
method reference

multicast delegate
MustInherit base class
MustOverride method
NotInheritable class
NotOverridable method
object-oriented programming (OOP)
Overridable method
Overrides keyword
polymorphic programming
polymorphism
reference type
references to abstract base class
Select Case logic
singlecast delegate

SELF-REVIEW EXERCISES

10.1 Fill in the blanks in each of the following statements:
 a) Treating a base-class object as a _____ can cause errors.
 b) Polymorphism helps eliminate _____ logic.
 c) If a class contains one or more **MustOverride** methods, it is an _____ class.
 d) Classes from which objects can be instantiated are called _____ classes.
 e) Classes declared with keyword _____ cannot be inherited.
 f) An attempt to cast an object to one of its derived types can cause an _____.
 g) Polymorphism involves using a base-class reference to manipulate _____.
 h) Abstract classes are declared with the _____ keyword.
 i) Class members can be overridden only with the _____ keyword.
 j) _____ are classes that encapsulate references to methods.

10.2 State whether each of the following is *true* or *false*. If *false*, explain why.
 a) All methods in a **MustInherit** base class must be declared **MustOverride**.
 b) Referring to a derived-class object with a base-class reference is dangerous.
 c) A class with a **MustOverride** method must be declared **MustInherit**.
 d) Methods that are declared **MustOverride** still must be implemented when they are declared.
 e) Classes declared with the **NotInheritable** keyword cannot be base classes.
 f) Polymorphism allows programmers to manipulate derived classes with references to base classes.
 g) Polymorphic programming can eliminate the need for unnecessary **Select-Case** logic.
 h) Use keyword **MustInherit** to declare an abstract method.

i) The delegate's declaration must specify its implementation.
j) Keyword **AddressOf** returns a reference to a delegate method.

ANSWERS TO SELF-REVIEW EXERCISES

10.1 a) derived-class object. b) **Select Case**. c) abstract. d) concrete. e) **NotInheritable**. f) **InvalidCastException**. g) derived-class objects. h) **MustInherit**. i) **Overrides**. j) Delegates

10.2 a) False. Not all methods in a **MustInherit** class must be declared **MustOverride**. b) False. Referring to a base-class object with a derived-class reference is dangerous. c) True. d) False. Methods that are declared **MustOverride** do not need to be implemented, except in the derived, concrete class. e) True. f) True. g) True. h) False. Use keyword **MustInherit** to declare an abstract class. i) False. The delegate's declaration specifies only a method signature (method name, parameters and return value). j) True.

EXERCISES

10.3 How is it that polymorphism enables you to program "in the general" rather than "in the specific"? Discuss the key advantages of programming "in the general."

10.4 Discuss the problems of programming with **Select**-**Case** logic. Explain why polymorphism is an effective alternative to using **Select**-**Case** logic.

10.5 Distinguish between inheriting services and inheriting implementation. How do inheritance hierarchies designed for inheriting services differ from those designed for inheriting implementation?

10.6 Modify the payroll system of Fig. 10.10–Fig. 10.14 to add **Private** instance variables **mBirthDate** (use class **CDay** from Fig 8.8) and **mDepartmentCode** (an **Integer**) to class **CEmployee**. Assume this payroll is processed once per month. Create an array of **CEmployee** references to store the various employee objects. In a loop, calculate the payroll for each **CEmployee** (polymorphically) and add a $100.00 bonus to the person's payroll amount if this is the month in which the **CEmployee**'s birthday occurs.

10.7 Implement the **CShape** hierarchy shown in Fig. 9.3. Each **CTwoDimensionalShape** should contain method **Area** to calculate the area of the two-dimensional shape. Each **CThreeDimensionalShape** should have methods **Area** and **Volume** to calculate the surface area and volume of the three-dimensional shape, respectively. Create a program that uses an array of **CShape** references to objects of each concrete class in the hierarchy. The program should output the **String** representation of each object in the array. Also, in the loop that processes all the shapes in the array, determine whether each shape is a **CTwoDimensionalShape** or a **CThreeDimensionalShape**. If a shape is a **CTwoDimensionalShape**, display its **Area**. If a shape is a **CThreeDimensionalShape**, display its **Area** and **Volume**.

10.8 Reimplement the program of Exercise 10.7 such that classes **CTwoDimensionalShape** and **CThreeDimensionalShape** implement an **IShape** interface, rather than extending **MustInherit** class **CShape**.

11

Exception Handling

Objectives

- To understand exceptions and error handling.
- To be able to use **Try** blocks to delimit code in which exceptions might occur.
- To be able to **Throw** exceptions.
- To use **Catch** blocks to specify exception handlers.
- To use the **Finally** block to release resources.
- To understand the Visual Basic exception class hierarchy.
- To create programmer-defined exceptions.

It is common sense to take a method and try it. If it fails, admit it frankly and try another. But above all, try something.
Franklin Delano Roosevelt

O! throw away the worser part of it,
And live the purer with the other half.
William Shakespeare

If they're running and they don't look where they're going I have to come out from somewhere and catch them.
Jerome David Salinger

And oftentimes excusing of a fault
Doth make the fault the worse by the excuse.
William Shakespeare

I never forget a face, but in your case I'll make an exception.
Groucho (Julius Henry) Marx

Outline

11.1 Introduction
11.2 Exception Handling Overview
11.3 Example: `DivideByZeroException`
11.4 .NET `Exception` Hierarchy
11.5 `Finally` Block
11.6 `Exception` Properties
11.7 Programmer-Defined Exception Classes
11.8 Handling Overflows

Summary • Terminology • Self-Review Exercises • Answers to Self-Review Exercises • Exercises

11.1 Introduction

In this chapter, we introduce *exception handling*. An *exception* is an indication of a problem that occurs during a program's execution. The name "exception" comes from the fact that, although the problem can occur, it occurs infrequently. If the "rule" is that a statement normally executes correctly, then the occurrence of the problem represents the "exception to the rule." Exception handling enables programmers to create applications that can resolve (or handle) exceptions. In many cases, the handling of an exception allows a program to continue executing as if no problems were encountered. However, more severe problems might prevent a program from continuing normal execution, instead requiring the program to notify the user of the problem and then terminate in a controlled manner. The features presented in this chapter enable programmers to write clear, robust and more *fault-tolerant programs*.

The style and details of exception handling in Visual Basic .NET are based in part on the work of Andrew Koenig and Bjarne Stroustrup, as presented in their paper, "Exception Handling for C++ (revised)."[1] Visual Basic's designers implemented an exception-handling mechanism similar to that used in C++, using Koenig's and Stroustrup's work as a model.

This chapter begins with an overview of exception-handling concepts and demonstrations of basic exception-handling techniques. The chapter also offers an overview of the exception-handling class hierarchy. Programs typically request and release resources (such as files on disk) during program execution. Often, the supply of these resources is limited, or the resources can be used by only one program at a time. We demonstrate a part of the exception-handling mechanism that enables a program to use a resource and then guarantees that the program releases the resource for use by other programs. The chapter continues with an example that demonstrates several properties of class `System.Exception` (the base class of all exception classes); this is followed by an example that shows programmers how to create and use their own exception classes. The chapter concludes with a practical application of exception handling, in which a program handles exceptions generated by arithmetic calculations that result in out-of-range values for a particular data type—a condition known as *arithmetic overflow*.

---

1. Koenig, A. and B. Stroustrup, "Exception Handling for C++ (revised)", *Proceedings of the Usenix C++ Conference*, 149–176, San Francisco, April 1990.

11.2 Exception Handling Overview

The logic of a program frequently tests conditions that determine how program execution proceeds. Consider the following pseudocode:

Perform a task

If the preceding task did not execute correctly
    Perform error processing

Perform next task

If the preceding task did not execute correctly
    Perform error processing

...

In this pseudocode, we begin by performing a task. We then test whether that task executed correctly. If not, we perform error processing. Otherwise, we continue on to the next task and start the entire process again. Although this form of error handling works, the intermixing of program logic with error-handling logic can make the program difficult to read, modify, maintain and debug. This is especially true in large applications. In fact, if many of the potential problems occur infrequently, the intermixing of program logic and error handling can degrade the performance of the program, because the program must test extra conditions to determine whether the next task can be performed.

Exception handling enables the programmer to remove error-handling code from the "main line" of the program's execution. This improves program clarity and enhances modifiability. Programmers can decide to handle whatever exceptions arise—all types of exceptions, all exceptions of a certain type or all exceptions of a group of related types. Such flexibility reduces the likelihood that errors will be overlooked, thereby increasing a program's robustness.

Testing and Debugging Tip 11.1
Exception handling helps improve a program's fault tolerance. If it is easy to write error-processing code, programmers are more likely to use it.

Software Engineering Observation 11.1
Although it is possible to do so, do not use exceptions for conventional flow of control. It is difficult to keep track of a large number of exception cases, and programs with a large number of exception cases are hard to read and maintain.

Good Programming Practice 11.1
Avoid using exception handling for purposes other than error handling, because such usage can reduce program clarity.

When using programming languages that do not support exception handling, programmers often postpone the writing of error-processing code and sometimes forget to include it. This results in less robust software products. Visual Basic enables the programmer to deal with exception handling in a convenient manner from the inception of a project. However, the programmer still must put considerable effort into incorporating an exception-handling strategy into software projects.

Software Engineering Observation 11.2

Try to incorporate an exception-handling strategy into a system from the inception of the design process. It can be difficult to add effective exception handling to a system after it has been implemented.

Software Engineering Observation 11.3

In the past, programmers used many techniques to implement error-processing code. Exception handling provides a single, uniform technique for processing errors. This helps programmers working on large projects to understand each other's error-processing code.

The exception-handling mechanism also is useful for processing problems that occur when a program interacts with software elements, such as methods, properties, assemblies and classes. Rather than handling all problems internally, such software elements often use exceptions to notify programs when problems occur. This enables programmers to implement error handling customized for each application.

Common Programming Error 11.1

Aborting a program could leave a resource—such as file stream or I/O device—in a state that causes the resource to be unavailable to other programs. This is known as a "resource leak."

Performance Tip 11.1

When no exceptions occur, exception-handling code does not hinder the program's performance. Thus, programs that implement exception handling operate more efficiently than do programs that perform error handling throughout the program logic.

Performance Tip 11.2

Exception-handling should be used only for problems that occur infrequently. As a "rule of thumb," if a problem occurs at least 30 percent of the time when a particular statement executes, the program should test for the error inline, because the overhead of exception handling will cause the program to execute more slowly.[2]

Software Engineering Observation 11.4

*Methods with common error conditions should return **Nothing** (or another appropriate value), rather than throwing exceptions. A program calling such a method can check the return value to determine the success or failure of the method call.*[3]

A complex application normally consists of predefined software components (such as those defined in the .NET Framework) and components specific to the application that uses the predefined components. When a predefined component encounters a problem, that component must have a mechanism by which it can communicate the problem to the application-specific component. This is because the predefined component cannot know in advance how a specific application will process a problem that occurs. Exception handling facilitates efficient collaboration between software components by enabling predefined components to communicate the occurrence of problems to application-specific components, which then can process the problems in an application-specific manner.

---

2. "Best Practices for Handling Exceptions [Visual Basic]," *.NET Framework Developer's Guide*, Visual Studio .NET Online Help.
3. "Best Practices for Handling Exceptions [Visual Basic]."

Exception handling is designed to process *synchronous errors*—errors that occur during the normal flow of program control. Common examples of these errors are out-of-range array subscripts, arithmetic overflow (i.e., the occurrence of a value that is outside the representable range of values), division by zero for integral types, invalid method parameters and running out of available memory. Exception handling is not designed to process *asynchronous* events, such as disk-I/O completions, network-message arrivals, mouse clicks and keystrokes.

Exception handling is geared toward situations in which the method that detects an error is unable to handle it. Such a method *throws an exception*. There is no guarantee that the program contains an *exception handler*—code that executes when the program detects an exception—to process that kind of exception. If an appropriate exception handler exists, the exception will be *caught* and *handled*. The result of an *uncaught exception* is dependant on whether the program is executing in debug mode or standard execution mode. In debug mode, when the runtime environment detects an uncaught exception, a dialog appears that enables the programmer to view the problem in the debugger or to continue program execution by ignoring the problem. In standard execution mode, a Windows application presents a dialog that allows the user to continue or terminate program execution. A console application presents a dialog that enables the user to open the program in the debugger or terminate program execution.

Visual Basic .NET uses **Try** blocks to enable exception handling. A **Try** block consists of keyword **Try**, followed by a block of code in which exceptions might occur. The **Try** block encloses statements that could cause exceptions and statements that should not execute if an exception occurs. Immediately following the **Try** block are zero or more **Catch** blocks (also called **Catch** handlers). Each **Catch** block specifies an exception parameter representing the type of exception that the **Catch** block can handle. If an exception parameter includes an optional parameter name, the **Catch** handler can use that parameter name to interact with a caught exception object. Optionally, programmers can include a *parameterless* **Catch** block that catches all exception types. After the last **Catch** block, an optional **Finally** block contains code that always executes, regardless of whether an exception occurs.

When a method called in a program detects an exception, or when the Common Language Runtime (CLR) detects a problem, the method or CLR *throws an exception*. The point in the program at which an exception occurs is called the *throw point*—an important location for debugging purposes (as we demonstrate in Section 11.6). Exceptions are objects of classes that extend class **Exception** of namespace **System**. If an exception occurs in a **Try** block, the **Try** block *expires* (i.e., terminates immediately), and program control transfers to the first **Catch** handler (if there is one) following the **Try** block. Visual Basic is said to use the *termination model of exception handling*, because the **Try** block enclosing a thrown exception expires immediately when that exception occurs.[4] As with any other block of code, when a **Try** block terminates, local variables defined in the block go out of scope. Next, the CLR searches for the first **Catch** handler that can process the type of exception that occurred. The CLR locates the matching **Catch** by comparing the thrown exception's type to each **Catch**'s exception-parameter type. A match occurs if

---

4. Some languages use the *resumption model of exception handling* in which, after handling the exception, control returns to the point at which the exception was thrown and execution resumes from that point.

the types are identical or if the thrown exception's type is a derived class of the exception-parameter type. Once an exception is matched to a **Catch** handler, the other **Catch** handlers are ignored.

Testing and Debugging Tip 11.2
If several handlers match the type of an exception, and if each of these handles the exception differently, then the order of the handlers will affect the manner in which the exception is handled.

Common Programming Error 11.2
It is a logic error if a catch that catches a base-class object is placed before a catch for that class's derived-class types.

If no exceptions occur in a **Try** block, the CLR ignores the exception handlers for that block. Program execution continues with the next statement after the **Try/Catch** sequence, regardless of whether an exception occurs. If an exception that occurs in a **Try** block has no matching **Catch** handler, or if an exception occurs in a statement that is not in a **Try** block, the method containing that statement terminates immediately, and the CLR attempts to locate an enclosing **Try** block in a calling method. This process is called *stack unwinding* and is discussed in Section 11.6.

11.3 Example: `DivideByZeroException`

Let us consider a simple example of exception handling. The application in Fig. 11.1 uses **Try** and **Catch** to specify a block of code that might throw exceptions and to handle those exceptions if they occur. The application displays two **TextBox**es in which the user can type integers. When the user presses the **Click To Divide** button, the program invokes **cmdDivide_Click** (lines 25–61), which obtains the user's input, converts the input values to type **Integer** and divides the first number (**numerator**) by the second number (**denominator**). Assuming that the user provides integers as input and does not specify **0** as the denominator for the division, **cmdDivide_Click** displays the division result in **lblOutput**. However, if the user inputs a non-integer value or supplies **0** as the denominator, exceptions occur. This program demonstrates how to catch such exceptions.

Before we discuss the details of this program, let us consider the sample output windows in Fig. 11.1. The first window shows a successful calculation, in which the user inputs the numerator **100** and the denominator **7**. Note that the result (**14**) is an **Integer**, because **Integer** division always yields an **Integer** result. The next two windows depict the result of inputting a non-**Integer** value—in this case, the user entered **"hello"** in the second **TextBox**. When the user presses **Click To Divide**, the program attempts to convert the input **String**s into **Integer** values using method **Convert.ToInt32**. If an argument passed to **Convert.ToInt32** does not represent an integer value, the method generates a *FormatException* (namespace **System**). The program detects the exception and displays an error message dialog, indicating that the user must enter two **Integers**. The last two output windows demonstrate the result after an attempt to divide by zero. In integer arithmetic, the CLR tests for division by zero and generates a *DivideByZeroException* (namespace **System**) if the denominator is zero.

Chapter 11   Exception Handling   447

The program detects the exception and displays an error message dialog, indicating that an attempt has been made to divide by zero.[5]

```vb
1    ' Fig. 11.1: DivideByZeroTest.vb
2    ' Basics of Visual Basic exception handling.
3
4    Imports System.Windows.Forms.Form
5
6    Public Class FrmDivideByZero
7       Inherits Form
8
9       ' Label and TextBox for specifying numerator
10      Friend WithEvents lblNumerator As Label
11      Friend WithEvents txtNumerator As TextBox
12
13      ' Label and TextBox for specifying denominator
14      Friend WithEvents lblDenominator As Label
15      Friend WithEvents txtDenominator As TextBox
16
17      ' Button for dividing numerator by denominator
18      Friend WithEvents cmdDivide As Button
19
20      Friend WithEvents lblOutput As Label ' output for division
21
22      ' Visual Studio .NET generated code
23
24      ' obtain integers from user and divide numerator by denominator
25      Private Sub cmdDivide_Click(ByVal sender As System.Object, _
26         ByVal e As System.EventArgs) Handles cmdDivide.Click
27
28         lblOutput.Text = ""
29
30         ' retrieve user input and call Quotient
31         Try
32
33            ' Convert.ToInt32 generates FormatException if argument
34            ' is not an integer
35            Dim numerator As Integer = _
36               Convert.ToInt32(txtNumerator.Text)
37
38            Dim denominator As Integer = _
39               Convert.ToInt32(txtDenominator.Text)
```

Fig. 11.1 Exception handlers for **FormatException** and **DivideByZeroException** (part 1 of 2).

---

5. The CLR allows floating-point division by zero, which produces a positive or negative infinity result, depending on whether the numerator is positive or negative. Dividing zero by zero is a special case that results in a value called "not a number." Programs can test for these results using constants for positive infinity (**PositiveInfinity**), negative infinity (**NegativeInfinity**) and not a number (**NaN**) that are defined in type **Double** (for **Double** calculations) and **Single** (for floating-point calculations).

```
40
41          ' division generates DivideByZeroException if
42          ' denominator is 0
43          Dim result As Integer = numerator \ denominator
44
45          lblOutput.Text = result.ToString()
46
47       ' process invalid number format
48       Catch formatExceptionParameter As FormatException
49          MessageBox.Show("You must enter two integers", _
50             "Invalid Number Format", MessageBoxButtons.OK, _
51             MessageBoxIcon.Error)
52
53       ' user attempted to divide by zero
54       Catch divideByZeroExceptionParameter As DivideByZeroException
55          MessageBox.Show(divideByZeroExceptionParameter.Message, _
56             "Attempted to Divide by Zero", _
57             MessageBoxButtons.OK, MessageBoxIcon.Error)
58
59       End Try
60
61    End Sub ' cmdDivide_Click
62
63 End Class ' FrmDivideByZero
```

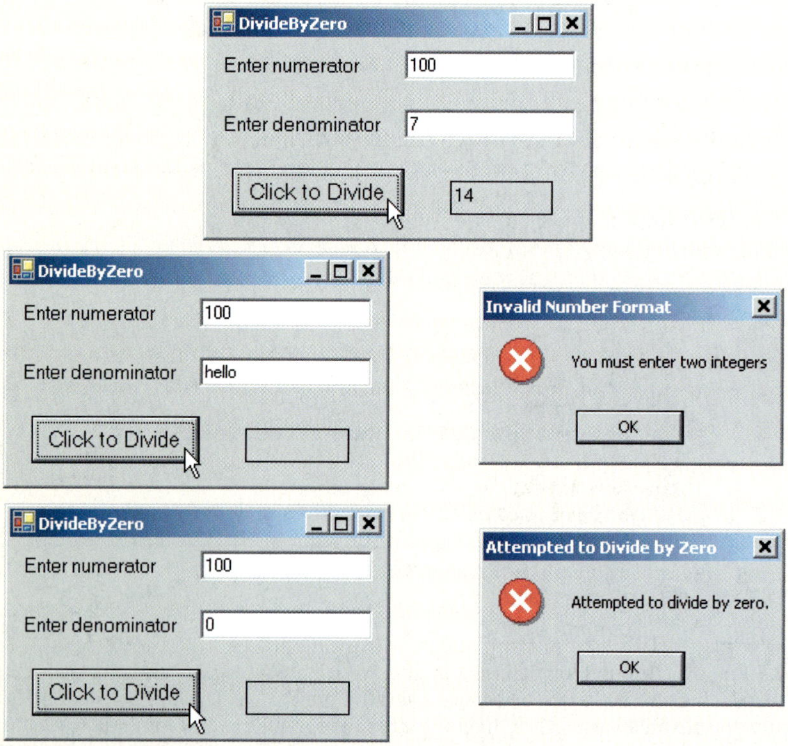

Fig. 11.1 Exception handlers for **FormatException** and **DivideByZeroException** (part 2 of 2).

Now, we consider the user interactions and flow of control that yield the results shown in the sample output windows. The user inputs values into the **TextBox**es that represent the numerator and denominator and then presses **Click To Divide**. At this point, the program invokes method **cmdDivide_Click**. Line 28 assigns the empty **String** to **lblOutput** to clear any prior result, because the program is about to attempt a new calculation. Lines 31–59 define a **Try** block enclosing the code that might throw exceptions, as well as the code that should not execute if an exception occurs. For example, the program should not display a new result in **lblOutput** (line 45) unless the calculation (line 43) completes successfully. Remember that the **Try** block terminates immediately if an exception occurs, so the remaining code in the **Try** block will not execute.

Software Engineering Observation 11.5

*Enclose in a **Try** block a significant logical section of the program in which several statements can throw exceptions, rather than using a separate **Try** block for every statement that might throw an exception. However, each **Try** block should enclose a small enough section of code such that when an exception occurs, the specific context is known, and the **Catch** handlers can process the exception properly.*

The two statements that read the **Integer**s from the **TextBox**es (lines 35–39) call method **Convert.ToInt32** to convert **String**s to **Integer** values. This method throws a **FormatException** if it cannot convert its **String** argument to an **Integer**. If lines 35–39 convert the values properly (i.e., no exceptions occur), then line 43 divides the **numerator** by the **denominator** and assigns the result to variable **result**. If the denominator is zero, line 43 causes the CLR to throw a **DivideByZeroException**. If line 43 does not cause an exception to be thrown, then line 45 displays the result of the division. If no exceptions occur in the **Try** block, the program successfully completes the **Try** block by ignoring the **Catch** handlers at lines 48–51 and 54–57 and reaching line 59. Then, the program executes the first statement following the **Try**/**Catch** sequence. In this example, the program reaches the end of event handler **cmdDivide_Click** (line 61), so the method terminates, and the program awaits the next user interaction.

Immediately following the **Try** block are two **Catch** handlers. Lines 48–51 define the **Catch** handler for a **FormatException**, and lines 54–57 define the **Catch** handler for the **DivideByZeroException**. Each **Catch** handler begins with keyword **Catch**, followed by an exception parameter that specifies the type of exception handled by the **Catch** block. The exception-handling code appears in the **Catch**-handler body. In general, when an exception occurs in a **Try** block, a **Catch** block catches the exception and handles it. In Fig. 11.1, the first **Catch** handler specifies that it catches **FormatException**s (thrown by method **Convert.ToInt32**), and the second **Catch** block specifies that it catches **DivideByZeroException**s (thrown by the CLR). If an exception occurs, the program executes only the matching **Catch** handler. Both the exception handlers in this example display an error message dialog. When program control reaches the end of a **Catch** handler, the program considers the exception to be handled, and program control continues with the first statement after the **Try**/**Catch** sequence (the end of the method, in this example).

In the second sample output, the user input **hello** as the denominator. When lines 38–39 execute, **Convert.ToInt32** cannot convert this **String** to an **Integer**, so **Convert.ToInt32** creates a **FormatException** object and throws it to indicate that the method was unable to convert the **String** to an **Integer**. When the exception occurs, the **Try** block expires (terminates). Any local variables defined in the **Try** block go out of scope; therefore, those variables are not available to the exception handlers. Next, the CLR attempts to locate a matching **Catch** handler. Starting with the **Catch** in line 48, the program compares the type of the thrown exception (**FormatException**) with the exception type in the **Catch**-block declaration (also **FormatException**). A match occurs, so the exception handler executes, and the program ignores all other exception handlers following the **Try** block. If a match did not occur, the program would compare the type of the thrown exception with the next **Catch** handler in sequence, repeating this process until a match is found.

Common Programming Error 11.3

*An attempt to access a **Try** block's local variables in one of that **Try** block's associated **Catch** handlers is a syntax error. Before a corresponding **Catch** handler can execute, the **Try** block expires, and its local variables go out of scope.*

Common Programming Error 11.4

*Specifying a comma-separated list of exception parameters in a **Catch** handler is a syntax error. Each **Catch** handler can have at most one exception parameter.*

In the third sample output, the user inputs **0** as the denominator. When line 43 executes, the CLR throws a **DivideByZeroException** object to indicate the occurrence of an attempt to divide by zero. Once again, the **Try** block terminates immediately upon encountering the exception, and the program attempts to locate a matching **Catch** handler. Starting from the **Catch** handler in line 48, the program compares the type of the thrown exception (**DivideByZeroException**) with the exception type in the **Catch**-handler declaration (**FormatException**). In this case, the first **Catch** handler does not produce a match. This is because the exception type in the **Catch**-handler declaration is not the same as the type of the thrown exception, and **FormatException** is not a base class of **DivideByZeroException**. Therefore, the program proceeds to line 54 and compares the type of the thrown exception (**DivideByZeroException**) with the exception type in the **Catch**-handler declaration (**DivideByZeroException**). A match occurs, which causes that exception handler to execute, using property *Message* of class **Exception** to display the error message. If there were additional **Catch** handlers, the program would ignore them.

11.4 .NET Exception Hierarchy

The exception-handling mechanism allows only objects of class **Exception** and its derived classes to be thrown and caught. This section overviews several of the .NET Framework's exception classes. In addition, we discuss how to determine whether a particular method throws exceptions.

Class **Exception** of namespace **System** is the base class of the .NET Framework exception hierarchy. Two of the most important classes derived from **Exception** are *ApplicationException* and *SystemException*. **ApplicationException** is a base class that programmers can extend to create exception data types that are specific to their applications. We discuss the creation of programmer-defined exception classes in Section 11.7. Programs can recover from most **ApplicationException**s and continue execution.

The CLR generates **`SystemException`**s, which can occur at any point during the execution of the program. Many of these exceptions can be avoided if applications are coded properly. These are called *runtime exceptions*. Runtime exceptions are are derived from class **`SystemException`**. For example, if a program attempts to access an out-of-range array subscript, the CLR throws an exception of type **`IndexOutOfRangeException`** (a derived class of **`SystemException`**). Similarly, a runtime exception occurs when a program uses an object reference to manipulate an object that does not yet exist (i.e., the reference has a **`Nothing`** value). Attempting to use a **`Nothing`** reference causes a **`NullReferenceException`** (another derived class of **`SystemException`**). According to Microsoft's "Best Practices for Handling Exceptions [Visual Basic],"[6] programs typically cannot recover from most exceptions that the CLR throws. Therefore, programs generally should not throw or catch **`SystemException`**s. [*Note:* For a complete list of the derived classes of **`Exception`**, search for "**`Exception`** class" in the **Index** of the Visual Studio .NET online documentation.]

A benefit of using the exception class hierarchy is that a **`Catch`** handler can catch exceptions of a particular type or can use a base-class type to catch exceptions in a hierarchy of related exception types. For example, Section 11.2 discussed the parameterless **`Catch`** handler, which catches exceptions of all types. A **`Catch`** handler that specifies an exception parameter of type **`Exception`** also can catch all exceptions, because **`Exception`** is the base class of all exception classes. The advantage of using this approach is that the exception handler can use the exception parameter to access the information of the caught exception.

The use of inheritance with exceptions enables an exception handler to catch related exceptions using a concise notation. An exception handler certainly could catch each derived-class exception type individually, but catching the base-class exception type is more concise. However, this makes sense only if the handling behavior is the same for a base class and all derived classes. Otherwise, catch each derived-class exception individually.

We know that many different exception types exist and we also know that methods, properties and the CLR can throw exceptions. But, how do we determine that an exception might occur in a program? For methods contained in the .NET Framework classes, programmers can investigate the detailed description of the methods in the online documentation. If a method throws an exception, its description contains a section called **Exceptions** that specifies the types of exceptions thrown by the method and briefly describes potential causes for the exceptions. For example, search for "**`Convert.ToInt32`** method" in the **Index** of the Visual Studio .NET online documentation. In the document that describes the method, click the link **Overloads Public Shared Function ToInt32(String) As Integer**. In the document that appears, the **Exceptions** section indicates that method **`Convert.ToInt32`** throws three exception types—**`ArgumentException`**, **`FormatException`** and **`OverflowException`**—and describes the reason why each exception type might occur.

Software Engineering Observation 11.6

*If a method throws exceptions, statements that invoke the method should be placed in **`Try`** blocks, and those exceptions should be caught and handled.*

---

6. "Best Practices for Handling Exceptions [Visual Basic]," *.NET Framework Developer's Guide*, Visual Studio .NET Online Help.

It is more difficult to determine when the CLR throws exceptions. Typically, such information appears in the *Visual Basic Language Specification*, which is located in the online documentation. To access the language specification, select **Help > Contents...** in Visual Studio. In the **Contents** dialogue, expand **Visual Studio .NET**, **Visual Basic and Visual C#**, **Reference**, **Visual Basic Language** and **Visual Basic .NET Language Specification**.

The language specification defines the syntax of the language and specifies cases in which exceptions are thrown. For example, in Fig. 11.1, we demonstrated that the CLR throws a `DivideByZeroException` when a program attempts to divide by zero in integer arithmetic. Section 10.5.4 of the language specification discusses the division operator. In this section, programmers find a detailed analysis of when a `DivideByZeroException` occurs.

11.5 `Finally` Block

Programs frequently request and release resources dynamically (i.e., at execution time). For example, a program that reads a file from disk first requests to open that file. If that request succeeds, the program reads the contents of the file. Operating systems typically prevent more than one program from manipulating a file at once. Therefore, when a program finishes processing a file, the program normally closes the file (i.e., releases the resource). This enables other programs to use the file. Closing the file helps prevent a *resource leak*; this occurs when the file resource is not available to other programs, because a program using the file never closed it. Programs that obtain certain types of resources (such as files) must return those resources explicitly to the system to avoid resource leaks.

In programming languages such as C and C++, in which the programmer is responsible for dynamic memory management, the most common type of resource leak is a *memory leak*. A memory leak occurs when a program allocates memory (as Visual Basic programmers do via keyword `New`), but does not deallocate the memory when the memory is no longer needed in the program. Normally, this is not an issue in Visual Basic, because the CLR performs "garbage collection" of memory that is no longer needed by an executing program. However, other kinds of resource leaks (such as the unclosed files that we mentioned previously) can occur in Visual Basic.

Testing and Debugging Tip 11.3
The CLR does not eliminate memory leaks completely. The CLR will not garbage collect an object until the program contains no more references to that object. Thus, memory leaks can occur if programmers erroneously keep references to unwanted objects.

Potential exceptions are associated with the processing of most resources that require explicit release. For example, a program that processes a file might receive `IOException`s during the processing. For this reason, file-processing code normally appears in a `Try` block. Regardless of whether a program successfully processes a file, the program should close the file when the file is no longer needed. Suppose a program places all resource-request and resource-release code in a `Try` block. If no exceptions occur, the `Try` block executes normally and releases the resources after using them. However, if an exception occurs, the `Try` block may expire before the resource-release code can execute. We could duplicate all resource-release code in the `Catch` handlers, but this would make the code more difficult to modify and maintain.

To address this problem, Visual Basic's exception handling mechanism provides the **`Finally`** block, which is guaranteed to execute if program control enters the corresponding **`Try`** block. The **`Finally`** block executes regardless of whether that **`Try`** block executes successfully or an exception occurs. This guarantee makes the **`Finally`** block an ideal location in which to place resource deallocation code for resources that are acquired and manipulated in the corresponding **`Try`** block. If the **`Try`** block executes successfully, the **`Finally`** block executes immediately after the **`Try`** block terminates. If an exception occurs in the **`Try`** block, the **`Finally`** block executes immediately after a **`Catch`** handler completes. If the exception is not caught by a **`Catch`** handler associated with that **`Try`** block, or if a **`Catch`** handler associated with that **`Try`** block throws an exception, the **`Finally`** block executes before the exception is processed by the next enclosing **`Try`** block (if there is one).

Testing and Debugging Tip 11.4

*A **`Finally`** block typically contains code to release resources acquired in the corresponding **`Try`** block; this makes the **`Finally`** block an effective way to eliminate resource leaks.*

Testing and Debugging Tip 11.5

*The only reason that a **`Finally`** block will not execute if program control enters the corresponding **`Try`** block is if the application terminates before **`Finally`** can execute.*

Performance Tip 11.3

As a rule, resources should be released as soon as it is apparent that they are no longer needed in a program. This makes the resources available for reuse, thus enhancing resource utilization in the program.

If one or more **`Catch`** handlers follow a **`Try`** block, the **`Finally`** block is optional. However, if no **`Catch`** handlers follow a **`Try`** block, a **`Finally`** block must appear immediately after the **`Try`** block. If any **`Catch`** handlers follow a **`Try`** block, the **`Finally`** block appears after the last **`Catch`** handler. Only whitespace and comments can separate the blocks in a **`Try/Catch/Finally`** sequence.

Common Programming Error 11.5

*Placing the **`Finally`** block before a **`Catch`** handler is a syntax error.*

The Visual Basic application in Fig. 11.2 demonstrates that the **`Finally`** block always executes, regardless of whether an exception occurs in the corresponding **`Try`** block. The program consists of method **`Main`** (lines 8–52) and four other **`Shared`** methods that **`Main`** invokes to demonstrate **`Finally`**. These methods are **`DoesNotThrowException`** (lines 55–73), **`ThrowExceptionWithCatch`** (lines 76–97), **`ThrowExceptionWithoutCatch`** (lines 100–118) and **`ThrowExceptionCatchRethrow`** (lines 121–149). [*Note:* We use **`Shared`** methods in this example so that **`Main`** can invoke these methods directly, without creating **`CUsingExceptions`** objects. This enables us to focus on the mechanics of the **`Try/Catch/Finally`** sequence.]

Line 12 of **`Main`** invokes method **`DoesNotThrowException`** (lines 55–73). The **`Try`** block (lines 58–70) for this method begins by outputting a message (line 59). Because the **`Try`** block does not throw any exceptions, program control ignores the **`Catch`** handler (lines 62–63) and executes the **`Finally`** block (lines 66–68), which outputs a message. At this point, program control continues with the first statement after the **End Try** statement (line 72), which outputs a message indicating that the end of the method has been reached. Then, program control returns to **Main**.

Line 18 of **Main** invokes method **ThrowExceptionWithCatch** (lines 76–97); which begins in its **Try** block (lines 79–94) by outputting a message. Next, the **Try** block creates an **Exception** object and uses a ***Throw*** *statement* to throw the exception object (lines 82–83). The **String** passed to the constructor becomes the exception object's error message. When a **Throw** statement in a **Try** block executes, the **Try** block expires immediately, and program control continues at the first **Catch** (lines 86–87) following the **Try** block. In this example, the type thrown (**Exception**) matches the type specified in the **Catch**, so line 87 outputs a message indicating the type of exception that occurred. Then, the **Finally** block (lines 90–92) executes and outputs a message. At this point, program control continues with the first statement after the **End Try** statement (line 96), which outputs a message indicating that the end of the method has been reached. Program control then returns to **Main**. In line 87, note that we use the exception object's ***Message*** *property* to retrieve the error message associated with the exception (i.e., the message passed to the **Exception** constructor). Section 11.6 discusses several properties of class **Exception**.

Lines 26–34 of **Main** define a **Try** block in which **Main** invokes method **ThrowExceptionWithoutCatch** (lines 100–118). The **Try** block enables **Main** to catch any exceptions thrown by **ThrowExceptionWithoutCatch**. The **Try** block in lines 103–114 of **ThrowExceptionWithoutCatch** begins by outputting a message. Next, the **Try** block throws an **Exception** (lines 106–107), and the **Try** block expires immediately.

```
1    ' Fig 11.2: UsingExceptions.vb
2    ' Using Finally blocks.
3
4    ' demonstrating that Finally always executes
5    Class CUsingExceptions
6
7       ' entry point for application
8       Shared Sub Main()
9
10         ' Case 1: No exceptions occur in called method
11         Console.WriteLine("Calling DoesNotThrowException")
12         DoesNotThrowException()
13
14         ' Case 2: Exception occurs and is caught in called method
15         Console.WriteLine(vbCrLf & _
16            "Calling ThrowExceptionWithCatch")
17
18         ThrowExceptionWithCatch()
19
20         ' Case 3: Exception occurs, but not caught in called method
21         ' because no Catch handler.
22         Console.WriteLine(vbCrLf & _
23            "Calling ThrowExceptionWithoutCatch")
24
```

Fig. 11.2 **Finally** statements always execute, regardless of whether an exception occurs (part 1 of 4).

```vbnet
25          ' call ThrowExceptionWithoutCatch
26          Try
27             ThrowExceptionWithoutCatch()
28
29          ' process exception returned from ThrowExceptionWithoutCatch
30          Catch
31             Console.WriteLine("Caught exception from " & _
32                "ThrowExceptionWithoutCatch in Main")
33
34          End Try
35
36          ' Case 4: Exception occurs and is caught in called method,
37          ' then rethrown to caller.
38          Console.WriteLine(vbCrLf & _
39             "Calling ThrowExceptionCatchRethrow")
40
41          ' call ThrowExceptionCatchRethrow
42          Try
43             ThrowExceptionCatchRethrow()
44
45          ' process exception returned from ThrowExceptionCatchRethrow
46          Catch
47             Console.WriteLine("Caught exception from " & _
48                "ThrowExceptionCatchRethrow in Main")
49
50          End Try
51
52       End Sub ' Main
53
54       ' no exceptions thrown
55       Public Shared Sub DoesNotThrowException()
56
57          ' Try block does not throw any exceptions
58          Try
59             Console.WriteLine("In DoesNotThrowException")
60
61          ' this Catch never executes
62          Catch
63             Console.WriteLine("This Catch never executes")
64
65          ' Finally executes because corresponding Try executed
66          Finally
67             Console.WriteLine( _
68                "Finally executed in DoesNotThrowException")
69
70          End Try
71
72          Console.WriteLine("End of DoesNotThrowException")
73       End Sub ' DoesNotThrowException
74
```

Fig. 11.2 `Finally` statements always execute, regardless of whether an exception occurs (part 2 of 4).

```vbnet
75     ' throws exception and catches it locally
76     Public Shared Sub ThrowExceptionWithCatch()
77
78        ' Try block throws exception
79        Try
80           Console.WriteLine("In ThrowExceptionWithCatch")
81
82           Throw New Exception( _
83              "Exception in ThrowExceptionWithCatch")
84
85        ' catch exception thrown in Try block
86        Catch exceptionParameter As Exception
87           Console.WriteLine("Message: " & exceptionParameter.Message)
88
89        ' Finally executes because corresponding Try executed
90        Finally
91           Console.WriteLine( _
92              "Finally executed in ThrowExceptionWithCatch")
93
94        End Try
95
96        Console.WriteLine("End of ThrowExceptionWithCatch")
97     End Sub ' ThrowExceptionWithCatch
98
99     ' throws exception and does not catch it locally
100    Public Shared Sub ThrowExceptionWithoutCatch()
101
102       ' throw exception, but do not catch it
103       Try
104          Console.WriteLine("In ThrowExceptionWithoutCatch")
105
106          Throw New Exception( _
107             "Exception in ThrowExceptionWithoutCatch")
108
109       ' Finally executes because corresponding Try executed
110       Finally
111          Console.WriteLine("Finally executed in " & _
112             "ThrowExceptionWithoutCatch")
113
114       End Try
115
116       ' unreachable code; logic error
117       Console.WriteLine("End of ThrowExceptionWithoutCatch")
118    End Sub ' ThrowExceptionWithoutCatch
119
120    ' throws exception, catches it and rethrows it
121    Public Shared Sub ThrowExceptionCatchRethrow()
122
123       ' Try block throws exception
124       Try
125          Console.WriteLine("In ThrowExceptionCatchRethrow")
126
```

Fig. 11.2 `Finally` statements always execute, regardless of whether an exception occurs (part 3 of 4).

```vbnet
127             Throw New Exception( _
128                 "Exception in ThrowExceptionCatchRethrow")
129
130         ' catch any exception and rethrow
131         Catch exceptionParameter As Exception
132             Console.WriteLine("Message: " & _
133                 exceptionParameter.Message)
134
135             ' rethrow exception for further processing
136             Throw exceptionParameter
137
138             ' unreachable code; logic error
139
140         ' Finally executes because corresponding Try executed
141         Finally
142             Console.WriteLine("Finally executed in " & _
143                 "ThrowExceptionCatchRethrow")
144
145         End Try
146
147         ' any code placed here is never reached
148         Console.WriteLine("End of ThrowExceptionCatchRethrow")
149     End Sub ' ThrowExceptionCatchRethrow
150
151 End Class ' UsingExceptions
```

```
Calling DoesNotThrowException
In DoesNotThrowException
Finally executed in DoesNotThrowException
End of DoesNotThrowException

Calling ThrowExceptionWithCatch
In ThrowExceptionWithCatch
Message: Exception in ThrowExceptionWithCatch
Finally executed in ThrowExceptionWithCatch
End of ThrowExceptionWithCatch

Calling ThrowExceptionWithoutCatch
In ThrowExceptionWithoutCatch
Finally executed in ThrowExceptionWithoutCatch
Caught exception from ThrowExceptionWithoutCatch in Main

Calling ThrowExceptionCatchRethrow
In ThrowExceptionCatchRethrow
Message: Exception in ThrowExceptionCatchRethrow
Finally executed in ThrowExceptionCatchRethrow
Caught exception from ThrowExceptionCatchRethrow in Main
```

Fig. 11.2 **Finally** statements always execute, regardless of whether an exception occurs (part 4 of 4).

Normally, program control would continue at the first **Catch** following this **Try** block. However, this **Try** block does not have any corresponding **Catch** handlers. Therefore, the exception is not caught in method **ThrowExceptionWithoutCatch**. Normal program control cannot continue until the exception is caught and processed. Thus, the CLR terminates **ThrowExceptionWithoutCatch**, and program control returns to **Main**. Before control returns to **Main**, the **Finally** block (lines 110–112) executes and outputs a message. At this point, program control returns to **Main**—any statements appearing after the **Finally** block (e.g., line 117) do not execute. In this example, such statements could cause logic errors, because the exception thrown in lines 106–107 is not caught. In **Main**, the **Catch** handler in lines 30–32 catches the exception and displays a message indicating that the exception was caught in **Main**.

Common Programming Error 11.6

*The argument of a **Throw**—an exception object—must be of class **Exception** or one of its derived classes.*

Lines 42–50 of **Main** define a **Try** block in which **Main** invokes method **ThrowExceptionCatchRethrow** (lines 121–149). The **Try** block enables **Main** to catch any exceptions thrown by **ThrowExceptionCatchRethrow**. The **Try** block in lines 124–145 of **ThrowExceptionCatchRethrow** begins by outputting a message. Next, the **Try** block throws an **Exception** (lines 127–128). The **Try** block expires immediately, and program control continues at the first **Catch** (lines 131–136) following the **Try** block. In this example, the type thrown (**Exception**) matches the type specified in the **Catch**, so lines 132–133 outputs a message indicating where the exception occurred. Line 136 uses the **Throw** statement to *rethrow* the exception. This indicates that the **Catch** handler performed partial processing of the exception and now is passing the exception back to the calling method (in this case, **Main**) for further processing. Note that the argument to the **Throw** statement is the reference to the exception that was caught. When rethrowing the original exception, you also can use the statement

Throw

with no argument. Section 11.6 demonstrates using a **Throw** statement with an argument from a **Catch** handler. After an exception is caught, such a **Throw** statement enables programmers to create an exception object then throw a different type of exception from the **Catch** handler. Class-library designers often do this to customize the exception types thrown from methods in their class libraries or to provide additional debugging information.

Software Engineering Observation 11.7

Before rethrowing an exception to a calling method, the method that rethrows the exception should release any resources it acquired before the exception occurred.[7]

Software Engineering Observation 11.8

Whenever possible, a method should handle exceptions that are thrown in that method, rather than passing the exceptions to another region of the program.

The exception handling in method **ThrowExceptionCatchRethrow** does not complete, because the program cannot run code in the **Catch** handler placed after the invocation of the **Throw** statement (line 136). Therefore, method **ThrowExceptionCatchRethrow** terminates and returns control to **Main**. Once again, the

---

7. "Best Practices for Handling Exceptions [Visual Basic]."

Finally block (lines 141–143) executes and outputs a message before control returns to **Main**. When control returns to **Main**, the **Catch** handler in lines 46–48 catches the exception and displays a message indicating that the exception was caught. Then, the program terminates.

Note that the location to which program control returns after the **Finally** block executes depends on the exception-handling state. If the **Try** block successfully completes, or if a **Catch** handler catches and handles an exception, control continues with the next statement after the **End Try** statement. However, if an exception is not caught, or if a **Catch** handler rethrows an exception, program control continues in the next enclosing **Try** block. The enclosing **Try** could be in the calling method or in one of its callers. It also is possible to nest a **Try**/**Catch** sequence in a **Try** block; in such a case, the outer **Try** block's **Catch** handlers would process any exceptions that were not caught in the inner **Try**/**Catch** sequence. If a **Try** block executes and has a corresponding **Finally** block, the **Finally** block always executes—even if the **Try** block terminates due to a **Return** statement. The **Return** occurs after the execution of the **Finally** block.

Common Programming Error 11.7

*Throwing an exception from a **Finally** block can be dangerous. If an uncaught exception is awaiting processing when the **Finally** block executes, and the **Finally** block throws a new exception that is not caught in the **Finally** block, the first exception is lost, and the new exception is passed to the next enclosing **Try** block.*

Testing and Debugging Tip 11.6

*When placing code that can throw an exception in a **Finally** block, always enclose that code in a **Try**/**Catch** sequence that catches the appropriate exception types. This prevents the loss of any uncaught and rethrown exceptions that occur before the **Finally** block executes.*

Software Engineering Observation 11.9

*Visual Basic's exception-handling mechanism removes error-processing code from the main line of a program to improve program clarity. Do not place **Try**/**Catch**/**Finally** around every statement that might throw an exception, because this can make programs difficult to read. Rather, place one **Try** block around a significant portion of code, and follow this **Try** block with **Catch** handlers that handle each of the possible exceptions. Then, follow the **Catch** handlers with a single **Finally** block.*

11.6 Exception Properties

As we discussed in Section 11.4, exception data types derive from class **Exception**, which has several properties. These properties frequently are used to formulate error messages indicating a caught exception. Two important properties are *Message* and *StackTrace*. Property **Message** stores the error message associated with an **Exception** object. This message can be a default message associated with the exception type or a customized message passed to an **Exception** object's constructor when the **Exception** object is thrown. Property **StackTrace** contains a **String** that represents the *method-call stack*. The runtime environment keeps a list of method calls that have been made up to a given moment. The **StackTrace String** represents this sequential list of methods that had not finished processing at the time the exception occurred. The exact location at which the exception occurs in the program is called the exception's *throw point*.

>
> **Testing and Debugging Tip 11.7**
> *A stack trace shows the complete method-call stack at the time an exception occurred. This enables the programmer to view the series of method calls that led to the exception. Information in the stack trace includes the names of the methods on the call stack at the time of the exception, names of the classes in which those methods are defined, names of the namespaces in which those classes are defined. The stack trace also includes line numbers; the first line number indicates the throw point, and subsequent line numbers indicate the locations from which the methods in the stack trace were called.*

Another property used frequently by class-library programmers is **InnerException**. Typically, programmers use this property to "wrap" exception objects caught in their code so that they then can throw new exception types that are specific to their libraries. For example, a programmer implementing an accounting system might have some account-number processing code in which account numbers are input as **String**s, but represented as **Integer**s in the code. Recall, a program can convert **String**s to **Integer** values with **Convert.ToInt32**, which throws a **FormatException** when it encounters an invalid number format. When an invalid account-number format occurs, the accounting-system programmer might wish employ a different error message than the default message supplied by **FormatException** or might wish to indicate a new exception type, such as **InvalidAccountNumberFormatException**. In these cases, the programmer would provide code to catch the **FormatException** and then would create an **Exception** object in the **Catch** handler, passing the original exception as one of the constructor arguments. The original exception object becomes the **InnerException** of the new exception object. When an **InvalidAccountNumberFormatException** occurs in code that uses the accounting-system library, the **Catch** block that catches the exception can obtain a reference to the original exception via property **InnerException**. Thus, the exception indicates both that the user specified an invalid account number and that the particular problem was an invalid number format.

Class **Exception** provides other properties, including *HelpLink*, *Source* and *TargetSite*. Property **HelpLink** specifies the location of the help file that describes the problem that occurred. This property is **Nothing** if no such file exists. Property **Source** specifies the name of the application where the exception occurred. Property **TargetSite** specifies the method where the exception originated.

Our next example (Fig. 11.3) demonstrates properties **Message**, **StackTrace** and **InnerException** and method **ToString** of class **Exception**. In addition, this example introduces *stack unwinding*, which is the process of attempting to locate an appropriate **Catch** handler for an uncaught exception. As we discuss this example, we keep track of the methods on the call stack so that we can discuss property **StackTrace** and the stack-unwinding mechanism.

Program execution begins with the invocation of **Main**, which becomes the first method on the method call stack. Line 13 of the **Try** block in **Main** invokes **Method1** (defined in lines 37–39), which becomes the second method on the stack. If **Method1** throws an exception, the **Catch** handler in lines 17–30 handles the exception and outputs information about the exception that occurred. Line 38 of **Method1** invokes **Method2** (lines 42–44), which becomes the third method on the stack. Then, line 43 of **Method2** invokes **Method3** (lines 47–61) which becomes the fourth method on the stack.

At this point, the method call stack for the program is:

```
Method3
Method2
Method1
Main
```

Notice the most recent method to be called (**Method3**) appears at the top of the list, whereas the first method called (**Main**) appears at the bottom. The **Try** block (lines 50–59) in **Method3** invokes method **Convert.ToInt32** (line 51), which attempts to convert a **String** to an **Integer**. At this point, **Convert.ToInt32** becomes the fifth and final method on the call stack.

Because the argument to **Convert.ToInt32** is not in **Integer** format, line 51 throws a **FormatException** that is caught in line 54 of **Method3**. The exception terminates the call to **Convert.ToInt32**, so the method is removed from the method-call stack. The **Catch** handler in **Method3** then creates and throws an **Exception** object. The first argument to the **Exception** constructor is the custom error message for our example, "**Exception occurred in Method3**." The second argument is the **InnerException**—the **FormatException** that was caught. The **StackTrace** for this new exception object reflects the point at which the exception was thrown (line 56). Now, **Method3** terminates, because the exception thrown in the **Catch** handler is not caught in the method body. Thus, control returns to the statement that invoked **Method3** in the prior method in the call stack (**Method2**). This removes, or *unwinds*, **Method3** from the method-call stack.

When control returns to line 42 in **Method2**, the CLR determines that line 42 is not in a **Try** block. Therefore, the exception cannot be caught in **Method2**, and **Method2** terminates. This unwinds **Method2** from the call stack and returns control to line 37 in **Method1**.

Here again, line 37 is not in a **Try** block, so the exception cannot be caught in **Method1**. The method terminates and unwinds from the call stack, returning control to line 13 in **Main**, which is located in a **Try** block. The **Try** block in **Main** expires and the **Catch** handler (lines 17–30) catches the exception. The **Catch** handler uses method **ToString** and properties **Message**, **StackTrace** and **InnerException** to create the output. Stack unwinding continues until a **Catch** handler catches the exception or the program terminates.

The first block of output (reformatted for readability) in Fig. 11.3 contains the exception's **String** representation, which is returned from method **ToString**. The **String** begins with the name of the exception class followed by the **Message** property value. The next ten lines present the **String** representation of the **InnerException** object. The remainder of the block of output shows the **StackTrace** for the exception thrown in **Method3**. Note that the **StackTrace** represents the state of the method-call stack at the throw point of the exception, rather than at the point where the exception eventually is caught. Each **StackTrace** line that begins with "**at**" represents a method on the call stack. These lines indicate the method in which the exception occurred, the file in which that method resides and the line number in the file where the exception is thrown (throw point). Also, note that the stack trace includes the inner exception stack trace.

Testing and Debugging Tip 11.8

When reading a stack trace, start from the top of the stack trace and read the error message first. Then, read the remainder of the stack trace, searching for the first line that references code from your program. Normally, this is the location that caused the exception.

```vbnet
1   ' Fig. 11.3: Properties.vb
2   ' Stack unwinding and Exception class properties.
3
4   ' demonstrates using properties Message, StackTrace and
5   ' InnerException
6   Class CProperties
7
8      Shared Sub Main()
9
10        ' call Method1; any Exception generated is caught
11        ' in Catch handler that follows
12        Try
13           Method1()
14
15        ' output String representation of Exception, then output
16        ' properties InnerException, Message and StackTrace
17        Catch exceptionParameter As Exception
18           Console.WriteLine("exceptionParameter.ToString: " & _
19              vbCrLf & "{0}" & vbCrLf, exceptionParameter.ToString())
20
21           Console.WriteLine("exceptionParameter.Message: " & _
22              vbCrLf & "{0}" & vbCrLf, exceptionParameter.Message)
23
24           Console.WriteLine("exceptionParameter.StackTrace: " & _
25              vbCrLf & "{0}" & vbCrLf, exceptionParameter.StackTrace)
26
27           Console.WriteLine( _
28              "exceptionParameter.InnerException: " & _
29              vbCrLf & "{0}" & vbCrLf, _
30              exceptionParameter.InnerException.ToString())
31
32        End Try
33
34     End Sub ' Main
35
36     ' calls Method2
37     Public Shared Sub Method1()
38        Method2()
39     End Sub
40
41     ' calls Method3
42     Public Shared Sub Method2()
43        Method3()
44     End Sub
45
46     ' throws an Exception containing InnerException
47     Public Shared Sub Method3()
48
49        ' attempt to convert String to Integer
50        Try
51           Convert.ToInt32("Not an integer")
52
```

Fig. 11.3 Exception properties and stack unwinding (part 1 of 3).

```vbnet
53             ' wrap FormatException in new Exception
54             Catch formatExceptionParameter As FormatException
55
56                Throw New Exception("Exception occurred in Method3", _
57                   formatExceptionParameter)
58
59             End Try
60
61         End Sub ' Method3
62
63     End Class ' CProperties
```

```
exceptionParameter.ToString:
System.Exception: Exception occurred in Method3 --->
   System.FormatException: Input string was not in a correct format.
   at System.Number.ParseInt32(String s, NumberStyles style,
      NumberFormatInfo info)
   at System.Int32.Parse(String s, NumberStyles style,
      IFormatProvider provider)
   at System.Int32.Parse(String s)
   at System.Convert.ToInt32(String value)
   at Properties.CProperties.Method3() in
 C:\Fig11_03\Properties\Properties.vb:line 51
   --- End of inner exception stack trace ---
   at Properties.CProperties.Method3() in
 C:\Fig11_03\Properties\Properties.vb:line 56
   at Properties.CProperties.Method2() in
 C:\Fig11_03\Properties\Properties.vb:line 43
   at Properties.CProperties.Method1() in
 C:\Fig11_03\Properties\Properties.vb:line 38
   at Properties.CProperties.Main() in
 C:\Fig11_03\Properties\Properties.vb:line 13

exceptionParameter.Message:
Exception occurred in Method3

exceptionParameter.StackTrace:
   at Properties.CProperties.Method3() in
 C:\Fig11_03\Properties\Properties.vb:line 56
   at Properties.CProperties.Method2() in
 C:\Fig11_03\Properties\Properties.vb:line 43
   at Properties.CProperties.Method1() in
 C:\Fig11_03\Properties\Properties.vb:line 38
   at Properties.CProperties.Main() in
 C:\Fig11_03\Properties\Properties.vb:line 13

exceptionParameter.InnerException:
System.FormatException: Input string was not in a correct format.
   at System.Number.ParseInt32(String s, NumberStyles style,
      NumberFormatInfo info)
```
(continued on next page)

Fig. 11.3 **Exception** properties and stack unwinding (part 2 of 3).

```
                                              (continued from previous page)
   at System.Int32.Parse(String s, NumberStyles style,
      IFormatProvider provider)
   at System.Int32.Parse(String s)
   at System.Convert.ToInt32(String value)
   at Properties.CProperties.Method3() in
C:\Fig11_03\Properties\Properties.vb:line 51
```

Fig. 11.3 **Exception** properties and stack unwinding (part 3 of 3).

Testing and Debugging Tip 11.9
*When catching and rethrowing an exception, provide additional debugging information in the rethrown exception. To do so, create an **Exception** object containing more specific debugging information and then pass the original caught exception to the new exception object's constructor to initialize the **InnerException** property.*[8]

The next block of output (two lines) simply displays the **Message** property's value (**Exception occurred in Method3**) of the exception thrown in **Method3**.

The third block of output displays the **StackTrace** property of the exception thrown in **Method3**. Note that this **StackTrace** property contains the stack trace starting from line 56 in **Method3**, because that is the point at which the **Exception** object was created and thrown. The stack trace always begins from the exception's throw point.

Finally, the last block of output displays the **ToString** representation of the **InnerException** property, which includes the namespace and class name of that exception object, as well as its **Message** property and **StackTrace** property.

11.7 Programmer-Defined Exception Classes

In many cases, programmers can use existing exception classes from the .NET Framework to indicate exceptions that occur in their programs. However, in some cases, programmers might wish to create new exception types that are specific to the problems that occur in their programs. *Programmer-defined exception classes* should derive directly or indirectly from class **ApplicationException** of namespace **System**.

Good Programming Practice 11.2
The association of each type of malfunction with an appropriately named exception class improves program clarity.

Software Engineering Observation 11.10
Before creating programmer-defined exception classes, investigate the existing exception classes in the .NET Framework to determine whether an appropriate exception type already exists.

Software Engineering Observation 11.11
Programmers should create exception classes only if they need to catch and handle the new exceptions in a different manner than other existing exception types.

---

8. "Best Practices for Handling Exceptions [Visual Basic]," *.NET Framework Developer's Guide*, Visual Studio .NET Online Help.

Figure 11.4 and Fig. 11.5 demonstrate a programmer-defined exception class. Class **NegativeNumberException** (Fig. 11.4) is a programmer-defined exception class representing exceptions that occur when a program performs an illegal operation on a negative number, such as attempting to calculate the square root of a negative number.

According to Microsoft,[9] programmer-defined exceptions should extend class **ApplicationException**, should have a class name that ends with "Exception" and should define three constructors—a default constructor, a constructor that receives a **String** argument (the error message) and a constructor that receives a **String** argument and an **Exception** argument (the error message and the inner exception object).

NegativeNumberExceptions most likely occur during arithmetic operations, so it seems logical to derive class **NegativeNumberException** from class **ArithmeticException**. However, class **ArithmeticException** derives from class **SystemException**—the category of exceptions thrown by the CLR. The base class for programmer-defined exception classes should inherit from **ApplicationException**, rather than **SystemException**.

Class **FrmSquareRoot** (Fig. 11.5) demonstrates our programmer-defined exception class. The application enables the user to input a numeric value and then invokes method **SquareRoot** (lines 23–34) to calculate the square root of that value. To perform this calculation, **SquareRoot** invokes class **Math**'s *Sqrt* method, which receives a **Double** value as its argument. Normally, if the argument is negative, method **Sqrt** returns constant **NaN** from class **Double**. In this program, we would like to prevent the user from calculating the square root of a negative number. If the numeric value that the user enters is negative, **SquareRoot** throws a **NegativeNumberException** (lines 27–28). Otherwise, **SquareRoot** invokes class **Math**'s method *Sqrt* to compute the square root (line 33).

When the user inputs a value and clicks the **Square Root** button, the program invokes event handler **cmdSquareRoot_Click** (lines 37–67). The **Try** block (lines 44–65) attempts to invoke **SquareRoot** using the value input by the user. If the user input is not a valid number, a **FormatException** occurs, and the **Catch** handler in lines 51–54 processes the exception. If the user inputs a negative number, method **SquareRoot** throws a **NegativeNumberException** (lines 27–28). The **Catch** handler in lines 57–63 catches and handles this type of exception.

```
1    ' Fig. 11.4: NegativeNumberExceptionDefinition.vb
2    ' NegativeNumberException represents exceptions caused by
3    ' illegal operations performed on negative numbers.
4
5    Public Class NegativeNumberException
6       Inherits ApplicationException
7
8       ' default constructor
9       Public Sub New()
10         MyBase.New("Illegal operation for a negative number")
11      End Sub ' New
```

Fig. 11.4 **ApplicationException** derived class thrown when a program performs an illegal operation on a negative number (part 1 of 2).

---

9. "Best Practices for Handling Exceptions [Visual Basic]," *.NET Framework Developer's Guide*, Visual Studio .NET Online Help.

```
12
13        ' constructor for customizing error message
14        Public Sub New(ByVal messageValue As String)
15           MyBase.New(messageValue)
16        End Sub ' New
17
18        ' constructor for customizing error message and specifying
19        ' InnerException object
20        Public Sub New(ByVal messageValue As String, _
21           ByVal inner As Exception)
22
23           MyBase.New(messageValue, inner)
24        End Sub ' New
25
26    End Class ' NegativeNumberException
```

Fig. 11.4 `ApplicationException` derived class thrown when a program performs an illegal operation on a negative number (part 2 of 2).

```
1     ' Fig. 11.5: SquareRootTest.vb
2     ' Demonstrating a programmer-defined exception class.
3
4     Imports System.Windows.Forms
5
6     Public Class FrmSquareRoot
7        Inherits Form
8
9        ' Label for showing square root
10       Friend WithEvents lblOutput As Label
11       Friend WithEvents lblInput As Label
12
13       ' Button invokes square-root calculation
14       Friend WithEvents cmdSquareRoot As Button
15
16       ' TextBox receives user's Integer input
17       Friend WithEvents txtInput As TextBox
18
19       ' Visual Studio .NET generated code
20
21       ' computes square root of parameter; throws
22       ' NegativeNumberException if parameter is negative
23       Public Function SquareRoot(ByVal value As Double) As Double
24
25          ' if negative operand, throw NegativeNumberException
26          If value < 0 Then
27             Throw New NegativeNumberException( _
28                "Square root of negative number not permitted")
29
30          End If
31
```

Fig. 11.5 `FrmSquareRoot` class throws an exception if an error occurs when calculating the square root (part 1 of 2).

```
32         ' compute square root
33         Return Math.Sqrt(value)
34      End Function ' SquareRoot
35
36      ' obtain user input, convert to Double, calculate square root
37      Private Sub cmdSquareRoot_Click( _
38         ByVal sender As System.Object, _
39         ByVal e As System.EventArgs) Handles cmdSquareRoot.Click
40
41         lblOutput.Text = ""
42
43         ' catch any NegativeNumberException thrown
44         Try
45            Dim result As Double = _
46               SquareRoot(Convert.ToDouble(txtInput.Text))
47
48            lblOutput.Text = result.ToString()
49
50         ' process invalid number format
51         Catch formatExceptionParameter As FormatException
52            MessageBox.Show(formatExceptionParameter.Message, _
53               "Invalid Number Format", MessageBoxButtons.OK, _
54               MessageBoxIcon.Error)
55
56         ' display MessageBox if negative number input
57         Catch negativeNumberExceptionParameter As _
58            NegativeNumberException
59
60            MessageBox.Show( _
61               negativeNumberExceptionParameter.Message, _
62               "Invalid Operation", MessageBoxButtons.OK, _
63               MessageBoxIcon.Error)
64
65         End Try
66
67      End Sub ' cmdSquareRoot_Click
68
69   End Class ' FrmSquareRoot
```

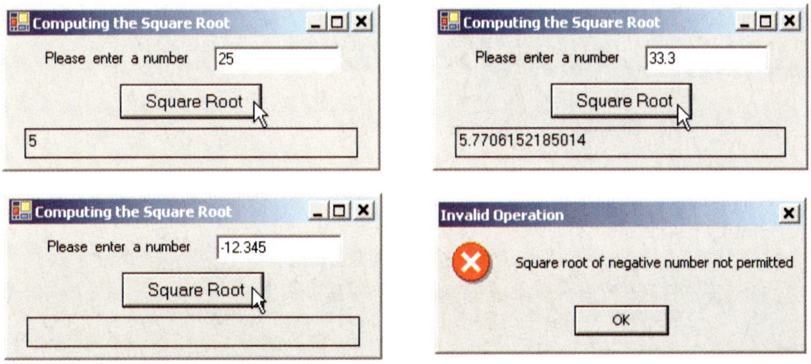

Fig. 11.5 **FrmSquareRoot** class throws an exception if an error occurs when calculating the square root (part 2 of 2).

11.8 Handling Overflows

In Visual Basic, primitive data types can represent values only within a fixed range. For instance, the maximum value of an **Integer** is 2,147,483,647. In **Integer** arithmetic, a value larger than 2,147,483,647 causes *overflow*—type **Integer** cannot represent such a number. Overflow also can occur with other Visual Basic primitive types. Overflows often cause programs to produce incorrect results.

Visual Basic enables the user to specify whether arithmetic occurs in a *checked context* or *unchecked context*. In a checked context, the CLR throws an **OverflowException** (namespace **System**) if overflow occurs during the evaluation of an arithmetic expression. In an unchecked context, overflow produces a truncated result.

By default, calculations occur in a checked context. However, the programmer can modify a project's properties to disable checking for arithmetic overflow—a dangerous practice. To do so, first select the project in the **Solution Explorer**. Next, select **View > Property Pages**. In the **Property Pages** dialog, select the **Configuration Properties** folder. Under **Optimizations**, select the checkbox named **Remove integer overflow checks** to disable checking for arithmetic overflow.

Performance Tip 11.4

The removal of integer-overflow checking improves runtime performance, but can yield faulty program results if an overflow occurs. Programmers should disable integer-overflow checking only if they have tested a program thoroughly and are certain that no overflows can occur.

The operators *****, **/**, **+** and **-** can cause overflow when used with integral data types (such as **Integer** and **Long**). In addition, conversions between integral data types can cause overflow. For example, the conversion of 1,000,000 from an **Integer** to a **Short** results in overflow because a **Short** can store a maximum value of 32,767. Figure 11.6 demonstrates overflows occurring in both checked and unchecked contexts. The first output depicts the program execution when integer-overflow checking is enabled, whereas the second output illustrates program execution without checking.

```
1    ' Fig. 11.6: Overflow.vb
2    ' Demonstrating overflows with and without checking.
3
4    ' demonstrates overflows with and without checking
5    Class COverflow
6
7       Shared Sub Main()
8
9          ' calculate sum of number1 and number 2
10         Try
11
12            Dim number1 As Integer = Int32.MaxValue ' 2,147,483,647
13            Dim number2 As Integer = Int32.MaxValue ' 2,147,483,647
14            Dim sum As Integer = 0
15
```

Fig. 11.6 **OverflowException** cannot occur if user disables integer-overflow checking (part 1 of 2).

```vbnet
16           ' output numbers
17           Console.WriteLine("number1: {0}" & vbCrLf & _
18              "number2: {1}", number1, number2)
19
20           Console.WriteLine(vbCrLf & _
21              "Sum integers in checked context:")
22
23           sum = number1 + number2  ' compute sum
24
25           ' this statement will not throw OverflowException if user
26           ' removes integer-overflow checks
27           Console.WriteLine(vbCrLf & _
28              "Sum after operation: {0}", sum)
29
30        ' catch overflow exception
31        Catch overflowExceptionParameter As OverflowException
32           Console.WriteLine(overflowExceptionParameter.ToString())
33
34        End Try
35
36     End Sub ' Main
37
38  End Class ' COverflow
```

```
number1: 2147483647
number2: 2147483647

Sum integers in checked context:
System.OverflowException: Arithmetic operation resulted in an overflow.
   at Overflow.COverflow.Main() in
C:\books\2001\vbhtp2\ch11\Overflow\Overflow.vb:line 23
```

```
number1: 2147483647
number2: 2147483647

Sum integers in checked context:

Sum after operation: -2
```

Fig. 11.6 **OverflowException** cannot occur if user disables integer-overflow checking (part 2 of 2).

The **Try** block in lines 10–34 begins by defining **Integer** variables **number1** and **number2** (lines 12–13), and assigning to each variable the maximum value for an **Integer**, which is 2,147,483,647. (This maximum is defined by *Int32.MaxValue*.) Next, line 23 calculates the total of **number1** and **number2** and stores the result in variable **sum**. Because variables **number1** and **number2** already contain the maximum value for an **Integer**, adding these values when integer-overflow checking is enabled causes an **OverflowException**. The **Catch** handler in lines 31–32 catches the exception and outputs its **String** representation. Note that, if integer-overflow checking is disabled (as represented by the second output window), line 23 does not generate an **OverflowException**. Lines 27–28 output the **sum** of **number1** and **number2**. The result of the calculation should be 4,294,967,294. However, this value is too large to be represented as an **Integer**, so Visual Basic truncates part of the value, resulting in a sum of **-2** in the output. The result of the unchecked calculation does not resemble the actual sum of the variables.

In this chapter, we demonstrated the exception-handling mechanism and discussed how to make applications more robust by writing exception handlers to process potential problems. As programmers develop applications, it is important that they investigate potential exceptions thrown by the methods that their program invokes or by the CLR. They then should implement appropriate exception-handling code to make their applications more robust. In the next chapter, we begin a more in-depth treatment of graphical user interfaces.

Testing and Debugging Tip 11.10

Use a checked context when performing calculations that can result in overflows. The programmer define exception handlers to deal with the overflow situations.

SUMMARY

- An exception is an indication of a problem that occurs during a program's execution.
- Exception handling enables programmers to create applications that can resolve exceptions, often allowing programs to continue execution as if no problems were encountered.
- Exception handling enables programmers to write clear, robust and more fault-tolerant programs.
- Exception handling also enables programmers to remove error-handling code from the "main line" of the program's execution. This improves program clarity and enhances modifiability.
- Exception handling is designed to process synchronous errors, such as out-of-range array subscripts, arithmetic overflow, division by zero and invalid method parameters.
- Exception handling is not designed to process asynchronous events, such as disk-I/O completions, network message arrivals, mouse clicks and keystrokes.
- When a method detects an error and is unable to handle it, the method throws an exception. There is no guarantee that there will be an exception handler to process that kind of exception. If there is, the exception will be caught and handled.
- In debug mode, when the runtime environment detects an uncaught exception, a dialog appears that enables the programmer to view the problem in the debugger or to continue program execution by ignoring the problem.
- Visual Basic uses **Try** blocks to enable exception handling. A **Try** block consists of keyword **Try** followed a block of code in which exceptions might occur.
- Immediately following the **Try** block are zero or more **Catch** handlers. Each **Catch** specifies an exception parameter representing the exception type that the **Catch** can handle.
- The **Catch** handler can use the exception-parameter name to interact with a caught exception object.
- A **Try** block can contain one parameterless **Catch** block that catches all exception types.
- After the last **Catch** block, an optional **Finally** block contains code that always executes, regardless of whether an exception occurs.
- When a method, property or the CLR detects a problem, the method, property or CLR throws an exception. The point in the program at which the exception occurs is called the throw point.
- Exceptions are objects of classes that inherit from class **System.Exception**.

- Visual Basic uses the termination model of exception handling. If an exception occurs in a **Try** block, the block expires and program control transfers to the first **Catch** handler following the **Try** block.
- The CLR searches for the first **Catch** handler that can process the type of exception that occurred. The appropriate handler is the first one in which the thrown exception's type matches, or is derived from, the exception type specified by the **Catch** block's exception parameter.
- If no exceptions occur in a **Try** block, the CLR ignores the exception handlers for that block.
- If no exception occurs or an exception is caught and handled, the program resumes execution with the next statement after the **Try/Catch/Finally** sequence.
- If an exception occurs in a statement that is not in a **Try** block, the method containing that statement terminates immediately, and the CLR attempts to locate an enclosing **Try** block in a calling method—a process called stack unwinding.
- When a **Try** block terminates, local variables defined in the block go out of scope.
- If an argument passed to method **Convert.ToInt32** is not an **Integer**, a **FormatException** occurs.
- In integer arithmetic, an attempt to divide by zero causes a **DivideByZeroException**.
- A **Try** block encloses a portion of code that might throw exceptions, as well as any code that should not execute if an exception occurs.
- Each **Catch** handler begins with keyword **Catch**, followed by an optional exception parameter that specifies the type of exception handled by the **Catch** handler. The exception-handling code appears in the body of the **Catch** handler.
- If an exception occurs, the program executes only the matching **Catch** handler. When program control reaches the end of a **Catch** handler, the CLR considers the exception to be handled, and program control continues with the first statement after the **Try/Catch** sequence.
- The exception-handling mechanism allows only objects of class **Exception** and its derived classes to be thrown and caught. Class **Exception** of namespace **System** is the base class of the .NET Framework exception hierarchy.
- **ApplicationException** is a base class that programmers can extend to create exception data types that are specific to their applications. Programs can recover from most **ApplicationException**s and continue execution.
- The CLR generates **SystemException**s. If a program attempts to access an out-of-range array subscript, the CLR throws an **IndexOutOfRangeException**. An attempt to manipulate an object through a **Nothing** reference causes a **NullReferenceException**.
- Programs typically cannot recover from most exceptions thrown by the CLR. Programs generally should not throw **SystemException**s nor attempt to catch them.
- A **Catch** handler can catch exceptions of a particular type or can use a base-class type to catch exceptions in a hierarchy of related exception types. A **Catch** handler that specifies an exception parameter of type **Exception** can catch all exceptions, because **Exception** is the base class of all exception classes.
- For methods in the .NET Framework classes, programmers should investigate the detailed description of the method in the online documentation to determine whether the method throws exceptions.
- Information on exceptions thrown by the CLR appears in the *Visual Basic Language Specification*, which is located in the online documentation.
- Many computer operating systems prevent more than one program from manipulating a resource at the same time. Therefore, when a program no longer needs a resource, the program normally

releases the resource to allow other programs to use the resource. This helps prevent resource leaks, and helps ensure that resources are available to other programs when needed.

- In C and C++, the most common resource leaks are memory leaks, which occur when a program allocates memory, but does not deallocate the memory when the memory is no longer needed in the program. In Visual Basic, however, the CLR performs garbage collection of memory that is no longer needed by an executing program, thus preventing most memory leaks.

- A program should release a resource when the resource is no longer needed. The **Finally** block is guaranteed to execute if program control enters the corresponding **Try** block, regardless of whether that **Try** block executes successfully or an exception occurs. This guarantee makes the **Finally** block an ideal location in which to place resource-deallocation code for resources acquired and manipulated in the corresponding **Try** block.

- A **Try** block that contains one or more **Catch** blocks does not require a **Finally** block—the **Finally** block is optional and appears after the last **Catch**. A **Try** block that does not contain any **Catch** blocks requires a **Finally** block.

- A **Throw** statement throws an exception object.

- A **Throw** statement can be used in a **Catch** handler to rethrow an exception. This indicates that the **Catch** handler has performed partial processing of the exception and now is passing the exception back to a calling method for further processing.

- **Exception** property **Message** stores the error message associated with an **Exception** object. This message can be a default message associated with the exception type or a customized message passed to an exception object's constructor when the program created the exception.

- **Exception** property **StackTrace** contains a **String** that represents the method-call stack at the throw point of the exception.

- **Exception** property **InnerException** typically is used to "wrap" a caught exception object in a new exception object and then throw the object of that new exception type.

- **Exception** property **HelpLink** specifies the location of the help file that describes the problem that occurred. This property is **Nothing** if no such file exists.

- **Exception** property **Source** specifies the name of the application that caused the exception.

- **Exception** property **TargetSite** specifies the method that caused the exception.

- When an exception is uncaught in a method, the method terminates. This removes, or unwinds, the method from the method-call stack.

- Programmer-defined exceptions should extend class **ApplicationException**, should have a class name that ends with "**Exception**" and should define three constructors. These are a default constructor, a constructor that receives a **String** argument (the error message) and a constructor that receives a **String** argument and an **Exception** argument (the error message and the inner exception object).

- Overflow occurs in integer arithmetic when the value of an expression is greater than the maximum value that can be stored in a particular data type.

- Visual Basic enables the user to specify whether arithmetic occurs in a *checked context* or *unchecked context*. In a checked context, the CLR throws an **OverflowException** if overflow occurs during the evaluation of an arithmetic expression. In an unchecked context, overflow produces a truncated result (normally, a dangerous thing to allow).

- The operators *****, **/**, **+** and **-** can cause overflow when used with integral data types (such as **Integer** and **Long**). Also, explicit conversions between integral data types can cause overflow.

TERMINOLOGY

`ApplicationException` class
arithmetic overflow
asynchronous event
call stack
`Catch` block
`Catch` handler
catch-related errors
checked context
disk-I/O completion
divide by zero
`DivideByZeroException` class
eliminate resource leak
error-processing code
exception
`Exception` class
exception handler
fault-tolerant program
`Finally` block
`FormatException` class
`HelpLink` property of `Exception`
`IndexOutOfRangeException` class
inheritance with exceptions
`InnerException` property of `Exception`
`MaxValue` constant of `Int32`
memory leak
`Message` property of `Exception`
method call stack

`NaN` constant of class `Double`
`NullReferenceException` class
out-of-range array subscript
overflow
`OverflowException` class
`ToInt32` method of `Convert`
parameterless `Catch` block
polymorphic processing of related errors
programmer-defined exception class
resource leak
resumption model of exception handling
rethrow an exception
runtime exception
`Source` property of `Exception`
stack unwinding
`StackTrace` property of `Exception`
synchronous error
`SystemException` class
`TargetSite` property of `Exception`
termination model of exception handling
throw an exception
throw point
`Throw` statement
`Try` block
`Try` block expires
unchecked context

SELF-REVIEW EXERCISES

11.1 Fill in the blanks in each of the following statements:
  a) Exception handling deals with _____ errors, but not _____ errors.
  b) A method is said to _____ an exception when that method detects that a problem occurred.
  c) When present, the _____ block associated with a `Try` block always executes.
  d) Exception objects are derived from class_____.
  e) The statement that throws an exception is called the _____ of the exception.
  f) Visual Basic uses the _____ model of exception handling.
  g) An uncaught exception in a method causes that method to _____ from the method call stack.
  h) Method `Convert.ToInt32` can throw a _____ exception if its argument is not a valid integer value.
  i) Runtime exceptions derive from class _____.
  j) In a _____ context, the CLR throws an `OverflowException` if overflow occurs during the evaluation of an arithmetic exception.

11.2 State whether each of the following is *true* or *false*. If *false*, explain why.
  a) Exceptions always are handled in the method that initially detects the exception.
  b) Programmer-defined exception classes should extend class `SystemException`.
  c) Accessing an out-of-bounds array index causes the CLR to throw an exception.

d) A **Finally** block is optional after a **Try** block that does not have any corresponding **Catch** handlers.
e) If a **Finally** block appears in a method, that **Finally** block is guaranteed to execute.
f) It is possible to return to the throw point of an exception using keyword **Return**.
g) Exceptions can be rethrown.
h) A checked context causes a syntax error when integral arithmetic overflow occurs.
i) Property **Message** returns a **String** indicating the method from which the exception was thrown.
j) Exceptions can be thrown only by methods explicitly called in a **Try** block.

ANSWERS TO SELF-REVIEW EXERCISES

11.1 a) synchronous, asynchronous. b) throw. c) **Finally**. d) **Exception**. e) throw point. f) termination. g) unwind. h) **FormatException**. i) **SystemException**. j) checked.

11.2 a) False. Exceptions can be handled by other methods on the method-call stack. b) False. Programmer-defined exception classes should extend class **ApplicationException**. c) True. d) False. A **Try** block that does not contain any **Catch** handler requires a **Finally** block. e) False. The **Finally** block executes only if program control enters the corresponding **Try** block. f) False. **Return** causes control to return to the caller. g) True. h) False. A checked context causes an **OverflowException** when arithmetic overflow occurs at execution time. i) False. Property **Message** returns a **String** representing the error message. j) False. Exceptions can be thrown by any method, regardless of whether it is called from a **Try** block. The CLR also can throw exceptions.

EXERCISES

11.3 Use inheritance to create an exception base class and various exception-derived classes. Write a program to demonstrate that the **Catch** specifying the base class catches derived-class exceptions.

11.4 Write a program that demonstrates how various exceptions are caught with

```
Catch exceptionParameter As Exception
```

11.5 Write a program demonstrating the importance of the order of exception handlers. Write two programs, one with correct ordering of **Catch** handlers (i.e., place the base-class exception handler after all derived-class exception handlers) and another with improper ordering (i.e., place the base-class exception handler before the derived-class exception handlers). Show that derived-class exceptions, when **Catch** handlers are ordered improperly, cause syntax errors.

11.6 Exceptions can be used to indicate problems that occur when an object is being constructed. Write a program that shows a constructor passing information about constructor failure to an exception handler. The exception thrown also should contain the arguments sent to the constructor.

11.7 Write a program that demonstrates rethrowing an exception.

11.8 Write a program demonstrating that a method with its own **Try** block does not have to **Catch** every possible exception that occurs within the **Try** block. Some exceptions can slip through to, and be handled in, other scopes.

12

Graphical User Interface Concepts: Part 1

Objectives

- To understand the design principles of graphical user interfaces.
- To be able to use events.
- To understand namespaces that contain graphical user interface components and event-handling classes.
- To be able to create graphical user interfaces.
- To be able to create and manipulate buttons, labels, lists, textboxes and panels.
- To be able to use mouse and keyboard events.

… The wisest prophets make sure of the event first.
Horace Walpole

…The user should feel in control of the computer; not the other way around. This is achieved in applications that embody three qualities: responsiveness, permissiveness, and consistency.
Inside Macintosh, Volume 1
Apple Computer, Inc. 1985

All the better to see you with, my dear.
The Big Bad Wolf to Little Red Riding Hood

Outline

12.1 Introduction
12.2 Windows Forms
12.3 Event-Handling Model
12.4 Control Properties and Layout
12.5 `Labels`, `TextBoxes` and `Buttons`
12.6 `GroupBoxes` and `Panels`
12.7 `CheckBoxes` and `RadioButtons`
12.8 `PictureBoxes`
12.9 Mouse-Event Handling
12.10 Keyboard-Event Handling

Summary • Terminology • Self-Review Exercises • Answers to Self-Review Exercises • Exercises

12.1 Introduction

A *graphical user interface* (*GUI*) allows a user to interact visually with a program. A GUI (pronounced "GOO-ee") gives a program a distinctive "look" and "feel." By providing different applications with a consistent set of intuitive user-interface components, GUIs enable users to spend less time trying to remember which keystroke sequences perform what functions, freeing up time that can be spent using the program in a productive manner.

Look-and-Feel Observation 12.1

Consistent user interfaces enable a user to learn new applications more quickly.

As an example of a GUI, Fig. 12.1 depicts an Internet Explorer window in which various *GUI components* have been labeled. Near the top of the window, there is a *menu bar* containing *menus*, including **File**, **Edit**, **View**, **Favorites**, **Tools** and **Help**. Below the menu bar is a set of *buttons*, each of which has a defined task in Internet Explorer. Below these buttons lies a *textbox*, in which users can type the locations of World Wide Web sites that they wish to visit. To the left of the textbox is a *label* that indicates the textbox's purpose. *Scrollbars are situated on the far right and bottom of the window. Usually, scrollbars are employed when a window contains* more information than can be displayed in the window's viewable area. By clicking the scrollbars, the user can view different portions of the window. These components form a user-friendly interface through which the user interacts with the Internet Explorer Web browser.

GUIs are built from GUI components (which are sometimes called *controls* or *widgets*—short for *window gadgets*). A GUI component is an object with which the user interacts via the mouse or keyboard. Several common GUI components are listed in Fig. 12.2. In the sections that follow, we discuss each of these GUI components in detail. The next chapter explores the features and properties of more advanced GUI components.

Chapter 12 Graphical User Interface Concepts: Part 1 477

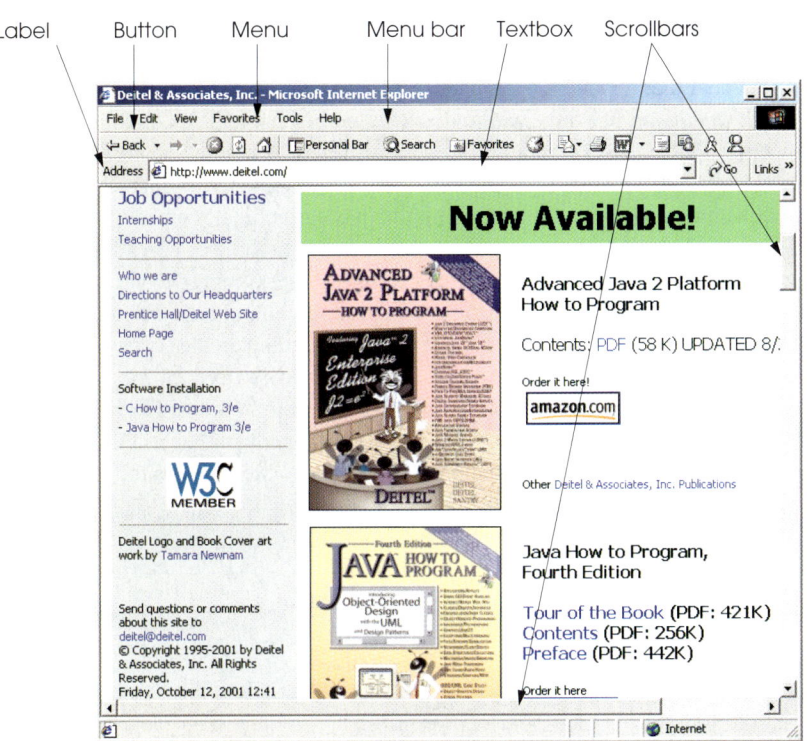

Fig. 12.1 GUI components in a sample Internet Explorer window.

Component	Description
`Label`	An area in which icons or uneditable text is displayed.
`Textbox`	An area in which the user inputs data from the keyboard. This area also can display information.
`Button`	An area that triggers an event when clicked.
`CheckBox`	A component that is either selected or unselected.
`ComboBox`	A drop-down list of items from which the user can make a selection either by clicking an item in the list or by typing into a box.
`ListBox`	An area in which a list of items is displayed. The user can make a selection from the list by clicking on any item. Multiple elements can be selected.
`Panel`	A container in which components can be placed.
`Scrollbar`	A component that allows the user to access a range of elements that normally cannot fit in the control's container.

Fig. 12.2 Some basic GUI components.

12.2 Windows Forms

Windows Forms (also called *WinForms*) are used to create the GUIs for programs. A *form* is a graphical element that appears on the desktop; it can be a dialog, a window or an *MDI window* (*multiple document interface window*, discussed in Chapter 13, Graphical User Interfaces Concepts: Part 2). A *component* is an instance of a class that implements the **IComponent** *interface*, which defines the behaviors that components must implement. A *control*, such as a button or label, is a component that has a graphical representation at runtime. Controls are visible, whereas components that lack the graphical representation (e.g., class **Timer** of namespace **System.Windows.Forms**, see Chapter 13) are not.

Figure 12.3 displays the Windows Forms controls and components that are contained in the **Toolbox**. The first two screenshots show the controls, and the last screenshot shows the components. To add a component or control to a Windows Form, a user selects that component or control from the **Toolbox** and drags it onto the Windows Form. Note that the **Pointer** (the icon at the top of the list) is not a component; rather it allows the programmer to use the mouse pointer and does not add an item to the form. In this chapter and the next, we discuss many of these controls.

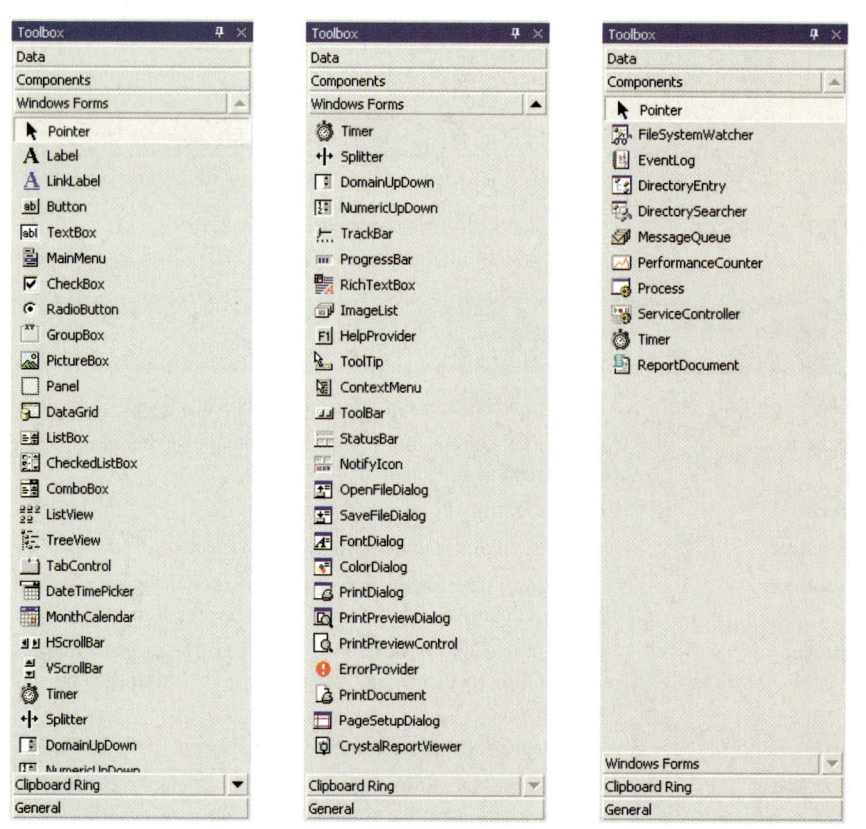

Fig. 12.3 Components and controls for Windows Forms.

In a series of windows, the *active window* is the frontmost window and has a highlighted title bar. A window becomes the active window when the user clicks somewhere inside it. During interaction with windows, the active Window is said to have the *focus*.

The form acts as a *container* for components and controls. As we saw in Chapter 4, Control Structures: Part 1, when we drag a control from the **Toolbox** onto the form, Visual Studio .NET generates this code for us, instantiating the component and setting its basic properties. Although we could write the code ourselves, it is much easier to create and modify controls using the **Toolbox** and **Properties** windows and allow Visual Studio .NET to handle the details. We introduced basic concepts relating to this kind of *visual programming* earlier in the book. In this chapter and the next, we use visual programming to build much richer and more complex GUIs.

When the user interacts with a control via the mouse or keyboard, events (discussed in Section 12.3) are generated. Typically, events are messages sent by a program to signal to an object or a set of objects that an action has occurred. Events are used most commonly used to signal user interactions with GUI components, but also can signal internal actions in a program. For example, clicking the **OK** button in a **MessageBox** generates an event. The **MessageBox** *handles* this event. The **MessageBox** component is designed to close when the event is handled, which occurs when the **OK** button is clicked. Section 12.3 describes how to design components so that they react differently to various types of events.

Each class we present in this chapter (i.e., form, component and control) is in the **System.Windows.Forms** namespace. Class **Form**, the basic window used by Windows applications, is fully qualified as **System.Windows.Forms.Form**. Likewise, class **Button** actually is **System.Windows.Forms.Button**.

The general design process for creating Windows applications requires generating a Windows Form, setting its properties, adding controls, setting their properties and implementing the *event handlers* (methods that are called in response to an event). Figure 12.4 lists common **Form** properties, methods and events.

Form Properties and Events	Description / Delegate and Event Arguments
Common Properties	
AcceptButton	Button that is clicked when *Enter* is pressed.
AutoScroll	**Boolean** value that allows or disallows scrollbars to appear when needed.
CancelButton	Button that is clicked when the *Escape* key is pressed.
FormBorderStyle	Border style for the form (e.g., **none**, **single**, **3D**, **sizable**).
Font	Font of text displayed on the form, and the default font of controls added to the form.
Text	Text in the form's title bar.
Common Methods	
Close	Closes a form and releases all resources. A closed form cannot be reopened.

Fig. 12.4 Common **Form** properties, methods and events (part 1 of 2).

Form Properties and Events	Description / Delegate and Event Arguments
`Hide`	Hides form (does not destroy the form or release its resources).
`Show`	Displays a hidden form.
Common Events	*(Delegate `EventHandler`, event arguments `EventArgs`)*
`Load`	Occurs before a form is displayed to the user. The handler for this event is displayed in the editor when the form is double-clicked in the Visual Studio .NET designer.

Fig. 12.4 Common `Form` properties, methods and events (part 2 of 2).

When we create controls and event handlers, Visual Studio .NET generates a large amount of the GUI–related code. Constructing GUIs can be performed graphically, by dragging and dropping components onto the form and setting properties via the **Properties** window. In visual programming, the IDE generally maintains GUI-related code and the programmer writes the necessary event handlers.

12.3 Event-Handling Model

GUIs are *event driven*—they *generate events* when a program's user interacts with the GUI. Typical interactions include moving the mouse, clicking the mouse, clicking a button, typing in a textbox, selecting an item from a menu and closing a window. Event information is passed to *event handlers*, which are methods that are called as a result of specific events. For example, consider a form that changes color when a button is clicked. Clicking the button generates an event and passes it to the button's event handler, causing the event-handler code to change the form's color.

Events are based on the notion of *delegates*, which are objects that reference methods (see Section 10.11). Event delegates are *multicast* (class **MulticastDelegate**), which means that they represent a set of delegates with the same signature. Multicast delegates enable event calls to be sent sequentially to all delegates contained within the multicast delegate. To learn more about delegates, see Chapter 10, Object-Oriented Programming: Polymorphism. In the event-handling model, delegates act as intermediaries between the objects creating (raising) events and the methods handling the events (Fig. 12.5).

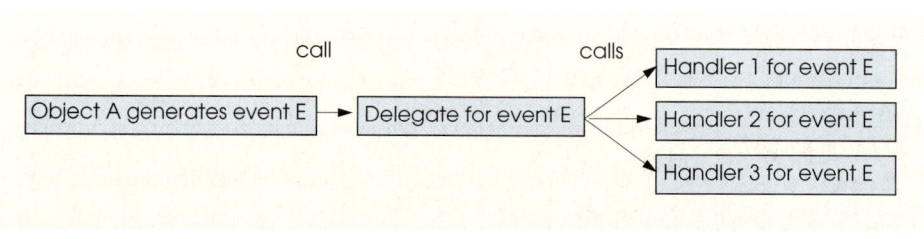

Fig. 12.5 Event-handling model using delegates.

Delegates enable classes to specify methods that will not be named or implemented until the class is instantiated. This is extremely helpful in creating event handlers. For example, the creator of the **Form** class does not need to name or define the method that will handle the **Click** event. Using delegates, the class can specify when such an event handler would be called. Programmers who create their own forms can then name and define this event handler. As long as the event handler has been registered with the proper delegate, the method will be called at the proper time.

Once an event is generated, the system calls every method (event handler) referenced by the delegate. Every method in the delegate must have the same signature, because all the methods are being passed the same information.

Many situations require handling events generated by .NET controls, such as buttons and scrollbars. These controls already have predefined delegates corresponding to every event they can generate. The programmer creates the event handler and registers it with the delegate; Visual Studio .NET helps automate this task. In the following example, we create a form that displays a message box when clicked. Afterwards, we analyze the event code generated by Visual Studio .NET.

Following the steps we outlined in Chapter 4, Control Structures: Part 1, create a **Form** containing a **Label**. First, create a new Windows application. Then, select the **Label** element from the **Windows Forms** list in the **Toolbox** window. Drag the **Label** element over the form to create a label. In the **Properties** window, set the **(Name)** property to **lblOutput** and the **Text** property to **"Click Me!"**.

We have been working in **Design** mode, which provides a graphical representation of our program. However, Visual Studio .NET has been creating code in the background, and that code can be accessed using the tab for the code or by right-clicking anywhere in the **Design** window and selecting **View Code**. To define and register an event handler for **lblOutput**, the IDE must be displaying the code listing for the Window application.

While viewing the code, notice the two drop-down menus above the editor window. (Fig. 12.6). The drop-down menu on the left-hand side, called the *Class Name* menu, contains a list of all components contained in our **Form** other than those elements that correspond to the **Form** base class. The Class Name drop-down menu for our **Form** should list one **Label**, named **lblOutput**. Select this element from the menu. On the right-hand side, the *Method Name* drop-down menu allows the programmer to access, modify and create event handlers for a component. This drop-down menu lists the events that the object can generate.

For the purposes of this exercise, we want the label to respond when clicked. Select the **Click** event in the Method Name drop-down menu. This creates an empty event handler inside the program code.

```
Private Sub lblOutput_Click(ByVal sender As Object, _
    ByVal e As System.EventArgs) Handles lblOutput.Click

End Sub
```

This is the method that is called when the form is clicked. We program the form to respond to the event by displaying a message box. To do this, insert the statement

```
MessageBox.Show("Label was clicked.")
```

into the event handler. The event handler now should appear as follows:

```
Private Sub lblOutput_Click(ByVal sender As Object, _
   ByVal e As System.EventArgs) Handles lblOutput.Click

   MessageBox.Show("Label was clicked.")
End Sub
```

Now we can compile and execute the program, which appears in Fig. 12.7. Whenever the label is clicked, a message box appears displaying the text **"Label was clicked"**. In previous examples, we commented out the code generated by the Visual Studio IDE. In this example, we present the complete code listing which we discuss in detail.

The Visual Studio .NET IDE generated the code pertaining to the creation and initialization of the application that we built through the GUI design window. The code generated by Visual Studio is contained within **#Region** and **#End Region** *preprocessor directives* (lines 7–69). In Visual Studio, these preprocessor directives allow code to be collapsed into a single line, enabling the programmer to focus on only certain portions of a program at a time. The only code that this example required us to write is the event-handling code (line 75).

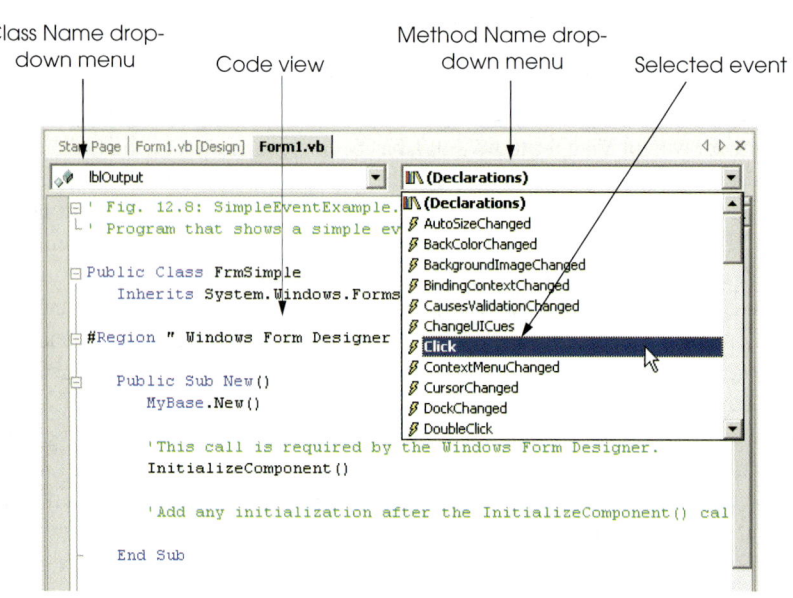

Fig. 12.6 Events section in the Method Name drop-down menu.

```
1   ' Fig. 12.7: SimpleEventExample.vb
2   ' Program demonstrating simple event handler.
3
4   Public Class FrmSimple
5       Inherits System.Windows.Forms.Form
```

Fig. 12.7 Simple event-handling example using visual programming (part 1 of 3).

```vb
 6
 7   #Region " Windows Form Designer generated code "
 8
 9      Public Sub New()
10         MyBase.New()
11
12         ' This call is required by the Windows Form Designer.
13         InitializeComponent()
14
15
16         ' Add any initialization after the
17         ' InitializeComponent() call
18      End Sub
19
20      ' Form overrides dispose to clean up the component list.
21      Protected Overloads Overrides Sub Dispose( _
22         ByVal disposing As Boolean)
23
24         If disposing Then
25
26            If Not (components Is Nothing) Then
27               components.Dispose()
28            End If
29
30         End If
31
32         MyBase.Dispose(disposing)
33      End Sub
34
35      Friend WithEvents lblOutput As System.Windows.Forms.Label
36
37      ' Required by the Windows Form Designer
38      Private components As System.ComponentModel.Container
39
40      ' NOTE: The following procedure is required by
41      ' the Windows Form Designer.
42      ' It can be modified using the Windows Form Designer.
43      ' Do not modify it using the code editor.
44      <System.Diagnostics.DebuggerStepThrough()> _
45      Private Sub InitializeComponent()
46         Me.lblOutput = New System.Windows.Forms.Label()
47         Me.SuspendLayout()
48         '
49         'lblOutput
50         '
51         Me.lblOutput.Location = New System.Drawing.Point(32, 48)
52         Me.lblOutput.Name = "lblOutput"
53         Me.lblOutput.Size = New System.Drawing.Size(168, 40)
54         Me.lblOutput.TabIndex = 0
55         Me.lblOutput.Text = "Click Me!"
56         '
57         'FrmSimple
58         '
```

Fig. 12.7 Simple event-handling example using visual programming (part 2 of 3).

```
59            Me.AutoScaleBaseSize = New System.Drawing.Size(5, 13)
60            Me.ClientSize = New System.Drawing.Size(272, 237)
61            Me.Controls.AddRange( _
62               New System.Windows.Forms.Control() {Me.lblOutput})
63
64            Me.Name = "FrmSimple"
65            Me.Text = "SimpleEventExample"
66            Me.ResumeLayout(False)
67        End Sub
68
69   #End Region
70
71        ' handler for click event on lblOutput
72        Private Sub lblOutput_Click(ByVal sender As Object, _
73           ByVal e As System.EventArgs) Handles lblOutput.Click
74
75           MessageBox.Show("Label was clicked")
76        End Sub ' lblOutput_Click
77
78   End Class ' FrmSimpleExample
```

Fig. 12.7 Simple event-handling example using visual programming (part 3 of 3).

The Visual Studio-generated code contains all references to the controls that we created through the GUI design window (in this case, **lblOutput**), the non-parameterized constructor (lines 9–18), the destructor (lines 21–33) and the initialization code for each of the controls (lines 44–67). The initialization code corresponds to the changes made to the **Properties** window for each control. Note that as we have learned in previous chapters, Visual Studio .NET adds comments to the code that it generates. The comments appear throughout the code, such as in lines 40–43. To make programs more concise and readable, we remove some of these generated comments in future examples, leaving only those comments that pertain to new concepts.

Lines 9–18 define the constructor. Because class **FrmSimpleExample** inherits from **System.Windows.Forms.Form**, line 10 of the default constructor calls the base-class constructor. This allows the base-class constructor to perform initialization before class **FrmSimpleExample** instantiates. Line 13 calls the Visual Studio-generated method **InitializeComponent** (lines 44–67), which regulates the property settings for all the controls that we created in the **Design** window. The property settings method **InitializeComponent** establishes such properties as the **Form** title, the **Form** size, component sizes and text within components. Visual Studio .NET examines this method to create the design view of the code. If we change this method, Visual Studio .NET might not recognize our modifications, in which case it would display the design improperly. It is important to note that the design view is based on the code, and not vice versa. A program can run even if its design view displays incorrectly.

Software Engineering Observation 12.1

*The complexity of the Visual Studio generated code favors a recommendation that programmers modify individual control's properties through the **Properties** window.*

Visual Studio also places within the **#Region** and **#End Region** preprocessor directives a declaration to each control that is created via the design window. Line 35 declares the **lblOutput** control. There are three things to note about the declaration of reference **lblOutput**. First, the declaration has a **Friend** access modifier. By default, all variable declarations for controls created through the design window have a **Friend** access modifier. Second, line 35 declares a member variable (**lblOutput**) to class **FrmSimpleExample**. Although **lblOutput** is declared within the **#Region** and **#End Region** preprocessor directives, it is still a class member to **FrmSimpleExample**. This is because the compiler does not consider the block of code encapsulated by the **#Region** and **#End Region** preprocessor directives to be a separate block of code. This means that the scope of variables declared within the **#Region** and **#End Region** preprocessor directives is not affected—the variables are included in the scope of the main class. Finally, the member variable **lblOutput** is declared with the keyword **WithEvents**.

The **WithEvents** keyword tells the compiler that methods handling events triggered by this component are identified by the inclusion of the suffix **Handles** *componentName.eventName* in their method declaration. When we selected event **Click** from the Method Name drop-down menu, the Visual Studio .NET IDE created a method signature that matched the **Click** event-handler delegate, placing the suffix **Handles lblOutput.Click** at the end of the method signature. This tells the Visual Basic compiler that the method will handle **Click** events triggered by **lblOutput**. However, it is possible to define additional methods that also handle **lblOutput Click** events. To register additional event handlers, we simply create a new method that has the same signature as the **Click** delegate and is accompanied by the method declaration suffix **Handles lblOutput.Click**.

The inclusion of multiple handlers for one event is called *event multicasting*. Although all event handlers are called when the event occurs, the order in which the event handlers are called is indeterminate.

Common Programming Error 12.1

The assumption that multiple event handlers registered for the same event are called in a particular order can lead to logic errors. If the order is important, register the first event handler and have it call the others in order, passing the event arguments to each handler.

As previously mentioned, every event handler must have a unique signature, which is specified by the event delegate. Two objects are passed to event handlers: A reference to the object that generated the event (**sender**) and an event arguments object (**e**). Argument **e** is of type **EventArgs**. Class **EventArgs** is the base class for objects that contain event information. We discuss the information contained in **EventArgs** objects later in the chapter.

To create the event handler, we first must find the delegate's signature. When we click an event name in the Method Name drop-down menu, Visual Studio .NET creates a method with the proper signature. The naming convention is *ControlName_EventName*; in our previous examples, the event handler is **lblOutput_Click**. Instead of using the Method Name drop-down menu, we also can look up the event-arguments class. Consult the documentation under each control's class (i.e., **Form class**), and click the **events** section (Fig. 12.8). This displays a list of all the events that the class can generate. Click the name of an event to bring up its delegate, its event argument type and a description (Fig. 12.9).

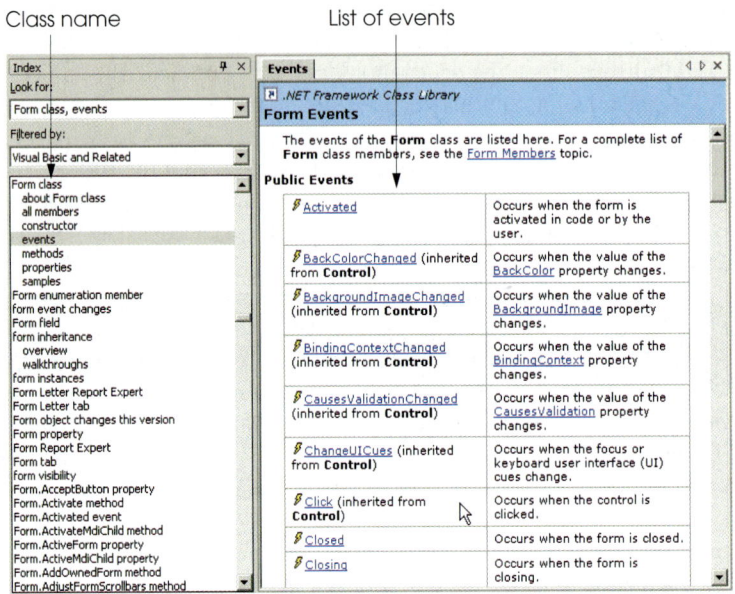

Fig. 12.8 List of `Form` events.

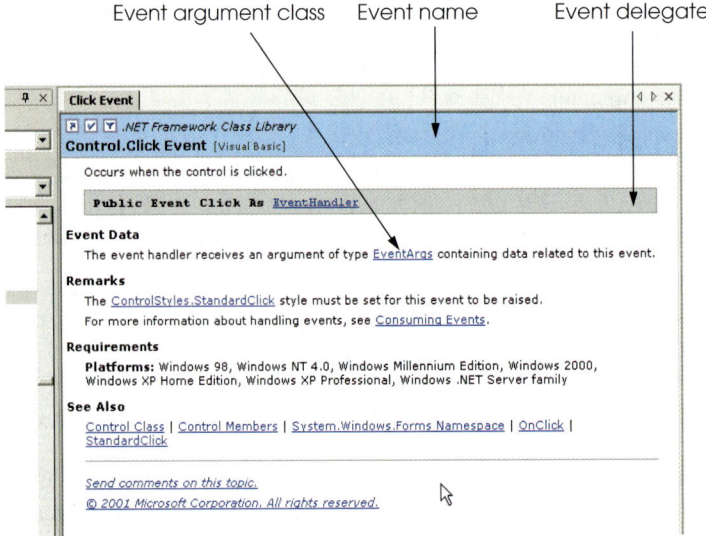

Fig. 12.9 `Click` event details.

In general, the format of the event-handling method is,

```
Private Sub ControlName_EventName(ByVal sender As Object, _
   ByVal e As System.EventArgs) Handles ControlName.EventName

      event-handling code
End Sub
```

where the name of the event handler is, by default, the name of the control, followed by an underscore (_) and the name of the event. Event handlers are methods that take two arguments: An **Object** (usually **sender**), and an instance of an **EventArgs** class. The differences between the various **EventArgs** classes are discussed later in this chapter.

Software Engineering Observation 12.2

*The handlers for predefined events (such as **Click**) are procedures. The programmer should not expect return values from event handlers; rather, event handlers are designed to execute code based on an action and then return control to the main program.*

Good Programming Practice 12.1

Use the event-handler naming convention ControlName_EventName, *so that method names are meaningful. Such names tell users what event a method handles, and for what control. Visual Studio .NET uses this naming convention when creating event handlers from the Method Name drop-down menu.*

In the upcoming sections, we indicate the *EventArgs* class and the *EventHandler* delegate that correspond to each event we present. To locate additional information about a particular type of event, review the help documentation under **ClassName class, events**.

12.4 Control Properties and Layout

This section overviews properties that are common to many controls. Controls derive from class **Control** (namespace **System.Windows.Forms**). Figure 12.10 lists some of class **Control**'s properties and methods; these properties can be set for many controls. The **Text** property determines the text that appears on a control. The appearance of this text can vary depending on the context. For example, the text of a Windows Form is its title bar, but the text of a button appears on its face.

Class **Control** Properties and Methods	Description
Common Properties	
BackColor	Sets the control's background color.
BackgroundImage	Sets the control's background image.
Enabled	Indicates whether the control is enabled (i.e., if the user can interact with it). A disabled control is displayed, but portions of the control appear in gray.

Fig. 12.10 Class **Control** properties and methods (part 1 of 2).

Class `Control` Properties and Methods	Description
`Focused`	Indicates whether a control has the focus.
`Font`	Sets the `Font` used to display the control's text.
`ForeColor`	Sets the control's foreground color. This usually determines the color of the `Text` property.
`TabIndex`	Sets the tab order of the control. When the *Tab* key is pressed, the focus transfers to various controls according to the tab order. This order can be set by the programmer.
`TabStop`	Indicates whether users can employ the *Tab* key to select the control. If `True`, then a user can select this control through the *Tab* key.
`Text`	Sets the text associated with the control. The location and appearance varies depending on the type of control.
`TextAlign`	Establishes the alignment of the text on the control—possibilities are one of three horizontal positions (left, center or right) and one of three vertical positions (top, middle or bottom).
`Visible`	Indicates whether the control is visible.
Common Methods	
`Focus`	Acquires the focus.
`Hide`	Hides the control (sets `Visible` to `False`).
`Show`	Shows the control (sets `Visible` to `True`).

Fig. 12.10 Class `Control` properties and methods (part 2 of 2).

The `Focus` method transfers the focus to a control. A control that has the focus is referred to as the *active control*. When the *Tab* key is pressed, controls are given the focus in the order specified by their `TabIndex` property. The `TabIndex` property is set by Visual Studio .NET, but can be changed by the programmer. `TabIndex` is helpful for users who enter information in many different locations—the user can enter information and quickly select the next control by pressing the *Tab* key. The `Enabled` property indicates whether a control can be used; often, if a control is disabled, it is because an option is unavailable to the user. In most cases, a disabled control's text appears in gray (rather than in black) when a control is disabled. However, a programmer can hide a control's text from the user without disabling the control by setting the `Visible` property to `False` or by calling method `Hide`. When a control's `Visible` property is set to `False`, the control still exists, but it is not shown on the form.

Visual Studio .NET enables control *anchoring* and *docking*, which allow the programmer to specify the layout of controls inside a container (such as a form). Anchoring causes controls to remain at a fixed distance from the sides of the container even when the control is resized. Docking sets the dimensions of a control to the dimensions of the parent container at all times.

For example, a programmer might want a control to appear in a certain position (top, bottom, left or right) in a form even if that form is resized. The programmer can specify this by *anchoring* the control to a side (top, bottom, left or right). The control then maintains a fixed distance between itself and the side to its parent container. Although most parent containers are forms, other controls also can act as parent containers.

When parent containers are resized, all controls move. Unanchored controls move relative to their original position on the form, whereas anchored controls move so that their distance from the sides to which they are anchored does not vary. For example, in Fig. 12.11, the top-most button is anchored to the top and left sides of the parent form. When the form is resized, the anchored button moves so that it remains a constant distance from the top and left sides of the form (its parent). By contrast, the unanchored button changes position as the form is resized.

To see the effects of anchoring a control, create a simple Windows application that contains two buttons (Fig. 12.12). Anchor one control to the right side by setting the **Anchor** property as shown in Fig. 12.12. Leave the other control unanchored. Now, enlarge the form by dragging its right side. Notice that both controls move. The anchored control moves so that it is always at the same distance from the top-right corner of the form, whereas the unanchored control adjusts its location relative to each side of the form.

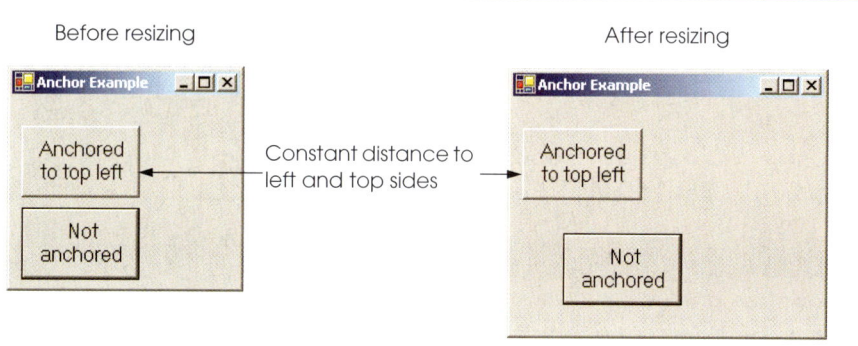

Fig. 12.11 Anchoring demonstration.

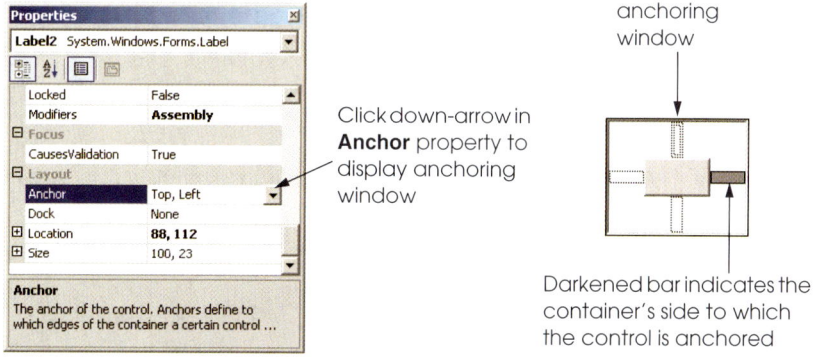

Fig. 12.12 Manipulating the **Anchor** property of a control.

Sometimes, it is desirable that a control span an entire side of the form, even when the form is resized. This is useful when we want one control, such as a status bar, to remain prevalent on the form. *Docking* allows a control span an entire side (left, right, top or bottom) of its parent container. When the parent is resized, the docked control resizes as well. In Fig. 12.13, a button is docked at the top of the form (it spans the top portion). When the form is resized horizontally, the button is resized to the form's new width. Windows Forms provide property **DockPadding**, which specifies the distance between the docked controls and the form edges. The default value is zero, which results in docked controls that are attached to the edge of the form. The control layout properties are summarized in the table in Fig. 12.14.

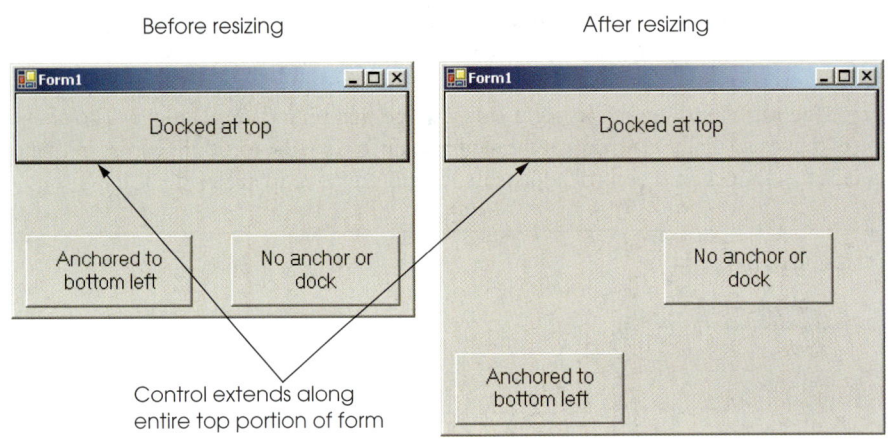

Fig. 12.13 Docking demonstration.

Common Layout Properties	Description
Anchor	Attaches control to the side of parent container. Used during resizing. Possible values include top, bottom, left and right.
Dock	Allows controls to span along the sides of their containers—values cannot be combined.
DockPadding (for containers)	Sets the space between a container's edges and docked controls. Default is zero, causing controls to appear flush with the sides of the container.
Location	Specifies the location of the upper-left corner of the control, in relation to its container.
Size	Specifies the size of the control. Takes a **Size** type, which has properties **Height** and **Width**.

Fig. 12.14 Control layout properties (part 1 of 2).

Common Layout Properties	Description
`MinimumSize`, `MaximumSize` (for Windows Forms)	Indicates the minimum and maximum size of the form.

Fig. 12.14 `Control` layout properties (part 2 of 2).

The docking and anchoring options refer to the parent container, which includes the form as well as other parent containers we discuss later in the chapter. The minimum and maximum form sizes can be set via properties `MinimumSize` and `MaximumSize`, respectively. Both properties use the `Size` type, which has properties `Height` and `Width`, to specify the size of the form. Properties `MinimumSize` and `MaximumSize` allow the programmer to design the GUI layout for a given size range. To set a form to a fixed size, set its minimum and maximum size to the same value.

Look-and-Feel Observation 12.2

Allow Windows Forms to be resized whenever possible—this enables users with limited screen space or multiple applications running at once to use the application more easily. Make sure that the GUI layout appears consistent across different permissible form sizes.

12.5 Labels, TextBoxes and Buttons

Labels provide text instructions or information and are defined with class `Label`, which is derived from class `Control`. A `Label` displays *read-only text* (i.e., text that the user cannot modify). At runtime, a `Label`'s text can be changed by setting `Label`'s `Text` property. Figure 12.15 lists common `Label` properties.

A *textbox* (class `TextBox`) is an area in which text can either be displayed by the program or be input by the user via the keyboard. A *password textbox* is a `TextBox` that hides the information entered by the user. As the user types in characters, the password textbox masks the user input by displaying characters (usually *****). If a value is provided for the `PasswordChar` property, the textbox becomes a password textbox. Otherwise it is a textbox.

Common `Label` Properties	Description / Delegate and Event Arguments
`Font`	The font used by the text on the `Label`.
`Text`	The text that appears on the `Label`.
`TextAlign`	The alignment of the `Label`'s text on the control. Possibilities are one of three horizontal positions (left, center or right) and one of three vertical positions (top, middle or bottom).

Fig. 12.15 Common `Label` properties.

Users often encounter both types of textboxes, when logging into a computer or Web site. The username textbox allows users to input their usernames; the password textbox allows users to enter their passwords. Figure 12.16 lists the common properties and events of **TextBox**es.

A *button* is a control that the user clicks to trigger a specific action. A program can employ several specific types of buttons, such as *checkboxes* and *radio buttons*. All the button types are derived from **ButtonBase** (namespace **System.Windows.Forms**), which defines common button features. In this section, we concentrate on the class **Button**, which initiates a command. The other button types are covered in subsequent sections. The text on the face of a **Button** is called a *button label*. Figure 12.17 lists the common properties and events of **Button**s.

Look-and-Feel Observation 12.3

*Although **Label**s, **TextBox**es and other controls can respond to mouse clicks, **Button**s more naturally convey this meaning. Use a **Button** (such as **OK**), rather than another type of control, to initiate a user action.*

The program in Fig. 12.18 uses a **TextBox**, a **Button** and a **Label**. The user enters text into a password box and clicks the **Button**, causing the text input to be displayed in the **Label**. Normally, we would not display this text—the purpose of password textboxes is to hide the text being entered by the user from anyone who might be looking over the user's shoulder. Figure 12.18 demonstrates that the text input into the password textbox is unaffected by property **PasswordChar**'s value.

First, we create the GUI by dragging the controls (a **Button**, a **Label** and a **TextBox**) onto the form. Once the controls are positioned, we change their names in the **Properties** window (by setting the **(Name)** property) from the default values—**TextBox1**, **Label1** and **Button1**—to the more descriptive **lblOutput**, **txtInput** and **cmdShow**. Visual Studio .NET creates the necessary code and places it inside method **InitializeComponent**. The **(Name)** property in the **Properties** window enables us to change the variable name of the object reference.

TextBox Properties and Events	Description / Delegate and Event Arguments
Common Properties	
`AcceptsReturn`	If **True**, pressing *Enter* creates a new line (if textbox is configured to contain multiple lines.) If **False**, pressing *Enter* clicks the default button of the form.
`Multiline`	If **True**, **Textbox** can span multiple lines. The default value is **False**.
`PasswordChar`	If a character is provided for this property, the **TextBox** becomes a password box, and the specified character masks each character typed by the user. If no character is specified, **Textbox** displays the typed text.

Fig. 12.16 **TextBox** properties and events (part 1 of 2).

Chapter 12　　　　　　　　　　Graphical User Interface Concepts: Part 1　　　493

TextBox Properties and Events	Description / Delegate and Event Arguments
ReadOnly	If **True**, **TextBox** has a gray background, and its text cannot be edited. The default value is **False**.
ScrollBars	For multiline textboxes, indicates which scrollbars appear (**none**, **horizontal**, **vertical** or **both**).
Text	The textbox's text content.
Common Events	*(Delegate **EventHandler**, event arguments **EventArgs**)*
TextChanged	Generated when text changes in **TextBox** (i.e., when the user adds or deletes characters). When a programmer double-clicks the **TextBox** control in **Design** view, an empty event handler for this event is generated.

Fig. 12.16 **TextBox** properties and events (part 2 of 2).

Button properties and events	Description / Delegate and Event Arguments
Common Properties	
Text	Specifies text displayed on the **Button** face.
Common Events	*(Delegate **EventHandler**, event arguments **EventArgs**)*
Click	Generated when user clicks the control. When a programmer double-clicks the **Button** control in design view, an empty event handler for this event is created.

Fig. 12.17 **Button** properties and events.

```
1   ' Fig. 12.18: LabelTextBoxButtonTest.vb
2   ' Using a textbox, label and button to display the hidden
3   ' text in a password box.
4
5   Imports System.Windows.Forms
6
7   Public Class FrmButtonTest
8      Inherits Form
9
10     Friend WithEvents txtInput As TextBox   ' input field
11     Friend WithEvents lblOutput As Label    ' display label
12     Friend WithEvents cmdShow As Button     ' activation button
13
14     ' Visual Studio .NET generated code
15
```

Fig. 12.18 Program to display hidden text in a password box (part 1 of 2).

```
16        ' handles cmdShow_Click events
17        Private Sub cmdShow_Click(ByVal sender As System.Object, _
18           ByVal e As System.EventArgs) Handles cmdShow.Click
19
20           lblOutput.Text = txtInput.Text
21        End Sub ' cmdShow_Click
22
23     End Class ' FrmButtonTest
```

Fig. 12.18 Program to display hidden text in a password box (part 2 of 2).

We then set **cmdShow**'s **Text** property to "**Show Me**" and clear the **Text** of **lblOutput** and **txtInput** so that they are blank when the program begins its execution. The **BorderStyle** property of **lblOutput** is set to **Fixed3D**, giving our **Label** a three-dimensional appearance. Notice that the **BorderStyle** property of all **TextBox**es is set to **Fixed3D** by default. The password character is set by assigning the asterisk character (*****) to the **PasswordChar** property. This property accepts only one character.

We create an event handler for **cmdShow** by selecting **cmdShow** from the Class Name drop-down menu and by selecting **Click** from the Method Name drop-down menu. This generates an empty event handler. We add line 20 to the event-handler code. When the user clicks **Button Show Me**, line 20 obtains user-input text in **txtInput** and displays it in **lblOutput**.

12.6 GroupBoxes and Panels

*GroupBox*es and *Panel*s arrange controls on a GUI. For example, buttons with similar functionality can be placed inside a **GroupBox** or **Panel** within the Visual Studio .NET Form Designer. All these buttons move together when the **GroupBox** or **Panel** is moved.

The main difference between the two classes is that **GroupBox**es can display a caption (i.e., text) and do not include scrollbars, whereas **Panel**s can include scrollbars and do not include a caption. **GroupBox**es have thin borders by default; **Panel**s can be set so that they also have borders, by changing their **BorderStyle** property.

Look-and-Feel Observation 12.4

Panels and GroupBoxes can contain other Panels and GroupBoxes.

Look-and-Feel Observation 12.5

Organize the GUI by anchoring and docking controls (of similar functionality) inside a GroupBox or Panel. The GroupBox or Panel then can be anchored or docked inside a form. This divides controls into functional "groups" that can be arranged easily.

To create a **GroupBox**, drag it from the toolbar and place it on a form. Then, create new controls and place them inside the **GroupBox**. These controls are added to the **GroupBox**'s **Controls** *property* and become part of the **GroupBox** class. The **GroupBox**'s **Text** property determines its caption. The following tables list the common properties of **GroupBox**es (Fig. 12.19) and **Panel**s (Fig. 12.20).

To create a **Panel**, drag it onto the form, and add controls to it. To enable the scrollbars, set the **Panel**'s **AutoScroll** property to **True**. If the **Panel** is resized and cannot display all of its controls, scrollbars appear (Fig. 12.21). The scrollbars then can be used to view all the controls in the **Panel** (both when running and designing the form). This allows the programmer to see the GUI exactly as it appears to the client.

GroupBox Properties	Description
Controls	Lists the controls that the **GroupBox** contains.
Text	Specifies text displayed at the top of the **GroupBox** (its caption).

Fig. 12.19 GroupBox properties.

Panel Properties	Description
AutoScroll	Indicates whether scrollbars appear when the **Panel** is too small to display all of its controls. Default is **False**.
BorderStyle	Sets the border of the **Panel** (default **None**; other options are **Fixed3D** and **FixedSingle**).
Controls	Lists the controls that the **Panel** contains.

Fig. 12.20 **Panel** properties.

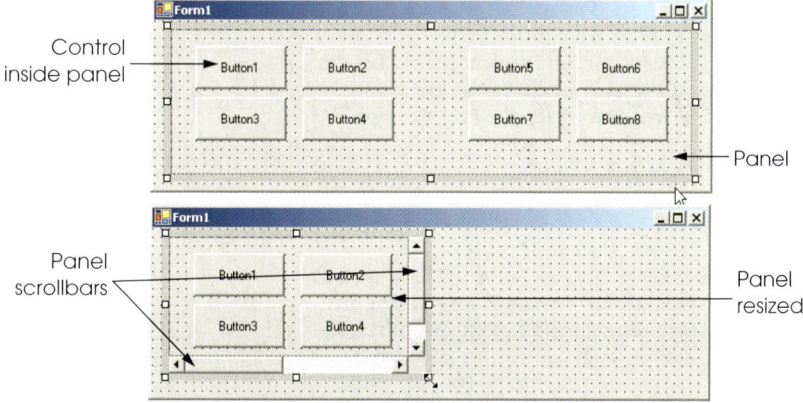

Fig. 12.21 Creating a **Panel** with scrollbars.

Look-and-Feel Observation 12.6

Use **Panel**s *with scrollbars to avoid cluttering a GUI and to reduce the GUI's size.*

The program in Fig. 12.22 uses a **GroupBox** and a **Panel** to arrange buttons. These buttons change the text on a **Label**.

The **GroupBox** (named **mainGroupBox**, line 10) has two buttons, **cmdHi** (labeled **Hi**, line 11) and **cmdBye** (labeled **Bye**, line 12). The **Panel** (named **mainPanel**, line 18) also has two buttons, **cmdLeft** (labeled **Far Left**, line19) and **cmdRight** (labeled **Far Right**, line 20). The **mainPanel** control has its **AutoScroll** property set to **True**, allowing scrollbars to appear when the contents of the **Panel** require more space than the **Panel**'s visible area. The **Label** (named **lblMessage**) is initially blank.

To add controls to **mainGroupBox**, Visual Studio .NET creates a **Windows.Forms.Control** array containing the controls. It then passes the array to method **AddRange** of the **Controls** collection in the **GroupBox**. Similarly, to add controls to **mainPanel**, Visual Studio .NET creates a **Windows.Forms.Control** array and passes it to the **mainPanel**'s **Controls.AddRange** method. Method **Controls.Add** adds a single control to a **Panel** or **GroupBox**.

The event handlers for the four buttons are located in lines 25–50. To create an empty **Click** event handler, double click the button in design mode (instead of using the Method Name drop-down menu). We then add a line in each handler to change the text of **lblMessage**.

```
1   ' Fig. 12.22: GroupBoxPanelExample.vb
2   ' Using GroupBoxes and Panels to hold buttons.
3
4   Imports System.Windows.Forms
5
6   Public Class FrmGroupBox
7      Inherits Form
8
9      ' top group box and controls
10     Friend WithEvents mainGroupBox As GroupBox
11     Friend WithEvents cmdHi As Button
12     Friend WithEvents cmdBye As Button
13
14     ' middle display
15     Friend WithEvents lblMessage As Label
16
17     ' bottom panel and controls
18     Private WithEvents mainPanel As Panel
19     Friend WithEvents cmdLeft As Button
20     Friend WithEvents cmdRight As Button
21
22     ' Visual Studio .NET generated code
23
```

Fig. 12.22 Using **GroupBox**es and **Panel**s to arrange **Button**s (part 1 of 2).

```
24      ' event handlers to change lblMessage
25      Private Sub cmdHi_Click(ByVal sender As System.Object, _
26         ByVal e As System.EventArgs) Handles cmdHi.Click
27
28         lblMessage.Text = "Hi pressed"
29      End Sub ' cmdHi_Click
30
31      ' bye button handler
32      Private Sub cmdBye_Click(ByVal sender As System.Object, _
33         ByVal e As System.EventArgs) Handles cmdBye.Click
34
35         lblMessage.Text = "Bye pressed"
36      End Sub ' cmdBye_Click
37
38      ' far left button handler
39      Private Sub cmdLeft_Click(ByVal sender As System.Object, _
40         ByVal e As System.EventArgs) Handles cmdLeft.Click
41
42         lblMessage.Text = "Far left pressed"
43      End Sub ' cmdLeft_Click
44
45      ' far right button handler
46      Private Sub cmdRight_Click(ByVal sender As System.Object, _
47         ByVal e As System.EventArgs) Handles cmdRight.Click
48
49         lblMessage.Text = "Far right pressed"
50      End Sub ' cmdRight_Click
51
52   End Class ' FrmGroupBox
```

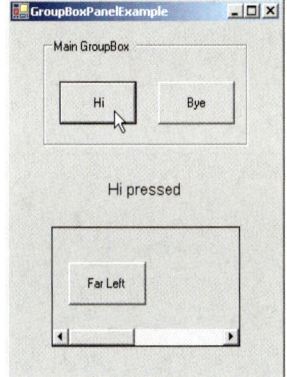
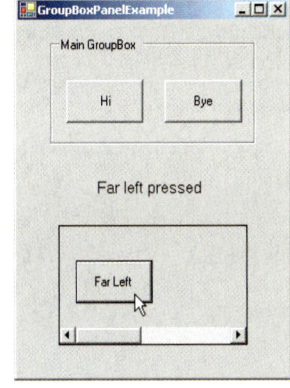
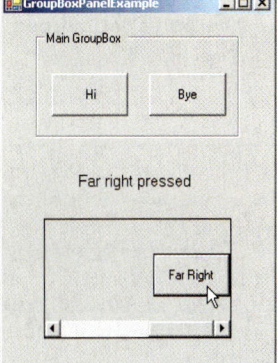

Fig. 12.22 Using **GroupBox**es and **Panel**s to arrange **Button**s (part 2 of 2).

12.7 CheckBoxes and RadioButtons

Visual Basic .NET has two types of *state buttons*—**CheckBox** and **RadioButton**—that can be in the on/off or true/false state. Classes **CheckBox** and **RadioButton** are derived from class **ButtonBase**. A **RadioButton** is different from a **CheckBox** in that **RadioButton**s are usually organized into groups and that only one of the **RadioButton**s in the group can be selected (**True**) at any time.

A checkbox is a small white square that either is blank or contains a checkmark. When a checkbox is selected, a black checkmark appears in the box. There are no restrictions on how checkboxes are used—any number of boxes can be selected at a time. The text that appears alongside a checkbox is referred to as the *checkbox label*. A list of common properties and events of class **Checkbox** appears in Fig. 12.23.

The program in Fig. 12.24 allows the user to select a **CheckBox** to change the font style of a **Label**. One **CheckBox** applies a bold style, whereas the other applies an italic style. If both **CheckBox**es are selected, the style of the font is both bold and italic. When the program initially executes, neither **CheckBox** is checked.

CheckBox events and properties	Description / Delegate and Event Arguments
Common Properties	
`Checked`	Indicates whether the **CheckBox** is checked (contains a black checkmark) or unchecked (blank).
`CheckState`	Indicates whether the **Checkbox** is checked or unchecked. An enumeration with values `Checked`, `Unchecked` or `Indeterminate` (checks and shades checkbox).
`Text`	Specifies the text displayed to the right of the **CheckBox** (called the label).
Common Events	*(Delegate `EventHandler`, event arguments `EventArgs`)*
`CheckedChanged`	Generated every time the **Checkbox** is either checked or unchecked. When a user double-clicks the **CheckBox** control in design view, an empty event handler for this event is generated.
`CheckStateChanged`	Generated when the **CheckState** property changes.

Fig. 12.23 CheckBox properties and events.

```
1    ' Fig. 12.24: CheckBoxTest.vb
2    ' Using CheckBoxes to toggle italic and bold styles.
3
4    Imports System.Windows.Forms
5
6    Public Class FrmCheckBox
7       Inherits Form
8
9       ' display label
10      Friend WithEvents lblOutput As Label
11
12      ' font checkboxes
13      Friend WithEvents chkBold As CheckBox
14      Friend WithEvents chkItalic As CheckBox
15
16      ' Visual Studio .NET generated code
17
```

Fig. 12.24 Using CheckBoxes to change font styles (part 1 of 2).

```vbnet
18      ' use Xor to toggle italic, keep other styles same
19      Private Sub chkItalic_CheckedChanged _
20         (ByVal sender As System.Object, ByVal e As System.EventArgs) _
21         Handles chkItalic.CheckedChanged
22
23         lblOutput.Font = New Font(lblOutput.Font.Name, _
24            lblOutput.Font.Size, lblOutput.Font.Style _
25            Xor FontStyle.Italic)
26      End Sub ' chkItalic_CheckedChanged
27
28      ' use Xor to toggle bold, keep other styles same
29      Private Sub chkBold_CheckedChanged _
30         (ByVal sender As System.Object, ByVal e As System.EventArgs) _
31         Handles chkBold.CheckedChanged
32
33         lblOutput.Font = New Font(lblOutput.Font.Name, _
34            lblOutput.Font.Size, lblOutput.Font.Style _
35            Xor FontStyle.Bold)
36      End Sub ' chkBold_CheckedChanged
37
38   End Class ' FrmCheckBox
```

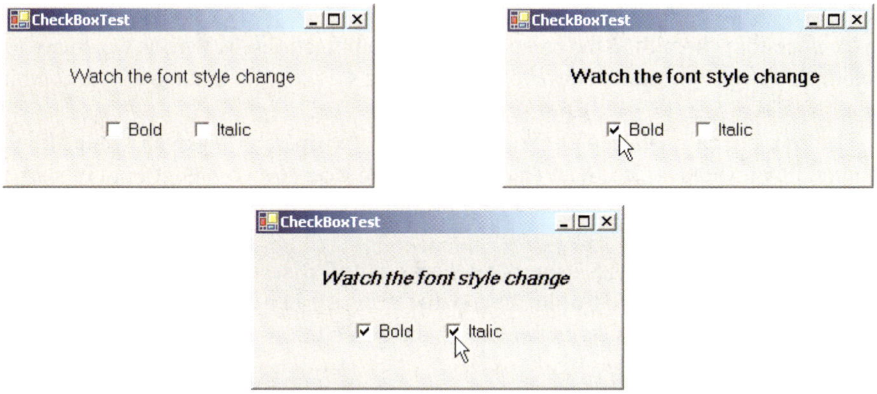

Fig. 12.24 Using **CheckBox**es to change font styles (part 2 of 2).

The first **CheckBox**, named **chkBold** (line 13), has its **Text** property set to **Bold**. The other **CheckBox** is named **chkItalic** (line 14) and labeled **Italic**. The **Text** property of the **Label**, named **lblOutput**, is set to **Watch the font style change**.

After creating the controls, we define their event handlers. Double clicking the **CheckBox** named **chkBold** at design time creates an empty **CheckedChanged** event handler (line 29). To understand the code added to the event handler, we first discuss the **Font** property of **lblOutput**.

To enable the font to be changed, the programmer must set the **Font** property to a **Font** object. The **Font** constructor (lines 23–25 and 33–35) that we use takes the font name, size and style. The first two arguments namely **lblOutput.Font.Name** and **lblOutput.Font.Size** (line 34), make use of **lblOutput**'s **Font** object. The style is a member of the **FontStyle** enumeration, which contains the font styles **Regular**, **Bold**, **Italic**, **Strikeout** and **Underline**. (The **Strikeout** style displays text with a line through it; the **Underline** style displays text with a line below it.) A **Font** object's **Style** property, which is read-only, is set when the **Font** object is created.

Styles can be combined via *bitwise operators*—operators that perform manipulation on bits. Recall from Chapter 1 that all data is represented on the computer as a series of 0s and 1s. Each 0 or 1 represents a bit. The FCL documentation indicates that **FontStyle** is a **System.FlagAttribute**, meaning that the **FontStyle** bit-values are selected in a way that allows us to combine different **FontStyle** elements to create compound styles, using bitwise operators. These styles are not mutually exclusive, so we can combine different styles and remove them without affecting the combination of previous **FontStyle** elements. We can combine these various font styles, using either the **Or** operator or the **Xor** operator. As a result of applying the **Or** operator to two bits, if at least one bit out of the two bits is 1, then the result is 1. The combination of styles using the **Or** operator works as follows. Assume that **FontStyle.Bold** is represented by bits **01** and that **FontStyle.Italic** is represented by bits **10**. When we **Or** both styles, we obtain the bitset **11**.

```
        01    = Bold
  Or    10    = Italic
        --
        11    = Bold and Italic
```

The **Or** operator is helpful in the creation of style combinations, as long as we do not need to undo the bitwise operation. However, what happens if we want to undo a style combination, as we did in Fig. 12.24?

The **Xor** operator enables us to accomplish the **Or** operator behavior while allowing us to undo compound styles. As a result of applying **Xor** to two bits, if both bits are the same ([1, 1] or [0, 0]), then the result is 0. If both bits are different ([1, 0] or [0, 1]), then the result is 1.

The combination of styles using **Xor** works as follows. Assume, again, that **FontStyle.Bold** is represented by bits **01** and that **FontStyle.Italic** is represented by bits **10**. When we **Xor** both styles, we obtain the bitset **11**.

```
        01    = Bold
  Xor   10    = Italic
        --
        11    = Bold and Italic
```

Now, suppose that we would like to remove the **FontStyle.Bold** style from the previous combination of **FontStyle.Bold** and **FontStyle.Italic**. The easiest way to do so is to reapply the **Xor** operator to the compound style and **FontStyle.Bold**.

```
        11    = Bold and Italic
  Xor   01    = Bold
        ----
        10    = Italic
```

This is a simple example. The advantages of using bitwise operators to combine **FontStyle** elements become more evident when we consider that there are five different **FontStyle** elements (**Bold**, **Italic**, **Regular**, **Strikeout** and **Underline**), resulting in 16 different **FontStyle** combinations. Using bitwise operators to combine font styles greatly reduces the amount of code required to check all possible font combinations.

In Fig. 12.24, we need to set the **FontStyle** so that the text appears bold if it was not bold originally, and vice versa. Notice that, in line 35, we use the bitwise **Xor** operator to do this. If **lblOutput.Font.Style** (line 34) is bold, then the resulting style is not bold. If the text is originally italicized, the resulting style is italicized and bold, rather than just bold. The same applies for **FontStyle.Italic** in line 25.

If we did not use bitwise operators to compound **FontStyle** elements, we would have to test for the current style and change it accordingly. For example, in the method **chkBold_CheckChanged**, we could test for the regular style and make it bold; test for the bold style and make it regular; test for the italic style and make it bold italic; and test for the italic bold style and make it italic. However, this method is cumbersome because, for every new style we add, we double the number of combinations. If we added a checkbox for underline, we would have to test for eight possible styles. To add a checkbox for strikeout then would require an additional 16 tests in each event handler. By using the bitwise **Xor** operator, we save ourselves from this trouble.

Radio buttons (defined with class **RadioButton**) are similar to checkboxes in that they also have two states—*selected* and *not selected* (also called *deselected*). However, radio buttons normally appear as a *group*, in which only one radio button can be selected at a time. The selection of one radio button in the group forces all other radio buttons in the group to be deselected. Therefore, radio buttons are used to represent a set of *mutually exclusive* options (i.e., a set in which multiple options cannot be selected at the same time).

Look-and-Feel Observation 12.7

Use **RadioButton**s *when the user should choose only one option in a group.*

Look-and-Feel Observation 12.8

Use **CheckBox**es *when the user should be able to choose multiple options in a group.*

All radio buttons added to a form become part of the same group. To separate radio buttons into several groups, the radio buttons must be added to **GroupBox**es or **Panel**s. The common properties and events of class **RadioButton** are listed in Fig. 12.25.

RadioButton properties and events	Description / Delegate and Event Arguments
Common Properties	
Checked	Indicates whether the **RadioButton** is checked.
Text	Specifies the text displayed to the right of the **RadioButton** (called the label).
Common Events	*(Delegate* **EventHandler**, *event arguments* **EventArgs**)
Click	Generated when user clicks the control.

Fig. 12.25 **RadioButton** properties and events (part 1 of 2).

RadioButton properties and events	Description / Delegate and Event Arguments
`CheckedChanged`	Generated every time the `RadioButton` is checked or unchecked. When a user double-clicks the `RadioButton` control in design view, an empty event handler for this event is generated.

Fig. 12.25 `RadioButton` properties and events (part 2 of 2).

Software Engineering Observation 12.3

Forms, *GroupBoxes*, and *Panels* can act as logical groups for radio buttons. The radio buttons within each group are mutually exclusive to each other, but not to radio buttons in different groups.

The program in Fig. 12.26 uses radio buttons to enable the selection of options for a **MessageBox**. After selecting the desired attributes, the user presses **Button Display**, causing the **MessageBox** to appear. A **Label** in the lower-left corner shows the result of the **MessageBox** (**Yes**, **No**, **Cancel** etc.). The different **MessageBox** icons and button types are illustrated and explained in Chapter 5, Control Structures: Part 2.

To store the user's choice of options, the objects **iconType** and **buttonType** are created and initialized (lines 9–10). Object **iconType** is a **MessageBoxIcon** enumeration that can have values **Asterisk**, **Error**, **Exclamation**, **Hand**, **Information**, **Question**, **Stop** and **Warning**. In this example, we use only **Error**, **Exclamation**, **Information** and **Question**.

```
1    ' Fig. 12.26: RadioButtonTest.vb
2    ' Using RadioButtons to set message window options.
3
4    Imports System.Windows.Forms
5
6    Public Class FrmRadioButton
7       Inherits Form
8
9       Private iconType As MessageBoxIcon
10      Private buttonType As MessageBoxButtons
11
12      ' button type group box and controls
13      Friend WithEvents buttonTypeGroupBox As GroupBox
14      Friend WithEvents radOk As RadioButton
15      Friend WithEvents radOkCancel As RadioButton
16      Friend WithEvents radAbortRetryIgnore As RadioButton
17      Friend WithEvents radYesNoCancel As RadioButton
18      Friend WithEvents radYesNo As RadioButton
19      Friend WithEvents radRetryCancel As RadioButton
20
21      ' icon group box and controls
22      Friend WithEvents iconGroupBox As GroupBox
23      Friend WithEvents radAsterisk As RadioButton
```

Fig. 12.26 Using **RadioButton**s to set message-window options (part 1 of 6).

```
24      Friend WithEvents radError As RadioButton
25      Friend WithEvents radExclamation As RadioButton
26      Friend WithEvents radHand As RadioButton
27      Friend WithEvents radInformation As RadioButton
28      Friend WithEvents radQuestion As RadioButton
29      Friend WithEvents radStop As RadioButton
30      Friend WithEvents radWarning As RadioButton
31
32      ' display button
33      Friend WithEvents cmdDisplay As Button
34
35      ' output label
36      Friend WithEvents lblDisplay As Label
37
38      ' Visual Studio .NET generated code
39
40      ' display message box and obtain dialogue button clicked
41      Private Sub cmdDisplay_Click(ByVal sender _
42         As System.Object, ByVal e As System.EventArgs) _
43         Handles cmdDisplay.Click
44
45         Dim dialog As DialogResult = MessageBox.Show( _
46            "This is Your Custom MessageBox", "Custom MessageBox", _
47            buttonType, iconType)
48
49         ' check for dialog result and display on label
50         Select Case dialog
51
52            Case DialogResult.OK
53               lblDisplay.Text = "OK was pressed"
54
55            Case DialogResult.Cancel
56               lblDisplay.Text = "Cancel was pressed"
57
58            Case DialogResult.Abort
59               lblDisplay.Text = "Abort was pressed"
60
61            Case DialogResult.Retry
62               lblDisplay.Text = "Retry was pressed"
63
64            Case DialogResult.Ignore
65               lblDisplay.Text = "Ignore was pressed"
66
67            Case DialogResult.Yes
68               lblDisplay.Text = "Yes was pressed"
69
70            Case DialogResult.No
71               lblDisplay.Text = "No was pressed"
72         End Select
73
74      End Sub ' cmdDisplay_Click
75
```

Fig. 12.26 Using **RadioButton**s to set message-window options (part 2 of 6).

```vbnet
76      ' set button type to OK
77      Private Sub radOk_CheckedChanged(ByVal sender _
78         As System.Object, ByVal e As System.EventArgs) _
79         Handles radOk.CheckedChanged
80
81         buttonType = MessageBoxButtons.OK
82      End Sub ' radOk_CheckedChanged
83
84      ' set button type to OkCancel
85      Private Sub radOkCancel_CheckedChanged(ByVal sender _
86         As System.Object, ByVal e As System.EventArgs) _
87         Handles radOkCancel.CheckedChanged
88
89         buttonType = MessageBoxButtons.OKCancel
90      End Sub ' radOkCancel_CheckedChanged
91
92      ' set button type to AbortRetryIgnore
93      Private Sub radAbortRetryIgnore_CheckedChanged(ByVal sender _
94         As System.Object, ByVal e As System.EventArgs) _
95         Handles radAbortRetryIgnore.CheckedChanged
96
97         buttonType = MessageBoxButtons.AbortRetryIgnore
98      End Sub ' radAbortRetryIgnore_CheckedChanged
99
100     ' set button type to YesNoCancel
101     Private Sub radYesNoCancel_CheckedChanged(ByVal sender _
102        As System.Object, ByVal e As System.EventArgs) _
103        Handles radYesNoCancel.CheckedChanged
104
105        buttonType = MessageBoxButtons.YesNoCancel
106     End Sub ' radYesNoCancel_CheckedChanged
107
108     ' set button type to YesNo
109     Private Sub radYesNo_CheckedChanged(ByVal sender _
110        As System.Object, ByVal e As System.EventArgs) _
111        Handles radYesNo.CheckedChanged
112
113        buttonType = MessageBoxButtons.YesNo
114     End Sub ' radYesNo_CheckedChanged
115
116     ' set button type to RetryCancel
117     Private Sub radRetryCancel_CheckedChanged(ByVal sender _
118        As System.Object, ByVal e As System.EventArgs) _
119        Handles radRetryCancel.CheckedChanged
120
121        buttonType = MessageBoxButtons.RetryCancel
122     End Sub ' radRetryCancel_CheckedChanged
123
124     ' set icon type to Asterisk when Asterisk checked
125     Private Sub radAsterisk_CheckedChanged(ByVal sender _
126        As System.Object, ByVal e As System.EventArgs) _
127        Handles radAsterisk.CheckedChanged
128
```

Fig. 12.26 Using `RadioButton`s to set message-window options (part 3 of 6).

```vbnet
129         iconType = MessageBoxIcon.Asterisk
130      End Sub ' radAsterisk_CheckedChanged
131
132      ' set icon type to Error when Error checked
133      Private Sub radError_CheckedChanged(ByVal sender _
134         As System.Object, ByVal e As System.EventArgs) _
135         Handles radError.CheckedChanged
136
137         iconType = MessageBoxIcon.Error
138      End Sub ' radError_CheckedChanged
139
140      ' set icon type to Exclamation when Exclamation checked
141      Private Sub radExclamation_CheckedChanged(ByVal sender _
142         As System.Object, ByVal e As System.EventArgs) _
143         Handles radExclamation.CheckedChanged
144
145         iconType = MessageBoxIcon.Exclamation
146      End Sub ' radExclamation_CheckedChanged
147
148      ' set icon type to Hand when Hand checked
149      Private Sub radHand_CheckedChanged(ByVal sender _
150         As System.Object, ByVal e As System.EventArgs) _
151         Handles radHand.CheckedChanged
152
153         iconType = MessageBoxIcon.Hand
154      End Sub ' radHand_CheckedChanged
155
156      ' set icon type to Information when Information checked
157      Private Sub radInformation_CheckedChanged(ByVal sender _
158         As System.Object, ByVal e As System.EventArgs) _
159         Handles radInformation.CheckedChanged
160
161         iconType = MessageBoxIcon.Information
162      End Sub ' radInformation_CheckedChanged
163
164      ' set icon type to Question when Question checked
165      Private Sub radQuestion_CheckedChanged(ByVal sender _
166         As System.Object, ByVal e As System.EventArgs) _
167         Handles radQuestion.CheckedChanged
168
169         iconType = MessageBoxIcon.Question
170      End Sub ' radQuestion_CheckedChanged
171
172      ' set icon type to Stop when Stop checked
173      Private Sub radStop_CheckedChanged(ByVal sender _
174         As System.Object, ByVal e As System.EventArgs) _
175         Handles radStop.CheckedChanged
176
177         iconType = MessageBoxIcon.Stop
178      End Sub ' radStop_CheckedChanged
179
```

Fig. 12.26 Using **RadioButton**s to set message-window options (part 4 of 6).

```
180         ' set icon type to Warning when Warning checked
181         Private Sub radWarning_CheckedChanged(ByVal sender _
182            As System.Object, ByVal e As System.EventArgs) _
183            Handles radWarning.CheckedChanged
184
185            iconType = MessageBoxIcon.Warning
186         End Sub ' radWarning_CheckedChanged
187
188   End Class ' FrmRadioButtons
```

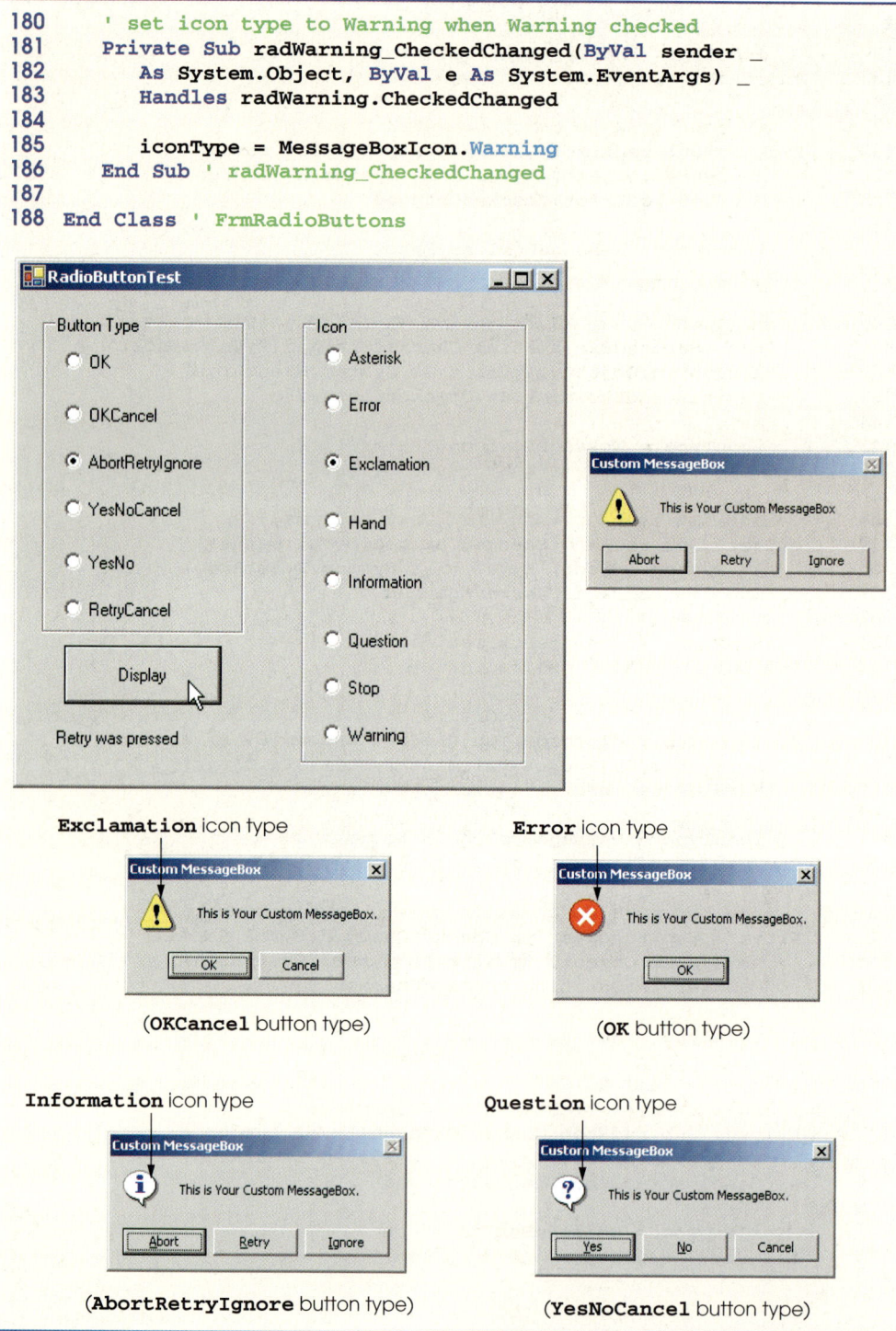

Fig. 12.26 Using `RadioButton`s to set message-window options (part 5 of 6).

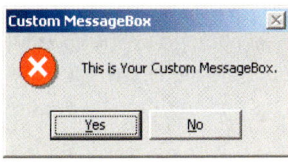
(**YesNo** button type)

(**RetryCancel** button type)

Fig. 12.26 Using **RadioButton**s to set message-window options (part 6 of 6).

Object **buttonType** is a **MessageBoxButton** enumeration with values **AbortRetryIgnore**, **OK**, **OKCancel**, **RetryCancel**, **YesNo** and **YesNoCancel**. The name indicates the options that are presented to the user. This example employs all **MessageBoxButton** enumeration values.

Two **GroupBox**es are created, one for each enumeration. Their captions are **Button Type** and **Icon**. There is also a button (**cmdDisplay**, line 33) labeled **Display**; when a user clicks it, a customized message box is displayed. A **Label** (**lblDisplay**, line 36) displays which button within the message box was pressed. **RadioButton**s are created for the enumeration options, and their labels are set appropriately. Because the radio buttons are grouped, only one **RadioButton** can be selected from each **GroupBox**.

Each radio button has an event handler that handles the radio button's **CheckedChanged** event. When a radio button contained in the **Button Type GroupBox** is checked, the checked radio button's corresponding event-handler sets **buttonType** to the appropriate value. Lines 77–122 contain the event handling for these radio buttons. Similarly, when the user checks the radio buttons belonging to the **Icon GroupBox**, the event handlers associated to these events (lines 125–186) sets **iconType** to its corresponding value.

To create the event handler for an event, it is necessary to use the functionality provided by Visual Studio. Note that each check box has its own event handler. This design has several advantages. First, it allows developers to modify the functionality of their code (i.e., by adding or removing check boxes) with minimal structural changes. The design structure also partitions the event-handling code to each respective event handler, reducing the potential for the accidental introduction of bugs into the code when an event handler for a particular check box must change. One common alternative design employs one event handler to handle all **CheckedChanged** events from a set of radio buttons. A "monolithic control structure" typically determines which code to execute on the basis of the control that triggered the event. This design offers the benefit that all event-handling code is localized to one event handler. However, the design complicates the process of extending the code for each event handler. Whenever the programmer modifies the event-handling code for a given **CheckBox**, a bug could be introduced into the monolithic control structure and could affect the code for the other, unmodified event handlers. This event-handling scheme is not recommended. It is always a good idea to separate unrelated sections of code from one another. This reduces the potential for bugs, thus decreasing development time.

The **Click** handler for **cmdDisplay** (lines 41–74) creates a **MessageBox** (lines 45–47). The **MessageBox** options are set by **iconType** and **buttonType**. The result of the message box is a **DialogResult** enumeration that has possible values **Abort**, **Cancel**, **Ignore**, **No**, **None**, **OK**, **Retry** or **Yes**. The **Select Case** statement on lines 50–72 tests for the result and sets **lblDisplay.Text** appropriately.

12.8 PictureBoxes

A picture box (class **PictureBox**) displays an image. The image, set by an object of class **Image**, can be in a bitmap, a *GIF (Graphics Interchange Format)*, a *JPEG (Joint Photographic Expert Group)*, icon or metafile format. (Images and multimedia are discussed in Chapter 16, Graphics and Multimedia.)

The **Image** property specifies the image that is displayed, and the **SizeMode** property indicates how the image is displayed (**Normal**, **StretchImage**, **Autosize** or **CenterImage**). Figure 12.27 describes important properties and events of class **PictureBox**.

The program in Fig. 12.28 uses **PictureBox picImage** to display one of three bitmap images—**image0**, **image1** or **image2**. These images are located in the directory **images** (in the **bin/images** directory of our project), where the executable file is also located. Whenever a user clicks **picImage**, the image changes. The **Label** (named **lblPrompt**) at the top of the form displays the text **Click On Picture Box to View Images**.

PictureBox properties and events	Description / Delegate and Event Arguments
Common Properties	
Image	Sets the image to display in the **PictureBox**.
SizeMode	Enumeration that controls image sizing and positioning. Values are **Normal** (default), **StretchImage**, **AutoSize** and **CenterImage**. **Normal** places image in top-left corner of **PictureBox**, and **CenterImage** puts image in middle (both truncate image if it is too large). **StretchImage** resizes image to fit in **PictureBox**. **AutoSize** resizes **PictureBox** to hold image.
Common Events	*(Delegate **EventHandler**, event arguments **EventArgs**)*
Click	Generated when user clicks the control. Default event when this control is double clicked in the designer.

Fig. 12.27 **PictureBox** properties and events.

```
1    ' Fig. 12.28: PictureBoxTest.vb
2    ' Using a PictureBox to display images.
3
4    Imports System.IO
5    Imports System.Windows.Forms
6
7    Public Class FrmPictureBox
8       Inherits Form
9
10      Private imageNumber As Integer = -1
11
12      ' instructions display label
13      Friend WithEvents lblPrompt As Label
```

Fig. 12.28 Using a **PictureBox** to display images (part 1 of 2).

```
14
15      ' image display area
16      Friend WithEvents picImage As Label
17
18      ' Visual Studio .NET generated code
19
20      ' replace image in picImage
21      Private Sub picImage_Click(ByVal sender As System.Object, _
22         ByVal e As System.EventArgs) Handles picImage.Click
23
24         ' imageNumber from 0 to 2
25         imageNumber = (imageNumber + 1) Mod 3
26
27         ' create Image object from file, display in PictureBox
28         picImage.Image = Image.FromFile _
29            (Directory.GetCurrentDirectory & "\images\image" & _
30            imageNumber & ".bmp")
31      End Sub ' picImage_Click
32
33   End Class ' FrmPictureBox
```

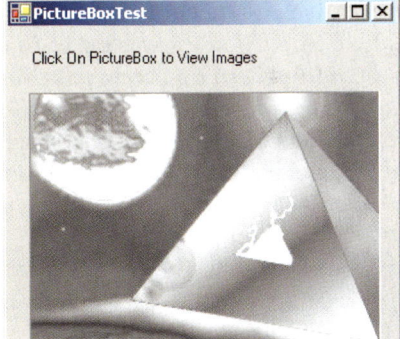
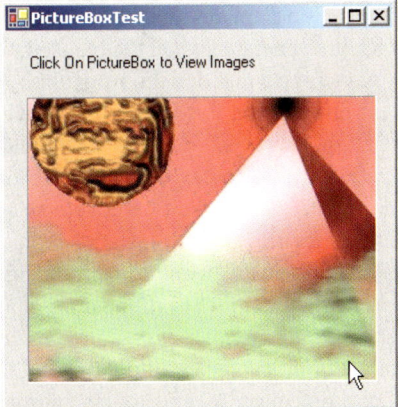
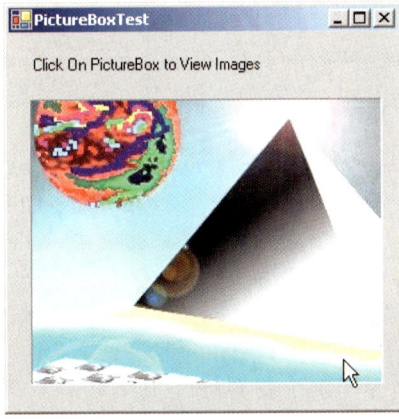

Fig. 12.28 Using a `PictureBox` to display images (part 2 of 2).

To respond to the user's clicks, the program must handle the **Click** event. Inside the event handler, **picImage_Click**, we use an **Integer** (**imageNumber**) to store the image we want to display. We then set the **Image** property of **picImage** to an **Image** (line 28–30). Although class **Image** is discussed in Chapter 16, Graphics and Multimedia, we now overview method **FromFile**, which takes a **String** (the image file) and creates an **Image** object.

To find the images, we use class **Directory** (namespace **System.IO**, specified on line 4) method **GetCurrentDirectory** (line 29). This returns the current directory of the executable file as a **String**. To access the **images** subdirectory, we append "**\images**" and the file name to the name of the current directory. We use **imageNumber** to append the proper number, enabling us to load either **image0**, **image1** or **image2**. The value of **Integer imageNumber** stays between **0** and **2** because of the modulus calculation in line 25. Finally, we append **".bmp"** to the filename. Thus, if we want to load **image0**, the **String** becomes "*CurrentDir***images****image0.bmp**", where *CurrentDir* is the directory of the executable.

12.9 Mouse-Event Handling

This section explains the handling of *mouse events,* such as *clicks*, *presses* and *moves*, which are generated when the mouse interacts with a control. Mouse events can be handled for any control that derives from class **System.Windows.Forms.Control**. Mouse-event information is passed through class **MouseEventArgs**, and the delegate used to create mouse-event handlers is **MouseEventHandler**. Each mouse-event-handling method requires an **Object** and a **MouseEventArgs** object as arguments. For example, the **Click** event, which we covered earlier, uses delegate **EventHandler** and event arguments **EventArgs**.

Class **MouseEventArgs** contains information related to the mouse event, such as the *x*- and *y*-coordinates of the mouse pointer, the mouse button pressed (**Right**, **Left** or **Middle**), the number of times the mouse was clicked and the number of notches through which the mouse wheel turned. Note that the *x*- and *y*-coordinates of the **MouseEventArgs** object are relative to the control that generated the event. Point *(0,0)* represents the upper-left corner of the control. Several mouse events are described in Fig. 12.29.

Mouse Events, Delegates and Event Arguments	
Mouse Events (Delegate **EventHandler***, event arguments* **EventArgs***)*	
MouseEnter	Generated if the mouse cursor enters the area of the control.
MouseLeave	Generated if the mouse cursor leaves the area of the control.
Mouse Events (Delegate **MouseEventHandler***, event arguments* **MouseEventArgs***)*	
MouseDown	Generated if the mouse button is pressed while its cursor is over the area of the control.
MouseHover	Generated if the mouse cursor hovers over the area of the control.

Fig. 12.29 Mouse events, delegates and event arguments (part 1 of 2).

Mouse Events, Delegates and Event Arguments	
`MouseMove`	Generated if the mouse cursor is moved while in the area of the control.
`MouseUp`	Generated if the mouse button is released when the cursor is over the area of the control.
Class `MouseEventArgs` *Properties*	
`Button`	Specifies the mouse button that was pressed (`left`, `right`, `middle` or `none`).
`Clicks`	Indicates the number of times that the mouse button was clicked.
`X`	The *x*-coordinate of the event, within the control.
`Y`	The *y*-coordinate of the event, within the control.

Fig. 12.29 Mouse events, delegates and event arguments (part 2 of 2).

The program in Fig. 12.30 uses mouse events to draw on a form. Whenever the user drags the mouse (i.e., moves the mouse while holding down a button), a line is drawn on the form.

In line 7, the program declares variable **shouldPaint**, which determines whether to draw on the form. We want the program to draw only while the mouse button is pressed (i.e., held down). Thus, in the event handler for event **MouseDown** (lines 28–33), **shouldPaint** is set to **True**. As soon as the mouse button is released, the program stops drawing: **shouldPaint** is set to **False** in the **FrmPainter_MouseUp** event handler (lines 36–41).

Whenever the mouse moves, the system generates a **MouseMove** event at a rate predefined by the operating system. Inside the **FrmPainter_MouseMove** event handler (lines 18–23), the program draws only if **shouldPaint** is **True** (indicating that the mouse button is pressed). Line 19 creates the form's **Graphics** object, which offers methods that draw various shapes. For example, method **FillEllipse** (lines 21–22) draws a circle at every point over which the mouse cursor moves (while the mouse button is pressed). The first parameter to method **FillEllipse** is a *SolidBrush* object, which specifies the color of the shape drawn. We create a new **SolidBrush** object by passing a **Color** value to the constructor. Type *Color* contains numerous predefined color constants—we selected **Color.BlueViolet** (line 22). The **SolidBrush** fills an elliptical region that lies inside a bounding rectangle. The bounding rectangle is specified by the *x*- and *y*-coordinates of its upper-left corner, its height and its width. These are the final four arguments to method **FillEllipse**. The *x*- and *y*-coordinates represent the location of the mouse event and can be taken from the mouse-event arguments (**e.X** and **e.Y**). To draw a circle, we set the height and width of the bounding rectangle so that they are equal—in this example, both are 4 pixels.

```
1    ' Fig. 12.30: Painter.vb
2    ' Using the mouse to draw on a form.
3
```

Fig. 12.30 Using the mouse to draw on a form (part 1 of 2).

```
4   Public Class FrmPainter
5      Inherits System.Windows.Forms.Form
6
7      Dim shouldPaint As Boolean = False
8
9      ' Visual Studio .NET generated code
10
11     ' draw circle if shouldPaint is True
12     Private Sub FrmPainter_MouseMove( _
13        ByVal sender As System.Object, _
14        ByVal e As System.Windows.Forms.MouseEventArgs) _
15        Handles MyBase.MouseMove
16
17        ' paint circle if mouse pressed
18        If shouldPaint Then
19           Dim graphic As Graphics = CreateGraphics()
20
21           graphic.FillEllipse _
22              (New SolidBrush(Color.BlueViolet), e.X, e.Y, 4, 4)
23        End If
24
25     End Sub ' FrmPainter_MouseMove
26
27     ' set shouldPaint to True
28     Private Sub FrmPainter_MouseDown(ByVal sender As Object, _
29        ByVal e As System.Windows.Forms.MouseEventArgs) _
30        Handles MyBase.MouseDown
31
32        shouldPaint = True
33     End Sub ' FrmPainter_MouseDown
34
35     ' set shouldPaint to False
36     Private Sub FrmPainter_MouseUp(ByVal sender As Object, _
37        ByVal e As System.Windows.Forms.MouseEventArgs) _
38        Handles MyBase.MouseUp
39
40        shouldPaint = False
41     End Sub ' FrmPainter_MouseUp
42
43  End Class ' FrmPainter
```

Fig. 12.30 Using the mouse to draw on a form (part 2 of 2).

Whenever the user clicks or holds down a mouse button, the system generates a **MouseDown** event. **FrmPainter_MouseDown** (lines 28–33) handles the **MouseDown** event. Line 32 sets **shouldPaint** to **True**. Unlike **MouseMove** events, the system generates a **MouseDown** event only once while the mouse button is down.

When the user releases the mouse button (to complete a "click" operation), the system generates a single **MouseUp** event. **FrmPainter_MouseUp** handles the **MouseUp** event (lines 36–41). Line 40 sets **shouldPaint** to **False**.

12.10 Keyboard-Event Handling

This section explains the handling of *key events*, which are generated when keys on the keyboard are pressed and released. Such events can be handled by any control that inherits from **System.Windows.Forms.Control**. There are two types of key events. The first is event **KeyPress**, which fires when a key representing an ASCII character is pressed (determined by **KeyPressEventArgs** property **KeyChar**). ASCII is a 128-character set of alphanumeric symbols, a full listing of which can be found in Appendix E, ASCII Character Set.

However the **KeyPress** event does not enable us to determine whether *modifier keys* (e.g., *Shift*, *Alt* and *Control*) were pressed. It is necessary to handle the second type of key events, the **KeyUp** or **KeyDown** events, to determine such actions. Class **KeyEventArgs** contains information about special modifier keys. The key's **Key** *enumeration* value can be returned, providing information about a wide range of non-ASCII keys. Often, modifier keys are used in conjunction with the mouse to select or highlight information. **KeyEventHandler** (event argument class **KeyEventArgs**) and **KeyPressEventHandler** (event argument class **KeyPressEventArgs**) are the delegates for the two classes. Figure 12.31 lists important information about key events.

Keyboard Events, Delegates and Event Arguments	
*Key Events (Delegate **KeyEventHandler**, event arguments **KeyEventArgs**)*	
KeyDown	Generated when key is initially pressed.
KeyUp	Generated when key is released.
*Key Events (Delegate **KeyPressEventHandler**, event arguments **KeyPressEventArgs**)*	
KeyPress	Generated when key is pressed. Occurs repeatedly while key is held down, at a rate specified by the operating system.
*Class **KeyPressEventArgs** Properties*	
KeyChar	Returns the ASCII character for the key pressed.
Handled	Indicates whether the **KeyPress** event was handled.
*Class **KeyEventArgs** Properties*	
Alt	Indicates whether the *Alt* key was pressed.
Control	Indicates whether the *Control* key was pressed.
Shift	Indicates whether the *Shift* key was pressed.

Fig. 12.31 Keyboard events, delegates and event arguments (part 1 of 2).

Keyboard Events, Delegates and Event Arguments

`Handled`	Indicates whether the event was handled.
`KeyCode`	Returns the key code for the key as a `Keys` enumeration. This does not include modifier-key information. Used to test for a specific key.
`KeyData`	Returns the key code for a key as a `Keys` enumeration, combined with modifier information. Contains all information about the pressed key.
`KeyValue`	Returns the key code as an `Integer`, rather than as a `Keys` enumeration. Used to obtain a numeric representation of the pressed key.
`Modifiers`	Returns a `Keys` enumeration for any modifier keys pressed (*Alt*, *Control* and *Shift*). Used to determine modifier-key information only.

Fig. 12.31 Keyboard events, delegates and event arguments (part 2 of 2).

Figure 12.32 demonstrates the use of the key-event handlers to display a key pressed by a user. The program is a form with two **Label**s. It displays the pressed key on one **Label** and modifier information on the other.

Initially, the two **Label**s (**lblCharacter** and **lblInformation**) are empty. The **lblCharacter** label displays the character value of the key pressed, whereas **lblInformation** displays information relating to the pressed key. Because the **KeyDown** and **KeyPress** events convey different information, the form (**FrmKeyDemo**) handles both.

The **KeyPress** event handler (lines 18–23) accesses the **KeyChar** property of the **KeyPressEventArgs** object. This returns the pressed key as a **Char** and displays the result in **lblCharacter** (line 22). If the pressed key is not an ASCII character, then the **KeyPress** event will not fire, and **lblCharacter** remains empty. ASCII is a common encoding format for letters, numbers, punctuation marks and other characters. It does not support keys such as the *function keys* (like *F1*) or the modifier keys (*Alt*, *Control* and *Shift*).

```
1    ' Fig. 12.32: KeyDemo.vb
2    ' Displaying information about a user-pressed key.
3
4    Imports System.Windows.Forms
5
6    Public Class FrmKeyDemo
7       Inherits Form
8
9       ' KeyPressEventArgs display label
10      Friend WithEvents lblCharacter As Label
11
12      ' KeyEventArgs display label
13      Friend WithEvents lblInformation As Label
14
```

Fig. 12.32 Demonstrating keyboard events (part 1 of 3).

```vbnet
15    ' Visual Studio .NET generated code
16
17    ' event handler for key press
18    Private Sub FrmKeyDemo_KeyPress(ByVal sender As System.Object, _
19       ByVal e As System.windows.Forms.KeyPressEventArgs) _
20       Handles MyBase.KeyPress
21
22       lblCharacter.Text = "Key pressed: " & e.KeyChar
23    End Sub
24
25    ' display modifier keys, key code, key data and key value
26    Private Sub FrmKeyDemo_KeyDown(ByVal sender As System.Object, _
27       ByVal e As System.Windows.Forms.KeyEventArgs) _
28       Handles MyBase.KeyDown
29
30       lblInformation.Text = ""
31
32       ' if key is Alt
33       If e.Alt Then
34          lblInformation.Text &= "Alt: Yes" & vbCrLf
35       Else
36          lblInformation.Text &= "Alt: No" & vbCrLf
37       End If
38
39       ' if key is Shift
40       If e.Shift Then
41          lblInformation.Text &= "Shift: Yes" & vbCrLf
42       Else
43          lblInformation.Text &= "Shift: No" & vbCrLf
44       End If
45
46       ' if key is Ctrl
47       If e.Control Then
48          lblInformation.Text &= "Ctrl: Yes" & vbCrLf
49       Else
50          lblInformation.Text &= "Ctrl: No" & vbCrLf
51       End If
52
53       lblInformation.Text &= "KeyCode: " & e.KeyCode.ToString & _
54          vbCrLf & "KeyData: " & e.KeyData.ToString & _
55          vbCrLf & "KeyValue: " & e.KeyValue
56    End Sub ' FrmKeyDemo_KeyDown
57
58    ' clear labels when key is released
59    Private Sub FrmKeyDemo_KeyUp(ByVal sender As System.Object, _
60       ByVal e As System.windows.Forms.KeyEventArgs) _
61       Handles MyBase.KeyUp
62
63       lblInformation.Text = ""
64       lblCharacter.Text = ""
65    End Sub ' FrmKeyDemo_KeyUp
66
67 End Class ' FrmKeyDemo
```

Fig. 12.32 Demonstrating keyboard events (part 2 of 3).

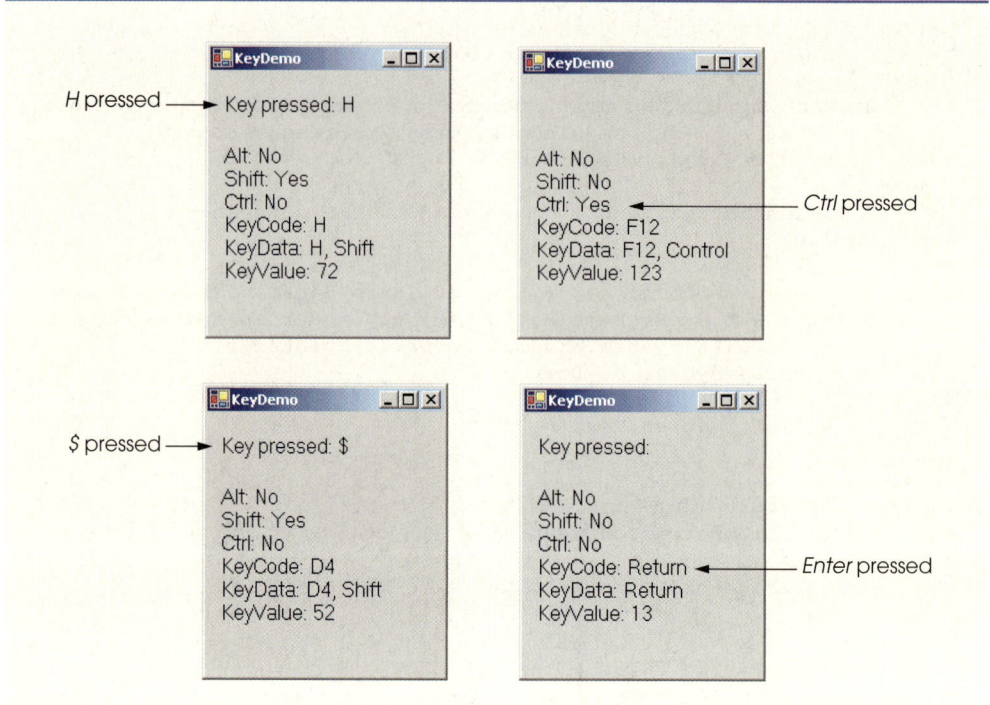

Fig. 12.32 Demonstrating keyboard events (part 3 of 3).

The **KeyDown** event handler (lines 26–56) displays information from its **KeyEventArgs** object. It tests for the *Alt*, *Shift* and *Control* keys by using the **Alt**, **Shift** and **Control** properties, each of which returns **Boolean**—**True** if their respective keys are pressed, **False** otherwise. It then displays the **KeyCode**, **KeyData** and **KeyValue** properties.

The **KeyCode** property returns a **Keys** enumeration, which is converted to a **String** via method **ToString** (line 53). The **KeyCode** property returns the pressed key, but does not provide any information about modifier keys. Thus, both a capital and a lowercase "a" are represented as the *A* key.

The **KeyData** property (line 54) also returns a **Keys** enumeration, but this property includes data about modifier keys. Thus, if "A" is input, the **KeyData** shows that the *A* key and the *Shift* key were pressed. Lastly, **KeyValue** (line 47) returns the key code of the pressed key as an **Integer**. This **Integer** is the *Windows virtual key code*, which provides an **Integer** value for a wide range of keys and for mouse buttons. The Windows virtual key code is useful when one is testing for non-ASCII keys (such as *F12*).

The **KeyUp** event handler (lines 59–65) clears both labels when the key is released. As we can see from the output, non-ASCII keys are not displayed in **lblCharacter**, because the **KeyPress** event is not generated. However, the **KeyDown** event still is generated, and **lblInformation** displays information about the key. The **Keys** enumeration can be used to test for specific keys by comparing the key pressed to a specific **KeyCode**. The Visual Studio .NET documentation contains a complete list of the **Keys** enumeration constants, under the topic **Keys enumeration**.

Chapter 12 — Graphical User Interface Concepts: Part 1

> **Software Engineering Observation 12.4**
>
> *To cause a control to react when a certain key is pressed (such as Enter), handle a key event and test for the pressed key. To cause a button to be clicked when the Enter key is pressed on a form, set the form's **AcceptButton** property.*

Throughout the chapter we introduced various GUI controls. We named the variables that referenced these controls according to their use in each program. We added a prefix that describes each control's type. This prefix enhances program readability by identifying a control's type. We include a table (Fig. 12.33) that contains the prefixes we use in this book.

In this chapter, we explored several GUI components in greater detail. In the next chapter, we continue our discussion of GUI components and GUI development by introducing additional controls.

SUMMARY

- A graphical user interface (GUI) presents a pictorial interface to a program. A GUI (pronounced "GOO-ee") gives a program a distinctive "look" and "feel."
- By providing different applications with a consistent set of intuitive user-interface components, GUIs allow the user to concentrate on using programs productively.
- GUIs are built from GUI components (sometimes called controls). A control is a visual object with which the user interacts via the mouse or keyboard.
- A **Form** is a graphical element that appears on the desktop. A form can be a dialog or a window.
- A component is a class that implements the **IComponent** interface.
- A control is a graphical component, such as a button.
- The active window has the focus. The active window is the frontmost window and has a highlighted title bar.
- A **Form** acts as a container for controls.
- When the user interacts with a control, an event is generated. This event can trigger methods that respond to the user's actions.
- All forms, components and controls are classes.
- The general design process for creating Windows applications involves creating a Windows Form, setting its properties, adding controls, setting their properties and configuring event handlers.

Prefix	Control
Frm	Form
lbl	Label
txt	TextBox
cmd	Button
chk	CheckBox
rad	RadioButton
pic	PictureBox

Fig. 12.33 Abbreviations for controls introduced in chapter.

- GUIs are event driven. When a user interaction occurs, an event is generated. The event information then is passed to event handlers.
- Events are based on the notion of delegates. Delegates act as an intermediate step between the object creating (raising) the event and the method handling it.
- Use the Class Name and Method Name drop-down menus to create and register event handlers.
- The information the programmer needs to register an event is the **EventArgs** class (to define the event handler) and the **EventHandler** delegate (to register the event handler).
- **Label**s (class **Label**) display read-only text to the user.
- A **TextBox** is a single-line area in which text can be input or displayed. A password textbox masks each character input by the user with another character (e.g., *****).
- A **Button** is a control that the user clicks to trigger a specific action. Buttons typically respond to the **Click** event.
- **GroupBox**es and **Panel**s help arrange controls on a GUI. The main difference between these classes is that **GroupBox**es can display text and **Panel**s can have scrollbars.
- Visual Basic .NET has two types of state buttons—**CheckBox**es and **RadioButton**s—that have on/off or true/false values.
- A checkbox is a small square that can be blank or contain a checkmark.
- Use the bitwise **Xor** operator to combine or negate a font style.
- Radio buttons (class **RadioButton**) have two states—selected, and not selected. Radio buttons appear as a group in which only one radio button can be selected at a time. To create new groups, radio buttons must be added to **GroupBox**es or **Panel**s. Each **GroupBox** or **Panel** is a group.
- Radio buttons and checkboxes generate the **CheckChanged** event.
- A picture box (class **PictureBox**) displays an image (class **Image**).
- Mouse events (such as clicks and presses) can be handled for any control that derives from **System.Windows.Forms.Control**. Mouse events use class **MouseEventArgs** (**MouseEventHandler** delegate) and **EventArgs** (**EventHandler** delegate).
- Class **MouseEventArgs** contains information about the *x*- and *y*-coordinates, the button used, the number of clicks and the number of notches through which the mouse wheel turned.
- Key events are generated when keyboard's keys are pressed and released. These events can be handled by any control that inherits from **System.Windows.Forms.Control**.
- Event **KeyPress** can return a **Char** for any ASCII character pressed. One cannot determine from a **KeyPress** event whether special modifier keys (such as *Shift*, *Alt* and *Control*) were pressed.
- Events **KeyUp** and **KeyDown** test for special modifier keys (using **KeyEventArgs**). The delegates are **KeyPressEventHandler** (**KeyPressEventArgs**) and **KeyEventHandler** (**KeyEventArgs**).
- Class **KeyEventArgs** has properties **KeyCode**, **KeyData** and **KeyValue**.
- The **KeyCode** property returns the key pressed, but does not give any information about modifier keys.
- The **KeyData** property includes data about modifier keys.
- The **KeyValue** property returns the key code for the key pressed as an **Integer**.

TERMINOLOGY

#Region (tag) and **#End Region**s preprocessor directive

active window
Alt property

ASCII character
background color
bitwise operator
button
Button class
button label
checkbox
CheckBox class
checkbox label
CheckedChanged event
click a button
click a mouse button
Click event
component
container
control
Control property
delegate
drag and drop
Enter key
Enter mouse event
event
event argument
event delegate
event driven
event handler
EventArgs class
event-handling model
Events window in Visual Studio
focus
Font property
font style
form
Form class
generate an event
GetCurrentDirectory method
graphical user interface (GUI)
GroupBox class
handle event
Image property
InitializeComponent method
input data from the keyboard
key code
key data
key event
key value
keyboard
KeyDown event
KeyEventArgs class
KeyPress event

KeyPressEventArgs class
KeyUp event
label
Label class
menu
menu bar
mouse
mouse click
mouse event
mouse move
mouse press
MouseDown event
MouseEventArgs class
MouseEventHandler delegate
MouseHover event
MouseLeave event
MouseMove event
MouseUp event
MouseWheel event
moving the mouse
multicast delegate
MulticastDelegate class
mutual exclusion
Name property
NewValue property
panel
Panel class
password box
PasswordChar property
picture box
PictureBox class
preprocessor directive
radio button
RadioButton class
radio-button group
read-only text
register an event handler
Scroll event
scrollbar
scrollbar on a panel
Shift property
SizeMode property
System.Windows.Forms namespace
text box
Text property
TextBox class
TextChanged event
trigger an event
uneditable text or icon
virtual key code

visual programming
widget
window gadget

Windows Form
Xor

SELF-REVIEW EXERCISES

12.1 State whether each of the following is *true* or *false*. If *false*, explain why.
  a) The **KeyData** property includes data about modifier keys.
  b) Windows Forms commonly are used to create GUIs.
  c) A form is an example of a container.
  d) All forms, components and controls are classes.
  e) Events are based on properties.
  f) A **Label** displays text that the user can edit.
  g) Button presses generate events.
  h) Checkboxes in the same group are mutually exclusive.
  i) All mouse events use the same event arguments class.
  j) Visual Studio can register an event and create an empty event handler.

12.2 Fill in the blanks in each of the following statements:
  a) The active control is said to have the _____.
  b) The form acts as a _____ for the controls that are added.
  c) GUIs are _____ driven.
  d) Every method that handles the same event must have the same_____.
  e) The information required when registering an event handler is the_____ class and the _____.
  f) A(n) _____ textbox masks user input with another character.
  g) Class _____ and class _____ help arrange controls on a GUI and provide logical groups for radio buttons.
  h) Typical mouse events include _____, _____ and _____.
  i) _____ events are generated when a key on the keyboard is pressed or released.
  j) The modifier keys are _____, _____ and _____.
  k) A(n) _____ event or delegate can call multiple methods.

ANSWERS TO SELF-REVIEW EXERCISES

12.1 a) True. b) True. c) True. d) True. e) False. Events are based on delegates. f) False. A **Label**'s text cannot be edited by the user. g) True. h) False. Radio buttons in the same group are mutually exclusive. i) False. Some mouse events use **EventArgs**, others **MouseEventArgs**. j) True.

12.2 a) focus. b) container. c) event. d) signature. e) event arguments, delegate. f) password. g) **GroupBox**, **Panel**. h) mouse clicks, mouse presses, mouse moves. i) Key. j) *Shift*, *Control*, *Alt*. k) multicast.

EXERCISES

12.1 Extend the program in Fig. 12.24 to include a **CheckBox** for every font style option. [*Hint*: Use **Xor** rather than testing for every bit explicitly.]

12.2 Create the following GUI:

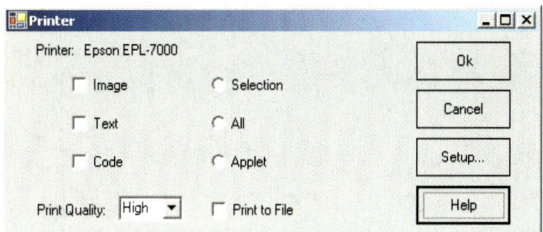

You do not have to provide any functionality.

12.3 Create the following GUI:

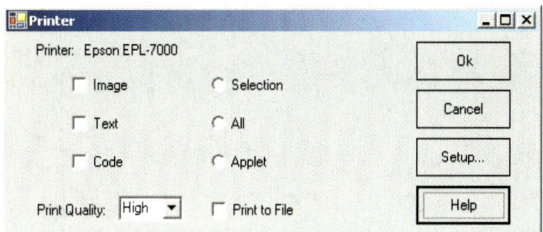

You do not have to provide any functionality.

12.4 Write a temperature conversion program that converts from Fahrenheit to Celsius. The Fahrenheit temperature should be entered from the keyboard (via a **TextBox**). A **Label** should be used to display the converted temperature. Use the following formula for the conversion:

$$Celsius = 5/9 \times (Fahrenheit - 32)$$

12.5 Extend the program of Fig. 12.30 to include options for changing the size and color of the lines drawn. Create a GUI similar to the one following.

12.6 Write a program that plays "guess the number" as follows: Your program chooses the number to be guessed by selecting an **Integer** at random in the range 1–1000. The program then displays the following text in a label:

> ```
> I have a number between 1 and 1000--can you guess my number?
> Please enter your first guess.
> ```

A **TextBox** should be used to input the guess. As each guess is input, the background color should change to red or blue. Red indicates that the user is getting "warmer," blue that the user is getting "colder." A **Label** should display either "**Too High**" or "**Too Low**," to help the user "zero-in" on the correct answer. When the user guesses the correct answer, display "**Correct!**" in a message box, change the form's background color to green and disable the **TextBox**. Provide a **Button** that allows the user to play the game again. When the **Button** is clicked, generate a new random number, change the background to the default color and enable the **TextBox**.

13

Graphical User Interface Concepts: Part 2

Objectives

- To be able to create menus, tabbed windows and multiple-document-interface (MDI) programs.
- To understand the use of the **ListView** and **TreeView** controls for displaying information.
- To be able to create hyperlinks using the **LinkLabel** control.
- To be able to display lists of information in **ListBox**es and **ComboBox**es.
- To create custom controls.

I claim not to have controlled events, but confess plainly that events have controlled me.
Abraham Lincoln

A good symbol is the best argument, and is a missionary to persuade thousands.
Ralph Waldo Emerson

Capture its reality in paint!
Paul Cézanne

But, soft! what light through yonder window breaks? It is the east, and Juliet is the sun!
William Shakespeare

An actor entering through the door, you've got nothing. But if he enters through the window, you've got a situation.
Billy Wilder

Outline

13.1 Introduction
13.2 Menus
13.3 `LinkLabels`
13.4 `ListBoxes` and `CheckedListBoxes`
    13.4.1 `ListBoxes`
    13.4.2 `CheckedListBoxes`
13.5 `ComboBoxes`
13.6 `TreeViews`
13.7 `ListViews`
13.8 Tab Control
13.9 Multiple-Document-Interface (MDI) Windows
13.10 Visual Inheritance
13.11 User-Defined Controls

Summary • Terminology • Self-Review Exercises • Answers to Self-Review Exercises • Exercises

13.1 Introduction

This chapter continues our study of GUIs. We begin our discussion of more advanced topics with a frequently used GUI component, the *menu*, which presents a user with several logically organized commands (or options). We discuss how to develop menus with the tools provided by Visual Studio .NET. We introduce `LinkLabel`s, powerful GUI components that enable the user to click the mouse to be taken to one of several destinations.

We consider GUI components that encapsulate smaller GUI components. We demonstrate how to manipulate a list of values via a `ListBox` and how to combine several checkboxes in a `CheckedListBox`. We also create drop-down lists using `ComboBox`es and display data hierarchically with a `TreeView` control. We present two important GUI components—tab controls and multiple-document-interface windows. These components enable developers to create real-world programs with sophisticated GUIs.

Visual Studio .NET provides a large set of GUI components, many of which are discussed in this chapter. Visual Studio .NET enables programmers to design custom controls and add those controls to the **ToolBox**. The techniques presented in this chapter form the groundwork for creating complex GUIs and custom controls.

13.2 Menus

Menus provide groups of related commands for Windows applications. Although these commands depend on the program, some—such as **Open** and **Save**—are common to many applications. Menus are an integral part of GUIs, because they organize commands without "cluttering" the GUI.

In Fig. 13.1, an expanded menu lists various commands (called *menu items*), plus *submenus* (menus within a menu). Notice that the top-level menus appear in the left portion of the figure, whereas any submenus or menu items are displayed to the right. The menu that contains a menu item is called that menu item's *parent menu*. A menu item that contains a submenu is considered to be the parent of that submenu.

All menu items can have *Alt* key shortcuts (also called *access shortcuts* or *hot keys*), which are accessed by pressing *Alt* and the underlined letter (for example, *Alt + F* expands the **File** menu). Menus that are not top-level menus can have shortcut keys as well (combinations of *Ctrl*, *Shift*, *Alt*, *F1*, *F2*, letter keys, etc.). Some menu items display checkmarks, usually indicating that multiple options on the menu can be selected at once.

To create a menu, open the **Toolbox** and drag a **MainMenu** control onto the form. This creates a menu bar on the top of the form and places a **MainMenu** icon at the bottom of the IDE. To select the **MainMenu**, click this icon. This configuration is known as the Visual Studio .NET Menu Designer, which allows the user to create and edit menus. Menus, like other controls, have properties, which can be accessed through the **Properties** window or the Menu Designer (Fig. 13.2), and events, which can be accessed through the **Class Name** and **Method Name** drop-down menus.

To add command names to the menu, click the **Type Here** textbox (Fig. 13.2) and type the menu command's name. Each entry in the menu is of type **MenuItem** from the **System.Windows.Forms** namespace. The menu itself is of type **MainMenu**. After the programmer presses the *Enter* key, the menu item name is added to the menu. Then, more **Type Here** textboxes appear, allowing the programmer to add items underneath or to the side of the original menu item (Fig. 13.3).

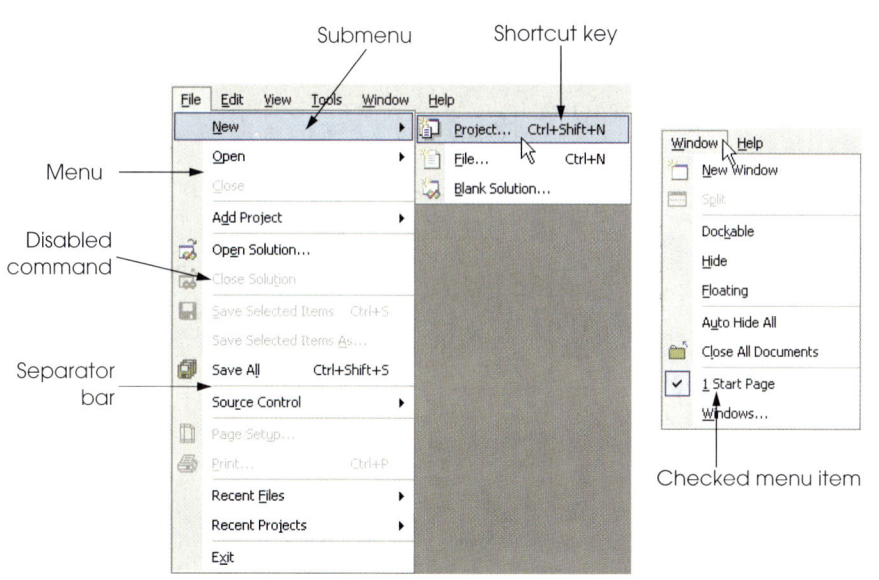

Fig. 13.1 Expanded and checked menus.

To create an *access shortcut* (or *keyboard shortcut*), type an ampersand (**&**) in front of the character to be underlined. For example, to create the **File** menu item, type **&File**. The ampersand character is displayed by typing **&&**. To add other shortcut keys (e.g., *Ctrl + F9*), set the **Shortcut** property of the **MenuItem**.

Look-and-Feel Observation 13.1

***Button**s also can have access shortcuts. Place the **&** symbol immediately before the desired character. To click the button, the user then presses* Alt *and the underlined character.*

Programmers can remove a menu item by selecting it with the mouse and pressing the *Delete* key. Menu items can be grouped logically by creating *separator bars*. Separator bars are inserted by right-clicking the menu and selecting **Insert Separator** or by typing "**-**" for the menu text.

Menu items generate a **Click** event when selected. To create an empty event handler, enter code-view mode and select the **MenuItem** instance from the Class Name drop-down menu. Then, select the desired event from the Method Name drop-down menu. Common menu actions include displaying dialogs an d setting properties. Menus also can display the names of open windows in multiple-document-interface (MDI) forms (see Section 13.9). Menu properties and events are summarized in Fig. 13.4.

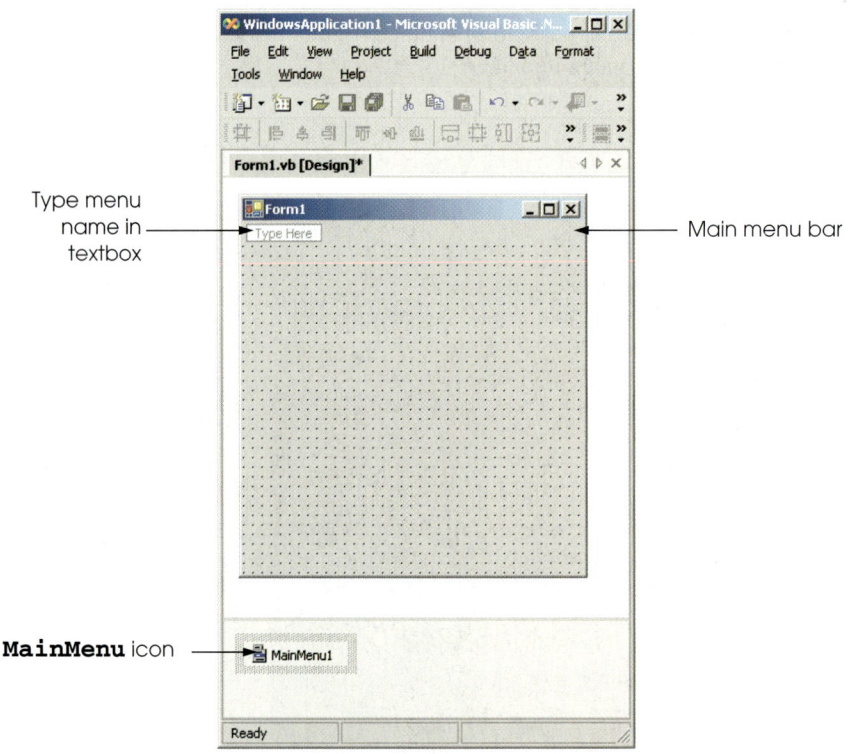

Fig. 13.2 Visual Studio .NET Menu Designer

Chapter 13 Graphical User Interface Concepts: Part 2 527

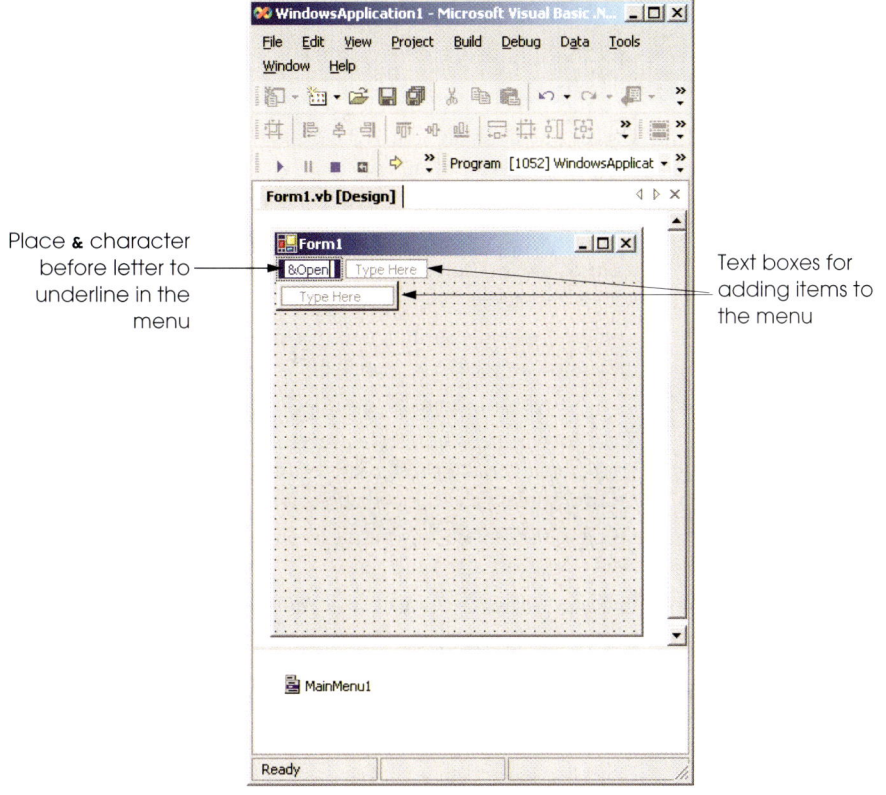

Fig. 13.3 Adding `MenuItem`s to `MainMenu`.

Look-and-Feel Observation 13.2
*It is convention to place an ellipsis (...) after a menu item that display a dialog (such as **Save As...**). Menu items that produce an immediate action without prompting the user (such as **Save**) should not have an ellipsis following their name.*

Look-and-Feel Observation 13.3
Using common Windows shortcuts (such as Ctrl+F for Find operations and Ctrl+S for Save operations) decreases an application's learning curve.

`MainMenu` and `MenuItem` events and properties	Description / Delegate and Event Arguments
`MainMenu` *Properties*	
`MenuItems`	Lists the `MenuItem`s that are contained in the `MainMenu`.

Fig. 13.4 `MainMenu` and `MenuItem` properties and events (part 1 of 2).

MainMenu and MenuItem events and properties	Description / Delegate and Event Arguments
`RightToLeft`	Causes text to display from right to left. Useful for languages, such as Arabic, that are read from right to left.
MenuItem Properties	
`Checked`	Indicates whether a menu item is checked (according to property `RadioCheck`). Default value is `False`, meaning that the menu item is unchecked.
`Index`	Specifies an item's position in its parent menu. A value of `0` places the `MenuItem` at the beginning of the menu.
`MenuItems`	Lists the submenu items for a particular menu item.
`RadioCheck`	Specifies whether a selected menu item appears as a radio button (black circle) or as a checkmark. `True` displays a radio button, and `False` displays a checkmark; default `False`.
`Shortcut`	Specifies the shortcut key for the menu item (e.g., *Ctrl* + *F9* is equivalent to clicking a specific item).
`ShowShortcut`	Indicates whether a shortcut key is shown beside menu item text. Default is `True`, which displays the shortcut key.
`Text`	Specifies the menu item's text. To create an *Alt* access shortcut, precede a character with `&` (e.g., `&File` for **File**).
Common Event	*(Delegate* `EventHandler`, *event arguments* `EventArgs`*)*
`Click`	Generated when item is clicked or shortcut key is used. This is the default event when the menu is double-clicked in designer.

Fig. 13.4 `MainMenu` and `MenuItem` properties and events (part 2 of 2).

Class `FrmMenu` (Fig. 13.5) creates a simple menu on a form. The form has a top-level **File** menu with menu items **About** (displays a message box) and **Exit** (terminates the program).The menu also includes a **Format** menu, which changes the text on a label. The **Format** menu has submenus **Color** and **Font**, which change the color and font of the text on a label.

```vb
1   ' Fig 13.5: MenuTest.vb
2   ' Using menus to change font colors and styles.
3
4   Imports System.Windows.Forms
5
6   Public Class FrmMenu
7      Inherits Form
8
9      ' display label
10     Friend WithEvents lblDisplay As Label
11
```

Fig. 13.5 Menus for changing text font and color (part 1 of 5).

```vb
12      ' main menu (contains file and format menus)
13      Friend WithEvents mnuMainMenu As MainMenu
14
15      ' file menu
16      Friend WithEvents mnuFile As MenuItem
17      Friend WithEvents mnuitmAbout As MenuItem
18      Friend WithEvents mnuitmExit As MenuItem
19
20      ' format menu (contains format and font submenus)
21      Friend WithEvents mnuFormat As MenuItem
22
23      ' color submenu
24      Friend WithEvents mnuitmColor As MenuItem
25      Friend WithEvents mnuitmBlack As MenuItem
26      Friend WithEvents mnuitmBlue As MenuItem
27      Friend WithEvents mnuitmRed As MenuItem
28      Friend WithEvents mnuitmGreen As MenuItem
29
30      ' font submenu
31      Friend WithEvents mnuitmFont As MenuItem
32      Friend WithEvents mnuitmTimes As MenuItem
33      Friend WithEvents mnuitmCourier As MenuItem
34      Friend WithEvents mnuitmComic As MenuItem
35      Friend WithEvents mnuitmDash As MenuItem
36      Friend WithEvents mnuitmBold As MenuItem
37      Friend WithEvents mnuitmItalic As MenuItem
38
39      ' Visual Studio .NET generated code
40
41      ' display MessageBox
42      Private Sub mnuitmAbout_Click( _
43         ByVal sender As System.Object, _
44         ByVal e As System.EventArgs) Handles mnuitmAbout.Click
45
46         MessageBox.Show("This is an example" & vbCrLf & _
47            "of using menus.", "About", MessageBoxButtons.OK, _
48            MessageBoxIcon.Information)
49      End Sub ' mnuitmAbout_Click
50
51      ' exit program
52      Private Sub mnuitmExit_Click( _
53         ByVal sender As System.Object, _
54         ByVal e As System.EventArgs) Handles mnuitmExit.Click
55
56         Application.Exit()
57      End Sub ' mnuitmExit_Click
58
59      ' reset font color
60      Private Sub ClearColor()
61
62         ' clear all checkmarks
63         mnuitmBlack.Checked = False
64         mnuitmBlue.Checked = False
```

Fig. 13.5 Menus for changing text font and color (part 2 of 5).

```vbnet
65            mnuitmRed.Checked = False
66            mnuitmGreen.Checked = False
67        End Sub ' ClearColor
68
69        ' update menu state and color display black
70        Private Sub mnuitmBlack_Click(ByVal sender As System.Object, _
71            ByVal e As System.EventArgs) Handles mnuitmBlack.Click
72
73            ' reset checkmarks for color menu items
74            ClearColor()
75
76            ' set color to black
77            lblDisplay.ForeColor = Color.Black
78            mnuitmBlack.Checked = True
79        End Sub ' mnuitmBlack_Click
80
81        ' update menu state and color display blue
82        Private Sub mnuitmBlue_Click(ByVal sender As System.Object, _
83            ByVal e As System.EventArgs) Handles mnuitmBlue.Click
84
85            ' reset checkmarks for color menu items
86            ClearColor()
87
88            ' set color to blue
89            lblDisplay.ForeColor = Color.Blue
90            mnuitmBlue.Checked = True
91        End Sub ' mnuitmBlue_Click
92
93        ' update menu state and color display red
94        Private Sub mnuitmRed_Click(ByVal sender As System.Object, _
95            ByVal e As System.EventArgs) Handles mnuitmRed.Click
96
97            ' reset checkmarks for color menu items
98            ClearColor()
99
100           ' set color to red
101           lblDisplay.ForeColor = Color.Red
102           mnuitmRed.Checked = True
103       End Sub ' mnuitmRed_Click
104
105       ' update menu state and color display green
106       Private Sub mnuitmGreen_Click(ByVal sender As System.Object, _
107           ByVal e As System.EventArgs) Handles mnuitmGreen.Click
108
109           ' reset checkmarks for color menu items
110           ClearColor()
111
112           ' set color to green
113           lblDisplay.ForeColor = Color.Green
114           mnuitmGreen.Checked = True
115       End Sub ' mnuitmGreen_Click
116
```

Fig. 13.5 Menus for changing text font and color (part 3 of 5).

```vb
117     ' reset font type
118     Private Sub ClearFont()
119
120         ' clear all checkmarks
121         mnuitmTimes.Checked = False
122         mnuitmCourier.Checked = False
123         mnuitmComic.Checked = False
124     End Sub ' ClearFont
125
126     ' update menu state and set font to Times
127     Private Sub mnuitmTimes_Click(ByVal sender As System.Object, _
128         ByVal e As System.EventArgs) Handles mnuitmTimes.Click
129
130         ' reset checkmarks for font menu items
131         ClearFont()
132
133         ' set Times New Roman font
134         mnuitmTimes.Checked = True
135         lblDisplay.Font = New Font("Times New Roman", 30, _
136             lblDisplay.Font.Style)
137     End Sub ' mnuitmTimes_Click
138
139     ' update menu state and set font to Courier
140     Private Sub mnuitmCourier_Click(ByVal sender As System.Object, _
141         ByVal e As System.EventArgs) Handles mnuitmCourier.Click
142
143         ' reset checkmarks for font menu items
144         ClearFont()
145
146         ' set Courier font
147         mnuitmCourier.Checked = True
148         lblDisplay.Font = New Font("Courier New", 30, _
149             lblDisplay.Font.Style)
150     End Sub ' mnuitmCourier_Click
151
152     ' update menu state and set font to Comic Sans MS
153     Private Sub mnuitmComic_Click(ByVal sender As System.Object, _
154         ByVal e As System.EventArgs) Handles mnuitmComic.Click
155
156         ' reset check marks for font menu items
157         ClearFont()
158
159         ' set Comic Sans font
160         mnuitmComic.Checked = True
161         lblDisplay.Font = New Font("Comic Sans MS", 30, _
162             lblDisplay.Font.Style)
163     End Sub ' mnuitmComic_Click
164
165     ' toggle checkmark and toggle bold style
166     Private Sub mnuitmBold_Click( _
167         ByVal sender As System.Object, _
168         ByVal e As System.EventArgs) Handles mnuitmBold.Click
169
```

Fig. 13.5 Menus for changing text font and color (part 4 of 5).

```
170         ' toggle checkmark
171         mnuitmBold.Checked = Not mnuitmBold.Checked
172
173         ' use Xor to toggle bold, keep all other styles
174         lblDisplay.Font = New Font( _
175            lblDisplay.Font.FontFamily, 30, _
176            lblDisplay.Font.Style Xor FontStyle.Bold)
177      End Sub ' mnuitmBold_Click
178
179      ' toggle checkmark and toggle italic style
180      Private Sub mnuitmItalic_Click( _
181         ByVal sender As System.Object, _
182         ByVal e As System.EventArgs) Handles mnuitmItalic.Click
183
184         ' toggle checkmark
185         mnuitmItalic.Checked = Not mnuitmItalic.Checked
186
187         ' use Xor to toggle italic, keep all other styles
188         lblDisplay.Font = New Font( _
189            lblDisplay.Font.FontFamily, 30, _
190            lblDisplay.Font.Style Xor FontStyle.Italic)
191      End Sub ' mnuitmItalic_Click
192
193 End Class ' FrmMenu
```

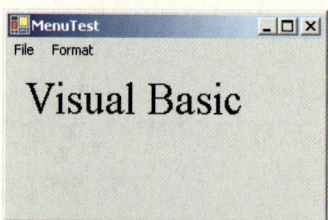

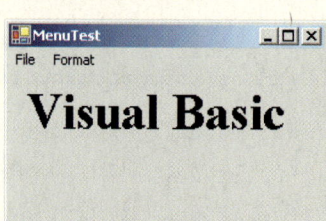
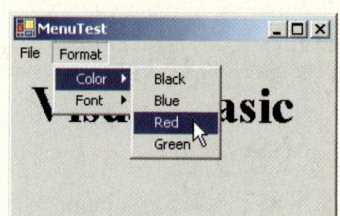
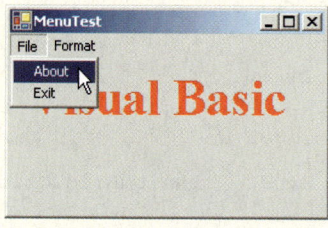
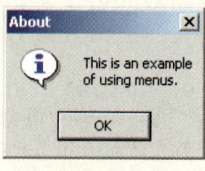

Fig. 13.5 Menus for changing text font and color (part 5 of 5).

We begin by dragging the **MainMenu** from the **ToolBox** onto the form. We then create our entire menu structure, using the Menu Designer. The **File** menu (**mnuFile**, line 16) has menu items **About** (**mnuitmAbout**, line 17) and **Exit** (**mnuitmExit**, line 18); the **Format** menu (**mnuFormat**, line 21) has two submenus. The first submenu, **Color** (**mnuitmColor**, line 24), contains menu items **Black** (**mnuitmBlack**, line 25), **Blue** (**mnuitmBlue**, line 26), **Red** (**mnuitmRed**, line 27) and **Green** (**mnuitmGreen**, line 28). The second submenu, **Font** (**mnuitmFont**, line 31), contains menu items **Times New Roman** (**mnuitmTimes**, line 32), **Courier** (**mnuitmCourier**, line 33), **Comic Sans** (**mnuitmComic**, line 34), a separator bar (**mnuitmDash**, line 35), **Bold** (**mnuitmBold**, line 36) and **Italic** (**mnuitmItalic**, line 37).

The **About** menu item in the **File** menu displays a **MessageBox** when clicked (lines 46–48). The **Exit** menu item closes the application through **Shared** method **Exit** of class **Application** (line 56). Class **Application**'s **Shared** methods control program execution. Method **Exit** causes our application to terminate.

We made the items in the **Color** submenu (**Black**, **Blue**, **Red** and **Green**) mutually exclusive—the user can select only one at a time (we explain how we did this shortly). To indicate this fact to the user, we set each **Color** menu item's **RadioCheck** properties to **True**. This causes a radio button to appear (instead of a checkmark) when a user selects a **Color**-menu item.

Each **Color** menu item has its own event handler. The method handler for color **Black** is **mnuitmBlack_Click** (lines 70–79). Similarly, the event handlers for colors **Blue**, **Red** and **Green** are **mnuitmBlue_Click** (lines 82–91), **mnuitmRed_Click** (lines 94–103) and **mnuitmGreen_Click** (lines 106–115), respectively. Each **Color** menu item must be mutually exclusive, so each event handler calls method **ClearColor** (lines 60–67) before setting its corresponding **Checked** property to **True**. Method **ClearColor** sets the **Checked** property of each color **MenuItem** to **False**, effectively preventing more than one menu item from being selected at a time.

Software Engineering Observation 13.1

*The mutual exclusion of menu items is not enforced by the **MainMenu**, even when the **RadioCheck** property is **True**. This behavior must be programmed.*

Look-and-Feel Observation 13.4
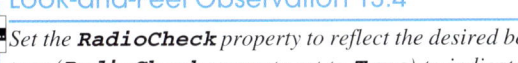
*Set the **RadioCheck** property to reflect the desired behavior of menu items. Use radio buttons (**RadioCheck** property set to **True**) to indicate mutually exclusive menu items. Use check marks (**RadioCheck** property set to **False**) for menu items that have no logical restriction.*

The **Font** menu contains three menu items for font types (**Courier**, **Times New Roman** and **Comic Sans**) and two menu items for font styles (**Bold** and **Italic**). We added a separator bar between the font-type and font-style menu items to indicate the distinction: Font types are mutually exclusive; styles are not. This means that a **Font** object can specify only one font type at a time but can set multiple styles at once (e.g., a font can be both bold and italic). We set the font-type menu items to display checks. As with the **Color** menu, we also must enforce mutual exclusion in our event handlers.

Event handlers for font-type menu items **TimesRoman**, **Courier** and **ComicSans** are **mnuitmTimes_Click** (lines 127–137), **mnuitmCourier_Click** (lines 140–150) and **mnuitmComic_Click** (lines 153–163), respectively. These event handlers behave in a manner similar to that of the event handlers for the **Color** menu items. Each event handler clears the **Checked** properties for all font-type menu items by calling method **ClearFont** (lines 118–124), then sets the **Checked** property of the menu item that raised the event to **True**. This enforces the mutual exclusion of the font-type menu items.

The event handlers for the **Bold** and **Italic** menu items (lines 166–191) use the bitwise **Xor** operator. For each font style, the **Xor** operator changes the text to include the style or, if that style is already applied, to remove it. The toggling behavior provided by the **Xor** operator is explained in Chapter 12, Graphical User Interfaces Concepts: Part 1. As explained in Chapter 12, this program's event-handling structure allows the programmer to add and remove menu entries while making minimal structural changes to the code.

13.3 LinkLabels

The ***LinkLabel*** control displays links to other resources, such as files or Web pages (Fig. 13.6). A **LinkLabel** appears as underlined text (colored blue by default). When the mouse moves over the link, the pointer changes to a hand; this is similar to the behavior of a hyperlink in a Web page. The link can change color to indicate whether the link is new, previously visited or active. When clicked, the **LinkLabel** generates a ***LinkClicked*** *event* (see Fig. 13.7). Class **LinkLabel** is derived from class **Label** and therefore inherits all of class **Label**'s functionality.

Look-and-Feel Observation 13.5

*Although other controls can perform actions similar to those of a **LinkLabel** (such as the opening of a Web page), **LinkLabel**s indicate that a link can be followed—a regular label or button does not necessarily convey that idea.*

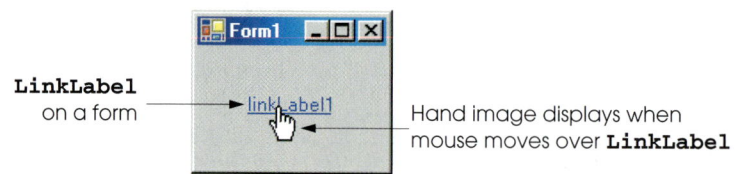

Fig. 13.6 **LinkLabel** control in running program.

LinkLabel properties and events	Description / Delegate and Event Arguments
Common Properties	
ActiveLinkColor	Specifies the color of the active link when clicked. Red is the default.
LinkArea	Specifies which portion of text in the **LinkLabel** is part of the link.

Fig. 13.7 **LinkLabel** properties and events (part 1 of 2).

LinkLabel properties and events	Description / Delegate and Event Arguments
`LinkBehavior`	Specifies the link's behavior, such as how the link appears when the mouse is placed over it.
`LinkColor`	Specifies the original color of all links before they have been visited. Blue is the default.
`Links`	Lists the `LinkLabel.Link` objects, which are the links contained in the `LinkLabel`.
`LinkVisited`	If `True`, link appears as though it were visited (its color is changed to that specified by property `VisitedLinkColor`). Default value is `False`.
`Text`	Specifies the control's text.
`UseMnemonic`	If `True`, `&` character in `Text` property acts as a shortcut (similar to the *Alt* shortcut in menus).
`VisitedLinkColor`	Specifies the color of visited links. Purple is the default.
Common Event	*(Delegate* `LinkLabelLinkClickedEventHandler`, *event arguments* `LinkLabelLinkClickedEventArgs`)
`LinkClicked`	Generated when the link is clicked. This is the default event when the control is double-clicked in designer.

Fig. 13.7 `LinkLabel` properties and events (part 2 of 2).

Class **FrmLinkLabel** (Fig. 13.8) uses three **LinkLabel**s, to link to the **C:** drive, the Deitel Web site (**www.deitel.com**) and the Notepad application, respectively. The **Text** properties of the **LinkLabel**'s **lnklblCDrive** (line 10), **lnklblDeitel** (line 11) and **lnklblNotepad** (line 12) describe each link's purpose.

The event handlers for the **LinkLabel** instances call method **Start** of class **Process** (namespace **System.Diagnostics**). This method allows us to execute other programs from our application. Method **Start** can take as arguments either the file to open (a **String**) or the application to run and its command-line arguments (two **String**s). Method **Start**'s arguments can be in the same form as if they were provided for input to the Windows **Run** command. For applications, full path names are not needed, and the **.exe** extension often can be omitted. To open a file that has a file type that Windows recognizes, simply insert the file's full path name. The Windows operating system must be able to use the application associated with the given file's extension to open the file.

The event handler for **lnklblCDrive**'s **LinkClicked** events browses the **C:** drive (lines 17–24). Line 22 sets the **LinkVisited** property to **True**, which changes the link's color from blue to purple (the **LinkVisited** colors are configured through the **Properties** window in Visual Studio). The event handler then passes **"C:\"** to method **Start** (line 23), which opens a **Windows Explorer** window.

The event handler for **lnklblDeitel**'s **LinkClicked** event (lines 27–35) opens the Web page **www.deitel.com** in Internet Explorer. We achieve this by passing the Web-page address as a **String** (lines 33–34), which opens Internet Explorer. Line 32 sets the **LinkVisited** property to **True**.

```vbnet
1    ' Fig. 13.8: LinkLabelTest.vb
2    ' Using LinkLabels to create hyperlinks.
3
4    Imports System.Windows.Forms
5
6    Public Class FrmLinkLabel
7       Inherits Form
8
9       ' linklabels to C:\ drive, www.deitel.com and Notepad
10      Friend WithEvents lnklblCDrive As LinkLabel
11      Friend WithEvents lnklblDeitel As LinkLabel
12      Friend WithEvents lnklblNotepad As LinkLabel
13
14      ' Visual Studio .NET generated code
15
16      ' browse C:\ drive
17      Private Sub lnklblCDrive_LinkClicked( _
18         ByVal sender As System.Object, ByVal e As _
19         System.Windows.Forms.LinkLabelLinkClickedEventArgs) _
20         Handles lnklblCDrive.LinkClicked
21
22         lnklblCDrive.LinkVisited = True
23         System.Diagnostics.Process.Start("C:\")
24      End Sub ' lnklblCDrive
25
26      ' load www.deitel.com in Web browser
27      Private Sub lnklblDeitel_LinkClicked( _
28         ByVal sender As System.Object, ByVal e As _
29         System.Windows.Forms.LinkLabelLinkClickedEventArgs) _
30         Handles lnklblDeitel.LinkClicked
31
32         lnklblDeitel.LinkVisited = True
33         System.Diagnostics.Process.Start( _
34            "IExplore", "http://www.deitel.com")
35      End Sub ' lnklblDeitel
36
37      ' run application Notepad
38      Private Sub lnklblNotepad_LinkClicked( _
39         ByVal sender As System.Object, ByVal e As _
40         System.Windows.Forms.LinkLabelLinkClickedEventArgs) _
41         Handles lnklblNotepad.LinkClicked
42
43         lnklblNotepad.LinkVisited = True
44
45         ' run notepad application
46         ' full path not needed
47         System.Diagnostics.Process.Start("notepad")
48      End Sub ' lnklblNotepad_LinkClicked
49
50   End Class ' LinkLabelList
```

Fig. 13.8 **LinkLabel**s used to link to a drive, a Web page and an application (part 1 of 2).

Chapter 13 Graphical User Interface Concepts: Part 2 537

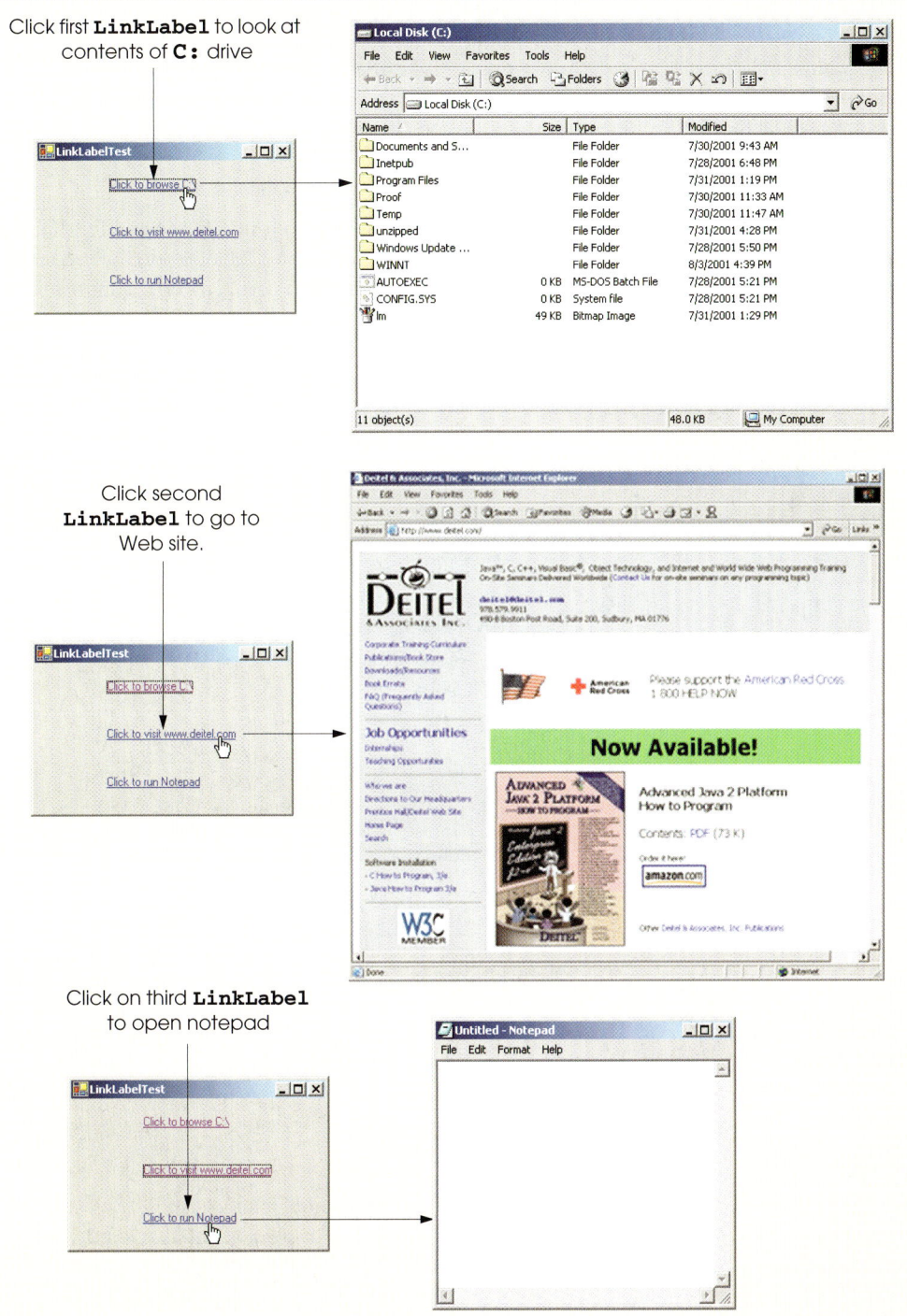

Fig. 13.8 LinkLabels used to link to a drive, a Web page and an application (part 2 of 2).

The event handler for **lnklblNotepad**'s **LinkClicked** events opens the specified Notepad application (lines 38–47). Line 43 sets the link to appear in the event handler as a visited link. Line 47 passes the argument **"notepad"** to method **Start**, which runs **notepad.exe**. Note that, in line 47, the **.exe** extension is not required—Windows can determine whether the argument given to method **Start** is an executable file.

13.4 ListBoxes and CheckedListBoxes

The **ListBox** control allows the user to view and select from multiple items in a list. **ListBox**es are static GUI entities, which means that users cannot add items to the list, unless the application adds items programmatically. The **CheckedListBox** control extends a **ListBox** by including check boxes next to each item in the list. This allows users to place checks on multiple items at once, as is possible in a **CheckBox** control (users also can select multiple items from a **ListBox**, but not by default). Figure 13.9 displays a **ListBox** and a **CheckedListBox**. In both controls, scrollbars appear if the number of items exceeds the **ListBox**'s viewable area. Figure 13.10 lists common **ListBox** properties, methods and events.

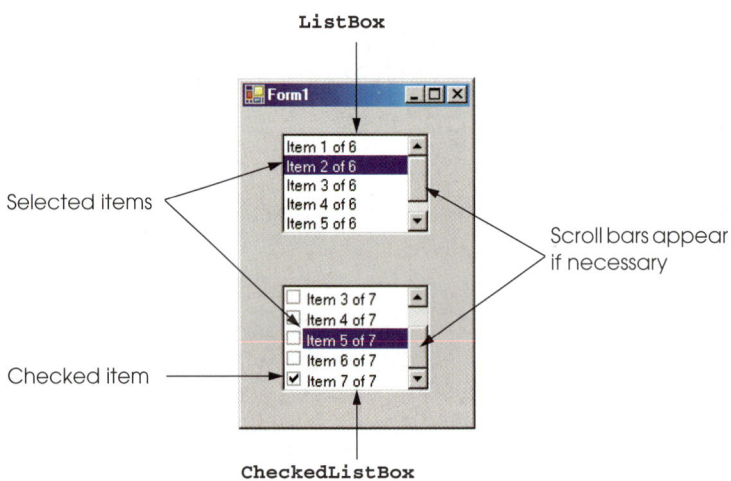

Fig. 13.9 **ListBox** and **CheckedListBox** on a form.

ListBox properties, methods and events	Description / Delegate and Event Arguments
Common Properties	
Items	The collection of items in the **ListBox**.

Fig. 13.10 **ListBox** properties, methods and events (part 1 of 2).

ListBox properties, methods and events	Description / Delegate and Event Arguments
`MultiColumn`	Indicates whether the `ListBox` can break a list into multiple columns. Multiple columns eliminate vertical scrollbars from the display.
`SelectedIndex`	Returns the index of the selected item. If the user selects multiple items, this property arbitrarily returns one of the selected indices; if no items have been selected, the property returns `-1`.
`SelectedIndices`	Returns a collection containing the indices for all selected items.
`SelectedItem`	Returns a reference to the selected item (if multiple items are selected, it returns the item with the lowest index number).
`SelectedItems`	Returns a collection of the selected item(s).
`SelectionMode`	Determines the number of items that can be selected, and the means through which multiple items can be selected. Values `None`, `One`, `MultiSimple` (multiple selection allowed) or `MultiExtended` (multiple selection allowed using a combination of arrow keys or mouse clicks and *Shift* and *Control* keys).
`Sorted`	Indicates whether items are sorted alphabetically. Setting this property's value to `True` sorts the items. The default value is `False`.
Common Method	
`GetSelected`	Takes an index as an argument, and returns `True` if the corresponding item is selected.
Common Event	*(Delegate* `EventHandler`, *event arguments* `EventArgs`*)*
`SelectedIndex-Changed`	Generated when selected index changes. This is the default event when the control is double-clicked in the designer.

Fig. 13.10 `ListBox` properties, methods and events (part 2 of 2).

The `SelectionMode` property determines the number of items that can be selected. This property has the possible values `None`, `One`, `MultiSimple` and `MultiExtended` (from the `SelectionMode` *enumeration*)—the differences among these settings are explained in Fig. 13.10. The `SelectedIndexChanged` event occurs when the user selects a new item.

Both the `ListBox` and `CheckedListBox` have properties `Items`, `SelectedItem` and `SelectedIndex`. Property `Items` returns all the list items as a collection. Collections are a common way of exposing lists of `Object`s in the .NET framework. Many .NET GUI components (e.g., `ListBox`es) use collections to expose lists of internal objects (e.g., items contained within a `ListBox`). We discuss collections further in Chapter 23, Data Structures and Collections. Property `SelectedItem` returns the `ListBox`'s currently selected item. If the user can select multiple items, use collection `SelectedItems` to return all the selected items as a collection. Property `SelectedIndex` returns the index of the selected item—if there could be more than one, use property `SelectedIndices`. If no items are selected, property `SelectedIndex` returns `-1`. Method `GetSelected` takes an index and returns `True` if the corresponding item is selected.

To add items to a **ListBox** or to a **CheckedListBox** we must add objects to its **Items** collection. This can be accomplished by calling method **Add** to add a **String** to the **ListBox**'s or **CheckedListBox**'s **Items** collection. For example, we could write

   myListBox.**Items.Add(** *myListItem* **)**

to add **String** *myListItem* to **ListBox** *myListBox*. To add multiple objects, programmers can either call method **Add** multiple times or call method **AddRange** to add an array of objects. Classes **ListBox** and **CheckedListBox** each call the submitted object's **ToString** method to determine the label for the corresponding object's entry in the list. This allows programmers to add different objects to a **ListBox** or a **CheckedListBox** that later can be returned through properties **SelectedItem** and **SelectedItems**.

Alternatively, we can add items to **ListBox**es and **CheckedListBox**es visually by examining the **Items** property in the **Properties** window. Clicking the ellipsis button opens the **String Collection Editor**, a text area in which programmers add items; each item appears on a separate line (Fig. 13.11). Visual Studio .NET then adds these **String**s to the **Items** collection inside method **InitializeComponent**.

13.4.1 ListBoxes

Figure 13.12 uses class **FrmListBox** to add, remove and clear items from **ListBox lstDisplay** (line 10). Class **FrmListBox** uses **TextBox txtInput** (line 13) to allow the user to type in a new item. When the user clicks the **Add** button (**cmdAdd** in line 16), the new item appears in **lstDisplay**. Similarly, if the user selects an item and clicks **Remove** (**cmdRemove** in line 17), the item is deleted. When clicked, **Clear** (**cmdClear** in line 18) deletes all entries in **lstDisplay**. The user terminates the application by clicking **Exit** (**cmdExit** in line 19).

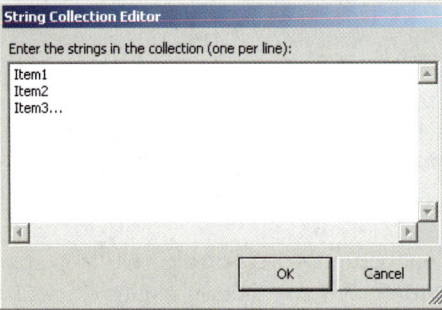

Fig. 13.11 String Collection Editor.

```
1    ' Fig. 13.12: ListBoxTest.vb
2    ' Program to add, remove and clear list box items.
3
4    Imports System.Windows.Forms
```

Fig. 13.12 Program that adds, removes and clears **ListBox** items (part 1 of 3).

```vbnet
 5
 6   Public Class FrmListBox
 7      Inherits Form
 8
 9      ' contains user-input list of elements
10      Friend WithEvents lstDisplay As ListBox
11
12      ' user-input textbox
13      Friend WithEvents txtInput As TextBox
14
15      ' add, remove, clear and exit command buttons
16      Friend WithEvents cmdAdd As Button
17      Friend WithEvents cmdRemove As Button
18      Friend WithEvents cmdClear As Button
19      Friend WithEvents cmdExit As Button
20
21      ' Visual Studio .NET generated code
22
23      ' add new item (text from input box) and clear input box
24      Private Sub cmdAdd_Click(ByVal sender As System.Object, _
25         ByVal e As System.EventArgs) Handles cmdAdd.Click
26
27         lstDisplay.Items.Add(txtInput.Text)
28         txtInput.Text = ""
29      End Sub ' cmdAdd_Click
30
31      ' remove item if one is selected
32      Private Sub cmdRemove_Click (ByVal sender As System.Object, _
33         ByVal e As System.EventArgs) Handles cmdRemove.Click
34
35         ' remove only if item is selected
36         If lstDisplay.SelectedIndex <> -1 Then
37            lstDisplay.Items.RemoveAt(lstDisplay.SelectedIndex)
38         End If
39
40      End Sub ' cmdRemove_Click
41
42      ' clear all items
43      Private Sub cmdClear_Click (ByVal sender As System.Object, _
44         ByVal e As System.EventArgs) Handles cmdClear.Click
45
46         lstDisplay.Items.Clear()
47      End Sub ' cmdClear_Click
48
49      ' exit application
50      Private Sub cmdExit_Click (ByVal sender As System.Object, _
51         ByVal e As System.EventArgs) Handles cmdExit.Click
52
53         Application.Exit()
54      End Sub ' cmdExit_Click
55
56   End Class ' FrmListBox
```

Fig. 13.12 Program that adds, removes and clears **ListBox** items (part 2 of 3).

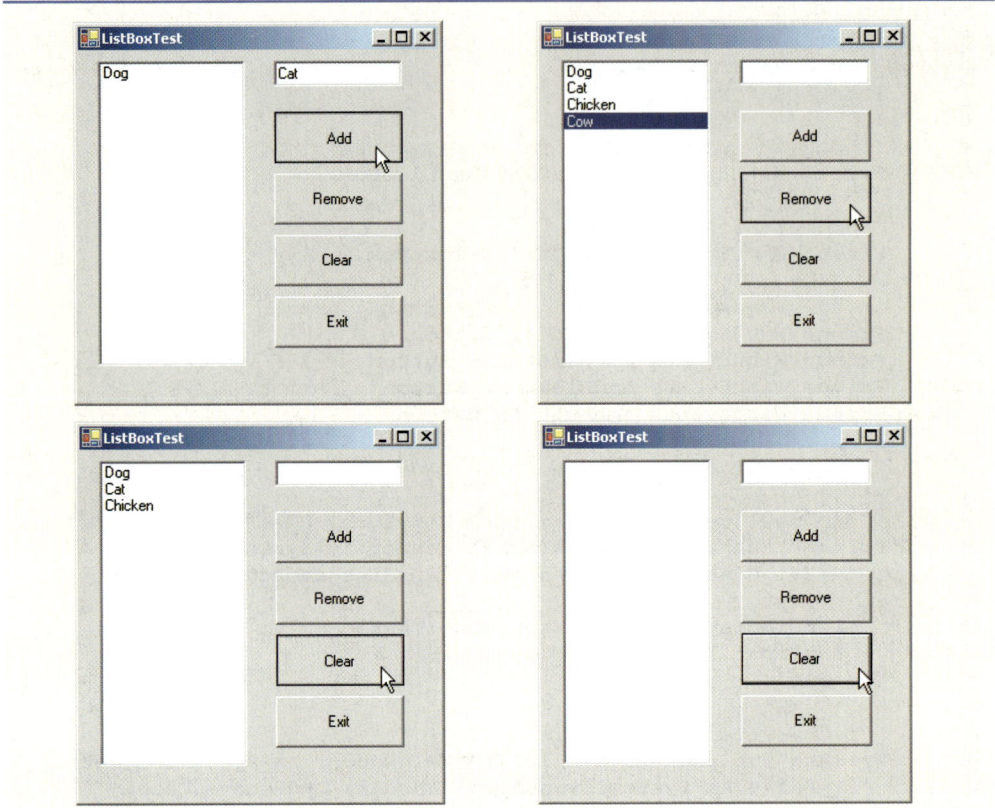

Fig. 13.12 Program that adds, removes and clears **ListBox** items (part 3 of 3).

The **cmdAdd_Click** event handler (lines 24–29) calls method **Add** of the **Items** collection in the **ListBox**. This method takes a **String** as the item to add to **lstDisplay**. In this case, the **String** used is the user-input text, or **txtInput.Text** (line 27). After the item is added, **txtInput.Text** is cleared (line 28).

The **cmdRemove_Click** event handler (lines 32–40) calls method **Remove** of the **Items** collection. Event handler **cmdRemove_Click** first uses property **SelectedIndex** to determine which index is selected. Unless **SelectedIndex** is empty (**-1**) (line 36), the handler removes the item that corresponds to the selected index.

The event handler for **cmdClear_Click** (lines 43–47) calls method **Clear** of the **Items** collection (line 46). This removes all the entries in **lstDisplay**. Finally, event handler **cmdExit_Click** (lines 50–54) terminates the application, by calling method **Application.Exit** (line 53).

13.4.2 CheckedListBoxes

The **CheckedListBox** control derives from class **ListBox** and includes a checkbox next to each item. As in **ListBox**es, items can be added via methods **Add** and **AddRange** or through the **String Collection Editor**. **CheckedListBox**es imply that multiple items can be selected, and the only possible values for the **SelectionMode** property are

None and **One**. **One** allows multiple selection, because checkboxes imply that there are no logical restrictions on the items—the user can select as many items as required. Thus, the only choice is whether to give the user multiple selection or no selection at all. This keeps the **CheckedListBox**'s behavior consistent with that of **CheckBox**es. The programmer is unable to set the last two **SelectionMode** values, **MultiSimple** and **MultiExtended**, because the only logical two selection modes are handled by **None** and **One**. Common properties and events of **CheckedListBox**es appear in Fig. 13.13.

Common Programming Error 13.1

*The IDE displays an error message if the programmer attempts to set the **SelectionMode** property to **MultiSimple** or **MultiExtended** in the **Properties** window of a **CheckedListBox**; If this value is set programmatically, a runtime error occurs.*

Event **ItemCheck** is generated whenever a user checks or unchecks a **CheckedListBox** item. Event argument properties **CurrentValue** and **NewValue** return **CheckState** values for the current and new state of the item, respectively. A comparison of these values allows the programmer to determine whether the **CheckedListBox** item was checked or unchecked. The **CheckedListBox** control retains the **SelectedItems** and **SelectedIndices** properties (it inherits them from class **ListBox**). However, it also includes properties **CheckedItems** and **CheckedIndices**, which return information about the checked items and indices.

CheckedListBox properties, methods and events	Description / Delegate and Event Arguments
Common Properties	*(All the **ListBox** properties and events are inherited by **CheckedListBox**.)*
CheckedItems	Contains the collection of items that are checked. This is distinct from the selected item, which is highlighted (but not necessarily checked). [*Note:* There can be at most one selected item at any given time.]
CheckedIndices	Returns indices for all checked items. This is not the same as the selected index.
SelectionMode	Determines how many items can be checked. Only possible values are **One** (allows multiple checks to be placed) or **None** (does not allow any checks to be placed).
Common Method	
GetItemChecked	Takes an index and returns **True** if the corresponding item is checked.
Common Event	*(Delegate **ItemCheckEventHandler**, event arguments **ItemCheckEventArgs**)*
ItemCheck	Generated when an item is checked or unchecked.
***ItemCheckEventArgs** Properties*	
CurrentValue	Indicates whether the current item is checked or unchecked. Possible values are **Checked**, **Unchecked** and **Indeterminate**.

Fig. 13.13 **CheckedListBox** properties, methods and events (part 1 of 2).

544 Graphical User Interface Concepts: Part 2   Chapter 13

CheckedListBox properties, methods and events	Description / Delegate and Event Arguments
`Index`	Returns index of the item that changed.
`NewValue`	Specifies the new state of the item.

Fig. 13.13 `CheckedListBox` properties, methods and events (part 2 of 2).

In Fig. 13.14, class **FrmCheckedListBox** uses a **CheckedListBox** and a **ListBox** to display a user's selection of books. The **CheckedListBox** named **chklstInput** (line 10), allows the user to select multiple titles. In the **String Collection Editor**, items were added for some Deitel™ books: C++, Java™, Visual Basic, Internet & WWW, Perl, Python, Wireless Internet and Advanced Java (the acronym HTP stands for "How to Program"). The **ListBox**, named **lstDisplay** (line 13), displays the user's selection. In the screenshots accompanying this example, the **CheckedListBox** appears to the left, the **ListBox** on the right.

When the user checks or unchecks an item in **CheckedListBox chklstInput**, an **ItemCheck** event is generated. Event handler **chklstInput_ItemCheck** (lines 18–34) handles the event. An **If/Else** control structure (lines 28–32) determines whether the user checked or unchecked an item in the **CheckedListBox**. Line 28 uses the **NewValue** property to determine whether the item is being checked (**CheckState.Checked**). If the user checks an item, line 29 adds the checked entry to the **ListBox lstDisplay**. If the user unchecks an item, line 31 removes the corresponding item from **lstDisplay**.

```vb
1   ' Fig. 13.14: CheckedListBoxTest.vb
2   ' Using the checked list boxes to add items to a list box.
3
4   Imports System.Windows.Forms
5
6   Public Class FrmCheckedListBox
7      Inherits Form
8
9      ' list of available book titles
10     Friend WithEvents chklstInput As CheckedListBox
11
12     ' user selection list
13     Friend WithEvents lstDisplay As ListBox
14
15     ' Visual Studio .NET generated code
16
17     ' item about to change, add or remove from lstDisplay
18     Private Sub chklstInput_ItemCheck( _
19        ByVal sender As System.Object, _
20        ByVal e As System.Windows.Forms.ItemCheckEventArgs) _
21        Handles chklstInput.ItemCheck
```

Fig. 13.14 `CheckedListBox` and `ListBox` used in a program to display a user selection (part 1 of 2).

```
22
23           ' obtain reference of selected item
24           Dim item As String = chklstInput.SelectedItem
25
26           ' if item checked add to listbox
27           ' otherwise remove from listbox
28           If e.NewValue = CheckState.Checked Then
29              lstDisplay.Items.Add(item)
30           Else
31              lstDisplay.Items.Remove(item)
32           End If
33
34       End Sub ' chklstInput_ItemCheck
35
36   End Class ' FrmCheckedListBox
```

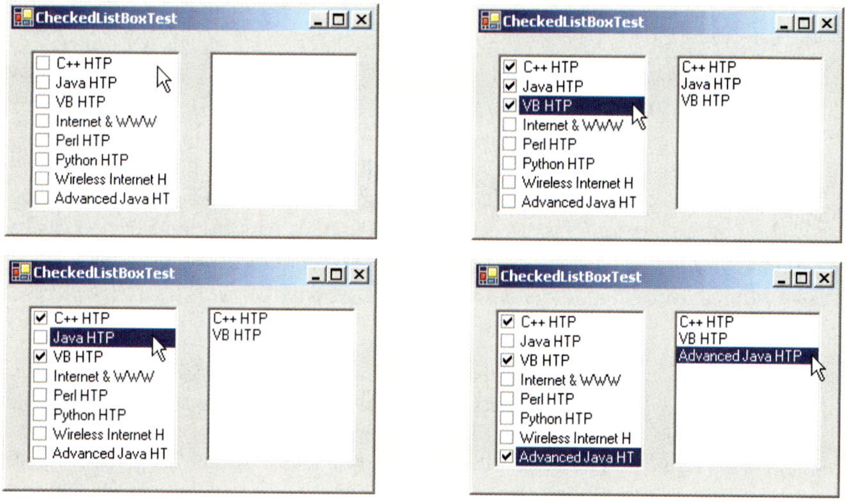

Fig. 13.14 **CheckedListBox** and **ListBox** used in a program to display a user selection (part 2 of 2).

13.5 ComboBoxes

The **ComboBox** control combines **TextBox** features with a *drop-down list*. A drop-down list is a GUI component that contains a list from which a value can be selected. It usually appears as a text box with a down arrow to its right. By default, the user can enter text into the text box or click the down arrow to display a list of predefined items. If a user chooses an element from this list, that element is displayed in the text box. If the list contains more elements than can be displayed in the drop-down list, a scrollbar appears. The maximum number of items that a drop-down list can display at one time is set by property **MaxDropDownItems**. Figure 13.15 shows a sample **ComboBox** in three different states.

As with the **ListBox** control, the programmer can add objects to collection **Items** programmatically, using methods **Add** and **AddRange**, or visually, with the **String Collection Editor**. Figure 13.16 lists common properties and events of class **ComboBox**.

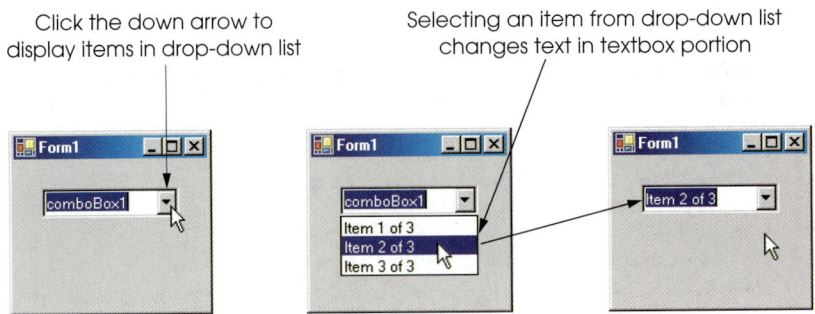

Fig. 13.15 **ComboBox** demonstration.

> **Look-and-Feel Observation 13.6**
> Use a **ComboBox** to save space on a GUI. The disadvantage is that, unlike with a **ListBox**, the user cannot see available items without expanding the drop-down list.

ComboBox events and properties	Description / Delegate and Event Arguments
Common Properties	
DropDownStyle	Determines the type of combo box. Value **Simple** means that the text portion is editable and the list portion is always visible. Value **DropDown** (the default) means that the text portion is editable, but the user must click an arrow button to see the list portion. Value **DropDownList** means that the text portion is not editable and the user must click the arrow button to see the list portion.
Items	The collection of items in the **ComboBox** control.
MaxDropDownItems	Specifies the maximum number of items (between **1** and **100**) that the drop-down list can display. If the number of items exceeds the maximum number of items to display, a scrollbar appears.
SelectedIndex	Returns the index of the selected item. If there is no selected item, **-1** is returned.
SelectedItem	Returns a reference to the selected item.
Sorted	Indicates whether items are sorted alphabetically. Setting this property's value to **True** sorts the items. Default is **False**.
Common Event	(Delegate **EventHandler**, event arguments **EventArgs**)
SelectedIndex-Changed	Generated when the selected index changes (such as when a different item is selected). This is the default event when control is double-clicked in designer.

Fig. 13.16 **ComboBox** properties and events.

Property **DropDownStyle** determines the type of **ComboBox**. Style **Simple** does not display a drop-down arrow. Instead, a scrollbar appears next to the control, allowing the user to select a choice from the list. The user also can type in a selection. Style **DropDown** (the default) displays a drop-down list when the down arrow is clicked (or the down-arrow key is pressed). The user can type a new item into the **ComboBox**. The last style is **Drop-DownList**, which displays a drop-down list but does not allow the user to enter a new item.

The **ComboBox** control has properties **Items** (a collection), **SelectedItem** and **SelectedIndex**, which are similar to the corresponding properties in **ListBox**. There can be at most one selected item in a **ComboBox** (if zero, then **SelectedIndex** is **-1**). When the selected item changes, event **SelectedIndexChanged** is generated.

Class **FrmComboBox** (Fig. 13.17) allows users to select a shape to draw—an empty or filled circle, ellipse, square or pie—by using a **ComboBox**. The combo box in this example is uneditable, so the user cannot input a custom item.

Look-and-Feel Observation 13.7

*Make lists (such as **ComboBox**es) editable only if the program is designed to accept user-submitted elements. Otherwise, the user might try to enter a custom item and be unable to use it.*

```vb
1   ' Fig. 13.17: ComboBoxTest.vb
2   ' Using ComboBox to select shape to draw.
3
4   Imports System.Windows.Forms
5   Imports System.Drawing
6
7   Public Class FrmComboBox
8      Inherits Form
9
10     ' contains shape list (circle, square, ellipse, pie)
11     Friend WithEvents cboImage As ComboBox
12
13     ' Visual Studio .NET generated code
14
15     ' get selected index, draw shape
16     Private Sub cboImage_SelectedIndexChanged( _
17        ByVal sender As System.Object, _
18        ByVal e As System.EventArgs) _
19        Handles cboImage.SelectedIndexChanged
20
21        ' create graphics object, pen and brush
22        Dim myGraphics As Graphics = MyBase.CreateGraphics()
23
24        ' create Pen using color DarkRed
25        Dim myPen As New Pen(Color.DarkRed)
26
27        ' create SolidBrush using color DarkRed
28        Dim mySolidBrush As New SolidBrush(Color.DarkRed)
29
30        ' clear drawing area by setting it to color White
31        myGraphics.Clear(Color.White)
```

Fig. 13.17 **ComboBox** used to draw a selected shape (part 1 of 3).

```vbnet
32
33            ' find index, draw proper shape
34            Select Case cboImage.SelectedIndex
35
36               Case 0 ' case circle is selected
37                  myGraphics.DrawEllipse(myPen, 50, 50, 150, 150)
38
39               Case 1 ' case rectangle is selected
40                  myGraphics.DrawRectangle(myPen, 50, 50, 150, 150)
41
42               Case 2 ' case ellipse is selected
43                  myGraphics.DrawEllipse(myPen, 50, 85, 150, 115)
44
45               Case 3 ' case pie is selected
46                  myGraphics.DrawPie(myPen, 50, 50, 150, 150, 0, 45)
47
48               Case 4 ' case filled circle is selected
49                  myGraphics.FillEllipse( _
50                     mySolidBrush, 50, 50, 150, 150)
51
52               Case 5 ' case filled rectangle is selected
53                  myGraphics.FillRectangle( _
54                     mySolidBrush, 50, 50, 150, 150)
55
56               Case 6 ' case filled ellipse is selected
57                  myGraphics.FillEllipse( _
58                     mySolidBrush, 50, 85, 150, 115)
59
60               Case 7 ' case filled pie is selected
61                  myGraphics.FillPie( _
62                     mySolidBrush, 50, 50, 150, 150, 0, 45)
63
64            End Select
65
66      End Sub ' cboImage_SelectedIndexChanged
67
68   End Class ' FrmComboBox
```

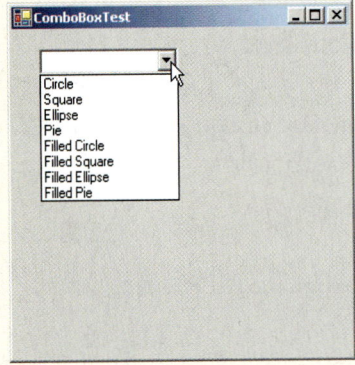
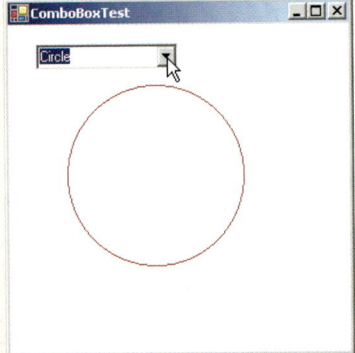

Fig. 13.17 **ComboBox** used to draw a selected shape (part 2 of 3).

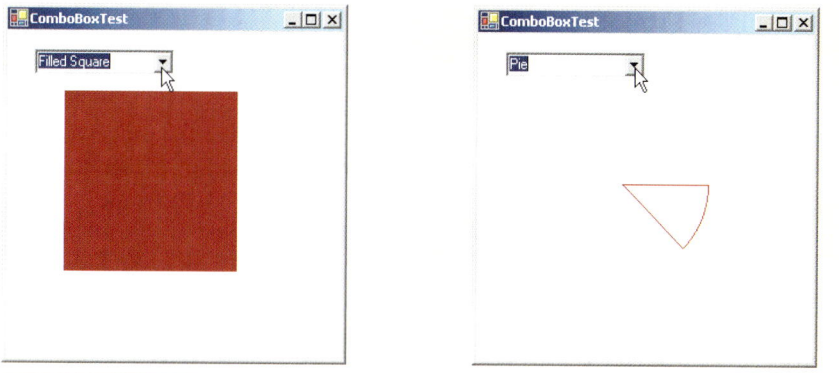

Fig. 13.17 ComboBox used to draw a selected shape (part 3 of 3).

After creating **ComboBox cboImage** (line 11), we make it uneditable by setting its **DropDownStyle** to **DropDownList** in the **Properties** window. Next, we add items **Circle**, **Square**, **Ellipse**, **Pie**, **Filled Circle**, **Filled Square**, **Filled Ellipse** and **Filled Pie** to the **Items** collection using the **String Collection Editor**. Whenever the user selects an item from **cboImage**, a **SelectedIndex-Changed** event is generated. Event handler **cboImage_SelectedIndexChanged** (lines 16–66) handles these events. Lines 22–28 create a **Graphics** object, a **Pen** and a **SolidBrush**, which are used to draw on the form. The **Graphics** object (line 22) allows a pen or brush to draw on a component using one of several **Graphics** methods. The **Pen** object is used by methods **drawEllipse**, **drawRectangle** and **drawPie** (lines 37, 40, 43 and 46) to draw the outlines of their corresponding shapes. The **Solid-Brush** object is used by methods **fillEllipse**, **fillRectangle** and **fillPie** (lines 49–50, 53–54, 57–58 and 61–62) to draw their corresponding solid shapes. Line 31 colors the entire form **White**, using **Graphics** method **Clear**. These methods are discussed in greater detail in Chapter 16, Graphics and Multimedia.

The application draws a particular shape on the basis of the selected item's index. The **Select Case** statement (lines 34–64) uses **cboImage.SelectedIndex** to determine which item the user selected. Class **Graphics** method *DrawEllipse* (line 37) takes a **Pen**, the *x*- and *y*- coordinates of the center and the width and height of the ellipse to draw. The origin of the coordinate system is in the upper-left corner of the form; the *x*-coordinate increases to the right, and the *y*-coordinate increases downward. A circle is a special case of an ellipse (the height and width are equal). Line 37 draws a circle. Line 43 draws an ellipse that has different values for height and width.

Class **Graphics** method *DrawRectangle* (line 40) takes a **Pen**, the *x*- and *y*-coordinates of the upper-left corner and the width and height of the rectangle to draw. Method *DrawPie* (line 46) draws a pie as a portion of an ellipse. The ellipse is bounded by a rectangle. Method *DrawPie* takes a **Pen**, the *x*- and *y*- coordinates of the upper-left corner of the rectangle, its width and height, the start angle (in degrees) and the sweep angle (in degrees) of the pie. Angles increase clockwise. The *FillEllipse* (lines 49–50 and 57–58), *FillRectangle* (lines 53–54) and *FillPie* (lines 61–62) methods are similar to their unfilled counterparts, except that they take a **SolidBrush** instead of a **Pen**. Some of the drawn shapes are illustrated in the screen shots at the bottom of Fig. 13.17.

13.6 TreeViews

The **TreeView** control displays *nodes* hierarchically in a *tree*. Traditionally, nodes are objects that contain values and can refer to other nodes. A *parent node* contains *child nodes*, and the child nodes can be parents to other nodes. Two child nodes that have the same parent node are considered *sibling nodes*. A tree is a collection of nodes, usually organized in hierarchical manner. The first parent node of a tree is the *root* node (a **TreeView** can have multiple roots). For example, the file system of a computer can be represented as a tree. The top-level directory (perhaps **C:**) would be the root, each subfolder of **C:** would be a child node and each child folder could have its own children. **TreeView** controls are useful for displaying hierarchal information, such as the file structure that we just mentioned. We cover nodes and trees in greater detail in Chapter 24, Data Structures. Figure 13.18 displays a sample **TreeView** control on a form.

A parent node can be expanded or collapsed by clicking the plus box or minus box to its left. Nodes without children do not have these boxes.

The nodes displayed in a **TreeView** are instances of class **TreeNode**. Each **TreeNode** has a **Nodes** *collection* (type **TreeNodeCollection**), which contains a list of other **TreeNode**s—its children. The **Parent** property returns a reference to the parent node (or **Nothing** if the node is a root node). Figure 13.19 and Fig. 13.20 list the common properties of **TreeView**s and **TreeNode**s, and a **TreeView** event.

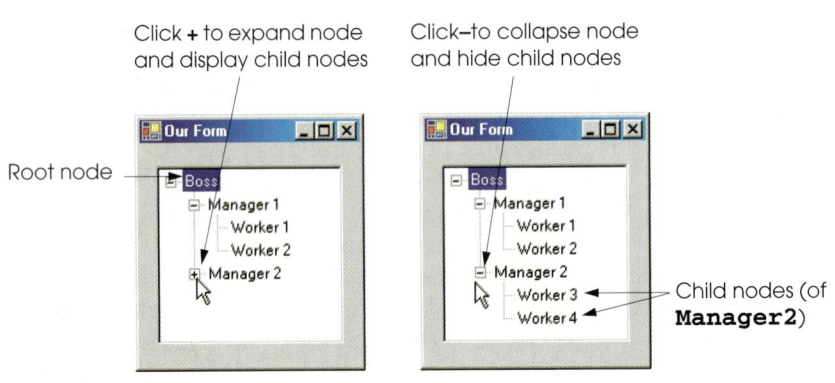

Fig. 13.18 **TreeView** displaying a sample tree.

TreeView properties and events	Description / Delegate and Event Arguments
Common Properties	
CheckBoxes	Indicates whether checkboxes appear next to nodes. A value of **True** displays checkboxes. The default value is **False**.

Fig. 13.19 **TreeView** properties and events (part 1 of 2).

TreeView properties and events	Description / Delegate and Event Arguments
`ImageList`	Specifies the `ImageList` containing the node icons. An `ImageList` is a collection that contains `Image` objects.
`Nodes`	Lists the collection of `TreeNode`s in the control. Contains methods `Add` (adds a `TreeNode` object), `Clear` (deletes the entire collection) and `Remove` (deletes a specific node). Removing a parent node deletes all its children.
`SelectedNode`	The selected node.
Common Event	*(Delegate `TreeViewEventHandler`, event arguments `TreeViewEventArgs`)*
`AfterSelect`	Generated after selected node changes. This is the default event when the control is double-clicked in the designer.

Fig. 13.19 `TreeView` properties and events (part 2 of 2).

TreeNode properties and methods	Description / Delegate and Event Arguments
Common Properties	
`Checked`	Indicates whether the `TreeNode` is checked (`CheckBoxes` property must be set to `True` in parent `TreeView`).
`FirstNode`	Specifies the first node in the `Nodes` collection (i.e., first child in tree).
`FullPath`	Indicates the path of the node, starting at the root of the tree.
`ImageIndex`	Specifies the index of the image shown when the node is deselected.
`LastNode`	Specifies the last node in the `Nodes` collection (i.e., last child in tree).
`NextNode`	Next sibling node.
`Nodes`	The collection of `TreeNode`s contained in the current node (i.e., all the children of the current node). Contains methods `Add` (adds a `TreeNode` object), `Clear` (deletes the entire collection) and `Remove` (deletes a specific node). Removing a parent node deletes all its children.
`PrevNode`	Indicates the previous sibling node.
`SelectedImageIndex`	Specifies the index of the image to use when the node is selected.
`Text`	Specifies the `TreeView`'s text.

Fig. 13.20 `TreeNode` properties and methods (part 1 of 2).

TreeNode properties and methods	Description / Delegate and Event Arguments
Common Methods	
`Collapse`	Collapses a node.
`Expand`	Expands a node.
`ExpandAll`	Expands all the children of a node.
`GetNodeCount`	Returns the number of child nodes.

Fig. 13.20 `TreeNode` properties and methods (part 2 of 2).

To add nodes to the **TreeView** visually, click the ellipsis by the **Nodes** property in the **Properties** window. This opens the ***TreeNode Editor***, which displays an empty tree representing the **TreeView** (Fig. 13.21). There are buttons to create a root, to add or delete a node, and to rename a node.

To add nodes programmatically, we first must create a root node. Create a new **TreeNode** object and pass it a **String** to display. Then, call method **Add** to add this new **TreeNode** to the **TreeView**'s **Nodes** collection. Thus, to add a root node to **TreeView** *myTreeView*, write

> *myTreeView*.**Nodes.Add(New TreeNode(***RootLabel***))**

where *myTreeView* is the **TreeView** to which we are adding nodes, and *RootLabel* is the text to display in *myTreeView*. To add children to a root node, add new **TreeNode**s to its **Nodes** collection. We select the appropriate root node from the **TreeView** by writing

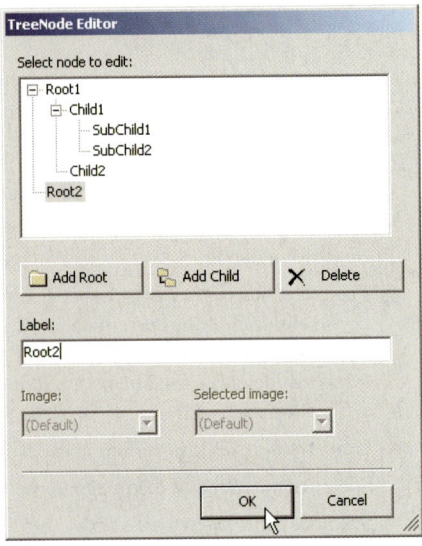

Fig. 13.21 TreeNode Editor.

Chapter 13   Graphical User Interface Concepts: Part 2   553

    myTreeView.**Nodes**(*myIndex*)

where *myIndex* is the root node's index in *myTreeView*'s **Nodes** collection. We add nodes to child nodes through the same process by which we added root nodes to *myTreeView*. To add a child to the root node at index *myIndex*, write

    myTreeView.**Nodes**(*myIndex*).**Nodes.Add**(**New TreeNode**(*ChildLabel*))

    Class **FrmTreeViewDirectory** (Fig. 13.22) uses a **TreeView** to display the directory file structure on a computer. The root node is the **C:** drive, and each subfolder of **C:** becomes a child. This layout is similar to that used in **Windows Explorer**. Folders can be expanded or collapsed by clicking the plus or minus boxes that appear to their left.

    When **FrmTreeViewDirectory** loads, a **Load** event is generated, that is handled by event handler **FrmTreeViewDirectory_Load** (lines 56–62). Line 60 adds a root node (**C:**) to our **TreeView**, named **treDirectory**. **C:** is the root folder for the entire directory structure. Line 61 calls method **PopulateTreeView** (lines 16–53), which takes a directory (a **String**) and a parent node. Method **PopulateTreeView** then creates child nodes corresponding to the subdirectories of the directory that was passed to it.

    Method **PopulateTreeView** (lines 16–53) obtains a list of subdirectories, using method *GetDirectories* of class **Directory** (namespace **System.IO**) on lines 23–24. Method **GetDirectories** takes a **String** (the current directory) and returns an array of **String**s (the subdirectories). If a directory is not accessible for security reasons, an **UnauthorizedAccessException** is thrown. Line 49 catches this exception and adds a node containing "**Access Denied**" instead of displaying the subdirectories.

```vb
1   ' Fig. 13.22: TreeViewDirectoryStructureTest.vb
2   ' Using TreeView to display directory structure.
3
4   Imports System.Windows.Forms
5   Imports System.IO
6
7   Public Class FrmTreeViewDirectory
8      Inherits Form
9
10     ' contains view of c:\ drive directory structure
11     Friend WithEvents treDirectory As TreeView
12
13     ' Visual Studio .NET generated code
14
15     ' add all subfolders of 'directoryValue' to 'parentNode'
16     Private Sub PopulateTreeView(ByVal directoryValue As String, _
17        ByVal parentNode As TreeNode)
18
19        ' populate current node with subdirectories
20        Try
21
22           ' get all subfolders
23           Dim directoryArray As String() = _
24              Directory.GetDirectories(directoryValue)
```

Fig. 13.22 **TreeView** used to display directories (part 1 of 3).

```vbnet
25
26             If directoryArray.Length <> 0 Then ' if at least one
27
28                Dim currentDirectory As String
29
30                ' for every subdirectory, create new TreeNode,
31                ' add as child of current node and
32                ' recursively populate child nodes with subdirectories
33                For Each currentDirectory In directoryArray
34
35                   ' create TreeNode for current directory
36                   Dim myNode As TreeNode = _
37                      New TreeNode(currentDirectory)
38
39                   ' add current directory node to parent node
40                   parentNode.Nodes.Add(myNode)
41
42                   ' recursively populate every subdirectory
43                   PopulateTreeView(currentDirectory, myNode)
44                Next
45
46             End If
47
48          ' catch exception
49          Catch unauthorized As UnauthorizedAccessException
50             parentNode.Nodes.Add("Access Denied")
51          End Try
52
53       End Sub ' PopulateTreeView
54
55       ' called by system when form loads
56       Private Sub FrmTreeViewDirectory_Load(ByVal sender As Object, _
57          ByVal e As System.EventArgs) Handles MyBase.Load
58
59          ' add c:\ drive to treDirectory and insert its subfolders
60          treDirectory.Nodes.Add("C:")
61          PopulateTreeView("C:\", treDirectory.Nodes(0))
62       End Sub ' FrmTreeViewDirectory_Load
63
64    End Class ' FrmTreeViewDirectory
```

Fig. 13.22 `TreeView` used to display directories (part 2 of 3).

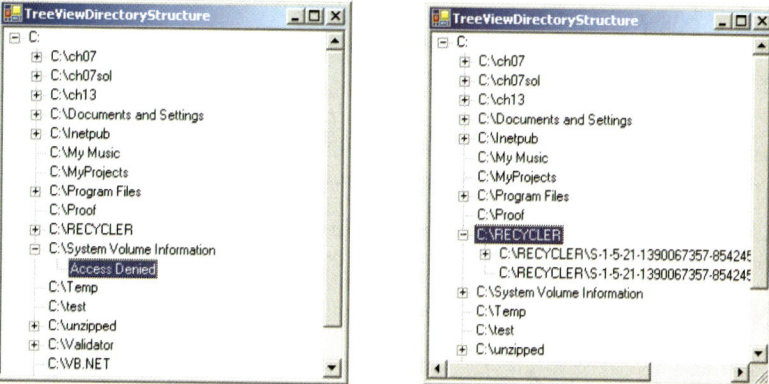

Fig. 13.22 `TreeView` used to display directories (part 3 of 3).

If there are accessible subdirectories, each **String** in the **directoryArray** is used to create a new child node (lines 36–37). We use method **Add** (line 40) to add each child node to the parent. Then, method **PopulateTreeView** is called recursively on every subdirectory (line 43) and eventually populates the entire directory structure. Our recursive algorithm causes our program to have an initial delay when it loads—it must create a tree for the entire **C:** drive. However, once the drive folder names are added to the appropriate **Nodes** collection, they can be expanded and collapsed without delay. In the next section, we present an alternate algorithm to solve this problem.

13.7 ListViews

The **ListView** control is similar to a **ListBox** in that both display lists from which the user can select one or more items (to see an example of a **ListView**, look ahead to the output of Fig. 13.25). The important difference between the two classes is that a **ListView** can display icons alongside the list items in a variety of ways (controlled by its **ImageList** property). Property **MultiSelect** (a boolean) determines whether multiple items can be selected. Checkboxes can be included by setting property **CheckBoxes** (a **Boolean**) to **True**, making the **ListView**'s appearance similar to that of a **CheckedListBox**. The **View** property specifies the layout of the **ListBox**. Property **Activation** determines the method by which the user selects a list item. The details of these properties are explained in Fig. 13.23.

ListView allows the programmer to define the images used as icons for **ListView** items. To display images, an **ImageList** component is required. Create one by dragging it onto a form from the **ToolBox**. Then, click the **Images** collection in the **Properties** window to display the **Image Collection Editor** (Fig. 13.24). Here, developers can browse for images that they wish to add to the **ImageList**, which contains an array of **Image**s. Once the images have been defined, set property **SmallImageList** of the **ListView** to the new **ImageList** object. Property **SmallImageList** specifies the image list for the small icons. Property **LargeImageList** sets the **ImageList** for large icons. Icons for the **ListView** items are selected by setting the item's **ImageIndex** property to the appropriate index.

ListView events and properties	Description / Delegate and Event Arguments
Common Properties	
Activation	Determines how the user activates an item. This property takes a value in the **ItemActivation** enumeration. Possible values are **OneClick** (single-click activation), **TwoClick** (double-click activation, item changes color when selected) and **Standard** (double-click activation).
CheckBoxes	Indicates whether items appear with checkboxes. **True** displays checkboxes. **False** is the default.
LargeImageList	Specifies the **ImageList** containing large icons for display.
Items	Returns the collection of **ListViewItem**s in the control.
MultiSelect	Determines whether multiple selection is allowed. Default is **True**, which enables multiple selection.
SelectedItems	Lists the collection of selected items.
SmallImageList	Specifies the **ImageList** containing small icons for display.
View	Determines appearance of **ListViewItem**s. Values **LargeIcon** (large icon displayed, items can be in multiple columns), **SmallIcon** (small icon displayed), **List** (small icons displayed, items appear in a single column) and **Details** (like **List**, but multiple columns of information can be displayed per item).
Common Event	*(Delegate **EventHandler**, event arguments **EventArgs**)*
ItemActivate	Raised when an item in the **ListView** is activated. Does not contain the specifics of which item is activated.

Fig. 13.23 ListView properties and events.

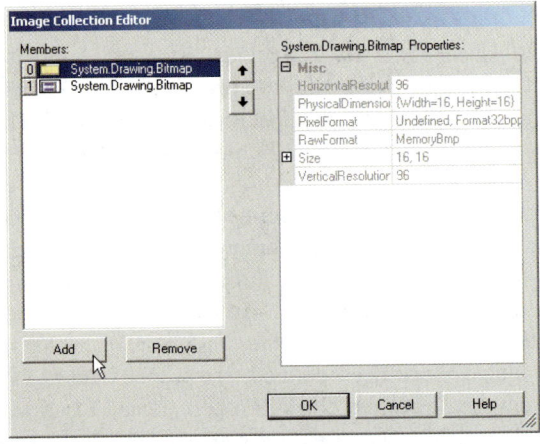

Fig. 13.24 Image Collection Editor window for an ImageList component.

Class **FrmListView** (Fig. 13.25) displays files and folders in a **ListView**, along with small icons representing each file or folder. If a file or folder is inaccessible because of permission settings, a message box appears. The program scans the contents of the directory as it browses, rather than indexing the entire drive at once.

To display icons beside list items, we must create an **ImageList** for the **ListView lvwBrowser** (line 15). First, drag and drop an **ImageList** onto the form and open the **Image Collection Editor**. Create two simple bitmap images—one for a folder (array index 0) and another for a file (array index 1). Then, set the object **lvwBrowser** property **SmallImageList** to the new **ImageList** in the **Properties** window. Developers can create such icons with any image software, such as Adobe® Photoshop™, Jasc® Paint Shop Pro™ or Microsoft® Paint.

```vb
1   ' Fig. 13.25: ListViewTest.vb
2   ' Displaying directories and their contents in ListView.
3
4   Imports System.Windows.Forms
5   Imports System.IO
6
7   Public Class FrmListView
8      Inherits Form
9
10     ' display labels for current location in directory tree
11     Friend WithEvents lblCurrent As Label
12     Friend WithEvents lblDisplay As Label
13
14     ' displays contents of current directory
15     Friend WithEvents lvwBrowser As ListView
16
17     ' specifies images for file icons and folder icons
18     Friend WithEvents ilsFileFolder As ImageList
19
20     ' Visual Studio .NET generated code
21
22     ' get current directory
23     Dim currentDirectory As String = _
24        Directory.GetCurrentDirectory()
25
26     ' browse directory user clicked or go up one level
27     Private Sub lvwBrowser_Click(ByVal sender As System.Object, _
28        ByVal e As System.EventArgs) Handles lvwBrowser.Click
29
30        ' ensure item selected
31        If lvwBrowser.SelectedItems.Count <> 0 Then
32
33           ' if first item selected, go up one level
34           If lvwBrowser.Items(0).Selected Then
35
36              ' create DirectoryInfo object for directory
37              Dim directoryObject As DirectoryInfo = _
38                 New DirectoryInfo(currentDirectory)
```

Fig. 13.25 **ListView** displaying files and folders (part 1 of 4).

```vbnet
39
40                  ' if directory has parent, load it
41                  If Not (directoryObject.Parent Is Nothing) Then
42                      LoadFilesInDirectory( _
43                          directoryObject.Parent.FullName)
44                  End If
45
46              ' selected directory or file
47              Else
48
49                  ' directory or file chosen
50                  Dim chosen As String = _
51                      lvwBrowser.SelectedItems(0).Text
52
53                  ' if item selected is directory
54                  If Directory.Exists(currentDirectory & _
55                      "\" & chosen) Then
56
57                      ' load subdirectory
58                      ' if in c:\, do not need "\", otherwise we do
59                      If currentDirectory = "C:\" Then
60                          LoadFilesInDirectory(currentDirectory & chosen)
61                      Else
62                          LoadFilesInDirectory(currentDirectory & _
63                              "\" & chosen)
64                      End If
65
66                  End If
67
68              End If
69
70              ' update lblDisplay
71              lblDisplay.Text = currentDirectory
72          End If
73
74      End Sub ' lvwBrowser_Click
75
76      ' display files/subdirectories of current directory
77      Public Sub LoadFilesInDirectory( _
78          ByVal currentDirectoryValue As String)
79
80          ' load directory information and display
81          Try
82
83              ' clear ListView and set first item
84              lvwBrowser.Items.Clear()
85              lvwBrowser.Items.Add("Go Up One Level")
86
87              ' update current directory
88              currentDirectory = currentDirectoryValue
89              Dim newCurrentDirectory As DirectoryInfo = _
90                  New DirectoryInfo(currentDirectory)
91
```

Fig. 13.25 `ListView` displaying files and folders (part 2 of 4).

```vbnet
 92              ' put files and directories into arrays
 93              Dim directoryArray As DirectoryInfo() = _
 94                 newCurrentDirectory.GetDirectories()
 95
 96              Dim fileArray As FileInfo() = _
 97                 newCurrentDirectory.GetFiles()
 98
 99              ' add directory names to ListView
100              Dim dir As DirectoryInfo
101
102              For Each dir In directoryArray
103
104                 ' add directory to listview
105                 Dim newDirectoryItem As ListViewItem = _
106                    lvwBrowser.Items.Add(dir.Name)
107
108                 ' set directory image
109                 newDirectoryItem.ImageIndex = 0
110              Next
111
112              ' add file names to ListView
113              Dim file As FileInfo
114
115              For Each file In fileArray
116
117                 ' add file to ListView
118                 Dim newFileItem As ListViewItem = _
119                    lvwBrowser.Items.Add(file.Name)
120
121                 newFileItem.ImageIndex = 1    ' set file image
122              Next
123
124           ' access denied
125           Catch exception As UnauthorizedAccessException
126              MessageBox.Show("Warning: Some files may " & _
127                 "not be visible due to permission settings", _
128                 "Attention", 0, MessageBoxIcon.Warning)
129           End Try
130
131        End Sub ' LoadFilesInDirectory
132
133        ' handle load event when Form displayed for first time
134        Private Sub FrmListView_Load(ByVal sender As System.Object, _
135           ByVal e As System.EventArgs) Handles MyBase.Load
136
137           ' set image list
138           Dim folderImage As Image = Image.FromFile _
139              (currentDirectory & "\images\folder.bmp")
140
141           Dim fileImage As Image = Image.FromFile _
142              (currentDirectory & "\images\file.bmp")
143
144           ilsFileFolder.Images.Add(folderImage)
```

Fig. 13.25 `ListView` displaying files and folders (part 3 of 4).

```
145         ilsFileFolder.Images.Add(fileImage)
146
147         ' load current directory into browserListView
148         LoadFilesInDirectory(currentDirectory)
149         lblDisplay.Text = currentDirectory
150     End Sub ' FrmListView_Load
151
152 End Class ' FrmListView
```

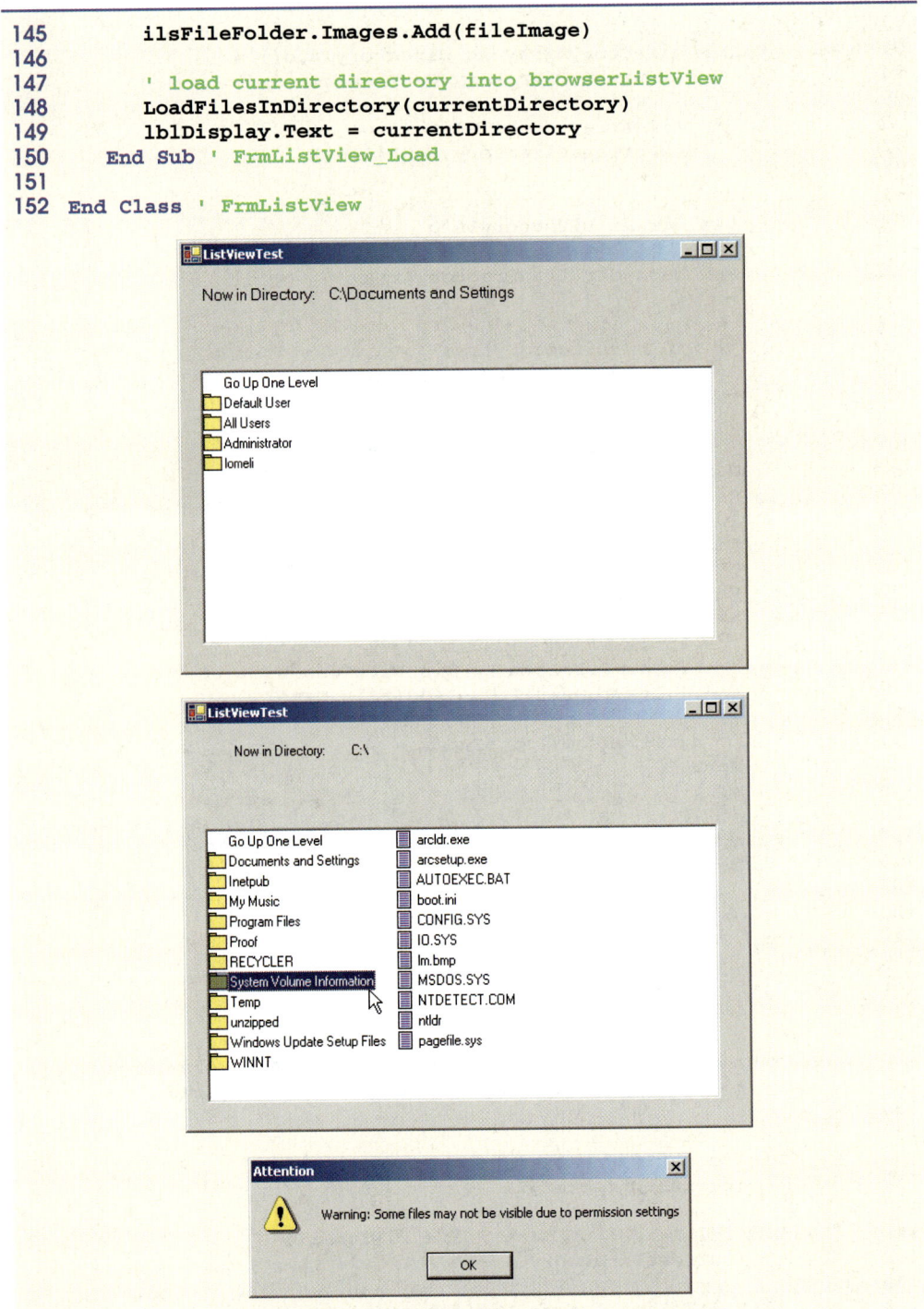

Fig. 13.25 `ListView` displaying files and folders (part 4 of 4).

Method **LoadFilesInDirectory** (lines 77–131) populates **lvwBrowser** with the directory passed to it (**currentDirectoryValue**). It clears **lvwBrowser** and adds the element **"Go Up One Level"**. When the user clicks this element, the program attempts to move up one level (we see how shortly). The method then creates a **DirectoryInfo** object initialized with the **String currentDirectory** (lines 89–90). If permission is not given to browse the directory, an exception is thrown (caught on line 125). Method **LoadFilesInDirectory** works differently from method **PopulateTreeView** in the previous program (Fig. 13.22). Instead of loading all the folders in the entire hard drive, method **LoadFilesInDirectory** loads only the folders in the current directory.

Class *DirectoryInfo* (namespace **System.IO**) enables us to browse or manipulate the directory structure easily. Method **GetDirectories** (lines 93–94) returns an array of **DirectoryInfo** objects containing the subdirectories of the current directory. Similarly, method **GetFiles** (lines 96–97) returns an array of class **FileInfo** objects containing the files in the current directory. Property *Name* (of both class **DirectoryInfo** and class **FileInfo**) contains only the directory or file name, such as **temp** instead of **C:\myfolder\temp**. To access the full name, use property *FullName*.

Lines 102–110 and lines 115–122 iterate through the subdirectories and files of the current directory and add them to **lvwBrowser**. Lines 109 and 121 set the **ImageIndex** properties of the newly created items. If an item is a directory, we set its icon to a directory icon (index 0); if an item is a file, we set its icon to a file icon (index 1).

Method **lvwBrowser_Click** (lines 27–74) responds when the user clicks control **lvwBrowser**. Line 31 checks whether anything is selected. If a selection has been made, line 34 determines whether the user chose the first item in **lvwBrowser**. The first item in **lvwBrowser** is always **Go up one level**; if it is selected, the program attempts to go up a level. Lines 37–38 create a **DirectoryInfo** object for the current directory. Line 41 tests property **Parent** to ensure that the user is not at the root of the directory tree. Property **Parent** indicates the parent directory as a **DirectoryInfo** object; if it exists **Parent** returns the value **Nothing**. If a parent directory exists, then lines 42–43 pass the full name of the parent directory to method **LoadFilesInDirectory**.

If the user did not select the first item in **lvwBrowser**, lines 47–68 allow the user to continue navigating through the directory structure. Lines 50–51 create **String chosen**, which receives the text of the selected item (the first item in collection **SelectedItems**). Lines 54–55 determine whether the user has selected a valid directory (rather than a file). The program combines variables **currentDirectory** and **chosen** (the new directory), separated by a slash (****), and passes this value to class **Directory**'s method *Exists*. Method **Exists** returns **True** if its **String** parameter is a directory. If this occurs, the program passes the **String** to method **LoadFilesInDirectory**. Because the **C:** directory already includes a slash, a slash is not needed when combining **currentDirectory** and **chosen** (line 60). However, other directories must include the slash (lines 62–63). Finally, **lblDisplay** is updated with the new directory (line 71).

This program loads quickly, because it indexes only the files in the current directory. This means that, rather than having a large delay in the beginning, a small delay occurs whenever a new directory is loaded. In addition, changes in the directory structure can be shown by reloading a directory. The previous program (Fig. 13.22) needs to be restarted to reflect any changes in the directory structure. This type of trade-off is typical in the software world. When designing applications that run for long periods of time, developers might choose a large initial delay to improve performance throughout the rest of the program. However, when creating applications that run for only short periods of time, developers often prefer fast initial loading times and a small delay after each action.

13.8 Tab Control

The **TabControl** control creates tabbed windows, such as the ones we have seen in the Visual Studio .NET IDE (Fig. 13.26). This allows the programmer to specify more information in the same space on a form, such as in the items of the Windows **Control Panel**.

TabControls contain **TabPage** objects, which are similar to **Panel**s and **GroupBox**es in that **TabPage**s also can contain controls. The programmer first adds controls to the **TabPage** objects, then adds the **TabPage**s to the **TabControl**. Only one **TabPage** is displayed at a time. To add objects to the **TabPage** and the **TabControl**, write

    myTabPage.**Controls.Add**(*myControl*)
    myTabControl.**Controls.Add**(*myTabPage*)

These statements call method **Add** of the **Controls** collection. The example adds **TabControl** *myControl* to **TabPage** *myTabPage*, then adds *myTabPage* to *myTabControl*. Alternatively, we can use method **AddRange** to add an array of **TabPage**s and an array of controls to **TabControl** and **TabPage** instances, respectively. Figure 13.27 depicts a sample **TabControl**.

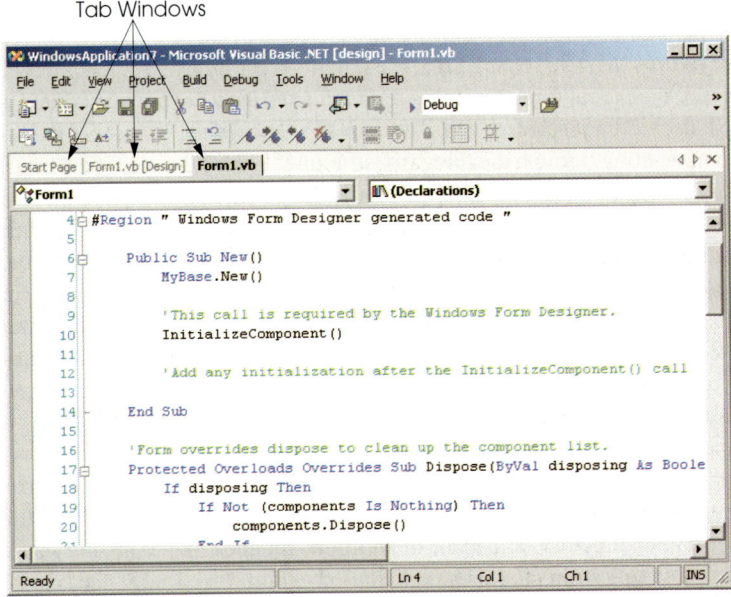

Fig. 13.26 Tabbed windows in Visual Studio .NET.

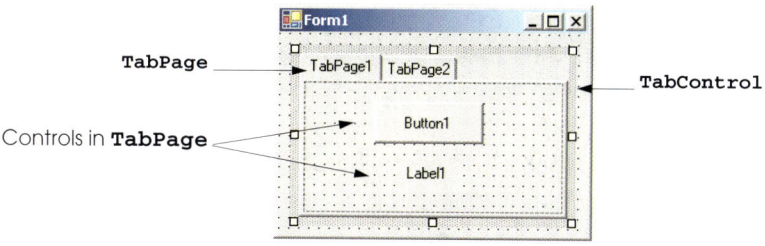

Fig. 13.27 **TabControl** with **TabPage**s example.

Programmers can add **TabControl**s visually by dragging and dropping them onto a form in design mode. To add **TabPage**s in the Visual Studio .NET designer, right-click the **TabControl**, and select **Add Tab** (Fig. 13.28). Alternatively, click the **TabPages** collection in the **Properties** window, and add tabs in the dialog that appears. To change a tab label, set the **Text** property of the **TabPage**. Note that clicking the tabs selects the **TabControl**—to select the **TabPage**, click the control area underneath the tabs. The programmer can add controls to the **TabPage** by dragging and dropping items from the **ToolBox**. To view different **TabPage**s, click the appropriate tab (in either design or run mode). Common properties and events of **TabControl**s are described in Fig. 13.28.

Each **TabPage** raises its own **Click** event when its tab is clicked. Remember, events for controls can be handled by any event handler that is registered with the control's event delegate. This also applies to controls contained in a **TabPage**. For convenience, Visual Studio .NET generates the empty event handlers for these controls.

Class **FrmTabs** (Fig. 13.30) uses a **TabControl** to display various options relating to the text on a label (**Color**, **Size** and **Message**). The last **TabPage** displays an **About** message, which describes the use of **TabControl**s.

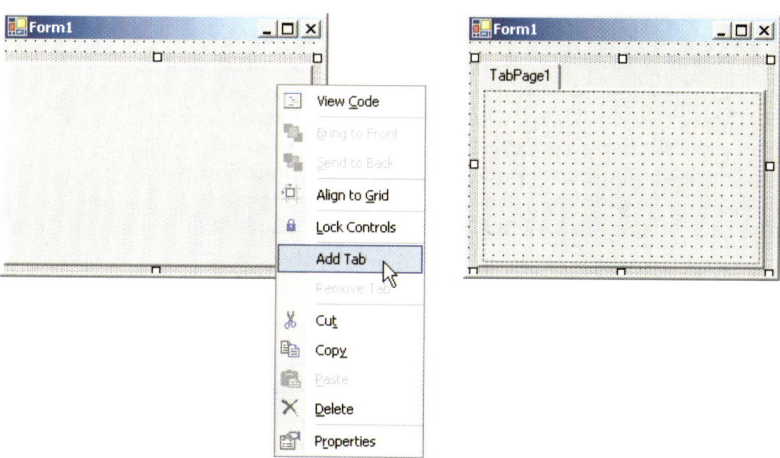

Fig. 13.28 **TabPage**s added to a **TabControl**.

564 Graphical User Interface Concepts: Part 2   Chapter 13

`TabControl` properties and events	**Description / Delegate and Event Arguments**
Common Properties	
`ImageList`	Specifies images to be displayed on tabs.
`ItemSize`	Specifies tab size.
`MultiLine`	Indicates whether multiple rows of tabs can be displayed.
`SelectedIndex`	Index of selected `TabPage`.
`SelectedTab`	The selected `TabPage`.
`TabCount`	Returns the number of tab pages.
`TabPages`	Collection of `TabPage`s within the `TabControl`.
Common Event	*(Delegate `EventHandler`, event arguments `EventArgs`)*
`SelectedIndexChanged`	Generated when `SelectedIndex` changes (i.e., another `TabPage` is selected).

Fig. 13.29 `TabControl` properties and events.

```vb
1   ' Fig. 13.30: UsingTabs.vb
2   ' Using TabControl to display various font settings.
3
4   Imports System.Windows.Forms
5
6   Public Class FrmTabs
7      Inherits Form
8
9      ' output label reflects text changes
10     Friend WithEvents lblDisplay As Label
11
12     ' table control containing table pages tbpColor,
13     ' tbpSize, tbpMessage and tbpAbout
14     Friend WithEvents tbcTextOptions As TabControl
15
16     ' table page containing color options
17     Friend WithEvents tbpColor As TabPage
18     Friend WithEvents radBlack As RadioButton
19     Friend WithEvents radRed As RadioButton
20     Friend WithEvents radGreen As RadioButton
21
22     ' table page containing font size options
23     Friend WithEvents tbpSize As TabPage
24     Friend WithEvents radSize12 As RadioButton
25     Friend WithEvents radSize16 As RadioButton
26     Friend WithEvents radSize20 As RadioButton
27
28     ' table page containing text display options
29     Friend WithEvents tbpMessage As TabPage
```

Fig. 13.30 `TabControl` used to display various font settings (part 1 of 3).

```
30        Friend WithEvents radHello As RadioButton
31        Friend WithEvents radGoodbye As RadioButton
32
33        ' table page containing about message
34        Friend WithEvents tbpAbout As TabPage
35        Friend WithEvents lblMessage As Label
36
37        ' Visual Studio .NET generated code
38
39        ' event handler for black radio button
40        Private Sub radBlack_CheckedChanged( _
41           ByVal sender As System.Object, ByVal e As System.EventArgs) _
42           Handles radBlack.CheckedChanged
43
44           lblDisplay.ForeColor = Color.Black
45        End Sub ' radBlack_CheckedChanged
46
47        ' event handler for red radio button
48        Private Sub radRed_CheckedChanged( _
49           ByVal sender As System.Object, ByVal e As System.EventArgs) _
50           Handles radRed.CheckedChanged
51
52           lblDisplay.ForeColor = Color.Red
53        End Sub ' radRed_CheckedChanged
54
55        ' event handler for green radio button
56        Private Sub radGreen_CheckedChanged( _
57           ByVal sender As System.Object, ByVal e As System.EventArgs) _
58           Handles radGreen.CheckedChanged
59
60           lblDisplay.ForeColor = Color.Green
61        End Sub ' radGreen_CheckedChanged
62
63        ' event handler for size 12 radio button
64        Private Sub radSize12_CheckedChanged( _
65           ByVal sender As System.Object, ByVal e As System.EventArgs) _
66           Handles radSize12.CheckedChanged
67
68           lblDisplay.Font = New Font(lblDisplay.Font.Name, 12)
69        End Sub ' radSize12_CheckedChanged
70
71        ' event handler for size 16 radio button
72        Private Sub radSize16_CheckedChanged( _
73           ByVal sender As System.Object, ByVal e As System.EventArgs) _
74           Handles radSize16.CheckedChanged
75
76           lblDisplay.Font = New Font(lblDisplay.Font.Name, 16)
77        End Sub ' radSize16_CheckedChanged
78
79        ' event handler for size 20 radio button
80        Private Sub radSize20_CheckedChanged( _
81           ByVal sender As System.Object, ByVal e As System.EventArgs) _
82           Handles radSize20.CheckedChanged
```

Fig. 13.30 `TabControl` used to display various font settings (part 2 of 3).

```
83
84            lblDisplay.Font = New Font(lblDisplay.Font.Name, 20)
85         End Sub ' radSize20_CheckedChanged
86
87         ' event handler for message "Hello!" radio button
88         Private Sub radHello_CheckedChanged( _
89            ByVal sender As System.Object, ByVal e As System.EventArgs) _
90            Handles radHello.CheckedChanged
91
92            lblDisplay.Text = "Hello!"
93         End Sub ' radHello_CheckedChanged
94
95         ' event handler for message "Goodbye!" radio button
96         Private Sub radGoodbye_CheckedChanged( _
97            ByVal sender As System.Object, ByVal e As System.EventArgs) _
98            Handles radGoodbye.CheckedChanged
99
100           lblDisplay.Text = "Goodbye!"
101        End Sub ' radGoodbye_CheckedChanged
102
103     End Class ' FrmTabs
```

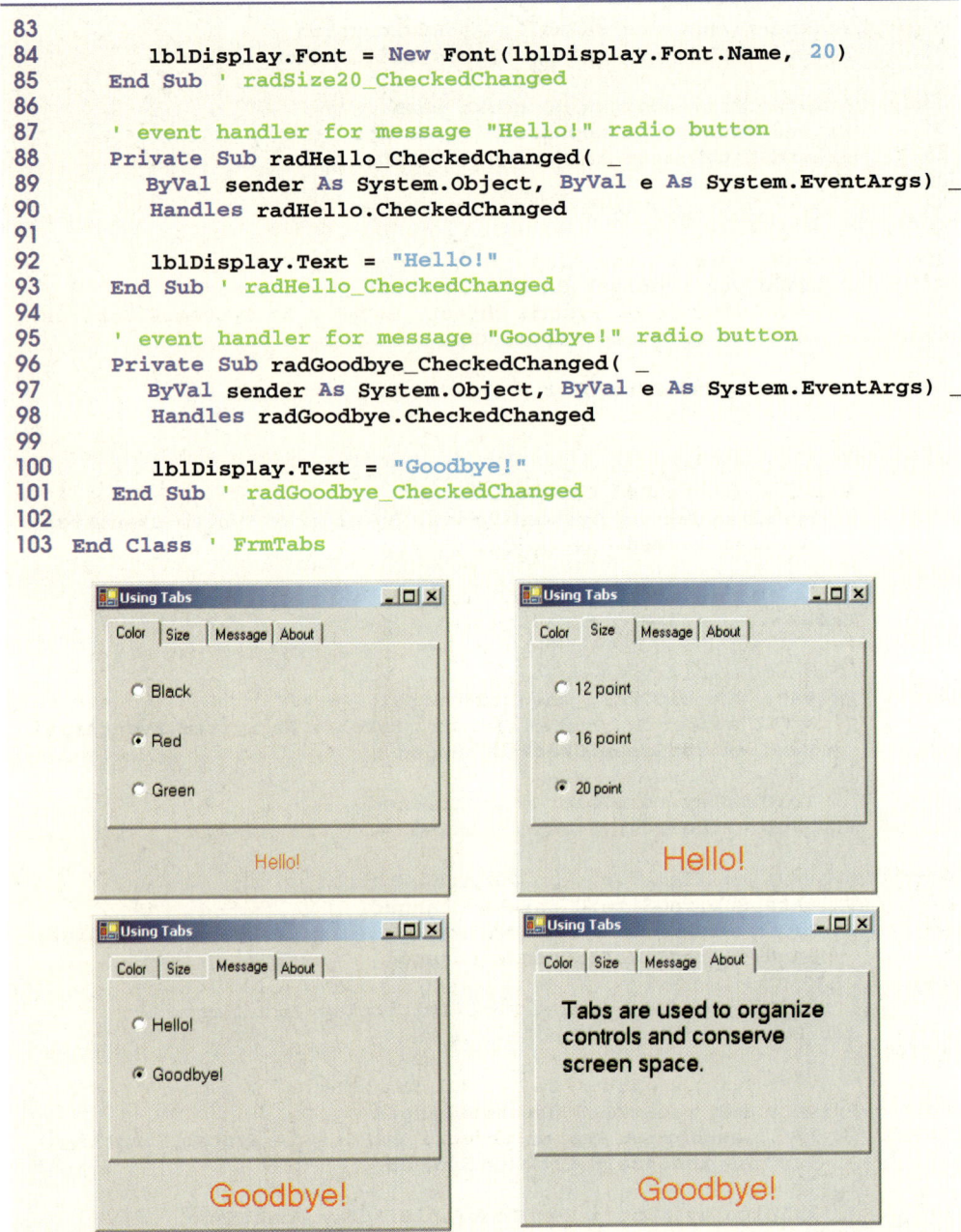

Fig. 13.30 **TabControl** used to display various font settings (part 3 of 3).

The **TabControl tbcTextOptions** (line 14) and **TabPage**s **tbpColor** (line 17), **tbpSize** (line 23), **tbpMessage** (line 29) and **tbpAbout** (line 34) are created in the designer (as described previously). **TabPage tbpColor** contains three radio buttons for the colors black (**radBlack**, line 18), red (**radRed**, line 19) and green (**radGreen**, line 20). The **CheckChanged** event handler for each button updates the color of the text in **lblDisplay** (lines 44, 52 and 60). **TabPage tbpSize** has three radio buttons, corresponding to font sizes **12** (**radSize12**, line 24), **16** (**radSize16**, line 25) and **20** (**radSize20**, line 26), which change the font size of **lblDisplay**—lines 68, 76 and 84, respectively. **TabPage tbpMessage** contains two radio buttons for the messages **Hello!** (**radHello**, line 30) and **Goodbye!** (**radGoodbye**, line 31). The two radio buttons determine the text on **lblDisplay** (lines 92 and 100, respectively). The last **TabPage** (**tbpAbout**, line 34) contains a **Label** (**lblMessage**, line 35) describing the purpose of **TabControl**s.

> **Software Engineering Observation 13.2**
>
> *A* **TabPage** *can act as a container for a single logical group of radio buttons and enforces their mutual exclusivity. To place multiple radio-button groups inside a single* **TabPage**, *programmers should group radio buttons within* **Panel***s or* **GroupBox***es contained within the* **TabPage**.

13.9 Multiple-Document-Interface (MDI) Windows

In previous chapters, we have built only *single-document-interface (SDI)* applications. Such programs (including Notepad or Paint) can support only one open window or document at a time. SDI applications usually have contracted abilities—Paint and Notepad, for example, have limited image- and text-editing features. To edit multiple documents, the user must create another instance of the SDI application.

Multiple document interface (MDI) programs (such as PaintShop Pro or Adobe Photoshop) enable users to edit multiple documents at once. MDI programs also tend to be more complex—PaintShop Pro and Photoshop have a greater number of image-editing features than does Paint. Until now, we had not mentioned that the applications we created were SDI applications. We define this here to emphasize the distinction between the two types of programs.

The application window of an MDI program is called the *parent window*, and each window inside the application is referred to as a *child window*. Although an MDI application can have many child windows, each has only one parent window. Furthermore, a maximum of one child window can be active at once. Child windows cannot be parents themselves and cannot be moved outside their parent. Otherwise, a child window behaves like any other window (with regard to closing, minimizing, resizing etc.). A child window's functionality can be different from the functionality of other child windows of the parent. For example, one child window might edit images, another might edit text and a third might display network traffic graphically, but all could belong to the same MDI parent. Figure 13.31 depicts a sample MDI application.

To create an MDI form, create a new **Form** and set its **IsMDIContainer** property to **True**. The form changes appearance, as in Fig. 13.32.

Next, create a child form class to be added to the form. To do this, right-click the project in the **Solution Explorer**, select **Add Windows Form...** and name the file. To add the child form to the parent, we must create a new child form object, set its **Mdi-Parent** property to the parent form and call method **Show**. In general, to add a child form to a parent, write

```
Dim frmChild As New ChildFormClass()
frmChild.MdiParent = frmParent
frmChild.Show()
```

In most cases, the parent form creates the child so that the *frmParent* reference is **Me**. The code to create a child usually lies inside an event handler, which creates a new window in response to a user action. Menu selections (such as **File** followed by a submenu option of **New** followed by a submenu option of **Window**) are common methods of creating new child windows.

Class **Form** property **MdiChildren** returns an array of child **Form** references. This is useful if the parent window wants to check the status of all its children (such as to ensure that all are saved before the parent closes). Property **ActiveMdiChild** returns a reference to the active child window; it returns **Nothing** if there are no active child windows. Other features of MDI windows are described in Fig. 13.33.

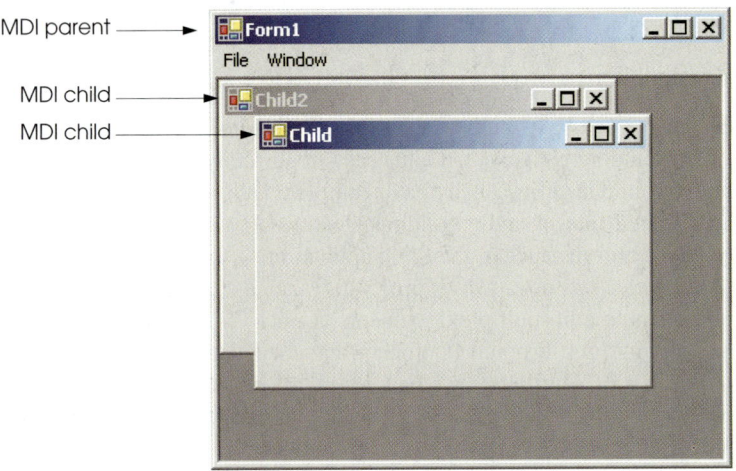

Fig. 13.31 MDI parent window and MDI child windows.

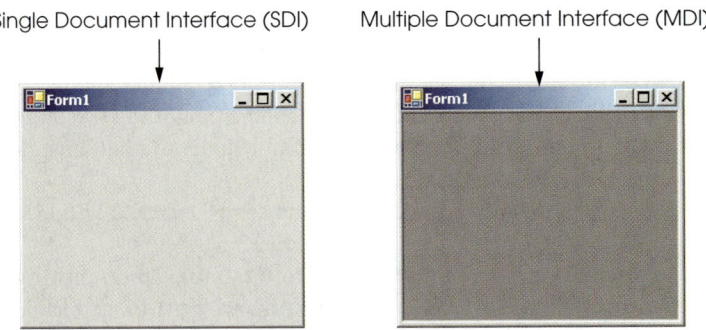

Fig. 13.32 SDI and MDI forms.

MDI Form events and properties	Description / Delegate and Event Arguments
Common MDI Child Properties	
`IsMdiChild`	Indicates whether the `Form` is an MDI child. If `True`, `Form` is an MDI child (read-only property).
`MdiParent`	Specifies the MDI parent `Form` of the child.
Common MDI Parent Properties	
`ActiveMdiChild`	Returns the `Form` that is the currently active MDI child (returns `Nothing` if no children are active).
`IsMdiContainer`	Indicates whether a `Form` can be an MDI parent. If `True`, the `Form` can be an MDI parent. The default value is `False`.
`MdiChildren`	Returns the MDI children as an array of `Form`s.
Common Method	
`LayoutMdi`	Determines the display of child forms on an MDI parent. Takes as a parameter an `MdiLayout` enumeration with possible values `ArrangeIcons`, `Cascade`, `TileHorizontal` and `TileVertical`. Figure 13.36 depicts the effects of these values.
Common Event	*(Delegate `EventHandler`, event arguments `EventArgs`)*
`MdiChildActivate`	Generated when an MDI child is closed or activated.

Fig. 13.33 MDI parent and MDI child events and properties.

Child windows can be minimized, maximized and closed independently of each other and of the parent window. Figure 13.34 shows two images, one containing two minimized child windows and a second containing a maximized child window. When the parent is minimized or closed, the child windows are minimized or closed as well. Notice that the title bar in the second image of Fig. 13.34 is **Parent Window - [Child]**. When a child window is maximized, its title bar is inserted into the parent window's title bar. When a child window is minimized or maximized, its title bar displays a restore icon, which can be used to return the child window to its previous size (its size before it was minimized or maximized).

The parent and child forms can have different menus, which are merged whenever a child window is selected. To specify how the menus merge, programmers can set the *MergeOrder* and the *MergeType* properties for each **MenuItem** (see Fig. 13.4). MergeOrder determines the order in which **MenuItem**s appear when two menus are merged. **MenuItem**s with a lower **MergeOrder** value appear first. For example, if **Menu1** has items **File**, **Edit** and **Window** (and their orders are 0, 10 and 20) and **Menu2** has items **Format** and **View** (and their orders are 7 and 15), then the merged menu contains menu items **File**, **Format**, **Edit**, **View** and **Window**, in that order.

Each **MenuItem** instance has its own **MergeOrder** property. It it likely that, at some point in an application, two **MenuItem**s with the same **MergeOrder** value will merge. Property **MergeType** resolves this conflict by determining the order in which the two menus are displayed.

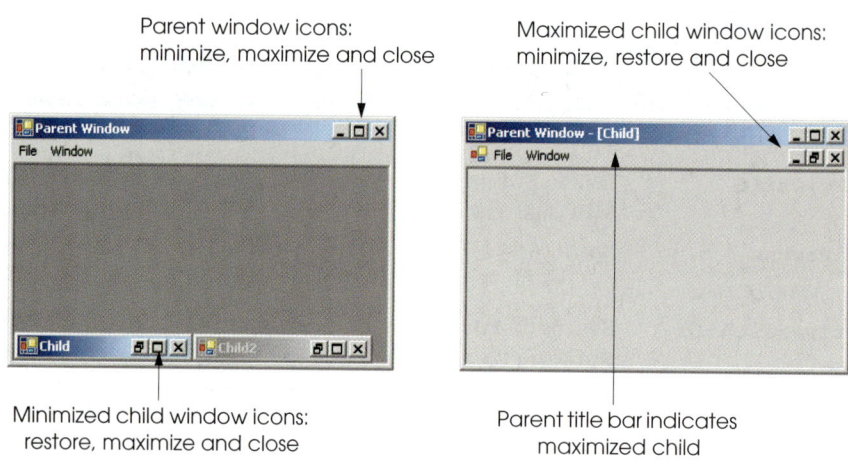

Fig. 13.34 Minimized and maximized child windows.

The **MergeType** property takes a **MenuMerge** enumeration value and determines which menu items are displayed when two menus are merged. A menu item with value **Add** is added to its parent's menu as a new menu on the menu bar (the parent's menu items come first). If a child form's menu item has value **Replace**, it attempts to take the place of its parent form's corresponding menu item during merging. A menu with value **MergeItems** combines its items with that of its parent's corresponding menu (if parent and child menus originally occupy the same space, their submenus are combined as one menu). A child's menu item with value **Remove** disappears when the menu is merged with that of its parent.

Value **MergeItems** acts passively—if the parent's menu has a **MergeType** that is different from the child menu's **MergeType**, the child's menu setting determines the outcome of the merge. When the child window is closed, the parent's original menu is restored.

Software Engineering Observation 13.3

*Set the parent's menu items' **MergeType** property to value **MergeItems**. This allows the child window to add most menu items according to its own settings. Parent menu items that must remain should have value **Add**, and those that must be removed should have value **Remove**.*

Visual Basic .NET provides a property that facilitates the tracking of which child windows are opened in an MDI container. Property **MdiList** (a **Boolean**) of class **MenuItem** determines whether a **MenuItem** displays a list of open child windows. The list appears at the bottom of the menu following a separator bar (first screen in Figure 13.35). When a new child window is opened, an entry is added to the list. If nine or more child windows are open, the list includes the option **More Windows...**, which allows the user to select a window from a list, using a scrollbar. Multiple **MenuItem**s can have their **MdiList** property set; each displays a list of open child windows.

Good Programming Practice 13.1

*When creating MDI applications, include a menu item with its **MdiList** property set to **True**. This helps the user select a child window quickly, rather than having to search for it in the parent window.*

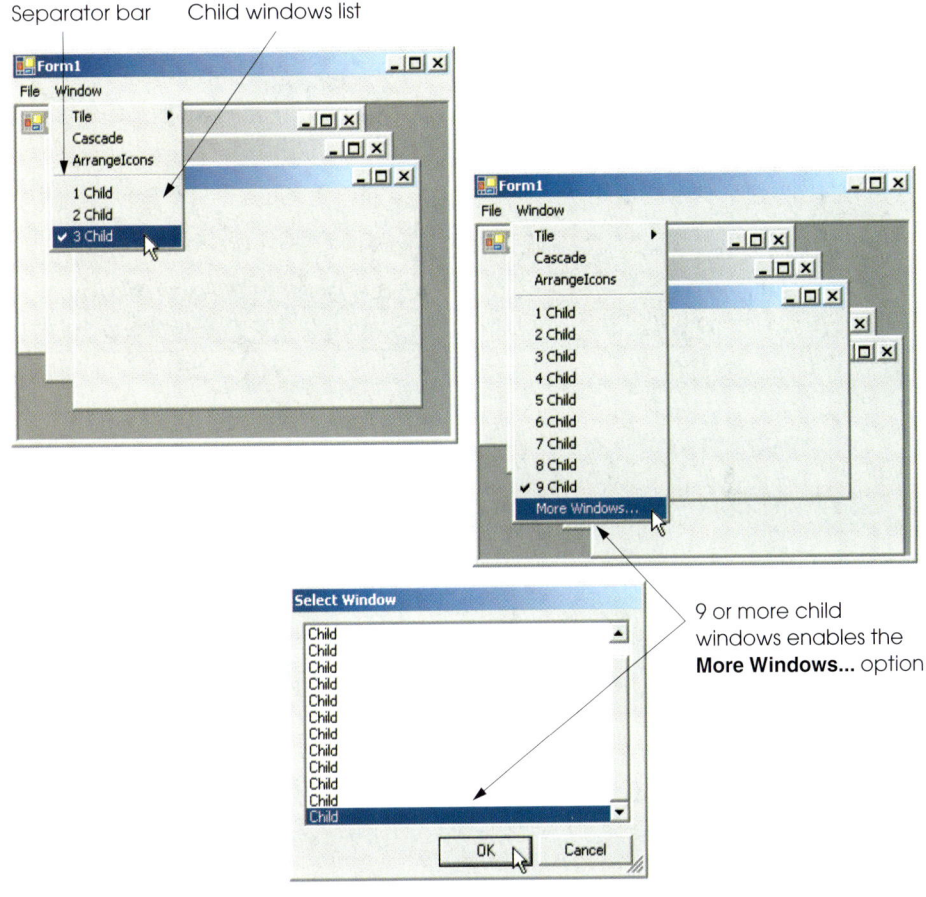

Fig. 13.35 `MenuItem` property `MdiList` example.

MDI containers allow developers to organize the placement of child windows. The child windows in an MDI application can be arranged by calling method **LayoutMdi** of the parent form. Method **LayoutMdi** takes a **MdiLayout** *enumeration*, which can have values **ArrangeIcons**, **Cascade**, **TileHorizontal** and **TileVertical**. *Tiled windows* completely fill the parent and do not overlap; such windows can be arranged horizontally (value **TileHorizontal**) or vertically (value **TileVertical**). *Cascaded windows* (value **Cascade**) overlap—each is the same size and displays a visible title bar, if possible. Value **ArrangeIcons** arranges the icons for any minimized child windows. If minimized windows are scattered around the parent window, value **ArrangeIcons** orders them neatly at the bottom-left corner of the parent window. Figure 13.36 illustrates the values of the **MdiLayout** enumeration.

Class **FrmUsingMDI** (Fig. 13.37) demonstrates the use of MDI windows. Class **FrmUsingMDI** uses three instances of child form **FrmChild** (Fig. 13.38), each containing a **PictureBox** that displays an image. The parent MDI form contains a menu enabling users to create and arrange child forms.

ArrangeIcons

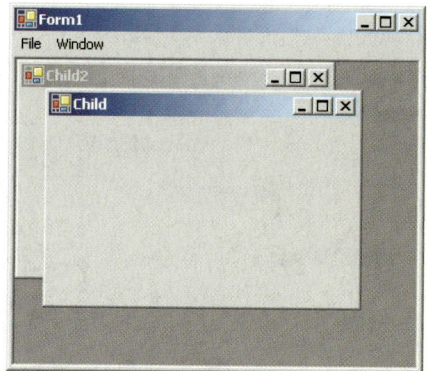
Cascade

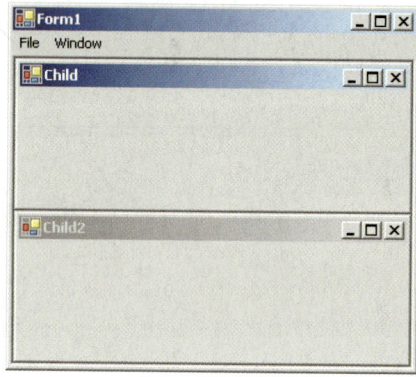
TileHorizontal

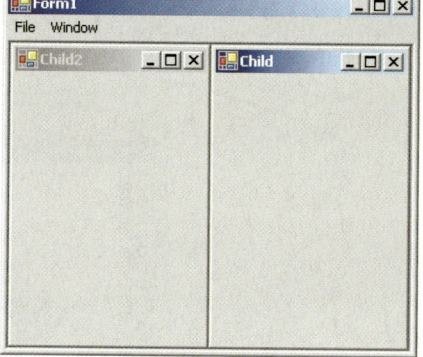
TileVertical

Fig. 13.36 `LayoutMdi` enumeration values.

```
1    ' Fig. 13.37: UsingMDI.vb
2    ' Demonstrating use of MDI parent and child windows.
3
4    Imports System.Windows.Forms
5
6    Public Class FrmUsingMDI
7       Inherits Form
8
9       ' main menu containing menu items File and Window
10      Friend WithEvents mnuMain As MainMenu
11
12      ' menu containing submenu New and menu item Exit
13      Friend WithEvents mnuitmFile As MenuItem
14      Friend WithEvents mnuitmExit As MenuItem
15
```

Fig. 13.37 MDI parent-window class (part 1 of 4).

```vbnet
16         ' submenu New
17         Friend WithEvents mnuitmNew As MenuItem
18         Friend WithEvents mnuitmChild1 As MenuItem
19         Friend WithEvents mnuitmChild2 As MenuItem
20         Friend WithEvents mnuitmChild3 As MenuItem
21
22         ' menu containing menu items Cascade, TileHorizontal and
23         ' TileVertical
24         Friend WithEvents mnuitmWindow As MenuItem
25         Friend WithEvents mnuitmCascade As MenuItem
26         Friend WithEvents mnuitmTileHorizontal As MenuItem
27         Friend WithEvents mnuitmTileVertical As MenuItem
28
29         ' Visual Studio .NET generated code
30
31         ' create Child1 when menu clicked
32         Private Sub mnuitmChild1_Click( _
33            ByVal sender As System.Object, _
34            ByVal e As System.EventArgs) Handles mnuitmChild1.Click
35
36            ' create image path
37            Dim imagePath As String = _
38               Directory.GetCurrentDirectory() & "\images\image0.jpg"
39
40            ' create new child
41            childWindow = New FrmChild(imagePath, "Child1")
42            childWindow.MdiParent = Me     ' set parent
43            childWindow.Show()             ' display child
44         End Sub ' mnuitmChild1_Click
45
46         ' create Child2 when menu clicked
47         Private Sub mnuitmChild2_Click( _
48            ByVal sender As System.Object, _
49            ByVal e As System.EventArgs) Handles mnuitmChild2.Click
50
51            ' create image path
52            Dim imagePath As String = _
53               Directory.GetCurrentDirectory() & "\images\image1.jpg"
54
55            ' create new child
56            childWindow = New FrmChild(imagePath, "Child2")
57            childWindow.MdiParent = Me     ' set parent
58            childWindow.Show()             ' display child
59         End Sub ' mnuitmChild2_Click
60
61         ' create Child3 when menu clicked
62         Private Sub mnuitmChild3_Click( _
63            ByVal sender As System.Object, _
64            ByVal e As System.EventArgs) Handles mnuitmChild3.Click
65
66            ' create image path
67            Dim imagePath As String = _
68               Directory.GetCurrentDirectory() & "\images\image2.jpg"
```

Fig. 13.37 MDI parent-window class (part 2 of 4).

```vbnet
69
70         ' create new child
71         childWindow = New FrmChild(imagePath, "Child3")
72         childWindow.MdiParent = Me   ' set parent
73         childWindow.Show()           ' display child
74      End Sub ' mnuitmChild3_Click
75
76      ' exit application
77      Private Sub mnuitmExit_Click(ByVal sender As System.Object, _
78         ByVal e As System.EventArgs) Handles mnuitmExit.Click
79
80         Application.Exit()
81      End Sub ' mnuitmExit_Click
82
83      ' set cascade layout
84      Private Sub mnuitmCascade_Click(ByVal sender As System.Object, _
85         ByVal e As System.EventArgs) Handles mnuitmCascade.Click
86
87         Me.LayoutMdi(MdiLayout.Cascade)
88      End Sub ' mnuitmCascade_Click
89
90      ' set TileHorizontal layout
91      Private Sub mnuitmTileHorizontal_Click( _
92         ByVal sender As System.Object, ByVal e As System.EventArgs) _
93         Handles mnuitmTileHorizontal.Click
94
95         Me.LayoutMdi(MdiLayout.TileHorizontal)
96      End Sub ' mnuitmTileHorizontal_Click
97
98      ' set TileVertical layout
99      Private Sub mnuitmTileVertical_Click( _
100        ByVal sender As System.Object, _
101        ByVal e As System.EventArgs) Handles mnuitmTileVertical.Click
102
103        Me.LayoutMdi(MdiLayout.TileVertical)
104     End Sub ' mnuitmTileVertical_Click
105
106  End Class ' FrmUsingMDI
```

Fig. 13.37 MDI parent-window class (part 3 of 4).

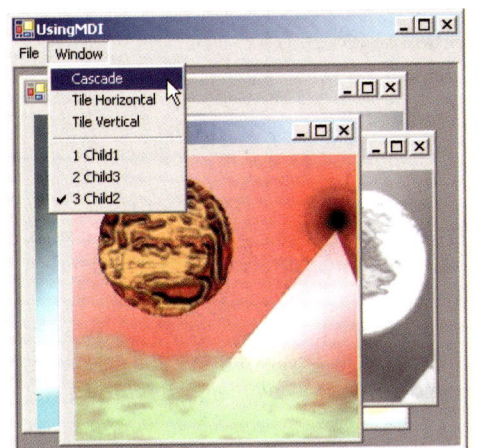
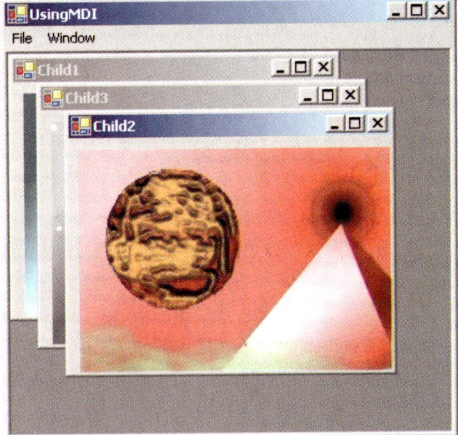

Fig. 13.37 MDI parent-window class (part 4 of 4).

The program in Fig. 13.37 is the application. The MDI parent form, which is created first, contains two top-level menus. The first of these menus, **File** (**mnuitmFile**, line 13), contains both an **Exit** item (**mnuitmExit**, line 14) and a **New** submenu (**mnuitmNew**, line 17) consisting of items for each child window. The second menu, **Window** (**mnuitmWindow**, line 24), provides options for laying out the MDI children, plus a list of the active MDI children.

```
1   ' Fig. 13.38: Child.vb
2   ' A child window of the MDI parent.
3
4   Imports System.Windows.Forms
5
6   Public Class FrmChild
7      Inherits Form
8
9      ' contains image loaded from disk
10     Friend WithEvents picDisplay As PictureBox
11
12     ' Visual Studio .NET generated code
13
14     ' constructor
15     Public Sub New(ByVal picture As String, _
16        ByVal name As String)
17
18        ' call Visual Studio generated default constructor
19        Me.New()
20
21        ' set title
22        Me.Text = name
23
```

Fig. 13.38 MDI child **FrmChild** (part 1 of 2).

```
24         ' set image for picture box
25         picDisplay.Image = Image.FromFile(picture)
26     End Sub ' New
27
28 End Class ' FrmChild
```

Fig. 13.38 MDI child `FrmChild` (part 2 of 2).

In the **Properties** window, we set the **Form**'s `IsMdiContainer` property to **True**, making the **Form** an MDI parent. In addition, we set the `mnuitmWindow MdiList` property to **True**. This enables `mnuitmWindow` to contain the list of child MDI windows.

The **Cascade** menu item (`mnuitmCascade`, line 25) has an event handler (`mnuitmCascade_Click`, lines 84–88) that arranges the child windows in a cascading manner. The event handler calls method `LayoutMdi` with the argument `Cascade` from the `MdiLayout` enumeration (line 87).

The **Tile Horizontal** menu item (`mnuitmTileHorizontal`, line 26) has an event handler (`mnuitmTileHorizontal_Click`, lines 91–96) that arranges the child windows in a horizontal manner. The event handler calls method `LayoutMdi` with the argument `TileHorizontal` from the `MdiLayout` enumeration (line 95).

Finally, the **Tile Vertical** menu item (`mnuitmTileVertical`, line 27) has an event handler (`mnuitmTileVertical_Click`, lines 99–104) that arranges the child windows in a vertical manner. The event handler calls method `LayoutMdi` with the argument `TileVertical` from the `MdiLayout` enumeration (line 103).

At this point the application is still incomplete—we must define the MDI child class. To do this, right-click the project in the **Solution Explorer** and select **Add**, then **Add Windows Form...**. Then, name the new class in the dialog as `FrmChild` (Fig. 13.38). Next, we add a `PictureBox` (`picDisplay`, line 10) to form `FrmChild`. We override the constructor generated by Visual Studio. Line 19 calls the default Visual Studio generated constructor to allow the form and all of its components to initialize. Line 22 sets the title bar text. Line 25 sets `FrmChild`'s `Image` property to an `Image`, using method `FromFile`. Method `FromFile` takes as a `String` argument the path of the image to load.

After the MDI child class is defined, the parent MDI form (Fig. 13.37) can create new instances of them. The event handlers in lines 32–74 create a new child form corresponding to the menu item clicked. Each event handler creates a `String` representing the image file path each `FrmChild` displays (lines 37–38, 52–53 and 67–68). Lines 41, 56 and 71 create new instances of `FrmChild`. Lines 42, 57 and 72 sets each `FrmChild`'s `MdiParent` property to the parent form. Lines 43, 58 and 73 call method `Show` to display each child form.

13.10 Visual Inheritance

In Chapter 9, Object-Oriented Programming: Inheritance, we discuss how to create classes by inheriting from other classes. In Visual Basic, we also can use inheritance to create **Form**s that display a GUI, because **Form**s are classes that derive from class `System.Windows.Forms.Form`. Visual inheritance allows us to create a new **Form** by inheriting from another **Form**. The derived **Form** class contains the functionality of its **Form** base class, including any base-class properties, methods, variables and controls. The derived class also inherits all visual aspects—such as sizing, component layout, spacing between GUI components, colors and fonts—from its base class.

Visual inheritance enables developers to achieve visual consistency across applications by reusing code. For example, a company could define a base form that contains a product's logo, a static background color, a predefined menu bar and other elements. Programmers then could use the base form throughout an application for purposes of uniformity and branding.

Class **FrmInheritance** (Fig. 13.39) is a derived class of class **Form**. The output depicts the workings of the program. The GUI contains two labels with text **Bugs, Bugs, Bugs** and **Copyright 2002, by Bug2Bug.com.**, as well as one button displaying the text **Learn More**. When a user presses the **Learn More** button, method **cmdLearn_Click** (lines 16–22) is invoked. This method displays a message box that provides some informative text.

To allow other forms to inherit from **FrmInheritance**, we must package **FrmInheritance** as a **.dll**. Right click the project's name in the **Solution Explorer** and choose **Properties**. Under **Common Properties > General**, change **Output Type** to **Class Library**. Building the project produces the **.dll**.

To visually inherit from **FrmInheritance**, we create an empty project. From the **Project** menu, select **Add Inherited Form...** to display the **Add New Item** dialog. Select **Inherited Form** from the **Templates** pane. Clicking **Open** displays the **Inheritance Picker** tool. The **Inheritance Picker** tool enables programmers to create a form which inherits from a specified form. Click button **Browse** and select the **.dll** file corresponding to **FrmInheritance**. This **.dll** file normally is located within the project's **bin** directory. Click **OK**. The Form Designer should now display the inherited form (Fig. 13.40). We can add components to the form.

```
1    ' Fig. 13.39: FrmInheritance.vb
2    ' Form template for use with visual inheritance.
3
4    Imports System.Windows.Forms
5
6    Public Class FrmInheritance
7       Inherits Form
8
9       Friend WithEvents lblBug As Label          ' top label
10      Friend WithEvents lblCopyright As Label    ' bottom label
11      Friend WithEvents cmdLearn As Button       ' left button
12
13      ' Visual Studio .NET generated code
14
15      ' invoked when user clicks Learn More button
16      Private Sub cmdLearn_Click(ByVal sender As System.Object, _
17         ByVal e As System.EventArgs) Handles cmdLearn.Click
18
19         MessageBox.Show("Bugs, Bugs, Bugs is a product of " & _
20            " Bug2Bug.com.", "Learn More", MessageBoxButtons.OK, _
21            MessageBoxIcon.Information)
22      End Sub ' cmdLearn_Click
23
24   End Class ' FrmInheritance
```

Fig. 13.39 Class **FrmInheritance**, which inherits from class **Form**, contains a button (**Learn More**) (part 1 of 2).

Fig. 13.39 Class `FrmInheritance`, which inherits from class `Form`, contains a button (**Learn More**) (part 2 of 2).

Fig. 13.40 Visual Inheritance through the Form Designer.

Class `FrmVisualTest` (Fig. 13.41) is a derived class of class `VisualForm.FrmInheritance`. The output illustrates the functionality of the program. The GUI contains those components derived from class `FrmInheritance`, as well as an additional button with text **Learn The Program**. When a user presses this button, method `cmdProgram_Click` (lines 13–20) is invoked. This method displays another message box providing different informative text.

Figure 13.41 demonstrates that the components, their layouts and the functionality of base-class `FrmInheritance` (Fig. 13.39) are inherited by `FrmVisualTest`. If a user clicks button **Learn More**, the base-class event handler `cmdLearn_Click` displays a `MessageBox`. `FrmInheritance` uses a `Friend` access modifier to declare its controls, so class `FrmVisualTest` cannot modify the controls inherited from class `FrmIn-`

heritance. As we discussed in Chapter 9, **Friend** access modifiers allow access only to other classes or modules belonging to the same assembly. In this example, **FrmVisualTest** does not belong to the assembly of **FrmInheritance** (**VisualForm**), so **FrmVisualTest** cannot modify the controls that it inherits from **FrmInheritance**.

```vb
1   ' Fig. 13.41: VisualTest.vb
2   ' A form that uses visual inheritance.
3
4   Public Class FrmVisualTest
5      Inherits VisualForm.FrmInheritance
6
7      ' new button added to form
8      Friend WithEvents cmdProgram As Button
9
10     ' Visual Studio .NET generated code
11
12     ' invoke when user clicks Learn the Program button
13     Private Sub cmdProgram_Click(ByVal sender As System.Object, _
14        ByVal e As System.EventArgs) Handles cmdProgram.Click
15
16        MessageBox.Show( _
17           "This program was created by Deitel & Associates", _
18           "Learn the Program", MessageBoxButtons.OK, _
19           MessageBoxIcon.Information)
20     End Sub ' cmdProgram_Click
21
22  End Class ' FrmVisualTest
```

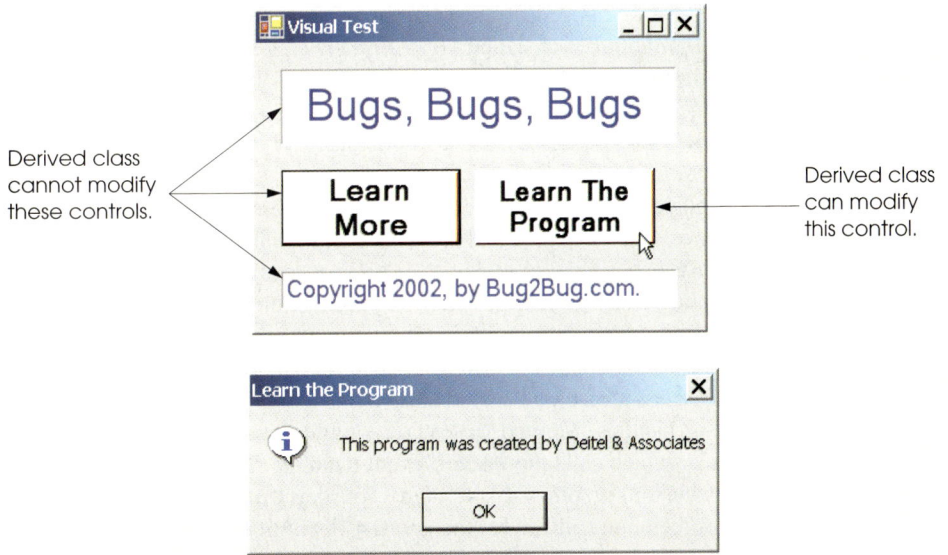

Fig. 13.41 Class **FrmVisualTest**, which inherits from class **VisualForm.FrmInheritance**, contains an additional button.

13.11 User-Defined Controls

The .NET Framework allows programmers to create *customized controls* or *custom controls* that inherit from a variety of classes. These customized controls appear in the user's **Toolbox** and can be added to **Form**s, **Panel**s or **GroupBox**es in the same way that we add **Button**s, **Label**s, and other predefined controls. The simplest way to create a customized control is to derive a class from an existing Windows Forms control, such as a **Label**. This is useful if the programmer wants to add functionality to an existing control, rather than having to reimplement the existing control in addition to including the desired functionality. For example, we can create a new type of label that behaves like a normal **Label** but has a different appearance. We accomplish this by inheriting from class **Label** and overriding method **OnPaint**.

Look-and-Feel Observation 13.8

*To change the appearance of any control, override method **OnPaint**.*

All controls contain method **OnPaint**, which the system calls when a component must be redrawn (such as when the component is resized). Method **OnPaint** is passed a **PaintEventArgs** object, which contains graphics information—property **Graphics** is the graphics object used to draw, and property **ClipRectangle** defines the rectangular boundary of the control. Whenever the system raises the **Paint** event, our control's base class catches the event. Through polymorphism, our control's **OnPaint** method is called. Our base class's **OnPaint** implementation is not called, so we must call it explicitly from our **OnPaint** implementation before we execute our custom-paint code. Alternately, if we do not wish to let our base class paint itself, we should not call our base class's **OnPaint** method implementation.

To create a new control composed of existing controls, use class **UserControl**. Controls added to a custom control are called *constituent controls*. For example, a programmer could create a **UserControl** composed of a button, a label and a text box, each associated with some functionality (such as if the button sets the label's text to that contained in the text box). The **UserControl** acts as a container for the controls added to it. The **UserControl** contains constituent controls, so it does not determine how these constituent controls are displayed. Method **OnPaint** cannot be overridden in these custom controls—their appearance can be added only by handling each constituent control's **Paint** event. The **Paint** event handler is passed a **PaintEventArgs** object, which can be used to draw graphics (lines, rectangles etc.) on the constituent controls.

Using another technique, a programmer can create a brand new control by inheriting from class **Control**. This class does not define any specific behavior; that task is left to the programmer. Instead, class **Control** handles the items associated with all controls, such as events and sizing handles. Method **OnPaint** should contain a call to the base class's **OnPaint** method, which calls the **Paint** event handlers. The programmer must then add code that adds custom graphics inside the overridden **OnPaint** method when drawing the control. This technique allows for the greatest flexibility, but also requires the most planning. All three approaches are summarized in Fig. 13.42.

We create a "clock" control in Fig. 13.43. This is a **UserControl** composed of a label and a timer—whenever the timer raises an event, the label is updated to reflect the current time.

Custom Control Techniques and `PaintEventArgs` Properties	Description
Inherit from Windows Forms control	Add functionality to a preexisting control. If overriding method `OnPaint`, call base class `OnPaint`. Can add only to the original control appearance, not redesign it.
Create a `UserControl`	Create a `UserControl` composed of multiple preexisting controls (and combine their functionality). Cannot override `OnPaint` methods of custom controls. Instead, add drawing code to a `Paint` event handler. Can add only to the original control appearance, not redesign it.
Inherit from class `Control`	Define a brand-new control. Override `OnPaint` method, call base class method `OnPaint` and include methods to draw the control. Can customize control appearance and functionality.
`PaintEventArgs` *Properties*	Use this object inside method `OnPaint` or `Paint` to draw on the control.
`Graphics`	The graphics object of the control. Used to draw on the control.
`ClipRectangle`	Specifies the rectangle indicating the boundary of the control.

Fig. 13.42 Custom control creation.

*Timer*s (`System.Windows.Forms` namespace) are non-visible components that reside on a form, generating `Tick` events at a set interval. This interval is set by the `Timer`'s `Interval` property, which defines the number of milliseconds (thousandths of a second) between events. By default, timers are disabled.

```
1    ' Fig 13.43: CClockUserControl.vb
2    ' User-defined control with timer and label.
3
4    Imports System.Windows.Forms
5
6    ' create clock control that inherits from UserControl
7    Public Class CClockUserControl
8       Inherits UserControl
9
10      ' displays time
11      Friend WithEvents lblDisplay As Label
12
13      ' non-visible event-triggering timer object
14      Friend WithEvents tmrClock As Timer
15
16      ' Visual Studio .NET generated code
17
```

Fig. 13.43 `UserControl`-defined clock (part 1 of 2).

```vbnet
18      ' update label at every tick
19      Private Sub tmrClock_Tick(ByVal sender As System.Object, _
20         ByVal e As System.EventArgs) Handles tmrClock.Tick
21
22         ' get current time (Now), convert to string
23         lblDisplay.Text = DateTime.Now.ToLongTimeString
24      End Sub ' tmrClock_Tick
25
26   End Class ' CClockUserControl
```

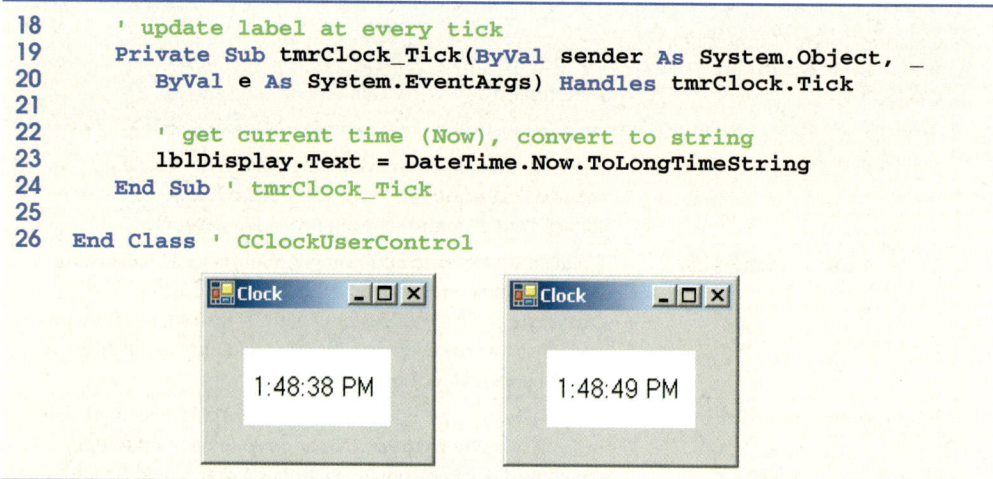

Fig. 13.43 `UserControl`-defined clock (part 2 of 2).

We create a **Form** that displays our custom control, **CClockUserControl** (Fig. 13.43). Next, we create a **UserControl** class for the project by selecting **Project > Add User Control...**. This displays a dialog from which we can select the type of control to add—user controls are already selected. We then name the file (and the class) **CClockUserControl**. This brings up our empty **CClockUserControl** as a grey rectangle.

We can treat this control like a Windows **Form**, meaning that we can add controls using the **ToolBox** and set properties, using the **Properties** window. However, instead of creating an application (notice there is no **Main** method in the **Control** class), we are simply creating a new control composed of other controls. We add a **Label** (**lblDisplay**, line 11) and a **Timer** (**tmrClock**, line 14) to the **UserControl**. We set the **Timer** interval to 100 milliseconds and set **lblDisplay**'s text with each event (lines 19–24). Note that **tmrClock** must be enabled by setting property **Enabled** to **True** in the **Properties** window.

Structure **DateTime** (namespace **System**) contains member **Now**, which is the current time. Method **ToLongTimeString** converts **Now** to a **String** containing the current hour, minute and second (along with AM or PM). We use this to set **lblDisplay** on line 23.

Once created, our clock control appears as an item on the **ToolBox**. To use the control, we can simply drag it onto a form and run the Windows application. The **CClockUserControl** object has a white background to make it stand out in the form. Figure 13.43 shows the output of **FrmClock**, which contains our **CClockUserControl**.

The above steps are useful when we need to define a custom control for the project on which we are working. Visual Studio .NET allows developers to share their custom controls with other developers. To create a **UserControl** that can be exported to other solutions, do the following:

1. Create a new **Windows Control Library** project.

2. Inside the project, add controls and functionality to the **UserControl** (Fig. 13.44).

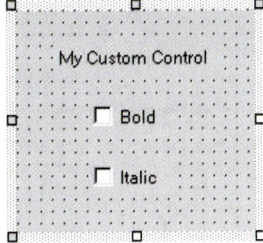

Fig. 13.44 Custom-control creation.

3. Build the project. Visual Studio .NET creates a **.dll** file for the **UserControl** in the output directory. The file is not executable: **Control** classes do not have a **Main** method. Select **Project > Properties** to find the output directory and output file (Fig. 13.45).

4. Create a new Windows application.

5. Import the **UserControl**. In the new Windows application, right click the **ToolBox**, and select **Customize Toolbox....** In the dialog that appears, select the **.NET Framework Components** tab. Browse for the **.dll** file, which is in the output directory for the Windows control library project. Click the checkbox next to the control, and click **OK** (Fig. 13.46).

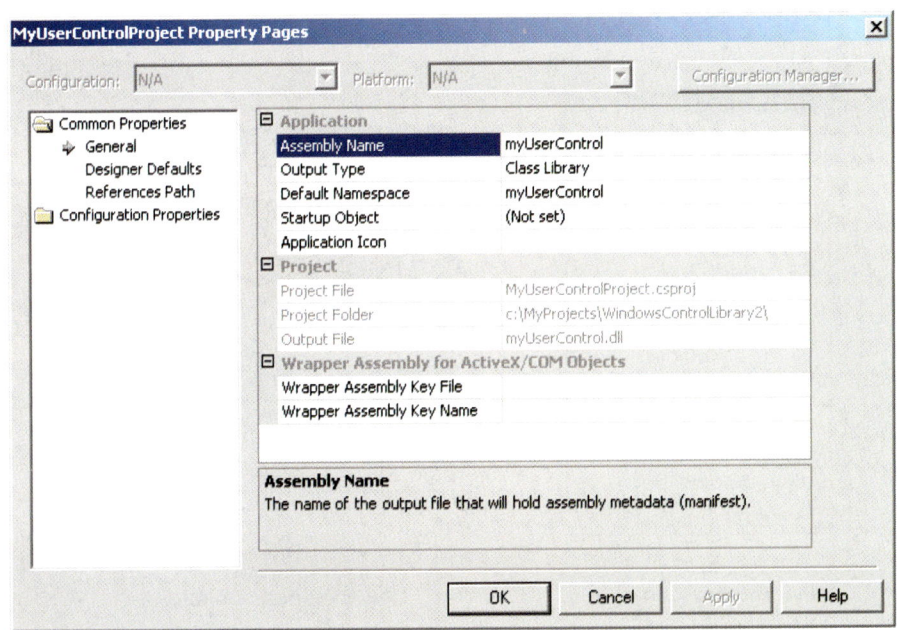

Fig. 13.45 Project properties dialog.

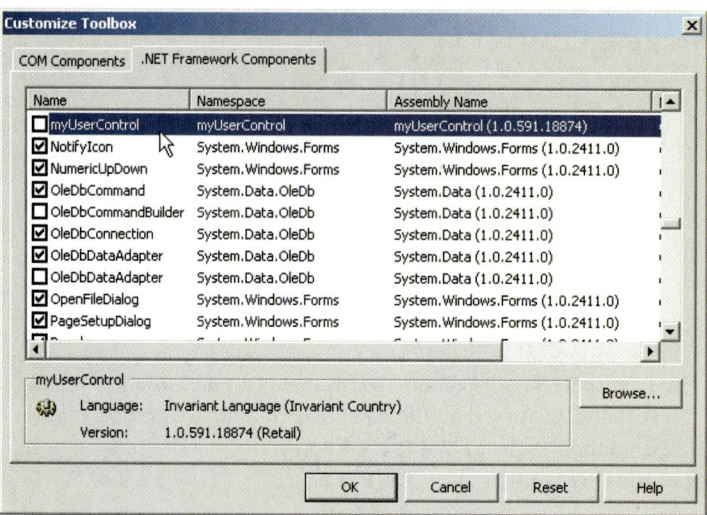

Fig. 13.46 Custom control added to the **ToolBox**.

6. The **UserControl** appears on the **ToolBox** and can be added to the form as if it were any other control (Fig. 13.47).

Testing and Debugging Tip 13.1

*Control classes do not have a **Main** method—they cannot be run by themselves. To test their functionality, add them to a sample Windows application and run them there.*

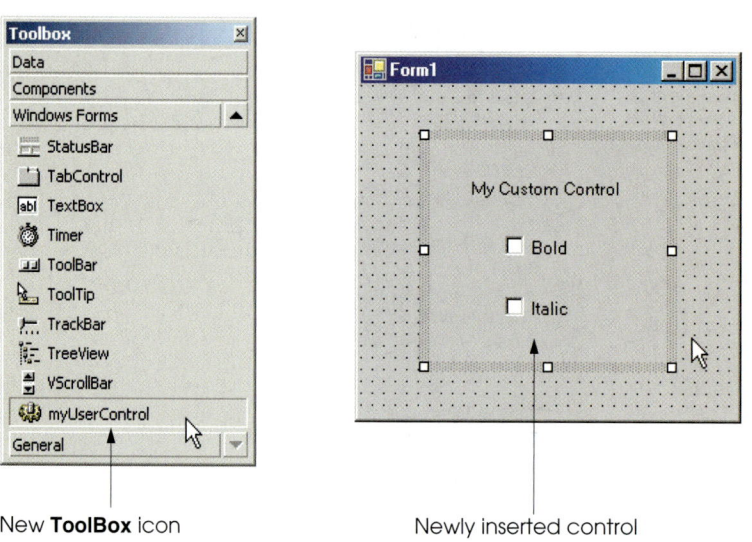

New **ToolBox** icon   Newly inserted control

Fig. 13.47 Custom control added to a **Form**.

As mentioned in Chapter 12, prefixing a variable name with an abbreviation of its type improves code readability. Figure 13.48 lists the abbreviations for the controls introduced in this chapter's code examples.

Many of today's most successful commercial programs provide GUIs that are easy to use and manipulate. Because of this demand for user-friendly GUIs, the ability to design sophisticated GUIs is an essential programming skill. Fortunately, Visual Studio .NET provides an IDE that makes GUI development quick and easy. In the last two chapters, we have presented the basic techniques required to add various GUI components to a program. The next chapter explores a more behind-the-scenes topic, *multithreading*. In many programming languages, the programmer can create multiple *threads*, enabling several processes to occur at once. By learning to create and manage multithreading in Visual Basic .NET, readers begin their study of a more mission-critical type of software.

SUMMARY

- Menus provide groups of related commands for Windows applications. Menus are an integral part of GUIs, because they enable user–application interaction without unnecessarily "cluttering" the GUI.
- Window's top-level menus appear on the left of the screen—any submenus or menu items are indented. All menu items can have *Alt* key shortcuts (also called access shortcuts).
- Sub menus can have shortcut keys (combinations of *Ctrl*, *Shift*, *Alt*, function keys *F1*, *F2*, letter keys etc.).
- To create a menu, open the **Toolbox** and drag a `MainMenu` control onto the form.
- To add entries to the menu, click the **Type Here** textbox and type the text that should appear in the menu. Remove a menu item by selecting it with the mouse and pressing the *Delete* key.
- Menus raise a `Click` event when selected.

Prefix	Control
mnu	Menu
mnuitm	MenuItem
lnklbl	LinkLabel
lst	ListBox
chklst	CheckedListBox
cbo	ComboBox
tre	TreeView
lvw	ListView
ils	ImageList
tbc	TabControl
tbp	TabPage
tmr	Timer

Fig. 13.48 Prefixes for controls used in chapter.

- Use the **Xor** (exclusive OR) operator to toggle single bits, such as those representing the bold and italic styles.
- The **LinkLabel** control displays links to other resources, such as files or Web pages. The links can change color to reflect whether each link is new, visited or active.
- When clicked, a **LinkLabel** generate a **LinkClicked** event.
- Method **Start** of class **Process** (namespace **System.Diagnostics**) can begin a new application. This method requires either the file to open (a **String**) or the application to run and the command line arguments (two **String**s).
- The **ListBox** control allows the user to view and select multiple items from a list. The user cannot create new list items in a **ListBox**.
- The **CheckedListBox** control extends a **ListBox** by preceding each item in the list with a checkbox. This allows multiple items to be selected with no logical restriction.
- The **SelectionMode** property determines how many items in a **CheckedListBox** can be selected.
- The **SelectedIndexChanged** event occurs when the user selects a new item in a **CheckedListBox**.
- **CheckBox**'s property **Items** returns all the objects in the list as a collection. Property **SelectedItem** returns the selected item. **SelectedIndex** returns the index of the selected item.
- Method **GetSelected** takes an index and returns **True** if the corresponding item is selected.
- Add items visually by examining the **Items** collection in the **Properties** window. Clicking the ellipsis opens the **String Collection Editor**, in which programmers can type the items to add.
- **CheckedListBox**es imply that multiple items can be selected—the **SelectionMode** property can only have values **None** or **One**. **One** allows multiple selection.
- Event **ItemCheck** is generated whenever a **CheckedListBox** item is about to change.
- The **ComboBox** control combines **TextBox** features with a drop-down list. The user can either select an option from the list or type one in (if allowed by the programmer). If the number of elements exceeds the maximum that can be displayed in the drop-down list, a scrollbar appears.
- Property **DropDownStyle** determines the type of **ComboBox**.
- The **ComboBox** control has properties **Items** (a collection), **SelectedItem** and **SelectedIndex**, which are similar to the corresponding properties in **ListBox**.
- When the selected item changes, event **SelectedIndexChanged** is raised.
- A **Graphics** object allows a pen or brush to draw on a component, using one of several **Graphics** methods.
- The **TreeView** control can display nodes hierarchically in a tree.
- A node is an element that contains a value and references to other nodes.
- A parent node contains child nodes, and the child nodes can be parents themselves.
- A tree is a collection of nodes, usually organized in some manner. The first parent node of a tree is often called the root node.
- Each node has a **Nodes** collection, which contains a list of the **Node**'s children.
- To add nodes to the **TreeView** visually, click the ellipsis by the **Nodes** property in the **Properties** window. This opens the **TreeNode Editor**, where there are buttons to create a root, and to add, delete and rename nodes.
- Method **GetDirectories** takes a **String** (the current directory) and returns an array of **String**s (the subdirectories).

- The **ListView** control is similar to a **ListBox**—it displays a list from which the user can select one or more items. However, a **ListView** can display icons alongside the list items.
- To display images, the programmer must use an **ImageList** component. Create one by dragging it onto the form from the **ToolBox**. Click the **Images** collection in the **Properties** window to display the **Image Collection Editor**.
- Class **DirectoryInfo** (namespace **System.IO**) allows programmers to browse or manipulate the directory structure easily. Method **GetDirectories** returns an array of **DirectoryInfo** objects containing the subdirectories of the current directory. Method **GetFiles** returns an array of class **FileInfo** objects containing the files in the current directory.
- The **TabControl** control creates tabbed windows. This allows the programmer to provide large quantities of information while saving screen space.
- **TabControl**s contain **TabPage** objects, which can contain controls.
- To add **TabPage**s in the Visual Studio .NET designer, right-click the **TabControl**, and select **Add Tab**.
- Each **TabPage** raises its own **Click** event when its tab is clicked. Events for controls inside the **TabPage** are still handled by the form.
- Single-document-interface (SDI) applications can support only one open window or document at a time. Multiple-document-interface (MDI) programs allows users to edit multiple documents at a time.
- Each window inside an MDI application is called a child window, and the application window is called the parent window.
- To create an MDI form, set the form's **IsMDIContainer** property to **True**.
- The parent and child windows of an application can have different menus, which are merged (combined) whenever a child window is selected.
- Class **MenuItem** property **MdiList** (a **Boolean**) allows a menu item to contain a list of open child windows.
- The child windows in an MDI application can be arranged by calling method **LayoutMdi** of the parent form.
- The .NET Framework allows the programmer to create customized controls. The most basic way to create a customized control is to derive a class from an existing Windows Forms control. If we inherit from an existing Windows Forms control, we can add to its appearance, but not redesign it. To create a new control composed of existing controls, use class **UserControl**. To create a new control from the ground up, inherit from class **Control**.
- **Timer**s are non-visible components that reside on a form and generate **Tick** events at a set interval.
- We create a **UserControl** class for the project by selecting **Project**, then **Add User Control...**. We can treat this control like a Windows Form, meaning that we can add controls, using the **ToolBox**, and set properties, using the **Properties** window.
- Structure **DateTime** (namespace **System**) contains member **Now**, which is the current time.

TERMINOLOGY

& (menu access shortcut)
access shortcut
Activation property of class **ListView**
ActiveLinkColor property of class **LinkLabel**
ActiveMdiChild property of class **Form**
Add member of enumeration **MenuMerge**
Add method of class **TreeNodeCollection**
Add Tab menu item
Add User Control... option in Visual Studio

Add Windows Form... option in Visual Studio
adding controls to **ToolBox**
`AfterSelect` event of class `TreeView`
`ArrangeIcons` value in `LayoutMdi` enumeration
boundary of a control
`Cascade` value in `LayoutMdi` enumeration
`CheckBoxes` property of class `ListView`
`CheckBoxes` property of class `TreeView`
`Checked` property of class `MenuItem`
`Checked` property of class `TreeNode`
`CheckedIndices` property of class `CheckedListBox`
`CheckedItems` property of class `CheckedListBox`
`CheckedListBox` class
child node
child window
child window maximized
child window minimized
`Clear` method of class `TreeNodeCollection`
`Click` event of class `MenuItem`
`ClipRectangle` property of class `PaintEventArgs`
`Collapse` method of class `TreeNode`
collapsing a node
`ComboBox` class
control boundary
`Control` class
`CurrentValue` event of class `CheckedListBox`
custom control
custom control being adding to **ToolBox**
Customize Toolbox... option in Visual Studio
`DateTime` structure
`DirectoryInfo` class
displaying files and folders in a `ListView`
draw on a control
`DrawEllipse` method of class `Graphics`
`DrawPie` method of class `Graphics`
`DrawRectangle` method of class `Graphics`
drop-down list
`DropDown` style for `ComboBox`
`DropDownList` style for `ComboBox`
`DropDownStyle` property of class `ComboBox`
events at an interval
`Exit` method of class `Application`
`Expand` method of class `TreeNode`
`ExpandAll` method of class `TreeNode`
expanding a node
`FillEllipse` method of class `Graphics`
`FillPie` method of class `Graphics`
`FillRectange` method of class `Graphics`
`FirstNode` property of class `TreeNode`
`FullName` property
`FullPath` property of class `TreeNode`
`GetDirectories` method of class `Directory`
`GetDirectories` method of class `DirectoryInfo`
`GetFiles` method of class `DirectoryInfo`
`GetItemChecked` method of class `CheckedListBox`
`GetNodeCount` method of class `TreeNode`
`GetSelected` method of class `ListBox`
`Graphics` class
`Graphics` property of class `PaintEventArgs`
Image Collection Editor
`ImageIndex` property of class `ListViewItem`
`ImageIndex` property of class `TreeNode`
`ImageList` class
`ImageList` collection
`ImageList` property of class `TabControl`
`ImageList` property of class `TreeView`
`Index` event of class `CheckedListBox`
`Index` property of class `MenuItem`
inherit from a Windows Form control
Insert Separator option
`Interval` property of class `Timer`
`IsMdiChild` property of class `Form`
`IsMdiContainer` property of class `Form`
`ItemActivate` event of class `ListView`
`ItemCheck` event of class `CheckedListBox`
`ItemCheckEventArgs` event of class `CheckedListBox`
`Items` property of class `ComboBox`
`Items` property of class `ListBox`
`Items` property of class `ListView`
`ItemSize` property of class `TabControl`
`LargeImageList` property of class `ListView`
`LastNode` property of class `TreeNode`
`LayoutMdi` enumeration
`LayoutMdi` method of class `Form`

`LinkArea` property of class `LinkLabel`
`LinkBehavior` property of class
    `LinkLabel`
`LinkClicked` event of class `LinkLabel`
`LinkColor` property of class `LinkLabel`
`LinkLabel` class
`Links` property of class `LinkLabel`
`LinkVisited` property of class `LinkLabel`
`ListBox` class
`ListView` class
`Main` method
`MainMenu` class
`MaxDropDownItems` property of class
    `ComboBox`
MDI form
MDI parent-window class
MDI title bar
`MdiChildActivate` event of class `Form`
`MdiChildren` property of class `Form`
`MdiList` property of class `MenuItem`
`MdiParent` property of class `Form`
menu
menu-access shortcut
Menu Designer in Visual Studio
menu, expanded and checked
menu item
`MenuItem` class
`MenuItems` property of class `MainMenu`
`MenuItems` property of class `MenuItem`
`MenuMerge` enumeration
`MergeItems` member of enumeration
    `MenuMerge`
`MergeOrder` property of class `MenuItem`
`MergeType` property of class `MenuItem`
More Windows... option in Visual Studio
`MultiColumn` property of class `ListBox`
`MultiExtended` value of `SelectionMode`
`MultiLine` property of class `TabControl`
multiple-document interface (MDI)
`MultiSelect` property of class `ListView`
`MultiSimple` value of `SelectionMode`
`Name` property of class `DirectoryInfo`
`Name` property of class `FileInfo`
`NewValue` event of class `CheckedListBox`
`NextNode` property of class `TreeNode`
`Nodes` property of class `TreeNode`
`Nodes` property of class `TreeView`
`None` value of `SelectionMode`
`Now` property of structure `DateTime`
`One` value of `SelectionMode`

`OnPaint` method
`PaintEventArgs` class
parent menu
parent node
parent window
`PictureBox` class
`PrevNode` property of class `TreeNode`
`Process` class
project properties dialog
project, Windows control library
radio buttons, using with `TabPage`
`RadioCheck` property of class `MenuItem`
`Remove` member of enumeration `MenuMerge`
`Remove` method of class
    `TreeNodeCollection`
`Replace` member of enumeration
    `MenuMerge`
`RightToLeft` property of class `MainMenu`
root node
`SelectedImageIndex` property of class
    `TreeNode`
`SelectedIndex` property of class
    `ComboBox`
`SelectedIndex` property of class `ListBox`
`SelectedIndex` property of class
    `TabControl`
`SelectedIndexChanged` event of class
    `ComboBox`
`SelectedIndexChanged` event of class
    `ListBox`
`SelectedIndexChanged` event of class
    `TabControl`
`SelectedIndices` property of class
    `ListBox`
`SelectedItem` property of class `ComboBox`
`SelectedItem` property of class `ListBox`
`SelectedItems` property of class `ListBox`
`SelectedItems` property of class
    `ListView`
`SelectedNode` property of class `TreeView`
`SelectedTab` property of class
    `TabControl`
`SelectionMode` enumeration
`SelectionMode` property of class
    `CheckedListBox`
`SelectionMode` property of class `ListBox`
separator bar
separator, menu
shortcut key
`Shortcut` property of class `MenuItem`

Show method of class **Form**
ShowShortcut property of class **MenuItem**
sibling node
Simple style for **ComboBox**
single-document interface (SDI)
SmallImageList property of class
    ListView
Solution Explorer in Visual Studio .NET
Sorted property of class **ComboBox**
Sorted property of class **ListBox**
Start method of class **Process**
String Collection Editor in Visual Studio .NET
submenu
TabControl, adding a **TabPage**
TabControl class
TabCount property of class **TabControl**
TabPage, add to **TabControl**
TabPage class
TabPage, using radio buttons
TabPages property of class **TabControl**
Text property of class **LinkLabel**
Text property of class **MenuItem**
Text property of class **TreeNode**
Tick event of class **Timer**
TileHorizontal value in **LayoutMdi**
    enumeration
TileVertical value in **LayoutMdi**
    enumeration
ToolBox customization
tree
TreeNode class
TreeNode Editor
TreeView class
UseMnemonic property of class **LinkLabel**
UserControl class
user-defined control
View property of class **ListView**
VisitedLinkColor property of class
    LinkLabel
Windows control library

SELF-REVIEW EXERCISES

13.1 State whether each of the following is *true* or *false*. If *false*, explain why.
    a) Menus provide groups of related classes.
    b) Menu items can display radio buttons, checkmarks and access shortcuts.
    c) The **ListBox** control allows only single selection (like a radio button), whereas the **CheckedListBox** allows multiple selection (like a check box).
    d) A **ComboBox** control has a drop-down list.
    e) Deleting a parent node in a **TreeView** control deletes its child nodes.
    f) The user can select only one item in a **ListView** control.
    g) A **TabPage** can act as a container for radio buttons.
    h) In general, multiple document interface (MDI) windows are used with simple applications.
    i) An MDI child window can have MDI children.
    j) MDI child windows can be moved outside the boundaries of their parent window.
    k) There are two basic ways to create a customized control.

13.2 Fill in the blanks in each of the following statements:
    a) Method _____ of class **Process** can open files and Web pages, similar to the **Run** menu in Windows.
    b) If more elements appear in a **ComboBox** than can fit, a _____ appears.
    c) The top-level node in a **TreeView** is the _____ node.
    d) A(n) _____ displays icons contained in **ImageList** control.
    e) The **MergeOrder** and **MergeType** properties determine how _____ merge.
    f) The _____ property allows a menu to display a list of active child windows.
    g) An important feature of the **ListView** control is the ability to display _____.
    h) Class _____ allows the programmer to combine several controls into a single, custom control.
    i) The _____ saves space by layering **TabPage**s on top of each other.

j) The _____ window layout option makes all windows the same size and layers them so every title bar is visible (if possible).
k) _____ are typically used to display hyperlinks to other resources, files or Web pages.

ANSWERS TO SELF-REVIEW EXERCISES

13.1 a) False. Menus provide groups of related commands. b) True. c) False. Both controls can have single or multiple selection. d) True. e) True. f) False. The user can select one or more items. g) True. h) False. MDI windows tend to be used with complex applications. i) False. Only an MDI parent window can have MDI children. An MDI parent window cannot be an MDI child. j) False. MDI child windows cannot be moved outside their parent window. k) False. There are three ways: 1) Derive from an existing control, 2) use a `UserControl` or 3) derive from `Control` and create a control from scratch.

13.2 a) `Start`. b) scrollbar. c) root. d) `ListView`. e) menus. f) `MdiList`. g) icons. h) `UserControl`. i) `TabControl`. j) `Cascade`. k) `LinkLabel`s.

EXERCISES

13.3 Write a program that displays the names of 15 states in a `ComboBox`. When an item is selected from the `ComboBox`, remove it.

13.4 Modify your solution to the previous exercise to add a `ListBox`. When the user selects an item from the `ComboBox`, remove the item from the `ComboBox` and add it to the `ListBox`. Your program should check to ensure that the `ComboBox` contains at least one item. If it does not, print a message, using a message box, and terminate program execution.

13.5 Write a program that allows the user to enter `String`s in a `TextBox`. Each `String` input is added to a `ListBox`. As each `String` is added to the `ListBox`, ensure that the `String`s are in sorted order. Any sorting method may be used. [*Note*: Do not use property `Sort`]

13.6 Create a file browser (similar to Windows Explorer) based on the programs in Fig. 13.8, Fig. 13.22 and Fig. 13.25. The file browser should have a `TreeView`, which allows the user to browse directories. There should also be a `ListView`, which displays the contents (all subdirectories and files) of the directory being browsed. Double-clicking a file in the `ListView` should open it, and double-clicking a directory in either the `ListView` or the `TreeView` should browse it. If a file or directory cannot be accessed, because of its permission settings, notify the user.

13.7 Create an MDI text editor. Each child window should contain a multiline `RichTextBox`. The MDI parent should have a **Format** menu, with submenus to control the size, font and color of the text in the active child window. Each submenu should have at least three options. In addition, the parent should have a **File** menu with menu items **New** (create a new child), **Close** (close the active child) and **Exit** (exit the application). The parent should have a **Window** menu to display a list of the open child windows and their layout options.

13.8 Create a `UserControl` called `LoginPasswordUserControl`. The `LoginPasswordUserControl` contains a `Label` (`lblLogin`) that displays `String "Login:"`, a `TextBox` (`txtLogin`) where the user inputs a login name, a `Label` (`lblPassword`) that displays the `String "Password:"` and finally, a `TextBox` (`txtPassword`) where a user inputs a password (do not forget to set property `PasswordChar` to `"*"` in the `TextBox`'s **Properties** window). `LoginPasswordUserControl` must provide `Public` read-only properties `Login` and `Password` that allow an application to retrieve the user input from `txtLogin` and `txtPassword`. The `UserControl` must be exported to an application that displays the values input by the user in `LoginPasswordUserControl`.

14

Multithreading

Objectives

- To understand the concept of multithreading.
- To appreciate how multithreading can improve program performance.
- To understand how to create, manage and destroy threads.
- To understand the life cycle of a thread.
- To understand thread synchronization.
- To understand thread priorities and scheduling.

The spider's touch, how exquisitely fine!
Feels at each thread, and lives along the line.
Alexander Pope

A person with one watch knows what time it is; a person with two watches is never sure.
Proverb

Learn to labor and to wait.
Henry Wadsworth Longfellow

The most general definition of beauty…Multeity in Unity.
Samuel Taylor Coleridge

Outline

14.1 Introduction
14.2 Thread States: Life Cycle of a Thread
14.3 Thread Priorities and Thread Scheduling
14.4 Thread Synchronization and Class `Monitor`
14.5 Producer/Consumer Relationship without Thread Synchronization
14.6 Producer/Consumer Relationship with Thread Synchronization
14.7 Producer/Consumer Relationship: Circular Buffer

Summary • Terminology • Self-Review Exercises • Answers to Self-Review Exercises • Exercises

14.1 Introduction

The human body performs a great variety of operations *in parallel*—or, as we will say throughout this chapter, *concurrently*. Respiration, blood circulation and digestion, for example, can occur concurrently. Similarly, all the senses—sight, touch, smell, taste and hearing—can occur at once. Computers, too, perform operations concurrently. It is common for a desktop personal computer to compile a program, send a file to a printer and receive electronic mail messages over a network concurrently.

Ironically, most programming languages do not enable programmers to specify concurrent activities. Rather, these programming languages provide only a simple set of control structures that allow programmers to organize successive actions; a program proceeds to the next action after the previous action is completed. Historically, the type of concurrency that computers perform today generally has been implemented as operating-system "primitives" available only to highly experienced "systems programmers."

The Ada programming language, developed by the United States Department of Defense, made concurrency primitives widely available to defense contractors building military command-and-control systems. However, Ada has not been widely adopted by universities or commercial industry.

The .NET Framework Class Library makes concurrency primitives available to applications programmers. A programmer can specify that an application contains "threads of execution," where each thread designates a portion of a program that might execute concurrently with other threads. This capability is called *multithreading*. Multithreading is available in all .NET programming languages, including Visual Basic, C# and Visual C++.

The .NET Framework Class Library, `System.Threading` *namespace, includes multithreading capabilities. These capabilities encourage the use of multithreading among a larger portion of the applications-programming community.*

In this chapter, we discuss various applications of concurrent programming. For example, when programs download large files, such as audio clips or video clips from the World Wide Web, users do not want to wait until an entire clip, downloads before starting the playback. To solve this problem, we can put multiple threads to work—one thread downloads a clip, and another plays the clip. This enables these activities, or *tasks*, to proceed concurrently. To avoid choppy playback, we *synchronize* the threads so that the player thread does not begin until the amount of the clip contained in memory is sufficient to keep the player thread busy while the downloading thread completes its execution.

Another example of multithreading is Visual Basic's automatic *garbage collection*. In C and C++, the programmer must assume responsibility for reclaiming dynamically allocated memory. By contrast, Visual Basic provides a *garbage-collector thread* that reclaims dynamically allocated memory when it is no longer needed.

Testing and Debugging Tip 14.1
In C and C++, programmers must provide statements explicitly for reclaiming dynamically allocated memory. When memory is not reclaimed (because a programmer forgets to do so, because of a logic error or because an exception diverts program control), an error called a memory leak *occurs. Overtime, memory leaks can exhaust the supply of free memory and even cause program termination. Visual Basic's automatic garbage collection eliminates the vast majority of memory leaks.*

Performance Tip 14.1
One reason that C and C++ have remained popular over the years is that these memory languages management techniques were more efficient than those of languages that used garbage collectors. However, memory management in Visual Basic often is faster than in C or C++.[1]

Good Programming Practice 14.1
Set an object reference to **Nothing** *when the program no longer needs that object. This enables the garbage collector to determine at the earliest possible moment that the object can be garbage collected. If the program retains other references to the object, that object cannot be collected.*

The writing of multithreaded programs can be tricky. Although the human mind can perform functions concurrently, people often find it difficult to jump between parallel "trains of thought." To perceive why multithreading can be difficult to program and understand, try the following experiment: Open three books to page one and try reading the books concurrently. Read a few words from the first book, then read a few words from the second book, then read a few words from the third book, then loop back and read the next few words from the first book, etc. After conducting this experiment, students will appreciate the challenges presented by multithreading. It is exceedingly difficult to switch between books, read each book briefly, remember your place in each book, move the book you are reading closer so you can see it and push books you are not reading aside. Moreover, it is nearly impossible to comprehend the content of the books amidst all this chaos!

Performance Tip 14.2
A problem with single-threaded applications is that lengthy activities must complete before other activities can begin. In a multithreaded application, threads can share a processor (or set of processors), enabling multiple tasks to be performed in parallel.

---

1. E. Schanzer, "Performance Considerations for Run-Time Technologies in the .NET Framework," August 2001 `<http://msdn.microsoft.com/library/default.asp?url=/library/en-us/dndotnet/html/dotnetperftechs.asp>`.

14.2 Thread States: Life Cycle of a Thread

At any time, a thread is said to be in one of several *thread states* (illustrated in Fig. 14.1). This section discusses the various states, as well as the transitions between states. Two classes that are essential to multithreaded applications are **Thread** and **Monitor** (**System.Threading** namespace). This section also discusses several methods of classes **Thread** and **Monitor** that cause state transitions.

When a program creates a new thread, the new thread begins its lifecycle in the *Unstarted* state. The thread remains in the *Unstarted* state until the program calls **Thread** method **Start**, which places the thread in the *Started* state (sometimes called the *Ready* or *Runnable* state) and then immediately returns control to the calling thread. At this point, the thread that invoked **Start**, the newly *Started* thread and any other threads in the program can execute concurrently.

The highest priority *Started* thread enters the *Running* state (i.e., begins executing) when the operating system assigns a processor to the thread (Section 14.3 discusses thread priorities). When a *Started* thread receives a processor for the first time and becomes a *Running* thread, the thread executes its **ThreadStart** delegate, which specifies the actions that the thread will perform during its lifecycle. When a program creates a new **Thread**, the program specifies the **Thread**'s **ThreadStart** delegate as an argument to the **Thread** constructor. The **ThreadStart** delegate must be a procedure that takes no arguments.

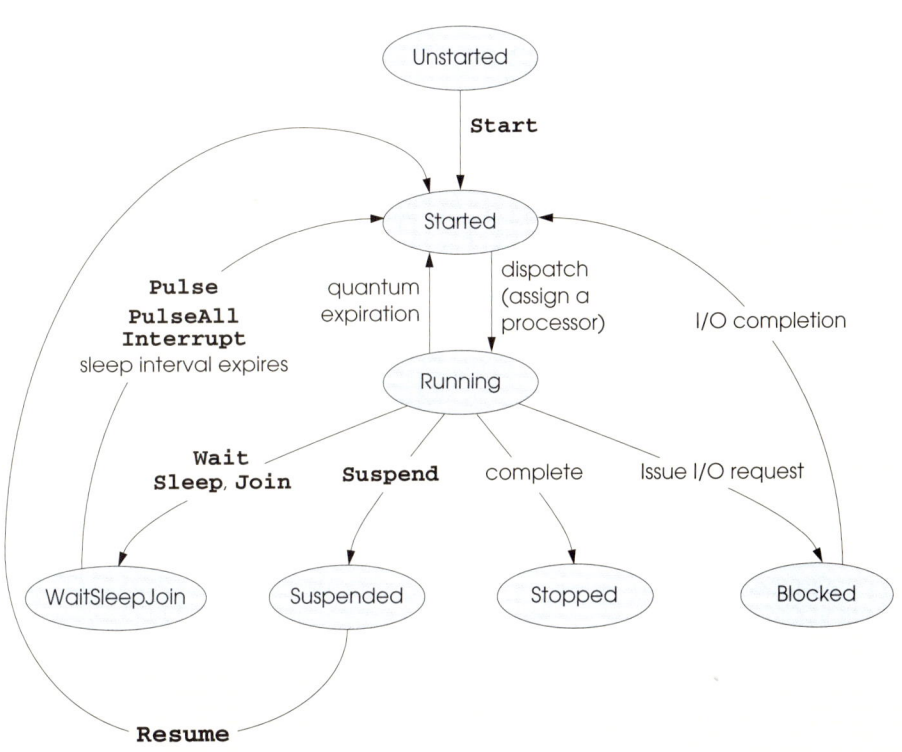

Fig. 14.1 Thread life cycle.

A *Running* thread enters the *Stopped* (or *Dead*) state when its **ThreadStart** delegate terminates. Note that a program can force a thread into the *Stopped* state by calling **Thread** method **Abort** on the appropriate **Thread** object. Method **Abort** throws a **ThreadAbortException** in the thread, normally causing the thread to terminate. When a thread is in the *Stopped* state and there are no references to the thread object remain in the program, the garbage collector can remove the thread object from memory.

A thread enters the *Blocked* state when the thread issues an input/output request. The operating system blocks the thread from executing until the operating system can complete the I/O for which the thread is waiting. Once the request is complete, the thread returns to the *Started* state and can resume execution. A *Blocked* thread cannot use a processor, even if one is available.

There are three ways in which a *Running* thread enters the *WaitSleepJoin* state. If a thread encounters code that it cannot execute yet (normally because a condition is not satisfied), the thread can call **Monitor** method **Wait** to enter the *WaitSleepJoin* state. Once in this state, a thread returns to the *Started* state when another thread invokes **Monitor** method **Pulse** or **PulseAll**. Method **Pulse** moves the next waiting thread back to the *Started* state. Method **PulseAll** moves all waiting threads back to the *Started* state.

Alternatively, a *Running* thread can call **Thread** method **Sleep** to enter the *WaitSleepJoin* state for a number of milliseconds specified as the argument to **Sleep**. A sleeping thread returns to the *Started* state when its designated sleep time expires. Like *Blocked* threads, sleeping threads cannot use a processor, even if one is available.

Any thread that enters the *WaitSleepJoin* state by calling **Monitor** method **Wait** or by calling **Thread** method **Sleep** leaves the *WaitSleepJoin* state and returns to the *Started* state if the sleeping or waiting **Thread**'s **Interrupt** method is called by another thread in the program.

If a thread (which we will call the dependent thread) cannot continue executing unless another thread terminates, the dependent thread calls the other thread's **Join** method to "join" the two threads. When two threads are "joined," the dependent thread leaves the *WaitSleepJoin* state when the other thread finishes execution (enters the *Stopped* state).

If a *Running* **Thread**'s **Suspend** method is called, the *Running* thread enters the *Suspended* state. A *Suspended* thread returns to the *Started* state when another thread in the program invokes the Suspended thread's **Resume** method.

14.3 Thread Priorities and Thread Scheduling

Every thread has a priority in the range from **ThreadPriority.Lowest** to **ThreadPriority.Highest**. These two values come from the **ThreadPriority** enumeration (namespace **System.Threading**), which consists of the values **Lowest**, **BelowNormal**, **Normal**, **AboveNormal** and **Highest**. By default, each thread has priority **Normal**. The *thread scheduler* determines when each thread executes based on the thread's priority.

The Windows platform supports a concept called *timeslicing, which* enables threads of equal priority to share a processor. Without timeslicing, each thread in a set of equal-priority threads runs to completion (unless the thread leaves the *Running* state and enters the *WaitSleepJoin*, *Suspended* or *Blocked* state) before the thread's peers get a chance to execute. With timeslicing, each thread receives a brief burst of processor time, called a *quantum*, during which the thread can execute. At the completion of the quantum, even if the thread has not finished executing, the processor is taken away from that thread and given to the next thread of equal priority, if one is available.

The job of the thread scheduler is to keep the highest-priority thread running at all times and, if there is more than one highest-priority thread, to ensure that all such threads execute for a quantum in round-robin fashion. Figure 14.2 illustrates the multilevel priority queue for threads. In Fig. 14.2, assuming that we are using a single-processor computer, threads A and B each execute for a quantum in round-robin fashion until both threads complete execution. This means that A gets a quantum of time to run, then B gets a quantum, then A gets another quantum and B gets another quantum. This continues until one thread completes. The processor then devotes all its power to the thread that remains (unless another thread of that priority is *Started*). Once A and B have finished executing, thread C runs to completion. Next threads D, E and F each execute for a quantum in round-robin fashion until they all complete execution. This process continues until all threads run to completion. Note that, depending on the operating system, new higher-priority threads could postpone—possibly indefinitely—the execution of lower-priority threads. Such *indefinite postponement* often is referred to more colorfully as *starvation*.

A thread's priority can be adjusted via the **Priority** property, which accepts values from the **ThreadPriority** enumeration. If the argument is not one of the valid thread-priority constants, an **ArgumentException** occurs.

A thread executes until it dies, becomes *Blocked* for input/output (or for some other reason), calls **Sleep**, calls **Monitor** methods **Wait** or **Join**, is preempted by a thread of higher priority or has its quantum expire. A thread with a higher priority than the *Running* thread can become *Started* (and hence preempt the *Running* thread) if a sleeping thread wakes up, if I/O completes for a thread that *Blocked* for that I/O, if either **Pulse** or **PulseAll** is called for an object on which a thread is waiting, or if a thread to which the high-priority thread was **Join**ed completes.

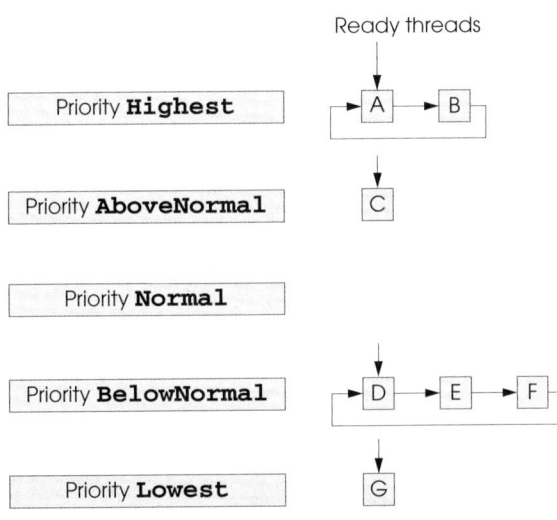

Fig. 14.2 Thread-priority scheduling.

Figure 14.3 and Figure 14.4 demonstrate basic threading techniques, including the construction of a **Thread** object and the use of the **Thread** class's **Shared** method **Sleep**. Module **modThreadTester** (Fig. 14.4) creates three threads that each have default priority **Normal**. Each thread displays a message indicating that it is going to sleep for a random interval between 0 and 5000 milliseconds and then goes to sleep. When each threads awakens, the thread displays message indicating its name and that it is done sleeping and enters the *Stopped* state. Readers will see that method **Main** (i.e., the *Main thread of execution*) terminates before the application terminates. The program consists of one module—**modThreadTester** (Fig. 14.4), which creates the three threads—and one class—**CMessagePrinter** (Fig. 14.3), which defines a **Print** method containing the actions that each thread will perform.

```vb
1   ' Fig. 14.3: MessagePrinter.vb
2   ' Thread control method prints verbose message,
3   ' sleeps and prints waking up verbose message.
4
5   Imports System.Threading
6
7   Public Class CMessagePrinter
8
9      Private sleepTime As Integer
10     Private Shared randomObject As New Random()
11
12     ' constructor to initialize a CMessagePrinter object
13     Public Sub New()
14
15        ' pick random sleep time between 0 and 5 seconds
16        sleepTime = randomObject.Next(5001)
17     End Sub ' New
18
19     ' method Print controls thread that prints messages
20     Public Sub Print()
21
22        ' obtain reference to currently executing thread
23        Dim current As Thread = Thread.CurrentThread
24
25        ' put thread to sleep for sleepTime amount of time
26        Console.WriteLine(current.Name & " going to sleep for " & _
27           sleepTime)
28
29        Thread.Sleep(sleepTime)
30
31        ' print thread name
32        Console.WriteLine(current.Name & " done sleeping")
33     End Sub ' Print
34
35  End Class ' CMessagePrinter
```

Fig. 14.3 **ThreadStart** delegate **Print** displays message and sleeps for arbitrary duration of time.

Objects of class **CMessagePrinter** (Fig. 14.3) control the lifecycle of each of the three threads that module **modThreadTester**'s **Main** method creates. Class **CMessagePrinter** consists of instance variable **sleepTime** (line 9), **Shared** variable **randomObject** (line 10), a constructor (lines 13–17) and a **Print** method (lines 20–33). Variable **sleepTime** stores a random **Integer** value chosen when a new **CMessagePrinter** object's constructor is called. Each thread controlled by a **CMessagePrinter** object sleeps for the amount of time specified by the corresponding **CMessagePrinter** object's **sleepTime**.

The **CMessagePrinter** constructor (lines 13–17) initializes **sleepTime** to a random **Integer** from 0 up to, but not including, 5001 (i.e., from 0 to 5000).

Method **Print** (lines 20–33) begins by obtaining a reference to the currently executing thread (line 23) via class **Thread**'s **Shared** property *CurrentThread*. The currently executing thread is the one that invokes method **Print**. Next, lines 26–27 display a message containing the name of the currently executing thread and an indicaton that the thread is going to sleep for a certain number of milliseconds. Note that line 26 uses the currently executing thread via the thread's **Name** property, which is set in method **Main** (Fig. 14.4, lines 8–35) when each thread is created. Line 29 invokes **Shared Thread** method **Sleep** to place the thread into the *WaitSleepJoin* state. At this point, the thread loses the processor, and the system allows another thread to execute. When the thread awakens, it reenters the *Started* state until the system assigns a processor to the thread. When the **CMessagePrinter** object enters the *Running* state again, line 32 outputs the thread's name in a message that indicates the thread is done sleeping, and method **Print** terminates.

Module **modThreadTester**'s **Main** method (Fig. 14.4, lines 8–35) creates three objects of class **CMessagePrinter**, in lines 11–13. Lines 17–19 create and initialize the three **Thread** objects that correspond to the **CMessagePrinter** objects created. Lines 22–24 set each **Thread**'s **Name** property, which we use for output purposes. Note that each **Thread**'s constructor receives a **ThreadStart** delegate as an argument. Remember that a **ThreadStart** delegate specifies the actions that a thread performs during its lifecycle. Line 17 specifies that the delegate for **thread1** will be method **Print** of the object to which **printer1** refers. When **thread1** enters the *Running* state for the first time, **thread1** invokes **printer1**'s **Print** method to perform the tasks specified in method **Print**'s body. Thus, **thread1** prints its name, displays the amount of time for which it will go to sleep, sleeps for that amount of time, wakes up and displays a message indicating that the thread is done sleeping. At that point, method **Print** terminates. A thread completes its task when the method specified by a **Thread**'s **ThreadStart** delegate terminates, placing the thread in the *Stopped* state. When **thread2** and **thread3** enter the *Running* state for the first time, they invoke the **Print** methods of **printer2** and **printer3**, respectively. Threads **thread2** and **thread3** perform the same tasks that **thread1** performs by executing the **Print** methods of the objects to which **printer2** and **printer3** refer (each of which has its own randomly chosen sleep time).

Testing and Debugging Tip 14.2

*The naming of threads assists in the debugging of a multithreaded program. Visual Studio .NET's debugger provides a **Threads** window that displays the name of each thread and enables programmers to view the execution of any thread in the program.*

Lines 30–32 invoke each **Thread**'s **Start** method to place the threads in the *Started* state (this process sometimes is called *launching a thread*). Method **Start** returns immediately from each invocation; line 34 then outputs a message indicating that the threads were started, and the **Main** thread of execution terminates. The program itself does not terminate, however, because it still contains threads that are alive (i.e., threads that were *Started* and have not reached the *Stopped* state yet). The program will not terminate until its last thread dies. When the system assigns a processor to a thread, the thread enters the *Running* state and calls the method specified by the thread's **ThreadStart** delegate. In this program, each thread invokes method **Print** of the appropriate **CMessagePrinter** object to perform the tasks discussed previously.

Note that the sample outputs for this program display the name and sleep time of each thread as the thread goes to sleep. The thread with the shortest sleep time normally awakens first, then indicates that it is done sleeping and terminates. Section 14.7 discusses multithreading issues that may prevent the thread with the shortest sleep time from awakening first.

```vb
1   ' Fig. 14.4: ThreadTester.vb
2   ' Shows multiple threads that print at different intervals.
3
4   Imports System.Threading
5
6   Module modThreadTester
7
8      Sub Main()
9
10        ' create CMessagePrinter instances
11        Dim printer1 As New CMessagePrinter()
12        Dim printer2 As New CMessagePrinter()
13        Dim printer3 As New CMessagePrinter()
14
15        ' Create each thread. Use CMessagePrinter's
16        ' Print method as argument to ThreadStart delegate
17        Dim thread1 As New Thread(AddressOf printer1.Print)
18        Dim thread2 As New Thread(AddressOf printer2.Print)
19        Dim thread3 As New Thread(AddressOf printer3.Print)
20
21        ' name each thread
22        thread1.Name = "thread1"
23        thread2.Name = "thread2"
24        thread3.Name = "thread3"
25
26        Console.WriteLine("Starting threads")
27
28        ' call each thread's Start method to place each
29        ' thread in Started state
30        thread1.Start()
31        thread2.Start()
32        thread3.Start()
33
34        Console.WriteLine("Threads started" & vbCrLf)
35     End Sub ' Main
36
37   End Module ' modThreadTester
```

Fig. 14.4 Threads sleeping and printing (part 1 of 2).

```
Starting threads
Threads started

thread1 going to sleep for 1977
thread2 going to sleep for 4513
thread3 going to sleep for 1261
thread3 done sleeping
thread1 done sleeping
thread2 done sleeping
```

```
Starting threads
Threads started

thread1 going to sleep for 1466
thread2 going to sleep for 4245
thread3 going to sleep for 1929
thread1 done sleeping
thread3 done sleeping
thread2 done sleeping
```

Fig. 14.4 Threads sleeping and printing (part 2 of 2).

14.4 Thread Synchronization and Class `Monitor`

Often, multiple threads of execution manipulate shared data. If threads that have access to shared data simply read that data, there is no need to prevent the data from being accessed by more than one thread at a time. However, when multiple threads share data and that data is modified by one or more of those threads, then indeterminate results might occur. If one thread is in the process of updating the data and another thread tries to update it too, the data will reflect the most recent update. If the data is an array or other data structure in which the threads could update separate parts of the data concurrently, it is possible that part of the data would reflect the information from one thread, whereas another part of the data would reflect information from a different thread. When this happens, it is difficult for the program to determine whether the data has been updated properly.

Programmers can solve this problem by giving any thread that is manipulating shared data exclusive access to that data during the manipulating. While one thread is manipulating the data, other threads desiring to access the data should be kept waiting. When the thread with exclusive access to the data completes its manipulation of the data, one of the waiting threads should be allowed to proceed. In this fashion, each thread accessing the shared data excludes all other threads from doing so simultaneously. This is called *mutual exclusion,* or *thread synchronization.*

Visual Basic uses the .NET Framework's monitors[2] to perform synchronization. Class **Monitor** provides methods for *locking objects,* which enables the implementation of synchronized access to shared data. The locking of an object means that only one thread can

---

2. Hoare, C. A. R. "Monitors: An Operating System Structuring Concept," *Communications of the ACM.* Vol. 17, No. 10, October 1974: 549–557. *Corrigendum, Communications of the ACM.* Vol. 18, No. 2, February 1975: 95.

access that object at a time. When a thread wishes to acquire exclusive control over an object, the thread invokes **Monitor** method **Enter** to acquire the lock on that data object. Each object has a *SyncBlock* that maintains the state of that object's lock. Methods of class **Monitor** use the data in an object's *SyncBlock* to determine the state of the lock for that object. After acquiring the lock for an object, a thread can manipulate that object's data. While the object is locked, all other threads attempting to acquire the lock on that object are blocked (i.e., they enter the *Blocked* state) from acquiring the lock. When the thread that locked the shared object no longer requires the lock, that thread invokes **Monitor** method **Exit** to release the lock. This updates the *SyncBlock* of the shared object to indicate that the lock for the object is available again. At this point, if there is a thread that was previously blocked from acquiring the lock on the shared object, that thread acquires the lock and can begin its processing of the object. If all threads with access to an object must acquire the object's lock before manipulating the object, only one thread at a time will be allowed to manipulate the object. This helps ensure the integrity of the data.

Common Programming Error 14.1

Make sure that all code that updates a shared object locks the object before doing so. Otherwise, a thread calling a method that does not lock the object can make the object unstable, even when another thread has acquired the lock for the object.

Common Programming Error 14.2

Deadlock occurs when a waiting thread (let us call this thread1*) cannot proceed, because it is waiting for another thread (let us call this* thread2*) to proceed. Similarly,* thread2 *cannot proceed, because it is waiting for* thread1 *to proceed. Because the two threads are waiting for each other, the actions that would enable each thread to continue execution never occur.*

Visual Basic also provides another means of manipulating an object's lock—keyword **SyncLock**. The placement of **SyncLock** before a block of code, as in:

```
SyncLock ( objectReference )
    ' code that requires synchronization goes here
End SyncLock
```

obtains the lock on the object to which the *objectReference* in parentheses refers. The *objectReference* is the same reference that normally would be passed to **Monitor** methods **Enter**, **Exit**, **Pulse** and **PulseAll**. When a **SyncLock** block terminates for any reason, Visual Basic releases the lock on the object to which the *objectReference* refers. We explain **SyncLock** further in Section 14.7.

If a thread determines that it cannot perform its task on a locked object, the thread can call **Monitor** method **Wait**, passing as an argument the object on which the thread will wait until the thread can perform its task. Calling method **Wait** from a thread releases the lock the thread has on the object that method **Wait** receives as an argument. Method **Wait** then places the calling thread into the *WaitSleepJoin* state for that object. A thread in the *WaitSleepJoin* state for an object leaves the *WaitSleepJoin* state when a separate thread invokes **Monitor** method **Pulse** or **PulseAll** with the object as an argument. Method **Pulse** transitions the object's first waiting thread from the *WaitSleepJoin* state to the *Started* state. Method **PulseAll** transitions all threads in the object's *WaitSleepJoin* state to the *Started* state. The transition to the *Started* state enables the thread (or threads) to prepare to continue executing.

There is a difference between threads waiting to acquire the lock for an object and threads waiting in an object's *WaitSleepJoin* state. Threads waiting in an object's *WaitSleepJoin* state call **Monitor** method **Wait** with the object as an argument. By contrast, threads that are waiting to acquire the lock enter the *Blocked* state and wait there until the object's lock becomes available. Then, one of the blocked threads can acquire the object's lock.

Common Programming Error 14.3

A thread in the WaitSleepJoin *state cannot reenter the* Started *state to continue execution until a separate thread invokes* **Monitor** *method* **Pulse** *or* **PulseAll** *with the appropriate object as an argument. If this does not occur, the waiting thread will wait forever and so can cause deadlock.*

Testing and Debugging Tip 14.3

When multiple threads manipulate a shared object using monitors, the programmer should ensure that, if one thread calls **Monitor** *method* **Wait** *to enter the* WaitSleepJoin *state for the shared object, a separate thread eventually will call* **Monitor** *method* **Pulse** *to transition the thread waiting on the shared object back to the* Started *state. If multiple threads might be waiting for the shared object, a separate thread can call* **Monitor** *method* **PulseAll** *as a safeguard to ensure that all waiting threads have another opportunity to perform their tasks.*

Performance Tip 14.3

Synchronization of threads in multithreaded programs can make programs run smore slowly, due to monitor overhead and the frequent transitioning of threads among the Running, *Wait-SleepJoin and* Started *states. There is not much to say, however, for highly efficient, incorrect multithreaded programs!*

Monitor methods **Enter**, **Exit**, **Wait**, **Pulse** and **PulseAll** all take a reference to an object—usually the keyword **Me**—as their argument.

14.5 Producer/Consumer Relationship without Thread Synchronization

In a *producer/consumer relationship*, the *producer* portion of an application generates data, and the *consumer* portion of the application uses that data. In a multithreaded producer/consumer relationship, a *producer thread* calls a *produce method* to generate data and place it into a shared region of memory, called a *buffer*. A *consumer thread* then calls a *consume method* to read that data. If the producer waiting to put the next data into the buffer determines that the consumer has not yet read the previous data from the buffer, the producer thread should call **Wait**; otherwise, the consumer never sees the previous data, and that data is lost to the application. When the consumer thread reads the data, it should call **Pulse** to allow a waiting producer to proceed. If a consumer thread finds the buffer empty or determines that it has already read the data in the buffer, the consumer should call **Wait**; otherwise, the consumer might read "garbage" from the buffer, or the consumer might process a previous data item more than once. Any of these possibilities results in a logic error in the application. When the producer places the next data into the buffer, the producer should call **Pulse** to allow the consumer thread to proceed.

Now, let us consider how logic errors can arise if we do not synchronize access among multiple threads manipulating shared data. Imagine a producer/consumer relationship in which a producer thread writes a sequence of numbers (we use 1–4) into a *shared buffer*— a memory location shared among multiple threads. The consumer thread reads this data from the shared buffer and then displays the data. We display in the program's output the values that the producer writes (produces) and that the consumer reads (consumes). Figure 14.8 demonstrates a producer and a consumer accessing a single shared cell (**Integer** variable **mBuffer**, Fig. 14.5 line 9) of memory without any synchronization. Both the consumer and the producer threads access this single cell: The producer thread writes to the cell, whereas the consumer thread reads from it. We would like each value that the producer thread writes to the shared cell to be consumed exactly once by the consumer thread. However, the threads in this example are not synchronized. Therefore, data can be lost if the producer places new data into the slot before the consumer consumes the previous data. In addition, data can be incorrectly repeated if the consumer consumes data again before the producer produces the next item. To illustrate these possibilities, the consumer thread in the following example keeps a total of all the values it reads. The producer thread produces values from 1 to 4. If the consumer reads each value once and only once, the total would be 10. However, if students execute this program several times, they will see that the total is rarely, if ever, 10. To emphasize our point, the producer and consumer threads in the example each sleep for random intervals of up to three seconds between performing their tasks. Thus, we do not know exactly when the producer thread will attempt to write a new value, nor do we know when the consumer thread will attempt to read a value.

The program consists of module **modSharedCell** (Fig. 14.8) and three classes—**CHoldIntegerUnsynchronized** (Fig. 14.5), **CProducer** (Fig. 14.6) and **CConsumer** (Fig. 14.7).

Class **CHoldIntegerUnsynchronized** (Fig. 14.5) consists of instance variable **mBuffer** (line 9) and property **Buffer** (lines 12–28), which provides **Get** and **Set** accessors. Property **Buffer**'s accessors do not synchronize access to instance variable **mBuffer**. Note that each accessor uses class **Thread**'s **Shared** property **CurrentThread** to obtain a reference to the currently executing thread and then uses that thread's property **Name** to obtain the thread's name.

```
1    ' Fig. 14.5: HoldIntegerUnsynchronized.vb
2    ' Definition of a shared integer without synchronization mechanisms.
3
4    Imports System.Threading
5
6    Public Class CHoldIntegerUnsynchronized
7
8       ' buffer shared by producer and consumer threads
9       Private mBuffer As Integer = -1
10
11      ' property Buffer
12      Property Buffer() As Integer
13
14         Get
15            Console.WriteLine(Thread.CurrentThread.Name & _
16               " reads " & mBuffer)
17
18            Return mBuffer
19         End Get
```

Fig. 14.5 Unsynchronized shared **Integer** buffer (part 1 of 2).

```
20
21          Set(ByVal Value As Integer)
22             Console.WriteLine(Thread.CurrentThread.Name & _
23                " writes " & Value)
24
25             mBuffer = Value
26          End Set
27
28       End Property ' Buffer
29
30    End Class ' CHoldIntegerUnsynchronized
```

Fig. 14.5 Unsynchronized shared **Integer** buffer (part 2 of 2).

Class **CProducer** (Fig. 14.6) consists of instance variable **sharedLocation** (line 8), instance variable **randomSleepTime** (line 9), a constructor (lines 12–17) to initialize the instance variables and a **Produce** method (lines 20–33). The constructor initializes instance variable **sharedLocation** so that it refers to the **CHoldIntegerUnsynchronized** object received from method **Main**. The producer thread in this program executes the tasks specified in method **Produce** of class **CProducer**. Method **Produce** contains a **For** structure (lines 25–28) that loops four times. Each iteration of the loop first invokes **Thread** method **Sleep** to place the producer thread into the *WaitSleepJoin* state for a random time interval of between 0 and 3 seconds (line 26). When the thread awakens, line 27 assigns the value of control variable **count** to the **CHoldIntegerUnsynchronized** object's **Buffer** property, which causes the **Set** accessor of **CHoldIntegerUnsynchronized** to modify the **mBuffer** instance variable of the **CHoldIntegerUnsynchronized** object. When the loop completes, lines 30–32 display a line of text in the command window to indicate that the thread finished producing data and is terminating. Then, the **Produce** method terminates, placing the producer thread in the *Stopped* state.

```
1   ' Fig. 14.6: Producer.vb
2   ' Produces integers from 1 to 4 and places them in
3   ' unsynchronized buffer.
4
5   Imports System.Threading
6
7   Public Class CProducer
8      Private sharedLocation As CHoldIntegerUnsynchronized
9      Private randomSleepTime As Random
10
11     ' constructor
12     Public Sub New(ByVal sharedObject As _
13        CHoldIntegerUnsynchronized, ByVal randomObject As Random)
14
15        sharedLocation = sharedObject
16        randomSleepTime = randomObject
17     End Sub ' New
18
```

Fig. 14.6 Producer places **Integer**s in unsynchronized shared buffer (part 1 of 2).

```
19        ' store values 1-4 in object sharedLocation
20        Public Sub Produce()
21           Dim count As Integer
22
23           ' sleep for random interval up to 3000 milliseconds
24           ' set sharedLocation's Buffer property
25           For count = 1 To 4
26              Thread.Sleep(randomSleepTime.Next(3000))
27              sharedLocation.Buffer = count
28           Next
29
30           Console.WriteLine(Thread.CurrentThread.Name & _
31              " done producing." & vbCrLf & "Terminating " & _
32              Thread.CurrentThread.Name & ".")
33        End Sub ' Produce
34
35     End Class ' CProducer
```

Fig. 14.6 Producer places **Integer**s in unsynchronized shared buffer (part 2 of 2).

Class **CConsumer** (Fig. 14.7) consists of instance variable **sharedLocation** (line 7), instance variable **randomSleepTime** (line 8), a constructor (lines 11–16) to initialize the instance variables and a **Consume** method (lines 19–32). The constructor initializes **sharedLocation** so that it refers to the **CHoldIntegerUnsynchronized** received from **Main** as the argument **sharedObject**. The consumer thread in this program performs the tasks specified in class **CConsumer**'s **Consume** method. The method contains a **For** structure (lines 24–27) that loops four times. Each iteration of the loop invokes **Thread** method **Sleep** to put the consumer thread into the *WaitSleepJoin* state for a random time interval of between 0 and 3 seconds (line 25). Next, line 26 gets the value of the **CHoldIntegerUnsynchronized** object's **Buffer** property and adds the value to the variable **sum**. When the loop completes, lines 29–31 display a line in the command window indicating the sum of all values that were read. Then the **Consume** method terminates, placing the consumer thread in the *Stopped* state.

```
1     ' Fig. 14.7: Consumer.vb
2     ' Consumes 4 integers from unsynchronized buffer.
3
4     Imports System.Threading
5
6     Public Class CConsumer
7        Private sharedLocation As CHoldIntegerUnsynchronized
8        Private randomSleepTime As Random
9
10       ' constructor
11       Public Sub New(ByVal sharedObject As _
12          CHoldIntegerUnsynchronized, ByVal randomObject As Random)
13
14          sharedLocation = sharedObject
15          randomSleepTime = randomObject
16       End Sub ' New
```

Fig. 14.7 Consumer reads **Integer**s from unsynchronized shared buffer (part 1 of 2).

```
17
18       ' store values 1-4 in object sharedLocation
19       Public Sub Consume()
20          Dim count, sum As Integer
21
22          ' sleep for random interval up to 3000 milliseconds
23          ' then add sharedLocation's Buffer property value to sum
24          For count = 1 To 4
25             Thread.Sleep(randomSleepTime.Next(3000))
26             sum += sharedLocation.Buffer
27          Next
28
29          Console.WriteLine(Thread.CurrentThread.Name & _
30             " read values totaling: " & sum & "." & vbCrLf & _
31             "Terminating " & Thread.CurrentThread.Name & ".")
32       End Sub ' Consume
33
34    End Class ' CConsumer
```

Fig. 14.7 Consumer reads **Integer**s from unsynchronized shared buffer (part 2 of 2).

Note: We use method **Sleep** in this example to emphasize the fact that, in multithreaded applications, it is unclear when each thread will perform its task and how long it will take to perform that task when it has the processor. Normally, dealing with these thread-scheduling issues is the job of the computer's operating system. In this program, our thread's tasks are quite simple—the producer must loop four times and perform an assignment statement;the consumer must loop four times and add a value to variable **sum**. If we omit the **Sleep** method call, and if the producer executes first, the producer would complete its task before the consumer ever gets a chance to execute. In the same situation, if the consumer executes first, it would consume **-1** four times and then terminate before the producer can produce the first real value.

Module **modSharedCell**'s **Main** method (Fig. 14.8) instantiates a shared **CHoldIntegerUnsynchronized** object (line 14) and a **Random** object (line 17) for generating random sleep times; it then passes these objects as arguments to the constructors for the objects of classes **CProducer** (**producer**, line 20) and **CConsumer** (**consumer**, line 21). The **CHoldIntegerUnsynchronized** object contains the data that will be shared between the producer and consumer threads. Line 25 creates **producerThread**. The **ThreadStart** delegate for **producerThread** specifies that the thread will execute method **Produce** of object **producer**. Line 26 creates the **consumerThread**. The **ThreadStart** delegate for the **consumerThread** specifies that the thread will execute method **Consume** of object **consumer**. Lines 29–30 name threads **producerThread** and **consumerThread**. Finally, lines 33–34 place the two threads in the *Started* state by invoking each thread's **Start** method. Then, the **Main** thread terminates.

Ideally, we would like every value produced by the **CProducer** object to be consumed exactly once by the **CConsumer** object. However, when we study the first output of Fig. 14.8, we see that the consumer retrieved a value (**-1**) before the producer ever placed a value in the shared buffer, and that the value **1** was consumed three times. The consumer finished executing before the producer had an opportunity to produce the values **2**, **3** and **4**. Therefore, those three values were lost. In the second output, we see that the

```vb
1   ' Fig. 14.8: SharedCell.vb
2   ' Creates producer and consumer threads which interact
3   ' with each other through common CHoldIntegerUnsynchronized
4   ' object.
5
6   Imports System.Threading
7
8   Module modSharedCell
9
10     ' create producer and consumer threads and start
11     Sub Main()
12
13        ' create shared object used by threads
14        Dim holdInteger As New CHoldIntegerUnsynchronized()
15
16        ' Random object used by each thread
17        Dim randomObject As New Random()
18
19        ' create Producer and Consumer objects
20        Dim producer As New CProducer(holdInteger, randomObject)
21        Dim consumer As New CConsumer(holdInteger, randomObject)
22
23        ' create threads for producer and consumer
24        ' set delegates for each thread
25        Dim producerThread As New Thread(AddressOf producer.Produce)
26        Dim consumerThread As New Thread(AddressOf consumer.Consume)
27
28        ' name each thread
29        producerThread.Name = "Producer"
30        consumerThread.Name = "Consumer"
31
32        ' start each thread
33        producerThread.Start()
34        consumerThread.Start()
35     End Sub ' Main
36
37   End Module ' modSharedCell
```

```
Consumer reads -1
Producer writes 1
Consumer reads 1
Consumer reads 1
Consumer reads 1
Consumer read values totaling: 2.
Terminating Consumer.
Producer writes 2
Producer writes 3
Producer writes 4
Producer done producing.
Terminating Producer.
```

Fig. 14.8 Producer and consumer threads accessing a shared object without synchronization (part 1 of 2).

```
Producer writes 1
Producer writes 2
Consumer reads 2
Producer writes 3
Consumer reads 3
Producer writes 4
Producer done producing.
Terminating Producer.
Consumer reads 4
Consumer reads 4
Consumer read values totaling: 13.
Terminating Consumer.
```

```
Producer writes 1
Consumer reads 1
Producer writes 2
Consumer reads 2
Producer writes 3
Consumer reads 3
Producer writes 4
Producer done producing.
Terminating Producer.
Consumer reads 4
Consumer read values totaling: 10.
Terminating Consumer.
```

Fig. 14.8 Producer and consumer threads accessing a shared object without synchronization (part 2 of 2).

value **1** was lost, because the values **1** and **2** were produced before the consumer thread could read the value **1**. In addition, the value **4** was consumed twice. The last sample output demonstrates that it is possible, with some luck, to achieve a proper output, in which each value that the producer produces is consumed once and only once by the consumer. This example clearly demonstrates that access to shared data by concurrent threads must be controlled carefully; otherwise, a program might produce incorrect results.

sTo solve the problems that occur in the previous example regarding lost and repeatedly consumed data, we will (in Fig. 14.9) synchronize the concurrent producer and consumer threads access to the shared data by using **Monitor** class methods **Enter**, **Wait**, **Pulse** and **Exit**. When a thread uses synchronization to access a shared object, the object is *locked*, and no other thread can acquire the lock for that shared object until the thread holding the lock releases it.

14.6 Producer/Consumer Relationship with Thread Synchronization

Figure 14.12 demonstrates a producer and a consumer accessing a shared cell of memory with synchronization. The consumer consumes only after the producer produces a value, and the producer produces a new value only after the consumer consumes the previously produced value. Classes **CProducer** (Fig. 14.10), **CConsumer** (Fig. 14.11) and module

modSharedCell (Fig. 14.12) are identical to those in Fig. 14.6, Fig. 14.7 and Fig. 14.8, respectively, except that they use the new class **CHoldIntegerSynchronized** (Fig. 14.9). [Note: In this example, we demonstrate synchronization with class **Monitor**'s **Enter** and **Exit** methods. In the next example, we demonstrate the same concepts using a **SyncLock** block.]

```vb
1   ' Fig. 14.9: HoldIntegerSynchronized.vb
2   ' Synchronizes access to an Integer.
3
4   Imports System.Threading
5
6   Public Class CHoldIntegerSynchronized
7
8      ' buffer shared by producer and consumer threads
9      Private mBuffer As Integer = -1
10
11     ' occupiedBufferCount maintains count of occupied buffers
12     Private occupiedBufferCount As Integer
13
14     Public Property Buffer() As Integer
15
16        Get
17
18           ' obtain lock on this object
19           Monitor.Enter(Me)
20
21           ' if there is no data to read, place invoking
22           ' thread in WaitSleepJoin state
23           If occupiedBufferCount = 0 Then
24              Console.WriteLine(Thread.CurrentThread.Name & _
25                 " tries to read.")
26
27              DisplayState("Buffer empty. " & _
28                 Thread.CurrentThread.Name & " waits.")
29
30              Monitor.Wait(Me)
31           End If
32
33           ' indicate that producer can store another value
34           ' because consumer just retrieved buffer value
35           occupiedBufferCount -= 1
36
37           DisplayState(Thread.CurrentThread.Name & " reads " & _
38              mBuffer)
39
40           ' tell waiting thread (if there is one) to
41           ' become ready to execute (Started state)
42           Monitor.Pulse(Me)
43
44           ' Get copy of buffer before releasing lock.
45           ' It is possible that the producer could be
46           ' assigned the processor immediately after the
```

Fig. 14.9 Synchronized shared **Integer** buffer (part 1 of 3).

```vb
47              ' monitor is released and before the return
48              ' statement executes. In this case, the producer
49              ' would assign a new value to buffer before the
50              ' return statement returns the value to the
51              ' consumer. Thus, the consumer would receive the
52              ' new value. Making a copy of buffer and
53              ' returning the copy helps ensure that the
54              ' consumer receives the proper value.
55              Dim bufferCopy As Integer = mBuffer
56
57              ' release lock on this object
58              Monitor.Exit(Me)
59
60              Return bufferCopy
61          End Get
62
63          Set(ByVal Value As Integer)
64
65              ' acquire lock for this object
66              Monitor.Enter(Me)
67
68              ' if there are no empty locations, place invoking
69              ' thread in WaitSleepJoin state
70              If occupiedBufferCount = 1 Then
71                  Console.WriteLine(Thread.CurrentThread.Name & _
72                      " tries to write.")
73
74                  DisplayState("Buffer full. " & _
75                      Thread.CurrentThread.Name & " waits.")
76
77                  Monitor.Wait(Me)
78              End If
79
80              ' set new buffer value
81              mBuffer = Value
82
83              ' indicate producer cannot store another value
84              ' until consumer retrieves current buffer value
85              occupiedBufferCount += 1
86
87              DisplayState(Thread.CurrentThread.Name & " writes " & _
88                  mBuffer)
89
90              ' tell waiting thread (if there is one) to
91              ' become ready to execute (Started state)
92              Monitor.Pulse(Me)
93
94              ' release lock on this object
95              Monitor.Exit(Me)
96          End Set
97
98      End Property ' Buffer
99
```

Fig. 14.9 Synchronized shared **Integer** buffer (part 2 of 3).

```vb
100     Public Sub DisplayState(ByVal operation As String)
101        Console.WriteLine("{0,-35}{1,-9}{2}" & vbCrLf, _
102           operation, mBuffer, occupiedBufferCount)
103     End Sub ' DisplayState
104
105  End Class ' CHoldIntegerSynchronized
```

Fig. 14.9 Synchronized shared `Integer` buffer (part 3 of 3).

```vb
1   ' Fig. 14.10: Producer.vb
2   ' Produce 4 integers and place them in synchronized buffer.
3
4   Imports System.Threading
5
6   Public Class CProducer
7      Private sharedLocation As CHoldIntegerSynchronized
8      Private randomSleepTime As Random
9
10     ' constructor
11     Public Sub New(ByVal sharedObject As _
12        CHoldIntegerSynchronized, ByVal randomObject As Random)
13
14        sharedLocation = sharedObject
15        randomSleepTime = randomObject
16     End Sub ' New
17
18     ' store values 1-4 in object sharedLocation
19     Public Sub Produce()
20        Dim count As Integer
21
22        ' sleep for random interval up to 3000 milliseconds
23        ' set sharedLocation's Buffer property
24        For count = 1 To 4
25           Thread.Sleep(randomSleepTime.Next(3000))
26           sharedLocation.Buffer = count
27        Next
28
29        Console.WriteLine(Thread.CurrentThread.Name & _
30           " done producing. " & vbCrLf & "Terminating " & _
31           Thread.CurrentThread.Name & "." & vbCrLf)
32     End Sub ' Produce
33
34  End Class ' CProducer
```

Fig. 14.10 Producer places `Integer`s in synchronized shared buffer.

```vb
1   ' Fig. 14.11: Consumer.vb
2   ' Consumes 4 Integers from synchronized buffer.
3
4   Imports System.Threading
5
```

Fig. 14.11 Consumer reads `Integer`s from synchronized shared buffer (part 1 of 2).

```vbnet
 6   Public Class CConsumer
 7      Private sharedLocation As CHoldIntegerSynchronized
 8      Private randomSleepTime As Random
 9
10      ' constructor
11      Public Sub New(ByVal sharedObject As _
12         CHoldIntegerSynchronized, ByVal randomObject As Random)
13
14         sharedLocation = sharedObject
15         randomSleepTime = randomObject
16      End Sub ' New
17
18      ' read sharedLocation's value four times
19      Public Sub Consume()
20         Dim count, sum As Integer
21
22         ' sleep for random interval up to 3000 milliseconds
23         ' add sharedLocation's Buffer property value to sum
24         For count = 1 To 4
25            Thread.Sleep(randomSleepTime.Next(3000))
26            sum += sharedLocation.Buffer
27         Next
28
29         Console.WriteLine(Thread.CurrentThread.Name & _
30            " read values totaling: " & sum & "." & vbCrLf & _
31            "Terminating " & Thread.CurrentThread.Name & "." & _
32            vbCrLf)
33      End Sub ' Consume
34
35   End Class ' CConsumer
```

Fig. 14.11 Consumer reads **Integer**s from synchronized shared buffer (part 2 of 2).

```vbnet
 1   ' Fig. 14.12: SharedCell.vb
 2   ' Create producer and consumer threads.
 3
 4   Imports System.Threading
 5
 6   Module modSharedCell
 7
 8      Sub Main()
 9
10         ' create shared object used by threads
11         Dim holdInteger As New CHoldIntegerSynchronized()
12
13         ' Random object used by each thread
14         Dim randomObject As New Random()
15
16         ' create CProducer and CConsumer objects
17         Dim producer As New CProducer(holdInteger, randomObject)
18         Dim consumer As New CConsumer(holdInteger, randomObject)
```

Fig. 14.12 Producer and consumer threads accessing a shared object with synchronization (part 1 of 3).

```vb
19
20          Console.WriteLine("{0,-35}{1,-9}{2}" & vbCrLf, _
21              "Operation", "Buffer", "Occupied Count")
22
23          holdInteger.DisplayState("Initial State")
24
25          ' create threads for producer and consumer
26          ' set delegates for each thread
27          Dim producerThread As _
28              New Thread(AddressOf producer.Produce)
29
30          Dim consumerThread As _
31              New Thread(AddressOf consumer.Consume)
32
33          ' name each thread
34          producerThread.Name = "Producer"
35          consumerThread.Name = "Consumer"
36
37          ' start each thread
38          producerThread.Start()
39          consumerThread.Start()
40      End Sub ' Main
41
42  End Module ' modSharedCell
```

Operation	Buffer	Occupied Count
Initial state	-1	0
Producer writes 1	1	1
Consumer reads 1	1	0
Consumer tries to read. Buffer empty. Consumer waits.	1	0
Producer writes 2	2	1
Consumer reads 2	2	0
Producer writes 3	3	1
Producer tries to write. Buffer full. Producer waits.	3	1
Consumer reads 3	3	0
Producer writes 4	4	1
Producer done producing. Terminating Producer.		
Consumer reads 4	4	0
Consumer read values totaling: 10. Terminating Consumer.		

Fig. 14.12 Producer and consumer threads accessing a shared object with synchronization (part 2 of 3).

```
Operation                              Buffer    Occupied Count
Initial state                          -1        0
Consumer tries to read.
Buffer empty. Consumer waits.          -1        0
Producer writes 1                      1         1
Consumer reads 1                       1         0
Producer writes 2                      2         1
Consumer reads 2                       2         0
Producer writes 3                      3         1
Producer tries to write.
Buffer full. Producer waits.           3         1
Consumer reads 3                       3         0
Producer writes 4                      4         1
Producer done producing.
Terminating Producer.
Consumer reads 4                       4         0
Consumer read values totaling: 10.
Terminating Consumer.
```

```
Operation                              Buffer    Occupied Count
Initial state                          -1        0
Producer writes 1                      1         1
Consumer reads 1                       1         0
Producer writes 2                      2         1
Consumer reads 2                       2         0
Producer writes 3                      3         1
Consumer reads 3                       3         0
Producer writes 4                      4         1
Producer done producing.
Terminating Producer.
Consumer reads 4                       4         0
Consumer read values totaling: 10.
Terminating Consumer.
```

Fig. 14.12 Producer and consumer threads accessing a shared object with synchronization (part 3 of 3).

Class **CHoldIntegerSynchronized** (Fig. 14.9) contains two instance variables—**mBuffer** (line 9) and **occupiedBufferCount** (line 12). Property **Buffer**'s **Get** (lines 16–61) and **Set** (lines 63–96) accessors now use methods of class **Monitor** to synchronize access to property **Buffer**. Thus, each object of class **CHoldIntegerSynchronized** has a *SyncBlock* to maintain synchronization. Instance variable **occupiedBufferCount** is known as a *condition variable*—property **Buffer**'s accessors use this **Integer** in conditions to determine whether it is the producer's turn to perform a task or the consumer's turn to perform a task. If **occupiedBufferCount** is **0**, property **Buffer**'s **Set** accessor can place a value into variable **mBuffer**, because the variable currently does not contain information. However, this means that property **Buffer**'s **Get** accessor currently cannot read the value of **mBuffer**. If **occupiedBufferCount** is **1**, the **Buffer** property's **Get** accessor can read a value from variable **mBuffer**, because the variable currently contains information. In this case, property **Buffer**'s **Set** accessor currently cannot place a value into **mBuffer**.

As in Fig. 14.6, the producer thread (Fig. 14.10) performs the tasks specified in the **producer** object's **Produce** method. When line 26 sets the value of **CHoldIntegerSynchronized** property **Buffer**, the producer thread invokes the **Set** accessor in lines 63–96 (Fig. 14.9). Line 66 invokes **Monitor** method **Enter** to acquire the lock on the **CHoldIntegerSynchronized** object. The **If** structure in lines 70–78 then determines whether **occupiedBufferCount** is **1**. If this condition is **True**, lines 71–72 output a message indicating that the producer thread tried to write a value, and lines 74–75 invoke method **DisplayState** (lines 100–103) to output another message indicating that the buffer is full and that the producer thread waits. Line 77 invokes **Monitor** method **Wait** to place the calling thread (i.e., the producer) in the *WaitSleepJoin* state for the **CHoldIntegerSynchronized** object and releases the lock on the object. The *WaitSleepJoin* state for an object is maintained by that object's *SyncBlock*. Now, another thread can invoke an accessor method of the **CHoldIntegerSynchronized** object's **Buffer** property.

The producer thread remains in state *WaitSleepJoin* until the thread is notified that it can proceed—at which point the thread returns to the *Started* state and waits to be assigned a processor. When the thread returns to the *Running* state, the thread implicitly reacquires the lock on the **CHoldIntegerSynchronized** object, and the **Set** accessor continues executing with the next statement after **Wait**. Line 81 assigns **Value** to **mBuffer**. Line 85 increments the **occupiedBufferCount** to indicate that the shared buffer now contains a value (i.e., a consumer can read the value, and a producer cannot yet put another value there). Lines 87–88 invoke method **DisplayState** to output a line to the command window indicating that the producer is writing a new value into the **mBuffer**. Line 92 invokes **Monitor** method **Pulse** with the **CHoldIntegerSynchronized** object as an argument. If there are any waiting threads in that object's *SyncBlock*, the first waiting thread enters the *Started* state; this thread can attempt its task again as soon as the thread is assigned a processor. The **Pulse** method returns immediately. Line 95 invokes **Monitor** method **Exit** to release the lock on the **CHoldIntegerSynchronized** object, and the **Set** accessor returns to its caller.

Common Programming Error 14.4
Failure to release the lock on an object when that lock is no longer needed is a logic error. This will prevent other threads that require the lock from acquiring the lock and proceeding with their tasks. These threads will be forced to wait (unnecessarily, because the lock is no longer needed). Such waiting can lead to deadlock and indefinite postponement.

The **Get** and **Set** accessors are implemented similarly. As in Fig. 14.7, the consumer thread (Fig. 14.11) performs the tasks specified in the **consumer** object's **Consume** method. The consumer thread gets the value of the **CHoldIntegerSynchronized** object's **Buffer** property (Fig. 14.11, line 26) by invoking the **Get** accessor at Fig. 14.9, lines 16–61. In Fig. 14.9, line 19 invokes **Monitor** method **Enter** to acquire the lock on the **CHoldIntegerSynchronized** object.

The **If** structure in lines 23–31 determines whether **occupiedBufferCount** is **0**. If this condition is **True**, lines 24–25 output a message indicating that the consumer thread tried to read a value, and lines 27–28 invoke method **DisplayState** to output another message indicating that the buffer is empty and that the consumer thread waits. Line 30 invokes **Monitor** method **Wait** to place the calling thread (i.e., the consumer) in the *WaitSleepJoin* state for the **CHoldIntegerSynchronized** object and releases the lock on the object. Now, another thread can invoke an accessor method of the **CHoldIntegerSynchronized** object's **Buffer** property.

The consumer thread object remains in the *WaitSleepJoin* state until the thread is notified that it can proceed—at which point the thread returns to the *Started* state and waits for the system to assign a processor to the thread. When the thread reenters the *Running* state, the thread implicitly reacquires the lock on the **CHoldIntegerSynchronized** object, and the **Get** accessor continues executing with the next statement after **Wait**. Line 35 decrements **occupiedBufferCount** to indicate that the shared buffer now is empty (i.e., a consumer cannot read the value, but a producer can place another value into the shared buffer). Lines 37–38 output a line to the command window specifying the value that the consumer is reading, and line 42 invokes **Monitor** method **Pulse** with the **CHoldIntegerSynchronized** object as an argument. If there are any waiting threads in that object's *SyncBlock*, the first waiting thread enters the *Started* state, indicating that the thread can attempt its task again as soon as the thread is assigned a processor. The **Pulse** method returns immediately. Line 55 creates a copy of **mBuffer** before releasing lock. It is possible that the producer could be assigned the processor immediately after the lock is released (line 58) and before the **Return** statement executes (line 60). In this case, the producer would assign a new value to **mBuffer** before the **Return** statement returns the value to the consumer. Thus, the consumer would receive the new value. By, making a copy of **mBuffer** and returning the copy, we ensure that the consumer receives the proper value. Line 58 invokes **Monitor** method **Exit** to release the lock on the **CHoldIntegerSynchronized** object, and the **Get** accessor returns **bufferCopy** to its caller.

Study the outputs depicted in Fig. 14.12. Observe that every **Integer** produced is consumed exactly once—no values are lost, and no values are consumed more than once. This occurs because the producer and consumer cannot perform tasks unless it is "their turn." The producer must go first; the consumer must wait if the producer has not produced a value since the consumer last consumed; and the producer must wait if the consumer has not yet consumed the value that the producer most recently produced. Execute this program several times to confirm that every **Integer** produced is consumed exactly once.

In the first and second sample outputs, notice the lines indicating when the producer and consumer must wait to perform their respective tasks. In the third sample output, notice that the producer and consumer were able to perform their tasks without waiting.

14.7 Producer/Consumer Relationship: Circular Buffer

Figure 14.9 uses thread synchronization to guarantee that two threads correctly manipulate data in a shared buffer. However, the application might not perform optimally. If the two threads operate at different speeds, one of the threads will spend more (or most) of its time waiting. For example, in Fig. 14.12, we shared a single **Integer** between the two threads. If the producer thread produces values faster than the consumer can consume those values, then the producer thread waits for the consumer, because there are no other memory locations in which to place the next value. Similarly, if the consumer consumes faster than the producer can produce values, the consumer waits until the producer places the next value into the shared location in memory. Even when we have threads that operate at the same relative speeds, over a period of time, those threads could become "out of sync," causing one of the threads to wait for the other. We cannot make assumptions about the relative speeds of asynchronous concurrent threads. Too many interactions occur among the operating system, the network, the user and other components, and these interactions can cause the threads to operate a different speeds. When this happens, threads wait. When threads wait, programs become less productive, user-interactive programs become less responsive and network applications suffer longer delays.

To minimize waiting by threads that share resources and operate at the same relative speeds, we can implement a *circular buffer*, which provides extra buffers into which the producer can place values and from which the consumer can retrieve those values. Let us assume the buffer is implemented as an array. The producer and consumer work from the beginning of the array. When either thread reaches the end of the array, it simply returns to the first element of the array to perform its next task. If the producer temporarily produces values faster than the consumer can consume them, the producer can write additional values into the extra buffers (if cells are available). This enables the producer to perform its task, even though the consumer is not ready to receive the value currently being produced. Similarly, if the consumer consumes faster than the producer produces new values, the consumer can read additional values from the buffer (if there are any). This enables the consumer to perform its task, even though the producer is not ready to produce additional values.

Readers should note that the circular buffer would be inappropriate if the producer and consumer operate at different speeds. If the consumer always executes faster than the producer, then a buffer with one location would suffice. Additional locations would waste memory. If the producer always executes faster, a buffer with an infinite number of locations would be required to absorb the extra production.

The key to using a circular buffer is to define it with enough extra cells so that it can handle the expected "extra" production. If, over a period of time, we determine that the producer often produces as many as three more values than the consumer can consume, we can define a buffer of at least three cells to handle the extra production. We do not want the buffer to be too small, because that would result in waiting threads. On the other hand, we do not want the buffer to be too large, because that would waste memory.

Performance Tip 14.4

Even when using a circular buffer, it is possible that a producer thread could fill the buffer, which would force the producer thread to wait until a consumer consumes a value to free an element in the buffer. Similarly, if the buffer is empty at any given time, the consumer thread must wait until the producer produces another value. The key to using a circular buffer to optimize the buffer size, thus minimizing the amount of thread-wait time.

Figure 14.16 demonstrates a producer and a consumer accessing a circular buffer (in this case, a shared array of three cells) with synchronization. In this version of the producer/consumer relationship, the consumer consumes a value only when the array is not empty, and the producer produces a value only when the array is not full. This program is implemented as a Windows application that sends its output to a **TextBox**. Classes **CProducer** (Fig. 14.14) and **CConsumer** (Fig. 14.15) perform the same tasks as in Fig. 14.10 and Fig. 14.11, respectively, except that they output messages to the **TextBox** in the application window. The statements that created and started the thread objects in the **Main** methods of module **modSharedCell** (Fig. 14.8 and Fig. 14.12) now appear in module **modCircularBuffer** (Fig. 14.16), where the **Load** event handler (lines 15–50) performs the statements.

The most significant differences between this and the previous synchronized example occur in class **CHoldIntegerSynchronized** (Fig. 14.13), which now contains five instance variables. Array **mBuffer** is a three-element **Integer** array that represents the circular buffer. Variable **occupiedBufferCount** is the condition variable used to determine whether a producer can write into the circular buffer (i.e., **occupiedBufferCount** is less than the number of elements in array **mBuffer**) and whether a consumer can read from the circular buffer (i.e., **occupiedBufferCount** is greater than **0**). Variable **readLocation** indicates the position from which the next value can be read by a consumer. Variable **writeLocation** indicates the next location in which a value can be placed by a producer. The program displays output in **txtOutput** (a **TextBox** control).

The **Set** accessor (lines 73–115) of property **Buffer** performs the same tasks that it did in Fig. 14.9, but with a few modifications. Rather than using **Monitor** methods **Enter** and **Exit** to acquire and release the lock on the **CHoldIntegerSynchronized** object, we use a block of code preceded by keyword **SyncLock** (line 77) to lock the **CHoldIntegerSynchronized** object. As program control enters the **SyncLock** block, the currently executing thread acquires the lock (assuming the lock currently is available) on the **CHoldIntegerSynchronized** object (i.e., **Me**). When the **SyncLock** block terminates, the thread releases the lock automatically.

Common Programming Error 14.5

*When using class **Monitor**'s **Enter** and **Exit** methods to manage an object's lock, **Exit** must be called explicitly to release the lock. If an exception occurs in a method before **Exit** can be called and that exception is not caught, the method could terminate without calling **Exit**. If so, the lock is not released. To avoid this error, place code that might throw exceptions in a **Try** block, and then place the call to **Exit** in the corresponding **Finally** block. This ensures that the lock is released.*

*Using a **SyncLock** block to manage the lock on a synchronized object eliminates the possibility of forgetting to release the lock via a call to **Monitor** method **Exit**. When a **SyncLock** block terminates for any reason, Visual Basic implicitly calls **Monitor** method **Exit**. Thus, even if an exception occurs in the block, the lock will be released.*

The **If** structure in lines 81–88 of the **Set** accessor determines whether the producer must wait (i.e., all buffers are full). If the producer thread must wait, lines 82–83 append text to the **txtOutput** indicating that the producer is waiting to perform its task, and line 87 invokes **Monitor** method **Wait** to place the producer thread in the *WaitSleepJoin* state of the **CHoldIntegerSynchronized** object. When execution continues at line 92 after the **If** structure, the value written by the producer is placed in the circular buffer at location **writeLocation**. Next, lines 94–96 append to the **TextBox** a message containing the produced value. Line 100 increments **occupiedBufferCount**, because the buffer now contains at least one value that the consumer can read. Then, lines 104–105 update **writeLocation** for the next call to the **Set** accessor of property **Buffer**. In line 107 method **CreateStateOutput** (lines 120–165) creates output indicating the number of occupied buffers, the contents of the buffers and the current **writeLocation** and **readLocation**. Finally, line 112 invokes **Monitor** method **Pulse** to indicate that a thread waiting on the **CHoldIntegerSynchronized** object (if there is a waiting thread) should transition to the *Started* state. Note that reaching the closing **SyncLock** statement (**End SyncLock**) in line 113 causes the thread to release the lock on the **CHoldIntegerSynchronized** object.

The **Get** accessor (lines 29–71) of property **Buffer** also performs the same tasks in this example that it did in Fig. 14.9, but with a few minor modifications. The **If** structure in lines 37–43 of the **Get** accessor determines whether the consumer must wait (i.e., all buffers are empty). If the consumer thread must wait, lines 38–39 append text to the **txtOutput** indicating that the consumer is waiting to perform its task, and line 42 invokes **Monitor** method **Wait** to place the consumer thread in the *WaitSleepJoin* state of the **CHoldIntegerSynchronized** object. Once again, we use a **SyncLock** block to acquire and release the lock on the **CHoldIntegerSynchronized** object, rather than using **Monitor** methods **Enter** and **Exit**. When execution continues at line 47 after the **If** structure, **readValue** is assigned the value at location **readLocation** in the circular buffer. Lines 49–51 appends the consumed value to the **TextBox**. Line 55 decrements the **occupiedBufferCount**, because the buffer contains at least one open position in which the producer thread can place a value. Then, line 59 update **readLocation** for the next call to the **Get** accessor of **Buffer**. Line 61 invokes method **CreateStateOutput** to output the number of occupied buffers, the contents of the buffers and the current **writeLocation** and **readLocation**. Finally, line 66 invokes method **Pulse** to transition the next thread waiting for the **CHoldIntegerSynchronized** object into the *Started* state, and line 68 returns the consumed value to the calling method.

```
1   ' Fig. 14.13: HoldIntegerSynchronized.vb
2   ' Synchronize access to circular Integer buffer.
3
4   Imports System.Threading
5   Imports System.Windows.Forms
6
7   Public Class CHoldIntegerSynchronized
8
9      ' each array element is a buffer
10     Private mBuffer As Integer() = {-1, -1, -1}
11
12     ' occupiedBufferCount maintains count of occupied buffers
13     Private occupiedBufferCount As Integer
14
15     ' maintains read and write buffer locations
16     Private readlocation, writeLocation As Integer
```

Fig. 14.13 Synchronized shared circular buffer (part 1 of 4).

```vbnet
17
18      ' GUI component to display output
19      Private txtOutput As TextBox
20
21      ' constructor
22      Public Sub New(ByVal output As TextBox)
23         txtOutput = output
24      End Sub ' New
25
26      ' property Buffer
27      Property Buffer() As Integer
28
29         Get
30
31            ' lock this object while getting value
32            ' from mBuffer array
33            SyncLock (Me)
34
35               ' if there is no data to read, place invoking
36               ' thread in WaitSleepJoin state
37               If occupiedBufferCount = 0 Then
38                  txtOutput.Text &= vbCrLf & "All buffers empty. " & _
39                     Thread.CurrentThread.Name & " waits."
40
41                  txtOutput.ScrollToCaret()
42                  Monitor.Wait(Me)
43               End If
44
45               ' obtain value at current readLocation
46               ' add string indicating consumed value to output
47               Dim readValue As Integer = mBuffer(readlocation)
48
49               txtOutput.Text &= vbCrLf & _
50                  Thread.CurrentThread.Name & " reads " & _
51                  mBuffer(readlocation) & " "
52
53               ' just consumed value, so decrement number of
54               ' occupied buffers
55               occupiedBufferCount -= 1
56
57               ' update readLocation for future read operation
58               ' add current state to output
59               readlocation = (readlocation + 1) Mod mBuffer.Length
60
61               txtOutput.Text &= CreateStateOutput()
62               txtOutput.ScrollToCaret()
63
64               ' return waiting thread (if there is one)
65               ' to Started state
66               Monitor.Pulse(Me)
67
68               Return readValue
69            End SyncLock
```

Fig. 14.13 Synchronized shared circular buffer (part 2 of 4).

```vbnet
70
71         End Get
72
73         Set(ByVal Value As Integer)
74
75            ' lock this object while setting value
76            ' in mBuffer array
77            SyncLock (Me)
78
79               ' if there are no empty locations, place invoking
80               ' thread in WaitSleepJoin state
81               If occupiedBufferCount = mBuffer.Length Then
82                  txtOutput.Text &= vbCrLf & "All buffers full. " & _
83                     Thread.CurrentThread.Name & " waits."
84
85                  txtOutput.ScrollToCaret()
86
87                  Monitor.Wait(Me)
88               End If
89
90               ' place value in writeLocation of mBuffer, then
91               ' add string indicating produced value to output
92               mBuffer(writeLocation) = Value
93
94               txtOutput.Text &= vbCrLf & _
95                  Thread.CurrentThread.Name & " writes " & _
96                  mBuffer(writeLocation) & " "
97
98               ' just produced value, so increment number of
99               ' occupied mBuffer elements
100              occupiedBufferCount += 1
101
102              ' update writeLocation for future write operation,
103              ' then add current state to output
104              writeLocation = (writeLocation + 1) Mod _
105                 mBuffer.Length
106
107              txtOutput.Text &= CreateStateOutput()
108              txtOutput.ScrollToCaret()
109
110              ' return waiting thread (if there is one)
111              ' to Started state
112              Monitor.Pulse(Me)
113           End SyncLock
114
115        End Set
116
117     End Property ' Buffer
118
119     ' create state output
120     Public Function CreateStateOutput() As String
121
122        Dim i As Integer
```

Fig. 14.13 Synchronized shared circular buffer (part 3 of 4).

```vb
123
124         ' display first line of state information
125         Dim output As String = "(buffers occupied: " & _
126            occupiedBufferCount & ")" & vbCrLf & "buffers: "
127
128         For i = 0 To mBuffer.GetUpperBound(0)
129            output &= " " & mBuffer(i) & "  "
130         Next
131
132         output &= vbCrLf
133
134         ' display second line of state information
135         output &= "            "
136
137         For i = 0 To mBuffer.GetUpperBound(0)
138            output &= "---- "
139         Next
140
141         output &= vbCrLf
142
143         ' display third line of state information
144         output &= "            "
145
146         For i = 0 To mBuffer.GetUpperBound(0)
147
148            If (i = writeLocation AndAlso _
149               writeLocation = readlocation) Then
150
151               output &= " WR  "
152            ElseIf i = writeLocation Then
153               output &= " W   "
154            ElseIf i = readlocation Then
155               output &= " R   "
156            Else
157               output &= "     "
158            End If
159
160         Next
161
162         output &= vbCrLf
163
164         Return output
165      End Function ' CreateStateOutput
166
167 End Class ' CHoldIntegerSynchronized
```

Fig. 14.13 Synchronized shared circular buffer (part 4 of 4).

```vb
1   ' Fig. 14.14: Producer.vb
2   ' Produce 10 Integers into synchronized Integer buffer.
3
4   Imports System.Threading
```

Fig. 14.14 Producer places **Integer**s in synchronized circular buffer (part 1 of 2).

```vbnet
 5   Imports System.Windows.Forms
 6
 7   Public Class CProducer
 8      Private sharedLocation As CHoldIntegerSynchronized
 9      Private randomSleepTime As Random
10      Private txtOutput As TextBox
11
12      ' constructor
13      Public Sub New(ByVal sharedObject As CHoldIntegerSynchronized, _
14         ByVal randomObject As Random, ByVal output As TextBox)
15
16         sharedLocation = sharedObject
17         randomSleepTime = randomObject
18         txtOutput = output
19      End Sub ' New
20
21      ' store values 11-20 and place them
22      ' in sharedLocation's buffer
23      Public Sub Produce()
24         Dim count As Integer
25
26         ' sleep for random interval up to 3000 milliseconds
27         ' set sharedLocation's Buffer property
28         For count = 11 To 20
29            Thread.Sleep(randomSleepTime.Next(1, 3000))
30            sharedLocation.Buffer = count
31         Next
32
33         txtOutput.Text &= vbCrLf & Thread.CurrentThread.Name & _
34            " done producing. " & vbCrLf & _
35            Thread.CurrentThread.Name & " terminated." & vbCrLf
36      End Sub ' Produce
37
38   End Class ' CProducer
```

Fig. 14.14 Producer places **Integer**s in synchronized circular buffer (part 2 of 2).

```vbnet
 1   ' Fig. 14.15: Consumer.vb
 2   ' Consume 10 Integers from synchronized circular buffer.
 3
 4   Imports System.Threading
 5   Imports System.Windows.Forms
 6
 7   Public Class CConsumer
 8      Private sharedLocation As CHoldIntegerSynchronized
 9      Private randomSleepTime As Random
10      Private txtOutput As TextBox
11
12      ' constructor
13      Public Sub New(ByVal sharedObject As CHoldIntegerSynchronized, _
14         ByVal randomObject As Random, ByVal output As TextBox)
15
```

Fig. 14.15 Consumer reads **Integer**s from synchronized circular buffer (part 1 of 2).

```
16            sharedLocation = sharedObject
17            randomSleepTime = randomObject
18            txtOutput = output
19         End Sub ' New
20
21         ' consume 10 Integers from buffer
22         Public Sub Consume()
23            Dim count, sum As Integer
24
25            ' loop 10 times and sleep for random interval up to
26            ' 3000 milliseconds
27            ' add sharedLocation's Buffer property value to sum
28            For count = 1 To 10
29               Thread.Sleep(randomSleepTime.Next(1, 3000))
30               sum += sharedLocation.Buffer
31            Next
32
33            txtOutput.Text &= vbCrLf & "Total " & _
34               Thread.CurrentThread.Name & " consumed: " & sum & vbCrLf & _
35               Thread.CurrentThread.Name & " terminated." & vbCrLf
36
37            txtOutput.ScrollToCaret()
38         End Sub ' Consume
39
40   End Class ' CConsumer
```

Fig. 14.15 Consumer reads **Integer**s from synchronized circular buffer (part 2 of 2).

```
1    ' Fig. 14.16: FrmCircularBuffer.vb
2    ' Create display form and start threads.
3
4    Imports System.Threading
5    Imports System.Windows.Forms
6
7    Public Class FrmCircularBuffer
8       Inherits Form
9
10      Friend WithEvents txtOutput As TextBox
11
12      ' Visual Studio .NET generated code
13
14      ' initialize threads upon loading
15      Private Sub FrmCircularBuffer_Load(ByVal sender As Object, _
16         ByVal e As System.EventArgs) Handles MyBase.Load
17
18         ' create shared object
19         Dim sharedLocation As _
20            New CHoldIntegerSynchronized(txtOutput)
21
22         ' display sharedLocation state before producer
23         ' and consumer threads begin execution
24         txtOutput.Text = sharedLocation.CreateStateOutput()
```

Fig. 14.16 Producer and consumer threads accessing a circular buffer (part 1 of 4).

```vbnet
25
26          ' Random object used by each thread
27          Dim randomObject As New Random()
28
29          ' create CProducer and CConsumer objects
30          Dim producer As New CProducer(sharedLocation, _
31             randomObject, txtOutput)
32
33          Dim consumer As New CConsumer(sharedLocation, _
34             randomObject, txtOutput)
35
36          ' create threads
37          Dim producerThread As _
38             New Thread(AddressOf producer.Produce)
39
40          Dim consumerThread As _
41             New Thread(AddressOf consumer.Consume)
42
43          ' name threads
44          producerThread.Name = "Producer"
45          consumerThread.Name = "Consumer"
46
47          ' start threads
48          producerThread.Start()
49          consumerThread.Start()
50       End Sub ' FrmCircularBuffer_Load
51
52    End Class ' FrmCircularBuffer
```

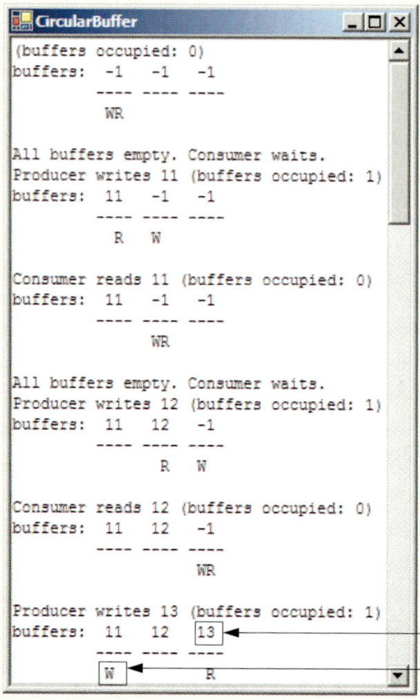

Fig. 14.16 Producer and consumer threads accessing a circular buffer (part 2 of 4).

Chapter 14 Multithreading 627

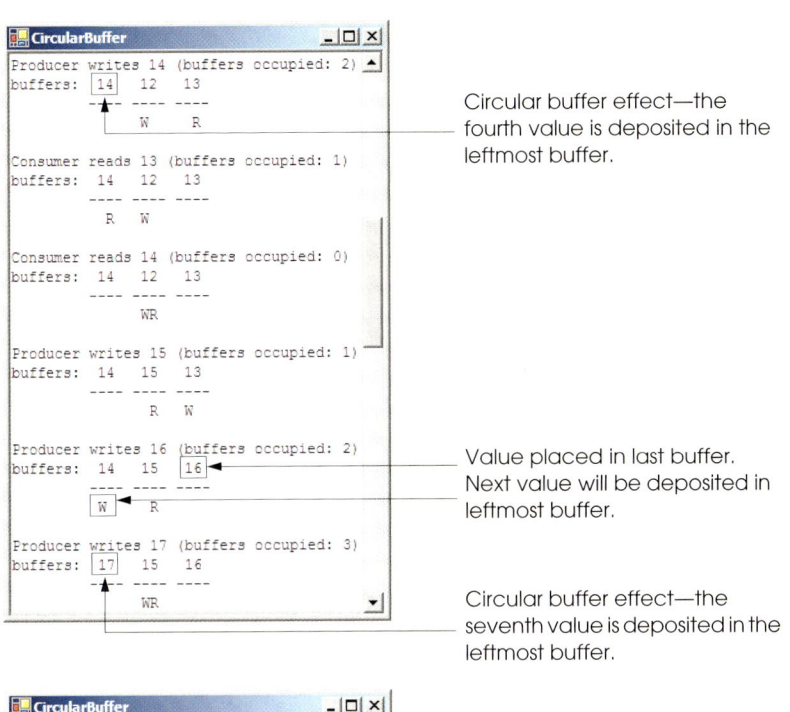

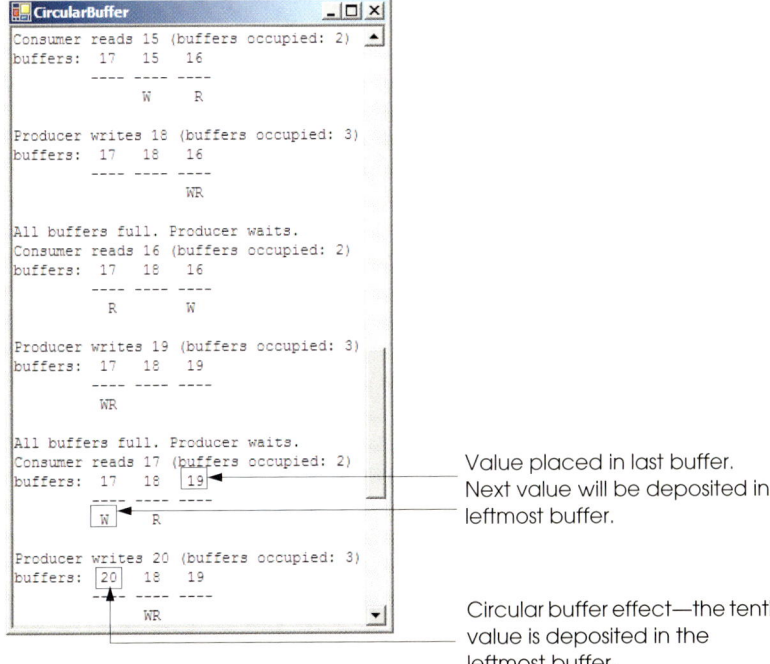

Fig. 14.16 Producer and consumer threads accessing a circular buffer (part 3 of 4).

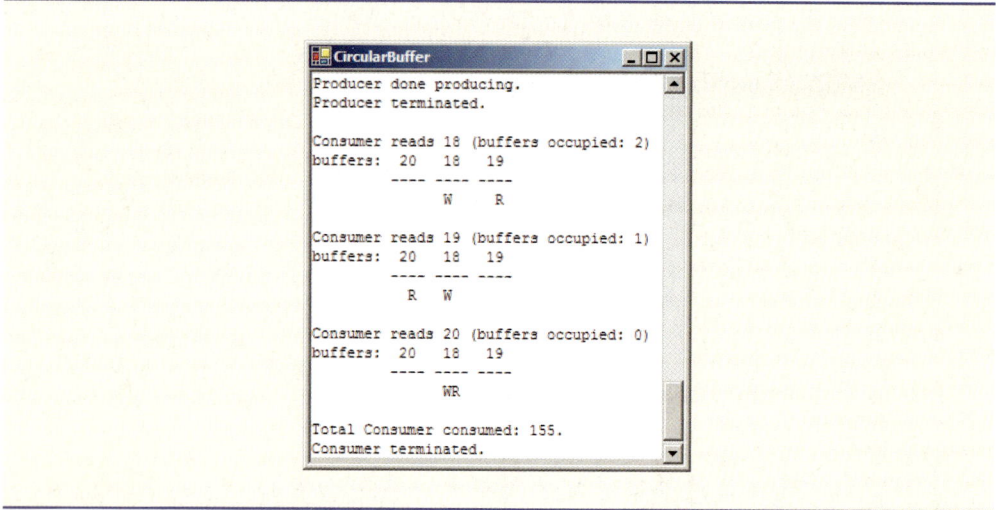

Fig. 14.16 Producer and consumer threads accessing a circular buffer (part 4 of 4).

In Fig. 14.16, the outputs include the current **occupiedBufferCount**, the contents of the buffers and the current **writeLocation** and **readLocation**. In the output, the letters **W** and **R** represent the current **writeLocation** and **readLocation**, respectively. Notice that, after the third value is placed in the third element of the buffer, the fourth value is inserted at the beginning of the array. This produces the circular buffer effect.

SUMMARY

- Computers can perform operations concurrently, such as compiling programs, printing files and receiving electronic mail messages over a network.
- Programming languages generally provide only a simple set of control structures that enable programmers to perform one action at a time, proceeding to the next action only after the previous one finishes.
- Historically, the type of concurrency that computers perform generally has been implemented as operating system "primitives" available only to highly experienced "systems programmers."
- The .NET Framework Class Library makes concurrency primitives available to the applications programmer. The programmer can specify that an application contains threads of execution, where each thread designates a portion of a program that might execute concurrently with other threads—this capability is called multithreading.
- A thread that was just created is in the *Unstarted* state. A thread is initialized using the **Thread** class's constructor, which receives a **ThreadStart** delegate. This delegate specifies the method that contains the tasks that a thread will perform.
- A thread remains in the *Unstarted* state until the thread's **Start** method is called; this causes the thread to enter the *Started* state (also known as the *Ready*, or *Runnable*, state).
- A thread in the *Started* state enters the *Running* state when the system assigns a processor to the thread. The system assigns the processor to the highest-priority *Started* thread.
- A thread enters the *Stopped* (or *Dead*) state when its **ThreadStart** delegate completes or terminates. A thread is forced into the *Stopped* state when its **Abort** method is called (by itself or by another thread).

- A *Running* thread enters the *Blocked* state when the thread issues an input/output request. A *Blocked* thread becomes *Started* when the I/O it is waiting for completes. A *Blocked* thread cannot use a processor, even if one is available.
- If a thread wants to go to sleep, it calls **Thread** method **Sleep**. A thread wakes up when the designated sleep interval expires.
- If a thread cannot continue executing (we will call this the dependent thread) unless another thread terminates, the dependent thread calls the other thread's **Join** method to "join" the two threads. When two threads are "joined," the dependent thread leaves the *WaitSleepJoin* state when the other thread finishes execution (enters the *Stopped* state).
- In thread synchronization, when a thread encounters code that it cannot yet run, the thread can call **Monitor** method **Wait** until certain actions occur that enable the thread to continue executing.
- Any thread in the *WaitSleepJoin* state can leave that state if another thread invokes **Thread** method **Interrupt** on the thread that is in the *WaitSleepJoin* state.
- If a thread calls **Monitor** method **Wait**, a corresponding call to the **Monitor** method **Pulse** or **PulseAll** by another thread in the program will transition the original thread from the *WaitSleepJoin* state to the *Started* state.
- If **Thread** method **Suspend** is called on a thread (by the thread itself or by another thread in the program), the thread enters the *Suspended* state. A thread leaves the *Suspended* state when a separate thread invokes **Thread** method **Resume** on the suspended thread.
- Every Visual Basic thread has a priority of **ThreadPriority.Lowest**, **ThreadPriority.BelowNormal**, **ThreadPriority.Normal**, **ThreadPriority.AboveNormal** or **ThreadPriority.Highest**.
- The job of the thread scheduler is to keep the highest-priority thread running at all times and, if there is more than one highest-priority thread, to ensure that all equally high-priority threads execute for a quantum at a time in round-robin fashion.
- A thread's priority can be adjusted with the **Priority** property, which accepts an argument from the **ThreadPriority** enumeration.
- A thread that updates shared data calls **Monitor** method **Enter** to acquire the lock on that data. It then updates the data and calls **Monitor** method **Exit** upon completion of the update. While that data is locked, all other threads attempting to acquire the lock on that data must wait.
- If a programmer places the **SyncLock** keyword before a block of code, the lock is acquired on the specified object as program control enters the block; the lock then is released when the block terminates for any reason.
- If a thread decides that it cannot continue execution, it can call **Wait**. This puts the thread into the *WaitSleepJoin* state. When the thread can continue execution again, **Pulse** or **PulseAll** is called to notify the thread to continue running.
- When the **SyncLock** keyword is used, Visual Basic implicitly calls the **Exit** method whenever we leave the scope of the block.

TERMINOLOGY

Abort method of class **Thread**
AboveNormal constant in **ThreadPriority**
accessing shared data with synchronization
acquire the lock for an object
automatic garbage collection
BelowNormal constant in **ThreadPriority**

Blocked state
Blocked thread
built-in multithreading
circular buffer
concurrency
concurrent producer and consumer threads

concurrent programming
condition variable
consumer
Dead state
deadlock
`DomainUpDown` control
`Enter` method of class `Monitor`
`Exit` method of class `Monitor`
garbage collection
garbage-collector thread
`Highest` constant in `ThreadPriority`
Hoare, C. A. R.
I/O completion
I/O request
indefinite postponement
input/output blocking
`Interrupt` method of class `Thread`
`Join` method of class `Thread`
life cycle of a thread
locking objects
`Lowest` constant in `ThreadPriority`
memory leak
`Monitor` class
multilevel priority queue
multithreading
`Name` property of class `Thread`
`Normal` constant in `ThreadPriority`
`Priority` property of class `Thread`
priority scheduling
producer
producer/consumer relationship
`Pulse` method of class `Monitor`
`PulseAll` method of class `Monitor`

quantum
quantum expiration
Ready state
release a lock
`Resume` method of class `Thread`
Runnable state
Running state
scheduling
shared buffer
sleep interval expires
`Sleep` method of class `Thread`
sleeping thread
`Start` method of class `Thread`
Started state
starvation
Stopped state
`Suspend` method of class `Thread`
SyncBlock
`SyncLock` keyword
synchronized block of code
`System.Threading` namespace
task
`Thread` class
thread of execution
thread-priority scheduling
thread state
`ThreadAbortException`
`ThreadPriority` enumeration
`ThreadStart` delegate
Unstarted state
`Wait` method of class `Monitor`
WaitSleepJoin state

SELF-REVIEW EXERCISES

14.1 Fill in the blanks in each of the following statements:
  a) Monitor methods _____ and _____ acquire and release the lock on an object.
  b) Among a group of equal-priority threads, each thread receives a brief burst of time called a _____, during which the thread has the processor and can perform its tasks.
  c) Visual Basic provides a _____ thread that reclaims dynamically allocated memory.
  d) Four reasons that a thread would be alive but not in the *Started* state are that the thread is _____, _____, _____ or _____.
  e) A thread enters the _____ state when the method that controls the thread's lifecycle terminates.
  f) A thread's priority must be one of the `ThreadPriority` constants _____, _____, _____, _____ and _____.
  g) To wait for a designated number of milliseconds and then resume execution, a thread should call the _____ method of class `Thread`.
  h) Method _____ of class `Monitor` transitions a thread from the *WaitSleepJoin* state to the *Started* state.

i) A _____ block automatically acquires the lock on an object as the program control enters the block and releases the lock on that object when the block terminates execution.
j) Class **Monitor** provides methods that _____ access to shared data.

14.2 State whether each of the following is *true* or *false*. If *false*, explain why.
a) A thread cannot execute if it is in the *Stopped* state.
b) In Visual Basic, a higher priority thread entering (or reentering) the *Started* state will pre-empt threads of lower priority.
c) The code that a thread executes is defined in its **Main** method.
d) A thread in the *WaitSleepJoin* state always returns to the *Started* state when **Monitor** method **Pulse** is called.
e) Method **Sleep** of class **Thread** does not consume processor time while a thread sleeps.
f) A blocked thread can be placed in the *Started* state by **Monitor** method **Pulse**.
g) Class **Monitor**'s **Wait**, **Pulse** and **PulseAll** methods can be used in any block of code.
h) The programmer must place a call to **Monitor** method **Exit** in a **SyncLock** block to relinquish the lock.
i) When **Monitor** class method **Wait** is called within a locked block, the lock for that block is released, and the thread that called **Wait** is placed in the *WaitSleepJoin* state.

ANSWERS TO SELF-REVIEW EXERCISES

14.1 a) **Enter**, **Exit**. b) timeslice or quantum. c) garbage collector. d) waiting, sleeping, suspended, blocked for input/output. e) *Stopped*. f) **Lowest**, **BelowNormal**, **Normal**, **AboveNormal**, **Highest**. g) **Sleep**. h) **Pulse**. i) **SyncLock**. j) synchronize.

14.2   a) True. b) True. c) False. The code that a thread executes is defined in the method specified by the thread's **ThreadStart** delegate. d) False. A thread might be in the *WaitSleepJoin* state for several reasons. Calling **Pulse** moves a thread from the *WaitSleepJoin* state to the *Started* state only if the thread entered the *WaitSleepJoin* state as the result of a call to **Monitor** method **Wait**. e) True. f) False. A thread is blocked by the operating system and returns to the *Started* state when the operating system determines that the thread can continue executing (e.g., when an I/O request completes or when a lock the thread attempted to acquire becomes available). g) False. Class **Monitor** methods can be called only if the thread performing the call currently owns the lock on the object that each method receives as an argument. h) False. A **SyncLock** block implicitly relinquishes the lock when the thread completes execution of the **SyncLock** block. i) True.

EXERCISES

14.3 The code that manipulates the circular buffer in Fig. 14.13 will work with a buffer of two or more elements. Try changing the buffer size to see how it affects the producer and consumer threads. In particular, notice that the producer waits to produce less frequently as the buffer grows in size.

14.4 Write a program to demonstrate that, as a high-priority thread executes, it will delay the execution of all lower-priority threads.

14.5 Write a program that demonstrates timeslicing among several equal-priority threads. Show that a lower-priority thread's execution is deferred by the timeslicing of the higher-priority threads.

14.6 Write a program that demonstrates a high-priority thread using **Sleep** to give lower-priority threads a chance to run.

14.7 Two problems that can occur in languages like Visual Basic that allow threads to wait are deadlock, in which one or more threads will wait forever for an event that cannot occur, and indefinite postponement, in which one or more threads will be delayed for some unpredictably long time, but might eventually complete. Give an example of how each of these problems can occur in a multi-threaded Visual Basic program.

14.8 (Readers and Writers) This exercise asks you to develop a Visual Basic monitor to solve a famous problem in concurrency control. This problem was first discussed and solved by P. J. Courtois, F. Heymans and D. L. Parnas in their research paper, "Concurrent Control with Readers and Writers," *Communications of the ACM*, Vol. 14, No. 10, October 1971, pp. 667–668. The interested student might also want to read C. A. R. Hoare's seminal research paper on monitors, "Monitors: An Operating System Structuring Concept," *Communications of the ACM*, Vol. 17, No. 10, October 1974, pp. 549–557. *Corrigendum, Communications of the ACM*, Vol. 18, No. 2, February 1975, p. 95. [The readers and writers problem is discussed at length in Chapter 5 of the author's book: Deitel, H. M., *Operating Systems*, Reading, MA: Addison-Wesley, 1990.]

With multithreading, many threads can access shared data; as we have seen, access to shared data must be synchronized to avoid corrupting the data.

Consider an airline-reservation system in which many clients are attempting to book seats on particular flights between particular cities. All the information about flights and seats is stored in a common database in memory. The database consists of many entries, each representing a seat on a particular flight for a particular day between particular cities. In a typical airline-reservation scenario, the client would probe the database, looking for the "optimal" flight to meet that client's needs. A client might probe the database many times before trying to book a particular flight. A seat that was available during this probing phase could easily be booked by someone else before the client has a chance to book it after deciding on it. In that case, when the client attempts to make the reservation, the client will discover that the data has changed, and the flight is no longer available.

The client probing the database is called a *reader*. The client attempting to book the flight is called a *writer*. Any number of readers can probe shared data at once, but each writer needs exclusive access to the shared data to prevent the data from being corrupted.

Write a multithreaded Visual Basic program that launches multiple reader threads and multiple writer threads, each attempting to access a single reservation record. A writer thread has two possible transactions, **MakeReservation** and **CancelReservation**. A reader has one possible transaction, **QueryReservation**.

First, implement a version of your program that allows unsynchronized access to the reservation record. Show how the integrity of the database can be corrupted. Next, implement a version of your program that uses Visual Basic monitor synchronization with **Wait** and **Pulse** to enforce a disciplined protocol for readers and writers accessing the shared reservation data. In particular, your program should allow multiple readers to access the shared data simultaneously when no writer is active—but, if a writer is active, then no reader should be allowed to access the shared data.

Be careful. This problem has many subtleties. For example, what happens when there are several active readers and a writer wants to write? If we allow a steady stream of readers to arrive and share the data, they could indefinitely postpone the writer (who might become tired of waiting and take his or her business elsewhere). To solve this problem, you might decide to favor writers over readers. But here, too, there is a trap, because a steady stream of writers could then indefinitely postpone the waiting readers, and they, too, might choose to take their business elsewhere! Implement your monitor with the following methods: **StartReading**, which is called by any reader who wants to begin accessing a reservation; **StopReading**, which is called by any reader who has finished reading a reservation; **StartWriting**, which is called by any writer who wants to make a reservation; and **StopWriting**, which is called by any writer who has finished making a reservation.

15

Strings, Characters and Regular Expressions

Objectives

- To be able to create and manipulate nonmodifiable character string objects of class **String**.
- To be able to create and manipulate modifiable character string objects of class **StringBuilder**.
- To be able to use regular expressions in conjunction with classes **Regex** and **Match**.

*The chief defect of Henry King
Was chewing little bits of string.*
Hilaire Belloc

Vigorous writing is concise. A sentence should contain no unnecessary words, a paragraph no unnecessary sentences.
William Strunk, Jr.

I have made this letter longer than usual, because I lack the time to make it short.
Blaise Pascal

The difference between the almost-right word & the right word is really a large matter—it's the difference between the lightning bug and the lightning.
Mark Twain

Mum's the word.
Miguel de Cervantes, *Don Quixote de la Mancha*

Outline

15.1 Introduction
15.2 Fundamentals of Characters and Strings
15.3 `String` Constructors
15.4 `String Length` and `Chars` Properties, and `CopyTo` Method
15.5 Comparing `Strings`
15.6 `String` Method `GetHashCode`
15.7 Locating Characters and Substrings in `Strings`
15.8 Extracting Substrings from `Strings`
15.9 Concatenating `Strings`
15.10 Miscellaneous `String` Methods
15.11 Class `StringBuilder`
15.12 `StringBuilder` Indexer, `Length` and `Capacity` Properties, and `EnsureCapacity` Method
15.13 `StringBuilder Append` and `AppendFormat` Methods
15.14 `StringBuilder Insert`, `Remove` and `Replace` Methods
15.15 `Char` Methods
15.16 Card Shuffling and Dealing Simulation
15.17 Regular Expressions and Class `Regex`

Summary • Terminology • Self-Review Exercises • Answers to Self-Review Exercises • Exercises

15.1 Introduction

This chapter introduces Visual Basic string and character processing capabilities and demonstrate using regular expressions to search for patterns in text. The techniques presented in this chapter can be employed to develop text editors, word processors, page-layout software, computerized typesetting systems and other kinds of text-processing software. Previous chapters have already presented several string-processing capabilities. In this chapter, we expand on this information by detailing the capabilities of class `String` and type `Char` from the `System` namespace, class `StringBuilder` from the `System.Text` namespace and classes `Regex` and `Match` from the `System.Text.RegularExpressions` namespace.

15.2 Fundamentals of Characters and Strings

Characters are the fundamental building blocks of Visual Basic source code. Every program is composed of characters that, when grouped together meaningfully, create a sequence that the compiler interprets as a series of instructions that describe how to accomplish a task. In addition to normal characters, a program also can contain *character constants*. A character constant is a character that is represented as an integer value, called a *character code*. For example, the integer value of `122` corresponds to the character constant `"z"c`. Character constants are established according to the *Unicode character set*, an international character set that contains many more symbols and letters than does the ASCII character set (see Appendix E, ASCII character set). To learn the integer equivalents of many common Unicode characters, see Appendix F, Unicode.

A string is a series of characters treated as a single unit. These characters can be uppercase letters, lowercase letters, digits and various *special characters*, such as **+**, **-**, *****, **/**, **$** and others. A string is an object of class **String** in the **System** namespace. We write *string literals*, or *string constants* (often called *literal **String** objects*), as sequences of characters in double quotation marks, as follows:

```
"John Q. Doe"
"9999 Main Street"
"Waltham, Massachusetts"
"(201) 555-1212"
```

A declaration can assign a **String** literal to a **String** reference. The declaration

```
Dim color As String = "blue"
```

initializes **String** reference **color** to refer to the **String** literal object **"blue"**.

Performance Tip 15.1

*If there are multiple occurrences of the same **String** literal object in an application, a single copy of the **String** literal object will be referenced from each location in the program that uses that **String** literal. It is possible to share the object in this manner, because **String** literal objects are implicitly constant. Such sharing conserves memory.*

15.3 String Constructors

Class **String** provides three constructors for initializing **String** objects in various ways. Figure 15.1 demonstrates the use of three of the constructors.

```
1   ' Fig. 15.1: StringConstructor.vb
2   ' Demonstrating String class constructors.
3
4   Imports System.Windows.Forms
5
6   Module modStringConstructor
7
8      Sub Main()
9         Dim characterArray As Char()
10        Dim output As String
11        Dim quotes As Char = ChrW(34)
12        Dim originalString, string1, string2, string3, _
13           string4 As String
14
15        characterArray = New Char() {"b"c, "i"c, "r"c, _
16           "t"c, "h"c, " "c, "d"c, "a"c, "y"c}
17
18        ' string initialization
19        originalString = "Welcome to VB.NET Programming!"
20        string1 = originalString
21        string2 = New String(characterArray)
```

Fig. 15.1 **String** constructors (part 1 of 2).

```
22          string3 = New String(characterArray, 6, 3)
23          string4 = New String("C"c, 5)
24
25          output = "string1 = " & quotes & string1 & quotes & _
26             vbCrLf & "string2 = " & quotes & string2 & quotes & _
27             vbCrLf & "string3 = " & quotes & string3 & quotes & _
28             vbCrLf & "string4 = " & quotes & string4 & quotes
29
30          MessageBox.Show(output, "String Class Constructors", _
31             MessageBoxButtons.OK, MessageBoxIcon.Information)
32       End Sub ' Main
33
34    End Module ' modStringConstructor
```

```
String Class Constructors
    string1 = "Welcome to VB.NET Programming!"
    string2 = "birth day"
    string3 = "day"
    string4 = "CCCCC"
            [ OK ]
```

Fig. 15.1 `String` constructors (part 2 of 2).

In line 11, we declare variable **quotes** and give it the value returned by function **ChrW** when **ChrW** is passed a value of **34**. The value passed to function **ChrW** is a Unicode character code. Function **ChrW** returns as a **Char** data type the character that corresponds to the specified Unicode character code. In this case, function **ChrW** returns a double quote character (**"**). (To learn more about character codes, see Appendix F, Unicode.)

Lines 15–16 allocate **Char** array **characterArray**, which contains nine characters. The **c** suffix that follows each **String** converts it to a character literal. We do this because **Option Strict** prohibits the implicit conversion from type **String** to type **Char**.

Line 19 assigns literal string **"Welcome to VB.NET Programming!"** to **String** reference **originalString**. Line 20 sets **string1** to reference **String** literal **originalString**.

Software Engineering Observation 15.1

*In most cases, it is not necessary to make a copy of an existing **String** object. All **String** objects are immutable—their character contents cannot be changed after they are created. Also, if there are one or more references to a **String** object (or any object for that matter), the object cannot be reclaimed by the garbage collector.*

Line 21 assigns to **string2** a new **String** object, using the **String** constructor that takes a character array as an argument. The new **String** object contains a copy of the characters in array **characterArray**.

Line 22 assigns to **string3** a new **String** object, using the **String** constructor that takes a **Char** array and two **Integer** arguments. The second argument specifies the starting index position (the *offset*) from which characters in the array are copied. The third argument specifies the number of characters (the *count*) to be copied from the specified starting position in the array. The new **String** object contains a copy of the specified characters in the array. If the specified offset or count indicates that the program should access an element outside the bounds of the character array, an **ArgumentOutOfRangeException** is thrown.

Line 23 assigns to **string4** a new **String** object, using the **String** constructor that takes as arguments a character and an **Integer** specifying the number of times to repeat that character in the **String**.

Each instance of variable **quotes** (lines 25–28) represents a double quote character (**"**). Visual Studio .NET treats double quotes as delimiters for **String**s and does not treat them as part of a **String**. We can represent a quotation mark within a **String** by using the numerical code of the character (e.g., line 11) or by placing consecutive double quote characters (**""**) in the **String**.

15.4 String Length and Chars Properties, and CopyTo Method

The application in Fig. 15.2 presents the **String** property **Chars**, which facilitates the retrieval of any character in the **String**, and the **String** property **Length**, which returns the length of the **String**. The **String** method **CopyTo** copies a specified number of characters from a **String** into a **Char** array.

```vb
1   ' Fig. 15.2: StringMiscellaneous.vb
2   ' Using properties Length and Chars, and method CopyTo
3   ' of class string.
4
5   Imports System.Windows.Forms
6
7   Module modMiscellaneous
8
9      Sub Main()
10        Dim string1, output As String
11        Dim characterArray As Char()
12        Dim i As Integer
13        Dim quotes As Char = ChrW(34)
14
15        string1 = "hello there"
16        characterArray = New Char(5) {}
17
18        ' output string
19        output = "string1: " & quotes & string1 & quotes
20
21        ' test Length property
22        output &= vbCrLf & "Length of string1: " & string1.Length
23
24        ' loop through characters in string1 and display
25        ' reversed
26        output &= vbCrLf & "The string reversed is: "
27
28        For i = string1.Length - 1 To 0 Step -1
29           output &= string1.Chars(i)
30        Next
```

Fig. 15.2 **String Length** and **Chars** properties, and **CopyTo** method (part 1 of 2).

```
31
32              ' copy characters from string1 into characterArray
33              string1.CopyTo(0, characterArray, 0, 5)
34              output &= vbCrLf & "The character array is: "
35
36              For i = 0 To characterArray.GetUpperBound(0)
37                 output &= characterArray(i)
38              Next
39
40              MessageBox.Show(output, "Demonstrating String" & _
41                 " properties Length and Chars", _
42                 MessageBoxButtons.OK, MessageBoxIcon.Information)
43         End Sub ' Main
44
45     End Module ' modMiscellaneous
```

Demonstrating String properties Length and Chars

string1: "hello there"
Length of string1: 11
The string reversed is: ereht olleh
The character array is: hello

OK

Fig. 15.2 `String Length` and `Chars` properties, and `CopyTo` method (part 2 of 2).

In this example, we create an application that determines the length of a **String**, reverses the order of the characters in the **String** and copies a series of characters from the **String** into a character array.

Line 22 uses **String** property **Length** to determine the number of characters in **String string1**. Like arrays, **String**s always know their own size.

Lines 28–30 append to **output** the characters of the **String string1** in reverse order. The **String** property **Chars** returns the character located in a specific index in the **String**. Property **Chars** takes an **Integer** argument specifying the index and returns the character at that index. As in arrays, the first element of a **String** is at index **0**.

Common Programming Error 15.1

*Attempting to access a character that is outside the bounds of a **String** (i.e., an index less than 0 or an index greater than or equal to the **String**'s length) results in an **IndexOutOfRangeException**.*

Line 33 uses **String** method **CopyTo** to copy the characters of a **String** (**string1**) into a character array (**characterArray**). The first argument given to method **CopyTo** is the index from which the method begins copying characters in the **String**. The second argument is the character array into which the characters are copied. The third argument is the index specifying the location at which the method places the copied characters in the character array. The last argument is the number of characters that the method will copy from the **String**. Lines 36–38 append the **Char** array contents to **String output** one character at a time.

15.5 Comparing `Strings`

The next two examples demonstrate the various methods that Visual Basic provides for comparing **String** objects. To understand how one **String** can be "greater than" or "less than" another **String**, consider the process of alphabetizing a series of last names. The reader would, no doubt, place **"Jones"** before **"Smith"**, because the first letter of **"Jones"** comes before the first letter of **"Smith"** in the alphabet. The alphabet is more than just a set of 26 letters—it is an ordered list of characters in which each letter occurs in a specific position. For example, **z** is more than just a letter of the alphabet; **z** is specifically the twenty-sixth letter of the alphabet.

Computers can order characters alphabetically because the characters are represented internally as Unicode numeric codes. When comparing two **String**s, computers simply compare the numeric codes of the characters in the **String**s.

Class **String** provides several ways to compare **String**s. The application in Fig. 15.3 demonstrates the use of method **Equals**, method **CompareTo** and the equality operator (**=**).

```vb
1   ' Fig. 15.3: StringCompare.vb
2   ' Comparing strings.
3
4   Imports System.Windows.Forms
5
6   Module modCompare
7
8      Sub Main()
9         Dim string1 As String = "hello"
10        Dim string2 As String = "good bye"
11        Dim string3 As String = "Happy Birthday"
12        Dim string4 As String = "happy birthday"
13        Dim output As String
14        Dim quotes As Char = ChrW(34)
15
16        ' output values of four Strings
17        output = "string1 = " & quotes & string1 & quotes & _
18           vbCrLf & "string2 = " & quotes & string2 & quotes & _
19           vbCrLf & "string3 = " & quotes & string3  & quotes & _
20           vbCrLf & "string4 = " & quotes & string4  & quotes & _
21           vbCrLf & vbCrLf
22
23        ' test for equality using Equals method
24        If (string1.Equals("hello")) Then
25           output &= "string1 equals " & quotes & "hello" & _
26              quotes & vbCrLf
27
28        Else
29           output &= "string1 does not equal " & quotes & _
30              "hello" & quotes & vbCrLf
31        End If
32
```

Fig. 15.3 **String** test to determine equality (part 1 of 2).

```vbnet
33         ' test for equality with =
34         If string1 = "hello" Then
35            output &= "string1 equals " & quotes & "hello" & _
36               quotes & vbCrLf
37
38         Else
39            output &= "string1 does not equal " & quotes & _
40               "hello" & quotes & vbCrLf
41         End If
42
43         ' test for equality comparing case
44         If (String.Equals(string3, string4)) Then
45            output &= "string3 equals string4" & vbCrLf
46         Else
47            output &= "string3 does not equal string4" & vbCrLf
48         End If
49
50         ' test CompareTo
51         output &= vbCrLf & "string1.CompareTo(string2) is " & _
52            string1.CompareTo(string2) & vbCrLf & _
53            "string2.CompareTo(string1) is " & _
54            string2.CompareTo(string1) & vbCrLf & _
55            "string1.CompareTo(string1) is " & _
56            string1.CompareTo(string1) & vbCrLf & _
57            "string3.CompareTo(string4) is " & _
58            string3.CompareTo(string4) & vbCrLf & _
59            "string4.CompareTo(string3) is " & _
60            string4.CompareTo(string3) & vbCrLf & vbCrLf
61
62         MessageBox.Show(output, "Demonstrating string" & _
63            " comparisons", MessageBoxButtons.OK, _
64            MessageBoxIcon.Information)
65      End Sub ' Main
66
67   End Module ' modCompare
```

```
Demonstrating string comparisons

   string1 = "hello"
   string2 = "good bye"
   string3 = "Happy Birthday"
   string4 = "happy birthday"

   string1 equals "hello"
   string1 equals "hello"
   string3 does not equal string4

   string1.CompareTo(string2) is 1
   string2.CompareTo(string1) is -1
   string1.CompareTo(string1) is 0
   string3.CompareTo(string4) is 1
   string4.CompareTo(string3) is -1

            OK
```

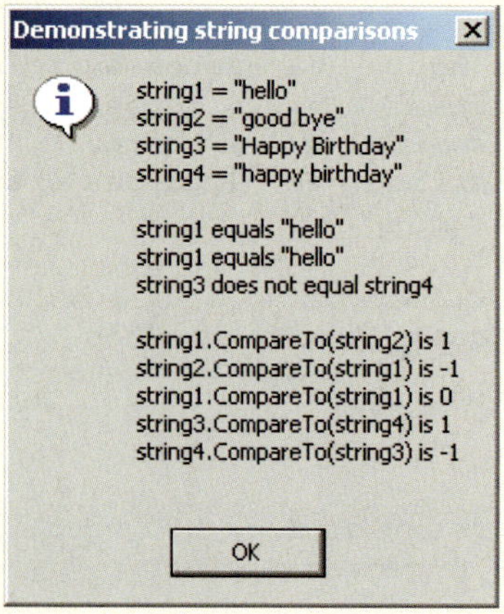

Fig. 15.3 **String** test to determine equality (part 2 of 2).

The **If** structure condition (line 24) uses method **Equals** to compare **string1** and literal **String "hello"** to determine whether they are equal. Method **Equals** (inherited by **String** from class **Object**) tests any two objects for equality (i.e., checks whether the objects contain identical contents). The method returns **True** if the objects are equal and **False** otherwise. In this instance, the preceding condition returns **True**, because **string1** references **String** literal object **"hello"**. Method **Equals** uses a *lexicographical comparison*—the integer Unicode values that represent each character in each **String** are compared. Method **Equals** compares the **Integer** Unicode values that represent the characters in each **String**. A comparison of the **String "hello"** with the **String "HELLO"** would return **False**, because the **Integer** representations of lowercase letters are different from the **Integer** representations of corresponding uppercase letters.

The condition in the second **If** structure (line 34) uses the equality operator (**=**) to compare **String string1** with the literal **String "hello"** for equality. In Visual Basic, the equality operator also uses a lexicographical comparison to compare two **String**s. Thus, the condition in the **If** structure evaluates to **True**, because the values of **string1** and **"hello"** are equal. As with any reference type, the **Is** operator may be used to determine whether two **String**s reference the same object.

We present the test for **String** equality between **string3** and **string4** (line 44) to illustrate that comparisons are indeed case sensitive. Here, **Shared** method **Equals** (as opposed to the instance method in line 24) is used to compare the values of two **String**s. **"Happy Birthday"** does not equal **"happy birthday"**, so the condition of the **If** structure fails, and the message **"string3 does not equal string4"** is added to the output message (line 47).

Lines 52–60 use the **String** method **CompareTo** to compare **String** objects. Method **CompareTo** returns **0** if the **String**s are equal, a **-1** if the **String** that invokes **CompareTo** is less than the **String** that is passed as an argument and a **1** if the **String** that invokes **CompareTo** is greater than the **String** that is passed as an argument. Method **CompareTo** uses a lexicographical comparison.

Notice that **CompareTo** considers **string3** to be larger than **string4**. The only difference between these two strings is that **string3** contains two uppercase letters. This example illustrates that an uppercase letter has a higher value in the Unicode character set than its corresponding lowercase letter.

The application in Fig. 15.4 shows how to test whether a **String** instance begins or ends with a given **String**. Method *StartsWith* determines if a **String** instance starts with the **String** text passed to it as an argument. Method *EndsWith* determines if a **String** instance ends with the **String** text passed to it as an argument. Application **modStartEnd**'s **Main** method defines an array of **String**s (called **strings**), which contains **"started"**, **"starting"**, **"ended"** and **"ending"**. The remainder of method **Main** tests the elements of the array to determine whether they start or end with a particular set of characters.

Line 20 uses method **StartsWith**, which takes a **String** argument. The condition in the **If** structure determines whether the **String** at index **i** of the array starts with the characters **"st"**. If so, the method returns **True** and appends **strings(i)** to **String output** for display purposes.

Line 32 uses method **EndsWith**, which also takes a **String** argument. The condition in the **If** structure determines whether the **String** at index **i** of the array ends with

```vbnet
1   ' Fig. 15.4: StringStartEnd.vb
2   ' Demonstrating StartsWith and EndsWith methods.
3
4   Imports System.Windows.Forms
5
6   Module modStartEnd
7
8      Sub Main()
9         Dim strings As String()
10        Dim output As String = ""
11        Dim i As Integer
12        Dim quotes As Char = ChrW(34)
13
14        strings = New String() {"started", "starting", _
15           "ended", "ending"}
16
17        ' test every string to see if it starts with "st"
18        For i = 0 To strings.GetUpperBound(0)
19
20           If strings(i).StartsWith("st") Then
21              output &= quotes & strings(i) & quotes & _
22                 " starts with " & quotes & "st" & quotes & vbCrLf
23           End If
24
25        Next
26
27        output &= vbCrLf
28
29        ' test every string to see if it ends with "ed"
30        For i = 0 To strings.GetUpperBound(0)
31
32           If strings(i).EndsWith("ed") Then
33              output &= quotes & strings(i) & quotes & _
34                 " ends with " & quotes & "ed" & quotes & vbCrLf
35           End If
36
37        Next
38
39        MessageBox.Show(output, "Demonstrating StartsWith and" & _
40           " EndsWith methods", MessageBoxButtons.OK, _
41           MessageBoxIcon.Information)
42     End Sub ' Main
43
44  End Module ' modStartEnd
```

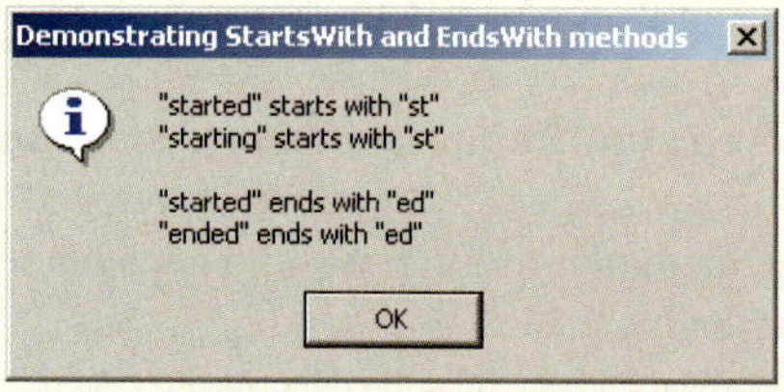

Demonstrating StartsWith and EndsWith methods

"started" starts with "st"
"starting" starts with "st"

"started" ends with "ed"
"ended" ends with "ed"

Fig. 15.4 **StartsWith** and **EndsWith** methods.

the characters **"ed"**. If so, the method returns **True**, and **strings(i)** is appended to **String output** for display purposes.

15.6 String Method GetHashCode

Often, it is necessary to store **String**s and other data types in a manner that enables the information to be found quickly. One of the best ways to make information easily accessible is to store it in a hash table. A *hash table* stores an object by performing a special calculation on that object, which produces a *hash code*. The object then is stored at a location in the hash table determined by the calculated hash code. When a program needs to retrieve the information, the same calculation is performed, generating the same hash code. Any object can be stored in a hash table. Class **Object** defines method **GetHashCode** to perform the hash-code calculation. Although all classes inherit this method from class **Object**, it is recommended that they override **Object**'s default implementation. **String Overrides** method **GetHashCode** to provide a good hash-code distribution based on the contents of the **String**. We will discuss hashing in detail in Chapter 24, Data Structures.

The example in Fig. 15.5 demonstrates the application of the **GetHashCode** method to two **String**s (**"hello"** and **"Hello"**). Here, the hash-code value for each **String** is different. However, **String**s that are not identical can have the same hash-code value.

```
1    ' Fig. 15.5: StringHashCode.vb
2    ' Demonstrating method GetHashCode of class String.
3
4    Imports System.Windows.Forms
5
6    Module modHashCode
7
8       Sub Main()
9          Dim string1 As String = "hello"
10         Dim string2 As String = "Hello"
11         Dim output As String
12         Dim quotes As Char = ChrW(34)
13
14         output = "The hash code for " & quotes & string1 & _
15            quotes & " is " & string1.GetHashCode() & vbCrLf
16
17         output &= "The hash code for " & quotes & string2 & _
18            quotes & " is " & string2.GetHashCode()
19
20         MessageBox.Show(output, _
21            "Demonstrating String Method GetHashCode")
22      End Sub ' Main
23
24   End Module ' modHashCode
```

Fig. 15.5 **GetHashCode** method demonstration (part 1 of 2).

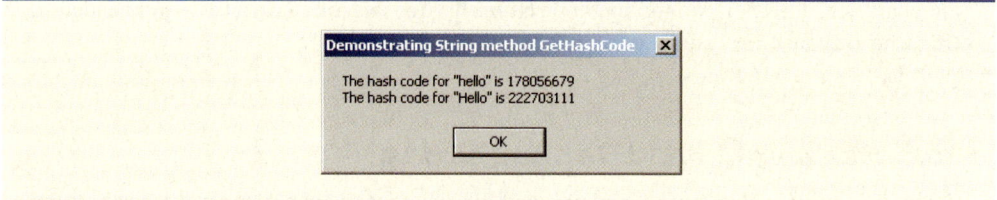

Fig. 15.5 `GetHashCode` method demonstration (part 2 of 2).

15.7 Locating Characters and Substrings in `Strings`

In many applications, it is necessary to search for a character or set of characters in a `String`. For example, a programmer creating a word processor would want to provide capabilities for searching through documents. The application in Fig. 15.6 demonstrates some of the many versions of `String` methods `IndexOf`, `IndexOfAny`, `LastIndexOf` and `LastIndexOfAny`, which search for a specified character or substring in a `String`. We perform all searches in this example on the `String letters` (initialized with `"abcdefghijklmabcdefghijklm"`) located in method `Main` of module `modIndexMethods`. Notice that this program makes use of adjacent quotation marks instead of creating a `quotes` variable with the value `ChrW(34)`.

Lines 14–21 use method `IndexOf` to locate the first occurrence of a character or substring in a `String`. If `IndexOf` finds a character, `IndexOf` returns the index of the specified character in the `String`; otherwise, `IndexOf` returns –1. The expression on line 18 uses a version of method `IndexOf` that takes two arguments—the character to search for and the starting index at which the search of the `String` should begin. The method does not examine any characters that occur prior to the starting index (in this case `1`). The expression in line 21 uses another version of method `IndexOf` which takes three arguments—the character to search for, the index at which to start searching and the number of characters to search.

```
1   ' Fig. 15.6: StringIndexMethods
2   ' Using String searching methods.
3
4   Imports System.Windows.Forms
5
6   Module modIndexMethods
7
8      Sub Main()
9         Dim letters As String = "abcdefghijklmabcdefghijklm"
10        Dim output As String
11        Dim searchLetters As Char() = New Char() {"c"c, "a"c, "$"c}
12
13        ' test IndexOf to locate a character in a string
14        output &= """c""" is located at index " & _
15           letters.IndexOf("c"c)
16
17        output &= vbCrLf & """a""" is located at index " & _
18           letters.IndexOf("a"c, 1)
```

Fig. 15.6 Searching for characters and substrings in `String`s (part 1 of 3).

```
19
20          output &= vbCrLf & """$""" is located at index " & _
21             letters.IndexOf("$"c, 3, 5)
22
23          ' test LastIndexOf to find a character in a string
24          output &= vbCrLf & vbCrLf & "Last ""c""" is located at " & _
25             "index " & letters.LastIndexOf("c"c)
26
27          output &= vbCrLf & "Last ""a""" is located at index " & _
28             letters.LastIndexOf("a"c, 25)
29
30          output &= vbCrLf & "Last ""$""" is located at index " & _
31             letters.LastIndexOf("$"c, 15, 5)
32
33          ' test IndexOf to locate a substring in a string
34          output &= vbCrLf & vbCrLf & """def""" is located at" & _
35             " index " & letters.IndexOf("def")
36
37          output &= vbCrLf & """def""" is located at index " & _
38             letters.IndexOf("def", 7)
39
40          output &= vbCrLf & """hello""" is located at index " & _
41             letters.IndexOf("hello", 5, 15)
42
43          ' test LastIndexOf to find a substring in a string
44          output &= vbCrLf & vbCrLf & "Last ""def""" is located " & _
45             "at index " & letters.LastIndexOf("def")
46
47          output &= vbCrLf & "Last ""def""" is located at " & _
48             letters.LastIndexOf("def", 25)
49
50          output &= vbCrLf & "Last ""hello""" is located at " & _
51             "index " & letters.LastIndexOf("hello", 20, 15)
52
53          ' test IndexOfAny to find first occurrence of character
54          ' in array
55          output &= vbCrLf & vbCrLf & "First occurrence of ""c""," & _
56             " ""a""" or ""$""" is located at " & _
57             letters.IndexOfAny(searchLetters)
58
59          output &= vbCrLf & "First occurrence of ""c"", ""a""" or " & _
60             """$""" is located at " & _
61             letters.IndexOfAny(searchLetters, 7)
62
63          output &= vbCrLf & "First occurrence of ""c"", ""a""" or " & _
64             """$""" is located at " & _
65             letters.IndexOfAny(searchLetters, 20, 5)
66
67          ' test LastIndexOfAny to find first occurrence of character
68          ' in array
69          output &= vbCrLf & vbCrLf & "Last occurrence of ""c""," & _
70             " ""a""" or ""$""" is located at " & _
71             letters.LastIndexOfAny(searchLetters)
```

Fig. 15.6 Searching for characters and substrings in **String**s (part 2 of 3).

```
72
73          output &= vbCrLf & "Last occurrence of ""c"", ""a"" or " & _
74             """$"" is located at " & _
75             letters.LastIndexOfAny(searchLetters, 1)
76
77          output &= vbCrLf & "Last occurrence of ""c"", ""a"" or " & _
78             """$"" is located at " & _
79             letters.LastIndexOfAny(searchLetters, 25, 5)
80
81          MessageBox.Show(output, _
82             "Demonstrating String class index methods")
83      End Sub ' Main
84
85   End Module ' modIndexMethods
```

```
Demonstrating String class index methods

"c" is located at index 2
"a" is located at index 13
"$" is located at index -1

Last "c" is located at index 15
Last "a" is located at index 13
Last "$" is located at index -1

"def" is located at index 3
"def" is located at index 16
"hello" is located at index -1

Last "def" is located at index 16
Last "def" is located at 16
Last "hello" is located at index -1

First occurrence of "c", "a" or "$" is located at 0
First occurrence of "c", "a" or "$" is located at 13
First occurrence of "c", "a" or "$" is located at -1

Last occurrence of "c", "a" or "$" is located at 15
Last occurrence of "c", "a" or "$" is located at 0
Last occurrence of "c", "a" or "$" is located at -1
```

Fig. 15.6 Searching for characters and substrings in **String**s (part 3 of 3).

Lines 24–31 use method **LastIndexOf** to locate the last occurrence of a character in a **String**. Method **LastIndexOf** performs the search from the end of the **String** toward the beginning of the **String**. If method **LastIndexOf** finds the character, **LastIndexOf** returns the index of the specified character in the **String**; otherwise, **LastIndexOf** returns **-1**. There are three versions of **LastIndexOf** that search for characters in a **String**. The expression in line 25 uses the version of method **LastIndexOf** that takes as an argument the character for which to search. The expression in line 28 uses the version of method **LastIndexOf** that takes two arguments—the character for which to search and the highest index from which to begin searching backward for the character. The expression in line 31 uses a third version of method **LastIndexOf** that takes three arguments—the character for which to search, the starting index from which to start searching backward and the number of characters (the portion of the **String**) to search.

Lines 34–51 use versions of **IndexOf** and **LastIndexOf** that take a **String** instead of a character as the first argument. These versions of the methods perform identically to those described above except that they search for sequences of characters (or substrings) that are specified by their **String** arguments.

Lines 55–79 use methods **IndexOfAny** and **LastIndexOfAny**, which take an array of characters as the first argument. These versions of the methods also perform identically to those described above except that they return the index of the first occurrence of any of the characters in the character array argument.

Common Programming Error 15.2

*In the overloaded methods **LastIndexOf** and **LastIndexOfAny** that take three parameters, the second argument must always be bigger than or equal to the third argument. This might seem counterintuitive, but remember that the search moves from the end of the string toward the start of the string.*

15.8 Extracting Substrings from **Strings**

Class **String** provides two ***Substring*** methods, which are used to create a new **String** object by copying part of an existing **String** object. Each method returns a new **String** object. The application in Fig. 15.7 demonstrates the use of both methods.

```vbnet
1   ' Fig. 15.7: SubString.vb
2   ' Demonstrating the String Substring method.
3
4   Imports System.Windows.Forms
5
6   Module modSubString
7
8      Sub Main()
9         Dim letters As String = "abcdefghijklmabcdefghijklm"
10        Dim output As String
11        Dim quotes As Char = ChrW(34)
12
13        ' invoke SubString method and pass it one parameter
14        output = "Substring from index 20 to end is " & _
15           quotes & letters.Substring(20) & quotes & vbCrLf
16
17        ' invoke SubString method and pass it two parameters
18        output &= "Substring from index 0 to 6 is " & _
19           quotes & letters.Substring(0, 6) & quotes
20
21        MessageBox.Show(output, _
22           "Demonstrating String method Substring")
23     End Sub ' Main
24
25  End Module ' modSubString
```

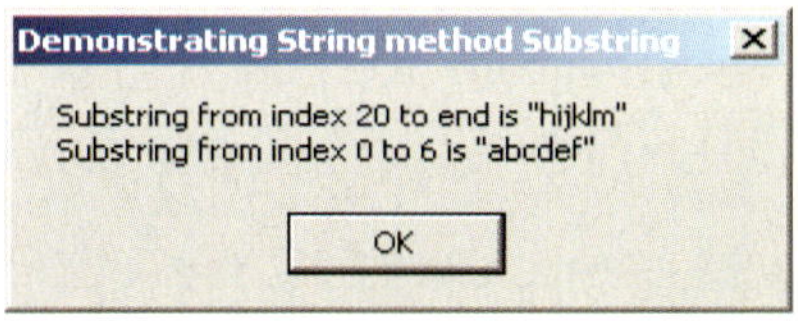

Demonstrating String method Substring

Substring from index 20 to end is "hijklm"
Substring from index 0 to 6 is "abcdef"

OK

Fig. 15.7 Substrings generated from **String**s.

The statement in lines 14–15 uses the **Substring** method that takes one **Integer** argument. The argument specifies the starting index from which the method copies characters in the original **String**. The substring returned contains a copy of the characters from the starting index to the end of the **String**. If the index specified in the argument is outside the bounds of the **String**, the program throws an **ArgumentOutOfRangeException**.

The second version of method **Substring** (line 19) takes two **Integer** arguments. The first argument specifies the starting index from which the method copies characters from the original **String**. The second argument specifies the length of the substring to be copied. The substring returned contains a copy of the specified characters from the original **String**.

15.9 Concatenating **Strings**

The **&** operator (discussed in Chapter 3, Introduction to Visual Basic Programming) is not the only way to perform **String** concatenation. The **Shared** method **Concat** of class **String** (Fig. 15.8) concatenates two **String** objects and returns a new **String** object containing the combined characters from both original **String**s. Line 18 appends the characters from **string2** to the end of **string1** using method **Concat**. The statement on line 18 does not modify the original **String**s.

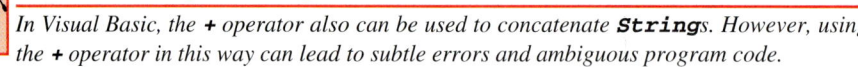

Common Programming Error 15.3

*In Visual Basic, the **+** operator also can be used to concatenate **String**s. However, using the **+** operator in this way can lead to subtle errors and ambiguous program code.*

```
1   ' Fig. 15.8: StringConcatination.vb
2   ' Demonstrating String class Concat method.
3
4   Imports System.Windows.Forms
5
6   Module modStringConcatenation
7
8      Sub Main()
9         Dim string1 As String = "Happy "
10        Dim string2 As String = "Birthday"
11        Dim output As String
12
13        output = "string1 = """ & string1 & """" & _
14           vbCrLf & "string2 = """ & string2 & """"
15
16        output &= vbCrLf & vbCrLf & _
17           "Result of String.Concat(string1, string2) = " & _
18           String.Concat(string1, string2)
19
20        MessageBox.Show(output, _
21           "Demonstrating String method Concat")
22     End Sub ' Main
23
24  End Module ' modStringConcatenation
```

Fig. 15.8 **Concat Shared** method (part 1 of 2).

Fig. 15.8 `Concat Shared` method (part 2 of 2).

15.10 Miscellaneous `String` Methods

Class **String** provides several methods that return modified copies of **String**s. The application in Fig. 15.9 demonstrates the use of these methods, which include **String** methods *Replace*, *ToLower*, *ToUpper*, *Trim* and *ToString*.

```
1    ' Fig. 15.9: StringMiscellaneous.vb
2    ' Demonstrating String methods Replace, ToLower, ToUpper, Trim,
3    ' and ToString.
4
5    Imports System.Windows.Forms
6
7    Module modStringMiscellaneous
8
9       Sub Main()
10          Dim string1 As String = "cheers!"
11          Dim string2 As String = "GOOD BYE "
12          Dim string3 As String = "   spaces   "
13          Dim output As String
14          Dim quotes As Char = ChrW(34)
15          Dim i As Integer
16
17          output = "string1 = " & quotes & string1 & quotes & _
18             vbCrLf & "string2 = " & quotes & string2 & quotes & _
19             vbCrLf & "string3 = " & quotes & string3 & quotes
20
21          ' call method Replace
22          output &= vbCrLf & vbCrLf & "Replacing " & quotes & "e" & _
23             quotes & " with " & quotes & "E" & quotes & _
24             " in string1: " & quotes & string1.Replace("e"c, "E"c) & _
25             quotes
26
27          ' call ToLower and ToUpper
28          output &= vbCrLf & vbCrLf & "string1.ToUpper() = " & _
29             quotes & string1.ToUpper() & quotes & vbCrLf & _
30             "string2.ToLower() = " & quotes & string2.ToLower() & _
31             quotes
32
```

Fig. 15.9 `String` methods `Replace`, `ToLower`, `ToUpper`, `Trim` and `ToString` (part 1 of 2).

```
33              ' call Trim method
34              output &= vbCrLf & vbCrLf & "string3 after trim = " & _
35                  quotes & string3.Trim() & quotes
36
37              ' call ToString method
38              output &= vbCrLf & vbCrLf & "string1 = " & _
39                  quotes & string1.ToString() & quotes
40
41              MessageBox.Show(output, _
42                  "Demonstrating miscellaneous String methods")
43          End Sub ' Main
44
45      End Module ' modStringMiscellaneous
```

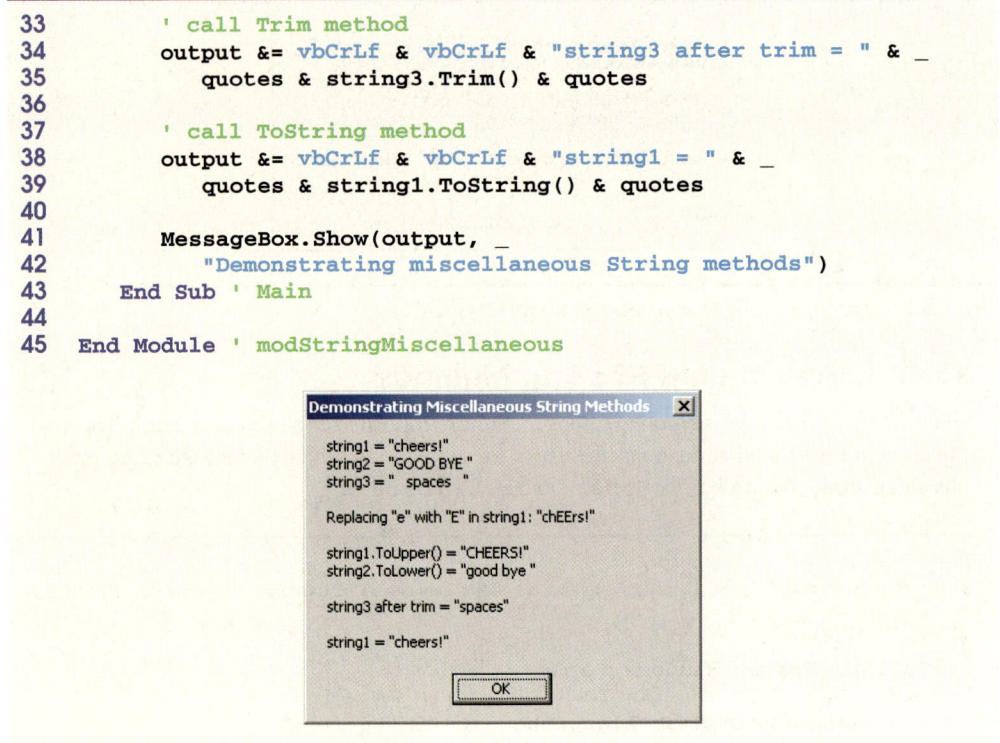

Fig. 15.9 `String` methods `Replace`, `ToLower`, `ToUpper`, `Trim` and `ToString` (part 2 of 2).

Line 24 uses **String** method **Replace** to return a new **String** object, replacing every occurrence in **string1** of character **"e"c** with character **"E"c**. Method **Replace** takes two arguments—a **String** for which to search and another **String** with which to replace all matching occurrences of the first argument. The original **String** remains unchanged. If there are no occurrences of the first argument in the **String**, the method returns the original **String**.

String method **ToUpper** generates a new **String** object (line 29) that replaces any lowercase letters in **string1** with their uppercase equivalent. The method returns a new **String** object containing the converted **String**; the original **String** remains unchanged. If there are no characters to convert to uppercase, the method returns the original **String**. Line 30 uses **String** method **ToLower** to return a new **String** in which any uppercase letters in **string2** are replaced by their lowercase equivalents. The original **String** is unchanged. As with **ToUpper**, if there are no characters to convert to lowercase, method **ToLower** returns the original **String**.

Line 35 uses **String** method **Trim** to remove all whitespace characters that appear at the beginning and end of a **String**. Without altering the original **String**, the method returns a new **String** object that contains the **String**, but omits leading or trailing whitespace characters. Another version of method **Trim** takes a character array, removes all whitespace characters from the beginning and end of the array and returns the result in a **String**.

Line 39 uses class **String**'s method **ToString** to show that the various other methods employed in this application have not modified **string1**. Why is the **ToString** method provided for class **String**? In Visual Basic .NET, all objects are derived from class **Object**, which defines **Overridable** method **ToString**. Thus, method **ToString** can be called to obtain a **String** representation any object. If a class that inherits from **Object** (such as **String**) does not override method **ToString**, the class uses the default version from class **Object**, which returns a **String** consisting of the object's class name. Classes usually override method **ToString** to express the contents of an object as text. Class **String** overrides method **ToString** so that, instead of returning the class name, it simply returns the **String**.

15.11 Class `StringBuilder`

The **String** class provides many capabilities for processing **String**s. However a **String**'s contents can never change. Operations which seem to concatenate **String**s are in fact assigning **String** references to newly created **String**s (e.g., the **&=** operator creates a new **String** and assigns the initial **String** reference to the newly created **String**).

The next several sections discuss the features of class **StringBuilder** (namespace **System.Text**), which is used to create and manipulate dynamic string information—i.e., modifiable strings. Every **StringBuilder** can store a certain number of characters that is specified by its capacity. Exceeding the capacity of a **StringBuilder** causes the capacity to expand to accommodate the additional characters. As we will see, members of class **StringBuilder**, such as methods **Append** and **AppendFormat**, can be used for concatenation like the operators **&** and **&=** for class **String**.

Software Engineering Observation 15.2

String objects are constant strings, whereas StringBuilder objects are modifiable strings. Visual Basic can perform certain optimizations involving String objects (such as the sharing of one String object among multiple references), because it knows these objects will not change.

Performance Tip 15.2

When given the choice between using a String object to represent a string and using a StringBuilder object to represent that string, always use a String object if the contents of the object will not change. When appropriate, using String objects instead of StringBuilder objects improves performance.

Class **StringBuilder** provides six overloaded constructors. Module **modBuilderConstructor** (Fig. 15.10) demonstrates the use of three of these overloaded constructors.

```
1   ' Fig. 15.10: StringBuilderConstructor.vb
2   ' Demonstrating StringBuilder class constructors.
3
4   Imports System.Text
5   Imports System.Windows.Forms
6
```

Fig. 15.10 **StringBuilder** class constructors (part 1 of 2).

```
 7   Module modBuilderConstructor
 8
 9      Sub Main()
10         Dim buffer1, buffer2, buffer3 As StringBuilder
11         Dim quotes As Char = ChrW(34)
12         Dim output As String
13
14         buffer1 = New StringBuilder()
15         buffer2 = New StringBuilder(10)
16         buffer3 = New StringBuilder("hello")
17
18         output = "buffer1 = " & quotes & buffer1.ToString() & _
19            quotes & vbCrLf
20
21         output &= "buffer2 = " & quotes & _
22            buffer2.ToString() & quotes & vbCrLf
23
24         output &= "buffer3 = " & quotes & _
25            buffer3.ToString() & quotes
26
27         MessageBox.Show(output, _
28            "Demonstrating StringBuilder class constructors")
29      End Sub ' Main
30
31   End Module ' modBuilderConstructor
```

Demonstrating StringBuilder class constructors

buffer1 = ""
buffer2 = ""
buffer3 = "hello"

OK

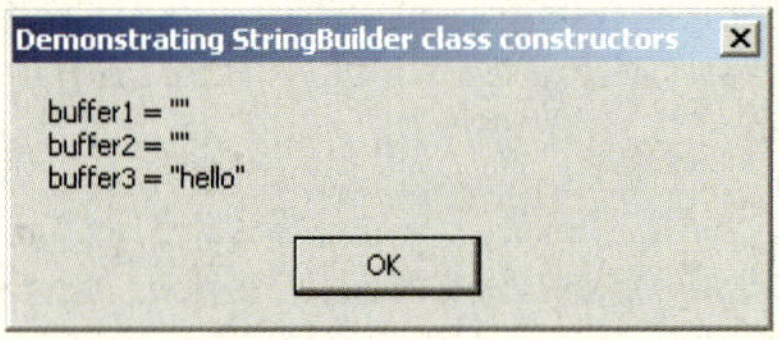

Fig. 15.10 `StringBuilder` class constructors (part 2 of 2).

Line 14 employs the no-argument **StringBuilder** constructor to create a **StringBuilder** that contains no characters and has a default initial capacity of 16 characters. Line 15 uses the **StringBuilder** constructor that takes an **Integer** argument to create a **StringBuilder** that contains no characters and has the initial capacity specified in the **Integer** argument (i.e., **10**). Line 16 uses the **StringBuilder** constructor that takes a **String** argument to create a **StringBuilder** containing the characters of the **String** argument. The initial capacity is the smallest power of two greater than the number of characters in the **String** passed as an argument.

Lines 18–25 use **StringBuilder** method **ToString** to obtain a **String** representation of the **StringBuilder**s' contents. This method returns the **StringBuilder**s' underlying string.

15.12 `StringBuilder` Indexer, `Length` and `Capacity` Properties, and `EnsureCapacity` Method

Class **StringBuilder** provides the *Length* and *Capacity* properties to return the number of characters currently in a **StringBuilder** and the number of characters that a **StringBuilder** can store without allocating more memory, respectively. These properties also can increase or decrease the length or the capacity of the **StringBuilder**.

Method ***EnsureCapacity*** allows programmers to guarantee that a **String-Builder** has a capacity that reduces the number of times the capacity must be increased. Method **EnsureCapacity** doubles the **StringBuilder** instance's current capacity. If this doubled value is greater than the value that the programmer wishes to ensure, it becomes the new capacity. Otherwise, **EnsureCapacity** alters the capacity to make it one more than the requested number. For example, if the current capacity is 17 and we wish to make it 40, 17 multiplied by 2 is not greater than 40, so the call will result in a new capacity of 41. If the current capacity is 23 and we wish to make it 40, 23 will be multiplied by 2 to result in a new capacity of 46. Both 41 and 46 are greater than 40, and so a capacity of 40 is indeed ensured by method **EnsureCapacity**. The program in Fig. 15.11 demonstrates the use of these methods and properties.

The program contains one **StringBuilder**, called **buffer**. Lines 11–12 of the program use the **StringBuilder** constructor that takes a **String** argument to instantiate the **StringBuilder** and initialize its value to **"Hello, how are you?"**. Lines 15–17 append to **output** the content, length and capacity of the **StringBuilder**. In the output window, notice that the capacity of the **StringBuilder** is initially 32. Remember, the **StringBuilder** constructor that takes a **String** argument creates a **StringBuilder** object with an initial capacity that is the smallest power of two greater than the number of characters in the **String** passed as an argument.

```vb
1   ' Fig. 15.11: StringBuilderFeatures.vb
2   ' Demonstrating some features of class StringBuilder.
3
4   Imports System.Text
5   Imports System.Windows.Forms
6
7   Module modBuilderFeatures
8
9      Sub Main()
10        Dim i As Integer
11        Dim buffer As StringBuilder = _
12           New StringBuilder("Hello, how are you?")
13
14        ' use Length and Capacity properties
15        Dim output As String = "buffer = " & buffer.ToString & _
16           vbCrLf & "Length = " & buffer.Length & vbCrLf & _
17           "Capacity = " & buffer.Capacity
18
19        ' use EnsureCapacity method
20        buffer.EnsureCapacity(75)
21
22        output &= vbCrLf & vbCrLf & "New capacity = " & _
23           buffer.Capacity
24
25        ' truncate StringBuilder by setting Length property
26        buffer.Length = 10
27
```

Fig. 15.11 **StringBuilder** size manipulation (part 1 of 2).

```
28              output &= vbCrLf & vbCrLf & "New Length = " & _
29                  buffer.Length & vbCrLf & "buffer = "
30
31              ' use StringBuilder Indexer
32              For i = 0 To buffer.Length - 1
33                  output &= buffer(i)
34              Next
35
36              MessageBox.Show(output, "StringBuilder features")
37          End Sub ' Main
38
39      End Module ' modBuilderFeatures
```

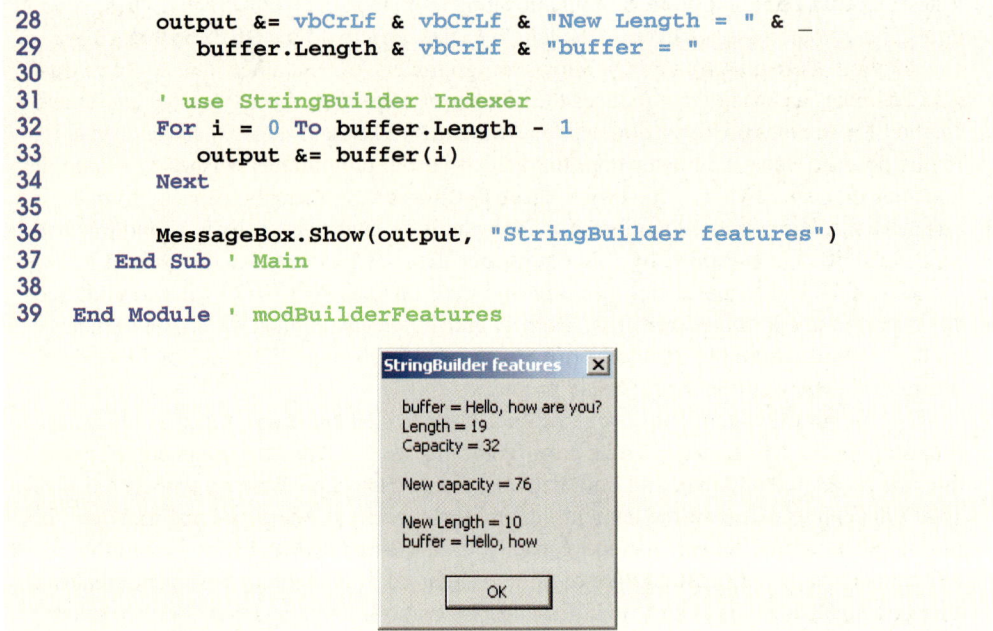

Fig. 15.11 `StringBuilder` size manipulation (part 2 of 2).

Line 20 expands the capacity of the **StringBuilder** to a minimum of 75 characters. The current capacity (**32**) multiplied by two is less than 75, so method **EnsureCapacity** increases the capacity to one greater than 75 (i.e., 76). If new characters are added to a **StringBuilder** so that its length exceeds its capacity, the capacity grows to accommodate the additional characters in the same manner as if method **EnsureCapacity** had been called.

Line 26 uses **Length**'s **Set** accessor to set the length of the **StringBuilder** to **10**. If the specified length is less than the current number of characters in the **StringBuilder**, the contents of **StringBuilder** are truncated to the specified length (i.e., the program discards all characters in the **StringBuilder** that occur after the specified length). If the specified length is greater than the number of characters currently in the **StringBuilder**, null characters (characters with the numeric representation **0** that signal the end of a **String**) are appended to the **StringBuilder** until the total number of characters in the **StringBuilder** is equal to the specified length.

 Common Programming Error 15.4

*Assigning **Nothing** to a **String** reference can lead to logic errors. The keyword **Nothing** is a null reference, not a **String**. Do not confuse **Nothing** with the empty string, **""** (the **String** that is of length 0 and contains no characters).*

15.13 `StringBuilder` `Append` and `AppendFormat` Methods

Class **StringBuilder** provides 19 overloaded **Append** methods that allow various data-type values to be added to the end of a **StringBuilder**. Visual Basic provides ver-

Chapter 15   Strings, Characters and Regular Expressions

sions for each of the primitive data types and for character arrays, **String**s and **Object**s. (Remember that method **ToString** produces a **String** representation of any **Object**.) Each of the methods takes an argument, converts it to a **String** and appends it to the **StringBuilder**. Figure 15.12 demonstrates the use of several **Append** methods.

```vb
 1   ' Fig. 15.12: StringBuilderAppend.vb
 2   ' Demonstrating StringBuilder Append methods.
 3
 4   Imports System.Text
 5   Imports System.Windows.Forms
 6
 7   Module modBuilderAppend
 8
 9      Sub Main()
10         Dim objectValue As Object = "hello"
11         Dim stringValue As String = "good bye"
12         Dim characterArray As Char() = {"a"c, "b"c, "c"c, _
13            "d"c, "e"c, "f"c}
14
15         Dim booleanValue As Boolean = True
16         Dim characterValue As Char = "Z"c
17         Dim integerValue As Integer = 7
18         Dim longValue As Long = 1000000
19         Dim singleValue As Single = 2.5
20         Dim doubleValue As Double = 33.333
21         Dim buffer As StringBuilder = New StringBuilder()
22
23         ' use method Append to append values to buffer
24         buffer.Append(objectValue)
25         buffer.Append("   ")
26         buffer.Append(stringValue)
27         buffer.Append("   ")
28         buffer.Append(characterArray)
29         buffer.Append("   ")
30         buffer.Append(characterArray, 0, 3)
31         buffer.Append("   ")
32         buffer.Append(booleanValue)
33         buffer.Append("   ")
34         buffer.Append(characterValue)
35         buffer.Append("   ")
36         buffer.Append(integerValue)
37         buffer.Append("   ")
38         buffer.Append(longValue)
39         buffer.Append("   ")
40         buffer.Append(singleValue)
41         buffer.Append("   ")
42         buffer.Append(doubleValue)
43
44         MessageBox.Show("buffer = " & buffer.ToString(), _
45            "Demonstrating StringBuilder Append methods", _
46            MessageBoxButtons.OK, MessageBoxIcon.Information)
47      End Sub ' Main
```

Fig. 15.12 Append methods of **StringBuilder** (part 1 of 2).

```
48
49    End Module ' modBuilderAppend
```

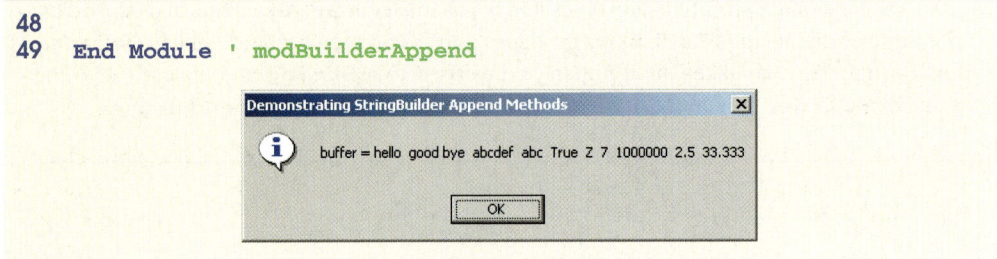

Fig. 15.12 Append methods of `StringBuilder` (part 2 of 2).

Lines 24–42 use 10 different overloaded **Append** methods to attach the objects created in lines 10–21 to the end of the **StringBuilder**. **Append** behaves similarly to the **&** operator which is used with **String**s. Just as **&** seems to append objects to a **String**, method **Append** can append data types to a **StringBuilder**'s underlying string.

Class **StringBuilder** also provides method **AppendFormat**, which converts a **String** to a specified format and then appends it to the **StringBuilder**. The example in Fig. 15.13 demonstrates the use of this method.

```vb
1    ' Fig. 15.13: StringBuilderAppendFormat.vb
2    ' Demonstrating method AppendFormat.
3
4    Imports System.Text
5    Imports System.Windows.Forms
6
7    Module modBuilderAppendFormat
8
9       Sub Main()
10          Dim buffer As StringBuilder = New StringBuilder()
11          Dim string1, string2 As String
12
13          ' formatted string
14          string1 = "This {0} costs: {1:C}." & vbCrLf
15
16          ' string1 argument array
17          Dim objectArray As Object() = New Object(1) {}
18
19          objectArray(0) = "car"
20          objectArray(1) = 1234.56
21
22          ' append to buffer formatted string with argument
23          buffer.AppendFormat(string1, objectArray)
24
25          ' formatted string
26          string2 = "Number:{0:D3}. " & vbCrLf & _
27             "Number right aligned with spaces:{0, 4}." & vbCrLf & _
28             "Number left aligned with spaces:{0, -4}."
29
30          ' append to buffer formatted string with argument
31          buffer.AppendFormat(string2, 5)
```

Fig. 15.13 `StringBuilder`'s `AppendFormat` method (part 1 of 2).

```
32
33            ' display formatted strings
34            MessageBox.Show(buffer.ToString(), "Using AppendFormat", _
35               MessageBoxButtons.OK, MessageBoxIcon.Information)
36       End Sub ' Main
37
38  End Module ' modBuilderAppendFormat
```

Using AppendFormat
This car costs: $1,234.56.
Number:005.
Number right aligned with spaces: 5.
Number left aligned with spaces:5   .

Fig. 15.13 `StringBuilder`'s `AppendFormat` method (part 2 of 2).

Line 14 creates a **String** that contains formatting information. The information enclosed within the braces determines how to format a specific piece of information. Formats have the form **{X[,Y][:FormatString]}**, where **X** is the number of the argument to be formatted, counting from zero. **Y** is an optional argument, which can be positive or negative, indicating how many characters should be in the result of formatting. If the resulting **String** is less than the number **Y**, the **String** will be padded with spaces to make up for the difference. A positive integer aligns the string to the right; a negative integer aligns it to the left. The optional **FormatString** applies a particular format to the argument: Currency, decimal, scientific, as well as others. In this case, "**{0}**" means the first argument will be printed out. "**{1:C}**" specifies that the second argument will be formatted as a currency value.

Line 23 shows a version of **AppendFormat**, which takes two parameters—a **String** specifying the format and an array of objects to serve as the arguments to the format **String**. The argument referred to by "**{0}**" is in the object array at index **0**, and so on.

Lines 26–28 define another **String** used for formatting. The first format "**{0:D3}**" specifies that the first argument will be formatted as a three-digit decimal, meaning any number that has fewer than three digits will have leading zeros placed in front to make up the difference. The next format, "**{0, 4}**" specifies that the formatted **String** should have four characters and should be right aligned. The third format, "**{0, -4}**" specifies that the **String**s should be aligned to the left. For more formatting options, please refer to the documentation.

Line 31 uses a version of **AppendFormat**, which takes two parameters: a **String** containing a format and an object to which the format is applied. In this case, the object is the number **5**. The output of Fig. 15.13 displays the result of applying these two version of **AppendFormat** with their respective arguments.

15.14 StringBuilder Insert, Remove and Replace Methods

Class **StringBuilder** provides 18 overloaded **Insert** methods to allow various data-type values to be inserted at any position in a **StringBuilder**. The class provides versions for each of the primitive data types and for character arrays, **String**s and **Object**s.

(Remember that method **ToString** produces a **String** representation of any **Object**.) Each method takes its second argument, converts it to a **String** and inserts the **String** in the **StringBuilder** in front of the index specified by the first argument. The index specified by the first argument must be greater than or equal to **0** and less than the length of the **StringBuilder**; otherwise, the program throws an **ArgumentOutOfRange-Exception**.

Class **StringBuilder** also provides method **Remove** for deleting any portion of a **StringBuilder**. Method **Remove** takes two arguments—the index at which to begin deletion and the number of characters to delete. The sum of the starting subscript and the number of characters to be deleted must always be less than the length of the **String-Builder**; otherwise, the program throws an **ArgumentOutOfRangeException**. The **Insert** and **Remove** methods are demonstrated in Fig. 15.14.

```vb
1   ' Fig. 15.14: StringBuilderInsertRemove.vb
2   ' Demonstrating methods Insert and Remove of the
3   ' StringBuilder class.
4
5   Imports System.Text
6   Imports System.Windows.Forms
7
8   Module modBuilderInsertRemove
9
10     Sub Main()
11        Dim objectValue As Object = "hello"
12        Dim stringValue As String = "good bye"
13        Dim characterArray As Char() = {"a"c, "b"c, "c"c, _
14           "d"c, "e"c, "f"c}
15
16        Dim booleanValue As Boolean = True
17        Dim characterValue As Char = "K"c
18        Dim integerValue As Integer = 7
19        Dim longValue As Long = 10000000
20        Dim singleValue As Single = 2.5
21        Dim doubleValue As Double = 33.333
22        Dim buffer As StringBuilder = New StringBuilder()
23        Dim output As String
24
25        ' insert values into buffer
26        buffer.Insert(0, objectValue)
27        buffer.Insert(0, " ")
28        buffer.Insert(0, stringValue)
29        buffer.Insert(0, " ")
30        buffer.Insert(0, characterArray)
31        buffer.Insert(0, " ")
32        buffer.Insert(0, booleanValue)
33        buffer.Insert(0, " ")
34        buffer.Insert(0, characterValue)
35        buffer.Insert(0, " ")
36        buffer.Insert(0, integerValue)
37        buffer.Insert(0, " ")
```

Fig. 15.14 **StringBuilder** text insertion and removal (part 1 of 2).

```
38          buffer.Insert(0, longValue)
39          buffer.Insert(0, " ")
40          buffer.Insert(0, singleValue)
41          buffer.Insert(0, " ")
42          buffer.Insert(0, doubleValue)
43          buffer.Insert(0, " ")
44
45          output = "buffer after inserts:" & vbCrLf & _
46             buffer.ToString() & vbCrLf & vbCrLf
47
48          buffer.Remove(12, 1) ' delete 5 in 2.5
49          buffer.Remove(2, 4)  ' delete 33.3 in 33.333
50
51          output &= "buffer after Removes:" & vbCrLf & _
52             buffer.ToString()
53
54          MessageBox.Show(output, "Demonstrating StringBuilder " & _
55             "Insert and Remove Methods", MessageBoxButtons.OK, _
56             MessageBoxIcon.Information)
57       End Sub ' Main
58
59    End Module ' modBuilderInsertRemove
```

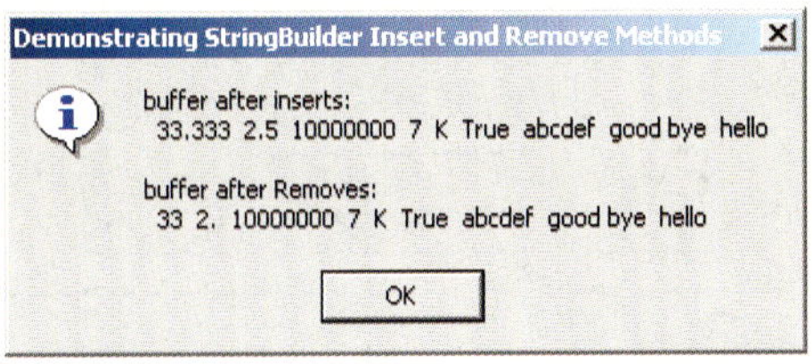

Fig. 15.14 `StringBuilder` text insertion and removal (part 2 of 2).

Another useful method included with **StringBuilder** is **Replace**. **Replace** searches for a specified **String** or character and substitutes another **String** or character in its place. Figure 15.15 demonstrates this method.

```
1  ' Fig. 15.15: StringBuilderReplace.vb
2  ' Demonstrating method Replace.
3
4  Imports System.Text
5  Imports System.Windows.Forms
6
7  Module modBuilderReplace
8
9     Sub Main()
10       Dim builder1 As StringBuilder = _
11          New StringBuilder("Happy Birthday Jane")
12
13       Dim builder2 As StringBuilder = _
14          New StringBuilder("good bye greg")
```

Fig. 15.15 `StringBuilder` text replacement (part 1 of 2).

```vbnet
15
16          Dim output As String = "Before Replacements:" & vbCrLf & _
17              builder1.ToString() & vbCrLf & builder2.ToString()
18
19          builder1.Replace("Jane", "Greg")
20          builder2.Replace("g"c, "G"c, 0, 5)
21
22          output &= vbCrLf & vbCrLf & "After Replacements:" & _
23              vbCrLf & builder1.ToString() & vbCrLf & _
24              builder2.ToString()
25
26          MessageBox.Show(output, _
27              "Using StringBuilder method Replace", _
28              MessageBoxButtons.OK, MessageBoxIcon.Information)
29      End Sub ' Main
30
31  End Module ' modBuilderReplace
```

Dialog output:
```
Using StringBuilder method Replace

Before Replacements:
Happy Birthday Jane
good bye greg

After Replacements:
Happy Birthday Greg
Good bye greg
```

Fig. 15.15 `StringBuilder` text replacement (part 2 of 2).

Line 19 uses method **Replace** to replace all instances of the **String "Jane"** with the **String "Greg"** in **builder1**. Another overload of this method takes two characters as parameters and replaces all occurrences of the first with the second. Line 20 uses an overload of **Replace** that takes four parameters, the first two of which are characters and the second two of which are **Integer**s. The method replaces all instances of the first character with the second, beginning at the index specified by the first **Integer** and continuing for a count specified by the second. Thus, in this case, **Replace** looks through only five characters starting with the character at index **0**. As the outputs illustrates, this version of **Replace** replaces **g** with **G** in the word **"good"**, but not in **"greg"**. This is because the **g**s in **"greg"** do not fall in the range indicated by the **Integer** arguments (i.e., between indexes **0** and **4**).

15.15 Char Methods

Visual Basic provides a program building block, called a *structure*, which is similar to a class. Although structures and classes are comparable in many ways, structures encapsulate value types. Like classes, structures include methods and properties. Both use the same modifiers (such as **Public**, **Private** and **Protected**) and access members via the member access operator (**.**). However, classes are created by using the keyword **Class**, and structures are created using the keyword *Structure*.

Many of the primitive data types that we have used in this book are actually aliases for different structures. For instance, an **Integer** is defined by structure **System.Int32**, a **Long** by **System.Int64**, and so on. These structures are derived from class **ValueType**, which in turn is derived from class **Object**. In this section, we present structure **Char**, which is the structure for characters.

Most **Char** methods are **Shared**, take at least one character argument and perform either a test or a manipulation on the character. We present several of these methods in the next example. Figure 15.16 demonstrates **Shared** methods that test characters to determine whether they are a specific character type and **Shared** methods that perform case conversions on characters.

```vb
1   ' Fig. 15.16: CharMethods.vb
2   ' Demonstrates Shared character testing methods
3   ' from Char structure
4
5   Public Class FrmCharacter
6      Inherits Form
7
8      Friend WithEvents lblEnter As Label    ' prompts for input
9
10     Friend WithEvents txtInput As TextBox  ' reads a Char
11     Friend WithEvents txtOutput As TextBox ' displays results
12
13     ' reads and displays information about input
14     Friend WithEvents cmdAnalyze As Button
15
16     ' Visual Studio .NET generated code
17
18     ' handle cmdAnalyze Click
19     Private Sub cmdAnalyze_Click(ByVal sender As System.Object, _
20        ByVal e As System.EventArgs) Handles cmdAnalyze.Click
21
22        Dim character As Char = Convert.ToChar(txtInput.Text)
23
24        BuildOutput(character)
25     End Sub ' cmdAnalyze_Click
26
27     ' display character information in txtOutput
28     Public Sub BuildOutput(ByVal inputCharacter As Char)
29        Dim output As String
30
31        output = "is digit: " & _
32           Char.IsDigit(inputCharacter) & vbCrLf
33
34        output &= "is letter: " & _
35           Char.IsLetter(inputCharacter) & vbCrLf
36
37        output &= "is letter or digit: " & _
38           Char.IsLetterOrDigit(inputCharacter) & vbCrLf
39
```

Fig. 15.16 **Char**'s **Shared** character-testing methods and case-conversion methods (part 1 of 2).

```
40          output &= "is lower case: " & _
41             Char.IsLower(inputCharacter) & vbCrLf
42
43          output &= "is upper case: " & _
44             Char.IsUpper(inputCharacter) & vbCrLf
45
46          output &= "to upper case: " & _
47             Char.ToUpper(inputCharacter) & vbCrLf
48
49          output &= "to lower case: " & _
50             Char.ToLower(inputCharacter) & vbCrLf
51
52          output &= "is punctuation: " & _
53             Char.IsPunctuation(inputCharacter) & vbCrLf
54
55          output &= "is symbol: " & Char.IsSymbol(inputCharacter)
56
57          txtOutput.Text = output
58       End Sub ' BuildOutput
59
60    End Class ' FrmCharacter
```

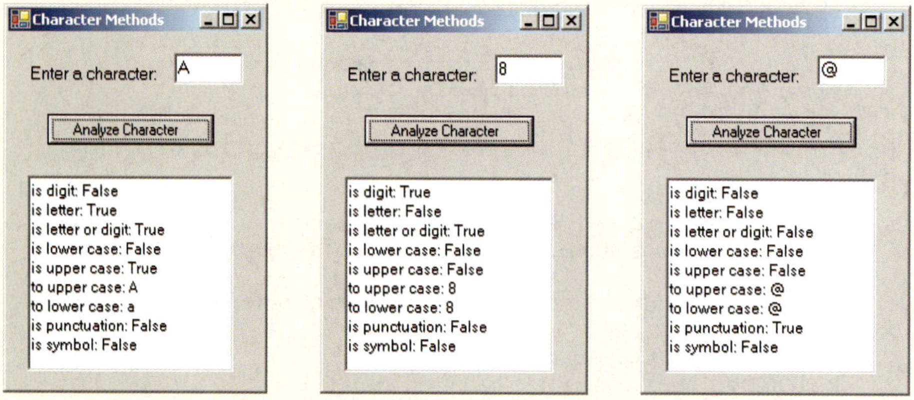

Fig. 15.16 Char's **Shared** character-testing methods and case-conversion methods (part 2 of 2).

This Windows application contains a prompt, a **TextBox** into which the user can input a character, a button that the user can press after entering a character and a second **TextBox** that displays the output of our analysis. When the user clicks the **Analyze Character** button, event handler **cmdAnalyze_Click** (lines 19–25) is invoked. This method converts the entered data from a **String** to a **Char** using method **Convert.ToChar** (line 22). On line 24, we call method **BuildOutput**, which is defined in lines 28–58.

Line 32 uses **Char** method *IsDigit* to determine whether character **inputCharacter** is defined as a digit. If so, the method returns **True**; otherwise, it returns **False**.

Line 35 uses **Char** method ***IsLetter*** to determine whether character **inputCharacter** is a letter. If so, the method returns **True**; otherwise, it returns **False**. Line 38 uses **Char** method ***IsLetterOrDigit*** to determine whether character **inputCharacter** is a letter or a digit. If so, the method returns **True**; otherwise, it returns **False**.

Line 41 uses **Char** method ***IsLower*** to determine whether character **inputCharacter** is a lowercase letter. If so, the method returns **True**; otherwise, it returns **False**. Line 44 uses **Char** method ***IsUpper*** to determine whether character **inputCharacter** is an uppercase letter. If so, the method returns **True**; otherwise, it returns **False**. Line 47 uses **Char** method ***ToUpper*** to convert the character **inputCharacter** to its uppercase equivalent. The method returns the converted character if the character has an uppercase equivalent; otherwise, the method returns its original argument. Line 50 uses **Char** method ***ToLower*** to convert the character **inputCharacter** to its lowercase equivalent. The method returns the converted character if the character has a lowercase equivalent; otherwise, the method returns its original argument.

Line 53 uses **Char** method ***IsPunctuation*** to determine whether character **inputCharacter** is a punctuation mark. If so, the method returns **True**; otherwise, it returns **False**. Line 55 uses **Char** method ***IsSymbol*** to determine whether character **inputCharacter** is a symbol. If so, the method returns **True**; otherwise it returns **False**.

Structure type **Char** also contains other methods not shown in this example. Many of the **Shared** methods are similar; for instance, ***IsWhiteSpace*** is used to determine whether a certain character is a whitespace character (e.g., newline, tab or space). The structure also contains several **Public** instance methods; many of these, such as methods **ToString** and **Equals**, are methods that we have seen before in other classes. This group includes method **CompareTo**, which is used to compare two character values with one another.

15.16 Card Shuffling and Dealing Simulation

In this section, we use random-number generation to develop a program that simulates the shuffling and dealing of cards. Once created, this program can be implemented in programs that imitate specific card games. We include several exercises at the end of this chapter that require card shuffling and dealing capabilities.

We develop application **DeckOfCards** (Fig. 15.18), which creates a deck of 52 playing cards using **CCard** objects. Users can deal each card by clicking the **Deal Card** button. Each dealt card is displayed in a **Label**. Users also can shuffle the deck at any time by clicking the **Shuffle Cards** button.

```
1   ' Fig. 15.17: Card.vb
2   ' Stores suit and face information on each card.
3
4   Public Class CCard
5      Private face As String
6      Private suit As String
7
```

Fig. 15.17 **CCard** class (part 1 of 2).

```vb
 8        Public Sub New(ByVal faceValue As String, _
 9           ByVal suitValue As String)
10
11           face = faceValue
12           suit = suitValue
13        End Sub ' New
14
15        Public Overrides Function ToString() As String
16           Return face & " of " & suit
17        End Function ' ToString
18
19     End Class ' CCard
```

Fig. 15.17 CCard class (part 2 of 2).

```vb
 1  ' Fig. 15.18: DeckOfCards.vb
 2  ' Simulating card dealing and shuffling.
 3
 4  Public Class FrmDeck
 5     Inherits Form
 6
 7     Friend WithEvents lblDisplay As Label ' displays dealt card
 8     Friend WithEvents lblStatus As Label  ' number of cards dealt
 9
10     Friend WithEvents cmdDeal As Button    ' deal one card
11     Friend WithEvents cmdShuffle As Button ' shuffle cards
12
13     ' Visual Studio .NET generated code
14
15     Private currentCard As Integer
16     Private randomObject As Random = New Random()
17     Private deck As CCard() = New CCard(51) {}
18
19     ' handles form at load time
20     Public Sub FrmDeck_Load(ByVal sender As System.Object, _
21        ByVal e As System.EventArgs) Handles MyBase.Load
22
23        Dim faces As String() = {"Ace", "Deuce", "Three", _
24           "Four", "Five", "Six", "Seven", "Eight", "Nine", _
25           "Ten", "Jack", "Queen", "King"}
26
27        Dim suits As String() = {"Hearts", "Diamonds", "Clubs", _
28           "Spades"}
29
30        Dim i As Integer
31
32        ' no cards have been drawn
33        currentCard = -1
34
```

Fig. 15.18 Card dealing and shuffling simulation (part 1 of 4).

```vbnet
35            ' initialize deck
36            For i = 0 To deck.GetUpperBound(0)
37               deck(i) = New CCard(faces(i Mod 13), suits(i Mod 4))
38            Next
39
40         End Sub ' FrmDeck_Load
41
42         ' handles cmdDeal Click
43         Private Sub cmdDeal_Click(ByVal sender As System.Object, _
44            ByVal e As System.EventArgs) Handles cmdDeal.Click
45
46            Dim dealt As CCard = DealCard()
47
48            ' if dealt card is Null, then no cards left
49            ' player must shuffle cards
50            If Not (dealt Is Nothing) Then
51               lblDisplay.Text = dealt.ToString()
52               lblStatus.Text = "Card #: " & currentCard
53            Else
54               lblDisplay.Text = "NO MORE CARDS TO DEAL"
55               lblStatus.Text = "Shuffle cards to continue"
56            End If
57
58         End Sub ' cmdDeal_Click
59
60         ' shuffle cards
61         Public Sub Shuffle()
62            Dim i As Integer
63            Dim j As Integer
64            Dim temporaryValue As CCard
65
66            currentCard = -1
67
68            ' swap each card with random card
69            For i = 0 To deck.GetUpperBound(0)
70               j = randomObject.Next(52)
71
72                ' swap cards
73               temporaryValue = deck(i)
74               deck(i) = deck(j)
75               deck(j) = temporaryValue
76            Next
77
78            cmdDeal.Enabled = True
79         End Sub ' Shuffle
80
81         Public Function DealCard() As CCard
82
83            ' if there is a card to deal then deal it
84            ' otherwise signal that cards need to be shuffled by
85            ' disabling cmdDeal and returning Nothing
86            If (currentCard + 1) < deck.GetUpperBound(0) Then
87               currentCard += 1
```

Fig. 15.18 Card dealing and shuffling simulation (part 2 of 4).

```vbnet
88
89              Return deck(currentCard)
90          Else
91              cmdDeal.Enabled = False
92
93              Return Nothing
94          End If
95
96      End Function ' DealCard
97
98      ' cmdShuffle_Click
99      Private Sub cmdShuffle_Click(ByVal sender As System.Object, _
100         ByVal e As System.EventArgs) Handles cmdShuffle.Click
101
102         lblDisplay.Text = "SHUFFLING..."
103
104         Shuffle()
105
106         lblDisplay.Text = "DECK IS SHUFFLED"
107     End Sub ' cmdShuffle_Click
108
109 End Class ' FrmDeck
```

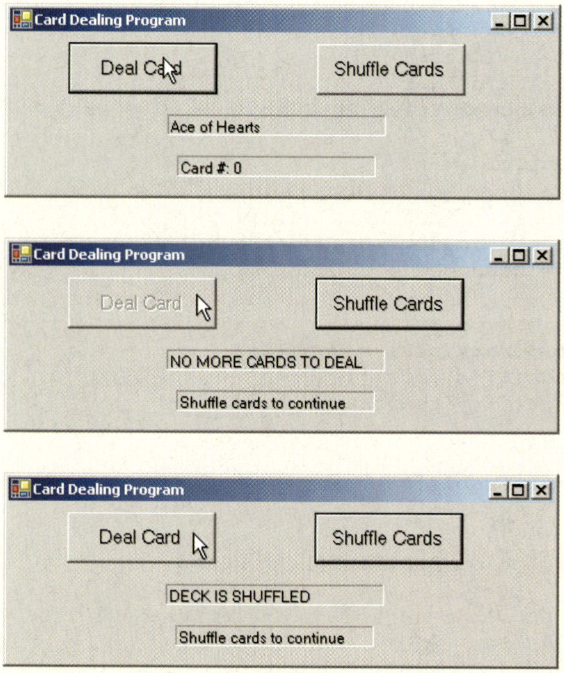

Fig. 15.18 Card dealing and shuffling simulation (part 3 of 4).

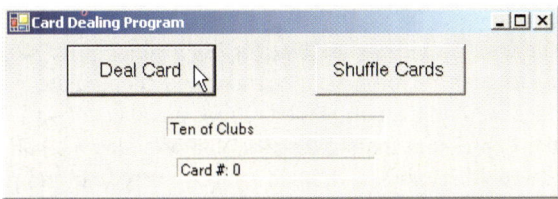

Fig. 15.18 Card dealing and shuffling simulation (part 4 of 4).

Class **CCard** (Fig. 15.17) contains two **String** instance variables—**face** and **suit**—that store references to the face name and suit name of a specific card. The constructor for the class receives two **String**s that it uses to initialize **face** and **suit**. Method **ToString** creates a **String** consisting of the **face** of the card and the **suit** of the card.

Method **FrmDeck_Load** (lines 20–40 of Fig. 15.18) uses the **For** structure (lines 36–38) to fill the **deck** array with **CCard**s. Note that each **CCard** is instantiated and initialized with two **String**s—one from the **faces** array (**String**s **"Ace"** through **"King"**) and one from the **suits** array (**"Hearts"**, **"Diamonds"**, **"Clubs"** or **"Spades"**). The calculation **i Mod 13** always results in a value from **0** to **12** (the thirteen subscripts of the **faces** array), and the calculation **i Mod 4** always results in a value from **0** to **3** (the four subscripts in the **suits** array). The initialized **deck** array contains the cards with faces ace through king for each suit.

When users click the **Deal Card** button, event handler **cmdDeal_Click** (line 43) invokes method **DealCard** (defined in lines 81–96) to get the next card in the **deck** array. If the **deck** is not empty, the method returns a **CCard** object reference; otherwise, it returns **Nothing**. If the reference is not **Nothing**, lines 51–52 display the **CCard** in **lblDisplay** and display the card number in the **lblStatus**.

If **dealCard** returns a **Nothing** reference, the **String** **"NO MORE CARDS TO DEAL"** is displayed in **lblDisplay**, and the **String** **"Shuffle cards to continue"** is displayed in **lblStatus**.

When users click the **Shuffle Cards** button, its event-handling method **cmdShuffle_Click** (lines 99–107) invokes method **Shuffle** (defined on line 61) to shuffle the cards. The method loops through all 52 cards (array subscripts **0**–**51**). For each card, the method randomly picks a number between **0** and **51**. Then the current **CCard** object and the randomly selected **CCard** object are swapped in the array. To shuffle the cards, method **Shuffle** makes a total of only 52 swaps during a single pass of the entire array. When the shuffling is complete, **lblDisplay** displays the **String** **"DECK IS SHUFFLED"**.

15.17 Regular Expressions and Class Regex

Regular expressions are specially formatted **String**s used to find patterns in text and can be useful during information validation, to ensure that data is in a particular format. For example, a ZIP code must consist of five digits, and a last name must start with a capital letter. One application of regular expressions is to facilitate the construction of a compiler. Often, a large and complex regular expression is used to validate the syntax of a program. If the program code does not match the regular expression, the compiler knows that there is a syntax error within the code.

The .NET Framework provides class **Regex** (**System.Text.RegularExpressions** namespace) to help developers recognize and manipulate regular expressions. Class **Regex** provides method **Match**, which returns an object of class **Match** that represents a single regular expression match. **RegEx** also provides method **Matches**, which finds all matches of a regular expression in an arbitrary **String** and returns a *MatchCollection* object—i.e., a set of **Match**es.

Common Programming Error 15.5
*When using regular expressions, do not confuse class **Match** with the method **Match**, which belongs to class **Regex**.*

Common Programming Error 15.6
*Visual Studio does not add **System.Text.RegularExpressions** to the list of namespaces imported in the project properties, so a programmer must import it manually with the statement **Imports System.Text.RegularExpressions**.*

The table in Fig. 15.19 specifies some *character classes* that can be used with regular expressions. A character class is an escape sequence that represents a group of characters.

A *word character* is any alphanumeric character or underscore. A *whitespace* character is a space, a tab, a carriage return, a newline or a form feed. A *digit* is any numeric character. Regular expressions are not limited to these character classes, however. The expressions employ various operators and other forms of notation to search for complex patterns. We discuss several of these techniques in the context of the next example.

Figure 15.20 presents a simple example that employs regular expressions. This program takes birthdays and tries to match them to a regular expression. The expression only matches birthdays that do not occur in April and that belong to people whose names begin with **"J"**.

Character	Matches	Character	Matches
\d	any digit	\D	any non-digit
\w	any word character	\W	any non-word character
\s	any whitespace	\S	any non-whitespace

Fig. 15.19 Character classes.

```
1    ' Fig. 15.20: RegexMatches.vb
2    ' Demonstrating Class Regex.
3
4    Imports System.Text.RegularExpressions
5    Imports System.Windows.Forms
6
7    Module modRegexMatches
8
```

Fig. 15.20 Regular expressions checking birthdays (part 1 of 2).

```
 9      Sub Main()
10         Dim output As String = ""
11         Dim myMatch As Match
12
13         ' create regular expression
14         Dim expression As Regex = _
15            New Regex("J.*\d[0-35-9]-\d\d-\d\d")
16
17         Dim string1 As String = "Jane's Birthday is 05-12-75" & _
18            vbCrLf & "Dave's Birthday is 11-04-68" & vbCrLf & _
19            "John's Birthday is 04-28-73" & vbCrLf & _
20            "Joe's Birthday is 12-17-77"
21
22         ' match regular expression to string and
23         ' print out all matches
24         For Each myMatch In expression.Matches(string1)
25            output &= myMatch.ToString() & vbCrLf
26         Next
27
28         MessageBox.Show(output, "Using Class Regex", _
29            MessageBoxButtons.OK, MessageBoxIcon.Information)
30      End Sub ' Main
31
32   End Module ' modRegexMatches
```

Fig. 15.20 Regular expressions checking birthdays (part 2 of 2).

Line 15 creates an instance of class **Regex** and defines the regular expression pattern for which **Regex** will search. The first character in the regular expression, **"J"**, is treated as a literal character. This means that any **String** matching this regular expression is required to start with **"J"**.

In a regular expression, the dot character **"."** matches any single character except a newline character. However, when the dot character is followed by an asterisk, as in the expression **".*"**, it matches any number of unspecified characters. In general, when the operator **"*"** is applied to any expression, the expression will match zero or more occurrences of the expression. By contrast, the application of the operator **"+"** to an expression causes the expression to match one or more occurrences of that expression. For example, both **"A*"** and **"A+"** will match **"A"**, but only **"A*"** will match an empty **String**.

As indicated in Fig. 15.19, **"\d"** matches any numeric digit. To specify sets of characters other than those that have a character class, characters can be listed in square brackets, **[]**. For example, the pattern **"[aeiou]"** can be used to match any vowel. Ranges of characters can be represented by placing a dash (**–**) between two characters. In the example, **"[0-35-9]"** matches only digits in the ranges specified by the pattern. In this case, the pattern matches any digit between **0** and **3** or between **5** and **9**; therefore, it matches any digit except **4**. If the first character in the brackets is the `"^"`, the expression accepts any character other than those indicated. However, it is important to note that `"[^4]"` is not the same as `"[0-35-9]"`, as the former matches any non-digit in addition to the digits other than **4**.

Although the `"-"` character indicates a range when it is enclosed in square brackets, instances of the `"-"` character outside grouping expressions are treated as literal characters. Thus, the regular expression in line 15 searches for a **String** that starts with the letter `"J"`, followed by any number of characters, followed by a two-digit number (of which the second digit cannot be **4**), followed by a dash, another two-digit number, a dash and another two-digit number.

Lines 24-26 use a **For Each** loop to iterate through each **Match** obtained from **expression.Matches**, which used **string1** as an argument. The output in Fig. 15.20 indicates the two matches that were found in **string1**. Notice that both matches conform to the patter specified by the regular expression.

The asterisk (*****) and plus (**+**) in the previous example are called *quantifiers*. Figure 15.21 lists various quantifiers and their uses.

We have already discussed how the asterisk (*****) and plus (**+**) work. The question mark (**?**) matches zero or one occurrences of the expression that it quantifies. A set of braces containing one number (**{n}**), matches exactly **n** occurrences of the expression it quantifies. We demonstrate this quantifier in the next example. Including a comma after the number enclosed in braces matches at least **n** occurrences of the quantified expression. The set of braces containing two numbers (**{n,m}**), matches between **n** and **m** occurrences of the expression that it qualifies. All of the quantifiers are *greedy*. This means that they will match as many occurrences as they can as long as the match is successful. However, if any of these quantifiers is followed by a question mark (**?**), the quantifier becomes *lazy*. It then will match as few occurrences as possible as long as the match is successful.

The Windows application in Fig. 15.22 presents a more involved example that validates user input via regular expressions.

Quantifier	Matches
*	Matches zero or more occurrences of the pattern.
+	Matches one or more occurrences of the pattern.
?	Matches zero or one occurrences of the pattern.
{n}	Matches exactly **n** occurrences.
{n,}	Matches at least **n** occurrences.
{n,m}	Matches between **n** and **m** (inclusive) occurrences.

Fig. 15.21 Quantifiers used in regular expressions.

```
1   ' Fig. 15.22: Validate.vb
2   ' Validate user information using regular expressions.
3
```

Fig. 15.22 Validating user information using regular expressions (part 1 of 5).

```vbnet
 4   Imports System.Text.RegularExpressions
 5
 6   Public Class FrmValid
 7      Inherits Form
 8
 9      ' field labels
10      Friend WithEvents lblLast As Label
11      Friend WithEvents lblFirst As Label
12      Friend WithEvents lblAddress As Label
13      Friend WithEvents lblCity As Label
14      Friend WithEvents lblState As Label
15      Friend WithEvents lblZip As Label
16      Friend WithEvents lblPhone As Label
17
18      ' field inputs
19      Friend WithEvents txtLast As TextBox
20      Friend WithEvents txtFirst As TextBox
21      Friend WithEvents txtAddress As TextBox
22      Friend WithEvents txtCity As TextBox
23      Friend WithEvents txtState As TextBox
24      Friend WithEvents txtZip As TextBox
25      Friend WithEvents txtPhone As TextBox
26
27      Friend WithEvents cmdOK As Button  ' validate all fields
28
29      ' Visual Studio .NET generated code
30
31      ' handles cmdOK Click event
32      Private Sub cmdOK_Click(ByVal sender As System.Object, _
33         ByVal e As System.EventArgs) Handles cmdOK.Click
34
35         ' ensures no textboxes are empty
36         If (txtPhone.Text = "" OrElse txtZip.Text = "" OrElse _
37            txtState.Text = "" OrElse txtCity.Text = "" OrElse _
38            txtAddress.Text = "" OrElse txtFirst.Text = "" OrElse _
39            txtLast.Text = "") Then
40
41            ' display popup box
42            MessageBox.Show("Please fill in all fields", "Error", _
43               MessageBoxButtons.OK, MessageBoxIcon.Error)
44
45            ' set focus to txtLast
46            txtLast.Focus()
47
48            Return
49         End If
50
51         ' if last name format invalid show message
52         If Not Regex.Match(txtLast.Text, _
53            "^[A-Z][a-zA-Z]*$").Success Then
54
55            ' last name was incorrect
56            MessageBox.Show("Invalid Last Name", "Message")
```

Fig. 15.22 Validating user information using regular expressions (part 2 of 5).

```
57              txtLast.Focus()
58
59              Return
60           End If
61
62           ' if first name format invalid show message
63           If Not Regex.Match(txtFirst.Text, _
64              "^[A-Z][a-zA-Z]*$").Success Then
65
66              ' first name was incorrect
67              MessageBox.Show("Invalid First Name", "Message")
68              txtFirst.Focus()
69
70              Return
71           End If
72
73           ' if address format invalid show message
74           If Not Regex.Match(txtAddress.Text, "^[0-9]+\s+([a-zA-Z]" & _
75              "+|[a-zA-Z]+\s[a-zA-Z]+)$").Success Then
76
77              ' address was incorrect
78              MessageBox.Show("Invalid Address", "Message")
79              txtAddress.Focus()
80
81              Return
82           End If
83
84           ' if city format invalid show message
85           If Not Regex.Match(txtCity.Text, "^([a-zA-Z]+|[a-zA-Z]" & _
86              "+\s[a-zA-Z]+)$").Success Then
87
88              ' city was incorrect
89              MessageBox.Show("Invalid City", "Message")
90              txtCity.Focus()
91
92              Return
93           End If
94
95           ' if state format invalid show message
96           If Not Regex.Match(txtState.Text, _
97              "^([a-zA-Z]+|[a-zA-Z]+\s[a-zA-Z]+)$").Success Then
98
99              ' state was incorrect
100             MessageBox.Show("Invalid State", "Message")
101             txtState.Focus()
102
103             Return
104          End If
105
106          ' if zip code format invalid show message
107          If Not Regex.Match(txtZip.Text, "^\d{5}$").Success Then
108
```

Fig. 15.22 Validating user information using regular expressions (part 3 of 5).

Chapter 15   Strings, Characters and Regular Expressions

```
109            ' zip code was incorrect
110            MessageBox.Show("Invalid zip code", "Message")
111            txtZip.Focus()
112
113            Return
114         End If
115
116         ' if phone number format invalid show message
117         If Not Regex.Match(txtPhone.Text, "^[1-9]" & _
118            "\d{2}-[1-9]\d{2}-\d{4}$").Success Then
119
120            ' phone was incorrect
121            MessageBox.Show("Invalid Phone Number", "Message")
122            txtPhone.Focus()
123
124            Return
125         End If
126
127         ' information is valid, signal user and exit application
128         Me.Hide()
129         MessageBox.Show("Thank you!", "Information Correct", _
130            MessageBoxButtons.OK, MessageBoxIcon.Information)
131
132         Application.Exit()
133      End Sub ' cmdOK_Click
134
135 End Class ' FrmValid
```

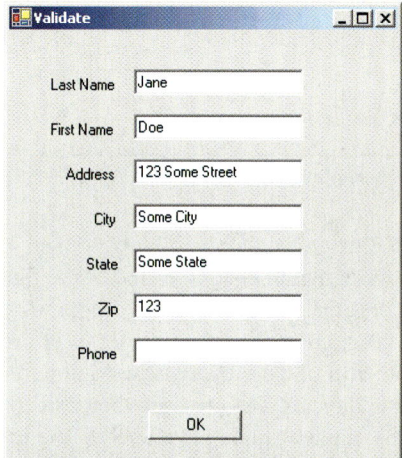

Fig. 15.22 Validating user information using regular expressions (part 4 of 5).

674 Strings, Characters and Regular Expressions   Chapter 15

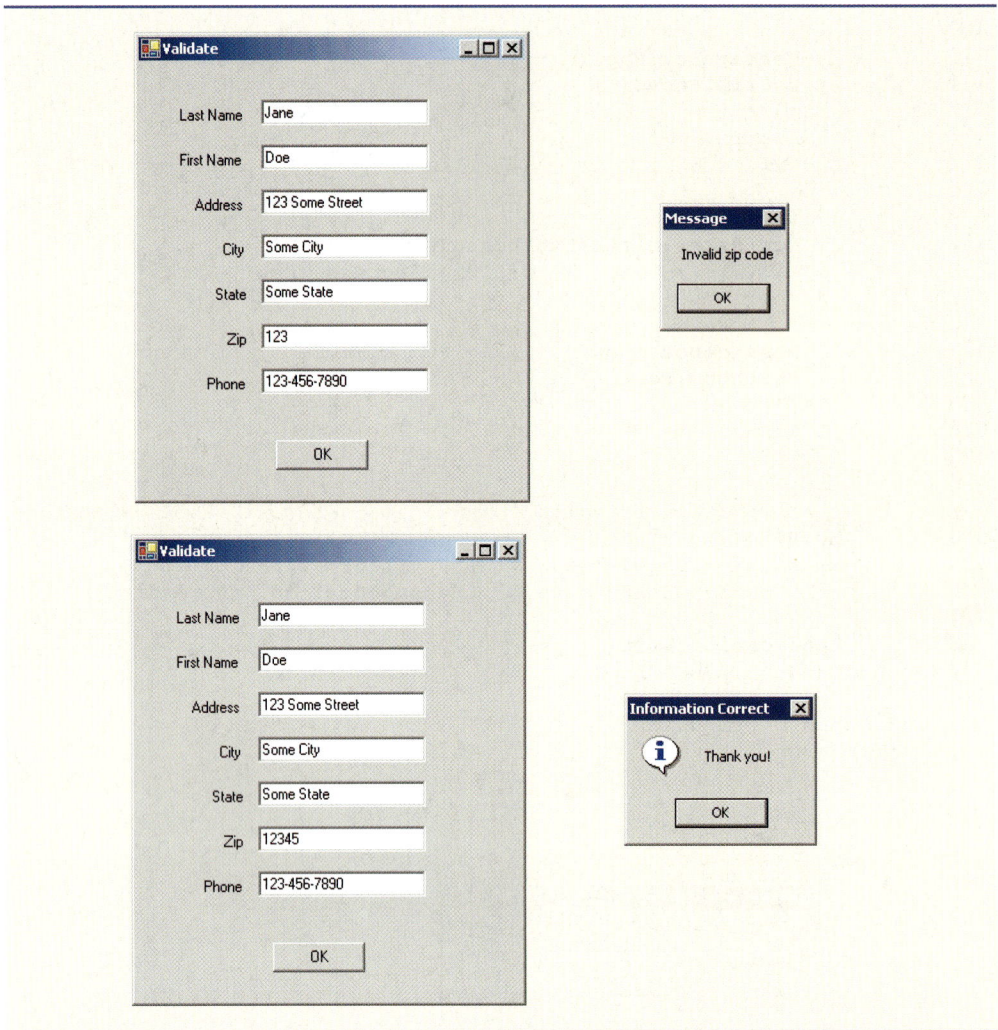

Fig. 15.22 Validating user information using regular expressions (part 5 of 5).

When a user clicks the **OK** button, the program checks to make sure that none of the fields are empty (lines 36–39). If one or more fields are empty, the program signals the user that all fields must be filled before the program can validate the input information (lines 42–43). Line 46 calls instance method **Focus** of class **TextBox**. Method **Focus** places the cursor within the **TextBox** that made the call. The program then exits the event handler (line 48). If there are no empty fields, the user input is validated. The **Last Name** is validated first (lines 52–60). If it passes the test (i.e., if the *Success* property of the **Match** instance is **True**), control moves on to validate the **First Name** (lines 63–71). This process continues until all **TextBox**es are validated, or until a test fails (*Success* is **False**) and the program sends an appropriate error message. If all fields contain valid information, success is signaled, and the program quits.

In the previous example, we searched for substrings that matched a regular expression. In this example, we want to check whether an entire **String** conforms to a regular expression. For example, we want to accept **"Smith"** as a last name, but not **"9@Smith#"**. We achieve this effect by beginning each regular expression with a **"^"** character and ending it with a **"$"** character. The **"^"** and **"$"** characters match the positions at the beginning and end of a **String**, respectively. This forces the regular expression to evaluate the entire **String** and not return a match if a substring matches successfully.

In this program, we use the **Shared** version of **Regex** method **Match**, which takes an additional parameter specifying the regular expression that we are trying to match. The expression in line 53 uses the square bracket and range notation to match an uppercase first letter, followed by letters of any case—**a-z** matches any lowercase letter, and **A-Z** matches any uppercase letter. The ***** quantifier signifies that the second range of characters may occur zero or more times in the **String**. Thus, this expression matches any **String** consisting of one uppercase letter, followed by zero or more additional letters.

The notation **\s** matches a single whitespace character (lines 74–75 and 86). The expression **\d{5}**, used in the **Zip** (zip code) field, matches any five digits (line 107). In general, an expression with a positive integer **x** in the curly braces will match any **x** digits. (Notice the importance of the **"^"** and **"$"** characters to prevent zip codes with extra digits from being validated.)

The character "**|**" matches the expression to its left or to its right. For example, **Hi (John|Jane)** matches both **Hi John** and **Hi Jane**. Note the use of parentheses to group parts of the regular expression. Quantifiers may be applied to patterns enclosed in parentheses to create more complex regular expressions.

The **Last Name** and **First Name** fields both accept **String**s of any length, which begin with an uppercase letter. The **Address** field matches a number of at least one digit, followed by a space and either one or more letters or one or more letters followed by a space and another series of one or more letters (lines 74–75). Therefore, **"10 Broadway"** and **"10 Main Street"** are both valid addresses. The **City** (lines 85–86) and **State** (lines 96–97) fields match any word of at least one character or, alternatively, any two words of at least one character if the words are separated by a single space. This means both **Waltham** and **West Newton** would match. As previously stated, the **Zip** code must be a five-digit number (line 107). The **Phone** number must be of the form **xxx-yyy-yyyy**, where the **x**s represent the area code and **y**s the number (lines 117–118). The first **x** and the first **y** may not be zero.

Sometimes it is useful to replace parts of a **String** with another, or split a **String** according to a regular expression. For this purpose, the **Regex** class provides **Shared** and instance versions of methods **Replace** and **Split**, which are demonstrated in Fig. 15.23.

```
1   ' Fig. 15.23: RegexSubstitution.vb
2   ' Using Regex method Replace.
3
4   Imports System.Text.RegularExpressions
5   Imports System.Windows.Forms
6
7   Module modRegexSubstitution
```

Fig. 15.23 **Regex** methods **Replace** and **Split** (part 1 of 3).

```vbnet
 8
 9      Sub Main()
10         Dim testString1 As String = _
11            "This sentence ends in 5 stars *****"
12
13         Dim testString2 As String = "1, 2, 3, 4, 5, 6, 7, 8"
14         Dim testRegex1 As Regex = New Regex("stars")
15         Dim testRegex2 As Regex = New Regex("\d")
16         Dim results As String()
17         Dim resultString As String
18         Dim output As String = "Original String 1" & vbTab & _
19            vbTab & vbTab & testString1
20
21         testString1 = Regex.Replace(testString1, "\*", "^")
22
23         output &= vbCrLf & "^ substituted for *" & vbTab & _
24            vbTab & vbTab & testString1
25
26         testString1 = testRegex1.Replace(testString1, "carets")
27
28         output &= vbCrLf & """carets"" substituted for " & _
29            """stars""" & vbTab & testString1
30
31         output &= vbCrLf & "Every word replaced by " & _
32            """word""" & vbTab & _
33            Regex.Replace(testString1, "\w+", "word")
34
35         output &= vbCrLf & vbCrLf & "Original String 2" & _
36            vbTab & vbTab & vbTab & testString2
37
38         output &= vbCrLf & "First 3 digits replaced by " & _
39            """digit""" & vbTab & _
40            testRegex2.Replace(testString2, "digit", 3)
41
42         output &= vbCrLf & "String split at commas" & vbTab & _
43            vbTab & "["
44
45         results = Regex.Split(testString2, ",\s*")
46
47         For Each resultString In results
48            output &= """" & resultString & """, "
49         Next
50
51         output = output.Substring(0, output.Length - 2) & "]"
52
53         MessageBox.Show(output, _
54            "Substitution using regular expressions")
55      End Sub ' Main
56
57   End Module ' modRegexSubstitution
```

Fig. 15.23 Regex methods Replace and Split (part 2 of 3).

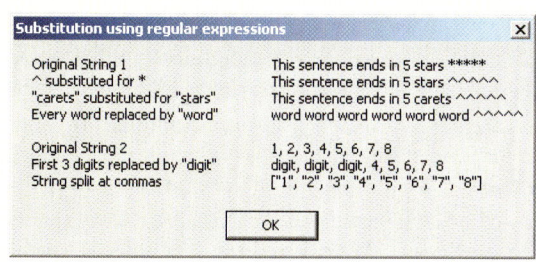

Fig. 15.23 `Regex` methods `Replace` and `Split` (part 3 of 3).

Method **Replace** replaces text in a **String** with new text wherever the original **String** matches a regular expression. We present two versions of this method in Fig. 15.23. The first version (line 21) is **Shared** and takes three parameters—the **String** to modify, the **String** containing the regular expression to match and the replacement **String**. Here, **Replace** replaces every instance of **"*"** in **testString1** with **"^"**. Notice that the regular expression (**"*"**) precedes character ***** with a backslash, ****. Normally, ***** is a quantifier indicating that a regular expression should match any number of occurrences of a preceding pattern. However, in line 21, we want to find all occurrences of the literal character *****; to do this, we must escape character ***** with character ****. By escaping a special regular expression character with a ****, we inform the regular-expression matching engine to find the actual character, as opposed to what it represents in a regular expression. The second version of method **Replace** (line 26) is an instance method that uses the regular expression passed to the constructor for **testRegex1** (line 14) to perform the replacement operation. In this case, every match for the regular expression **"stars"** in **testString1** is replaced with **"carets"**.

Line 15 instantiates **testRegex2** with argument **"\d"**. The call to instance method **Replace** in line 40 takes three arguments—a **String** to modify, a **String** containing the replacement text and an **Integer** specifying the number of replacements to make. In other words, this version of **Replace** replaces the first three instances of a digit (**"\d"**) in **testString2** with the text **"digit"** (line 40).

Method **Split** divides a **String** into several substrings. The original **String** is broken in any location that matches a specified regular expression. Method **Split** returns an array containing the substrings between matches for the regular expression. In line 45, we use the **Shared** version of method **Split** to separate a **String** of comma-separated integers. The first argument is the **String** to split, and the second argument is the regular expression. In this case, we use the regular expression **",\s*"** to separate the substrings wherever a comma occurs. By matching any whitespace characters, we eliminate extra spaces from the resulting substrings.

SUMMARY

- Characters are the fundamental building blocks of Visual Basic program code. Every program is composed of a sequence of characters that is interpreted by the compiler as a series of instructions used to accomplish a task.

- A **String** is a series of characters treated as a single unit. A **String** may include letters, digits and various special characters, such as **+**, **-**, *****, **/**, **$** and others.
- All characters correspond to numeric codes (see Appendix E). When the computer compares two **String**s, it actually compares the numeric codes of the characters in the **String**s.
- Method **Equals** uses a lexicographical comparison, meaning that if a certain **String** has a higher value than another **String**, it would be found later in a dictionary. Method **Equals** compares the integer Unicode values that represent each character in each **String**.
- Method **CompareTo** returns **0** if the **String**s are equal, a negative number if the **String** that invokes **CompareTo** is less than the **String** passed as an argument and a positive number if the **String** that invokes **CompareTo** is greater than the **String** passed as an argument. Method **CompareTo** uses a lexicographical comparison.
- A hash table stores information, using a special calculation on the object to be stored that produces a hash code. The hash code is used to choose the location in the table at which to store the object.
- Class **Object** defines method **GetHashCode** to perform the hash-code calculation. This method is inherited by all subclasses of **Object**. Method **GetHashCode** is overridden by **String** to provide a good hash-code distribution based on the contents of the **String**.
- Class **String** provides two **Substring** methods to enable a new **String** object to be created by copying part of an existing **String** object.
- **String** method **IndexOf** locates the first occurrence of a character or a substring in a **String**. Method **LastIndexOf** locates the last occurrence of a character or a substring in a **String**.
- **String** method **StartsWith** determines whether a **String** starts with the characters specified as an argument. **String** method **EndsWith** determines whether a **String** ends with the characters specified as an argument.
- The **Shared** method **Concat** of class **String** concatenates two **String** objects and returns a new **String** object containing the characters from both original **String**s.
- Methods **Replace**, **ToUpper**, **ToLower**, **Trim** and **Remove** are provided for more advanced **String** manipulation.
- The **String** class provides many capabilities for processing **String**s. However, once a **String** object is created, its contents can never change. Class **StringBuilder** is available for creating and manipulating dynamic **String**s, i.e., **String**s that can change.
- Class **StringBuilder** provides **Length** and **Capacity** properties to return the number of characters currently in a **StringBuilder** and the number of characters that can be stored in a **StringBuilder** without allocating more memory, respectively. These properties also can be used to increase or decrease the length or the capacity of the **StringBuilder**.
- Method **EnsureCapacity** allows programmers to guarantee that a **StringBuilder** has a minimum capacity. Method **EnsureCapacity** attempts to double the capacity. If this value is greater than the value that the programmer wishes to ensure, this will be the new capacity. Otherwise, **EnsureCapacity** alters the capacity to make it one more than the requested number.
- Class **StringBuilder** provides 19 overloaded **Append** methods to allow various data-type values to be added to the end of a **StringBuilder**. Versions are provided for each of the primitive data types and for character arrays, **String**s and **Object**s.
- The braces in a format **String** specify how to format a specific piece of information. Formats have the form **{X[,Y][:FormatString]}**, where **X** is the number of the argument to be formatted, counting from zero. **Y** is an optional argument, which can be positive or negative. **Y** indicates how many characters should be in the result of formatting, if the resulting **String** is less than this number it will be padded with spaces to make up for the difference. A positive integer means the **String** will be right aligned, a negative one means it will be left aligned. The optional

Chapter 15   Strings, Characters and Regular Expressions   679

- **FormatString** indicates what kind of formatting should be applied to the argument: Currency, decimal, scientific, as well as others.
- Class **StringBuilder** provides 19 overloaded **Insert** methods to allow various data-type values to be inserted at any position in a **StringBuilder**. Versions are provided for each of the primitive data types and for character arrays, **String**s and **Object**s.
- Class **StringBuilder** also provides method **Remove** for deleting any portion of a **StringBuilder**.
- Another useful method included with **StringBuilder** is **Replace**. **Replace** searches for a specified **String** or character and substitutes another in its place.
- Visual Basic provides **Structure**s, a program building block similar to classes.
- Structures are in many ways similar to classes, the largest difference between them being that structures encapsulate value types, whereas classes encapsulate reference types.
- Many of the primitive data types that we have been using are actually aliases for different structures. These structures are derived from class **ValueType**, which in turn is derived from class **Object**.
- **Char** is a structure that represents characters.
- Method **Char.Parse** converts data into a character.
- Method **Char.IsDigit** determines whether a character is a defined Unicode digit.
- Method **Char.IsLetter** determines whether a character is a letter.
- Method **Char.IsLetterOrDigit** determines whether a character is a letter or a digit.
- Method **Char.IsLower** determines whether a character is a lowercase letter.
- Method **Char.IsUpper** determines whether a character is an uppercase letter.
- Method **Char.ToUpper** converts a character to its uppercase equivalent.
- Method **Char.ToLower** converts a character to its lowercase equivalent.
- Method **Char.IsPunctuation** determines whether a character is a punctuation mark.
- Method **Char.IsSymbol** determines whether a character is a symbol.
- Method **Char.IsWhiteSpace** determines whether a character is a white-space character.
- **Char** method **CompareTo** compares two character values.
- Regular expressions find patterns in text.
- The .NET Framework provides class **Regex** to aid developers in recognizing and manipulating regular expressions. **Regex** provides method **Match**, which returns an object of class **Match**. This object represents a single match in a regular expression. **Regex** also provides the method **Matches**, which finds all matches of a regular expression in an arbitrary **String** and returns a **MatchCollection**—a set of **Match**es.
- Both classes **Regex** and **Match** are in **System.Text.RegularExpressions** namespace.
- In general, applying the quantifier ***** to any expression will match zero or more occurrences of that expression, and applying the quantifier **+** will match one or more occurrences of that expression.
- The pattern **"[0-35-9]"** is a regular expression that matches one in a range of characters. This **String** will match any digit **0**-**3** and **5**-**9**, so it will match any digit except **4**.
- The character "**|**" matches the expression to its left or to its right. For example, **"Hi (John|Jane)"** matches both **"Hi John"** and **"Hi Jane"**.
- Method **Replace** replaces substrings in a **String** that match a certain regular expression with a specified **String**.

TERMINOLOGY

& operator
&= concatenation operator
= comparison operator
alphabetizing
Append method of class **StringBuilder**
AppendFormat method of class **StringBuilder**
ArgumentOutOfRangeException
Capacity property of class **StringBuilder**
Char array
Char structure
Chars property of class **String**
character
character class
CompareTo method of class **String**
CompareTo method of structure **Char**
Concat method of class **String**
CopyTo method of class **String**
Enabled property of class **Control**
EndsWith method of class **String**
EnsureCapacity method of class **StringBuilder**
Equals method of class **String**
format string
garbage collector
GetHashCode
greedy quantifier
hash code
hash table
immutable **String**
IndexOf method of class **String**
IndexOfAny method of class **String**
IsDigit method of structure **Char**
IsLetter method of structure **Char**
IsLetterOrDigit method of structure **Char**
IsLower method of structure **Char**
IsPunctuation method of structure **Char**
IsSymbol method of structure **Char**
IsUpper method of structure **Char**
IsWhiteSpace method of structure **Char**
LastIndexOf method of class **String**
LastIndexOfAny method of class **String**

lazy quantifier
Length property of class **String**
Length property of class **StringBuilder**
lexicographical comparison
literal **String** objects
Match class
MatchCollection class
Parse method of structure **Char**
page-layout software
quantifier
random-number generation
Regex class
Remove method of class **StringBuilder**
Replace method of class **Regex**
Replace method of class **String**
Replace method of class **StringBuilder**
special characters
Split method of class **Regex**
StartsWith method of class **String**
String class
string literal
String reference
StringBuilder class
Structure
Substring method of class **String**
Success property of class **Match**
System namespace
System.Text namespace
System.Text.RegularExpressions namespace
text editor
ToLower method of class **String**
ToLower method of structure **Char**
ToString method of class **String**
ToString method of class **StringBuilder**
ToUpper method of class **String**
ToUpper method of structure **Char**
trailing whitespace characters
Trim method of class **String**
Unicode character set
ValueType class
whitespace characters
word character

SELF-REVIEW EXERCISES

15.1 State whether each of the following is *true* or *false*. If *false*, explain why.
   a) When **String** objects are compared with **=**, the result is *true* if the **String**s contain the same values.

b) A **String** can be modified after it is created.
c) Class **String** has no **ToString** method.
d) **StringBuilder EnsureCapacity** method sets the capacity to its argument.
e) The method **Equals** and the equality operator work the same for **String**s.
f) Method **Trim** removes all whitespace at the beginning and the end of a **String**.
g) A regular expression matches a **String** to a pattern.
h) It is always better to use **String**s rather than **StringBuilder**s because **String**s containing the same value will reference the same object in memory.
i) Class **String** method **ToUpper** capitalizes just the first letter of the **String**.
j) The expression **\d** in a regular expression denotes all letters.

15.2 Fill in the blanks in each of the following statements:
a) To concatenate strings, use the _____ operator or class _____ method _____.
b) Method **Compare** of class **String** uses a _____ comparison of **String**s.
c) Class **Regex** is located in namespace _____.
d) **StringBuilder** method _____ first formats the specified **String** then concatenates it to the end of the **StringBuilder**.
e) If the arguments to a **Substring** method call are out of range, an _____ exception is thrown.
f) **Regex** method _____ changes all occurrences of a pattern in a **String** to a specified **String**.
g) Method _____ is inherited by every object and calculates its hash code.
h) A **C** in a format means to output the number as _____.
i) Regular expression quantifier _____ matches zero or more occurrences of an expression.
j) Regular expression operator _____ inside square brackets will not match any of the characters in that set of brackets.

ANSWERS TO SELF-REVIEW EXERCISES

15.1 a) True. b) False. **String** objects are immutable and cannot be modified after they are created. **StringBuilder** objects can be modified after they are created. c) False. Class **String** inherits a **ToString** method from class **Object**. d) **AppendFormat**. e) True. f) True. g) True. h) False. **StringBuilder** should be used if the **String** is to be modified. i) False. Class **String** method **ToUpper** capitalizes all letters in the **String**. j) False. The expression **\d** denotes all decimals in a regular expression.

15.2 a) **&**, **StringBuilder**, **Append**. b) lexicographical. c) **System.Text.RegularExpressions**. d) **AppendFormat** e) **ArgumentOutOfRangeException**. f) **Replace**. g) **GetHashCode**. h) currency. i) *****. j) **^**.

EXERCISES

15.3 Modify the program in Fig. 15.18 so that the card-dealing method deals a five-card poker hand. Then write the following additional methods:
a) Determine if the hand contains a pair.
b) Determine if the hand contains two pairs.
c) Determine if the hand contains three of a kind (e.g., three jacks).
d) Determine if the hand contains four of a kind (e.g., four aces).
e) Determine if the hand contains a flush (i.e., all five cards of the same suit).
f) Determine if the hand contains a straight (i.e., five cards of consecutive face values).

g) Determine if the hand contains a full house (i.e., two cards of one face value and three cards of another face value).

15.4 Use the methods developed in Exercise 15.3 to write a program that deals two five-card poker hands, evaluates each hand and determines which is the better hand.

15.5 Write an application that uses `String` method `CompareTo` to compare two `String`s input by the user. Output whether the first `String` is less than, equal to or greater than the second.

15.6 Write an application that uses random-number generation to create sentences. Use four arrays of `String`s called `article`, `noun`, `verb` and `preposition`. Create a sentence by selecting a word at random from each array in the following order: `article`, `noun`, `verb`, `preposition`, `article` and `noun`. As each word is picked, concatenate it to the previous words in the sentence. The words should be separated by spaces. When the final sentence is output, it should start with a capital letter and end with a period. The program should generate 20 sentences and output them to a text area.

The arrays should be filled as follows: the `article` array should contain the articles `"the"`, `"a"`, `"one"`, `"some"` and `"any"`; the `noun` array should contain the nouns `"boy"`, `"girl"`, `"dog"`, `"town"` and `"car"`; the `verb` array should contain the past-tense verbs `"drove"`, `"jumped"`, `"ran"`, `"walked"` and `"skipped"`; the `preposition` array should contain the prepositions `"to"`, `"from"`, `"over"`, `"under"` and `"on"`.

After the preceding program is written, modify the program to produce a short story consisting of several of these sentences. (How about the possibility of a random term-paper writer!)

15.7 *(Pig Latin)* Write an application that encodes English language phrases into pig Latin. Pig Latin is a form of coded language often used for amusement. Many variations exist in the methods used to form pig Latin phrases. For simplicity, use the following algorithm:

To translate each English word into a pig Latin word, place the first letter of the English word at the end of the word and add the letters "`ay`." Thus, the word "`jump`" becomes "`umpjay`," the word "`the`" becomes "`hetay`" and the word "`computer`" becomes "`omputercay`." Blanks between words remain as blanks. Assume the following: The English phrase consists of words separated by blanks, there are no punctuation marks, and all words have two or more letters. Enable the user to input a sentence. Use techniques discussed in this chapter to divide the sentence into separate words. Method `GetPigLatin` should translate a single word into pig Latin. Keep a running display of all the converted sentences in a text area.

15.8 Write a program that reads a five-letter word from the user and produces all possible three-letter words that can be derived from the letters of the five-letter word. For example, the three-letter words produced from the word "bathe" include the commonly used words "ate," "bat," "bet," "tab," "hat," "the" and "tea."

16

Graphics and Multimedia

Objectives

- To understand graphics contexts and graphics objects.
- To be able to manipulate colors and fonts.
- To understand and be able to use GDI+ **Graphics** methods to draw lines, rectangles, **String**s and images.
- To be able to use class **Image** to manipulate and display images.
- To be able to draw complex shapes from simple shapes with class **GraphicsPath**.
- To be able to use Windows Media Player and Microsoft Agent in a Visual Basic application.

One picture is worth ten thousand words.
Chinese proverb

Treat nature in terms of the cylinder, the sphere, the cone, all in perspective.
Paul Cezanne

Nothing ever becomes real till it is experienced—even a proverb is no proverb to you till your life has illustrated it.
John Keats

A picture shows me at a glance what it takes dozens of pages of a book to expound.
Ivan Sergeyevich

Outline

16.1 Introduction
16.2 Graphics Contexts and Graphics Objects
16.3 Color Control
16.4 Font Control
16.5 Drawing Lines, Rectangles and Ovals
16.6 Drawing Arcs
16.7 Drawing Polygons and Polylines
16.8 Advanced Graphics Capabilities
16.9 Introduction to Multimedia
16.10 Loading, Displaying and Scaling Images
16.11 Animating a Series of Images
16.12 Windows Media Player
16.13 Microsoft Agent

Summary • Terminology • Self-Review Exercises • Answers to Self-Review Exercises • Exercises

16.1 Introduction

In this chapter, we overview Visual Basic's tools for drawing two-dimensional shapes and for controlling colors and fonts. Visual Basic supports graphics that enable programmers to enhance their Windows applications visually. The language contains many sophisticated drawing capabilities as part of namespace **System.Drawing** and the other namespaces that make up the .NET resource *GDI+*. GDI+, an extension of the Graphical Device Interface, is an application programming interface (API) that provides classes for creating two-dimensional vector graphics (a high-performance technique for creating graphics), manipulating fonts and inserting images. GDI+ expands GDI by simplifying the programming model and introducing several new features, such as graphics paths, extended image file format support and alpha blending. Using the GDI+ API, programmers can create images without worrying about the platform-specific details of their graphics hardware.

We begin with an introduction to Visual Basic's drawing capabilities. We then present more powerful drawing capabilities, such as changing the styles of lines used to draw shapes and controlling the colors and patterns of filled shapes.

Figure 16.1 depicts a portion of the **System.Drawing** class hierarchy, which includes several of the basic graphics classes and structures covered in this chapter. The most commonly used components of GDI+ reside in the **System.Drawing** and **System.Drawing.Drawing2D** namespaces.

Class **Graphics** contains methods used for drawing **String**s, lines, rectangles and other shapes on a **Control**. The drawing methods of class **Graphics** usually require a **Pen** or **Brush** object to render a specified shape. The **Pen** draws shape outlines; the **Brush** draws solid objects.

Structure **Color** contains numerous **Shared** properties, which set the colors of various graphical components, as well as methods that allow users to create new colors. Class

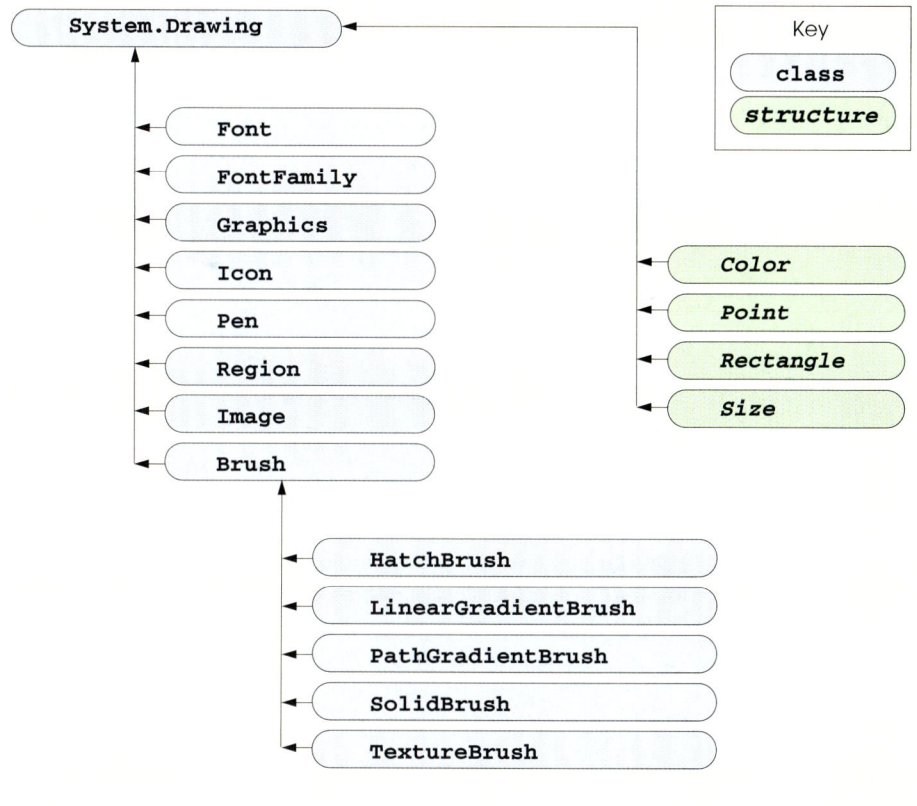

Fig. 16.1 `System.Drawing` namespace's Classes and Structures.

Font contains properties that define unique fonts. Class *FontFamily* contains methods for obtaining font information.

To begin drawing in Visual Basic, we first must understand GDI+'s *coordinate system* (Fig. 16.2), a scheme for identifying every point on the screen. By default, the upper-left corner of a GUI component (such as a `Panel` or a `Form`) has the coordinates (0, 0). A coordinate pair has both an *x-coordinate* (the *horizontal coordinate*) and a *y-coordinate* (the *vertical coordinate*). The *x*-coordinate is the horizontal distance (to the right) from the upper-left corner. The *y*-coordinate is the vertical distance (downward) from the upper-left corner. The *x-axis* defines every horizontal coordinate, and the *y-axis* defines every vertical coordinate. Programmers position text and shapes on the screen by specifying their (*x*,*y*) coordinates. Coordinate units are measured in *pixels* ("picture elements"), which are the smallest units of resolution on a display monitor.

Portability Tip 16.1

Different display monitors have different resolutions, so the density of pixels on such monitors will vary. This might cause the sizes of graphics to appear different on different monitors.

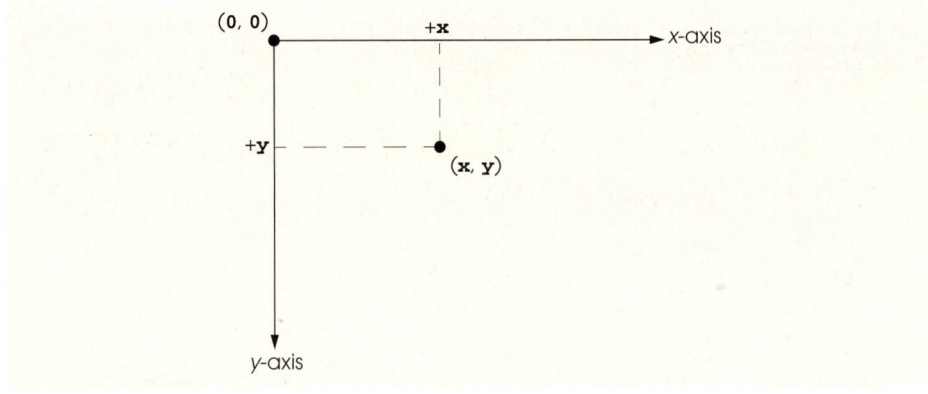

Fig. 16.2 GDI+ coordinate system. Units are measured in pixels.

The **System.Drawing** namespace provides structures **Rectangle** and **Point**. The *Rectangle* structure defines rectangular shapes and dimensions. The *Point* structure represents the *x-y* coordinates of a point on a two-dimensional plane.

In the remainder of this chapter, we explore techniques of manipulating images and creating smooth animations. We also discuss class *Image*, which can store and manipulate images from many file formats. Later, we explain how to combine the graphical rendering capabilities covered in the early sections of the chapter with those for image manipulation.

16.2 Graphics Contexts and Graphics Objects

A Visual Basic *graphics context* represents a drawing surface and enables drawing on the screen. A **Graphics** object manages a graphics context by controlling how information is drawn. **Graphics** objects contain methods for drawing, font manipulation, color manipulation and other graphics-related actions. Every Windows application that derives from class **System.Windows.Forms.Form** inherits an **Overridable** *OnPaint* method where most graphics operations are performed. The arguments to the **OnPaint** method include a **PaintEventArgs** object from which we can obtain a **Graphics** object for the control. We must obtain the **Graphics** object on each call to the method, because the properties of the graphics context that the graphics object represents could change. The **OnPaint** method triggers the **Control**'s *Paint* event.

When displaying graphical information on a **Form**'s client area, programmers can override the **OnPaint** method to retrieve a **Graphics** object from argument **PaintEventArgs** or to create a new **Graphics** object associated with the appropriate surface. We demonstrate these techniques of drawing in applications later in the chapter.

To override the inherited **OnPaint** method, use the following method definition:

```
Protected Overrides Sub OnPaint(ByVal e As PaintEventArgs)
```

Next, extract the incoming **Graphics** object from the **PaintEventArgs** argument:

```
Dim graphicsObject As Graphics = e.Graphics
```

Variable **graphicsObject** now is available to draw shapes and **String**s on the form.

Calling the `OnPaint` method raises the `Paint` event. Instead of overriding the `OnPaint` method, programmers can add an event handler for the `Paint` event. First, write the code for the `Paint` event handler in this form:

```
Public Sub MyEventHandler_Paint( _
   ByVal sender As Object, ByVal e As PaintEventArgs) _
   Handles MyBase.Paint
```

Programmers seldom call the `OnPaint` method directly, because the drawing of graphics is an *event-driven process*. An event—such as the covering, uncovering or resizing of a window—calls the `OnPaint` method of that form. Similarly, when any control (such as a `TextBox` or `Label`) is displayed, the program calls that control's `Paint` method.

If programmers need to invoke method `OnPaint` explicitly, they can call the `Invalidate` method (inherited from `Control`). This method refreshes a control's client area and repaints all graphical components. Visual Basic contains several overloaded `Invalidate` methods that allow programmers to update portions of the client area.

Performance Tip 16.1

Calling the `Invalidate` method to refresh the `Control` often is inefficient. Instead, call `Invalidate` with a `Rectangle` parameter to refresh only the area designated by the rectangle. This improves program performance.

Controls, such as `Label`s and `Button`s, also have their own graphics contexts. To draw on a control, first obtain its graphics object by invoking the `CreateGraphics` method:

```
Dim graphicsObject As Graphics = label1.CreateGraphics()
```

Then, you can use the methods provided in class `Graphics` to draw on the control.

16.3 Color Control

Colors can enhance a program's appearance and help convey meaning. For example, a red traffic light indicates stop, yellow indicates caution and green indicates go.

Structure `Color` defines methods and constants used to manipulate colors. Because it is a lightweight object that performs only a handful of operations and stores `Shared` fields, `Color` is implemented as a structure, rather than as a class.

Every color can be created from a combination of alpha, red, green and blue components. Together, these components are called *ARGB values*. All four ARGB components are `Byte`s that represent integer values in the range from 0 to 255. The alpha value determines the intensity of the color. For example, the alpha value 0 results in a transparent color, whereas the value 255 results in an opaque color. Alpha values between 0 and 255 result in a weighted blending effect of the color's RGB value with that of any background color, causing a semi-transparent effect. The first number in the RGB value defines the amount of red in the color, the second defines the amount of green and the third defines the amount of blue. The larger the value, the greater the amount of that particular color. Visual Basic enables programmers to choose from almost 17 million colors. If a particular computer cannot display all these colors, it will display the color closest to the one specified. Figure 16.3 summarizes some predefined color constants, and Fig. 16.4 describes several `Color` methods and properties.

Constants in structure `Color` (all are `Public Shared`)	RGB value	Constants in structure `Color` (all are `Public Shared`)	RGB value
`Orange`	255, 200, 0	`White`	255, 255, 255
`Pink`	255, 175, 175	`Gray`	28, 128, 128
`Cyan`	0, 255, 255	`DarkGray`	64, 64, 64
`Magenta`	255, 0, 255	`Red`	255, 0, 0
`Yellow`	255, 255, 0	`Green`	0, 255, 0
`Black`	0, 0, 0	`Blue`	0, 0, 255

Fig. 16.3 `Color` structure `Shared` constants and their RGB values.

Structure `Color` methods and properties	Description
Common Methods	
`Shared FromArgb`	Creates a color based on red, green and blue values expressed as `Integers` from 0 to 255. Overloaded version allows specification of alpha, red, green and blue values.
`Shared FromName`	Creates a color from a name, passed as a `String`.
Common Properties	
`A`	`Integer` between 0 and 255, representing the alpha component.
`R`	`Integer` between 0 and 255, representing the red component.
`G`	`Integer` between 0 and 255, representing the green component.
`B`	`Integer` between 0 and 255, representing the blue component.

Fig. 16.4 `Color` structure members.

The table in Fig. 16.4 describes two **`FromArgb`** method calls. One takes three **`Integer`** arguments, and one takes four **`Integer`** arguments (all argument values must be between 0 and 255). Both take **`Integer`** arguments specifying the amount of red, green and blue. The overloaded version takes four arguments and allows the user to specify alpha; the three-argument version defaults the alpha to 255. Both methods return a **`Color`** object representing the specified values. **`Color`** properties **`A`**, **`R`**, **`G`** and **`B`** return **`Byte`**s that represent **`Integer`** values from 0 to 255, corresponding to the amounts of alpha, red, green and blue, respectively.

Programmers draw shapes and **`String`**s using **`Brush`**es and **`Pen`**s. A **`Pen`**, which functions similarly to an ordinary pen, is used to draw lines. Most drawing methods require a **`Pen`** object. The overloaded **`Pen`** constructors allow programmers to specify the colors and widths of the lines that they wish to draw. The **`System.Drawing`** namespace also provides a **`Pens`** collection containing predefined **`Pen`**s.

All classes derived from abstract class **Brush** define objects that color the interiors of graphical shapes (for example, the **SolidBrush** constructor takes a **Color** object—the color to draw). In most **Fill** methods, **Brush**es fill a space with a color, pattern or image. Figure 16.5 summarizes various **Brush**es and their functions.

The application in Fig. 16.6 demonstrates several of the methods described in Fig. 16.4. It displays two overlapping rectangles, allowing the user to experiment with color values and color names.

Class	Description
`HatchBrush`	Uses a rectangular brush to fill a region with a pattern. The pattern is defined by a member of the `HatchStyle` enumeration, a foreground color (with which the pattern is drawn) and a background color.
`LinearGradient-Brush`	Fills a region with a gradual blend of one color into another. Linear gradients are defined along a line. They can be specified by the two colors, the angle of the gradient and either the width of a rectangle or two points.
`SolidBrush`	Fills a region with one color. Defined by a `Color` object.
`TextureBrush`	Fills a region by repeating a specified `Image` across the surface.

Fig. 16.5 Classes that derive from class **Brush**.

```vb
1   ' Fig. 16.6: ShowColors.vb
2   ' Using different colors in Visual Basic.
3
4   Public Class FrmColorForm
5      Inherits System.Windows.Forms.Form
6
7      ' input text boxes
8      Friend WithEvents txtColorName As TextBox
9      Friend WithEvents txtGreenBox As TextBox
10     Friend WithEvents txtRedBox As TextBox
11     Friend WithEvents txtAlphaBox As TextBox
12     Friend WithEvents txtBlueBox As TextBox
13
14     ' set color command buttons
15     Friend WithEvents cmdColorName As Button
16     Friend WithEvents cmdColorValue As Button
17
18     ' color labels
19     Friend WithEvents lblBlue As Label
20     Friend WithEvents lblGreen As Label
21     Friend WithEvents lblRed As Label
22     Friend WithEvents lblAlpha As Label
23
24     ' group boxes
25     Friend WithEvents nameBox As GroupBox
26     Friend WithEvents colorValueGroup As GroupBox
```

Fig. 16.6 Color value and alpha demonstration (part 1 of 3).

```vb
27
28         ' Visual Studio .NET generated code
29
30         ' color for back rectangle
31         Private mBehindColor As Color = Color.Wheat
32
33         ' color for front rectangle
34         Private mFrontColor As Color = Color.FromArgb(100, 0, 0, 255)
35
36         ' overrides Form OnPaint method
37         Protected Overrides Sub OnPaint(ByVal e As PaintEventArgs)
38            Dim graphicsObject As Graphics = e.Graphics ' get graphics
39
40            Dim textBrush As SolidBrush = _
41               New SolidBrush(Color.Black) ' create text brush
42
43            Dim brush As SolidBrush = _
44               New SolidBrush(Color.White) ' create solid brush
45
46            ' draw white background
47            graphicsObject.FillRectangle(brush, 4, 4, 275, 180)
48
49            ' display name of behindColor
50            graphicsObject.DrawString(mBehindColor.Name, Me.Font, _
51               textBrush, 40, 5)
52
53            ' set brush color and display back rectangle
54            brush.Color = mBehindColor
55
56            graphicsObject.FillRectangle(brush, 45, 20, 150, 120)
57
58            ' display Argb values of front color
59            graphicsObject.DrawString("Alpha: " & mFrontColor.A & _
60               " Red: " & mFrontColor.R & " Green: " & mFrontColor.G _
61               & " Blue: " & mFrontColor.B, Me.Font, textBrush, _
62               55, 165)
63
64            ' set brush color and display front rectangle
65            brush.Color = mFrontColor
66
67            graphicsObject.FillRectangle(brush, 65, 35, 170, 130)
68         End Sub ' OnPaint
69
70         ' handle cmdColorValue click event
71         Private Sub cmdColorValue_Click(ByVal sender As _
72            System.Object, ByVal e As System.EventArgs) _
73            Handles cmdColorValue.Click
74
75            ' obtain new front color from text boxes
76            mFrontColor = Color.FromArgb(txtAlphaBox.Text, _
77               txtRedBox.Text, txtGreenBox.Text, txtBlueBox.Text)
78
```

Fig. 16.6 Color value and alpha demonstration (part 2 of 3).

```
79          Invalidate() ' refresh Form
80       End Sub ' cmdColorValue_Click
81
82       Private Sub cmdColorName_Click(ByVal sender As _
83          System.Object, ByVal e As System.EventArgs) _
84          Handles cmdColorName.Click
85
86          ' set behindColor to color specified in text box
87          mBehindColor = Color.FromName(txtColorName.Text)
88
89          Invalidate() ' refresh Form
90       End Sub ' cmdColorName_Click
91
92    End Class ' FrmColorForm
```

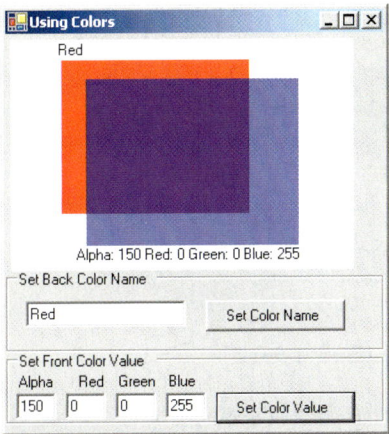

Fig. 16.6 Color value and alpha demonstration (part 3 of 3).

When the application begins its execution, it calls class **ShowColors**' **OnPaint** method to paint the window. Line 38 gets a reference to **PaintEventArgs e**'s **Graphics** object and assigns it to **Graphics** object **graphicsObject**. Lines 40–44 create a black and a white **SolidBrush** for drawing on the form. Class **SolidBrush** derives from abstract base class **Brush**; programmers can draw solid shapes with the **SolidBrush**.

Graphics method *FillRectangle* draws a solid white rectangle with the **Brush** supplied as a parameter (line 47). It takes as parameters a brush, the *x*- and *y*-coordinates of a point and the width and height of the rectangle to draw. The point represents the upper-left corner of the rectangle. Lines 50–51 display the **String Name** property of the **Brush**'s **Color** property with the **Graphics DrawString** method. The programmer has access to several overloaded **DrawString** methods; the version demonstrated in lines 50–51 takes a **String** to display, the display **Font**, a **Brush** and the x- and y-coordinates of the location for the **String**'s first character.

Lines 54–56 assign the **Color mBehindColor** value to the **Brush**'s **Color** property and display a rectangle. Lines 59–62 extract and display the ARGB values of **Color mFrontColor** and then display a filled rectangle that overlaps the first.

Button event-handler method **cmdColorValue_Click** (lines 71–80) uses **Color** method **FromARGB** to construct a new **Color** object from the ARGB values that a user specifies via text boxes. It then assigns the newly created **Color** to **mFrontColor**. **Button** event-handler method **cmdColorName_Click** (lines 82–90) uses the **Color** method **FromName** to create a new **Color** object from the **colorName** that a user enters in a text box. This **Color** is assigned to **mBehindColor**.

If the user assigns an alpha value between 0 and 255 for the **mFrontColor**, the effects of alpha blending are apparent. In the screenshot output, the red back rectangle blends with the blue front rectangle to create purple where the two overlap.

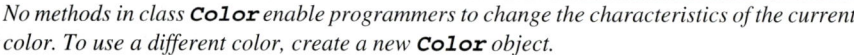

> *No methods in class **Color** enable programmers to change the characteristics of the current color. To use a different color, create a new **Color** object.*

The predefined GUI component **ColorDialog** is a dialog box that allows users to select from a palette of available colors. It also offers the option of creating custom colors. The program in Fig. 16.7 demonstrates the use of such a dialog. When a user selects a color and presses **OK**, the application retrieves the user's selection via the **ColorDialog**'s **Color** property.

```
1    ' Fig. 16.7: ShowColorsComplex.vb
2    ' Change the background and text colors of a form.
3
4    Imports System.Windows.Forms
5
6    Public Class FrmColorDialogTest
7       Inherits System.Windows.Forms.Form
8
9       Friend WithEvents cmdBackgroundButton As Button
10      Friend WithEvents cmdTextButton As Button
11
12      ' Visual Studio .NET generated code
13
14      ' change text color
15      Private Sub cmdTextButton_Click(ByVal sender As System.Object, _
16         ByVal e As System.EventArgs) Handles cmdTextButton.Click
17
18         ' create ColorDialog object
19         Dim colorBox As ColorDialog = New ColorDialog()
20         Dim result As DialogResult
21
22         ' get chosen color
23         result = colorBox.ShowDialog()
24
25         If result = DialogResult.Cancel Then
26            Return
27         End If
28
```

Fig. 16.7 **ColorDialog** used to change background and text color (part 1 of 2).

```
29         ' assign forecolor to result of dialog
30         cmdBackgroundButton.ForeColor = colorBox.Color
31         cmdTextButton.ForeColor = colorBox.Color
32      End Sub ' cmdTextButton_Click
33
34      ' change background color
35      Private Sub cmdBackgroundButton_Click( _
36         ByVal sender As System.Object, _
37         ByVal e As System.EventArgs) _
38         Handles cmdBackgroundButton.Click
39
40         ' create ColorDialog object
41         Dim colorBox As ColorDialog = New ColorDialog()
42         Dim result As DialogResult
43
44         ' show ColorDialog and get result
45         colorBox.FullOpen = True
46         result = colorBox.ShowDialog()
47
48         If result = DialogResult.Cancel Then
49            Return
50         End If
51
52         ' set background color
53         Me.BackColor = colorBox.Color
54      End Sub  ' cmdBackgroundButton_Click
55
56   End Class ' FrmColorDialogTest
```

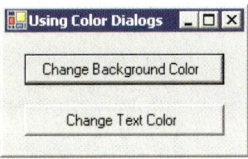
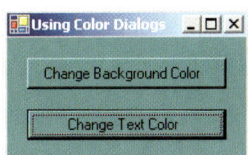
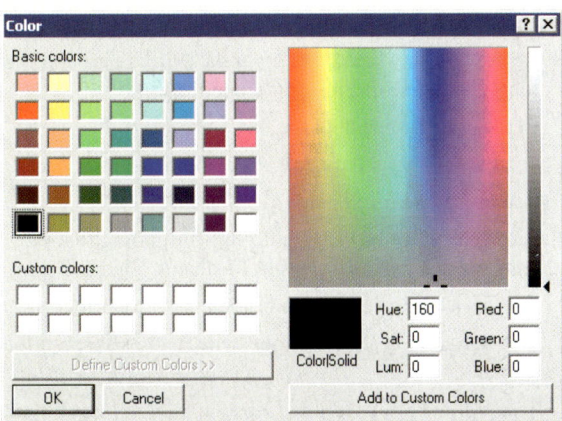

Fig. 16.7 `ColorDialog` used to change background and text color (part 2 of 2).

The GUI for this application contains two **Button**s. The top one, **cmdBackground**, allows the user to change the form and button background colors. The bottom one, **cmdTextButton**, allows the user to change the button text colors.

Lines 15–32 define **Button cmdTextButton**'s event handler, which creates a new **ColorDialog** named **colorBox** and invokes its **ShowDialog** method to display the window. Property **Color** of **colorBox** stores users' selections. Lines 30–31 set the text color of both buttons to the selected color.

Lines 35–54 define the event handler for button **cmdBackgroundButton**. The method modifies the background color of the form by setting **BackColor** equal to the dialog's **Color** property. The method creates a new **ColorDialog** and sets the dialog's **FullOpen** property to **True**. The dialog now displays all available colors, as shown in the screen capture in Fig. 16.7. The regular color display does not show the right-hand portion of the screen.

Users are not restricted to the **ColorDialog**'s 48 colors. To create a custom color, users can click anywhere in the **ColorDialog**'s large rectangle—this displays the various color shades. Adjust the slider, hue and other features to refine the color. When finished, click the **Add to Custom Colors** button, which adds the custom color to a square in the custom colors section of the dialog. Clicking **OK** sets the **Color** property of the **ColorDialog** to that color. Selecting a color and pressing the dialog's **OK** button causes the application's background color to change.

16.4 Font Control

This section introduces methods and constants that are related to font control. Once a **Font** has been created, its properties cannot be modified. If programmers require a different **Font**, they must create a new **Font** object—there are many overloaded versions of the **Font** constructor for creating custom **Font**s. Some properties of class **Font** are summarized in Fig. 16.8.

Property	Description
Bold	Tests a font for a bold font style. Returns **True** if the font is bold.
FontFamily	Represents the **FontFamily** of the **Font** (a grouping structure to organize fonts and define their similar properties).
Height	Represents the height of the font.
Italic	Tests a font for an italic font style. Returns **True** if the font is italic.
Name	Represents the font's name as a **String**.
Size	Returns a **Single** value indicating the current font size measured in design units (design units are any specified units of measurement for the font).
SizeInPoints	Returns a **Single** value indicating the current font size measured in points.
Strikeout	Tests a font for a strikeout font style. Returns **True** if the font is in strikeout format.
Underline	Tests a font for a underline font style. Returns **True** if the font is underlined.

Fig. 16.8 **Font** class read-only properties.

Note that property **Size** returns the font size as measured in design units, whereas **SizeInPoints** returns the font size as measured in points (the more common measurement). When we say that the **Size** property measures the size of the font in *design units*, we mean that the font size can be specified in a variety of ways, such as inches or millimeters. Some versions of the **Font** constructor accept a **GraphicsUnit** argument—an enumeration that allows users to specify the unit of measurement employed to describe the font size. Members of the **GraphicsUnit** enumeration include **Point** (1/72 inch), **Display** (1/75 inch), **Document** (1/300 inch), **Millimeter**, **Inch** and **Pixel**. If this argument is provided the **Size** property contains the size of the font as measured in the specified design unit, and the **SizeInPoints** property converts the size of the font into points. For example, if we create a **Font** with a size of **1** and specify that **GraphicsUnit.Inch** be used to measure the font, the **Size** property will be **1**, and the **SizeInPoints** property will be **72**. If we employ a constructor that does not accept a member of the **GraphicsUnit**, the default measurement for the font size is **GraphicsUnit.Point** (thus, the **Size** and **SizeInPoints** properties will be equal).

Class **Font** has a number of constructors. Most require a *font name*, which is a **String** representing the default font currently supported by the system. Common fonts include Microsoft *SansSerif* and *Serif*. Constructors also usually require the *font size* as an argument. Lastly, **Font** constructors usually require the *font style*, which is a member of the ***FontStyle*** enumeration: ***Bold***, ***Italic***, ***Regular***, ***Strikeout***, ***Underline***. Font styles can be combined via the **Or** operator (for example, **FontStyle.Italic Or FontStyle.Bold**, makes a font both italic and bold).

Graphics method ***DrawString*** sets the current drawing font—the font in which the text displays—to its **Font** argument.

Common Programming Error 16.1
Specifying a font that is not available on a system is a logic error. If this occurs, Visual Basic will substitute that system's default font.

The program in Fig. 16.9 displays text in four different fonts, each of a different size. The program uses the **Font** constructor to initialize **Font** objects (lines 17–29). Each call to the **Font** constructor passes a font name (e.g., Arial, Times New Roman, Courier New or Tahoma) as a **String**, a font size (a **Single**) and a **FontStyle** object (**style**). **Graphics** method **DrawString** sets the font and draws the text at the specified location. Note that line 14 creates a **DarkBlue SolidBrush** object (**brush**), causing all **String**s drawn with that brush to appear in **DarkBlue**.

Software Engineering Observation 16.2
*There is no way to change the properties of a **Font** object—to use a different font, programmers must create a new **Font** object.*

```
1   ' Fig. 16.9: UsingFonts.vb
2   ' Demonstrating various font settings.
3
4   Public Class FrmFonts
5      Inherits System.Windows.Forms.Form
6
```

Fig. 16.9 **Font**s and **FontStyle**s (part 1 of 2).

```vbnet
 7        ' Visual Studio .NET generated code
 8
 9        ' demonstrate various font and style settings
10        Protected Overrides Sub OnPaint( _
11           ByVal paintEvent As PaintEventArgs)
12
13           Dim graphicsObject As Graphics = paintEvent.Graphics
14           Dim brush As SolidBrush = New SolidBrush(Color.DarkBlue)
15
16           ' arial, 12 pt bold
17           Dim style As FontStyle = FontStyle.Bold
18           Dim arial As Font = New Font( _
19              New FontFamily("Arial"), 12, style)
20
21           ' times new roman, 12 pt regular
22           style = FontStyle.Regular
23           Dim timesNewRoman As Font = New Font( _
24              "Times New Roman", 12, style)
25
26           ' courier new, 16 pt bold and italic
27           style = FontStyle.Bold Or FontStyle.Italic
28           Dim courierNew As Font = New Font("Courier New", _
29              16, style)
30
31           ' tahoma, 18 pt strikeout
32           style = FontStyle.Strikeout
33           Dim tahoma As Font = New Font("Tahoma", 18, style)
34
35           graphicsObject.DrawString(arial.Name & " 12 point bold.", _
36              arial, brush, 10, 10)
37
38           graphicsObject.DrawString(timesNewRoman.Name & _
39              " 12 point plain.", timesNewRoman, brush, 10, 30)
40
41           graphicsObject.DrawString(courierNew.Name & _
42              " 16 point bold and italic.", courierNew, brush, 10, 54 )
43
44           graphicsObject.DrawString(tahoma.Name & _
45              " 18 point strikeout.", tahoma, brush, 10, 75)
46        End Sub ' OnPaint
47
48     End Class ' FrmFonts
```

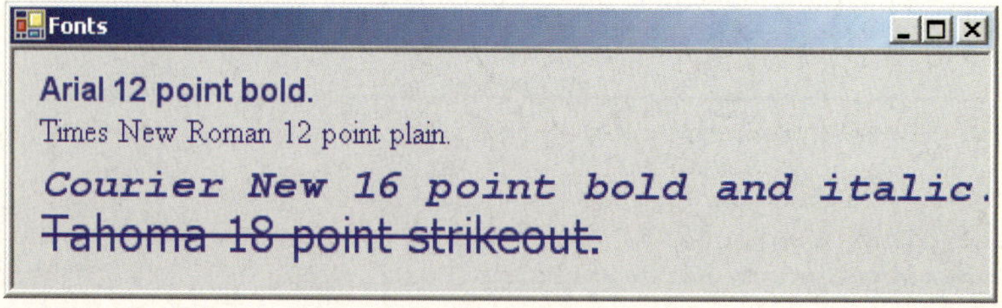

Fig. 16.9 Fonts and FontStyles (part 2 of 2).

Programmers can define precise information about a font's *metrics* (or properties), such as *height*, *descent* (the amount that characters dip below the baseline), *ascent* (the amount that characters rise above the baseline) and *leading* (the difference between the ascent of one line and the decent of the previous line). Figure 16.10 illustrates these properties.

Class **FontFamily** defines characteristics common to a group of related fonts. Class **FontFamily** provides several methods used to determine the font metrics that are shared by members of a particular family. These methods are summarized in Fig. 16.11.

The program shown in Fig. 16.12 calls method **ToString** to display the metrics of two fonts. Line 21 creates **Font arial** and sets it to 12-point Arial font. Line 22 uses class **Font** property **FontFamily** to obtain object **arial**'s **FontFamily** object. Lines 30–31 call **ToString** to output the **String** representation of the font. Lines 33–47 then use methods of class **FontFamily** to return integers specifying the ascent, descent, height and leading of the font. Lines 50–67 repeat this process for font **sansSerif**, a **Font** object derived from the MS Sans Serif **FontFamily**.

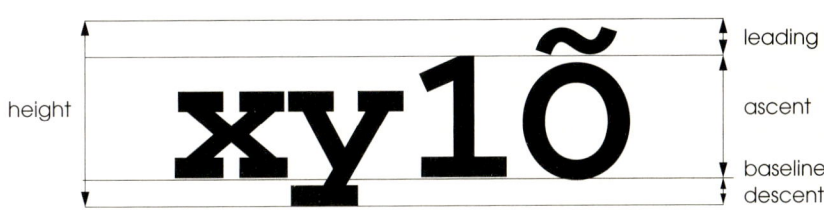

Fig. 16.10 An illustration of font metrics.

Method	Description
`GetCellAscent`	Returns an **Integer** representing the ascent of a font as measured in design units.
`GetCellDescent`	Returns an **Integer** representing the descent of a font as measured in design units.
`GetEmHeight`	Returns an **Integer** representing the height of a font as measured in design units.
`GetLineSpacing`	Returns an **Integer** representing the distance between two consecutive lines of text as measured in design units.

Fig. 16.11 **FontFamily** methods that return font-metric information.

```
1   ' Fig. 16.12: UsingFontMetrics.vb
2   ' Displaying font metric information.
3
4   Imports System
5   Imports System.Drawing
6   Imports System.Drawing.Text
```

Fig. 16.12 **FontFamily** class used to obtain font-metric information (part 1 of 3).

```vbnet
 7
 8   Public Class FrmFontMetrics
 9       Inherits System.Windows.Forms.Form
10
11       ' Visual Studio .NET generated code
12
13       Protected Overrides Sub OnPaint( _
14          ByVal paintEvent As PaintEventArgs)
15
16          Dim graphicsObject As Graphics = paintEvent.Graphics
17          Dim brush As SolidBrush = New SolidBrush(Color.Red)
18          Dim pen As Pen = New Pen(brush, Convert.ToSingle(2.5))
19
20          ' Arial font metrics
21          Dim arial As Font = New Font("Arial", 12)
22          Dim family As FontFamily = arial.FontFamily
23          Dim sanSerif As Font = New Font("Microsoft Sans Serif", _
24             14, FontStyle.Italic)
25
26          pen.Color = brush.Color
27          brush.Color = Color.DarkBlue
28
29          ' display Arial font metrics
30          graphicsObject.DrawString("Current Font: " & arial.ToString, _
31             arial, brush, 10, 10)
32
33          graphicsObject.DrawString("Ascent: " & _
34             family.GetCellAscent(FontStyle.Regular), arial, brush, _
35             10, 30)
36
37          graphicsObject.DrawString("Descent: " & _
38             family.GetCellDescent(FontStyle.Regular), arial, brush, _
39             10, 50)
40
41          graphicsObject.DrawString("Height: " & _
42             family.GetEmHeight(FontStyle.Regular), _
43             arial, brush, 10, 70)
44
45          graphicsObject.DrawString("Leading: " & _
46             family.GetLineSpacing(FontStyle.Regular), arial, brush, _
47             10, 90)
48
49          ' display Sans Serif font metrics
50          family = sanSerif.FontFamily
51
52          graphicsObject.DrawString("Current Font: " & _
53             sanSerif.ToString(), sanSerif, brush, 10, 130)
54
55          graphicsObject.DrawString("Ascent: " & _
56             family.GetCellAscent(FontStyle.Italic), _
57             sanSerif, brush, 10, 150)
58
```

Fig. 16.12 `FontFamily` class used to obtain font-metric information (part 2 of 3).

```
59              graphicsObject.DrawString("Descent: " & _
60                  family.GetCellDescent(FontStyle.Italic), sanSerif, _
61                  brush, 10, 170)
62
63              graphicsObject.DrawString("Height: " & family.GetEmHeight _
64                  (FontStyle.Italic), sanSerif, brush, 10, 190)
65
66              graphicsObject.DrawString("Leading: " & _
67                  family.GetLineSpacing(FontStyle.Italic), sanSerif, _
68                  brush, 10, 210)
69       End Sub    ' OnPaint
70
71   End Class    ' FrmFontMetrics
```

```
Metrics                                                              _ □ ×
Current Font: [Font: Name=Arial, Size=12, Units=3, GdiCharSet=1, GdiVerticalFont=False]
Ascent: 1854
Descent: 434
Height: 2048
Leading: 2355


Current Font: [Font: Name=Microsoft Sans Serif, Size=14, Units=3, GdiCharSet=1, GdiVerticalFont=False]
Ascent: 1888
Descent: 430
Height: 2048
Leading: 2318
```

Fig. 16.12 **FontFamily** class used to obtain font-metric information (part 3 of 3).

16.5 Drawing Lines, Rectangles and Ovals

This section presents a variety of **Graphics** methods for drawing lines, rectangles and ovals. Each of the drawing methods has several overloaded versions. When employing methods that draw shape outlines, we use versions that take a **Pen** and four **Integer**s; when employing methods that draw solid shapes, we use versions that take a **Brush** and four **Integer**s. In both instances, the first two **Integer** arguments represent the coordinates of the upper-left corner of the shape or its enclosing area, and the last two **Integer**s indicate the shape's width and height. Figure 16.13 summarizes the **Graphics** methods and their parameters.

Graphics Drawing Methods and Descriptions.
Note: Many of these methods are overloaded—consult the documentation for a full listing.
DrawLine(ByVal p As Pen, ByVal x1 As Integer, ByVal y1 As Integer, ByVal x2 As Integer, ByVal y2 As Integer) Draws a line from (**x1, y1**) to (**x2, y2**). The **Pen** determines the color, style and width of the line.

Fig. 16.13 **Graphics** methods that draw lines, rectangles and ovals (part 1 of 2).

Graphics Drawing Methods and Descriptions.
`DrawRectangle(ByVal p As Pen, ByVal x As Integer, ByVal y As Integer, ByVal width As Integer, ByVal height As Integer)` Draws a rectangle of the specified width and height. The top-left corner of the rectangle is at point (**x**, **y**). The **Pen** determines the color, style, and border width of the rectangle.
`FillRectangle(ByVal b As Brush, ByVal x As Integer, ByVal y As Integer, ByVal width As Integer, ByVal height As Integer)` Draws a solid rectangle of the specified width and height. The top-left corner of the rectangle is at point (**x**, **y**). The **Brush** determines the fill pattern inside the rectangle.
`DrawEllipse(ByVal p As Pen, ByVal x As Integer, ByVal y As Integer, ByVal width As Integer, ByVal height As Integer)` Draws an ellipse inside a rectangle. The width and height of the rectangle are as specified, and its top-left corner is at point (**x**, **y**). The **Pen** determines the color, style and border width of the ellipse.
`FillEllipse(ByVal b As Brush, ByVal x As Integer, ByVal y As Integer, ByVal width As Integer, ByVal height As Integer)` Draws a filled ellipse inside a rectangle. The width and height of the rectangle are as specified, and its top-left corner is at point (**x**, **y**). The **Brush** determines the pattern inside the ellipse.

Fig. 16.13 **Graphics** methods that draw lines, rectangles and ovals (part 2 of 2).

The application in Fig. 16.14 draws lines, rectangles and ellipses. In this application, we also demonstrate methods that draw filled and unfilled shapes.

```
1   ' Fig. 16.14: LinesRectanglesOvals.vb
2   ' Demonstrating lines, rectangles, and ovals.
3
4   Public Class FrmDrawing
5      Inherits System.Windows.Forms.Form
6
7      ' Visual Studio .NET generated code
8
9      ' display ovals lines, and rectangles
10     Protected Overrides Sub OnPaint( _
11        ByVal paintEvent As PaintEventArgs)
12
13        ' get graphics object
14        Dim g As Graphics = paintEvent.Graphics
15        Dim brush As SolidBrush = New SolidBrush(Color.Blue)
16        Dim pen As Pen = New Pen(Color.AliceBlue)
17
18        ' create filled rectangle
19        g.FillRectangle(brush, 90, 30, 150, 90)
20
21        ' draw lines to connect rectangles
22        g.DrawLine(pen, 90, 30, 110, 40)
```

Fig. 16.14 Drawing lines, rectangles and ellipses (part 1 of 2).

```
23          g.DrawLine(pen, 90, 120, 110, 130)
24          g.DrawLine(pen, 240, 30, 260, 40)
25          g.DrawLine(pen, 240, 120, 260, 130)
26
27          ' draw top rectangle
28          g.DrawRectangle(pen, 110, 40, 150, 90)
29
30          ' set brush to red
31          brush.Color = Color.Red
32
33          ' draw base Ellipse
34          g.FillEllipse(brush, 280, 75, 100, 50)
35
36          ' draw connecting lines
37          g.DrawLine(pen, 380, 55, 380, 100)
38          g.DrawLine(pen, 280, 55, 280, 100)
39
40          ' draw Ellipse outline
41          g.DrawEllipse(pen, 280, 30, 100, 50)
42      End Sub ' OnPaint
43
44  End Class ' FrmDrawing
```

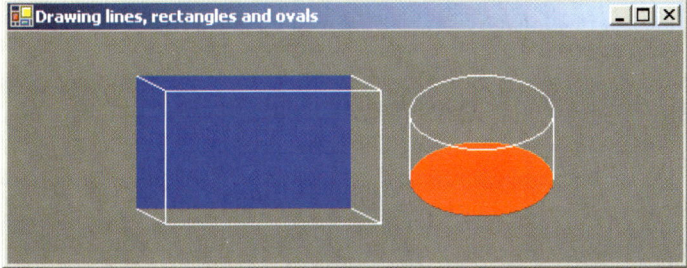

Fig. 16.14 Drawing lines, rectangles and ellipses (part 2 of 2).

Methods **DrawRectangle** and **FillRectangle** (lines 19 and 28) draw rectangles on the screen. For each method, the first argument specifies the drawing object to use. The **DrawRectangle** method uses a **Pen** object, whereas the **FillRectangle** method uses a **Brush** object (in this case, an instance of **SolidBrush**—a class that derives from **Brush**). The next two arguments specify the coordinates of the upper-left corner of the *bounding rectangle*, which represents the area in which the rectangle will be drawn. The fourth and fifth arguments specify the rectangle's width and height. Method **DrawLine** (lines 22–25) takes a **Pen** and two pairs of **Integer**s, specifying the start and endpoint of the line. The method then draws a line, using the **Pen** object passed to it.

Methods **DrawEllipse** and **FillEllipse** each provide overloaded versions that take five arguments. In both methods, the first argument specifies the drawing object to use. The next two arguments specify the upper-left coordinates of the bounding rectangle representing the area in which the ellipse will be drawn. The last two arguments specify the bounding rectangle's width and height, respectively. Figure 16.15 depicts an ellipse bounded by a rectangle. The ellipse touches the midpoint of each of the four sides of the bounding rectangle. The bounding rectangle is not displayed on the screen.

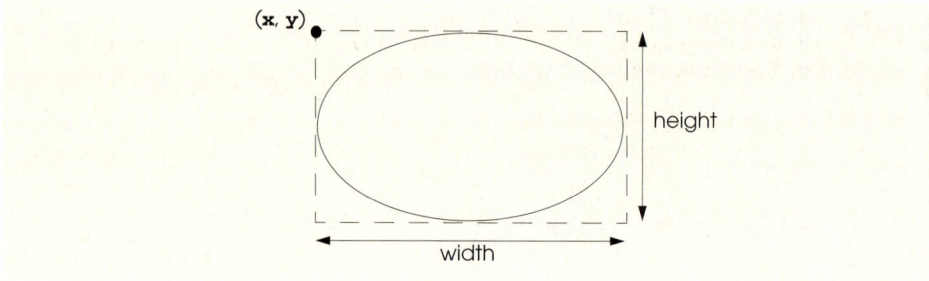

Fig. 16.15 Ellipse bounded by a rectangle.

16.6 Drawing Arcs

Arcs are portions of ellipses and are measured in degrees, beginning at a *starting angle* and continuing for a specified number of degrees (called the *arc angle*). An arc is said to *sweep* (traverse) its arc angle, beginning from its starting angle. Arcs that sweep in a clockwise direction are measured in positive degrees, whereas arcs that sweep in a counterclockwise direction are measured in negative degrees. Figure 16.16 depicts two arcs. Note that the left portion of the figure sweeps downward from zero degrees to approximately 110 degrees. Similarly, the arc in the right portion of the figure sweeps upward from zero degrees to approximately –110 degrees.

Notice the dashed boxes around the arcs in Fig. 16.16. We draw each arc as part of an oval (the rest of which is not visible). When drawing an oval, we specify the oval's dimensions in the form of a bounding rectangle that encloses the oval. The boxes in Fig. 16.16 correspond to these bounding rectangles. The **Graphics** methods used to draw arcs—**DrawArc**, **DrawPie** and **FillPie**—are summarized in Fig. 16.17.

The program in Fig. 16.18 draws six images (three arcs and three filled pie slices) to demonstrate the arc methods listed in Fig. 16.17. To illustrate the bounding rectangles that determine the sizes and locations of the arcs, the arcs are displayed inside red rectangles that have the same *x*-coordinates, *y*-coordinates, width and height arguments as those that define the bounding rectangles for the arcs.

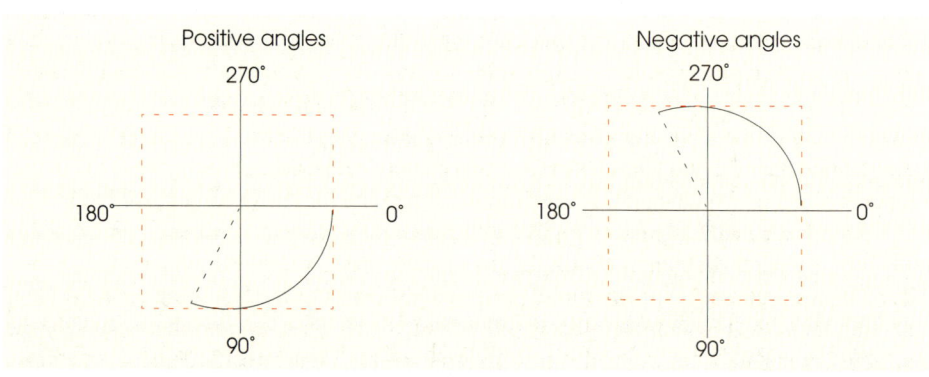

Fig. 16.16 Positive and negative arc angles.

Graphics Methods And Descriptions

Note: Many of these methods are overloaded—consult the documentation for a full listing.

DrawArc(ByVal p As Pen, ByVal x As Integer, ByVal y As Integer,
  ByVal width As Integer, ByVal height As Integer,
  ByVal startAngle As Integer, ByVal sweepAngle As Integer)
Draws an arc of an ellipse, beginning from angle **startAngle** (in degrees) and sweeping **sweepAngle** degrees. The ellipse is defined by a bounding rectangle of width **w**, height **h** and upper-left corner (**x,y**). The **Pen** determines the color, border width and style of the arc.

DrawPie(ByVal p As Pen, ByVal x As Integer, ByVal y As Integer,
  ByVal width As Integer, ByVal height As Integer,
  ByVal startAngle As Integer, ByVal sweepAngle As Integer)
Draws a pie section of an ellipse, beginning from angle **startAngle** (in degrees) and sweeping **sweepAngle** degrees. The ellipse is defined by a bounding rectangle of width **w**, height **h** and upper-left corner (**x,y**). The **Pen** determines the color, border width and style of the arc.

FillPie(ByVal b As Brush, ByVal x As Integer, ByVal y As Integer,
  ByVal width As Integer, ByVal height As Integer,
  ByVal startAngle As Integer, ByVal sweepAngle As Integer)
Functions similarly to **DrawPie**, except draws a solid arc (i.e., a sector). The **Brush** determines the fill pattern for the solid arc.

Fig. 16.17 Graphics methods for drawing arcs.

```vb
1   ' Fig. 16.18: DrawArcs.vb
2   ' Drawing various arcs on a form.
3
4   Public Class FrmArcTest
5      Inherits System.Windows.Forms.Form
6
7      ' Visual Studio .NET generated code
8
9      Protected Overrides Sub OnPaint( _
10        ByVal paintEvent As PaintEventArgs)
11
12        ' get graphics object
13        Dim graphicsObject As Graphics = paintEvent.Graphics
14        Dim rectangle1 As Rectangle = New Rectangle(15, 35, 80, 80)
15        Dim brush1 As SolidBrush = New SolidBrush(Color.FireBrick)
16        Dim pen1 As Pen = New Pen(brush1, 1)
17        Dim brush2 As SolidBrush = New SolidBrush(Color.DarkBlue)
18        Dim pen2 As Pen = New Pen(brush2, 1)
19
20        ' start at 0 and sweep 360 degrees
21        graphicsObject.DrawRectangle(pen1, rectangle1)
22        graphicsObject.DrawArc(pen2, rectangle1, 0, 360)
23
```

Fig. 16.18 Arc method demonstration (part 1 of 2).

```vbnet
24          ' start at 0 and sweep 110 degrees
25          rectangle1.Location = New Point(100, 35)
26          graphicsObject.DrawRectangle(pen1, rectangle1)
27          graphicsObject.DrawArc(pen2, rectangle1, 0, 110)
28
29          ' start at 0 and sweep -270 degrees
30          rectangle1.Location = New Point(185, 35)
31          graphicsObject.DrawRectangle(pen1, rectangle1)
32          graphicsObject.DrawArc(pen2, rectangle1, 0, -270)
33
34          ' start at 0 and sweep 360 degrees
35          rectangle1.Location = New Point(15, 120)
36          rectangle1.Size = New Size(80, 40)
37          graphicsObject.DrawRectangle(pen1, rectangle1)
38          graphicsObject.FillPie(brush2, rectangle1, 0, 360)
39
40          ' start at 270 and sweep -90 degrees
41          rectangle1.Location = New Point(100, 120)
42          graphicsObject.DrawRectangle(pen1, rectangle1)
43          graphicsObject.FillPie(brush2, rectangle1, 270, -90)
44
45          ' start at 0 and sweep -270 degrees
46          rectangle1.Location = New Point(185, 120)
47          graphicsObject.DrawRectangle(pen1, rectangle1)
48          graphicsObject.FillPie(brush2, rectangle1, 0, -270)
49       End Sub ' OnPaint
50
51    End Class ' FrmArcTest
```

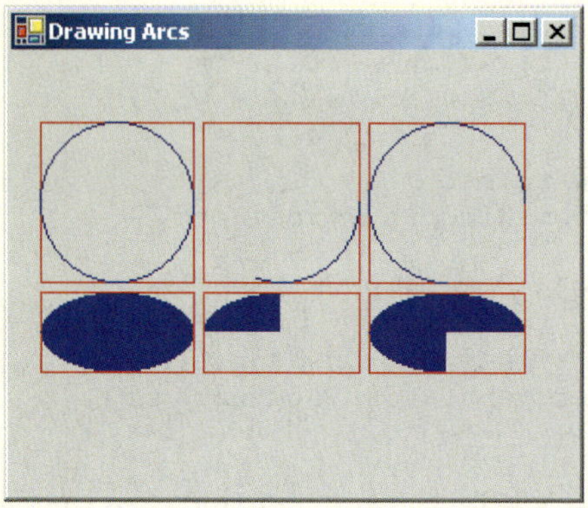

Fig. 16.18 Arc method demonstration (part 2 of 2).

Lines 13–16 create the objects that we need to draw various arcs: **Graphics** objects, **Rectangle**s, **SolidBrush**es and **Pen**s. Lines 21–22 then draw a rectangle and an arc inside the rectangle. The arc sweeps 360 degrees, becoming a circle. Line 25 changes the location of the **Rectangle** by setting its **Location** property to a new **Point**. The **Point** constructor takes the *x*- and *y*-coordinates of the new point. The **Location** property determines the upper-left corner of the **Rectangle**. After drawing the rectangle, the program draws an arc that starts at 0 degrees and sweeps 110 degrees. Because angles in Visual Basic increase in a clockwise direction, the arc sweeps downward.

Lines 30–32 perform similar functions, except that the specified arc sweeps -270 degrees. The **Size** property of a **Rectangle** determines the arc's height and width. Line 36 sets the **Size** property to a new **Size** object, which changes the size of the rectangle.

The remainder of the program is similar to the portions described above, except that a **SolidBrush** is used with method **FillPie**. The resulting arcs, which are filled, can be seen in the bottom half of the screenshot Fig. 16.18.

16.7 Drawing Polygons and Polylines

Polygons are multisided shapes. There are several **Graphics** methods used to draw polygons: **DrawLines** draws a series of connected points, **DrawPolygon** draws a closed polygon and **FillPolygon** draws a solid polygon. These methods are described in Fig. 16.19. The program in Fig. 16.20 allows users to draw polygons and connected lines via the methods listed in Fig. 16.19.

Method	Description
`DrawLines`	Draws a series of connected lines. The coordinates of each point are specified in an array of **Point**s. If the last point is different from the first point, the figure is not closed.
`DrawPolygon`	Draws a polygon. The coordinates of each point are specified in an array of **Point** objects. This method draws a closed polygon, even if the last point is different from the first point.
`FillPolygon`	Draws a solid polygon. The coordinates of each point are specified in an array of **Points**. This method draws a closed polygon, even if the last point is different from the first point.

Fig. 16.19 **Graphics** methods for drawing polygons.

```
1    ' Fig. 16.20: DrawPolygons.vb
2    ' Demonstrating polygons.
3
4    Public Class FrmPolygon
5       Inherits System.Windows.Forms.Form
6
7       ' polygon type options
8       Friend WithEvents filledPolygonRadio As RadioButton
9       Friend WithEvents lineRadio As RadioButton
10      Friend WithEvents polygonRadio As RadioButton
11
12      ' command buttons
13      Friend WithEvents cmdClear As Button
14      Friend WithEvents cmdNewColor As Button
15
16      Friend WithEvents drawWindow As Panel
17      Friend WithEvents typeGroup As GroupBox
```

Fig. 16.20 Polygon drawing demonstration (part 1 of 4).

```vbnet
18
19        ' Visual Studio .NET generated code
20
21        ' contains list of polygon points
22        Private mPoints As ArrayList = New ArrayList()
23
24        ' initialize default pen and brush
25        Dim mPen As Pen = New Pen(Color.DarkBlue)
26        Dim mBrush As SolidBrush = New SolidBrush(Color.DarkBlue)
27
28        ' draw panel mouse down event handler
29        Private Sub drawWindow_MouseDown(ByVal sender _
30           As Object, ByVal e As _
31           System.Windows.Forms.MouseEventArgs) _
32           Handles drawWindow.MouseDown
33
34           ' Add mouse position to vertex list
35           mPoints.Add(New Point(e.X, e.Y))
36           drawWindow.Invalidate() ' refresh panel
37        End Sub ' drawWindow_MouseDown
38
39        ' draw panel paint event handler
40        Private Sub drawWindow_Paint(ByVal sender As Object, _
41           ByVal e As System.Windows.Forms.PaintEventArgs) _
42           Handles drawWindow.Paint
43
44           ' get graphics object for panel
45           Dim graphicsObject As Graphics = e.Graphics
46
47           ' if arraylist has 2 or more points, display shape
48           If mPoints.Count > 1 Then
49
50              ' get array for use in drawing functions
51              Dim pointArray() As Point = _
52                 mPoints.ToArray(mPoints(0).GetType())
53
54              If polygonRadio.Checked Then ' draw polygon
55                 graphicsObject.DrawPolygon(mPen, pointArray)
56
57              ElseIf lineRadio.Checked Then ' draw lines
58                 graphicsObject.DrawLines(mPen, pointArray)
59
60              ElseIf filledPolygonRadio.Checked Then ' draw filled
61                 graphicsObject.FillPolygon(mBrush, pointArray)
62              End If
63
64           End If
65
66        End Sub ' drawWindow_Paint
67
68        ' handle cmdClear click event
69        Private Sub cmdClear_Click(ByVal sender As System.Object, _
70           ByVal e As System.EventArgs) Handles cmdClear.Click
```

Fig. 16.20 Polygon drawing demonstration (part 2 of 4).

```vbnet
71
72          mPoints = New ArrayList() ' remove points
73
74          drawWindow.Invalidate() ' refresh panel
75       End Sub ' cmdClear_Click
76
77       ' handle polygon radio button CheckedChange event
78       Private Sub polygonRadio_CheckedChanged(ByVal sender As _
79          System.Object, ByVal e As System.EventArgs) _
80          Handles polygonRadio.CheckedChanged
81
82          drawWindow.Invalidate() ' refresh panel
83       End Sub ' polygonRadio_CheckedChanged
84
85       ' handle line radio button CheckChanged event
86       Private Sub lineRadio_CheckedChanged(ByVal sender As _
87          System.Object, ByVal e As System.EventArgs) _
88          Handles lineRadio.CheckedChanged
89
90          drawWindow.Invalidate() ' refresh panel
91       End Sub ' lineRadio_CheckedChanged
92
93       ' handle filled polygon radio button CheckChanged event
94       Private Sub filledPolygonRadio_CheckedChanged(ByVal sender _
95          As System.Object, ByVal e As System.EventArgs) _
96          Handles filledPolygonRadio.CheckedChanged
97
98          drawWindow.Invalidate() ' refresh panel
99       End Sub ' filledPolygonRadio_CheckedChanged
100
101      ' handle cmdNewColor click event
102      Private Sub cmdNewColor_Click(ByVal sender As _
103         System.Object, ByVal e As System.EventArgs) _
104         Handles cmdNewColor.Click
105
106         ' create new color dialog
107         Dim colorBox As ColorDialog = New ColorDialog()
108
109         ' show dialog and obtain result
110         Dim result As DialogResult = colorBox.ShowDialog()
111
112         ' return if user cancels
113         If result = DialogResult.Cancel Then
114            Return
115         End If
116
117         mPen.Color = colorBox.Color ' set pen to new color
118         mBrush.Color = colorBox.Color ' set brush
119         drawWindow.Invalidate() ' refresh panel
120      End Sub ' cmdNewColor_Click
121
122 End Class ' FrmPolygon
```

Fig. 16.20 Polygon drawing demonstration (part 3 of 4).

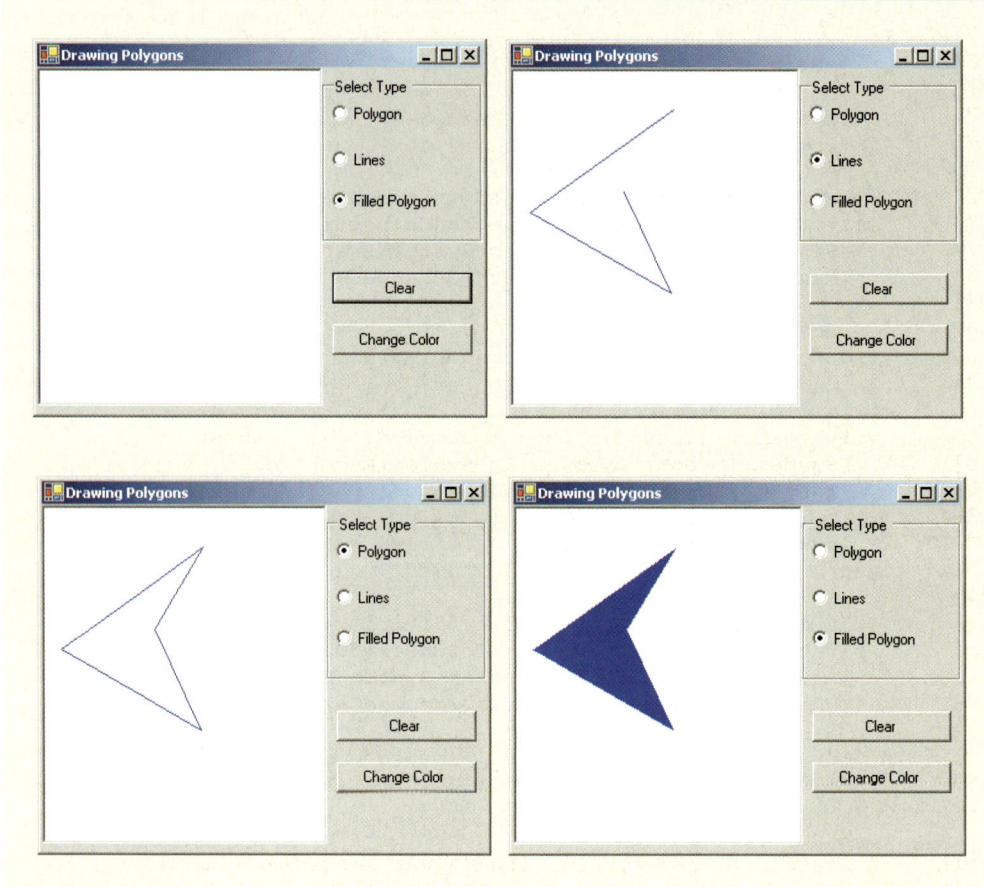

Fig. 16.20 Polygon drawing demonstration (part 4 of 4).

To allow the user to specify a variable number of points, line 22 declares **ArrayList mPoints** as a container for our **Point** objects. Lines 25–25 declare the **Pen** and **Brush** used to color our shapes. The **MouseDown** event handler (lines 29–37) for **Panel drawWindow** stores mouse-click locations in the **mPoints ArrayList**. It then calls method **Invalidate** of **drawWindow** to ensure that the panel refreshes to accommodate the new point. Method **drawWindow_Paint** (lines 40–66) handles the **Panel**'s **Paint** event. It obtains the panel's **Graphics** object (line 45) and, if the **ArrayList mPoints** contains two or more **Point**s, displays the polygon using the method that the user selected via the GUI radio buttons (lines 54–62). In lines 51–52, we extract an **Array** from the **ArrayList** via method **ToArray**. Method **ToArray** can take a single argument to determine the type of the returned array; we obtain the type from the first element in the **ArrayList**.

Method **cmdClear_Click** (lines 69–75) handles the **Clear** button's click event, creates an empty **ArrayList** (causing the old list to be erased) and refreshes the display. Lines 78–99 define the event handlers for the radio buttons' **CheckedChanged** event. Each method refreshes **Panel drawWindow** to ensure that the panel display reflects the selected drawing type. Event method **cmlNewColor_Click** (102–120) allows the user to select a new drawing color with a **ColorDialog**, using the same technique demonstrated in Fig. 16.7.

16.8 Advanced Graphics Capabilities

Visual Basic offers many additional graphics capabilities. The **Brush** hierarchy, for example, also includes *HatchBrush*, *LinearGradientBrush*, *PathGradientBrush* and *TextureBrush*.

The program in Fig. 16.21 demonstrates several graphics features, such as dashed lines, thick lines and the ability to fill shapes with patterns. These represent just a few of the additional capabilities of the **System.Drawing** namespace.

Lines 12–82 define the overridden **OnPaint** method for our form. Lines 19–21 create **LinearGradientBrush** (namespace **System.Drawing.Drawing2D**) object **brush**. A **LinearGradientBrush** enables users to draw with a color gradient. The **LinearGradientBrush** used in this example takes four arguments: A **Rectangle**, two **Color**s and a member of enumeration **LinearGradientMode**. In Visual Basic, all linear gradients are defined along a line that determines the gradient endpoint. This line can be specified either by starting and ending points or by the diagonal of a rectangle. The first argument, **Rectangle boundingRectangle**, specifies the defining line for **LinearGradientBrush brush**. This **Rectangle** argument represents the endpoints of the linear gradient—the upper-left corner is the starting point, and the bottom-right corner is the ending point. The second and third arguments specify the colors that the gradient will use. In this case, the color of the ellipse will gradually change from **Color.Blue** to **Color.Yellow**. The last argument, a type from the enumeration *LinearGradientMode*, specifies the linear gradient's direction. In our case, we use *LinearGradientMode.ForwardDiagonal*, which creates a gradient from the upper-left to the lower-right corner. We then use **Graphics** method **FillEllipse** in line 38 to draw an ellipse with **brush**; the color gradually changes from blue to yellow, as described above.

```
1   ' Fig. 16.21: DrawShapes.vb
2   ' Drawing various shapes on a form.
3
4   Imports System.Drawing.Drawing2D
5
6   Public Class FrmDrawShapes
7      Inherits System.Windows.Forms.Form
8
9      ' Visual Studio .NET generated code
10
11     ' draw various shapes on form
12     Protected Overrides Sub OnPaint(ByVal e As PaintEventArgs)
13
14        ' references to object we will use
15        Dim graphicsObject As Graphics = e.Graphics
16
17        ' ellipse rectangle and gradient brush
18        Dim drawArea1 As Rectangle = New Rectangle(5, 35, 30, 100)
```

Fig. 16.21 Shapes drawn on a form (part 1 of 3).

```vbnet
19         Dim linearBrush As LinearGradientBrush = _
20            New LinearGradientBrush(drawArea1, Color.Blue, _
21            Color.Yellow, LinearGradientMode.ForwardDiagonal)
22
23         ' pen and location for red outline rectangle
24         Dim thickRedPen As Pen = New Pen(Color.Red, 10)
25         Dim drawArea2 As Rectangle = New Rectangle(80, 30, 65, 100)
26
27         ' bitmap texture
28         Dim textureBitmap As Bitmap = New Bitmap(10, 10)
29         Dim graphicsObject2 As Graphics = _
30            Graphics.FromImage(textureBitmap) ' get bitmap graphics
31
32         ' brush and pen used throughout program
33         Dim solidColorBrush As SolidBrush = _
34            New SolidBrush(Color.Red)
35         Dim coloredPen As Pen = New Pen(solidColorBrush)
36
37         ' draw ellipse filled with a blue-yellow gradient
38         graphicsObject.FillEllipse(linearBrush, 5, 30, 65, 100)
39
40         ' draw thick rectangle outline in red
41         graphicsObject.DrawRectangle(thickRedPen, drawArea2)
42
43         ' fill textureBitmap with yellow
44         solidColorBrush.Color = Color.Yellow
45         graphicsObject2.FillRectangle(solidColorBrush, 0, 0, 10, 10)
46
47         ' draw small black rectangle in textureBitmap
48         coloredPen.Color = Color.Black
49         graphicsObject2.DrawRectangle(coloredPen, 1, 1, 6, 6)
50
51         ' draw small blue rectangle in textureBitmap
52         solidColorBrush.Color = Color.Blue
53         graphicsObject2.FillRectangle(solidColorBrush, 1, 1, 3, 3)
54
55         ' draw small red square in textureBitmap
56         solidColorBrush.Color = Color.Red
57         graphicsObject2.FillRectangle(solidColorBrush, 4, 4, 3, 3)
58
59         ' create textured brush and display textured rectangle
60         Dim texturedBrush As TextureBrush = _
61            New TextureBrush(textureBitmap)
62
63         graphicsObject.FillRectangle( _
64            texturedBrush, 155, 30, 75, 100)
65
66         ' draw pie-shaped arc in white
67         coloredPen.Color = Color.White
68         coloredPen.Width = 6
69         graphicsObject.DrawPie( _
70            coloredPen, 240, 30, 75, 100, 0, 270)
71
```

Fig. 16.21 Shapes drawn on a form (part 2 of 3).

```vbnet
72          ' draw lines in green and yellow
73          coloredPen.Color = Color.Green
74          coloredPen.Width = 5
75          graphicsObject.DrawLine(coloredPen, 395, 30, 320, 150)
76
77          ' draw a rounded, dashed yellow line
78          coloredPen.Color = Color.Yellow
79          coloredPen.DashCap = LineCap.Round
80          coloredPen.DashStyle = DashStyle.Dash
81          graphicsObject.DrawLine(coloredPen, 320, 30, 395, 150)
82      End Sub ' OnPaint
83
84  End Class ' FrmDrawShapes
```

Fig. 16.21 Shapes drawn on a form (part 3 of 3).

In line 24, we create a **Pen** object **pen**. We pass to **pen**'s constructor **Color.Red** and **Integer** argument **10**, indicating that we want **pen** to draw red lines that are 10 pixels wide.

Line 28 creates a new **Bitmap** image, which initially is empty. Class **Bitmap** can produce images in color and gray scale; this particular **Bitmap** is 10 pixels wide and 10 pixels tall. Method **FromImage** (line 29–30) is a **Shared** member of class **Graphics** and retrieves the **Graphics** object associated with an **Image**, which may be used to draw on an image. Lines 44–53 draw on the **Bitmap** a pattern consisting of black, blue, red and yellow rectangles and lines. A **TextureBrush** is a brush that fills the interior of a shape with an image, rather than a solid color. In line 63–64, **TextureBrush** object **textureBrush** fills a rectangle with our **Bitmap**. The **TextureBrush** constructor version that we use takes as an argument an image that defines its texture.

Next, we draw a pie-shaped arc with a thick white line. Lines 67–69 set **pen**'s color to **White** and modify its width to be six pixels. We then draw the pie on the form by specifying the **Pen**, *x*-coordinate, *y*-coordinate, length and width of the bounding rectangle, start angle and sweep angle.

Finally, lines 79–80 make use of **System.Drawing.Drawing2D** enumerations **DashCap** and **DashStyle** to draw a diagonal dashed line. Line 79 sets the **DashCap** property of **pen** (not to be confused with the **DashCap** enumeration) to a member of the **DashCap** enumeration. The **DashCap** enumeration specifies the styles for the start and end of a dashed line. In this case, we want both ends of the dashed line to be rounded, so we use **DashCap.Round**. Line 80 sets the **DashStyle** property of **pen** (not to be confused with the **DashStyle** enumeration) to **DashStyle.Dash**, indicating that we want our line to consist entirely of dashes.

Our next example demonstrates the use of a *general path*. A general path is a shape constructed from straight lines and complex curves. An object of class **GraphicsPath** (**System.Drawing.Drawing2D** namespace) represents a general path. The **GraphicsPath** class provides functionality that enables the creation of complex shapes from vector-based primitive graphics objects. A **GraphicsPath** object consists of figures defined by simple shapes. The start point of each vector-graphics object (such as a line or arc) that is added to the path is connected by a straight line to the end point of the previous object. When called, the **CloseFigure** method attaches the final graphic object endpoint to the initial starting point for the current figure by a straight line then starts a new figure. Method **StartFigure** begins a new figure within the path without closing the previous figure.

The program of Fig. 16.22 draws general paths in the shape of five-pointed stars. Line 29 sets the origin of the **Graphics** object. The arguments to method **TranslateTransform** indicate that the origin should be translated to the coordinates (150, 150). Lines 20–23 define two **Integer** arrays, representing the *x*- and *y*-coordinates of the points in the star, and line 26 defines **GraphicsPath** object **star**. A **For** loop then creates lines to connect the points of the star and adds these lines to **star**. We use **GraphicsPath** method **AddLine** to append a line to the shape. The arguments of **AddLine** specify the coordinates for the line's endpoints; each new call to **AddLine** adds a line from the previous point to the current point. Line 38 uses **GraphicsPath** method **CloseFigure** to complete the shape.

```vb
1    ' Fig. 16.22: DrawStars.vb
2    ' Using paths to draw stars on a form.
3
4    Imports System.Drawing.Drawing2D
5
6    Public Class FrmDrawStars
7       Inherits System.Windows.Forms.Form
8
9       ' Visual Studio .NET generated code
10
11      ' create path and draw stars along it
12      Protected Overrides Sub OnPaint(ByVal e As PaintEventArgs)
13         Dim graphicsObject As Graphics = e.Graphics
14         Dim i As Integer
15         Dim random As Random = New Random()
16         Dim brush As SolidBrush = _
17            New SolidBrush(Color.DarkMagenta)
18
19         ' x and y points of path
20         Dim xPoints As Integer() = _
21            {55, 67, 109, 73, 83, 55, 27, 37, 1, 43}
22         Dim yPoints As Integer() = _
23            {0, 36, 36, 54, 96, 72, 96, 54, 36, 36}
24
25         ' create graphics path for star
26         Dim star As GraphicsPath = New GraphicsPath()
27
```

Fig. 16.22 Paths used to draw stars on a form (part 1 of 2).

```
28          ' translate origin to (150, 150)
29          graphicsObject.TranslateTransform(150, 150)
30
31          ' create star from series of points
32          For i = 0 To 8 Step 2
33             star.AddLine(xPoints(i), yPoints(i), _
34                xPoints(i + 1), yPoints(i + 1))
35          Next
36
37          ' close shape
38          star.CloseFigure()
39
40          ' rotate origin and draw stars in random colors
41          For i = 1 To 18
42             graphicsObject.RotateTransform(20)
43
44             brush.Color = Color.FromArgb(random.Next(200, 255), _
45                random.Next(255), random.Next(255), random.Next(255))
46
47             graphicsObject.FillPath(brush, star)
48          Next
49
50       End Sub ' OnPaint
51
52    End Class ' FrmDrawStars
```

Fig. 16.22 Paths used to draw stars on a form (part 2 of 2).

The **For** structure in lines 41–48 draws the **star** 18 times, rotating it around the origin. Line 42 uses **Graphics** method ***RotateTransform*** to move to the next position on the form; the argument specifies the rotation angle in degrees. **Graphics** method **FillPath** (line 47) then draws a filled version of the **star** with the **Brush** created on lines 44–45. The application determines the **SolidBrush**'s color randomly, using **Random** variable **random**'s method **Next**.

16.9 Introduction to Multimedia

Visual Basic offers many convenient ways to include images and animations in programs. People who entered the computing field decades ago used computers primarily to perform arithmetic calculations. As the discipline evolves, we are beginning to realize the importance of computers' data-manipulation capabilities. We are seeing a wide variety of exciting new three-dimensional applications. Multimedia programming is an entertaining and innovative field, but one that presents many challenges

Multimedia applications demand extraordinary computing power. Until recently, affordable computers with this amount of power were not available. However, today's ultrafast processors are making multimedia-based applications commonplace. As the market for multimedia explodes, users are purchasing faster processors, larger memories and wider communications bandwidths needed to support multimedia applications. This benefits the computer and communications industries, which provide the hardware, software and services fueling the multimedia revolution.

In the remaining sections of this chapter, we introduce the use and manipulation of images, as well as other multimedia features and capabilities. Section 16.10 discusses how to load, display and scale images; Section 16.11 demonstrates image animation; Section 16.12 presents the video capabilities of the Windows Media Player control; and Section 16.13 explores Microsoft Agent technology.

16.10 Loading, Displaying and Scaling Images

Visual Basic's multimedia capabilities include graphics, images, animations and video. Previous sections demonstrated Visual Basic's vector-graphics capabilities; this section concentrates on image manipulation. The Windows form that we create in Fig. 16.23 demonstrates the loading of an **Image** (**System.Drawing** namespace). The application allows users to enter a desired height and width for the **Image**, which then is displayed in the specified size.

```
1   ' Fig. 16.23: DisplayLogo.vb
2   ' Displaying and resizing an image.
3
4   Public Class FrmDisplayLogo
5      Inherits System.Windows.Forms.Form
6
7      ' width controls
8      Friend WithEvents txtWidth As TextBox
9      Friend WithEvents lblWidth As Label
10
11     ' height controls
12     Friend WithEvents lblHeight As Label
13     Friend WithEvents txtHeight As TextBox
14
15     Private mGraphicsObject As Graphics
16     Private mImage As Image
17
```

Fig. 16.23 Image resizing (part 1 of 3).

```
18      ' sets member variables on form load
19      Private Sub FrmDisplayLogo_Load(ByVal sender As _
20         System.Object, ByVal e As System.EventArgs) _
21         Handles MyBase.Load
22
23         ' get Form's graphics object
24         mGraphicsObject = Me.CreateGraphics
25
26         ' load image
27         mImage = Image.FromFile("images/Logo.gif")
28
29      End Sub ' FrmDisplayLogo_Load
30
31      ' Visual Studio .NET generated code
32
33      Private Sub cmdSetButton_Click (ByVal sender As System.Object, _
34         ByVal e As System.EventArgs) Handles cmdSetButton.Click
35
36         ' get user input
37         Dim width As Integer = Convert.ToInt32(txtWidth.Text)
38         Dim height As Integer = Convert.ToInt32(txtHeight.Text)
39
40         ' if specified dimensions are too large display problem
41         If (width > 375 OrElse height > 225) Then
42            MessageBox.Show("Height or Width too large")
43
44            Return
45         End If
46         mGraphicsObject.Clear(Me.BackColor) ' clear Windows Form
47
48         ' draw image
49         mGraphicsObject.DrawImage(mImage, 5, 5, width, height)
50      End Sub ' cmdSetButton_Click
51
52   End Class ' FrmDisplayLogo
```

Fig. 16.23 Image resizing (part 2 of 3).

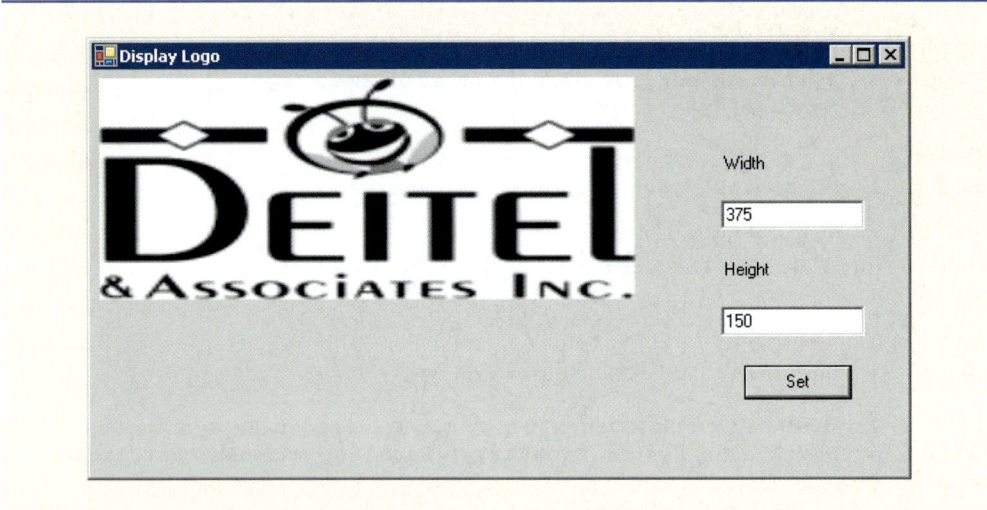

Fig. 16.23 Image resizing (part 3 of 3).

Line 16 declares **Image** reference **mImage**. The **Shared Image** method **FromFile** then retrieves an image stored on disk and assigns it to **mImage** (line 27). Line 24 uses **Form** method **CreateGraphics** to create a **Graphics** object associated with the **Form**; we use this object to draw on the **Form**. Method **CreateGraphics** is inherited from class **Control**; all Windows controls, such as **Button**s and **Panel**s, also provide this method. When users click **Set**, the width and height parameters are validated to ensure that they are not too large. If the parameters are valid, line 46 calls **Graphics** method **Clear** to paint the entire **Form** in the current background color. Line 49 calls **Graphics** method **DrawImage** with the following parameters: the image to draw, the *x*-coordinate of the upper-left corner, the *y*-coordinate of the upper-left corner, the width of the image and the height of the image. If the width and height do not correspond to the image's original dimensions, the image is scaled to fit the new specifications.

16.11 Animating a Series of Images

The next example animates a series of images stored in an array. The application uses the same techniques to load and display **Image**s as those illustrated in Fig. 16.23. The images were created with Adobe Photoshop.

The animation in Fig. 16.24 uses a **PictureBox**, which contains the images that we animate. We use a **Timer** to cycle through the images, causing a new image to display every 50 milliseconds. Variable **count** keeps track of the current image number and increases by one every time we display a new image. The array includes 30 images (numbered 0–29); when the application reaches image 29, it returns to image 0. The 30 images were prepared in advance with a graphics software package and placed in the **images** folder inside the **bin/Debug** directory of the project.

Lines 19–22 load each of 30 images and place them in an **ArrayList**. **ArrayList** method **Add** allows us to add objects to the **ArrayList**; we use this method in lines 20–21 to add each **Image**. Line 25 places the first image in the **PictureBox**, using the

ArrayList indexer. Line 28 modifies the size of the **PictureBox** so that it is equal to the size of the **Image** it is displaying. The event handler for **timer**'s **Tick** event (line 38–46) then displays the next image from the **ArrayList**.

```vbnet
1   ' Fig. 16.24: LogoAnimator.vb
2   ' Program that animates a series of images.
3
4   Public Class FrmLogoAnimator
5      Inherits System.Windows.Forms.Form
6
7      Private mImages As ArrayList = New ArrayList()
8      Private mCount As Integer = 1
9
10     Public Sub New()
11        MyBase.New()
12
13        ' This call is required by Windows Form Designer.
14        InitializeComponent()
15
16        ' load all images
17        Dim i As Integer
18
19        For i = 0 To 29
20           mImages.Add(Image.FromFile("images/deitel" & i _
21              & ".gif"))
22        Next
23
24        ' load first image
25        logoPictureBox.Image = CType(mImages(0), Image)
26
27        ' set PictureBox to be same size as Image
28        logoPictureBox.Size = logoPictureBox.Image.Size
29     End Sub ' New
30
31     Friend WithEvents timer As System.Windows.Forms.Timer
32
33     Friend WithEvents logoPictureBox As _
34        System.Windows.Forms.PictureBox
35
36     ' Visual Studio .NET generated code
37
38     Private Sub timer_Tick(ByVal sender As System.Object, _
39        ByVal e As System.EventArgs) Handles timer.tick
40
41        ' increment counter
42        mCount = (mCount + 1) Mod 30
43
44        ' load next image
45        logoPictureBox.Image = CType(mImages(mCount), Image)
46     End Sub ' Timer_Tick
47
48  End Class ' FrmLogoAnimator
```

Fig. 16.24 Animation of a series of images (part 1 of 2).

Fig. 16.24 Animation of a series of images (part 2 of 2).

Performance Tip 16.2
It is more efficient to load an animation's frames as one image than to load each image separately. (A painting program, such as Adobe Photoshop®, Jasc® or Paint Shop Pro™, can be used to combine the animation's frames into one image.) If the images are being loaded separately from the Web, each loaded image requires a separate connection to the site on which the images are stored; this process can result in poor performance.

Performance Tip 16.3
Loading animation frames can cause program delays, because the program waits for all frames to load before displaying them.

The following chess example demonstrates the capabilities of GDI+ as they pertain to a chess-game application. These include techniques for two-dimensional *collision detection*, the selection of single frames from a multi-frame image and *regional invalidation* (refreshing only the required parts of the screen) to increase performance. Two-dimensional collision detection is the detection of an overlap between two shapes. In the next example, we demonstrate the simplest form of collision detection, which determines whether a point (the mouse-click location) is contained within a rectangle (a chess-piece image).

Class **CChessPiece** (Fig. 16.25) is a container class for the individual chess pieces. Lines 7–14 define a public enumeration of constants that identify each chess-piece type. The constants also serve to identify the location of each piece in the chess-piece image file. **Rectangle** object **mLocationRectangle** (lines 20–21) identifies the image location on the chess board. The **x** and **y** properties of the rectangle are assigned in the **CChessPiece** constructor, and all chess-piece images have heights and widths of **75**.

```
1    ' Fig. 16.25 : Chesspiece.vb
2    ' Storage class for chess piece attributes.
3
4    Public Class CChessPiece
5
6       ' define chess-piece type constants
7       Public Enum Types
8          KING
9          QUEEN
10         BISHOP
11         KNIGHT
12         ROOK
```

Fig. 16.25 Container class for chess pieces (part 1 of 2).

```vbnet
13          PAWN
14      End Enum
15
16      Private mCurrentType As Integer ' this object's type
17      Private mPieceImage As Bitmap ' this object's image
18
19      ' default display location
20      Private mLocationRectangle As Rectangle = _
21          New Rectangle(0, 0, 75, 75)
22
23      ' construct piece
24      Public Sub New(ByVal type As Integer, _
25          ByVal xLocation As Integer, ByVal yLocation As Integer, _
26          ByVal sourceImage As Bitmap)
27
28          mCurrentType = type ' set current type
29          mLocationRectangle.X = xLocation ' set current x location
30          mLocationRectangle.Y = yLocation ' set current y location
31
32          ' obtain pieceImage from section of sourceImage
33          mPieceImage = sourceImage.Clone(New Rectangle(type * 75, _
34              0, 75, 75), Drawing.Imaging.PixelFormat.DontCare)
35      End Sub ' constructor
36
37      ' draw this piece
38      Public Sub Draw(ByVal graphicsObect As Graphics)
39          graphicsObect.DrawImage(mPieceImage, mLocationRectangle)
40      End Sub ' Draw
41
42      ' obtain this piece's location rectangle
43      Public Readonly Property LocationRectangle As Rectangle
44          Get
45              Return mLocationRectangle
46          End Get
47      End Property ' LocationRectangle
48
49      ' set this piece's location
50      Public Sub SetLocation(ByVal xLocation As Integer, _
51          ByVal yLocation As Integer)
52
53          mLocationRectangle.X = xLocation
54          mLocationRectangle.Y = yLocation
55      End Sub ' SetLocation
56
57  End Class ' CChesspiece
```

Fig. 16.25 Container class for chess pieces (part 2 of 2).

The **CChessPiece** constructor (lines 24–35) requires that the calling class define a chess-piece type, its **x** and **y** location and the **Bitmap** containing all chess-piece images. Rather than loading the chess-piece image within the class, we allow the calling class to pass the image. This avoids the image-loading overhead for each piece. It also increases the flexibility of the class by allowing the user to change images; for example, in this case, we use the class for both black and white chess-piece images. Lines 33–34 extract a subimage that contains only the current piece's bitmap data. Our chess-piece images are defined in a specific manner: One image contains six chess-piece images, each defined within a 75-pixel block, resulting in a total image size of 450-by-75. We obtain a single image via **Bitmap**'s **Clone** method, which allows us to specify a rectangle image location and the desired pixel format. The location is a 75-by-75 pixel block with its upper-left corner **x** equal to **75 * type** and the corresponding **y** equal to **0**. For the pixel format, we specify constant **DontCare**, causing the format to remain unchanged.

Method **Draw** (lines 38–40) causes the **CChessPiece** to draw **mPieceImage** in **mLocationRectangle** on the passed **Graphics** object. **Readonly Property LocationRectangle** returns the object **mLocationRectangle** for use in collision detection, and **SetLocation** allows the calling class to specify a new piece location.

Class **FrmChessSurface** (Fig. 16.26) defines the game and graphics code for our chess game. Lines 20–30 define class-scope variables that are required by the program. **ArrayList mChessTile** (line 20) stores the board tile images; it contains four images: Two light tiles and two dark tiles (to increase board variety). **ArrayList mChessPieces** (line 23) stores all active **CChessPiece** objects, and **Integer mSelectedIndex** (line 26) identifies the index in **mChessPieces** of the currently selected piece. The **mBoard** (line 27) is an 8-by-8, two-dimensional **Integer** array corresponding to the squares of a Chess board. Each board element is an integer from 0 to 3 that corresponds to an index in **mChessTile** and is used to specify the Chess-board square image. **Integer TILESIZE** (line 30) is a constant defining the size of each tile in pixels.

```
1   ' Fig. 16.26: ChessGame.vb
2   ' Chess Game graphics code.
3
4   Imports System.Drawing.Drawing2D
5
6   Public Class FrmChessSurface
7       Inherits System.Windows.Forms.Form
8
9       ' display box
10      Friend WithEvents pieceBox As PictureBox
11
12      ' game menu
13      Friend WithEvents gameMenu As MainMenu
14      Friend WithEvents gameItem As MenuItem
15      Friend WithEvents newGame As MenuItem
16
17      ' Visual Studio .NET generated code
18
19      ' ArrayList for board tile images
20      Dim mChessTile As ArrayList = New ArrayList()
21
22      ' ArrayList for chess pieces
23      Dim mChessPieces As ArrayList = New ArrayList()
24
25      ' define index for selected piece
26      Dim mSelectedIndex As Integer = -1
27      Dim mBoard As Integer(,) = New Integer(7,7) {} ' board array
```

Fig. 16.26 Chess-game code (part 1 of 9).

```vbnet
28
29       ' define chess tile size in pixels
30       Private Const TILESIZE As Integer = 75
31
32       ' load tile bitmaps and reset game
33       Private Sub FrmChessSurface_Load(ByVal sender _
34          As System.Object, ByVal e As System.EventArgs) _
35          Handles MyBase.Load
36
37          ' load chess board tiles
38          mChessTile.Add(Bitmap.FromFile("lightTile1.png"))
39          mChessTile.Add(Bitmap.FromFile("lightTile2.png"))
40          mChessTile.Add(Bitmap.FromFile("darkTile1.png"))
41          mChessTile.Add(Bitmap.FromFile("darkTile2.png"))
42
43          ResetBoard() ' initialize board
44          Invalidate() ' refresh form
45       End Sub ' FrmChessSurface_Load
46
47       ' initialize pieces to start positions and rebuild board
48       Private Sub ResetBoard()
49          Dim column As Integer = 0
50          Dim row As Integer = 0
51          Dim current As Integer
52          Dim piece As CChessPiece
53          Dim random As Random = New Random()
54          Dim light As Boolean = False
55          Dim type As Integer
56
57          ' ensure empty arraylist
58          mChessPieces = New ArrayList()
59
60          ' load whitepieces image
61          Dim whitePieces As Bitmap = _
62             Bitmap.FromFile("whitePieces.png")
63
64          ' load blackpieces image
65          Dim blackPieces As Bitmap = _
66             Bitmap.FromFile("blackPieces.png")
67
68          ' set whitepieces drawn first
69          Dim selected As Bitmap = whitePieces
70
71          ' traverse board rows in outer loop
72          For row = 0 To mBoard.GetUpperBound(0)
73
74             ' if at bottom rows, set to black piece images
75             If row > 5 Then
76                selected = blackPieces
77             End If
78
```

Fig. 16.26 Chess-game code (part 2 of 9).

```vbnet
 79            ' traverse board columns in inner loop
 80            For column = 0 To mBoard.GetUpperBound(1)
 81
 82               ' if first or last row, organize pieces
 83               If (row = 0 OrElse row = 7) Then
 84
 85                  Select Case column
 86
 87                     Case 0, 7 ' set current piece to rook
 88                        current = CChessPiece.Types.ROOK
 89
 90                     Case 1, 6 ' set current piece to knight
 91                        current = CChessPiece.Types.KNIGHT
 92
 93                     Case 2, 5 ' set current piece to bishop
 94                        current = CChessPiece.Types.BISHOP
 95
 96                     Case 3 ' set current piece to king
 97                        current = CChessPiece.Types.KING
 98
 99                     Case 4 ' set current piece to queen
100                        current = CChessPiece.Types.QUEEN
101                  End Select
102
103                  ' create current piece at start position
104                  piece = New CChessPiece(current, _
105                     column * TILESIZE, row * TILESIZE, selected)
106
107                  ' add piece to ArrayList
108                  mChessPieces.Add(piece)
109               End If
110
111               ' if second or seventh row, organize pawns
112               If (row = 1 OrElse row = 6) Then
113                  piece = New CChessPiece(CChessPiece.Types.PAWN, _
114                     column * TILESIZE, row * TILESIZE, selected)
115
116                  mChessPieces.Add(piece)
117               End If
118
119               ' determine board piece type
120               type = random.Next(0, 2)
121
122               If light Then ' set light tile
123                  mBoard(row, column) = type
124                  light = False
125               Else ' set dark tile
126                  mBoard(row, column) = type + 2
127                  light = True
128               End If
129
130            Next ' next column
131
```

Fig. 16.26 Chess-game code (part 3 of 9).

```vbnet
132                ' account for new row tile color switch
133                light = Not light
134          Next ' next row
135
136       End Sub ' ResetBoard
137
138       ' display board in form OnPaint event
139       Protected Overrides Sub OnPaint(ByVal paintEvent _
140          As PaintEventArgs)
141
142          ' obtain graphics object
143          Dim graphicsObject As Graphics = paintEvent.Graphics
144          Dim row, column As Integer
145
146          For row = 0 To mBoard.GetUpperBound(0)
147
148             For column = 0 To mBoard.GetUpperBound(1)
149
150                ' draw image specified in board array
151                graphicsObject.DrawImage( _
152                   CType(mChessTile(mBoard(row, column)), _
153                   Image), New Point(TILESIZE * column, _
154                   TILESIZE * row))
155             Next
156
157          Next
158
159       End Sub ' OnPaint
160
161       ' return index of piece that intersects point
162       ' optionally exclude a value
163       Private Function CheckBounds(ByVal point As Point, _
164          Optional ByVal exclude As Integer = -1) As Integer
165
166          Dim rectangle As Rectangle ' current bounding rectangle
167          Dim i As Integer
168
169          For i = 0 To mChessPieces.Count - 1
170
171             ' get piece rectangle
172             rectangle = Getpiece(i).LocationRectangle()
173
174             ' check if rectangle contains point
175             If (rectangle.Contains(point) AndAlso i <> exclude) Then
176                Return i
177             End If
178
179          Next
180
181          Return -1
182       End Function ' CheckBounds
183
```

Fig. 16.26 Chess-game code (part 4 of 9).

```vbnet
184     ' handle pieceBox paint event
185     Private Sub pieceBox_Paint(ByVal sender As System.Object, _
186        ByVal e As System.Windows.Forms.PaintEventArgs) _
187        Handles pieceBox.Paint
188
189        Dim i As Integer
190
191        ' draw all pieces
192        For i = 0 To mChessPieces.Count - 1
193           Getpiece(i).Draw(e.Graphics)
194        Next
195
196     End Sub ' pieceBox_Paint
197
198     ' on MouseDown event, select chess piece
199     Private Sub pieceBox_MouseDown(ByVal sender As System.Object, _
200        ByVal e As System.Windows.Forms.MouseEventArgs) _
201        Handles pieceBox.MouseDown
202
203        ' determine selected piece
204        mSelectedIndex = CheckBounds(New Point(e.X, e.Y))
205     End Sub ' pieceBox_MouseDown
206
207     ' if piece is selected, move it
208     Private Sub pieceBox_MouseMove(ByVal sender As System.Object, _
209        ByVal e As System.Windows.Forms.MouseEventArgs) _
210        Handles pieceBox.MouseMove
211
212        If mSelectedIndex > -1 Then
213
214           Dim region As Rectangle = New Rectangle(e.X - _
215              TILESIZE * 2, e.Y - TILESIZE * 2, TILESIZE * 4, _
216              TILESIZE * 4)
217
218           ' set piece center to mouse
219           Getpiece(mSelectedIndex).SetLocation(e.X - _
220              TILESIZE / 2, e.Y - TILESIZE / 2)
221
222           ' refresh immediate area
223           pieceBox.Invalidate(region)
224        End If
225
226     End Sub ' pieceBox_MouseMove
227
228     ' on mouse up, deselect chess piece and remove taken piece
229     Private Sub pieceBox_MouseUp(ByVal sender As _
230        System.Object, ByVal e As _
231        System.Windows.Forms.MouseEventArgs) _
232        Handles pieceBox.MouseUp
233
234        Dim remove As Integer = -1
235
```

Fig. 16.26 Chess-game code (part 5 of 9).

```vbnet
236         If mSelectedIndex > -1 Then ' if chess piece was selected
237
238             Dim current As Point = New Point(e.X, e.Y)
239             Dim newPoint As Point = New Point(current.X - _
240                 current.X Mod TILESIZE, current.Y - _
241                 current.Y Mod TILESIZE)
242
243             ' check bounds with point, exclude selected piece
244             remove = CheckBounds(current, mSelectedIndex)
245
246             ' snap piece into center of closest square
247             Getpiece(mSelectedIndex).SetLocation(newPoint.X, _
248                 newPoint.Y)
249
250             mSelectedIndex = -1 ' deselect piece
251
252             ' remove taken piece
253             If remove > -1 Then
254                 mChessPieces.RemoveAt(remove)
255             End If
256
257         End If
258
259         ' refresh pieceBox to ensure artifact removal
260         pieceBox.Invalidate()
261     End Sub ' pieceBox_MouseUp
262
263     ' helper function to convert ArrayList object as CChesspiece
264     Private Function Getpiece(ByVal i As Integer) _
265         As CChessPiece
266
267         Return CType(mChessPieces(i), CChessPiece)
268     End Function ' Getpiece
269
270     ' handle NewGame menu option click
271     Private Sub NewGame_Click(ByVal sender As Object, _
272         ByVal e As System.EventArgs) Handles NewGame.Click
273
274         ResetBoard() ' re-initialize board
275         Invalidate() ' refresh form
276     End Sub ' NewGame_Click
277
278 End Class ' FrmChessSurface
```

Fig. 16.26 Chess-game code (part 6 of 9).

The chess game GUI consists of **Form FrmChessSurface**, the area in which we draw the tiles; **PictureBox pieceBox**, the window in which we draw the pieces (note that **pieceBox** background color is set to **"transparent"**); and a **Menu** that allows the user to begin a new game. Although the pieces and tiles could have been drawn on the same form, doing so would decrease performance. We would be forced to refresh the board as well as the pieces every time we refreshed the control.

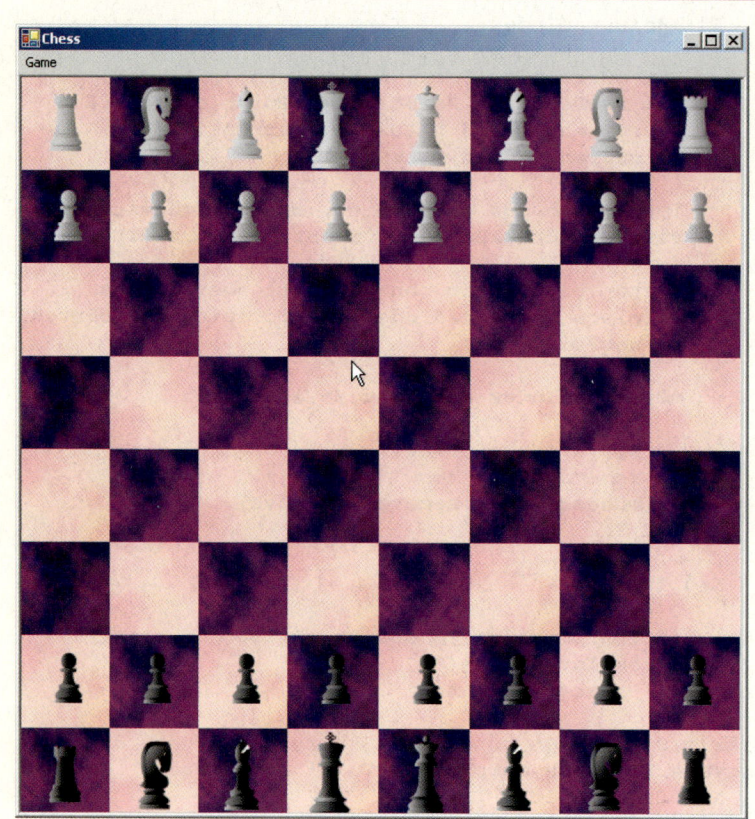

Fig. 16.26 Chess-game code (part 7 of 9).

The **FrmChessSurface Load** event (lines 33–45) loads each tile image into **mChessTile**. It then calls method **ResetBoard** to refresh the **Form** and begin the game. Method **ResetBoard** (lines 48–136) assigns **mChessPieces** to a new **ArrayList**, loading images for both the black and white chess-piece sets, and creates **Bitmap selected** to define the currently selected **Bitmap** set. Lines 72–134 loop through 64 positions on the chess board, setting the tile color and piece for each tile. Lines 75–77 cause the currently selected image to switch to the **blackPieces** after the fifth row. If the row counter is on the first or last row, lines 83–109 add a new piece to **mChessPieces**. The type of the piece is based on the current column we are initializing. Pieces in chess are positioned in the following order, from left to right: Rook, knight, bishop, queen, king, bishop, knight and rook. Lines 112–117 add a new pawn at the current location if the current **row** is second or seventh.

A chess board is defined by alternating light and dark tiles across a row in a pattern where the color that starts each row is equal to the color of the last tile of the previous row. Lines 122–128 assign the current board-tile color as an index in the **mBoard** array. Based on the alternating value of **Boolean** variable **light** and the results of the random operation on line 120, **0** and **1** are light tiles, whereas **2** and **3** are dark tiles. Line 133 inverts the value of **light** at the end of each row to maintain the staggered effect of a chess board.

Chapter 16 Graphics and Multimedia

Fig. 16.26 Chess-game code (part 8 of 9).

Method **OnPaint** (lines 139–159) overrides class **Form**'s **OnPaint** method and draws the tiles according to their values in the board array. Method **pieceBox_Paint**, which handles the **pieceBox PictureBox paint** event, iterates through each element of the **mChessPiece ArrayList** and calls its **Draw** method.

The **MouseDown** event handler (lines 199–205) calls method **CheckBounds** with the location of the user's click to determine whether the user selected a piece. **Check-Bounds** returns an integer locating a collision from a given point.

The **MouseMove** event handler (lines 208–226) moves the currently selected piece with the mouse. Lines 219–220 set the selected piece location to the mouse cursor position, adjusting the location by half a tile to center the image on the mouse. Lines 214–215 define and refresh a region of the **PictureBox** that spans two tiles in every direction from the mouse. As mentioned earlier in the chapter, the **Invalidate** method is slow. This means that the **MouseMove** event handler might be called again several times before the **Invalidate** method completes. If a user working on a slow computer moves the mouse quickly, the application could leave behind *artifacts*. An artifact is any unintended visual abnormality in a graphical program. By causing the program to refresh a two-square rectangle, which should suffice in most cases, we achieve a significant performance enhancement over an entire component refresh during each **MouseMove** event.

Fig. 16.26 Chess-game code (part 9 of 9).

Lines 229–261 define the **MouseUp** event handler. If a piece has been selected, lines 236–257 determine the index in **mChessPieces** of any piece collision, remove the collided piece, snap (align) the current piece into a valid location and deselect the piece. We check for piece collisions to allow the chess piece to "take" other chess pieces. Line 244 checks whether any piece (excluding the currently selected piece) is beneath the current mouse location. If a collision is detected, the returned piece index is assigned to **Integer remove**. Lines 247–248 determine the closest valid chess tile and "snap" the selected piece to that location. If **remove** contains a positive value **mChessPieces**, line 254 removes it from the **mChessPieces ArrayList**. Finally, the entire **PictureBox** is **Invalidate**d in line 260 to display the new piece location and remove any artifacts created during the move.

Method **CheckBounds** (lines 163–182) is a collision-detection helper method; it iterates through the **mChessPieces ArrayList** and returns the index of any piece rectangle containing the point value passed to the method (the mouse location, in this example). Method **CheckBounds** optionally can exclude a single piece index (to ignore the selected index in the **MouseUp** event handler, in this example).

Lines 264–268 define helper function **GetPiece**, which simplifies the conversion from **Object**s in the **ArrayList mChessPieces** to **CChessPiece** types. Method

NewGame_Click handles the **NewGame** menu item click event, calls **RefreshBoard** to reset the game and **Invalidate**s the entire form.

16.12 Windows Media Player

The Windows Media Player control enables an application to play video and sound in many multimedia formats. These include MPEG (Motion Pictures Experts Group) audio and video, AVI (audio–video interleave) video, WAV (Windows wave-file format) audio and MIDI (Musical Instrument Digital Interface) audio. Users can find preexisting audio and video on the Internet, or they can create their own files using available sound and graphics packages.

The application in Fig. 16.27 demonstrates the Windows Media Player control, which enables users to play multimedia files. To use the Windows Media Player control, programmers must add the control to the **Toolbox**. This is accomplished by first selecting **Customize Toolbox** from the **Tool** menu to display the **Customize Toolbox** dialog box. In the dialog box, scroll down and select the option **Windows Media Player**. Then, click the **OK** button to dismiss the dialog box. The icon for the Windows Media Player control now should appear at the bottom of the **Toolbox**.

```vb
1   ' Fig 16.27: MediaPlayerTest.vb
2   ' Demonstrates the Windows Media Player control
3
4   Public Class FrmMediaPlayer
5      Inherits System.Windows.Forms.Form
6
7      ' action menus
8      Friend WithEvents applicationMenu As MainMenu
9      Friend WithEvents fileItem As MenuItem
10     Friend WithEvents openItem As MenuItem
11     Friend WithEvents exitItem As MenuItem
12     Friend WithEvents aboutItem As MenuItem
13     Friend WithEvents aboutMessageItem As MenuItem
14
15     ' media player control
16     Friend WithEvents player As AxMediaPlayer.AxMediaPlayer
17     Friend WithEvents openMediaFileDialog As OpenFileDialog
18
19     ' Visual Studio .NET generated code
20
21     ' open new media file in Windows Media Player
22     Private Sub openItem_Click(ByVal sender As System.Object, _
23        ByVal e As System.EventArgs) Handles openItem.Click
24
25        openMediaFileDialog.ShowDialog()
26
27        player.FileName = openMediaFileDialog.FileName
28
29        ' adjust the size of the Media Player control and the
30        ' Form according to the size of the image
31        player.Size = New Size( _
32           player.ImageSourceWidth, player.ImageSourceHeight)
```

Fig. 16.27 Windows Media Player demonstration (part 1 of 2).

```vbnet
33
34          Me.Size = New Size(player.Size.Width + 20, _
35             player.Size.Height + 60)
36       End Sub ' openItem_Click
37
38       ' exit application
39       Private Sub exitItem_Click(ByVal sender As System.Object, _
40          ByVal e As System.EventArgs) Handles exitItem.Click
41
42          Application.Exit()
43       End Sub ' exitItem_Click
44
45       ' show the About box for Windows Media Player
46       Private Sub aboutMessageItem_Click(ByVal sender As _
47          System.Object, ByVal e As System.EventArgs) _
48          Handles aboutMessageItem.Click
49
50          player.AboutBox()
51       End Sub ' aboutMessageItem_Click
52
53    End Class ' FrmMediaPlayer
```

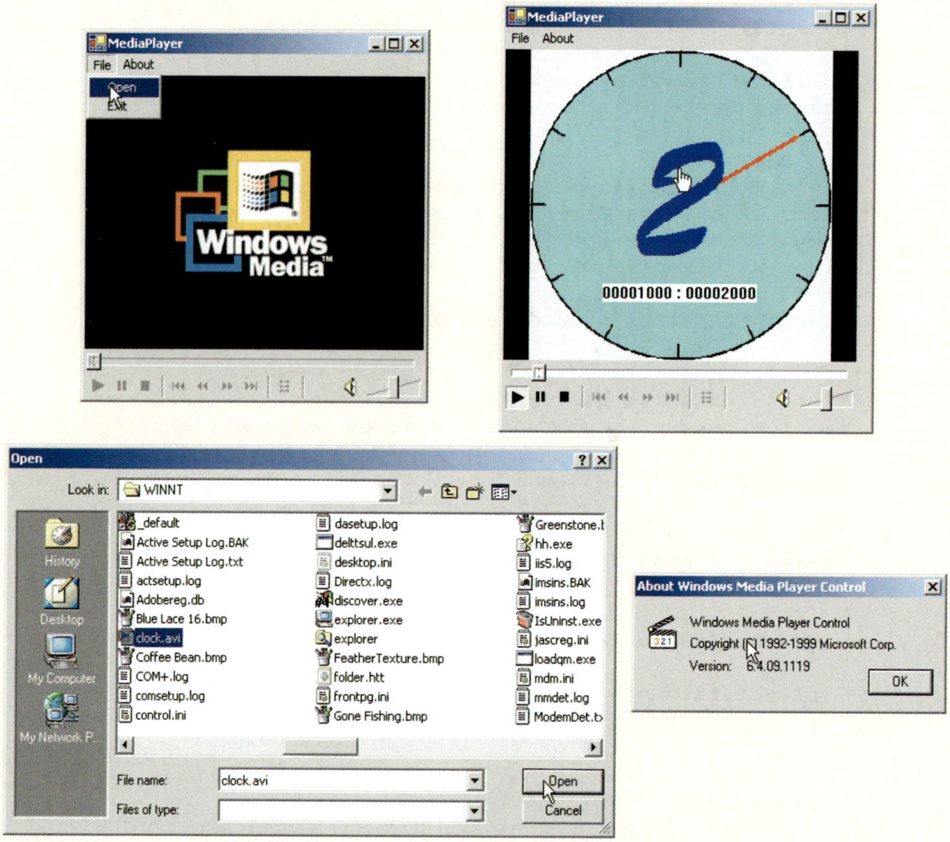

Fig. 16.27 Windows Media Player demonstration (part 2 of 2).

The Windows Media Player control provides several buttons that allow the user to play the current file, pause, stop, play the previous file, rewind, forward and play the next file. The control also includes a volume control and trackbars to select a specific position in the media file.

The application provides a **MainMenu**, which includes **File** and **About** menus. The **File** menu contains the **Open** and **Exit** menu items; the **About** menu contains the **About Windows Media Player** menu item.

When a user chooses **Open** from the **File** menu, the **openMenuItem_Click** event handler (lines 22–36) executes. An **OpenFileDialog** box displays (line 25), allowing the user to select a file. The program then sets the **FileName** property of the player (the Windows Media Player control object of type **AxMediaPlayer**) to the name of the file chosen by the user. The **FileName** property specifies the file that Windows Media Player currently is using. Lines 31–35 adjust the size of **player** and the application to reflect the size of the media contained in the file.

The event handler that executes when the user selects **Exit** from the **File** menu (lines 39–43) simply calls **Application.Exit** to terminate the application. The event handler that executes when the user chooses **About Windows Media Player** from the **About** menu (lines 46–51) calls the **AboutBox** method of the player. **AboutBox** simply displays a preset message box containing information about Windows Media Player.

16.13 Microsoft Agent

Microsoft Agent is a technology used to add *interactive animated characters* to Windows applications or Web pages. Interactivity is the key function of Microsoft Agent technology: Microsoft Agent characters can speak and respond to user input via speech recognition and synthesis. Microsoft employs its Agent technology in applications such as Word, Excel and PowerPoint. Agents in these programs aid users in finding answers to questions and in understanding how the applications function.

The Microsoft Agent control provides programmers with access to four predefined characters—*Genie* (a genie), *Merlin* (a wizard), *Peedy* (a parrot) and *Robby* (a robot). Each character has a unique set of animations that programmers can use in their applications to illustrate different points and functions. For instance, the Peedy character-animation set includes different flying animations, which the programmer might use to move Peedy on the screen. Microsoft provides basic information on Agent technology at its Web site:

www.microsoft.com/msagent

Microsoft Agent technology enables users to interact with applications and Web pages through speech, the most natural form of human communication. When the user speaks into a microphone, the control uses a *speech recognition engine,* an application that translates vocal sound input from a microphone into language that the computer understands. The Microsoft Agent control also uses a *text-to-speech engine*, which generates characters' spoken responses. A text-to-speech engine is an application that translates typed words into audio sound that users hear through headphones or speakers connected to a computer. Microsoft provides speech recognition and text-to-speech engines for several languages at its Web site:

www.microsoft.com/products/msagent/downloads.htm

732 Graphics and Multimedia   Chapter 16

Programmers can even create their own animated characters with the help of the *Microsoft Agent Character Editor* and the *Microsoft Linguistic Sound Editing Tool*. These products are available free for download from:

www.microsoft.com/products/msagent/devdownloads.htm

This section introduces the basic capabilities of the Microsoft Agent control. For complete details on downloading this control, visit:

www.microsoft.com/products/msagent/downloads.htm

The following example, Peedy's Pizza Palace, was developed by Microsoft to illustrate the capabilities of the Microsoft Agent control. Peedy's Pizza Palace is an online pizza shop where users can place their orders via voice input. The Peedy character interacts with users by helping them choose toppings and then calculating the totals for their orders.

Readers can view this example at:

agent.microsoft.com/agent2/sdk/samples/html/peedypza.htm

To run this example, students must download the Peedy character file, a text-to-speech engine and a speech-recognition engine. When the page loads, the browser prompts for these downloads. Follow the directions provided by Microsoft to complete installation.

When the window opens, Peedy introduces himself (Fig. 16.28), and the words he speaks appear in a cartoon bubble above his head. Notice that Peedy's animations correspond to the words he speaks.

Bubble contains text equivalent to words Peedy speaks

Fig. 16.28 Peedy introducing himself when the window opens.

Programmers can synchronize character animations with speech output to illustrate a point or to convey a character's mood. For instance, Fig. 16.29 depicts Peedy's *Pleased* animation. The Peedy character-animation set includes eighty-five different animations, each of which is unique to the Peedy character.

Look-and-Feel Observation 16.1

Agent characters remain on top of all active windows while a Microsoft Agent application is running. Their motions are not limited to within the boundaries of the browser or application window.

Peedy also responds to input from the keyboard and mouse. Figure 16.30 shows what happens when a user clicks Peedy with the mouse pointer. Peedy jumps up, ruffles his feathers and exclaims, "Hey that tickles!" or, "Be careful with that pointer!" Users can relocate Peedy on the screen by clicking and dragging him with the mouse. However, even when the user moves Peedy to a different part of the screen, he continues to perform his pre-set animations and location changes.

Many location changes involve animations. For instance, Peedy can hop from one screen location to another, or he can fly (Fig. 16.31).

Once Peedy completes the ordering instructions, a text box appears beneath him indicating that he is listening for a voice command (Fig. 16.32). Users can enter the type of pizza they wish to order either by speaking the style name into a microphone or by clicking the radio button corresponding to their choice.

Fig. 16.29 Peedy's *Pleased* animation.

734 Graphics and Multimedia   Chapter 16

Fig. 16.30 Peedy's reaction when he is clicked.

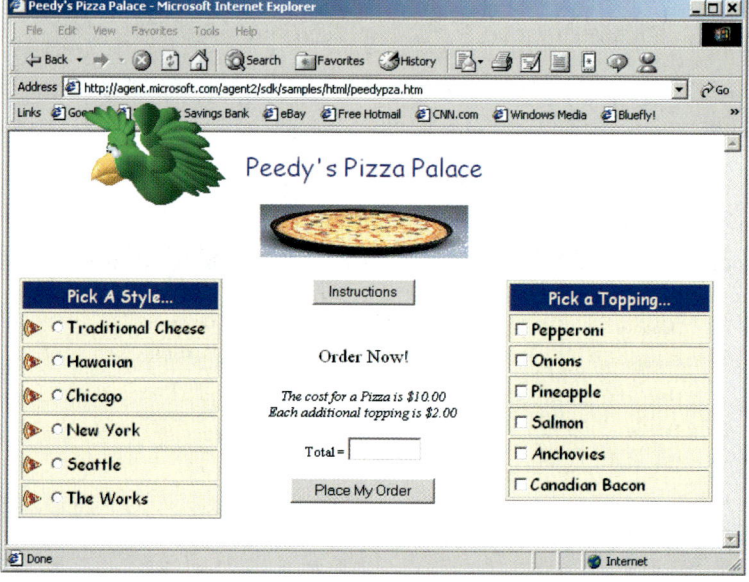

Fig. 16.31 Peedy flying animation

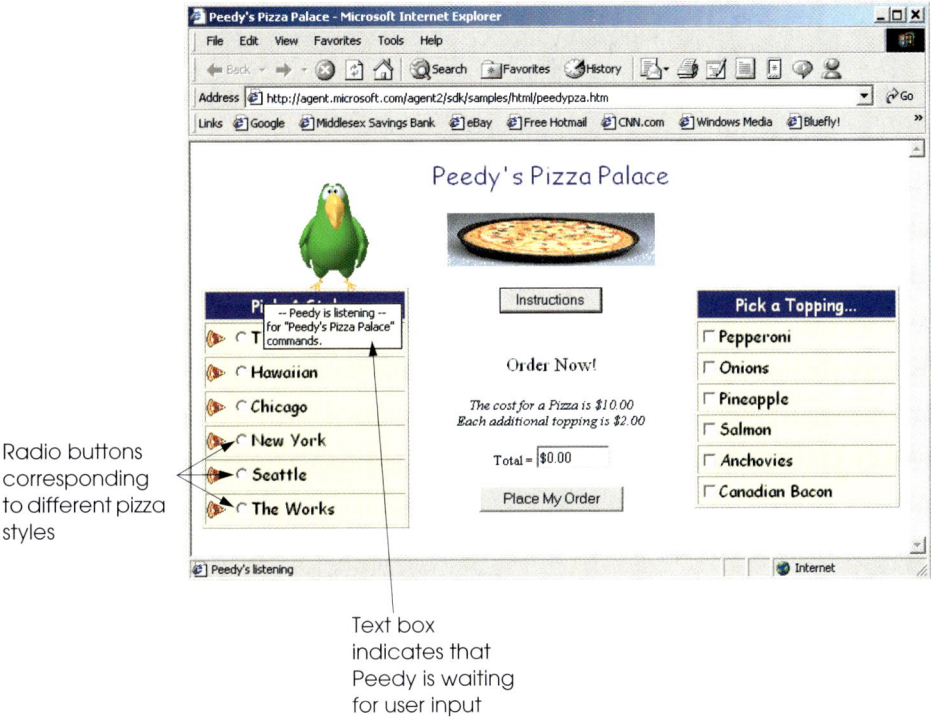

Fig. 16.32 Peedy waiting for speech input.

If a user chooses speech input, a box appears below Peedy displaying the words that Peedy "heard" (i.e., the words translated to the program by the speech-recognition engine). Once he recognizes the user input, Peedy gives the user a description of the selected pizza. Figure 16.33 shows what happens when the user chooses **Seattle** as the pizza style.

Peedy then asks the user to choose additional toppings. Again, the user can either speak or use the mouse to make a selection. Check boxes corresponding to toppings that come with the selected pizza style are checked for the user. Figure 16.34 shows what happens when a user chooses anchovies as an additional topping. Peedy makes a wisecrack about the user's choice.

The user can submit the order either by pressing the **Place My Order** button or by speaking, "Place order" into the microphone. Peedy recounts the order while writing down the order items on his notepad (Fig. 16.35). He then calculates the figures on his calculator and reports the total to the user (Fig. 16.36).

736 Graphics and Multimedia Chapter 16

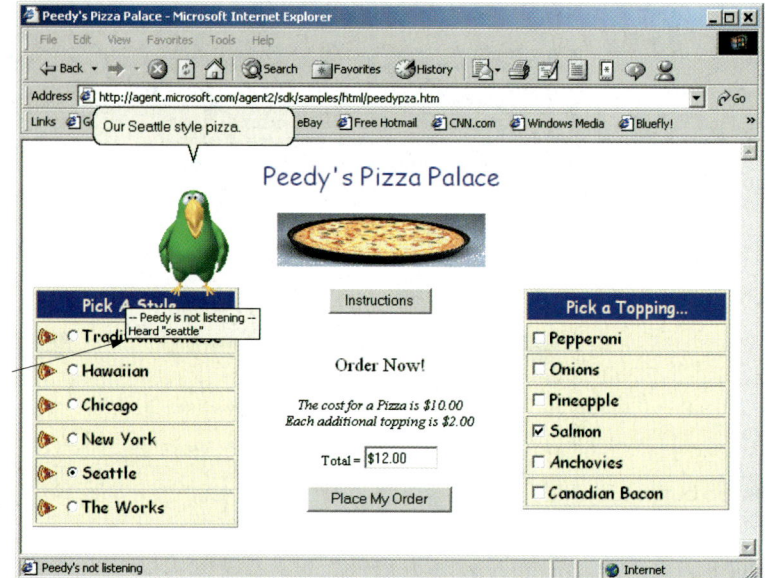

Fig. 16.33 Peedy repeating the user's request for Seattle style pizza.

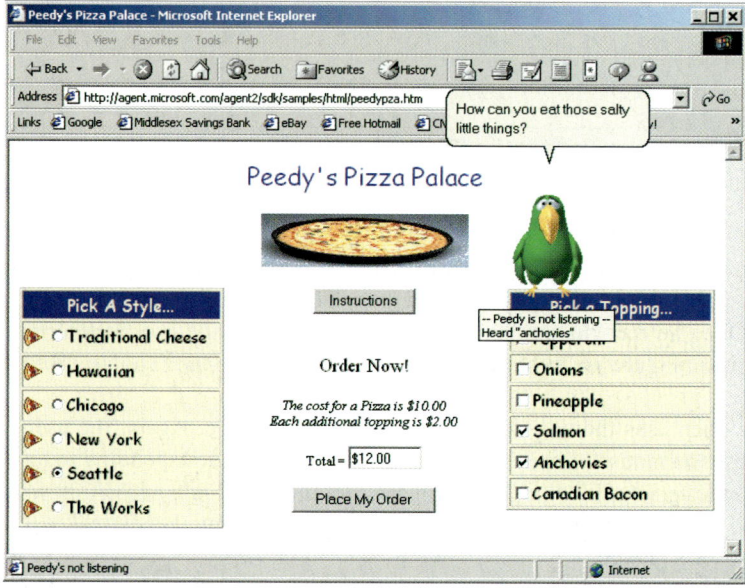

Fig. 16.34 Peedy repeating the user's request for anchovies as an additional topping.

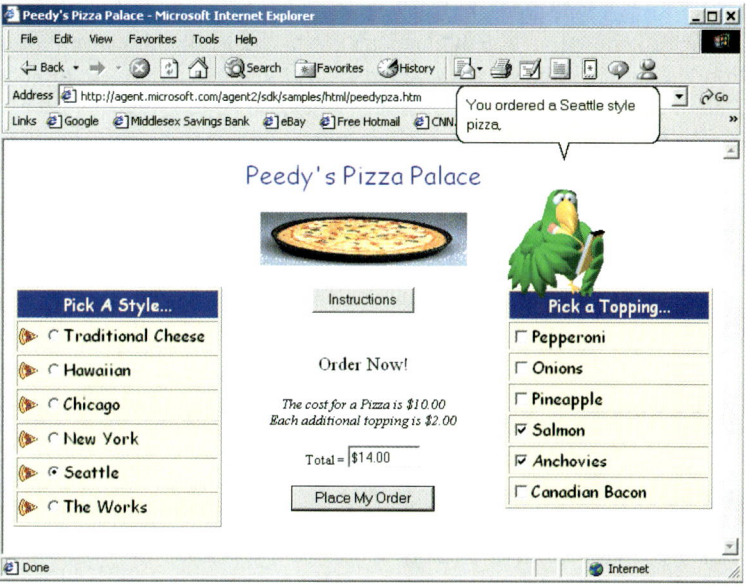

Fig. 16.35 Peedy recounting the order.

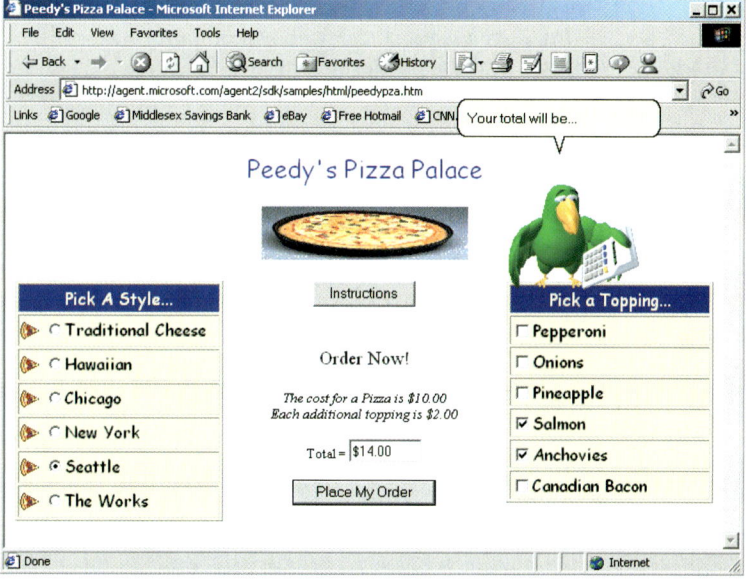

Fig. 16.36 Peedy calculating the total.

The following example (Fig. 16.37) demonstrates how to build a simple application using the Microsoft Agent control. This application contains two drop-down lists from which the user can choose an Agent character and a character animation. When the user chooses from these lists, the chosen character appears and performs the chosen animation. The application uses speech recognition and synthesis to control the character animations and speech: Users can tell the character which animation to perform by pressing the *Scroll Lock* key and then speaking the animation name into a microphone. The example also allows the user to switch to a new character by speaking its name, and also creates a custom command, **MoveToMouse**. In addition, the characters also speak any text that a user enters into the text box. Before running this example, readers first must download and install the control, speech recognition engine, text to speech engine and the character definitions from the Microsoft Agent Web site listed previously.

```vb
1    ' Fig. 16.37: Agent.vb
2    ' Demonstrating Microsoft Agent.
3
4    Imports System.IO
5    Imports System.Collections
6    Imports System.Windows.Forms
7
8    Public Class FrmAgent
9       Inherits System.Windows.Forms.Form
10
11      ' options
12      Friend WithEvents characterCombo As ComboBox
13      Friend WithEvents actionsCombo As ComboBox
14
15      Friend WithEvents GroupBox1 As GroupBox
16      Friend WithEvents cmdSpeak As Button
17      Friend WithEvents mainAgent As AxAgentObjects.AxAgent
18
19      ' input boxes
20      Friend WithEvents txtLocation As TextBox
21      Friend WithEvents txtSpeech As TextBox
22
23      ' current agent object
24      Private mSpeaker As AgentObjects.IAgentCtlCharacter
25
26      ' Visual Studio .NET generated code
27
28      ' keyDown event handler for locationTextBox
29      Private Sub txtLocation_KeyDown(ByVal sender As _
30         Object, ByVal e As System.Windows.Forms.KeyEventArgs)_
31         Handles txtLocation.KeyDown
32
33         If e.KeyCode = Keys.Enter Then
34
35            ' set character location to text box value
36            Dim location As String = txtLocation.Text
37
```

Fig. 16.37 Microsoft Agent demonstration (part 1 of 6).

```vb
38            ' initialize characters
39            Try
40
41               ' load characters into agent object
42               mainAgent.Characters.Load( _
43                  "Genie", location & "Genie.acs")
44
45               mainAgent.Characters.Load( _
46                  "Merlin", location & "Merlin.acs")
47
48               mainAgent.Characters.Load( _
49                  "Peedy", location & "Peedy.acs")
50
51               mainAgent.Characters.Load( _
52                  "Robby", location & "Robby.acs")
53
54               ' disable TextBox location and enable other controls
55               txtLocation.Enabled = False
56               txtSpeech.Enabled = True
57               cmdSpeak.Enabled = True
58               characterCombo.Enabled = True
59               actionsCombo.Enabled = True
60
61               ' set current character to Genie and show
62               mSpeaker = mainAgent.Characters("Genie")
63               GetAnimationNames() ' obtain animation name list
64               mSpeaker.Show(0)
65
66            Catch fileNotFound As FileNotFoundException
67               MessageBox.Show("Invalid character location", _
68                  "Error", MessageBoxButtons.OK, _
69                  MessageBoxIcon.Error)
70            End Try
71
72         End If
73
74      End Sub ' txtLocation_KeyDown
75
76      ' speak button event handler
77      Private Sub cmdSpeak_Click(ByVal sender As System.Object, _
78         ByVal e As System.EventArgs) Handles cmdSpeak.Click
79
80         ' if TextBox is empty, have character ask
81         ' user to type words into TextBox, otherwise
82         ' have character say words in TextBox
83         If txtSpeech.Text = "" Then
84            mSpeaker.Speak( _
85               "Please type the words you want me to speak", "")
86         Else
87            mSpeaker.Speak(txtSpeech.Text, "")
88         End If
89
90      End Sub ' cmdSpeak_Click
```

Fig. 16.37 Microsoft Agent demonstration (part 2 of 6).

```vbnet
 91
 92       ' click event for agent
 93       Private Sub mainAgent_ClickEvent(ByVal sender As Object _
 94          Object, ByVal e As AxAgentObjects._AgentEvents_ClickEvent)_
 95          Handles mainAgent.ClickEvent
 96
 97          mSpeaker.Play("Confused")
 98          mSpeaker.Speak("Why are you poking me?", "")
 99          mSpeaker.Play("RestPose")
100       End Sub ' mainAgent_ClickEvent
101
102       ' comboBox changed event, switch active agent
103       Private Sub characterCombo_SelectedIndexChanged(ByVal _
104          sender As System.Object, ByVal e As System.EventArgs) _
105          Handles characterCombo.SelectedIndexChanged
106
107          ChangeCharacter(characterCombo.Text)
108       End Sub ' characterCombo_SelectedIndexChanged
109
110       ' hide current character and show new
111       Private Sub ChangeCharacter(ByVal name As String)
112          mSpeaker.Hide(0)
113          mSpeaker = mainAgent.Characters(name)
114          GetAnimationNames() ' regenerate animation name list
115          mSpeaker.Show(0)
116       End Sub ' ChangeCharacter
117
118       ' get animation names and store in arraylist
119       Private Sub GetAnimationNames()
120
121          ' ensure thread safety
122          SyncLock (Me)
123
124             ' get animation names
125             Dim enumerator As IEnumerator = _
126                mainAgent.Characters.Character( _
127                mSpeaker.Name).AnimationNames.GetEnumerator()
128
129             Dim voiceString As String
130
131             ' clear cboActions combo box
132             actionsCombo.Items.Clear()
133             mSpeaker.Commands.RemoveAll()
134
135             ' copy enumeration to ArrayList
136             While enumerator.MoveNext()
137
138                ' remove underscores in speech string
139                voiceString = Convert.ToString(enumerator.Current)
140                voiceString = voiceString.Replace("_", "underscore")
141
142                actionsCombo.Items.Add(enumerator.Current)
143
```

Fig. 16.37 Microsoft Agent demonstration (part 3 of 6).

```vbnet
144                    ' add all animations as voice enabled commands
145                    mSpeaker.Commands.Add(Convert.ToString( _
146                       enumerator.Current, , voiceString, True, False)
147             End While
148
149             ' add custom command
150             mSpeaker.Commands.Add("MoveToMouse", "MoveToMouse", _
151                "MoveToMouse", True, True)
152         End SyncLock
153
154     End Sub ' GetAnimationNames
155
156     ' user selects new action
157     Private Sub actionsCombo_SelectedIndexChanged(ByVal sender _
158        As System.Object, ByVal e As System.EventArgs) _
159        Handles actionsCombo.SelectedIndexChanged
160
161        mSpeaker.Stop()
162        mSpeaker.Play(actionsCombo.Text)
163        mSpeaker.Play("RestPose")
164     End Sub ' actionsCombo_SelectedIndexChanged
165
166     ' handles agent commands
167     Private Sub mainAgent_Command(ByVal sender As System.Object, _
168        ByVal e As AxAgentObjects._AgentEvents_CommandEvent) _
169        Handles mainAgent.Command
170
171        ' get UserInput object
172        Dim command As AgentObjects.IAgentCtlUserInput = _
173           CType(e.userInput, AgentObjects.IAgentCtlUserInput)
174
175        ' change character if user speaks character name
176        If (command.Voice = "Peedy" OrElse _
177           command.Voice = "Robby" OrElse _
178           command.Voice = "Merlin" OrElse _
179           command.Voice = "Genie") Then
180           ChangeCharacter(command.Voice)
181
182           Return
183        End If
184
185        ' send agent to mouse
186        If command.Name = "MoveToMouse" Then
187           mSpeaker.MoveTo(Convert.ToInt16( _
188              Cursor.Position.X - 60), Convert.ToInt16( _
189              Cursor.Position.Y - 60))
190
191           Return
192        End If
193
194        ' play new animation
195        mSpeaker.Stop()
196        mSpeaker.Play(command.Name)
```

Fig. 16.37 Microsoft Agent demonstration (part 4 of 6).

```
197
198     End Sub ' mainAgent_Command
199
200 End Class ' FrmAgent
```

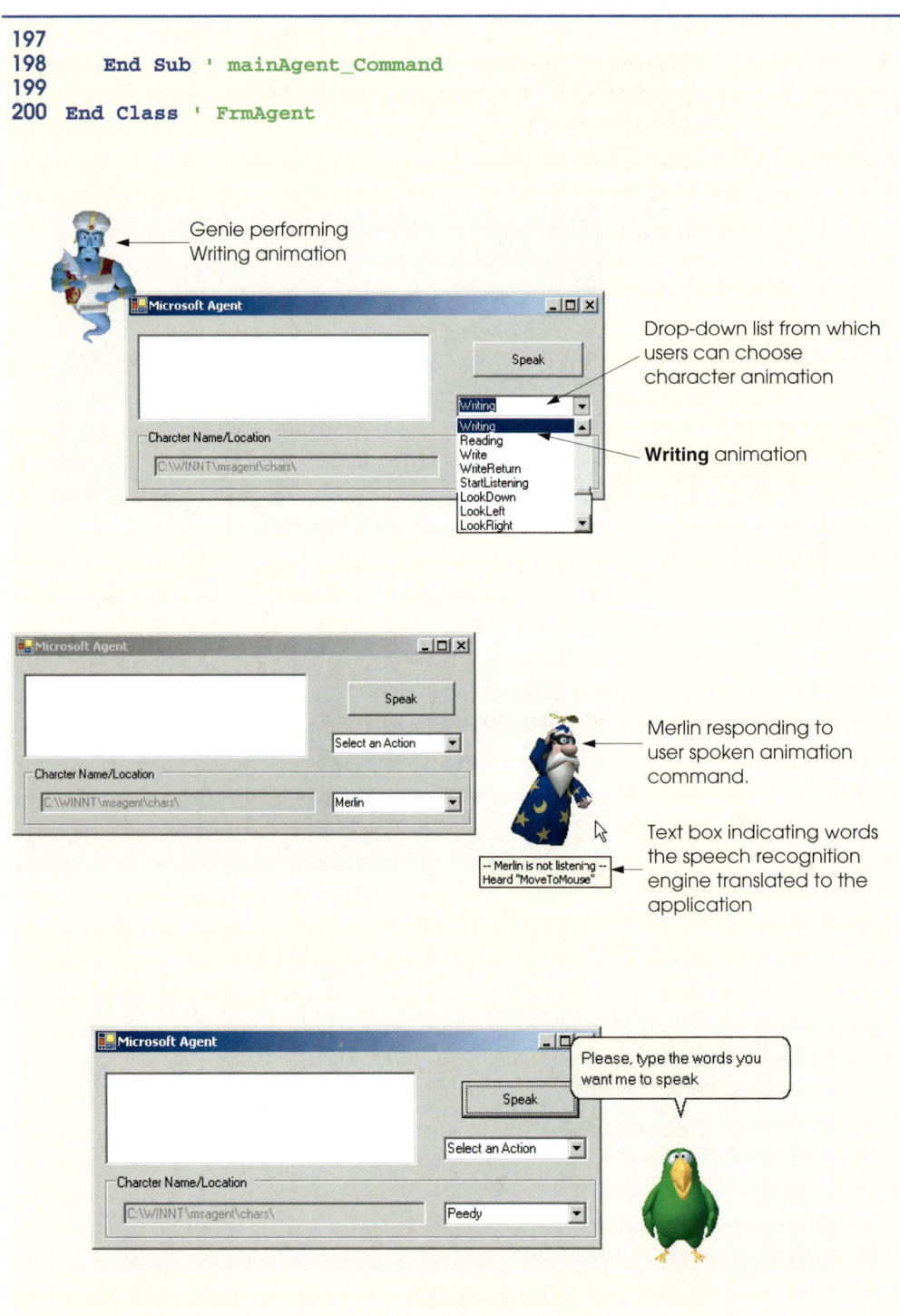

Fig. 16.37 Microsoft Agent demonstration (part 5 of 6).

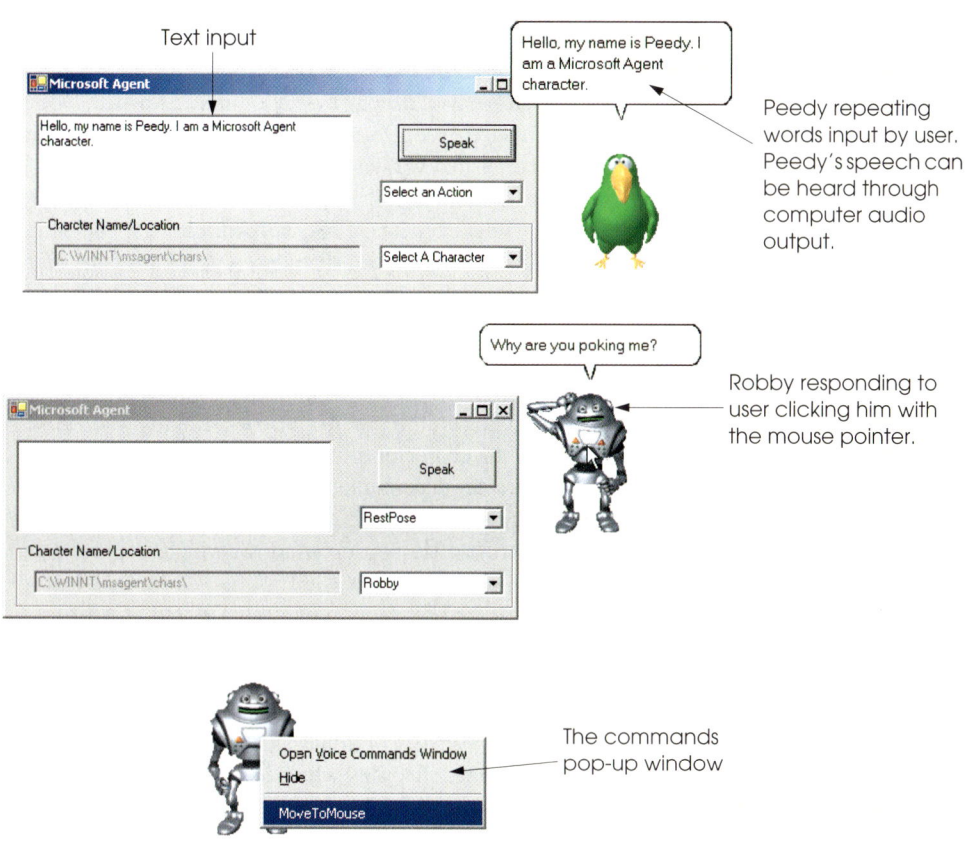

Fig. 16.37 Microsoft Agent demonstration (part 6 of 6).

To use the Microsoft Agent control, the programmer first must add it to the **Toolbox**. Begin by selecting **Customize Toolbox** from the **Tools** menu to display the **Customize Toolbox** dialog. In the dialog, scroll down and select the option **Microsoft Agent Control 2.0**. When this option is selected properly, a small check mark appears in the box to the left of the option. Then, click **OK** to dismiss the dialog. The icon for the Microsoft Agent control now should appear at the bottom of the **Toolbox**.

In addition to the Microsoft Agent object **mainAgent** (of type **AxAgent**) that manages all the characters, we also need an object (of type **IAgentCtlCharacter**) to represent the current character. We create this object, named **mSpeaker**, in line 24.

When the program begins, the only enabled control is the **txtLocation**. This text box contains the default location for the character files, but the user can change this location if the files are located elsewhere on the user's computer. Once the user presses *Enter* in the **TextBox**, event handler **txtLocation_KeyDown** (lines 29–74) executes. Lines 42–52 load the character descriptions for the predefined animated characters. If the specified location of the characters is incorrect, or if any character is missing, a **FileNotFoundException** is thrown.

Lines 55–59 disable **txtLocation** and enable the rest of the controls. Lines 62–64 set Genie as the default character, obtain all animation names via method **GetAnimationNames** and then call **IAgentCtlCharacter** method *Show* to display the character. We access characters through property *Characters* of **mainAgent**, which contains all characters that have been loaded. We use the indexer of the **Characters** property to specify the name of the character that we wish to load (Genie).

When a user clicks the character (i.e., pokes it with the mouse), event handler **mainAgent_ClickEvent** (lines 93–100) executes. First, **mSpeaker** method *Play* plays an animation. This method accepts as an argument a **String** representing one of the predefined animations for the character (a list of animations for each character is available at the Microsoft Agent Web site; each character provides over 70 animations). In our example, the argument to *Play* is "Confused"—this animation is defined for all four characters, each of which expresses this emotion in a unique way. The character then speaks, "Why are you poking me?" via a call to method *Speak*. Finally, the *RestPose* animation is played, which returns the character to its neutral, resting pose.

The list of valid commands for a character is contained in the **Commands** property of the **IAgentCtlCharacter** object (**mSpeaker**, in this example). The commands for an Agent character can be viewed in the **Commands** pop-up window, which displays when the user right-clicks an Agent character (the last screenshot in Fig. 16.37). Method **Add** of the **Commands** property adds a new command to the command list. Method **Add** takes three **String** arguments and two **Boolean** arguments. The first **String** argument identifies the name of the command, which we use to identify the command programmatically. The second **String** is optional and defines the command name as it appears in the **Commands** pop-up window. The third **String** also is optional and defines the voice input that triggers the command. The first **Boolean** specifies whether the command is active, and the second **Boolean** indicates whether the command is visible in the **Commands** pop-up window. A command is triggered when the user selects the command from the **Commands** pop-up window or speaks the voice input into a microphone. Command logic is handled in the **Command** event of the **AxAgent** control (**mainAgent**, in this example). In addition, Agent defines several global commands that have predefined functions (for example, speaking a character name causes that character to appear).

Method **GetAnimationNames** (lines 119–154) fills the **actionsCombo ComboBox** with the current character's animation listing and defines the valid commands that can be used with the character. The method contains a **SyncLock** block to prevent errors resulting from rapid character changes. The method obtains the current character's animations as an enumerator (125–127), then clears the existing items in the **ComboBox** and character's **Commands** property. Lines 136–147 iterate through all items in the animation name enumerator. For each animation, in line 139, we assign the animation name to **String voiceString**. Line 140 removes any underscore characters (_) and replaces them with the **String "underscore"**; this changes the **String** so that a user can pronounce and employ it as a command activator. The **Add** method (lines 145–146) of the **Commands** property adds a new command to the current character. The **Add** method adds all animations as commands by providing the following arguments: the animation name as the new command's **name** and **voiceString** for the voice activation **String**. The method's **Boolean** arguments enable the command, but make it unavailable in the **Commands** pop-up window. Thus, the command can be activated only by voice input. Lines

150–151 create a new command, named **MoveToMouse**, which is visible in the **Commands** pop-up window.

After the **GetAnimationNames** method has been called, the user can select a value from the **actionsCombo ComboBox**. Event-handler method **actionsCombo.SelectedIndexChanged** stops any current animation and then displays the animation that the user selected from the **ComboBox**.

The user also can type text into the **TextBox** and click **Speak**. This causes event handler **cmdSpeak_Click** (line 77–90) to call **mSpeaker**'s method **Speak**, supplying as an argument the text in **txtSpeech**. If the user clicks **Speak** without providing text, the character speaks, **"Please, type the words you want me to speak"**.

At any point in the program, the user can choose to display a different character from the **ComboBox**. When this happens, the **SelectedIndexChanged** event handler for **characterCombo** (lines 103–108) executes. The event handler calls method **ChangeCharacter** (lines 111–116) with the text in the **characterCombo ComboBox** as an argument. Method **ChangeCharacter** calls the **Hide** method of **mSpeaker** (line 112) to remove the current character from view. Line 113 assigns the newly selected character to **mSpeaker**, line 114 generates the character's animation names and commands, and line 115 displays the character via a call to method **Show**.

Each time a user presses the *Scroll Lock* key and speaks into a microphone or selects a command from the **Commands** pop-up window, event handler **mainAgent_Command** is called. This method is passed an argument of type **AxAgentObjects._AgentEvents_CommandEvent**, which contains a single method, **userInput**. The **userInput** method returns an **Object** that can be converted to type **AgentObjects.IAgentCtlUserInput**. The **userInput** object is assigned to a **IAgentCtlUserInput** object **command**, which is used to identify the command and then take appropriate action. Lines 176–180 use method **ChangeCharacter** to change the current Agent character if the user speaks a character name. Microsoft Agent always will show a character when a user speaks its name; however, by controlling the character change, we can ensure that only one Agent character is displayed at a time. Lines 186–192 move the character to the current mouse location if the user invokes the **MoveToMouse** command. The Agent method ***MoveTo*** takes x- and y-coordinate arguments and moves the character to the specified screen position, applying appropriate movement animations. For all other commands, we **Play** the command name as an animation on line 196.

In this chapter, we explored various graphics capabilities of GDI+, including pens, brushes and images, as well as some multimedia capabilities of the .NET Famework Class Library. In the next chapter, we cover the reading, writing and accessing of sequential- and random-access files. We also explore several types of streams included in Visual Studio .NET.

SUMMARY

- A coordinate system is used to identify every possible point on the screen.
- The upper-left corner of a GUI component has coordinates *(0, 0)*. A coordinate pair is composed of an *x*-coordinate (the horizontal coordinate) and a *y*-coordinate (the vertical coordinate).
- Coordinate units are measured in pixels. A pixel is the smallest unit of resolution on a display monitor.

- A graphics context represents a drawing surface on the screen. A **Graphics** object provides access to the graphics context of a control.
- An instance of the **Pen** class is used to draw lines.
- An instance of one of the classes that derive from abstract class **Brush** is used to draw solid shapes.
- The **Point** structure can be used to represent a point in a two-dimensional plane.
- **Graphics** objects contain methods for drawing, font manipulation, color manipulation and other graphics-related actions.
- Method **OnPaint** normally is called in response to an event, such as the uncovering of a window. This method, in turn, triggers a **Paint** event.
- Structure **Color** defines constants for manipulating colors in a Visual Basic program.
- **Color** properties **R**, **G** and **B** return **Integer** values from 0 to 255, representing the amounts of red, green and blue, respectively, that exist in a **Color**. The larger the value, the greater the amount of that particular color.
- Visual Basic provides class **ColorDialog** to display a dialog that allows users to select colors.
- **Component** property **BackColor** (one of the many **Component** properties that can be called on most GUI components) changes the component's background color.
- Class **Font**'s constructors all take at least three arguments—the font name, the font size and the font style. The font name is any font currently supported by the system. The font style is a member of the **FontStyle** enumeration.
- Class **FontMetrics** defines several methods for obtaining font metrics.
- Class **Font** provides the **Bold**, **Italic**, **Strikeout** and **Underline** properties, which return **True** if the font is bold, italic, strikeout or underlined, respectively.
- Class **Font** provides the **Name** property, which returns a **String** representing the name of the font.
- Class **Font** provides the **Size** and **SizeInPoints** properties, which return the size of the font in design units and points, respectively.
- The **FontFamily** class provides information about such font metrics as the family's spacing and height information.
- The **FontFamily** class provides the **GetCellAscent**, **GetCellDescent**, **GetEmHeight** and **GetLineSpacing** methods, which return the ascent of a font, descent of a font, the font's height in points and the distance between two consecutive lines of text, respectively.
- Class **Graphics** provides methods **DrawLine**, **DrawRectangle**, **DrawEllipse**, **DrawArc**, **DrawLines**, **DrawPolygon** and **DrawPie**, which draw lines and shape outlines.
- Class **Graphics** provides methods **FillRectangle**, **FillEllipse**, **FillPolygon** and **FillPie**, which draw solid shapes.
- Classes **HatchBrush**, **LinearGradientBrush**, **PathGradientBrush** and **TextureBrush** all derive from class **Brush** and represent shape-filling styles.
- **Graphics** method **FromImage** retrieves the **Graphics** object associated with the image file that is its argument.
- The **DashStyle** and **DashCap** enumerations define the style of dashes and their ends, respectively.
- Class **GraphicsPath** represents a shape constructed from straight lines and curves.
- **GraphicsPath** method **AddLine** appends a line to the shape that is encapsulated by the object.

- **GraphicsPath** method **CloseFigure** completes the shape that is represented by the **GraphicsPath** object.
- Class **Image** is used to manipulate images.
- Class **Image** provides method **FromFile** to retrieve an image stored on disk and load it into an instance of class **Image**.
- **Graphics** method **Clear** paints the entire **Control** with the color that the programmer provides as an argument.
- **Graphics** method **DrawImage** draws the specified **Image** on the **Control**.
- Using Visual Studio .NET and Visual Basic, programmers can create applications that use components such as Windows Media Player and Microsoft Agent.
- The Windows Media Player allows programmers to create applications that can play multimedia files.
- Microsoft Agent is a technology that allows programmers to include interactive animated characters in their applications.

TERMINOLOGY

A property of structure **Color**
AboutBox method of class **AxMediaPlayer**
Add method of class **ArrayList**
AddLine method of class **GraphicsPath**
animated characters
animating a series of images
animation
arc angle
arc method
ARGB values
ArrayList class
ascent of a font
audio–video interleave (AVI)
AxAgent class
AxMediaPlayer class
B property of structure **Color**
bandwidth
Bitmap class
Black Shared property of structure **Color**
Blue Shared property of structure **Color**
Bold member of enumeration **FontStyle**
Bold property of class **Font**
bounding rectangle
bounding rectangle for an oval
Brush class
Characters property of class **AxAgent**
closed polygon
CloseFigure method of class **GraphicsPath**
color constants
color manipulation
Color methods and properties

Color property of class **ColorDialog**
Color structure
ColorDialog class
complex curve
connected lines
coordinate system
coordinates (0, 0)
curve
customizing the **Toolbox**
Cyan Shared property of structure **Color**
DarkBlue Shared property of structure **Color**
DarkGray Shared property of structure **Color**
Dash member of enumeration **DashStyle**
DashCap enumeration
DashCap property of class **Pen**
dashed lines
DashStyle enumeration
DashStyle property of class **Pen**
default font
degree
descent of a font
Display member of enumeration **GraphicsUnit**
display monitor
Document member of enumeration **GraphicsUnit**
DrawArc method of class **Graphics**
DrawEllipse method of class **Graphics**
DrawLine method of class **Graphics**
DrawLines method of class **Graphics**

`DrawPie` method of class `Graphics`
`DrawPolygon` method of class `Graphics`
`DrawRectangle` method of class `Graphics`
`DrawString` method of class `Graphics`
event-driven process
`FileName` property of class
    `AxMediaPlayer`
fill a shape with color
`Fill` method of class `Graphics`
fill shape
`FillEllipse` method of class `Graphics`
`FillPie` method of class `Graphics`
`FillPolygon` method of class `Graphics`
`FillRectangle` method of class `Graphics`
`FillRectangles` method of class
    `Graphics`
five-pointed star
font
font ascent
`Font` class
font control
font descent
font height
font leading
font manipulation
font metrics
font name
font size
font style
`FontFamily` class
`FontFamily` property of class `Font`
`FontStyle` enumeration
`ForwardDiagonal` member of enumeration
    `LinearGradientMode`
`FromArgb` method of structure `Color`
`FromImage` method of class `Graphics`
`FromName` method
`G` property of structure `Color`
GDI+
general path
Genie `Microsoft Agent` character
`GetCellAscent` method of class
    `FontFamily`
`GetCellDescent` method of class
    `FontFamily`
`GetEmHeight` method of class `FontFamily`
`GetLineSpacing` method of class
    `FontFamily`
graphics
`Graphics` class

graphics context
`GraphicsPath` class
`GraphicsUnit`
`Gray Shared` property of structure `Color`
`Green Shared` property of structure `Color`
`HatchBrush` class
`HatchStyle` enumeration
`Height` property of class `Font`
horizontal coordinate
`IAgentCtlCharacter` interface
`Inch` member of enumeration
    `GraphicsUnit`
interactive animated character
`Invalidate` method of class `Control`
`Italic` member of enumeration `FontStyle`
`Italic` property of class `Font`
line
`LinearGradientBrush` class
`LinearGradientMode` enumeration
`Magenta Shared` property of
    structure `Color`
Merlin `Microsoft Agent` character
`Microsoft Agent`
Microsoft Agent Character Editor
Microsoft Linguistic Sound Editing Tool
Microsoft Sans Serif font
Microsoft Serif font
MIDI
`Millimeter` member of
    enumeration `GraphicsUnit`
Motion Pictures Experts Group (MPEG)
multimedia
Musical Instrument Digital Interface (MIDI)
`Name` property of class `Font`
`Name` property of structure `Color`
negative arc angles
`OnPaint` method of class `Control`
`Orange Shared` property of structure `Color`
`PaintEventArgs` class
`Panel` class
`PathGradientBrush` class
pattern
Peedy `Microsoft Agent` character
`Pen` class
`Pink Shared` property of structure `Color`
pixel
`Pixel` member of enumeration
    `GraphicsUnit`
`Play` method of interface
    `IAgentCtlCharacter`

`Point` member of enumeration `GraphicsUnit`	style of a font
`Point` structure	sweep
positive and negative arc angles	sweep counterclockwise
`R` property of structure `Color`	`System.Drawing` namespace
rectangle	`System.Drawing.Drawing2D` namespace
`Rectangle` structure	`TextureBrush` class
`Red Shared` property of structure `Color`	thick line
`Regular` member of enumeration `FontStyle`	thin line
resolution	three-dimensional application
RGB values	`Tick` event of class `Timer`
Robby the Robot `Microsoft Agent` character	`Timer` class
`RotateTransform` method of class `Graphics`	`TranslateTransform` method of class `Graphics`
`Round` member of enumeration `DashCap`	two-dimensional shape
sector	`Underline` member of enumeration `FontStyle`
`Show` method of interface `IAgentCtlCharacter`	`Underline` property of class `Font`
`Size` property of class `Font`	upper-left corner of a GUI component
`SizeInPoints` property of class `Font`	vertical coordinate
solid arc	WAV
solid polygon	`White Shared` property of structure `Color`
solid rectangle	Windows Media Player
`SolidBrush` class	Windows wave file format (WAV)
starting angle	x-axis
straight line	x-coordinate
`Strikeout` member of enumeration `FontStyle`	y-axis
`Strikeout` property of class `Font`	y-coordinate
	yellow
	`Yellow Shared` property of structure `Color`

SELF-REVIEW EXERCISES

16.1 State whether each of the following is *true* or *false*. If *false*, explain why.
 a) A `Font` object's size can be changed by setting its `Size` property.
 b) In the Visual Basic coordinate system, *x*-values increase from left to right.
 c) Method `FillPolygon` draws a solid polygon with a specified `Brush`.
 d) Method `DrawArc` allows negative angles.
 e) `Font` property `Size` returns the size of the current font in centimeters.
 f) Pixel coordinate (0, 0) is located at the exact center of the monitor.
 g) A `HatchBrush` is used to draw lines.
 h) A `Color` is defined by its alpha, red, green and violet content.
 i) Every `Control` has an associated `Graphics` object.
 j) Method `OnPaint` is inherited by every `Form`.

16.2 Fill in the blanks in each of the following statements:
 a) Class _____ is used to draw lines of various colors and thicknesses.
 b) Classes_____ and _____ define the fill for a shape in such a way that the fill gradually changes from one color to another.

c) The _____ method of class **Graphics** draws a line between two points.
d) ARGB is short for _____, _____, _____ and _____.
e) Font sizes usually are measured in units called _____.
f) Class_____ fills a shape using a pattern drawn in a **Bitmap**.
g) _____ _____ _____ allows an application to play multimedia files.
h) Class _____ defines a path consisting of lines and curves.
i) Visual Basic's drawing capabilities are part of the namespaces _____ and _____.
j) Method _____ loads an image from a disk into an **Image** object.

ANSWERS TO SELF-REVIEW EXERCISES

16.1 a) False. **Size** is a read-only property. b) True. c) True. d) True. e) False. It returns the size of the current **Font** in design units. f) False. The coordinate (0,0) corresponds to the upper-left corner of a GUI component on which drawing occurs. g) False. A **Pen** is used to draw lines, a HatchBrush fills a shape with a hatch pattern. h) False. A color is defined by its alpha, red, green and blue content. i) True. j) True.

16.2 a) **Pen**. b) **LinearGradientBrush**, **PathGradientBrush**. c) **DrawLine**. d) alpha, red, green, blue. e) points. f) **TextureBrush**. g) Windows Media Player h) **GraphicsPath** i) **System.Drawing**, **System.Drawing.Drawing2D**. j) **FromFile**.

EXERCISES

16.3 Write a program that draws eight concentric circles. The circles should be separated from one another by 10 pixels. Use the **DrawArc** method.

16.4 Write a program that draws 100 lines with random lengths, positions, thicknesses and colors.

16.5 Write a program that draws a tetrahedron (a pyramid). Use class **GraphicsPath** and method **DrawPath**.

16.6 Write a program that allows the user to draw "free-hand" images with the mouse in a **PictureBox**. Allow the user to change the drawing color and width of the pen. Provide a button that allows the user to clear the **PictureBox**.

16.7 Write a program that repeatedly flashes an image on the screen. Do this by interspersing the image with a plain background-color image.

16.8 If you want to emphasize an image, you might place a row of simulated light bulbs around the image. Write a program which an image is emphasized this way. You can let the light bulbs flash in unison or you can let them fire on and off in sequence, one after another.

16.9 (*Eight Queens*) A puzzler for chess buffs is the Eight Queens problem. Simply stated: Is it possible to place eight queens on an empty chessboard so that no queen is "attacking" any other (i.e., so that no two queens are in the same row, the same column or along the same diagonal)?

Create a GUI that allows the user to drag-and-drop each queen on the board. Use the graphical features of Fig. 16.26. Provide eight queen images to the right of the board (Fig. 16.38), which the user can drag-and-drop onto the board. When a queen is dropped on the board, its corresponding image to the right should not be visible. If a queen is in conflict with another queen when placed on the board, display a message box and remove the queen from the board.

Chapter 16 Graphics and Multimedia 751

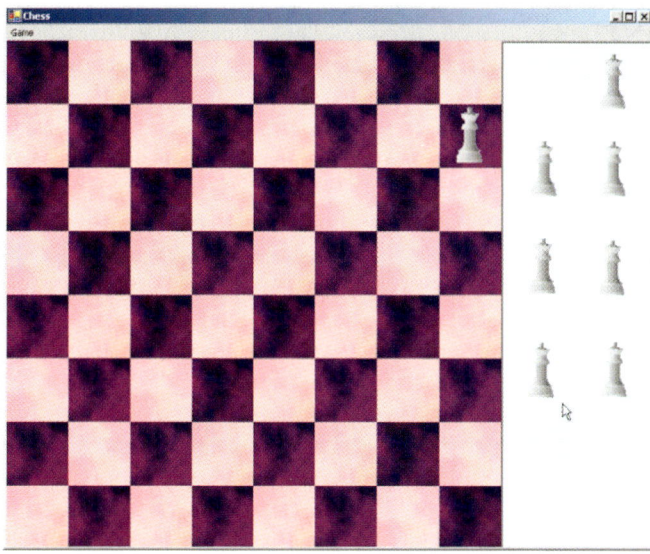

Fig. 16.38 GUI for eight queens exercise.

17

Files and Streams

Objectives

- To be able to create, read, write and update files.
- To understand the Visual Basic streams class hierarchy.
- To be able to use classes **File** and **Directory**.
- To be able to use the **FileStream** and **BinaryFormatter** classes to read objects from, and write objects to, files.
- To become familiar with sequential-access and random-access file processing.

I can only assume that a "Do Not File" document is filed in a "Do Not File" file.
Senator Frank Church
Senate Intelligence Subcommittee Hearing, 1975

Consciousness ... does not appear to itself chopped up in bits. ... A "river" or a "stream" are the metaphors by which it is most naturally described.
William James

I read part of it all the way through.
Samuel Goldwyn

Chapter 17 — Files and Streams

Outline

17.1 Introduction
17.2 Data Hierarchy
17.3 Files and Streams
17.4 Classes **File** and **Directory**
17.5 Creating a Sequential-Access File
17.6 Reading Data from a Sequential-Access File
17.7 Random-Access Files
17.8 Creating a Random-Access File
17.9 Writing Data Randomly to a Random-Access File
17.10 Reading Data Sequentially from a Random-Access File
17.11 Case Study: A Transaction-Processing Program

Summary • Terminology • Self-Review Exercises • Answers to Self-Review Exercises • Exercises

17.1 Introduction

Variables and arrays offer only temporary storage of data—the data are lost when a local variable "goes out of scope" or when the program terminates. By contrast, *files* are used for long-term retention of large amounts of data, even after the program that created the data terminates. Data maintained in files often are called *persistent data*. Computers store files on *secondary storage devices*, such as magnetic disks, optical disks and magnetic tapes. In this chapter, we explain how to create, update and process data files in Visual Basic programs. We consider both "sequential-access" files and "random-access" files, indicating the kinds of applications for which each is best suited. We have two goals in this chapter: To introduce the sequential-access and random-access file-processing paradigms and to provide the reader with sufficient stream-processing capabilities to support the networking features that we introduce in Chapter 22, Networking: Streams-Based Sockets and Datagrams.

File processing is one of a programming language's most important capabilities, because it enables a language to support commercial applications that typically process massive amounts of persistent data. This chapter discusses Visual Basic's powerful and abundant file-processing and stream-input/output features.

17.2 Data Hierarchy

Ultimately, all data items processed by a computer are reduced to combinations of zeros and ones. This occurs because it is simple and economical to build electronic devices that can assume two stable states—**0** represents one state, and **1** represents the other. It is remarkable that the impressive functions performed by computers involve only the most fundamental manipulations of **0**s and **1**s.

The smallest data item that computers support are called *bits* (short for "*binary digit*"—a digit that can assume one of two values). Each data item, or bit, can assume either the value **0** or the value **1**. Computer circuitry performs various simple bit manipulations, such as examining the value of a bit, setting the value of a bit and reversing a bit (from **1** to **0** or from **0** to **1**).

Programming with data in the low-level form of bits is cumbersome. It is preferable to program with data in forms such as *decimal digits* (i.e., 0, 1, 2, 3, 4, 5, 6, 7, 8 and 9), *letters* (i.e., A through Z and a through z) and *special symbols* (i.e., $, @, %, &, *, (,), -, +, ", :, ?, / and many others). Digits, letters and special symbols are referred to as *characters.* The set of all characters used to write programs and represent data items on a particular computer is called that computer's *character set.* Because computers can process only **1**s and **0**s, every character in a computer's character set is represented as a pattern of **1**s and **0**s. *Bytes* are composed of eight bits (characters in Visual Basic are *Unicode* characters, which are composed of 2 bytes). Programmers create programs and data items with characters; computers manipulate and process these characters as patterns of bits.

Just as characters are composed of bits, *fields* are composed of characters. A field is a group of characters that conveys some meaning. For example, a field consisting of uppercase and lowercase letters can represent a person's name.

Data items processed by computers form a *data hierarchy* (Fig. 17.1) in which data items become larger and more complex in structure as we progress from bits, to characters, to fieldsand up to larger data structures.

Typically, a *record* (i.e., a **Class** in Visual Basic) is composed of several fields (called member variables in Visual Basic). In a payroll system, for example, a record for a particular employee might include the following fields:

1. Employee identification number
2. Name
3. Address
4. Hourly pay rate
5. Number of exemptions claimed
6. Year-to-date earnings
7. Amount of taxes withheld

Thus, a record is a group of related fields. In the preceding example, each field is associated with the same employee. A *file* is a group of related records.[1] A company's payroll file normally contains one record for each employee. Thus, a payroll file for a small company might contain only 22 records, whereas a payroll file for a large company might contain 100,000 records. It is not unusual for a company to have many files, some containing millions, billions, or even trillions of characters of information.

To facilitate the retrieval of specific records from a file, at least one field in each record is chosen as a *record key.* A record key identifies a record as belonging to a particular person or entity and distiguishes that record from all other records. In the payroll record described previously, the employee identification number normally would be chosen as the record key.

---

1. Generally, a file can contain arbitrary data in arbitrary formats. In some operating systems, a file is viewed as nothing more than a collection of bytes. In such an operating system, any organization of the bytes in a file (such as organizing the data into records) is a view created by the applications programmer.

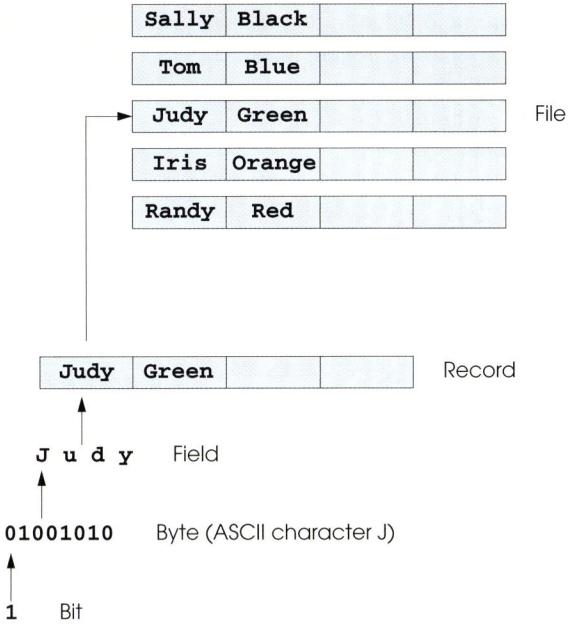

Fig. 17.1 Data hierarchy.

There are many ways of organizing records in a file. The most common type of organization is called a *sequential file*, in which records typically are stored in order by the record-key field. In a payroll file, records usually are placed in order by employee identification number. The first employee record in the file contains the lowest employee identification number, and subsequent records contain increasingly higher employee identification numbers.

Most businesses use many different files to store data. For example, a company might have payroll files, accounts receivable files (listing money due from clients), accounts payable files (listing money due to suppliers), inventory files (listing facts about all the items handled by the business) and many other types of files. Sometimes, a group of related files is called a *database*. A collection of programs designed to create and manage databases is called a *database management system* (DBMS). We discuss databases in detail in Chapter 19, Databases, SQL and ADO.NET.

17.3 Files and Streams

Visual Basic views each file as a sequential *stream* of bytes (Fig. 17.2). Each file ends either with an *end-of-file marker* or at a specific byte number that is recorded in a system-maintained administrative data structure. When a file is *opened*, Visual Basic creates an object and then associates a stream with that object. The runtime environment creates three stream objects upon program execution, each accessible via properties **Console.Out**, **Console.In** and **Console.Error**, respectively. These objects facilitate communication between a program and a particular file or device. Property **Console.In** returns the *standard input stream object*, which enables a program to input data from the keyboard. Property **Console.Out** returns the *standard output stream object*, which enables a program to output data to the screen. Property **Console.Error** returns the *standard error stream object*, which enables a program to output error messages to the screen. We have been using **Console.Out** and **Console.In** in our console applications—**Console** methods **Write** and **WriteLine** use **Console.Out** to perform output, and methods **Read** and **ReadLine** use **Console.In** to perform input.

To perform file processing in Visual Basic, namespace **System.IO** must be referenced. This namespace includes definitions for stream classes such as **StreamReader** (for text input from a file), **StreamWriter** (for text output to a file) and **FileStream** (for both input and output to a file). Files are opened by creating objects of these stream classes, which inherit from **MustInherit** classes **TextReader**, **TextWriter** and **Stream**, respectively. Actually, **Console.In** and **Console.Out** are properties of class **TextReader** and **TextWriter**, respectively. These classes are **MustInherit**; **StreamReader** and **StreamWriter** are classes that derive from classes **TextReader** and **TextWriter**.

Visual Basic provides class ***BinaryFormatter***, which is used in conjunction with a **Stream** object to perform input and output of objects. *Serialization* involves converting an object into a format that can be written to a file without losing any of that object's data. *Deserialization* consists of reading this format from a file and reconstructing the original object from it. A **BinaryFormatter** can serialize objects to, and deserialize objects from, a specified **Stream**.

Class ***System.IO.Stream*** provides functionality for representing streams as bytes. This class is **MustInherit**, so objects of this class cannot be instantiated. Classes ***FileStream***, ***MemoryStream*** and ***BufferedStream*** (all from namespace **System.IO**) inherit from class **Stream**. Later in the chapter, we use **FileStream** to read data to, and write data from, sequential-access and random-access files. Class **MemoryStream** enables the transferal of data directly to and from memory—this type of transfer is much faster than other types of data transfer (e.g., to and from disk). Class **BufferedStream** uses *buffering* to transfer data to or from a stream. Buffering is an I/O-performance-enhancement technique, in which each output operation is directed to a region in memory called a *buffer* that is large enough to hold the data from many output operations. Then, actual transfer to the output device is performed in one large *physical output operation* each time the buffer fills. The output operations directed to the output buffer in memory often are called *logical output operations*.

Visual Basic offers many classes for performing input and output. In this chapter, we use several key stream classes to implement a variety of file-processing programs that create, manipulate and destroy sequential-access files and random-access files. In Chapter 22, Networking: Streams-Based Sockets and Datagrams, we use stream classes extensively to implement networking applications.

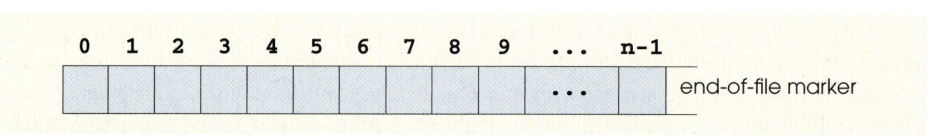

Fig. 17.2 Visual Basic's view of an *n-byte* file.

17.4 Classes `File` and `Directory`

Information on computers is stored in files, which are organized in directories. Class **`File`** is provided for manipulating files, and class **`Directory`** is provided for manipulating directories. Class **`File`** cannot write to or read from files directly; we discuss methods for reading and writing files in the following sections.

Note that the **** *separator character* separates directories and files in a path. On UNIX systems, the separator character is **/**. Visual Basic actually processes both characters as identical in a path name. This means that, if we specified the path **c:\VisualBasic/README**, which uses one of each separator character, Visual Basic still processes the file properly.

Figure 17.3 lists some methods in class **`File`** for manipulating and determining information about particular files. Class **`File`** contains only **`Shared`** methods—you cannot instantiate objects of type **`File`**. We use several of these methods in the example of Fig. 17.5.

Class **`Directory`** provides the capabilities for manipulating directories with the .NET framework. Figure 17.4 lists some methods that can be used for directory manipulation. We use several of these methods in the example of Fig. 17.5.

The **`DirectoryInfo`** object returned by method **`CreateDirectory`** contains information about a directory. Much of the information contained in this class also can be accessed via the **`Directory`** methods.

`Shared` Method	Description
`AppendText`	Returns a `StreamWriter` that appends to an existing file or creates a file if one does not exist.
`Copy`	Copies a file to a new file.
`Create`	Returns a `FileStream` associated with the file just created.
`CreateText`	Returns a `StreamWriter` associated with the new text file.
`Delete`	Deletes the specified file.
`GetCreationTime`	Returns a `DateTime` object representing the time that the file was created.
`GetLastAccessTime`	Returns a `DateTime` object representing the time that the file was last accessed.
`GetLastWriteTime`	Returns a `DateTime` object representing the time that the file was last modified.
`Move`	Moves the specified file to a specified location.
`Open`	Returns a `FileStream` associated with the specified file and equipped with the specified read/write permissions.
`OpenRead`	Returns a read-only `FileStream` associated with the specified file.
`OpenText`	Returns a `StreamReader` associated with the specified file.
`OpenWrite`	Returns a read/write `FileStream` associated with the specified file.

Fig. 17.3 `File` class methods (partial list).

`Shared` Method	Description
`CreateDirectory`	Returns the `DirectoryInfo` object associated with the newly created directory.
`Delete`	Deletes the specified directory.
`Exists`	Returns `True` if the specified directory exists; otherwise, it returns `False`.
`GetLastWriteTime`	Returns a `DateTime` object representing the time that the directory was last modified.
`GetDirectories`	Returns `String` array representing the names of the directories in the specified directory.
`GetFiles`	Returns `String` array representing the names of the files in the specified directory.
`GetCreationTime`	Returns a `DateTime` object representing the time that the directory was created.
`GetLastAccessTime`	Returns a `DateTime` object representing the time that the directory was last accessed.
`GetLastWriteTime`	Returns a `DateTime` object representing the time that items were last written to the directory.
`Move`	Moves the specified directory to specified location.

Fig. 17.4 `Directory` class methods (partial list).

Class **FrmFileTest** (Fig. 17.5) uses various the methods described in Fig. 17.3 and Fig. 17.4 to access file and directory information. This class contains **TextBox txtInput** (line 15), which enables the user to input a file or directory name. For each key that the user presses in the text box, the program calls method **txtInput_KeyDown** (lines 20–84). If the user presses the *Enter* key (line 25), this method displays either file or directory contents, depending on the text the user input in the **TextBox**. (Note that, if the user does not press the *Enter* key, this method returns without displaying any content.) Line 33 uses method **Exists** of class **File** to determine whether the user-specified text is a file. If the user specifies an existing file, line 36 invokes **Private** method **GetInformation** (lines 87–108), which calls methods **GetCreationTime** (line 97), **GetLastWriteTime** (line 101) and **GetLastAccessTime** (line 105) of class **File** to access information on the file. When method **GetInformation** returns, lines 42–43 instantiate a **StreamReader** for reading text from the file. The **StreamReader** constructor takes as an argument a **String** containing the name of the file to open. Line 44 calls method **ReadToEnd** of the **StreamReader** to read the file content from the file and then displays the content.

If line 33 determines that the user-specified text is not a file, line 56 determines whether it is a directory using method **Exists** of class **Directory**. If the user specified an existing directory, line 62 invokes method **GetInformation** to access the directory information. Line 65 calls method **GetDirectories** of class **Directory** to obtain a

String array containing the names of subdirectories in the specified directory. Lines 71–73 display each element in the **String** array. Note that, if line 56 determines that the user-specified text is neither a file nor a directory, lines 77–79 notify the user (via a **MessageBox**) that the file or directory does not exist.

```vb
1    ' Fig 17.5: FileTest.vb
2    ' Using classes File and Directory.
3
4    Imports System.IO
5    Imports System.Windows.Forms
6
7    Public Class FrmFileTest
8       Inherits Form
9
10      ' label that gives directions to user
11      Friend WithEvents lblDirections As Label
12
13      ' text boxes for inputting and outputting data
14      Friend WithEvents txtOutput As TextBox
15      Friend WithEvents txtInput As TextBox
16
17      ' Visual Studio .NET generated code
18
19      ' invoked when user presses key
20      Protected Sub txtInput_KeyDown(ByVal sender As Object, _
21         ByVal e As System.Windows.Forms.KeyEventArgs) Handles _
22         txtInput.KeyDown
23
24         ' determine whether user pressed Enter key
25         If e.KeyCode = Keys.Enter Then
26
27            Dim fileName As String ' name of file or directory
28
29            ' get user-specified file or directory
30            fileName = txtInput.Text
31
32            ' determine whether fileName is a file
33            If File.Exists(fileName) Then
34
35               ' get file's creation date, modification date, etc.
36               txtOutput.Text = GetInformation(fileName)
37
38               ' display file contents through StreamReader
39               Try
40
41                  ' obtain reader and file contents
42                  Dim stream As StreamReader
43                  stream = New StreamReader(fileName)
44                  txtOutput.Text &= stream.ReadToEnd()
45
```

Fig. 17.5 **FrmFileTest** class tests classes **File** and **Directory** (part 1 of 3).

```vbnet
46              ' handle exception if StreamReader is unavailable
47              Catch exceptionCatch As IOException
48
49                 ' display error
50                 MessageBox.Show("FILE ERROR", "FILE ERROR", _
51                    MessageBoxButtons.OK, MessageBoxIcon.Error)
52
53              End Try
54
55           ' determine whether fileName is a directory
56           ElseIf Directory.Exists(fileName) Then
57
58              Dim directoryList As String() ' array for directories
59              Dim i As Integer
60
61              ' get directory's creation date, modification date, etc
62              txtOutput.Text = GetInformation(fileName)
63
64              ' obtain directory list of specified directory
65              directoryList = Directory.GetDirectories(fileName)
66
67              txtOutput.Text &= vbCrLf & vbCrLf & _
68                 "Directory contents:" & vbCrLf
69
70              ' output directoryList contents
71              For i = 0 To directoryList.Length - 1
72                 txtOutput.Text &= directoryList(i) & vbCrLf
73              Next
74
75           ' notify user that neither file nor directory exists
76           Else
77              MessageBox.Show(txtInput.Text & " does not exist", _
78                 "FILE ERROR", MessageBoxButtons.OK, _
79                 MessageBoxIcon.Error)
80           End If
81
82        End If ' determine whether user pressed Enter key
83
84     End Sub ' txtInput_KeyDown
85
86     ' get information on file or directory
87     Private Function GetInformation(ByRef fileName As String) _
88        As String
89
90        Dim information As String
91
92        ' output that file or directory exists
93        information = fileName & " exists" & vbCrLf & vbCrLf
94
95        ' output when file or directory was created
96        information &= "Created : " & _
97           File.GetCreationTime(fileName) & vbCrLf
98
```

Fig. 17.5 **FrmFileTest** class tests classes **File** and **Directory** (part 2 of 3).

```
 99            ' output when file or directory was last modified
100            information &= "Last modified: " & _
101               File.GetLastWriteTime(fileName) & vbCrLf
102
103            ' output when file or directory was last accessed
104            information &= "Last accessed: " & _
105               File.GetLastAccessTime(fileName) & vbCrLf & vbCrLf
106
107            Return information
108        End Function ' GetInformation
109
110 End Class ' FrmFileTest
```

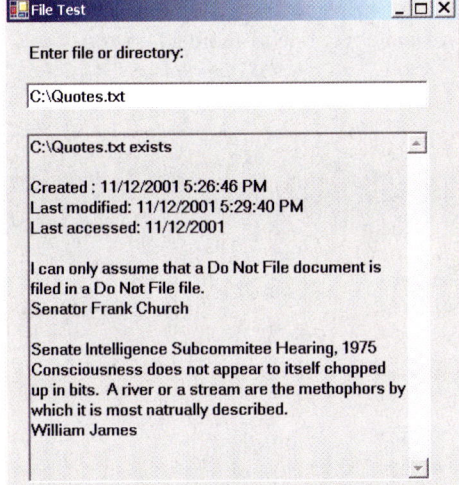
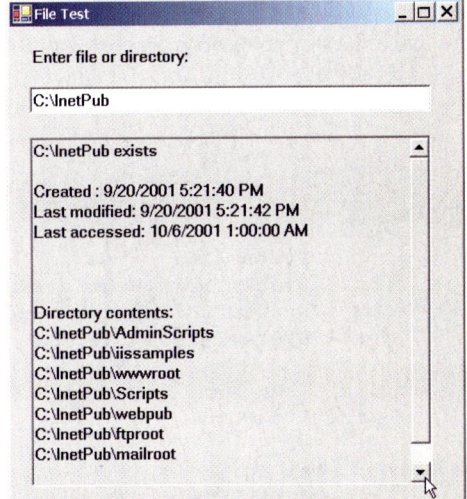

Fig. 17.5 `FrmFileTest` class tests classes `File` and `Directory` (part 3 of 3).

We now consider another example that uses Visual Basic's file and directory-manipulation capabilities. Class **FrmFileSearch** (Fig. 17.6) uses classes **File** and **Directory** in conjunction with classes for performing regular expressions to report the number of files of each file type in the specified directory path. The program also serves as a "cleanup" utility—when the program encounters a file that has the **.bak** extension (i.e., a backup file), the program displays a **MessageBox** asking if that file should be removed and then responds appropriately to the user's input.

When the user presses the *Enter* key or clicks the **Search Directory** button, the program invokes method `cmdSearch_Click` (lines 47–88), which searches recursively through the directory path that the user provides. If the user inputs text in the `TextBox`, line 56 calls method `Exists` of class `Directory` to determine whether that text indicates a valid directory. If the user specifies an invalid directory, lines 65–66 notify the user of the error.

If the user specifies a valid directory, line 78 passes the directory name as an argument to `Private` method `SearchDirectory` (lines 91–181). This method locates files on the basis of the regular expression defined in lines 100–101 by the `Regex` object, which matches any sequence of numbers or letters followed by a period and one or more letters. Notice an unfamiliar substring of format (`?<extension>`*regular-expression*) contained in the argument to the `Regex` constructor (line 101). All `String`s with the substring *regular-expression* are tagged with the name `extension`. In this program, we assign to the variable `extension` any `String` matching one or more characters.

```vb
1   ' Fig 17.6: FileSearch.vb
2   ' Using regular expressions to determine file types.
3
4   Imports System.IO
5   Imports System.Text.RegularExpressions
6   Imports System.Collections.Specialized
7   Imports System.Windows.Forms
8
9   Public Class FrmFileSearch
10      Inherits Form
11
12      ' label that displays current directory
13      Friend WithEvents lblDirectory As Label
14
15      ' label that displays directions to user
16      Friend WithEvents lblDirections As Label
17
18      ' button that activates search
19      Friend WithEvents cmdSearch As Button
20
21      ' text boxes for inputting and outputting data
22      Friend WithEvents txtInput As TextBox
23      Friend WithEvents txtOutput As TextBox
24
25      ' Visual Studio .NET generated code
26
27      Dim currentDirectory As String = Directory.GetCurrentDirectory
28      Dim directoryList As String() ' subdirectories
29      Dim fileArray As String() ' files in current directory
30
31      ' store extensions found and number found
32      Dim found As NameValueCollection = New NameValueCollection()
```

Fig. 17.6 `FrmFileSearch` class uses regular expressions to determine file types (part 1 of 5).

```vbnet
33
34        ' invoked when user types in text box
35        Private Sub txtInput_KeyDown(ByVal sender As System.Object, _
36           ByVal e As System.Windows.Forms.KeyEventArgs) _
37           Handles txtInput.KeyDown
38
39           ' determine whether user pressed Enter
40           If (e.KeyCode = Keys.Enter) Then
41              cmdSearch_Click(sender, e)
42           End If
43
44        End Sub ' txtInput_KeyDown
45
46        ' invoked when user clicks "Search Directory" button
47        Private Sub cmdSearch_Click(ByVal sender As System.Object, _
48           ByVal e As System.EventArgs) Handles cmdSearch.Click
49
50           Dim current As String
51
52           ' check for user input; default is current directory
53           If txtInput.Text <> "" Then
54
55              ' verify that user input is a valid directory name
56              If Directory.Exists(txtInput.Text) Then
57                 currentDirectory = txtInput.Text
58
59                 ' reset input text box and update display
60                 lblDirectory.Text = "Current Directory:" & vbCrLf & _
61                    currentDirectory
62
63                 ' show error if user does not specify valid directory
64              Else
65                 MessageBox.Show("Invalid Directory", "Error", _
66                    MessageBoxButtons.OK, MessageBoxIcon.Error)
67
68                 Return
69              End If
70
71           End If
72
73           ' clear text boxes
74           txtInput.Text = ""
75           txtOutput.Text = ""
76
77           ' search directory
78           SearchDirectory(currentDirectory)
79
80           ' summarize and print results
81           For Each current In found
82              txtOutput.Text &= "* Found " & found(current) & " " _
83                 & current & " files." & vbCrLf
84           Next
```

Fig. 17.6 **FrmFileSearch** class uses regular expressions to determine file types (part 2 of 5).

```vbnet
85
86         ' clear output for new search
87         found.Clear()
88      End Sub ' cmdSearch_Click
89
90      ' search directory using regular expression
91      Private Sub SearchDirectory(ByVal currentDirectory As String)
92
93         ' for file name without directory path
94         Try
95            Dim fileName As String = ""
96            Dim myFile As String
97            Dim myDirectory As String
98
99            ' regular expression for extensions matching pattern
100           Dim regularExpression As Regex = _
101              New Regex("([a-zA-Z0-9]+\.(?<extension>\w+))")
102
103           ' stores regular-expression-match result
104           Dim matchResult As Match
105
106           Dim fileExtension As String ' holds file extensions
107
108           ' number of files with given extension in directory
109           Dim extensionCount As Integer
110
111           ' get directories
112           directoryList = _
113              Directory.GetDirectories(currentDirectory)
114
115           ' get list of files in current directory
116           fileArray = Directory.GetFiles(currentDirectory)
117
118           ' iterate through list of files
119           For Each myFile In fileArray
120
121              ' remove directory path from file name
122              fileName = myFile.Substring( _
123                 myFile.LastIndexOf("\") + 1)
124
125              ' obtain result for regular-expression search
126              matchResult = regularExpression.Match(fileName)
127
128              ' check for match
129              If (matchResult.Success) Then
130                 fileExtension = matchResult.Result("${extension}")
131              Else
132                 fileExtension = "[no extension]"
133              End If
```

Fig. 17.6 `FrmFileSearch` class uses regular expressions to determine file types (part 3 of 5).

```vb
134
135                    ' store value from container
136                    If (found(fileExtension) = Nothing) Then
137                       found.Add(fileExtension, "1")
138                    Else
139                       extensionCount = _
140                          Convert.ToInt32(found(fileExtension)) + 1
141
142                       found(fileExtension) = extensionCount.ToString()
143                    End If
144
145                    ' search for backup(.bak) files
146                    If fileExtension = "bak" Then
147
148                       ' prompt user to delete (.bak) file
149                       Dim result As DialogResult = _
150                          MessageBox.Show("Found backup file " & _
151                          fileName & ". Delete?", "Delete Backup", _
152                          MessageBoxButtons.YesNo, _
153                          MessageBoxIcon.Question)
154
155                       ' delete file if user clicked 'yes'
156                       If (result = DialogResult.Yes) Then
157                          File.Delete(myFile)
158                          extensionCount = _
159                             Convert.ToInt32(found("bak")) - 1
160
161                          found("bak") = extensionCount.ToString()
162                       End If
163
164                    End If
165
166                 Next
167
168                 ' recursive call to search files in subdirectory
169                 For Each myDirectory In directoryList
170                    SearchDirectory(myDirectory)
171                 Next
172
173              ' handle exception if files have unauthorized access
174              Catch unauthorizedAccess As UnauthorizedAccessException
175                 MessageBox.Show("Some files may not be visible due to" _
176                    & " permission settings", "Warning", _
177                    MessageBoxButtons.OK, MessageBoxIcon.Information)
178
179           End Try
180
181        End Sub ' SearchDirectory
182
183 End Class ' FrmFileSearch
```

Fig. 17.6 **FrmFileSearch** class uses regular expressions to determine file types (part 4 of 5).

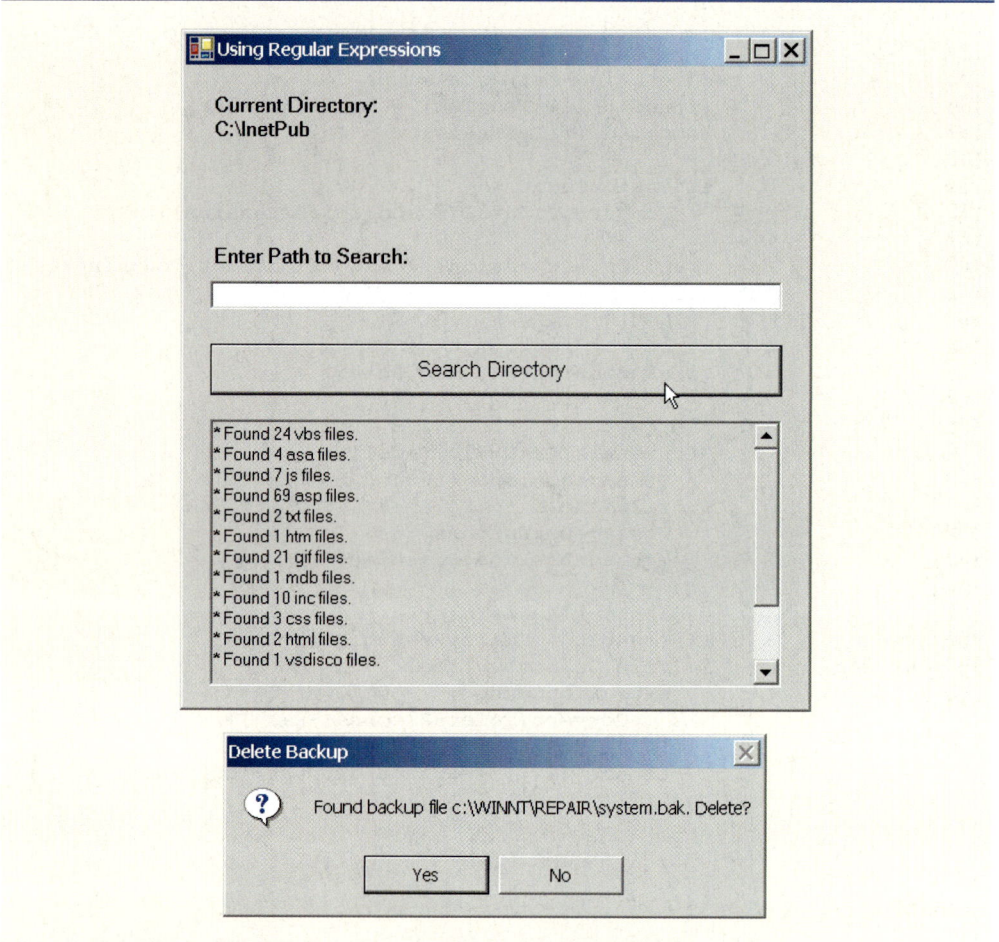

Fig. 17.6 **FrmFileSearch** class uses regular expressions to determine file types (part 5 of 5).

Lines 112–113 call method **GetDirectories** of class **Directory** to retrieve the names of all directories that belong to the current directory. Line 116 calls method **GetFiles** of class **Directory** to store the names of all current-directory files in **String** array **fileArray**. The **For Each** loop in line 119 searches for files with extension **bak**; it then calls **SearchDirectory** recursively for each subdirectory in the current directory. Lines 122–123 eliminate the directory path, so the program can test only the file name when using the regular expression. Lines 126 uses method **Match** of the **Regex** object to match the regular expression with the file name and then returns the result to object **matchResult** of type **Match**. If the match is successful, line 130 uses method **Result** of object **matchResult** to store the extension **String** from object **matchResult** in **fileExtension** (the **String** that will contain the current file's extension). If the match is unsuccessful, line 132 sets **fileExtension** to hold a value of **"[no extension]"**.

Class **FrmFileSearch** uses an instance of class **NameValueCollection** (declared in line 32) to store each file-extension type and the number of files for each type.

A **NameValueCollection** contains a collection of key/value pairs, each of which is a **String**, and provides method **Add** to add a key/value pair. The indexer for this pair can index according to the order that the items were added or according to the entry key—both means of indexing return the value corresponding to that key. Line 136 uses **NameValueCollection** variable **found** to determine whether this is the first occurrence of the file extension. If so, line 137 adds to **found** that extension as a key with the value **1**. Otherwise, lines 139–142 increment the value associated with the extension in **found** to indicate another occurrence of that file extension.

Line 146 determines whether **fileExtension** equals "**bak**"—i.e., the file is a backup file. Lines 149–153 prompt the user to indicate whether the file should be removed—if the user clicks **Yes** (line 156), lines 157–159 delete the file and decrement the value for the "**bak**" file type in **found**.

Lines 169–171 call method **SearchDirectory** for each subdirectory. Using recursion, we ensure that the program performs the same logic for finding **bak** files on each subdirectory. After each subdirectory has been checked for **bak** files, method **SearchDirectory** returns to the event handler (i.e., method **cmdSearch_Click**), and lines 81–84 display the results.

17.5 Creating a Sequential-Access File

Visual Basic imposes no structure on a file. Thus, concepts like that of a "record" do not exist in Visual Basic files. This means that, the programmer must structure files to meet the requirements of applications. In this example, we use text and special characters to organize our own concept of a "record."

As we will see, the GUIs for most of the programs in this chapter are similar; therefore, we created class **FrmBankUI** (Fig. 17.7) to encapsulate this GUI (see the screen capture in Fig. 17.7). Class **FrmBankUI** contains four **Label**s (lines 10–13) and four **TextBox**es (lines 16–19). Methods **ClearTextBoxes** (lines 35–52), **SetTextBoxValues** (lines 55–72) and **GetTextBoxValues** (lines 75–86) clear, set the values of, and get the values of the text in the **TextBox**es, respectively.

```
1   ' Fig 17.7: BankUI.vb
2   ' A reusable windows form for the examples in this chapter.
3
4   Imports System.Windows.Forms
5
6   Public Class FrmBankUI
7      Inherits Form
8
9      ' labels for TextBoxes
10     Public WithEvents lblAccount As Label
11     Public WithEvents lblFirstName As Label
12     Public WithEvents lblLastName As Label
13     Public WithEvents lblBalance As Label
14
```

Fig. 17.7 **FrmBankUI** class is the base class for GUIs in our file-processing applications (part 1 of 3).

```vb
15         ' text boxes that receive user input
16         Public WithEvents txtAccount As TextBox
17         Public WithEvents txtFirstName As TextBox
18         Public WithEvents txtLastName As TextBox
19         Public WithEvents txtBalance As TextBox
20
21         ' Visual Studio .NET generated code
22
23         ' number of TextBoxes on Form
24         Protected TextBoxCount As Integer = 4
25
26         ' enumeration constants specify TextBox indices
27         Public Enum TextBoxIndices
28            ACCOUNT
29            FIRST
30            LAST
31            BALANCE
32         End Enum
33
34         ' clear all TextBoxes
35         Public Sub ClearTextBoxes()
36            Dim myControl As Control ' current GUI component
37            Dim i As Integer
38
39            ' iterate through every Control on form
40            For i = 0 To Controls.Count - 1
41               myControl = Controls(i) ' get Control
42
43               ' determine whether Control is TextBox
44               If (TypeOf myControl Is TextBox) Then
45
46                  ' clear Text property (set to empty String)
47                  myControl.Text = ""
48               End If
49
50            Next
51
52         End Sub ' ClearTextBoxes
53
54         ' set TextBox values to String-array values
55         Public Sub SetTextBoxValues(ByVal values As String())
56
57            ' determine whether String array has correct length
58            If (values.Length <> TextBoxCount) Then
59
60               ' throw exception if not correct length
61               Throw New ArgumentException("There must be " & _
62                  TextBoxCount + 1 & " strings in the array")
63
64            ' else set array values to TextBox values
65            Else
66               txtAccount.Text = values(TextBoxIndices.ACCOUNT)
```

Fig. 17.7 `FrmBankUI` class is the base class for GUIs in our file-processing applications (part 2 of 3).

```
67              txtFirstName.Text = values(TextBoxIndices.FIRST)
68              txtLastName.Text = values(TextBoxIndices.LAST)
69              txtBalance.Text = values(TextBoxIndices.BALANCE)
70           End If
71
72        End Sub ' SetTextBoxValues
73
74        ' return TextBox values as String array
75        Public Function GetTextBoxValues() As String()
76
77           Dim values(TextBoxCount) As String
78
79           ' copy TextBox fields to String array
80           values(TextBoxIndices.ACCOUNT) = txtAccount.Text
81           values(TextBoxIndices.FIRST) = txtFirstName.Text
82           values(TextBoxIndices.LAST) = txtLastName.Text
83           values(TextBoxIndices.BALANCE) = txtBalance.Text
84
85           Return values
86        End Function ' GetTextBoxValues
87
88    End Class ' FrmBankUI
```

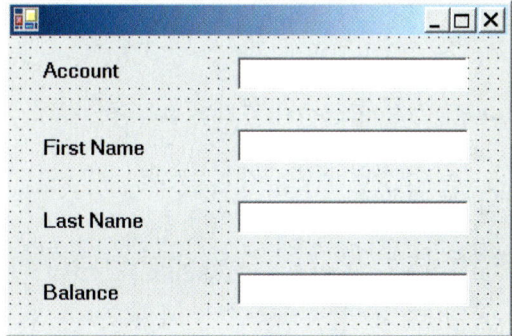

Fig. 17.7 **FrmBankUI** class is the base class for GUIs in our file-processing applications (part 3 of 3).

To reuse class **FrmBankUI**, we compile the GUI into a DLL library by creating a project of type **Windows Control Library** (the DLL we create is called **BankLibrary**). This library, as well as all the code in this book, can be found on the CD accompanying this book and at our Web site, **www.deitel.com**. However, students might need to change the reference to this library, as it most likely resides in a different location on their systems.

Figure 17.8 contains the **CRecord** class that the programs of Fig. 17.9, Fig. 17.11 and Fig. 17.12 use for reading records from, and writing records to, a file sequentially. This class also belongs to the **BankLibrary** DLL, which means that it is located in the same project as is class **FrmBankUI**. (When students add class **CRecord** to the project containing **FrmBankUI**, they must remember to rebuild the project.)

```vbnet
1   ' Fig. 17.8: CRecord.vb
2   ' Serializable class that represents a data record.
3
4   <Serializable()> Public Class CRecord
5
6      Private mAccount As Integer
7      Private mFirstName As String
8      Private mLastName As String
9      Private mBalance As Double
10
11     ' default constructor sets members to default values
12     Public Sub New()
13        Me.New(0, "", "", 0.0)
14     End Sub ' New
15
16     ' overloaded constructor sets members to parameter values
17     Public Sub New(ByVal accountValue As Integer, _
18        ByVal firstNameValue As String, _
19        ByVal lastNameValue As String, _
20        ByVal balanceValue As Double)
21
22        Account = accountValue
23        FirstName = firstNameValue
24        LastName = lastNameValue
25        Balance = balanceValue
26     End Sub ' New
27
28     ' property Account
29     Public Property Account() As Integer
30
31        Get
32           Return mAccount
33        End Get
34
35        Set(ByVal accountValue As Integer)
36           mAccount = accountValue
37        End Set
38
39     End Property ' Account
40
41     ' property FirstName
42     Public Property FirstName() As String
43
44        Get
45           Return mFirstName
46        End Get
47
48        Set(ByVal firstNameValue As String)
49           mFirstName = firstNameValue
50        End Set
51
52     End Property ' FirstName
```

Fig. 17.8 **CRecord** class represents a record for sequential-access file-processing applications (part 1 of 2).

```
53
54        ' property LastName
55        Public Property LastName() As String
56
57           Get
58              Return mLastName
59           End Get
60
61           Set(ByVal lastNameValue As String)
62              mLastName = lastNameValue
63           End Set
64
65        End Property ' LastName
66
67        ' property Balance
68        Public Property Balance() As Double
69
70           Get
71              Return mBalance
72           End Get
73
74           Set(ByVal balanceValue As Double)
75              mBalance = balanceValue
76           End Set
77
78        End Property ' Balance
79
80     End Class ' CRecord
```

Fig. 17.8 **CRecord** class represents a record for sequential-access file-processing applications (part 2 of 2).

The **Serializable** attribute (line 4) indicates to the compiler that objects of class **CRecord** can be *serialized*, or represented as sets of bytes—we then either can write these bytes to streams or store stream data into these sets. Objects that we wish to write to or read from a stream must include this attribute tag before their class definitions.

Class **CRecord** contains **Private** data members **mAccount**, **mFirstName**, **mLastName** and **mBalance** (lines 6–9), which collectively represent all information necessary to store record data. The default constructor (lines 12–14) sets these members to their default (i.e., empty) values, and the overloaded constructor (lines 17–26) sets these members to specified parameter values. Class **CRecord** also provides properties **Account** (lines 29–39), **FirstName** (lines 42–52), **LastName** (lines 55–65) and **Balance** (lines 68–78) for accessing the account number, first name, last name and balance of each customer, respectively.

Class **FrmCreateSequentialAccessFile** (Fig. 17.9) uses instances of class **CRecord** to create a sequential-access file that might be used in an accounts-receivable system—i.e., a program that organizes data regarding money owed by a company's credit clients. For each client, the program obtains an account number and the client's first name, last name and balance (i.e., the amount of money that the client owes to the company for previously received goods or services). The data obtained for each client constitutes a record for that client. In this application, the account number represents the record key—

files are created and maintained in account-number order. This program assumes that the user enters records in account-number order. However, in a comprehensive accounts-receivable system would provide a sorting capability. The user could enter the records in any order, and the records then could be sorted and written to the file in order. (Note that all outputs in this chapter should be read row by row, from left to right in each row.)

Figure 17.9 contains the code for class **FrmCreateSequentialAccessFile**, which either creates or opens a file (depending on whether one exists) and then allows the user to write bank information to that file. Line 11 imports the **BankLibrary** namespace; this namespace contains class **FrmBankUI**, from which class **FrmCreateSequentialAccessFile** inherits (line 14). Because of this inheritance relationship, the **FrmCreateSequentialAccessFile** GUI is similar to that of class **FrmBankUI** (shown in the Fig. 17.9 output), except that the inherited class contains buttons **Save As**, **Enter** and **Exit**.

```vb
1   ' Fig 17.9: CreateSequentialAccessFile.vb
2   ' Creating a sequential-access file.
3
4   ' Visual Basic namespaces
5   Imports System.IO
6   Imports System.Runtime.Serialization.Formatters.Binary
7   Imports System.Runtime.Serialization
8   Imports System.Windows.Forms
9
10  ' Deitel namespaces
11  Imports BankLibrary
12
13  Public Class FrmCreateSequentialAccessFile
14     Inherits FrmBankUI
15
16     ' GUI buttons to save file, enter data and exit program
17     Friend WithEvents cmdSave As Button
18     Friend WithEvents cmdEnter As Button
19     Friend WithEvents cmdExit As Button
20
21     ' Visual Studio .NET generated code
22
23     ' serializes CRecord in binary format
24     Private formatter As BinaryFormatter = New BinaryFormatter()
25
26     ' stream through which serializable data is written to file
27     Private output As FileStream
28
29     ' invoked when user clicks Save button
30     Protected Sub cmdSave_Click(ByVal sender As Object, _
31        ByVal e As System.EventArgs) Handles cmdSave.Click
32
33        ' create dialog box enabling user to save file
34        Dim fileChooser As SaveFileDialog = New SaveFileDialog()
35        Dim result As DialogResult = fileChooser.ShowDialog()
36        Dim fileName As String ' name of file to save data
```

Fig. 17.9 **FrmCreateSequentialAccessFile** class creates and writes to sequential-access files (part 1 of 5).

```vb
37
38         ' allow user to create file
39         fileChooser.CheckFileExists = False
40
41         ' exit event handler if user clicked "Cancel"
42         If result = DialogResult.Cancel Then
43            Return
44         End If
45
46         fileName = fileChooser.FileName ' get specified file name
47
48         ' show error if user specified invalid file
49         If (fileName = "" OrElse fileName = Nothing) Then
50            MessageBox.Show("Invalid File Name", "Error", _
51               MessageBoxButtons.OK, MessageBoxIcon.Error)
52         Else
53
54            ' save file via FileStream if user specified valid file
55            Try
56
57               ' open file with write access
58               output = New FileStream(fileName, _
59                  FileMode.OpenOrCreate, FileAccess.Write)
60
61               cmdSave.Enabled = False ' disable Save button
62               cmdEnter.Enabled = True ' enable Enter button
63
64            ' notify user if file does not exist
65            Catch fileException As FileNotFoundException
66               MessageBox.Show("File Does Not Exits", "Error", _
67                  MessageBoxButtons.OK, MessageBoxIcon.Error)
68
69            End Try
70
71         End If
72
73      End Sub ' cmdSave_Click
74
75      ' invoked when user clicks Enter button
76      Protected Sub cmdEnter_Click(ByVal sender As Object, _
77         ByVal Be As System.EventArgs) Handles cmdEnter.Click
78
79         ' account-number value from TextBox
80         Dim accountNumber As Integer
81
82         ' store TextBox-values String array
83         Dim values As String() = GetTextBoxValues()
84
85         ' CRecord containing TextBox values to serialize
86         Dim record As New CRecord()
87
```

Fig. 17.9 `FrmCreateSequentialAccessFile` class creates and writes to sequential-access files (part 2 of 5).

```vbnet
 88            ' determine whether TextBox account field is empty
 89            If values(TextBoxIndices.ACCOUNT) <> "" Then
 90
 91               ' store TextBox values in CRecord and serialize CRecord
 92               Try
 93
 94                  ' get account-number value from TextBox
 95                  accountNumber = _
 96                     Convert.ToInt32(values(TextBoxIndices.ACCOUNT))
 97
 98                  ' determine whether accountNumber is valid
 99                  If accountNumber > 0 Then
100
101                     ' store TextBox fields in CRecord
102                     record.Account = accountNumber
103                     record.FirstName = values(TextBoxIndices.FIRST)
104                     record.LastName = values(TextBoxIndices.LAST)
105                     record.Balance = Convert.ToDouble( _
106                        values(TextBoxIndices.BALANCE))
107
108                     ' write CRecord to FileStream (Serialize object)
109                     formatter.Serialize(output, record)
110
111                     ' notify user if invalid account number
112                  Else
113                     MessageBox.Show("Invalid Account Number", _
114                        "Error", MessageBoxButtons.OK, _
115                        MessageBoxIcon.Error)
116                  End If
117
118                  ' notify user if error occurs in serialization
119               Catch serializableException As SerializationException
120                  MessageBox.Show("Error Writing to File", "Error", _
121                     MessageBoxButtons.OK, MessageBoxIcon.Error)
122
123                  ' notify user if error occurs regarding parameter format
124               Catch formattingException As FormatException
125                  MessageBox.Show("Invalid Format", "Error", _
126                     MessageBoxButtons.OK, MessageBoxIcon.Error)
127
128               End Try
129
130            End If
131
132            ClearTextBoxes() ' clear TextBox values
133         End Sub ' cmdEnter_Click
134
135         ' invoked when user clicks Exit button
136         Protected Sub cmdExit_Click(ByVal sender As Object, _
137            ByVal e As System.EventArgs) Handles cmdExit.Click
138
```

Fig. 17.9 `FrmCreateSequentialAccessFile` class creates and writes to sequential-access files (part 3 of 5).

```vb
139         ' determine whether file exists
140         If (output Is Nothing) = False Then
141
142            ' close file
143            Try
144               output.Close()
145
146            ' notify user of error closing file
147            Catch fileException As IOException
148               MessageBox.Show("Cannot close file", "Error", _
149                  MessageBoxButtons.OK, MessageBoxIcon.Error)
150
151            End Try
152
153         End If
154
155         Application.Exit()
156      End Sub ' cmdExit_Click
157
158 End Class ' FrmCreateSequentialAccessFile
```

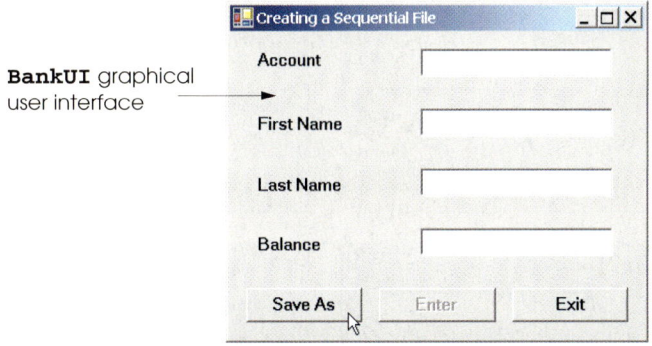

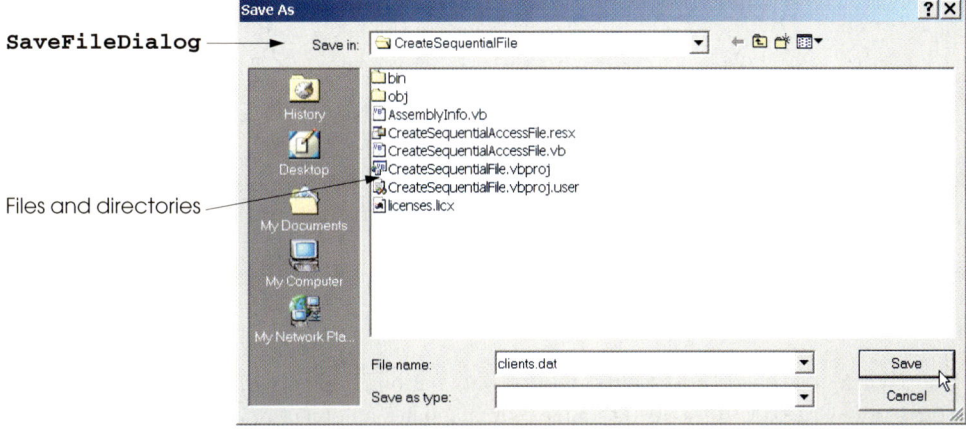

Fig. 17.9 `FrmCreateSequentialAccessFile` class creates and writes to sequential-access files (part 4 of 5).

776 Files and Streams Chapter 17

Fig. 17.9 `FrmCreateSequentialAccessFile` class creates and writes to sequential-access files (part 5 of 5).

When the user clicks the **Save As** button, the program invokes method `cmdSave_Click` (lines 30–73). Line 34 instantiates an object of class `SaveFileDialog`, which belongs to the `System.Windows.Forms` namespace. Objects of this class are used for selecting files (see the second screen in Fig. 17.9). Line 36 calls method `ShowDialog` of the `SaveFileDialog` object to display the `SaveFileDialog`.

When displayed, a **SaveFileDialog** prevents the user from interacting with any other window in the program until the user closes the **SaveFileDialog** by clicking either **Save** or **Cancel**. Dialogs that behave in this fashion are called *modal dialogs*. The user selects the appropriate drive, directory and file name and then clicks **Save**. Method **Show-Dialog** returns an integer specifying which button (**Save** or **Cancel**) the user clicked to close the dialog. In this example, the **Form** property **DialogResult** receives the integer. Line 42 tests whether the user clicked **Cancel** by comparing the value returned by property **DialogResult** to **Const** *DialogResult.Cancel*. If the values are equai, method **cmdSave_Click** returns (line 43). If the values are unequal (i.e., the user clicked **Save**, instead of clicking **Cancel**), line 46 uses property *FileName* of class **SaveFileDialog** to obtain the user-selected file.

As we stated previously in this chapter, we can open files to perform text manipulation by creating objects of classes **FileStream**. In this example, we want the file to be opened for output, so lines 58–59 instantiate a **FileStream** object. The **FileStream** constructor that we use receives three arguments—a **String** containing the name of the file to be opened, a **Const** describing how to open the file and a **Const** describing the file permissions. Line 59 passes **Const FileMode.OpenOrCreate** to the **FileStream** constructor as the constructor's second argument. This constant indicates that the **FileStream** object should open the file, if the file exists, or create the file if the file does not exist. Visual Basic offers other **FileMode** constants describing how to open files; we introduce these constants as we use them in examples. Line 59 passes **Const FileAccess.Write** to the **FileStream** constructor as the constructor's third argument. This constant ensures that the program can perform write-only operations on the **FileStream** object. Visual Basic provides two other constants for this parameter—**FileAccess.Read** for read-only access and **FileAccess.ReadWrite** for both read and write access.

Good Programming Practice 17.1

*When opening files, use the **FileAccess** enumeration to control user access.*

After the user types information in each **TextBox**, the user clicks the **Enter** button, which calls method **cmdEnter_Click** (lines 76–133) to save the **TextBox** data in the user-specified file. If the user entered a valid account number (i.e., an integer greater than zero), lines 102–106 store the **TextBox** values into an object of type **CRecord**. If the user entered invalid data in one of the **TextBox**es (such as entering a **String** in the **Balance** field), the program throws a **FormatException**. The **Catch** statement in line 124 handles such an exception by notifying the user (via a **MessageBox**) of the improper format. If the user entered valid data, line 109 writes the record to the file by invoking method **Serialize** of the **BinaryFormatter** object (instantiated in line 24). Class **BinaryFormatter** uses methods *Serialize* and *Deserialize* to write and read objects into streams, respectively. Method **Serialize** writes the object's representation to a file. Method **Deserialize** reads this representation from a file and reconstructs the original object. Both methods throw **SerializationException**s if an error occurs during serialization or deserialization (errors results when the methods attempt to access streams or records that do not exist). Both methods **Serialize** and **Deserialize** require a **Stream** object (e.g., the **FileStream**) as a parameter so that the **BinaryFormatter** can access the correct file; the **BinaryFormatter** must receive an instance of a class that derives from class **Stream**, because **Stream** is **MustInherit**. Class **BinaryFor-**

matter belongs the ***System.Runtime.Serialization.Formatters.Binary*** namespace.

Common Programming Error 17.1
Failure to open a file before attempting to reference it in a program is a logic error.

When the user clicks the **Exit** button, the program invokes method **cmdExit_Click** (lines 136–156) to exit the application. Line 144 closes the **FileStream** if one has been opened, and line 155 exits the program.

Performance Tip 17.1
Close each file explicitly when the program no longer needs to reference the file. This can reduce resource usage in programs that continues executing long after they finish using a specific file. The practice of explicitly closing files also improves program clarity.

Performance Tip 17.2
Releasing resources explicitly when they are no longer needed makes them immediately available for reuse by the program, thus improving resource utilization.

In the sample execution for the program of Fig. 17.9, we entered information for five accounts (Fig. 17.10). The program does not depict how the data records are rendered in the file. To verify that the file has been created successfully, in the next section we create a program to read and display the file.

17.6 Reading Data from a Sequential-Access File

Data are stored in files so that they can be retrieved for processing when they are needed. The previous section demonstrated how to create a file for sequential access. In this section, we discuss how to read (or retrieve) data sequentially from a file.

Class ***FrmReadSequentialAccessFile*** (Fig. 17.11) reads records from the file created by the program in Fig. 17.9 and then displays the contents of each record. Much of the code in this example is similar to that of Fig. 17.9, so we discuss only the unique aspects of the application.

When the user clicks the **Open File** button, the program calls method **cmdOpen_Click** (lines 29–58). Line 33 instantiates an object of class ***OpenFileDialog***, and line 34 calls the object's ***ShowDialog*** method to display the **Open** dialog (see the second screenshot in Fig. 17.11). The behavior and GUI between the two dialog types are the same (except that **Save** is replaced by **Open**). If the user inputs a valid file name, lines 52–53 create a **FileStream** object and assign it to reference **input**. We pass **Const FileMode.Open** as the second argument to the **FileStream** constructor. This constant indicates that the **FileStream** should open the file if one exists and throw a **FileNotFoundException** if the file does not exist. (In this example, the **FileStream** constructor will not throw a **FileNotFoundException**, because the **OpenFileDialog** requires the user to enter a file that exists.) In the last example (Fig. 17.9), we wrote text to the file using a **FileStream** object with write-only access. In this example, (Fig. 17.11), we specify read-only access to the file by passing **Const FileAccess.Read** as the third argument to the **FileStream** constructor.

Account Number	First Name	Last Name	Balance
100	Nancy	Brown	-25.54
200	Stacey	Dunn	314.33
300	Doug	Barker	0.00
400	Dave	Smith	258.34
500	Sam	Stone	34.98

Fig. 17.10 Sample data for the program of Fig. 17.9.

```vb
1    ' Fig. 17.11: ReadSequentialAccessFile.vb
2    ' Reading a sequential-access file.
3
4    ' Visual Basic namespaces
5    Imports System.IO
6    Imports System.Runtime.Serialization.Formatters.Binary
7    Imports System.Runtime.Serialization
8    Imports System.Windows.Forms
9
10   ' Deitel namespaces
11   Imports BankLibrary
12
13   Public Class FrmReadSequentialAccessFile
14      Inherits FrmBankUI
15
16      ' GUI buttons for opening file and reading records
17      Friend WithEvents cmdOpen As Button
18      Friend WithEvents cmdNext As Button
19
20      ' Visual Studio .NET generated code
21
22      ' stream through which serializable data is read from file
23      Private input As FileStream
24
25      ' object for deserializing CRecord in binary format
26      Private reader As BinaryFormatter = New BinaryFormatter()
27
28      ' invoked when user clicks Open button
29      Protected Sub cmdOpen_Click(ByVal sender As Object, _
30         ByVal e As EventArgs) Handles cmdOpen.Click
31
32         ' create dialog box enabling user to open file
33         Dim fileChooser As OpenFileDialog = New OpenFileDialog()
34         Dim result As DialogResult = fileChooser.ShowDialog()
35         Dim fileName As String ' name of file containing data
36
```

Fig. 17.11 `FrmReadSequentialAccessFile` class reads sequential-access files (part 1 of 4).

```vb
37         ' exit event handler if user clicked Cancel
38         If result = DialogResult.Cancel Then
39            Return
40         End If
41
42         fileName = fileChooser.FileName ' get specified file name
43         ClearTextBoxes()
44
45         ' show error if user specified invalid file
46         If (fileName = "" OrElse fileName = Nothing) Then
47            MessageBox.Show("Invalid File Name", "Error", _
48               MessageBoxButtons.OK, MessageBoxIcon.Error)
49         Else ' open file if user specified valid file
50
51            ' create FileStream to obtain read access to file
52            input = New FileStream(fileName, FileMode.Open, _
53               FileAccess.Read)
54
55            cmdNext.Enabled = True ' enable Next Record button
56
57         End If
58      End Sub ' cmdOpen_Click
59
60      ' invoked when user clicks Next button
61      Protected Sub cmdNext_Click(ByVal sender As Object, _
62         ByVal e As EventArgs) Handles cmdNext.Click
63
64         ' deserialize CRecord and store data in TextBoxes
65         Try
66
67            ' get next CRecord available in file
68            Dim record As CRecord = _
69               CType(reader.Deserialize(input), CRecord)
70
71            ' store CRecord values in temporary String array
72            Dim values As String() = New String() { _
73               record.Account.ToString(), _
74               record.FirstName.ToString(), _
75               record.LastName.ToString(), _
76               record.Balance.ToString()}
77
78            ' copy String-array values to TextBox values
79            SetTextBoxValues(values)
80
81         ' handle exception when no CRecords in file
82         Catch serializableException As SerializationException
83
84            input.Close() ' close FileStream if no CRecords in file
85
86            cmdOpen.Enabled = True ' enable Open Record button
87            cmdNext.Enabled = False ' disable Next Record button
88
```

Fig. 17.11 `FrmReadSequentialAccessFile` class reads sequential-access files (part 2 of 4).

Chapter 17 — Files and Streams

```
89            ClearTextBoxes()
90
91            ' notify user if no CRecords in file
92            MessageBox.Show("No more records in file", "", _
93               MessageBoxButtons.OK, MessageBoxIcon.Information)
94         End Try
95
96      End Sub ' cmdNext_Click
97
98   End Class ' FrmReadSequentialAccessFile
```

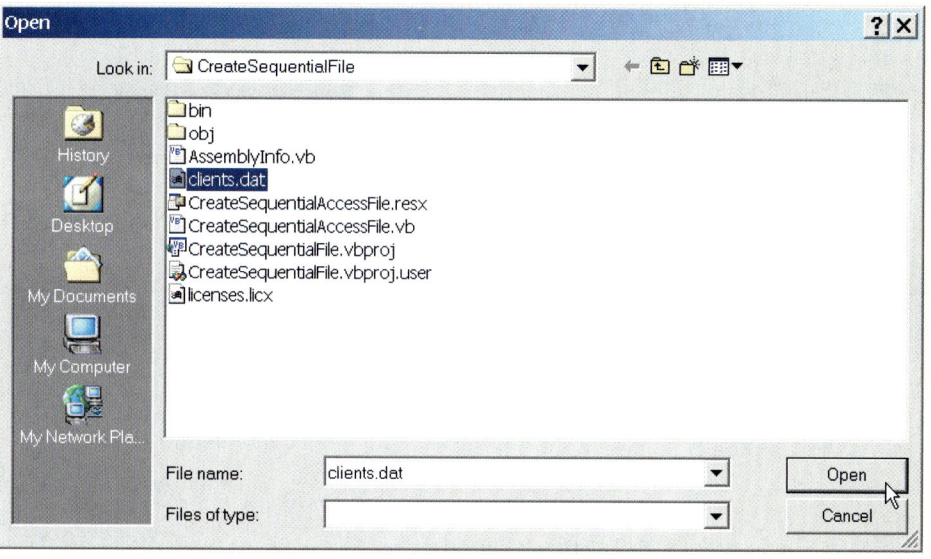

Fig. 17.11 `FrmReadSequentialAccessFile` class reads sequential-access files (part 3 of 4).

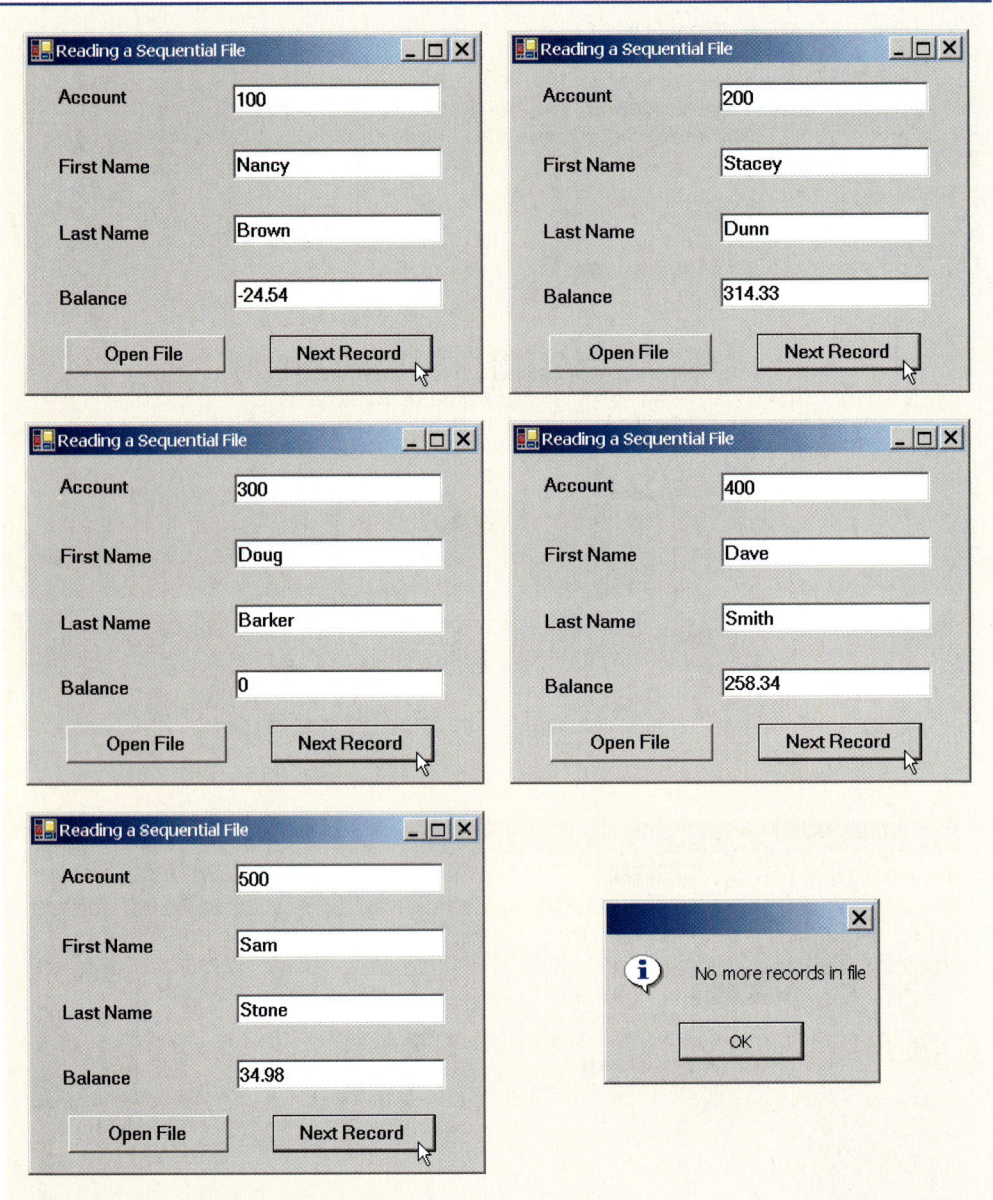

Fig. 17.11 `FrmReadSequentialAccessFile` class reads sequential-access files (part 4 of 4).

Testing and Debugging Tip 17.1

Open a file with the `FileAccess.Read` file-open mode if the contents of the file should not be modified. This prevents unintentional modification of the file's contents.

When the user clicks the **Next Record** button, the program calls method `cmdNext_Click` (lines 61–96), which reads the next record from the user-specified file.

(The user must click **Next Record** to view the first record after opening the file.) Lines 68–69 call method **Deserialize** of the **BinaryFormatter** object to read the next record. Method **Deserialize** reads the data and casts the result to a **CRecord**—this cast is necessary, because **Deserialize** returns a reference to an instance of class **Object** (not of **BinaryFormatter**). Lines 72–79 then display the **CRecord** values in the **TextBox**es. When method **Deserialize** attempts to deserialize a record that does not exist in the file (i.e., the program has displayed all file records), the method throws a **SerializationException**. The **Catch** block (defined in line 82) that handles this exception closes the **FileStream** object (line 84) and notifies the user that there are no more records (lines 92–93).

To retrieve data sequentially from a file, programs normally start from the beginning of the file, reading data consecutively until the desired data are found. It sometimes is necessary to process a file sequentially several times (from the beginning of the file) during the execution of a program. A **FileStream** object can reposition its *file-position pointer* (which contains the byte number of the next byte to be read from or written to the file) to any position in the file—we show this feature when we introduce random-access file-processing applications. When a **FileStream** object is opened, its file-position pointer is set to zero (i.e., the beginning of the file)

Performance Tip 17.3

It is time-consuming to close and reopen a file for the purpose of moving the file-position pointer to the file's beginning. Doing so frequently could slow program performance.

We now present a more substantial program that builds on the the concepts employed in Fig. 17.11. Class **FrmCreditInquiry** (Fig. 17.12) is a credit-inquiry program that enables a credit manager to display account information for those customers with credit balances (i.e., customers to whom the company owes money), zero balances (i.e., customers who do not owe the company money) and debit balances (i.e., customers who owe the company money for previously received goods and services). Note that line 18 declares a **RichTextBox** that will display the account information. **RichTextBox**es provide more functionality than do regular **TextBox**es—for example, **RichTextBox**es offers method **Find** for searching individual **String**s and method **LoadFile** for displaying file contents. Class **RichTextBox** does not inherit from class **TextBox**; rather, both classes inherit directly from **MustInherit** class *System.Windows.Forms.TextBoxBase*. We use a **RichTextBox** in this example, because, by default, a **RichTextBox** displays multiple lines of text, whereas a regular **TextBox** displays only one. Alternatively, we could have specified multiple lines of text for a **TextBox** object by setting its **Multiline** property to **True**.

```
1   ' Fig. 17.12: CreditInquiry.vb
2   ' Read a file sequentially and display contents based on account
3   ' type specified by user (credit, debit or zero balances).
4
5   ' Visual Basic namespaces
6   Imports System.IO
```

Fig. 17.12 FrmCreditInquiry class is a program that displays credit inquiries (part 1 of 7).

```vbnet
 7      Imports System.Runtime.Serialization.Formatters.Binary
 8      Imports System.Runtime.Serialization
 9      Imports System.Windows.Forms
10
11      ' Deitel namespaces
12      Imports BankLibrary
13
14      Public Class FrmCreditInquiry
15         Inherits Form
16
17         ' displays several lines of output
18         Friend WithEvents txtDisplay As RichTextBox
19
20         ' buttons to open file, read records and exit program
21         Friend WithEvents cmdOpen As Button
22         Friend WithEvents cmdCredit As Button
23         Friend WithEvents cmdDebit As Button
24         Friend WithEvents cmdZero As Button
25         Friend WithEvents cmdDone As Button
26
27         ' Visual Studio .NET generated code
28
29         ' stream through which serializable data is read from file
30         Private input As FileStream
31
32         ' object for deserializing CRecord in binary format
33         Dim reader As BinaryFormatter = New BinaryFormatter()
34
35         ' name of file that stores credit, debit and zero balances
36         Private fileName As String
37
38         ' invoked when user clicks Open File button
39         Protected Sub cmdOpen_Click(ByVal sender As Object, _
40            ByVal e As System.EventArgs) Handles cmdOpen.Click
41
42            ' create dialog box enabling user to open file
43            Dim fileChooser As OpenFileDialog = New OpenFileDialog()
44            Dim result As DialogResult = fileChooser.ShowDialog()
45
46            ' exit event handler if user clicked Cancel
47            If result = DialogResult.Cancel Then
48               Return
49            End If
50
51            fileName = fileChooser.FileName ' get file name from user
52
53            ' enable buttons allowing user to display balances
54            cmdCredit.Enabled = True
55            cmdDebit.Enabled = True
56            cmdZero.Enabled = True
57
```

Fig. 17.12 `FrmCreditInquiry` class is a program that displays credit inquiries (part 2 of 7).

```vbnet
58            ' show error if user specified invalid file
59            If (fileName = "" OrElse fileName = Nothing) Then
60               MessageBox.Show("Invalid File Name", "Error", _
61                  MessageBoxButtons.OK, MessageBoxIcon.Error)
62
63            ' else enable all GUI buttons, except for Open File button
64            Else
65               cmdOpen.Enabled = False
66               cmdCredit.Enabled = True
67               cmdDebit.Enabled = True
68               cmdZero.Enabled = True
69            End If
70
71      End Sub ' cmdOpen_Click
72
73         ' invoked when user clicks Credit Balances, Debit Balances
74         ' or Zero Balances button
75         Protected Sub cmdGet_Click(ByVal senderObject As Object, _
76            ByVal e As System.EventArgs) Handles cmdCredit.Click, _
77            cmdZero.Click, cmdDebit.Click
78
79            ' convert senderObject explicitly to object of type Button
80            Dim senderButton As Button = CType(senderObject, Button)
81
82            ' get text from clicked Button, which stores account type
83            Dim accountType As String = senderButton.Text
84
85            ' used to store each record read from file
86            Dim record As CRecord
87
88            ' read and display file information
89            Try
90
91               ' close file from previous operation
92               If (input Is Nothing) = False Then
93                  input.Close()
94               End If
95
96               ' create FileStream to obtain read access to file
97               input = New FileStream(fileName, FileMode.Open, _
98                  FileAccess.Read)
99
100              txtDisplay.Text = "The accounts are:" & vbCrLf
101
102              ' traverse file until end of file
103              While True
104
105                 ' get next CRecord available in file
106                 record = CType(reader.Deserialize(input), CRecord)
107
108                 ' store record's last field in balance
109                 Dim balance As Double = record.Balance
```

Fig. 17.12 `FrmCreditInquiry` class is a program that displays credit inquiries (part 3 of 7).

```vb
110
111            ' determine whether to display balance
112            If ShouldDisplay(balance, accountType) = True Then
113
114               ' display record
115               Dim output As String = record.Account & vbTab & _
116                  record.FirstName & vbTab & record.LastName & _
117                  Space(6) & vbTab
118
119               ' display balance with correct monetary format
120               output &= _
121                  String.Format("{0:F}", balance) & vbCrLf
122
123               txtDisplay.Text &= output ' copy output to screen
124            End If
125
126         End While
127
128      ' handle exception when file cannot be closed
129      Catch fileException As IOException
130         MessageBox.Show("Cannot Close File", "Error", _
131            MessageBoxButtons.OK, MessageBoxIcon.Error)
132
133      ' handle exception when no more records
134      Catch serializableException As SerializationException
135         input.Close() ' close FileStream if no CRecords in file
136
137      End Try
138
139   End Sub ' cmdGet_Click
140
141   ' determine whether to display given record
142   Private Function ShouldDisplay(ByVal balance As Double, _
143      ByVal accountType As String) As Boolean
144
145      If balance > 0 Then
146
147         ' display Credit Balances
148         If accountType = "Credit Balances" Then
149            Return True
150         End If
151
152      ElseIf balance < 0 Then
153
154         ' display Debit Balances
155         If accountType = "Debit Balances" Then
156            Return True
157         End If
158
```

Fig. 17.12 `FrmCreditInquiry` class is a program that displays credit inquiries (part 4 of 7).

```
159          Else ' balance = 0
160
161             ' display Zero Balances
162             If accountType = "Zero Balances" Then
163                Return True
164             End If
165
166          End If
167
168          Return False
169       End Function ' ShouldDisplay
170
171       ' invoked when user clicks Done button
172       Protected Sub cmdDone_Click(ByVal sender As Object, _
173          ByVal e As System.EventArgs) Handles cmdDone.Click
174
175          ' determine whether file exists
176          If input Is Nothing = False Then
177
178             ' close file
179             Try
180                input.Close()
181
182             ' notify user of error closing file
183             Catch fileException As IOException
184                MessageBox.Show("Cannot close file", "Error", _
185                   MessageBoxButtons.OK, MessageBoxIcon.Error)
186
187             End Try
188
189          End If
190
191          Application.Exit()
192       End Sub ' cmdDone_Click
193
194    End Class ' FrmCreditInquiry
```

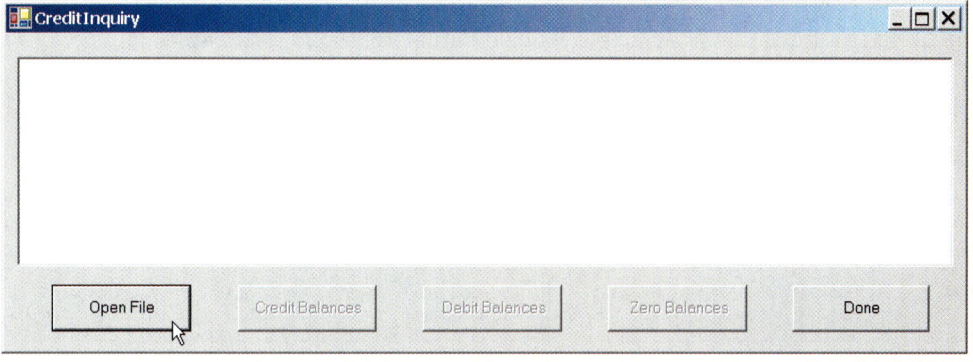

Fig. 17.12 `FrmCreditInquiry` class is a program that displays credit inquiries (part 5 of 7).

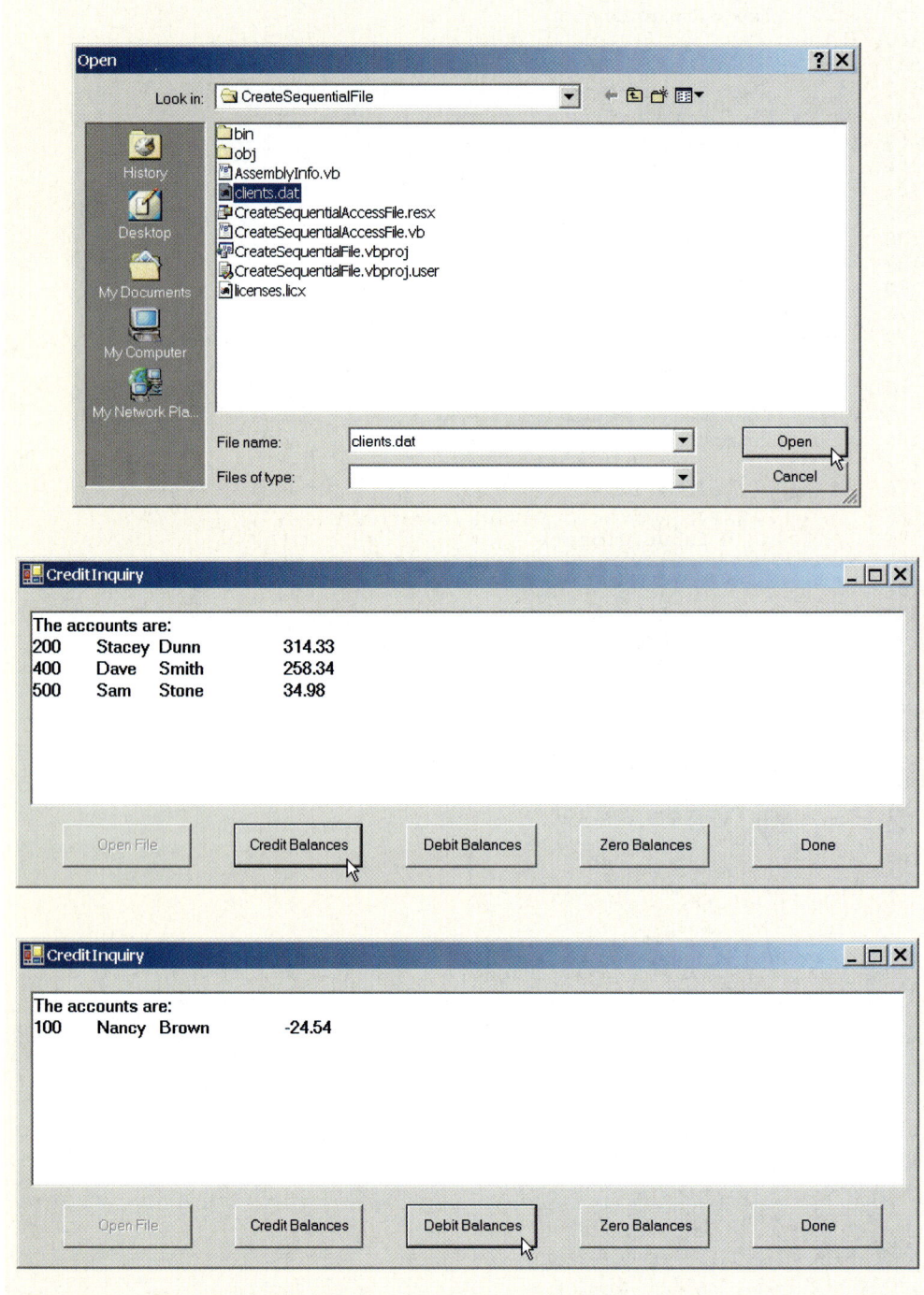

Fig. 17.12 `FrmCreditInquiry` class is a program that displays credit inquiries (part 6 of 7).

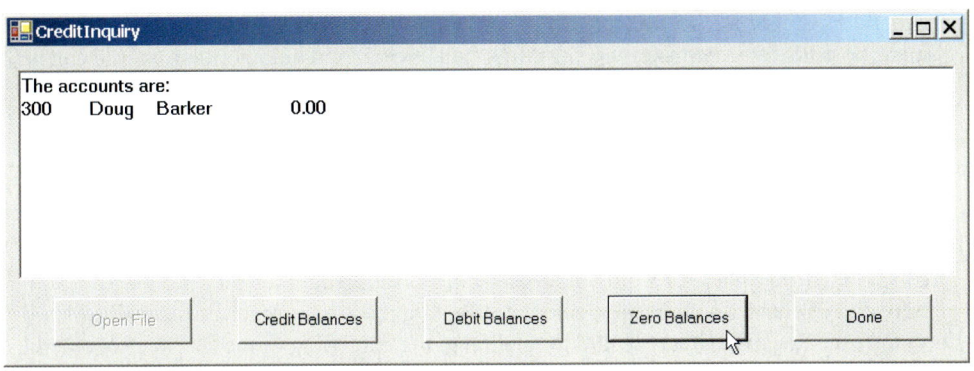

Fig. 17.12 `FrmCreditInquiry` class is a program that displays credit inquiries (part 7 of 7).

The program displays buttons that enable a credit manager to obtain credit information. The **Open File** button opens a file for gathering data. The **Credit Balances** button produces a list of accounts that have credit balances. The **Debit Balances** button produces a list of accounts that have debit balances. The **Zero Balances** button produces a list of accounts that have zero balances. The **Done** button exits the application.

When the user clicks the **Open File** button, the program calls method `cmdOpen_Click` (lines 39–71). Line 43 instantiates an object of class `OpenFileDialog`, and line 44 calls the object's `ShowDialog` method to display the **Open** dialog, in which the user inputs the name of the file to open.

When user clicks **Credit Balances**, **Debit Balances** or **Zero Balances**, the program invokes method `cmdGet_Click` (lines 75–139). Line 80 casts the `senderObject` parameter, which contains information on the object that sent the event, to a `Button` object. Line 83 extracts the `Button` object's text, which the program uses to determine which GUI `Button` the user clicked. Lines 97–98 create a `FileStream` object with read-only file access and assign it to reference `input`. Lines 103–126 define a `While` loop that uses `Private` method `ShouldDisplay` (lines 142–169) to determine whether to display each record in the file. The `While` loop obtains the each record by calling method `Deserialize` of the `FileStream` object repeatedly (line 106). When the file-position pointer reaches the end of file, method `Deserialize` throws a `SerializationException`, which the **Catch** statement in line 134 handles—line 135 calls the **Close** method of `FileStream` to close the file, and method `cmdGet_Click` returns.

17.7 Random-Access Files

So far, we have explained how to create sequential-access files and how to search through such files to locate particular information. However, sequential-access files are inappropriate for so-called *"instant-access" applications*, in which a particular record of information must be located immediately. Popular instant-access applications include airline-reservation systems, banking systems, point-of-sale systems, automated-teller machines and other kinds of *transaction-processing systems* that require rapid access to specific data. The bank at which an individual has an account might have hundreds of thousands or even millions of other customers, however, when that individual uses an automated teller machine, the appropriate account is checked for sufficient funds in seconds. This type of instant access is made possible by *random-access files*. Individual records of a random-access file can be accessed directly (and quickly) without searching through potentially large numbers of other records, as is necessary with sequential-access files. Random-access files sometimes are called *direct-access files*.

As we discussed earlier in this chapter, Visual Basic does not impose structure on files, so applications that use random-access files must create the random-access capability. There are a variety of techniques for creating random-access files. Perhaps the simplest involves requiring that all records in a file be of uniform fixed length. The use of fixed-length records enables a program to calculate (as a function of the record size and the record key) the exact location of any record in relation to the beginning of the file. We soon demonstrate how this facilitates immediate access to specific records, even in large files.

Figure 17.13 illustrates the view we will create of a random-access file composed of fixed-length records (each record in this figure is 100 bytes long). Students can consider a random-access file as analogous to a railroad train with many cars, some of which are empty and some of which contain contents.

Data can be inserted into a random-access file without destroying other data in the file. In addition, previously stored data can be updated or deleted without rewriting the entire file. In the following sections, we explain how to create a random-access file, write data to that file, read the data both sequentially and randomly, update the data and delete data that is no longer needed.

Figure 17.14 contains class **CRandomAccessRecord**, which is used in the random-access file-processing applications in this chapter. This class also belongs to the **Bank-Library** DLL—i.e., it is part of the project that contains classes **FrmBankUI** and **CRecord**. (When adding class **CRandomAccessRecord** to the project containing **FrmBankUI** and **CRecord**, remember to rebuild the project.)

Like class **CRecord** (Fig. 17.8), class **CRandomAccessRecord** contains **Private** data members (lines 18–21) for storing record information, two constructors for setting these members to default and parameter-specified values, and properties for accessing these members. However, class **CRandomAccessRecord** does not contain attribute **<Serializable>** before its class definition. We do not serialize this class, because Visual Basic does not provide a means to obtain an object's size at runtime. This means that we cannot guarantee a fixed-length record size.

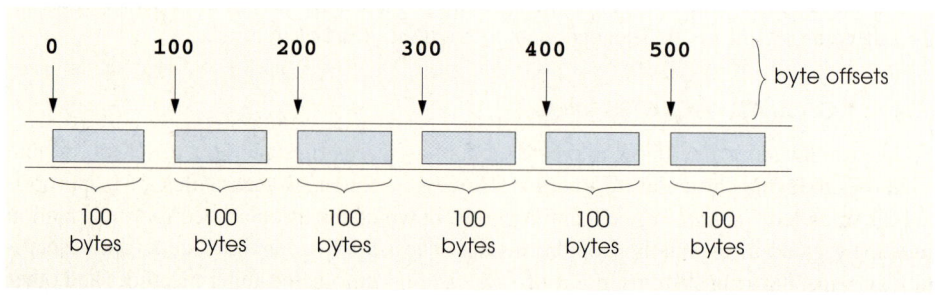

Fig. 17.13 Random-access file with fixed-length records.

```vb
1    ' Fig. 17.14: CRandomAccessRecord.vb
2    ' Data-record class for random-access applications.
3
4    Public Class CRandomAccessRecord
5
6       ' length of mFirstName and mLastName
7       Private Const CHAR_ARRAY_LENGTH As Integer = 15
8
9       Private Const SIZE_OF_CHAR As Integer = 2
10      Private Const SIZE_OF_INT32 As Integer = 4
11      Private Const SIZE_OF_DOUBLE As Integer = 8
12
13      ' length of record
14      Public Const SIZE As Integer = SIZE_OF_INT32 + _
15         2 * (SIZE_OF_CHAR * CHAR_ARRAY_LENGTH) + SIZE_OF_DOUBLE
16
17      ' record data
18      Private mAccount As Integer
19      Private mFirstName(CHAR_ARRAY_LENGTH) As Char
20      Private mLastName(CHAR_ARRAY_LENGTH) As Char
21      Private mBalance As Double
22
23      ' default constructor sets members to default values
24      Public Sub New()
25         Me.New(0, "", "", 0.0)
26      End Sub ' New
27
28      ' overloaded constructor sets members to parameter values
29      Public Sub New(ByVal accountValue As Integer, _
30         ByVal firstNameValue As String, _
31         ByVal lastNameValue As String, _
32         ByVal balanceValue As Double)
33
34         Account = accountValue
35         FirstName = firstNameValue
36         LastName = lastNameValue
37         Balance = balanceValue
38      End Sub ' New
39
40      ' property Account
41      Public Property Account() As Integer
42
43         Get
44            Return mAccount
45         End Get
46
47         Set(ByVal accountValue As Integer)
48            mAccount = accountValue
49         End Set
50
51      End Property ' Account
52
```

Fig. 17.14 **CRandomAccessRecord** class represents a record for random-access file-processing applications (part 1 of 3).

```
53         ' property FirstName
54         Public Property FirstName() As String
55
56            Get
57               Return mFirstName
58            End Get
59
60            Set(ByVal firstNameValue As String)
61
62               ' determine length of String parameter
63               Dim stringSize As Integer = firstNameValue.Length()
64
65               ' mFirstName String representation
66               Dim recordFirstNameString As String = firstNameValue
67
68               ' append spaces to String parameter if too short
69               If CHAR_ARRAY_LENGTH >= stringSize Then
70                  recordFirstNameString = firstNameValue & _
71                     Space(CHAR_ARRAY_LENGTH - stringSize)
72
73               ' remove characters from String parameter if too long
74               Else
75                  recordFirstNameString = _
76                     firstNameValue.Substring(0, CHAR_ARRAY_LENGTH)
77               End If
78
79               ' convert String parameter to Char array
80               mFirstName = recordFirstNameString.ToCharArray()
81
82            End Set
83
84         End Property ' FirstName
85
86         ' property LastName
87         Public Property LastName() As String
88
89            Get
90               Return mLastName
91            End Get
92
93            Set(ByVal lastNameValue As String)
94
95               ' determine length of String parameter
96               Dim stringSize As Integer = lastNameValue.Length()
97
98               ' mLastName String representation
99               Dim recordLastNameString As String = lastNameValue
100
101              ' append spaces to String parameter if too short
102              If CHAR_ARRAY_LENGTH >= stringSize Then
103                 recordLastNameString = lastNameValue & _
104                    Space(CHAR_ARRAY_LENGTH - stringSize)
```

Fig. 17.14 `CRandomAccessRecord` class represents a record for random-access file-processing applications (part 2 of 3).

```
105
106              ' remove characters from String parameter if too long
107              Else
108                 recordLastNameString = _
109                    lastNameValue.Substring(0, CHAR_ARRAY_LENGTH)
110              End If
111
112              ' convert String parameter to Char array
113              mLastName = recordLastNameString.ToCharArray()
114
115           End Set
116
117        End Property ' LastName
118
119        ' property Balance
120        Public Property Balance() As Double
121
122           Get
123              Return mBalance
124           End Get
125
126           Set(ByVal balanceValue As Double)
127              mBalance = balanceValue
128           End Set
129
130        End Property ' Balance
131
132     End Class ' CRandomAccessRecord
```

Fig. 17.14 `CRandomAccessRecord` class represents a record for random-access file-processing applications (part 3 of 3).

Instead of serializing the class, we fix the length of the **Private** data members and then write those data as a byte stream to the file. To fix this length, the **Set** accessors of properties **FirstName** (lines 60–82) and **LastName** (lines 93–115) ensure that members **mFirstName** and **mLastName** are **Char** arrays of exactly 15 elements. Each **Set** accessor receives as an argument a **String** representing the first name and last name, respectively. If the **String** parameter contains fewer than 15 **Char**s, the property's **Set** accessor copies the **String**'s values to the **Char** array and then populates the remainder with spaces. If the **String** parameter contains more than 15 **Char**s, the **Set** accessor stores only the first 15 **Char**s of the **String** parameter into the **Char** array.

Lines 14–15 declare **Const SIZE**, which specifies the record's length. Each record contains **mAccount** (4-byte **Integer**), **mFirstName** and **mLastName** (two 15-element **Char** arrays, where each **Char** occupies two bytes, resulting in a total of 60 bytes) and **mBalance** (8-byte **Double**). In this example, each record (i.e., the four **Private** data members that our programs will read to and write from files) occupies 72 bytes (4 bytes + 60 bytes + 8 bytes).

17.8 Creating a Random-Access File

Consider the following problem statement for a credit-processing application:

> Create a transaction-processing program capable of storing a maximum of 100 fixed-length records for a company that can have a maximum of 100 customers. Each record consists of an account number (that acts as the record key), a last name, a first name and a balance. The program can update an account, create an account and delete an account.

The next several sections introduce the techniques necessary to create this credit-processing program. We now discuss the program used to create the random-access file that the programs of Fig. 17.16 and Fig. 17.17 and the transaction-processing application use to manipulate data. Class **FrmCreateRandomAccessFile** (Fig. 17.15) creates a random-access file.

```vb
1   ' Fig. 17.15: CreateRandomAccessFile.vb
2   ' Creating a random file.
3
4   ' Visual Basic namespaces
5   Imports System.IO
6   Imports System.Windows.Forms
7
8   ' Deitel namespaces
9   Imports BankLibrary
10
11  Public Class CCreateRandomAccessFile
12
13     ' number of records to write to disk
14     Private Const NUMBER_OF_RECORDS As Integer = 100
15
16     ' start application
17     Shared Sub Main()
18
19        ' create random file, then save to disk
20        Dim file As CCreateRandomAccessFile = _
21           New CCreateRandomAccessFile()
22
23        file.SaveFile()
24     End Sub ' Main
25
26     ' write records to disk
27     Private Sub SaveFile()
28
29        ' record for writing to disk
30        Dim blankRecord As CRandomAccessRecord = _
31           New CRandomAccessRecord()
32
33        ' stream through which serializable data is written to file
34        Dim fileOutput As FileStream
35
36        ' stream for writing bytes to file
37        Dim binaryOutput As BinaryWriter
```

Fig. 17.15 **FrmCreateRandomAccessFile** class creates files for random-access file-processing applications (part 1 of 3).

```vbnet
38
39         ' create dialog box enabling user to save file
40         Dim fileChooser As SaveFileDialog = New SaveFileDialog()
41         Dim result As DialogResult = fileChooser.ShowDialog
42
43         ' get file name from user
44         Dim fileName As String = fileChooser.FileName
45         Dim i As Integer
46
47         ' exit event handler if user clicked Cancel
48         If result = DialogResult.Cancel Then
49            Return
50         End If
51
52         ' show error if user specified invalid file
53         If (fileName = "" OrElse fileName = Nothing) Then
54            MessageBox.Show("Invalid File Name", "Error", _
55               MessageBoxButtons.OK, MessageBoxIcon.Error)
56         Else
57
58            ' write records to file
59            Try
60
61               ' create FileStream to hold records
62               fileOutput = New FileStream(fileName, _
63                  FileMode.Create, FileAccess.Write)
64
65               ' set length of file
66               fileOutput.SetLength( _
67                  CRandomAccessRecord.SIZE * NUMBER_OF_RECORDS)
68
69               ' create object for writing bytes to file
70               binaryOutput = New BinaryWriter(fileOutput)
71
72               ' write empty records to file
73               For i = 0 To NUMBER_OF_RECORDS - 1
74
75                  ' set file-position pointer in file
76                  fileOutput.Position = i * CRandomAccessRecord.SIZE
77
78                  ' write blank record to file
79                  binaryOutput.Write(blankRecord.Account)
80                  binaryOutput.Write(blankRecord.FirstName)
81                  binaryOutput.Write(blankRecord.LastName)
82                  binaryOutput.Write(blankRecord.Balance)
83               Next
84
85               ' notify user of success
86               MessageBox.Show("File Created", "Success", _
87                  MessageBoxButtons.OK, MessageBoxIcon.Information)
88
```

Fig. 17.15 `FrmCreateRandomAccessFile` class creates files for random-access file-processing applications (part 2 of 3).

```vbnet
89              ' show error if error occurs during writing
90              Catch fileException As IOException
91                 MessageBox.Show("Cannot write to file", "Error", _
92                    MessageBoxButtons.OK, MessageBoxIcon.Error)
93
94              End Try
95
96           End If
97
98           ' close FileStream
99           If (fileOutput Is Nothing) <> False Then
100             fileOutput.Close()
101          End If
102
103          ' close BinaryWriter
104          If (binaryOutput Is Nothing) <> False Then
105             binaryOutput.Close()
106          End If
107
108       End Sub ' SaveFile
109
110    End Class ' FrmCreateRandomAccessFile
```

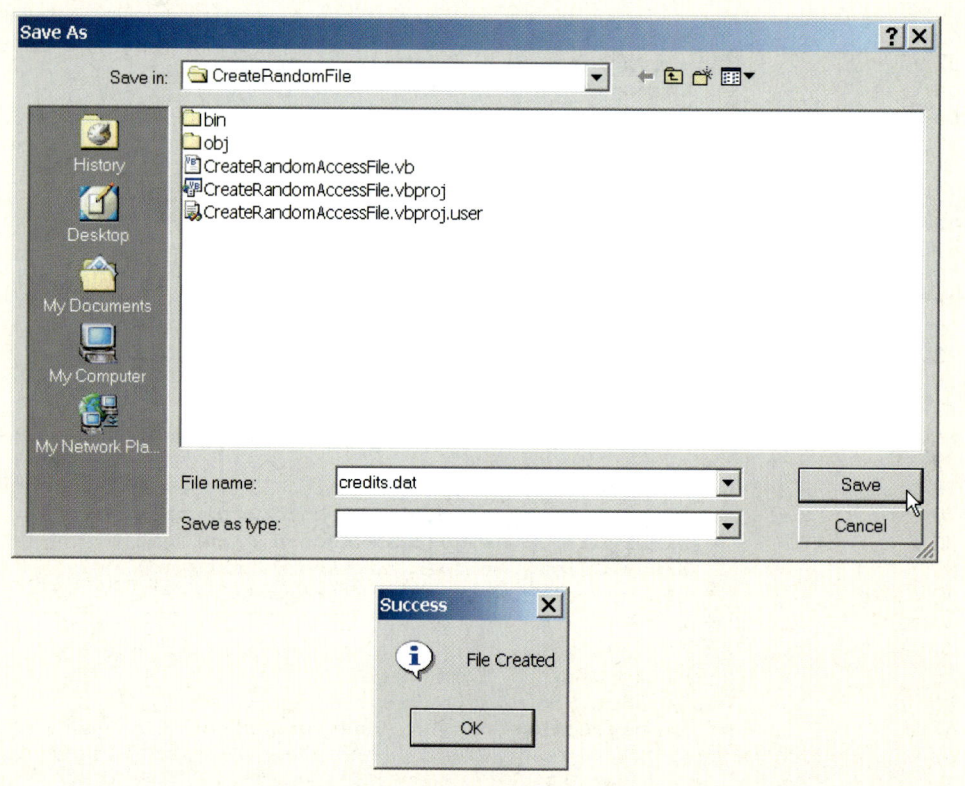

Fig. 17.15 `FrmCreateRandomAccessFile` class creates files for random-access file-processing applications (part 3 of 3).

Method **Main** (lines 17–24) starts the application, which creates a random-access file by calling user-defined method **SaveFile** (lines 27–108). Method **SaveFile** populates a file with 100 copies of the default (i.e., empty) values for **Private** data members **mAccount**, **mFirstName**, **mLastName** and **mBalance** of class **CRandomAccessRecord**. Lines 40–41 create and display the **SaveFileDialog**, which enables a user to specify the file to which the program writes data. Using this file, lines 62–63 instantiate the **FileStream**—note that lines 63 passes **Const FileMode.Create**, which either creates the specified file, if the file does not exist, or overwrites the specified file if it does exist. Lines 66–67 sets the **FileStream**'s length, which is equal to the size of an individual **CRandomAccessRecord** (obtained through constant **CRandomAccessRecord.SIZE**) multiplied by the number of records we want to copy (obtained through constant **NUMBER_OF_RECORDS** in line 14, which we set to value **100**).

We now require a means to write bytes to a file. Class ***BinaryWriter*** of namespace **System.IO** provides methods for writing bytes to streams, rather than files. The **BinaryWriter** constructor receives as an argument a reference to an instance of class **System.IO.Stream** through which the **BinaryWriter** can write bytes. Because class **FileStream** provides methods for writing streams to files and inherits from class **Stream**, we can pass the **FileStream** object as an argument to the **BinaryWriter** constructor (line 70). Now, we can use the **BinaryWriter** to write bytes directly to the file.

Lines 73–83 define the **For** loop that populates the file with 100 copies of the empty record values (i.e., default values for **Private** data members of class **CRandomAccessRecord**). Line 76 changes the file-position pointer to specify the location in the file in which to write the next empty record. Now that we are working with a random-access file, we must set the file-pointer explicitly using the **Set** accessor of the **FileStream** object's **Position** property. This method receives as an argument a **Long** value describing where to position the pointer relative to the beginning of the file—in this example, we set the pointer so that it advances a number of bytes that is equal to the record size (obtained by **CRandomAccessRecord.SIZE**). Lines 79–82 call method **Write** of the **BinaryWriter** object to write the data. Method **Write** is an overloaded method that receives as an argument any primitive data type and then writes that type to a stream of bytes. After the **For** loop exits, lines 99–106 close the **FileStream** and **BinaryWriter** objects.

17.9 Writing Data Randomly to a Random-Access File

Now that we have created a random-access file, we use class **FrmWriteRandomAccessFile** (Fig. 17.16) to write data to that file. When a user clicks the **Open File** button, the program invokes method **cmdOpen_Click** (lines 30–75), which displays the **OpenFileDialog** for specifying the file to serialize data (lines 34–35), and then uses the specified file to create **FileStream** object with write-only access (lines 57–58). Line 61 uses the **FileStream** reference to instantiate an object of class **BinaryWriter**, enabling the program to write bytes to files. We used the same approach with class **FrmCreateRandomAccessFile** (Fig. 17.15).

The user enters values in the **TextBox**es for the account number, first name, last name and balance. When the user clicks the **Enter** button, the program invokes method **cmdEnter_Click** (lines 78–131), which writes the data in the **TextBox**es to the file. Line 85 calls method **GetTextBoxValues** (provided by base class **FrmBankUI**) to retrieve the data. Lines 98–99 determine whether the **Account Number TextBox** holds valid information (i.e., the account number is in the **1–100** range).

```vb
1   ' Fig 17.16: WriteRandomAccessFile.vb
2   ' Write data to a random-access file.
3
4   ' Visual Basic namespaces
5   Imports System.IO
6   Imports System.Windows.Forms
7
8   ' Deitel namespaces
9   Imports BankLibrary
10
11  Public Class FrmWriteRandomAccessFile
12      Inherits FrmBankUI
13
14      ' buttons for opening file and entering data
15      Friend WithEvents cmdOpen As Button
16      Friend WithEvents cmdEnter As Button
17
18      ' Visual Studio .NET generated code
19
20      ' number of CRandomAccessRecords to write to disk
21      Private Const NUMBER_OF_RECORDS As Integer = 100
22
23      ' stream through which data is written to file
24      Private fileOutput As FileStream
25
26      ' stream for writing bytes to file
27      Private binaryOutput As BinaryWriter
28
29      ' invoked when user clicks Open button
30      Public Sub cmdOpen_Click(ByVal sender As System.Object, _
31          ByVal e As System.EventArgs) Handles cmdOpen.Click
32
33          ' create dialog box enabling user to open file
34          Dim fileChooser As OpenFileDialog = New OpenFileDialog()
35          Dim result As DialogResult = fileChooser.ShowDialog()
36
37          ' get file name from user
38          Dim fileName As String = fileChooser.FileName
39
40          ' exit event handler if user clicked Cancel
41          If result = DialogResult.Cancel Then
42              Return
43          End If
44
```

Fig. 17.16 FrmWriteRandomAccessFile class writes records to random-access files (part 1 of 5).

```vb
45         ' show error if user specified invalid file
46         If (fileName = "" OrElse fileName = Nothing) Then
47            MessageBox.Show("Invalid File Name", "Error", _
48               MessageBoxButtons.OK, MessageBoxIcon.Error)
49
50         ' open file if user specified valid file
51         Else
52
53            ' open file if file already exists
54            Try
55
56               ' create FileStream to hold records
57               fileOutput = New FileStream(fileName, FileMode.Open, _
58                  FileAccess.Write)
59
60               ' create object for writing bytes to file
61               binaryOutput = New BinaryWriter(fileOutput)
62
63               cmdOpen.Enabled = False ' disable Open button
64               cmdEnter.Enabled = True ' enable Enter button
65
66            ' notify user if file does not exist
67            Catch fileException As IOException
68               MessageBox.Show("File Does Not Exits", "Error", _
69                  MessageBoxButtons.OK, MessageBoxIcon.Error)
70
71            End Try
72
73         End If
74
75      End Sub ' cmdOpen_Click
76
77      ' invoked when user clicks Enter button
78      Private Sub cmdEnter_Click(ByVal sender As System.Object, _
79         ByVal e As System.EventArgs) Handles cmdEnter.Click
80
81         ' account-number value from TextBox
82         Dim accountNumber As Integer
83
84         ' TextBox-values String array
85         Dim values As String() = GetTextBoxValues()
86
87         ' determine whether TextBox account field is empty
88         If (values(TextBoxIndices.ACCOUNT) <> "") Then
89
90            ' write record to file at appropriate position
91            Try
92
93               ' get account-number value from TextBox
94               accountNumber = _
95                  Convert.ToInt32(values(TextBoxIndices.ACCOUNT))
96
```

Fig. 17.16 `FrmWriteRandomAccessFile` class writes records to random-access files (part 2 of 5).

```vbnet
97              ' determine whether accountNumber is valid
98              If (accountNumber > 0 AndAlso _
99                 accountNumber <= NUMBER_OF_RECORDS) Then
100
101                ' move file-position pointer
102                fileOutput.Seek((accountNumber - 1) * _
103                   CRandomAccessRecord.SIZE, SeekOrigin.Begin)
104
105                ' write data to file
106                binaryOutput.Write(accountNumber)
107                binaryOutput.Write(values(TextBoxIndices.FIRST))
108                binaryOutput.Write(values(TextBoxIndices.LAST))
109                binaryOutput.Write( Convert.ToDouble( _
110                   values(TextBoxIndices.BALANCE)))
111
112             ' notify user if invalid account number
113             Else
114                MessageBox.Show("Invalid Account Number", _
115                   "Error", MessageBoxButtons.OK, _
116                   MessageBoxIcon.Error)
117             End If
118
119             ClearTextBoxes()
120
121          ' notify user if error occurs when formatting numbers
122          Catch formattingException As FormatException
123             MessageBox.Show("Invalid Balance", "Error", _
124                MessageBoxButtons.OK, MessageBoxIcon.Error)
125
126          End Try
127
128       End If
129
130       ClearTextBoxes() ' clear TextBox values
131    End Sub ' cmdEnter_Click
132
133 End Class ' FrmWriteRandomAccessFile
```

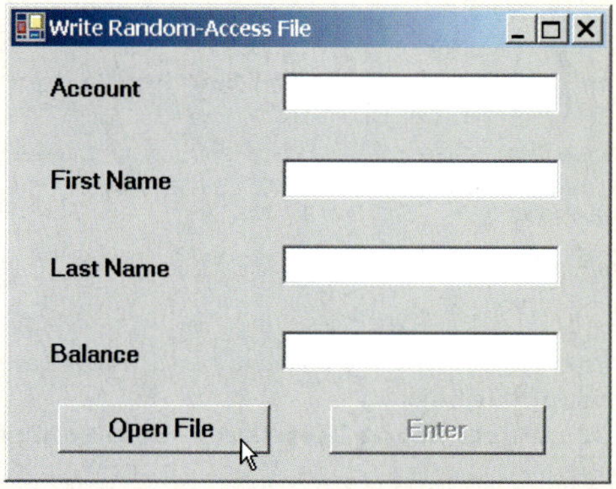

Fig. 17.16 FrmWriteRandomAccessFile class writes records to random-access files (part 3 of 5).

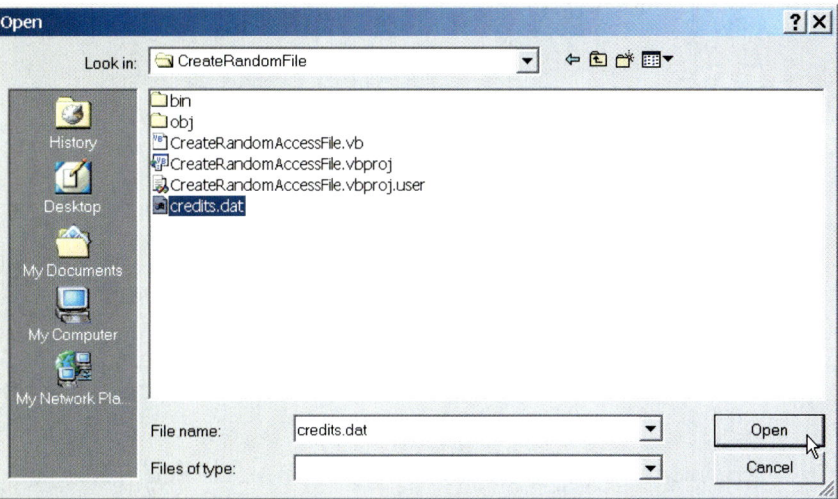

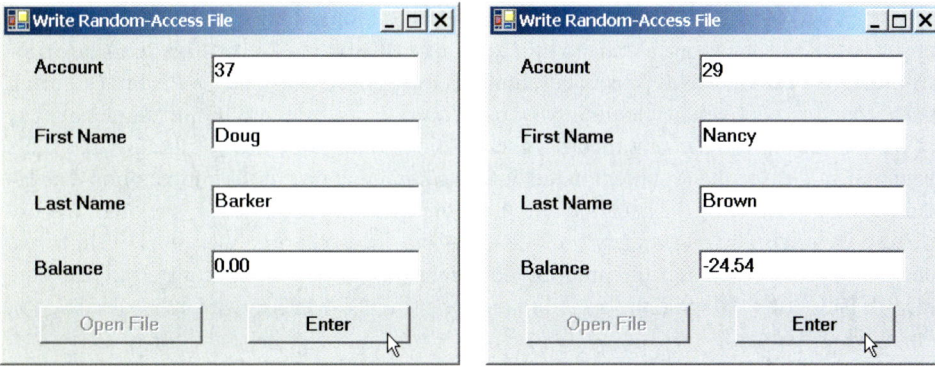

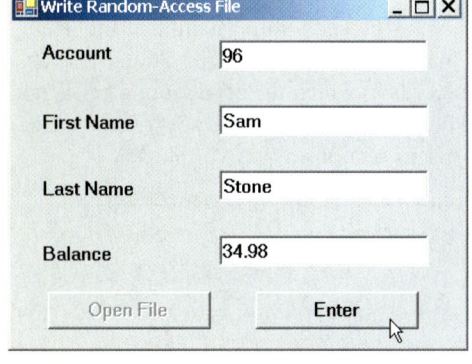
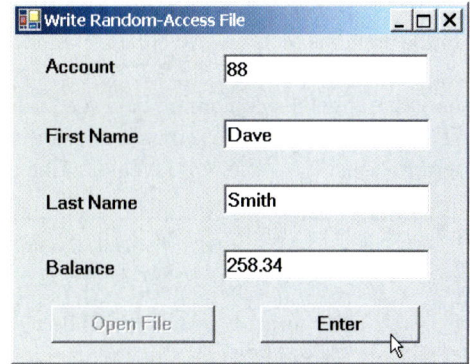

Fig. 17.16 `FrmWriteRandomAccessFile` class writes records to random-access files (part 4 of 5).

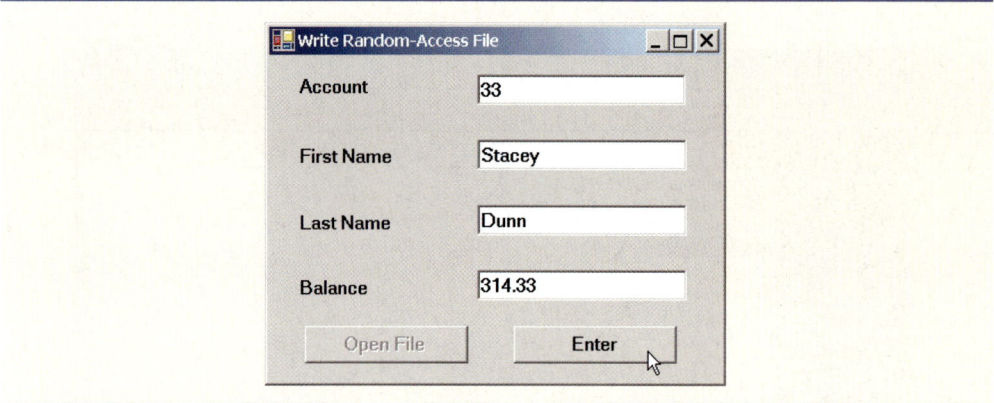

Fig. 17.16 `FrmWriteRandomAccessFile` class writes records to random-access files (part 5 of 5).

Class **FrmWriteRandomAccessFile** must determine the position in the **FileStream** in which to insert the data from the **TextBox**es. Lines 102–103 use method **Seek** of the **FileStream** object to locate an exact location in the file. In this case, method **Seek** sets the position of the file-position pointer for the **FileStream** object to the byte location calculated by **(accountNumber - 1) * CRandomAccessRecord.SIZE**. Because the account numbers range from **1** to **100**, we subtract **1** from the account number when calculating the byte location of the record. For example, our use of method **Seek** sets the first record's file-position pointer to byte 0 of the file (the file's beginning). The second argument to method **Seek** is a member of the enumeration *SeekOrigin* and specifies the location in which the method should begin seeking. We use **Const SeekOrigin.Begin**, because we want the method to seek in relation to the beginning of the file. After the program determines the file location at which to place the record, lines 106–110 write the record to the file using the **BinaryWriter** (discussed in the previous section).

17.10 Reading Data Sequentially from a Random-Access File

In the previous sections, we created a random-access file and wrote data to that file. Here, we develop a program (Fig. 17.17) that opens the file, reads records from it and displays only those records containing data (i.e., those records in which the account number is not zero). This program also provides an additional benefit. Students should see if they can determine what it is—we will reveal it at the end of this section.

```
1   ' Fig 17.17: ReadRandomAccessFile.vb
2   ' Reads and displays random-access file contents.
3
4   ' Visual Basic namespaces
5   Imports System.IO
6   Imports System.Windows.Forms
```

Fig. 17.17 `FrmReadRandomAccessFile` class reads records from random-access files sequentially (part 1 of 5).

```vbnet
 7
 8    ' Deitel namespaces
 9    Imports BankLibrary
10
11    Public Class FrmReadRandomAccessFile
12       Inherits FrmBankUI
13
14       ' buttons for opening file and reading records
15       Friend WithEvents cmdOpen As Button
16       Friend WithEvents cmdNext As Button
17
18       ' Visual Studio .NET generated code
19
20       ' stream through which data is read from file
21       Private fileInput As FileStream
22
23       ' stream for reading bytes from file
24       Private binaryInput As BinaryReader
25
26       ' index of current record to be displayed
27       Private currentRecordIndex As Integer
28
29       ' invoked when user clicks Open button
30       Protected Sub cmdOpen_Click(ByVal sender As System.Object, _
31          ByVal e As System.EventArgs) Handles cmdOpen.Click
32
33          ' create dialog box enabling user to open file
34          Dim fileChooser As OpenFileDialog = New OpenFileDialog()
35          Dim result As DialogResult = fileChooser.ShowDialog()
36
37          ' get file name from user
38          Dim fileName As String = fileChooser.FileName
39
40          ' exit event handler if user clicked Cancel
41          If result = DialogResult.Cancel Then
42             Return
43          End If
44
45          ' show error if user specified invalid file
46          If (fileName = "" OrElse fileName = Nothing) Then
47             MessageBox.Show("Invalid File Name", "Error", _
48                MessageBoxButtons.OK, MessageBoxIcon.Error)
49
50          ' open file if user specified valid file
51          Else
52
53             ' create FileStream to obtain read access to file
54             fileInput = New FileStream(fileName, FileMode.Open, _
55                FileAccess.Read)
56
57             ' use FileStream for BinaryWriter to read bytes from file
58             binaryInput = New BinaryReader(fileInput)
```

Fig. 17.17 `FrmReadRandomAccessFile` class reads records from random-access files sequentially (part 2 of 5).

```
59
60              cmdOpen.Enabled = False  ' disable Open button
61              cmdNext.Enabled = True   ' enable Next button
62
63              currentRecordIndex = 0
64              ClearTextBoxes()
65          End If
66
67      End Sub ' cmdOpen_Click
68
69      ' invoked when user clicks Next button
70      Protected Sub cmdNext_Click(ByVal sender As System.Object, _
71          ByVal e As System.EventArgs) Handles cmdNext.Click
72
73          ' record to store file data
74          Dim record As CRandomAccessRecord = _
75              New CRandomAccessRecord()
76
77          ' read record and store data in TextBoxes
78          Try
79              Dim values As String()  ' for storing TextBox values
80
81              ' get next record available in file
82              While (record.Account = 0)
83
84                  ' set file-position pointer to next record in file
85                  fileInput.Seek( _
86                      currentRecordIndex * CRandomAccessRecord.SIZE, 0)
87
88                  currentRecordIndex += 1
89
90                  ' read data from record
91                  record.Account = binaryInput.ReadInt32()
92                  record.FirstName = binaryInput.ReadString()
93                  record.LastName = binaryInput.ReadString()
94                  record.Balance = binaryInput.ReadDouble()
95              End While
96
97              ' store record values in temporary String array
98              values = New String() { _
99                  record.Account.ToString(), _
100                 record.FirstName.ToString(), _
101                 record.LastName.ToString(), _
102                 record.Balance.ToString()}
103
104             ' copy String-array values to TextBox values
105             SetTextBoxValues(values)
106
107         ' handle exception when no records in file
108         Catch fileException As IOException
109
```

Fig. 17.17 `FrmReadRandomAccessFile` class reads records from random-access files sequentially (part 3 of 5).

```
110            ' close streams if no records in file
111            fileInput.Close()
112            binaryInput.Close()
113
114            cmdOpen.Enabled = True   ' enable Open button
115            cmdNext.Enabled = False  ' disable Next button
116            ClearTextBoxes()
117
118            ' notify user if no records in file
119            MessageBox.Show("No more records in file", "", _
120               MessageBoxButtons.OK, MessageBoxIcon.Information)
121
122         End Try
123
124      End Sub ' cmdNext_Click
125
126   End Class ' FrmReadRandomAccessFile
```

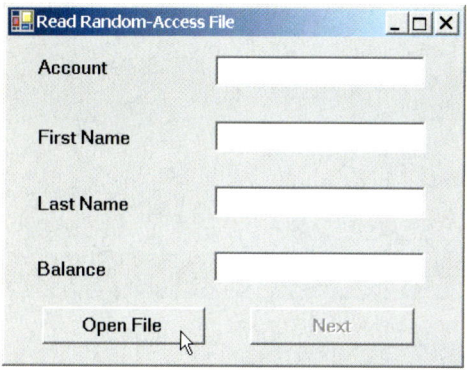

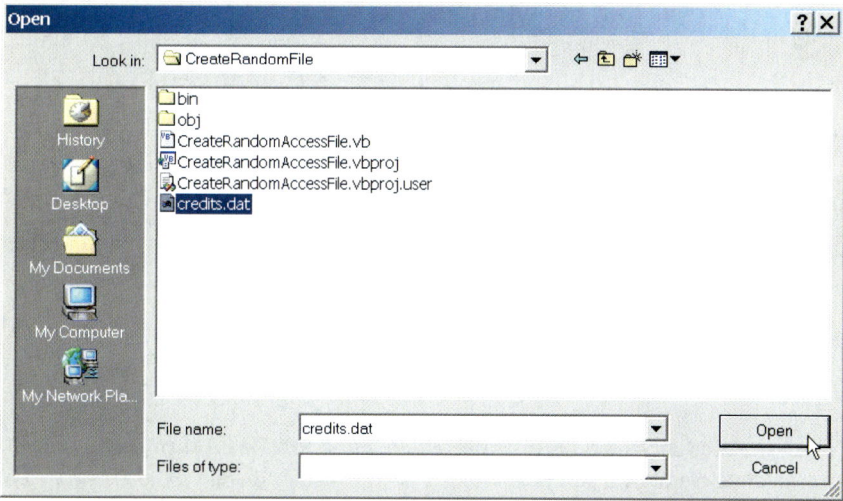

Fig. 17.17 `FrmReadRandomAccessFile` class reads records from random-access files sequentially (part 4 of 5).

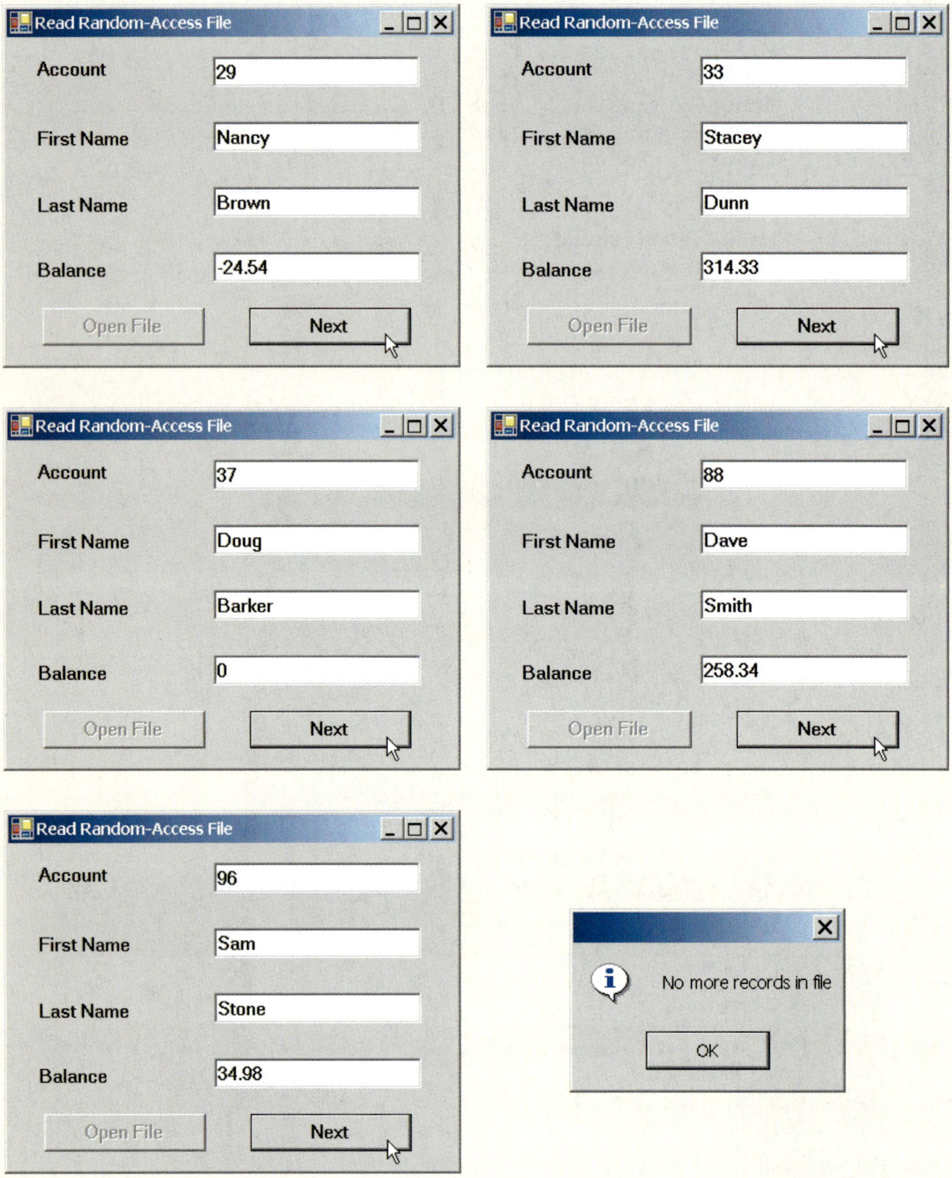

Fig. 17.17 `FrmReadRandomAccessFile` class reads records from random-access files sequentially (part 5 of 5).

When the user clicks the **Open File** button, class `FrmReadRandomAccessFile` invokes method `cmdOpen_Click` (lines 30–67), which displays the `OpenFileDialog` for specifying the file from which to read data. Lines 54–55 instantiate a `FileStream` object that opens a file with read-only access. Line 58 creates an instance of class `BinaryReader`, which reads bytes from a stream. We pass the `FileStream` object as an argument to the **BinaryReader** constructor, thus enabling the **BinaryReader** to read bytes from the file created by the **BinaryWriter** in Fig. 17.9.

When the user clicks the **Next** button, the program calls method **cmdNext_Click** (lines 70–124), which reads the next record in the file. Lines 74–75 instantiate a **CRandomAccessRecord** for storing the record data from the file. Lines 82–95 define a **While** loop that reads from the file until it reaches a record that has a non-zero account number (**0** is the initial value for the account). Lines 85–86 call method **Seek** of the **FileStream** object, which moves the file-position pointer to the appropriate place in the file where the record must be read. To accomplish this, method **Seek** uses **Integer currentRecordIndex**, which stores the number of records that have been read. Lines 91–94 use the **BinaryReader** object to store the file data in the **CRandomAccessRecord** object. Recall that class **BinaryWriter** provides overloaded **Write** methods for writing data. However, class **BinaryReader** does not provide overloaded **Read** methods to read data. This means that we must use method **ReadInt32** to read an **Integer**, method **ReadString** to read a **String** and method **ReadDouble** to read a **Double**. Note that the order of these method invocations must correspond to the order in which the **BinaryWriter** object wrote each data type. When the **BinaryReader** reads a valid account number (i.e., a non-zero value), the loop terminates, and lines 98–105 display the record values in the **TextBox**es. When the program has displayed all records, method **Seek** throws an **IOException** (because method **Seek** tries to position the file-position pointer to a location that is beyond the end-of-file marker). The **Catch** statement (defined in line 108) handles this exception by closing the **FileStream** and **BinaryReader** objects (lines 111–112) and notifying the user that no more records exist (lines 119–120).

What about that additional benefit that we promised? If students examine the GUI as the program executes, they will notice that the program displays the records in ascending order by account number! This is a simple consequence of using our direct-access techniques to store these records in the file. Sorting with direct-access techniques is much faster than sorting with the bubble sort presented in Chapter 7, Arrays. We achieve this speed by making the file large enough to hold every possible record that a user might create. Of course, this means that the file could be sparsely occupied most of the time, resulting in a waste of storage. Here is yet another example of the space/time trade-off: By using large amounts of space, we are able to develop a faster sorting algorithm.

17.11 Case Study: A Transaction-Processing Program

We now develop a substantial transaction-processing program (Fig. 17.18–Fig. 17.23) using a random- access file to achieve "instant-access" processing. The program maintains a bank's account information. Users of this program can add new accounts, update existing accounts and delete accounts that are no longer needed. First, we discuss the transaction-processing behavior (i.e., the class enables the addition, updating and removal of accounts). We then discuss the GUI, which contains windows that display the account information and enable the user to invoke the application's transaction-processing behavior.

Transaction-Processing Behavior
In this case study, we create class **CTransaction** (Fig. 17.18), which acts as a *proxy* to handle all transaction processing. The objects in this application do not provide the transaction-processing behavior—rather, these objects use an instance of **CTransaction** to pro-

vide this functionality. The use of a proxy enables us to encapsulate transaction-processing behavior in only one class, enabling various classes in our application to reuse it. Furthermore, if we decide to modify this behavior, we modify only the proxy (i.e., class **CTransaction**), rather than having to modify the behavior of each class that uses the proxy.

```vbnet
1    ' Fig. 17.18: CTransaction.vb
2    ' Handles record transactions.
3
4    ' Visual Basic namespaces
5    Imports System.IO
6    Imports System.Windows.Forms
7
8    ' Deitel namespaces
9    Imports BankLibrary
10
11   Public Class CTransaction
12
13      ' number of records to write to disk
14      Private Const NUMBER_OF_RECORDS As Integer = 100
15
16      ' stream through which data moves to and from file
17      Private file As FileStream
18
19      ' stream for reading bytes from file
20      Private binaryInput As BinaryReader
21
22      ' stream for writing bytes to file
23      Private binaryOutput As BinaryWriter
24
25      ' create/open file containing empty records
26      Public Sub OpenFile(ByVal fileName As String)
27
28         ' write empty records to file
29         Try
30
31            ' create FileStream from new file or existing file
32            file = New FileStream(fileName, FileMode.OpenOrCreate)
33
34            ' use FileStream for BinaryWriter to read bytes from file
35            binaryInput = New BinaryReader(file)
36
37            ' use FileStream for BinaryWriter to write bytes to file
38            binaryOutput = New BinaryWriter(file)
39
40            ' determine whether file has just been created
41            If file.Length = 0 Then
42
43               ' record to be written to file
44               Dim blankRecord As CRandomAccessRecord = _
45                  New CRandomAccessRecord()
46
```

Fig. 17.18 **CTransaction** class handles record transactions for the transaction-processor case study (part 1 of 4).

```vbnet
47              Dim i As Integer ' counter
48
49              ' new record can hold NUMBER_OF_RECORDS records
50              file.SetLength( _
51                 CRandomAccessRecord.SIZE * NUMBER_OF_RECORDS)
52
53              ' write blank records to file
54              For i = 0 To NUMBER_OF_RECORDS - 1
55
56                 ' move file-position pointer to next position
57                 file.Position = i * CRandomAccessRecord.SIZE
58
59                 ' write blank record to file
60                 binaryOutput.Write(blankRecord.Account)
61                 binaryOutput.Write(blankRecord.FirstName)
62                 binaryOutput.Write(blankRecord.LastName)
63                 binaryOutput.Write(blankRecord.Balance)
64              Next
65
66           End If
67
68        ' notify user of error during writing of blank records
69        Catch fileException As IOException
70           MessageBox.Show("Cannot create file", "Error", _
71              MessageBoxButtons.OK, MessageBoxIcon.Error)
72
73        End Try
74
75     End Sub ' OpenFile
76
77     ' retrieve record depending on whether account is valid
78     Public Function GetRecord(ByVal accountValue As String) _
79        As CRandomAccessRecord
80
81        ' store file data associated with account in record
82        Try
83
84           ' record to store file data
85           Dim record As CRandomAccessRecord = _
86              New CRandomAccessRecord()
87
88           ' get value from TextBox's account field
89           Dim accountNumber As Integer = _
90              Convert.ToInt32(accountValue)
91
92           ' if account is invalid, do not read data
93           If (accountNumber < 1 OrElse _
94              accountNumber > NUMBER_OF_RECORDS) Then
95
96              ' set record's account field with account number
97              record.Account = accountNumber
98
```

Fig. 17.18 `CTransaction` class handles record transactions for the transaction-processor case study (part 2 of 4).

```vbnet
99            ' get data from file if account is valid
100           Else
101
102              ' locate position in file where record exists
103              file.Seek( _
104                 (accountNumber - 1) * CRandomAccessRecord.SIZE, 0)
105
106              ' read data from record
107              record.Account = binaryInput.ReadInt32()
108              record.FirstName = binaryInput.ReadString()
109              record.LastName = binaryInput.ReadString()
110              record.Balance = binaryInput.ReadDouble()
111           End If
112
113           Return record
114
115        ' notify user of error during reading
116        Catch fileException As IOException
117           MessageBox.Show("Cannot read file", "Error", _
118              MessageBoxButtons.OK, MessageBoxIcon.Error)
119
120        ' notify user of error in parameter mismatch
121        Catch formattingException As FormatException
122           MessageBox.Show("Invalid Account", "Error", _
123              MessageBoxButtons.OK, MessageBoxIcon.Error)
124
125        End Try
126
127        Return Nothing
128     End Function ' GetRecord
129
130     ' add record to file at position determined by accountNumber
131     Public Function AddRecord(ByVal record As CRandomAccessRecord, _
132        ByVal accountNumber As Integer) As Boolean
133
134        ' write record to file
135        Try
136
137           ' move file-position pointer to appropriate position
138           file.Seek( _
139              (accountNumber - 1) * CRandomAccessRecord.SIZE, 0)
140
141           ' write data to file
142           binaryOutput.Write(record.Account)
143           binaryOutput.Write(record.FirstName)
144           binaryOutput.Write(record.LastName)
145           binaryOutput.Write(record.Balance)
146
147        ' notify user if error occurs during writing
148        Catch fileException As IOException
149           MessageBox.Show("Error Writing To File", "Error", _
150              MessageBoxButtons.OK, MessageBoxIcon.Error)
```

Fig. 17.18 **CTransaction** class handles record transactions for the transaction-processor case study (part 3 of 4).

```
151
152             Return False ' failure
153         End Try
154
155         Return True ' success
156     End Sub ' AddRecord
157
158 End Class ' CTransaction
```

Fig. 17.18 CTransaction class handles record transactions for the transaction-processor case study (part 4 of 4).

Class **CTransaction** contains methods **OpenFile**, **GetRecord** and **AddRecord**. Method **OpenFile** (lines 26–75) uses **Const FileMode.OpenOrCreate** (line 32) to create a **FileStream** object from either an existing file or one not yet created. Lines 35–38 use this **FileStream** to create **BinaryReader** and **BinaryWriter** objects for reading and writing bytes to the file. If the file is new, lines 54–64 populate the **FileStream** object with empty records. Students might recall that we used these techniques in Section 17.8.

Method **GetRecord** (lines 78–128) returns the record associated with the account-number parameter. Lines 85–86 instantiate a **CRandomAccessRecord** object that will store the file data. If the account parameter is valid, lines 103–104 call method **Seek** of the **FileStream** object, which uses the parameter to determine the position of the specified record in the file. Lines 107–110 then call methods **ReadInt32**, **ReadString** and **ReadDouble** of the **BinaryReader** object to store the file data in the **CRandomAccessRecord** object. Line 113 returns the **CRandomAccessRecord** object. We used these techniques in Section 17.10.

Method **AddRecord** (lines 131–156) inserts a record into the file. Lines 138–139 call method **Seek** of the **FileStream** object, which uses the account-number parameter to locate the position which to insert the record in the file. Lines 142–145 call the overloaded **Write** methods of the **BinaryWriter** object to write the **CRandomAccessRecord** object's data to the file. We used these techniques in Section 17.9. Note that, if an error occurs when adding the record (i.e., either the **FileStream** or the **BinaryWriter** throws an **IOException**), lines 149–152 notify the user of the error and return **False** (failure).

Transaction-Processor GUI
The GUI for this program consists of a window containing internal frames (an MDI). Class **FrmTransactionProcessor** (Fig. 17.19) is the parent window, which acts as the driver for the application and displays one of its children windows—an object of type **FrmStartDialog** (Fig. 17.20), **FrmNewDialog** (Fig. 17.21), **FrmUpdateDialog** (Fig. 17.22) or **FrmDeleteDialog** (Fig. 17.23). **FrmStartDialog** allows the user to open a file containing account information and provides access to the **FrmNewDialog**, **FrmUpdateDialog** and **FrmDeleteDialog** internal frames. These frames allow us-

ers to update, create and delete records, respectively (using a reference to the **CTransaction** object).

Initially, **FrmTransactionProcessor** displays the **FrmStartDialog** object, this window provides the user with various options. It contains four buttons that enable the user to create or open a file, create a record, update an existing record or delete an existing record.

Before the user can modify records, the user must either create or open a file. When the user clicks the **New/Open File** button, the program calls method **cmdOpen_Click** (lines 36–94 of Fig. 17.20), which opens a file that the application uses for modifying records. Lines 40–48 display the **OpenFileDialog** for specifying the file from which to read data and then uses this file to create the **FileStream** object. Note that line 46 sets property **CheckFileExists** of the **OpenFileDialog** object to **False**—this enables the user to create a file if the specified file does not exist. If this property were **True** (its default value), the dialog would notify the user that the specified file does not exist, thus preventing the user from creating a file.

If the user specifies a file name, line 67 instantiates an object of class **CTransaction** (Fig. 17.18), which acts as the proxy for creating, reading records from and writing records to random-access files. Line 68 calls its method **OpenFile**, which either creates or opens the specified file, depending on whether the file exists.

Class **FrmStartDialog** also creates internal windows that enable the user to create, update and delete records. We do not use the default constructor created by Visual Studio .NET for these classes; instead, we use an overloaded constructor that takes as arguments the **CTransaction** object and a delegate object that references method **ShowStartDialog** (lines 121–123). Each child window uses the second delegate parameter to display the **FrmStartDialog** GUI when the user closes a child window. Lines 77–86 instantiate objects of classes **FrmUpdateDialog**, **FrmNewDialog** and **FrmDeleteDialog**, which serve as the child windows.

```
1    ' Fig. 17.19: TransactionProcessor.vb
2    ' MDI parent for transaction-processor application.
3
4    Imports System.Windows.Forms
5
6    Public Class FrmTransactionProcessor
7       Inherits Form
8
9       ' Visual Studio .NET generated code
10
11      ' reference to Multiple-Document-Interface client
12      Private childForm As MdiClient
13
14      ' reference to StartDialog
15      Private startDialog As FrmStartDialog
16
17   End Class ' FrmTransactionProcessor
```

Fig. 17.19 **FrmTransactionProcessor** class runs the transaction-processor application.

```vb
 1    ' Fig. 17.20: StartDialog.vb
 2    ' Initial dialog box displayed to user. Provides buttons for
 3    ' creating/opening file and for adding, updating and removing
 4    ' records from file.
 5
 6    ' Visual Basic namespaces
 7    Imports System.Windows.Forms
 8
 9    ' Deitel namespaces
10    Imports BankLibrary
11
12    Public Class FrmStartDialog
13       Inherits Form
14
15       ' buttons for displaying other dialogs
16       Friend WithEvents cmdOpen As Button
17       Friend WithEvents cmdNew As Button
18       Friend WithEvents cmdUpdate As Button
19       Friend WithEvents cmdDelete As Button
20
21       ' Visual Studio .NET generated code
22
23       ' reference to dialog box for adding record
24       Private newDialog As FrmNewDialog
25
26       ' reference to dialog box for updating record
27       Private updateDialog As FrmUpdateDialog
28
29       ' reference to dialog box for removing record
30       Private deleteDialog As FrmDeleteDialog
31
32       ' reference to object that handles transactions
33       Private transactionProxy As CTransaction
34
35       ' invoked when user clicks New/Open File button
36       Protected Sub cmdOpen_Click(ByVal sender As System.Object, _
37          ByVal e As System.EventArgs) Handles cmdOpen.Click
38
39          ' create dialog box enabling user to create or open file
40          Dim fileChooser As OpenFileDialog = New OpenFileDialog()
41          Dim result As DialogResult
42          Dim fileName As String
43
44          ' enable user to create file if file does not exist
45          fileChooser.Title = "Create File / Open File"
46          fileChooser.CheckFileExists = False
47
48          result = fileChooser.ShowDialog()  ' show dialog box to user
49
50          ' exit event handler if user clicked Cancel
51          If result = DialogResult.Cancel Then
52             Return
```

Fig. 17.20 `FrmStartDialog` class enables users to access dialog boxes associated with various transactions (part 1 of 4).

```vbnet
53          End If
54
55          ' get file name from user
56          fileName = fileChooser.FileName
57
58          ' show error if user specified invalid file
59          If (fileName = "" OrElse fileName = Nothing) Then
60             MessageBox.Show("Invalid File Name", "Error", _
61                MessageBoxButtons.OK, MessageBoxIcon.Error)
62
63          ' open or create file if user specified valid file
64          Else
65
66             ' create CTransaction with specified file
67             transactionProxy = New CTransaction()
68             transactionProxy.OpenFile(fileName)
69
70             ' enable GUI buttons except for New/Open File button
71             cmdNew.Enabled = True
72             cmdUpdate.Enabled = True
73             cmdDelete.Enabled = True
74             cmdOpen.Enabled = False
75
76             ' instantiate dialog box for creating records
77             newDialog = New FrmNewDialog(transactionProxy, _
78                AddressOf ShowStartDialog)
79
80             ' instantiate dialog box for updating records
81             updateDialog = New FrmUpdateDialog(transactionProxy, _
82                AddressOf ShowStartDialog)
83
84             ' instantiate dialog box for removing records
85             deleteDialog = New FrmDeleteDialog(transactionProxy, _
86                AddressOf ShowStartDialog)
87
88             ' set StartDialog as MdiParent for dialog boxes
89             newDialog.MdiParent = Me.MdiParent
90             updateDialog.MdiParent = Me.MdiParent
91             deleteDialog.MdiParent = Me.MdiParent
92          End If
93
94       End Sub ' cmdOpen_Click
95
96       ' invoked when user clicks New Record button
97       Protected Sub cmdNew_Click(ByVal sender As System.Object, _
98          ByVal e As System.EventArgs) Handles cmdNew.Click
99
100         Hide() ' hide StartDialog
101         newDialog.Show() ' show NewDialog
102      End Sub ' cmdNew_Click
103
```

Fig. 17.20 `FrmStartDialog` class enables users to access dialog boxes associated with various transactions (part 2 of 4).

```
104         ' invoked when user clicks Update Record button
105         Protected Sub cmdUpdate_Click(ByVal sender As System.Object, _
106            ByVal e As System.EventArgs) Handles cmdUpdate.Click
107
108            Hide() ' hide StartDialog
109            updateDialog.Show() ' show UpdateDialog
110         End Sub ' cmdUpdate_Click
111
112         ' invoked when user clicks Delete Record button
113         Protected Sub cmdDelete_Click(ByVal sender As System.Object, _
114            ByVal e As System.EventArgs) Handles cmdDelete.Click
115
116            Hide() ' hide StartDialog
117            deleteDialog.Show() ' show DeleteDialog
118         End Sub ' cmdDelete_Click
119
120         ' displays StartDialog
121         Protected Sub ShowStartDialog()
122            Show()
123         End Sub ' ShowStartDialog
124
125   End Class ' FrmStartDialog
```

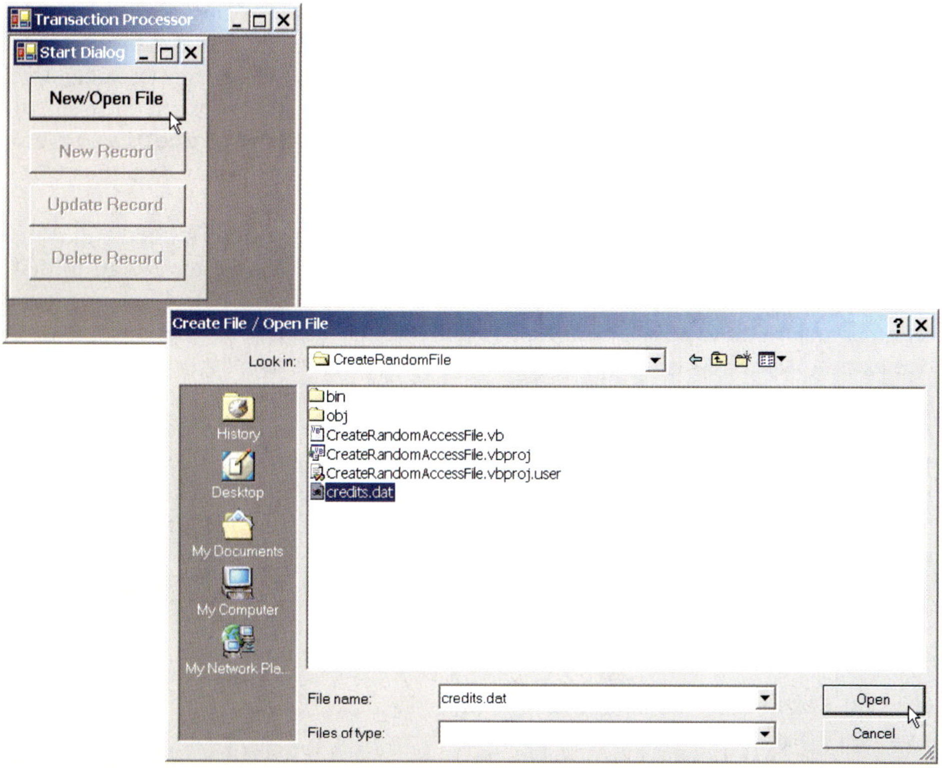

Fig. 17.20 `FrmStartDialog` class enables users to access dialog boxes associated with various transactions (part 3 of 4).

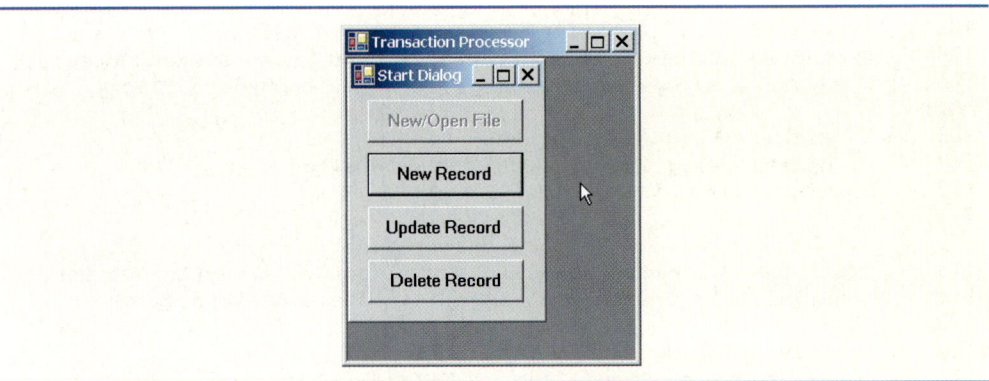

Fig. 17.20 **FrmStartDialog** class enables users to access dialog boxes associated with various transactions (part 4 of 4).

When the user clicks the **New Record** button in the **Start Dialog**, the program invokes method **cmdNew_Click** of class **FrmStartDialog** (Fig. 17.20, lines 97–102), which displays the **FrmNewDialog** internal frame. Class **FrmNewDialog** (Fig. 17.21) enables the user to create records in the file that **FrmStartDialog** opened (or created). Line 23 defines **MyDelegate** as a delegate to a method that does not return a value and has no parameters—method **ShowStartDialog** of class **FrmStartDialog** (Fig. 17.20, lines 121–123) conforms to these requirements. Class **FrmNewDialog** receives a **MyDelegate** object, which references this method as a parameter—therefore, **FrmNewDialog** can invoke this method to display the start window when the user exits the **FrmNewDialog**. Classes **FrmUpdateDialog** and **FrmDeleteDialog** also receive **MyDelegate** references as arguments, enabling them to display **FrmStartDialog** after completing their tasks.

After the user enters data in the **TextBox**es and clicks the **Save Record** button, the program invokes method **cmdSave_Click** (lines 47–62) to write the record to disk. Lines 50–52 call method **GetRecord** of the **CTransaction** object, which should return an empty **CRandomAccessRecord**. If method **GetRecord** returns a **CRandomAccessRecord** that contains content, the user is attempting to overwrite that **CRandomAccessRecord** with a new one. Line 56 calls **Private** method **InsertRecord** (lines 65–108). If the **CRandomAccessRecord** is empty, method **InsertRecord** calls method **AddRecord** of the **CTransaction** object (lines 93–94), which inserts the newly created **CRandomAccessRecord** into the file. If the user is attempting to overwrite an existing file, lines 76–80 notify the user that the file already exists and return from the method.

```
1    ' Fig. 17.21: NewDialog.vb
2    ' Enables user to insert new record into file.
3
4    ' Visual Basic namespaces
5    Imports System.Windows.Forms
6
```

Fig. 17.21 **FrmNewDialog** class enables users to create records in transaction-processor case study (part 1 of 4).

```vb
 7     ' Deitel namespaces
 8     Imports BankLibrary
 9
10     Public Class FrmNewDialog
11        Inherits FrmBankUI
12
13        ' buttons for creating record and canceling action
14        Friend WithEvents cmdSave As Button
15        Friend WithEvents cmdCancel As Button
16
17        ' Windows Form Designer generated code
18
19        ' reference to object that handles transactions
20        Private transactionProxy As CTransaction
21
22        ' delegate for method that displays previous window
23        Delegate Sub MyDelegate()
24        Public showPreviousWindow As MyDelegate
25
26        ' initialize components and set members to parameter values
27        Public Sub New(ByVal transactionProxyValue As CTransaction, _
28           ByVal delegateValue As MyDelegate)
29
30           InitializeComponent()
31           showPreviousWindow = delegateValue
32
33           ' instantiate object that handles transactions
34           transactionProxy = transactionProxyValue
35        End Sub ' New
36
37        ' invoked when user clicks Cancel button
38        Protected Sub cmdCancel_Click(ByVal sender As System.Object, _
39           ByVal e As System.EventArgs) Handles cmdCancel.Click
40
41           Hide()
42           ClearTextBoxes()
43           showPreviousWindow()
44        End Sub ' cmdCancel_Click
45
46        ' invoked when user clicks Save As button
47        Protected Sub cmdSave_Click(ByVal sender As System.Object, _
48           ByVal e As System.EventArgs) Handles cmdSave.Click
49
50           Dim record As CRandomAccessRecord = _
51              transactionProxy.GetRecord( _
52                 GetTextBoxValues(TextBoxIndices.ACCOUNT))
53
54           ' if record exists, add it to file
55           If (record Is Nothing) = False Then
56              InsertRecord(record)
57           End If
58
```

Fig. 17.21 `FrmNewDialog` class enables users to create records in transaction-processor case study (part 2 of 4).

```vbnet
59         Hide()
60         ClearTextBoxes()
61         showPreviousWindow()
62      End Sub ' cmdSave_Click
63
64      ' insert record in file at position specified by accountNumber
65      Private Sub InsertRecord(ByVal record As CRandomAccessRecord)
66
67         ' store TextBox values in String array
68         Dim textBoxValues As String() = GetTextBoxValues()
69
70         ' store TextBox account field
71         Dim accountNumber As Integer = _
72            Convert.ToInt32(textBoxValues(TextBoxIndices.ACCOUNT))
73
74         ' notify user and return if record account is not empty
75         If record.Account <> 0 Then
76            MessageBox.Show( _
77               "Record Already Exists or Invalid Number", "Error", _
78               MessageBoxButtons.OK, MessageBoxIcon.Error)
79
80            Return
81         End If
82
83         ' store values in record
84         record.Account = accountNumber
85         record.FirstName = textBoxValues(TextBoxIndices.FIRST)
86         record.LastName = textBoxValues(TextBoxIndices.LAST)
87         record.Balance = Convert.ToDouble( _
88            textBoxValues(TextBoxIndices.BALANCE))
89
90         ' add record to file
91         Try
92
93            If (transactionProxy.AddRecord( _
94               record, accountNumber) = False ) Then
95
96               Return ' if error
97            End If
98
99         ' notify user if error occurs in parameter mismatch
100         Catch formattingException As FormatException
101            MessageBox.Show("Invalid Balance", "Error", _
102               MessageBoxButtons.OK, MessageBoxIcon.Error)
103
104         End Try
105
106         MessageBox.Show("Record Created", "Success", _
107            MessageBoxButtons.OK, MessageBoxIcon.Information)
108      End Sub ' InsertRecord
109
110 End Class ' FrmNewDialog
```

Fig. 17.21 `FrmNewDialog` class enables users to create records in transaction-processor case study (part 3 of 4).

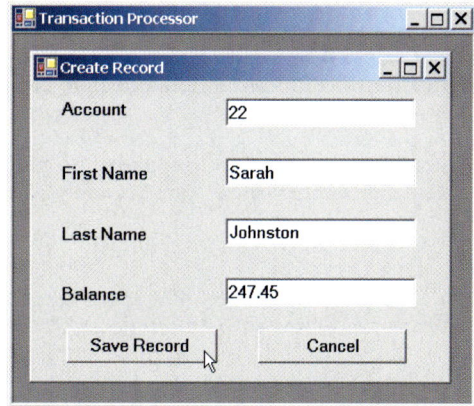

Fig. 17.21 FrmNewDialog class enables users to create records in transaction-processor case study (part 4 of 4).

When the user clicks the **Update Record** button in the **Start Dialog**, the program invokes method **cmdUpdate_Click** of class **FrmStartDialog** (Fig. 17.20, lines 105–110), which displays the **FrmUpdateDialog** internal frame (Fig. 17.22). Class **FrmUpdateDialog** enables the user to update existing records in the file. To update a record, users must enter the account number associated with the record they wish to update. When the user presses *Enter*, **FrmUpdateDialog** calls method **txtAccount-Number_KeyDown** (lines 42–82) to display the record contents. This method calls method **GetRecord** of the **CTransaction** object (lines 51–53) to retrieve the specified **CRandomAccessRecord**. If the record is not empty, lines 64–67 populate the **Text-Box**es with the **CRandomAccessRecord** values.

```
1   ' Fig. 17.22: UpdateDialog.vb
2   ' Enables user to update records in file.
3
4   ' Visual Basic namespaces
5   Imports System.Windows.Forms
6
7   ' Deitel namespaces
8   Imports BankLibrary
9
10  Public Class FrmUpdateDialog
11      Inherits FrmBankUI
```

Fig. 17.22 FrmUpdateDialog class enables users to update records in transaction-processor case study (part 1 of 6).

```vbnet
12
13        ' label and textbox for user to enter transaction data
14        Friend WithEvents lblTransaction As Label
15        Friend WithEvents txtTransaction As TextBox
16
17        ' buttons for saving data to file and canceling save
18        Friend WithEvents cmdSave As Button
19        Friend WithEvents cmdCancel As Button
20
21        ' Visual Studio .NET generated code
22
23        ' reference to object that handles transactions
24        Private transactionProxy As CTransaction
25
26        ' delegate for method that displays previous window
27        Delegate Sub MyDelegate()
28        Public showPreviousWindow As MyDelegate
29
30        ' initialize components and set members to parameter values
31        Public Sub New(ByVal transactionProxyValue As CTransaction, _
32           ByVal delegateValue As MyDelegate)
33
34           InitializeComponent()
35           showPreviousWindow = delegateValue
36
37           ' instantiate object that handles transactions
38           transactionProxy = transactionProxyValue
39        End Sub ' New
40
41        ' invoked when user enters text in Account TextBox
42        Protected Sub txtAccountNumber_KeyDown( _
43           ByVal sender As System.Object, _
44           ByVal e As System.Windows.Forms.KeyEventArgs) _
45           Handles txtAccount.KeyDown
46
47           ' determine whether user pressed Enter Key
48           If e.KeyCode = Keys.Enter Then
49
50              ' retrieve record associated with account from file
51              Dim record As CRandomAccessRecord = _
52                 transactionProxy.GetRecord( _
53                    GetTextBoxValues(TextBoxIndices.ACCOUNT))
54
55              ' return if record does not exist
56              If (record Is Nothing) = True Then
57                 Return
58              End If
59
60              ' determine whether record is empty
61              If record.Account <> 0 Then
62
```

Fig. 17.22 `FrmUpdateDialog` class enables users to update records in transaction-processor case study (part 2 of 6).

```
63                       ' store record values in String array
64                       Dim values As String() = {record.Account.ToString(), _
65                          record.FirstName.ToString(), _
66                          record.LastName.ToString(), _
67                          record.Balance.ToString()}
68
69                       ' copy String-array value to TextBox values
70                       SetTextBoxValues(values)
71                       txtTransaction.Text = "[Charge or Payment]"
72
73                    ' notify user if record does not exist
74                    Else
75                       MessageBox.Show("Record Does Not Exist", "Error", _
76                          MessageBoxButtons.OK, MessageBoxIcon.Error)
77
78                    End If
79
80            End If
81
82      End Sub ' txtAccountNumber_KeyDown
83
84      ' invoked when user enters text in Transaction TextBox
85      Protected Sub txtTransactionNumber_KeyDown( _
86         ByVal sender As System.Object, _
87         ByVal e As System.Windows.Forms.KeyEventArgs) _
88         Handles txtTransaction.KeyDown
89
90         ' determine whether user pressed Enter key
91         If e.KeyCode = Keys.Enter Then
92
93            ' calculate balance using Transaction TextBox value
94            Try
95
96               ' retrieve record associated with account from file
97               Dim record As CRandomAccessRecord = _
98                  transactionProxy.GetRecord( _
99                     GetTextBoxValues(TextBoxIndices.ACCOUNT))
100
101              ' get Transaction TextBox value
102              Dim transactionValue As Double = _
103                 Convert.ToDouble(txtTransaction.Text)
104
105              ' calculate new balance (old balance + transaction)
106              Dim newBalance As Double = _
107                 record.Balance + transactionValue
108
109              ' store record values in String array
110              Dim values As String() = {record.Account.ToString(), _
111                 record.FirstName.ToString(), _
112                 record.LastName.ToString(), newBalance.ToString()}
113
```

Fig. 17.22 `FrmUpdateDialog` class enables users to update records in transaction-processor case study (part 3 of 6).

```vbnet
114              ' copy String-array value to TextBox values
115              SetTextBoxValues(values)
116
117              ' clear txtTransactionNumber
118              txtTransaction.Text = ""
119
120           ' notify user if error occurs in parameter mismatch
121           Catch formattingException As FormatException
122              MessageBox.Show("Invalid Transaction", "Error", _
123                 MessageBoxButtons.OK, MessageBoxIcon.Error)
124
125           End Try
126
127        End If
128
129     End Sub ' txtTransactionNumber_KeyDown
130
131     ' invoked when user clicks Save button
132     Protected Sub cmdSave_Click(ByVal sender As System.Object, _
133        ByVal e As System.EventArgs) Handles cmdSave.Click
134
135        Dim record As CRandomAccessRecord = _
136           transactionProxy.GetRecord( _
137              GetTextBoxValues(TextBoxIndices.ACCOUNT))
138
139        ' if record exists, update in file
140        If (record Is Nothing) = False Then
141           UpdateRecord(record)
142        End If
143
144        Hide()
145        ClearTextBoxes()
146        showPreviousWindow()
147     End Sub ' cmdSave_Click
148
149     ' invoked when user clicks Cancel button
150     Protected Sub cmdCancel_Click(ByVal sender As System.Object, _
151        ByVal e As System.EventArgs) Handles cmdCancel.Click
152
153        Hide()
154        ClearTextBoxes()
155        showPreviousWindow()
156     End Sub ' cmdCancel_Click
157
158     ' update record in file at position specified by accountNumber
159     Public Sub UpdateRecord(ByVal record As CRandomAccessRecord)
160
161        ' store TextBox values in record and write record to file
162        Try
163           Dim accountNumber As Integer = record.Account
164           Dim values As String() = GetTextBoxValues()
165
```

Fig. 17.22 `FrmUpdateDialog` class enables users to update records in transaction-processor case study (part 4 of 6).

```
166             ' store values in record
167             record.Account = accountNumber
168             record.FirstName = values(TextBoxIndices.FIRST)
169             record.LastName = values(TextBoxIndices.LAST)
170             record.Balance = _
171                Double.Parse(values(TextBoxIndices.BALANCE))
172
173             ' add record to file
174             If (transactionProxy.AddRecord( _
175                record, accountNumber) = False ) Then
176
177                Return ' if error
178             End If
179
180          ' notify user if error occurs in parameter mismatch
181          Catch formattingException As FormatException
182             MessageBox.Show("Invalid Balance", "Error", _
183                MessageBoxButtons.OK, MessageBoxIcon.Error)
184
185             Return
186          End Try
187
188          MessageBox.Show("Record Updated", "Success", _
189             MessageBoxButtons.OK, MessageBoxIcon.Information)
190       End Sub ' UpdateRecord
191
192 End Class ' FrmUpdateDialog
```

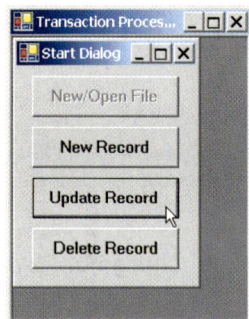

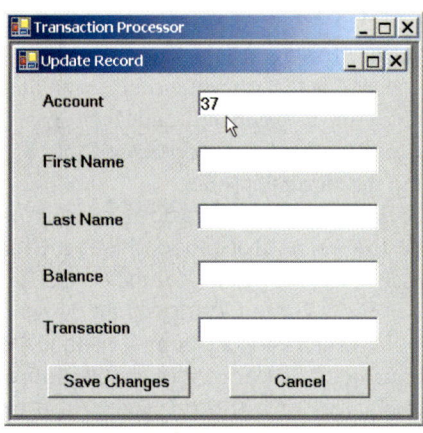

Fig. 17.22 FrmUpdateDialog class enables users to update records in transaction-processor case study (part 5 of 6).

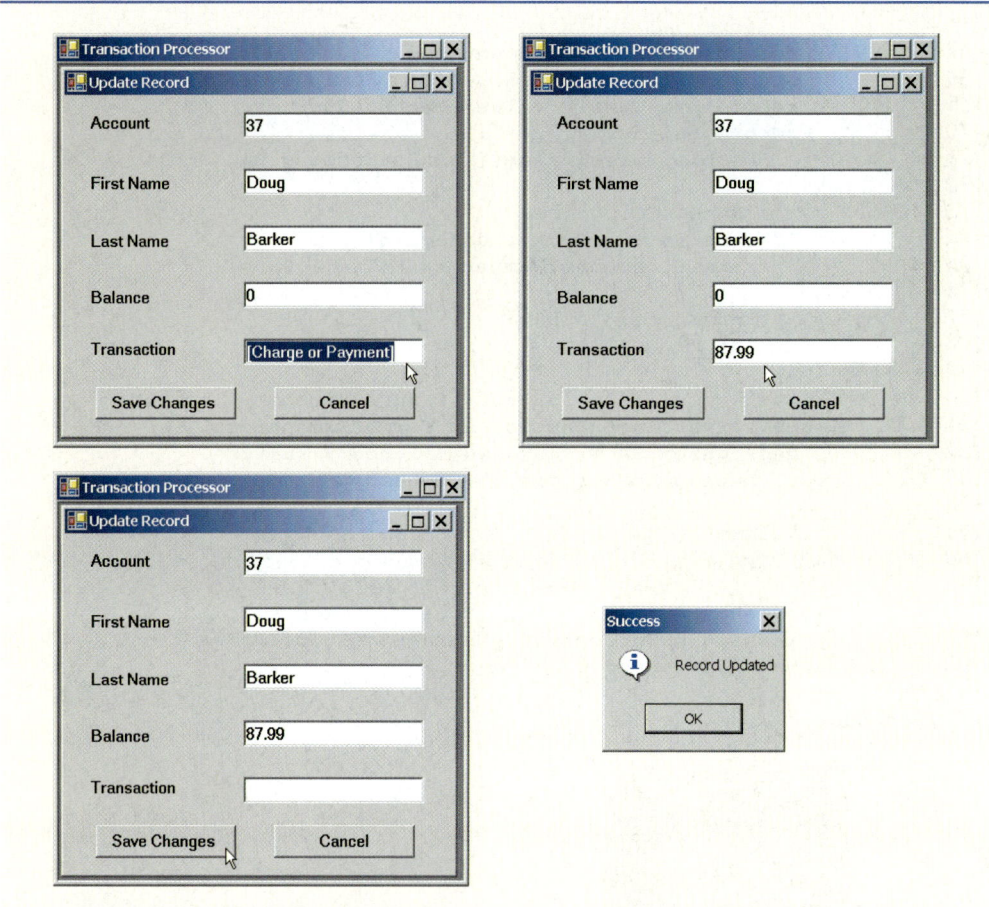

Fig. 17.22 `FrmUpdateDialog` class enables users to update records in transaction-processor case study (part 6 of 6).

The **Transaction TextBox** initially contains the string **Charge or Payment**. The user should select this text, type the transaction amount (a positive value for a charge or a negative value for a payment) and then press *Enter*. The program calls method `txtTransactionNumber_KeyDown` (lines 85–129) to add the user-specified transaction amount to the current balance.

The user clicks the **Save Changes** button to write the altered contents of the **TextBox**es to the file. (Note that pressing **Save Changes** does not update the **Balance** field—the user must press *Enter* to update this field before pressing **Save Changes**.) When the user clicks **Save Changes**, the program invokes method `cmdSave_Click` (lines 132–147), which calls `Private` method `UpdateRecord` (lines 159–190). This method calls method `AddRecord` of the `CTransaction` object (lines 174–175) to store the **TextBox** values in a `CRandomAccessRecord` and overwrite the existing file record with the `CRandomAccessRecord` containing the new data.

When the user clicks the **Delete Record** button of the **Start Dialog**, the program invokes method `cmdDelete_Click` of class `FrmStartDialog` (Fig. 17.20, lines

113–118), which displays the **FrmDeleteDialog** internal frame (Fig. 17.23). Class **FrmDeleteDialog** enables the user to remove existing records from the file. To remove a record, users must enter the account number associated with the record they wish to delete. When the user clicks the **Delete Record** button (now, from the **FrmDeleteDialog** internal frame), **FrmDeleteDialog** calls method **cmdDelete_Click** (lines 42–55). This method calls method **DeleteRecord** (lines 66–97), which ensures that the record to be deleted exists and then calls method **AddRecord** of the **CTransaction** object (lines 83–84) to overwrite the file record with an empty one.

```vb
1   ' Fig. 17.23: DeleteDialog.vb
2   ' Enables user to delete records in file.
3
4   ' Visual Basic namespaces
5   Imports System.Windows.Forms
6
7   ' Deitel namespaces
8   Imports BankLibrary
9
10  Public Class FrmDeleteDialog
11     Inherits Form
12
13     ' label and TextBox enabling user to input account number
14     Friend WithEvents lblAccount As Label
15     Friend WithEvents txtAccount As TextBox
16
17     ' buttons for deleting record and canceling action
18     Friend WithEvents cmdDelete As Button
19     Friend WithEvents cmdCancel As Button
20
21     ' Visual Studio .NET generated code
22
23     ' reference to object that handles transactions
24     Private transactionProxy As CTransaction
25
26     ' delegate for method that displays previous window
27     Delegate Sub MyDelegate()
28     Public showPreviousWindow As MyDelegate
29
30     ' initialize components and set members to parameter values
31     Public Sub New(ByVal transactionProxyValue As CTransaction, _
32        ByVal delegateValue As MyDelegate)
33
34        InitializeComponent()
35        showPreviousWindow = delegateValue
36
37        ' instantiate object that handles transactions
38        transactionProxy = transactionProxyValue
39     End Sub ' New
40
```

Fig. 17.23 **FrmDeleteDialog** class enables users to remove records from files in transaction-processor case study (part 1 of 3).

```vb
41     ' invoked when user clicks Delete Record button
42     Protected Sub cmdDelete_Click(ByVal sender As System.Object, _
43        ByVal e As System.EventArgs) Handles cmdDelete.Click
44
45        Dim record As CRandomAccessRecord = _
46           transactionProxy.GetRecord(txtAccount.Text)
47
48        ' if record exists, delete it in file
49        If (record Is Nothing) = False Then
50           DeleteRecord(record)
51        End If
52
53        Me.Hide()
54        showPreviousWindow()
55     End Sub ' cmdDelete_Click
56
57     ' invoked when user clicks Cancel button
58     Protected Sub cmdCancel_Click(ByVal sender As System.Object, _
59        ByVal e As System.EventArgs) Handles cmdCancel.Click
60
61        Me.Hide()
62        showPreviousWindow()
63     End Sub ' cmdCancel_Click
64
65     ' delete record in file at position specified by accountNumber
66     Public Sub DeleteRecord(ByVal record As CRandomAccessRecord)
67
68        Dim accountNumber As Integer = record.Account
69
70        ' display error message if record does not exist
71        If record.Account = 0 Then
72           MessageBox.Show("Record Does Not Exist", "Error", _
73              MessageBoxButtons.OK, MessageBoxIcon.Error)
74           txtAccount.Clear()
75
76           Return
77        End If
78
79        ' create blank record
80        record = New CRandomAccessRecord()
81
82        ' write over file record with empty record
83        If (transactionProxy.AddRecord( _
84           record, accountNumber) = True) Then
85
86           ' notify user of successful deletion
87           MessageBox.Show("Record Deleted", "Success", _
88              MessageBoxButtons.OK, MessageBoxIcon.Information)
89        Else
90
91           ' notify user of failure
92           MessageBox.Show("Record could not be deleted", "Error", _
```

Fig. 17.23 `FrmDeleteDialog` class enables users to remove records from files in transaction-processor case study (part 2 of 3).

```
93                MessageBoxButtons.OK, MessageBoxIcon.Error)
94         End If
95
96         txtAccount.Clear() ' clear text box
97      End Sub ' DeleteRecord
98
99   End Class ' FrmDeleteDialog
```

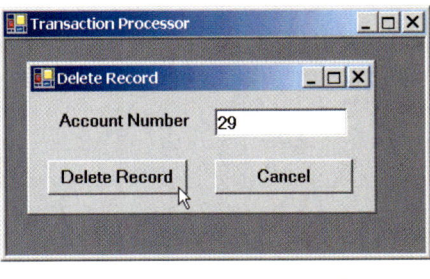

Fig. 17.23 `FrmDeleteDialog` class enables users to remove records from files in transaction-processor case study (part 3 of 3).

SUMMARY

- All data items processed by a computer ultimately are reduced to combinations of zeros and ones.
- The smallest data items that computers support are called bits and can assume either the value **0** or the value **1**.
- Digits, letters and special symbols are referred to as characters. The set of all characters used to write programs and represent data items on a particular computer is called that computer's character set. Every character in a computer's character set is represented as a pattern of **1**s and **0**s (characters in Visual Basic are Unicode characters, which are composed of 2 bytes).
- A field is a group of characters (or bytes) that conveys some meaning.
- A record is a group of related fields.
- At least one field in a record is chosen as a record key, which identifies that record as belonging to a particular person or entity and distinguishes that record from all other records in the file.
- Files are used for long-term retention of large amounts of data and can store those data even after the program that created the data terminates.
- A file is a group of related records.
- Data maintained in files is often called persistent data.
- Class **File** enables programs to obtain information about a file.
- Class **Directory** enables programs to obtain information about a directory.
- Class **FileStream** provides method **Seek** for repositioning the file-position pointer (the byte number of the next byte in the file to be read or written) to any position in the file.
- The most common type of file organization is a sequential file, in which records typically are stored in order by the record-key field.
- When a file is opened, an object is created, and a stream is associated with the object.

- Visual Basic imposes no structure on a file. This means that concepts like that of a "record" do not exist in Visual Basic. The programmer must structure a file appropriately to meet the requirements of an application.
- A collection of programs designed to create and manage databases is called a database management system (DBMS).
- Visual Basic views each file as a sequential stream of bytes.
- Each file ends in some machine-dependent form of end-of-file marker.
- Objects of classes **OpenFileDialog** and **SaveFileDialog** are used for selecting files to open and save, respectively. Method **ShowDialog** of these classes displays that dialog.
- When displayed, both an **OpenFileDialog** and a **SaveFileDialog** prevent the user from interacting with any other program window until the dialog is closed. Dialogs that behave in this fashion are called modal dialogs.
- Streams provide communication channels between files and programs.
- To perform file processing in Visual Basic, the namespace **System.IO** must be referenced. This namespace includes definitions for stream classes such as **StreamReader**, **StreamWriter** and **FileStream**. Files are opened by instantiating objects of these classes.
- To retrieve data sequentially from a file, programs normally start from the beginning of the file, reading all data consecutively until the desired data are found.
- With a sequential-access file, each successive input/output request reads or writes the next consecutive set of data in the file.
- Instant data access is possible with random-access files. A program can access individual records of a random-access file directly (and quickly) without searching through other records. Random-access files sometimes are called direct-access files.
- With a random-access file, each successive input/output request can be directed to any part of the file, which can be any distance from the part of the file referenced in the previous request.
- Programmers can use members of the **FileAccess** enumeration to control users' access to files.
- Only classes with the **Serializable** attribute can be serialized to and deserialized from files.
- There are a variety of techniques for creating random-access files. Perhaps the simplest involves requiring that all records in a file are of the same fixed length.
- The use of fixed-length records makes it easy for a program to calculate (as a function of the record size and the record key) the exact location of any record in relation to the beginning of the file
- A random-access file is like a railroad train with many cars—some empty and some with contents.
- Data can be inserted into a random-access file without destroying other data in the file. Users can also update or delete previously stored data without rewriting the entire file.
- **BinaryFormatter** uses methods **Serialize** and **Deserialize** to write and read objects, respectively. Method **Serialize** writes the object's representation to a file. Method **Deserialize** reads this representation from a file and reconstructs the original object.
- Methods **Serialize** and **Deserialize** require **Stream** objects as parameters, enabling the **BinaryFormatter** to access the correct file.
- Class **BinaryReader** and **BinaryWriter** provide methods for reading and writing bytes to streams, respectively. The **BinaryReader** and **BinaryWriter** constructors receive as arguments references to instances of class **System.IO.Stream**.
- Class **FileStream** inherits from class **Stream**, so we can pass the **FileStream** object as an argument to either the **BinaryReader** or **BinaryWriter** constructor to create object that can transfer bytes directly to and from a file.

- Random-access file-processing programs rarely write a single field to a file. Normally, they write one object at a time.
- Sorting with direct-access techniques is fast. This speed is achieved by making the file large enough to hold every possible record that might be created. Of course, this means that the file could be sparsely occupied most of the time, possibly wasting memory.

TERMINOLOGY

binary digit (bit)
`BinaryFormatter` class
`BinaryReader` class
`BinaryWriter` class
`BufferedStream` class
character
character set
`Close` method of class `StreamReader`
closing a file
`Console` class
`Copy` method of class `File`
`Create` method of class `File`
`CreateDirectory` method of class `Directory`
`CreateText` method of class `File`
data hierarchy
database
database management system (DBMS)
`Delete` method of class `Directory`
`Delete` method of class `File`
`Deserialize` method of class `BinaryFormatter`
direct-access files
`Directory` class
`DirectoryInfo` class
end-of-file marker
`Error` property of class `Console`
escape sequence
`Exists` method of class `Directory`
field
file
`File` class
file-processing programs
`FileAccess` enumeration
file-position pointer
`FileStream` class
fixed-length records
`GetCreationTime` method of class `Directory`
`GetCreationTime` method of class `File`
`GetDirectories` method of class `Directory`
`GetFiles` method of class `Directory`
`GetLastAccessTime` method of class `Directory`
`GetLastAccessTime` method of class `File`
`GetLastWriteTime` method of class `Directory`
`GetLastWriteTime` method of class `File`
`In` property of class `Console`
"instant-access" application
`IOException`
`MemoryStream` class
modal dialog
`Move` method of class `Directory`
`Move` method of class `File`
`Open` method of class `File`
`OpenFileDialog` class
`OpenRead` method of class `File`
`OpenText` method of class `File`
`OpenWrite` method of class `File`
`Out` property of class `Console`
pattern of `1`s and `0`s
persistent data
random-access file
`Read` method of class `Console`
`ReadDouble` method of class `BinaryReader`
`ReadInt32` method of class `BinaryReader`
`ReadLine` method of class `Console`
`ReadLine` method of class `StreamReader`
`ReadString` method of class `BinaryReader`
record
record key
regular expression
`SaveFileDialog` class
secondary storage devices
`Seek` method of class `FileStream`
`SeekOrigin` enumeration
separation character
sequential-access file
`Serializable` attribute
`SerializationException`

Serialize method of class
  BinaryFormatter
ShowDialog method of class
  OpenFileDialog
ShowDialog method of class
  SaveFileDialog
standard error stream object
standard input stream object
standard output stream object
Stream class
stream of bytes
stream processing
StreamReader class

StreamWriter class
System.IO namespace
System.Runtime.Serialization.
  Formatters.Binary namespace
TextReader class
TextWriter class
transaction-processing system
Windows Control Library project
Write method of class **BinaryWriter**
Write method of class **Console**
Write method of class **StreamWriter**
WriteLine method of class **Console**
WriteLine method of class **StreamWriter**

SELF-REVIEW EXERCISES

17.1 State whether each of the following is *true* or *false*. If *false*, explain why.
  a) Creating instances of classes **File** and **Directory** is impossible.
  b) Typically, a sequential file stores records in order by the record-key field.
  c) Class **StreamReader** inherits from class **Stream**.
  d) Any class can be serialized to a file.
  e) Searching a random-access file sequentially to find a specific record is unnecessary.
  f) Method **Seek** of class **FileStream** always seeks relative to the beginning of a file.
  g) Visual Basic provides class **Record** to store records for random-access file-processing applications.
  h) Banking systems, point-of-sale systems and automated-teller machines are types of transaction-processing systems.
  i) Classes **StreamReader** and **StreamWriter** are used with sequential-access files.
  j) Instantiating objects of type **Stream** is impossible.

17.2 Fill in the blanks in each of the following statements:
  a) Ultimately, all data items processed by a computer are reduced to combinations of _____ and _____.
  b) The smallest data item a computer can process is called a _____.
  c) A _____ is a group of related records.
  d) Digits, letters and special symbols are referred to as _____.
  e) A group of related files is called a _____.
  f) **StreamReader** method _____ reads a line of text from the file.
  g) **StreamWriter** method _____ writes a line of text to the file.
  h) Method **Serialize** of class **BinaryFormatter** takes a(n) _____ and a(n) _____ as arguments.
  i) The _____ namespace contains most of Visual Basic's file-processing classes.
  j) The _____ namespace contains the **BinaryFormatter** class.

ANSWERS TO SELF-REVIEW EXERCISES

17.1 a) True. b) True. c) False. **StreamReader** inherits from **TextReader**. d) False. Only classes with the **Serializable** attribute can be serialized. e) True. f) False. It seeks relative to the **SeekOrigin** enumeration member that is passed as one of the arguments. g) False. Visual Basic imposes no structure on a file, so the concept of a "record" does not exist. h) True. i) True. j) True.

17.2 a) **1**s, **0**s. b) bit. c) file. d) characters. e) database. f) `ReadLine`. g) `WriteLine`. h) `Stream`, `Object`. i) `System.IO`. j) `System.Runtime.Serialization.Formatters.Binary`.

EXERCISES

17.3 Create a program that stores student grades in a text file. The file should contain the name, ID number, class taken and grade of every student. Allow the user to load a grade file and display its contents in a read-only textbox. The entries should be displayed as follows:

```
LastName, FirstName:  ID#  Class   Grade
```

We list some sample data below:

```
Jones, Bob: 1 "Introduction to Computer Science" "A-"
Johnson, Sarah: 2 "Data Structures" "B+"
Smith, Sam: 3 "Data Structures" "C"
```

17.4 Modify the previous program to use objects of class that can be serialized to and deserialized from a file. Ensure fixed-length records by fixing the length of fields `LastName`, `FirstName`, `Class` and `Grade`.

17.5 Extend classes `StreamReader` and `StreamWriter`. Allow the class that derives from `StreamReader` to have methods `ReadInteger`, `ReadBoolean` and `ReadString`. Allow the class that derives from `StreamWriter` to have methods `WriteInteger`, `WriteBoolean` and `WriteString`. Think about how to design the writing methods so that the reading methods will be able to read what was written. Design `WriteInteger` and `WriteBoolean` to write `String`s of uniform size so that `ReadInteger` and `ReadBoolean` can read those values accurately. Make sure `ReadString` and `WriteString` use the same character(s) to separate `String`s.

17.6 Create a program that combines the ideas of Fig. 17.9 and Fig. 17.11 to allow the user to write records to and read records from a file. Add an extra field of type `Boolean` to the record indicating whether the account has overdraft protection.

17.7 In commercial data processing, it is common to have several files in each application system. In an accounts-receivable system, for example, there is generally a master file containing detailed information about each customer, such as the customer's name, address, telephone number, outstanding balance, credit limit, discount terms, contract arrangements and possibly a condensed history of recent purchases and cash payments.

As transactions occur (i.e., sales are made and cash payments arrive in the mail), they are entered into a file. At the end of each business period (i.e., a month for some companies, a week for others and a day in some cases), the file of transactions (`trans.dat`) is applied to the master file (`oldmast.dat`), thus updating each account's record of purchases and payments. During an updating run, the master file is rewritten as a new file (`newmast.dat`), which then is used at the end of the next business period to begin the updating process again.

File-matching programs must deal with certain problems that do not exist in single-file programs. For example, a match does not always occur. A customer on the master file might not have made any purchases or cash payments in the current business period, and, therefore, no record for this customer will appear on the transaction file. Similarly, a customer who did make some purchases or cash payments might have just moved to the community, and the company might not have had a chance to create a master record for this customer.

When a match occurs (i.e., records with the same account number appear on both the master file and the transaction file), add the dollar amount on the transaction file to the current balance on the master file and write the `newmast.dat` record. (Assume that purchases are indicated by positive amounts on the transaction file and that payments are indicated by negative amounts.) When there is a master record for a particular account, but no corresponding transaction record, merely write the master record to **newmast.dat**. When there is a transaction record, but no corresponding master record, print the message "**Unmatched transaction record for account number...**" (fill in the account number from the transaction record).

17.8 You are the owner of a hardware store and need to keep an inventory of the different tools you sell, how many of each are currently in stock and the cost of each. Write a program that initializes the random-access file **hardware.dat** to 100 empty records, lets you input the data concerning each tool, enables you to list all your tools, lets you delete a record for a tool that you no longer have and lets you update any information in the file. The tool identification number should be the record number. Use the information in Fig. 17.24 to start your file.

Record #	Tool name	Quantity	Price
3	Electric sander	18	35.99
19	Hammer	128	10.00
26	Jig saw	16	14.25
39	Lawn mower	10	79.50
56	Power saw	8	89.99
76	Screwdriver	236	4.99
81	Sledge hammer	32	19.75
88	Wrench	65	6.48

Fig. 17.24 Inventory of a hardware store.

18

Extensible Markup Language (XML)

Objectives

- To be able to mark up data using XML.
- To understand the concept of an XML namespace.
- To understand the relationship between DTDs, Schemas and XML.
- To be able to create Schemas.
- To be able to create and use simple XSLT documents.
- To be able to transform XML documents into XHTML using class **XslTransform**.
- To become familiar with BizTalk™.

*Knowing trees, I understand the meaning of patience.
Knowing grass, I can appreciate persistence.*
Hal Borland

Like everything metaphysical, the harmony between thought and reality is to be found in the grammar of the language.
Ludwig Wittgenstein

I played with an idea, and grew willful; tossed it into the air; transformed it; let it escape and recaptured it; made it iridescent with fancy, and winged it with paradox.
Oscar Wilde

Outline

18.1 Introduction
18.2 XML Documents
18.3 XML Namespaces
18.4 Document Object Model (DOM)
18.5 Document Type Definitions (DTDs), Schemas and Validation
    18.5.1 Document Type Definitions
    18.5.2 Microsoft XML Schemas
18.6 Extensible Stylesheet Language and `XslTransform`
18.7 Microsoft BizTalk™
18.8 Internet and World Wide Web Resources

Summary • Terminology • Self-Review Exercises • Answers to Self-Review Exercises • Exercises

18.1 Introduction

The *Extensible Markup Language* (XML) was developed in 1996 by the *World Wide Web Consortium's (W3C's) XML Working Group*. XML is a portable, widely supported, *open technology* (i.e., non-proprietary technology) for describing data. XML is becoming the standard for storing data that exchanged is between applications. Using XML, document authors can describe any type of data, including mathematical formulas, software-configuration instructions, music, recipes and financial reports. XML documents are readable by both humans and machines.

The .NET Framework uses XML extensively. The Framework Class Library provides an extensive set of XML-related classes. Much of Visual Studio's internal implementation also employs XML. In this chapter, we introduce XML, XML-related technologies and key classes for creating and manipulating XML documents.

18.2 XML Documents

In this section, we present our first XML document, which describes an article (Fig. 18.1). The line numbers shown are not part of the XML document.

```
1   <?xml version = "1.0"?>
2
3   <!-- Fig. 18.1: article.xml      -->
4   <!-- Article structured with XML -->
5
6   <article>
7
8       <title>Simple XML</title>
9
```

Fig. 18.1 XML used to mark up an article (part 1 of 2).

```
10      <date>December 6, 2001</date>
11
12      <author>
13         <firstName>John</firstName>
14         <lastName>Doe</lastName>
15      </author>
16
17      <summary>XML is pretty easy.</summary>
18
19      <content>In this chapter, we present a wide variety of examples
20         that use XML.
21      </content>
22
23   </article>
```

Fig. 18.1 XML used to mark up an article (part 2 of 2).

This document begins with an optional *XML declaration* (line 1), which identifies the document as an XML document. The **version** *information parameter* specifies the version of XML that is used in the document. XML comments (lines 3–4), which begin with `<!--` and end with `-->`, can be placed almost anywhere in an XML document. As in a Visual Basic program, comments are used in XML for documentation purposes.

Common Programming Error 18.1

The placement of any characters, including whitespace, before the XML declaration is a syntax error.

Portability Tip 18.1

Although the XML declaration is optional, documents should include the declaration to identify the version of XML used. Otherwise, in the future, a document that lacks an XML declaration might be assumed to conform to the latest version of XML, and errors could result.

In XML, data are marked up using *tags*, which are names enclosed in *angle brackets* (`<>`). Tags are used in pairs to delimit character data (e.g., **Simple XML**). A tag that begins *markup* (i.e., XML data) is called a *start tag*, whereas a tag that terminates markup is called an *end tag*. Examples of start tags are `<article>` and `<title>` (lines 6 and 8, respectively). End tags differ from start tags in that they contain a *forward slash* (`/`) character immediately after the `<` character. Examples of end tags are `</title>` and `</article>` (lines 8 and 23, respectively). XML documents can contain any number of tags.

Common Programming Error 18.2

Failure to provide a corresponding end tag for a start tag is a syntax error.

Individual units of markup (i.e., everything included between a start tag and its corresponding end tag) are called *elements*. An XML document includes one element (called a *root element*) that contains every other element. The root element must be the first elemnent after the XML declaration. In Fig. 18.1, **article** (line 6) is the root element. Elements are *nested* within each other to form hierarchies—with the root element at the top of the hierarchy. This allows document authors to create explicit relationships between data. For example, elements **title**, **date**, **author**, **summary** and **content** then are nested within **article**. Elements **firstName** and **lastName** are nested within **author**.

Common Programming Error 18.3

Attempting to create more than one root element in an XML document is a syntax error.

Element **title** (line 8) contains the title of the article, **Simple XML**, as character data. Similarly, **date** (line 10), **summary** (line 17) and **content** (lines 19–21) contain as character data the date, summary and content, respectively. XML element names can be of any length and may contain letters, digits, underscores, hyphens and periods—they must begin with a letter or an underscore.

Common Programming Error 18.4

XML is case sensitive. The use of the wrong case for an XML element name is a syntax error.

By itself, this document is simply a text file named **article.xml**. Although it is not required, most XML documents end in the file extension **.xml**. The processing of XML documents requires a program called an *XML parser*. Parsers are responsible for checking an XML document's syntax and making the XML document's data available to applications. Often, XML parsers are built into applications such as Visual Studio or available for download over the Internet. Popular parsers include Microsoft's *msxml*, the Apache Software Foundation's *Xerces* and IBM's *XML4J*. In this chapter, we use msxml.

When the user loads **article.xml** into Internet Explorer (IE),[1] msxml parses the document and passes the parsed data to IE. IE then uses a built-in *style sheet* to format the data. Notice that the resulting format of the data (Fig. 18.2) is similar to the format of the XML document shown in Fig. 18.1. As we soon demonstrate, style sheets play an important and powerful role in the transformation of XML data into formats suitable for display.

Notice the minus (**–**) and plus (**+**) signs in Fig. 18.2. Although these are not part of the XML document, IE places them next to all *container elements* (i.e., elements that contain other elements). Container elements also are called *parent elements*. A minus sign indicates that the parent element's *child elements* (i.e., nested elements) are being displayed. When clicked, a minus sign becomes a plus sign (which collapses the container element and hides all children). Conversely, clicking a plus sign expands the container element and changes the plus sign to a minus sign. This behavior is similar to the viewing of the directory structure on a Windows system using Windows Explorer. In fact, a directory structure often is modeled as a series of tree structures, in which each drive letter (e.g., **C:**, etc.) represents the *root* of a tree. Each folder is a *node* in the tree. Parsers often place XML data into trees to facilitate efficient manipulation, as discussed in Section 18.4.

Common Programming Error 18.5

Nesting XML tags improperly is a syntax error. For example, **<x><y>hello</x></y>** *is an error, because the* **</y>** *tag must precede the* **</x>** *tag.*

We now present a second XML document (Fig. 18.3), which marks up a business letter. This document contains significantly more data than did the previous XML document.

---

1. IE 5 and higher.

Chapter 18 Extensible Markup Language (XML) 837

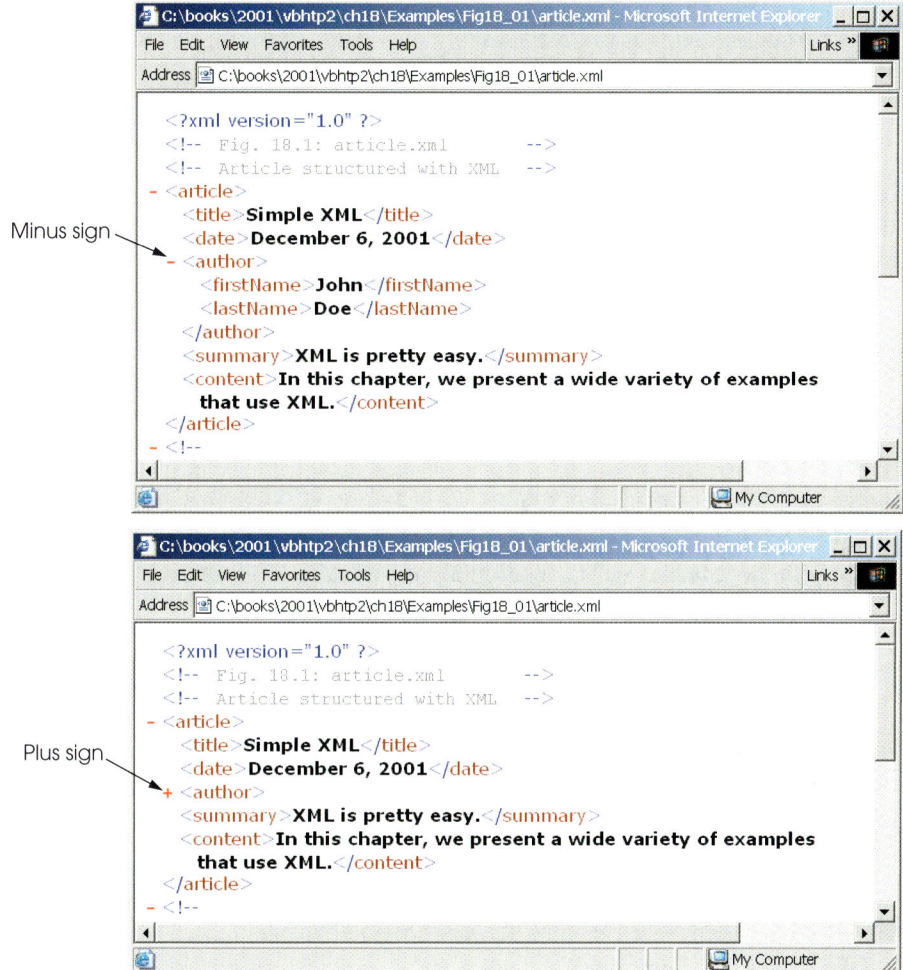

Fig. 18.2 `article.xml` displayed by Internet Explorer.

```
1   <?xml version = "1.0"?>
2
3   <!-- Fig. 18.3: letter.xml              -->
4   <!-- Business letter formatted with XML -->
5
6   <letter>
7      <contact type = "from">
8         <name>Jane Doe</name>
9         <address1>Box 12345</address1>
10        <address2>15 Any Ave.</address2>
11        <city>Othertown</city>
12        <state>Otherstate</state>
```

Fig. 18.3 XML to mark up a business letter (part 1 of 2).

```
13              <zip>67890</zip>
14              <phone>555-4321</phone>
15              <flag gender = "F" />
16          </contact>
17
18          <contact type = "to">
19              <name>John Doe</name>
20              <address1>123 Main St.</address1>
21              <address2></address2>
22              <city>Anytown</city>
23              <state>Anystate</state>
24              <zip>12345</zip>
25              <phone>555-1234</phone>
26              <flag gender = "M" />
27          </contact>
28
29          <salutation>Dear Sir:</salutation>
30
31              <paragraph>It is our privilege to inform you about our new
32              database managed with <technology>XML</technology>. This
33              new system allows you to reduce the load on
34              your inventory list server by having the client machine
35              perform the work of sorting and filtering the data.
36              </paragraph>
37
38              <paragraph>Please visit our Web site for availability
39              and pricing.
40              </paragraph>
41
42          <closing>Sincerely</closing>
43
44          <signature>Ms. Doe</signature>
45      </letter>
```

Fig. 18.3 XML to mark up a business letter (part 2 of 2).

Root element **letter** (lines 6–45) contains the child elements **contact** (lines 7–16 and 18–27), **salutation**, **paragraph**, **closing** and **signature**. In addition to being placed between tags, data also can be placed in *attributes*, which are name-value pairs in start tags. Elements can have any number of attributes in their start tags. The first **contact** element (lines 7–16) has attribute **type** with attribute *value* **"from"**, which indicates that this contact element marks up information about the letter's sender. The second **contact** element (lines 18–27) has attribute **type** with value **"to"**, which indicates that this contact element marks up information about the letter's recipient. Like element names, attribute names are case sensitive, can be any length; may contain letters, digits, underscores, hyphens and periods; and must begin with either a letter or underscore character. A **contact** element stores a contact's name, address and phone number. Element **salutation** (line 29) marks up the letter's salutation. Lines 31–40 mark up the letter's body with **paragraph** elements. Elements **closing** (line 42) and **signature** (line 44) mark up the closing sentence and the signature of the letter's author, respectively.

Common Programming Error 18.6

Failure to enclose attribute values in double (`" "`) or single (`' '`) quotes is a syntax error.

In line 15, we introduce *empty element* **flag**, which is used to indicate the gender of the contact. Empty elements do not contain character data (i.e., they do not contain text between the start and end tags). Such elements are closed either by placing a slash at the end of the element (as shown in line 15) or by explicitly writing a closing tag, as in

```
<flag gender = "F"></flag>
```

18.3 XML Namespaces

Object-oriented programming languages, such as C++ and Visual Basic, provide massive class libraries that group their features into namespaces. These namespaces prevent *naming collisions* between programmer-defined identifiers and identifiers in class libraries. For example, we might use class **CBook** to represent information on one of our publications; however, a stamp collector might use class **CBook** to represent a book of stamps. A naming collision would occur if we use these two classes in the same assembly, without using namespaces to differentiate them.

Like Visual Basic, XML also provides *namespaces*, which provide a means of uniquely identifying XML elements. In addition, XML-based languages—called *vocabularies*, such as XML Schema (Section 18.5), Extensible Stylesheet Language (Section 18.6) and BizTalk (Section 18.7)—often use namespaces to identify their elements.

Elements are differentiated via *namespace prefixes*, which identify the namespace to which an element belongs. For example,

```
<deitel:book>Visual Basic How to Program</deitel:book>
```

qualifies element **book** with namespace prefix **deitel**. This indicates that element **book** is part of namespace **deitel**. Document authors can use any name for a namespace prefix except the reserved namespace prefix *xml*.

Common Programming Error 18.7

*Attempting to create a namespace prefix named **xml** in any mixture of case is a syntax error.*

The mark up in Fig. 18.4 demonstrates the use of namespaces. This XML document contains two **file** elements that are differentiated using namespaces.

```
1  <?xml version = "1.0"?>
2
3  <!-- Fig. 18.4: namespace.xml -->
4  <!-- Demonstrating namespaces -->
5
6  <text:directory xmlns:text = "urn:deitel:textInfo"
7     xmlns:image = "urn:deitel:imageInfo">
8
```

Fig. 18.4 XML namespaces demonstration (part 1 of 2).

```
 9      <text:file filename = "book.xml">
10         <text:description>A book list</text:description>
11      </text:file>
12
13      <image:file filename = "funny.jpg">
14         <image:description>A funny picture</image:description>
15         <image:size width = "200" height = "100" />
16      </image:file>
17
18   </text:directory>
```

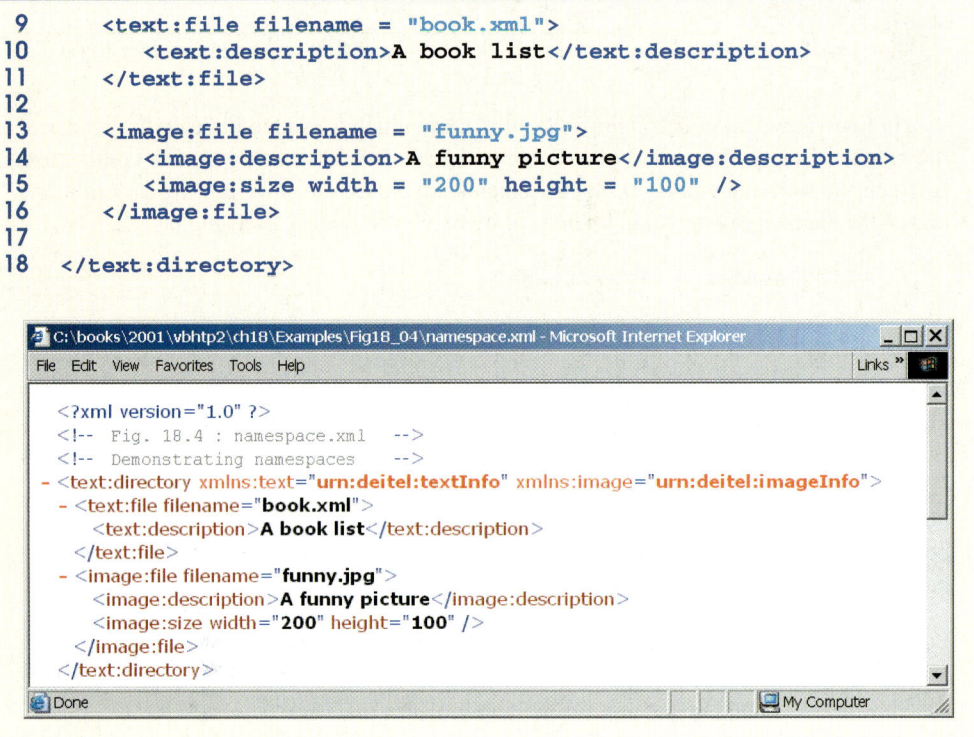

Fig. 18.4 XML namespaces demonstration (part 2 of 2).

Software Engineering Observation 18.1

Attributes need not be qualified with namespace prefixes, because they always are associated with elements.

Lines 6–7 use attribute **xmlns** to create two namespace prefixes: **text** and **image**. Each namespace prefix is bound to a series of characters called a *uniform resource identifier (URI)* that uniquely identifies the namespace. Document authors create their own namespace prefixes and URIs.

To ensure that namespaces are unique, document authors must provide unique URIs. Here, we use the text **urn:deitel:textInfo** and **urn:deitel:imageInfo** as URIs. A common practice is to use *Universal Resource Locators (URLs)* for URIs, because the domain names (such as, **www.deitel.com**) used in URLs are guaranteed to be unique. For example, lines 6–7 could have been written as

```
<text:directory xmlns:text =
   "http://www.deitel.com/xmlns-text"
   xmlns:image = "http://www.deitel.com/xmlns-image">
```

In this example, we use URLs related to the Deitel & Associates, Inc, domain name to identify namespaces. The parser never visits these URLs—they simply represent a series of characters used to differentiate names. The URLs need not refer to actual Web pages or be formed properly .

Lines 9–11 use the namespace prefix **text** to describe elements **file** and **description**. Notice that the namespace prefix **text** is applied to the end tags as well. Lines 13–16 apply namespace prefix **image** to elements **file**, **description** and **size**.

To eliminate the need to precede each element with a namespace prefix, document authors can specify a *default namespace*. Figure 18.5 demonstrates the creation and use of default namespaces.

Line 6 declares a default namespace using attribute **xmlns** with a URI as its value. Once we define this default namespace, child elements belonging to the namespace need not be qualified by a namespace prefix. Element **file** (line 9–11) is in the namespace corresponding to the URI **urn:deitel:textInfo**. Compare this to Fig. 18.4, where we prefixed **file** and **description** with **text** (lines 9–11).

```xml
 1  <?xml version = "1.0"?>
 2
 3  <!-- Fig. 18.5: defaultnamespace.xml -->
 4  <!-- Using default namespaces        -->
 5
 6  <directory xmlns = "urn:deitel:textInfo"
 7     xmlns:image = "urn:deitel:imageInfo">
 8
 9     <file filename = "book.xml">
10        <description>A book list</description>
11     </file>
12
13     <image:file filename = "funny.jpg">
14        <image:description>A funny picture</image:description>
15        <image:size width = "200" height = "100" />
16     </image:file>
17
18  </directory>
```

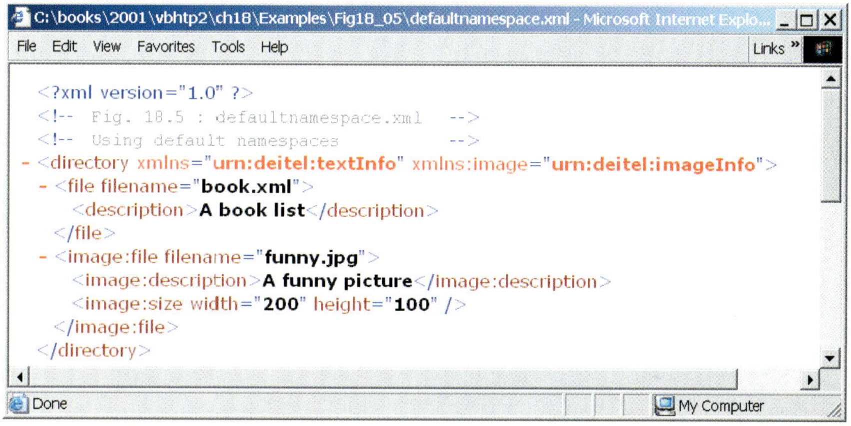

Fig. 18.5 Default namespaces demonstration.

The default namespace applies to the **directory** element and all elements that are not qualified with a namespace prefix. However, we can use a namespace prefix to specify a different namespace for particular elements. For example, the **file** element in line 13 is prefixed with **image** to indicate that it is in the namespace corresponding to the URI **urn:deitel:imageInfo**, rather than the default namespace.

18.4 Document Object Model (DOM)

Although XML documents are text files, retrieving data from them via sequential-file access techniques is neither practical nor efficient, especially in situations where data must be added or deleted dynamically.

Upon successful parsing of documents, some XML parsers store document data as tree structures in memory. Figure 18.6 illustrates the tree structure for the document **article.xml** discussed in Fig. 18.1. This hierarchical tree structure is called a *Document Object Model (DOM)* tree, and an XML parser that creates this type of structure is known as a *DOM parser*. The DOM tree represents each component of the XML document (e.g., **article**, **date**, **firstName**, etc.) as a node in the tree. Nodes (such as, **author**) that contain other nodes (called *child nodes*) are called *parent nodes*. Nodes that have the same parent (such as, **firstName** and **lastName**) are called *sibling nodes*. A node's *descendant nodes* include that node's children, its children's children and so on. Similarly, a node's *ancestor nodes* include that node's parent, its parent's parent and so on. Every DOM tree has a single *root node* that contains all other nodes in the document.

Classes for creating, reading and manipulating XML documents are located in the Visual Basic namespace **System.Xml**. This namespace also contains additional namespaces that contain other XML-related operations.

In this section, we present several examples that use DOM trees. Our first example, the program in Fig. 18.7, loads the XML document presented in Fig. 18.1 and displays its data in a text box. This example uses an **XmlReader** derived class named **XmlNodeReader**, which iterates through each node in the XML document. Class **XmlReader** is an **MustInherit** class that defines the interface for reading XML documents.

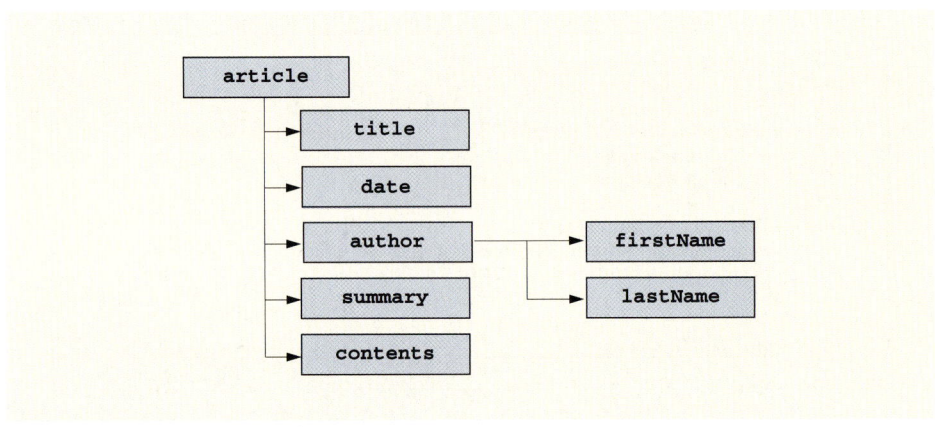

Fig. 18.6 Tree structure for Fig. 18.1.

Line 4 includes the **System.Xml** namespace, which contains the XML classes used in this example. Line 23 creates a reference to an ***XmlDocument*** object that conceptually represents an empty XML document. The XML document **article.xml** is parsed and loaded into this **XmlDocument** object when method ***Load*** is invoked in line 24. Once an XML document is loaded into an **XmlDocument**, its data can be read and manipulated programmatically. In this example, we read each node in the **XmlDocument**, which is the DOM tree. In successive examples, we demonstrate how to manipulate node values.

```vb
1   ' Fig. 18.7: XmlReaderTest.vb
2   ' Reading an XML document.
3
4   Imports System.Xml
5   Imports System.Windows.Forms
6
7   Public Class FrmXMLReaderTest
8      Inherits Form
9
10     ' TextBox displays XML output
11     Friend WithEvents txtOutput As TextBox
12
13     Public Sub New()
14        MyBase.New()
15
16        ' This call is required by the Windows Form Designer.
17        InitializeComponent()
18
19        ' Add any initialization after the
20        ' InitializeComponent() call
21
22        ' reference to "XML document"
23        Dim document As XmlDocument = New XmlDocument()
24        document.Load("article.xml")
25
26        ' create XmlNodeReader for document
27        Dim reader As XmlNodeReader = New XmlNodeReader(document)
28
29        ' show form before txtOutput is populated
30        Me.Show()
31
32        ' tree depth is -1, no indentation
33        Dim depth As Integer = -1
34
35        ' display each node's content
36        While reader.Read
37
38           Select Case reader.NodeType
39
40              ' if Element, display its name
41              Case XmlNodeType.Element
42
43                 ' increase tab depth
44                 depth += 1
```

Fig. 18.7 **XmlNodeReader** iterates through an XML document (part 1 of 3).

```vbnet
45                     TabOutput(depth)
46                     txtOutput.Text &= "<" & reader.Name & ">" & _
47                        vbCrLf
48
49                     ' if empty element, decrease depth
50                     If reader.IsEmptyElement Then
51                        depth -= 1
52                     End If
53
54                  Case XmlNodeType.Comment ' if Comment, display it
55                     TabOutput(depth)
56                     txtOutput.Text &= "<!--" & reader.Value & _
57                        "-->" & vbCrLf
58
59                  Case XmlNodeType.Text ' if Text, display it
60                     TabOutput(depth)
61                     txtOutput.Text &= vbTab & reader.Value & vbCrLf
62
63                     ' if XML declaration, display it
64                  Case XmlNodeType.XmlDeclaration
65                     TabOutput(depth)
66                     txtOutput.Text &= "<?" & reader.Name & " " & _
67                        reader.Value & "?>" & vbCrLf
68
69                     ' if EndElement, display it and decrement depth
70                  Case XmlNodeType.EndElement
71                     TabOutput(depth)
72                     txtOutput.Text &= "</" & reader.Name & ">/" & _
73                        vbCrLf
74
75                     depth -= 1
76
77               End Select
78
79            End While
80
81     End Sub ' New
82
83     ' Visual Studio .NET generated code
84
85     ' insert tabs
86     Private Sub TabOutput(ByVal number As Integer)
87        Dim i As Integer
88
89        For i = 0 To number - 1
90           txtOutput.Text &= vbTab
91        Next
92
93     End Sub ' TabOutput
94
95  End Class ' FrmXmlReaderTest
```

Fig. 18.7 **XmlNodeReader** iterates through an XML document (part 2 of 3).

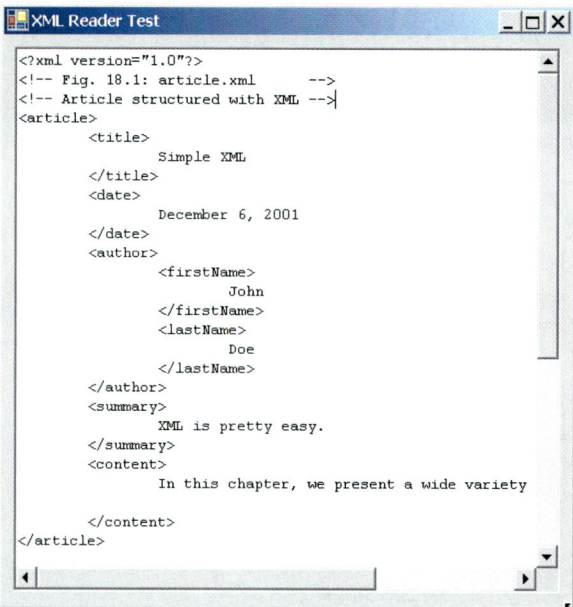

Fig. 18.7 **XmlNodeReader** iterates through an XML document (part 3 of 3).

In line 27, we create an **XmlNodeReader** and assign it to reference **reader**, which enables us to read each node sequentially from the **XmlDocument**. Method **Read** of **XmlReader** reads one node from the DOM tree. By placing this statement in the **While** loop (lines 36–79), **reader Read**s all the document nodes. The **Select Case** statement (lines 38–77) processes each node. Either the **Name** property (line 46), which contains the node's name, or the **Value** property (line 56), which contains the node's data, is formatted and concatenated to the **String** assigned to the text box **Text** property. The **NodeType** property contains the node type (specifying whether the node is an element, comment, text etc.). Notice that each **Case** specifies a node type using **XmlNodeType** enumeration constants. Note that our line breaks use the Visual Basic constant **vbCrLf**, which denotes a carriage return followed by a line feed. This is the standard line break for Windows-based applications and controls.

The displayed output emphasizes the structure of the XML document. Variable **depth** (line 33) sets the number of tab characters for indenting each element. The depth is incremented each time an **Element** type is encountered and is decremented each time an **EndElement** or empty element is encountered. We use a similar technique in the next example to emphasize the tree structure of the XML document in the display.

The Visual Basic program in Fig. 18.8 demonstrates how to manipulate DOM trees programmatically. This program loads **letter.xml** (Fig. 18.3) into the DOM tree and then creates a second DOM tree that duplicates the DOM tree containing **letter.xml**'s contents. The GUI for this application contains a text box, a **TreeView** control and three buttons—**Build**, **Print** and **Reset**. When clicked, **Build** copies **letter.xml** and displays the document's tree structure in the **TreeView** control, **Print** displays the XML element values and names in a text box and **Reset** clears the **TreeView** control and text-box content.

```vb
1   ' Fig. 18.8: XmlDom.vb
2   ' Demonstrates DOM tree manipulation.
3
4   Imports System.Xml
5   Imports System.Windows.Forms
6   Imports System.CodeDom.Compiler ' contains TempFileCollection
7
8   Public Class FrmXmlDom
9      Inherits Form
10
11     ' TextBox and TreeView for displaying data
12     Friend WithEvents txtConsole As TextBox
13     Friend WithEvents treXml As TreeView
14
15     ' Buttons for building, printing and reseting DOM tree
16     Friend WithEvents cmdBuild As Button
17     Friend WithEvents cmdPrint As Button
18     Friend WithEvents cmdReset As Button
19
20     Private source As XmlDocument ' reference to "XML document"
21
22     ' reference copy of source's "XML document"
23     Private copy As XmlDocument
24
25     Private tree As TreeNode ' TreeNode reference
26
27     Public Sub New()
28        MyBase.New()
29
30        ' This call is required by the Windows Form Designer.
31        InitializeComponent()
32
33        ' Add any initialization after the
34        ' InitializeComponent() call
35
36        ' create XmlDocument and load letter.xml
37        source = New XmlDocument()
38        source.Load("letter.xml")
39
40        ' initialize references to Nothing
41        copy = Nothing
42        tree = Nothing
43
44     End Sub ' New
45
46     ' Visual Studio .NET generated code
47
48     ' event handler for cmdBuild click event
49     Private Sub cmdBuild_Click(ByVal sender As System.Object, _
50        ByVal e As System.EventArgs) Handles cmdBuild.Click
51
52        ' determine if copy has been built already
53        If Not copy Is Nothing Then
```

Fig. 18.8 DOM structure of an XML document (part 1 of 5).

```vbnet
54            Return ' document already exists
55         End If
56
57         ' instantiate XmlDocument and TreeNode
58         copy = New XmlDocument()
59         tree = New TreeNode()
60
61         ' add root node name to TreeNode and add
62         ' TreeNode to TreeView control
63         tree.Text = source.Name ' assigns #root
64         treXml.Nodes.Add(tree)
65
66         ' build node and tree hierarchy
67         BuildTree(source, copy, tree)
68      End Sub ' cmdBuild_Click
69
70      ' event handler for cmdPrint click event
71      Private Sub cmdPrint_Click(ByVal sender As System.Object, _
72         ByVal e As System.EventArgs) Handles cmdPrint.Click
73
74         ' exit if copy does not reference an XmlDocument
75         If copy Is Nothing Then
76            Return
77         End If
78
79         ' create temporary XML file
80         Dim file As TempFileCollection = New TempFileCollection()
81
82         ' create file that is deleted at program termination
83         file.AddExtension("xml", False)
84         Dim filename As String() = New String(0) {}
85         file.CopyTo(filename, 0)
86
87         ' write XML data to disk
88         Dim writer As XmlTextWriter = _
89            New XmlTextWriter(filename(0), _
90            System.Text.Encoding.UTF8)
91
92         copy.WriteTo(writer)
93         writer.Close()
94
95         ' parse and load temporary XML document
96         Dim reader As XmlTextReader = _
97            New XmlTextReader(filename(0))
98
99         ' read, format and display data
100        While reader.Read
101
102           If reader.NodeType = XmlNodeType.EndElement Then
103              txtConsole.Text &= "/"
104           End If
105
```

Fig. 18.8 DOM structure of an XML document (part 2 of 5).

```vbnet
106              If reader.Name <> String.Empty Then
107                  txtConsole.Text &= reader.Name & vbCrLf
108              End If
109
110              If reader.Value <> String.Empty Then
111                  txtConsole.Text &= vbTab & reader.Value & vbCrLf
112              End If
113
114          End While
115
116          reader.Close()
117      End Sub ' cmdPrint_Click
118
119      ' handle cmdReset click event
120      Private Sub cmdReset_Click(ByVal sender As System.Object, _
121          ByVal e As System.EventArgs) Handles cmdReset.Click
122
123          ' remove TreeView nodes
124          If Not tree Is Nothing Then
125              treXml.Nodes.Remove(tree)
126          End If
127
128          treXml.Refresh() ' force TreeView update
129
130          ' delete XmlDocument and tree
131          copy = Nothing
132          tree = Nothing
133
134          txtConsole.Clear() ' clear text box
135      End Sub ' cmdReset_Click
136
137      ' construct DOM tree
138      Private Sub BuildTree(ByVal xmlSourceNode As XmlNode, _
139          ByVal documentValue As XmlNode, _
140          ByVal treeNode As TreeNode)
141
142          ' create XmlNodeReader to access XML document
143          Dim nodeReader As XmlNodeReader = _
144              New XmlNodeReader(xmlSourceNode)
145
146          ' represents current node in DOM tree
147          Dim currentNode As XmlNode = Nothing
148
149          ' treeNode to add to existing tree
150          Dim newNode As TreeNode = New TreeNode()
151
152          ' references modified node type for CreateNode
153          Dim modifiedNodeType As XmlNodeType
154
155          While nodeReader.Read
156
157              ' get current node type
158              modifiedNodeType = nodeReader.NodeType
```

Fig. 18.8 DOM structure of an XML document (part 3 of 5).

```vb
159
160            ' check for EndElement, store as Element
161            If modifiedNodeType = XmlNodeType.EndElement Then
162               modifiedNodeType = XmlNodeType.Element
163            End If
164
165            ' create node copy
166            currentNode = copy.CreateNode(modifiedNodeType, _
167               nodeReader.Name, nodeReader.NamespaceURI)
168
169            ' build tree based on node type
170            Select Case nodeReader.NodeType
171
172               ' if Text node, add its value to tree
173               Case XmlNodeType.Text
174                  newNode.Text = nodeReader.Value
175                  treeNode.Nodes.Add(newNode)
176
177                  ' append Text node value to currentNode data
178                  CType(currentNode, XmlText).AppendData _
179                     (nodeReader.Value)
180
181                  documentValue.AppendChild(currentNode)
182
183               ' if EndElement, move up tree
184               Case XmlNodeType.EndElement
185                  documentValue = documentValue.ParentNode
186                  treeNode = treeNode.Parent
187
188               ' if new element, add name and traverse tree
189               Case XmlNodeType.Element
190
191                  ' determine if element contains content
192                  If Not nodeReader.IsEmptyElement Then
193
194                     ' assign node text, add newNode as child
195                     newNode.Text = nodeReader.Name
196                     treeNode.Nodes.Add(newNode)
197
198                     ' set treeNode to last child
199                     treeNode = newNode
200
201                     documentValue.AppendChild(currentNode)
202                     documentValue = documentValue.LastChild
203
204                  Else ' do not traverse empty elements
205
206                     ' assign NodeType string to newNode
207                     newNode.Text = nodeReader.NodeType.ToString
208
209                     treeNode.Nodes.Add(newNode)
210                     documentValue.AppendChild(currentNode)
211                  End If
```

Fig. 18.8 DOM structure of an XML document (part 4 of 5).

```
212
213            Case Else ' all other types, display node type
214               newNode.Text = nodeReader.NodeType.ToString
215               treeNode.Nodes.Add(newNode)
216               documentValue.AppendChild(currentNode)
217
218         End Select
219
220         newNode = New TreeNode()
221      End While
222
223      ' update TreeView control
224      treXml.ExpandAll()
225      treXml.Refresh()
226   End Sub ' BuildTree
227
228 End Class ' FrmXmlDom
```

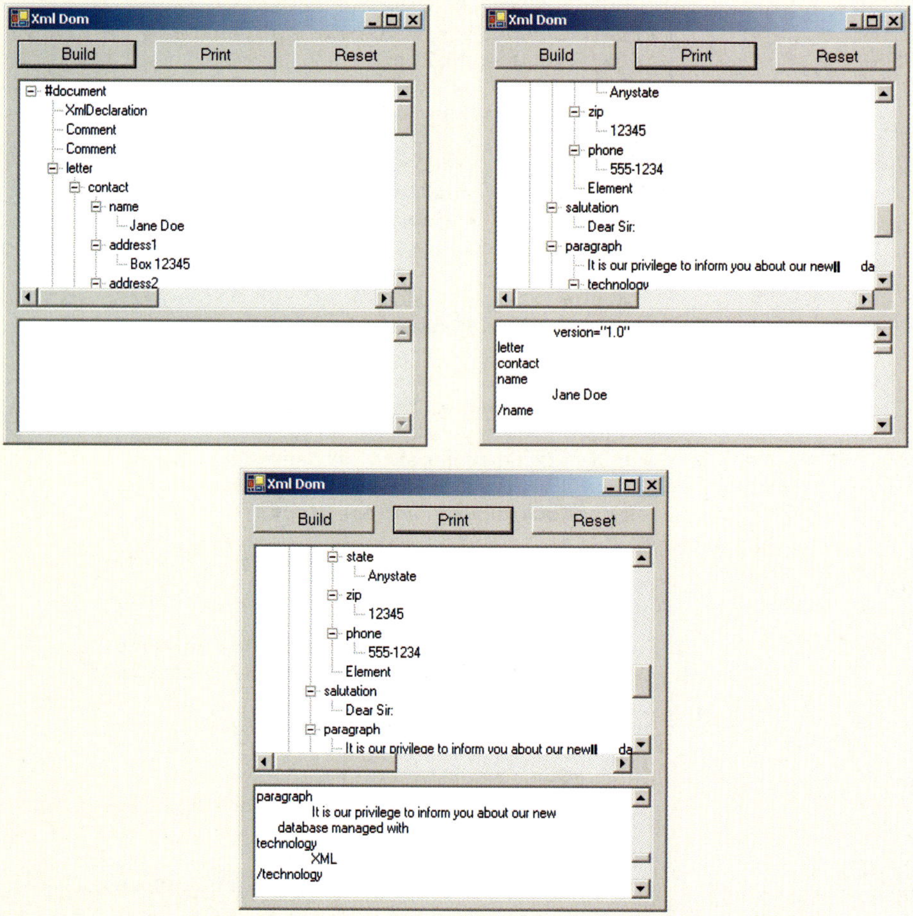

Fig. 18.8 DOM structure of an XML document (part 5 of 5).

Lines 20 and 23 create references to **XmlDocument**s **source** and **copy**. Line 37 assigns a new **XmlDocument** object to reference **source**. Line 38 then invokes method **Load** to parse and load **letter.xml**. We discuss reference **copy** shortly.

Unfortunately, **XmlDocument**s do not provide any features for displaying their content graphically. In this example, we display the document's contents using a *TreeView* control. We use class *TreeNode* to represent each node in the tree. Class **TreeView** and class **TreeNode** are part of the **System.Windows.Forms.Form** namespace. **TreeNode**s are added to the **TreeView** to emphasize the structure of the XML document.

When clicked, the **Build** button triggers the event handler **cmdBuild_Click** (lines 49–68), which creates a copy of **letter.xml** dynamically. Lines 58–59 create the **XmlDocument** and **TreeNode**s (i.e., the nodes for graphical representation in the **TreeView**). Line 63 retrieves the **Name** of the node referenced by **source** (i.e., **#root**, which represents the document root) and assigns it to **tree**'s **Text** property. This **TreeNode** then is inserted into the **TreeView** control's node list. Method **Add** is called to add each new **TreeNode** to the **TreeView**'s **Nodes** collection. Line 67 calls method **BuildTree** to copy the **XMLDocument** referenced by **source** and to update the **TreeView**.

Method **BuildTree** (line 138–226) receives an **XmlNode** representing the source node, an empty **XmlNode** and a **treeNode** to place in the DOM tree. Parameter **treeNode** references the current location in the tree (i.e., the **TreeNode** most recently added to the **TreeView** control). Lines 143–144 instantiate an **XmlNodeReader** for iterating through the DOM tree. Lines 147–150 declare **XmlNode** and **TreeNode** references that indicate the next nodes added to **document** (i.e., the DOM tree referenced by **copy**) and **treeNode**. Lines 155–221 iterate through each node in the tree.

Lines 158–167 create a node containing a copy of the current **nodeReader** node. Method *CreateNode* of **XmlDocument** takes a **NodeType**, a **Name** and a *NamespaceURI* as arguments. The **NodeType** cannot be an **EndElement**. If the **NodeType** is an **EndElement** type, lines 161–162 assign **modifiedNodeType** type **Element**.

The **Select Case** statement in lines 170–218 determines the node type, creates and adds nodes to the **TreeView** and updates the DOM tree. When a text node is encountered, the new **TreeNode**'s **newNode**'s **Text** property is assigned the current node's value. This **TreeNode** is added to the **TreeView** control. In lines 178–179, we downcast **currentNode** to **XmlText** and append the node's value. The **currentNode** then is appended to the **document**. Lines 184–186 match an **EndElement** node type. This **case** moves up the tree, because the end of an element has been encountered. The *ParentNode* and *Parent* properties retrieve the **documentValue**'s and **treeNode**'s parents, respectively.

Line 189 matches **Element** node types. Each non-empty **Element NodeType** (line 192) increases the depth of the tree; thus, we assign the current **nodeReader Name** to the **newNode**'s **Text** property and add the **newNode** to the **treeNode** node list. Lines 199–202 reorder the nodes in the node list to ensure that **newNode** is the last **TreeNode** in the node list. **XmlNode currentNode** is appended to **documentValue** as the last child, and **document** is set to its *LastChild*, which is the child we just added. If it is an empty element (line 204), we assign to the **newNode**'s **Text** property the **String** representation of the **NodeType**. Next, the **newNode** is added to the **treeNode** node list. Line 216 appends the **currentNode** to the **documentValue**. The **default** case assigns the

String representation of the node type to the **NewNode Text** property, adds the **newNode** to the **TreeNode** node list and appends the **currentNode** to the **document**.

After the DOM trees are built, the **TreeNode** node list is displayed in the **TreeView** control. The clicking of the nodes (i.e., the **+** or **−** boxes) in the **TreeView** either expands or collapses them. When **Print** is clicked, the event handler method **cmdPrint_Click** (lines 71–117) is invoked. Lines 80–85 create a temporary file for storing the XML. Lines 88–90 create an **XmlTextWriter** for streaming the XML data to disk. Method **WriteTo** is called to write the XML representation to the **XmlTextWriter** stream (line 92). Lines 96–97 create an **XmlTextReader** to read from the file. The **While** loop (line 100–114) reads each node in the DOM tree and writes tag names and character data to the text box. If it is an end element, a slash is concatenated. If the node has a **Name** or **Value**, that name or value is concatenated to the text box text.

The **Reset** button's event handler, **cmdReset_Click**, deletes both dynamically generated trees and updates the **TreeView** control's display. Reference **copy** is assigned **Nothing** (to allow its tree to be garbage collected in line 131), and the **TreeNode** node list reference **tree** is assigned **Nothing**.

Although **XmlReader** includes methods for reading and modifying node values, it is not the most efficient means of locating data in a DOM tree. Microsoft .NET provides class **XPathNavigator** in the **System.Xml.XPath** namespace for iterating through node lists that match search criteria, which are written as an *XPath expression*. XPath (XML Path Language) provides a syntax for locating specific nodes in XML documents effectively and efficiently. XPath is a string-based language of expressions used by XML and many of its related technologies (such as, XSLT, discussed in Section 18.6).

Figure 18.9, demonstrates how to navigate through an XML document using an **XPathNavigator**. Like Fig. 18.8, this program uses a **TreeView** control and **TreeNode** objects to display the XML document's structure. However, instead of displaying the entire DOM tree, the **TreeNode** node list is updated each time the **XPathNavigator** is positioned to a new node. Nodes are added to and deleted from the **TreeView** to reflect the **XPathNavigator**'s location in the DOM tree. The XML document **games.xml** that we use in this example is presented in Fig. 18.10.

```vb
 1    ' Fig. 18.9: PathNavigator.vb
 2    ' Demonstrates Class XPathNavigator
 3
 4    Imports System.Windows.Forms
 5    Imports System.Xml.XPath ' contains XPathNavigator
 6
 7    Public Class FrmPathNavigator
 8       Inherits Form
 9
10       ' GroupBox contains Controls for locating XML file
11       Friend WithEvents locateGroupBox As GroupBox
12       Friend WithEvents cmdSelect As Button
13       Friend WithEvents cboSelect As ComboBox
14       Friend WithEvents txtSelect As TextBox
15
```

Fig. 18.9 **XPathNavigator** class navigates selected nodes (part 1 of 7).

```vb
16      ' GroupBox contains Controls for navigating DOM tree
17      Friend WithEvents navigateGroupBox As GroupBox
18      Friend WithEvents cmdNext As Button
19      Friend WithEvents cmdPrevious As Button
20      Friend WithEvents cmdParent As Button
21      Friend WithEvents cmdFirstChild As Button
22
23      ' TreeView displays DOM-tree results
24      Friend WithEvents trePath As TreeView
25
26      ' navigator to traverse document
27      Private xPath As XPathNavigator
28
29      ' references document for use by XPathNavigator
30      Private document As XPathDocument
31
32      ' references TreeNode list used by TreeView control
33      Private tree As TreeNode
34
35      Public Sub New()
36         MyBase.New()
37
38         ' This call is required by the Windows Form Designer.
39         InitializeComponent()
40
41         ' Add any initialization after the
42         ' InitializeComponent() call
43
44         ' load in XML document
45         document = New XPathDocument("sports.xml")
46
47         ' create nagivator
48         xPath = document.CreateNavigator
49
50         ' create root node for TreeNodes
51         tree = New TreeNode()
52
53         tree.Text = xPath.NodeType.ToString    ' #root
54         trePath.Nodes.Add(tree)                ' add tree
55
56         ' update TreeView control
57         trePath.ExpandAll()
58         trePath.Refresh()
59         trePath.SelectedNode = tree            ' highlight root
60      End Sub ' New
61
62      ' Visual Studio .NET generated code
63
64      ' traverse to first child
65      Private Sub cmdFirstChild_Click( _
66         ByVal sender As System.Object, _
67         ByVal e As System.EventArgs) Handles cmdFirstChild.Click
```

Fig. 18.9 `XPathNavigator` class navigates selected nodes (part 2 of 7).

```vbnet
68
69          Dim newTreeNode As TreeNode
70
71          ' move to first child
72          If xPath.MoveToFirstChild Then
73             newTreeNode = New TreeNode() ' create new node
74
75             ' set node's Text property to either
76             ' navigator's name or value
77             DetermineType(newTreeNode, xPath)
78
79             ' add node to TreeNode node list
80             tree.Nodes.Add(newTreeNode)
81             tree = newTreeNode ' assign tree newTreeNode
82
83             ' update TreeView control
84             trePath.ExpandAll()
85             trePath.Refresh()
86             trePath.SelectedNode = tree
87
88          Else ' node has no children
89             MessageBox.Show("Current Node has no children.", _
90                "", MessageBoxButtons.OK, MessageBoxIcon.Information)
91          End If
92
93       End Sub ' cmdFirstChild_Click
94
95       ' traverse to node's parent on cmdParent_Click event
96       Private Sub cmdParent_Click(ByVal sender As System.Object, _
97          ByVal e As System.EventArgs) Handles cmdParent.Click
98
99          ' move to parent
100         If xPath.MoveToParent Then
101
102            tree = tree.Parent
103
104            ' get number of child nodes, not including sub trees
105            Dim count As Integer = tree.GetNodeCount(False)
106
107            ' remove all children
108            Dim i As Integer
109            For i = 0 To count - 1
110               tree.Nodes.Remove(tree.FirstNode)
111            Next
112
113            ' update TreeView control
114            trePath.ExpandAll()
115            trePath.Refresh()
116            trePath.SelectedNode = tree
117
```

Fig. 18.9 **XPathNavigator** class navigates selected nodes (part 3 of 7).

```vbnet
118         Else ' if node has no parent (root node)
119             MessageBox.Show("Current node has no parent.", "", _
120                 MessageBoxButtons.OK, MessageBoxIcon.Information)
121
122         End If
123
124     End Sub ' cmdParent_Click
125
126     ' find next sibling on cmdNext_Click event
127     Private Sub cmdNext_Click(ByVal sender As System.Object, _
128         ByVal e As System.EventArgs) Handles cmdNext.Click
129
130         Dim newTreeNode As TreeNode = Nothing
131         Dim newNode As TreeNode = Nothing
132
133         ' move to next sibling
134         If xPath.MoveToNext Then
135
136             newTreeNode = tree.Parent ' get parent node
137
138             newNode = New TreeNode() ' create new node
139             DetermineType(newNode, xPath)
140             newTreeNode.Nodes.Add(newNode)
141
142             ' set current position for display
143             tree = newNode
144
145             ' update TreeView control
146             trePath.ExpandAll()
147             trePath.Refresh()
148             trePath.SelectedNode = tree
149
150         Else ' node has no additional siblings
151             MessageBox.Show("Current node is last sibling.", "", _
152                 MessageBoxButtons.OK, MessageBoxIcon.Information)
153
154         End If
155
156     End Sub ' cmdNext_Click
157
158     ' get previous sibling on cmdPrevious_Click
159     Private Sub cmdPrevious_Click( _
160         ByVal sender As System.Object, _
161         ByVal e As System.EventArgs) Handles cmdPrevious.Click
162
163         Dim parentTreeNode As TreeNode = Nothing
164
165         ' move to previous sibling
166         If xPath.MoveToPrevious Then
167
168             parentTreeNode = tree.Parent ' get parent node
169
```

Fig. 18.9 **XPathNavigator** class navigates selected nodes (part 4 of 7).

```vbnet
170             ' delete current node
171             parentTreeNode.Nodes.Remove(tree)
172
173             ' move to previous node
174             tree = parentTreeNode.LastNode
175
176             ' update TreeView control
177             trePath.ExpandAll()
178             trePath.Refresh()
179             trePath.SelectedNode = tree
180
181         Else ' if current node has no previous siblings
182             MessageBox.Show("Current node is first sibling.", "", _
183                 MessageBoxButtons.OK, MessageBoxIcon.Information)
184
185         End If
186
187     End Sub ' cmdPrevious_Click
188
189     ' process cmdSelect_Click event
190     Private Sub cmdSelect_Click(ByVal sender As System.Object, _
191         ByVal e As System.EventArgs) Handles cmdSelect.Click
192
193         Dim iterator As XPathNodeIterator ' enables node iteration
194
195         ' get specified node from ComboBox
196         Try
197             iterator = xPath.Select(cboSelect.Text)
198             DisplayIterator(iterator) ' print selection
199
200             ' catch invalid expressions
201         Catch argumentException As System.ArgumentException
202             MessageBox.Show(argumentException.Message, "Error", _
203                 MessageBoxButtons.OK, MessageBoxIcon.Error)
204
205         End Try
206
207     End Sub ' cmdSelect_Click
208
209     ' print values for XPathNodeIterator
210     Private Sub DisplayIterator( _
211         ByVal iterator As XPathNodeIterator)
212
213         txtSelect.Clear()
214
215         ' prints selected node's values
216         While iterator.MoveNext
217             txtSelect.Text &= iterator.Current.Value.Trim & vbCrLf
218         End While
219
220     End Sub ' DisplayIterator
221
```

Fig. 18.9 **XPathNavigator** class navigates selected nodes (part 5 of 7).

```
222     ' determine if TreeNode should display current node
223     ' name or value
224     Private Sub DetermineType(ByVal node As TreeNode, _
225        ByVal xPath As XPathNavigator)
226
227        ' determine NodeType
228        Select Case xPath.NodeType
229
230           Case XPathNodeType.Element ' if Element, get its name
231
232              ' get current node name, and remove whitespaces
233              node.Text = xPath.Name.Trim
234
235           Case Else   ' obtain node values
236
237              ' get current node value and remove whitespaces
238              node.Text = xPath.Value.Trim
239
240        End Select
241
242     End Sub ' DetermineType
243
244  End Class ' FrmPathNavigator
```

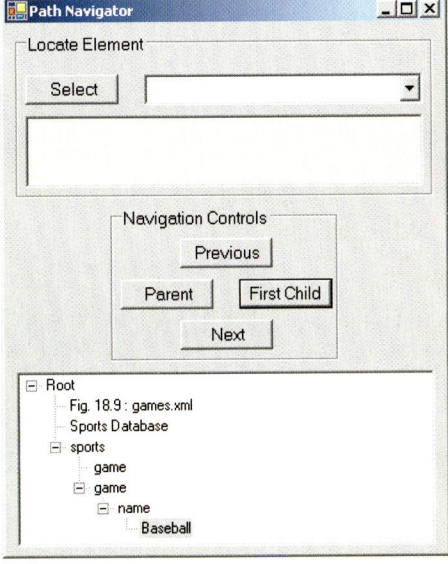
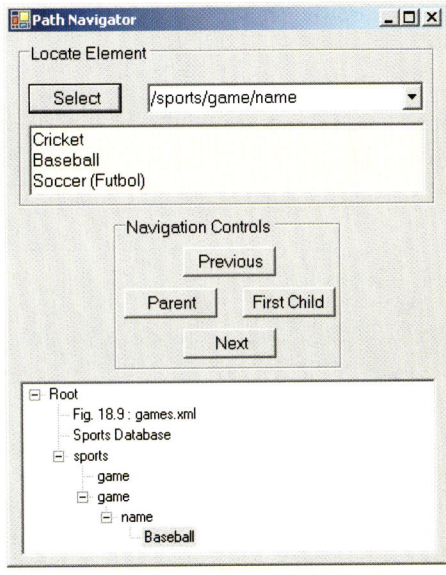

Fig. 18.9 **XPathNavigator** class navigates selected nodes (part 6 of 7).

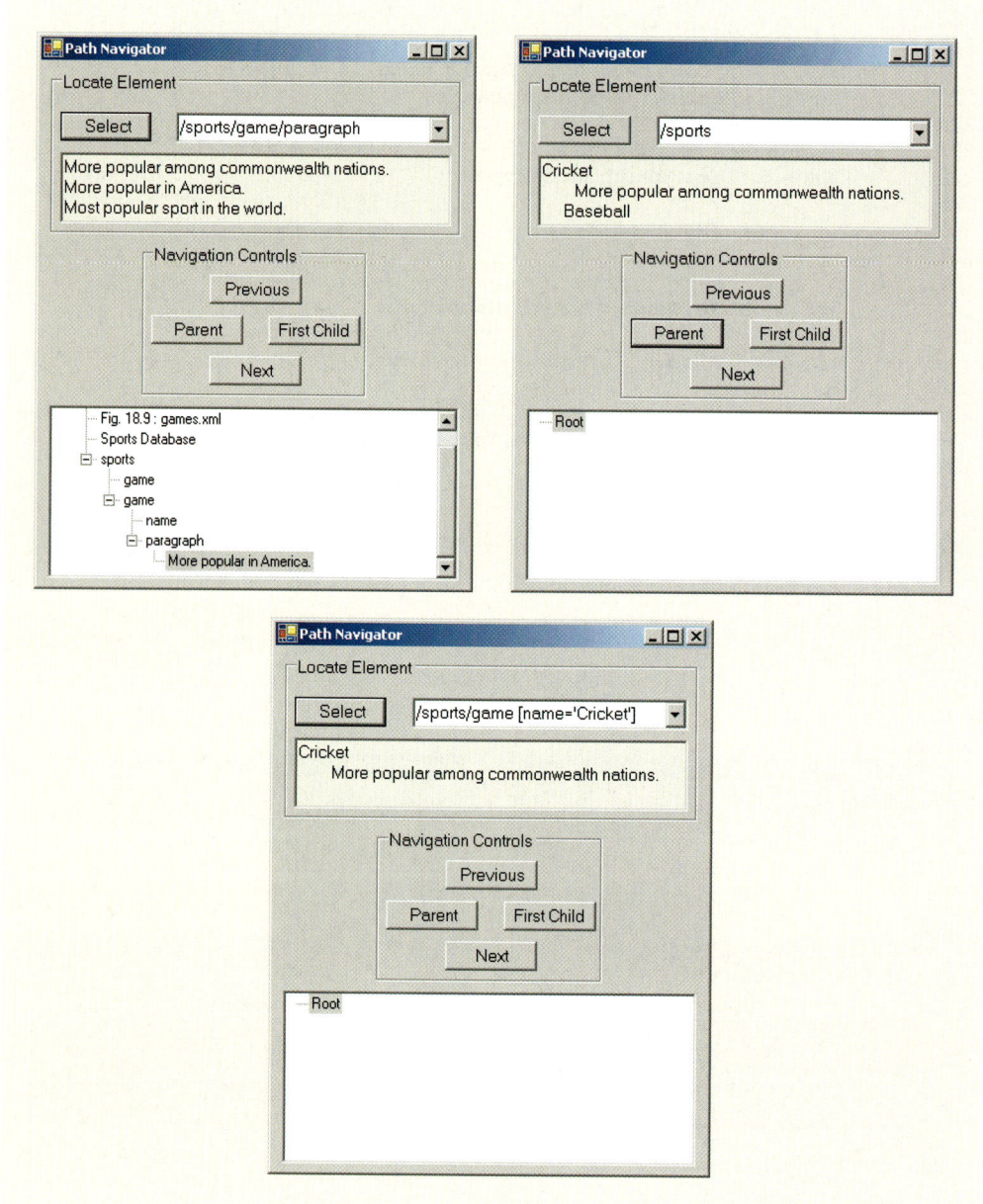

Fig. 18.9 **XPathNavigator** class navigates selected nodes (part 7 of 7).

This program loads XML document **sports.xml** into an **XPathDocument** object by passing the document's file name to the **XPathDocument** constructor (line 45). Method **CreateNavigator** (line 48) creates and returns an **XPathNavigator** reference to the **XPathDocument**'s tree structure.

```xml
1   <?xml version = "1.0"?>
2
3   <!-- Fig. 18.10: games.xml -->
4   <!-- Sports Database        -->
5
6   <sports>
7
8     <game id = "783">
9         <name>Cricket</name>
10
11        <paragraph>
12           More popular among commonwealth nations.
13        </paragraph>
14    </game>
15
16    <game id = "239">
17        <name>Baseball</name>
18
19        <paragraph>
20           More popular in America.
21        </paragraph>
22    </game>
23
24    <game id = "418">
25        <name>Soccer(Futbol)</name>
26        <paragraph>Most popular sport in the world</paragraph>
27    </game>
28  </sports>
```

Fig. 18.10 XML document that describes various sports.

The navigation methods of **XPathNavigator** in Fig. 18.9 are *MoveToFirstChild* (line 72), *MoveToParent* (line 100), *MoveToNext* (line 134) and *MoveToPrevious* (line 166). Each method performs the action that its name implies. Method **MoveToFirstChild** moves to the first child of the node referenced by the **XPathNavigator**, **MoveToParent** moves to the parent node of the node referenced by the **XPathNavigator**, **MoveToNext** moves to the next sibling of the node referenced by the **XPathNavigator** and **MoveToPrevious** moves to the previous sibling of the node referenced by the **XPathNavigator**. Each method returns a **Boolean** indicating whether the move was successful. In this example, we display a warning in a **MessageBox**, whenever a move operation fails. Furthermore, each method is called in the event handler of the button that matches its name (e.g., button **First Child** triggers **cmdFirstChild_Click**, which calls **MoveToFirstChild**).

Whenever we move forward using the **XPathNavigator**, as with **MoveToFirstChild** and **MoveToNext**, nodes are added to the **TreeNode** node list. **Private** Method **DetermineType** (lines 224–242) determines whether to assign the **Node**'s *Name* property or *Value* property to the **TreeNode** (lines 233 and 238). Whenever **MoveToParent** is called, all children of the parent node are removed from the display. Similarly, a call to **MoveToPrevious** removes the current sibling node. Note that the nodes are removed only from the **TreeView**, not from the tree representation of the document.

The other event handler corresponds to button **Select** (line 190–207). Method **Select** (line 197) takes search criteria in the form of either an *XPathExpression* or a **String** that represents an XPath expression and returns as an **XPathNodeIterator** object any nodes that match the search criteria. Figure 18.11 summarizes the XPath expressions provided by this program's combo box.

Method **DisplayIterator** (defined in lines 210–220) appends the node values from the given **XPathNodeIterator** to the **txtSelect** text box. Note that we call the **String** method **Trim** to remove unnecessary whitespace. Method *MoveNext* (line 216) advances to the next node, which property *Current* (line 217) can access.

18.5 Document Type Definitions (DTDs), Schemas and Validation

XML documents can reference optional documents that specify how the XML documents should be structured. These optional documents are called *Document Type Definitions (DTDs)* and *Schemas*. When a DTD or Schema document is provided, some parsers (called *validating parsers*) can read the DTD or Schema and check the XML document's structure against it. If the XML document conforms to the DTD or Schema, then the XML document is *valid*. Parsers that cannot check for document conformity against the DTD or Schema and are called *non-validating parsers*. If an XML parser (validating or non-validating) is able to process an XML document (that does not reference a DTD or Schema), the XML document is considered to be *well formed* (i.e., it is syntactically correct). By definition, a valid XML document is also a well-formed XML document. If a document is not well formed, parsing halts, and the parser issues an error.

 Software Engineering Observation 18.2

DTD and Schema documents are essential components for XML documents used in business-to-business (B2B) transactions and mission-critical systems. These documents help ensure that XML documents are valid.

Expression	Description
`/sports`	Matches all **sports** nodes that are child nodes of the document root node.
`/sports/game/name`	Matches all **name** nodes that are child nodes of **game**. The **game** is a child of **sports**, which is a child of the document root.
`/sports/game/paragraph`	Matches all **paragraph** nodes that are child nodes of **game**. The **game** is a child of **sports**, which is a child of the document root.
`/sports/game[name='Cricket']`	Matches all **game** nodes that contain element **name** whose name is **Cricket**. The **game** is a child of **sports**, which is a child of the document root.

Fig. 18.11 XPath expressions and descriptions.

Software Engineering Observation 18.3

Because XML document content can be structured in many different ways, an application cannot determine whether the document data it receives is complete, missing data or ordered properly. DTDs and Schemas solve this problem by providing an extensible means of describing a document's contents. An application can use a DTD or Schema document to perform a validity check on the document's contents.

18.5.1 Document Type Definitions

Document type definitions (DTDs) provide a means for type checking XML documents and thus verifying their *validity* (confirming that elements contain the proper attributes, elements are in the proper sequence, etc.). DTDs use *EBNF* (*Extended Backus-Naur Form*) *grammar* to describe an XML document's content. XML parsers need additional functionality to read EBNF grammar, because it is not XML syntax. Although DTDs are optional, they are recommended to ensure document conformity. The DTD in Fig. 18.12 defines the set of rules (i.e., the grammar) for structuring the business letter document contained in Fig. 18.13.

Portability Tip 18.2

DTDs can ensure consistency among XML documents generated by different programs.

Line 4 uses the **ELEMENT** *element type declaration* to define rules for element **letter**. In this case, **letter** contains one or more **contact** elements, one **salutation** element, one or more **paragraph** elements, one **closing** element and one **signature** element, in that sequence. The *plus sign* (**+**) *occurrence indicator* specifies that an element must occur one or more times. Other indicators include the *asterisk* (*****), which indicates an optional element that can occur any number of times, and the *question mark* (**?**), which indicates an optional element that can occur at most once. If an occurrence indicator is omitted, exactly one occurrence is expected.

```
1   <!-- Fig. 18.12: letter.dtd    -->
2   <!-- DTD document for letter.xml -->
3
4   <!ELEMENT letter ( contact+, salutation, paragraph+,
5      closing, signature )>
6
7   <!ELEMENT contact ( name, address1, address2, city, state,
8      zip, phone, flag )>
9   <!ATTLIST contact type CDATA #IMPLIED>
10
11  <!ELEMENT name ( #PCDATA )>
12  <!ELEMENT address1 ( #PCDATA )>
13  <!ELEMENT address2 ( #PCDATA )>
14  <!ELEMENT city ( #PCDATA )>
15  <!ELEMENT state ( #PCDATA )>
16  <!ELEMENT zip ( #PCDATA )>
17  <!ELEMENT phone ( #PCDATA )>
18  <!ELEMENT flag EMPTY>
```

Fig. 18.12 Document Type Definition (DTD) for a business letter (part 1 of 2).

```
19    <!ATTLIST flag gender (M | F) "M">
20
21    <!ELEMENT salutation ( #PCDATA )>
22    <!ELEMENT closing ( #PCDATA )>
23    <!ELEMENT paragraph ( #PCDATA )>
24    <!ELEMENT signature ( #PCDATA )>
```

Fig. 18.12 Document Type Definition (DTD) for a business letter (part 2 of 2).

The **contact** element definition (line 7) specifies that it contains the **name**, **address1**, **address2**, **city**, **state**, **zip**, **phone** and **flag** elements—in that order. Exactly one occurrence of each is expected.

Line 9 uses the **ATTLIST** *element type declaration* to define an attribute (i.e., **type**) for the **contact** element. Keyword **#IMPLIED** specifies that, if the parser finds a **contact** element without a **type** attribute, the application can provide a value or ignore the missing attribute. The absence of a **type** attribute cannot invalidate the document. Other types of default values include **#REQUIRED** and **#FIXED**. Keyword **#REQUIRED** specifies that the attribute must be present in the document and the keyword **#FIXED** specifies that the attribute (if present) must always be assigned a specific value. For example,

<!ATTLIST address zip #FIXED "01757">

indicates that the value **01757** must be used for attribute **zip**; otherwise, the document is invalid. If the attribute is not present, then the parser, by default, uses the fixed value that is specified in the **ATTLIST** declaration. Flag **CDATA** specifies that attribute **type** contains a **String** that is not processed by the parser, but instead is passed to the application as is.

Software Engineering Observation 18.4

DTD syntax does not provide any mechanism for describing an element's (or attribute's) data type.

Flag **#PCDATA** (line 11) specifies that the element can store *parsed character data* (i.e., text). Parsed character data cannot contain markup. The characters less than (**<**) and ampersand (**&**) must be replaced by their *entities* (i.e., **<** and **&**). However, the ampersand character can be inserted when used with entities. See Appendix L (on CD) for a list of pre-defined entities.

Line 18 defines an empty element named **flag**. Keyword **EMPTY** specifies that the element cannot contain character data. Empty elements commonly are used for their attributes.

Common Programming Error 18.8

Any element, attribute or relationship not explicitly defined by a DTD results in an invalid document.

XML documents must explicitly reference a DTD. Figure 18.13 is an XML document that conforms to **letter.dtd** (Fig. 18.12).

This XML document is similar to that in Fig. 18.3. Line 6 references a DTD file. This markup contains three pieces: The name of the root element (**letter** in line 8) to which the DTD is applied, the keyword **SYSTEM** (which in this case denotes an *external DTD*—a DTD defined in a separate file) and the DTD's name and location (i.e., **letter.dtd** in the current directory). Though almost any file extension can be used, DTD documents typically end with the *.dtd* extension.

```xml
 1  <?xml version = "1.0"?>
 2
 3  <!-- Fig. 18.13: letter2.xml          -->
 4  <!-- Business letter formatted with XML -->
 5
 6  <!DOCTYPE letter SYSTEM "letter.dtd">
 7
 8  <letter>
 9     <contact type = "from">
10        <name>Jane Doe</name>
11        <address1>Box 12345</address1>
12        <address2>15 Any Ave.</address2>
13        <city>Othertown</city>
14        <state>Otherstate</state>
15        <zip>67890</zip>
16        <phone>555-4321</phone>
17        <flag gender = "F" />
18     </contact>
19
20     <contact type = "to">
21        <name>John Doe</name>
22        <address1>123 Main St.</address1>
23        <address2></address2>
24        <city>Anytown</city>
25        <state>Anystate</state>
26        <zip>12345</zip>
27        <phone>555-1234</phone>
28        <flag gender = "M" />
29     </contact>
30
31     <salutation>Dear Sir:</salutation>
32
33     <paragraph>It is our privilege to inform you about our new
34        database managed with XML. This new system
35        allows you to reduce the load on your inventory list
36        server by having the client machine perform the work of
37        sorting and filtering the data.
38     </paragraph>
39
40     <paragraph>Please visit our Web site for availability
41        and pricing.
42     </paragraph>
43     <closing>Sincerely</closing>
44     <signature>Ms. Doe</signature>
45  </letter>
```

Fig. 18.13 XML document referencing its associated DTD.

Various tools (many of which are free) check document conformity against DTDs and Schemas (discussed momentarily). The output in Fig. 18.14 shows the results of the validation of **letter2.xml** using Microsoft's *XML Validator*. Visit **www.w3.org/XML/Schema.html** for a list of validating tools. Microsoft XML Validator is available free for download from **msdn.microsoft.com/downloads/samples/Internet/xml/xml_validator/sample.asp**.

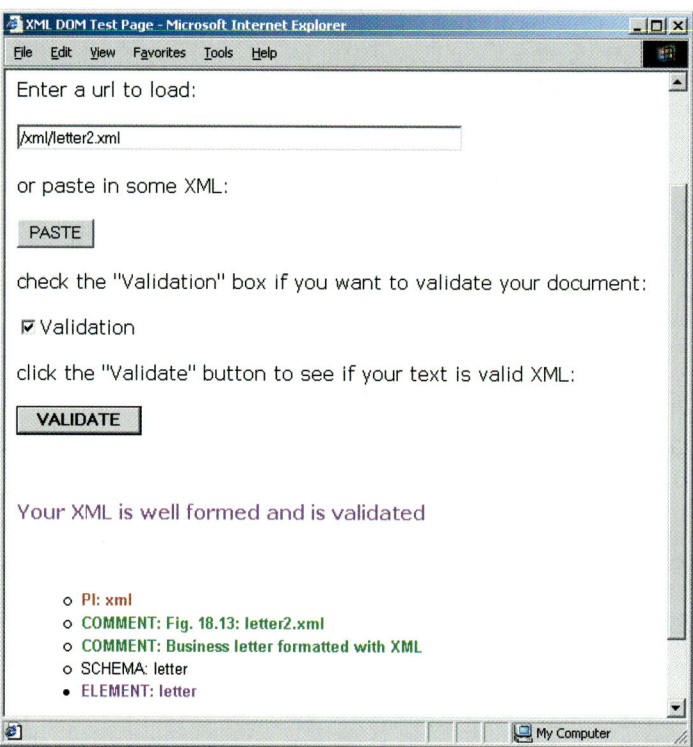

Fig. 18.14 XML Validator validates an XML document against a DTD.

Microsoft XML Validator can validate XML documents against DTDs locally or by uploading the documents to XML Validator Web site. Here, **letter2.xml** and **letter.dtd** are placed in folder **C:\XML**. This XML document (**letter2.xml**) is well formed and conforms to **letter.dtd**.

XML documents that fail validation are still well-formed documents. When a document fails to conform to a DTD or Schema, Microsoft XML Validator displays an error message. For example, the DTD in Fig. 18.12 indicates that the **contacts** element must contain child element **name**. If the document omits this child element, the document is well formed, but not valid. In such a scenario, Microsoft XML Validator displays the error message shown in Fig. 18.15.

Visual Basic programs can use msxml to validate XML documents against DTDs. For information on how to accomplish this, visit:

```
msdn.microsoft.com/library/default.asp?
url=/library/en-us/cpguidnf/html/
cpconvalidationagainstdtdwithxmlvalidatingreader.asp
```

As mentioned earlier, Schemas are the preferred means of defining structures for XML documents in .NET. Although, several types of Schemas exist, the two most popular are Microsoft Schema and W3C Schema. We begin our discussion of Schemas in the next section.

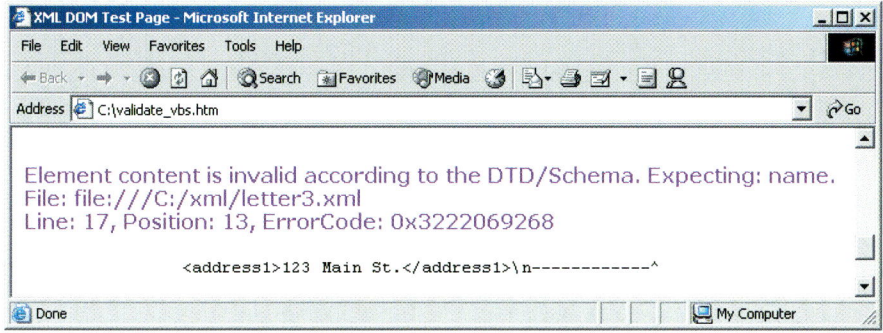

Fig. 18.15 XML Validator displaying an error message.

18.5.2 Microsoft XML Schemas

In this section, we introduce an alternative to DTDs—called Schemas—for defining XML document structures. Many developers in the XML community feel that DTDs are not flexible enough to meet today's programming needs. For example, DTDs cannot be manipulated (e.g., searched, programmatically modified, etc.) in the same manner that XML documents can, because DTDs are not XML documents.

Unlike DTDs, Schemas do not use Extended Backus-Naur Form (EBNF) grammar. Instead, Schemas are XML documents that can be manipulated (e.g., elements can be added or removed, etc.) like any other XML document. As with DTDs, Schemas require validating parsers.

In this section, we focus on Microsoft's *XML Schema* vocabulary.[2] Figure 18.16 presents an XML document that conforms to the Microsoft Schema document shown in Figure 18.17. By convention, Microsoft XML Schema documents use the file extension **.xdr**. Line 6 (Fig. 18.16) references the Schema document **book.xdr**.

```
1   <?xml version = "1.0"?>
2
3   <!-- Fig. 18.16: book.xml          -->
4   <!-- XML file that marks up book data -->
5
6   <books xmlns = "x-schema:book.xdr">
7      <book>
8         <title>C# How to Program</title>
9      </book>
10
11     <book>
12        <title>Java How to Program, 4/e</title>
13     </book>
```

Fig. 18.16 XML document that conforms to a Microsoft Schema document (part 1 of 2).

---

2. For those readers who are interested in W3C Schema, we provide such examples on our Web site, **www.deitel.com**. We also provide a detailed treatment of W3C Schema in *XML How to Program, 2/e*.

```
14
15      <book>
16         <title>Visual Basic .NET How to Program</title>
17      </book>
18
19      <book>
20         <title>Advanced Java 2 Platform How to Program</title>
21      </book>
22
23      <book>
24         <title>Python How to Program</title>
25      </book>
26   </books>
```

Fig. 18.16 XML document that conforms to a Microsoft Schema document (part 2 of 2).

```
1    <?xml version = "1.0"?>
2
3    <!-- Fig. 18.17: book.xdr                           -->
4    <!-- Schema document to which book.xml conforms -->
5
6    <Schema xmlns = "urn:schemas-microsoft-com:xml-data">
7       <ElementType name = "title" content = "textOnly"
8          model = "closed" />
9
10      <ElementType name = "book" content = "eltOnly" model = "closed">
11         <element type = "title" minOccurs = "1" maxOccurs = "1" />
12      </ElementType>
13
14      <ElementType name = "books" content = "eltOnly" model = "closed">
15         <element type = "book" minOccurs = "0" maxOccurs = "*" />
16      </ElementType>
17   </Schema>
```

Fig. 18.17 Schema file that contains structure to which **book.xml** conforms.

Software Engineering Observation 18.5

Schemas are XML documents that conform to DTDs, which define the structure of a Schema. These DTDs, which are bundled with the parser, are used to validate the Schemas that authors create.

Software Engineering Observation 18.6

Many organizations and individuals are creating DTDs and Schemas for a broad range of categories (e.g., financial transactions, medical prescriptions, etc.). Often, these collections—called repositories—are available free for download from the Web.[3]

In line 6, root element **Schema** begins the Schema markup. Microsoft Schema use the namespace URI **"urn:schemas-microsoft-com:data"**. Line 7 uses the **ElementType** element to define element **title**. Attribute **content** specifies that this element contains parsed character data (i.e., text only). Element **title** is not permitted to

---

3. See, for example, **opengis.net/schema.htm**.

contain child elements. Setting the *model* attribute to **"closed"** specifies that a conforming XML document can contain only elements defined in this Schema. Line 10 defines element **book**; this element's **content** is "elements only" (i.e., *eltOnly*). This means that the element cannot contain mixed content (i.e., text and other elements). Within the **ElementType** element named **book**, the *element* element indicates that **title** is a **child** element of **book**. Attributes *minOccurs* and *maxOccurs* are set to **"1"**, indicating that a **book** element must contain exactly one **title** element. The asterisk (*) in line 15 indicates that the Schema permits any number of **book** elements in element **books**.

Class *XmlValidatingReader* validates an XML document against a Schema. The program in Fig. 18.18 validates an XML document that the user provides (such as, Fig. 18.16 or Fig. 18.19) against a Microsoft Schema document (Fig. 18.17).

Line 17 creates an *XmlSchemaCollection* reference named **schemas**. Line 33 calls its *Add* method to add an *XmlSchema* object to the Schema collection. Method **Add** receives as arguments a name that identifies the Schema (e.g., **"book"**) and the name of the Schema file (e.g., **"book.xdr"**).

The XML document to be validated against the Schema(s) contained in the **XmlSchemaCollection** must be passed to the **XmlValidatingReader** constructor (line 48–49). Lines 44–45 create an **XmlReader** for the file that the user selected from **filesComboBox**. The **XmlReader** passed to this constructor is created using the file name selected from **cboFiles** (lines 44–45).

Line 52 **Add**s the Schema collection referenced by **Schemas** to the *Schemas* property. This property sets the Schema(s) used to validate the document. The *ValidationType* property (line 55) is set to the *ValidationType* enumeration constant for Microsoft Schema. Lines 58–59 register method **ValidationError** with *ValidationEventHandler*. Method **ValidationError** (lines 79–84) is called if the document is invalid or an error occurs, such as if the document cannot be found. Failure to register a method with **ValidationEventHandler** causes an exception to be thrown when the document is missing or invalid.

```
1    ' Fig. 18:18: ValidationTest.vb
2    ' Validating XML documents against Schemas.
3
4    Imports System.Windows.Forms
5    Imports System.Xml
6    Imports System.Xml.Schema   ' contains Schema classes
7
8    ' determines XML document Schema validity
9    Public Class FrmValidationTest
10      Inherits Form
11
12      ' Controls for validating XML document
13      Friend WithEvents cboFiles As ComboBox
14      Friend WithEvents cmdValidate As Button
15      Friend WithEvents lblConsole As Label
16
17      Private schemas As XmlSchemaCollection  ' Schemas
18      Private valid As Boolean  ' validation result
```

Fig. 18.18 Schema-validation example (part 1 of 3).

```vbnet
19
20     Public Sub New()
21        MyBase.New()
22
23        ' This call is required by the Windows Form Designer.
24        InitializeComponent()
25
26        ' Add any initialization after the
27        ' InitializeComponent() call
28
29        valid = True ' assume document is valid
30
31        ' get Schema(s) for validation
32        schemas = New XmlSchemaCollection()
33        schemas.Add("book", "book.xdr")
34     End Sub ' New
35
36     ' Visual Studio .NET generated code
37
38     ' handle cmdValidate click event
39     Private Sub cmdValidate_Click( _
40        ByVal sender As System.Object, _
41        ByVal e As System.EventArgs) Handles cmdValidate.Click
42
43        ' get XML document
44        Dim reader As XmlTextReader = _
45           New XmlTextReader(cboFiles.Text)
46
47        ' get validator
48        Dim validator As XmlValidatingReader = _
49           New XmlValidatingReader(reader)
50
51        ' assign Schema(s)
52        validator.Schemas.Add(schemas)
53
54        ' Microsoft XDR validation
55        validator.ValidationType = ValidationType.XDR
56
57        ' register event handler for validation error(s)
58        AddHandler validator.ValidationEventHandler, _
59           AddressOf ValidationError
60
61        ' validate document node-by-node
62        While validator.Read
63
64           ' empty body
65        End While
66
67        ' check validation result
68        If valid Then
69           lblConsole.Text = "Document is valid"
70        End If
71
```

Fig. 18.18 Schema-validation example (part 2 of 3).

```
72          valid = True   ' reset variable
73
74          ' close reader stream
75          validator.Close()
76      End Sub ' cmdValidate_Click
77
78      ' event handler for validation error
79      Private Sub ValidationError(ByVal sender As Object, _
80          ByVal arguments As ValidationEventArgs)
81
82          lblConsole.Text = arguments.Message
83          valid = False ' validation failed
84      End Sub ' ValidationError
85
86  End Class ' FrmValidationTest
```

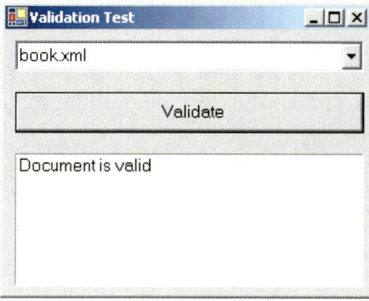

Fig. 18.18 Schema-validation example (part 3 of 3).

Validation is performed node-by-node by calling method **Read** of the **ValidatingReader** object (line 62). Each call to **Read** validates the next node in the document. The loop terminates either when all nodes have been validated successfully or if a node fails validation.

When validated against the Schema, the XML document in Fig. 18.16 validates successfuly. However, when the XML document of Fig. 18.19 is provided, validation fails, because the **book** element defined by lines 19–22 contains more than one **title** element.

```
1   <?xml version = "1.0"?>
2
3   <!-- Fig. 18.19: fail.xml                                      -->
4   <!-- XML file that does not conform to Schema book.xdr -->
5
6   <books xmlns = "x-schema:book.xdr">
7      <book>
8         <title>XML How to Program</title>
9      </book>
10
11     <book>
12        <title>Java How to Program, 4/e</title>
13     </book>
```

Fig. 18.19 XML file that does not conform to the Schema in Fig. 18.17 (part 1 of 2).

```
14
15      <book>
16         <title>Visual Basic .NET How to Program</title>
17      </book>
18
19      <book>
20         <title>C++ How to Program, 3/e</title>
21         <title>Python How to Program</title>
22      </book>
23
24      <book>
25         <title>C# How to Program</title>
26      </book>
27   </books>
```

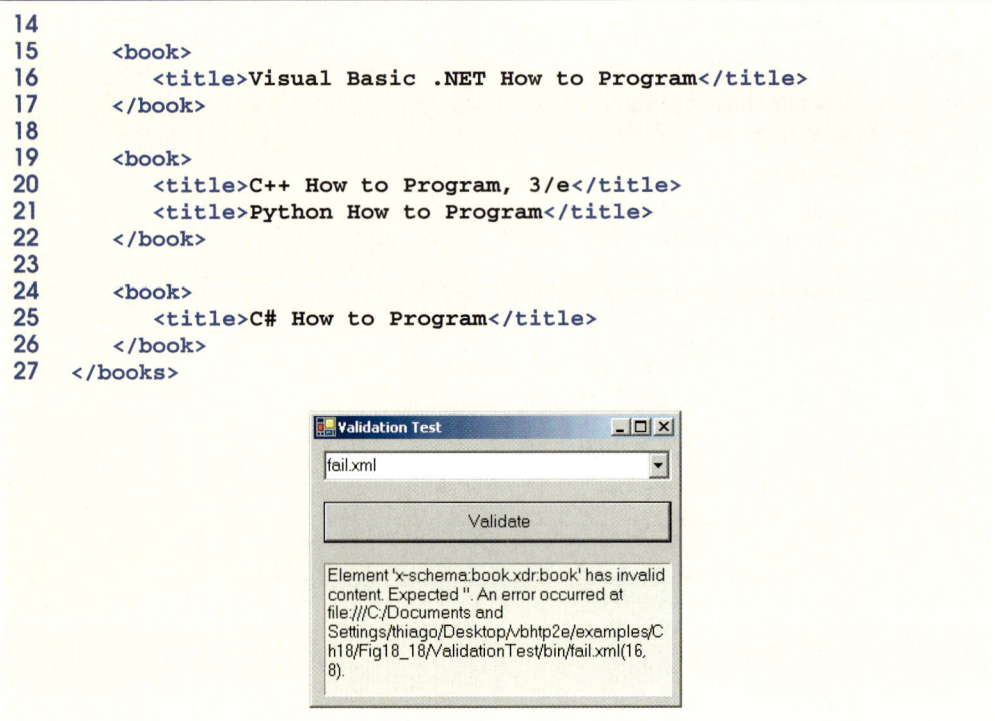

Fig. 18.19 XML file that does not conform to the Schema in Fig. 18.17 (part 2 of 2).

18.6 Extensible Stylesheet Language and `XslTransform`

Extensible Stylesheet Language (XSL) is an XML vocabulary for formatting XML data. In this section, we discuss the portion of XSL—called *XSL Transformations* (*XSLT*)—that creates formatted text-based documents from XML documents. This process is called a *transformation* and involves two tree structures: the *source tree*, which is the XML document being transformed, and the *result tree*, which is the result (e.g., *Extensible Hypertext Markup Language or XHTML*) of the transformation.[4] The source tree is not modified when a transformation occurs.

To perform transformations, an XSLT processor is required. Popular XSLT processors include Microsoft's msxml and the Apache Software Foundation's *Xalan 2*. The XML document, shown in Fig. 18.20, is transformed by msxml into an XHTML document (Fig. 18.21).

Line 6 is a *processing instruction* (*PI*), which contains application-specific information that is embedded into the XML document. In this particular case, the processing instruction is specific to IE and specifies the location of an XSLT document with which to transform the XML document. The characters **<?** and **?>** delimit a processing instruction,

---

4. XHTML is the W3C technical recommendation that replaces HTML for marking up content for the Web. For more information on XHTML, see the XHTML Appendices J and K on the CD and visit **www.w3.org**.

which consists of a *PI target* (e.g., **xml:stylesheet**) and *PI value* (e.g., **type = "text/xsl" href = "sorting.xsl"**). The portion of this particular PI value that follows **href** specifies the name and location of the style sheet to apply—in this case, **sorting.xsl**, which is located in the same directory as this XML document.

Fig. 18.21 presents the XSLT document (**sorting.xsl**) that transforms **sorting.xml** (Fig. 18.20) to XHTML.

Performance Tip 18.1

Using Internet Explorer on the client to process XSLT documents conserves server resources by using the client's processing power (instead of having the server process XSLT documents for multiple clients).

Line 1 of Fig. 18.21 contains the XML declaration. Recall that an XSL document is an XML document. Line 6 is the **xsl:stylesheet** root element. Attribute **version** specifies the version of XSLT to which this document conforms. Namespace prefix **xsl** is defined and bound to the XSLT URI defined by the W3C. When processed, lines 11–13 write the document type declaration to the result tree. Attribute **method** is assigned **"xml"**, which indicates that XML is being output to the result tree. Attribute **omit-xml-declaration** is assigned **"no"**, which outputs an XML declaration to the result tree. Attribute **doctype-system** and **doctype-public** write the **Doctype** DTD information to the result tree.

```
1   <?xml version = "1.0"?>
2
3   <!-- Fig. 18.20: sorting.xml                    -->
4   <!-- XML document containing book information   -->
5
6   <?xml:stylesheet type = "text/xsl" href = "sorting.xsl"?>
7
8   <book isbn = "999-99999-9-X">
9      <title>Deitel&apos;s XML Primer</title>
10
11     <author>
12        <firstName>Paul</firstName>
13        <lastName>Deitel</lastName>
14     </author>
15
16     <chapters>
17        <frontMatter>
18           <preface pages = "2" />
19           <contents pages = "5" />
20           <illustrations pages = "4" />
21        </frontMatter>
22
23        <chapter number = "3" pages = "44">
24           Advanced XML</chapter>
25        <chapter number = "2" pages = "35">
26           Intermediate XML</chapter>
27        <appendix number = "B" pages = "26">
28           Parsers and Tools</appendix>
```

Fig. 18.20 XML document containing book information (part 1 of 2).

```
29            <appendix number = "A" pages = "7">
30               Entities</appendix>
31            <chapter number = "1" pages = "28">
32               XML Fundamentals</chapter>
33         </chapters>
34
35         <media type = "CD" />
36      </book>
```

Fig. 18.20 XML document containing book information (part 2 of 2).

```
1     <?xml version = "1.0"?>
2
3     <!-- Fig. 18.21 : sorting.xsl                          -->
4     <!-- Transformation of book information into XHTML     -->
5
6     <xsl:stylesheet version = "1.0"
7        xmlns:xsl = "http://www.w3.org/1999/XSL/Transform">
8
9        <!-- write XML declaration and DOCTYPE DTD information -->
10       <xsl:output method = "xml" omit-xml-declaration = "no"
11          doctype-system =
12             "http://www.w3.org/TR/xhtml1/DTD/xhtml1-strict.dtd"
13          doctype-public = "-//W3C//DTD XHTML 1.0 Strict//EN"/>
14
15       <!-- match document root -->
16       <xsl:template match = "/">
17          <html xmlns = "http://www.w3.org/1999/xhtml">
18             <xsl:apply-templates/>
19          </html>
20       </xsl:template>
21
22       <!-- match book -->
23       <xsl:template match = "book">
24          <head>
25             <title>ISBN <xsl:value-of select = "@isbn" /> -
26                <xsl:value-of select = "title" /></title>
27          </head>
28
29          <body>
30             <h1 style = "color: blue">
31                <xsl:value-of select = "title"/></h1>
32
33             <h2 style = "color: blue">by <xsl:value-of
34                select = "author/lastName" />,
35                <xsl:value-of select = "author/firstName" /></h2>
36
37             <table style =
38                "border-style: groove; background-color: wheat">
39
```

Fig. 18.21 XSL document that transforms **sorting.xml** into XHTML (part 1 of 3).

```
40            <xsl:for-each select = "chapters/frontMatter/*">
41               <tr>
42                  <td style = "text-align: right">
43                     <xsl:value-of select = "name()" />
44                  </td>
45
46                  <td>
47                     ( <xsl:value-of select = "@pages" /> pages )
48                  </td>
49               </tr>
50            </xsl:for-each>
51
52            <xsl:for-each select = "chapters/chapter">
53               <xsl:sort select = "@number" data-type = "number"
54                  order = "ascending" />
55               <tr>
56                  <td style = "text-align: right">
57                     Chapter <xsl:value-of select = "@number" />
58                  </td>
59
60                  <td>
61                     ( <xsl:value-of select = "@pages" /> pages )
62                  </td>
63               </tr>
64            </xsl:for-each>
65
66            <xsl:for-each select = "chapters/appendix">
67               <xsl:sort select = "@number" data-type = "text"
68                  order = "ascending" />
69               <tr>
70                  <td style = "text-align: right">
71                     Appendix <xsl:value-of select = "@number" />
72                  </td>
73
74                  <td>
75                     ( <xsl:value-of select = "@pages" /> pages )
76                  </td>
77               </tr>
78            </xsl:for-each>
79         </table>
80
81         <br /><p style = "color: blue">Pages:
82            <xsl:variable name = "pagecount"
83               select = "sum(chapters//*/@pages)" />
84            <xsl:value-of select = "$pagecount" />
85         <br />Media Type:
86            <xsl:value-of select = "media/@type" /></p>
87      </body>
88   </xsl:template>
89
90 </xsl:stylesheet>
```

Fig. 18.21 XSL document that transforms `sorting.xml` into XHTML (part 2 of 3).

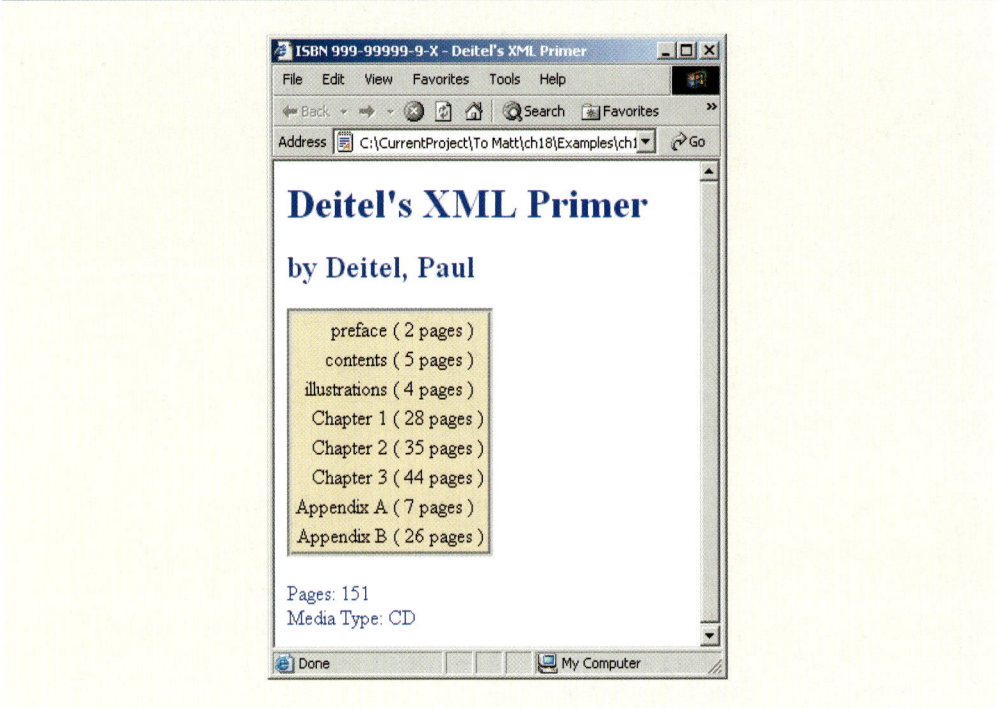

Fig. 18.21 XSL document that transforms `sorting.xml` into XHTML (part 3 of 3).

XSLT documents contain one or more **xsl:template** elements that specify which information is outputted to the result tree. The template on line 16 **match**es the source tree's document root. When the document root is encountered in the transformation, this template is applied, and any text marked up by this element that is not in the namespace referenced by **xsl** is outputted to the result tree. Line 18 calls for all the **template**s that match children of the document root to be applied. Line 23 specifies a **template** that **match**es element **book**.

Lines 25–26 create the title for the XHTML document. We use the ISBN of the book from attribute **isbn** and the contents of element **title** to create the title **String ISBN 999-99999-9-X - Deitel's XML Primer**. Element **xsl:value-of** selects the **book** element's **isbn** attribute.

Lines 33–35 create a header element that contains the book's author. Because the *context node* (i.e., the current node being processed) is **book**, the XPath expression **author/lastName** selects the author's last name, and the expression **author/firstName** selects the author's first name.

Line 40 selects each element (indicated by an asterisk) that is a child of element **frontMatter**. Line 43 calls *node-set function* **name** to retrieve the current node's element name (e.g., **preface**). The current node is the context node specified in the **xsl:for-each** (line 40).

Lines 53–54 sort **chapter**s by number in ascending order. Attribute **select** selects the value of context node **chapter**'s attribute **number**. Attribute *data-type* with value **"number"**, specifies a numeric sort and attribute *order* specifies **"ascending"** order. Attribute **data-type** also can, be assigned the value *"text"* (line 67) and attribute **order** also may be assigned the value *"descending"*.

Lines 82–83 use an *XSL variable* to store the value of the book's page count and output it to the result tree. Attribute **name** specifies the variable's name, and attribute **select** assigns it a value. Function *sum* totals the values for all **page** attribute values. The two slashes between **chapters** and ***** indicate that all descendent nodes of **chapters** are searched for elements that contain an attribute named **pages**.

Figure 18.22 applies a style sheet (**games.xsl**) to **games.xml** (Fig. 18.10). The transformation result is written to a text box and to a file. We also show the transformation results rendered in IE.

Line 7 imports the *System.Xml.Xsl* namespace, which contains classes for applying XSLT style sheets to XML documents. Specifically, an object of class *Xsl-Transform* performs the transformation.

Line 19 declares **XslTransform** reference **transformer**. An object of this type is necessary to transform the XML data to another format. In line 33, the XML document is parsed and loaded into memory by calling method **Load** of the **XMLDocument** object. Method **CreateNavigator** of the **XMLDocument** object is called in line 36 to create an **XPathNavigator** object for navigating the XML document during the transformation. A call to method *Load* of the **XslTransform** object (line 40) parses and loads the style sheet that this application uses. The argument that is passed contains the name and location of the style sheet.

Event handler **cmdTransform_Click** (lines 46–66) calls method *Transform* of class **XslTransform** to apply the style sheet (**games.xsl**) to **games.xml** (line 51). This method takes three arguments: an **XPathNavigator** (created from **games.xml**'s **XmlDocument**); an instance of class *XsltArgumentList*, which is a list of **String** parameters that can be applied to a style sheet (**Nothing** in this case); and an instance of a derived class of **TextWriter** (in this example, an instance of class **StringWriter**). The results of the transformation are stored in the **StringWriter** object referenced by **output**. Lines 57–61 write the transformation results to disk. The third screen shot depicts the created XHTML document rendered in IE.

```
1   ' Fig. 18.22: TransformTest.vb
2   ' Applying a sytle to an XML document.
3
4   Imports System.Windows.Forms
5   Imports System.Xml
6   Imports System.Xml.XPath
7   Imports System.Xml.Xsl
8   Imports System.IO
9
10  Public Class FrmTransformTest
11      Inherits Form
12
13      ' Controls for starting and displaying transformation
14      Friend WithEvents cmdTransform As Button
15      Friend WithEvents txtConsole As TextBox
16
```

Fig. 18.22 XSL style sheet applied to an XML document (part 1 of 3).

```vbnet
17      Private document As XmlDocument        ' Xml document root
18      Private navigator As XPathNavigator    ' navigate document
19      Private transformer As XslTransform    ' transform document
20      Private output As StringWriter         ' display document
21
22      Public Sub New()
23         MyBase.New()
24
25         ' This call is required by the Windows Form Designer.
26         InitializeComponent()
27
28         ' Add any initialization after the
29         ' InitializeComponent() call
30
31         ' load XML data
32         document = New XmlDocument()
33         document.Load("games.xml")
34
35         ' create navigator
36         navigator = document.CreateNavigator
37
38         ' load style sheet
39         transformer = New XslTransform()
40         transformer.Load("games.xsl")
41      End Sub ' New
42
43      ' Visual Studio .NET generated code
44
45      ' cmdTransform click event
46      Private Sub cmdTransform_Click( ByVal sender As System.Object, _
47         ByVal e As System.EventArgs) Handles cmdTransform.Click
48
49         ' transform XML data
50         output = New StringWriter()
51         transformer.Transform(navigator, Nothing, output)
52
53         ' display transformation in text box
54         txtConsole.Text = output.ToString
55
56         ' write transformation result to disk
57         Dim stream As FileStream = _
58            New FileStream("games.html", FileMode.Create)
59
60         Dim writer As StreamWriter = New StreamWriter(stream)
61         writer.Write(output.ToString)
62
63         ' close streams
64         writer.Close()
65         output.Close()
66      End Sub ' cmdTransform_Click
67
68   End Class ' FrmTransformTest
```

Fig. 18.22 XSL style sheet applied to an XML document (part 2 of 3).

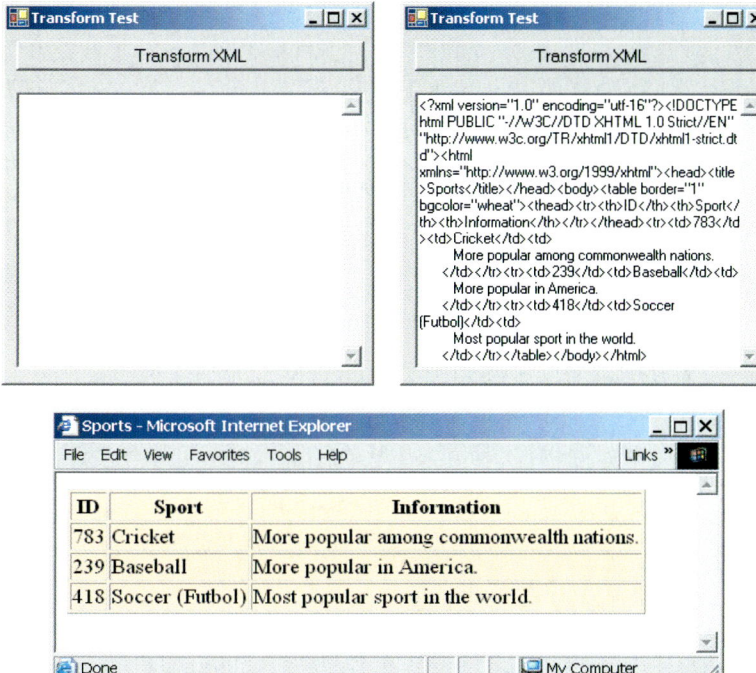

Fig. 18.22 XSL style sheet applied to an XML document (part 3 of 3).

18.7 Microsoft BizTalk™

Increasingly, organizations are using the Internet to exchange critical data. However, transfering data between these organizations can become difficult, because organizations often use different platforms, applications and data specifications that complicate data transfer. To help resolve this complication, Microsoft developed *BizTalk* ("business talk"), an XML-based technology that helps to manage and facilitate business transactions.

BizTalk consists of three parts: The BizTalk Server, the BizTalk Framework and the BizTalk Schema Library. The *BizTalk Server* (*BTS*) parses and translates all inbound and outbound messages (or documents) that are sent to and from a business. The *BizTalk Framework* is a Schema for structuring those messages. The *BizTalk Schema Library* is a collection of Framework Schemas. Businesses can design their own Schemas or choose existing Schemas from the BizTalk Schema Library. Figure 18.23 summarizes BizTalk terminology.

BizTalk	Description
Framework	A specification that defines a format for messages.
Schema library	A repository of Framework XML Schemas.

Fig. 18.23 BizTalk terminology (part 1 of 2).

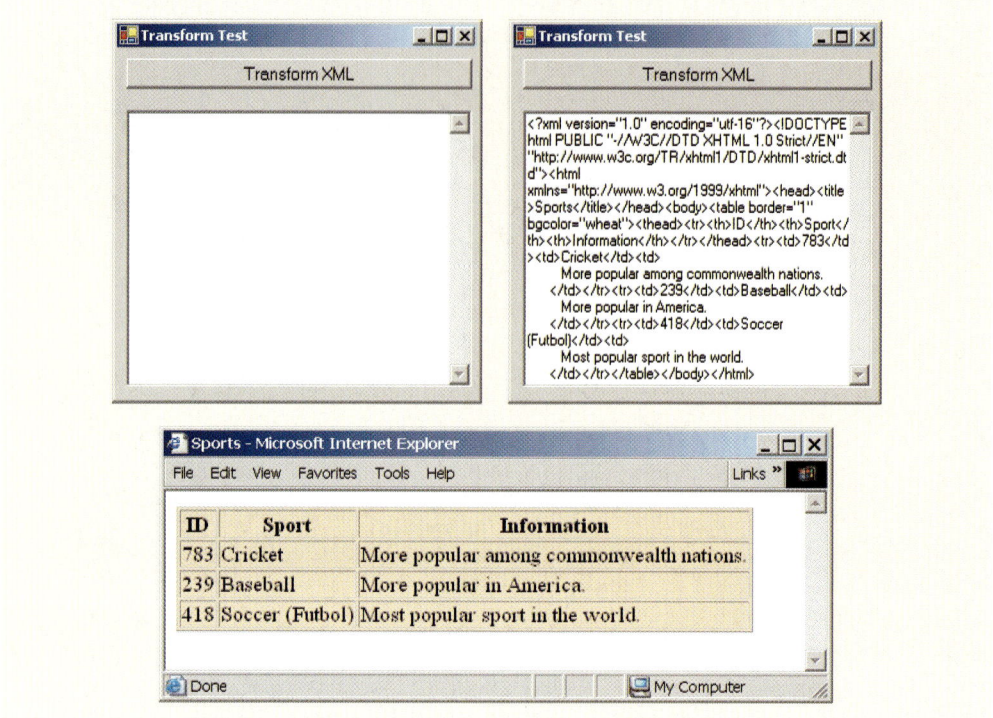

Fig. 18.22 XSL style sheet applied to an XML document (part 3 of 3).

18.7 Microsoft BizTalk™

Increasingly, organizations are using the Internet to exchange critical data. However, transfering data between these organizations can become difficult, because organizations often use different platforms, applications and data specifications that complicate data transfer. To help resolve this complication, Microsoft developed *BizTalk* ("business talk"), an XML-based technology that helps to manage and facilitate business transactions.

BizTalk consists of three parts: The BizTalk Server, the BizTalk Framework and the BizTalk Schema Library. The *BizTalk Server* (*BTS*) parses and translates all inbound and outbound messages (or documents) that are sent to and from a business. The *BizTalk Framework* is a Schema for structuring those messages. The *BizTalk Schema Library* is a collection of Framework Schemas. Businesses can design their own Schemas or choose existing Schemas from the BizTalk Schema Library. Figure 18.23 summarizes BizTalk terminology.

BizTalk	Description
Framework	A specification that defines a format for messages.
Schema library	A repository of Framework XML Schemas.

Fig. 18.23 BizTalk terminology (part 1 of 2).

```
37
38              <ReferenceImageURL>
39                 http://www.Example.com/clothes/index.jpg
40              </ReferenceImageURL>
41
42              <OfferName>Clearance sale</OfferName>
43
44              <OfferDescription>
45                 This is a clearance sale
46              </OfferDescription>
47
48              <PromotionalText>Free Shipping</PromotionalText>
49
50              <Comments>
51                 Clothes that you would love to wear.
52              </Comments>
53
54              <IconType value = "BuyNow" />
55
56              <ActionURL>
57                 http://www.example.com/action.htm
58              </ActionURL>
59
60              <AgeGroup1 value = "Infant" />
61              <AgeGroup2 value = "Adult" />
62
63              <Occasion1 value = "Birthday" />
64              <Occasion2 value = "Anniversary" />
65              <Occasion3 value = "Christmas" />
66
67           </Offer>
68        </Offers>
69     </Body>
70  </BizTalk>
```

Fig. 18.24 BizTalk markup using an offer Schema (part 2 of 2).

All Biztalk documents have the root element **BizTalk** (line 2). Line 3 defines a default namespace for the **BizTalk** framework elements. Element **Route** (lines 8–14) contains the routing information, which is mandatory for all BizTalk documents. Element **Route** also contains elements **To** and **From** (lines 9–12), which specify the document's destination and source, respectively. This makes it easier for the receiving application to communicate with the sender. Attribute **locationType** specifies the type of business that sends or receives the information, and attribute **locationID** specifies a business identity (the unique identifier for a business). These attributes facilitate source and destination organization. Attribute **handle** provides information to routing applications that handle the document.

Element **Body** (lines 16–69) contains the actual message, whose Schema is defined by the businesses themselves. Lines 17–18 specify the default namespace for element **Offers** (lines 17–68), which is contained in element **Body** (note that line 18 wraps—if we split this line, Internet Explorer cannot locate the namespace). Each offer is marked up using an **Offer** element (lines 19–67) that contains elements describing the offer. For additional information on BizTalk, visit **www.biztalk.com**.

In this chapter, we studied the Extensible Markup Language and several of its related technologies. In Chapter 19, we begin our discussion of databases, which are crucial to the development of multi-tier Web-based applications.

18.8 Internet and World Wide Web Resources

www.w3.org/xml
The W3C (World Wide Web Consortium) facilitates the development of common protocols to ensure interoperability on the Web. Their XML page includes information about upcoming events, publications, software and discussion groups. Visit this site to read about the latest developments in XML.

www.xml.org
xml.org is a reference for XML, DTDs, schemas and namespaces.

www.w3.org/style/XSL
This W3C page provides information on XSL, including the topics such as XSL development, learning XSL, XSL-enabled tools, the XSL specification, FAQs and XSL history.

www.w3.org/TR
This is the W3C technical reports and publications page. It contains links to working drafts, proposed recommendations and other resources.

www.xmlbooks.com
This site provides a list of XML books recommended by Charles Goldfarb, one of the original designers of GML (General Markup Language), from which SGML was derived.

www.xml-zone.com
The Development Exchange XML Zone is a complete resource for XML information. This site includes a FAQ, news, articles and links to other XML sites and newsgroups.

wdvl.internet.com/Authoring/Languages/XML
Web Developer's Virtual Library XML site includes tutorials, a FAQ, the latest news and extensive links to XML sites and software downloads.

www.xml.com
This site provides the latest news and information about XML, conference listings, links to XML Web resources organized by topic, tools and other resources.

msdn.microsoft.com/xml/default.asp
The MSDN Online XML Development Center features articles on XML, Ask-the-Experts chat sessions, samples, demos, newsgroups and other helpful information.

msdn.microsoft.com/downloads/samples/Internet/xml/xml_validator/sample.asp
The Microsoft XML validator, which can be downloaded from this site, can validate both online and offline documents.

www.oasis-open.org/cover/xml.html
The SGML/XML Web Page is an extensive resource that includes links to several FAQs, online resources, industry initiatives, demos, conferences and tutorials.

www.gca.org/whats_xml/default.htm
The GCA site offers an XML glossary, list of books, brief descriptions of the draft standards for XML and links to online drafts.

www-106.ibm.com/developerworks/xml
The IBM XML Zone site is a great resource for developers. It provides news, tools, a library, case studies and information about events and standards.

developer.netscape.com/tech/xml/index.html
The XML and Metadata Developer Central site has demos, technical notes and news articles related to XML.

www.projectcool.com/developer/xmlz
The Project Cool Developer Zone site includes several tutorials covering introductory through advanced XML topics.

www.ucc.ie/xml
This site is a detailed XML FAQ. Developers can check out responses to some popular questions or submit their own questions through the site.

SUMMARY

- XML is a widely supported, open technology (i.e., non-proprietary technology) for data exchange.
- XML is highly portable. Any text editor that supports ASCII or Unicode characters can render or display XML documents. Because XML elements describe the data they contain, they are both machine and human readable.
- XML permits document authors to create custom markup for virtually any type of information. This extensibility enables document authors to create entirely new markup languages that describe specific types of data, including mathematical formulas, chemical molecular structures, music, recipes, etc.
- The processing of XML documents—which programs typically store in files whose names end with the **.xml** extension—requires a program called an XML parser. A parser is responsible for identifying components of XML documents, then storing those components in a data structure for manipulation.
- An XML document can reference another optional document that defines the XML document's structure. Two types of optional structure-defining documents are Document Type Definitions (DTDs) and schemas.
- An XML document begins with an optional XML declaration, which identifies the document as an XML document. The **version** information parameter specifies the version of XML syntax that is used in the document.
- XML comments begin with **<!--** and end with **-->**. Data is marked up using tags whose names are enclosed in angle brackets (**<>**). Tags are used in pairs to delimit markup. A tag that begins markup is called a start tag, and a tag that terminates markup is called an end tag. End tags differ from start tags in that they contain a forward slash (**/**) character.
- Individual units of markup are called elements, which are the most fundamental XML building blocks. XML documents contain one element called a root element that contains every other element in the document. Elements are embedded or nested within each other to form hierarchies, with the root element at the top of the hierarchy.
- XML element names can be of any length and can contain letters, digits, underscores, hyphens and periods. However, they must begin with either a letter or an underscore.
- When a user loads an XML document into Internet Explorer (IE), msxml parses the document and passes the parsed data to IE. IE then uses a style sheet to format the data.
- IE displays minus (**–**) and plus (**+**) signs next to all container elements (i.e., elements that contain other elements). A minus sign indicates that all child elements (i.e., nested elements) are being displayed. When clicked, a minus sign becomes a plus sign (which collapses the container element and hides all children), and vice versa.
- In addition to being placed between tags, data also can be placed in attributes, which are name-value pairs in start tags. Elements can have any number of attributes.

- Because XML allows document authors to create their own tags, naming collisions (i.e., two different elements that have the same name) can occur. As in Visual Basic, XML namespaces provide a means for document authors to prevent collisions.
- Each namespace prefix is bound to a uniform resource identifier (URI) that uniquely identifies the namespace. A URI is a series of characters that differentiate names. Document authors create their own namespace prefixes. Virtually any name can be used as a namespace prefix except the reserved namespace prefix **xml**.
- To eliminate the need to place a namespace prefix in each element, authors can specify a default namespace for an element and its children. We declare a default namespace using keyword **xmlns** with a URI (Universal Resource Indicator) as its value.
- When an XML parser successfully parses a document, the parser stores a tree structure containing the document's data in memory. This hierarchical tree structure is called a Document Object Model (DOM) tree. The DOM tree represents each component of the XML document as a node in the tree. Nodes that contain other nodes (called child nodes) are called parent nodes. Nodes that have the same parent are called sibling nodes. A node's descendant nodes include that node's children, its children's children and so on. A node's ancestor nodes include that node's parent, its parent's parent and so on. The DOM tree has a single root node that contains all other nodes in the document.
- Namespace **System.Xml**, contains classes for creating, reading and manipulating XML documents.
- **XmlReader** derived class **XmlNodeReader** iterates through each node in the XML document.
- Class **XmlReader** is an **MustInherit** class that defines the interface for reading XML documents.
- A new **XmlDocument** object conceptually represents an empty XML document.
- The XML documents are parsed and loaded into an **XmlDocument** object when method **Load** is invoked. Once an XML document is loaded into an **XmlDocument**, its data can be read and manipulated programmatically.
- An **XmlNodeReader** allows us to read one node at a time from an **XmlDocument**.
- Method **Read** of **XmlReader** reads one node from the DOM tree.
- The **Name** property contains the node's name, the **Value** property contains the node's data and the **NodeType** property contains the node type (i.e., element, comment, text, etc.).
- Line breaks use the constant **vbCrLf**, which denotes a carriage return followed by a line feed. This is the standard line break for Windows-based applications and controls.
- Method **CreateNode** of **XmlDocument** takes a **NodeType**, a **Name** and a **NamespaceURI** as arguments.
- An **XmlTextWriter** streams XML data to disk. Method **WriteTo** writes an XML representation to an **XmlTextWriter** stream.
- An **XmlTextReader** reads XML data from a file.
- Class **XPathNavigator** in the **System.Xml.XPath** namespace can iterate through node lists that match search criteria, written as an XPath expression.
- XPath (XML Path Language) provides a syntax for locating, specific nodes in XML documents effectively and efficiently. XPath is a string-based language of expressions used by XML and many of its related technologies.
- Navigation methods of **XPathNavigator** are **MoveToFirstChild**, **MoveToParent**, **MoveToNext** and **MoveToPrevious**. Each method performs the action that its name implies.
- Method **MoveToFirstChild** moves to the first child of the node referenced by the **XPathNavigator**, **MoveToParent** moves to the parent node of the node referenced by the **XPath-**

Navigator. **MoveToNext** moves to the next sibling of the node referenced by the **XPathNavigator** and **MoveToPrevious** moves to the previous sibling of the node referenced by the **XPathNavigator**.

- Whereas XML contains only data, XSL is capable of converting XML into any text-based document. XSL documents have the extension **.xsl**.
- XSL stylesheets can be connected directly to an XML document by adding an **xml:stylesheet** element to the XML document.
- When transforming an XML document using XSLT, two tree structures are involved: The source tree, which is the XML document being transformed, and the result tree, which is the result (e.g., XHTML) of the transformation.
- XSL specifies the use of element **value-of** to retrieve an attribute's value. The symbol, **@** specifies an attribute node.
- The XSL node-set function **name** retrieves the current node's element name.
- Attribute **select** selects the value of context node's attribute.
- XML documents can be transformed programmatically through Visual Basic. The **System.Xml.Xsl** namespace facilities the application of XSL stylesheets to XML documents.
- Class **XsltArgumentList** is a list of **String** parameters that can be applied to a stylesheet.
- BizTalk consists of three parts: The BizTalk Server, the BizTalk Framework and the BizTalk Schema Library.

TERMINOLOGY

@ character
Add method
ancestor node
asterisk (*****) occurrence indicator
ATTLIST element
attribute
attribute node
attribute value
BizTalk Framework
BizTalk Schema Library
BizTalk Server (BTS)
CDATA character data
child element
child node
container element
context node
CreateNavigator method
CreateNode method
Current property
data-type attribute
default namespace
descendent node
doctype-public attribute
doctype-system attribute
document root
Document Type Definition (DTD)
DOM (Document Object Model)

EBNF (Extended Backus-Naur Form) grammar
ELEMENT element type declaration
empty element
EMPTY keyword
end tag
Extensible Stylesheet Language (XSL)
external DTD
forward slash
#IMPLIED flag
invalid document
IsEmptyElement property
LastChild property
Load method
markup
match attribute
maxOccurs attribute
method attribute
minOccurs attribute
MoveToFirstChild property
MoveToNext property
MoveToParent property
MoveToPrevious property
MoveToRoot property
msxml parser
name attribute
name node-set function
Name property

namespace prefix
node
Nodes collection
node-set function
NodeType property
nonvalidating XML parser
occurrence indicator
`omit-xml-declaration` attribute
`order` attribute
parent node
Parent property
ParentNode property
parsed character data
parser
`#PCDATA` flag
PI (processing instruction)
PI target
PI value
plus sign (**+**) occurrence indicator
processing instruction
question mark (**?**) occurrence indicator
Read method
reserved namespace prefix **xml**
result tree
root element
root node
Schema element
Schemas property
`select` attribute
Select method
sibling node
single-quote character (**'**)
source tree
style sheet
sum function
SYSTEM flag
System.Xml namespace
System.Xml.Schema namespace
text node
Transform method
tree-based model
`type` attribute
validating XML parser
ValidatingReader class
ValidationEventHandler class
ValidationType property

`ValidationType.XDR` constant
`value` property
`version` attribute
`version` information parameter
well-formed document
`.xdr` extension
XML (Extensible Markup Language)
XML declaration
`.xml` file extension
`xml` namespace
XML node
XML processor
XML Schema
XML Validator
`XmlDocument` class
`XmlNodeReader` class
`XmlNodeType` enumeration
`XmlNodeType.Comment` constant
`XmlNodeType.Document` constant
`XmlNodeType.DocumentType` constant
`XmlNodeType.Element` constant
`XmlNodeType.EndElement` constant
`XmlNodeType.Text` constant
`XmlNodeType.XmlDeclaration` constant
`xmlns` attribute
`XmlPathNodeIterator` class
`XmlReader` class
`XmlSchema` class
`XmlSchemaCollection` collection
`XmlTextWriter` class
`XPathExpression` class
`XPathNavigator` class
`xs:output` element
XSL (Extensible Stylesheet Language)
`.xsl` extension
XSL Transformations (XSLT)
XSL variable
`xsl:apply-templates` element
`xsl:for-each` element
`xsl:output` element
`xsl:sort` element
`xsl:stylesheet` element
`xsl:template` element
`xsl:value-of` element
`XslTransform` class
`XsltTextWriter` class

SELF-REVIEW EXERCISES

18.1 Which of the following are valid XML element names?
    a) `yearBorn`

b) `year.Born`
c) `year Born`
d) `year-Born1`
e) `2_year_born`
f) `--year/born`
g) `year*born`
h) `.year_born`
i) `_year_born_`
j) `y_e-a_r-b_o-r_n`

18.2 State whether the following are *true* or *false*. If *false*, explain why.
a) XML is a technology for creating markup languages.
b) XML markup is delimited by forward and backward slashes (`/` and `\`).
c) All XML start tags must have corresponding end tags.
d) Parsers check an XML document's syntax.
e) XML does not support namespaces.
f) When creating XML elements, document authors must use the set of XML tags provided by the W3C.
g) The pound character (`#`), the dollar sign (`$`), ampersand (`&`), greater-than (`>`) and less-than (`<`) are examples of XML reserved characters.

18.3 Fill in the blanks for each of the following:
a) _____ help prevent naming collisions.
b) _____ embed application–specific information into an XML document.
c) _____ is Microsoft's XML parser.
d) XSL element _____ writes a `DOCTYPE` to the result tree.
e) XML Schema documents have root element _____.
f) XSL element _____ is the root element in an XSL document.
g) XSL element _____ selects specific XML elements using repetition.

18.4 State which of the following statements are *true* and which are *false*. If *false*, explain why.
a) XML is not case sensitive.
b) Visual Basic architecture supports W3C Schema.
c) DTDs are a vocabulary of XML.
d) Schema is a technology for locating information in an XML document.

18.5 In Fig. 18.1, we subdivided the `author` element into more detailed pieces. How might you subdivide the `date` element?

18.6 Write a processing instruction that includes stylesheet `wap.xsl` for use in Internet Explorer.

18.7 Fill in the blanks:
a) Nodes that contain other nodes are called _____ nodes.
b) Nodes that are peers are called _____ nodes.
c) Class `XmlDocument` is analogous to the _____ of a tree.
d) To add an `XmlNode` to an `XmlTree` as a child of the current node, use method _____.

18.8 Write an XPath expression that locates `contact` nodes in `letter.xml` (Fig. 18.3).

18.9 Describe method `Select` of class `XPathNavigator`.

ANSWERS TO SELF-REVIEW EXERCISES

18.1 a, b, d, i, j. [Choice c is incorrect because it contains a space; Choice e is incorrect because the first character is a number; Choice f is incorrect because it contains a division symbol (`/`) and does not begin with a letter or underscore; Choice g is incorrect because it contains an asterisk (*****); Choice h is incorrect because the first character is a period (**.**) and does not begin with a letter or underscore.]

18.2 a) True. b) False. In an XML document, markup text is delimited by angle brackets (**<** and **>**) with a forward slash in the end tag. c) True. d) True. e) False. XML does support namespaces. f) False. When creating tags, document authors can use any valid name except the reserved word **xml** (also **XML**, **Xml**, etc.). g) False. XML reserved characters include the ampersand (**&**), the left-angle bracket (**<**) and the right-angle bracket (**>**), but not **#** and **$**.

18.3 a) namespaces. b) processing instructions. c) msxml. d) **xsl:output**. e) **Schema**. f) **xsl:stylesheet**. g) **xsl:for-each**.

18.4 a) False. XML is case sensitive. b) True. c) False. DTDs use EBNF grammar which is not XML syntax. d) False. XPath is a technology for locating information in an XML document.

18.5
```
<date>
    <month>December</month>
    <day>6</day>
    <year>2001</year>
</date>.
```

18.6 `<?xsl:stylesheet type = "text/xsl" href = "wap.xsl"?>`

18.7 a) parent. b) sibling. c) root. d) **AppendChild**.

18.8 **/letter/contact**.

18.9 Method **Select** receives as an argument either an **XPathExpression** or a **String** containing an **XPathExpression** to select nodes referenced by the navigator.

EXERCISES

18.10 Create an XML document that marks up the nutrition facts for a package of cookies. A package of cookies has a serving size of 1 package and the following nutritional value per serving: 260 calories, 100 fat calories, 11 grams of fat, 2 grams of saturated fat, 5 milligrams of cholesterol, 210 milligrams of sodium, 36 grams of total carbohydrates, 2 grams of fiber, 15 grams of sugars and 5 grams of protein. Name this document **nutrition.xml**. Load the XML document into Internet Explorer [*Hint*: Your markup should contain elements describing the product name, serving size/amount, calories, sodium, cholesterol, proteins, etc. Mark up each nutrition fact/ingredient listed above.]

18.11 Write an XSL style sheet for your solution to Exercise 18.10 that displays the nutritional facts in an XHTML table. Modify Fig. 18.22 (**TransformTest.vb**) to output an XHTML file, **nutrition.html**. Render **nutrition.html** in a Web browser.

18.12 Write a Microsoft Schemas for Fig. 18.20 and Exercise 18.10.

18.13 Alter Fig. 18.18 (**ValidationTest.vb**) to include a list of schema in a drop-down box along with the list of XML files. Allow the user to test whether any XML file on the list satisfies a specific schema. Use **books.xml**, **books.xdr**, **sorting.xml**, **sorting.xdr**, **nutrition.xml**, **nutrition.xdr** and **fail.xml**.

18.14 Modify **XmlReaderTest** (Fig. 18.7) to display **letter.xml** (Fig. 18.3) in a **TreeView**, instead of in a text box.

18.15 Modify Fig. 18.21 (**sorting.xsl**) to sort by page number, rather than by chapter number. Save the modified document as **sorting_byPage.xsl**.

18.16 Modify **TransformTest.vb** (Fig. 18.22) to take in **sorting.xml** (Fig. 18.20), **sorting.xsl** (Fig. 18.21) and **sorting_byChapter.xsl** and print the XHTML document resulting from the transform of **sorting.xml** into two XHTML files, **sorting_byPage.html** and **sorting_byChapter.html**.

19

Database, SQL and ADO .NET

Objectives

- To understand the relational database model.
- To understand basic database queries written in Structured Query Language (SQL).
- To use the classes and interfaces of namespace **System.Data** to manipulate databases.
- To understand and use ADO .NET's disconnected model.
- To use the classes and interfaces of namespace **System.Data.OleDb**.

It is a capital mistake to theorize before one has data.
Arthur Conan Doyle

Now go, write it before them in a table, and note it in a book, that it may be for the time to come for ever and ever.
The Holy Bible: The Old Testament

Let's look at the record.
Alfred Emanuel Smith

Get your facts first, and then you can distort them as much as you please.
Mark Twain

I like two kinds of men: domestic and foreign.
Mae West

Outline

19.1 Introduction
19.2 Relational Database Model
19.3 Relational Database Overview: `Books` Database
19.4 Structured Query Language (SQL)
    19.4.1 Basic `SELECT` Query
    19.4.2 `WHERE` Clause
    19.4.3 `ORDER BY` Clause
    19.4.4 Merging Data from Multiple Tables: `INNER JOIN`
    19.4.5 Joining Data from Tables `Authors`, `AuthorISBN`, `Titles` and `Publishers`
    19.4.6 `INSERT` Statement
    19.4.7 `UPDATE` Statement
    19.4.8 `DELETE` Statement
19.5 ADO .NET Object Model
19.6 Programming with ADO .NET: Extracting Information from a Database
    19.6.1 Connecting to and Querying an Access Data Source
    19.6.2 Querying the `Books` Database
19.7 Programming with ADO .NET: Modifying a Database
19.8 Reading and Writing XML Files

Summary • Terminology • Self-Review Exercises • Answers to Self-Review Exercises • Exercises • Bibliography

19.1 Introduction

A *database* is an integrated collection of data. Many different strategies exist for organizing data in databases to facilitate easy access to and manipulation of the data. A *database management system* (*DBMS*) provides mechanisms for storing and organizing data in a manner that is consistent with the database's format. Database management systems enable programmers to access and store data without worrying about the internal representation of databases.

Today's most popular database systems are *relational databases*. Almost universally, relational databases use a language called *Structured Query Language* (*SQL*—pronounced as its individual letters or as "sequel") to perform *queries* (i.e., to request information that satisfies given criteria) and to manipulate data. [*Note*: The writing in this chapter assumes that SQL is pronounced as its individual letters. For this reason, we often precede SQL with the article "an" as in "an SQL database" or "an SQL statement."]

Some popular, enterprise-level relational database systems include Microsoft SQL Server, Oracle™, Sybase™, DB2™, Informix™ and MySQL™. This chapter presents examples using *Microsoft Access*—a relational database system that comes with *Microsoft Office*.

19.2 Relational Database Model

A programming language connects to, and interacts with, a relational database via an *interface*—software that facilitates communication between a database management system and a program. Visual Basic .NET programmers communicate with databases and manipulate their data through *Microsoft ActiveX Data Objects*™ (ADO), *ADO .NET*.

19.2 Relational Database Model

The *relational database model* is a logical representation of data that allows relationships among data to be considered without concern for the physical structure of the data. A relational database is composed of *tables*. Figure 19.1 illustrates an example table that might be used in a personnel system. The table name is **Employee**, and its primary purpose is to illustrate the specific attributes of various employees. A particular row of the table is called a *record* (or *row*). This table consists of six records. The **number** *field* (or *column*) of each record in the table is the *primary key* for referencing data in the table. A primary key is a field (or fields) in a table that contain(s) unique data, or data that is not duplicated in other records of that table. This guarantees that each record can be identified by at least one unique value. Examples of primary-key fields are columns that contain social security numbers, employee IDs and part numbers in an inventory system. The records of Fig. 19.1 are *ordered* by primary key. In this case, the records are listed in increasing order (they also could be in decreasing order).

Each column of the table represents a different field. Records normally are unique (by primary key) within a table, but particular field values might be duplicated in multiple records. For example, three different records in the **Employee** table's **Department** field contain the number 413.

Often, different users of a database are interested in different data and different relationships among those data. Some users require only subsets of the table columns. To obtain table subsets, we use SQL statements to specify certain data to *select* from a table. SQL provides a complete set of commands (including **SELECT**) that enable programmers to define complex *queries* to select data from a table. The results of a query commonly are called *result sets* (or *record sets*). For example, we might select data from the table in Fig. 19.1 to create a new result set containing only the location of each department. This result set appears in Fig. 19.2. SQL queries are discussed in Section 19.4.

number	name	department	salary	location
23603	Jones	413	1100	New Jersey
24568	Kerwin	413	2000	New Jersey
34589	Larson	642	1800	Los Angeles
35761	Myers	611	1400	Orlando
47132	Neumann	413	9000	New Jersey
78321	Stephens	611	8500	Orlando

Record/Row — Primary key (number), Field/Column (department)

Fig. 19.1 Relational-database structure of an **Employee** table.

department	location
413	New Jersey
611	Orlando
642	Los Angeles

Fig. 19.2   Result set formed by selecting **Department** and **Location** data from the **Employee** table.

19.3 Relational Database Overview: Books Database

This section provides an overview of SQL in the context of a sample **Books** database we created for this chapter. Before we discuss SQL, we explain the various tables of the **Books** database. We use this database to introduce various database concepts, including the use of SQL to manipulate and obtain useful information from the database.

The database consists of four tables: **Authors**, **Publishers**, **AuthorISBN** and **Titles**. The **Authors** table (described in Fig. 19.3) consists of three fields (or columns) that maintain each author's unique ID number, first name and last name. Figure 19.4 contains the data from the **Authors** table of the **Books** database.

Field	Description
authorID	Author's ID number in the database. In the **Books** database, this **Integer** field is defined as an *auto-incremented field*. For each new record inserted in this table, the database increments the **authorID** value, ensuring that each record has a unique **authorID**. This field represents the table's primary key.
firstName	Author's first name (a **String**).
lastName	Author's last name (a **String**).

Fig. 19.3   **Authors** table from **Books**.

authorID	firstName	lastName
1	Harvey	Deitel
2	Paul	Deitel
3	Tem	Nieto
4	Kate	Steinbuhler
5	Sean	Santry

Fig. 19.4   Data from the **Authors** table of **Books** (part 1 of 2).

authorID	firstName	lastName
6	Ted	Lin
7	Praveen	Sadhu
8	David	McPhie
9	Cheryl	Yaeger
10	Marina	Zlatkina
11	Ben	Wiedermann
12	Jonathan	Liperi

Fig. 19.4 Data from the **Authors** table of **Books** (part 2 of 2).

The **Publishers** table (Fig. 19.5) consists of two fields, representing each publisher's unique ID and name. Figure 19.6 contains the data from the **Publishers** table of the **Books** database.

The **AuthorISBN** table (Fig. 19.7) consists of two fields, which maintain ISBN numbers for each book and their corresponding authors' ID numbers. This table helps associate the names of the authors with the titles of their books. Figure 19.8 contains the data from the **AuthorISBN** table of the **Books** database. ISBN is an abbreviation for "International Standard Book Number"—a numbering scheme by which publishers worldwide give every book a unique identification number. [*Note*: To save space, we have split the contents of this figure into two columns, each containing the **authorID** and **isbn** fields.]

Field	Description
publisherID	The publisher's ID number in the database. This auto-incremented **Integer** field is the table's primary-key field.
publisherName	The name of the publisher (a **String**).

Fig. 19.5 **Publishers** table from **Books**.

publisherID	publisherName
1	Prentice Hall
2	Prentice Hall PTG

Fig. 19.6 Data from the **Publishers** table of **Books**.

Field	Description
`authorID`	The author's ID number, which allows the database to associate each book with a specific author. The integer ID number in this field must also appear in the **Authors** table.
`isbn`	The ISBN number for a book (a **String**).

Fig. 19.7 **AuthorISBN** table from **Books**.

The **Titles** table (Fig. 19.9) consists of seven fields, which maintain general information about the books in the database. This information includes each book's ISBN number, title, edition number, copyright year and publisher's ID number, as well as the name of a file containing an image of the book cover, and finally, each book's price. Figure 19.10 contains the data from the **Titles** table.

authorID	isbn	authorID	isbn
1	0130895725	2	0139163050
1	0132261197	2	013028419x
1	0130895717	2	0130161438
1	0135289106	2	0130856118
1	0139163050	2	0130125075
1	013028419x	2	0138993947
1	0130161438	2	0130852473
1	0130856118	2	0130829277
1	0130125075	2	0134569555
1	0138993947	2	0130829293
1	0130852473	2	0130284173
1	0130829277	2	0130284181
1	0134569555	2	0130895601
1	0130829293	3	013028419x
1	0130284173	3	0130161438
1	0130284181	3	0130856118
1	0130895601	3	0134569555
2	0130895725	3	0130829293
2	0132261197	3	0130284173
2	0130895717	3	0130284181
2	0135289106	4	0130895601

Fig. 19.8 Data from **AuthorISBN** table in **Books**.

Field	Description
`isbn`	ISBN number of the book (a `String`).
`title`	Title of the book (a `String`).
`editionNumber`	Edition number of the book (a `String`).
`copyright`	Copyright year of the book (an `Integer`).
`publisherID`	Publisher's ID number (an `Integer`). This value must correspond to an ID number in the `Publishers` table.
`imageFile`	Name of the file containing the book's cover image (a `String`).
`price`	Suggested retail price of the book (a real number). [*Note*: The prices shown in this database are for example purposes only.]

Fig. 19.9 `Titles` table from `Books`.

isbn	title	edition-Number	publish-erID	copy-right	imageFile	price
0130923613	Python How to Program	1	1	2002	`python.jpg`	$69.95
0130622214	C# How to Program	1	1	2002	`cshtp.jpg`	$69.95
0130341517	Java How to Program	4	1	2002	`jhtp4.jpg`	$69.95
0130649341	The Complete Java Training Course	4	2	2002	`javactc4.jpg`	$109.95
0130895601	Advanced Java 2 Platform How to Program	1	1	2002	`advjhtp1.jpg`	$69.95
0130308978	Internet and World Wide Web How to Program	2	1	2002	`iw3htp2.jpg`	$69.95
0130293636	Visual Basic .NET How to Program	2	1	2002	`vbnet.jpg`	$69.95
0130895636	The Complete C++ Training Course	3	2	2001	`cppctc3.jpg`	$109.95
0130895512	The Complete e-Business & e-Commerce Programming Training Course	1	2	2001	`ebecctc.jpg`	$109.95
013089561X	The Complete Internet & World Wide Web Programming Training Course	2	2	2001	`iw3ctc2.jpg`	$109.95

Fig. 19.10 Data from the `Titles` table of `Books` (part 1 of 3).

isbn	title	edition-Number	copy-right	publish-erID	imageFile	price
0130895547	The Complete Perl Training Course	1	2	2001	`perl.jpg`	$109.95
0130895563	The Complete XML Programming Training Course	1	2	2001	`xmlctc.jpg`	$109.95
0130895725	C How to Program	3	1	2001	`chtp3.jpg`	$69.95
0130895717	C++ How to Program	3	1	2001	`cpphtp3.jpg`	$69.95
013028419X	e-Business and e-Commerce How to Program	1	1	2001	`ebechtp1.jpg`	$69.95
0130622265	Wireless Internet and Mobile Business How to Program	1	1	2001	`wireless.jpg`	$69.95
0130284181	Perl How to Program	1	1	2001	`perlhtp1.jpg`	$69.95
0130284173	XML How to Program	1	1	2001	`xmlhtp1.jpg`	$69.95
0130856118	The Complete Internet and World Wide Web Programming Training Course	1	2	2000	`iw3ctc1.jpg`	$109.95
0130125075	Java How to Program (Java 2)	3	1	2000	`jhtp3.jpg`	$69.95
0130852481	The Complete Java 2 Training Course	3	2	2000	`javactc3.jpg`	$109.95
0130323640	e-Business and e-Commerce for Managers	1	1	2000	`ebecm.jpg`	$69.95
0130161438	Internet and World Wide Web How to Program	1	1	2000	`iw3htp1.jpg`	$69.95
0130132497	Getting Started with Visual C++ 6 with an Introduction to MFC	1	1	1999	`gsvc.jpg`	$49.95
0130829293	The Complete Visual Basic 6 Training Course	1	2	1999	`vbctc1.jpg`	$109.95
0134569555	Visual Basic 6 How to Program	1	1	1999	`vbhtp1.jpg`	$69.95

Fig. 19.10 Data from the **Titles** table of **Books** (part 2 of 3).

isbn	title	edition-Number	publisherID	copyright	imageFile	price
0132719746	Java Multimedia Cyber Classroom	1	2	1998	`javactc.jpg`	$109.95
0136325890	Java How to Program	1	1	1998	`jhtp1.jpg`	$69.95
0139163050	The Complete C++ Training Course	2	2	1998	`cppctc2.jpg`	$109.95
0135289106	C++ How to Program	2	1	1998	`cpphtp2.jpg`	$49.95
0137905696	The Complete Java Training Course	2	2	1998	`javactc2.jpg`	$109.95
0130829277	The Complete Java Training Course (Java 1.1)	2	2	1998	`javactc2.jpg`	$99.95
0138993947	Java How to Program (Java 1.1)	2	1	1998	`jhtp2.jpg`	$49.95
0131173340	C++ How to Program	1	1	1994	`cpphtp1.jpg`	$69.95
0132261197	C How to Program	2	1	1994	`chtp2.jpg`	$49.95
0131180436	C How to Program	1	1	1992	`chtp.jpg`	$69.95

Fig. 19.10 Data from the **Titles** table of **Books** (part 3 of 3).

Figure 19.11 illustrates the relationships among the tables in the **Books** database. The first line in each table is the table's name. The field whose name appears in italics contains that table's primary key. A table's primary key uniquely identifies each record in the table. Every record must have a value in the primary-key field, and the value must be unique. This is known as the *Rule of Entity Integrity*. Note that the **AuthorISBN** table contains two fields whose names are italicized. This indicates that these two fields form a *compound primary key*—each record in the table must have a unique **authorID**–**isbn** combination. For example, several records might have an **authorID** of **2**, and several records might have an **isbn** of **0130895601**, but only one record can have both an **authorID** of **2** and an **isbn** of **0130895601**.

Common Programming Error 19.1
Failure to provide a value for a primary-key field in every record breaks the Rule of Entity Integrity and causes the DBMS to report an error.

Common Programming Error 19.2
Providing duplicate values for the primary-key field in multiple records causes the DBMS to report an error.

The lines connecting the tables in Fig. 19.11 represent the *relationships* among the tables. Consider the line between the **Publishers** and **Titles** tables. On the **Publishers** end of the line, there is a **1**, and on the **Titles** end, there is an infinity (∞) symbol. This line indicates a *one-to-many relationship*, in which every publisher in the

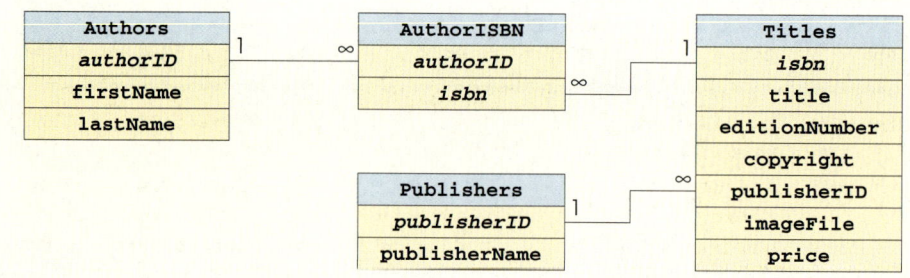

Fig. 19.11 Table relationships in **Books**.

Publishers table can have an arbitrarily large number of books in the **Titles** table. Note that the relationship line links the **publisherID** field in the **Publishers** table to the **publisherID** field in **Titles** table. In the **Titles** table, the **publisherID** field is a *foreign key*—a field for which every entry has a unique value in another table and where the field in the other table is the primary key for that table (e.g., **publisherID** in the **Publishers** table). Programmers specify foreign keys when creating a table. The foreign key helps maintain the *Rule of Referential Integrity*: Every foreign-key field value must appear in another table's primary-key field. Foreign keys enable information from multiple tables to be *joined* together for analysis purposes. There is a one-to-many relationship between a primary key and its corresponding foreign key. This means that a foreign-key field value can appear many times in its own table, but must appear exactly once as the primary key of another table. The line between the tables represents the link between the foreign key in one table and the primary key in another table.

Common Programming Error 19.3

Providing a foreign-key value that does not appear as a primary-key value in another table breaks the Rule of Referential Integrity and causes the DBMS to report an error.

The line between the **AuthorISBN** and **Authors** tables indicates that, for each author in the **Authors** table, there can be an arbitrary number of ISBNs for books written by that author in the **AuthorISBN** table. The **authorID** field in the **AuthorISBN** table is a forcign kcy of the **authorID** field (the primary key) of the **Authors** table. Note, again, that the line between the tables links the foreign key in table **AuthorISBN** to the corresponding primary key in table **Authors**. The **AuthorISBN** table links information in the **Titles** and **Authors** tables.

Finally, the line between the **Titles** and **AuthorISBN** tables illustrates a one-to-many relationship; a title can be written by any number of authors. In fact, the sole purpose of the **AuthorISBN** table is to represent a many-to-many relationship between the **Authors** and **Titles** tables; an author can write any number of books, and a book can have any number of authors.

19.4 Structured Query Language (SQL)

In this section, we provide an overview of Structured Query Language (SQL) in the context of our **Books** sample database. The SQL queries discussed here form the foundation for the SQL used in the chapter examples.

Figure 19.12 lists SQL keywords programmers use in the context of complete SQL queries. In the next several subsections, we discuss these SQL keywords in the context of complete SQL queries. Other SQL keywords exist, but are beyond the scope of this text. [*Note*: To locate additional information on SQL, please refer to the bibliography at the end of this chapter.]

19.4.1 Basic SELECT Query

Let us consider several SQL queries that extract information from database **Books**. A typical SQL query "selects" information from one or more tables in a database. Such selections are performed by **SELECT** *queries*. The simplest format for a **SELECT** query is:

> **SELECT * FROM** *tableName*

In this query, the asterisk (*****) indicates that all columns from the *tableName* table of the database should be selected. For example, to select the entire contents of the **Authors** table (i.e., all the data in Fig. 19.13), use the query:

> **SELECT * FROM Authors**

To select specific fields from a table, replace the asterisk (*****) with a comma-separated list of the field names to select. For example, to select only the fields **authorID** and **lastName** for all rows in the **Authors** table, use the query

> **SELECT authorID, lastName FROM Authors**

This query only returns the data presented in Fig. 19.13. [*Note*: If a field name contains spaces, the entire field name must be enclosed in square brackets (**[ ]**) in the query. For example, if the field name is **first name**, it must appear in the query as **[first name]**.]

SQL keyword	Description
SELECT	Selects (retrieves) fields from one or more tables.
FROM	Specifies tables from which to get fields or delete records. Required in every **SELECT** and **DELETE** statement.
WHERE	Specifies criteria that determines the rows to be retrieved.
INNER JOIN	Joins records from multiple tables to produce a single set of records.
GROUP BY	Specifies criteria for grouping records.
ORDER BY	Specifies criteria for ordering records.
INSERT	Inserts data into a specified table.
UPDATE	Updates data in a specified table.
DELETE	Deletes data from a specified table.

Fig. 19.12 SQL query keywords.

authorID	lastName	authorID	lastName
1	Deitel	7	Sadhu
2	Deitel	8	McPhie
3	Nieto	9	Yaeger
4	Steinbuhler	10	Zlatkina
5	Santry	11	Wiedermann
6	Lin	12	Liperi

Fig. 19.13 `authorID` and `lastName` from the `Authors` table.

Common Programming Error 19.4

If a program assumes that an SQL statement using the asterisk (*) to select fields always returns those fields in the same order, the program could process the result set incorrectly. If the field order in the database table(s) changes, the order of the fields in the result set would change accordingly.

Performance Tip 19.1

If a program does not know the order of fields in a result set, the program must process the fields by name. This could require a linear search of the field names in the result set. If users specify the field names that they wish to select from a table (or several tables), the application receiving the result set can know the order of the fields in advance. When this occurs, the program can process the data more efficiently, because fields can be accessed directly by column number.

19.4.2 WHERE Clause

In most cases, users search a database for records that satisfy certain *selection criteria*. Only records that match the selection criteria are selected. SQL uses the optional **WHERE** clause in a **SELECT** query to specify the selection criteria for the query. The simplest format of a **SELECT** query that includes selection criteria is:

> **SELECT** *fieldName1*, *fieldName2*, ... **FROM** *tableName* **WHERE** *criteria*

For example, to select the `title`, `editionNumber` and `copyright` fields from those rows of table `Titles` in which the `copyright` date is greater than `1999`, use the query

```
SELECT title, editionNumber, copyright
FROM Titles
WHERE copyright > 1999
```

Figure 19.14 shows the result set of the preceding query. [*Note*: When we construct a query for use in Visual Basic .NET, we simply create a **String** containing the entire query. However, when we display queries in the text, we often use multiple lines and indentation to enhance readability.]

Title	editionNumber	copyright
Internet and World Wide Web How to Program	2	2002
Java How to Program	4	2002
The Complete Java Training Course	4	2002
The Complete e-Business & e-Commerce Programming Training Course	1	2001
The Complete Internet & World Wide Web Programming Training Course	2	2001
The Complete Perl Training Course	1	2001
The Complete XML Programming Training Course	1	2001
C How to Program	3	2001
C++ How to Program	3	2001
The Complete C++ Training Course	3	2001
e-Business and e-Commerce How to Program	1	2001
Internet and World Wide Web How to Program	1	2000
The Complete Internet and World Wide Web Programming Training Course	1	2000
Java How to Program (Java 2)	3	2000
The Complete Java 2 Training Course	3	2000
XML How to Program	1	2001
Perl How to Program	1	2001
Advanced Java 2 Platform How to Program	1	2002
e-Business and e-Commerce for Managers	1	2000
Wireless Internet and Mobile Business How to Program	1	2001
C# How To Program	1	2002
Python How to Program	1	2002
Visual Basic .NET How to Program	2	2002

Fig. 19.14 Titles with copyrights after 1999 from table **Titles**.

Performance Tip 19.2

Using selection criteria improves performance, because queries that involve such criteria normally select a portion of the database that is smaller than the entire database. Working with a smaller portion of the data is more efficient than working with the entire set of data stored in the database.

The **WHERE** clause condition can contain operators <, >, <=, >=, =, <> and **LIKE**. Operator **LIKE** is used for *pattern matching* with wildcard characters *asterisk* (*) and *question mark* (?). Pattern matching allows SQL to search for similar strings that "match a pattern."

A pattern that contains an asterisk (*****) searches for strings in which zero or more characters take the asterisk character's place in the pattern. For example, the following query locates the records of all authors whose last names start with the letter **D**:

```
SELECT authorID, firstName, lastName
FROM Authors
WHERE lastName LIKE 'D*'
```

The preceding query selects the two records shown in Fig. 19.15, because two of the authors in our database have last names that begin with the letter **D** (followed by zero or more characters). The ***** in the **WHERE** clause's **LIKE** pattern indicates that any number of characters can appear after the letter **D** in the **lastName** field. Notice that the pattern string is surrounded by single-quote characters.

Portability Tip 19.1
*Not all database systems support the **LIKE** operator, so be sure to read the database system's documentation carefully before employing this operator.*

Portability Tip 19.2
*Most databases use the **%** character in place of the ***** character in **LIKE** expressions.*

Portability Tip 19.3
In some databases, string data is case sensitive.

Portability Tip 19.4
In some databases, table names and field names are case sensitive.

Good Programming Practice 19.1
By convention, SQL keywords should be written entirely in uppercase letters on systems that are not case sensitive. This emphasizes the SQL keywords in an SQL statement.

A pattern string including a question mark (**?**) character searches for strings in which exactly one character takes the question mark's place in the pattern. For example, the following query locates the records of all authors whose last names start with any character (specified with **?**), followed by the letter **i**, followed by any number of additional characters (specified with *****):

```
SELECT authorID, firstName, lastName
FROM Authors
WHERE lastName LIKE '?i*'
```

authorID	firstName	lastName
1	Harvey	Deitel
2	Paul	Deitel

Fig. 19.15 Authors from the **Authors** table whose last names start with **D**.

The preceding query produces the records listed in Fig. 19.16; four authors in our database have last names that contain the letter **i** as the second letter.

 Portability Tip 19.5

Most databases use the _ character in place of the ? character in **LIKE** *expressions.*

19.4.3 ORDER BY Clause

The results of a query can be arranged in ascending or descending order using the optional **ORDER BY** *clause*. The simplest form of an **ORDER BY** clause is:

```
SELECT fieldName1, fieldName2, ... FROM tableName ORDER BY field ASC
SELECT fieldName1, fieldName2, ... FROM tableName ORDER BY field DESC
```

where **ASC** specifies ascending order (lowest to highest), **DESC** specifies descending order (highest to lowest) and *field* specifies the field that determines the sorting order.

For example, to obtain the list of authors that is arranged in ascending order by last name (Fig. 19.17), use the query:

```
SELECT authorID, firstName, lastName
FROM Authors
ORDER BY lastName ASC
```

Note that the default sorting order is ascending; therefore **ASC** is optional.

authorID	firstName	lastName
3	Tem	Nieto
6	Ted	Lin
11	Ben	Wiedermann
12	Jonathan	Liperi

Fig. 19.16 Authors from table **Authors** whose last names contain **i** as their second letter.

authorID	firstName	lastName
2	Paul	Deitel
1	Harvey	Deitel
6	Ted	Lin
12	Jonathan	Liperi
8	David	McPhie

Fig. 19.17 Authors from table **Authors** in ascending order by **lastName** (part 1 of 2).

authorID	firstName	lastName
3	Tem	Nieto
7	Praveen	Sadhu
5	Sean	Santry
4	Kate	Steinbuhler
11	Ben	Wiedermann
9	Cheryl	Yaeger
10	Marina	Zlatkina

Fig. 19.17 Authors from table **Authors** in ascending order by **lastName** (part 2 of 2).

To obtain the same list of authors arranged in descending order by last name (Fig. 19.18), use the query:

```
SELECT authorID, firstName, lastName
FROM Authors
ORDER BY lastName DESC
```

The **ORDER BY** clause also can be used to order records by multiple fields. Such queries are written in the form:

> **ORDER BY** *field1 sortingOrder*, *field2 sortingOrder*, ...

where *sortingOrder* is either **ASC** or **DESC**. Note that the *sortingOrder* does not have to be identical for each field.

authorID	firstName	lastName
10	Marina	Zlatkina
9	Cheryl	Yaeger
11	Ben	Wiedermann
4	Kate	Steinbuhler
5	Sean	Santry
7	Praveen	Sadhu
3	Tem	Nieto
8	David	McPhie
12	Jonathan	Liperi
6	Ted	Lin
2	Paul	Deitel
1	Harvey	Deitel

Fig. 19.18 Authors from table **Authors** in descending order by **lastName**.

For example, the query:

```
SELECT authorID, firstName, lastName
FROM Authors
ORDER BY lastName, firstName
```

sorts all authors in ascending order by last name, then by first name. This means that, if any authors have the same last name, their records are returned sorted by first name (Fig. 19.19).

The **WHERE** and **ORDER BY** clauses can be combined in one query. For example, the query

```
SELECT isbn, title, editionNumber, copyright, price
FROM Titles
WHERE title
LIKE '*How to Program' ORDER BY title ASC
```

returns the ISBN, title, edition number, copyright and price of each book in the **Titles** table that has a **title** ending with "**How to Program**"; it lists these records in ascending order by **title**. The results of the query are depicted in Fig. 19.20.

19.4.4 Merging Data from Multiple Tables: INNER JOIN

Database designers often split related data into separate tables to ensure that a database does not store data redundantly. For example, the **Books** database has tables **Authors** and **Titles**. We use an **AuthorISBN** table to provide "links" between authors and titles. If we did not separate this information into individual tables, we would need to include author information with each entry in the **Titles** table. This would result in the database storing duplicate author information for authors who wrote multiple books.

authorID	firstName	lastName
1	Harvey	Deitel
2	Paul	Deitel
6	Ted	Lin
12	Jonathan	Liperi
8	David	McPhie
3	Tem	Nieto
7	Praveen	Sadhu
5	Sean	Santry
4	Kate	Steinbuhler
11	Ben	Wiedermann
9	Cheryl	Yaeger
10	Marina	Zlatkina

Fig. 19.19 Authors from table **Authors** in ascending order by **lastName** and by **firstName**.

isbn	title	edition-Number	copy-right	price
0130895601	Advanced Java 2 Platform How to Program	1	2002	$69.95
0131180436	C How to Program	1	1992	$69.95
0130895725	C How to Program	3	2001	$69.95
0132261197	C How to Program	2	1994	$49.95
0130622214	C# How To Program	1	2002	$69.95
0135289106	C++ How to Program	2	1998	$49.95
0131173340	C++ How to Program	1	1994	$69.95
0130895717	C++ How to Program	3	2001	$69.95
013028419X	e-Business and e-Commerce How to Program	1	2001	$69.95
0130308978	Internet and World Wide Web How to Program	2	2002	$69.95
0130161438	Internet and World Wide Web How to Program	1	2000	$69.95
0130341517	Java How to Program	4	2002	$69.95
0136325890	Java How to Program	1	1998	$0.00
0130284181	Perl How to Program	1	2001	$69.95
0130923613	Python How to Program	1	2002	$69.95
0130293636	Visual Basic .NET How to Program	2	2002	$69.95
0134569555	Visual Basic 6 How to Program	1	1999	$69.95
0130622265	Wireless Internet and Mobile Business How to Program	1	2001	$69.95
0130284173	XML How to Program	1	2001	$69.95

Fig. 19.20 Books from table **Titles** whose titles end with **How to Program** in ascending order by **title**.

Often, it is necessary for analysis purposes to merge data from multiple tables into a single set of data. Referred to as *joining* the tables, this is accomplished via an **INNER JOIN** operation in the **SELECT** query. An **INNER JOIN** merges records from two or more tables by testing for matching values in a field that is common to the tables. The simplest format of an **INNER JOIN** clause is:

```
SELECT fieldName1, fieldName2, …
FROM table1
INNER JOIN table2
    ON table1.fieldName = table2.fieldName
```

The **ON** part of the **INNER JOIN** clause specifies the fields from each table that are compared to determine which records are joined. For example, the following query produces a list of authors accompanied by the ISBN numbers for books written by each author:

```
SELECT firstName, lastName, isbn
FROM Authors
INNER JOIN AuthorISBN
    ON Authors.authorID = AuthorISBN.authorID
ORDER BY lastName, firstName
```

The query merges the **firstName** and **lastName** fields from table **Authors** and the **isbn** field from table **AuthorISBN**, sorting the results in ascending order by **lastName** and **firstName**. Notice the use of the syntax *tableName.fieldName* in the **ON** part of the **INNER JOIN**. This syntax (called a *fully qualified name*) specifies the fields from each table that should be compared to join the tables. The "*tableName.*" syntax is required if the fields have the same name in both tables. The same syntax can be used in any query to distinguish among fields in different tables that have the same name. Fully qualified names that start with the database name can be used to perform cross-database queries.

Software Engineering Observation 19.1

*If an SQL statement includes fields from multiple tables that have the same name, the statement must precede those field names with their table names and the dot operator (e.g., **Authors.authorID**).*

Common Programming Error 19.5

In a query, failure to provide fully qualified names for fields that have the same name in two or more tables is an error.

As always, the query can contain an **ORDER BY** clause. Figure 19.21 depicts the results of the preceding query, ordered by **lastName** and **firstName**. [*Note*: To save space, we split the results of the query into two columns, each containing the **firstName**, **lastName** and **isbn** fields.]

firstName	lastName	isbn	firstName	lastName	isbn
Harvey	Deitel	0130895601	Harvey	Deitel	0130856118
Harvey	Deitel	0130284181	Harvey	Deitel	0130161438
Harvey	Deitel	0130284173	Harvey	Deitel	013028419x
Harvey	Deitel	0130829293	Harvey	Deitel	0139163050
Harvey	Deitel	0134569555	Harvey	Deitel	0135289106
Harvey	Deitel	0130829277	Harvey	Deitel	0130895717
Harvey	Deitel	0130852473	Harvey	Deitel	0132261197
Harvey	Deitel	0138993947	Harvey	Deitel	0130895725
Harvey	Deitel	0130125075	Paul	Deitel	0130895601

Fig. 19.21 Authors from table **Authors** and ISBN numbers of the authors' books, sorted in ascending order by **lastName** and **firstName** (part 1 of 2).

firstName	lastName	isbn	firstName	lastName	isbn
Paul	Deitel	0130284181	Paul	Deitel	0135289106
Paul	Deitel	0130284173	Paul	Deitel	0130895717
Paul	Deitel	0130829293	Paul	Deitel	0132261197
Paul	Deitel	0134569555	Paul	Deitel	0130895725
Paul	Deitel	0130829277	Tem	Nieto	0130284181
Paul	Deitel	0130852473	Tem	Nieto	0130284173
Paul	Deitel	0138993947	Tem	Nieto	0130829293
Paul	Deitel	0130125075	Tem	Nieto	0134569555
Paul	Deitel	0130856118	Tem	Nieto	0130856118
Paul	Deitel	0130161438	Tem	Nieto	0130161438
Paul	Deitel	013028419x	Tem	Nieto	013028419x
Paul	Deitel	0139163050	Sean	Santry	0130895601

Fig. 19.21 Authors from table `Authors` and ISBN numbers of the authors' books, sorted in ascending order by `lastName` and `firstName`.

19.4.5 Joining Data from Tables `Authors`, `AuthorISBN`, `Titles` and `Publishers`

The `Books` database contains one predefined query (`TitleAuthor`), which selects as its results the title, ISBN number, author's first name, author's last name, copyright year and publisher's name for each book in the database. For books that have multiple authors, the query produces a separate composite record for each author. The `TitleAuthor` query is shown in Fig. 19.22. Figure 19.23 contains a portion of the query results.

```
1   SELECT Titles.title, Titles.isbn, Authors.firstName,
2          Authors.lastName, Titles.copyright,
3          Publishers.publisherName
4   FROM
5      ( Publishers INNER JOIN Titles
6          ON Publishers.publisherID = Titles.publisherID )
7      INNER JOIN
8      ( Authors INNER JOIN AuthorISBN
9          ON Authors.authorID = AuthorISBN.authorID )
10     ON Titles.isbn = AuthorISBN.isbn
11  ORDER BY Titles.title
```

Fig. 19.22 Joining tables to produce a result set in which each record contains an author, title, ISBN number, copyright and publisher name.

Title	isbn	first-Name	last-Name	copy-right	publisher-Name
Advanced Java 2 Platform How to Program	0130895601	Paul	Deitel	2002	Prentice Hall
Advanced Java 2 Platform How to Program	0130895601	Harvey	Deitel	2002	Prentice Hall
Advanced Java 2 Platform How to Program	0130895601	Sean	Santry	2002	Prentice Hall
C How to Program	0131180436	Harvey	Deitel	1992	Prentice Hall
C How to Program	0131180436	Paul	Deitel	1992	Prentice Hall
C How to Program	0132261197	Harvey	Deitel	1994	Prentice Hall
C How to Program	0132261197	Paul	Deitel	1994	Prentice Hall
C How to Program	0130895725	Harvey	Deitel	2001	Prentice Hall
C How to Program	0130895725	Paul	Deitel	2001	Prentice Hall
C# How To Program	0130622214	Tem	Nieto	2002	Prentice Hall
C# How To Program	0130622214	Paul	Deitel	2002	Prentice Hall
C# How To Program	0130622214	Cheryl	Yaeger	2002	Prentice Hall
C# How To Program	0130622214	Marina	Zlatkina	2002	Prentice Hall
C# How To Program	0130622214	Harvey	Deitel	2002	Prentice Hall
C++ How to Program	0130895717	Paul	Deitel	2001	Prentice Hall
C++ How to Program	0130895717	Harvey	Deitel	2001	Prentice Hall
C++ How to Program	0131173340	Paul	Deitel	1994	Prentice Hall
C++ How to Program	0131173340	Harvey	Deitel	1994	Prentice Hall
C++ How to Program	0135289106	Harvey	Deitel	1998	Prentice Hall
C++ How to Program	0135289106	Paul	Deitel	1998	Prentice Hall
e-Business and e-Commerce for Managers	0130323640	Harvey	Deitel	2000	Prentice Hall
e-Business and e-Commerce for Managers	0130323640	Kate	Stein-buhler	2000	Prentice Hall
e-Business and e-Commerce for Managers	0130323640	Paul	Deitel	2000	Prentice Hall
e-Business and e-Commerce How to Program	013028419X	Harvey	Deitel	2001	Prentice Hall
e-Business and e-Commerce How to Program	013028419X	Paul	Deitel	2001	Prentice Hall
e-Business and e-Commerce How to Program	013028419X	Tem	Nieto	2001	Prentice Hall

Fig. 19.23 Portion of the result set produced by the query in Fig. 19.22.

We added indentation to the query of Fig. 19.22 to make the query more readable. Let us now break down the query into its various parts. Lines 1–3 contain a comma-separated list of the fields that the query returns; the order of the fields from left to right specifies the fields' order in the returned table. This query selects fields **title** and **isbn** from table **Titles**, fields **firstName** and **lastName** from table **Authors**, field **copyright** from table **Titles** and field **publisherName** from table **Publishers**. For the purpose of clarity, we fully qualified each field name with its table name (e.g., **Titles.isbn**).

Lines 5–10 specify the **INNER JOIN** operations used to combine information from the various tables. There are three **INNER JOIN** operations. It is important to note that, although an **INNER JOIN** is performed on two tables, either of those two tables can be the result of another query or another **INNER JOIN**. We use parentheses to nest the **INNER JOIN** operations; SQL evaluates the innermost set of parentheses first then moves outward. We begin with the **INNER JOIN**:

```
( Publishers INNER JOIN Titles
   ON Publishers.publisherID = Titles.publisherID )
```

which joins the **Publishers** table and the **Titles** table **ON** the condition that the **publisherID** number in each table matches. The resulting temporary table contains information about each book and its publisher.

The other nested set of parentheses contains the **INNER JOIN**:

```
( Authors INNER JOIN AuthorISBN ON
   Authors.AuthorID = AuthorISBN.AuthorID )
```

which joins the **Authors** table and the **AuthorISBN** table **ON** the condition that the **authorID** field in each table matches. Remember that the **AuthorISBN** table has multiple entries for **ISBN** numbers of books that have more than one author.

The third **INNER JOIN**:

```
( Publishers INNER JOIN Titles
   ON Publishers.publisherID = Titles.publisherID )
INNER JOIN
( Authors INNER JOIN AuthorISBN
   ON Authors.authorID = AuthorISBN.authorID )
ON Titles.isbn = AuthorISBN.isbn
```

joins the two temporary tables produced by the prior inner joins **ON** the condition that the **Titles.isbn** field for each record in the first temporary table matches the corresponding **AuthorISBN.isbn** field for each record in the second temporary table. The result of all these **INNER JOIN** operations is a temporary table from which the appropriate fields are selected to produce the results of the query.

Finally, line 11 of the query:

```
ORDER BY Titles.title
```

indicates that all the titles should be sorted in ascending order (the default).

19.4.6 INSERT Statement

The *INSERT* statement inserts a new record in a table. The simplest form for this statement is:

    INSERT INTO *tableName* **(** *fieldName1*, *fieldName2*, ..., *fieldNameN* **)**
        VALUES (*value1*, *value2*, ..., *valueN* **)**

where *tableName* is the table in which to insert the record. The *tableName* is followed by a comma-separated list of field names in parentheses. The list of field names is followed by the SQL keyword **VALUES** and a comma-separated list of values in parentheses. The specified values in this list must match the field names listed after the table name in both order and type (for example, if *fieldName1* is specified as the **firstName** field, then *value1* should be a string in single quotes representing the first name). The **INSERT** statement:

    INSERT INTO Authors (firstName, lastName)
        VALUES ('Sue', 'Smith')

inserts a record into the **Authors** table. The first comma-separated list indicates that the statement provides data for the **firstName** and **lastName** fields. The corresponding values to insert, which are contained in the second comma-separated list, are **'Sue'** and **'Smith'**. We do not specify an **authorID** in this example, because **authorID** is an auto-increment field in the database. Every new record that we add to this table is assigned a unique **authorID** value that is the next value in the auto-increment sequence (i.e., 1, 2, 3, etc.). In this case, **Sue Smith** would be assigned **authorID** number 13. Figure 19.24 shows the **Authors** table after we perform the **INSERT** operation.

authorID	firstName	lastName
1	Harvey	Deitel
2	Paul	Deitel
3	Tem	Nieto
4	Kate	Steinbuhler
5	Sean	Santry
6	Ted	Lin
7	Praveen	Sadhu
8	David	McPhie
9	Cheryl	Yaeger
10	Marina	Zlatkina
11	Ben	Wiedermann
12	Jonathan	Liperi
13	Sue	Smith

Fig. 19.24 Table **Authors** after an **INSERT** operation to add a record.

> **Common Programming Error 19.6**
>
> *SQL statements use the single-quote (* **'** *) character as a delimiter for strings. To specify a string containing a single quote (such as O'Malley) in an SQL statement, the string must include two single quotes in the position where the single-quote character should appear in the string (e.g.,* **'O''Malley'** *). The first of the two single-quote characters acts as an escape character for the second. Failure to escape single-quote characters in a string that is part of an SQL statement is an SQL syntax error.*

19.4.7 UPDATE Statement

An **UPDATE** statement modifies data in a table. The simplest form for an **UPDATE** statement is:

```
UPDATE tableName
    SET fieldName1 = value1, fieldName2 = value2, …, fieldNameN = valueN
    WHERE criteria
```

where *tableName* is the table in which to update a record (or records). The *tableName* is followed by keyword **SET** and a comma-separated list of field name/value pairs written in the format, *fieldName = value*. The **WHERE** clause specifies the criteria used to determine which record(s) to update. For example, the **UPDATE** statement:

```
UPDATE Authors
    SET lastName = 'Jones'
    WHERE lastName = 'Smith' AND firstName = 'Sue'
```

updates a record in the **Authors** table. The statement indicates that the **lastName** will be assigned the new value **Jones** for the record in which **lastName** currently is equal to **Smith** and **firstName** is equal to **Sue**. If we know the **authorID** in advance of the **UPDATE** operation (possibly because we searched for the record previously), the **WHERE** clause could be simplified as follows:

```
WHERE AuthorID = 13
```

Figure 19.25 depicts the **Authors** table after we perform the **UPDATE** operation.

authorID	firstName	lastName
1	Harvey	Deitel
2	Paul	Deitel
3	Tem	Nieto
4	Kate	Steinbuhler
5	Sean	Santry
6	Ted	Lin

Fig. 19.25 Table **Authors** after an **UPDATE** operation to change a record (part 1 of 2).

authorID	firstName	lastName
7	Praveen	Sadhu
8	David	McPhie
9	Cheryl	Yaeger
10	Marina	Zlatkina
11	Ben	Wiedermann
12	Jonathan	Liperi
13	Sue	Jones

Fig. 19.25 Table **Authors** after an **UPDATE** operation to change a record (part 2 of 2).

Common Programming Error 19.7

*Failure to use a **WHERE** clause with an **UPDATE** statement could lead to logic errors.*

19.4.8 DELETE Statement

An SQL **DELETE** statement removes data from a table. The simplest form for a **DELETE** statement is:

```
DELETE FROM tableName WHERE criteria
```

where *tableName* is the table from which to delete a record (or records). The **WHERE** clause specifies the criteria used to determine which record(s) to delete. For example, the **DELETE** statement:

```
DELETE FROM Authors
    WHERE lastName = 'Jones' AND firstName = 'Sue'
```

deletes the record for **Sue Jones** from the **Authors** table.

Common Programming Error 19.8

***WHERE** clauses can match multiple records. When deleting records from a database, be sure to define a **WHERE** clause that matches only the records to be deleted.*

Figure 19.26 shows the **Authors** table after we perform the **DELETE** operation.

authorID	firstName	lastName
1	Harvey	Deitel
2	Paul	Deitel

Fig. 19.26 Table **Authors** after a **DELETE** operation to remove a record (part 1 of 2).

authorID	firstName	lastName
3	Tem	Nieto
4	Kate	Steinbuhler
5	Sean	Santry
6	Ted	Lin
7	Praveen	Sadhu
8	David	McPhie
9	Cheryl	Yaeger
10	Marina	Zlatkina
11	Ben	Wiedermann
12	Jonathan	Liperi

Fig. 19.26 Table **Authors** after a **DELETE** operation to remove a record (part 2 of 2).

19.5 ADO .NET Object Model

The ADO .NET object model provides an API for accessing database systems programmatically. ADO .NET was created for the .NET framework and is the next generation of *ActiveX Data Objects*™ (ADO), which was designed to interact with Microsoft's *Component Object Model*™ (COM) framework.

The primary namespaces for ADO .NET are **System.Data**, **System.Data.OleDb** and **System.Data.SqlClient**. These namespaces contain classes for working with databases and other types of datasources (such as, XML files). Namespace **System.Data** is the root namespace for the ADO .NET API. Namespaces **System.Data.OleDb** and **System.Data.SqlClient** contain classes that enable programs to connect with and modify datasources. Namespace **System.Data.OleDb** contains classes that are designed to work with any datasource, whereas the **System.Data.SqlClient** namespace contains classes that are optimized to work with Microsoft SQL Server 2000 databases.

Instances of class **System.Data.DataSet**, which consist of a set of **DataTable**s and relationships among those **DataTable**s, represent a *cache* of data—data that a program stores temporarily in local memory. The structure of a **DataSet** mimics the structure of a relational database. An advantage of using class **DataSet** is that it is *disconnected*—the program does not need a persistent connection to the datasource to work with data in a **DataSet**. The program connects to the datasource only during the initial population of the **DataSet** initially and then to store any changes made in the **DataSet**. Hence, the program does not require any active, permanent connection to the datasource.

Instances of class **OleDbConnection** of namespace **System.Data.OleDb** represent a connection to a datasource. Instances of class **OleDbDataAdapter** connect to a datasource through an instance of class **OleDbConnection** and can populate **DataSet**s with data from a datasource. We discuss the details of creating and populating **DataSet**s later in this chapter.

Instances of class **OleDbCommand** of namespace **System.Data.OleDb** represent an arbitrary SQL command to be executed on a datasource. A program can use instances of class **OleDbCommand** to manipulate a datasource through an **OleDbConnection**. The programmer must close the active connection to the datasource explicitly once no further changes are to be made. Unlike **DataSet**s, **OleDbCommand** objects do not cache data in local memory.

19.6 Programming with ADO .NET: Extracting Information from a Database

In this section, we present two examples that introduce how to connect to a database, query the database and display the results of the query. The database used in these examples is the Microsoft Access **Books** database that we have discussed throughout this chapter. It can be found in the project directory for the application of Fig. 19.27. Every program employing this database must specify the database's location on the computer's hard drive. When executing these examples, this location must be updated for each program. For example, before readers can run the application in Fig. 19.27 on their computers, they must change lines 230–246 so that the code specifies the correct location for the database file.

19.6.1 Connecting to and Querying an Access Data Source

The first example (Fig. 19.27) performs a simple query on the **Books** database that retrieves the entire **Authors** table and displays the data in a *DataGrid* (a component from namespace **System.Windows.Forms** that can display a datasource in a GUI). The program illustrates the process of connecting to the database, querying the database and displaying the results in a **DataGrid**. The discussion following the example presents the key aspects of the program. [*Note*: We present all of Visual Studio's auto-generated code in Fig. 19.27 so that readers are aware of what Visual Studio generates for the example.]

```
1   ' Fig. 19.27: DisplayTable.vb
2   ' Displaying data from a database table.
3
4   Public Class FrmTableDisplay
5      Inherits System.Windows.Forms.Form
6
7   #Region " Windows Form Designer generated code "
8
9      Public Sub New()
10        MyBase.New()
11
12        ' This call is required by the Windows Form Designer.
13        InitializeComponent()
14
15        ' Add any initialization after the
16        ' InitializeComponent call
17
18        ' fill DataSet1 with data
19        OleDbDataAdapter1.Fill(DataSet1, "Authors")
20
```

Fig. 19.27 Database access and information display (part 1 of 7).

```vbnet
21         ' bind data in Users table in dataSet1 to dgdAuthors
22         dgdAuthors.SetDataBinding(DataSet1, "Authors")
23      End Sub ' New
24
25      ' Form overrides dispose to clean up the component list.
26      Protected Overloads Overrides Sub Dispose( _
27         ByVal disposing As Boolean)
28
29         If disposing Then
30            If Not (components Is Nothing) Then
31               components.Dispose()
32            End If
33         End If
34         MyBase.Dispose(disposing)
35      End Sub ' Dispose
36
37      Friend WithEvents dgdAuthors As System.Windows.Forms.DataGrid
38      Friend WithEvents OleDbSelectCommand1 As _
39         System.Data.OleDb.OleDbCommand
40
41      Friend WithEvents OleDbInsertCommand1 As _
42            System.Data.OleDb.OleDbCommand
43
44      Friend WithEvents OleDbUpdateCommand1 As _
45         System.Data.OleDb.OleDbCommand
46
47      Friend WithEvents OleDbDeleteCommand1 As _
48         System.Data.OleDb.OleDbCommand
49
50      Friend WithEvents OleDbConnection1 As _
51         System.Data.OleDb.OleDbConnection
52
53      Friend WithEvents OleDbDataAdapter1 As _
54         System.Data.OleDb.OleDbDataAdapter
55
56      Friend WithEvents DataSet1 As System.Data.DataSet
57
58      ' Required by the Windows Form Designer
59      Private components As System.ComponentModel.Container
60
61      ' NOTE: The following procedure is required by the
62      ' Windows Form Designer
63      ' It can be modified using the Windows Form Designer.
64      ' Do not modify it using the code editor.
65      <System.Diagnostics.DebuggerStepThrough()> _
66      Private Sub InitializeComponent()
67
68         Me.dgdAuthors = New System.Windows.Forms.DataGrid()
69         Me.OleDbSelectCommand1 = _
70            New System.Data.OleDb.OleDbCommand()
71
72         Me.OleDbInsertCommand1 = _
73            New System.Data.OleDb.OleDbCommand()
```

Fig. 19.27 Database access and information display (part 2 of 7).

```
74
75          Me.OleDbUpdateCommand1 = _
76              New System.Data.OleDb.OleDbCommand()
77
78          Me.OleDbDeleteCommand1 = _
79              New System.Data.OleDb.OleDbCommand()
80
81          Me.OleDbConnection1 = _
82              New System.Data.OleDb.OleDbConnection()
83
84          Me.OleDbDataAdapter1 = _
85              New System.Data.OleDb.OleDbDataAdapter()
86
87          Me.DataSet1 = New System.Data.DataSet()
88          CType(Me.dgdAuthors, _
89              System.ComponentModel.ISupportInitialize).BeginInit()
90
91          CType(Me.DataSet1, _
92              System.ComponentModel.ISupportInitialize).BeginInit()
93
94          Me.SuspendLayout()
95
96          '
97          ' dgdAuthors
98          '
99          Me.dgdAuthors.DataMember = ""
100         Me.dgdAuthors.Location = New System.Drawing.Point(8, 8)
101         Me.dgdAuthors.Name = "dgdAuthors"
102         Me.dgdAuthors.Size = New System.Drawing.Size(304, 256)
103         Me.dgdAuthors.TabIndex = 0
104
105         '
106         ' OleDbSelectCommand1
107         '
108         Me.OleDbSelectCommand1.CommandText = _
109             "SELECT authorID, firstName, lastName FROM Authors"
110
111         Me.OleDbSelectCommand1.Connection = Me.OleDbConnection1
112
113         '
114         ' OleDbInsertCommand1
115         '
116         Me.OleDbInsertCommand1.CommandText = _
117             "INSERT INTO Authors(authorID, firstName, lastName)" & _
118             "VALUES (?, ?, ?)"
119
120         Me.OleDbInsertCommand1.Connection = _
121             Me.OleDbConnection1
122
123         Me.OleDbInsertCommand1.Parameters.Add _
124             (New System.Data.OleDb.OleDbParameter("authorID", _
125             System.Data.OleDb.OleDbType.Numeric, 0, _
126             System.Data.ParameterDirection.Input, False, _
```

Fig. 19.27 Database access and information display (part 3 of 7).

```vbnet
127         CType(10, Byte), CType(0, Byte), "authorID", _
128         System.Data.DataRowVersion.Current, Nothing))
129
130      Me.OleDbInsertCommand1.Parameters.Add _
131         (New System.Data.OleDb.OleDbParameter("firstName", _
132         System.Data.OleDb.OleDbType.Char, 50, _
133         System.Data.ParameterDirection.Input, False, _
134         CType(0, Byte), CType(0, Byte), "firstName", _
135         System.Data.DataRowVersion.Current, Nothing))
136
137      Me.OleDbInsertCommand1.Parameters.Add _
138         (New System.Data.OleDb.OleDbParameter("lastName", _
139         System.Data.OleDb.OleDbType.Char, 50, _
140         System.Data.ParameterDirection.Input, False, _
141         CType(0, Byte), CType(0, Byte), "lastName", _
142         System.Data.DataRowVersion.Current, Nothing))
143
144      '
145      ' OleDbUpdateCommand1
146      '
147      Me.OleDbUpdateCommand1.CommandText = _
148         "UPDATE Authors SET authorID = ?, firstName = ?, " & _
149         "lastName = ? WHERE (authorID = ?)" & _
150         " AND (firstName = ?) AND (lastName = ?)"
151
152      Me.OleDbUpdateCommand1.Connection = Me.OleDbConnection1
153      Me.OleDbUpdateCommand1.Parameters.Add ( _
154         New System.Data.OleDb.OleDbParameter("authorID", _
155         System.Data.OleDb.OleDbType.Numeric, 0, _
156         System.Data.ParameterDirection.Input, False, _
157         CType(10, Byte), CType(0, Byte), "authorID", _
158         System.Data.DataRowVersion.Current, Nothing))
159
160      Me.OleDbUpdateCommand1.Parameters.Add _
161         (New System.Data.OleDb.OleDbParameter("firstName", _
162         System.Data.OleDb.OleDbType.Char, 50, _
163         System.Data.ParameterDirection.Input, False, _
164         CType(0, Byte), CType(0, Byte), "firstName", _
165         System.Data.DataRowVersion.Current, Nothing))
166
167      Me.OleDbUpdateCommand1.Parameters.Add _
168         (New System.Data.OleDb.OleDbParameter("lastName", _
169         System.Data.OleDb.OleDbType.Char, 50, _
170         System.Data.ParameterDirection.Input, False, _
171         CType(0, Byte), CType(0, Byte), "lastName", _
172         System.Data.DataRowVersion.Current, Nothing))
173
174      Me.OleDbUpdateCommand1.Parameters.Add _
175         (New System.Data.OleDb.OleDbParameter _
176         ("Original_authorID", _
177         System.Data.OleDb.OleDbType.Numeric, 0, _
178         System.Data.ParameterDirection.Input, False, _
```

Fig. 19.27 Database access and information display (part 4 of 7).

```vbnet
179                 CType(10, Byte), CType(0, Byte), "authorID", _
180                 System.Data.DataRowVersion.Original, Nothing))
181
182             Me.OleDbUpdateCommand1.Parameters.Add _
183                 (New System.Data.OleDb.OleDbParameter _
184                 ("Original_firstName", _
185                 System.Data.OleDb.OleDbType.Char, 50, _
186                 System.Data.ParameterDirection.Input, False, _
187                 CType(0, Byte), CType(0, Byte), "firstName", _
188                 System.Data.DataRowVersion.Original, Nothing))
189
190             Me.OleDbUpdateCommand1.Parameters.Add _
191                 (New System.Data.OleDb.OleDbParameter _
192                 ("Original_lastName", _
193                 System.Data.OleDb.OleDbType.Char, 50, _
194                 System.Data.ParameterDirection.Input, False, _
195                 CType(0, Byte), CType(0, Byte), "lastName", _
196                 System.Data.DataRowVersion.Original, Nothing))
197
198             '
199             ' OleDbDeleteCommand1
200             '
201             Me.OleDbDeleteCommand1.CommandText = _
202                 "DELETE FROM Authors WHERE (authorID = ?) AND " & _
203                 "(firstName = ?) AND (lastName = ?)"
204
205             Me.OleDbDeleteCommand1.Connection = Me.OleDbConnection1
206             Me.OleDbDeleteCommand1.Parameters.Add _
207                 (New System.Data.OleDb.OleDbParameter("authorID", _
208                 System.Data.OleDb.OleDbType.Numeric, 0, _
209                 System.Data.ParameterDirection.Input, False, _
210                 CType(10, Byte), CType(0, Byte), "authorID", _
211                 System.Data.DataRowVersion.Original, Nothing))
212
213             Me.OleDbDeleteCommand1.Parameters.Add _
214                 (New System.Data.OleDb.OleDbParameter("firstName", _
215                 System.Data.OleDb.OleDbType.Char, 50, _
216                 System.Data.ParameterDirection.Input, False, _
217                 CType(0, Byte), CType(0, Byte), "firstName", _
218                 System.Data.DataRowVersion.Original, Nothing))
219
220             Me.OleDbDeleteCommand1.Parameters.Add _
221                 (New System.Data.OleDb.OleDbParameter("lastName", _
222                 System.Data.OleDb.OleDbType.Char, 50, _
223                 System.Data.ParameterDirection.Input, False, _
224                 CType(0, Byte), CType(0, Byte), "lastName", _
225                 System.Data.DataRowVersion.Original, Nothing))
226
227             '
228             'OleDbConnection1
229             '
230             Me.OleDbConnection1.ConnectionString = _
231                 "Provider=Microsoft.Jet.OLEDB.4.0;Password=""""; " & _
```

Fig. 19.27 Database access and information display (part 5 of 7).

```
232             "User ID=Admin;Data Source=C:\Documen" & _
233             "ts and Settings\thiago\Desktop\vbhtp2e\examples\" & _
234             "Ch19\Fig19_27\Books.mdb;Mode=Sha" & _
235             "re Deny None;Extended Properties="""";" & _
236             "Jet OLEDB:System database="""";Jet OLEDB:Regis" & _
237             "try Path="""";Jet OLEDB:Database Password="""";" & _
238             "Jet OLEDB:Engine Type=5;Jet OLEDB:Dat" & _
239             "abase Locking Mode=1;Jet OLEDB:Global Partial " & _
240             "Bulk Ops=2;Jet OLEDB:Global Bulk T" & _
241             "ransactions=1;Jet OLEDB:New Database " & _
242             "Password="""";Jet OLEDB:Create System Databas" & _
243             "e=False;Jet OLEDB:Encrypt Database=False;" & _
244             "Jet OLEDB:Don't Copy Locale on Compact=" & _
245             "False;Jet OLEDB:Compact Without Replica " & _
246             "Repair=False;Jet OLEDB:SFP=False"
247
248         '
249         ' OleDbDataAdapter1
250         '
251         Me.OleDbDataAdapter1.DeleteCommand = _
252             Me.OleDbDeleteCommand1
253
254         Me.OleDbDataAdapter1.InsertCommand = _
255             Me.OleDbInsertCommand1
256
257         Me.OleDbDataAdapter1.SelectCommand = _
258             Me.OleDbSelectCommand1
259
260         Me.OleDbDataAdapter1.TableMappings.AddRange _
261             (New System.Data.Common.DataTableMapping() _
262             {New System.Data.Common.DataTableMapping("Table", _
263             "Authors", New System.Data.Common.DataColumnMapping() _
264             {New System.Data.Common.DataColumnMapping("authorID", _
265             "authorID"), New System.Data.Common.DataColumnMapping _
266             ("firstName", "firstName"), _
267             New System.Data.Common.DataColumnMapping("lastName", _
268             "lastName")})})
269
270         Me.OleDbDataAdapter1.UpdateCommand = _
271             Me.OleDbUpdateCommand1
272
273         '
274         ' DataSet1
275         '
276         Me.DataSet1.DataSetName = "NewDataSet"
277         Me.DataSet1.Locale = _
278             New System.Globalization.CultureInfo("en-US")
279
280         '
281         ' FrmTableDisplay
282         '
283         Me.AutoScaleBaseSize = New System.Drawing.Size(5, 13)
284         Me.ClientSize = New System.Drawing.Size(320, 273)
```

Fig. 19.27 Database access and information display (part 6 of 7).

```
285            Me.Controls.AddRange(New System.Windows.Forms.Control() _
286                {Me.dgdAuthors})
287
288            Me.Name = "FrmTableDisplay"
289            Me.Text = "Table Display"
290            CType(Me.dgdAuthors, System.ComponentModel. _
291                ISupportInitialize).EndInit()
292
293            CType(Me.DataSet1, System.ComponentModel. _
294                ISupportInitialize).EndInit()
295
296            Me.ResumeLayout(False)
297
298        End Sub ' InitializeComponent
299
300  #End Region
301
302  End Class ' FrmTableDisplay
```

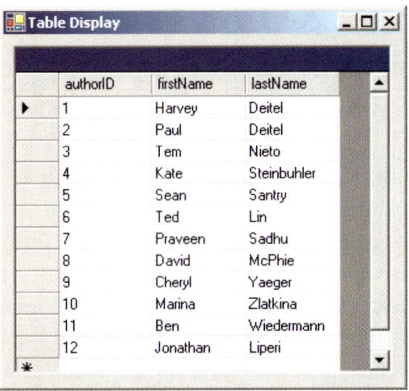

Fig. 19.27 Database access and information display (part 7 of 7).

This example uses an Access database. To register the **Books** database as a datasource, right click the **Data Connections** node in the **Server Explorer** and then click **Add Connection**. In the **Provider** tab of the window that appears, choose "**Microsoft Jet 4.0 OLE DB Provider**", which is the driver for Access databases. In the **Connection** tab, click the ellipses button (**...**) to the right of the textbox for the database name; this opens the **Select Access Database** window. Go to the appropriate folder, select the **Books** database and click **OK**. Then, click the **Add Connection** window's **OK** button. Now, the database is listed as a connection in the **Server Explorer**. Drag the database node onto the Windows Form. This creates an **OleDbConnection** to the source, which the Windows Form designer shows as **OleDbConnection1**.

Next, drag an **OleDbDataAdapter** from the **Toolbox**'s *Data* subheading onto the Windows Form designer. This displays the **Data Adapter Configuration Wizard**, which configures the **OleDbDataAdapter** instance with a custom query for populating a **DataSet**. Click **Next** to display a drop-down list of possible connections. Select the connection created in the previous step from the drop-down list and click **Next**. The resulting screen allows us to choose how the **OleDbDataAdapter** should access the database. Keep the default **Use SQL Statement** option and click **Next**. Click the "**Query Builder**" button, then select the **Authors** table from the "**Add**" menu and then **Close** that menu. Place a check mark in the "***All Columns**" box from the small "**Authors**" window. Note how that particular window lists all columns of the **Authors** table. Click **OK** and then **Finish**.

Next, we create a **DataSet** to store the query results. To do so, drag **DataSet** from the **Data** tab in the **Toolbox** onto the form. This displays the **Add DataSet** window. Choose the "**Untyped DataSet (no schema)**"—the query with which we populate the **DataSet** dictates the **DataSet**'s *schema*, or structure (i.e., the tables that comprise the **DataSet** and the relationships among those tables. Finally, add **DataGrid dgdAuthors** to the **Form**.

Figure 19.27 includes all of the auto-generated code. Normally, we omit this code from examples, because this code consists solely of GUI components. In this case, however, we must discuss database functionality that is contained in the auto-generated code. Furthermore, we have left Visual Studio's default naming conventions in this example to show exactly the code Visual Studio creates. Normally, we would change these names to conform to our programming conventions and style.

> ### Good Programming Practice 19.2
> *Use clear, descriptive variable names in code. This makes programs easier to understand.*

Lines 230–246 initialize the **OleDbConnection** for this program. Property **ConnectionString** specifies the path to the database file on the computer's hard drive.

An instance of class **OleDbDataAdapter** populates the **DataSet** in this example with data from the **Books** database. The instance properties ***DeleteCommand*** (lines 251–252), ***InsertCommand*** (lines 254–255), ***SelectCommand*** (lines 257–258) and ***UpdateCommand*** (lines 270–271) are **OleDbCommand** objects that specify how the **OleDbDataAdapter** deletes, inserts, selects and updates data in the database.

Each **OleDbCommand** object must have an **OleDbConnection** through which the **OleDbCommand** can communicate with the database. Property **Connection** is set to the **OleDbConnection** to the **Books** database. For **OleDbUpdateCommand1**, line 152 sets the **Connection** property, and lines 147–150 set the **CommandText**.

Although Visual Studio .NET generates most of this program's code, we manually enter code in the **FrmTableDisplay** constructor (lines 9–23); this code populates **dataSet1** using an **OleDbDataAdapter**. Line 19 calls **OleDbDataAdapter** method ***Fill*** to retrieve information from the database associated with the **OleDbConnection**, placing this information in the **DataSet** provided as an argument. The second argument to method **Fill** is a **String** specifying the name of the table in the database from which to **Fill** the **DataSet**.

Line 22 invokes **DataGrid** method **SetDataBinding** to bind the **DataGrid** to a datasource. The first argument is the **DataSet**—in this case, **DataSet1**—whose data the **DataGrid** should display. The second argument is a **String** representing the name of the table within the datasource that we want to bind to the **DataGrid**. Once this line executes, the **DataGrid** is filled with the information in the **DataSet**. The information in **DataSet1** is used to set the correct number of rows and columns in the **DataGrid** and to provide the columns with default names.

19.6.2 Querying the Books Database

The code example in Fig. 19.28 demonstrates how to execute SQL **SELECT** statements on a database and display the results. Although Fig. 19.28 uses only **SELECT** statements to query the data, the application could be used to execute many different SQL statements with a few minor modifications.

```vb
1   ' Fig. 19.28: DisplayQueryResults.vb
2   ' Displays the contents of the authors database.
3
4   Imports System.Windows.Forms
5
6   Public Class FrmDisplayQueryResult
7      Inherits Form
8
9      ' SQL query input textbox and submit button
10     Friend WithEvents txtQuery As TextBox
11     Friend WithEvents cmdSubmit As Button
12
13     ' dataset display grid
14     Friend WithEvents dgdResults As DataGrid
15
16     ' database connection
17     Friend WithEvents BooksConnection As _
18        System.Data.OleDb.OleDbConnection
19
20     ' database adapter
21     Friend WithEvents BooksDataAdapter As _
22        System.Data.OleDb.OleDbDataAdapter
23
24     ' query dataset
25     Friend WithEvents BooksDataSet As System.Data.DataSet
26
27     ' Visual Studio .NET generated code
28
29     ' perform SQL query on data
30     Private Sub cmdSubmit_Click(ByVal sender As System.Object, _
31        ByVal e As System.EventArgs) Handles cmdSubmit.Click
32
33        Try
34
35           ' set text of SQL query to what user typed
36           BooksDataAdapter.SelectCommand.CommandText = _
37              txtQuery.Text
38
39           ' clear DataSet from previous operation
40           BooksDataSet.Clear()
41
42           ' fill data set with information that results
43           ' from SQL query
44           BooksDataAdapter.Fill(BooksDataSet, "Authors")
45
```

Fig. 19.28 SQL statements executed on a database (part 1 of 2).

```
46             ' bind DataGrid to contents of DataSet
47             dgdResults.SetDataBinding(BooksDataSet, "Authors")
48
49          ' display database connection message
50          Catch oleDbExceptionParameter As _
51             System.Data.OleDb.OleDbException
52
53             MessageBox.Show("Invalid Query")
54          End Try
55
56       End Sub ' cmdSubmit_Click
57
58    End Class ' FrmDisplayQueryResults
```

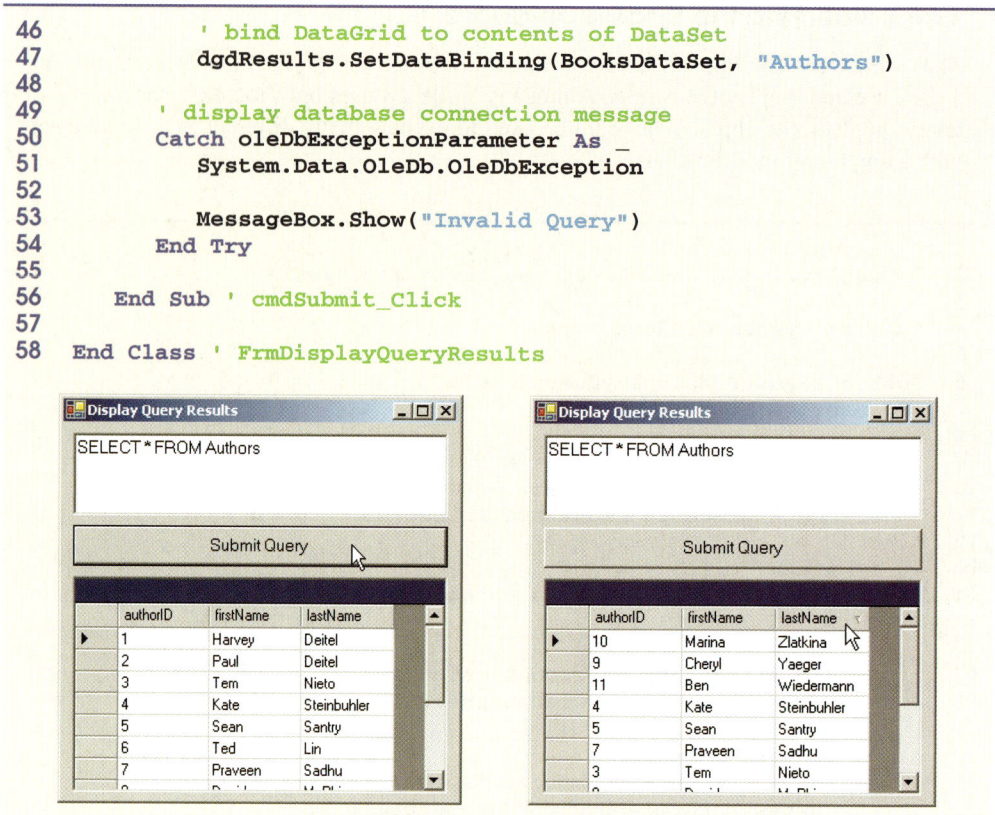

Fig. 19.28 SQL statements executed on a database (part 2 of 2).

Form **FrmDisplayQueryResult** (Fig. 19.28) contains **TextBox txtQuery** (line 10), in which users input **SELECT** statements. After entering a query, the user clicks **Button cmdSubmit** (line 11), labeled **Submit Query**, to view the results of the query. The results then are displayed in **DataGrid dgdResults** (line 14).

Event handler **cmdSubmit_Click** (lines 30–56) is the key part of this program. When the program invokes this event handler in response to a button click, lines 36–37 assign the **SELECT** query that the user typed in **txtQuery** as the value of the **OleDb-DataAdapter**'s **SelectCommand** property. This **String** is parsed into an SQL query and executed on the database via the **OleDbDataAdapter**'s method **Fill** (line 44). This method, as discussed in the previous section, places the data from the database into **BooksDataSet**. Line 40 calls method **Clear** of class **DataSet**. Method **Clear** removes all previous information contained within a **DataSet**.

Common Programming Error 19.9

*If a **DataSet** already has been **Fill**ed at least once, failure to call the **DataSet**'s **Clear** method before calling the **Fill** method will lead to logic errors.*

To display or redisplay contents in the **DataGrid**, use method **SetDataBinding**. Again, the first argument to this method is the datasource to be displayed in the table—a **DataSet**, in this case. The second argument is the **String** name of the datasource member to be displayed (line 47)—a table name, in this case. Readers can try entering their own queries in the text box and then pressing the **Submit Query** button to execute the query.

Fig. 19.28 displays the output for `FrmDisplayQueryResults`. The first screenshot demonstrates the query results of retrieving all records from the `Authors` table. As the second screen capture demonstrates, clicking any column sorts the rows according to the contents of that column in either ascending or descending order.

19.7 Programming with ADO .NET: Modifying a DBMS

Our next example implements a simple address-book application that enables users to insert records into, locate records from and update the Microsoft Access database `Addressbook`.

The `Addressbook` application (Fig. 19.29) provides a GUI through which users can execute SQL statements on the database. Earlier in the chapter, we presented examples explaining the use of `SELECT` statements to query a database. This example provides that same functionality.

Event handler `cmdFind_Click` (lines 72–119) performs the `SELECT` query on the database for the record associated with the `String` entered in `txtLast`. This represents the last name of the person whose record the user wishes to retrieve. Line 81 invokes method `Clear` of class `DataSet` to empty the `DataSet` of any prior data. Lines 85–87 modify the text of the SQL query to perform the appropriate `SELECT` operation. The `OleDbDataAdapter` method `Fill` then executes this statement (line 91). Notice how a different overload of method `Fill` from the previous example has been used in this situation. Only the `DataSet` to be filled is passed as an argument. Finally, the `TextBox`es are updated with a call to method `Display` (line 94).

Methods `cmdAdd_Click` (lines 122–173) and `cmdUpdate_Click` (lines 176–232) perform `INSERT` and `UPDATE` operations, respectively. Each method uses members of class `OleDbCommand` to perform operations on a database. The instance properties `InsertCommand` and `UpdateCommand` of class `OleDbDataAdapter` are instances of class `OleDbCommand`.

```vbnet
1   ' Fig. 19.29: AddressBook.vb
2   ' Using SQL statements to manipulate a database.
3
4   Imports System.Windows.Forms
5
6   Public Class FrmAddressBook
7      Inherits Form
8
9      ' top set of command buttons
10     Friend WithEvents cmdFind As Button
11     Friend WithEvents cmdAdd As Button
12     Friend WithEvents cmdUpdate As Button
13     Friend WithEvents cmdClear As Button
14     Friend WithEvents cmdHelp As Button
15
16     ' textbox identifier labels
17     Friend WithEvents lblId As Label
```

Fig. 19.29 Database modification demonstration (part 1 of 9).

```vb
18      Friend WithEvents lblFirst As Label
19      Friend WithEvents lblLast As Label
20      Friend WithEvents lblAddress As Label
21      Friend WithEvents lblCity As Label
22      Friend WithEvents lblState As Label
23      Friend WithEvents lblZip As Label
24      Friend WithEvents lblCountry As Label
25      Friend WithEvents lblEmail As Label
26      Friend WithEvents lblPhone As Label
27      Friend WithEvents lblFax As Label
28
29      ' input textboxes
30      Friend WithEvents txtId As TextBox
31      Friend WithEvents txtFirst As TextBox
32      Friend WithEvents txtLast As TextBox
33      Friend WithEvents txtAddress As TextBox
34      Friend WithEvents txtCity As TextBox
35      Friend WithEvents txtState As TextBox
36      Friend WithEvents txtZip As TextBox
37      Friend WithEvents txtCountry As TextBox
38      Friend WithEvents txtEmail As TextBox
39      Friend WithEvents txtPhone As TextBox
40      Friend WithEvents txtFax As TextBox
41
42      ' query status display textbox
43      Friend WithEvents txtStatus As TextBox
44
45      ' database connection
46      Friend WithEvents AddressBookConnection As _
47         System.Data.OleDb.OleDbConnection
48
49      ' database adapter
50      Friend WithEvents AddressBookDataAdapter As _
51         System.Data.OleDb.OleDbDataAdapter
52
53      ' query dataset
54      Friend WithEvents AddressBookDataSet As System.Data.DataSet
55
56      ' constructor
57      Public Sub New()
58         MyBase.New()
59
60         ' This call is required by the Windows Form Designer.
61         InitializeComponent()
62
63         ' Add any initialization after the InitializeComponent call
64
65         ' open connection
66         AddressBookConnection.Open()
67      End Sub ' New
68
69      ' Visual Studio .NET generated code
70
```

Fig. 19.29 Database modification demonstration (part 2 of 9).

```vbnet
71        ' finds record in database
72        Private Sub cmdFind_Click(ByVal sender As System.Object, _
73           ByVal e As System.EventArgs) Handles cmdFind.Click
74
75           Try
76
77              ' ensure user input last name
78              If txtLast.Text <> "" Then
79
80                 ' clear DataSet from last operation
81                 AddressBookDataSet.Clear()
82
83                 ' create SQL query to find contact
84                 ' with specified last name
85                 AddressBookDataAdapter.SelectCommand.CommandText = _
86                    "SELECT * FROM addresses WHERE " & _
87                    "lastname = '" & txtLast.Text & "' "
88
89                 ' fill AddressBookDataSet with the rows resulting
90                 ' from the query
91                 AddressBookDataAdapter.Fill(AddressBookDataSet)
92
93                 ' display information
94                 Display(AddressBookDataSet)
95                 txtStatus.Text &= vbCrLf & "Query Successful " & _
96                    vbCrLf
97
98              ' prompt user for last name
99              Else
100                txtLast.Text = _
101                   "Enter last name here then press Find"
102             End If
103
104          ' display verbose information with database exception
105          Catch oleDbExceptionParameter As _
106             System.Data.OleDb.OleDbException
107
108             Console.WriteLine(oleDbExceptionParameter.StackTrace)
109             txtStatus.Text &= oleDbExceptionParameter.ToString
110
111          ' display message box when invalid operation
112          Catch invalidOperationExceptionParameter As _
113             InvalidOperationException
114
115             MessageBox.Show( _
116                invalidOperationExceptionParameter.Message)
117          End Try
118
119       End Sub ' cmdFind_Click
120
```

Fig. 19.29 Database modification demonstration (part 3 of 9).

```vbnet
121         ' adds record to database
122         Private Sub cmdAdd_Click(ByVal sender As System.Object, _
123            ByVal e As System.EventArgs) Handles cmdAdd.Click
124
125            Try
126
127               ' ensure first and last name input
128               If (txtLast.Text <> "" AndAlso txtFirst.Text <> "") Then
129
130                  ' create the SQL query to insert a row
131                  AddressBookDataAdapter.InsertCommand.CommandText = _
132                     "INSERT INTO addresses(firstname, " & _
133                     "lastname, address, city, " & _
134                     "stateorprovince, postalcode, country, " & _
135                     "emailaddress, homephone, faxnumber) " & _
136                     "VALUES('" & txtFirst.Text & "' , " & _
137                     "'" & txtLast.Text & "' , " & _
138                     "'" & txtAddress.Text & "' , " & _
139                     "'" & txtCity.Text & "' , " & _
140                     "'" & txtState.Text & "' , " & _
141                     "'" & txtZip.Text & "' , " & _
142                     "'" & txtCountry.Text & "' , " & _
143                     "'" & txtEmail.Text & "' , " & _
144                     "'" & txtPhone.Text & "' , " & _
145                     "'" & txtFax.Text & "')"
146
147                  ' notify the user the query is being sent
148                  txtStatus.Text &= vbCrLf & "Sending query: " & _
149                     AddressBookDataAdapter.InsertCommand. _
150                        CommandText & vbCrLf
151
152                  ' send query
153                  AddressBookDataAdapter.InsertCommand. _
154                     ExecuteNonQuery()
155
156                  txtStatus.Text &= vbCrLf & "Query successful"
157
158               ' prompt user to input first and last name
159               Else
160                  txtStatus.Text &= vbCrLf & _
161                     "Enter at least first and last name then " & _
162                     "press Add" & vbCrLf
163               End If
164
165            ' display verbose information when database exception
166            Catch oleDbExceptionParameter As _
167               System.Data.OleDb.OleDbException
168
169               Console.WriteLine(oleDbExceptionParameter.StackTrace)
170               txtStatus.Text &= oleDbExceptionParameter.ToString
171            End Try
172
173         End Sub ' cmdAdd_Click
```

Fig. 19.29 Database modification demonstration (part 4 of 9).

```vb
174
175         ' updates entry in database
176         Private Sub cmdUpdate_Click(ByVal sender As System.Object, _
177            ByVal e As System.EventArgs) Handles cmdUpdate.Click
178
179            Try
180
181               ' make sure user has already found
182               ' record to update
183               If txtId.Text <> "" Then
184
185                  ' set SQL query to update all fields in
186                  ' table where id number matches id in
187                  ' idTextBox
188                  AddressBookDataAdapter.UpdateCommand.CommandText = _
189                     "UPDATE addresses SET firstname=" & _
190                     "'" & txtFirst.Text & "' , " & _
191                     "lastname = '" & txtLast.Text & "' , " & _
192                     "address='" & txtAddress.Text & "' , " & _
193                     "city='" & txtCity.Text & "' , " & _
194                     "stateorprovince= " & _
195                     "'" & txtState.Text & "', " & _
196                     "postalcode='" & txtZip.Text & "', " & _
197                     "country='" & txtCountry.Text & "' , " & _
198                     "emailaddress='" & txtEmail.Text & "' , " & _
199                     "homephone='" & txtPhone.Text & "' , " & _
200                     "faxnumber='" & txtFax.Text & "' " & _
201                     "WHERE id=" & txtId.Text & " ; "
202
203                  ' notify user that query is being sent
204                  txtStatus.Text &= vbCrLf & "Sending query: " & _
205                     AddressBookDataAdapter.UpdateCommand. _
206                        CommandText & vbCrLf
207
208                  ' execute query
209                  AddressBookDataAdapter.UpdateCommand. _
210                     ExecuteNonQuery()
211
212                  txtStatus.Text &= vbCrLf & "Query Successful" & _
213                     vbCrLf
214
215               ' prompt user to input existing record
216               Else
217                  txtStatus.Text &= vbCrLf & _
218                     "You may only update an existing record. " & _
219                     "Use Find to locate the record, then " & _
220                     "modify the information and press Update." & _
221                     vbCrLf
222               End If
223
224            ' display verbose information when database exception
225            Catch oleDbExceptionParameter As _
226               System.Data.OleDb.OleDbException
```

Fig. 19.29 Database modification demonstration (part 5 of 9).

```vbnet
227
228                Console.WriteLine(oleDbExceptionParameter.StackTrace)
229                txtStatus.Text &= oleDbExceptionParameter.ToString
230         End Try
231
232      End Sub ' cmdUpdate_Click
233
234      ' clears all information in textboxes
235      Private Sub cmdClear_Click(ByVal sender As System.Object, _
236         ByVal e As System.EventArgs) Handles cmdClear.Click
237
238         txtId.Clear()
239         ClearTextBoxes()
240      End Sub ' cmdClear_Click
241
242      ' displays information on application use
243      Private Sub cmdHelp_Click(ByVal sender As System.Object, _
244         ByVal e As System.EventArgs) Handles cmdHelp.Click
245
246         txtStatus.AppendText(vbCrLf & _
247            "Click Find to locate a record" & vbCrLf & _
248            "Click Add to insert a new record." & vbCrLf & _
249            "Click Update to update the information in a " & _
250            "record " & vbCrLf & "Click Clear to empty the " & _
251            "textboxes")
252      End Sub ' cmdHelp_Click
253
254      ' displays data in dataset
255      Private Sub Display(ByVal dataset As DataSet)
256
257         Try
258
259            ' get first DataTable - there will be one
260            Dim dataTable As DataTable = dataset.Tables(0)
261
262            ' ensure dataTable not empty
263            If dataTable.Rows.Count <> 0 Then
264               Dim recordNumber As Integer = _
265                  Convert.ToInt32(dataTable.Rows(0)(0))
266
267               txtId.Text = recordNumber.ToString
268               txtFirst.Text = _
269                  Convert.ToString(dataTable.Rows(0)(1))
270
271               txtLast.Text = _
272                  Convert.ToString(dataTable.Rows(0)(2))
273
274               txtAddress.Text = _
275                  Convert.ToString(dataTable.Rows(0)(3))
276
277               txtCity.Text = _
278                  Convert.ToString(dataTable.Rows(0)(4))
279
```

Fig. 19.29 Database modification demonstration (part 6 of 9).

```
280                txtState.Text = _
281                   Convert.ToString(dataTable.Rows(0)(5))
282
283                txtZip.Text = _
284                   Convert.ToString(dataTable.Rows(0)(6))
285
286                txtCountry.Text = _
287                   Convert.ToString(dataTable.Rows(0)(7))
288
289                txtEmail.Text = _
290                   Convert.ToString(dataTable.Rows(0)(8))
291
292                txtPhone.Text = _
293                   Convert.ToString(dataTable.Rows(0)(9))
294
295                txtFax.Text = _
296                   Convert.ToString(dataTable.Rows(0)(10))
297
298            ' display not-found message
299            Else
300               txtStatus.Text &= vbCrLf & "No record found" & vbCrLf
301            End If
302
303         ' display verbose information when database exception
304         Catch oleDbExceptionParameter As _
305            System.Data.OleDb.OleDbException
306
307            Console.WriteLine(oleDbExceptionParameter.StackTrace)
308            txtStatus.Text &= oleDbExceptionParameter.ToString
309         End Try
310
311      End Sub ' Display
312
313      ' clears text boxes
314      Private Sub ClearTextBoxes()
315         txtFirst.Clear()
316         txtLast.Clear()
317         txtAddress.Clear()
318         txtCity.Clear()
319         txtState.Clear()
320         txtZip.Clear()
321         txtCountry.Clear()
322         txtEmail.Clear()
323         txtPhone.Clear()
324         txtFax.Clear()
325      End Sub  ' ClearTextBoxes
326
327   End Class ' FrmAddressBook
```

Fig. 19.29 Database modification demonstration (part 7 of 9).

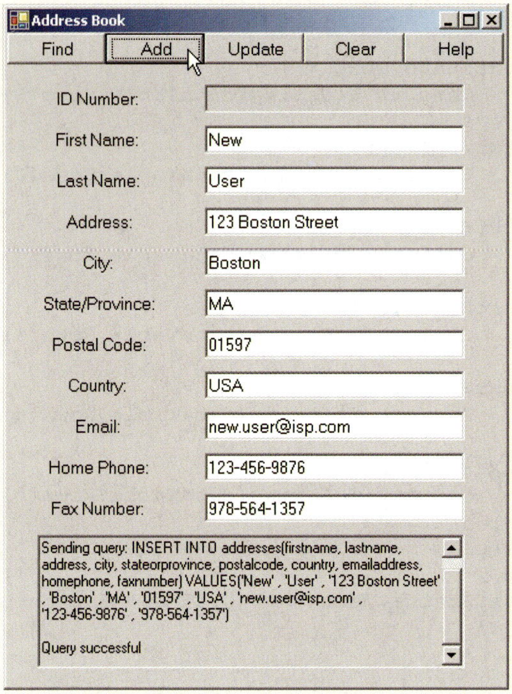

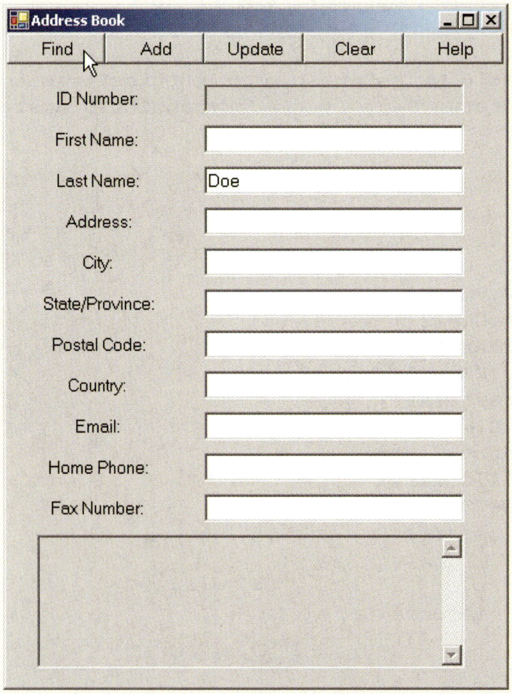

Fig. 19.29 Database modification demonstration (part 8 of 9).

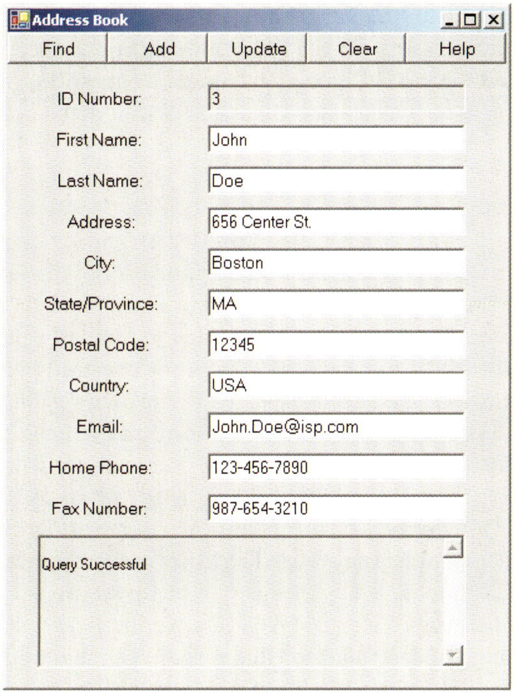

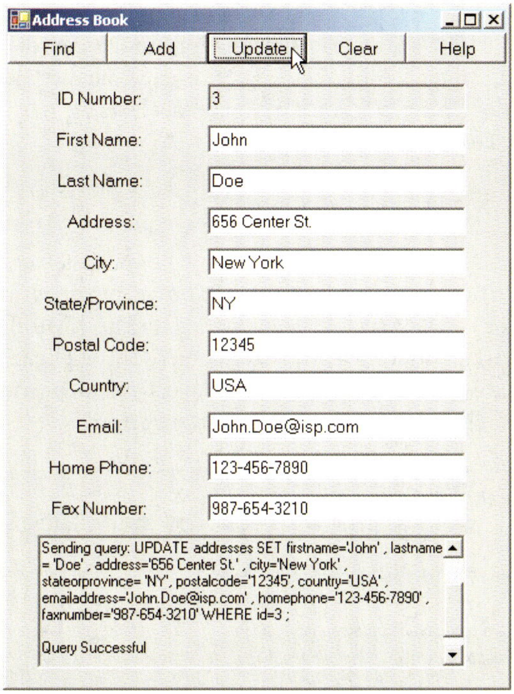

Fig. 19.29 Database modification demonstration (part 9 of 9).

Property **CommandText** of class **OleDbCommand** is a **String** representing the SQL statement that the **OleDbCommand** object executes. Event handler **cmdAdd_Click** sets property **CommandText** of the **OleDbCommand** object (accessed through **AddressBookDataAdapter**'s property **InsertCommand**) to execute the appropriate **INSERT** statement on the database (lines 131–145). Method **cmdUpdate_Click** sets this property of **UpdateCommand** to execute the appropriate **UPDATE** statement on the database (lines 188–201).

The *ExecuteNonQuery* method of class **OleDbCommand** performs the action specified by **CommandText**. Hence, the **INSERT** statement defined by **AddressBookDataAdapter.InsertCommand.CommandText** in the **cmdAdd_Click** event handler is executed when lines 153–154 invoke method **AddressBookDataAdapter.InsertCommand.ExecuteNonQuery**. Similarly, the **UPDATE** statement defined by **AddressBookDataAdapter.UpdateCommand.CommandText** in the event handler **cmdUpdate_Click** is executed by invoking method **AddressBookDataAdapter.UpdateCommand.ExecuteNonQuery** (lines 209–210).

Method **Display** (lines 255-311) updates the user interface with data from the newly retrieved address book record. Line 260 obtains a **DataTable** from the **DataSet**'s **Tables** collection. This **DataTable** contains the results of our SQL query. Line 263 checks whether the query returned any rows. The **Rows** property in class **DataTable** provides access to all records retrieved by the query. The **Rows** property is much like a two-dimensional rectangular array. Lines 264–265 retrieve the field with index *0, 0* (i.e., the first record's first column of data) and store the value in variable **recordNumber**. Lines 267–296 then retrieve the remaining fields of data from the **DataTable** to populate the user interface.

The application's **Help** button prints instructions in the console at the bottom of the application window (lines 246–251). The event handler for this button is **cmdHelp_Click** (lines 243–252). The **Clear** button clears the text from the **TextBox**es using method **ClearTextBoxes** (line 314).

19.8 Reading and Writing XML Files

A powerful feature of ADO .NET is its ability to convert data stored in a datasource to XML. Class **DataSet** of namespace **System.Data** provides methods *WriteXml*, *ReadXml* and *GetXml*, which enable developers to create XML documents from datasources and to convert data from XML into datasources. The application of Fig. 19.30 populates a **DataSet** with statistics about baseball players and then writes the data to files as XML. The application also displays the XML in a **TextBox**.

```
1    ' Fig. 19.30: XMLWriter.vb
2    ' Demonstrates generating XML from an ADO .NET DataSet.
3
4    Imports System.Windows.Forms
5
6    Public Class FrmXMLWriter
7        Inherits Form
8
```

Fig. 19.30 XML representation of a **DataSet** written to a file (part 1 of 3).

```vbnet
 9        ' constructor
10        Public Sub New()
11           MyBase.New()
12
13           ' This call is required by the Windows Form Designer.
14           InitializeComponent()
15
16           ' Add any initialization after the
17           ' InitializeComponent() call
18
19           ' open database connection
20           BaseballConnection.Open()
21
22           ' fill DataSet with data from OleDbDataAdapter
23           BaseballDataAdapter.Fill(BaseballDataSet, "Players")
24
25           ' bind DataGrid to DataSet
26           dgdPlayers.SetDataBinding(BaseballDataSet, "Players")
27        End Sub
28
29        ' form controls
30        Friend WithEvents cmdWrite As Button
31        Friend WithEvents dgdPlayers As DataGrid
32        Friend WithEvents txtOutput As TextBox
33
34        ' database connection
35        Friend WithEvents BaseballConnection As _
36           System.Data.OleDb.OleDbConnection
37
38        ' database adapter
39        Friend WithEvents BaseballDataAdapter As _
40           System.Data.OleDb.OleDbDataAdapter
41
42        ' results dataset
43        Friend WithEvents BaseballDataSet As System.Data.DataSet
44
45        ' Visual Studio .NET generated code
46
47        ' write XML representation of DataSet when button clicked
48        Private Sub cmdWrite_Click(ByVal sender As System.Object, _
49           ByVal e As System.EventArgs) Handles cmdWrite.Click
50
51           ' write XML representation of DataSet to file
52           BaseballDataSet.WriteXml("Players.xml")
53
54           ' display XML in TextBox
55           txtOutput.Text &= "Writing the following XML:" & _
56              vbCrLf & BaseballDataSet.GetXml() & vbCrLf
57        End Sub ' cmWrite_Click
58
59     End Class ' FrmXMLWriter
```

Fig. 19.30 XML representation of a **DataSet** written to a file (part 2 of 3).

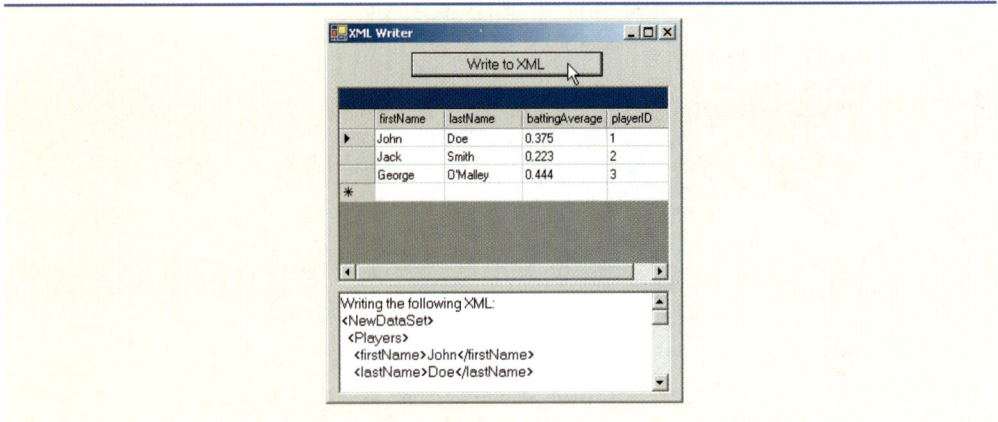

Fig. 19.30 XML representation of a **DataSet** written to a file (part 3 of 3).

The **FrmXMLWriter** constructor (lines 10–27) establishes a connection to the **Baseball** database in line 20. Line 23 calls method **Fill** of class **OleDbDataAdapter** to populate **BaseballDataSet** with data from the **Players** table in the **Baseball** database. Line 26 binds the **dgdPlayers** to **BaseballDataSet** to display the information to the user.

Event handler **cmdWrite_Click** (lines 48–57) defines the event handler for the **Write to XML** button. When the user clicks this button, line 52 invokes **DataSet** method **WriteXml**, which generates an XML representation of the data contained in the **DataSet** and then writes the XML to the specified file. Figure 19.31 depicts this XML representation. Each **Players** element represents a record in the **Players** table. The **firstName**, **lastName**, **battingAverage** and **playerID** elements correspond to the fields that have these names in the **Players** database table.

```
1   <?xml version="1.0" standalone="yes"?>
2   <NewDataSet>
3      <Players>
4         <firstName>John</firstName>
5         <lastName>Doe</lastName>
6         <battingAverage>0.375</battingAverage>
7         <playerID>1</playerID>
8      </Players>
9
10     <Players>
11        <firstName>Jack</firstName>
12        <lastName>Smith</lastName>
13        <battingAverage>0.223</battingAverage>
14        <playerID>2</playerID>
15     </Players>
16
17     <Players>
18        <firstName>George</firstName>
19        <lastName>O'Malley</lastName>
```

Fig. 19.31 XML document generated from **WriteXML** (part 1 of 2).

```
20          <battingAverage>0.444</battingAverage>
21          <playerID>3</playerID>
22       </Players>
23    </NewDataSet>
```

Fig. 19.31 XML document generated from `DataSet` in `XMLWriter` (part 2 of 2).

SUMMARY

- A database is an integrated collection of data. A database management system (DBMS) provides mechanisms for storing and organizing data.
- Today's most popular database systems are relational databases.
- A language called Structured Query Language (SQL) is used almost universally with relational-database systems to perform queries and manipulate data.
- A programming language connects to, and interacts with, relational databases via an interface—software that facilitates communications between a database management system and a program.
- Visual Basic programmers communicate with databases and manipulate their data via ADO .NET.
- A relational database is composed of tables. A row of a table is called a record.
- A primary key is a field that contains unique data, or data that is not duplicated in other records of that table.
- Each column of the table represents a different field (or attribute).
- The primary key can be composed of more than one column (or field) in the database.
- SQL provides a complete set of commands enabling programmers to define complex queries to select data from a table. The results of a query commonly are called result sets (or record sets).
- A one-to-many relationship between tables indicates that a record in one table can have many corresponding records in a separate table.
- A foreign key is a field for which every entry in one table has a unique value in another table and where the field in the other table is the primary key for that table.
- The simplest format for a **SELECT** query is

    SELECT * **FROM** *tableName*

  where the asterisk (*) indicates that all columns from *tableName* should be selected, and *tableName* specifies the table in the database from which the data will be selected.
- To select specific fields from a table, replace the asterisk (*) with a comma-separated list of the field names to select.
- Programmers process result sets by knowing in advance the order of the fields in the result set. Specifying the field names to select guarantees that the fields are returned in the specified order, even if the actual order of the fields in the database table(s) changes.
- The optional **WHERE** clause in a **SELECT** query specifies the selection criteria for the query. The simplest format for a **SELECT** query with selection criteria is

    SELECT *fieldName1*, *fieldName2*, ... **FROM** *tableName* **WHERE** *criteria*

- The **WHERE** clause condition can contain operators <, >, <=, >=, =, <> and **LIKE**. Operator **LIKE** is used for pattern matching with wildcard characters asterisk (*) and question mark (?).
- A pattern that contains an asterisk character (*) searches for strings in which zero or more characters appear in the asterisk character's location in the pattern.

- A pattern string containing a question mark (**?**) searches for strings in which exactly one character appears in the question mark's position in the pattern.
- The results of a query can be arranged in ascending or descending order via the optional **ORDER BY** clause. The simplest form of an **ORDER BY** clause is

    SELECT *fieldName1*, *fieldName2*, ... **FROM** *tableName* **ORDER BY** *field* **ASC**
    SELECT *fieldName1*, *fieldName2*, ... **FROM** *tableName* **ORDER BY** *field* **DESC**

    where **ASC** specifies ascending order, **DESC** specifies descending order, and *field* specifies the field to be sorted. The default sorting order is ascending, so **ASC** is optional.
- An **ORDER BY** clause also can sort records by multiple fields. Such queries are written in the form:

    ORDER BY *field1 sortingOrder*, *field2 sortingOrder*, ...

- The **WHERE** and **ORDER BY** clauses can be combined in one query.
- A join merges records from two or more tables by testing for matching values in a field that is common to both tables. The simplest format of a join is

    SELECT *fieldName1*, *fieldName2*, ...
       FROM *table1*, **INNER JOIN** *table2*
       ON *table1.fieldName* = *table2.fieldName*

    in which the **ON** clause specifies the fields from each table that should be compared to determine which records are joined. These fields normally represent the primary key in one table and the corresponding foreign key in the other table.
- If an SQL statement uses fields that have the same name in multiple tables, the statement must fully qualify the field name by preceding it with its table name and the dot operator (**.**).
- An **INSERT** statement inserts a new record in a table. The simplest form for this statement is:

    INSERT INTO *tableName* (*fieldName1*, *fieldName2*, ..., *fieldNameN*)
       VALUES (*value1*, *value2*, ..., *valueN*)

    where *tableName* is the table in which to insert the record. The *tableName* is followed by a comma-separated list of field names in parentheses. The list of field names is followed by the SQL keyword **VALUES** and a comma-separated list of values in parentheses.
- SQL statements use a single quote (**'**) as a delimiter for strings. To specify a string containing a single quote in an SQL statement, the single quote must be escaped with another single quote.
- An **UPDATE** statement modifies data in a table. The simplest form for an **UPDATE** statement is:

    UPDATE *tableName*
       SET *fieldName1* = *value1*, *fieldName2* = *value2*, ..., *fieldNameN* = *valueN*
       WHERE *criteria*

    where *tableName* is the table in which to update a record (or records). The *tableName* is followed by keyword **SET** and a comma-separated list of field-name/value pairs written in the format *fieldName* = *value*. The **WHERE** *criteria* determine the record(s) to update.
- A **DELETE** statement removes data from a table. The simplest form for a **DELETE** statement is:

    DELETE FROM *tableName* **WHERE** *criteria*

    where *tableName* is the table from which to delete a record (or records). The **WHERE** *criteria* determine which record(s) to delete.

- Microsoft Access 2000™ is an easy-to-use Office 2000™ database program.
- **System.Data**, **System.Data.OleDb** and **System.Data.SqlClient** are the three main namespaces in ADO .NET.
- Class **DataSet** is from the **System.Data** namespace. Instances of this class represent in-memory caches of data.
- The advantage of using class **DataSet** is that it is a way to modify the contents of a datasource without having to maintain an active connection.
- One approach to ADO .NET programming uses **OleDbCommand** of the **System.Data.OleDb** namespace. In this approach, SQL statements are executed directly on the datasource.
- Use the **Add Connection** option to create a database connection in the **Data Link Properties** window.
- Use the **Data Adapter Configuration Wizard** to set up an **OleDbDataAdapter** and generate queries.
- If a **DataSet** needs to be named, use the instance property **DataSetName**.
- **OleDbCommands** commands are what the **OleDbDataAdapter** executes on the database in the form of SQL queries.
- **DataColumnMapping**s converts data from a database to a **DataSet** and vice versa.
- Instance property **Parameters** of class **OleDbCommand** is a collection of **OleDbParameter** objects. Adding them to an **OleDbCommand** is an optional way to add parameters in a command, instead of creating a lengthy, complex command string.
- **OleDbCommand** instance property **Connection** is set to the **OleDbConnection** that the command will be executed on, and the instance property **CommandText** is set to the SQL query that will be executed on the database.
- **OleDbDataAdapter** method **Fill** retrieves information from the database associated with the **OleDbConnection** and places this information in the **DataSet** provided as an argument.
- **DataGrid** method **SetDataBinding** binds a **DataGrid** to a data source.
- Method **Clear** of class **DataSet** is called to empty the **DataSet** of any prior data.
- The instance properties **InsertCommand** and **UpdateCommand** of class **OleDbDataAdapter** are instances of class **OleDbCommand**.
- Property **CommandText** of class **OleDbCommand** is the **String** representing the SQL statement to be executed.
- Method **ExecuteNonQuery** of class **OleDbCommand** is called to perform the action specified by **CommandText** on the database.
- A powerful feature of ADO .NET is its ability to readily convert data stored in a datasource to XML, and vice versa.
- Method **WriteXml** of class **DataSet** writes the XML representation of the **DataSet** instance to the first argument passed to it. This method has several overloaded versions that allow programmers to specify an output source and a character encoding for the data.
- Method **ReadXml** of class **DataSet** reads the XML representation of the first argument passed to it into its own **DataSet**. This method has several overloaded versions that allow programmers to specify an input source and a character encoding for the data.

TERMINOLOGY

% SQL wildcard character
_ SQL wildcard character
* SQL wildcard character
? SQL wildcard character

ADO .NET
AND
Application Programming Interface
ASC (ascending order)
asterisk (*)
attribute
cache
Clear method of **DataSet**
column
column number
column number in a result set
CommandText method of **OleDbCommand**
CommandText property of **OleDbCommand**
connect to a database
data attribute
database
database management system (DBMS)
database table
DataColumn class
DataGrid class
DataRow class
DataRowCollection class
DataSet class
DataSetName property of **DataSet**
DataTable class
DB2
DELETE
DELETE FROM
DeleteCommand property of
    OleDbAdapter
DESC
disconnected
distributed computing system
escape character
ExecuteNonQuery method of
    OleDbCommand
ExecuteNonQuery property of
    OleDbCommand
field
Fill method of **OleDbAdapter**
FROM
fully qualified name
GetXml method of **DataSet**
GROUP BY
Informix
in-memory cache
INSERT INTO
InsertCommand property of
    OleDbAdapter
interface

ItemArray property of **DataRow**
joining tables
LIKE
locate records in a database
match the selection criteria
merge records from tables
Microsoft SQL Server
MySQL
OleDbCommand class
OleDbConnection class
OleDbDataAdapter class
Oracle
ORDER BY
ordered
ordering of records
Parameters property of **OleDbParameter**
pattern matching
primary key
query a database
ReadXml method of **DataSet**
record
record set
Refresh method of **DataGrid**
relational database
relational database model
relational database table
result set
roll back a transaction
row
Rows property of **DataTable**
rows to be retrieved
SELECT
select all fields from a table
SelectCommand property of
    OleDbAdapter
selecting data from a table
selection criteria
SET
SetDataBinding method of **DataGrid**
single-quote character
SQL keyword
SQL statement
SqlConnection class
square brackets in a query
Structured Query Language (SQL)
Sybase
System.Data namespace
System.Data.OleDb namespace
System.Data.Sqlclient namespace
table

table column
table row
TableMappings property of
   OleDbAdapter
Tables property of **DataSet**
UPDATE
Update method of **OleDbDataAdapter**

UpdateCommand property of
   OleDbAdapter
VALUES
WHERE
WriteXml method of **DataSet**
XML document

SELF-REVIEW EXERCISES

19.1 Fill in the blanks in each of the following statements:
a) The most popular database query language is _____.
b) A table in a database consists of _____ and _____.
c) Databases can be manipulated in Visual Basic as _____ objects.
d) Use class _____ to map a **DataSet**'s data graphically in Visual Basic.
e) SQL keyword(s) _____ is followed by selection criteria that specify the records to select in a query.
f) SQL keyword(s) _____ specifies the order in which records are sorted in a query.
g) Selecting data from multiple database tables is called _____ the data.
h) A _____ is an integrated collection of data that is centrally controlled.
i) A _____ is a field in a table for which every entry has a unique value in another table and where the field in the other table is the primary key for that table.
j) Namespace _____ contains special classes and interfaces for manipulating SQLServer databases in Visual Basic.
k) Visual Basic marks up data as _____ for transmission between datasources.
l) Namespace _____ is Visual Basic's general interface to a database.

19.2 State which of the following are *true* or *false*. If *false*, explain why.
a) In general, ADO .NET is a disconnected model.
b) SQL can implicitly convert fields with the same name from two or mores tables to the appropriate field.
c) Only the **UPDATE** SQL statement can commit changes to a database.
d) Providing a foreign-key value that does not appear as a primary-key value in another table breaks the Rule of Referential Integrity.
e) The **VALUES** keyword in an **INSERT** statement inserts multiple records in a table.
f) **SELECT** statements can merge data from multiple tables.
g) The **DELETE** statement deletes only one record in a table.
h) An **OleDbDataAdapter** can **Fill** a **DataSet**.
i) Class **DataSet** of namespace **System.Data** provides methods that enable developers to create XML documents from datasources.
j) SQLServer is an example of a managed provider.
k) Because Visual Basic uses a disconnected model, **OleDbConnection**s are optional.
l) It is always faster to assign a value to a variable than to instantiate a new **Object**.

ANSWERS TO SELF-REVIEW EXERCISES

19.3 a) SQL. b) rows, columns. c) **DataSet**. d) **DataGrid**. e) **WHERE**. f) **ORDER BY**. g) joining. h) database. i) foreign key. j) **System.Data.SqlClient**. k) XML. l) **System.Data.OleDb**.

19.4 a) True. b) False. In a query, failure to provide fully qualified names for fields with the same name from two or more tables is an error. c) False. **INSERT** and **DELETE** change the database, as well. Do not confuse the SQL **UPDATE** statement with method **OleDbDataAdapter.Update**. d) True. e) False. An **INSERT** statement inserts one record in the table. The **VALUES** keyword specifies the comma-separated list of values of which the record is composed. f) True. g) False. The **DELETE** statement deletes all records matching its **WHERE** clause. h) True. i) True. j) True. k) False. This class is required to connect to a database. l) True.

EXERCISES

19.5 Using the techniques shown in this chapter, define a complete query application for the **Authors.mdb** database. Provide a series of predefined queries with an appropriate name for each query displayed in a **System.Windows.Forms.ComboBox**. Also, allow users to supply their own queries and add them to the **ComboBox**. Provide any queries you feel are appropriate.

19.6 Using the techniques shown in this chapter, define a complete query application for the **Books.mdb** database. Provide a series of predefined queries with an appropriate name for each query displayed in a **System.Windows.Forms.ComboBox**. Also, allow users to supply their own queries and add them to the **ComboBox**. Provide the following predefined queries:
    a) Select all authors from the **Authors** table.
    b) Select all publishers from the **Publishers** table.
    c) Select a specific author and list all books for that author. Include the title, year and ISBN number. Order the information alphabetically by title.
    d) Select a specific publisher and list all books published by that publisher. Include the title, year and ISBN number. Order the information alphabetically by title.
    e) Provide any other queries you feel are appropriate.

19.7 Modify Exercise 19.6 to define a complete database-manipulation application for the **Books.mdb** database. In addition to the querying capabilities, the application should enable users to edit existing data and add new data to the database. Allow the user to edit the database in the following ways:
    a) Add a new author.
    b) Edit the existing information for an author.
    c) Add a new title for an author (remember that the book must have an entry in the **AuthorISBN** table). Be sure to specify the publisher of the title.
    d) Add a new publisher.
    e) Edit the existing information for a publisher.

For each of the preceding database manipulations, design an appropriate GUI to allow the user to perform the data manipulation.

19.8 Modify the address-book example of Fig. 19.29 to enable each address-book entry to contain multiple addresses, phone numbers and e-mail addresses. The user should be able to view multiple addresses, phone numbers and e-mail addresses. [*Note:* This is a large exercise that requires substantial modifications to the original classes in the address-book example.]

19.9 Write a GUI application that enables users to retrieve records from the **Books.mdb** database. The application must provide a GUI front-end which allows users to select the fields and criteria on which to display authors' titles.

19.10 Write a program that allows the user to modify a database graphically through an XML text editor. The GUI should be able to display the contents of the database and commit any changes to the XML text to the database.

ASP .NET, Web Forms and Web Controls

Objectives

- To become familiar with Web Forms in ASP .NET.
- To be able to create Web Forms.
- To be able to create an ASP .NET application consisting of multiple Web Forms.
- To be able to control user access to Web applications through forms authentication.
- To be able to use files and databases in an ASP .NET application.
- To learn how to use tracing with Web Forms.

If any man will draw up his case, and put his name at the foot of the first page, I will give him an immediate reply. Where he compels me to turn over the sheet, he must wait my leisure.
Lord Sandwich

Rule One: Our client is always right
Rule Two: If you think our client is wrong, see Rule One.
Anonymous

A fair question should be followed by a deed in silence.
Dante Alighieri

You will come here and get books that will open your eyes, and your ears, and your curiosity, and turn you inside out or outside in.
Ralph Waldo Emerson

Outline

20.1 Introduction
20.2 Simple HTTP Transaction
20.3 System Architecture
20.4 Creating and Running a Simple Web-Form Example
20.5 Web Controls
    20.5.1 Text and Graphics Controls
    20.5.2 `AdRotator` Control
    20.5.3 Validation Controls
20.6 Session Tracking
    20.6.1 Cookies
    20.6.2 Session Tracking with `HttpSessionState`
20.7 Case Study: Online Guest book
20.8 Case Study: Connecting to a Database in ASP .NET
20.9 Tracing
20.10 Internet and World Wide Web Resources

Summary • Terminology • Self-Review Exercises • Answers to Self-Review Exercises • Exercises

20.1 Introduction

In previous chapters, we used Windows Forms and Windows controls to develop Windows applications. In this chapter, we introduce *Web-based application development*, which employs Microsoft's ASP .NET technology. Web-based applications create Web content for Web browser clients. This Web content includes HyperText Markup Language (HTML),[1] client-side scripting, images and binary data.

We present several examples that demonstrate Web-based applications development using *Web Forms* (also known as *Web Form pages*), *Web controls* (also known as *ASP .NET server controls*) and Visual Basic programming. Web Form files have the file extension **.aspx** and contain the Web page's GUI. Programmers customize Web Forms by adding Web controls, which include labels, textboxes, images, buttons and other GUI components. The Web Form file represents the Web page that is sent to the client browser. [*Note*: From this point onward, we refer to Web Form files as *ASPX files*.]

Every ASPX file created in Visual Studio has a corresponding class written in a .NET language, such as Visual Basic; this class includes event handlers, initialization code, utility methods and other supporting code. The Visual Basic file that contains this class is called the *code-behind file* and provides the ASPX file's programmatic implementation.

---

1. Readers not familiar with HTML should first read Appendices H–I before studying this chapter.

20.2 Simple HTTP Transaction

Before exploring Web-based applications development further, a basic understanding of networking and the World Wide Web is necessary. In this section, we examine the inner workings of the *HyperText Transfer Protocol (HTTP)* and discuss what occurs behind the scenes when a browser displays a Web page. HTTP specifies a set of *methods* and *headers* that allow clients and servers to interact and exchange information in a uniform and predictable way.

In its simplest form, a Web page is nothing more than a HTML document. This document is a plain text file containing markings (*markup* or *tags*) that describe to a Web browser how to display and format the document's information. For example, the HTML markup

```
<title>My Web Page</title>
```

indicates to the browser that the text contained between the `<title>` *start tag* and the `</title>` *end tag* is the Web page's title. HTML documents also can contain *hypertext* data (usually called *hyperlinks*), which create links to different pages or to other parts of the same page. When the user activates a hyperlink (usually by clicking it with the mouse), the requested Web page (or different part of the same Web page) is loaded into the user's browser window.

Any HTML document available for viewing over the Web has a corresponding *Uniform Resource Locator (URL)*, which is an address indicating the location of a resource. The URL contains information that directs a browser to the resource document that the user wishes to access. Computers that run *Web server* software provide such resources. When developing ASP .NET Web applications, Micorsoft *Internet Information Services* (*IIS*) is the Web server.

Let us examine the components of the URL

```
http://www.deitel.com/books/downloads.htm
```

The `http://` indicates that the resource is to be obtained using HTTP. The middle portion, `www.deitel.com`, is the fully qualified *hostname* of the server. The hostname is the name of the computer on which the resource resides. This computer usually is referred to as the *host*, because it houses and maintains resources. The hostname `www.deitel.com` is translated into an *IP address* (`207.60.134.230`), which identifies the server in a manner similar to that in which a telephone number uniquely defines a particular phone line. The translation of the hostname into an IP address normally is performed by a *domain name server (DNS)*, a computer that maintains a database of hostnames and their corresponding IP addresses. This translation operation is called a *DNS lookup*.

The remainder of the URL provides the name of the requested resource, `/books/downloads.htm` (an HTML document). This portion of the URL specifies both the name of the resource (`downloads.htm`) and its path, or location (`/books`), on the Web server. The path could specify the location of an actual directory on the Web server's file system. However, for security reasons, the path often specifies the location of a *virtual directory*. In such systems, the server translates the virtual directory into a real location on the server (or on another computer on the server's network), thus hiding the true location of the resource. Furthermore, some resources are created dynamically and do not reside anywhere on the server computer. The hostname in the URL for such a resource specifies the correct server, and the path and resource information identify the location of the resource with which to respond to the client's request.

When given a URL, a browser performs a simple HTTP transaction to retrieve and display a Web page. Figure 20.1 illustrates the transaction in detail. This transaction consists of interaction between the Web browser (the client side) and the Web-server application (the server side).

In Fig. 20.1, the Web browser sends an HTTP request to the server. The request (in its simplest form) is

GET /books/downloads.htm HTTP/1.1

The word ***GET*** is an HTTP method indicating that the client wishes to obtain a resource from the server. The remainder of the request provides the path name of the resource (an HTML document) and the protocol's name and version number (**HTTP/1.1**).

Any server that understands HTTP (version 1.1) can translate this request and respond appropriately. Figure 20.2 depicts the results of a successful request. The server first responds by sending a line of text that indicates the HTTP version, followed by a numeric code and phrase describing the status of the transaction. For example,

HTTP/1.1 200 OK

indicates success, whereas

HTTP/1.1 404 Not found

informs the client that the Web server could not locate the requested resource.

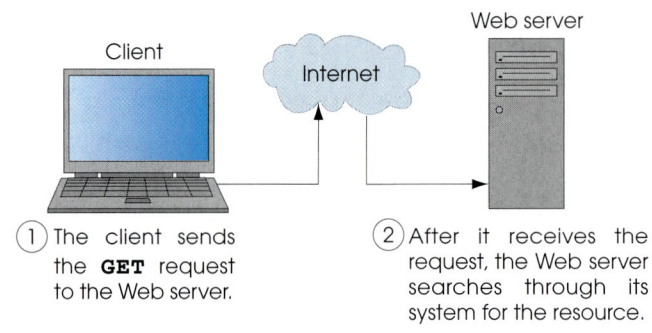

Fig. 20.1 Client interacting with Web server. Step 1: The **GET** request, **GET /books/downloads.htm HTTP/1.1**.

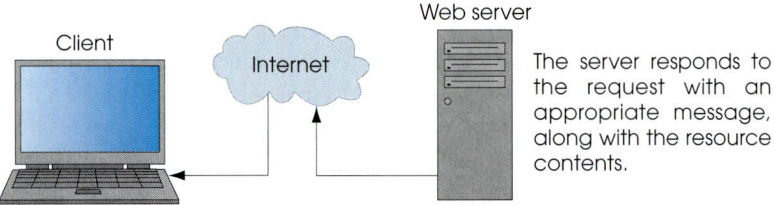

Fig. 20.2 Client interacting with Web server. Step 2: The HTTP response, **HTTP/1.1 200 OK**.

The server then sends one or more *HTTP headers,* which provide additional information about the data that will be sent. In this case, the server is sending an HTML text document, so the HTTP header for this example reads:

```
Content-type: text/html
```

The information provided in this header specifies the *Multipurpose Internet Mail Extensions (MIME)* type of the content that the server is transmitting to the browser. MIME is an Internet standard that specifies the way in which certain data must be formatted so that programs can interpret the data correctly. For example, the MIME type **text/plain** indicates that the sent information is text that can be displayed directly, without any interpretation of the content as HTML markup. Similarly, the MIME type **image/gif** indicates that the content is a GIF image. When the browser receives this MIME type, it attempts to display the image.

The header or set of headers is followed by a blank line, which indicates to the client that the server is finished sending HTTP headers. The server then sends the contents of the requested HTML document (**downloads.htm**). The server terminates the connection when the transfer of the resource is complete. At this point, the client-side browser parses the HTML it has received and *renders* (or displays) the results.

20.3 System Architecture

Web-based applications are *multi-tier applications*, which sometimes are referred to as *n-tier applications*. Multi-tier applications divide functionality into separate *tiers* (i.e., logical groupings of functionality). Although tiers can be located on the same computer, the tiers of Web-based applications typically reside on separate computers. Figure 20.3 presents the basic structure of a three-tier Web-based application.

The *information tier* (also called the *data tier* or the *bottom tier*) maintains data pertaining to the application. This tier typically stores data in a *relational database management system (RDBMS)*. We discussed RDBMSs in Chapter 19. For example, a retail store might have a database for storing product information, such as descriptions, prices and quantities in stock. The same database also might contain customer information, such as user names, billing addresses and credit-card numbers. This tier can be comprised of multiple databases, which together contain the data needed for our application.

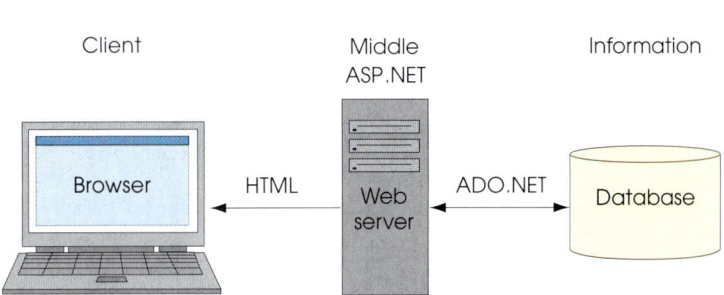

Fig. 20.3 Three-tier architecture.

The *middle tier* implements *business logic*, *controller logic* and *presentation logic* to control interactions between application clients and application data. The middle tier acts as an intermediary between data in the information tier and the application's clients. The middle-tier controller logic processes client requests (such as requests to view a product catalog) and retrieves data from the database. The middle-tier presentation logic then processes data from the information tier and presents the content to the client. Web applications typically present data to clients in the form of HTML documents.

Business logic in the middle tier enforces *business rule*s and ensures that data are reliable before the server application updates the database or presents data to users. Business rules dictate how clients can and cannot access application data and how applications process data.

The *client tier*, or *top tier*, is the application's user interface, which is typically a Web browser. Users interact directly with the application through the user interface. The client tier interacts with the middle tier to make requests and to retrieve data from the information tier. The client tier then displays to the user the data retrieved from the middle tier.

20.4 Creating and Running a Simple Web-Form Example

In this section, we present our first example, which displays the time of day as maintained on the Web server in a browser window. When run, this program displays the text **A Simple Web Form Example**, followed by the Web server's time. As mentioned previously, the program consists of two related files—an ASPX file (Fig. 20.4) and a Visual Basic code-behind file (Fig. 20.5). We display the markup, code and output first; then, we carefully guide the reader through the step-by-step process of creating this program. [*Note*: The markup in Fig. 20.4 and other ASPX file listings in this chapter have been reformatted for presentation purposes.]

```
1  <%-- Fig. 20.4: WebTime.aspx            --%>
2  <%-- A page that contains two labels. --%>
3
4  <%@ Page Language="vb" AutoEventWireup="false"
5     Codebehind="WebTime.aspx.vb" Inherits="WebTime.WebTimer"
6     enableViewState="False" EnableSessionState="False" %>
7
8  <!DOCTYPE HTML PUBLIC "-//W3C//DTD HTML 4.0 Transitional//EN">
9  <HTML>
10    <HEAD>
11      <title>WebTime</title>
12      <meta name="GENERATOR"
13        content="Microsoft Visual Studio.NET 7.0">
14      <meta name="CODE_LANGUAGE" content="Visual Basic 7.0">
15      <meta name="vs_defaultClientScript" content="JavaScript">
16      <meta name="vs_targetSchema"
17        content="http://schemas.microsoft.com/intellisense/ie5">
18    </HEAD>
19    <body MS_POSITIONING="GridLayout">
20      <form id="Form1" method="post" runat="server">
21
```

Fig. 20.4 ASPX page that displays the Web server's time (part 1 of 2).

```
22          <asp:Label id="displayLabel" style="Z-INDEX: 101;
23             LEFT: 42px; POSITION: absolute; TOP: 36px"
24             runat="server" Width="186px">
25             A Simple Web Form Example
26          </asp:Label>
27
28          <asp:Label id="timeLabel" style="Z-INDEX: 102;
29             LEFT: 33px; POSITION: absolute; TOP: 84px"
30             runat="server" Width="225px" Height="55px"
31             ForeColor="#C0FFC0" BackColor="Black"
32             Font-Size="XX-Large">
33          </asp:Label>
34
35       </form>
36    </body>
37 </HTML>
```

Fig. 20.4 ASPX page that displays the Web server's time (part 2 of 2).

Visual Studio generates the markup shown in Fig. 20.4 when the programmer drags two **Label**s onto the Web Form and sets their properties. Notice that the ASPX file contains other information in addition to HTML.

Lines 1–2 of Fig. 20.4 are *ASP .NET comments* that indicate the figure number, the file name and the purpose of the file. ASP.NET comments begin with **<%--** and terminate with **--%>**. We added these comments to the file. Lines 4–5 use a *<%@ Page...%> directive* to specify information needed by the Common Language Runtime (CLR) to process this file. The **language** of the code-behind file is specified as **vb**; the code-behind file is named **WebTime.aspx.vb**.

The **AutoEventWireup** attribute determines how Web Form events are handled. When the **AutoEventWireup** is set to **true**, ASP .NET determines which methods in the class are called in response to an event generated by the **Page**. For example, ASP .NET will call methods **Page_Load** and **Page_Init** in the code-behind file to handle the **Page**'s **Load** and **Init** events respectively, without the use of the **Handles** keyword. When Visual Studio .NET generates an **aspx** file it sets **AutoEventWireup** to **false**. This is because Visual Studio .NET generates the **Page_Load** and **Page_Init** event handlers using the **Handles** keyword when the project is created. For this reason, always set **AutoEventWireup false** when using Visual Studio.

The **Inherits** attribute specifies the class in the code-behind file from which this ASP .NET class inherits—in this case, **WebTimer**. We say more about **Inherits** momemtarily. [*Note*: We explicitly set the **EnableViewState** attribute and the **EnableSessionState** attribute to **false**. We explain the significance of these attributes later in the chapter.]

For this first ASPX file, we provide a brief discussion of the HTML markup. We do not discuss the **HTML** contained in subsequent ASPX files. Line 7 is called the *document type declaration*, which specifies the document element name (**HTML**) and the **PUBLIC** Uniform Resource Identifier (URI) for the DTD.

Lines 8–9 contain the **<HTML>** and **<HEAD>** start tags, respectively. **HTML** documents have root element HTML and mark up information about the document in the **HEAD** element. Line 10 sets the title for this Web page. Lines 11–16 are a series of **meta** elements, which contain information about the document. Two important **meta**-element attributes are **name**, which identifies the **meta** element, and **content**, which stores the **meta** element's data. Visual Studio generates these **meta** elements when an ASPX file is created.

Line 18 contains the **<body>** start tag, which begins the HTML body; the body contains the main content that the browser displays. The **Form** that contains our controls is defined in lines 19–34. Notice the **runat** attribute in line 19, which is set to **"server"**. This attribute indicates that the **form** executes on the server. The corresponding HTML will be generated and sent to the client.

Lines 21–25 and 27–32 mark up two label Web controls. The properties that we set in the **Properties** window, such as **Font-Size** and **Text**, are attributes here. The *asp: tag prefix* in the declaration of the *Label* tag indicates that the label is an ASP .NET Web control. Each Web control maps to a corresponding HTML element.

Portability Tip 20.1

The same Web control can map to different HTML elements, depending on the client browser and the Web control's property settings.

In this example, the **asp:Label** control maps to the HTML **span** element. A **span** element contains text that is displayed in a Web page. This particular element is used because **span** elements facilitate the application of styles to text. Several of the property values that were applied to our labels are represented as part of the **style** of the **span** element. Soon we will see the **span** elements that are created.

Each of the Web controls in our example contains the **runat="server"** attribute-value pair, because these controls must be processed on the server. If this attribute pair is not present, the **asp:Label** element is written as text to the client (i.e., the control would not be converted into a **span** element and would not be rendered properly).

Figure 20.5 presents the code-behind file. Recall that the ASPX file in Fig. 20.4 references this file in line 4. To explain the code, we present the entire code-behind file for this example.

```
1    ' Fig. 20.5: WebTime.aspx.vb
2    ' The code-behind file for a page
3    ' that displays the current time.
4
5    Imports System
6    Imports System.Web
7    Imports System.Web.UI
8    Imports System.Web.UI.WebControls
9
10   Public Class WebTimer
11      Inherits System.Web.UI.Page
12
13      Protected WithEvents displayLabel As _
14         System.Web.UI.WebControls.Label
15
16      Protected WithEvents timeLabel As _
17         System.Web.UI.WebControls.Label
18
```

Fig. 20.5 Code-behind file for a page that displays the Web server's time (part 1 of 2).

```
19      ' This call is required by the Web Form Designer
20      Private Sub InitializeComponent()
21      End Sub
22
23      Private Sub Page_Init(ByVal sender As System.Object, _
24         ByVal e As System.EventArgs) Handles MyBase.Init
25
26         InitializeComponent()
27
28         timeLabel.Text = _
29            String.Format("{0:D2}:{1:D2}:{2:D2}", _
30            DateTime.Now.Hour, DateTime.Now.Minute, _
31            DateTime.Now.Second)
32      End Sub ' Page_Init
33
34      Private Sub Page_Load(ByVal sender As System.Object, _
35         ByVal e As System.EventArgs) Handles MyBase.Load
36         ' Put user code to initialize the page here
37      End Sub ' Page_Load
38   End Class ' WebTimer
```

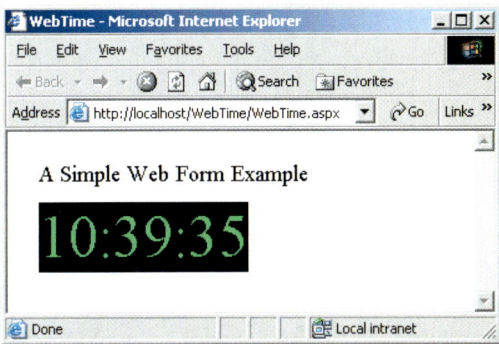

Fig. 20.5 Code-behind file for a page that displays the Web server's time (part 2 of 2).

Notice the **Imports** statements in lines 5–8. These statements specify namespaces that contain classes for developing Web-based applications. The key namespace on which we initially focus is **System.Web**, which contains classes that manage client requests and server responses. The other namespaces define the controls available and how they can be manipulated; these are discussed throughout the chapter as they become more relevant.

Line 10 begins the class definition for **WebTimer**, which inherits from class **Page**. This class defines the requested Web page and is located in the **System.Web.UI** namespace (line 7), which contains classes pertinent to the creation of Web-based applications and controls. Class **Page** also provides event handlers and objects necessary for creating Web-based applications. In addition to the **Page** class (from which all Web applications directly or indirectly inherit), **System.Web.UI** also includes the **Control** class. This class is the base class that provides common functionality for all Web controls.

Lines 13–17 declare references to two **Label**s. These **Label**s are Web controls, defined in namespace ***System.Web.UI.WebControls*** (line 8). This namespace contains Web controls employed in the design of the page's user interface. Web controls in this namespace derive from class ***WebControl***.

Lines 23–32 define method ***Page_Init***, which handles the page's **Init** event. This event, which is the first event raised, indicates that the page is ready to be initialized. Method ***Page_Init*** calls method ***InitializeComponent*** (line 20–21). Like Windows Forms, this method is used to programmatically set some initial properties of the application's components. After this call, **timeLabel**'s **Text** property is set to the Web server's time (lines 28–31).

How are the ASPX file and the code-behind file used to create the Web page that is sent to the client? First, recall that class **WebTimer** is the base class specified in line 5 of the ASPX file (Fig. 20.4). This class inherits from **Page**, which defines the general functionality of a Web page. Class **WebTimer** inherits this functionality and defines some of its own (i.e., displaying the current time). The code-behind file is the file that defines this functionality, whereas the ASPX file defines the GUI. When a client requests an ASPX file, a class is created behind the scenes that contains both the visual aspect of our page (defined in the ASPX file) and the logic of our page (defined in the code-behind file). This new class inherits from **Page**. The first time that our Web page is requested, this class is compiled, and an instance is created. This instance represents our page—it creates the HTML that is sent to the client. The assembly created from our compiled class is placed in the project's **bin** directory.

Performance Tip 20.1

Once an instance of the Web page has been created, multiple clients can use it to access the page—no recompilation is necessary. The project will be recompiled only when a programmer modifies the application; changes are detected by the runtime environment, and the project is recompiled to reflect the altered content.

Let us look briefly at how the code in our Web page executes. When an instance of our page is created, the **Init** event occurs first, invoking method ***Page_Init***. This method calls ***InitializeComponent***. In addition to this call, method ***Page_Init*** might contain code needed to initialize objects. After this occurs, the **Load** event is generated and the ***Page_Load*** event handler executes any processing that is necessary to restore data from previous requests. After this event handler has finished executing, the page processes any events raised by the page's controls. This includes the handling of any events generated by the user, such as button clicks. When the Web-Form object is ready for garbage collection, an ***Unload*** event is generated. Although not present, event handler ***Page_Unload*** is inherited from class **Page**. This event handler contains any code that releases resources, especially any *unmanaged resources* (i.e., resources not managed by the CLR).

Figure 20.6 shows the HTML generated by the ASP .NET application. To view this HTML, select **View > Source** in Internet Explorer.

The contents of this page are similar to those of the ASPX file. Lines 7–15 define a document header comparable to that in Fig. 20.4. Lines 17–35 define the body of the document. Line 18 begins the form, which is a mechanism for collecting user information and sending it to the Web server. In this particular program, the user does not submit data to the Web server for processing; however, this is a crucial part of many applications and is facilitated by the form.

```
1   <!-- Fig. 20.6: WebTime.html                        -->
2   <!-- The HTML generated when WebTime is loaded. -->
3
4   <!DOCTYPE HTML PUBLIC "-//W3C//DTD HTML 4.0 Transitional//EN" >
5
6   <HTML>
7      <HEAD>
8         <title>WebTime</title>
9         <meta name="GENERATOR"
10            Content="Microsoft Visual Studio 7.0">
11        <meta name="CODE_LANGUAGE" Content="Visual Basic 7.0">
12        <meta name="vs_defaultClientScript" content="JavaScript">
13        <meta name="vs_targetSchema"
14           content="http://schemas.microsoft.com/intellisense/ie5">
15     </HEAD>
16
17     <body MS_POSITIONING="GridLayout">
18        <form name="Form1" method="post"
19           action="WebTime.aspx" id="Form1">
20           <input type="hidden" name="__VIEWSTATE"
21              value="dDw1OTc3ODM2Mzk7Oz4=" />
22
23           <span id="displayLabel"
24              style="width:186px;Z-INDEX: 101;
25              LEFT: 42px; POSITION: absolute; TOP: 36px">
26              A Simple Web Form Example
27           </span>
28           <span id="timeLabel" style="color:#C0FFC0;
29              background-color:Black;font-size:XX-Large;
30              height:55px;width:225px;Z-INDEX: 102;
31              LEFT: 33px; POSITION: absolute; TOP: 84px">
32              10:39:35
33           </span>
34        </form>
35     </body>
36  </HTML>
```

Fig. 20.6 HTML response when the browser requests **WebTime.aspx**.

HTML forms can contain visual and nonvisual components. Visual components include clickable buttons and other GUI components with which users interact. Nonvisual components, called *hidden inputs*, store any data that the document author specifies, such as e-mail addresses. One of these hidden inputs is defined in lines 20–21. We discuss the precise meaning of this hidden input later in the chapter. Attribute **method** specifies the method by which the Web browser submits the form to the server. The **action** attribute in the **<form>** tag identifies the name and location of the resource that will be requested when this form is submitted; in this case, **WebTime.aspx**. Recall that the ASPX file's **form** elements contained the **runat="server"** attribute-value pair. When the **form** is processed on the server, the **name="Form1"** and **action="WebTime.aspx"** attribute-value pairs are added to the HTML **form** sent to the client browser.

In the ASPX file, the form's labels were Web controls. Here, we are viewing the HTML created by our application, so the **form** contains **span** elements to represent the text in our labels. In this particular case, ASP .NET maps the label Web controls to HTML **span** elements. Each **span** element contains formatting information, such as size and placement, for the text being displayed. Most of the information specified as properties for **timeLabel** and **displayLabel** are specified by the **style** attribute of each **span**.

Now that we have presented the ASPX file and the code-behind file[2], we outline the process by which we created this application. To create the application, perform the following steps:

1. *Create the project.* Select **File > New > Project...** to display the **New Project** dialog (Fig. 20.7). In this dialog, select **Visual Basic Projects** in the left pane and then **ASP.NET Web Application** in the right pane. Notice that the field for the project name is grayed out. Rather than using this field, we specify the name and location of the project in the **Location** field. We want our project to be located in **http://localhost**, which is the URL for IIS' root directory (typically **C:\InetPub\wwwroot**). The name *localhost* indicates that the client and server reside on the same machine. If the Web server were located on a different machine, localhost would be replaced with the appropriate IP address or hostname. By default, Visual Studio assigns the project name **WebApplication1**, which we change to **WebTime**. IIS must be running for this project to be created successfully. IIS can be started by executing **inetmgr.exe**, right-clicking **Default Web Site** and selecting **Start**. [*Note*: You might need to expand the node representing your computer to display the **Default Web Site**.] Below the **Location** textbox, the text "**Project will be created at http://localhost/VB/WebTime**" appears. This indicates that the project's folder is located in the root directory on the Web server. When the developer clicks **OK**, the project is created; this action also produces a virtual directory, which is linked to the project folder. The **Create New Web** dialog is displayed next, while Visual Studio is creating the Web site on the server (Fig. 20.8).

2. *Examine the newly created project.* The next several figures describe the new project's content; we begin with the **Solution Explorer** shown in Fig. 20.9. As occurs with Windows applications, Visual Studio creates several files when a new project is created. **WebForm1.aspx** is the Web Form (**WebForm1** is the default name for this file). As mentioned previously, a code-behind file is included as part of the project. To view the ASPX file's code-behind file, right click the ASPX file, and select **View Code**. Alternatively, the programmer can click an icon to display all files, then expand the node for our ASPX page (see Fig. 20.9.)

   Figure 20.10, shows the **Web Forms** controls listed in the **Toolbox**. The left figure displays the beginning of the Web controls list, and the right figure displays the remaining Web controls. Notice that some controls are similar to the Windows controls presented earlier in the book.

   Figure 20.11 shows the Web Form designer for **WebForm1.aspx**. It consists of a grid on which users drag and drop components, such as buttons and labels, from the **Toolbox**.

---

2. To run the examples included on this book's, CD you must create a virtual directory in Microsoft Internet Information Services. For instructions visit the **Downloads/Resources** link at **www.deitel.com**.

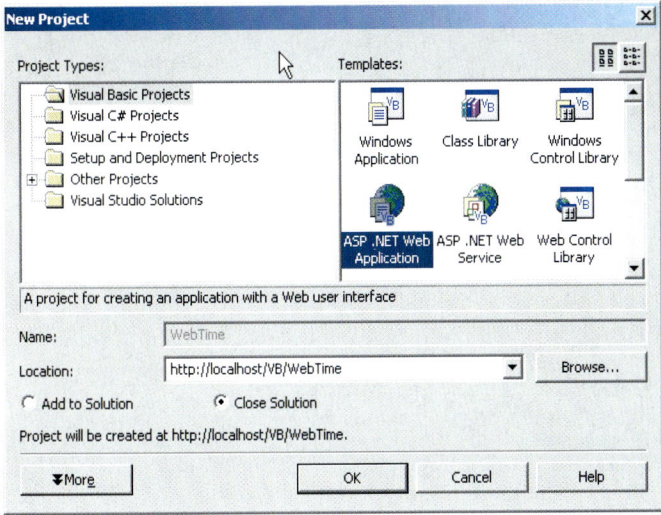

Fig. 20.7 Creating an **ASP.NET Web Application** in Visual Studio.

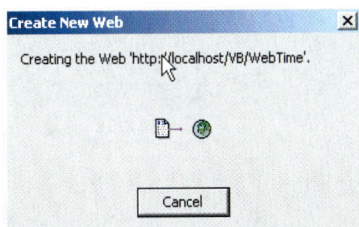

Fig. 20.8 Visual Studio creating and linking a virtual directory for the **WebTime** project folder.

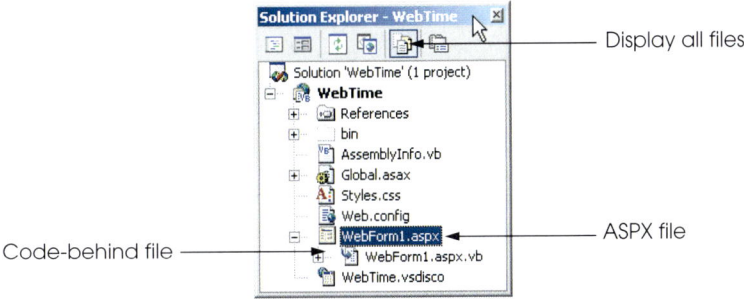

Fig. 20.9 **Solution Explorer** window for project **WebTime**.

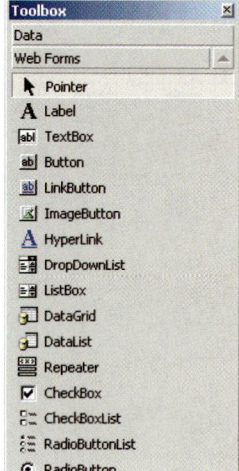 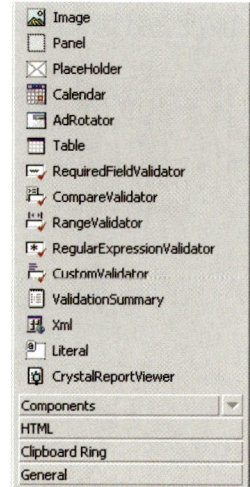

Fig. 20.10 Web Forms menu in the Toolbox.

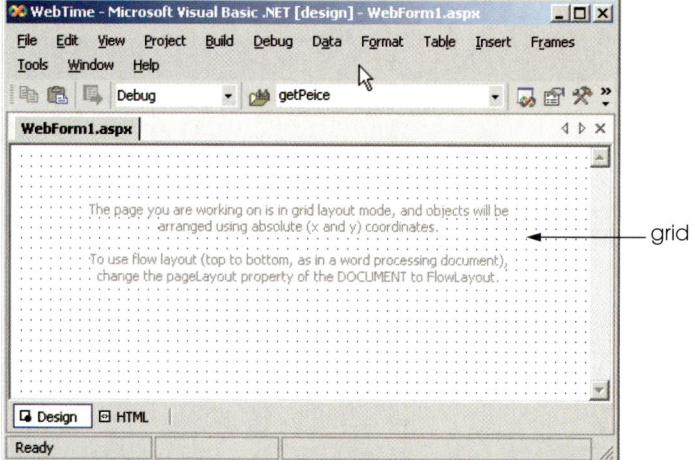

Fig. 20.11 Design mode of Web Form designer.

Figure 20.12 portrays the Web Form designer in **HTML** mode, which allows the programmer to view the markup that represents the user interface shown in design mode. When a developer clicks the **HTML** button in the lower-left corner of the Web Form designer, the Web Form designer switches to HTML mode. Similarly, the clicking of the **Design** button (to the left of the **HTML** button) returns the Web Form designer to design mode.

The next figure (Fig. 20.13) displays `WebForm1.aspx.vb`—the code-behind file for `WebForm1.aspx`. Recall that Visual Studio .NET generates this code-behind file when the project is created; it has been reformatted for presentation.

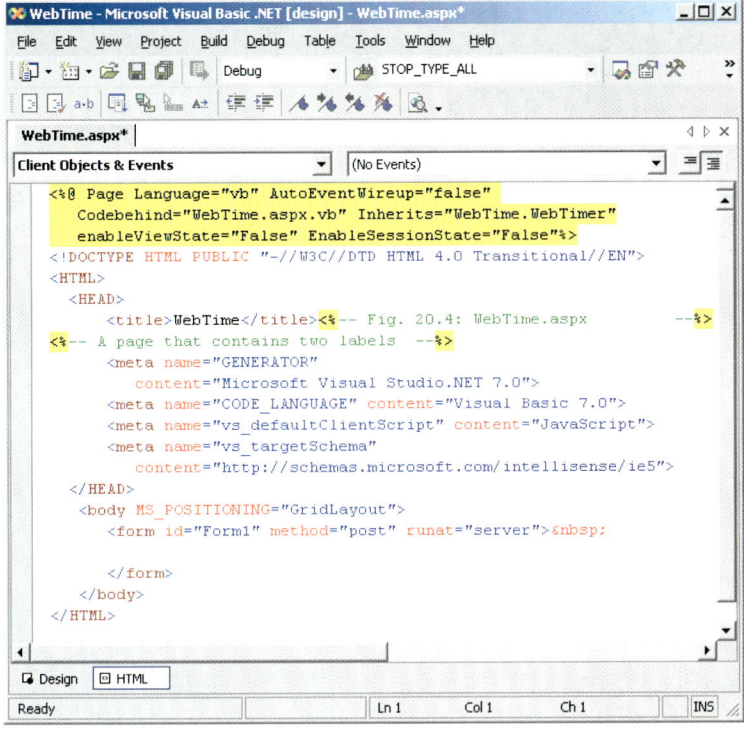

Fig. 20.12 **HTML** mode of Web-Form designer.

3. *Rename the ASPX file.* We have displayed the contents of the default ASPX and code-behind files. We now rename these files. Right click the ASPX file in the **Solution Explorer** and select **Rename**. Enter the new file name and hit *Enter*. This updates the name of both the ASPX file and the code-behind file. In this example, we use the name **WebTime.aspx**.

4. *Design the page.* Designing a Web Form is as simple as designing a Windows Form. To add controls to the page, drag and drop them from the **Toolbox** onto the Web Form. Like the Web Form itself, each control is an object that has properties, methods and events. Developers can set these properties and events, using the **Properties** window.

The **PageLayout** property determines how controls are arranged on the form (Fig. 20.15). By default, property **PageLayout** is set to **GridLayout**, which specifies that all controls are located exactly where they are dropped on the Web Form. This is called *absolute positioning*. Alternatively, the developer can set the Web Form's **PageLayout** property to **FlowLayout**, which causes controls to be placed sequentially on the Web Form. To view the Web Form's properties, select **Document** from the drop-down list in the **Properties** window; **Document** is the name used to represent the Web Form in the **Properties** window. This is called *relative positioning*, because the controls' positions are relative to the Web Form's upper-left corner. We use **GridLayout** for many of our examples.

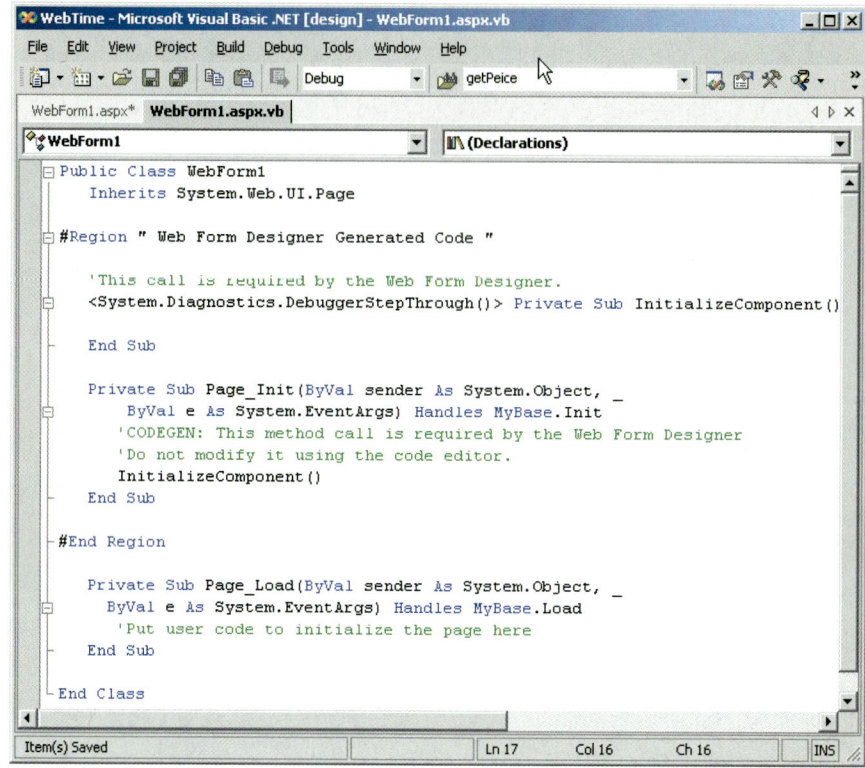

Fig. 20.13 Code-behind file for **WebForm1.aspx** generated by Visual Studio .NET.

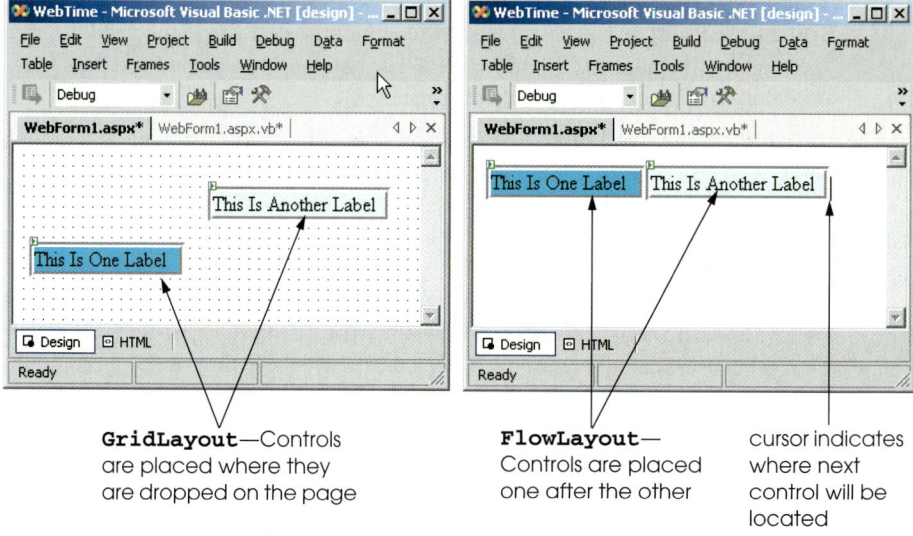

Fig. 20.14 FlowLayout and **GridLayout** illustration.

In this example, we use two **Label**s, which developers can place on the Web Form either by drag-and-drop or by double-clicking the **Toolbox**'s **Label** control. Name the first **Label displayLabel** and the second **timeLabel**. We delete **timeLabel**'s text, because this text is set in the code-behind file. When a **Label** does not contain text, the name is displayed in square brackets in the Web Form designer, but is not displayed at run time (Fig. 20.15). We set the text for **promptLabel** to **A Simple Web Form Example**.

We set **timeLabel**'s **BackColor**, **ForeColor** and **Font-Size** properties to **Black**, **LimeGreen** and **XX-Large**, respectively. To change font properties, the programmer must expand the **Font** node in the **Properties** window, then change each relevant property individually. We also set the labels' locations and sizes by dragging the controls. Finally, we set the Web Form's **EnableSessionState** and **EnableViewState** properties to **false** (we discuss these properties later in the chapter). Once the **Label**s' properties are set in the **Properties** window, Visual Studio updates the ASPX file's contents. Figure 20.15 shows the IDE after these properties are set.

5. *Add page logic.* Once the user interface has been designed, Visual Basic code must be added to the code-behind file. In this example, lines 28–31 of Fig. 20.5 are added to the code-behind file. The statement retrieves the current time and formats it so that the time is in the format *HH*:*MM*:*SS*. For example, 9 a.m. is formatted as **09:00:00**.

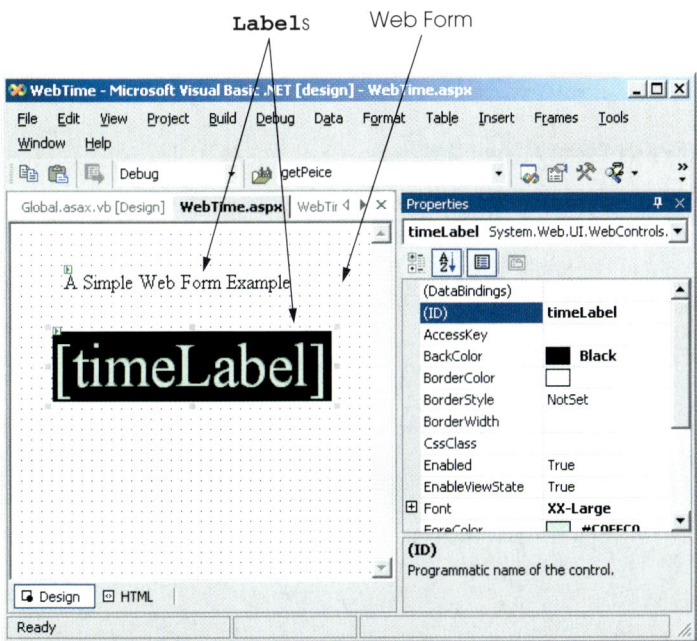

Fig. 20.15 **WebForm.aspx** after adding two **Label**s and setting their properties.

6. *Run the program.* Select **Start > Debug**. An Internet Explorer window opens and loads the Web page (the ASPX file). Notice that the URL is `http://localhost/VB/WebTime/WebTime.aspx` (Fig. 20.4), indicating that our ASPX file is located within the directory `WebTime`, which is located in the Web server's `VB` directory.

   After the Web Form is created, the programmer can view it four different ways. First, the programmer can select **Start > Debug** (as described previously), which runs the application by opening a browser window. The IDE exits **Run** or **Debug** mode when the browser is closed.

   The programmer also can right-click either the Web Form designer or the ASPX file name (in the **Solution Explorer**) and select **Build and Browse** or **View In Browser**. These each open a browser window within Visual Studio and displays preview of the page. This preview shows the user what the page would look like when requested by a client. The third way to run an ASP .NET application is to open a browser window and type in the Web page's URL. When testing an ASP .NET application on the same computer, type `http://localhost/`*ProjectFolder*`/`*PageName*`.aspx`, where *ProjectFolder* is the folder in which the page resides (usually the name of the project), and *PageName* is the name of the ASP .NET page. The first two methods of running the application compile the project for the programmer. The third and fourth methods require that the programmer compile the project by selecting **Build > Build Solution** in Visual Studio.

20.5 Web Controls

This section introduces some of the Web controls located on the **Web Form** tab in the **Toolbox** (Fig. 20.10). Figure 20.16 summarizes some of the Web controls used in the chapter examples.

20.5.1 Text and Graphics Controls

Figure 20.17 depicts a simple form for gathering user input. This example uses all the controls listed in Fig. 20.16. [*Note*: This example does not contain any functionality (i.e., no action occurs when the user clicks **Register**). We ask the reader to provide the functionality as an exercise. In successive examples, we demonstrate how to add functionality to many of these Web controls.]

Web Control	Description
`Label`	Displays text that the user cannot edit.
`Button`	Triggers an event when clicked.
`TextBox`	Gathers user input and displays text.
`Image`	Displays images (e.g., GIF and JPG).

Fig. 20.16 Commonly used Web controls (part 1 of 2).

Web Control	Description
`RadioButtonList`	Groups radio buttons.
`DropDownList`	Displays a drop-down list of choices from which a user can select one item.

Fig. 20.16 Commonly used Web controls (part 2 of 2).

Lines 50–54 define an **Image** control, which inserts an image into a Web page, the image is located in the Chapter 20 examples directory on the CD that accompanies this book. The **ImageUrl** property (line 53) specifies the file location of the image to display. To specify an image, click the ellipsis next to the **ImageUrl** property and use the resulting dialog to browse for the desired image. The top of this dialog displays the contents of this application. If the image is not explicitly part of the project, the programmer will need to use the **Browse** button. When the programmer right-clicks the image in the **Solution Explorer** and selects **Include in Project**, this image will be displayed in the top portion of the dialog.

```
1   <%-- Fig. 20.17: Controls.aspx   --%>
2   <%-- Demonstrates web controls.  --%>
3
4   <%@ Page Language="vb" AutoEventWireup="false"
5      Codebehind="Controls.aspx.vb"
6      Inherits="Controls.WebForm1"
7      enableViewState="False" EnableSessionState="False" %>
8
9   <!DOCTYPE HTML PUBLIC "-//W3C//DTD HTML 4.0 Transitional//EN">
10  <HTML>
11     <HEAD>
12        <title>WebForm1</title>
13        <meta name="GENERATOR"
14           content="Microsoft Visual Studio.NET 7.0">
15        <meta name="CODE_LANGUAGE" content="Visual Basic 7.0">
16        <meta name="vs_defaultClientScript" content="JavaScript">
17        <meta name="vs_targetSchema"
18           content="http://schemas.microsoft.com/intellisense/ie5">
19     </HEAD>
20     <body MS_POSITIONING="GridLayout">
21        <form id="Form1" method="post" runat="server">
22
23           <asp:Label id="WelcomeLabel" style="Z-INDEX: 101;
24              LEFT: 44px; POSITION: absolute; TOP: 27px"
25              runat="server" Width="451px" Height="28px"
26              Font-Size="X-Large">
27              This is a simple registration form.
28           </asp:Label>
29
```

Fig. 20.17 Web-controls demonstration (part 1 of 5).

```
30      <asp:Label id="RegisterLabel" style="Z-INDEX: 102;
31         LEFT: 48px; POSITION: absolute; TOP: 71px"
32         runat="server" Width="376px" Height="26px"
33         Font-Italic="True" Font-Size="Medium">
34         Please fill in all fields and click Register.
35      </asp:Label>
36
37      <asp:Image id="UserLabel" style="Z-INDEX: 103;
38         LEFT: 42px; POSITION: absolute; TOP: 135px"
39         runat="server" Width="439px" Height="28px"
40         ImageUrl="images/user.png">
41      </asp:Image>
42
43      <asp:Label id="FillLabel" style="Z-INDEX: 104;
44         LEFT: 50px; POSITION: absolute; TOP: 189px"
45         runat="server" Width="225px" ForeColor="Lime"
46         Font-Size="Medium">
47         Please fill out the fields below.
48      </asp:Label>
49
50      <asp:Image id="FirstImage" style="Z-INDEX: 105;
51         LEFT: 49px; POSITION: absolute; TOP: 224px"
52         runat="server" Width="84px" Height="36px"
53         ImageUrl="images/fname.png">
54      </asp:Image>
55
56      <asp:Image id="EmailImage" style="Z-INDEX: 106;
57         LEFT: 49px; POSITION: absolute; TOP: 280px"
58         runat="server" Width="86px" Height="29px"
59         ImageUrl="images/email.png">
60      </asp:Image>
61
62      <asp:TextBox id="FirstTextBox" style="Z-INDEX: 107;
63         LEFT: 145px; POSITION: absolute; TOP: 231px"
64         runat="server" Width="115px" Height="20px">
65      </asp:TextBox>
66
67      <asp:TextBox id="EmailTextBox" style="Z-INDEX: 108;
68         LEFT: 147px; POSITION: absolute; TOP: 284px"
69         runat="server" Width="112px" Height="18px">
70      </asp:TextBox>
71
72      <asp:Image id="LastImage" style="Z-INDEX: 109;
73         LEFT: 292px; POSITION: absolute; TOP: 227px"
74         runat="server" Width="77px" Height="33px"
75         ImageUrl="images/lname.png">
76      </asp:Image>
77
78      <asp:Image id="PhoneImage" style="Z-INDEX: 110;
79         LEFT: 292px; POSITION: absolute; TOP: 273px"
80         runat="server" Width="80px" Height="30px"
81         ImageUrl="images/phone.png">
82      </asp:Image>
```

Fig. 20.17 Web-controls demonstration (part 2 of 5).

```
 83
 84            <asp:TextBox id="LastTextBox" style="Z-INDEX: 111;
 85               LEFT: 400px; POSITION: absolute; TOP: 232px"
 86               runat="server" Width="109px" Height="20px">
 87            </asp:TextBox>
 88
 89            <asp:TextBox id="PhoneTextBox" style="Z-INDEX: 112;
 90               LEFT: 399px; POSITION: absolute; TOP: 277px"
 91               runat="server" Width="108px" Height="18px">
 92            </asp:TextBox>
 93
 94            <asp:Label id="PhoneLabel" style="Z-INDEX: 113;
 95               LEFT: 309px; POSITION: absolute; TOP: 318px"
 96               runat="server" Width="223px" Height="18px">
 97               Must be in the form (555)555-5555.
 98            </asp:Label>
 99
100            <asp:Image id="PublicationImage" style="Z-INDEX: 114;
101               LEFT: 50px; POSITION: absolute; TOP: 356px"
102               runat="server" Width="435px" Height="27px"
103               ImageUrl="images/downloads.png">
104            </asp:Image>
105
106            <asp:Label id="Booklabel" style="Z-INDEX: 115;
107               LEFT: 54px; POSITION: absolute; TOP: 411px"
108               runat="server" Width="348px" Height="23px"
109               ForeColor="Lime" Font-Size="Medium">
110               Which book would you like information about?
111            </asp:Label>
112
113            <asp:DropDownList id="BookDropDownList"
114               style="Z-INDEX: 116; LEFT: 60px; POSITION:
115               absolute; TOP: 448px" runat="server"
116               Width="326px" Height="29px">
117
118               <asp:ListItem Value="XML How to Program 1e">
119                  XML How to Program 1e
120               </asp:ListItem>
121               <asp:ListItem Value="C# How to Program 1e">
122                  C# How to Program 1e
123               </asp:ListItem>
124               <asp:ListItem Value="Java How to Program 4e">
125                  Java How to Program 4e
126               </asp:ListItem>
127               <asp:ListItem Value=
128                  "Advanced Java How to Program 1e">
129                     Advanced Java How to Program 1e
130               </asp:ListItem>
131               <asp:ListItem Value=
132                  "Visual Basic .NET How to Program 2e">
133                     Visual Basic .NET How to Program 2e
134               </asp:ListItem>
```

Fig. 20.17 Web-controls demonstration (part 3 of 5).

```
135              <asp:ListItem Value="C++ How to Program 3e">
136                 C++ How to Program 3e
137              </asp:ListItem>
138           </asp:DropDownList>
139
140           <asp:HyperLink id="BooksHyperLink"
141              style="Z-INDEX: 117; LEFT: 64px; POSITION:
142              absolute; TOP: 486px" runat="server"
143              Width="385px" Height="22px"
144              NavigateUrl="http://www.deitel.com">
145              Click here to view more information about our books.
146           </asp:HyperLink>
147
148           <asp:Image id="OperatingImage" style="Z-INDEX: 118;
149              LEFT: 53px; POSITION: absolute; TOP: 543px"
150              runat="server" Width="431px" Height="32px"
151              ImageUrl="images/os.png">
152           </asp:Image>
153
154           <asp:Label id="OperatingLabel" style="Z-INDEX: 119;
155              LEFT: 63px; POSITION: absolute; TOP: 591px"
156              runat="server" Width="328px" Height="29px"
157              ForeColor="Lime" Font-Size="Medium">
158              Which operating system are you using?
159           </asp:Label>
160
161           <asp:Button id="RegisterButton" style="Z-INDEX: 124;
162              LEFT: 69px; POSITION: absolute; TOP: 760px"
163              runat="server" Width="120px" Height="33px"
164              Text="Register">
165           </asp:Button>
166
167           <asp:RadioButtonList id="OperatingRadioButtonList"
168              style="Z-INDEX: 125; LEFT: 65px; POSITION:
169              absolute; TOP: 624px" runat="server"
170              Height="122px" Width="155px">
171
172              <asp:ListItem Value="Windows NT">
173                 Windows NT
174              </asp:ListItem>
175              <asp:ListItem Value="Windows 2000">
176                 Windows 2000
177              </asp:ListItem>
178              <asp:ListItem Value="Windows XP">
179                 Windows XP
180              </asp:ListItem>
181              <asp:ListItem Value="Linux">
182                 Linux
183              </asp:ListItem>
184              <asp:ListItem Value="Other">
185                 Other
186              </asp:ListItem>
187           </asp:RadioButtonList>
```

Fig. 20.17 Web-controls demonstration (part 4 of 5).

```
188
189        </form>
190    </body>
191 </HTML>
```

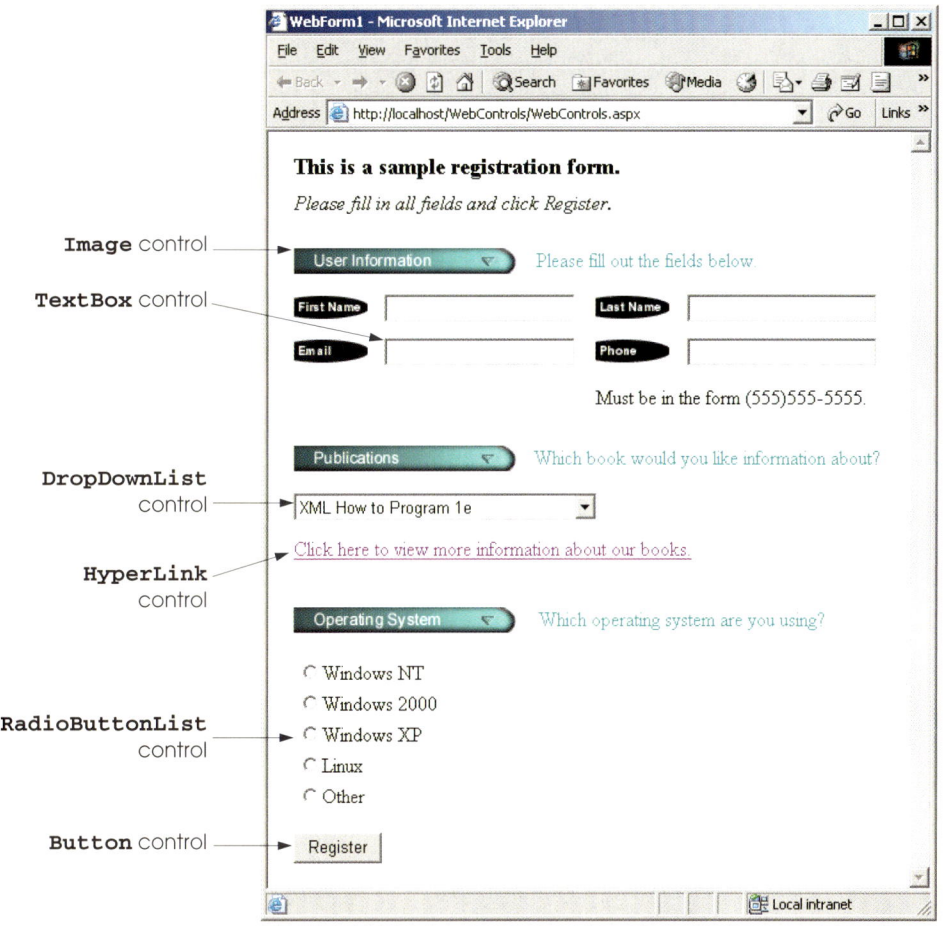

Fig. 20.17 Web-controls demonstration (part 5 of 5).

Lines 62–65 define a **TextBox** control, which allows the programmer to read and display text. Lines 167–187 define a **RadioButtonList** control, which provides a series of radio buttons from which the user can select only one. Each radio button is defined by a **ListItem** element (lines 172–186). The **HyperLink** control (lines 140–146) adds a hyperlink to a Web page. The **NavigateUrl** property (line 144) of this control specifies the resource that is requested (i.e., **http://www.deitel.com**) when a user clicks the hyperlink. Lines 113–138 define a **DropDownList**. This control is similar to a **RadioButtonList**, in that it allows the user to select exactly one option. When a user clicks the drop-down list, it expands and displays a list from which the user can make a selection. Lines 118–137 define the **ListItem**s that display when the drop-down list is expanded. Like the **Button** Windows control, the **Button** Web control (lines 161–165) represents a button; a button Web control typically maps to an **input** HTML element that has attribute **type** and value **"button"**.

20.5.2 `AdRotator` Control

Web pages often contain product or service advertisements, and these advertisements usually consist of images. Although Web site authors want to include as many sponsors as possible, Web pages can display only a limited number of advertisements. To address this problem, ASP .NET provides the **AdRotator** Web control for displaying advertisements. Using advertisement data located in an XML file, the **AdRotator** control randomly selects an image to display and then generates a hyperlink to the Web page associated with that image. Browsers that do not support images instead display alternate text that is specified in the XML document. If a user clicks the image or substituted text, the browser loads the Web page associated with that image.

Figure 20.18 demonstrates the **AdRotator** Web control. In this example, our advertisements that we rotate are the flags of eleven countries. When a user clicks the displayed flag image, the browser is redirected to a Web page containing information about the country that the flag represents. If a user clicks refresh or re-requests the page, one of the eleven flags is again chosen at random and displayed.

```
1   <%-- Fig 20.18: CountryRotator.aspx            --%>
2   <%-- A Web Form that demonstrates class AdRotator. --%>
3
4   <%@ Page Language="vb" AutoEventWireup="false"
5      Codebehind="CountryRotator.aspx.vb"
6      Inherits="AdRotator.AdRotator"
7      enableViewState="False" EnableSessionState="False" %>
8
9   <!DOCTYPE HTML PUBLIC "-//W3C//DTD HTML 4.0 Transitional//EN">
10  <HTML>
11     <HEAD>
12        <title>WebForm1</title>
13        <meta content="Microsoft Visual Studio.NET 7.0"
14           name="GENERATOR">
15        <meta content="Visual Basic 7.0" name="CODE_LANGUAGE">
16        <meta content="JavaScript" name="vs_defaultClientScript">
17        <meta name="vs_targetSchema"
18           content="http://schemas.microsoft.com/intellisense/ie5">
19     </HEAD>
20     <body background=
21        "images/background.png"
22        MS_POSITIONING="GridLayout">
23        <form id="Form1" method="post" runat="server">
24
25           <asp:label id="displayLabel" style="Z-INDEX: 101;
26              LEFT: 36px; POSITION: absolute; TOP: 22px"
27              runat="server" Font-Size="Medium" Height="28px"
28              Width="268px">AdRotator Example
29           </asp:label>
```

Fig. 20.18 `AdRotator` class demonstrated on a Web form (part 1 of 2).

```
30
31              <asp:adrotator id="countryRotator" style="Z-INDEX: 102;
32                 LEFT: 36px; POSITION: absolute; TOP: 47px"
33                 runat="server" Height="72px" Width="108px"
34                 AdvertisementFile="AdRotatorInformation.xml">
35              </asp:adrotator>
36
37         </form>
38      </body>
39   </HTML>
```

Fig. 20.18 **AdRotator** class demonstrated on a Web form (part 2 of 2).

The ASPX file in Fig. 20.18 is similar to that in Fig. 20.4. However, instead of two **Label**s, this page contains one **Label** and one **AdRotator** control named **countryRotator**. The **background** property for our page is set to display the image **background.png**. To specify this file, click the ellipsis provided next to the **Background** property and use the resulting dialog to browse for **background.png**.

In the **Properties** window, we set the **AdRotator** control's **AdvertisementFile** property to **AdRotatorInformation.xml** (line 33). The Web control determines which advertisement to display from this file. We present the contents of this XML file momentarily. As illustrated in Fig. 20.19, the programmer does not need to add any additional code to the code-behind file, because the **adRotator** control does "all the work." The output depicts two different requests—the first time the page is requested, the American flag is shown, and, in the second request, the Latvian flag is displayed. The last image depicts the Web page that loads when the Latvian flag is clicked.

```vb
1    ' Fig. 20.19: CountryRotator.aspx.vb
2    ' The code-behind file for a page that
3    ' demonstrates the AdRotator class.
4
5    Public Class AdRotator
6       Inherits System.Web.UI.Page
7
8       Protected WithEvents displayLabel As _
9          System.Web.UI.WebControls.Label
10
11      Protected WithEvents countryRotator As _
12         System.Web.UI.WebControls.AdRotator
13
14      ' This call is required by the Web Form Designer.
15      Private Sub InitializeComponent()
16      End Sub
17
18      Private Sub Page_Init(ByVal sender As System.Object, _
19         ByVal e As System.EventArgs) Handles MyBase.Init
20
```

Fig. 20.19 Code-behind file for page demonstrating the **AdRotator** class (part 1 of 2).

```
21         ' CODEGEN: This method call is required by the Web Form Designer
22         ' Do not modify it using the code editor.
23            InitializeComponent()
24        End Sub ' Page_Init
25
26        Private Sub Page_Load(ByVal sender As System.Object, _
27            ByVal e As System.EventArgs) Handles MyBase.Load
28            ' Put user code to initialize the page here
29        End Sub
30   End Class ' AdRotator
```

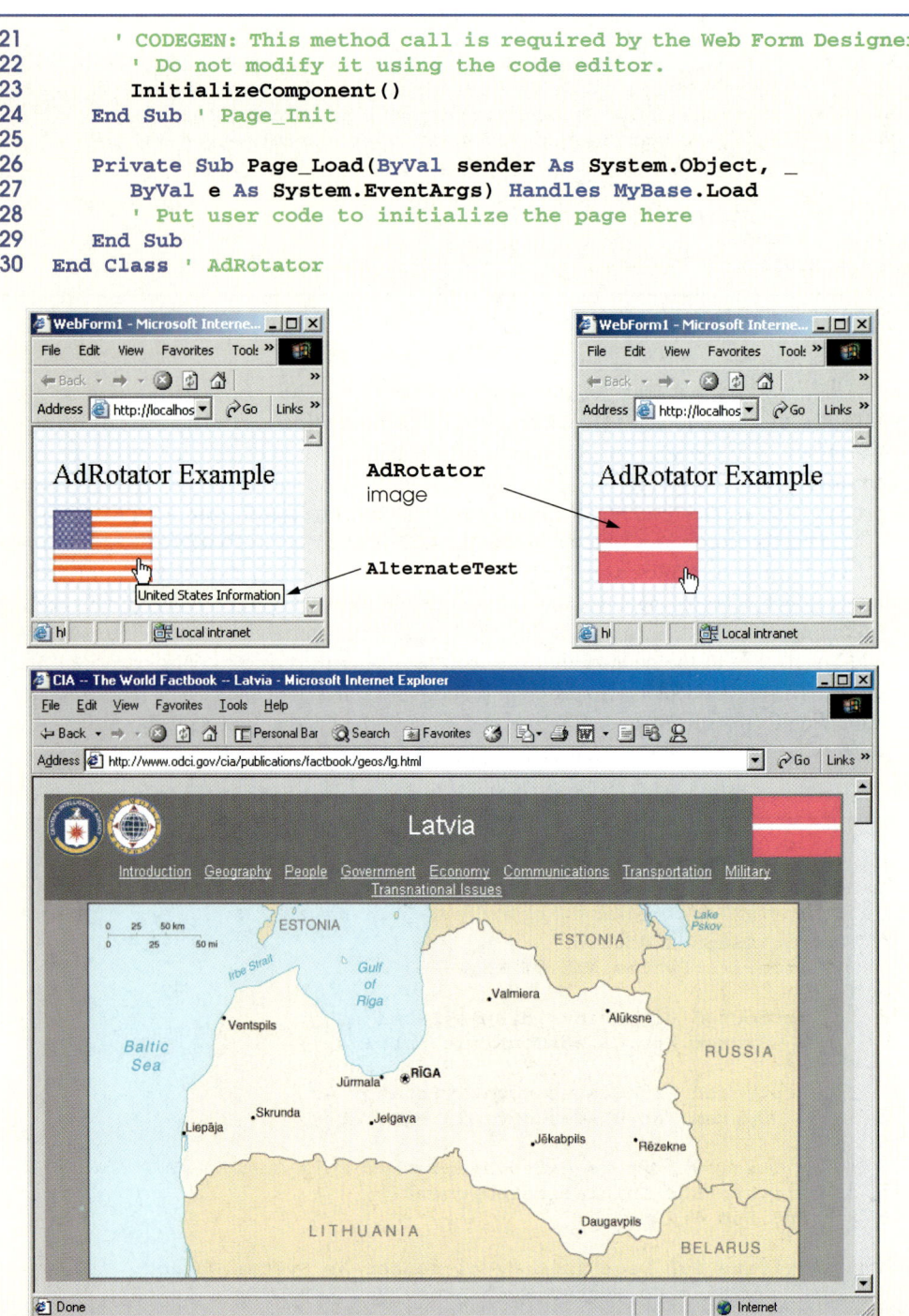

Fig. 20.19 Code-behind file for page demonstrating the **AdRotator** class (part 2 of 2).

XML document **AdRotatorInformation.xml** (Fig. 20.20) contains several **Ad** elements, each of which provides information about a different advertisement. Element **ImageUrl** specifies the path (location) of the advertisement's image, and element **NavigateUrl** specifies the URL for the web page that loads when a user clicks the advertisement. The **AlternateText** element contains text that displays in place of the image when the browser cannot locate or render the image for some reason (i.e., because the file is missing, or the browser is not capable of displaying it). The **AlternateText** element's text is also a *tooltip* that Internet Explorer displays when a user places the mouse pointer over the image (Fig. 20.19). A tooltip is a caption that appears when the mouse hovers over a control and provides the user with information about that control. The **Impressions** element specifies how often a particular image appears, relative to the other images. An advertisement that has a higher **Impressions** value displays more frequently than an advertisement with a lower value. In our example, the advertisements display with equal probability, because each **Impressions**' value is set to **1**.

```xml
1   <?xml version="1.0" encoding="utf-8"?>
2
3   <!-- Fig. 20.20: AdRotatorInformation.xml           -->
4   <!-- XML file containing advertisement information. -->
5
6   <Advertisements>
7      <Ad>
8         <ImageUrl>images/us.png</ImageUrl>
9         <NavigateUrl>
10           http://www.odci.gov/cia/publications/factbook/geos/us.html
11        </NavigateUrl>
12        <AlternateText>United States Information</AlternateText>
13        <Impressions>1</Impressions>
14     </Ad>
15
16     <Ad>
17        <ImageUrl>images/france.png</ImageUrl>
18        <NavigateUrl>
19           http://www.odci.gov/cia/publications/factbook/geos/fr.html
20        </NavigateUrl>
21        <AlternateText>France Information</AlternateText>
22        <Impressions>1</Impressions>
23     </Ad>
24
25     <Ad>
26        <ImageUrl>images/germany.png</ImageUrl>
27        <NavigateUrl>
28           http://www.odci.gov/cia/publications/factbook/geos/gm.html
29        </NavigateUrl>
30        <AlternateText>Germany Information</AlternateText>
31        <Impressions>1</Impressions>
32     </Ad>
33
34     <Ad>
35        <ImageUrl>images/italy.png</ImageUrl>
```

Fig. 20.20 AdvertisementFile used in **AdRotator** example (part 1 of 3).

```
36          <NavigateUrl>
37             http://www.odci.gov/cia/publications/factbook/geos/it.html
38          </NavigateUrl>
39          <AlternateText>Italy Information</AlternateText>
40          <Impressions>1</Impressions>
41       </Ad>
42
43       <Ad>
44          <ImageUrl>images/spain.png</ImageUrl>
45          <NavigateUrl>
46             http://www.odci.gov/cia/publications/factbook/geos/sp.html
47          </NavigateUrl>
48          <AlternateText>Spain Information</AlternateText>
49          <Impressions>1</Impressions>
50       </Ad>
51
52       <Ad>
53          <ImageUrl>images/latvia.png</ImageUrl>
54          <NavigateUrl>
55             http://www.odci.gov/cia/publications/factbook/geos/lg.html
56          </NavigateUrl>
57          <AlternateText>Latvia Information</AlternateText>
58          <Impressions>1</Impressions>
59       </Ad>
60
61       <Ad>
62          <ImageUrl>images/peru.png</ImageUrl>
63          <NavigateUrl>
64             http://www.odci.gov/cia/publications/factbook/geos/pe.html
65          </NavigateUrl>
66          <AlternateText>Peru Information</AlternateText>
67          <Impressions>1</Impressions>
68       </Ad>
69
70       <Ad>
71          <ImageUrl>images/senegal.png</ImageUrl>
72          <NavigateUrl>
73             http://www.odci.gov/cia/publications/factbook/geos/sg.html
74          </NavigateUrl>
75          <AlternateText>Senegal Information</AlternateText>
76          <Impressions>1</Impressions>
77       </Ad>
78
79       <Ad>
80          <ImageUrl>images/sweden.png</ImageUrl>
81          <NavigateUrl>
82             http://www.odci.gov/cia/publications/factbook/geos/sw.html
83          </NavigateUrl>
84          <AlternateText>Sweden Information</AlternateText>
85          <Impressions>1</Impressions>
86       </Ad>
87
```

Fig. 20.20 `AdvertisementFile` used in `AdRotator` example (part 2 of 3).

```
88          <Ad>
89              <ImageUrl>images/thailand.png</ImageUrl>
90              <NavigateUrl>
91                  http://www.odci.gov/cia/publications/factbook/geos/th.html
92              </NavigateUrl>
93              <AlternateText>Thailand Information</AlternateText>
94              <Impressions>1</Impressions>
95          </Ad>
96
97          <Ad>
98              <ImageUrl>images/unitedstates.png</ImageUrl>
99              <NavigateUrl>
100                 http://www.odci.gov/cia/publications/factbook/geos/us.html
101             </NavigateUrl>
102             <AlternateText>United States Information</AlternateText>
103             <Impressions>1</Impressions>
104         </Ad>
105     </Advertisements>
```

Fig. 20.20 `AdvertisementFile` used in `AdRotator` example (part 3 of 3).

20.5.3 Validation Controls

This section introduces a different type of Web control, called a *validation control* (or *validator*), which detremines whether the data in another Web control are in the proper format. For example, validators could determine whether a user has provided information in a required field or whether a ZIP-code field contains exactly five digits. Validators provide a mechanism for validating user input on the client. When the HTML for our page is created, the validator is converted into *ECMAScript*[3] that performs the validation. ECMAScript is a scripting language that enhances the functionality and appearance of Web pages. ECMAScript is typically executed on the client. However, if the client does not support scripting or scripting is disabled, validation is performed on the server.

The example in this section prompts the user to input a phone number, in the form 555–4567. After the user enters a number, validators ensure that the phone-number field is filled and that the number is in the correct format before the program sends the number to the Web server. Once the phone number is submitted, the Web Server responds by sending an HTML page containing all possible letter combinations that represent the phone number. The letters used for each digit are the letters found on a phone's key pad. For instance, the 5-button displays the letters j, k and l. For the position in the phone number where there is a 5, we can substitute one of these three letters. Businesses often use this technique to make their phone numbers easy to remember. Figure 20.21 presents the ASPX file.

The HTML page sent to the client browser accepts a phone number in the form **555–4567** and then lists all the possible words that can be generated from both the first three digits and the last four digits. This example uses a **RegularExpressionValidator**

---

3. ECMAScript (commonly known as JavaScript) is a scripting standard created by the ECMA (European Computer Manufacturer's Association). Both Netscape's JavaScript and Microsoft's JScript implement the ECMAScript standard, but each provides additional features beyond the specification. For information on the current ECMAScript standard, visit **www.ecma.ch/stand/ecma-262.htm**.

```
1   <%-- Fig. 20.21: Generator.aspx                          --%>
2   <%-- A Web Form demonstrating the use of validators. --%>
3
4   <%@ Page Language="vb" AutoEventWireup="false"
5      Codebehind="Generator.aspx.vb"
6      Inherits="WordGenerator.Generator"
7      enableViewState="False" EnableSessionState="False" %>
8
9   <!DOCTYPE HTML PUBLIC "-//W3C//DTD HTML 4.0 Transitional//EN">
10  <HTML>
11     <HEAD>
12        <title>WebForm1</title>
13        <meta name="GENERATOR"
14           content="Microsoft Visual Studio.NET 7.0">
15        <meta name="CODE_LANGUAGE" content="Visual Basic 7.0">
16        <meta name="vs_defaultClientScript" content="JavaScript">
17        <meta name="vs_targetSchema"
18           content="http://schemas.microsoft.com/intellisense/ie5">
19     </HEAD>
20     <body MS_POSITIONING="GridLayout">
21        <form id="Form1" method="post" runat="server">
22
23           <asp:Label id="promptLabel" style="Z-INDEX: 101;
24              LEFT: 32px; POSITION: absolute; TOP: 17px"
25              runat="server">
26              Please enter a phone number in the form 555-4567.
27           </asp:Label>
28
29           <asp:TextBox id="outputTextBox" style="Z-INDEX: 106;
30              LEFT: 40px; POSITION: absolute; TOP: 118px"
31              runat="server" Width="451px" Height="342px"
32              TextMode="MultiLine" Visible="False">
33           </asp:TextBox>
34
35           <asp:RegularExpressionValidator id="phoneNumberValidator"
36              style="Z-INDEX: 105; LEFT: 204px; POSITION: absolute;
37              TOP: 44px" runat="server" ErrorMessage=
38              "The phone number must be in the form 555-4567."
39              ControlToValidate="phoneTextBox"
40              ValidationExpression="^\d{3}-\d{4}$">
41           </asp:RegularExpressionValidator>
42
43           <asp:RequiredFieldValidator id="phoneInputValidator"
44              style="Z-INDEX: 104; LEFT: 207px; POSITION:
45              absolute; TOP: 81px" runat="server"
46              ErrorMessage=
47                 "Please enter a phone number."
48              ControlToValidate="phoneTextBox">
49           </asp:RequiredFieldValidator>
50
```

Fig. 20.21 Validators used in a Web Form that generates possible letter combinations from a phone number (part 1 of 2).

```
51              <asp:Button id="submitButton" style="Z-INDEX: 103;
52                 LEFT: 38px; POSITION: absolute; TOP: 77px"
53                 runat="server" Text="Submit">
54              </asp:Button>
55
56              <asp:TextBox id="phoneTextBox" style="Z-INDEX: 102;
57                 LEFT: 34px; POSITION: absolute; TOP: 42px"
58                 runat="server">
59              </asp:TextBox>
60
61          </form>
62      </body>
63  </HTML>
```

Fig. 20.21 Validators used in a Web Form that generates possible letter combinations from a phone number (part 2 of 2).

to match another Web control's content against a regular expression. (The use of regular expressions is introduced in Chapter 15, Strings, Characters and Regular Expressions.) Lines 35–41 create a **RegularExpressionValidator** named **phoneNumberValidator**. Property **ErrorMessage**'s text (lines 37–38) is displayed on the Web Form if the validation fails. The regular expression that validates the input is assigned to property **ValidationExpression** in line 38. The input is valid if it matches the regular expression **^\d{3}-\d{4}$** (i.e., if exactly 3 digits are followed by a hyphen and exactly 4 digits, where the 3 digits are at the beginning of the string and the 4 digits are at the end of the string).

The clicking of property **ValidationExpression** in the **Properties** window displays a dialog that contains a list of common regular expressions for phone numbers, ZIP codes and other formatted information. However, we write our own regular expression in this example, because the phone number input should not contain an area code. Line 39 associates **phoneTextBox** with **phoneNumberValidator** by setting property **ControlToValidate** to **phoneTextBox**. This indicates that **phoneNumberValidator** verifies the **phoneTextBox**'s contents. If the user inputs text that does not have the correct format and attempts to submit the form, the **ErrorMessage** text is displayed in red.

This example also uses a **RequiredFieldValidator** to ensure that the text box is not empty when the HTML form is submitted. Lines 43–49 define **RequiredFieldValidator phoneInputValidator**, which confirms that **phoneTextBox**'s content is not empty. If the user does not input any data in **phoneTextBox** and attempts to submit the form, validation fails, and the **ErrorMessage** for this validator is displayed in red. If the validator is successful, a multiline **TextBox** named **outputTextBox** (lines 29–33) displays the words generated from the phone number. Notice that the **Visible** property initially is set to **False** when the server returns its HTML response.

Figure 20.22 depicts the code-behind file for the ASPX file in Fig. 20.21. Notice that this code-behind file does not contain any implementation related to the validators. We say more about this soon.

```vb
1   ' Fig. 20.22: Generator.aspx.vb
2   ' The code-behind file for a page that
3   ' generates words when given a phone number.
4
5   Imports System.Web.UI.WebControls
6
7   Public Class Generator
8      Inherits System.Web.UI.Page
9
10     Protected WithEvents phoneInputValidator As _
11        RequiredFieldValidator
12
13     Protected WithEvents phoneNumberValidator As _
14        RegularExpressionValidator
15
16     Protected WithEvents promptLabel As Label
17     Protected WithEvents outputTextBox As TextBox
18     Protected WithEvents submitButton As Button
19     Protected WithEvents phoneTextBox As TextBox
20
21     ' Web Form Designer generated code
22
23     Private Sub Page_Load(ByVal sender As System.Object, _
24        ByVal e As System.EventArgs) Handles MyBase.Load
25
26        ' if not first time page loads
27        If IsPostBack Then
28           Dim number As String
29
30           outputTextBox.Text() = ""
31
32           ' retrieve number and remove "-"
33           number = Request.Form("phoneTextBox")
34           number = number.Remove(3, 1)
35
36           ' generate words for first 3 digits
37           outputTextBox.Text &= "Here are the words for the " & _
38              "first three digits" & vbCrLf
39
40           ComputeWords(number.Substring(0, 3), "")
41           outputTextBox.Text &= vbCrLf
42
43           ' generate words for last 4 digits
44           outputTextBox.Text &= "Here are the words for the " & _
45              "last 4 digits" & vbCrLf
46
47           ComputeWords(number.Substring(3), "")
48
49           outputTextBox.Visible = True
50        End If
51
52     End Sub ' Page_Load
53
```

Fig. 20.22 Code-behind file for the word-generator page (part 1 of 4).

```vbnet
54      Private Sub ComputeWords(ByVal number As String, _
55         ByVal temporaryWord As String)
56
57         Dim current As Integer
58
59         ' if number is empty, print word
60         If number = "" Then
61            outputTextBox.Text &= temporaryWord & vbCrLf
62            Return
63         End If
64
65         ' retrieve first number and convert to Integer
66         current = Convert.ToInt32(number.Substring(0, 1))
67
68         ' delete first number
69         number = number.Remove(0, 1)
70
71         ' determine number, call ComputeWord recursively
72         Select Case current
73
74            ' 0 can be q or z
75            Case 0
76               ComputeWords(number, temporaryWord & "q")
77               ComputeWords(number, temporaryWord & "z")
78
79            ' 1 has no letter associated with it
80            Case 1
81               ComputeWords(number, temporaryWord & "")
82
83            ' 2 can be a, b or c
84            Case 2
85               ComputeWords(number, temporaryWord & "a")
86               ComputeWords(number, temporaryWord & "b")
87               ComputeWords(number, temporaryWord & "c")
88
89            ' 3 can be d, e or f
90            Case 3
91               ComputeWords(number, temporaryWord & "d")
92               ComputeWords(number, temporaryWord & "e")
93               ComputeWords(number, temporaryWord & "f")
94
95            ' 4 can be g, h or i
96            Case 4
97               ComputeWords(number, temporaryWord & "g")
98               ComputeWords(number, temporaryWord & "h")
99               ComputeWords(number, temporaryWord & "i")
100
101           ' 5 can be j, k or l
102           Case 5
103              ComputeWords(number, temporaryWord & "j")
104              ComputeWords(number, temporaryWord & "k")
105              ComputeWords(number, temporaryWord & "l")
106
```

Fig. 20.22 Code-behind file for the word-generator page (part 2 of 4).

```vbnet
107              ' 6 can be m, n or o
108          Case 6
109              ComputeWords(number, temporaryWord & "m")
110              ComputeWords(number, temporaryWord & "n")
111              ComputeWords(number, temporaryWord & "o")
112
113              ' 7 can be p, r or s
114          Case 7
115              ComputeWords(number, temporaryWord & "p")
116              ComputeWords(number, temporaryWord & "r")
117              ComputeWords(number, temporaryWord & "s")
118
119              ' 8 can be t, u or v
120          Case 8
121              ComputeWords(number, temporaryWord & "t")
122              ComputeWords(number, temporaryWord & "u")
123              ComputeWords(number, temporaryWord & "v")
124
125              ' 9 can be w, x or y
126          Case 9
127              ComputeWords(number, temporaryWord & "w")
128              ComputeWords(number, temporaryWord & "x")
129              ComputeWords(number, temporaryWord & "y")
130          End Select
131
132      End Sub ' ComputeWords
133 End Class ' Generator
```

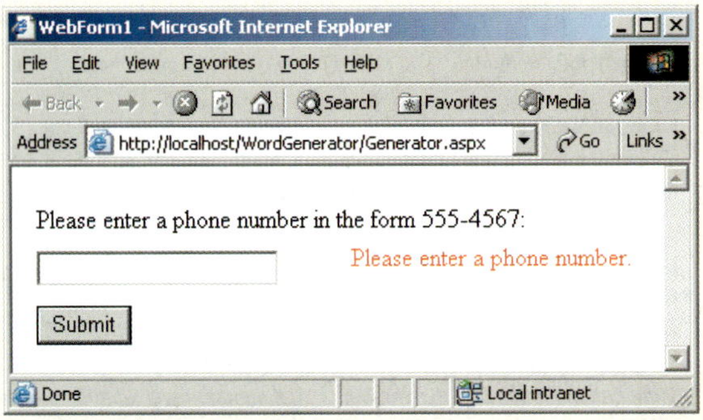

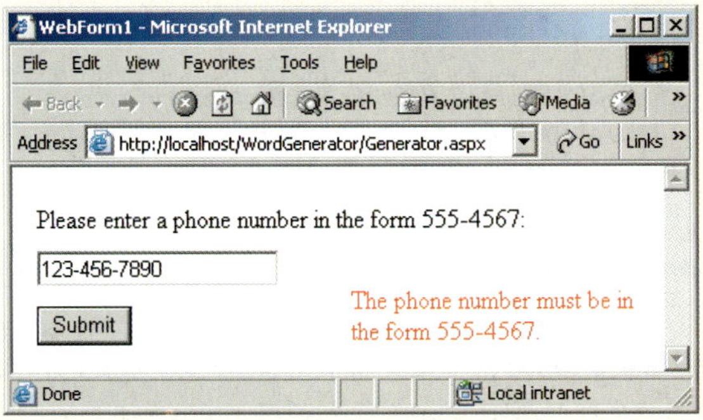

Fig. 20.22 Code-behind file for the word-generator page (part 3 of 4).

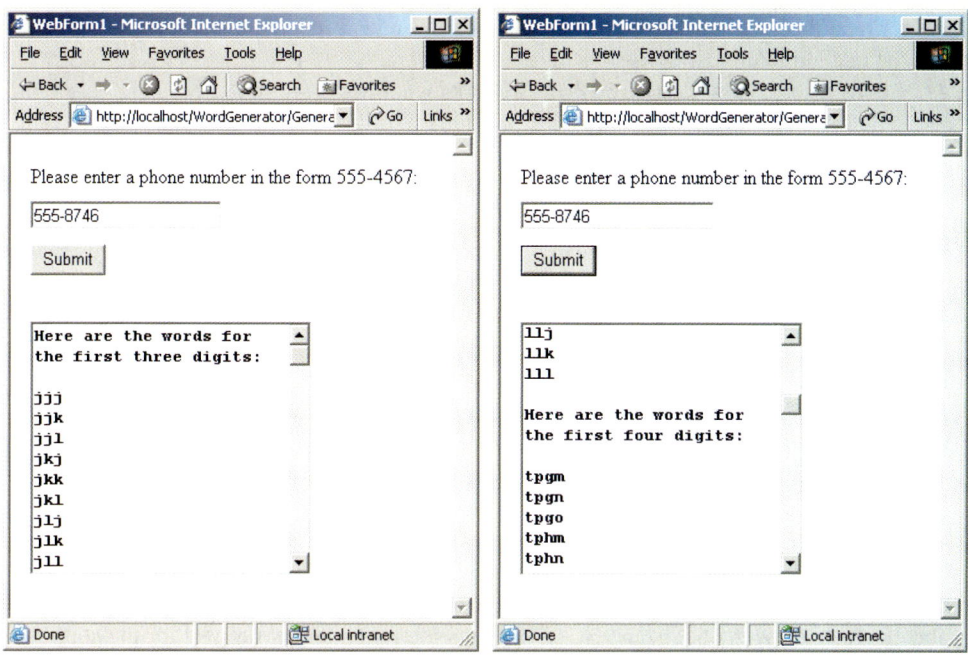

Fig. 20.22 Code-behind file for the word-generator page (part 4 of 4).

Web programmers using ASP .NET often design their Web pages so that the current page reloads when the user submits the form; this enables the program to receive input, process it as necessary and display the results in the same page when it is reloaded. These pages usually contain a form that, when submitted, causes the current page to be requested again. This event is known as a *postback*. Line 27 uses the **IsPostBack** property of class **Page** to determine whether the page is being loaded due to a postback. The first time that the Web page is requested, **IsPostBack** is **False**. When the postback occurs (from the users clicking of **Submit**), **IsPostBack** is **True**. To prepare the **outputTextBox** for display, its **Text** property is set to an empty string (**""**) in line 30. Line 33 then uses the **Request** object to retrieve **phoneTextBox**'s value from the **Form** array. When data is posted to the Web server, the HTML **form**'s data is accessible to the Web application through the **Request** object's **Form** array. The hyphen is **Remove**d from the phone number string in line 34. Method **ComputeWords** is passed a substring containing the first three numbers and an empty **String** (line 40). Line 49 sets the **outputTextBox**'s **Visible** property to **True**.

Method **ComputeWords**, defined in lines 54–132, is a recursive method that generates the list of words from the **String** containing the digits of the phone number, minus the hyphen. The first argument, **number**, contains the digits that are being converted to letters. The first call to this method (line 40) passes in the first three digits, and the second call (line 47) passes in the last four digits. The second argument, **temporaryWord**, builds up the list that is displayed by the program. Each time this method is called, as we will see shortly, **number** contains one character fewer than on the previous call and **temporaryWord** contains one character more than on the previous call. Lines 60–63 define the base case, which occurs when **number** equals the empty string. When this occurs, the **temporaryWord** that has been built up from the previous calls is added to **outputTextBox**, and the method returns.

Let us discuss how **ComputeWords** works when we do not have the base case. On line 57, we declare variable **current** and initialize its value to the first character in **number**. We then remove this character from **number**. The remainder of the method uses a **Select Case** structure (lines 72–130) to make the correct recursive calls based on the number in **current**. For each digit, we wish to add the appropriate letter to **temporaryWord**. For most of the digits, there are two or three letters that can be represented by the number in **current**. The keypad button for the number 3, for instance, also represents the letters d, e or f. In this example we want to exhaust all possible letter combinations, so we make a recursive call to **ComputeWords** for each option (lines 91–93). Each call passes **number** as the first argument (which contains one digit fewer, as a result of the call to method **Remove** on line 69). The second argument contains **temporaryWord**, concatenated with the new letter. Each call continues to add a letter for the current number, until all the numbers have been processed. At this point we reach the base case, and **temporaryWord** is appended to **outputTextBox**.

Figure 20.23 shows the HTML sent to the client browser. Notice that lines 25–28 and lines 71–113 contain ECMAScript, which provides the implementation for the validation controls. Visual Studio generates this ECMAScript. The programmer does not need to be able to create or even understand ECMAScript—the functionality defined for the controls in our application is converted to working ECMAScript for us.

```
1    <!-- Fig. 20.23: Generator.html                        -->
2    <!-- The HTML page that is sent to the client browser. -->
3
4    <!DOCTYPE HTML PUBLIC "-//W3C//DTD HTML 4.0 Transitional//EN" >
5    <HTML>
6       <HEAD>
7          <title>WebForm1</title>
8          <meta name="GENERATOR"
9             content="Microsoft Visual Studio 7.0">
10         <meta name="CODE_LANGUAGE" content="Visual Basic 7.0" >
11         <meta name="vs_defaultClientScript"
12            content="JavaScript">
13         <meta name="vs_targetSchema"
14            content="http://schemas.microsoft.com/intellisense/ie5">
15      </HEAD>
16
17      <body MS_POSITIONING="GridLayout">
18
19         <form name="Form1" method="post"
20            action="Generator.aspx" language="javascript"
21            onsubmit="ValidatorOnSubmit();" id="FORM1">
22            <input type="hidden" name="__VIEWSTATE"
23               value="dDwxMjgyMzM3ozs+" />
24
25            <script language="javascript"
```

Fig. 20.23 HTML and JavaScript sent to the client browser (part 1 of 3).

```html
        src=
"/aspnet_client/system_web/1_0_3215_11/WebUIValidation.js">
     </script>

     <span id="phoneNumberValidator"
        controltovalidate="phoneTextBox"
        errormessage=
           "The phone number must be in the form 555-4567."
        evaluationfunction=
           "RegularExpressionValidatorEvaluateIsValid"
        validationexpression="^\d{3}-\d{4}$"
        style="color:Red;Z-INDEX:106;LEFT:217px;
           POSITION:absolute;TOP:73px;visibility:hidden;">
        The phone number must be in the form 555-4567.
     </span>

     <input name="phoneTextBox" type="text"
        id="phoneTextBox"
        style="Z-INDEX: 102; LEFT: 16px;
        POSITION: absolute; TOP: 52px" />

     <input type="submit" name="submitButton"
        value="Submit"
        onclick= "if ( " +
           "typeof(Page_ClientValidate) == 'function') " +
           "Page_ClientValidate(); " language="javascript"
           id="submitButton" style="Z-INDEX: 103;
        LEFT: 16px;
        POSITION: absolute;
        TOP: 86px" />

     <span id="phoneInputValidator"
        controltovalidate="phoneTextBox"
        errormessage="Please enter a phone number."
        evaluationfunction=
           "RequiredFieldValidatorEvaluateIsValid"
        initialvalue="" style="color:Red;Z-INDEX:105;
           LEFT:217px;POSITION:absolute;TOP:47px;
           visibility:hidden;">Please enter a phone number.
     </span>

     <span id="promptLabel" style="Z-INDEX: 101;
        LEFT: 16px; POSITION: absolute; TOP: 23px">
        Please enter a phone number in the form 555-4567:
     </span>

     <script language="javascript">
     <!--
        var Page_Validators = new Array(
           document.all["phoneNumberValidator"],
           document.all["phoneInputValidator"] );
     // -->
     </script>
```

Fig. 20.23 HTML and JavaScript sent to the client browser (part 2 of 3).

```
 79
 80            <script language="javascript">
 81            <!--
 82               var Page_ValidationActive = false;
 83
 84               if (
 85                  typeof(clientInformation) != "undefined" &&
 86                  clientInformation.appName.indexOf("Explorer")
 87                  != -1 ) {
 88
 89                  if ( typeof(Page_ValidationVer) == "undefined" )
 90                     alert(
 91                        "Unable to find script library " +
 92                        "'/aspnet_client/system_web/'"+
 93                        "'1_0_3215_11/WebUIValidation.js'. " +
 94                        "Try placing this file manually, or " +
 95                        "reinstall by running 'aspnet_regiis -c'.");
 96                  else if ( Page_ValidationVer != "125" )
 97                     alert(
 98                        "This page uses an incorrect version " +
 99                        "of WebUIValidation.js. The page " +
100                        "expects version 125. " +
101                        "The script library is " +
102                        Page_ValidationVer + ".");
103                  else
104                     ValidatorOnLoad();
105               }
106
107               function ValidatorOnSubmit() {
108                  if (Page_ValidationActive) {
109                     ValidatorCommonOnSubmit();
110                  }
111               }
112               // -->
113            </script>
114        </form>
115     </body>
116 </HTML>
```

Fig. 20.23 HTML and JavaScript sent to the client browser (part 3 of 3).

In earlier ASPX files, we explicitly set the **EnableViewState** attribute to **false**. This attribute determines whether a Web control's value persists (i.e., is retained) when a postback occurs. By default, this attribute is **true**, which indicates that control values persist. In the screen shots (Fig. 20.22), notice that the phone number input still appears in the text box after the postback occurs. A **hidden** input in the HTML document (line 22–23) contains the data of the controls on this page. This element is always named **__VIEWSTATE** and stores the controls' data as an encoded string.

Performance Tip 20.2

The setting of **EnabledViewState** *to* **false** *reduces the amount of data passed to the Web server.*

20.6 Session Tracking

Originally, critics accused the Internet and e-business of failing to provide the kind of customized service typically experienced in bricks-and-mortar stores. To address this problem, e-businesses began to establish mechanisms by which they could personalize users' browsing experiences, tailoring content to individual users while enabling them to bypass irrelevant information. Businesses achieve this level of service by tracking each customer's movement through the Internet and combining the collected data with information provided by the consumer, including billing information, personal preferences, interests and hobbies.

Personalization makes it possible for e-businesses to communicate effectively with their customers and also improves users' ability to locate desired products and services. Companies that provide content of particular interest to users can establish relationships with customers and build on those relationships over time. Furthermore, by targeting consumers with personal offers, advertisements, promotions and services, e-businesses create customer loyalty. At such Web sites as **MSN.com** and **CNN.com**, sophisticated technology allows visitors to customize home pages to suit their individual needs and preferences. Similarly, online shopping sites often store personal information for customers and target them with notifications and special offers tailored to their interests. Such services can create customer bases that visit sites more frequently and make purchases from those sites more regularly.

A trade-off exists, however, between personalized e-business service and protection of *privacy*. Whereas some consumers embrace the idea of tailored content, others fear that the release of information that they provide to e-business or that is collected about them by tracking technologies will have adverse consequences on their lives. Consumers and privacy advocates ask: What if the e-business to which we give personal data sells or gives that information to another organization without our knowledge? What if we do not want our actions on the Internet—a supposedly anonymous medium—to be tracked and recorded by unknown parties? What if unauthorized parties gain access to sensitive private data, such as credit-card numbers or medical history? All of these are questions that must be debated and addressed by consumers, e-businesses and lawmakers alike.

To provide personalized services to consumers, e-businesses must be able to recognize clients when they request information from a site. As we have discussed, the request/response system on which the Web operates is facilitated by HTTP. Unfortunately, HTTP is a stateless protocol—it does not support persistent connections that would enable Web servers to maintain state information regarding particular clients. This means that Web servers have no capacity to determine whether a request comes from a particular client or whether the same or different clients generate a series of requests. To circumvent this problem, sites such as **MSN.com** and **CNN.com** provide mechanisms by which they identify individual clients. A session represents a unique client on the Internet. If the client leaves a site and then returns later, the client will still be recognized as the same user. To help the server distinguish among clients, each client must identify itself to the server. The tracking of individual clients, known as *session tracking*, can be achieved in a number of ways. One popular technique involves the use of cookies (Section 20.6.1); another employs .NET's **HttpSessionState** object (Section 20.6.2). Additional session-tracking techniques include the use of input form elements of type **"hidden"** and URL rewriting. Using **"hidden"** form elements, a Web Form can write session-tracking data into a **form** in the Web page that it returns to the client in response to a prior request. When the user submits the form in the new Web page, all the form data, including the **"hidden"** fields, are sent to the form handler on the Web server. When a Web site employs URL rewriting, the Web Form embeds session-tracking information directly in the URLs of hyperlinks that the user clicks to send subsequent requests to the Web server.

The reader should note that, in previous examples, we usually set the Web Form's **EnableSessionState** property to **false**. However, because we wish to use session tracking in the following examples, we leave this property in its default mode, which is **true**.

20.6.1 Cookies

A popular way to customize interactions with Web pages is via *cookies*. A cookie is a text file stored by a Web site on an individual's computer that allows the site to track the actions of the visitor. The first time that a user visits the Web site, the user's computer might receive a cookie; this cookie is then reactivated each time the user revisits that site. The collected information is intended to be an anonymous record containing data that are used to personalize the user's future visits to the site. For example, cookies in a shopping application might store unique identifiers for users. When a user adds items to an on-line shopping cart or performs another task resulting in a request to the Web server, the server receives a cookie containing the user's unique identifier. The server then uses the unique identifier to locate the shopping cart and perform any necessary processing.

In addition to identifying users, cookies also can indicate clients' shopping preferences. When a Web Form receives a request from a client, the Web Form could examine the cookie(s) it sent to the client during previous communications, identify the client's preferences and immediately display products that are of interest to the client.

Every HTTP-based interaction between a client and a server includes a header containing information either about the request (when the communication is from the client to the server) or about the response (when the communication is from the server to the client). When a Web Form receives a request, the header includes information such as the request type (e.g., **Get**) and any cookies that have been sent previously from the server to be stored on the client machine. When the server formulates its response, the header information includes any cookies the server wants to store on the client computer and other information, such as the MIME type of the response.

If the programmer of a cookie does not set an *expiration date*, the Web browser maintains the cookie for the duration of the browsing session. Otherwise, the Web browser maintains the cookie until the expiration date occurs. When the browser requests a resource from a Web server, cookies previously sent to the client by that Web server are returned to the Web server as part of the request formulated by the browser. Cookies are deleted when they *expire*. The expiration date of a cookie can be set in that cookie's **Expires** property.

The next Web application demonstrates the use of cookies. The example contains two pages. In the first page (Fig. 20.24 and Fig. 20.25), users select a favorite programming language from a group of radio buttons and then submit the HTML **form** to the Web server for processing. The Web server responds by creating a cookie that stores a record of the chosen language, as well as the ISBN number for a book on that topic. The server then returns an HTML document to the browser, allowing the user either to select another favorite programming language or to view the second page in our application (Fig. 20.26 and Fig. 20.27), which lists recommended books pertaining to the programming language that the user selected previously. When the user clicks the hyperlink, the cookies previously stored on the client are read and used to form the list of book recommendations.

```aspx
 1  <%-- Fig 20.24: OptionsPage.aspx                     --%>
 2  <%-- allows clients to select a programming language --%>
 3  <%-- to get recommendations.                         --%>
 4
 5  <%@ Page Language="vb" AutoEventWireup="false"
 6     Codebehind="OptionsPage.aspx.vb"
 7     Inherits="Cookies.Cookie"%>
 8
 9  <!DOCTYPE HTML PUBLIC "-//W3C//DTD HTML 4.0 Transitional//EN">
10  <HTML>
11     <HEAD>
12        <title>Cookies</title>
13        <meta content="Microsoft Visual Studio.NET 7.0"
14           name="GENERATOR">
15        <meta content="Visual Basic 7.0" name="CODE_LANGUAGE">
16        <meta content="JavaScript" name="vs_defaultClientScript">
17        <meta name="vs_targetSchema"
18           content="http://schemas.microsoft.com/intellisense/ie5">
19     </HEAD>
20     <body MS_POSITIONING="GridLayout">
21        <form id="Form1" method="post" runat="server">
22
23           <asp:label id="promptLabel" style="Z-INDEX: 101;
24              LEFT: 42px; POSITION: absolute; TOP: 22px"
25              runat="server" Font-Bold="True" Font-Size="Large">
26              Select a programming language.
27           </asp:label>
28
29           <asp:radiobuttonlist id="LanguageList"
30              style="Z-INDEX: 111; LEFT: 42px; POSITION:
31              absolute; TOP: 52px" runat="server">
32
33              <asp:ListItem Value="Visual Basic .NET"
34                 >Visual Basic .NET</asp:ListItem>
35
36              <asp:ListItem Value="C#">C#</asp:ListItem>
37              <asp:ListItem Value="C">C</asp:ListItem>
38              <asp:ListItem Value="C++">C++</asp:ListItem>
39              <asp:ListItem Value="Python">Python</asp:ListItem>
40           </asp:radiobuttonlist>
41
42           <asp:hyperlink id="recommendationsLink"
43              style="Z-INDEX: 110; LEFT: 42px; POSITION:
44              absolute; TOP: 90px" runat="server"
45              Visible="False" NavigateUrl=
46              "RecommendationPage.aspx">
47              Click here to get book recommendations
48           </asp:hyperlink>
49
50           <asp:hyperlink id="languageLink" style="Z-INDEX:
51              109; LEFT: 42px; POSITION: absolute;
52              TOP: 55px" runat="server" Visible="False"
53              NavigateUrl="OptionsPage.aspx">
```

Fig. 20.24 ASPX file that presents a list of programming languages (part 1 of 2).

```
54              Click here to choose another language
55          </asp:hyperlink>
56
57          <asp:label id="welcomeLabel" style="Z-INDEX: 108;
58              LEFT: 42px; POSITION: absolute; TOP: 23px"
59              runat="server" Visible="False" Font-Bold="True"
60              Font-Size="Large">Welcome to cookies! You selected
61          </asp:label>
62
63          <asp:button id="submitButton" style="Z-INDEX: 107;
64              LEFT: 42px; POSITION: absolute; TOP: 196px"
65              runat="server" Text="Submit">
66          </asp:button>
67
68      </form>
69   </body>
70 </HTML>
```

Fig. 20.24 ASPX file that presents a list of programming languages (part 2 of 2)x.

The ASPX file in Fig. 20.24 contains five radio buttons (lines 29–40), having the values **Visual Basic .NET**, **C#**, **C**, **C++**, and **Python**. A programmer sets these values by clicking the **Items** property in the **Properties** window and then adding items via the **List Item Collection Editor**. This process is similar to the customizing of a **ListBox** in a Windows application. The user selects a programming language by clicking one of the radio buttons. The page contains a **Submit** button, which, when clicked, creates a cookie containing a record of the selected language. Once created, this cookie is added to the HTTP response header, and a postback occurs. Each time the user chooses a language and clicks **Submit**, a cookie is written to the client.

When the postback occurs, certain components are hidden and others are displayed. Towards the bottom of the page, two hyperlinks are displayed: One that requests this page (lines 50–55), and one that requests **Recommendations.aspx** (lines 42–48). Notice that clicking the first hyperlink (the one that requests the current page) does not cause a postback to occur. The file **OptionsPage.aspx** is specified in the **NavigateUrl** property of the hyperlink. When the hyperlink is clicked, this page is requested as a completely new request.

Figure 20.25 presents the code-behind file. Line 14 defines **books** as a **Hashtable** (namespace **System.Collections**), which is a data structure that stores *key–value pairs* (we introduced hash tables briefly in Chapter 15, String, Characters and Regular Expressions). The program uses the key to store and retrieve the associated value in the **Hashtable**. In this example, the keys are **String**s containing the programming language name's and the values are **String**s containing the ISBN numbers for the recommended books. Class **Hashtable** provides method **Add**, which takes as arguments a key and a value. A value that is added via method **Add** is placed in the **Hashtable** at a location determined by the key. The value for a specific **Hashtable** entry can be determined by indexing the hash table with that value's key. For instance,

HashtableName (*keyName*)

returns the value in the key-value pair in which *keyName* is the key. An example of this is shown in line 65; **books(language)** returns the value that corresponds to the key contained in **language**. Class **Hashtable** is discussed in detail in Chapter 23, Data Structures.

```vb
1    ' Fig. 20.25: OptionsPage.aspx.vb
2    ' Page that allows the user to choose a different language.
3
4    Imports System.Web.UI.WebControls
5
6    Public Class Cookie
7       Inherits System.Web.UI.Page
8       Protected WithEvents languageLink As HyperLink
9       Protected WithEvents recommendationsLink As HyperLink
10      Protected WithEvents promptLabel As Label
11      Protected WithEvents LanguageList As RadioButtonList
12      Protected WithEvents welcomeLabel As Label
13      Protected WithEvents submitButton As Button
14      Private books = New Hashtable()
15
16      ' Visual Studio .NET generated code
17
18      Private Sub Page_Init(ByVal sender As System.Object, _
19         ByVal e As System.EventArgs) Handles MyBase.Init
20
21         InitializeComponent()
22
23         ' add values to Hastable
24         books.Add("Visual Basic .NET", "0-13-456955-5")
25         books.Add("C#", "0-13-062221-4")
26         books.Add("C", "0-13-089572-5")
27         books.Add("C++", "0-13-089571-7")
28         books.Add("Python", "0-13-092361-3")
29      End Sub ' Page_Init
30
31      Private Sub Page_Load(ByVal sender As System.Object, _
32         ByVal e As System.EventArgs) Handles MyBase.Load
33
34         If IsPostBack Then
35
36            ' if postback is True, user has submitted information
37            ' display welcome message and appropriate hyperlinks
38            welcomeLabel.Visible = True
39            languageLink.Visible = True
40            recommendationsLink.Visible = True
41
42            ' hide option information
43            submitButton.Visible = False
44            promptLabel.Visible = False
45            LanguageList.Visible = False
46
47            If (LanguageList.SelectedItem Is Nothing) = False Then
48               welcomeLabel.Text &= " " & _
49                  LanguageList.SelectedItem.Text.ToString & "."
```

Fig. 20.25 Code-behind file that writes cookies to the client (part 1 of 3).

```vbnet
50            Else
51               welcomeLabel.Text &= "no language."
52            End If
53         End If
54      End Sub ' Page_Load
55
56      Private Sub submitButton_Click(ByVal sender As System.Object, _
57         ByVal e As System.EventArgs) Handles submitButton.Click
58
59         Dim language, ISBN As String
60         Dim cookie As HttpCookie
61
62         ' if choice was made by user
63         If (LanguageList.SelectedItem Is Nothing) = False Then
64            language = LanguageList.SelectedItem.ToString()
65            ISBN = books(language).ToString()
66
67            ' create cookie, name/value pair is
68            ' language chosen and ISBN number from Hashtable
69            cookie = New HttpCookie(language, ISBN)
70
71            ' add cookie to response,
72            ' thus placing it on user's machine
73            Response.Cookies.Add(cookie)
74         End If
75
76      End Sub ' submitButton_Click
77   End Class ' Cookie
```

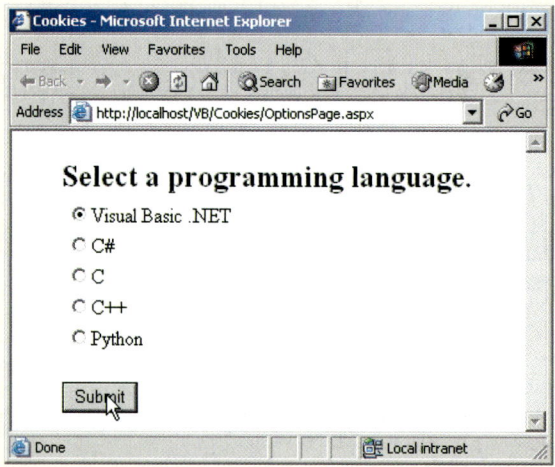

Fig. 20.25 Code-behind file that writes cookies to the client (part 2 of 3).

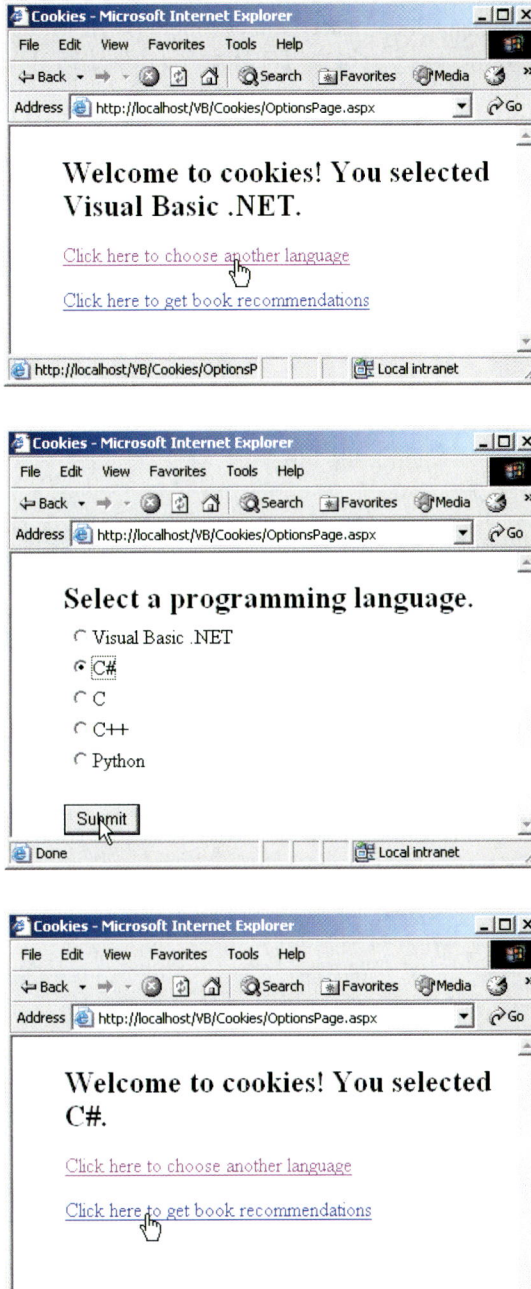

Fig. 20.25 Code-behind file that writes cookies to the client (part 3 of 3).

Clicking the **Submit** button creates a cookie if a language is selected and causes a postback to occur. A new cookie object (of type **HttpCookie**) is created to store the **language** and its corresponding **ISBN** number (line 69). This cookie is then **Add**ed to the **Cookies** collection sent as part of the HTTP response header (line 73). The postback causes the condition in the **If** structure of **Page_Load** (line 34) to evaluate to **True**, and lines 38–53 execute. Line 47 determines whether the user selected a language. If so, that language is displayed in **welcomeLabel** (lines 48–49). Otherwise, text indicating that a language was not selected is displayed in **welcomeLabel** (line 51). The two hyperlinks are made visible on lines 38–39.

After the postback request, the user may request a book recommendation. The book recommendation hyperlink forwards the user to **RecomendationPage.aspx** (Fig. 20.26) to display a recommendation.

```
1   <%-- Fig 20.26: RecommendationPage.aspx          --%>
2   <%-- Displays book recommendations using cookies. --%>
3
4   <%@ Page Language="vb" AutoEventWireup="false"
5      Codebehind="RecommendationPage.aspx.vb"
6      Inherits="Cookies.Recommendations"%>
7
8   <!DOCTYPE HTML PUBLIC "-//W3C//DTD HTML 4.0 Transitional//EN">
9   <HTML>
10     <HEAD>
11        <title>Book recommendations</title>
12        <meta content="Microsoft Visual Studio.NET 7.0"
13           name="GENERATOR">
14        <meta content="Visual Basic 7.0" name="CODE_LANGUAGE">
15        <meta content="JavaScript" name="vs_defaultClientScript">
16        <meta name="vs_targetSchema"
17           content="http://schemas.microsoft.com/intellisense/ie5">
18     </HEAD>
19     <body MS_POSITIONING="GridLayout">
20        <form id="Form1" method="post" runat="server">
21
22           <asp:label id="recommendationsLabel"
23              style="Z-INDEX: 101; LEFT: 55px; POSITION:
24              absolute; TOP: 38px" runat="server"
25              Font-Size="X-Large">Recommendations
26           </asp:label>
27
28           <asp:listbox id="booksListBox" style="Z-INDEX: 102;
29              LEFT: 50px; POSITION: absolute; TOP: 80px"
30              runat="server" Width="442px" Height="125px">
31           </asp:listbox>
32
33        </form>
34     </body>
35  </HTML>
```

Fig. 20.26 ASPX page that displays book information.

RecommendationsPage.aspx contains a label (lines 22–26) and a list box (lines 28–31). The label displays the text **Recommendations** if the user has selected one or more languages; otherwise, it displays **No Recommendations**. The list box displays the recommendations created by the code-behind file, which is shown in Fig. 20.27.

Method **Page_Init** (lines 13–43) retrieves the cookies from the client, using the **Request** object's **Cookies** property (line 22). This returns a collection of type **HttpCookieCollection**, containing cookies that have previously been written to the client. Cookies can be read by an application only if they were created in the domain in which our application is running—a Web server can never access cookies created outside the domain associated with that server. For example, a cookie created by a Web server in the **deitel.com** domain cannot be downloaded by a Web server in the **bug2bug.com** domain.

```
1    ' Fig. 20.27: RecommendationsPage.aspx.vb
2    ' Reading cookie data from the client.
3
4    Imports System.Web.UI.WebControls
5
6    Public Class Recommendations
7       Inherits Page
8       Protected WithEvents recommendationsLabel As Label
9       Protected WithEvents booksListBox As ListBox
10
11      ' Visual Studio .NET generated code
12
13      Private Sub Page_Init(ByVal sender As System.Object, _
14         ByVal e As System.EventArgs) Handles MyBase.Init
15
16         InitializeComponent()
17
18         ' retrieve client's cookies
19         Dim cookies As HttpCookieCollection
20         Dim i As Integer
21
22         cookies = Request.Cookies
23
24         ' if there are cookies besides the ID cookie,
25         ' list appropriate books and ISBN numbers
26         If (((cookies Is Nothing) = False) _
27            AndAlso cookies.Count <> 1) Then
28
29            For i = 1 To cookies.Count - 1
30               booksListBox.Items.Add(cookies(i).Name & _
31                  " How to Program. ISBN#: " & _
32                  cookies(i).Value)
33            Next
34
35            ' if no cookies besides ID, no options were
36            ' chosen. no recommendations made
```

Fig. 20.27 Cookies being read from a client in an ASP .NET application (part 1 of 2).

```
37          Else
38              recommendationsLabel.Text = "No Recommendations"
39              booksListBox.Items.Clear()
40              booksListBox.Visible = False
41          End If
42
43      End Sub ' Page_Init
44
45      Private Sub Page_Load(ByVal sender As System.Object, _
46          ByVal e As System.EventArgs) Handles MyBase.Load
47
48          ' Put user code to initialize the page here
49      End Sub ' Page_Load
50  End Class ' Recommendations
```

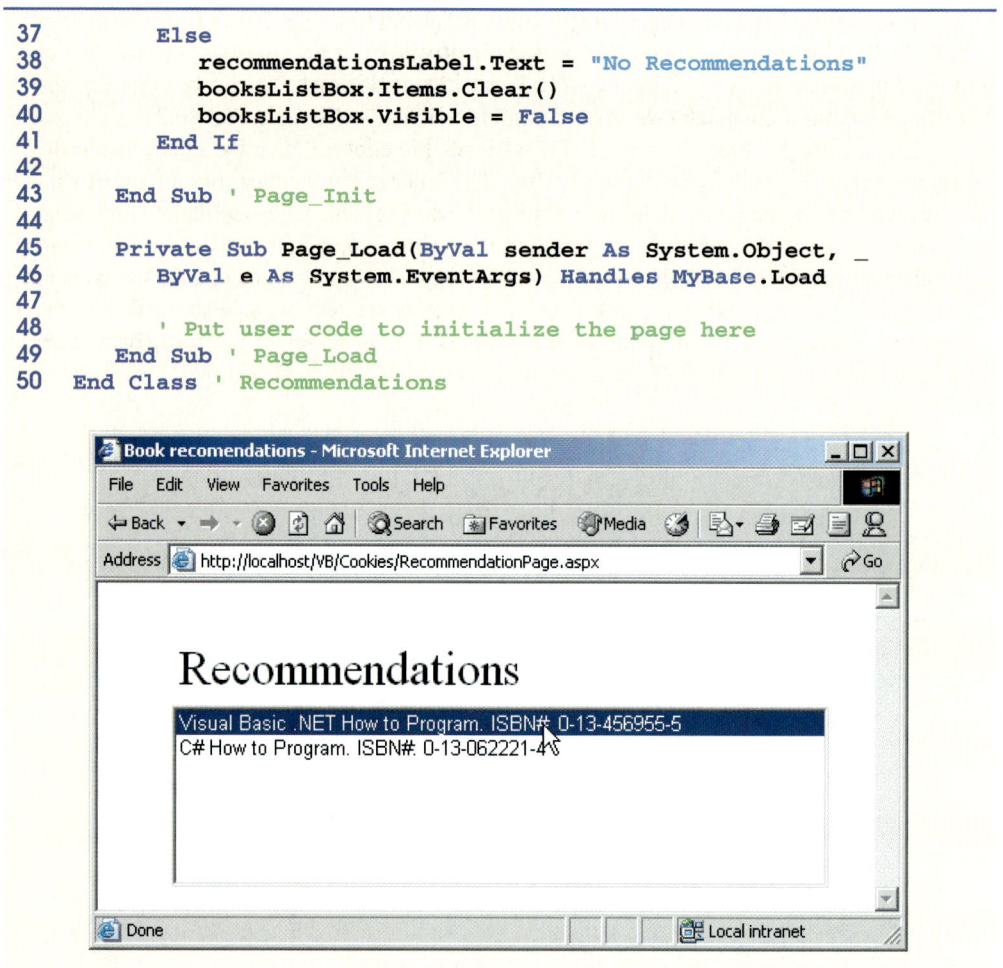

Fig. 20.27 Cookies being read from a client in an ASP .NET application (part 2 of 2).

Lines 26–27 determines whether at least two cookies exist. ASP .NET always adds a cookie named **ASP.NET_SessionId** to the response, so lines 26–27 ensure that there is at least one cookie besides the **ASP.NET_SessionId** cookie. Lines 29–33 add the information in the other cookie(s) to our list box. The **For** structure iterates through all the cookies except for the first one, the **ASP.NET_SessionID** cookie. The application retrieves the name and value of each cookie by using **i**, the control variable in our **For** structure, to determine the current value in our cookie collection. The **Name** and **Value** properties of class **HttpCookie** contain the language and corresponding ISBN, respectively, are concatenated with **" How to Program. ISBN# "** and added to the **ListBox**. The list box displays a maximum of five books. Lines 38–40 execute if no language was selected. We summarize some commonly used **HttpCookie** properties in Fig. 20.28.

Properties	Description
`Domain`	Returns a `String` containing the cookie's domain (i.e., the domain of the Web server from which the cookie was downloaded). This determines which Web servers can receive the cookie. By default, cookies are sent to the Web server that originally sent the cookie to the client.
`Expires`	Returns a `DateTime` object indicating when the browser can delete the cookie.
`Name`	Returns a `String` containing the cookie's name.
`Path`	Returns a `String` containing the URL prefix for the cookie. Cookies can be "targeted" to specific URLs that include directories on the Web server, enabling the programmer to specify the location of the cookie. By default, a cookie is returned to services operating in the same directory as the service that sent the cookie or a subdirectory of that directory.
`Secure`	Returns a `Boolean` value indicating whether the cookie should be transmitted through a secure protocol. The value `True` causes a secure protocol to be used.
`Value`	Returns a `String` containing the cookie's value.

Fig. 20.28 `HttpCookie` properties.

20.6.2 Session Tracking with `HttpSessionState`

Visual Basic provides session-tracking capabilities in the Framework Class Library's `HttpSessionState` class. To demonstrate basic session-tracking techniques, we modified Fig. 20.27 so that it employs `HttpSessionState` objects. Figure 20.29 presents the ASPX file, and Fig. 20.30 presents the code-behind file. The ASPX file is similar to that presented in Fig. 20.24.

```
1   <%-- Fig. 20.29: OptionsPage.aspx    --%>
2   <%-- displays a list of book options --%>
3
4   <%@ Page Language="vb" AutoEventWireup="false"
5      Codebehind="OptionsPage.aspx.vb"
6      Inherits="Sessions.Options2"%>
7
8   <!DOCTYPE HTML PUBLIC "-//W3C//DTD HTML 4.0 Transitional//EN">
9   <HTML>
10     <HEAD>
11        <title>Session Tracking</title>
12        <meta name="GENERATOR"
13           content="Microsoft Visual Studio.NET 7.0">
14        <meta name="CODE_LANGUAGE" content="Visual Basic 7.0">
15        <meta name="vs_defaultClientScript" content="JavaScript">
16        <meta name="vs_targetSchema"
17           content="http://schemas.microsoft.com/intellisense/ie5">
18     </HEAD>
```

Fig. 20.29 Options supplied on an ASPX page (part 1 of 3).

```
19      <body MS_POSITIONING="GridLayout">
20         <form id="Form1" method="post" runat="server">
21
22            <asp:label id="promptLabel" style="Z-INDEX: 106;
23               LEFT: 43px; POSITION: absolute; TOP: 32px"
24               runat="server" Font-Bold="True" Font-Size="Large">
25               Select a programming language.
26            </asp:label>
27
28            <asp:Label id="timeOutLabel" style="Z-INDEX: 108;
29               LEFT: 42px; POSITION: absolute; TOP: 100px"
30               runat="server">
31            </asp:Label>
32
33            <asp:Label id="idLabel" style="Z-INDEX: 107;
34               LEFT: 42px; POSITION: absolute; TOP: 66px"
35               runat="server">
36            </asp:Label>
37
38         <asp:radiobuttonlist id="LanguageList" style="Z-INDEX: 105;
39            LEFT: 43px; POSITION: absolute; TOP: 69px" runat="server">
40
41            <asp:ListItem Value="Visual Basic .NET"
42               Selected="True">Visual Basic .NET</asp:ListItem>
43
44            <asp:ListItem Value="C#">C#</asp:ListItem>
45            <asp:ListItem Value="C">C</asp:ListItem>
46            <asp:ListItem Value="C++">C++</asp:ListItem>
47            <asp:ListItem Value="Python">Python</asp:ListItem>
48         </asp:radiobuttonlist>
49
50         <asp:hyperlink id="recommendationsLink" style="Z-INDEX: 104;
51            LEFT: 42px; POSITION: absolute; TOP: 172px"
52            runat="server" NavigateUrl="RecommendationPage.aspx"
53            Visible="False">
54            Click here to get book recommendations
55         </asp:hyperlink>
56
57         <asp:hyperlink id="languageLink" style="Z-INDEX: 103;
58            LEFT: 42px; POSITION: absolute; TOP: 137px"
59            runat="server" NavigateUrl="OptionsPage.aspx"
60            Visible="False">
61            Click here to choose another language
62         </asp:hyperlink>
63
64            <asp:label id="welcomeLabel" style="Z-INDEX: 102;
65               LEFT: 42px; POSITION: absolute; TOP: 32px"
66               runat="server" Visible="False" Font-Bold="True"
67               Font-Size="Large">Welcome to sessions! You selected
68            </asp:label>
69
```

Fig. 20.29 Options supplied on an ASPX page (part 2 of 3).

```
70              <asp:button id="submitButton" style="Z-INDEX: 101;
71                 LEFT: 42px; POSITION: absolute; TOP: 207px"
72                 runat="server" Text="Submit">
73              </asp:button>
74
75          </form>
76      </body>
77  </HTML>
```

Fig. 20.29 Options supplied on an ASPX page (part 3 of 3).

Every Web Form includes an **HttpSessionState** object, which is accessible through property **Session** of class **Page**. Throughout this section, we use property **Session** to manipulate our page's **HttpSessionState** object. When the Web page is requested, an **HttpSessionState** object is created and assigned to the **Page**'s **Session** property. As a result, we often refer to property **Session** as the **Session** object. When the user presses **Submit**, **submitButton_Click** is invoked in the code-behind file (Fig. 20.30). Method **submitButton_Click** responds by adding a key-value pair to our **Session** object, specifying the language chosen and the ISBN number for a book on that language. These key-value pairs are often referred to as *session items*. Next, a postback occurs. Each time the user clicks **Submit**, **submitButton_Click** adds a new session item to the **HttpSessionState** object. Because much of this example is identical to the last example, we concentrate on the new features.

```
1   ' Fig. 20.30: OptionsPage.aspx.vb
2   ' A listing of programming languages,
3   ' cookie is created based on choice made.
4
5   Imports System.Web.UI.WebControls
6
7   Public Class Options2
8       Inherits System.Web.UI.Page
9       Protected WithEvents languageLink As HyperLink
10      Protected WithEvents recommendationsLink As HyperLink
11      Protected WithEvents LanguageList As RadioButtonList
12      Protected WithEvents idLabel As Label
13      Protected WithEvents timeOutLabel As Label
14      Protected WithEvents promptLabel As Label
15      Protected WithEvents welcomeLabel As Label
16      Protected WithEvents submitButton As Button
17      Private books = New Hashtable()
18
19      ' Visual Studio .NET generated code
20
21      Private Sub Page_Init(ByVal sender As System.Object, _
22         ByVal e As System.EventArgs) Handles MyBase.Init
23
24         InitializeComponent()
25
```

Fig. 20.30 Sessions are created for each user in an ASP .NET Web application (part 1 of 4).

```vb
26            ' add values to Hastable
27            books.Add("Visual Basic .NET", "0-13-456955-5")
28            books.Add("C#", "0-13-062221-4")
29            books.Add("C", "0-13-089572-5")
30            books.Add("C++", "0-13-089571-7")
31            books.Add("Python", "0-13-092361-3")
32         End Sub ' Page_Init
33
34         Private Sub Page_Load(ByVal sender As System.Object, _
35            ByVal e As System.EventArgs) Handles MyBase.Load
36
37            If IsPostBack Then
38
39               ' if postback is True, user has submitted information
40               ' display welcome message and appropriate hyperlinks
41               welcomeLabel.Visible = True
42               languageLink.Visible = True
43               recommendationsLink.Visible = True
44
45               ' hide option information
46               submitButton.Visible = False
47               promptLabel.Visible = False
48               LanguageList.Visible = False
49
50               If (LanguageList.SelectedItem Is Nothing) = False Then
51                  welcomeLabel.Text &= " " & _
52                     LanguageList.SelectedItem.Text.ToString & "."
53               Else
54                  welcomeLabel.Text &= "no language."
55               End If
56
57               idLabel.Text = "Your unique session ID is: " & _
58                  Session.SessionID
59
60               timeOutLabel.Text = "Timeout: " & Session.Timeout & _
61                  " minutes."
62
63            End If
64
65         End Sub ' Page_Load
66
67         Private Sub submitButton_Click(ByVal sender As System.Object, _
68            ByVal e As System.EventArgs) Handles submitButton.Click
69
70            Dim language, ISBN As String
71
72            ' if choice was made by user
73            If (LanguageList.SelectedItem Is Nothing) = False Then
74               language = LanguageList.SelectedItem.ToString()
75               ISBN = books(language).ToString()
76
```

Fig. 20.30 Sessions are created for each user in an ASP .NET Web application (part 2 of 4).

```
77                ' add name/value pair to Session
78            Session.Add(language, ISBN)
79        End If
80
81    End Sub ' submitButton_Click
82 End Class ' Options2
```

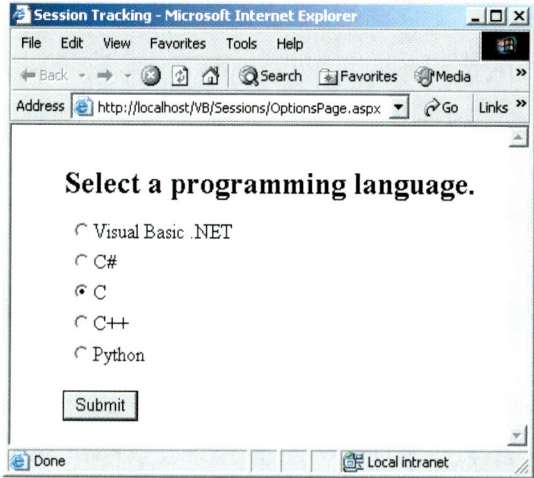

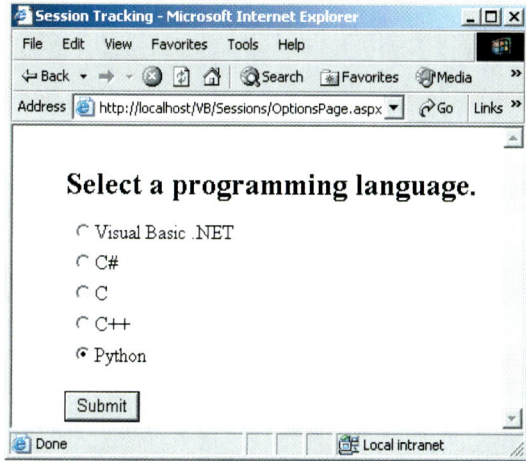

Fig. 20.30 Sessions are created for each user in an ASP .NET Web application (part 3 of 4).

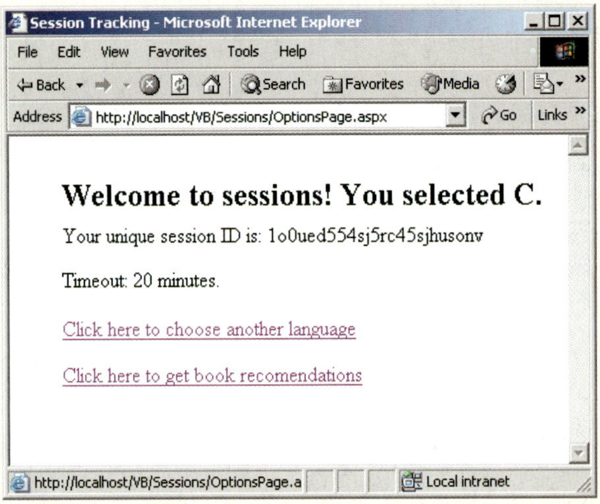

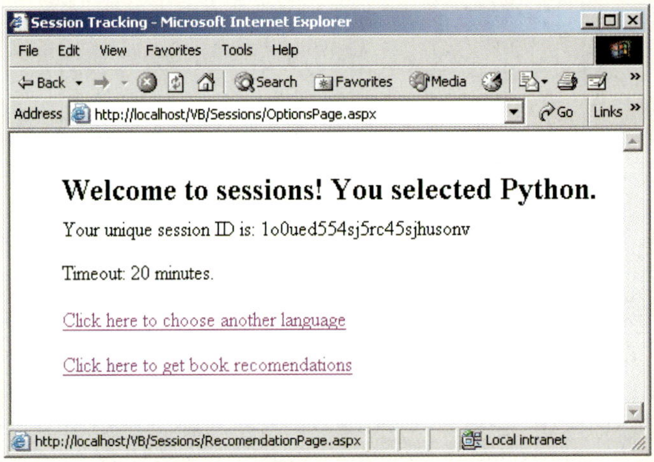

Fig. 20.30 Sessions are created for each user in an ASP .NET Web application (part 4 of 4).

> **Software Engineering Observation 20.1**
>
> *A Web Form should not use instance variables to maintain client state information, because clients accessing that Web Form in parallel might overwrite the shared instance variables. Web Forms should maintain client state information in **HttpSessionState** objects, because such objects are specific to each client.*

Like a cookie, an **HttpSessionState** object can store name-value pairs. These session items are placed into an **HttpSessionState** object by calling method **Add**. Line 78 calls **Add** to place the language and its corresponding recommended book's ISBN number into the **HttpSessionState** object. One of the primary benefits of using **HttpSessionState** objects (rather than cookies) is that **HttpSessionState** objects can store any type of object (not just **String**s) as attribute values. This provides Visual Basic programmers with increased flexibility in determining the type of state information they wish to maintain for their clients. If the application calls method **Add** to add an attribute that has the same name as an attribute previously stored in a session, the object associated with that attribute is replaced.

After the values are added to the **HttpSessionState** object, the application handles the postback event (lines 37–63) in method **Page_Load**. Here, we retrieve information about the current client's session from the **Session** object's properties and display this information in the Web page. The ASP .NET application contains information about the **HttpSessionState** object for the current client. Property ***SessionID*** (lines 57–58) contains the *session's unique ID*. The first time a client connects to the Web server, a unique session ID is created for that client. When the client makes additional requests, the client's session ID is compared with the session IDs stored in the Web server's memory. Property ***Timeout*** (line 60) specifies the maximum amount of time that an **HttpSessionState** object can be inactive before it is discarded. Figure 20.31 lists some common **HttpSessionState** properties.

As in the cookies example, this application provides a link to **RecommendationsPage.aspx** (Fig. 20.32), which displays a list of book recommendations that is based on the user's language selections. Lines 28–31 define a **ListBox** Web control that is used to present the recommendations to the user. Figure 20.33 presents the code-behind file for this ASPX file.

Properties	Description
`Count`	Specifies the number of key-value pairs in the **Session** object.
`IsNewSession`	Indicates whether this is a new session (i.e., whether the session was created during loading of this page).
`IsReadOnly`	Indicates whether the **Session** object is read only.
`Keys`	Returns a collection containing the **Session** object's keys.
`SessionID`	Returns the session's unique ID.
`Timeout`	Specifies the maximum number of minutes during which a session can be inactive (i.e., no requests are made) before the session expires. By default, this property is set to 20 minutes.

Fig. 20.31 `HttpSessionState` properties.

```
1   <%-- Fig. 20.32: RecommendationPage.aspx            --%>
2   <%-- Displays book recommendations based on session --%>
3   <%-- information       .                            --%>
4
5   <%@ Page Language="vb" AutoEventWireup="false"
6      Codebehind="RecommendationPage.aspx.vb"
7      Inherits="Sessions.Recommendations" %>
8
9   <!DOCTYPE HTML PUBLIC "-//W3C//DTD HTML 4.0 Transitional//EN">
```

Fig. 20.32 Session information displayed in a `ListBox` (part 1 of 2).

```
10    <HTML>
11       <HEAD>
12          <meta content="Microsoft Visual Studio.NET 7.0"
13             name="GENERATOR">
14          <meta content="Visual Basic 7.0" name="CODE_LANGUAGE">
15          <meta content="JavaScript" name="vs_defaultClientScript">
16          <meta name="vs_targetSchema"
17             content="http://schemas.microsoft.com/intellisense/ie5">
18       </HEAD>
19       <body MS_POSITIONING="GridLayout">
20          <form id="Form1" method="post" runat="server">
21
22             <asp:label id="recommendationLabel"
23                style="Z-INDEX: 101; LEFT: 55px;
24                POSITION: absolute; TOP: 38px" runat="server"
25                Font-Size="X-Large">Recommendations
26             </asp:label>
27
28             <asp:listbox id="booksListBox" style="Z-INDEX: 102;
29                LEFT: 50px; POSITION: absolute; TOP: 80px"
30                runat="server" Width="442px" Height="125px">
31             </asp:listbox>
32
33          </form>
34       </body>
35    </HTML>
```

Fig. 20.32 Session information displayed in a **ListBox** (part 2 of 2).

```
1     ' Fig. 20.33: RecommendationPage.aspx.vb
2     ' Reading cookie data from the client
3
4     Imports System.Web.UI.WebControls
5
6     Public Class Recommendations
7        Inherits Page
8        Protected WithEvents recommendationLabel As Label
9        Protected WithEvents booksListBox As ListBox
10
11       ' Visual Studio .NET generated code
12
13       Private Sub Page_Init(ByVal sender As System.Object, _
14          ByVal e As System.EventArgs) Handles MyBase.Init
15
16          InitializeComponent()
17
18          Dim i As Integer
19          Dim keyName As String
20
```

Fig. 20.33 Session data read by an ASP .NET Web application to provide recommendations for the user (part 1 of 2).

```
21         ' determine if Session contains information
22         If Session.Count <> 0 Then
23
24            ' iterate through Session values,
25            ' display in ListBox
26            For i = 0 To Session.Count - 1
27
28               ' store current key in sessionName
29               keyName = Session.Keys(i)
30
31               ' use current key to display
32               ' Session's name/value pairs
33               booksListBox.Items.Add(keyName & _
34                  " How to Program. ISBN#: " & _
35                  Session(keyName))
36            Next
37         Else
38            recommendationLabel.Text = "No Recommendations"
39            booksListBox.Visible = False
40         End If
41      End Sub ' Page_Init
42
43      Private Sub Page_Load(ByVal sender As System.Object, _
44         ByVal e As System.EventArgs) Handles MyBase.Load
45
46         ' Put user code to initialize the page here
47      End Sub ' Page_Load
48   End Class ' Recommendations
```

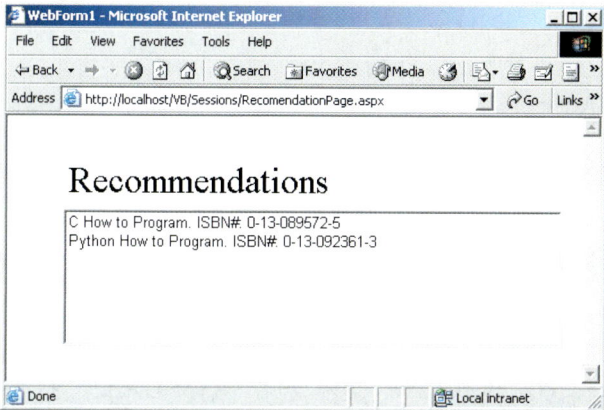

Fig. 20.33 Session data read by an ASP .NET Web application to provide recommendations for the user (part 2 of 2).

Event handler **Page_Init** (lines 13–41) retrieves the session information. If a user has not selected any language during any visit to this site, our **Session** object's **Count** property will be zero. This property provides the number of session items contained in a **Session** object. If **Session** object's **Count** property is zero (i.e., no language was ever selected) then we display the text **No Recommendations**.

If the user has chosen a language, the **For** structure (lines 26–36) iterates through our **Session** object's session items (line 29). The value in a key-value pair is retrieved from the **Session** object by indexing the **Session** object with the key name, using the same process by which we retrieved a value from our hash table in the last section.

We then access the **Keys** property of class **HttpSessionState** (line 29), which returns a collection containing all the keys inthe session. Line 29 indexes our collection to retrieve the current key. Lines 33–35 concatenate **keyName**'s value to the **String " How to Program. ISBN#: "** and to the value from the session object for which **keyName** is the key. This **String** is the recommendation that appears in the **ListBox**.

20.7 Case Study: Online Guest book

Many Web sites allow users to provide feedback about the Web site in a *guest book*. Typically, users click a link on the Web site's home page to request the guest-book page. This page usually consists of an HTML **form** that contains fields for the user's name, e-mail address, message/feedback and so on. Data submitted on the guest-book **form** often are stored in a database located on the Web server's machine. In this section, we create a guest-book Web Form application. The GUI is slightly more complex, containing a **DataGrid**, as shown in Fig. 20.34.

The HTML **form** presented to the user consists of a user-name field, an e-mail address field and a message field. Figure 20.35 presents the ASPX file and Fig. 20.36 presents the code–behind file for the guest-book application. For the sake of simplicity, we write the guest-book information to a text file. However, in the exercises, we ask the reader to modify this example so that the application stores the guest-book information in a database.

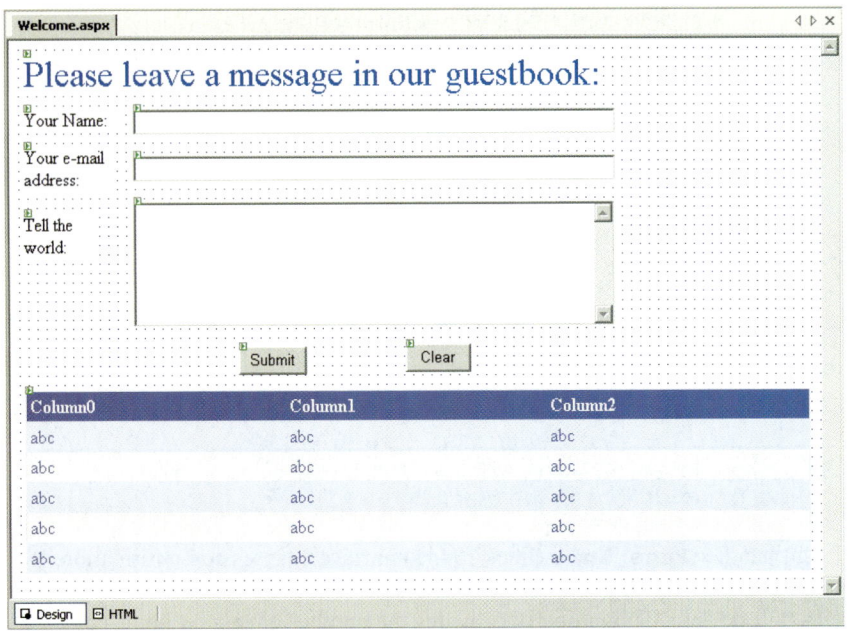

Fig. 20.34 Guest-book application GUI.

```
1   <%-- Fig. 20.35: GuestbookPage.aspx                   --%>
2   <%-- Controls and layout for guestbook application. --%>
3
4   <%@ Page Language="vb" AutoEventWireup="false"
5      Codebehind="GuestbookPage.aspx.vb"
6      Inherits="Guestbook.Guestbook"%>
7
8   <!DOCTYPE HTML PUBLIC "-//W3C//DTD HTML 4.0 Transitional//EN">
9   <HTML>
10     <HEAD>
11        <title>GuestBook</title>
12        <meta content="Microsoft Visual Studio.NET 7.0"
13           name="GENERATOR">
14        <meta content="Visual Basic 7.0" name="CODE_LANGUAGE">
15        <meta content="JavaScript" name="vs_defaultClientScript">
16        <meta content=
17           "http://schemas.microsoft.com/intellisense/ie5"
18           name="vs_targetSchema">
19     </HEAD>
20     <body MS_POSITIONING="GridLayout">
21        <form id="Form1" method="post" runat="server">
22
23           <asp:Label id="promptLabel" style="Z-INDEX: 101;
24              LEFT: 39px; POSITION: absolute; TOP: 20px"
25              runat="server" Font-Size="X-Large"
26              ForeColor="Blue">
27              Please leave a message in our guestbook:
28           </asp:Label>
29
30           <asp:Button id="clearButton" style="Z-INDEX: 110;
31              LEFT: 383px; POSITION: absolute; TOP: 318px"
32              runat="server" Width="56px" Text="Clear">
33           </asp:Button>
34
35           <asp:Button id="submitButton" style="Z-INDEX: 109;
36              LEFT: 187px; POSITION: absolute; TOP: 319px"
37              runat="server" Text="Submit">
38           </asp:Button>
39
40           <asp:DataGrid id="DataGrid1" style="Z-INDEX: 108;
41              LEFT: 39px; POSITION: absolute; TOP: 372px"
42              runat="server" Width="541px" Height="95px"
43              HorizontalAlign="Left" BorderColor="#E7E7FF"
44              BorderWidth="1px" GridLines="None" CellPadding="3"
45              PageSize="5">
46
47              <SelectedItemStyle ForeColor="#F7F7F7"
48                 BackColor="#738A9C">
49              </SelectedItemStyle>
50              <AlternatingItemStyle BackColor="#F7F7F7">
51              </AlternatingItemStyle>
```

Fig. 20.35 ASPX file for the guest-book application (part 1 of 2).

```
52              <ItemStyle HorizontalAlign="Left" Width="100px"
53                 ForeColor="#4A3C8C" BackColor="#E7E7FF">
54              </ItemStyle>
55              <HeaderStyle ForeColor="#F7F7F7"
56                 BackColor="#4A3C8C">
57              </HeaderStyle>
58              <FooterStyle ForeColor="#4A3C8C"
59                 BorderColor="#B5C7DE">
60              </FooterStyle>
61              <PagerStyle HorizontalAlign="Right"
62                 ForeColor="#4A3C8C" BackColor="#E7E7FF"
63                 Mode="NumericPages">
64              </PagerStyle>
65           </asp:DataGrid>
66
67           <asp:TextBox id="messageTextBox" style="Z-INDEX: 107;
68              LEFT: 135px; POSITION: absolute; TOP: 181px"
69              runat="server" Width="449px" Height="113px"
70              TextMode="MultiLine">
71           </asp:TextBox>
72
73           <asp:TextBox id="emailTextBox" style="Z-INDEX: 106;
74              LEFT: 135px; POSITION: absolute; TOP: 132px"
75              runat="server" Width="449px">
76           </asp:TextBox>
77
78           <asp:TextBox id="nameTextBox" style="Z-INDEX: 105;
79              LEFT: 135px; POSITION: absolute; TOP: 85px"
80              runat="server" Width="449px">
81           </asp:TextBox>
82
83           <asp:Label id="messageLabel" style="Z-INDEX: 104;
84              LEFT: 39px; POSITION: absolute; TOP: 167px"
85              runat="server" Width="51px">Tell the world:
86           </asp:Label>
87
88           <asp:Label id="emailLabel" style="Z-INDEX: 103;
89              LEFT: 39px; POSITION: absolute; TOP: 118px"
90              runat="server" Width="69px">Your email address:
91           </asp:Label>
92
93           <asp:Label id="nameLabel" style="Z-INDEX: 102;
94              LEFT: 39px; POSITION: absolute; TOP: 90px"
95              runat="server">Your name:
96           </asp:Label>
97
98        </form>
99     </body>
100 </HTML>
```

Fig. 20.35 ASPX file for the guest-book application (part 2 of 2).

The ASPX file generated by the GUI is shown in Fig. 20.35. After dragging the two buttons onto the form, double-click each button to create its corresponding event handler.

Visual Studio adds the event handlers to the code-behind file (Fig. 20.36). A **DataGrid** named **dataGrid** displays all guest-book entries. This control can be added from the **Toolbox**, just as could a button or label. The colors for the **DataGrid** are specified through the **Auto Format...** link that is located near the bottom of the **Properties** window when we are looking at the properties of our **DataGrid**. A dialog will open with several choices. In this example, we chose **Colorful 4**. We discuss adding information to this **DataGrid** shortly.

The event handler for **clearButton** (lines 35–41) clears each **TextBox** by setting its **Text** property to an empty string. Lines 84–107 contain the event-handling code for **submitButton**, which will add the user's information to **guestbook.txt**, a text file stored in our project. The various entries in this file will be displayed in the **DataGrid**, including the newest entry. Let us look at how this is done in the code.

Lines 90–92 create a **StreamWriter** that references the file containing the guest-book entries. We use the **Request** object's *PhysicalApplicationPath* property to retrieve the path of the application's root directory (this will be the path of the project folder for the current application) and then concatenate to it the file name (i.e., **guestbook.txt**). The second argument (**True**) specifies that new information will be appended to the file (i.e., added at the end). Lines 95–98 append the appropriate message to the guest-book file. Before the event handler exits, it calls method **FillMessageTable** (line 106).

```
1    ' Fig. 20.36: GuestbookPage.aspx.vb
2    ' The code-behind file for the guest book page.
3
4    Imports System.Web.UI.WebControls
5    Imports System.Data
6    Imports System.IO
7
8    ' allows users to leave message
9    Public Class Guestbook
10       Inherits System.Web.UI.Page
11
12       Protected WithEvents promptLabel As Label
13       Protected WithEvents nameLabel As Label
14       Protected WithEvents emailLabel As Label
15       Protected WithEvents messageLabel As Label
16       Protected WithEvents dataGrid As DataGrid
17       Protected WithEvents submitButton As Button
18       Protected WithEvents messageTextBox As TextBox
19       Protected WithEvents emailTextBox As TextBox
20       Protected WithEvents nameTextBox As TextBox
21       Protected WithEvents clearButton As Button
22       Protected WithEvents dataView As System.Data.DataView
23
24       ' Visual Studio .NET generated code
25
26       Private Sub Page_Load(ByVal sender As System.Object, _
27          ByVal e As System.EventArgs) Handles MyBase.Load
28
```

Fig. 20.36 Code-behind file for the guest-book application (part 1 of 4).

```vbnet
29            'Put user code to initialize the page here
30            dataView = New DataView(New DataTable())
31
32         End Sub
33
34         ' clear text boxes; user can enter new input
35         Private Sub clearButton_Click(ByVal sender As System.Object, _
36            ByVal e As System.EventArgs) Handles clearButton.Click
37
38            nameTextBox.Text = ""
39            emailTextBox.Text = ""
40            messageTextBox.Text = ""
41         End Sub ' clearButton_Click
42
43         Public Sub FillMessageTable()
44            Dim table As New DataTable()
45            Dim reader As StreamReader
46            Dim separator As Char()
47            Dim message As String
48            Dim parts As String()
49
50            table = dataView.Table
51
52            table.Columns.Add("Date")
53            table.Columns.Add("FirstName")
54            table.Columns.Add("email")
55            table.Columns.Add("Message")
56
57            ' open guestbook file for reading
58            reader = New StreamReader( _
59               Request.PhysicalApplicationPath & "guestbook.txt")
60
61            separator = New Char() {vbTab}
62
63            ' read one line from file
64            message = reader.ReadLine()
65
66            While message <> ""
67
68               ' split String into four parts
69               parts = message.Split(separator)
70
71               ' load data into table
72               table.LoadDataRow(parts, True)
73
74               ' read one line from file
75               message = reader.ReadLine()
76            End While
77
78            dataGrid.DataBind() ' update grid
79
80            reader.Close()
81         End Sub ' FillMessageTable
```

Fig. 20.36 Code-behind file for the guest-book application (part 2 of 4).

```vbnet
82
83       ' add user's entry to guestbook
84       Private Sub submitButton_Click(ByVal sender As System.Object, _
85          ByVal e As System.EventArgs) Handles submitButton.Click
86
87          Dim guestbook As StreamWriter
88
89          ' open stream for appending to file
90          guestbook = New StreamWriter( _
91             Request.PhysicalApplicationPath & _
92             "guestbook.txt", True)
93
94          ' write new message to file
95          guestbook.WriteLine( _
96             DateTime.Now.Date.ToString().Substring(0, 10) & _
97             vbTab & nameTextBox.Text & vbTab & emailTextBox.Text & _
98             vbTab & messageTextBox.Text)
99
100         ' clear textboxes and close stream
101         nameTextBox.Text = ""
102         emailTextBox.Text = ""
103         messageTextBox.Text = ""
104         guestbook.Close()
105
106         FillMessageTable()
107      End Sub ' submitButton_Click
108 End Class ' Guestbook
```

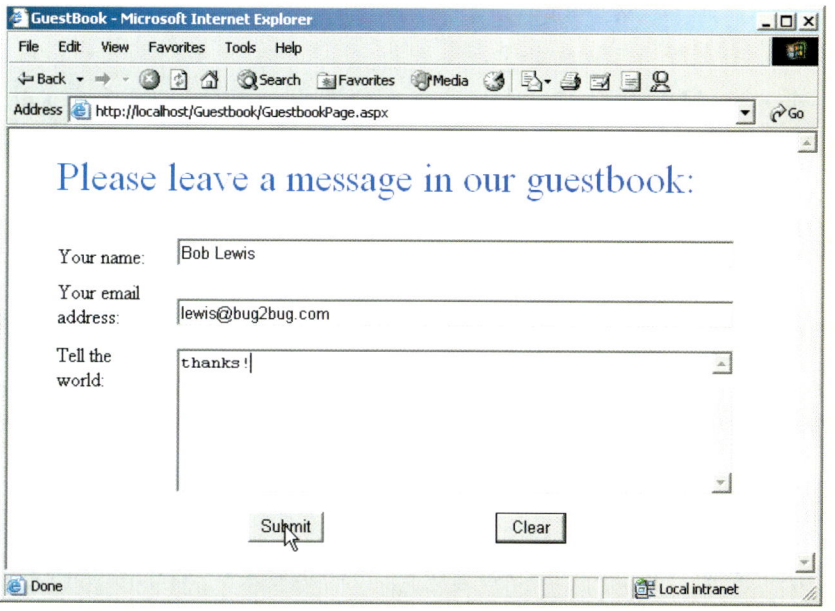

Fig. 20.36 Code-behind file for the guest-book application (part 3 of 4).

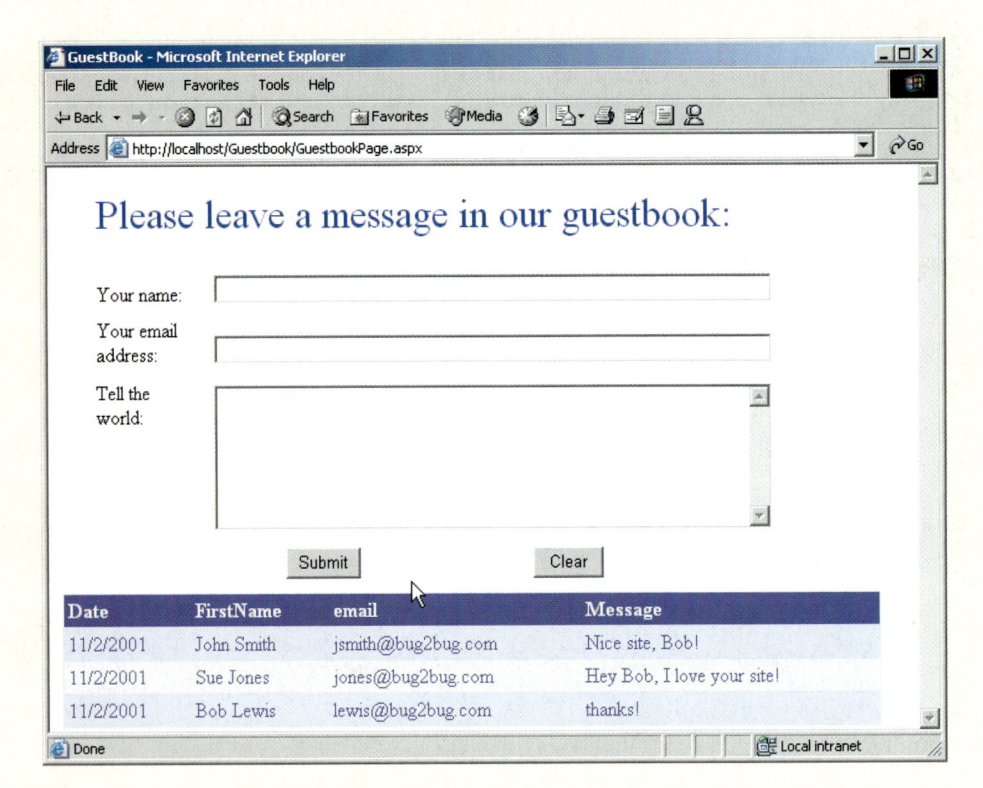

Fig. 20.36 Code-behind file for the guest-book application (part 4 of 4).

Method **FillMessageTable** (lines 43–81) places the guest-book entries in **DataTable table**. Lines 50–55 create a **DataTable** object from our **DataView**'s **Table** property and then form the necessary columns, using the **Columns** collection's **Add** method. Lines 66–76 read each line in the text file. Method **Split** breaks each line read from the file into four tokens, which are added to the **table** by calling method **LoadDataRow** (line 72). The second argument to method **LoadDataRow** is **True**, indicating that any changes resulting from the addition will be accepted. The **DataTable** places one piece of data in each column. After the **DataTable** is populated, the data are bound to the **DataGrid**. Method **DataBind** is called to refresh the **DataView**. [*Note*: **DataView dataView** was assigned to the **DataSource** property of the **DataGrid** in the Web Form designer, after it was declared in the code.]

20.8 Case Study: Connecting to a Database in ASP .NET

This case study presents a Web-based application in which a user can view a list of publications by an author. This program consists of two Web Forms. The first page that a user requests is **Login.aspx** (Fig. 20.37). After accessing this page, users select their names from the drop-down list and then enter their passwords. If their passwords are valid, they are redirected to **Authors.aspx** (Fig. 20.40), which provides a list of authors. When the user chooses an author and clicks the **Select** button, a postback occurs, and the updated page displays a table containing the titles, ISBNs and publishers of books by the selected author.

Much of the information provided by this Web page is accessed through databases stored in our project. **Login.aspx** retrieves valid user names for this site through **Login.mdb**, and all the author information is retrieved from the **Books.mdb** database. The reader can view these databases by opening the **Database** project for this chapter.

```
1    <%-- Fig. 20.37: login.aspx                        --%>
2    <%-- Controls and formatting for login page. --%>
3
4    <%@ Register TagPrefix="Header" TagName="ImageHeader"
5       Src="ImageHeader.ascx" %>
6
7    <%@ Page Language="vb" AutoEventWireup="false"
8       Codebehind="login.aspx.vb"
9       Inherits="Database.Login"%>
10
11   <!DOCTYPE HTML PUBLIC "-//W3C//DTD HTML 4.0 Transitional//EN">
12   <HTML>
13      <HEAD>
14         <title></title>
15         <meta content="Microsoft Visual Studio.NET 7.0"
16            name="GENERATOR">
17         <meta content="Visual Basic 7.0" name="CODE_LANGUAGE">
18         <meta content="JavaScript" name="vs_defaultClientScript">
19         <meta name="vs_targetSchema"
20            content="http://schemas.microsoft.com/intellisense/ie5">
21      </HEAD>
22      <body bgColor="#ffebff" MS_POSITIONING="GridLayout">
23         <form id="Form1" method="post" runat="server">
24
25            <asp:label id="promptLabel" style="Z-INDEX: 108;
26               LEFT: 20px; POSITION: absolute; TOP: 144px"
27               runat="server">Please select your name and enter
28                  your password to log in:
29            </asp:label>
30
31            <asp:label id="nameLabel" style="Z-INDEX: 101;
32               LEFT: 15px; POSITION: absolute; TOP: 188px"
33               runat="server">Name
34            </asp:label>
35
36            <asp:dropdownlist id="nameList" style="Z-INDEX: 105;
37               LEFT: 92px; POSITION: absolute; TOP: 185px"
38               runat="server" Width="154px">
39            </asp:dropdownlist>
40
41            <asp:label id="passwordLabel" style="Z-INDEX: 102;
42               LEFT: 15px; POSITION: absolute; TOP: 220px"
43               runat="server">Password
44            </asp:label>
45
```

Fig. 20.37 Login Web Form (part 1 of 2).

```
46              <asp:textbox id="passwordTextBox" style="Z-INDEX: 103;
47                 LEFT: 92px; POSITION: absolute; TOP: 221px"
48                 runat="server" TextMode="Password">
49              </asp:textbox>
50
51              <asp:customvalidator id="invalidPasswordValidator"
52                 style="Z-INDEX: 107; LEFT: 262px; POSITION:
53                 absolute; TOP: 221px" runat="server"
54                 ControlToValidate="passwordTextBox" Font-Bold="True"
55                 ForeColor="DarkCyan" ErrorMessage="Invalid password!">
56              </asp:customvalidator>
57
58              <asp:requiredfieldvalidator id=
59                 "requiredPasswordValidator" style="Z-INDEX: 106;
60                 LEFT: 262px; POSITION: absolute; TOP: 221px"
61                 runat="server" ControlToValidate="passwordTextBox"
62                 Font-Bold="True" ForeColor="DarkCyan"
63                 ErrorMessage="Please enter a password!">
64              </asp:requiredfieldvalidator>
65
66              <asp:button id="submitButton" style="Z-INDEX: 104;
67                 LEFT: 92px; POSITION: absolute; TOP: 263px"
68                 runat="server" Text="Submit">
69              </asp:button>
70
71              <Header:ImageHeader id="ImageHeader1" runat="server">
72              </Header:ImageHeader>
73
74          </form>
75       </body>
76    </HTML>
```

Fig. 20.37 Login Web Form (part 2 of 2).

Lines 4–5 add one *Web user control* to the ASPX file. Readers might recall that we covered the definition of user controls for Windows applications in Chapter 13, Graphical User Interface: Part 2; we can define user controls for Web Forms by a similar technique. Because the ASPX files that users request do not define user controls for Web Forms, such controls do not have **HTML** or **BODY** elements. Rather, programmers specify these controls via the *<%@ Register...%>* directive. For example, a programmer might want to include a *navigation bar* (i.e., a series of buttons for navigating a Web site) on every page of a site. If the site encompasses a large number of pages, the addition of markup to create the navigation bar for each page can be time consuming. Moreover, if the programmer subsequently modifies the navigation bar, every page on the site that uses it must be updated. By creating a user control, the programmer can specify where on each page the navigation bar is placed with only a few lines of markup. If the navigation bar changes, the pages that use it are updated the next time the page is requested.

Like Web Forms, most Web user controls consist of two pages: An *ASCX file* and a code-behind file. Lines 4–5 define the user control's *tag name* (the name of this instance of the control) and tag prefix, which are **ImageHeader** and **Header**, respectively. The **ImageHeader** element is added to the file in lines 71–72. The tag definition is located in the **Src** file `HeaderImage.ascx` (Fig. 20.38). The programmer can create this file by right clicking the project name in the **Solution Explorer** and selecting **Add > Add New Item...**. From the dialog that opens, select **Web User Control**, and a new ASCX file will be added to the solution. At this point, the programmer can add items to this file as if it were an ASPX document, defining any functionality in the Web user control's code-behind file. After creating the user control, the programmer can drag it from the **Solution Explorer** directly onto an open ASPX file. An instance of the control then will be created and added to the Web Form.

The form (Fig. 20.37) includes several **Label**s, a **TextBox** (`passwordTextbox`) and a **DropDownList** (`nameList`), which is populated in the code-behind file, `Login.aspx.vb` (Fig. 20.39), with user names retrieved from a database. We also include two validators: A `RequiredFieldValidator`, and a *CustomValidator*. A `CustomValidator` allows us to specify the circumstances under which a field is valid. We define these circumstances in the event handler for the *ServerValidate* event of the `CustomValidator`. The event-handling code is placed in the code-behind file for `Login.aspx.vb` and is discussed shortly. Both validators' `ControlToValidate` properties are set to `passwordTextbox`.

```
1   <%-- Fig. 20.38: ImageHeader.ascx         --%>
2   <%-- Listing for the header user control. --%>
3
4   <%@ Control Language="vb" AutoEventWireup="false"
5       Codebehind="ImageHeader.ascx.vb"
6       Inherits="Database.ImageHeader"
7       TargetSchema="http://schemas.microsoft.com/intellisense/ie5" %>
8
9   <asp:Image id="Image1" runat="server"
10      ImageUrl="http://localhost/VB/Database/bug2bug.png">
11  </asp:Image>
```

Fig. 20.38 ASCX code for the header.

```
1   ' Fig. 20.39: Login.aspx.vb
2   ' The code-behind file for the page that logs the user in.
3
4   Imports System
5   Imports System.Collections
6   Imports System.ComponentModel
7   Imports System.Data
8   Imports System.Data.OleDb
9   Imports System.Drawing
10  Imports System.Web
11  Imports System.Web.SessionState
12  Imports System.Web.UI
13  Imports System.Web.UI.WebControls
14  Imports System.Web.UI.HtmlControls
15  Imports System.Web.Security
16
```

Fig. 20.39 Code-behind file for the login page for authors application (part 1 of 5).

```vbnet
17   Public Class Login
18      Inherits System.Web.UI.Page
19
20      Protected WithEvents requiredPasswordValidator As _
21      RequiredFieldValidator
22
23      Protected WithEvents invalidPasswordValidator As _
24         CustomValidator
25
26      Protected WithEvents submitButton As Button
27      Protected WithEvents passwordTextBox As TextBox
28      Protected WithEvents passwordLabel As Label
29      Protected WithEvents nameList As DropDownList
30      Protected WithEvents nameLabel As Label
31      Protected WithEvents OleDbDataAdapter1 As OleDbDataAdapter
32      Protected WithEvents OleDbSelectCommand1 As OleDbCommand
33      Protected WithEvents OleDbInsertCommand1 As OleDbCommand
34      Protected WithEvents OleDbUpdateCommand1 As OleDbCommand
35      Protected WithEvents OleDbDeleteCommand1 As OleDbCommand
36      Protected WithEvents OleDbConnection1 As OleDbConnection
37      Protected WithEvents promptLabel As Label
38      Protected dataReader As OleDbDataReader
39
40      ' Visual Studio .NET generated code
41
42      Private Sub Page_Init(ByVal sender As System.Object, _
43         ByVal e As System.EventArgs) Handles MyBase.Init
44
45         InitializeComponent()
46
47         ' if page loads due to postback, process information
48         ' otherwise, page is loading for first time, so
49         ' do nothing
50         If Not IsPostBack Then
51
52            ' open database and read data
53            Try
54               ' open database connection
55               OleDbConnection1.Open()
56
57               ' execute query
58               dataReader = _
59                  OleDbDataAdapter1.SelectCommand.ExecuteReader()
60
61               ' while we can read row from query result,
62               ' add first item to drop-down list
63               While (dataReader.Read())
64                  nameList.Items.Add(dataReader.GetString(0))
65               End While
66
67            ' catch error if database cannot be opened
68            Catch exception As OleDbException
69               Response.Write("Unable to open database!")
```

Fig. 20.39 Code-behind file for the login page for authors application (part 2 of 5).

```vbnet
70
71               ' close database
72               Finally
73                  ' close database connection
74                  OleDbConnection1.Close()
75               End Try
76           End If
77       End Sub ' Page_Init
78
79       ' validate user name and password
80       Private Sub invalidPasswordValidator_ServerValidate( _
81          ByVal source As Object, _
82          ByVal args As ServerValidateEventArgs) _
83          Handles invalidPasswordValidator.ServerValidate
84
85           ' open database and check password
86           Try
87              ' open database connection
88              OleDbConnection1.Open()
89
90              ' set select command to find password of username
91              ' from drop-down list
92              OleDbDataAdapter1.SelectCommand.CommandText = _
93                 "SELECT * FROM Users WHERE loginID = '" & _
94                 Request.Form("nameList").ToString() & "'"
95
96              dataReader = _
97                 OleDbDataAdapter1.SelectCommand.ExecuteReader()
98
99              dataReader.Read()
100
101             ' if password user provided is correct create
102             ' authentication ticket for user and redirect
103             ' user to Authors.aspx; otherwise set IsValid to false
104             If args.Value = dataReader.GetString(1) Then
105                FormsAuthentication.SetAuthCookie( _
106                   Request.Form("namelist"), False)
107                Session.Add("name", _
108                      Request.Form("nameList").ToString())
109                Response.Redirect("Authors.aspx")
110             Else
111                args.IsValid = False
112
113             End If
114
115          ' display error if unable to open database
116          Catch exception As OleDbException
117             Response.Write("Unable to open database!")
118
119          ' close database
120          Finally
121             ' close database connection
122             OleDbConnection1.Close()
```

Fig. 20.39 Code-behind file for the login page for authors application (part 3 of 5).

```
123         End Try
124      End Sub ' InvalidPasswordValidator_ServerValidate
125 End Class ' Login
```

Fig. 20.39 Code-behind file for the login page for authors application (part 4 of 5).

Fig. 20.39 Code-behind file for the login page for authors application (part 5 of 5).

In Fig. 20.39, the **Page_Init** event handler is defined in lines 42–77. If the page is being loaded for the first time, lines 50–76 execute. The database code is contained within a **Try/Catch/Finally** block (lines 53–74) to handle any database connectivity exceptions and to ensure that the database is closed. Lines 58–59 execute the SQL query that Visual Studio generates at design time—this query simply retrieves all the rows from the **Users** table of the **Login** database. Lines 63–65 iterate through the rows, placing the item in the first column of each row (the user name) into **nameList**.

The reader might notice that we use an *OleDbDataReader*, an object that reads data from a database. We did not use an object of this type before, because the **OleDbDataReader** is not as flexible as other readers we discussed in Chapter 19. The object can read data, but cannot update it. However, we use **OleDbDataReader** in this example because we need only read the users' names; this object provides a fast and simple way to do so.

In this example, we use a **CustomValidator** to validate the user's password. We define a handler (lines 80–124) for the *ServerValidate* event of the **CustomValidator**, which executes every time the user clicks **Submit**. This event handler contains a *ServerValidateEventArgs* parameter called **args**. The object referenced by **args** has two important properties: *Value*, which contains the value of the control that the **CustomValidator** is validating, and *IsValid*, which contains a **Boolean** representing the validation result. Once the event handler completes, if **IsValid** is **True**, the HTML form is submitted to the Web server; if **IsValid** is **False**, the **CustomValidator**'s **ErrorMessage** is displayed, and the HTML **form** is not submitted to the Web server.

To create and attach an event handler for the **ServerValidate** event, double-click **CustomValidator**. The definition for this event handler (lines 80–124) tests the selected user name against the password provided by the user. If they match, the user is *authenticated* (i.e., the user's identity is confirmed), and the browser is redirected to **Authors.aspx** (Fig. 20.40). Lines 104–110 authenticate the user and provide access to **Authors.aspx** by calling method **SetAuthCookie** of class **FormsAuthentication**. This class is in the **System.Web.Security** namespace (line 15). Method **SetAuthCookie** writes to the client an *encrypted* cookie containing information necessary to authenticate the user. Encrypted data is data translated into a code that only the sender and receiver can understand thereby keeping it private. Method **SetAuthCookie** takes two arguments: A **String** containing the user name, and a **Boolean** value that specifies whether this cookie should persist (i.e., remain on the client's computer) beyond the current session. Because we want the application to authenticate the user only for the current session, we set this value to **False**. After the user is authenticated, the user's Web browser is redirected to **Authors.aspx**. If the database query did not verify the user's identity, property *IsValid* of the **CustomValidator** is set to **False**; the **ErrorMessage** is displayed, and the user can attempt to log in again.

This example uses a technique known as *forms authentication*, which protects a page so that only authenticated users can access it. Authentication is a crucial tool for sites that allow only members to enter the site or a portion of the site. Authentication and denial of access to unauthorized users involves the placement of several lines in **Web.config** (a file used for application configuration). This XML file is a part of every ASP .NET application created in Visual Studio. If readers open this file, they will see the default authentication element, which is only one line and appears as follows:

```
<authentication mode="None" />
```

To deny access to unauthorized users, replace this line with

```
<authentication mode="Forms">
   <forms name="DatabaseCookie"
      loginUrl="Login.aspx" protection="Encryption" />
</authentication>

<authorization>
   <deny users="?" />
</authorization>
```

This replacement alters the value of the *mode* attribute in the **authentication** element from **"None"** to **"Forms"**, specifying that we want to use forms authentication. The *forms* element defines the way in which users are validated. Inside the forms element, **name** attribute sets the name of the cookie that is created on the user's machine—in this case, we named it **DatabaseCookie**. Attribute *loginUrl* specifies the login page for our application; users who attempt to access any page in our application without logging in are redirected to this page. Attribute *protection* specifies whether the value of the cookie is encrypted. In this case, we set the value of **protection** to **"Encryption"** to encrypt the cookie's data.

Element *authorization* indicates the type of access that specific users can have. In this application, we want to allow authenticated users access to all pages on the site. We place the *deny* element inside the **authorization** element to specify to what users we wish to deny access. When we set this attribute's value to **"?"**, all anonymous (i.e., unauthenticated) users are denied access to the site.

A user who has been authenticated will be redirected to **Authors.aspx** (Fig. 20.40). This page provides a list of authors, from which the user can choose one. After a choice has been made, a table is displayed with information about books that author has written.

```
1   <%-- Fig. 20.40: Authors.aspx                      --%>
2   <%-- Displays book titles based on author name     --%>
3   <%-- from database.                                --%>
4
5   <%@ Page Language="vb" AutoEventWireup="false"
6      Codebehind="Authors.aspx.vb"
7      Inherits="Database.Authors"%>
8
9   <%@ Register TagPrefix="Header" TagName="ImageHeader"
10     Src="ImageHeader.ascx" %>
11
12  <!DOCTYPE HTML PUBLIC "-//W3C//DTD HTML 4.0 Transitional//EN">
13  <HTML>
14     <HEAD>
15        <title>Authors</title>
16        <meta name="GENERATOR"
17           content="Microsoft Visual Studio.NET 7.0">
18        <meta name="CODE_LANGUAGE" content="Visual Basic 7.0">
19        <meta name="vs_defaultClientScript" content="JavaScript">
20        <meta name="vs_targetSchema"
21           content="http://schemas.microsoft.com/intellisense/ie5">
22     </HEAD>
23     <body MS_POSITIONING="GridLayout" bgColor="#ffebff">
24        <form id="Form1" method="post" runat="server">
25
26           <asp:DataGrid id="dataGrid" style="Z-INDEX: 106;
27              LEFT: 15px; POSITION: absolute; TOP: 131px"
28              runat="server" ForeColor="Black" AllowPaging="True"
29              DataSource="<%# dataView %>" AllowSorting="True"
30              Visible="False" Width="700px" Height="23px">
31
32              <EditItemStyle BackColor="White"></EditItemStyle>
33              <AlternatingItemStyle ForeColor="Black"
34                 BackColor="LightGoldenrodYellow">
35              </AlternatingItemStyle>
36              <ItemStyle BackColor="White"></ItemStyle>
37              <HeaderStyle BackColor="LightGreen"></HeaderStyle>
38              <PagerStyle NextPageText="Next &amp;gt; "
39                 PrevPageText="&amp;lt; Previous">
40              </PagerStyle>
41           </asp:DataGrid>
42
43           <asp:Button id="Button1" style="Z-INDEX: 104;
44              LEFT: 29px; POSITION: absolute; TOP: 188px"
45              runat="server" Width="78px" Text="Select">
46           </asp:Button>
```

Fig. 20.40 ASPX file that allows a user to select an author from a drop-down list (part 1 of 2).

```
47
48              <asp:DropDownList id="nameList" style="Z-INDEX: 103;
49                 LEFT: 90px; POSITION: absolute; TOP: 157px"
50                 runat="server" Width="158px" Height="22px">
51              </asp:DropDownList>
52
53              <asp:Label id="Label2" style="Z-INDEX: 102;
54                 LEFT: 28px; POSITION: absolute; TOP: 157px"
55                 runat="server" Width="48px" Height="22px">
56                 Authors:
57              </asp:Label>
58
59              <asp:Label id="Label3" style="Z-INDEX: 105;
60                 LEFT: 19px; POSITION: absolute; TOP: 127px"
61                 runat="server" Visible="False" Width="210px">
62                 You chose
63              </asp:Label>
64
65              <Header:ImageHeader id="ImageHeader1" runat="server">
66              </Header:ImageHeader>
67
68           </form>
69        </body>
70     </HTML>
```

Fig. 20.40 ASPX file that allows a user to select an author from a drop-down list (part 2 of 2).

The ASPX file for this page creates a number of controls: A **DropDownList**, three **Label**s, a **Button** and a **DataGrid**. Notice that some of the controls—one of the **Label**s and the **DataGrid**—have their **Visible** properties set to **false** (line 30 and line 61). This means that the controls are not visible when the page first loads, because there is no author information to display because the user has not yet chosen an author. Users select an author from the **DropDownList** and click **Submit**, causing a postback to occur. When the postback is handled, the **DataGrid** is filled and displayed. Figure 20.41 lists the code-behind file for this ASPX file.

Method **Page_Load** (lines 34–106) contains most of the code for this example. The condition (line 38) determines whether the page was loaded as a result of a postback event. If it is not a postback, line 41 adds a session item to the **Session** object to help us sort the data. Line 45 then opens the database connection, and lines 48–49 execute the database command, which retrieves all the authors' first and last names from the database. Lines 53–56 iterate through the result set and add the authors' first and last names to **nameList**.

```
1    ' Fig. 20.41: Authors.aspx.vb
2    ' The code-behind file for a page that allows a user to choose
3    ' an author and then view that author's books.
4
5    Imports System
6    Imports System.Data.OleDb
```

Fig. 20.41 Database information being inputted into a **DataGrid** (part 1 of 5).

```vb
7    Imports System.Collections
8    Imports System.ComponentModel
9    Imports System.Data
10   Imports System.Drawing
11   Imports System.Web
12   Imports System.Web.SessionState
13   Imports System.Web.UI
14   Imports System.Web.UI.WebControls
15   Imports System.Web.UI.HtmlControls
16
17   Public Class Authors
18      Inherits System.Web.UI.Page
19
20      Protected WithEvents Label3 As Label
21      Protected WithEvents Label2 As Label
22      Protected WithEvents nameList As DropDownList
23      Protected WithEvents Button1 As Button
24      Protected WithEvents dataGrid As dataGrid
25      Protected WithEvents OleDbDataAdapter1 As OleDbDataAdapter
26      Protected WithEvents OleDbSelectCommand1 As OleDbCommand
27      Protected WithEvents OleDbConnection1 As OleDbConnection
28      Protected WithEvents dataView As DataView
29      Protected dataTable As New DataTable()
30      Protected dataReader As OleDbDataReader
31
32      ' Visual Studio .NET generated code
33
34      Private Sub Page_Load(ByVal sender As System.Object, _
35         ByVal e As System.EventArgs) Handles MyBase.Load
36
37         ' test if the page was loaded due to a post back
38         If Not IsPostBack Then
39
40            ' add data sort string
41            Session.Add("sortString", "Title")
42
43            ' open database connection
44            Try
45               OleDbConnection1.Open()
46
47               ' execute query
48               dataReader = _
49                  OleDbDataAdapter1.SelectCommand.ExecuteReader()
50
51               ' while we can read a row from the result of the
52               ' query, add the first item to the dropdown list
53               While (dataReader.Read())
54                  nameList.Items.Add(dataReader.GetString(0) & _
55                     " " & dataReader.GetString(1))
56               End While
57
```

Fig. 20.41 Database information being inputted into a **DataGrid** (part 2 of 5).

```
58            ' if database cannot be found
59            Catch exception As System.Data.OleDb.OleDbException
60               Label3.Text = "Server Error: Unable to load database!"
61
62            Finally ' close database connection
63               OleDbConnection1.Close()
64            End Try
65         Else
66            ' set some controls to be invisible
67            nameList.Visible = False
68            Button1.Visible = False
69            Label2.Visible = False
70
71            ' set other controls to be visible
72            Label3.Visible = True
73            dataGrid.Visible = True
74
75            ' add author name to label
76            Label3.Text = "You Chose " & nameList.SelectedItem.Text _
77               & "."
78            Dim authorID As Integer = nameList.SelectedIndex + 1
79
80            Try
81               ' open database connection
82               OleDbConnection1.Open()
83
84               ' grab the title, ISBN and publisher name for each book
85               OleDbDataAdapter1.SelectCommand.CommandText = _
86                  "SELECT Titles.Title, Titles.ISBN, " & _
87                  "Publishers.PublisherName FROM AuthorISBN " & _
88                  "INNER JOIN Titles ON AuthorISBN.ISBN = " & _
89                  "Titles.ISBN, Publishers WHERE " & _
90                  "(AuthorISBN.AuthorID = " & authorID & ")"
91
92               ' fill dataset with results
93               OleDbDataAdapter1.Fill(dataTable)
94               dataView = New DataView(dataTable)
95               dataView.Sort = Session("sortString")
96               dataGrid.DataBind() ' bind grid to data source
97
98            ' if database cannot be found
99            Catch exception As System.Data.OleDb.OleDbException
100
101               Label3.Text = "Server Error: Unable to load database!"
102            Finally ' close database connection
103               OleDbConnection1.Close()
104            End Try
105        End If
106     End Sub ' Page_Load
107
```

Fig. 20.41 Database information being inputted into a **DataGrid** (part 3 of 5).

```vb
108     ' handles DataGrid page changed event
109     Private Sub OnNewPage(ByVal sender As Object, _
110        ByVal e As DataGridPageChangedEventArgs) _
111        Handles dataGrid.PageIndexChanged
112
113        ' set current page to next page
114        dataGrid.CurrentPageIndex = e.NewPageIndex
115
116        dataView.Sort = Session("sortString")
117        dataGrid.DataBind() ' rebind data
118
119     End Sub ' OnNewPage
120
121     ' handles Sort event
122     Private Sub dataGrid_SortCommand(ByVal source As Object, _
123        ByVal e As DataGridSortCommandEventArgs) _
124        Handles dataGrid.SortCommand
125
126        ' get table to sort
127        Session.Add("sortString", e.SortExpression.ToString())
128        dataView.Sort = Session("sortString") ' sort
129        dataGrid.DataBind() ' rebind data
130
131     End Sub ' dataGrid_SortCommand
132 End Class ' Authors
```

Fig. 20.41 Database information being inputted into a **DataGrid** (part 4 of 5).

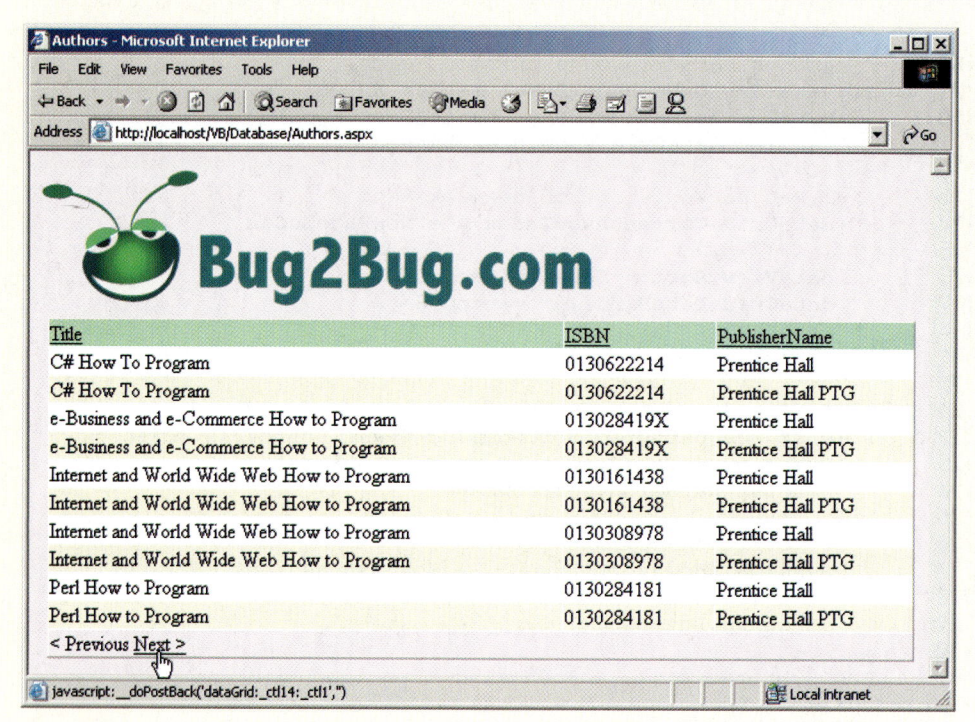

Fig. 20.41 Database information being inputted into a **DataGrid** (part 5 of 5).

Once the user has selected an author and submitted the form, the condition (line 38) is **False**, which causes lines 65–105 to execute. The initial set of controls displayed to the user (i.e., the label, drop-down list and button) are hidden in the postback. However, the label and the data grid that previously were invisible are made visible. Line 76 adds the selected author's name to the label control.

Lines 85–90 create a database query to retrieve the title, ISBN and publisher name for each of the author's books and assign them to the command's **CommandText** property. Method **Fill** (line 93) populates its **DataTable** argument with the rows returned by our query on 85–90. The **DataView** class's **Sort** property sorts its data by the **String** assigned to it (this value is stored in the **Session** object with key value **sortString**). This value is set initially to **"Title"** on line 41, indicating that rows in our table are to be sorted by title, in ascending order. Ascending order is the default. If the session value were **"TitleDESC"**, the rows in our table would also be sorted by title, but in descending order.

Method **OnNewPage** (lines 109–119) handles the **DataGrid**'s **PageIndex-Changed** event, which is fired when the user clicks the **Next** link at the bottom of the **DataGrid** control to display the next page of data. To enable paging, the **AllowPaging** property of the **DataGrid** is set to **True** in the Web-Form designer. **DataGrid**'s **PageSize** property determines the number of entries per page, and its **PagerStyle** property customizes the display of our **DataGrid** during paging. This **DataGrid** control displays ten books per page. After the **DataGrid**'s **CurrentPageIndex** property is assigned the event argument **NewPageIndex** (line 114), we sort the data and rebind it, so that the next page of data can be displayed (lines 116–117). This technique for displaying data makes the site more readable and enables pages to load more quickly (because less data is displayed at one time).

Method **dataGrid_SortCommand** (lines 122–131) handles the **Sort** event of the **DataGrid** control. When the **AllowSorting** property in the Web-Form designer is enabled, the **DataGrid** displays all table headings as **LinkButton** controls (i.e., buttons that act as hyperlinks). The **SortCommand** event is raised when the user clicks a column header name. On line 127, we use the **SortExpression** property of **e**. This property indicates the column by which the data is sorted. This value is added to the current **Session** object's **sortString** key, which is then assigned to our **DataView**'s **Sort** property on line 128. On line 129, we rebind the sorted data to our **DataGrid**.

20.9 Tracing

ASP .NET provides a *tracing* feature for the debugging of Web-based applications. Tracing is the process of placing statements throughout the code-behind file that output information during execution about the program's status.

In Windows applications, message boxes can be used as an aid in debugging; in Web Forms, a programmer might use **Response.Write** for this purpose. However, the employment of **Response.Write** for tracing in ASP .NET has several drawbacks.

One of these drawbacks is that, once an application is executing correctly, the programmer must remove all **Response.Write** statements from the program. This is time-consuming and can introduce errors, because the programmer must differentiate between statements that are part of the program's logic and statements that are used for testing purposes. ASP .NET provides the programmer with two forms of built-in tracing: *page tracing* and *application tracing*.

Page tracing involves the tracing of the actions of an individual page. Setting the **Trace** property of the page to **True** in the **Properties** window enables tracing for that page. Instead of calling the **Response** object's **Write** method, we call the **Trace** object's **Write** method. Object **Trace** is an instance of the *TraceContext* class and provides tracing capabilities. In addition to method **Write**, the **Trace** object includes method **Warn**, which prints warning statements in red. When tracing is disabled by setting the **Trace** property to **False**, **Trace** statements are not executed.

Figure 20.42 depicts a simple page that displays a sentence (we do not show the code for this page, as it is quite simplistic). The **Page_Load** event for this page includes the statement **Trace.Warn("Using warnings")**. Notice that **"Using warnings"** is not displayed on the page; we will see shortly when and where trace statements are displayed.

Figure 20.43 displays the same page when the **Trace** property is set to **True**. The top of the figure depicts the original page, and the tracing information generated by ASP .NET appears below. The ***Request Details*** section provides information about the request. The ***Trace Information*** section contains the information output by calling the **Write** and **Warn** methods. The second row contains the message, which displays in red.

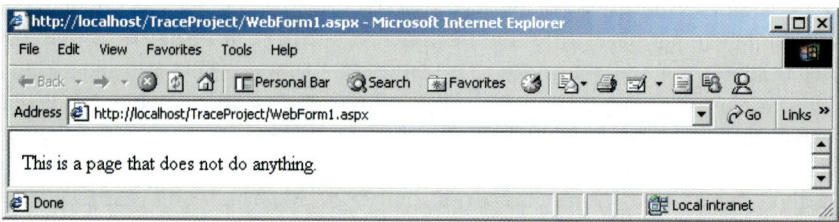

Fig. 20.42 ASPX page with tracing turned off.

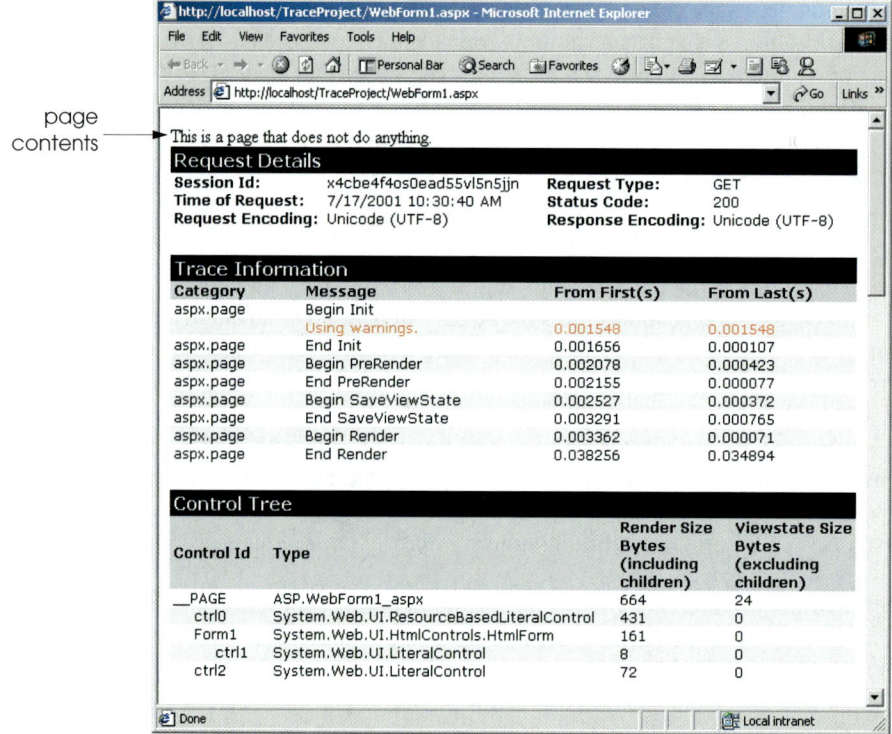

Fig. 20.43 Tracing enabled on a page.

The **Control Tree** section lists all the controls contained on the page. Several additional tables also appear in this page. The **Cookies Collection** section contains information about the program's cookies, the **Headers Collection** section catalogs the HTTP headers for the page and the **Server Variables** section provides a list of server variables (i.e., information sent by the browser with each request) and their values.

Tracing for the entire project is also available. To turn on application-level tracing, open the **Web.config** file for the project. Set the **Enabled** property to **True** in the **trace** element. To view the project's tracing information, navigate the browser to the

trace.axd file in the project folder. This file does not actually exist on the hard drive; it is generated when the user requests **trace.axd**. Figure 20.44 shows the Web page that is generated when the programmer views the **trace.axd** file.

This page lists all the requests made to this application and the times when the pages were accessed. The clicking of one of the **View Details** links directs the browser to a page similar to the one portrayed in Fig. 20.43.

20.10 Internet and World Wide Web Resources

www.asp.net

The Microsoft site overviews ASP .NET and provides a link for downloading ASP .NET. This site includes the IBuy Spy e-commerce storefront example that uses ASP .NET. Links to the Amazon and Barnes & Noble Web sites where the user can purchase books also are included.

www.asp101.com/aspplus

This site overviews ASP .NET, and includes articles, code examples and links to ASP .NET resources. The code samples demonstrate the use of cookies in an ASP .NET application and show how to establish a connection to a database—two key capabilities of multi-tier applications.

www.411asp.net

This resource site provides programmers with ASP .NET tutorials and code samples. The community pages allows programmers to ask questions, answer questions and post messages.

www.aspfree.com

This site provides free ASP .NET demos and source code. The site also provides a list of articles for various topics and a frequently asked questions (FAQs) page.

www.aspng.com

This site offers tutorials, links and recommendations for books on ASP.NET. Links to different mailing lists are also provides. These links are organized by topic. This site also contains articles related to many ASP.NET topics, such as "Performance Tips and Tricks."

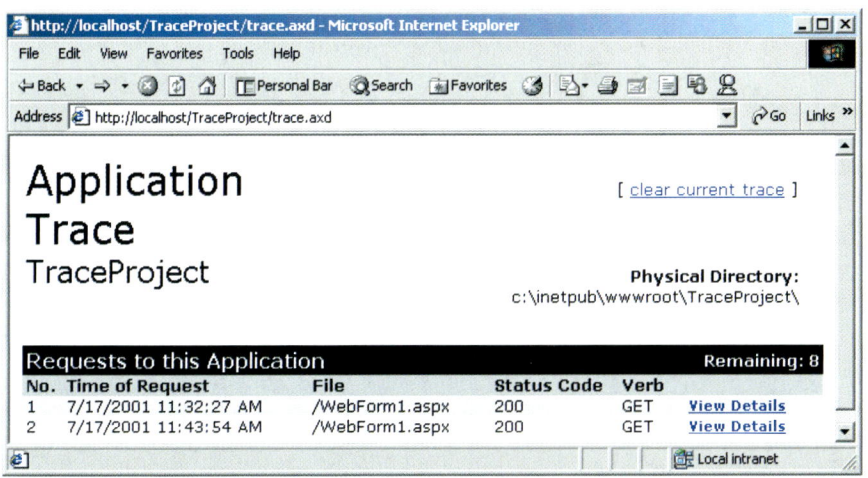

Fig. 20.44 Tracing information for a project.

www.aspnetfaq.com
This site provides answers to frequently asked questions (FAQs) about ASP.NET.

www.123aspx.com
This site offers a directory of links to ASP .NET resources. The site also includes daily and weekly newsletters.

SUMMARY

- Microsoft's ASP .NET technology is used for Web-based application development.
- Web-based applications are used to create Web content for Web browsers.
- The Web-Form file represents the Web page that is sent to the client browser.
- Web-Form files have the file extension **.aspx** and contain the GUI of the Web page currently being developed.
- Programmers customize Web Forms by adding Web controls, which include labels, text boxes, images and buttons.
- Every ASPX file created in Visual Studio has a corresponding class written in a .NET-compliant language. The file that contains this class is called the code-behind file and provides the ASPX file's programmatic implementation.
- HTTP specifies a set of methods and headers that allow clients and servers to interact and exchange information in a uniform and predictable way.
- In its simplest form, a Web page is nothing more than a HTML document. This document is a plain text file containing markings (markup or tags) that describe to a Web browser how to display and format the document's information.
- Any HTML document available for viewing over the Web has a corresponding Uniform Resource Locator (URL), which is an address indicating the location of a resource.
- Computers that run Web-server software provide resources for download over the Internet.
- The hostname is the name of the computer on which the resource resides. This computer usually is referred to as the host, because it houses and maintains resources.
- An IP address identifies a server in a manner similar to that by which a telephone number uniquely defines a particular phone line.
- MIME is an Internet standard that specifies the way in which certain data must be formatted so that programs can interpret the data correctly.
- Web-based applications are multi-tier applications, which sometimes are referred to as *n*-tier applications. Multi-tier applications divide functionality into separate tiers (i.e., logical groupings of functionality).
- The information tier maintains data pertaining to the application.
- The middle tier implements business logic, controller logic and presentation logic to control interactions between application clients and application data.
- The client tier, or top tier, is the application's user interface, which is typically a Web browser.
- Visual Studio generates the markup in our ASPX page when controls are dragged onto the Web Form.
- A **<%@ Page…%>** directive specifies information needed by the CLR to process this file.
- The **Inherits** attribute specifies the class in the code-behind file from which this ASP .NET class inherits.
- When a control's **runat** attribute is set to **"server"**, we are indicating that this control is executed on a server, generating an HTML equivalent.

- The **asp:** tag prefix in the declaration of a control indicates that the control is an ASP .NET Web control.
- Each Web control maps to a corresponding HTML element.
- The same Web control can map to different HTML elements, depending on the client browser and the Web control's property settings.
- Namespace **System.Web** contains classes that manage client requests and server responses.
- Namespace **System.Web.UI** contains classes for the creation of Web-based applications and controls.
- Class **Page** defines a standard Web page, providing event handlers and objects necessary for creating Web-based applications. All code-behind classes for ASPX forms inherit from class **Page**.
- Class **Control** is the base class that provides common functionality for all Web controls.
- Namespace **System.Web.UI.WebControls** contains Web controls employed in the design of the page's user interface.
- Method **Page_Init** is called when the **Init** event is raised. This event indicates that the page is ready to be initialized.
- The **Load** event is raised when the page loads. (This event occurs after all the Web controls on the page have been initialized and loaded.)
- When a client requests an ASPX file, a class is created behind the scenes that contains both the visual aspect of our page (defined in the ASPX file) and the logic of our page (defined in the code-behind file). This new class inherits from **Page**. The first time that our Web page is requested, this class will be compiled, and an instance will be created. This instance represents our page—it will create the HTML that is sent to the client. The assembly created from our compiled class will be placed in the project's **bin** directory.
- Changes to the Web application can be detected by the runtime, and the project is recompiled to reflect the altered content.
- The **Page_Load** event handler is usually used to execute any processing that is necessary to restore data from previous requests.
- After **Page_Load** has finished executing, the page processes any events raised by the page's controls.
- When a Web Form object is ready for garbage collection, an **Unload** event is raised. Event handler **Page_Unload** is inherited from class **Page** and contains any code that releases resources.
- A form is a mechanism for collecting user information and sending it to the Web server.
- HTML forms can contain visual and nonvisual components. Visual components include clickable buttons and other graphical user interface components with which users interact.
- Nonvisual components in an HTML form, called hidden inputs, store any data that the document author specifies.
- The name **localhost** indicates that the client and server reside on the same machine. If the Web server were located on a different machine, **localhost** would be replaced with the appropriate IP address or hostname.
- The Web-Form designer can display **HTML** mode, allowing the programmer to view the markup that represents the user interface of this page. The **Design** mode allows the programmer to view the page as it will look and modify it using the drag-and-drop technique.
- The **PageLayout** property determines how controls are arranged on the form.
- By default, property **PageLayout** is set to **GridLayout**, which means that all controls remain exactly where they are dropped on the Web Form. This is called absolute positioning.

- Alternatively, the developer can set the Web Form's **PageLayout** property to **FlowLayout**, which causes controls to be placed sequentially on the Web Form. This is called relative positioning, because the controls' positions are relative to the Web Form's upper-left corner.
- **Image** controls insert an image into a Web page. The **ImageUrl** property specifies the file location of the image to display.
- A **TextBox** control allows the programmer to read and display text.
- A **RadioButtonList** control provides a series of radio buttons for the user.
- A **DropDownList** control provides a list of options to the user.
- The **HyperLink** control adds a hyperlink to a Web page. The **NavigateUrl** property of this control specifies the resource that is requested when a user clicks the hyperlink.
- ASP .NET provides the **AdRotator** Web control for displaying advertisements. One advertisement is chosen at random from the advertisements stored in an XML file, specified by property **AdvertisementFile**.
- The advertisement file used for an **AdRotator** control contains **Ad** elements, each of which provides information about a different advertisement.
- Element **ImageUrl** in an advertisement file specifies the path (location) of the advertisement's image, and element **NavigateUrl** specifies the URL for the Web page that loads when a user clicks the advertisement.
- The **AlternateText** element contains text that displays in place of the image when the browser cannot locate or render the image for some reason.
- Element **Impressions** specifies how often an image appears, relative to the other images.
- A validation control checks whether the data in another Web control is in the proper format.
- When the HTML for our page is created, a validator is converted into ECMAScript.
- ECMAScript is a scripting language that facilitates a disciplined approach to designing computer programs that enhance the functionality and appearance of Web pages.
- A **RegularExpressionValidator** matches a Web control's content against a regular expression. The regular expression that validates the input is assigned to property **ValidationExpression**.
- A validator's **ControlToValidate** property indicates which control will be validated.
- A **RequiredFieldValidator** is used to ensure that a control receives input from the user when the form is submitted.
- Web programmers using ASP .NET often design their Web pages so that, when submitted, the current page is requested again. This event is known as a postback.
- The **Page**'s **IsPostBack** property can be used to determine whether the page is being loaded as a result of a postback.
- The **EnableViewState** attribute determines whether a Web control's state persists (i.e., is retained) when a postback occurs.
- Personalization makes it possible for e-businesses to communicate effectively with their customers and also improves users' ability to locate desired products and services.
- To provide personalized services to consumers, e-businesses must be able to recognize clients when they request information from a site.
- The request/response system on which the Web operates is facilitated by HTTP. Unfortunately, HTTP is a stateless protocol—it does not support persistent connections that would enable Web servers to maintain state information regarding particular clients.

- A session represents a unique client on the Internet. If the client leaves a site and then returns later, the client should still be recognized as the same user. To help the server distinguish among clients, each client must identify itself to the server.
- The tracking of individual clients is known as session tracking.
- A cookie is a text file stored by a Web site on an individual's computer that allows the site to track the actions of the visitor.
- When a Web Form receives a request, the header includes such information as the request type and any cookies that have been sent previously from the server to be stored on the client machine.
- When the server formulates its response, the header information includes any cookies the server wants to store on the client computer and other information, such as the MIME type of the response.
- The expiration date of a cookie can be set using in cookie's **Expires** property. Cookies are deleted when they expire.
- If the programmer of a cookie does not set an expiration date, the Web browser maintains the cookie for the duration of the browsing session.
- A cookie object is of type **HttpCookie**.
- Cookies are sent and received in the form of a collection of cookies, of type **HttpCookieCollection**.
- Cookies can be read by an application only if they were created in the domain in which the application is running—a Web server can never access cookies created outside the domain associated with that server.
- The **Name** and **Value** properties of class **HttpCookie** can be used to retrieve the key and value of the key-value pair in a cookie.
- Visual Basic provides session-tracking capabilities in the Framework Class Library's **HttpSessionState** class.
- Every Web Form includes an **HttpSessionState** object, which is accessible through property **Session** of class **Page**.
- When the Web page is requested, an **HttpSessionState** object is created and is assigned to the **Page**'s **Session** property.
- **Page** property **Session** is known as the **Session** object.
- **Session** object key-value pairs are often referred to as session items.
- A Web Form should not use shared instance variables to maintain client state information, because clients accessing that Web Form in parallel might overwrite the shared instance variables.
- Web Forms should maintain client state information in **HttpSessionState** objects, because such objects are specific to each client.
- Like a cookie, an **HttpSessionState** object can store name-value pairs. These session items are placed into an **HttpSessionState** object via a call to method **Add**.
- **HttpSessionState** objects can store any type of object (not just **String**s) as attribute values. This provides Visual Basic programmers with increased flexibility in determining the type of state information they wish to maintain for their clients.
- If the application calls method **Add** to add an attribute that has the same name as an attribute previously stored in a session, the object associated with that attribute is replaced.
- Property SessionID contains the session's unique ID. The first time a client connects to the Web server, a unique session ID is created for that client. When the client makes additional requests, the client's session ID is compared with the session IDs stored in the Web server's memory.

- Property **Timeout** specifies the maximum amount of time that an **HttpSessionState** object can be inactive before it is discarded.
- **Session** object's **Count** property provides the number of session items contained in a **Session** object.
- A value in a key-value pair is retrieved from the **Session** object by indexing the **Session** object with the key name, using the same process by which a value can be retrieved from a hash table.
- The **Keys** property of class **HttpSessionState** returns a collection containing all the keys in the session.
- The colors for a **DataGrid** can be specified through the **Auto Format...** link that is located near the bottom of the **Properties** window when we are looking at the properties of our **DataGrid**. A dialog will open with several choices.
- The **Request** object's **PhysicalApplicationPath** property retrieves the path of the application's root directory.
- Columns can be added to a **DataTable** object via the **Columns** collection's **Add** method.
- Information can be added to a **DataTable** via method **LoadDataRow**.
- Method **DataBind** is called to refresh the information in a **DataView**.
- Programmers can define their own Web control, known as a Web user control.
- Web user controls usually consist of two pages: An ASCX file, and a code-behind file.
- A **CustomValidator** allows us to specify the circumstances under which a field is valid. We define these circumstances in the event handler for the **ServerValidate** event of the **CustomValidator**.
- An **OleDbDataReader** is an object that can be used to read data from a database.
- When a user's identity is confirmed, we say that the user has been authenticated.
- Method **SetAuthCookie** writes to the client an encrypted cookie containing information necessary to authenticate the user.
- Encrypted data is data translated into a code that only the sender and receiver can understand.
- A technique known as forms authentication protects a page so that only authenticated users can access it.
- Authentication and denial of access to unauthorized users involves the placement of several lines in **Web.config** (a file used for application configuration). This file is a part of every ASP .NET application created in Visual Studio.
- We can modify this file so that a user who is not authenticated will not be allowed to view any of the pages in the application. One who attempts to view a later page will be forced back to the login page.
- The **DataView** class's **Sort** property sorts its data by the **String** assigned it.
- To enable paging, the **AllowPaging** property of a **DataGrid** is set to **True**.
- When the **AllowSorting** property in the Web Form designer is enabled, a **DataGrid** displays all table headings as **LinkButton** controls (i.e., buttons that act as hyperlinks). The **SortCommand** event is raised when the user clicks a column header name.
- ASP .NET provides a tracing feature for the debugging of Web-based applications. Tracing is the process of placing statements throughout the code-behind file that output information during execution about the program's status.
- ASP .NET provides the programmer with two forms of built-in tracing: Page tracing, and application tracing.
- Page tracing involves the tracing of the actions of an individual page. Setting the **Trace** property of the page to **True** in the **Properties** window enables tracing for that page.

- Object **`Trace`** is an instance of the **`TraceContext`** class and provides tracing capabilities.
- In addition to method **`Write`**, the **`Trace`** object includes method **`Warn`**, which prints warning statements in red.
- When tracing is disabled by setting the **`Trace`** property to **`False`**, **`Trace`** statements are not executed.
- The **Request Details** section that appears when tracing information is displayed in an ASPX page provides information about the request.
- The **Trace Information** section contains the information output by calling the **`Write`** and **`Warn`** methods.
- The **Control Tree** section lists all the controls contained on the page.
- The **Cookies Collection** section contains information about the program's cookies, the **Headers Collection** section catalogs the HTTP headers for the page and the **Server Variables** section provides a list of server variables and their values.
- Tracing for an entire project is also available. To turn on application-level tracing, open file **`Web.config`** for the project. Set the **`Enabled`** property to **`true`** in the **`trace`** element. To view the project's tracing information, navigate the browser to the **`trace.axd`** file in the project folder.

TERMINOLOGY

%> tag
<% tag
`Ad` attribute in XML file
`AdRotator` class
`AdRotatorInformation.xml`
`AdvertisementFile` property of class
    `AdRotator`
`AlternateText` attribute in XML file
application tracing
ASCX file
ASP .NET
ASP .NET Web Application project
ASPX file
`authentication` element in **`Web.config`**
`authorization` element in **`Web.config`**
`AutoEventWireup` attribute of
    ASP .NET page
code-behind file
`CompareValidator` class
`ControlToValidate` property of class
    `RegularExpressionValidator`
cookie
`CustomValidator` class
`deny` element in **`Web.config`**
DNS
Document
domain-name server
`DropDownList` class
dynamic Web content
enabling application tracing

`FlowLayout`
forms authentication
`forms` element in **`Web.config`**
`FormsAuthentication` class
`GridLayout`
host
hostname
HTML
HTML tag
HTTP
HTTP header
HTTP method
HTTP request type
HTTP response
HTTP transaction
`HttpRequest` class
`HttpResponse` class
`HttpSessionState` class
hyperlink
`HyperLink` class
hypertext
IIS Web server
`ImageUrl` attribute in XML file
`Impressions` attribute in XML file
`Inherits` attribute of ASP .NET page
`Init` event of class **`Page`**
IP address
`IsValid` property of class
    `ServerValidateEventArgs`
`LinkButton` class

`LiteralControl` class
`Load` event of class `Page`
`loginUrl` attribute of `forms` element in `Web.config`
MIME type
`mode` attribute of `forms` element in `Web.config`
`name` attribute of `forms` element in `Web.config`
`NavigateUrl` attribute in XML file
`NavigateUrl` property of class `HyperLink`
.NET Framework
`Page` class
page tracing
`pageLayout` property of ASP .NET page
path to a resource
`PhysicalApplicationPath` property of class `HttpRequest`
postback
processing directives in ASP .NET page
`protection` attribute in `forms` element in `Web.config`
`RegularExpressionValidator` class
request method
`Request` property of class `Page`
`RequiredFieldValidator` class
`Response` property of class `Page`
`ServerValidate` event of class `CustomValidator`
`ServerValidateEventArgs` class
`Session` property of class `Page`
session variable
`sessionState` element of `Web.config`
`SetAuthCookie` method of class `FormsAuthentication`
`StreamReader` class
`StreamWriter` class
`System.Web.Security` namespace
`System.Web.UI`
`System.Web.UI.WebControls` namespace
`System.Windows.Forms` namespace
tag
`Text` property of class `HyperLink`
`TextBox` class of namespace `System.Web.UI.WebControls`
`title` HTML element
Toolbox
`trace` element in `Web.config`
`trace` property of an ASP .NET page
`trace` property of class `Page`
`trace.axd` file
`TraceContext` class
tracing
Uniform Resource Locator (URL)
user control
`users` attribute of `deny` element in `Web.config`
validating information
`ValidationExpression` property of class `RegularExpressionValidator`
validator
`Value` property of class `ServerValidateEventArgs`
viewing a page with tracing enabled
viewing the tracing information for a project
virtual directory
`Warn` method of class `TraceContext`
Web Form
`Web.config` file

SELF-REVIEW EXERCISES

20.1 State whether each of the following is *true* or *false*. If *false*, explain why.
  a) `FlowLayout` is the default setting of the `PageLayout` property.
  b) It is possible to enable tracing in an individual page or in an entire application in ASP .NET.
  c) Web Form file names typically end in **.aspx**.
  d) If no expiration data is set for a cookie, that cookie will be destroyed at the end of the session.
  e) A maximum of one validator control can be placed on a Web Form.
  f) The `TextBox` Web control is not the same `TextBox` Windows control.
  g) An `AdRotator` always displays all ads with equal frequency.
  h) The file that contains image information for an `AdRotator` can be in a format other than XML.
  i) `HttpResponse` method `Redirect` can redirect the browser only to an ASP .NET page within the same folder.

j) Changes made to properties of controls in the **Properties** window are reflected in the `InitializeComponent` method in the code-behind file.

20.2 Fill in the blanks in each of the following statements:
a) Web applications contain three basic tiers: _____, _____, and _____.
b) A control that validates the data format in another control is called a _____.
c) A _____ occurs when a page requests itself.
d) Every ASP .NET page inherits from class _____ .
e) When a page loads, the _____ event occurs first, followed by the _____ event.
f) The _____ file contains the functionality for an ASP.NET page.
g) Method _____ of the _____ object of class **Page** outputs HTML to a client.
h) `AdRotator`'s _____ property points to the file containing information in _____ format about all the ads that will be displayed.
i) The _____ property in the Web Form designer organizes controls either by lining them up or by placing them on a grid.
j) Code generated by Visual Studio during the design of an ASP .NET page is placed in the _____ method.

ANSWERS TO SELF-REVIEW EXERCISES

20.1 a) False. `GridLayout` is the default setting of the `PageLayout` property. b) True. c) True. d) True. e) False. An unlimited number of validation controls can be placed on one control. f) True. g) False. The frequency with which the `AdRotator` displays ads is specified in the `AdvertisementFile`. h) False. The `AdvertisementFile` must be an XML file. i) False. `Redirect` can redirect the user to any page. j) False. Changes to properties of controls can be seen in the ASPX file.

20.2 a) information, middle, client. b) validator. c) postback. d) **Page**. e) `Init`, `Load`. f) code-behind. g) `Write`, `Response`. h) `AdvertisementFile`, XML. i) `PageLayout`. j) `InitializeComponent`.

EXERCISES

20.3 Modify the `WebTime` example so that it allows a user to select a time zone from a `DropDownList`. The Web Form then should redirect the user to a page that displays the time in the selected zone. Update the time every thirty seconds.

20.4 Modify the first exercise to contain drop-down lists for such `Label` properties as `BgColor`, `ForeColor` and `Font`. Allow the user to select from these lists and submit the selections; then, reload the page so that it reflects the specified changes to the properties of the `Label` displaying the time.

20.5 Create an ASP .NET page that uses a file on disk to keep track of how many hits the page has received. Display the number of hits every time the page loads.

20.6 Provide functionality for the example in Section 20.5.1. When users click **Submit**, store their information in a file. On postback, thank the user for providing the information.

20.7 Using the same techniques as those covered in the guest-book case study in Section 20.7, develop an ASP .NET application for a discussion group. Allow new links to be created for new topics.

20.8 Create a set of ASP .NET pages that allows users to manipulate a database. Create a database for a book seller with the following fields: `BookName`, `Price`, `Quantity`. The main ASP .NET page should allow users to select from a drop-down list, which will contain options to enter more information into the database, view the entire database, update a row from the database, and delete an item from the database. After completing an operation, the user should be able to return to the main page via a link to begin another operation.

21

ASP .NET and Web Services

Objectives

- To understand what a Web service is.
- To be able to create Web services.
- To understand the elements that compose a Web service, such as service descriptions and discovery files.
- To be able to create a client that uses a Web service.
- To be able to use Web services with Windows and Web applications.
- To understand session tracking in Web services.
- To be able to pass user-defined data types to a Web service.

A client is to me a mere unit, a factor in a problem.
Sir Arthur Conan Doyle

...if the simplest things of nature have a message that you understand, rejoice, for your soul is alive.
Eleonora Duse

Protocol is everything.
Francoise Giuliani

They also serve who only stand and wait.
John Milton

Chapter 21

Outline

21.1 Introduction
21.2 Web Services
21.3 Simple Object Access Protocol (SOAP) and Web Services
21.4 Publishing and Consuming Web Services
21.5 Session Tracking in Web Services
21.6 Using Web Forms and Web Services
21.7 Case Study: Temperature Information Application
21.8 User-Defined Types in Web Services
21.9 Internet and World Wide Web Resources

Summary • Terminology • Self-Review Exercises • Answers to Self-Review Exercises • Exercises

21.1 Introduction[1]

Throughout this book, we have created dynamic link libraries (DLLs) to facilitate software reusability and modularity—the cornerstones of good object-oriented programming. However, the use of DLLs is limited, because a DLL must reside on the same machine as the program that uses it. This chapter introduces the use of Web services (sometimes called *XML Web services*) to promote software reusability over distributed systems. Distributed-systems technologies allow applications to execute across multiple computers on a network. A Web service is a class that enables distributed computing by allowing one machine to call methods on other machines via common data formats and protocols, such as XML and HTTP. In .NET, the method calls are implemented through The Simple Object Access Protocol (SOAP), an XML-based protocol describing how to mark up requests and responses so that they can be transferred via protocols such as HTTP. Using SOAP, applications represent and transmit data in a standardized format—XML. The underlying implementation of the Web service is usually not relevant to the client using the Web service.

Microsoft is encouraging software vendors and e-businesses toward the deployment of Web services. As larger numbers of people worldwide connect to the Internet, the concept of applications that call methods across a network becomes more practical. Earlier in this text, we delineated the merits of object-oriented programming. Web services represents the next step in object-oriented programming: Instead of developing software from a small number of class libraries provided at one location, programmers can access countless libraries in multiple locations. This technology also makes it easier for businesses to collaborate and grow together. By purchasing Web services that are relevant to their businesses, companies that create applications can spend less time coding and more time developing new products. In addition, e-businesses can employ Web services to provide their customers with an enhanced shopping experience. Let us look at an online music store as a simple example. The store's Web site provides links to various CDs, enabling users to purchase the CDs or to obtain information about the artists. Another company that sells concert tickets provides a Web service that displays the dates of upcoming concerts by var-

---

1. IIS must be running in order to create a Web service in Visual Studio.

ious artists then allows users to buy concert tickets. By deploying the concert-ticket Web service on its site, the online music store can provide an additional service to its customers that will likely result in increased traffic to its site. The company that sells concert tickets also benefits from the business relationship. In addition to selling more tickets, it receives revenue from the online music store for the use of its Web service.

Visual Studio and the .NET framework provide a simple, user-friendly way to create Web services like the one discussed in this example. In this chapter, we explore the steps involved in both the creation and the use of Web services. For each example, we provide the code for the Web service, then give an example of an application that might use the Web service. Our first examples are designed to offer an in-depth analysis of Web services and how they work in Visual Studio. Then, we move on to demonstrate more sophisticated Web services that use session tracking and complex data types.

21.2 Web Services

A Web service is a class stored on one machine that can be accessed on another machine over a network. Because of this relationship, the machine on which the Web service resides commonly is referred to as a *remote machine*. The application that desires access to the Web service sends a method call and its arguments to the remote machine, which processes the call and sends a response to the caller. This kind of distributed computing can benefit various systems, including slow systems, those with limited amounts of memory or resources, those without access to certain data and those lacking the code necessary to perform specific computations. Another advantage of Web services is that code and data can be stored on another computer. For instance, a Web service can be defined at one location to execute several common queries to a database. Not only does the Web service define the necessary code for the client, but the database is stored on the same machine as is the Web service. The client does not need to access or store the database on its machine.

A Web service is, in its simplest form, a class. In previous chapters, when we wanted to include a class in a project, we would have to either define the class in our project or add a reference to the compiled DLL. This compiled DLL is placed in the **bin** directory of our application by default. As a result, all pieces of our application reside on one machine. When we are using Web services, the class we wish to include in our project is instead stored on a remote machine—a compiled version of this class will not be placed in the current application. What actually does happen is discussed shortly.

Methods in a Web service are executed through a *Remote Procedure Call* (*RPC*). These methods, which are marked with the **WebMethod** attribute, are often referred to as *Web-service methods*. Declaring a method with this attribute makes the method accessible to other classes through an RPC. The declaration of a Web-service method with attribute **WebMethod** is known as *exposing* a Web-service method.

Common Programming Error 21.1

Trying to call a remote method in a Web service where the method is not declared with the **WebMethod** *attribute is a compile-time error.*

Method calls to and responses from Web services are transmitted via SOAP. This means that any client capable of generating and processing SOAP messages can use a Web service, regardless of the language in which the Web service is written.

Web services have important implications for *business-to-business (B2B) transactions*—ones that occur between two or more businesses. Now, businesses are able to conduct their transactions via Web services, rather than via custom-created applications—a much simpler and more efficient means of conducting business. Because Web services and SOAP are platform independent, companies can collaborate and use each others' Web services without worrying about the compatibility of technologies or programming languages. In this way, Web services are an inexpensive, readily-available solution to facilitate B2B transactions.

A Web service in .NET has two parts: An *ASMX* file, and a code-behind file. The ASMX file can be viewed in any Web browser and contains valuable information about the Web service, such as descriptions of Web-service methods and ways to test these methods. The code-behind file provides the implementation for the methods that the Web service encompasses. Figure 21.1 depicts Internet Explorer rendering an ASMX file.

The top of the page provides a link to the Web service's **Service Description**. A service description is an XML document that conforms to the *Web Service Description Language (WSDL)*, an XML vocabulary that describes how a Web service behaves. A WSDL document defines the methods that the Web service makes available and the ways in which clients can interact with those methods. The document also specifies lower-level information that clients might need, such as the required format in which to send requests to the Web service and the format of the Web service's response. Visual Studio .NET generates the WSDL service description. Client programs can use the service description to confirm the correctness of method calls when those client programs are compiled.

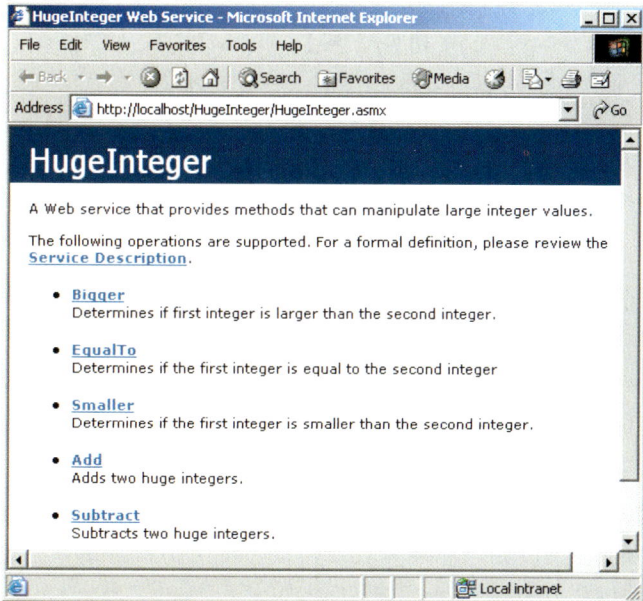

Fig. 21.1 ASMX file rendered in Internet Explorer.

The programmer should not alter this document, for it defines how a Web service works. When a user clicks the **Service Description** link at the top of the ASMX page, WSDL is displayed that defines the service description for this Web service (Fig. 21.2).

Below the **Service Description** link, the Web page shown in Fig. 21.1 lists the methods that the Web service provides (i.e., all methods in the application that are declared with `WebMethod` attributes). Clicking any method name requests a test page that describes the method (Fig. 21.3). After explaining the method's arguments, the page allows users to execute a test run of the method by entering the proper parameters and clicking **Invoke**. (We discuss the process of testing a Web-service method shortly.) Below the **Invoke** button, the page displays sample request and response messages, using SOAP, HTTP GET and HTTP POST. These protocols are the three options for sending and receiving messages in Web services. The protocol used for request and response messages is sometimes known as the Web service's *wire protocol* or *wire format*, because the wire format specifies how information is sent "along the wire." Notice that Fig. 21.3 uses the HTTP GET protocol to test a method. Later in this chapter, when we use Web services in our Visual Basic programs, we instead employ SOAP, because SOAP is the default protocol for Web services in Visual Studio. As we will demonstrate, the use of SOAP to execute calls to Web-service methods can be quite advantageous.

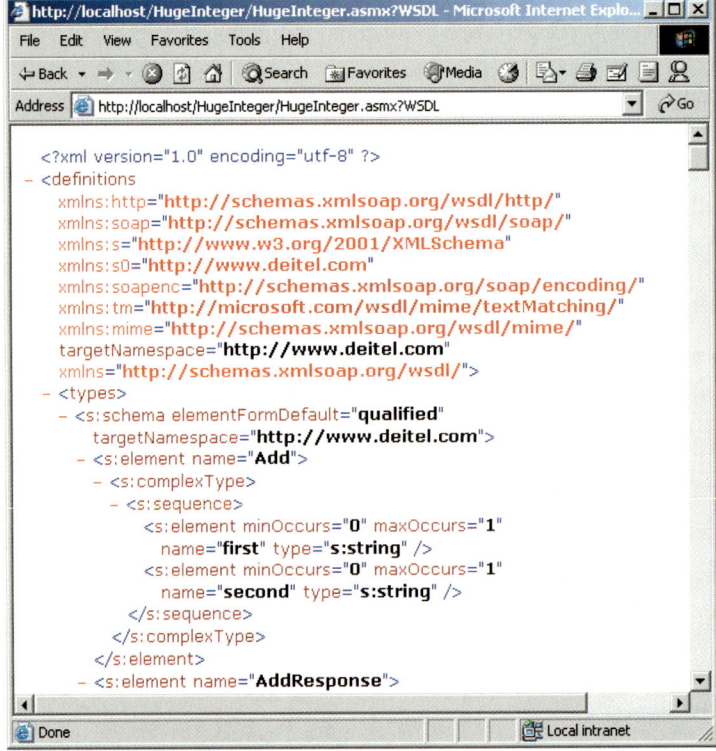

Fig. 21.2 Service description for a Web service.

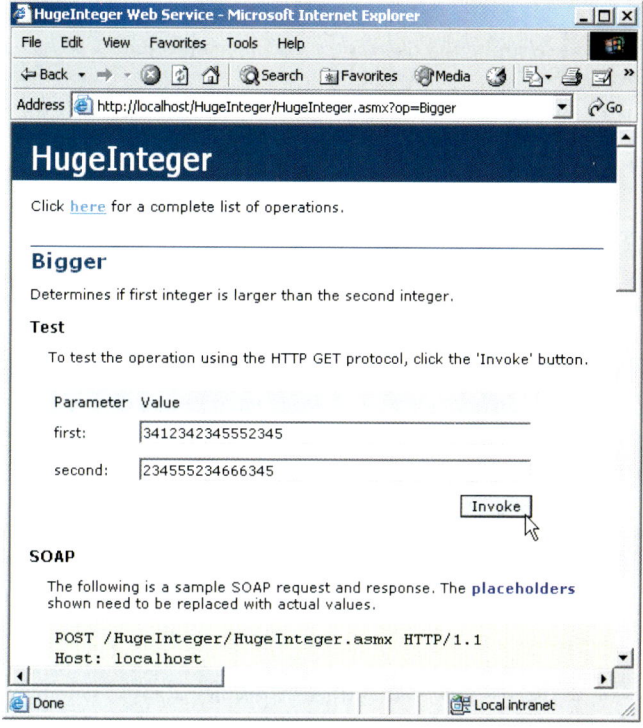

Fig. 21.3 Invoking a method of a Web service from a Web browser.

Users can test the method above by entering **Value**s in the **first:** and **second:** fields and then clicking **Invoke**. The method executes, and a new Web-browser window opens to display an XML document containing the result (Fig. 21.4). Now that we have introduced a simple example using a Web service, the next several sections explore the role of XML in Web services, as well as other aspects of Web services' functionality.

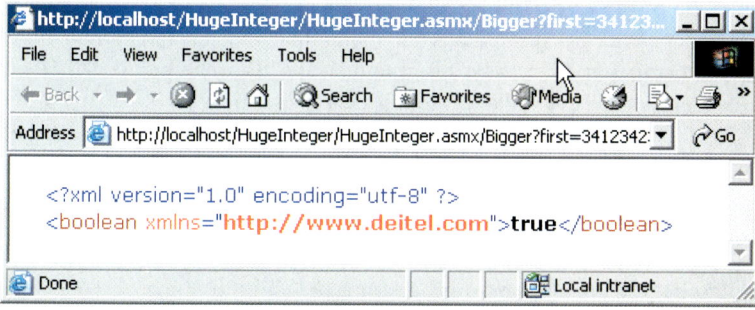

Fig. 21.4 Results of invoking a Web-service method from a Web browser.

>
> **Testing and Debugging Tip 21.1**
>
> *Using the ASMX page of a Web service to test and debug methods makes that Web service more reliable and robust; it also reduces the likelihood that others who use the Web service will encounter errors.*

21.3 Simple Object Access Protocol (SOAP) and Web Services

Simple Object Access Protocol (SOAP) is a platform-independent protocol that uses XML to make remote procedure calls over HTTP. Each call and response is packaged in a *SOAP message*—an XML message containing all the information necessary to process its contents. SOAP messages are quite popular, because they are written in the easy-to-understand and platform-independent XML. Similarly, HTTP was chosen to transmit SOAP messages because HTTP is a standard protocol for sending information across the Internet. The use of XML and HTTP enables different operating systems to send and receive SOAP messages. Another benefit of HTTP is that it can be used with networks that contain *firewalls*—security barriers that restrict communication among networks.

Another reason that programmers creating Web services use SOAP is its extensive set of supported data types. Readers should note that the wire format used to transmit requests and responses must support all data types passed between the applications. Web services that use SOAP support a wider variety of data types than do Web services that employ other wire formats. The data types supported by SOAP include the basic data types, **DataSet**, **DateTime**, **XmlNode** and several others. SOAP also permits transmission of arrays of all these types. In addition, user-defined types can be used; we demonstrate how to do this in Section 21.8.

ASP .NET Web services send requests and responses to and from Web services via SOAP. When a program invokes a Web-service method, the request and all relevant information is packaged in a SOAP request message and sent to the appropriate destination. When the Web service receives this SOAP message, it begins to process the contents called the *SOAP envelope*, which specifies the method that the client wishes to execute and the arguments the client is passing to that method. After the Web service receives this request and parses it, the proper method is called with the specified arguments (if there are any), and the response is sent back to the client in a SOAP response message. The client parses the response to retrieve the result of the method call.

The SOAP response message portrayed in Fig. 21.5 was taken directly from the **Bigger** method of the **HugeInteger** Web service (Fig. 21.3). This Web service provides programmers with several methods that manipulate integers larger than those that can be stored as a **Long** variable. Most programmers do not manipulate SOAP messages, allowing the Web service to handle the details of transmission.

```
1   POST /HugeInteger/HugeInteger.asmx HTTP/1.1
2   Host: localhost
3   Content-Type: text/xml; charset=utf-8
4   Content-Length: length
5   SOAPAction: "http://www.deitel.com/Bigger"
6
```

Fig. 21.5 SOAP request message for the **HugeInteger** Web service (part 1 of 2).

```
 7    <?xml version="1.0" encoding="utf-8"?>
 8
 9    <soap:Envelope
10       xmlns:xsi="http://www.w3.org/2001/XMLSchema-instance"
11       xmlns:xsd="http://www.w3.org/2001/XMLSchema"
12       xmlns:soap="http://schemas.xmlsoap.org/soap/envelope/">
13
14       <soap:Body>
15          <Bigger xmlns="http://www.deitel.com">
16             <first>string</first>
17             <second>string</second>
18          </Bigger>
19       </soap:Body>
20    </soap:Envelope>
```

Fig. 21.5 SOAP request message for the **HugeInteger** Web service (part 2 of 2).

Figure 21.5 displays a standard SOAP request message, which is created when a client wishes to execute the **HugeInteger** Web service's method **Bigger**. When a request to a Web service causes such a SOAP request message to be created, the MIME **content-length**'s value (**length**) and elements **first** and **second**'s character data (**String**s) would contain the actual values entered by the user (line 4 and lines 16–17, respectively). If this envelope were transmitting the request from Fig. 21.3, element **first** and element **second** instead would be the numbers represented in the figure. Placeholder "**length**" would contain the length of this SOAP request message.

21.4 Publishing and Consuming Web Services

This section presents several examples of creating (also known as *publishing*) and using (also known as *consuming*) a Web service. An application that consumes a Web service actually consists of two parts: A *proxy* class representing the Web service and a client application that accesses the Web service via an instance of the proxy class. A proxy class handles the transferal of the arguments for a Web-service method from the client application to the Web service and the transferal of the result from the Web-service method back to the client application. Visual Studio can generate a proxy class—we demonstrate how to do this momentarily.

Figure 21.6 presents the code-behind file for the **HugeInteger** Web service (Fig. 21.1). This Web service is designed to perform calculations with integers that contain a maximum of 100 digits. As we mentioned earlier, **Long** variables cannot handle integers of this size (i.e., an overflow occurs). The Web service provides a client with methods that take two "huge integers" and immediately determines which one is larger or smaller, whether the two numbers are equal, their sum and their difference. The reader can think of these methods as services that one application provides for the programmers of other applications (hence the term, Web services). Any programmer can access this Web service, use the methods and thus avoid writing over 200 lines of code. We hide portions of the Visual Studio generated code in the code-behind files. We do this for both brevity and presentation purposes.

Line 14 assigns the Web service namespace to **www.deitel.com** to uniquely identify this Web service. This namespace is specified in the **Namespace** property of a **WebService** attribute. In lines 15–16, we use property **Description** to provide information about our Web service that appears in the ASMX file. In line 18, notice that our class derives from **System.Web.Services.WebService**—by default, Visual Studio defines our Web service so that it inherits from the **WebService** class. Although a Web service is not required to derive from **WebService**, this class provides members that are useful in determining information about the client and the Web service itself. Several methods in class **HugeInteger** are tagged with the **WebMethod** attribute, which exposes a method so that it can be called remotely. When this attribute is absent, the method is not accessible through the Web service. Notice that this attribute, like the **WebService** attribute, contains a **Description** property, which provides information about the method to our ASMX page. Readers can see these descriptions in the output of Fig. 21.6.

```vb
1   ' Fig. 21.6: HugeInteger.asmx.vb
2   ' HugeInteger WebService.
3
4   Imports System
5   Imports System.Collections
6   Imports System.ComponentModel
7   Imports System.Data
8   Imports System.Diagnostics
9   Imports System.Web
10  Imports System.Web.Services ' contains Web service classes
11
12  ' performs operation on large integers
13
14  <WebService(Namespace:="http://www.deitel.com", _
15     Description := "A Web service that provides methods that" _
16     & " can manipulate large integer values." ) > _
17  Public Class HugeInteger
18     Inherits System.Web.Services.WebService
19
20     Private Const MAXIMUM As Integer = 100
21     Public number() As Integer
22
23     ' default constructor
24     Public Sub New()
25
26        ' CODEGEN: This call is required by the ASP.NET Web
27        ' Services Designer
28        InitializeComponent()
29
30        number = New Integer(MAXIMUM) {}
31     End Sub ' New
32
33     ' Visual Studio .NET generated code
34
35     ' property that accepts an integer parameter
36     Public Property Digits(ByVal index As Integer) As Integer
37        Get
38           Return number(index)
39        End Get
40
```

Fig. 21.6 **HugeInteger** Web service (part 1 of 5).

```vb
41         Set(ByVal Value As Integer)
42            number(index) = Value
43         End Set
44
45      End Property ' Property
46
47      ' returns String representation of HugeInteger
48      Public Overrides Function ToString() As String
49         Dim returnString As String = ""
50
51         Dim digit As Integer
52         For Each digit In number
53            returnString = digit & returnString
54         Next
55
56         Return returnString
57      End Function
58
59
60      ' creates HugeInteger based on argument
61      Public Shared Function FromString(ByVal value As String) _
62         As HugeInteger
63
64         Dim parsedInteger As New HugeInteger()
65         Dim i As Integer
66
67         For i = 0 To value.Length - 1
68            parsedInteger.Digits(i) = Int32.Parse( _
69               value.Chars(value.Length - i - 1).ToString())
70         Next
71
72
73         Return parsedInteger
74      End Function
75
76      ' WebMethod that performs the addition of integers
77      'represented by the string arguments
78      <WebMethod( Description := "Adds two huge integers." )> _
79      Public Function Add(ByVal first As String, _
80         ByVal second As String) As String
81
82         Dim carry As Integer = 0
83         Dim i As Integer
84
85         Dim operand1 As HugeInteger = _
86            HugeInteger.FromString(first)
87
88         Dim operand2 As HugeInteger = _
89            HugeInteger.FromString(second)
90
91         ' store result of addition
92         Dim result As New HugeInteger()
93
```

Fig. 21.6 `HugeInteger` Web service (part 2 of 5).

```vb
 94            ' perform addition algorithm for each digit
 95            For i = 0 To MAXIMUM
 96
 97               ' add two digits in same column
 98               ' result is their sum, plus carry from
 99               ' previous operation modulo 10
100               result.Digits(i) = _
101                  (operand1.Digits(i) + operand2.Digits(i)) _
102                     Mod 10 + carry
103
104               ' set carry to remainder of dividing
105               ' sums of two digits by 10
106               carry = (operand1.Digits(i) + operand2.Digits(i)) \ 10
107            Next
108
109            Return result.ToString()
110
111         End Function ' Add
112
113         ' WebMethod that performs the subtraction of integers
114         ' represented by the String arguments
115         <WebMethod( Description := "Subtracts two huge integers." )> _
116         Public Function Subtract(ByVal first As String, _
117            ByVal second As String) As String
118
119            Dim i As Integer
120            Dim operand1 As HugeInteger = _
121               HugeInteger.FromString(first)
122
123            Dim operand2 As HugeInteger = _
124               HugeInteger.FromString(second)
125
126            Dim result As New HugeInteger()
127
128            ' subtract top digit from bottom digit
129            For i = 0 To MAXIMUM
130               ' if top digit is smaller than bottom
131               ' digit we need to borrow
132               If operand1.Digits(i) < operand2.Digits(i) Then
133                  Borrow(operand1, i)
134               End If
135
136               ' subtract bottom from top
137               result.Digits(i) = operand1.Digits(i) - _
138                  operand2.Digits(i)
139            Next
140
141            Return result.ToString()
142         End Function ' Subtract
143
```

Fig. 21.6 `HugeInteger` Web service (part 3 of 5).

```vbnet
144         ' borrows 1 from next digit
145         Private Sub Borrow(ByVal hugeInteger As HugeInteger, _
146            ByVal place As Integer)
147
148            ' if no place to borrow from, signal problem
149            If place >= MAXIMUM - 1 Then
150               Throw New ArgumentException()
151
152            ' otherwise if next digit is zero,
153            ' borrow from digit to left
154            ElseIf hugeInteger.Digits(place + 1) = 0 Then
155               Borrow(hugeInteger, place + 1)
156            End If
157
158            ' add ten to current place because we borrowed
159            ' and subtract one from previous digit -
160            ' this is digit borrowed from
161            hugeInteger.Digits(place) += 10
162            hugeInteger.Digits(place + 1) -= 1
163
164         End Sub ' Borrow
165
166         ' WebMethod that returns true if first integer is
167         ' bigger than second
168         <WebMethod( Description := "Determines if first integer is " & _
169            "larger than the second integer." )> _
170         Public Function Bigger(ByVal first As String, _
171            ByVal second As String) As Boolean
172
173            Dim zeroes As Char() = {"0"}
174
175            Try
176               ' if elimination of all zeroes from result
177               ' of subtraction is an empty string,
178               ' numbers are equal, so return false,
179               ' otherwise return true
180               If Subtract(first, second).Trim(zeroes) = "" Then
181                  Return False
182               Else
183                  Return True
184               End If
185
186               ' if ArgumentException occurs, first number
187               ' was smaller, so return False
188            Catch exception As ArgumentException
189               Return False
190            End Try
191         End Function ' Bigger
192
```

Fig. 21.6 `HugeInteger` Web service (part 4 of 5).

```
193     ' WebMethod returns True if first integer is
194     ' smaller than second
195     <WebMethod( Description := "Determines if the first integer " & _
196        "is smaller than the second integer.")> _
197     Public Function Smaller(ByVal first As String, _
198        ByVal second As String) As Boolean
199
200        ' if second is bigger than first, then first is
201        ' smaller than second
202        Return Bigger(second, first)
203     End Function
204
205     ' WebMethod that returns true if two integers are equal
206     <WebMethod( Description := "Determines if the first integer " & _
207        "is equal to the second integer" )> _
208     Public Function EqualTo(ByVal first As String, _
209        ByVal second As String) As Boolean
210
211        ' if either first is bigger than second, or first is
212        ' smaller than second, they are not equal
213        If (Bigger(first, second) OrElse _
214           Smaller(first, second)) Then
215           Return False
216        Else
217           Return True
218        End If
219     End Function ' EqualTo
220  End Class ' HugeInteger
```

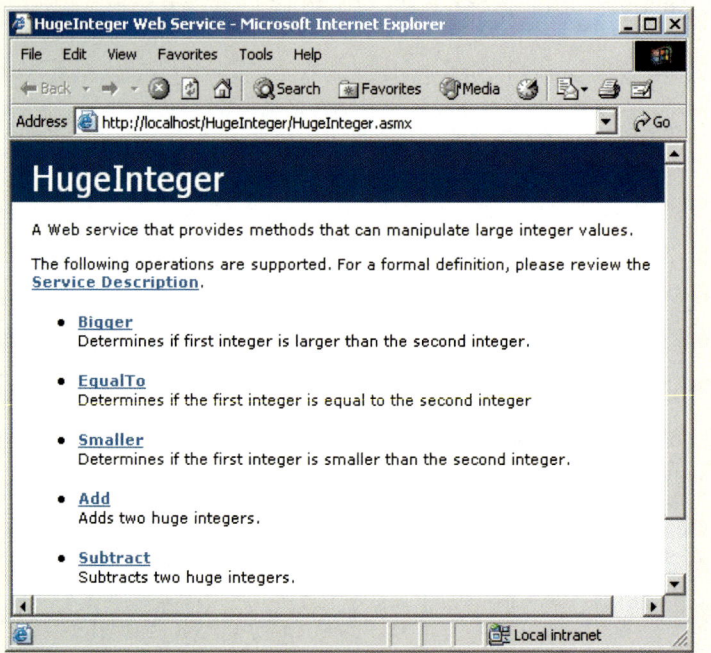

Fig. 21.6 `HugeInteger` Web service (part 5 of 5).

Good Programming Practice 21.1

Specify a namespace for each Web service so that it can be uniquely identified.

Good Programming Practice 21.2

Specify descriptions for all Web services and Web-service methods so that clients can obtain additional information about the Web service and its contents.

Common Programming Error 21.2

No method with the `WebMethod` *attribute can be declared* `Shared`*—for a client to access a Web-service method, an instance of that Web service must exist.*

Lines 36–45 define a `Property` that enables us to access any digit in a `HugeInteger` through property `Digits`. Lines 78 and 115 define `WebMethod`s `Add` and `Subtract`, which perform addition and subtraction, respectively. Method `Borrow` (defined in lines 145–162) handles the case in which the digit that we are currently looking at in the left operand is smaller than the corresponding digit in the right operand. For instance, when we subtract 19 from 32, we usually go digit by digit, starting from the right. The number 2 is smaller than 9, so we add 10 to 2 (resulting in 12), which subtracts 9, resulting in 3 for the right most digit in the solution. We then subtract 1 from the next digit over (3), making it 2. The corresponding digit in the right operand is now the "1" in 19. The subtraction of 1 from 2 is 1, making the corresponding digit in the result 1. The final result, when the resulting digits are put together, is 13. Method `Borrow` is the method that adds ten to the appropriate digits and subtracts 1 from the digits to the left. Because this is a utility method that is not intended to be called remotely, it is not qualified with attribute `WebMethod`.

The screen capture in Fig. 21.6 is identical to the one in Fig. 21.1. A client application can invoke only the five methods listed in the screen shot (i.e., the methods qualified with the `WebMethod` attribute).

Let us demonstrate how to create this.[2] To begin, we must create a project of type **ASP.NET Web Service**. Like Web Forms, Web services are stored in the Web server's `wwwroot` directory on the server (e.g., `localhost`). By default, Visual Studio places the solution file (`.sln`) in the `Visual Studio Projects` folder.

Notice that, when the project is created, the code-behind file is displayed by default in design view (Fig. 21.7). If this file is not open, it can be opened by double-clicking `Service1.asmx`. The file that will be opened, however, is `Service1.asmx.vb` (the code-behind file for our Web service). This is because, when creating Web services in Visual Studio, programmers work almost exclusively in the code-behind file. In fact, if a programmer were to open the ASMX file, it would contain only the lines

```
<%@ WebService Language="vb" Codebehind="Service1.asmx.vb"
    Class="WebService1.Service1" %>
```

indicating the name of the code-behind file, the programming language in which the code-behind file is written and the class that defines our Web service. This is the extent of the information that this file must contain. [*Note*: By default, the code-behind file is not listed

---

2. Visit the **Downloads/Resources** link at `www.deitel.com` for step-by-step configuration instructions for the Web Services included on this book's CD.

in the **Solution Explorer**. It is displayed when the ASMX file is double clicked. It can be listed in the **Solution Explorer** if the icon to show all files is clicked.]

It may seem strange that there is a design view for a Web service, when a Web service does not have a graphical user interface. The answer is that more sophisticated Web services contain methods that manipulate more than just strings or numbers. For example, a Web-service method could manipulate a database. Instead of typing all the code necessary to create a database connection, we simply drop the proper ADO .NET components into the design view and manipulate them as we would in a Windows or Web application. We will see an example of this in Section 21.6.

Now that we have defined our Web service, we demonstrate how to use it. First, a client application must be created. In this first example, we create a Windows application as our client. Once this application has been created, the client must add a proxy class that can be used to access the Web service. A proxy class (or *proxy*) is a class created from the Web service's WSDL file that enables the client to call Web-service methods over the Internet. The proxy class handles all the "plumbing" required for method calls to Web-service methods. Whenever a call is made in the client application to a Web-service method, the application actually calls a corresponding method in the proxy class. This method takes the method name and arguments and then formats them so that they can be sent as a request in a SOAP envelope. The Web service receives this request and executes the method call, sending back the result in another SOAP envelope. When the client application receives the SOAP envelope containing the response, the proxy class decodes it and formats the results so that they are understandable to the client. This information then is returned to the client. It is important to note that the proxy class essentially is hidden from the program. We cannot, in fact, view it in the **Solution Explorer** unless we choose to show all the files. The purpose of the proxy class is to make it seem to clients as if they are calling the Web-service methods directly— the client should have no need to view or manipulate the proxy class.

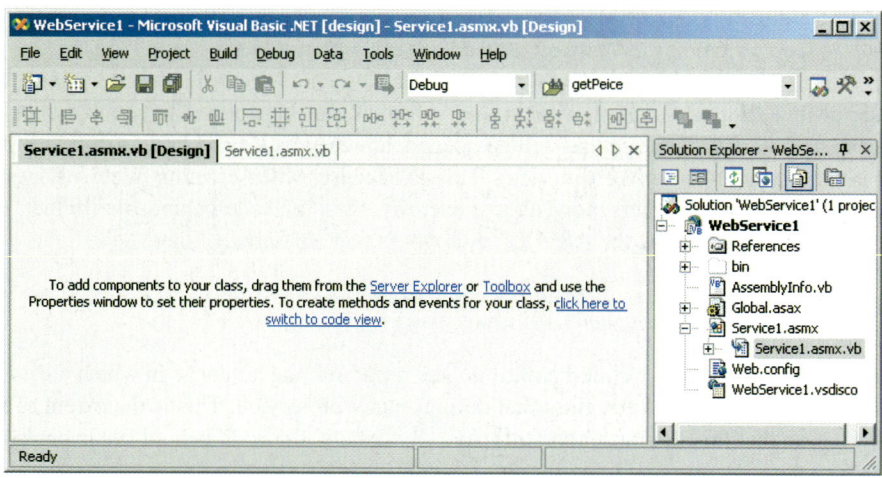

Fig. 21.7 Design view of a Web service.

The next example demonstrates how to create a Web-service client and its corresponding proxy class. We must begin by creating a project and then adding a *Web reference* to the project. When we add a Web reference to a client application, the proxy class is created. The client then creates an instance of the proxy class, which is in turn used to call methods included in the Web service.

To create a proxy in Visual Studio, right click the **References** folder in **Solution Explorer**, and select **Add Web Reference** (Fig. 21.8). In the **Add Web Reference** dialog that appears (Fig. 21.9), enter the Web address of the Web service, and press *Enter*. In this chapter, we store the Web service in the root directory of our local Web server (**http://localhost**, whose physical location is **C:\Inetpub\wwwroot**). We do not store the services in the **VB** directory used in the previous chapter. For simplicity, we have instead stored them directly in the root of our Web server. This allows us to add a Web reference without typing in the whole address, by clicking the link **Web References on Local Web Server** (Fig. 21.9). Next, we select the appropriate Web service from the list of Web services located on **localhost** (Fig. 21.10). Notice that each Web service is listed as a file with the extension **.vsdisco**, located in the directory for the Web service project. Files with the extension **.disco** and **.vsdisco** are known as discovery files. We discuss discovery files, as well as the distinction between discovery files with the **.disco** and **.vsdisco** extension later in this section. When the description of the Web service appears, click **Add Reference** (Fig. 21.11). This adds to the **Solution Explorer** (Fig. 21.12) a **Web References** folder with a node named after the domain name where the Web service is located. In this case, the name is **localhost**, because we are using the local Web server. This means that, when we reference class **HugeInteger**, we will be doing so through class **HugeInteger** in namespace **localhost** (the Web service class and proxy class have the same name). Visual Studio generates a proxy for the Web service and adds it as a reference (Fig. 21.12).

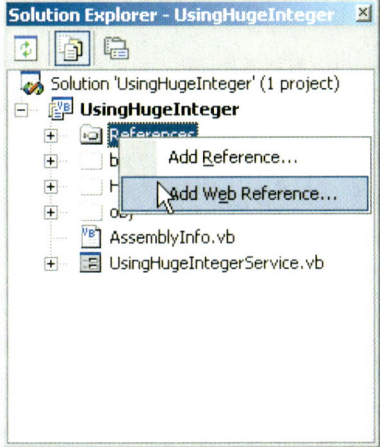

Fig. 21.8 Adding a Web service reference to a project.

1046 ASP .NET and Web Services Chapter 21

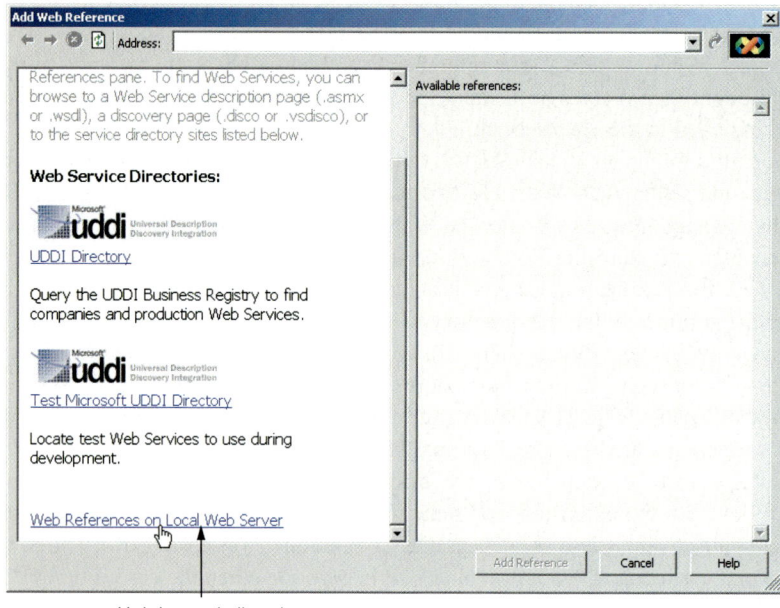

Fig. 21.9 Add Web Reference dialog.

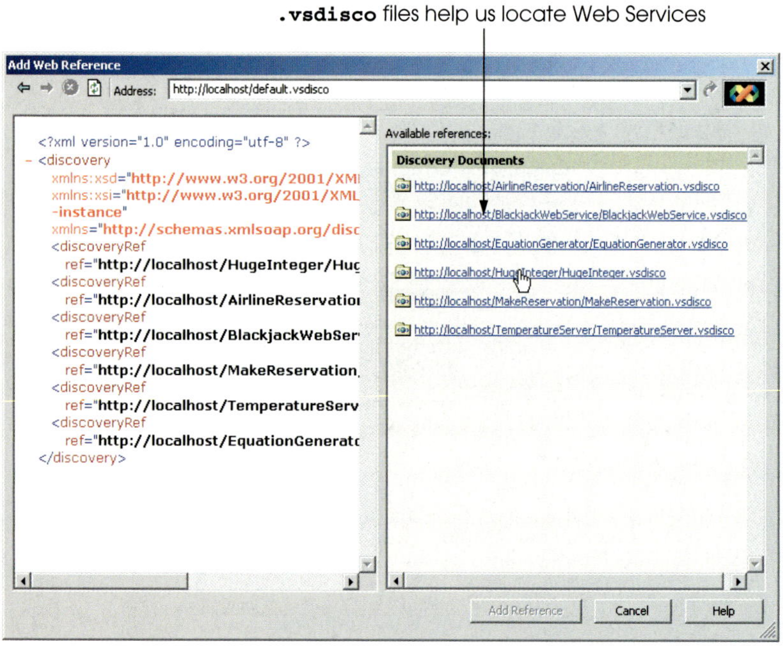

Fig. 21.10 Web services located on `localhost`.

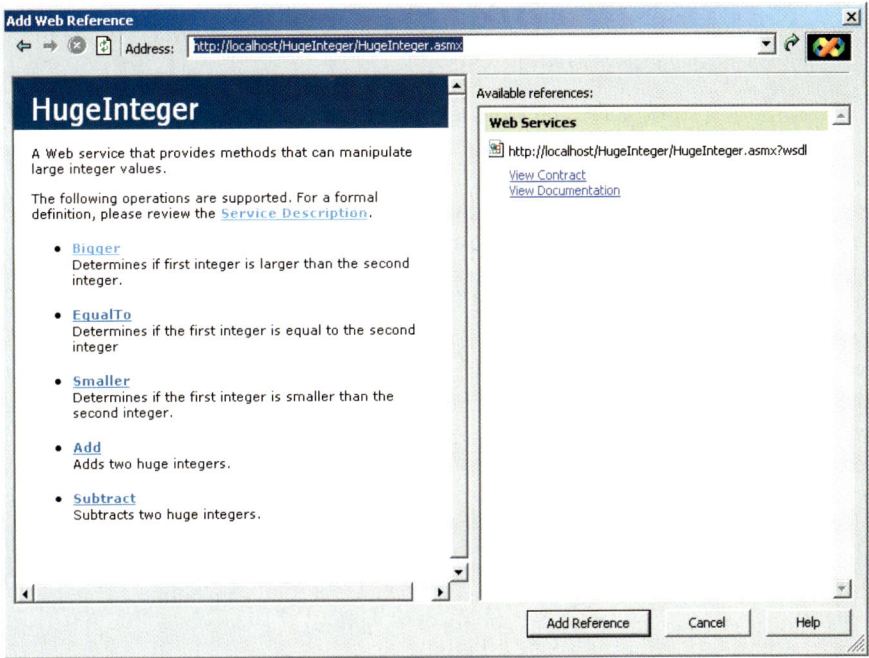

Fig. 21.11 Web reference selection and description.

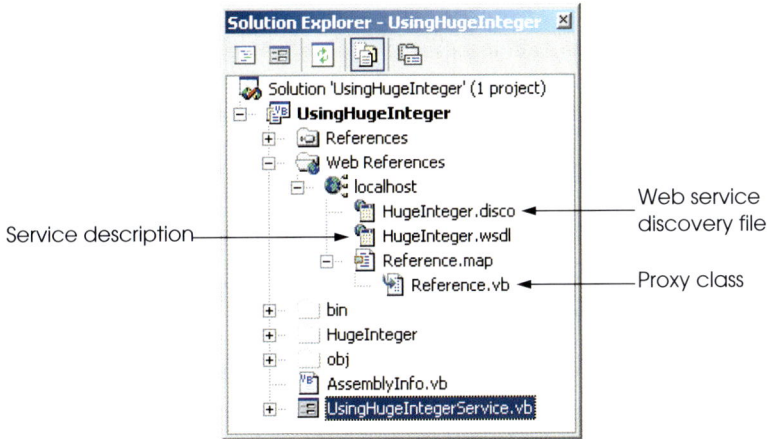

Fig. 21.12 Solution Explorer after adding a Web reference to a project.

Good Programming Practice 21.3

When creating a program that uses Web services, add the Web reference first. This enables Visual Studio to recognize an instance of the Web-service class, allowing Intellisense to help developers use the Web service.

The steps that we described previously work well if the programmer knows the appropriate Web-services reference. However, what if we are trying to locate a new Web service? There are two technologies that can facilitate this process: *Universal Description, Discovery and Integration (UDDI)* and *Discovery files (DISCO)*. UDDI is a project for developing a set of specifications that define how Web services should be exposed, so that programmers searching for Web services can find them. Microsoft began an ongoing project to facilitate the locating of Web services that conform to certain specifications, allowing programmers to find different Web services through search engines. UDDI organizes and describes Web services and then places this information in a central location. Although UDDI is beyond the scope of what we are teaching, the reader can learn more about this project and view a demonstration by visiting `www.uddi.org` and `uddi.microsoft.com`. Both of these sites contain search tools that make finding Web services fast and easy.

A DISCO file catalogs any Web services that are available in the current directory. There are two types of discovery files: *Dynamic discovery* files (`.vsdisco` extension) and *static discovery* files (`.disco` extension). These files indicate both the location of the ASMX file and the service description (a WSDL file) for each Web service in the current directory. When a programmer creates a Web service, Visual Studio generates a dynamic discovery file for that Web service. When a client is adding a Web reference, the dynamic discovery file is then used to point out the Web service, as was demonstrated in Fig. 21.10. Once the Web reference is created, a static discovery file is placed in the client's project. The static discovery file hard-codes the location for the ASMX and WSDL files (by "hard code," we mean that the location is entered directly into the file). Dynamic discovery files, on the other hand, are created such that the list of Web services are created dynamically on the server when a client is searching for Web services. The use of dynamic discovery enables certain extra options, such as the hiding of certain Web services in subdirectories. Discovery files are a Microsoft-specific technology, whereas UDDI is not. The two can work together, though, to enable a client to find a Web service. Using both technologies, the client can use a search engine to find a location with various Web services on a topic, and then use discovery files to view all the Web services in that location.

Once the Web reference is added, the client can access the Web service through a proxy. Because `HugeInteger` is located as a proxy class in namespace `localhost`, we must use `localhost.HugeInteger` to reference this class. The Windows Form in Fig. 21.13 uses the `HugeInteger` Web service to perform computations with positive integers that are up to `100` digits long.

The user inputs two integers, each up to 100 digits long. Clicking any button invokes a remote method to perform the appropriate calculation and return the result. The return value of each operation is displayed, and all leading zeroes are eliminated by `String` method `TrimStart`. Note that `UsingHugeInteger` does not have the capability to perform operations with 100-digit numbers. It instead creates `String` representations of these numbers and passes them as arguments to Web-service methods that handle such tasks for us.

```vbnet
1   ' Fig. 21.13: UsingHugeIntegerService.vb
2   ' Using the HugeInteger Web Service.
3
4   Imports System
5   Imports System.Drawing
6   Imports System.Collections
7   Imports System.ComponentModel
8   Imports System.Windows.Forms
9   Imports System.Web.Services.Protocols
10
11  ' allows user to perform operations on large integers
12  Public Class FrmUsingHugeInteger
13     Inherits Windows.Forms.Form
14
15     ' declare a reference Web service
16     Private remoteInteger As localhost.HugeInteger
17
18     ' HugeInteger operation buttons
19     Friend WithEvents cmdAdd As Button
20     Friend WithEvents cmdEqual As Button
21     Friend WithEvents cmdSmaller As Button
22     Friend WithEvents cmdLarger As Button
23     Friend WithEvents cmdSubtract As Button
24
25     ' input text boxes
26     Friend WithEvents txtSecond As TextBox
27     Friend WithEvents txtFirst As TextBox
28
29     ' question and answer labels
30     Friend WithEvents lblPrompt As Label
31     Friend WithEvents lblResult As Label
32
33     Private zeroes() As Char = {"0"}
34
35     ' default constructor
36     Public Sub New()
37        MyBase.New()
38
39        InitializeComponent()
40
41        ' instantiate remoteInteger
42        remoteInteger = New localhost.HugeInteger()
43     End Sub
44
45     ' Visual Studio .NET generated code
46
47     Public Shared Sub Main()
48        Application.Run(New FrmUsingHugeInteger())
49     End Sub ' Main
50
```

Fig. 21.13 Using the **HugeInteger** Web service (part 1 of 5).

```vbnet
51     ' checks if two numbers user input are equal
52     Private Sub cmdEqual_Click(ByVal sender As System.Object, _
53        ByVal e As System.EventArgs) Handles cmdEqual.Click
54
55        ' make sure HugeIntegers do not exceed 100 digits
56        If SizeCheck(txtFirst, txtSecond) Then
57           Return
58        End If
59
60        ' call Web-service method to determine if integers are equal
61        If remoteInteger.EqualTo( _
62           txtFirst.Text, txtSecond.Text) Then
63
64           lblResult.Text = _
65              txtFirst.Text.TrimStart(zeroes) & _
66              " is equal to " & _
67              txtSecond.Text.TrimStart(zeroes)
68        Else
69           lblResult.Text = _
70              txtFirst.Text.TrimStart(zeroes) & _
71              " is NOT equal to " & _
72              txtSecond.Text.TrimStart(zeroes)
73        End If
74
75     End Sub ' cmdEqual_Click
76
77     ' checks if first integer input
78     ' by user is smaller than second
79     Private Sub cmdSmaller_Click(ByVal sender As System.Object, _
80        ByVal e As System.EventArgs) Handles cmdSmaller.Click
81
82        ' make sure HugeIntegers do not exceed 100 digits
83        If SizeCheck(txtFirst, txtSecond) Then
84           Return
85        End If
86
87        ' call Web-service method to determine if first
88        ' integer is smaller than second
89        If remoteInteger.Smaller( _
90           txtFirst.Text, txtSecond.Text) Then
91
92           lblResult.Text = _
93              txtFirst.Text.TrimStart(zeroes) & _
94              " is smaller than " & _
95              txtSecond.Text.TrimStart(zeroes)
96        Else
97           lblResult.Text = _
98              txtFirst.Text.TrimStart(zeroes) & _
99              " is NOT smaller than " & _
100             txtSecond.Text.TrimStart(zeroes)
101       End If
102
103    End Sub ' cmdSmaller_Click
```

Fig. 21.13 Using the **HugeInteger** Web service (part 2 of 5).

```vbnet
104
105     ' checks if first integer input
106     ' by user is bigger than second
107     Private Sub cmdLarger_Click(ByVal sender As System.Object, _
108        ByVal e As System.EventArgs) Handles cmdLarger.Click
109
110        ' make sure HugeIntegers do not exceed 100 digits
111        If SizeCheck(txtFirst, txtSecond) Then
112           Return
113        End If
114
115        ' call Web-service method to determine if first
116        ' integer is larger than the second
117        If remoteInteger.Bigger(txtFirst.Text, _
118           txtSecond.Text) Then
119
120           lblResult.Text = _
121              txtFirst.Text.TrimStart(zeroes) & _
122              " is larger than " & _
123              txtSecond.Text.TrimStart(zeroes)
124        Else
125           lblResult.Text = _
126              txtFirst.Text.TrimStart(zeroes) & _
127              " is NOT larger than " & _
128              txtSecond.Text.TrimStart(zeroes)
129        End If
130
131     End Sub ' cmdLarger_Click
132
133     ' subtract second integer from first
134     Private Sub cmdSubtract_Click(ByVal sender As System.Object, _
135        ByVal e As System.EventArgs) Handles cmdSubtract.Click
136
137        ' make sure HugeIntegers do not exceed 100 digits
138        If SizeCheck(txtFirst, txtSecond) Then
139           Return
140        End If
141
142        ' perform subtraction
143        Try
144           Dim result As String = remoteInteger.Subtract( _
145              txtFirst.Text, txtSecond.Text).TrimStart(zeroes)
146
147           If result = "" Then
148              lblResult.Text = "0"
149           Else
150              lblResult.Text = result
151           End If
152
153        ' if WebMethod throws an exception, then first
154        ' argument was smaller than second
```

Fig. 21.13 Using the **HugeInteger** Web service (part 3 of 5).

```vbnet
155             Catch exception As SoapException
156                 MessageBox.Show( _
157                     "First argument was smaller than the second")
158             End Try
159
160         End Sub ' cmdSubtract_Click
161
162         ' adds two integers input by user
163         Private Sub cmdAdd_Click(ByVal sender As System.Object, _
164             ByVal e As System.EventArgs) Handles cmdAdd.Click
165
166             ' make sure HugeInteger does not exceed 100 digits
167             ' and be sure both are not 100 digits long
168             ' which would result in overflow
169
170             If txtFirst.Text.Length > 100 OrElse _
171                 txtSecond.Text.Length > 100 OrElse _
172                 (txtFirst.Text.Length = 100 AndAlso _
173                 txtSecond.Text.Length = 100) Then
174
175                 MessageBox.Show("HugeIntegers must not be more " _
176                     & "than 100 digits" & vbCrLf & "Both integers " _
177                     & "cannot be of length 100: this causes an overflow", _
178                     "Error", MessageBoxButtons.OK, _
179                     MessageBoxIcon.Information)
180                 Return
181             End If
182
183             ' perform addition
184             lblResult.Text = _
185                 remoteInteger.Add(txtFirst.Text, _
186                 txtSecond.Text).TrimStart(zeroes)
187
188         End Sub ' cmdAdd_Click
189
190         ' determines if size of integers are too big
191         Private Function SizeCheck(ByVal first As TextBox, _
192             ByVal second As TextBox) As Boolean
193
194             If first.Text.Length > 100 OrElse _
195                 second.Text.Length > 100 Then
196
197                 MessageBox.Show("HugeIntegers must be less than 100" _
198                     & " digits", "Error", MessageBoxButtons.OK, _
199                     MessageBoxIcon.Information)
200
201                 Return True
202             End If
203
204             Return False
205         End Function ' SizeCheck
206 End Class ' FrmUsingHugeInteger
```

Fig. 21.13 Using the **HugeInteger** Web service (part 4 of 5).

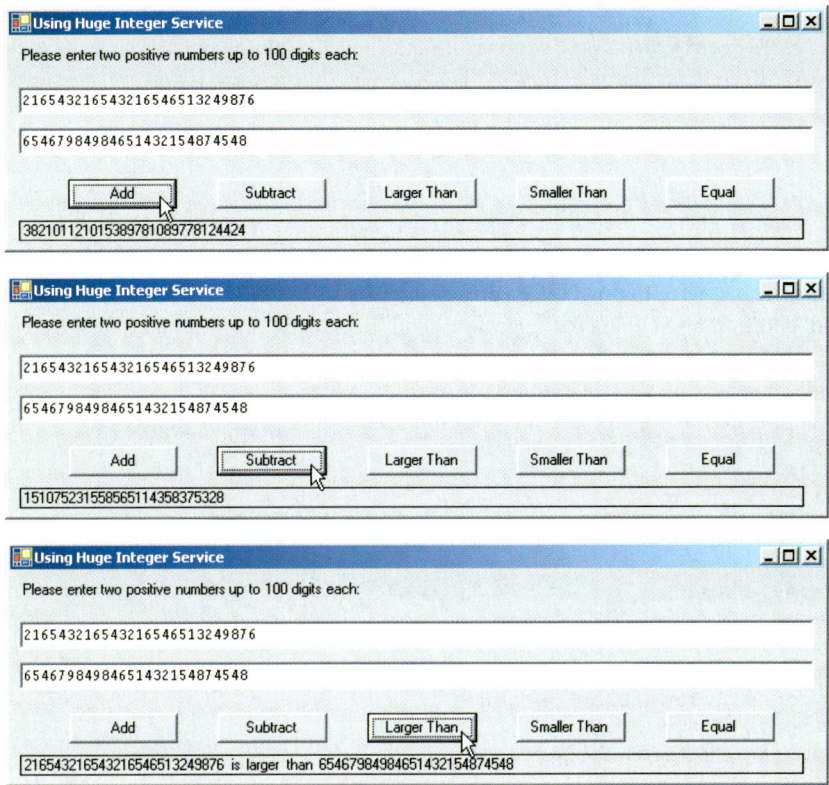

Fig. 21.13 Using the **HugeInteger** Web service (part 5 of 5).

21.5 Session Tracking in Web Services

In Chapter 20, we described the importance of maintaining information about users to personalize their experiences. In the context of that discussion, we explored session tracking using cookies and sessions. In this section, we incorporate session tracking into a Web service. Sometimes, it makes sense that a client application would call several methods from the same Web service, and it might call some methods possibly several times. It would be beneficial for such a Web service to maintain state information for the client. Using session tracking can be beneficial because information that is stored as part of the session will not need to be passed back and forth between the Web service and the client. This will not only cause the client application to run faster, but also require less effort on the part of the programmer (who likely will have to pass less information to a method).

Storing session information also can provide for a more intuitive Web service. In the following example, we create a Web service designed to assist with the computations involved in playing a game of Blackjack (Fig. 21.14). We will then use this Web service to create a dealer for a game of Blackjack. This dealer handles the details for our deck of cards. The information is stored as part of the session, so that one deck of cards does not get mixed up with another deck being used by another client application. Our example uses casino Blackjack rules:

Two cards each are dealt to the dealer and the player. The player's cards are dealt face up. Only one of the dealer's cards is dealt face up. Then, the player can begin taking additional cards one at a time. These cards are dealt face up, and the player decides when to stop taking cards. If the sum of the player's cards exceeds 21, the game is over, and the player loses. When the player is satisfied with the current set of cards, the player "stays" (i.e., stops taking cards) and the dealer's hidden card is revealed. If the dealer's total is less than 17, the dealer must take another card; otherwise, the dealer must stay. The dealer must continue to take cards until the sum of the dealer's cards is greater than or equal to 17. If the dealer exceeds 21, the player wins. Otherwise, the hand with the higher point total wins. If both sets of cards have the same point total, the game is a push (i.e., a tie) and no one wins.

The Web service that we create provides methods to deal a card and to count cards in a hand, determining a value for a specific hand. Each card is represented by a **String** in the form "**face suit**" where **face** is a digit representing the face of the card, and **suit** is a digit representing the suit of the card. After the Web service is created, we create a Windows application that uses these methods to implement a game of Blackjack.

```vb
1   ' Fig. 21.15: BlackjackService.asmx.vb
2   ' Blackjack Web Service which deals and counts cards.
3
4   Imports System
5   Imports System.Collections
6   Imports System.ComponentModel
7   Imports System.Data
8   Imports System.Diagnostics
9   Imports System.Web
10  Imports System.Web.Services
11
12  <WebService(Namespace:="http://www.deitel.com", Description := _
13      "A Web service that provides methods to manipulate a deck " _
14      & "of cards" )> _
15  Public Class BlackjackService
16      Inherits System.Web.Services.WebService
17
18      ' Visual Studio .NET generated code
19
20      ' deals card that has not yet been dealt
21      <WebMethod(EnableSession:=True, Description := "Deal a new " _
22          & "card from the deck." )> _
23      Public Function DealCard() As String
24
25          Dim card As String = "2 2"
26
27          ' get client's deck
28          Dim deck As ArrayList = CType(Session("deck"), ArrayList)
29          card = Convert.ToString(deck(0))
30          deck.RemoveAt(0)
31          Return card
32
33      End Function ' DealCard
34
```

Fig. 21.14 Blackjack Web service (part 1 of 3).

```vbnet
35      <WebMethod(EnableSession:=True, Description := "Create and " _
36         & "shuffle a deck of cards." )> _
37      Public Sub Shuffle()
38
39         Dim temporary As Object
40         Dim randomObject As New Random()
41         Dim newIndex As Integer
42         Dim i, j As Integer
43
44         Dim deck As New ArrayList()
45
46         ' generate all possible cards
47         For i = 1 To 13
48            For j = 0 To 3
49               deck.Add(i & " " & j)
50            Next
51         Next
52
53         ' swap each card with another card randomly
54         For i = 0 To deck.Count - 1
55
56            newIndex = randomObject.Next(deck.Count - 1)
57            temporary = deck(i)
58            deck(i) = deck(newIndex)
59            deck(newIndex) = temporary
60         Next
61
62         ' add this deck to user's session state
63         Session.Add("deck", deck)
64      End Sub ' Shuffle
65
66      ' computes value of hand
67      <WebMethod( Description := "Compute a numerical value" _
68         & " for the current hand." )> _
69      Public Function CountCards(ByVal dealt As String) As Integer
70
71         ' split string containing all cards
72         Dim tab As Char() = {vbTab}
73         Dim cards As String() = dealt.Split(tab)
74         Dim drawn As String
75         Dim total As Integer = 0
76         Dim face, numAces As Integer
77         numAces = 0
78
79         For Each drawn In cards
80
81            ' get face of card
82            face = Int32.Parse( _
83               drawn.Substring(0, drawn.IndexOf(" ")))
84
85            Select Case face
86               Case 1 ' if ace, increment numAces
87                  numAces += 1
```

Fig. 21.14 `Blackjack` Web service (part 2 of 3).

```
88                Case 11 To 13 ' if jack, queen or king, add 10
89                    total += 10
90                Case Else ' otherwise, add value of face
91                    total += face
92            End Select
93        Next
94
95        ' if there are any aces, calculate optimum total
96        If numAces > 0 Then
97
98            ' if it is possible to count one Ace as 11, and rest
99            ' 1 each, do so; otherwise, count all Aces as 1 each
100           If (total + 11 + numAces - 1 <= 21) Then
101               total += 11 + numAces - 1
102           Else
103               total += numAces
104           End If
105       End If
106
107       Return total
108
109   End Function ' CountCards
110
111 End Class ' BlackjackService
```

Fig. 21.14 `Blackjack` Web service (part 3 of 3).

Lines 21–23 define method **DealCard** as a **WebMethod**, with property **EnableSession** set to **True**. This property needs to be set to **True** for session information to be maintained. This simple step provides an important advantage to our Web service. The Web service can now use an **HttpSessionState** object (called **Session**) to maintain the deck of cards for each client application that wishes to use this Web service (line 28). We can use **Session** to store objects for a specific client between method calls. We discussed session state in detail in Chapter 20, ASP .NET, Web Forms and Web Controls.

As we discuss shortly, method **DealCard** removes a card from the deck and returns it to the client. Without using a session variable, the deck of cards would need to be passed back and forth with each method call. Not only does the use of session state make the method easy to call (it requires no arguments), but we avoid the overhead that would occur from sending this information back and forth. This makes our Web service faster.

Right now, we simply have methods that use session variables. The Web service, however, still cannot determine which session variables belong to which user. This is an important point—if the Web service cannot uniquely identify a user, it has failed to perform session tracking properly. If two clients successfully call the **DealCard** method, the same deck would be manipulated. In order to identify various users, the Web service creates a cookie for each user. A client application that wishes to use this Web service will need to accept this cookie in a **CookieContainer** object. We discuss this in more detail shortly, when we look into the client application that uses the Blackjack Web service.

Method **DealCard** (lines 21–33) obtains the current user's deck as an **ArrayList** from the Web service's **Session** object (line 28). You can think of an **ArrayList** as a dynamic array (i.e., its size can change at runtime). Class **ArrayList** is discussed in greater detail in Chapter 24, Data Structures. The class' method **Add** places an **Object** in the **ArrayList**. Method **DealCard** then removes the top card from the deck (line 30) and returns the card's value as a **String** (line 31).

Method **Shuffle** (lines 35–64) generates an **ArrayList** representing a card deck, shuffles it and stores the shuffled cards in the client's **Session** object. Lines 47–51 include **For** loops to generate **String**s in the form "**face suit**" to represent each possible card in a deck. Lines 54–60 shuffle the recreated deck by swapping each card with another random card in the deck. Line 63 adds the **ArrayList** to the **Session** object to maintain the deck between method calls.

Method **CountCards** (lines 67–109) counts the values of the cards in a hand by trying to attain the highest score possible without going over 21. Precautions need to be taken when calculating the value of the cards, because an ace can be counted as either 1 or 11, and all face cards count as 10.

The **String dealt** is tokenized into its individual cards by calling **String** method **Split** and passing it an array containing the tab character. The **For Each** loop (line 79) counts the value of each card. Lines 82–83 retrieve the first integer—the face—and uses that value as input to the **Select Case** statement in line 85. If the card is 1 (an ace), the program increments variable **aceCount**. Because an ace can have two values, additional logic is required to process aces. If the card is an 13, 12 or 11 (King, Queen or Jack), the program adds 10 to the total. If the card is anything else, the program increases the total by that value.

In lines 96–104, the aces are counted after all the other cards. If several aces are included in a hand, only one can be counted as 11 (e.g., if two were counted as 11 we would already have a hand value of 22, which is a losing hand). We then determine whether counting one ace as 11 and the rest as 1 will result in a total that does not exceed 21. If this is possible, line 101 adjusts the total accordingly. Otherwise, line 103 adjusts the total, counting each ace as 1 point.

CountCards attempts to maximize the value of the current cards without exceeding 21. Imagine, for example, that the dealer has a 7 and then receives an ace. The new total could be either 8 or 18. However, **CountCards** always tries the maximize the value of the cards without going over 21, so the new total is 18.

Now, we use the Blackjack Web service in a Windows application called **Game** (Fig. 21.15). This program uses an instance of **BlackjackWebService** to represent the dealer, calling its **DealCard** and **CountCards** methods. The Web service keeps track of both the player's and the dealer's cards (i.e., all the cards that have been dealt).

Each player has eleven **PictureBox**es—the maximum number of cards that can be dealt without automatically exceeding 21. These **PictureBox**es are placed in an **ArrayList**, allowing us to index the **ArrayList** to determine which **PictureBox** will display the card image.

```
1    ' Fig. 21.16: Blackjack.vb
2    ' Blackjack game that uses the Blackjack Web service.
3
```

Fig. 21.15 Blackjack game that uses the **Blackjack** Web service (part 1 of 9).

```vb
4   Imports System
5   Imports System.Drawing
6   Imports System.Collections
7   Imports System.ComponentModel
8   Imports System.Windows.Forms
9   Imports System.Data
10  Imports System.Net ' for cookieContainer
11
12  ' game that uses Blackjack Web Service
13  Public Class FrmBlackJack
14      Inherits System.Windows.Forms.Form
15
16      Private dealer As localhost.BlackjackService
17      Private dealersCards, playersCards As String
18      Private cardBoxes As ArrayList
19      Private playerCard, dealerCard As Integer
20      Friend WithEvents pbStatus As System.Windows.Forms.PictureBox
21
22      Friend WithEvents cmdStay As System.Windows.Forms.Button
23      Friend WithEvents cmdHit As System.Windows.Forms.Button
24      Friend WithEvents cmdDeal As System.Windows.Forms.Button
25
26      Friend WithEvents lblDealer As System.Windows.Forms.Label
27      Friend WithEvents lblPlayer As System.Windows.Forms.Label
28
29      Public Enum GameStatus
30          PUSH
31          LOSE
32          WIN
33          BLACKJACK
34      End Enum
35
36
37      Public Sub New()
38
39          InitializeComponent()
40
41          dealer = New localhost.BlackjackService()
42
43          ' allow session state
44          dealer.CookieContainer = New CookieContainer()
45
46          cardBoxes = New ArrayList()
47
48          ' put PictureBoxes into ArrayList
49          cardBoxes.Add(pictureBox1)
50          cardBoxes.Add(pictureBox2)
51          cardBoxes.Add(pictureBox3)
52          cardBoxes.Add(pictureBox4)
53          cardBoxes.Add(pictureBox5)
54          cardBoxes.Add(pictureBox6)
55          cardBoxes.Add(pictureBox7)
56          cardBoxes.Add(pictureBox8)
```

Fig. 21.15 Blackjack game that uses the **Blackjack** Web service (part 2 of 9).

```vbnet
57              cardBoxes.Add(pictureBox9)
58              cardBoxes.Add(pictureBox10)
59              cardBoxes.Add(pictureBox11)
60              cardBoxes.Add(pictureBox12)
61              cardBoxes.Add(pictureBox13)
62              cardBoxes.Add(pictureBox14)
63              cardBoxes.Add(pictureBox15)
64              cardBoxes.Add(pictureBox16)
65              cardBoxes.Add(pictureBox17)
66              cardBoxes.Add(pictureBox18)
67              cardBoxes.Add(pictureBox19)
68              cardBoxes.Add(pictureBox20)
69              cardBoxes.Add(pictureBox21)
70              cardBoxes.Add(pictureBox22)
71          End Sub ' New
72
73          ' Visual Studio .NET generated code
74
75          ' deals cards to dealer while dealer's total is
76          ' less than 17, then computes value of each hand
77          ' and determines winner
78          Private Sub cmdStay_Click(ByVal sender As System.Object, _
79              ByVal e As System.EventArgs) Handles cmdStay.Click
80              cmdStay.Enabled = False
81              cmdHit.Enabled = False
82              cmdDeal.Enabled = True
83              DealerPlay()
84          End Sub ' cmdStay_Click
85
86          ' process dealers turn
87          Private Sub DealerPlay()
88
89              ' while value of dealer's hand is below 17,
90              ' dealer must take cards
91              While dealer.CountCards(dealersCards) < 17
92                  dealersCards &= vbTab & dealer.DealCard()
93                  DisplayCard(dealerCard, "")
94                  dealerCard += 1
95                  MessageBox.Show("Dealer takes a card")
96              End While
97
98
99              Dim dealersTotal As Integer = _
100                 dealer.CountCards(dealersCards)
101             Dim playersTotal As Integer = _
102                 dealer.CountCards(playersCards)
103
104             ' if dealer busted, player wins
105             If dealersTotal > 21 Then
106                 GameOver(GameStatus.WIN)
107                 Return
108             End If
109
```

Fig. 21.15 Blackjack game that uses the **Blackjack** Web service (part 3 of 9).

```vbnet
110         ' if dealer and player have not exceeded 21,
111         ' higher score wins; equal scores is a push
112         If dealersTotal > playersTotal Then
113            GameOver(GameStatus.LOSE)
114         ElseIf playersTotal > dealersTotal Then
115            GameOver(GameStatus.WIN)
116         Else
117            GameOver(GameStatus.PUSH)
118         End If
119
120      End Sub 'DealerPlay
121
122      ' deal another card to player
123      Private Sub cmdHit_Click(ByVal sender As System.Object, _
124         ByVal e As System.EventArgs) Handles cmdHit.Click
125
126         ' get player another card
127         Dim card As String = dealer.DealCard()
128         playersCards &= vbTab & card
129         DisplayCard(playerCard, card)
130         playerCard += 1
131
132         Dim total As Integer = _
133            dealer.CountCards(playersCards)
134
135         ' if player exceeds 21, house wins
136         If total > 21 Then
137            GameOver(GameStatus.LOSE)
138         End If
139         ' if player has 21, they cannot take more cards
140         ' the dealer plays
141         If total = 21 Then
142            cmdHit.Enabled = False
143            DealerPlay()
144         End If
145
146
147      End Sub ' cmdHit_Click
148
149      ' deal two cards each to dealer and player
150      Private Sub cmdDeal_Click(ByVal sender As System.Object, _
151         ByVal e As System.EventArgs) Handles cmdDeal.Click
152
153         Dim card As String
154         Dim cardImage As PictureBox
155
156         ' clear card images
157         For Each cardImage In cardBoxes
158            cardImage.Image = Nothing
159         Next
160
161         pbStatus.Image = Nothing
162
```

Fig. 21.15 Blackjack game that uses the **Blackjack** Web service (part 4 of 9).

```vbnet
163        dealer.Shuffle()
164
165        ' deal two cards to player
166        playersCards = dealer.DealCard()
167        DisplayCard(0, playersCards)
168        card = dealer.DealCard()
169        DisplayCard(1, card)
170        playersCards &= vbTab & card
171
172        ' deal two cards to dealer, only display face
173        ' of first card
174        dealersCards = dealer.DealCard()
175        DisplayCard(11, dealersCards)
176        card = dealer.DealCard()
177        DisplayCard(12, "")
178        dealersCards &= vbTab & card
179
180        cmdStay.Enabled = True
181        cmdHit.Enabled = True
182        cmdDeal.Enabled = False
183
184        Dim dealersTotal As Integer = _
185           dealer.CountCards(dealersCards)
186
187        Dim playersTotal As Integer = _
188           dealer.CountCards(playersCards)
189
190        ' if hands equal 21, it is a push
191        If dealersTotal = playersTotal AndAlso _
192           dealersTotal = 21 Then
193           GameOver(GameStatus.PUSH)
194
195        ' if dealer has 21, dealer wins
196        ElseIf dealersTotal = 21 Then
197           GameOver(GameStatus.LOSE)
198
199        ' if player has 21, the player has blackjack
200        ElseIf playersTotal = 21 Then
201           GameOver(GameStatus.BLACKJACK)
202        End If
203
204        playerCard = 2
205        dealerCard = 13
206
207     End Sub ' cmdDeal_Click
208
209     ' displays card represented by card value in
210     ' PictureBox with number card
211     Public Sub DisplayCard(ByVal card As Integer, _
212        ByVal cardValue As String)
213
```

Fig. 21.15 Blackjack game that uses the **Blackjack** Web service (part 5 of 9).

```
214            ' retrieve appropriate PictureBox from ArrayList
215            Dim displayBox As PictureBox = _
216                CType(cardBoxes(card), PictureBox)
217
218            ' if String representing card is empty,
219            ' set displayBox to display back of card
220            If cardValue = "" Then
221                displayBox.Image = _
222                    Image.FromFile("blackjack_images\\cardback.png")
223                Return
224            End If
225
226            ' retrieve face value of card from cardValue
227            Dim faceNumber As Integer = Int32.Parse( _
228                cardValue.Substring(0, cardValue.IndexOf(" ")))
229
230            Dim face As String = faceNumber.ToString()
231
232            ' retrieve the suit of the card from cardValue
233            Dim suit As String = cardValue.Substring( _
234                cardValue.IndexOf(" ") + 1)
235
236            Dim suitLetter As Char
237
238            ' determine if suit is other then clubs
239            Select Case (Convert.ToInt32(suit))
240                Case 0 ' suit is clubs
241                    suitLetter = "c"
242                Case 1 ' suit is diamonds
243                    suitLetter = "d"
244                Case 2 ' suit is hearts
245                    suitLetter = "h"
246                Case Else 'suit is spades
247                    suitLetter = "s"
248            End Select
249
250            ' set displayBox to display appropriate image
251            displayBox.Image = Image.FromFile( _
252                "blackjack_images\\" & face & suitLetter & ".png")
253
254        End Sub ' DisplayCard
255
256        ' displays all player cards and shows
257        ' appropriate game status message
258        Public Sub GameOver(ByVal winner As GameStatus)
259
260            Dim tab As Char() = {vbTab}
261            Dim cards As String() = dealersCards.Split(tab)
262            Dim i As Integer
263
264            For i = 0 To cards.Length - 1
265                DisplayCard(i + 11, cards(i))
266            Next
```

Fig. 21.15 Blackjack game that uses the **Blackjack** Web service (part 6 of 9).

```vbnet
            ' push
            If winner = GameStatus.PUSH Then
               pbStatus.Image = _
                  Image.FromFile("blackjack_images\\tie.png")

            ' player loses
            ElseIf winner = GameStatus.LOSE Then
               pbStatus.Image = _
                  Image.FromFile("blackjack_images\\lose.png")

            ' player has blackjack
            ElseIf winner = GameStatus.BLACKJACK Then
               pbStatus.Image = _
                  Image.FromFile("blackjack_images\\blackjack.png")

            ' player wins
            Else
               pbStatus.Image = _
                  Image.FromFile("blackjack_images\\win.png")
            End If

            cmdStay.Enabled = False
            cmdHit.Enabled = False
            cmdDeal.Enabled = True

      End Sub ' GameOver

End Class ' Blackjack
```

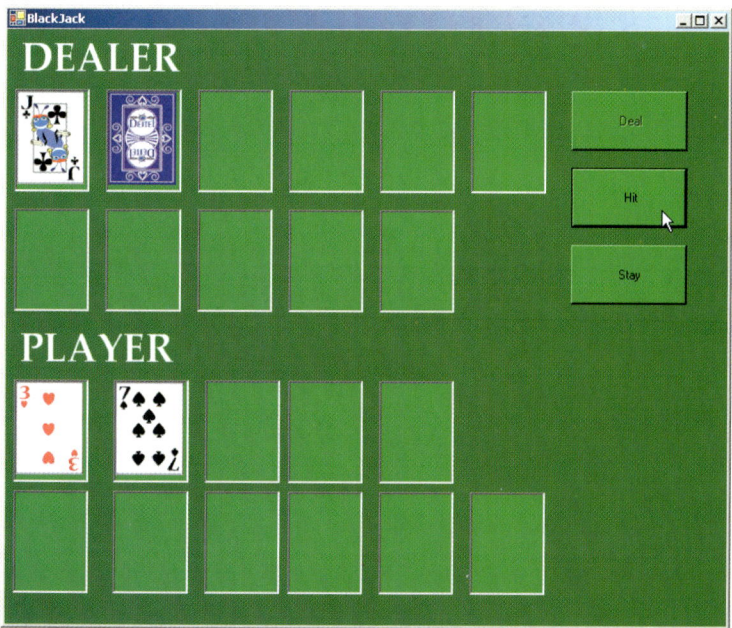

Fig. 21.15 Blackjack game that uses the **Blackjack** Web service (part 7 of 9).

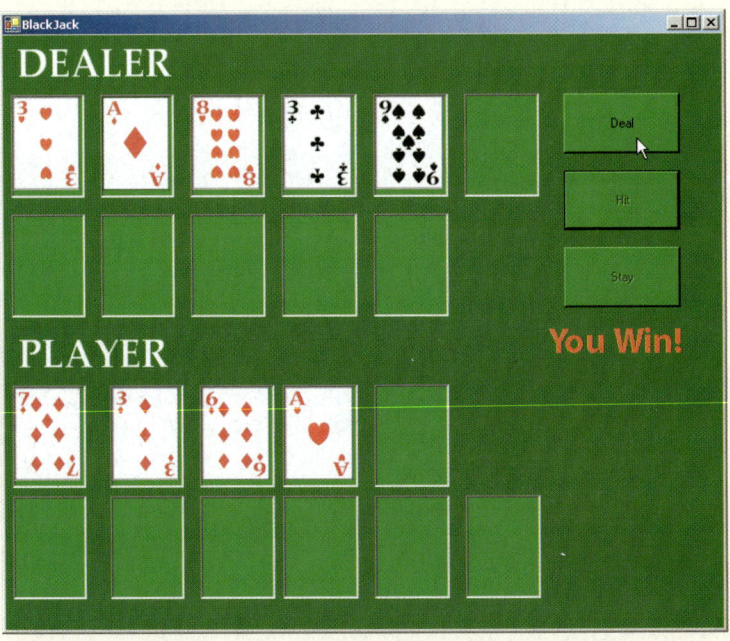

Fig. 21.15 Blackjack game that uses the `Blackjack` Web service (part 8 of 9).

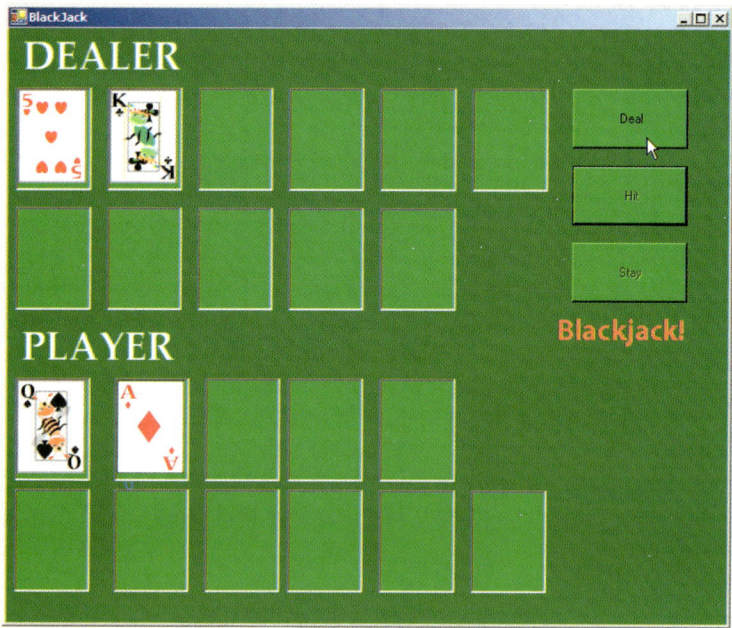

Fig. 21.15 Blackjack game that uses the **Blackjack** Web service (part 9 of 9).

Previously we mentioned that the client must provide a way to accept any cookies created by the Web service to identify users. Line 44 in the constructor creates a new **CookieContainer** object for the **CookieContainer** property of **dealer**. Class **CookieContainer** (defined in namespace **System.Net**) acts as a storage space for an object of the **HttpCookie** class. Creating the **CookieContainer** allows the Web service to maintain a session state for this client. This **CookieContainer** contains a **Cookie** with a unique identifier that the server can use to recognize the client when the client makes future requests. By default, the **CookieContainer** is **Nothing**, and a new **Session** object is created by the Web Service for each request.

Method **GameOver** (line 258–293) displays all the dealer's cards (many of which are face-down during the game) and shows the appropriate message in the status **PictureBox**. Method **GameOver** receives as an argument a member of the **GameStatus** enumeration (defined in lines 29–34). The enumeration represents whether the player tied, lost or won the game; its four members are: **PUSH**, **LOSE**, **WIN** and **BLACKJACK**.

When the player clicks the **Deal** button (event handler on lines 150–207), all the **PictureBox**es are cleared, the deck is shuffled and the player and dealer receive two cards each. If both obtain scores of 21, method **GameOver** is called and is passed **GameStatus.PUSH**. If only the player has 21 after the first two cards are dealt, **GameOver** is called and is passed **GameStatus.BLACKJACK**. If only the dealer has 21, method **GameOver** is called and is passed **GameStatus.LOSE**.

If **GameOver** is not called, the player can take additional cards by clicking the **Hit** button (event handler on line 123–147). Each time a player clicks **HIT**, the player is dealt one card, which is displayed in the GUI. If the player exceeds 21, the game is over, and the player loses. If the player has exactly 21, the player is not allowed to take any more cards.

Players can click the **Stay** button to indicate that they do not want to risk being dealt another card. In the event handler for this event (lines 78–84), all the **Hit** and **Stay** buttons are disabled, and method **DealerPlay** is called. This method (lines 87–120) causes the dealer to keep taking cards until the dealer's hand is worth 17 or more. If the dealer exceeds 21, the player wins; otherwise, the values of the hands are compared, and **GameOver** is called with the appropriate argument.

Method **DisplayCard** (lines 211–254) retrieves the appropriate card image. It takes as arguments an integer representing the index of the **PictureBox** in the **ArrayList** that must have its image set and a **String** representing the card. An empty **String** indicates that we wish to display the back of a card; otherwise, the program extracts the face and suit from the **String** and uses this information to find the correct image. The **Select Case** statement (lines 239–248) converts the number representing the suit into an integer and assigns the appropriate character to **suitLetter** (**c** for Clubs, **d** for Diamonds, **h** for Hearts and **s** for Spades). The character **suitLetter** is used to complete the image's file name.

21.6 Using Web Forms and Web Services

In the previous examples, we have accessed Web services from Windows applications. However, we can just as easily use them in Web applications. Because Web-based businesses are becoming more and more prevalent, it often is more practical for programmers to design Web services as part of Web applications. Figure 21.16 presents an airline reservation Web service that receives information regarding the type of seat the customer wishes to reserve and then makes a reservation if such a seat is available.

```
1   ' Fig. 21.16: Reservation.asmx.vb
2   ' Airline reservation Web Service.
3
4   Imports System
5   Imports System.Data
6   Imports System.Diagnostics
7   Imports System.Web
8   Imports System.Web.Services
9   Imports System.Data.OleDb
10
11  ' performs reservation of a seat
12  <WebService(Namespace:="http://www.deitel.com/", Description := _
13      "Service that enables a user to reserve a seat on a plane.")> _
14  Public Class Reservation
15      Inherits System.Web.Services.WebService
16
17      Friend WithEvents oleDbDataAdapter1 As _
18          System.Data.OleDb.OleDbDataAdapter
```

Fig. 21.16 Airline reservation Web service (part 1 of 3).

```vbnet
19
20      Friend WithEvents oleDbDeleteCommand1 As _
21         System.Data.OleDb.OleDbCommand
22
23      Friend WithEvents oleDbConnection1 As _
24         System.Data.OleDb.OleDbConnection
25
26      Friend WithEvents oleDbInsertCommand1 As _
27         System.Data.OleDb.OleDbCommand
28
29      Friend WithEvents oleDbSelectCommand1 As _
30         System.Data.OleDb.OleDbCommand
31
32      Friend WithEvents oleDbUpdateCommand1 As _
33         System.Data.OleDb.OleDbCommand
34
35      ' Visual Studio .NET generated code
36
37      ' checks database to determine if matching seat is available
38      <WebMethod(Description := "Method to reserve a seat.")> _
39      Public Function Reserve(ByVal seatType As String, _
40         ByVal classType As String) As Boolean
41
42         ' try database connection
43         Try
44            Dim dataReader As OleDbDataReader
45
46            ' open database connection
47            oleDbConnection1.Open()
48
49            ' set and execute SQL query
50            oleDbDataAdapter1.SelectCommand.CommandText = _
51               "SELECT Number FROM Seats WHERE Type = '" & _
52               seatType & "' AND Class = '" & classType & _
53               "' AND Taken = '0'"
54            dataReader = _
55               oleDbDataAdapter1.SelectCommand.ExecuteReader()
56
57            ' if there were results, seat is available
58            If dataReader.Read() Then
59
60               Dim seatNumber As String = dataReader.GetString(0)
61               dataReader.Close()
62
63               ' update the first available seat to be taken
64               oleDbDataAdapter1.UpdateCommand.CommandText = _
65                  "Update Seats Set Taken = '1' WHERE Number = '" _
66                  & seatNumber & "'"
67
68               oleDbDataAdapter1.UpdateCommand.ExecuteNonQuery()
69
70               Return True
71            End If
```

Fig. 21.16 Airline reservation Web service (part 2 of 3).

```
72
73                dataReader.Close()
74
75           Catch exception As OleDbException   ' if connection problem
76               Return False
77
78           Finally
79               oleDbConnection1.Close()
80           End Try
81
82           ' no seat was reserved
83           Return False
84
85       End Function   ' Reserve
86
87   End Class   ' Reservation
```

Fig. 21.16 Airline reservation Web service (part 3 of 3).

The airline reservation Web service has a single **WebMethod**—**Reserve** (line 38–85)—which searches its seat database to locate a seat matching a user's request. If it finds an appropriate seat, **Reserve** updates the database, makes the reservation, and returns **True**; otherwise, no reservation is made, and the method returns **False**.

Reserve takes two arguments—a **String** representing the desired seat type (the choices are window, middle and aisle) and a **String** representing the desired class type (the choices are economy and first class). Our database contains four columns: The seat number, the seat type, the class type and a column containing either 0 or 1 to indicate whether the seat is taken. Lines 50–53 define an SQL command that retrieves the number of available seats matching the requested seat and class type. The statement in lines 54–55 executes the query. If the result of the query is not empty, the application reserves the first seat number that the query returns. The database is updated with an **UPDATE** command, and **Reserve** returns **True**, indicating that the reservation was successful. If the result of the **SELECT** query is not successful, **Reserve** returns **False**, indicating that no seats available matched the request.

Earlier in the chapter, we displayed a Web service in design view (Fig. 21.7), and we explained that design view allows the programmer to add components to a Web service in a visual manner. In our airline reservation Web service (Fig. 21.16), we used various data components. Figure 21.17 shows these components in design view. Notice that it is easier to drop these components into our Web service using the **Toolbox** rather than typing the equivalent code.

Figure 21.18 presents the ASPX listing for the Web Form through which users can select seat types. This page allows users to reserve a seat on the basis of its class and location in a row of seats. The page then uses the airline-reservation Web service to carry out users' requests. If the database request is not successful, the user is instructed to modify the request and try again.

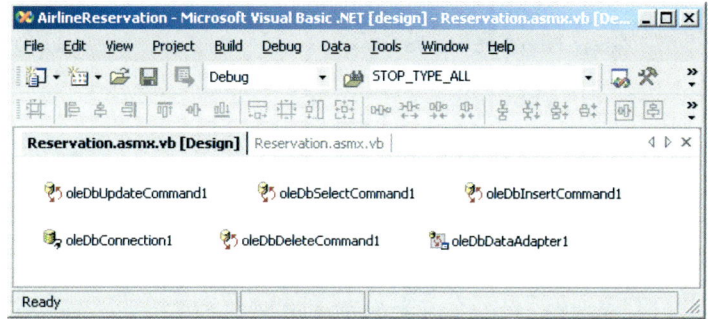

Fig. 21.17 Airline Web Service in design view.

```
1   <%-- Fig. 21.18: TicketReservation.aspx          --%>
2   <%-- A Web Form to allow users to select the kind of seat --%>
3   <%-- they wish to reserve.                       --%>
4
5   <%@ Page Language="vb" AutoEventWireup="false"
6      Codebehind="TicketReservation.aspx.vb"
7      Inherits="MakeReservation.TicketReservation"%>
8
9   <!DOCTYPE HTML PUBLIC "-//W3C//DTD HTML 4.0 Transitional//EN">
10  <HTML>
11     <HEAD>
12       <title>Ticket Reservation</title>
13      <meta content="Microsoft Visual Studio.NET 7.0" name=GENERATOR>
14       <meta content="Visual Basic 7.0" name=CODE_LANGUAGE>
15       <meta content=JavaScript name=vs_defaultClientScript>
16       <meta name=vs_targetSchema content=
17          http://schemas.microsoft.com/intellisense/ie5>
18     </HEAD>
19     <body MS_POSITIONING="GridLayout">
20
21        <form id=Form1 method=post runat="server">
22
23           <asp:DropDownList id=seatList style="Z-INDEX: 105;
24              LEFT: 23px; POSITION: absolute; TOP: 43px"
25              runat="server" Width="105px" Height="22px">
26
27              <asp:ListItem Value="Aisle">Aisle</asp:ListItem>
28              <asp:ListItem Value="Middle">Middle</asp:ListItem>
29              <asp:ListItem Value="Window">Window</asp:ListItem>
30
31           </asp:DropDownList>
32
33           <asp:DropDownList id=classList style="Z-INDEX: 102;
34              LEFT: 145px; POSITION: absolute; TOP: 43px"
35              runat="server" Width="98px" Height="22px">
36
```

Fig. 21.18 ASPX file that takes reservation information (part 1 of 2).

```
37            <asp:ListItem Value="Economy">Economy</asp:ListItem>
38            <asp:ListItem Value="First">First</asp:ListItem>
39
40         </asp:DropDownList>
41
42         <asp:Button id=reserveButton style="Z-INDEX: 103;
43            LEFT: 21px; POSITION: absolute; TOP: 83px"
44            runat="server" Text="Reserve">
45         </asp:Button>
46
47         <asp:Label id=Label1 style="Z-INDEX: 104;
48            LEFT: 17px; POSITION: absolute; TOP: 13px"
49            runat="server">Please select the type of seat and
50            class you wish to reserve:
51         </asp:Label>
52
53      </form>
54   </body>
55 </HTML>
```

Fig. 21.18 ASPX file that takes reservation information (part 2 of 2).

This page defines two **DropDownList** objects and a **Button**. One **DropDownList** displays all the seat types from which users can select. The second lists choices for the class type. Users click the **Button**, named **reserveButton**, to submit requests after making selections from the **DropDownList**s. The code-behind file (Fig. 21.19) attaches an event handler for this button.

```
1  ' Fig. 21.19: TicketReservation.aspx.vb
2  ' Making a reservation using a Web Service.
3
4  Imports System
5  Imports System.Collections
6  Imports System.ComponentModel
7  Imports System.Data
8  Imports System.Drawing
9  Imports System.Web
10 Imports System.Web.SessionState
11 Imports System.Web.UI
12 Imports System.Web.UI.WebControls
13 Imports System.Web.UI.HtmlControls
14
15 ' allows visitors to select seat type to reserve, and
16 ' then make the reservation
17 Public Class TicketReservation
18    Inherits System.Web.UI.Page
19
20    Protected WithEvents Label1 As Label
21    Protected WithEvents reserveButton As Button
22    Protected WithEvents classList As DropDownList
23    Protected WithEvents seatList As DropDownList
```

Fig. 21.19 Code-behind file for the reservation page (part 1 of 3).

```
24      Private Agent As New localhost.Reservation()
25
26      ' Visual Studio .NET generated code
27
28      Private Sub Page_Load(ByVal sender As System.Object, _
29         ByVal e As System.EventArgs) Handles MyBase.Load
30
31         If IsPostBack
32            classList.Visible = False
33            seatList.Visible = False
34            reserveButton.Visible = False
35            Label1.Visible = False
36         End If
37      End Sub
38
39      ' calls Web Service to try to reserve the specified seat
40      Private Sub reserveButton_Click(ByVal sender As _
41         System.Object, ByVal e As System.EventArgs) _
42         Handles reserveButton.Click
43
44         ' if WebMethod returned true, signal success
45         If Agent.Reserve(seatList.SelectedItem.Text, _
46            classList.SelectedItem.Text.ToString) Then
47
48            Response.Write("Your reservation has been made." _
49               & "  Thank you.")
50
51            ' WebMethod returned False, so signal failure
52         Else
53            Response.Write("This seat is not available, " & _
54               "please hit the back button on your browser " & _
55               "and try again.")
56         End If
57
58      End Sub ' reserveButton_Click
59
60   End Class ' TicketReservation
```

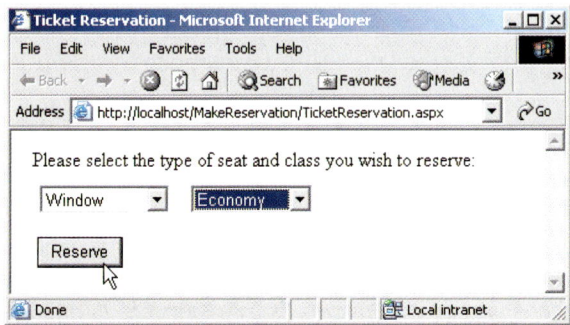

Fig. 21.19 Code-behind file for the reservation page (part 2 of 3).

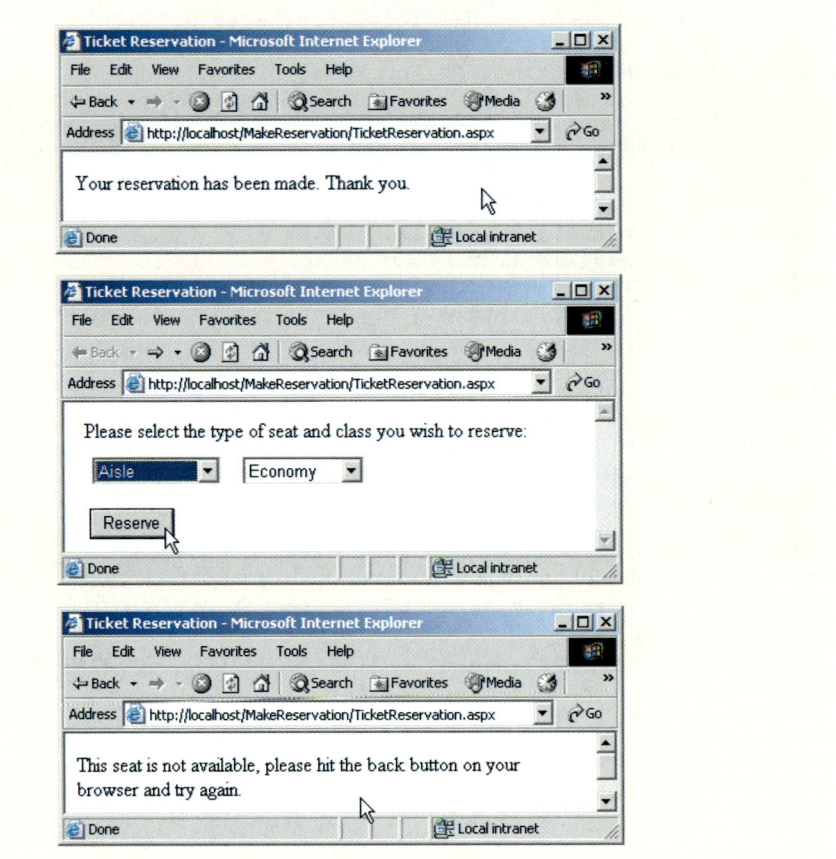

Fig. 21.19 Code-behind file for the reservation page (part 3 of 3).

Line 24 creates a **Reservation** object. When the user clicks **Reserve**, the **reserveButton_Click** event handler executes, and the page reloads. The event handler (lines 46–56) calls the Web service's **Reserve** method and passes it the selected seat and class type as arguments. If **Reserve** returns **True**, the application displays a message thanking the user for making a reservation; otherwise, the user is notified that the type of seat requested is not available, and the user is instructed to try again.

21.7 Case Study: Temperature Information Application

This case study discusses both a Web service that presents weather forecasts for various cities around the United States and a Windows application that employs the Web service. The Web service uses networking capabilities to display the forecasts; it parses a Web page containing the required information and then extracts weather forecast information.

First, we present Web service **TemperatureServer**, in Fig. 21.20. This Web service reads a Web page and collects information about the temperature and weather conditions in an assortment of American cities. [*Note*: At the time of publication, this program runs in the manner that we depict. However, if changes are made to the Web page from which the program retrieves data, the program might work differently or not at all. Please check our Web site at **www.deitel.com** for updates.]

```vbnet
1    ' Fig. 21.20: TemperatureServer.asmx.vb
2    ' TemperatureServer Web Service that extract weather
3    ' information from a Web page.
4
5    Imports System
6    Imports System.Collections
7    Imports System.ComponentModel
8    Imports System.Data
9    Imports System.Diagnostics
10   Imports System.Web
11   Imports System.Web.Services
12   Imports System.IO
13   Imports System.Net
14
15   <WebService(Namespace:="http://www.deitel.com", Description := _
16      "A Web service that provides information from the " _
17      & "National Weather Service.")> _
18   Public Class TemperatureServer
19      Inherits System.Web.Services.WebService
20
21      Dim cityList As ArrayList
22
23      Public Sub New()
24         MyBase.New()
25
26         'This call is required by the Web Services Designer.
27         InitializeComponent()
28      End Sub
29
30      ' Visual Studio .Net generated code
31
32      <WebMethod(EnableSession := true, Description := "Method to " _
33         & "read information from the National Weather Service.")> _
34      Public Sub UpdateWeatherConditions()
35         ' create a WebClient to get access to the web
36         ' page
37         Dim myClient As New WebClient()
38         Dim cityList As New ArrayList()
39
40         ' get a StreamReader for response so we can read
41         ' the page
42         Dim input As New StreamReader( _
43            myClient.OpenRead( _
44            "http://iwin.nws.noaa.gov/iwin/us/" & _
45            "traveler.html"))
46
47         Dim separator As String = "TAV12"
48
49         'locate first horizontal line on Web page
```

Fig. 21.20 TemperatureServer Web service (part 1 of 3).

```vb
50         While Not input.ReadLine().StartsWith( _
51            separator)
52            ' do nothing
53         End While
54
55         ' s1 is the day format and s2 is the night format
56         Dim dayFormat As String = _
57            "CITY             WEA    HI/LO   WEA       HI/LO"
58         Dim nightFormat As String = _
59            "CITY             WEA    LO/HI   WEA       LO/HI"
60
61         Dim inputLine As String = ""
62
63         ' locate header that begins weather information
64         Do
65            inputLine = input.ReadLine()
66         Loop While (Not inputLine.Equals(dayFormat)) AndAlso _
67            (Not inputLine.Equals(nightFormat))
68
69         ' get first city's info
70         inputLine = input.ReadLine()
71
72         While inputLine.Length > 28
73
74            ' create WeatherInfo object for city
75            Dim cityWeather As New CityWeather( _
76               inputLine.Substring(0, 16), _
77               inputLine.Substring(16, 7), _
78               inputLine.Substring(23, 7))
79
80            ' add to List
81            cityList.Add(cityWeather)
82
83            ' get next city's info
84            inputLine = input.ReadLine()
85         End While
86
87         ' close connection to NWS server
88         input.Close()
89
90         ' add city list to user session
91         Session.Add("cityList", cityList)
92
93      End Sub 'UpdateWeatherConditions
94
95      <WebMethod(EnableSession := true, Description := "Method to " _
96         & "retrieve a list of cities.")> _
97      Public Function Cities() As String()
98
99         Dim cityList As ArrayList = _
100           Ctype(Session("cityList"), ArrayList)
101
102        Dim currentCities(cityList.Count-1) As String
```

Fig. 21.20 TemperatureServer Web service (part 2 of 3).

```vbnet
103        Dim i As Integer
104
105        ' retrieve the names of all cities
106        For i = 0 To cityList.Count - 1
107           Dim weather As CityWeather = _
108              CType(cityList(i), CityWeather)
109           currentCities(i) = weather.CityName
110        Next
111
112        Return currentCities
113     End Function ' Cities
114
115     <WebMethod(EnableSession := true, Description := "Method to " _
116        & "retrieve a list of weather descriptions for cities.")> _
117     Public Function Descriptions() As String()
118
119        Dim cityList As ArrayList = _
120           Ctype(Session("cityList"), ArrayList)
121
122        Dim cityDescriptions(cityList.Count-1) As String
123        Dim i As Integer
124        ' retrieve weather descriptions of all cities
125        For i = 0 To cityList.Count - 1
126
127           Dim weather As CityWeather = _
128              CType(cityList(i), CityWeather)
129           cityDescriptions(i) = weather.Description
130        Next
131
132        Return cityDescriptions
133     End Function ' Descriptions
134
135     <WebMethod(EnableSession := true, Description := "Method to " _
136        & "retrieve a list of temperatures for a list of cities.")> _
137     Public Function Temperatures() As String()
138
139        Dim cityList As ArrayList = _
140           Ctype(Session("cityList"), ArrayList)
141
142        Dim cityTemperatures(cityList.Count-1) As String
143        Dim i As Integer
144
145        ' retrieve temperatures for all cities
146        For i = 0 To cityList.Count - 1
147
148           Dim weather As CityWeather = _
149              CType(cityList(i), CityWeather)
150           cityTemperatures(i) = weather.Temperature
151        Next
152
153        Return cityTemperatures
154     End Function ' Temperatures
155 End Class ' TemperatureServer
```

Fig. 21.20 TemperatureServer Web service (part 3 of 3).

Method **UpdateWeatherConditions**, which gathers weather data from a Web page, is the first **WebMethod** that a client must call from the Web service. The service also provides the **WebMethod**s **Cities**, **Descriptions** and **Temperatures**, which return different kinds of forecast-related information.

When **UpdateWeatherConditions** (line 32–93) is invoked, the method connects to a Web site containing the traveler's forecasts from the National Weather Service (NWS). Line 37 creates a *WebClient* object, which we use because the **WebClient** class is designed for interaction with a source specified by a URL. In this case, the URL for the NWS page is **http://iwin.nws.noaa.gov/iwin/us/traveler.html**. Lines 43–54 call **WebClient** method *OpenRead*; the method retrieves a **Stream** from the URL containing the weather information and then uses this **Stream** to create a **StreamReader** object. Using a **StreamReader** object, the program can read the Web page's HTML markup line-by-line.

The section of the Web page in which we are interested starts with the **String** "**TAV12**." Therefore, lines 50–53 read the HTML markup one line at a time until this **String** is encountered. Once the string "**TAV12**" is reached, the **Do/Loop While** structure (lines 64–67) continues to read the page one line at a time until it finds the header line (i.e., the line at the beginning of the forecast table). This line starts with either **dayFormat**, indicating day format, or **nightFormat**, indicating night format. Because the line could be in either format, the structure checks for both. Line 70 reads the next line from the page, which is the first line containing temperature information.

The **While** structure (lines 72–85) creates a new **CityWeather** object to represent the current city. It parses the **String** containing the current weather data, separating the city name, the weather condition and the temperature. The **CityWeather** object is added to **cityList** (an **ArrayList** that contains a list of the cities, their descriptions and their current temperatures); then, the next line from the page is read and is stored in **inputLine** for the next iteration. This process continues until the length of the **String** read from the Web page is less than or equal to **28**. This signals the end of the temperature section. Line 91 adds the **ArrayList cityList** to the **Session** object so that the values are maintained between method calls.

Method **Cities** (line 95–113) creates an array of **String**s that can contain as many **String**s as there are elements in **cityList**. Lines 99–100 obtain the list of cities from the **Session** object. Lines 106–110 iterate through each **CityWeather** object in **cityList** and insert the city name into the array that is returned in line 109. Methods **Descriptions** (lines 115–133) and **Temperatures** (lines 135–154) behave similarly, except that they return weather descriptions and temperatures, respectively.

Figure 21.21 contains the code listing for the **CityWeather** class. The constructor takes three arguments: The city's name, the weather description and the current temperature. The class provides the properties **CityName**, **Temperature** and **Description**, so that these values can be retrieved by the Web service.

```
1   ' Fig. 21.21: CityWeather.vb
2   ' Class representing the weather information for one city.
3
4   Imports System
```

Fig. 21.21 Class that stores weather information about a city (part 1 of 2).

```
5
6   Public Class CityWeather
7
8      Private mCityName, mTemperature, mDescription As String
9
10     Public Sub New(ByVal city As String, ByVal description _
11        As String, ByVal temperature As String)
12        mCityName = city
13        mDescription = description
14        mTemperature = temperature
15     End Sub
16
17     ' name of city
18     Public ReadOnly Property CityName() As String
19        Get
20           Return mCityName
21        End Get
22     End Property
23
24     ' temperature of city
25     Public ReadOnly Property Temperature() As String
26        Get
27           Return mTemperature
28        End Get
29     End Property
30
31     ' description of forecast
32     Public ReadOnly Property Description() As String
33        Get
34           Return mDescription
35        End Get
36     End Property
37   End Class
```

Fig. 21.21 Class that stores weather information about a city (part 2 of 2).

The Windows application in Fig. 21.22 uses the **TemperatureServer** Web service to display weather information in a user-friendly format.

```
1    ' Fig. 21.22: Client.vb
2    ' Class that displays weather information which it receives
3    ' from a Web Service.
4
5    Imports System
6    Imports System.Drawing
7    Imports System.Collections
8    Imports System.ComponentModel
9    Imports System.Windows.Forms
10   Imports System.Net
11
12   Public Class FrmClient
13      Inherits System.Windows.Forms.Form
```

Fig. 21.22 Receiving temperature and weather data from a Web service (part 1 of 4).

```vbnet
14
15      Public Sub New()
16         MyBase.New()
17
18         ' This call is required by the Windows Form Designer.
19         InitializeComponent()
20
21         Dim client As New localhost.TemperatureServer()
22         client.CookieContainer = New CookieContainer()
23         client.UpdateWeatherConditions()
24
25         Dim cities As String() = client.Cities()
26         Dim descriptions As String() = client.Descriptions()
27         Dim temperatures As String() = client.Temperatures()
28
29         label35.BackgroundImage = New Bitmap( _
30            "images/header.jpg")
31         label36.BackgroundImage = New Bitmap( _
32            "images/header.jpg")
33
34         ' create Hashtable and populate with every label
35         Dim cityLabels As New Hashtable()
36         cityLabels.Add(1, label1)
37         cityLabels.Add(2, label2)
38         cityLabels.Add(3, label3)
39         cityLabels.Add(4, label4)
40         cityLabels.Add(5, label5)
41         cityLabels.Add(6, label6)
42         cityLabels.Add(7, label7)
43         cityLabels.Add(8, label8)
44         cityLabels.Add(9, label9)
45         cityLabels.Add(10, label10)
46         cityLabels.Add(11, label11)
47         cityLabels.Add(12, label12)
48         cityLabels.Add(13, label13)
49         cityLabels.Add(14, label14)
50         cityLabels.Add(15, label15)
51         cityLabels.Add(16, label16)
52         cityLabels.Add(17, label17)
53         cityLabels.Add(18, label18)
54         cityLabels.Add(19, label19)
55         cityLabels.Add(20, label20)
56         cityLabels.Add(21, label21)
57         cityLabels.Add(22, label22)
58         cityLabels.Add(23, label23)
59         cityLabels.Add(24, label24)
60         cityLabels.Add(25, label25)
61         cityLabels.Add(26, label26)
62         cityLabels.Add(27, label27)
63         cityLabels.Add(28, label28)
64         cityLabels.Add(29, label29)
65         cityLabels.Add(30, label30)
66         cityLabels.Add(31, label31)
```

Fig. 21.22 Receiving temperature and weather data from a Web service (part 2 of 4).

```vbnet
67         cityLabels.Add(32, label32)
68         cityLabels.Add(33, label33)
69         cityLabels.Add(34, label34)
70
71         ' create Hashtable and populate with all weather
72         ' conditions
73         Dim weather As New Hashtable()
74         weather.Add("SUNNY", "sunny")
75         weather.Add("PTCLDY", "pcloudy")
76         weather.Add("CLOUDY", "mcloudy")
77         weather.Add("MOCLDY", "mcloudy")
78         weather.Add("TSTRMS", "rain")
79         weather.Add("RAIN", "rain")
80         weather.Add("SNOW", "snow")
81         weather.Add("VRYHOT", "vryhot")
82         weather.Add("FAIR", "fair")
83         weather.Add("RNSNOW", "rnsnow")
84         weather.Add("SHWRS", "showers")
85         weather.Add("WINDY", "windy")
86         weather.Add("NOINFO", "noinfo")
87         weather.Add("MISG", "noinfo")
88         weather.Add("DRZL", "rain")
89         weather.Add("HAZE", "noinfo")
90         weather.Add("SMOKE", "mcloudy")
91         weather.Add("FOG", "mcloudy")
92
93         Dim i As Integer
94         Dim background As New Bitmap("images/back.jpg")
95         Dim font As New Font("Courier New", 8, _
96            FontStyle.Bold)
97
98         ' for every city
99         For i = 0 To cities.Length - 1
100
101            ' use Hashtable to find the next Label
102            Dim currentCity As Label = _
103               CType(cityLabels(i + 1), Label)
104
105            ' set current Label's image to the image
106            ' corresponding to its weather condition -
107            ' find correct image name in Hashtable weather
108            currentCity.Image = New Bitmap("images/" & _
109               weather(descriptions(i).Trim()).ToString & ".jpg")
110
111            ' set background image, font and forecolor
112            ' of Label
113            currentCity.BackgroundImage = background
114            currentCity.Font = font
115            currentCity.ForeColor = Color.White
116
```

Fig. 21.22 Receiving temperature and weather data from a Web service (part 3 of 4).

```
117                ' set label's text to city name
118                currentCity.Text = vbCrLf & cities(i) & " " & _
119                    temperatures(i)
120         Next
121
122     End Sub ' New
123
124     ' Visual Studio .NET generated code
125 End Class ' Client
```

Fig. 21.22 Receiving temperature and weather data from a Web service (part 4 of 4).

TemperatureClient (Fig. 21.22) is a Windows application that uses the **TemperatureServer** Web service to display weather information in a graphical and easy-to-read manner. This application consists of 36 **Label**s, placed in two columns. Each **Label** displays the weather information for a different city.

Lines 21–23 of the constructor instantiate a **TemperatureServer** object, create a new **CookieContainer** object and update the weather data by calling method **UpdateWeatherConditions**. Lines 25–27 call **TemperatureServer** methods **Cities**, **Descriptions** and **Temperatures** to retrieve the city's weather and description information. Because the application presents weather data for so many cities, we must establish a way to organize the information in the **Label**s and to ensure that each weather description is accompanied by an appropriate image. To address these concerns, the program uses class **Hashtable** (discussed further in Chapter 24, Data Structures and Collections) to store all the **Label**s, the weather descriptions and the names of their corresponding images. A **Hashtable** stores key–value pairs, in which both the key and the value can be any type of object. Method **Add** adds key-value pairs to a **Hashtable**. The class also provides an indexer to return the key value on which the **Hashtable** is indexed. Line 35 creates a **Hashtable** object, and lines 36–69 add the **Label**s to the **Hashtable**, using the numbers **1** through **36** as keys. Then, line 73 creates a second **Hashtable** object (**weather**) to contain pairs of weather conditions and the images associated with those conditions. Note that a given weather description does not necessarily correspond to the name of the PNG file containing the correct image. For example, both "**TSTRMS**" and "**RAIN**" weather conditions use the **rain.png** file.

Lines 74–91 set each **Label** so that it contains a city name, the current temperature in the city and an image corresponding to the weather condition for that city. Line 103 uses the **Hashtable** indexer to retrieve the next **Label** by passing as an argument the current value of **i** plus **1**. We do this because the **Hashtable** indexer begins at 0, despite the fact that both the labels and the **Hashtable** keys are numbered from 1–36.

Lines 108–109 set the **Label**'s image to the PNG image that corresponds to the city's weather condition. The application does this by retrieving the name of the PNG image from the **weather Hashtable**. The program eliminates any spaces in the description **String** by calling **String** method **Trim**. Lines 113–119 set several **Label**s' properties to achieve the visual effect seen in the output. For each label, we specify a blue-and-black background image (line 113). Lines 118–119 set each label's text so that it displays the correct information for each city (i.e., the city name and temperature information).

21.8 User-Defined Types in Web Services

Notice that the Web service discussed in the previous section returns arrays of **String**s. It would be much more convenient if **TemperatureServer** could return an array of **CityWeather** objects, instead of an array of **String**s. Fortunately, it is possible to define and use user-defined types in a Web service. These types can be passed into or returned from Web-service methods. Web-service clients also can use user-defined types, because the proxy class created for the client contains these type definitions. There are, however, some subtleties to keep in mind when using user-defined types in Web services; we point these out as we encounter them in the next example.

The case study in this section presents a math tutoring program. The Web service generates random equations of type **Equation**. The client inputs information about the kind of mathematical example that the user wants (addition, subtraction or multiplication) and the skill level of the user (1 creates equations using 1-digit numbers, 2 for more difficult equations, involving 2 digits, and 3 for the most difficult equations, containing 3-digit numbers); it then generates an equation consisting of random numbers that have the proper number of digits. The client receives the **Equation** and uses a Windows form to display the sample questions to the user.

We mentioned earlier that all data types passed to and from Web services must be supported by SOAP. How, then, can SOAP support a type that is not even created yet? In Chapter 17, Files and Streams, we discussed the serializing of data types, which enables them to be written to files. Similarly, custom types that are sent to or from a Web service are serialized, so that they can be passed in XML format. This process is referred to as *XML serialization*.

In this example, we define class **Equation** (Fig. 21.23). This class is included in the Web-service project and contains fields, properties and methods. Before explaining class **Equation**, we briefly discuss the process of returning objects from Web-service methods. Any object returned by a Web-service method must have a default constructor. Although all objects can be instantiated by a default **Public** constructor (even if this constructor is not defined explicitly), a class returned from a Web service must have an explicitly defined constructor, even if its body is empty.

```vb
1   ' Fig. 21.23: Equation.vb
2   ' Class Equation that contains
3   ' information about an equation.
4
5   Imports System
6
7   Public Class Equation
8
9      Private mLeft, mRight, mResult As Integer
10     Private mOperation As String
11
12     ' required default constructor
13     Public Sub New()
14        Me.New(0, 0, "+")
15     End Sub ' New
16
17     ' constructor for class Equation
18     Public Sub New(ByVal leftValue As Integer, _
19        ByVal rightValue As Integer, _
20        ByVal operationType As String)
21
22        mLeft = leftValue
23        mRight = rightValue
24        mOperation = operationType
25
26        Select Case operationType
27
28           Case "+" ' addition operator
29              mResult = mLeft + mRight
30           Case "-" ' subtraction operator
31              mResult = mLeft - mRight
32           Case "*" ' multiplication operator
33              mResult = mLeft * mRight
34        End Select
35     End Sub ' New
```

Fig. 21.23 Class that stores equation information (part 1 of 3).

```
36
37      Public Overrides Function ToString() As String
38
39         Return Left.ToString() & " " & mOperation & " " & _
40            mRight.ToString() & " = " & mResult.ToString()
41      End Function ' ToString
42
43      ' readonly property returning a string representing
44      ' left-hand side
45      Public Property LeftHandSide() As String
46         Get
47            Return mLeft.ToString() & " " & mOperation & " " & _
48               mRight.ToString()
49         End Get
50         Set(ByVal Value As String)
51         End Set
52      End Property
53
54      ' readonly property returning a string representing
55      ' the right hand side
56      Public Property RightHandSide() As String
57         Get
58            Return mResult.ToString()
59         End Get
60         Set(ByVal Value As String)
61         End Set
62      End Property
63
64      ' left operand get and set property
65      Public Property Left() As Integer
66         Get
67            Return mLeft
68         End Get
69         Set(ByVal value As Integer)
70
71            mLeft = value
72         End Set
73      End Property
74
75      ' right operand get and set property
76      Public Property Right() As Integer
77         Get
78            Return mRight
79         End Get
80
81         Set(ByVal Value As Integer)
82            mRight = Value
83         End Set
84      End Property
85
```

Fig. 21.23 Class that stores equation information (part 2 of 3).

```
86         ' get and set property of result of applying
87         ' operation to left and right operands
88         Public Property Result() As Integer
89            Get
90               Return mResult
91            End Get
92            Set(ByVal Value As Integer)
93               mResult = Value
94            End Set
95         End Property
96
97         ' get and set property for the operation
98         Public Property Operation() As String
99            Get
100              Return mOperation
101           End Get
102           Set(ByVal Value As String)
103              Operation = Value
104           End Set
105        End Property
106    End Class 'Equation
```

Fig. 21.23 Class that stores equation information (part 3 of 3).

Common Programming Error 21.3
Failure to define explicitly a **Public** *constructor for a type being used in a Web service results in a runtime error.*

A few additional requirements apply to custom types in Web services. Any variables of our custom type that we wish to access during runtime must be declared **Public**. We also must define both the **Get** and **Set** accessors of any properties that we wish to access at run time. The Web service needs to have a way both to retrieve and to manipulate such properties, because objects of the custom type will be converted into XML (when the objects are serialized) then converted back to objects (when they are deserialized). During serialization, the property value must be read (through the **Get** accessor); during deserialization, the property value of the new object must be set (through the **Set** accessor). If only one of the accessors is present, the client application will not have access to the property.

Common Programming Error 21.4
Defining only the **Get** *or* **Set** *accessor of a property for a custom type being used in a Web service results in a property that is inaccessible to the client.*

Common Programming Error 21.5
Clients of a Web service can access only that service's **Public** *members. To allow access to* **Private** *data, the programmer should provide* **Public** *properties.*

Now, let us discuss class **Equation** (Fig. 21.23). Lines 18–35 define a constructor that takes three arguments—two **Integers** representing the left and right operands and a **String** that represents the algebraic operation to carry out. The constructor sets the **mLeft**, **mRight** and **mOperation** fields, then calculates the appropriate result. The default constructor (line 13–15) calls the other constructor and passes some default values. We do not use the default constructor, but it must be defined in the program.

Class **Equation** defines properties **LeftHandSide**, **RightHandSide**, **Left**, **Right**, **Operation** and **Result**. The program does not need to modify the values of these properties, but an implementation for the **Set** accessor must be provided. **LeftHandSide** returns a **String** representing everything to the left of the "=" sign, and **RightHandSide** returns a **String** representing everything to the right of the "=" sign. **Left** returns the **Integer** to the left of the operator (known as the left operand), and **Right** returns the **Integer** to the right of the operator (known as the right operand). **Result** returns the answer to the equation, and **Operation** returns the operator. The program does not actually need the **RightHandSide** property, but we have chosen to include it in case other clients choose to use it. Figure 21.24 presents the **EquationGenerator** Web service that creates random, customized **Equation**s.

```vb
1   ' Fig. 21.24: Generator.asmx.vb
2   ' Web Service to generate random equations based on the
3   ' operation and difficulty level.
4
5   Imports System
6   Imports System.Collections
7   Imports System.ComponentModel
8   Imports System.Data
9   Imports System.Diagnostics
10  Imports System.Web
11  Imports System.Web.Services
12
13  <WebService(Namespace:="http://www.deitel.com/", Description:= _
14     "Web service that generates a math equation.")> _
15  Public Class Generator
16     Inherits System.Web.Services.WebService
17
18     ' Visual Studio .NET generated code
19
20     <WebMethod(Description:="Method to generate a " _
21        & "math equation.")> _
22     Public Function GenerateEquation(ByVal operation As String, _
23        ByVal level As Integer) As Equation
24
25        ' find maximum and minimum number to be used
26        Dim maximum As Integer = Convert.ToInt32( _
27           Math.Pow(10, level))
28
29        Dim minimum As Integer = Convert.ToInt32( _
30           Math.Pow(10, level - 1))
31
32        Dim randomObject As New Random()
33
34        ' create equation consisting of two random numbers
35        ' between minimum and maximum parameters
36        Dim equation As New Equation( _
37           randomObject.Next(minimum, maximum), _
38           randomObject.Next(minimum, maximum), operation)
39
```

Fig. 21.24 Web service that generates random equations (part 1 of 2).

```
40          Return equation
41      End Function ' Generate Equation
42  End Class ' Generator
```

Fig. 21.24 Web service that generates random equations (part 2 of 2).

Web service **Generator** contains only one method, **GenerateEquation**. This method takes as arguments a **String** representing the operation we wish to perform and an **Integer** representing the difficulty level. Figure 21.25 demonstrates the result of executing a test call of this Web service. Notice that the return value from our Web service method is XML. However, this example differs from previous ones in that the XML specifies the values for all **Public** properties and fields of the object that is being returned. The return object has been serialized into XML. Our proxy class takes this return value and deserializes it into an object that then is passed back to the client.

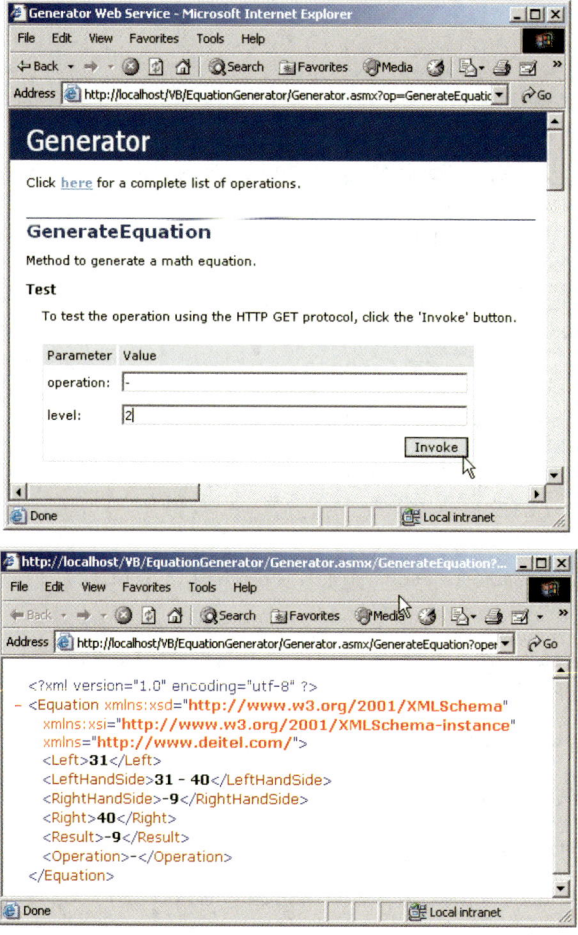

Fig. 21.25 Returning an object from a Web-service method.

Lines 26–30 define the lower and upper bounds for the random numbers that the method generates. To set these limits, the program first calls **Shared** method **Pow** of class **Math**—this method raises its first argument to the power of its second argument. **Integer maximum** represents the upper bound for a randomly generated number. The program raises **10** to the power of the specified **level** argument and then passes this value as the upper bound. For instance, if **level** is **1**, **maximum** is **10**; if **level** is **2**, **minimum** is **100**; and so on. Variable **minimum**'s value is determined by raising **10** to a power one less than **level**. This calculates the smallest number with **level** digits. If **level** is **2**, **min** is **10**; if **level** is **3**, **minimum** is **100**; and so on.

Lines 36–38 create a new **Equation** object. The program calls **Random** method **Next**, which returns an **Integer** that is greater than or equal to a specified lower bound, but less than a specified upper bound. This method generates a left operand value that is greater than or equal to **minimum** but less than **maximum** (i.e., a number with **level** digits). The right operand is another random number with the same characteristics. The operation passed to the **Equation** constructor is the **String operation** that was received by **GenerateEquation**. The new **Equation** object is returned.

Figure 21.26 lists the math-tutoring application that uses the **Generator** Web service. The application calls **Generator**'s **GenerateEquation** method to create an **Equation** object. The tutor then displays the left-hand side of the **Equation** and waits for user input. In this example, the program accesses both class **Generator** and class **Equation** from within the **localhost** namespace—both are placed in this namespace when the proxy is generated.

The math-tutor application displays a question and waits for input. The default setting for the difficulty level is **1**, but the user can change this at any time by choosing a level from among the bottom row of **RadioButton**s. Clicking any of the levels invokes its click event handler (lines 78–94), which sets integer **level** to the level selected by the user. Although the default setting for the question type is **Addition**, the user also can change this at any time by selecting one of the top-row **RadioButton**s. Doing so invokes the radio-button event handlers on lines 97–121, which set **String operation** so that it contains the symbol corresponding to the user's selection.

```
1    ' Fig. 21.26: Tutor.vb
2    ' Math Tutor program.
3
4    Public Class FrmTutor
5       Inherits System.Windows.Forms.Form
6
7       Friend WithEvents cmdGenerate As Button
8       Friend WithEvents cmdOk As Button
9
10      Friend WithEvents txtAnswer As TextBox
11      Friend WithEvents lblQuestion As Label
12
13      Friend WithEvents pnlOperations As Panel
14      Friend WithEvents pnlLevel As Panel
```

Fig. 21.26 Math-tutor application (part 1 of 4).

```vbnet
15
16      ' select math operation
17      Friend WithEvents subtractRadio As RadioButton
18      Friend WithEvents addRadio As RadioButton
19      Friend WithEvents multiplyRadio As RadioButton
20
21      ' select question level radio buttons
22      Friend WithEvents levelOne As RadioButton
23      Friend WithEvents levelTwo As RadioButton
24      Friend WithEvents levelThree As RadioButton
25
26      Private operation As String = "+"
27      Private level As Integer = 1
28      Private equation As localhost.Equation
29      Private generator As New localhost.Generator()
30
31      ' Visual Studio .NET generated code
32
33      ' generates new equation on click event
34      Private Sub cmdGenerate_Click(ByVal sender As _
35         System.Object, ByVal e As System.EventArgs) _
36         Handles cmdGenerate.Click
37
38         ' generate equation using current operation
39         ' and level
40         equation = generator.GenerateEquation(operation, _
41            level)
42
43         ' display left-hand side of equation
44         lblQuestion.Text = equation.LeftHandSide
45
46         cmdOk.Enabled = True
47         txtAnswer.Enabled = True
48      End Sub ' cmdGenerate_Click
49
50      ' check user's answer
51      Private Sub cmdOk_Click(ByVal sender As _
52         System.Object, ByVal e As System.EventArgs) _
53         Handles cmdOk.Click
54
55         ' determine correct result from Equation object
56         Dim answer As Integer = equation.Result
57
58         If txtAnswer.Text = "" Then
59            Return
60         End If
61
62         ' get user's answer
63         Dim myAnswer As Integer = Int32.Parse( _
64            txtAnswer.Text)
65
```

Fig. 21.26 Math-tutor application (part 2 of 4).

```vbnet
66         ' test if user's answer is correct
67         If answer = myAnswer Then
68
69            lblQuestion.Text = ""
70            txtAnswer.Text = ""
71            cmdOk.Enabled = False
72            MessageBox.Show("Correct! Good job!")
73         Else
74            MessageBox.Show("Incorrect. Try again.")
75         End If
76      End Sub ' cmdOk_Click
77
78      Private Sub levelOne_Click(ByVal sender As Object, _
79         ByVal e As System.EventArgs) Handles levelOne.Click
80
81         level = 1
82      End Sub ' levelOne_Click
83
84      Private Sub levelTwo_Click(ByVal sender As Object, _
85         ByVal e As System.EventArgs) Handles levelTwo.Click
86
87         level = 2
88      End Sub ' levelTwo_Click
89
90      Private Sub levelThree_Click(ByVal sender As Object, _
91         ByVal e As System.EventArgs) Handles levelThree.Click
92
93         level = 3
94      End Sub ' levelThree_Click
95
96      ' set the add operation
97      Private Sub addRadio_Click(ByVal sender As Object, _
98         ByVal e As System.EventArgs) Handles addRadio.Click
99
100        operation = "+"
101        cmdGenerate.Text = "Generate " & addRadio.Text & _
102           " Example"
103     End Sub ' addRadio_Click
104
105     ' set the subtract operation
106     Private Sub subtractRadio_Click(ByVal sender As Object, _
107        ByVal e As System.EventArgs) Handles subtractRadio.Click
108
109        operation = "-"
110        cmdGenerate.Text = "Generate " & subtractRadio.Text & _
111           " Example"
112     End Sub ' subtractRadio_Click
113
114     ' set the multiply operation
115     Private Sub multiplyRadio_Click(ByVal sender As Object, _
116        ByVal e As System.EventArgs) Handles multiplyRadio.Click
117
118        operation = "*"
```

Fig. 21.26 Math-tutor application (part 3 of 4).

```
119         cmdGenerate.Text = "Generate " & multiplyRadio.Text & _
120            " Example"
121      End Sub ' multiplyRadio_Click
122   End Class ' FrmTutor
```

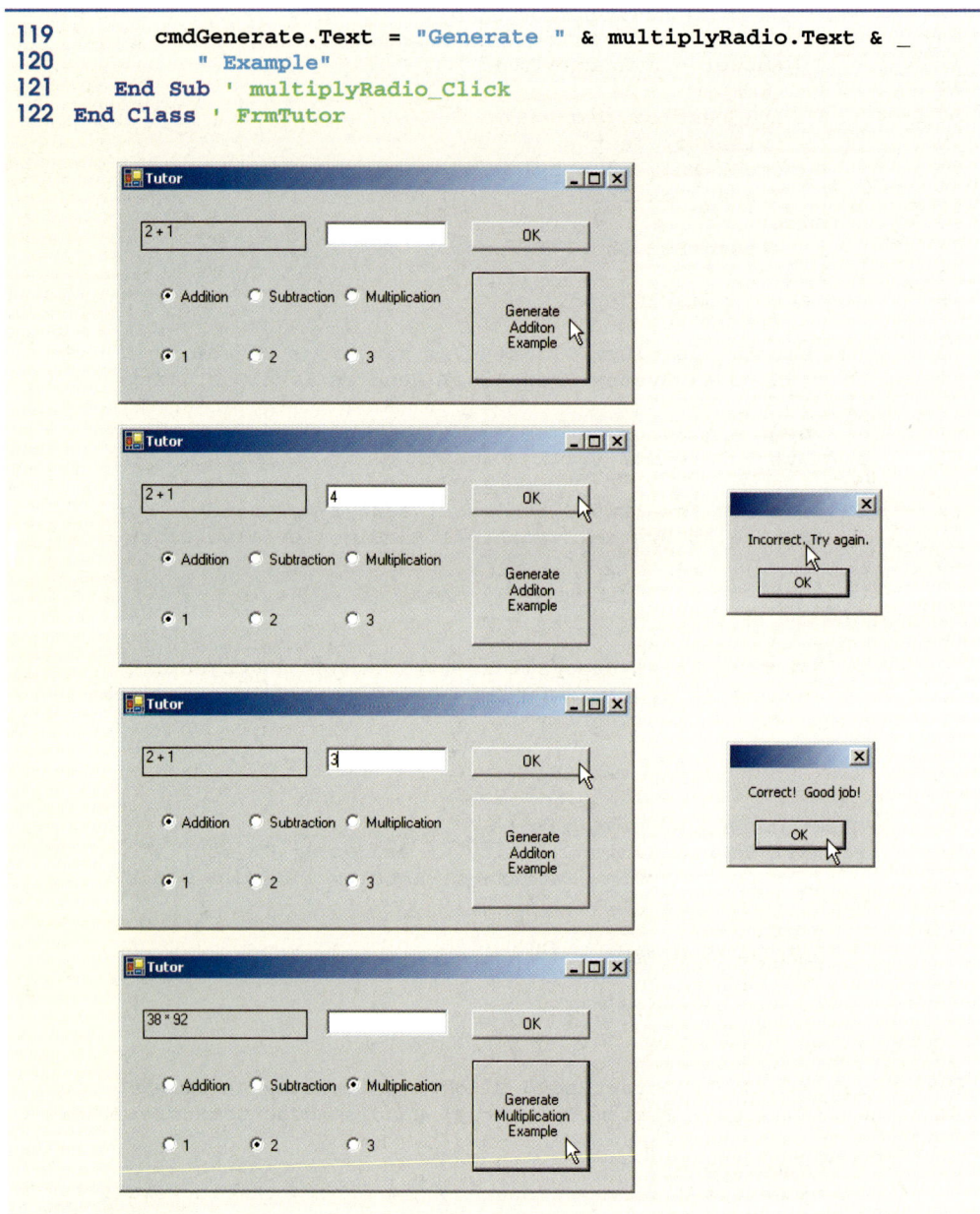

Fig. 21.26 Math-tutor application (part 4 of 4).

Event handler **cmdGenerate_Click** (line 34–48) invokes **Generator** method **GenerateEquation**. The left-hand side of the equation is displayed in **lblQuestion** (line 44), and **cmdOk** is enabled so that the user can enter an answer. When the user clicks **OK**, **cmdOk_Click** (line 51–76) checks whether the user provided the correct answer.

The last two chapters familiarized the user with the creation of Web applications and Web services, both of which enable users to request and receive data via the Internet. In the next chapter, we discuss the low-level details of how data is sent from one location to another (networking). Topics discussed in the next chapter include the implementation of servers and clients and the sending of data via sockets.

21.9 Internet and World Wide Web Resources

msdn.microsoft.com/webservices
This Microsoft site includes .NET Web service technology specifications and white papers with XML/SOAP articles, columns and links.

www.webservices.org
This site provides industry related news, articles, resources and links.

www.w3.org/TR/wsdl
This site provides extensive documentation on WSDL. It provides a thorough discussion of Web Service related technologies such as XML, SOAP, HTTP and MIME types in the context of WSDL.

www-106.ibm.com/developerworks/library/w-wsdl.html
This IBM site discusses WSDL. The page demonstrates the current WSDL XML Web Service specification with XML examples.

www.devxpert.com/tutors/wsdl/wsdl.asp
This site presents a high-level introduction to Web Services. The discussion includes several diagrams and examples.

msdn.microsoft.com/soap
This Microsoft site includes documentation, headlines and overviews SOAP. ASP .NET examples that use SOAP are available at this site.

www.w3.org/TR/SOAP
This site provides extensive SOAP documentation. The site describes SOAP messages, using SOAP with HTTP and SOAP security issues.

www.uddi.com
The Universal Description, Discovery and Integration site provides discussions, specifications, white pages and general information on UDDI.

SUMMARY

- A Web service is a class that is stored on a remote machine and accessed through a remote procedure call.
- Web-services method calls are implemented through Simple Object Access Protocol (SOAP)—an XML-based protocol describing how requests and responses are marked up so that they can be transferred via protocols such as HTTP.
- Methods are executed through a Remote Procedure Call (RPC). These methods are marked with the **WebMethod** attribute and are often referred to as Web-service methods.
- Method calls and responses sent to and from Web services use SOAP by default. As long as a client can create and understand SOAP messages, the client can use Web services, regardless of the programming languages in which the Web services are written.
- A Web service in .NET has two parts: An ASMX file, and a code-behind file.
- The ASMX file can be viewed in any Web browser and displays information about the Web service.
- The code-behind file contains the definition for the methods in the Web service.

- A service description is an XML document that conforms to the Web Service Description Language (WSDL).
- WSDL is an XML vocabulary that describes how Web services behave.
- The service description can be used by a client program to confirm the correctness of method calls at compile time.
- The ASMX file also provides a way for clients to execute test runs of the Web-service methods.
- SOAP, HTTP GET and HTTP POST are the three different ways of sending and receiving messages in Web services. The format used for these request and response messages is sometimes known as the wire protocol or wire format, because the format defines how information is sent "along the wire."
- The Simple Object Access Protocol (SOAP) is a platform-independent protocol that uses XML to make remote-procedure calls over HTTP.
- Requests to and responses from a Web-service method are packaged by default in a SOAP envelope—an XML message containing all the information necessary to process its contents.
- SOAP allows Web services to use a variety of data types, including user-defined data types.
- When a program invokes a Web service method, the request and all relevant information is packaged in a SOAP envelope and sent to the appropriate destination.
- When a Web service receives a SOAP message, it processes the message's contents, which specify the method that the client wishes to execute and the arguments the client is passing to that method.
- When the Web service receives a request this request is parsed, and the proper method is called with the specified arguments (if there are any). The response is sent back to the client as another SOAP message.
- An application that uses a Web service consists of two parts: A proxy class for the Web service, and a client application that accesses the Web service via the proxy.
- A proxy class handles the task of transferring the arguments passed from the client into a SOAP message, which is sent to the Web service. The proxy likewise handles the transferring of information in the response back to the client.
- The **Namespace** property of a **WebService** attribute uniquely identifies a Web service.
- The **Description** property of a **WebService** attribute adds a description of the Web service when the Web service is displayed in a browser.
- Class **WebService** provides members that determine information about the user, the application and other topics relevant to the Web service.
- A Web service is not required to inherit from class **WebService**.
- A programmer specifies a method as a Web-service method by tagging it with a **WebMethod** attribute.
- Visual Studio provides a design view for each Web service, which allows the programmer to add components to the application.
- A proxy class is created from the Web service's WSDL file that enables the client to call Web-service methods over the Internet.
- Whenever a call is made in a client application to a Web-service method, a method in the proxy class is called. This method takes the method name and arguments passed by the client and formats them so that they can be sent as a request in a SOAP message.
- A Web-service method that is called sends the result back to the client in a SOAP message.
- By default, the namespace of a proxy class is the name of the domain in which the Web service resides.

- UDDI is a project for developing a set of specifications that define how Web services should be exposed, so that programmers searching for Web services can find them.
- A DISCO file is a file that specifies any Web services that are available in the current directory.
- There are two types of discovery files: Dynamic discovery files (**.vsdisco** extension) and static discovery files (**.disco** extension).
- Once a Web reference is created, a static discovery file is placed in the client's project. The static discovery file hard-codes the location for the ASMX and WSDL files (by "hard code," we mean that the location is entered directly into the file).
- Dynamic discovery files are created such that the list of Web services is created dynamically on the server when a client is searching for Web services.
- The reader should note that, to store session information, we must set the **EnableSession** property of the **WebMethod** attribute to **True**.
- The use of session state in a Web service can make coding easier and reduce overhead.
- When storing session information, a Web service must have a way of identifying users between method calls. This is implemented by cookies, which are stored in a **CookieContainer**.
- We can use Web services in Web applications and in Windows applications.
- User-defined types can be defined and used in a Web service. These types can be passed into or returned from Web-service methods.
- User-defined types can be sent to or returned from Web-service methods, because the types are defined in the proxy class created for the client.
- Custom types that are sent to or from a Web service are serialized so that they can be passed in XML format.
- Any object returned by a Web-service method must have a default constructor.
- Any variables of a custom type that we wish to make available to clients must be declared **Public**.
- Properties of a custom type that we wish to make available to clients must have both **Get** and **Set** accessors defined.
- When an object is returned from a Web service, all its public properties and fields are marked up in XML. This information can then be transferred back into an object on the client side.

TERMINOLOGY

Add Web Reference dialog
ASMX file
ASP.NET Web Service project type
code-behind file in Web services
consuming a Web service
CookieContainer class
CookieContainer property
creating a proxy class for a Web service
Description property for a
    WebMethod attribute
Description property of a
    WebService attribute
.disco file extension
discovery (DISCO) files
distributed computing

distributed system
EnableSession property of
    WebMethod attribute
exposing a Web-service method
firewall
Invoke button
Invoking a method of a Web service from
    a Web browser
Namespace property of
    WebService attribute
OpenRead method of class **WebClient**
proxy class
publishing a Web service
remote machine
Remote Procedure Call (RPC)

session tracking in Web services
Simple Object Access Protocol (SOAP)
SOAP envelope
SOAP message
SOAP request
`System.Net`
Uniform Resource Locator (URL)
Universal Description, Discovery
 and Integration (UDDI)
`.vsdisco` file extension
Web service
Web Service Description Language (WSDL)
Web-service method
`WebClient` class
`WebMethod` attribute
`WebService` attribute
`WebService` class
wire format
wire protocol
XML serialization

SELF-REVIEW EXERCISES

21.1 State whether each of the following is *true* or *false*. If *false*, explain why.
 a) The purpose of a Web service is to create objects of a class located on a remote machine. This class then can be instantiated and used on the local machine.
 b) A Web server is required to create Web services and make them available.
 c) If the Web service is referenced by adding a Web reference, a proxy class is not created.
 d) A program communicating with a Web service uses SOAP to send and receive messages.
 e) An application can use only Web-service methods that are tagged with the `WebMethod` attribute.
 f) To enable session tracking in a Web-service method, no other action is required the programmer sets the `EnableSession` property to `True` in the `WebMethod` attribute.
 g) The `EnableSession` property of `WebMethod` attributes enables session tracking in Web services.
 h) An application can use only one Web service.
 i) Not all primitive data types can be returned from a Web service.
 j) `WebMethod`s methods cannot be declared `Shared`.
 k) A user-defined type used in a Web service must define both `Get` and `Set` accessors for any property that will be accessed in an application.

21.2 Fill in the blanks for each of the following statements:
 a) When messages are sent between an application and a Web service, each message is placed in a _____.
 b) A Web service can inherit from class _____.
 c) The class that defines a Web service usually is located in the _____ file for that Web service.
 d) Class _____ is designed for interaction with resources identified by a URL.
 e) Web-service requests are sent over the Internet via the _____ protocol.
 f) To add a description for a Web service method in an ASMX page, the _____ property of the `WebService` attribute is used.
 g) Sending objects between a Web service and a client requires _____ of the object.
 h) A proxy class is defined in a namespace whose name is that of the _____ in which the Web service is defined.

ANSWERS TO SELF-REVIEW EXERCISES

21.1 a) False. Web services are used to execute methods on remote machines. The Web service receives the parameters it needs to execute a particular method, executes the method and returns the result to the caller. b) True. c) False. The proxy is created by Visual Studio—its creation is hidden from the programmer. d) True. e) True. f) False. A `CookieContainer` also must be created on the client side. g) True. h) False. An application can use as many Web services as it needs. i) True. j) True. k) True.

21.2 a) SOAP message. b) `WebService`. c) code-behind. d) `WebClient`. e) HTTP. f) `Description`. g) XML serialization. h) domain.

EXERCISES

21.3 Create a Web service that stores phone-book entries in a database. Give the user the capability to enter new contacts and to find contacts by last name. Pass only primitive types as arguments to the Web service.

21.4 Modify Exercise 21.3 so that it uses a class named `PhoneBookEntry`. The client application should provide objects of type `PhoneBookEntry` to the Web service when adding contacts and should receive objects of type `PhoneBookEntry` when searching for contacts.

21.5 Modify the Blackjack Web service example in Section 21.5 to include a class `Card`. Have `DealCard` return an object of type `Card`. Also have the client application keep track of what cards have been dealt, using `Card`s. Your card class should include properties to determine the face and suit of the card.

21.6 Modify the airline reservation example in Section 21.6 so that it contains two separate Web methods—one that allows users to view all available seats, and another that allows them to reserve seats. Use an object of type `Ticket` to pass information to and from the Web service. This Web application should list all available seats in a `ListBox` and then allow the user to click a seat to reserve it. Your application must be able to handle cases where two users view available seats, one reserves a seat, and then the second user tries to reserve the same seat not knowing that the database has changed since the page was loaded.

21.7 Modify the `TemperatureServer` example in Section 21.7 so that it returns an array of `CityWeather` objects that the client application uses to display the weather information.

21.8 Modify the Web service in the math-tutor example in Section 21.8 so that it includes a method that calculates how "close" the player is to the correct answer. The client application should provide the correct answer only after a user has offered numerous answers that were far from the correct one. Use your best judgement regarding what constitutes being "close" to the right answer. Remember that there should be a different formula for 1-digit, 2-digit and 3-digit numbers. Also, give the program the capability to suggest to users that they try a lower difficulty level if the users are consistently wrong.

22

Networking: Streams-Based Sockets and Datagrams

Objectives

- To be able to implement Visual Basic networking applications using sockets and datagrams.
- To understand how to create clients and servers that communicate with one another.
- To understand the implementation of network-based applications.
- To construct a multithreaded server.

If the presence of electricity can be made visible in any part of a circuit, I see no reason why intelligence may not be transmitted instantaneously by electricity.
Samuel F. B. Morse

Mr. Watson, come here, I want you.
Alexander Graham Bell

What networks of railroads, highways and canals were in another age, the networks of telecommunications, information and computerization ... are today.
Bruno Kreisky, Austrian Chancellor

Science may never come up with a better office-communication system than the coffee break.
Earl Wilson

Chapter 22   Networking: Streams-Based Sockets and Datagrams   1097

Outline

22.1 Introduction
22.2 Establishing a Simple Server (Using Stream Sockets)
22.3 Establishing a Simple Client (Using Stream Sockets)
22.4 Client/Server Interaction via Stream-Socket Connections
22.5 Connectionless Client/Server Interaction via Datagrams
22.6 Client/Server Tic-Tac-Toe Using a Multithreaded Server

Summary • Terminology • Self-Review Exercises • Answers to Self-Review Exercises • Exercises

22.1 Introduction

The Internet and the World Wide Web have generated a great deal of excitement in the business and computing communities. The Internet ties the "information world" together; the Web makes the Internet easy to use while providing the flair of multimedia. Organizations see both the Internet and the Web as crucial to their information-systems strategies. Visual Basic and the .NET Framework offer a number of built-in networking capabilities that facilitate Internet-based and Web-based applications development. Visual Basic not only can specify parallelism through multithreading, but also can enable programs to search the Web for information and collaborate with programs running on other computers internationally.

In Chapters 20 and 21, we began our presentation of Visual Basic's networking and distributed-computing capabilities. We discussed Web Forms and Web Services, two high-level networking technologies that enable programmers to develop distributed applications in Visual Basic. In this chapter, we focus on the networking technologies that support Visual Basic's ASP.NET capabilities and can be used to build distributed applications.

Our discussion of networking focuses on both sides of a *client–server relationship*. The *client* requests that some action be performed; the *server* performs the action and responds to the client. A common implementation of this request–response model is between Web browsers and Web servers. When users select Web sites that they wish to view through a browser (the client application), the browser makes a request to the appropriate Web server (the server application). The server normally responds to the client by sending the appropriate HTML Web pages.

Visual Basic's networking capabilities are grouped into several namespaces. The fundamental networking capabilities are defined by classes and interfaces of namespace **System.Net.Sockets**. Through this namespace, Visual Basic offers *socket-based communications*, which enable developers to view networking as if it were file I/O. This means that a program can read from a *socket* (network connection) or write to a socket as easily as it can read from or write to a file. Sockets are the fundamental way to perform network communications in the .NET Framework. The term "socket" refers to the Berkeley Sockets Interface, which was developed in 1978 for network programming with UNIX and was popularized by C and C++ programmers.

The classes and interfaces of namespace **System.Net.Sockets** also offer *packet-based communications*, through which individual *packets* of information are transmitted— this is a common method of transmitting audio and video over the Internet. In this chapter, we show how to create and manipulate sockets and how to communicate via packets of data.

Socket-based communications in Visual Basic employ *stream sockets*. With stream sockets, a *process* (running program) establishes a *connection* to another process. While the connection is in place, data flows between the processes in continuous *streams*. For this reason, stream sockets are said to provide a *connection-oriented service*. The popular *TCP (Transmission Control Protocol)* facilitates stream-socket transmission.

By contrast, packet-based communications in Visual Basic employ *datagram sockets*, through which individual *packets* of information are transmitted. Unlike TCP, the protocol used to enable datagram sockets—*UDP*, the *User Datagram Protocol*—is a *connectionless service* and does not guarantee that packets will arrive in any particular order. In fact, packets can be lost or duplicated and can arrive out of sequence. Applications that use UDP often require significant extra programming to deal with these problems. UDP is most appropriate for network applications that do not require the error checking and reliability of TCP. Stream sockets and the TCP protocol will be the most desirable method of communication for the vast majority of Visual Basic programmers.

Performance Tip 22.1

Connectionless services generally offer better performance but less reliability than do connection-oriented services.

Portability Tip 22.1

The TCP protocol and its related set of protocols enable intercommunication among a wide variety of heterogeneous computer systems (i.e., computer systems with different processors and different operating systems).

22.2 Establishing a Simple Server (Using Stream Sockets)

Typically, with TCP and stream sockets, a server "waits" for a connection request from a client. Often, the server program contains a control structure or block of code that executes continuously until the server receives a request. On receiving a request, the server establishes a connection with the client. The server then uses this connection to handle future requests from that client and to send data to the client.

The establishment of a simple server with TCP and stream sockets in Visual Basic requires five steps. The first step is to create an object of class **TcpListener**, which belongs to namespace **System.Net.Sockets**. This class represents a TCP stream socket through which a server can listen for requests. A call to the **TcpListener** constructor, such as

```
Dim server As TcpListener = New TcpListener( port )
```

binds (assigns) the server to the specified *port number*. A port number is a numeric identifier that a process uses to identify itself at a given *network address*, also known as an *Internet Protocol Address (IP Address)*. IP addresses identify computers on the Internet. In fact, Web-site names, such as **www.deitel.com**, are aliases for IP addresses. Any process that performs networking identifies itself via an *IP address/port number pair*. Hence, no two processes can have the same port number at a given IP address. The explicit binding of a socket to a port (using method **Bind** of class **Socket**) is usually unnecessary, because class **TcpListener** and other classes discussed in this chapter hide this binding (i.e., bind sockets to ports implicitly), plus they perform other socket-initialization operations.

Software Engineering Observation 22.1

Port numbers can have values between 0 and 65535. Many operating systems reserve port numbers below 1024 for system services (such as e-mail and Web servers). Applications must be granted special privileges to use these reserved port numbers. Usually, a server-side application should not specify port numbers below 1024 as connection ports, because some operating systems might reserve these numbers.

Common Programming Error 22.1

Attempting to bind an already assigned port at a given IP address is a logic error.

To receive requests, the **TcpListener** first must listen for them. The second step in our connection process is to call **TcpListener**'s **Start** method, which causes the **TcpListener** object to begin listening for connection requests. The third step establishes the connection between the server and client. The server listens indefinitely for a request—i.e., the execution of the server-side application waits until some client attempts to connect with it. The server creates a connection to the client upon receipt of a connection request. An object of class **System.Net.Sockets.Socket** manages each connection to the client. Method **AcceptSocket** of class **TcpListener** waits for a connection request, then creates a connection when a request is received. This method returns a **Socket** object upon connection, as in the statement

```
Dim connection As Socket = server.AcceptSocket()
```

When the server receives a request, method **AcceptSocket** calls method **Accept** of the **TcpListener**'s underlying **Socket** to make the connection. This is an example of Visual Basic's hiding networking complexity from the programmer. The programmer can write the preceding statement into a server-side program, then allow the classes of namespace **System.Net.Sockets** to handle the details of accepting requests and establishing connections.

Step four is the processing phase, in which the server and the client communicate via methods **Receive** and **Send** of class **Socket**. These methods return references to **Socket** objects for reading from, and writing to, respectively. Note that these methods, as well as TCP and stream sockets, can be used only when the server and client are connected. By contrast, through **Socket** methods **SendTo** and **ReceiveFrom**, UDP and datagram sockets can be used when no connection exists.

The fifth step is the connection-termination phase. When the client and server have finished communicating, the server uses method **Close** of the **Socket** object to close the connection. Most servers then return to step two (i.e., wait for another client's connection request).

One problem associated with the server scheme described in this section is that step four *blocks* other requests while processing a client's request, so that no other client can connect with the server while the code that defines the processing phase is executing. The most common technique for addressing this problem is to use multithreaded servers, which place the processing-phase code in a separate thread. When the server receives a connection request, the server *spawns*, or creates, a **Thread** to process the connection, leaving its **TcpListener** (or **Socket**) free to receive other connections.

Software Engineering Observation 22.2

Using Visual Basic's multithreading capabilities, we can create servers that can manage simultaneous connections with multiple clients. This multithreaded-server architecture is precisely what popular UNIX and Windows network servers use.

Software Engineering Observation 22.3

*A multithreaded server can be implemented to create a thread that manages network I/O across a reference to a **Socket** object returned by method **AcceptSocket**. A multithreaded server also can be implemented to maintain a pool of threads that manage network I/O across newly created **Socket**s.*

Performance Tip 22.2

*In high-performance systems with abundant memory, a multithreaded server can be implemented to create a pool of threads. These threads can be assigned quickly to handle network I/O across each newly created **Socket**. Thus, when a connection is received, the server does not incur the overhead of thread creation.*

22.3 Establishing a Simple Client (Using Stream Sockets)

We create TCP-stream-socket clients via a process that requires four steps. In the first step, we create an object of class **TcpClient** (which belongs to namespace **System.Net.Sockets**) to connect to the server. This connection is established through method **Connect** of class **TcpClient**. One overloaded version of this method receives two arguments—the server's IP address and the port number—as in the following:

```
Dim client As TcpClient = New TcpClient()
client.Connect( serverAddress, serverPort )
```

Here, **serverPort** is an **Integer** that represents the server's port number; **serverAddress** can be either an **IPAddress** instance (that encapsulates the server's IP address) or a **String** that specifies the server's hostname. Alternatively, the programmer could pass an object reference of class **IPEndPoint**, which represents an IP address/port number pair, to a different overload of method **Connect**. Method **Connect** of class **TcpClient** calls method **Connect** of class **Socket** to establish the connection. If the connection is successful, method **TcpClient.Connect** returns a positive integer; otherwise, it returns **0**.

In step two, the **TcpClient** uses its method **GetStream** to get a **NetworkStream** so that it can write to and read from the server. **NetworkStream** methods **WriteByte** and **Write** can be used to output individual bytes or sets of bytes to the server, respectively; similarly, **NetworkStream** methods **ReadByte** and **Read** can be used to input individual bytes or sets of bytes from the server, respectively.

The third step is the processing phase, in which the client and the server communicate. In this phase, the client uses methods **Read**, **ReadByte**, **Write** and **WriteByte** of class **NetworkStream** to perform the appropriate communications. Using a process similar to that used by servers, a client can employ threads to prevent blocking of communications with other servers while processing data from one connection.

After the transmission is complete, step four requires the client to close the connection by calling method **Close** of the **NetworkStream** object. This closes the underlying **Socket** (if the **NetworkStream** has a reference to that **Socket**). Then, the client calls method **Close** of class **TcpClient** connection to terminate the TCP connection. At this point, a new connection can be established through method **Connect**, as we have described.

22.4 Client/Server Interaction via Stream-Socket Connections

The applications in Fig. 22.1 and Fig. 22.2 use the classes and techniques discussed in the previous two sections to construct a simple *client/server chat application*. The server waits for a client's request to make a connection. When a client application connects to the server, the server application sends an array of bytes to the client, indicating that the connection was successful. The client then displays a message notifying the user that a connection has been established.

Both the client and the server applications contain **TextBox**es that enable users to type messages and send them to the other application. When either the client or the server sends message "**TERMINATE**," the connection between the client and the server terminates. The server then waits for another client to request a connection. Figure 22.1 and Fig. 22.2 provide the code for classes **Server** and **Client**, respectively. Figure 22.2 also contains screen captures displaying the execution between the client and the server.

```vb
1   ' Fig. 22.1: Server.vb
2   ' Set up a Server that receives connections from clients and sends
3   ' String data to clients.
4
5   Imports System.Windows.Forms
6   Imports System.Threading
7   Imports System.Net.Sockets
8   Imports System.IO
9
10  Public Class FrmServer
11     Inherits Form
12
13     ' TextBoxes for receiving user input and displaying information
14     Friend WithEvents txtInput As TextBox
15     Friend WithEvents txtDisplay As TextBox
16
17     Private connection As Socket ' Socket object handles connection
18     Private readThread As Thread ' server thread
19
20     ' Stream through which to transfer data
21     Private socketStream As NetworkStream
22
23     ' objects for writing and reading data
24     Private writer As BinaryWriter
25     Private reader As BinaryReader
26
27     Public Sub New()
28        MyBase.New()
29
30        ' equired by the Windows Form Designer.
31        InitializeComponent()
```

Fig. 22.1 Server portion of a client/server stream-socket connection (part 1 of 4).

```vb
32
33          ' add any initialization after the
34          ' InitializeComponent call
35
36          ' create thread from server
37          readThread = New Thread(AddressOf RunServer)
38          readThread.Start()
39       End Sub ' New
40
41       ' Visual Studio .NET generated code
42
43       ' invoked when user closes server
44       Private Sub FrmServer_Closing( _
45          ByVal sender As System.Object, _
46          ByVal e As system.ComponentModel.CancelEventArgs) _
47          Handles MyBase.Closing
48
49          System.Environment.Exit(System.Environment.ExitCode)
50       End Sub ' FrmServer_Closing
51
52       ' send server text to client
53       Private Sub txtInput_KeyDown( ByVal sender As System.Object, _
54          ByVal e As system.Windows.Forms.KeyEventArgs) _
55          Handles txtInput.KeyDown
56
57          ' send text to client
58          Try
59
60             ' send text if user pressed Enter and connection exists
61             If (e.KeyCode = Keys.Enter AndAlso _
62                Not connection Is Nothing) Then
63
64                writer.Write("SERVER>>> " & txtInput.Text) ' send data
65
66                txtDisplay.Text &= vbCrLf & "SERVER>>> " & _
67                   txtInput.Text
68
69                ' close connection if server's user signals termination
70                If txtInput.Text = "TERMINATE" Then
71                   connection.Close()
72                End If
73
74                txtInput.Clear()
75             End If
76
77          ' handle exception if error occurs when server sends data
78          Catch exception As SocketException
79             txtDisplay.Text &= vbCrLf & "Error writing object"
80
81          End Try
82
83       End Sub ' txtInput_KeyDown
84
```

Fig. 22.1 Server portion of a client/server stream-socket connection (part 2 of 4).

```vbnet
85          ' allow client to connect and display text sent by user
86      Public Sub RunServer()
87          Dim listener As TcpListener
88          Dim counter As Integer = 1
89
90              ' wait for request, then establish connection
91          Try
92
93              ' Step 1: create TcpListener
94              listener = New TcpListener(5000)
95
96              ' Step 2: TcpListener waits for connection request
97              listener.Start()
98
99              ' Step 3: establish connection upon client request
100             While True
101                 txtDisplay.Text = "Waiting for connection" & vbCrLf
102
103                 ' accept an incoming connection
104                 connection = listener.AcceptSocket()
105
106                 ' create NetworkStream object associated with socket
107                 socketStream = New NetworkStream(connection)
108
109                 ' create objects for transferring data across stream
110                 writer = New BinaryWriter(socketStream)
111                 reader = New BinaryReader(socketStream)
112
113                 txtDisplay.Text &= "Connection " & counter & _
114                     " received." & vbCrLf
115
116                 ' inform client that connection was successfull
117                 writer.Write("SERVER>>> Connection successful")
118
119                 txtInput.ReadOnly = False
120                 Dim theReply As String = ""
121
122                 ' Step 4: read String data sent from client
123                 Try
124
125                     ' loop until client signals termination
126                     Do
127                         theReply = reader.ReadString() ' read data
128
129                         ' display message
130                         txtDisplay.Text &= vbCrLf & theReply
131
132                     Loop While (theReply <> "CLIENT>>> TERMINATE" _
133                         AndAlso connection.Connected)
134
135                     ' handle exception if error reading data
136                 Catch inputOutputException As IOException
137                     MessageBox.Show("Client application closing")
```

Fig. 22.1 Server portion of a client/server stream-socket connection (part 3 of 4).

```
138             ' close connections
139         Finally
140
141             txtDisplay.Text &= vbCrLf & _
142                 "User terminated connection"
143
144             txtInput.ReadOnly = True
145
146             ' Step 5: close connection
147             writer.Close()
148             reader.Close()
149             socketStream.Close()
150             connection.Close()
151
152             counter += 1
153         End Try
154
155     End While
156
157     ' handle exception if error occurs in establishing connection
158     Catch inputOutputException As IOException
159         MessageBox.Show("Server application closing")
160
161     End Try
162
163  End Sub ' RunServer
164
165 End Class ' FrmServer
```

Fig. 22.1 Server portion of a client/server stream-socket connection (part 4 of 4).

```
1   ' Fig. 22.2: Client.vb
2   ' Set up a client that reads and displays data sent from server.
3
4   Imports System.Windows.Forms
5   Imports System.Threading
6   Imports System.Net.Sockets
7   Imports System.IO
8
9   Public Class FrmClient
10      Inherits Form
11
12      ' TextBoxes for inputting and displaying information
13      Friend WithEvents txtInput As TextBox
14      Friend WithEvents txtDisplay As TextBox
15
16      ' stream for sending data to server
17      Private output As NetworkStream
18
19      ' objects for writing and reading bytes to streams
20      Private writer As BinaryWriter
```

Fig. 22.2 Client portion of a client/server stream-socket connection (part 1 of 5).

```vbnet
21      Private reader As BinaryReader
22
23      Private message As String = "" ' message sent to server
24
25      ' thread prevents client from blocking data transfer
26      Private readThread As Thread
27
28      Public Sub New()
29         MyBase.New()
30
31         ' equired by the Windows Form Designer.
32         InitializeComponent()
33
34         ' add any initialization after the
35         ' InitializeComponent call
36
37         readThread = New Thread(AddressOf RunClient)
38         readThread.Start()
39      End Sub ' New
40
41      ' Visual Studio .NET generated code
42
43      ' invoked when user closes application
44      Private Sub FrmClient_Closing(ByVal sender As System.Object, _
45         ByVal e As System.ComponentModel.CancelEventArgs) _
46         Handles MyBase.Closing
47
48         System.Environment.Exit(System.Environment.ExitCode)
49      End Sub
50
51      ' send user input to server
52      Private Sub txtInput_KeyDown(ByVal sender As System.Object, _
53         ByVal e As System.windows.Forms.KeyEventArgs) _
54         Handles txtInput.KeyDown
55
56         ' send user input if user pressed Enter
57         Try
58
59            ' determine whether user pressed Enter
60            If e.KeyCode = Keys.Enter Then
61
62               ' send data to server
63               writer.Write("CLIENT>>> " & txtInput.Text)
64
65               txtDisplay.Text &= vbCrLf & "CLIENT>>> " & _
66                  txtInput.Text
67
68               txtInput.Clear()
69            End If
70
```

Fig. 22.2 Client portion of a client/server stream-socket connection (part 2 of 5).

```vbnet
71             ' handle exception if error occurs in sending data to server
72          Catch exception As SocketException
73             txtDisplay.Text &= vbCrLf & "Error writing object"
74          End Try
75
76       End Sub ' txtInput_KeyDown
77
78       ' connect to server and display server-generated text
79       Public Sub RunClient()
80          Dim client As TcpClient
81
82          ' instantiate TcpClient for sending data to server
83          Try
84
85             txtDisplay.Text &= "Attempting connection" & vbCrLf
86
87             ' Step 1: create TcpClient and connect to server
88             client = New TcpClient()
89             client.Connect("localhost", 5000)
90
91             ' Step 2: get NetworkStream associated with TcpClient
92             output = client.GetStream()
93
94             ' create objects for writing and reading across stream
95             writer = New BinaryWriter(output)
96             reader = New BinaryReader(output)
97
98             txtDisplay.Text &= vbCrLf & "Got I/O streams" & vbCrLf
99
100            txtInput.ReadOnly = False
101
102            ' Step 3: processing phase
103            Try
104
105               ' loop until server signals termination
106               Do
107
108                  ' read message from server
109                  message = reader.ReadString
110                  txtDisplay.Text &= vbCrLf & message
111
112               Loop While message <> "SERVER>>> TERMINATE"
113
114               ' handle exception if error in reading server data
115            Catch inputOutputException As IOException
116               MessageBox.Show("Client application closing")
117
118               ' Step 4: close connection
119            Finally
120
121               txtDisplay.Text &= vbCrLf & "Closing connection." & _
122                  vbCrLf
123
```

Fig. 22.2 Client portion of a client/server stream-socket connection (part 3 of 5).

```
124                writer.Close()
125                reader.Close()
126                output.Close()
127                client.Close()
128
129             End Try
130
131             Application.Exit()
132
133          ' handle exception if error in establishing connection
134          Catch inputOutputException As Exception
135             MessageBox.Show("Client application closing")
136
137          End Try
138
139       End Sub ' RunClient
140
141    End Class ' FrmClient
```

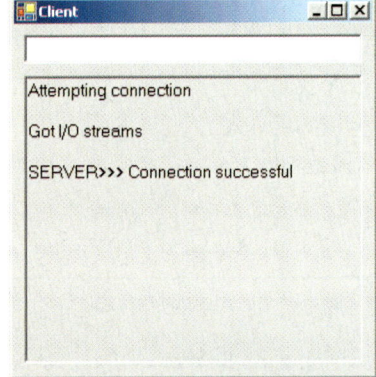
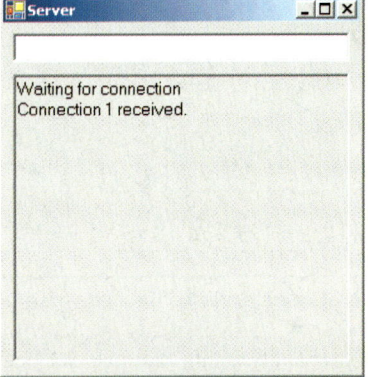
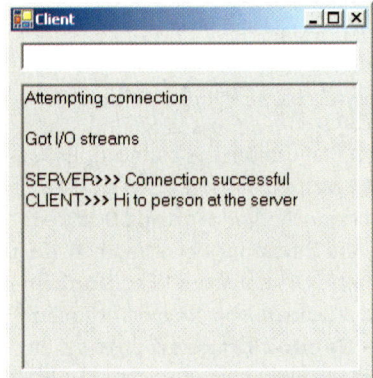
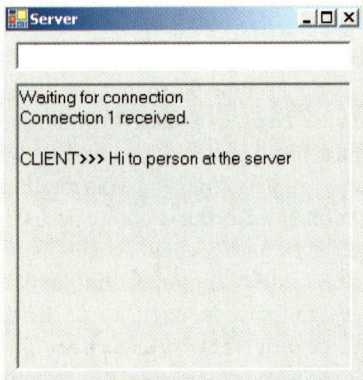

Fig. 22.2 Client portion of a client/server stream-socket connection (part 4 of 5).

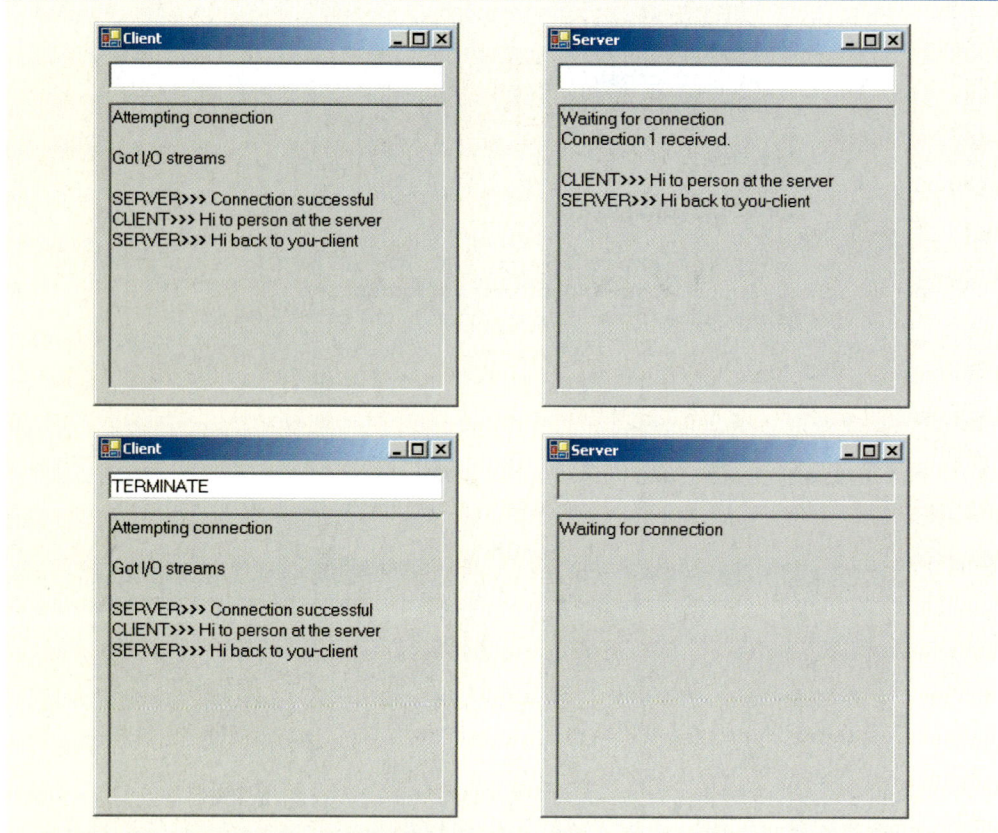

Fig. 22.2 Client portion of a client/server stream-socket connection (part 5 of 5).

As we analyze this example, we begin by discussing class **Server** (Fig. 22.1). In the constructor, line 37 creates a **Thread** that will accept connections from clients. Line 38 starts the **Thread**, which invokes method **RunServer** (lines 86–164). Method **RunServer** initializes the server to receive connection requests and process connections. Line 94 instantiates the **TcpListener** to listen for a connection request from a client at port **5000** (Step 1). Line 97 then calls method **Start** of the **TcpListener** object, which requires the **TcpListener** to wait for requests (Step 2).

Lines 100–156 declare an infinite **While** loop that establishes connections requested by clients (Step 3). Line 104 calls method **AcceptSocket** of the **TcpListener** object, which returns a **Socket** upon successful connection. Method **AcceptSocket** blocks other services until a client request is made (i.e., the thread in which method **AcceptSocket** is called stops executing until a connection is established). The **Socket** object will manage the connection. Line 107 passes this **Socket** object as an argument to the constructor of a **NetworkStream** object. Class **NetworkStream** provides access to streams across a network—in this example, the **NetworkStream** object provides access to the **Socket** connection. Lines 110–111 create instances of the *BinaryWriter* and *BinaryReader* classes for writing and reading data. We pass the **NetworkStream** object as an argument to each constructor; **BinaryWriter** can write bytes to the **Net-**

workStream, and **BinaryReader** can read bytes from **NetworkStream**. Lines 113–114 append text to the **TextBox**, indicating that a connection was received.

BinaryWriter method *Write* has many overloaded versions, which enable the method to write various types to a stream. (You might remember that we used these overloaded methods in Chapter 17 to write record data to files.) Line 117 uses method **Write** to send to the client a **String** notifying the user of a successful connection. Lines 126–133 declare a **Do/Loop While** structure that executes until the server receives a message indicating connection termination (i.e., **CLIENT>>> TERMINATE**). Line 127 uses **BinaryReader** method *ReadString* to read a **String** from the stream (Step 4). (You might remember that we also used this method in Chapter 17 to read records' first-name and last-name **String**s from files.) Method **ReadString** blocks until a **String** is read. To prevent the whole server from blocking, we use a separate **Thread** to handle the transfer of information. The **While** statement loops until there is more information to read—this results in I/O blocking, which causes the program always to appear frozen. However, if we run this portion of the program in a separate **Thread**, the user can interact with the Windows **Form** and send messages while the program waits in the background for incoming messages.

When the chat is complete, lines 148–151 close the **BinaryWriter**, **BinaryReader**, **NetworkStream** and **Socket** (Step 5) by invoking their respective **Close** methods. The server then waits for another client connection request by returning to the beginning of the **While** loop (line 100).

When the user of the server application enters a **String** in the **TextBox** and presses the *Enter* key, event handler **txtInput_KeyDown** (lines 53–83) reads the **String** and sends it via method **Write** of class **BinaryWriter**. If a user terminates the server application, line 71 calls method **Close** of the **Socket** object to close the connection.

Lines 44–50 define the **frmServer_Closing** event handler for the **Closing** event. The event closes the application and uses **System.Environment.Exit** method with parameter **System.Environment.ExitCode** to terminate all threads. Method **Exit** of class **Environment** closes all threads associated with the application.

Figure 22.2 depicts the code for the **Client** object. Like the **Server** object, the **Client** object creates a **Thread** (lines 37–38) in its constructor to handle all incoming messages. **Client** method **RunClient** (lines 79–139) connects to the **Server**, receives data from the **Server** and sends data to the **Server** (when the user presses *Enter*). Lines 88–89 instantiate a **TcpClient** object, then call its method **Connect** to establish a connection (Step 1). The first argument to method **Connect** is the name of the server—in our case, the server's name is **"localhost"**, meaning that the server is located on the same machine as the client. The **localhost** is also known as the *loopback IP address* and is equivalent to the IP address **127.0.0.1**. This value sends the data transmission back to the sender's IP address. [*Note*: We chose to demonstrate the client/server relationship by connecting between programs that are executing on the same computer (**localhost**). Normally, this argument would contain the Internet address of another computer.] The second argument to method **Connect** is the server port number. This number must match the port number at which the server waits for connections.

The **Client** uses a **NetworkStream** to send data to and receive data from the server. The client obtains the **NetworkStream** on line 92 through a call to **TcpClient** method **GetStream** (Step 2). The **Do/Loop While** structure in lines 106–112 loops until the client receives the connection-termination message (**SERVER>>> TERMINATE**). Line 109 uses

BinaryReader method **ReadString** to obtain the next message from the server (Step 3). Lines 121–122 display the message and lines 124–127 close the **BinaryWriter**, **BinaryReader**, **NetworkStream** and **TcpClient** objects (Step 4).

When the user of the client application enters a **String** in the **TextBox** and presses the *Enter* key, the event handler **txtInput_KeyDown** (lines 52–76) reads the **String** from the **TextBox** and sends it via **BinaryWriter** method **Write**. Notice that, here, the **Server** receives a connection, processes it, closes it and waits for the next one. In a real-world application, a server would likely receive a connection, set up the connection to be processed as a separate thread of execution and wait for new connections. The separate threads that process existing connections can continue to execute while the **Server** concentrates on new connection requests.

22.5 Connectionless Client/Server Interaction via Datagrams

Up to this point, we have discussed connection-oriented, streams-based transmission. Now, we consider connectionless transmission using datagrams.

Connection-oriented transmission is similar to interaction over a telephone system, in which a user dials a number and is *connected* to the telephone of the party they wish to connect. The system maintains the connection for the duration of the phone call, regardless of whether the users are speaking.

By contrast, connectionless transmission via *datagrams* more closely resembles the method by which the postal service carries and delivers mail. Connectionless transmission bundles and sends information in *packets* called datagrams, which can be thought of as similar to posted letters. If a large message will not fit in one envelope, that message is broken into separate message pieces and placed in separate, sequentially numbered envelopes. All the letters are mailed at once. The letters might arrive in order, out of order or not at all. The person at the receiving end reassembles the message pieces into sequential order before attempting to interpret the message. If the message is small enough to fit in one envelope, the sequencing problem is eliminated, but it is still possible that the message will never arrive. (Unlike with posted mail, duplicates of datagrams could reach a receiving computers.) Visual Basic provides the **UdpClient** class for connectionless transmission. Like **TcpListener** and **TcpClient**, **UdpClient** uses methods from class **Socket**. The **UdpClient** methods *Send* and *Receive* are used to transmit data with **Socket**'s **SendTo** method and to read data with **Socket**'s **ReceiveFrom** method, respectively.

The programs in Fig. 22.3 and Fig. 22.4 use datagrams to send *packets* of information between a client and server application. In the **Client** application, the user types a message into a **TextBox** and presses *Enter*. The client converts the message to a **Byte** array and sends it to the server. The server receives the packet and displays the packet's information, then *echoes*, or returns, the packet back to the client. When the client receives the packet, the client displays the packet's information. In this example, the implementations of the **Client** and **Server** classes are similar.

```
1    ' Fig. 22.3: Server.vb
2    ' Server receives packets from a client, then echoes packets back
3    ' to clients.
```

Fig. 22.3 Server-side portion of connectionless client/server computing (part 1 of 3).

```vb
4
5   Imports System.Windows.Forms
6   Imports System.Net
7   Imports System.Net.Sockets
8   Imports System.Threading
9
10  Public Class FrmDatagramServer
11     Inherits Form
12
13     ' TextBox displays packet information
14     Friend WithEvents txtDisplay As TextBox
15
16     ' reference to client that will send packet information
17     Private client As UdpClient
18
19     ' client IP address/port number pair
20     Private receivePoint As IPEndPoint
21
22     Public Sub New()
23        MyBase.New()
24
25        ' equired by the Windows Form Designer.
26        InitializeComponent()
27
28        ' add any initialization after the
29        ' InitializeComponent call
30
31        ' instantiate UdpClient listening for requests at port 5000
32        client = New UdpClient(5000)
33
34        ' hold IP address and port number of client
35        receivePoint = New IPEndPoint(New IPAddress(0), 0)
36
37        Dim readThread As Thread = New Thread _
38           (New ThreadStart(AddressOf WaitForPackets))
39
40        readThread.Start() ' wait for packets
41     End Sub ' New
42
43     ' Visual Studio .NET generated code
44
45     ' invoked when user closes server
46     Protected Sub Server_Closing(ByVal sender As system.Object, _
47        ByVal e As System.ComponentModel.CancelEventArgs) _
48        Handles MyBase.Closing
49
50        System.Environment.Exit(System.Environment.ExitCode)
51     End Sub ' Server_Closing
52
53     ' wait for packets to arrive from client
54     Public Sub WaitForPackets()
55
```

Fig. 22.3 Server-side portion of connectionless client/server computing (part 2 of 3).

```vbnet
56          ' use infinite loop to wait for data to arrive
57          While True
58
59             ' receive byte array from client
60             Dim data As Byte() = client.Receive(receivePoint)
61
62             ' output packet data to TextBox
63             txtDisplay.Text &= vbCrLf & "Packet received:" & _
64                vbCrLf & "Length: " & data.Length & vbCrLf & _
65                "Containing: " & _
66                System.Text.Encoding.ASCII.GetString(data)
67
68             txtDisplay.Text &= vbCrLf & vbCrLf & _
69                "Echo data back to client..."
70
71             ' echo information from packet back to client
72             client.Send(data, data.Length, receivePoint)
73             txtDisplay.Text &= vbCrLf & "Packet sent" & _
74                vbCrLf
75
76          End While
77
78       End Sub ' WaitForPackets
79
80    End Class ' FrmDatagramServer
```

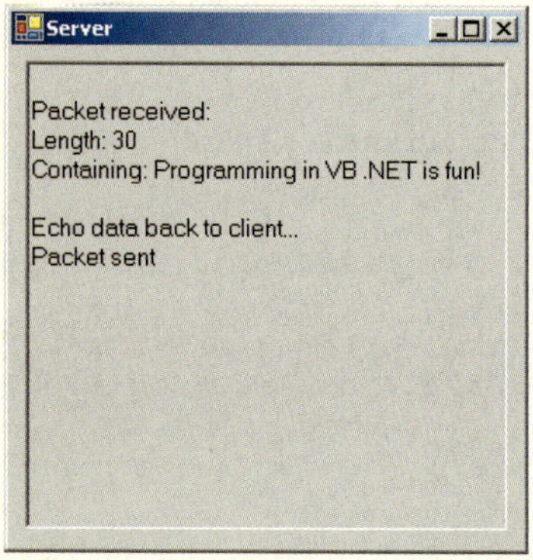

Fig. 22.3 Server-side portion of connectionless client/server computing (part 3 of 3).

```vbnet
1     ' Fig. 22.4: Client.vb
2     ' Client sends packets to, and receives packets from, a server.
3
4     Imports System.Windows.Forms
5     Imports System.Net
6     Imports System.Net.Sockets
7     Imports System.Threading
8
9     Public Class FrmDatagramClient
10       Inherits Form
```

Fig. 22.4 Client-side portion of connectionless client/server computing (part 1 of 3).

```vb
11
12       ' TextBoxes for inputting and displaying packet information
13       Friend WithEvents txtInput As TextBox
14       Friend WithEvents txtDisplay As TextBox
15
16       ' UdpClient that sends packets to server
17       Private client As UdpClient
18
19       ' hold IP address and port number of clients
20       Private receivePoint As IPEndPoint
21
22       Public Sub New()
23          MyBase.New()
24
25          ' equired by the Windows Form Designer.
26          InitializeComponent()
27
28          ' add any initialization after the
29          ' InitializeComponent() call
30
31          receivePoint = New IPEndPoint(New IPAddress(0), 0)
32
33          ' instantiate UdpClient to listen on port 5001
34          client = New UdpClient(5001)
35
36          Dim thread As Thread = New Thread _
37             (New ThreadStart(AddressOf WaitForPackets))
38
39          thread.Start() ' wait for packets
40       End Sub ' New
41
42       ' Visual Studio .NET generated code
43
44       ' invoked when user closes client
45       Private Sub FrmDatagramClient_Closing( _
46          ByVal sender As System.Object, _
47          ByVal e As System.ComponentModel.CancelEventArgs) _
48          Handles MyBase.Closing
49
50          System.Environment.Exit(System.Environment.ExitCode)
51       End Sub ' FrmDatagramClient_Closing
52
53       ' invoked when user presses key
54       Private Sub txtInput_KeyDown( ByVal sender As System.Object, _
55          ByVal e As System.Windows.Forms.KeyEventArgs) _
56          Handles txtInput.KeyDown
57
58          ' determine whether user pressed Enter
59          If e.KeyCode = Keys.Enter Then
60
61             ' create packet (datagram) as String
62             Dim packet As String = txtInput.Text
63
```

Fig. 22.4 Client-side portion of connectionless client/server computing (part 2 of 3).

```vbnet
64           txtDisplay.Text &= vbCrLf & _
65              "Sending packet containing: " & packet
66
67           ' convert packet to byte array
68           Dim data As Byte() = _
69              System.Text.Encoding.ASCII.GetBytes(packet)
70
71           ' send packet to server on port 5000
72           client.Send(data, data.Length, "localhost", 5000)
73
74           txtDisplay.Text &= vbCrLf & "Packet sent" & vbCrLf
75           txtInput.Clear()
76        End If
77
78     End Sub ' txtInput_KeyDown
79
80     ' wait for packets to arrive
81     Public Sub WaitForPackets()
82
83        While True
84
85           ' receive byte array from client
86           Dim data As Byte() = client.Receive(receivePoint)
87
88           ' output packet data to TextBox
89           txtDisplay.Text &= vbCrLf & "Packet received:" & _
90              vbCrLf & "Length: " & data.Length & vbCrLf & _
91              System.Text.Encoding.ASCII.GetString(data)
92
93        End While
94
95     End Sub ' WaitForPackets
96
97  End Class ' FrmDatagramClient
```

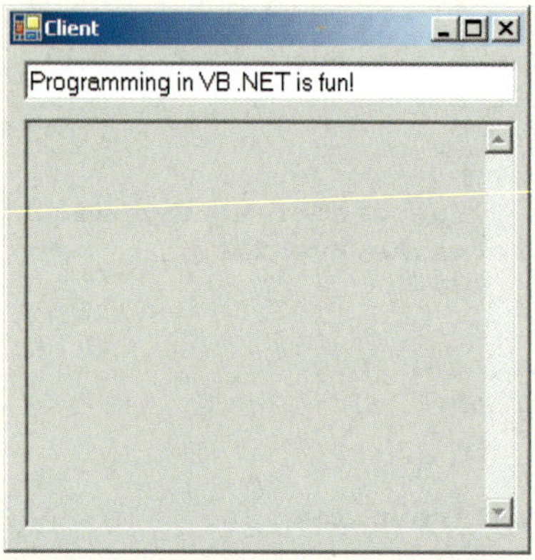

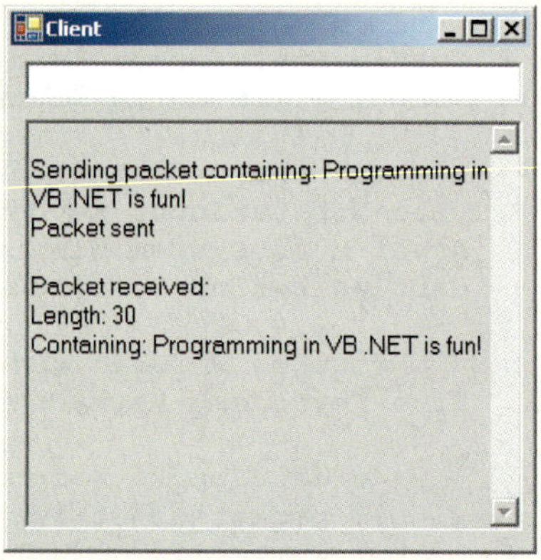

Fig. 22.4 Client-side portion of connectionless client/server computing (part 3 of 3).

The code in Fig. 22.3 defines the **Server** for this application. Line 32 in the constructor for class **Server** creates an instance of the **UdpClient** class that receives data at port **5000**. This initializes the underlying **Socket** for communications. Line 35 creates an instance of class **IPEndPoint** to hold the IP address and port number of the client(s) that transmit to **Server**. The first argument to the constructor of **IPEndPoint** is an **IPAddress** object; the second argument to the constructor for **IPEndPoint** is the port number of the endpoint. These values are both **0**, because we need only instantiate an empty **IPEndPoint** object. The IP addresses and port numbers of clients are copied into the **IPEndPoint** when datagrams are received from clients.

Server method **WaitForPackets** (lines 54–78) executes an infinite loop while waiting for data to arrive at the **Server**. When information arrives, the **UdpClient** method **Receive** (line 60) receives a byte array from the client. We include **Receive** in the **IPEndPoint** object created in the constructor; this provides the method with a reference to an **IPEndPoint** into which the program copies the client's IP address and port number. This program will compile and run without an exception even if the reference to the **IPEndPoint** object is **Nothing**, because method **Receive** (or some method that method **Receive** subsequently calls) initializes the **IPEndPoint** if it is **Nothing**.

Good Programming Practice 22.1

*Initialize all references to objects (to a value other than **Nothing**). This protects code from methods that do not check their parameters for **Nothing** references.*

Lines 63–66 update the **Server**'s display to include the packet's information and content. Line 72 echoes the data back to the client, using **UdpClient** method **Send**. This version of **Send** takes three arguments: The byte array to send, an **Integer** representing the array's length and the **IPEndPoint** to which to send the data. We use array **Byte()** returned by method **Receive** as the data, the length of array **Byte()** as the length and the **IPEndPoint** passed to method **Receive** as the data's destination. The IP address and port number of the client that sent the data to **Server** are stored in **receivePoint**, so merely passing **receivePoint** to **Send** allows **Server** to respond to the client.

Class **Client** (Fig. 22.4) works similarly to class **Server**, except that the **Client** object sends packets only when the user types a message in a **TextBox** and presses the *Enter* key. When this occurs, the program calls event handler **txtInput_KeyDown** (lines 54–78). Lines 68–69 convert the **String** that the user entered in the **TextBox** to a **Byte** array. Line 72 calls **UdpClient** method **Send** to send the **Byte** array to the **Server** that is located on **localhost** (i.e., the same machine). We specify the port as **5000**, which we know to be **Server**'s port.

Line 34 instantiates a **UdpClient** object to receive packets at port **5001**—we choose port **5001**, because the **Server** already occupies port **5000**. Method **WaitForPackets** of class **Client** (lines 81–95) uses an infinite loop to wait for these packets. The **UdpClient** method **Receive** blocks until a packet of data is received (line 86). However, this does not prevent the user from sending a packet, because Visual Basic provides a separate thread for handling GUI events. The blocking performed by method **Receive** does not prevent class **Client** from performing other services (e.g., handling user input), because a separate thread runs method **WaitForPackets**.

When a packet arrives, lines 89–91 display its contents in the **TextBox**. The user can type information into the **Client** window's **TextBox** and press the *Enter* key at any

1116 Networking: Streams-Based Sockets and Datagrams   Chapter 22

time, even while a packet is being received. The event handler for the **TextBox** processes the event and sends the data to the server.

22.6 Client/Server Tic-Tac-Toe Using a Multithreaded Server

In this section, we present our capstone networking example—the popular game Tic-Tac-Toe, implemented with stream sockets and client/server techniques. The program consists of a **FrmServer** application (Fig. 22.5) and two **FrmClient** applications (Fig. 22.7); **FrmServer** allows the **FrmClient**s to connect to the server and play Tic-Tac-Toe. We depict the output in Fig. 22.7. When the server receives a client connection, lines 67–78 of Fig. 22.5 create an instance of class **CPlayer** to process the client in a separate thread of execution. This enables the server to handle requests from both clients. The server assigns value **"X"** to the first client that connects (player **X** makes the first move), then assigns value **"O"** to the second client. Throughout the game, the server maintains information regarding the status of the board so that the server can validate players' requested moves. However, neither the server nor the client can establish whether a player has won the game—in this application, method **GameOver** (lines 166–170) always returns **False**. Exercise 22.7 asks the reader to implement functionality that enables the application to determine a winner. Each **FrmClient** maintains its own GUI version of the Tic-Tac-Toe board to display the game. The clients can place marks only in empty squares on the board. Class **CSquare** (Fig. 22.8) is used to define squares on the Tic-Tac-Toe board.

```
1   ' Fig. 22.5: Server.vb
2   ' Server maintains a Tic-Tac-Toe game for two client applications.
3
4   Imports System.Windows.Forms
5   Imports System.Net.Sockets
6   Imports System.Threading
7
8   Public Class FrmServer
9      Inherits Form
10
11     ' TextBox for displaying results
12     Friend WithEvents txtDisplay As TextBox
13
14     Private board As Char() ' Tic-Tac-Toe game board
15
16     Private players As CPlayer() ' player-client applications
17     Private playerThreads As Thread() ' Threads that run clients
18
19     ' indicates current player ("X" or "O")
20     Private currentPlayer As Integer
21
22     ' indicates whether server has disconnected
23     Private disconnect As Boolean = False
24
25     Public Sub New()
26        MyBase.New()
27
```

Fig. 22.5 Server side of client/server Tic-Tac-Toe program (part 1 of 4).

```vb
28         ' required by the Windows Form Designer
29         InitializeComponent()
30
31         ' add any initialization after the
32         ' InitializeComponent call
33
34         board = New Char(8) {} ' create board with nine squares
35
36         players = New CPlayer(1) {} ' create two players
37
38         ' create one thread for each player
39         playerThreads = New Thread(1) {}
40         currentPlayer = 0
41
42         ' use separate thread to accept connections
43         Dim getPlayers As Thread = New Thread(New ThreadStart( _
44            AddressOf SetUp))
45
46         getPlayers.Start()
47      End Sub ' New
48
49      ' Visual Studio .NET generated code
50
51      ' invoked when user closes server window
52      Private Sub FrmServer_Closing(ByVal sender As System.Object, _
53         ByVal e As System.ComponentModel.CancelEventArgs) _
54         Handles MyBase.Closing
55
56         disconnect = True
57      End Sub ' FrmServer_Closing
58
59      ' accept connections from two client applications
60      Public Sub SetUp()
61
62         ' server listens for requests on port 5000
63         Dim listener As TcpListener = New TcpListener(5000)
64         listener.Start()
65
66         ' accept first client (player) and start its thread
67         players(0) = New CPlayer(listener.AcceptSocket(), Me, "X"c)
68         playerThreads(0) = _
69            New Thread(New ThreadStart(AddressOf players(0).Run))
70
71         playerThreads(0).Start()
72
73         ' accept second client (player) and start its thread
74         players(1) = New CPlayer(listener.AcceptSocket, Me, "O"c)
75         playerThreads(1) = _
76            New Thread(New ThreadStart(AddressOf players(1).Run))
77
78         playerThreads(1).Start()
79
```

Fig. 22.5 Server side of client/server Tic-Tac-Toe program (part 2 of 4).

```
 80            ' inform first player of other player's connection to server
 81            SyncLock (players(0))
 82
 83               players(0).threadSuspended = False
 84               Monitor.Pulse(players(0))
 85            End SyncLock
 86
 87         End Sub ' SetUp
 88
 89         ' display message argument in txtDisplay
 90         Public Sub Display(ByVal message As String)
 91            txtDisplay.Text &= message & vbCrLf
 92         End Sub ' Display
 93
 94         ' determine whether move is valid
 95         Public Function ValidMove(ByVal location As Integer, _
 96            ByVal player As Char) As Boolean
 97
 98            ' prevent other threads from making moves
 99            SyncLock(Me)
100
101               Dim playerNumber As Integer = 0
102
103               ' playerNumber = 0 if player = "X", else playerNumber = 1
104               If player = "O"c
105                  playerNumber = 1
106               End If
107
108               ' wait while not current player's turn
109               While playerNumber <> currentPlayer
110                  Monitor.Wait(Me)
111               End While
112
113               ' determine whether desired square is occupied
114               If Not IsOccupied(location) Then
115
116                  ' place either an "X" or an "O" on board
117                  If currentPlayer = 0 Then
118                     board(location) = "X"c
119                  Else
120                     board(location) = "O"c
121                  End If
122
123                  ' set currentPlayer as other player (change turns)
124                  currentPlayer = (currentPlayer + 1) Mod 2
125
126                  ' notify other player of move
127                  players(currentPlayer).OtherPlayerMoved(location)
128
129                  ' alert other player to move
130                  Monitor.Pulse(Me)
131
132                  Return True
```

Fig. 22.5 Server side of client/server Tic-Tac-Toe program (part 3 of 4).

```
133                Else
134                    Return False
135                End If
136
137           End SyncLock
138
139       End Function ' ValidMove
140
141       ' determine whether specified square is occupied
142       Public Function IsOccupied(ByVal location As Integer) _
143           As Boolean
144
145           ' return True if board location contains "X" or "O"
146           If (board(location) = "X"c OrElse _
147               board(location) = "O"c) Then
148
149               Return True
150           Else
151               Return False
152           End If
153
154       End Function ' IsOccupied
155
156       ' allow clients to see if server has disconnected
157       Public ReadOnly Property Disconnected() As Boolean
158
159           Get
160               Return disconnect
161           End Get
162
163       End Property ' Disconnected
164
165       ' determine whether game is over
166       Public Function GameOver() As Boolean
167
168           ' place code here to test for winner of game
169           Return False
170       End Function ' GameOver
171
172  End Class ' FrmServer
```

Fig. 22.5 Server side of client/server Tic-Tac-Toe program (part 4 of 4).

```
1   ' Fig. 22.6: Player.vb
2   ' Represents a Tic-Tac-Toe player.
3
4   Imports System.Threading
5   Imports System.Net.Sockets
6   Imports System.IO
7
8   Public Class CPlayer
9
```

Fig. 22.6 **CPlayer** class represents a Tic-Tac-Toe player (part 1 of 4).

```vb
10      Private connection As Socket   ' connection to server
11      Private server As FrmServer    ' reference to Tic-Tac-Toe server
12
13      ' object for sending data to server
14      Private socketStream As NetworkStream
15
16      ' objects for writing and reading bytes to streams
17      Private writer As BinaryWriter
18      Private reader As BinaryReader
19
20      Private mark As Char    ' "X" or "O"
21      Friend threadSuspended As Boolean = True
22
23      Sub New(ByVal socketValue As Socket, _
24         ByVal serverValue As FrmServer, ByVal markValue As Char)
25
26         ' assign argument values to class-member values
27         connection = socketValue
28         server = serverValue
29         mark = markValue
30
31         ' use Socket to create NetworkStream object
32         socketStream = New NetworkStream(connection)
33
34         ' create objects for writing and reading bytes across streams
35         writer = New BinaryWriter(socketStream)
36         reader = New BinaryReader(socketStream)
37      End Sub ' New
38
39      ' inform other player that move was made
40      Public Sub OtherPlayerMoved(ByVal location As Integer)
41
42         ' notify opponent
43         writer.Write("Opponent moved")
44         writer.Write(location)
45      End Sub ' OtherPlayerMoved
46
47      ' inform server of move and receive move from other player
48      Public Sub Run()
49
50         Dim done As Boolean = False   ' indicates whether game is over
51
52         ' indicate successful connection and send mark to server
53         If mark = "X"c Then
54            server.Display("Player X connected")
55            writer.Write(mark)
56            writer.Write("Player X connected" & vbCrLf)
57         Else
58            server.Display("Player O connected")
59            writer.Write(mark)
60            writer.Write("Player O connected, please wait" & vbCrLf)
61         End If
62
```

Fig. 22.6 `CPlayer` class represents a Tic-Tac-Toe player (part 2 of 4).

```vbnet
63           ' wait for other player to connect
64          If mark = "X"c Then
65             writer.Write("Waiting for another player")
66
67             ' wait for notification that other player has connected
68             SyncLock (Me)
69
70                While ThreadSuspended
71                   Monitor.Wait(Me)
72                End While
73
74             End SyncLock
75
76             writer.Write("Other player connected. Your move")
77          End If
78
79          ' play game
80          While Not done
81
82             ' wait for data to become available
83             While connection.Available = 0
84                Thread.Sleep(1000)
85
86                ' end loop if server disconnects
87                If server.Disconnected Then
88                   Return
89                End If
90
91             End While
92
93             ' receive other player's move
94             Dim location As Integer = reader.ReadInt32()
95
96             ' determine whether move is valid
97             If server.ValidMove(location, mark) Then
98
99                ' display move on server
100               server.Display("loc: " & location)
101
102               ' notify server of valid move
103               writer.Write("Valid move.")
104
105            Else  ' notify server of invalid move
106               writer.Write("Invalid move, try again")
107            End If
108
109            ' exit loop if game over
110            If server.GameOver Then
111               done = True
112            End If
113
114         End While
115
```

Fig. 22.6 `CPlayer` class represents a Tic-Tac-Toe player (part 3 of 4).

```
116             ' close all connections
117             writer.Close()
118             reader.Close()
119             socketStream.Close()
120             connection.Close()
121         End Sub ' Run
122
123 End Class ' CPlayer
```

Fig. 22.6 `CPlayer` class represents a Tic-Tac-Toe player (part 4 of 4).

```
1   ' Fig. 22.7: Client.vb
2   ' Client for the Tic-Tac-Toe program.
3
4   Imports System.Windows.Forms
5   Imports System.Net.Sockets
6   Imports System.Threading
7   Imports System.IO
8
9   Public Class FrmClient
10      Inherits Form
11
12      ' board contains nine panels where user can place "X" or "O"
13      Friend WithEvents Panel1 As Panel
14      Friend WithEvents Panel2 As Panel
15      Friend WithEvents Panel3 As Panel
16      Friend WithEvents Panel4 As Panel
17      Friend WithEvents Panel5 As Panel
18      Friend WithEvents Panel6 As Panel
19      Friend WithEvents Panel7 As Panel
20      Friend WithEvents Panel8 As Panel
21      Friend WithEvents Panel9 As Panel
22
23      ' TextBox displays game status and other player's moves
24      Friend WithEvents txtDisplay As TextBox
25      Friend WithEvents lblId As Label ' Label displays player
26
27      Private board As CSquare(,) ' Tic-Tac-Toe board
28
29      ' square that user previously clicked
30      Private mCurrentSquare As CSquare
31
32      Private connection As TcpClient ' connection to server
33      Private stream As NetworkStream ' stream to tranfser data
34
35      ' objects for writing and reader bytes to streams
36      Private writer As BinaryWriter
37      Private reader As BinaryReader
38
39      Private mark As Char ' "X" or "O"
40      Private turn As Boolean ' indicates which player should move
41
```

Fig. 22.7 Client side of client/server Tic-Tac-Toe program (part 1 of 7).

```vb
42      Private brush As SolidBrush ' brush for painting board
43
44      Private done As Boolean = False ' indicates whether game is over
45
46      Public Sub New()
47         MyBase.New()
48
49         ' required by the Windows Form Designer
50         InitializeComponent()
51
52         ' add any initialization after the
53         ' InitializeComponent call
54
55         board = New CSquare(2, 2) {} ' create 3 x 3 board
56
57         ' create nine CSquare's and place their Panels on board
58         board(0, 0) = New CSquare(Panel1, " ", 0)
59         board(0, 1) = New CSquare(Panel2, " ", 1)
60         board(0, 2) = New CSquare(Panel3, " ", 2)
61         board(1, 0) = New CSquare(Panel4, " ", 3)
62         board(1, 1) = New CSquare(Panel5, " ", 4)
63         board(1, 2) = New CSquare(Panel6, " ", 5)
64         board(2, 0) = New CSquare(Panel7, " ", 6)
65         board(2, 1) = New CSquare(Panel8, " ", 7)
66         board(2, 2) = New CSquare(Panel9, " ", 8)
67
68         ' create SolidBrush for writing on Squares
69         brush = New SolidBrush(Color.Black)
70
71         ' make connection request to server at port 5000
72         connection = New TcpClient("localhost", 5000)
73         stream = connection.GetStream()
74
75         ' create objects for writing and reading bytes to streams
76         writer = New BinaryWriter(stream)
77         reader = New BinaryReader(stream)
78
79         ' create thread for sending and receiving messages
80         Dim outputThread As Thread = New Thread(AddressOf Run)
81         outputThread.Start()
82      End Sub ' New
83
84      ' Visual Studio .NET generated code
85
86      ' invoked on screen redraw
87      Private Sub FrmClient_Paint(ByVal sender As System.Object, _
88         ByVal e As System.Windows.Forms.PaintEventArgs) _
89         Handles MyBase.Paint
90
91         PaintSquares()
92      End Sub
93
```

Fig. 22.7 Client side of client/server Tic-Tac-Toe program (part 2 of 7).

```vbnet
 94       ' invoked when user closes client application
 95       Private Sub FrmClient_Closing(ByVal sender As System.Object, _
 96          ByVal e As System.ComponentModel.CancelEventArgs) _
 97          Handles MyBase.Closing
 98
 99          done = True
100       End Sub
101
102       ' redraw Tic-Tac-Toe board
103       Public Sub PaintSquares()
104          Dim graphics As Graphics
105
106          ' counters for traversing Tic-Tac-Toe board
107          Dim row As Integer
108          Dim column As Integer
109
110          ' draw appropriate mark on each panel
111          For row = 0 To 2
112
113             For column = 0 To 2
114
115                ' get Graphics for each Panel
116                graphics = board(row, column).Panel.CreateGraphics()
117
118                ' draw appropriate letter on panel
119                graphics.DrawString(board(row, _
120                   column).Mark.ToString(), Me.Font, brush, 8, 8)
121             Next
122          Next
123
124       End Sub ' PaintSquares
125
126       ' invoked when user clicks Panels
127       Private Sub square_MouseUp(ByVal sender As System.Object, _
128          ByVal e As System.Windows.Forms.MouseEventArgs) Handles _
129          Panel1.MouseUp, Panel2.MouseUp, Panel3.MouseUp, _
130          Panel4.MouseUp, Panel5.MouseUp, Panel6.MouseUp, _
131          Panel7.MouseUp, Panel8.MouseUp, Panel9.MouseUp
132
133          ' counters for traversing Tic-Tac-Toe board
134          Dim row As Integer
135          Dim column As Integer
136
137          For row = 0 To 2
138
139             For column = 0 To 2
140
141                ' determine which Panel was clicked
142                If board(row, column).Panel Is sender Then
143                   mCurrentSquare = board(row, column)
144
```

Fig. 22.7 Client side of client/server Tic-Tac-Toe program (part 3 of 7).

```vbnet
145                       ' send move to server
146                       SendClickedSquare(board(row, column).Location)
147                End If
148
149            Next
150        Next
151
152    End Sub ' square_MouseUp
153
154    ' continuously update TextBox display
155    Public Sub Run()
156
157        Dim quote As Char = ChrW(34) ' single quote
158
159        ' get player's mark ("X" or "O")
160        mark = Convert.ToChar(stream.ReadByte())
161        lblId.Text = "You are player " & quote & mark & quote
162
163        ' determine which player should move
164        If mark = "X" Then
165            turn = True
166        Else
167            turn = False
168        End If
169
170        ' process incoming messages
171        Try
172
173            ' receive messages sent to client
174            While True
175                ProcessMessage(reader.ReadString())
176            End While
177
178            ' notify user if server closes connection
179        Catch exception As EndOfStreamException
180            txtDisplay.Text = "Server closed connection.  Game over."
181
182        End Try
183
184    End Sub ' Run
185
186    ' process messages sent to client
187    Public Sub ProcessMessage(ByVal messageValue As String)
188
189        ' if valid move, set mark to clicked square
190        If messageValue = "Valid move." Then
191            txtDisplay.Text &= "Valid move, please wait." & vbCrLf
192            mCurrentSquare.Mark = mark
193            PaintSquares()
194
```

Fig. 22.7 Client side of client/server Tic-Tac-Toe program (part 4 of 7).

```vbnet
195             ' if invalid move, inform user to try again
196          ElseIf messageValue = "Invalid move, try again" Then
197             txtDisplay.Text &= messageValue & vbCrLf
198             turn = True
199
200             ' if opponent moved, mark opposite mark on square
201          ElseIf messageValue = "Opponent moved" Then
202
203             ' find location of opponent's move
204             Dim location As Integer = reader.ReadInt32()
205
206             ' mark that square with opponent's mark
207             If mark = "X" Then
208                board(location \ 3, location Mod 3).Mark = "O"c
209             Else
210                board(location \ 3, location Mod 3).Mark = "X"c
211             End If
212
213             PaintSquares()
214
215             txtDisplay.Text &= "Opponent moved. Your turn." & vbCrLf
216
217             turn = True ' change turns
218
219             ' display message as default case
220          Else
221             txtDisplay.Text &= messageValue & vbCrLf
222          End If
223
224       End Sub ' ProcessMessage
225
226       ' send square position to server
227       Public Sub SendClickedSquare(ByVal location As Integer)
228
229          ' send location to the server if current turn
230          If turn Then
231             writer.Write(location)
232             turn = False ' change turns
233          End If
234
235       End Sub ' SendClickedSquare
236
237       ' Property CurrentSquare
238       Public WriteOnly Property CurrentSquare() As CSquare
239
240          Set(ByVal Value As CSquare)
241             mCurrentSquare = Value
242          End Set
243
244       End Property ' CurrentSquare
245
246    End Class ' FrmClient
```

Fig. 22.7 Client side of client/server Tic-Tac-Toe program (part 5 of 7).

Chapter 22 Networking: Streams-Based Sockets and Datagrams 1127

1.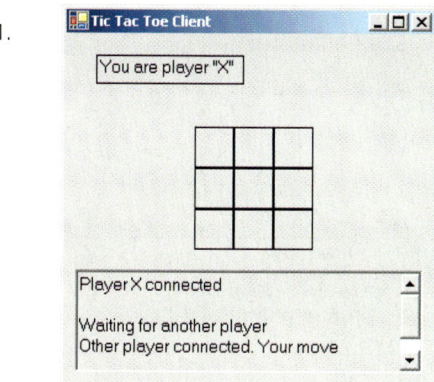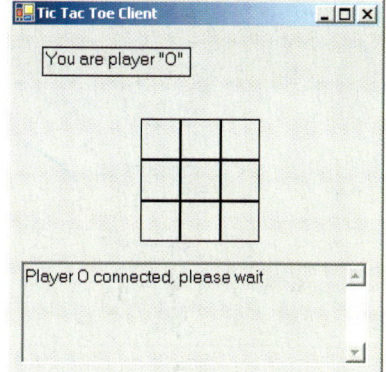

2.

3.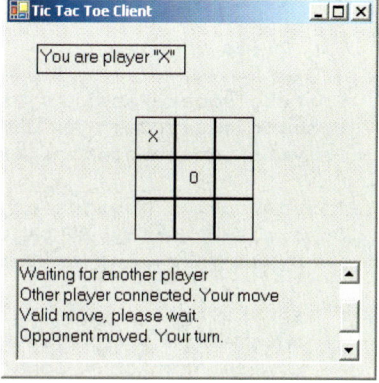

Fig. 22.7 Client side of client/server Tic-Tac-Toe program (part 6 of 7).

1128 Networking: Streams-Based Sockets and Datagrams Chapter 22

4.

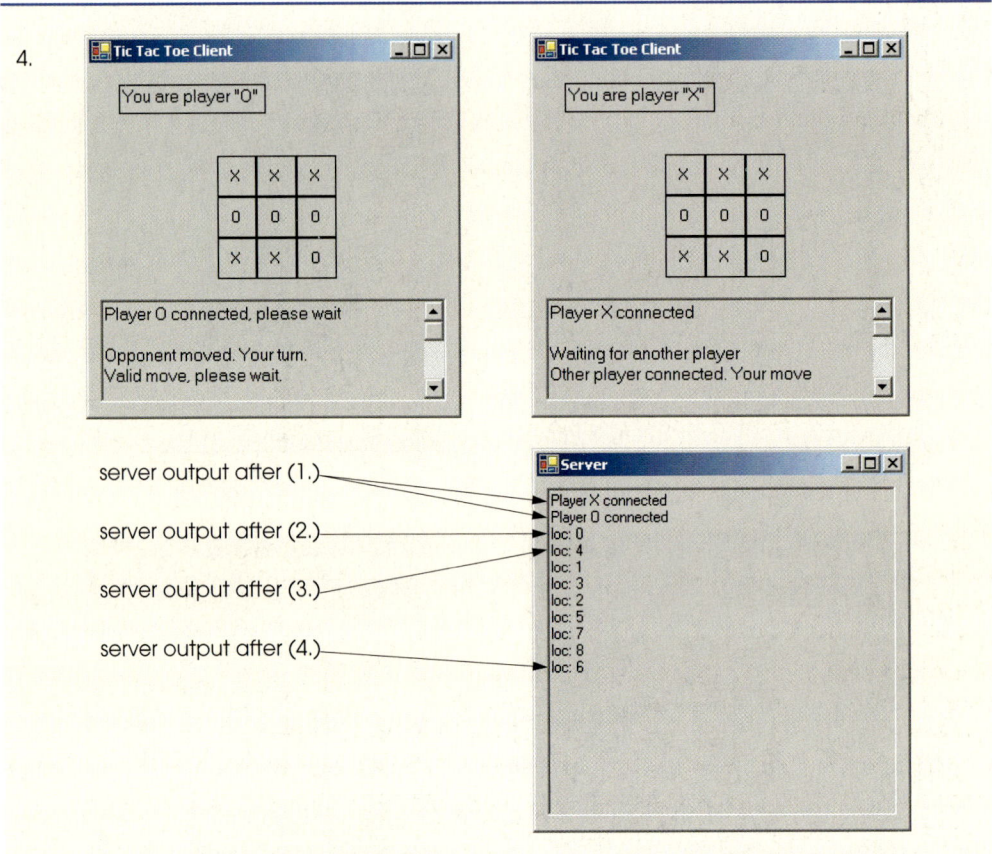

Fig. 22.7 Client side of client/server Tic-Tac-Toe program (part 7 of 7).

```
1   ' Fig. 22.8: Square.vb
2   ' Represents a square on the Tic-Tac-Toe board.
3
4   Public Class CSquare
5
6      Private squarePanel As Panel ' panel on which user clicks
7      Private squareMark As Char ' "X" or "O"
8      Private squareLocation As Integer ' position on board
9
10     ' constructor assigns argument values to class-member values
11     Public Sub New(ByVal panelValue As Panel, _
12        ByVal markValue As Char, ByVal locationValue As Integer)
13
14        squarePanel = panelValue
15        squareMark = markValue
16        squareLocation = locationValue
17     End Sub ' New
18
```

Fig. 22.8 **CSquare** class represents a square on the Tic-Tac-Toe board (part 1 of 2).

```vb
19         ' return panel on which user can click
20         Public ReadOnly Property Panel() As Panel
21
22            Get
23               Return squarePanel
24            End Get
25
26         End Property ' Panel
27
28         ' set and get squareMark ("X" or "O")
29         Public Property Mark() As Char
30
31            Get
32               Return squareMark
33            End Get
34
35            Set(ByVal Value As Char)
36               squareMark = Value
37            End Set
38
39         End Property ' Mark
40
41         ' return squarePanel position on Tic-Tac-Toe board
42         Public ReadOnly Property Location() As Integer
43
44            Get
45               Return squareLocation
46            End Get
47
48         End Property ' Location
49
50   End Class ' CSquare
```

Fig. 22.8 **CSquare** class represents a square on the Tic-Tac-Toe board (part 2 of 2).

FrmServer (Fig. 22.5) uses its constructor (lines 25–47) to create a **Char** array to store the moves the players have made (line 34). The program creates an array of two references to **CPlayer** objects (line 36) and an array of two references to **Thread** objects (line 39). Each element in both arrays corresponds to a Tic-Tac-Toe player. Variable **currentPlayer** is set to **0**, which corresponds to player **"X."** In our program, player **"X"** makes the first move (line 40). Lines 43–46 create and start **Thread getPlayers**, which the **FrmServer** uses to accept connections so that the current **Thread** does not block while awaiting players.

Thread **getPlayers** executes method **SetUp** (lines 60–87), which creates a **TcpListener** object to listen for requests on port **5000** (lines 63–64). This object then listens for connection requests from the first and second players. Lines 67 and 74 instantiate **CPlayer** objects representing the players, and lines 68–69 and 75–76 create two **Thread**s that execute the **Run** methods of each **CPlayer** object.

The **CPlayer** constructor (Fig. 22.6, lines 23–37) receives as arguments a reference to the **Socket** object (i.e., the connection to the client), a reference to the **FrmServer** object and a **Char** indicating the mark (**"X"** or **"O"**) used by that player. In this case study, **FrmServer** calls method **Run** (lines 48–121) after instantiating a **CPlayer** object. Lines 52–

61 notify the server of a successful connection and send to the client the **Char** that the client will place on the board when making a move. If **Run** is executing for **CPlayer "X"**, lines 65–76 execute, causing **CPlayer "X"** to wait for a second player to connect. Lines 70–72 define a **While** loop that suspends the **CPlayer "X" Thread** until the server signals that **CPlayer "O"** has connected. The server notifies the **CPlayer** of the connection by setting the **CPlayer**'s **threadSuspended** variable to **False** (Fig. 22.5, lines 81–85). When **threadSuspended** becomes **False**, **CPlayer** exits the **While** loop of lines 70–72.

Method **Run** executes the **While** structure (lines 80–114), enabling the user to play the game. Each iteration of this structure waits for the client to send an **Integer** specifying where on the board to place the **"X"** or **"O"**—the **CPlayer** then places the mark on the board, if the specified mark location is valid (e.g., that location does not already contain a mark). Note that the **While** structure continues execution only if **Boolean** variable **done** is **False**. This variable is set to **True** by event handler **FrmServer_Closing** of class **FrmServer**, which is invoked when the server closes the connection.

Line 83 of Fig. 22.6 begins a **While** that loops until **Socket** property **Available** indicates that there is information to receive from the **Socket** (or until the server disconnects from the client). If there is no information, the thread goes to sleep for one second. Upon awakening, the thread uses property **Disconnected** to check for whether server variable **disconnect** is **True** (lines 83–91). If the value is **True**, the **Thread** exits the method (thus terminating the **Thread**); otherwise, the **Thread** loops again. However, if property **Available** indicates that there is data to receive, the **While** loop of lines 83–91 terminates, enabling the information to be processed.

This information contains an **Integer** representing the location in which the client wants to place a mark. Line 94 calls method **ReadInt32** of the **BinaryReader** object (which reads from the **NetworkStream** created with the **Socket**) to read this **Integer**. Line 97 then passes the **Integer** to **Server** method **ValidMove**. If this method validates the move, the **CPlayer** places the mark in the desired location.

Method **ValidMove** (Fig. 22.5, lines 95–139) sends to the client a message indicating whether the move was valid. Locations on the board correspond to numbers from **0**–**8** (**0**–**2** for the first row, **3**–**5** for the second and **6**–**8** for the third). All statements in method **ValidMove** are enclosed in a **SyncLock** statement that allows only one move to be attempted at a time. This prevents two players from modifying the game's state information simultaneously. If the **CPlayer** attempting to validate a move is not the current player (i.e., the one allowed to make a move), that **CPlayer** is placed in a *wait* state until it is that **CPlayer**'s turn to move. If the user attempts to place a mark on a location that already contains a mark, method **ValidMove** returns **False**. However, if the user has selected an unoccupied location (line 114), lines 117–121 place the mark on the local representation of the board. Line 127 notifies the other **CPlayer** that a move has been made, and line 130 invokes the **Pulse** method so that the waiting **CPlayer** can validate a move. The method then returns **True** to indicate that the move is valid.

When a **FrmClient** application (Fig. 22.7) executes, it creates a **TextBox** to display messages from the server and the Tic-Tac-Toe board representation. The board is created out of nine **CSquare** objects (Fig. 22.8) that contain **Panel**s on which the user can click, indicating the position on the board in which to place a mark. The **FrmClient**'s constructor (line 46–82) opens a connection to the server (line 72) and obtains a reference to the connection's associated **NetworkStream** object from **TcpClient** (line 73). Lines 80–81 start a thread to read messages sent from the server to the client. The server passes messages (for example, whether each move is valid) to method **ProcessMessage** (lines 187–224). If the message indicates that a move is valid (line 190), the client sets its mark to the current square (the square that the user clicked) and repaints the board. If the message indicates that a move is invalid (line 196), the client notifies the user to click a different square. If the message indicates that the opponent made a move (line 201), line 204 reads from the server an **Integer** specifying where on the board the client should place the opponent's mark.

In this chapter, we discussed how to use Visual Basic's networking technologies by providing both connection-oriented (i.e., streams-based) transmission and connectionless (i.e., packet-based) transmission. We showed how to create a simple server and client via stream sockets, then showed how to create a multithreaded server. In Chapter 23, Data Structures and Collections, we discuss how to store data dynamically and discuss several of the key classes that belong to the Visual Basic **System.Collections** namespace.

SUMMARY

- Sockets are the fundamental way to perform network communications in the .NET Framework. The term "socket" refers to the Berkeley Sockets Interface, which was developed in 1978 to facilitate network programming with UNIX and was popularized by C and C++ programmers.
- The two most popular types of sockets are stream sockets and datagram sockets.
- Stream sockets provide a connection-oriented service, meaning that one process establishes a connection to another process, and data can flow between the processes in continuous streams.
- Datagram sockets provide a connectionless service that uses messages to transmit data.
- Connectionless services generally offer greater performance but less reliability than connection-oriented services.
- Transmission Control Protocol (TCP) is the preferred protocol for stream sockets. It is a reliable and relatively fast way to send data through a network.
- The User Datagram Protocol (UDP) is the preferred protocol for datagram sockets. UDP is unreliable. There is no guarantee that packets sent with UDP will arrive in the order in which they were sent or that they will arrive at all.
- The establishment of a simple server with TCP and stream sockets in Visual Basic requires five steps. Step 1 is to create a **TcpListener** object. This class represents a TCP stream socket that a server can use to receive connections.
- To receive connections, the **TcpListener** must be listening for them. For the **TcpListener** to listen for client connections, its **Start** method must be called (Step 2).
- **TcpListener** method **AcceptSocket** blocks indefinitely until a connection is established, at which point it returns a **Socket** (Step 3).
- Step 4 is the processing phase, in which the server and the client communicate via methods **Read** and **Write** via a **NetworkStream** object.
- When the client and server have finished communicating, the server closes the connection with the **Close** method on the **Socket** (Step 5). Most servers will then, by means of a control loop, return to the **AcceptSocket** call step to wait for another client's connection.
- A port number is a numeric ID number that a process uses to identify itself at a given network address, also known as an Internet Protocol Address (IP Address).
- An individual process running on a computer is identified by an IP address/port number pair. Hence, no two processes can have the same port number at a given IP address.

- The establishment of a simple client requires four steps. In Step 1, we create a **TcpClient** to connect to the server. This connection is established through a call to the **TcpClient** method **Connect** containing two arguments—the server's IP address and the port number
- In Step 2, the **TcpClient** uses method **GetStream** to get a **Stream** to write to and read from the server.
- Step 3 is the processing phase, in which the client and the server communicate.
- Step 4 has the client close the connection by calling the **Close** method on the **NetworkStream**.
- **NetworkStream** methods **WriteByte** and **Write** can be used to output individual bytes or sets of bytes to the server, respectively.
- **NetworkStream** methods **ReadByte** and **Read** can be used to input individual bytes or sets of bytes from the server, respectively.
- Method **GetBytes** of the **System.Text.Encoding**'s **Shared ASCII** property retrieves the bytes that make up a string. This method returns an array of bytes.
- Class **UdpClient** is provided for connectionless transmission of data.
- Class **UdpClient** methods **Send** and **Receive** are used to transmit data.
- Class **IPEndPoint** represents an endpoint on a network.
- Class **IPAddress** represents an Internet Protocol address.
- Multithreaded servers can manage many simultaneous connections with multiple clients.

TERMINOLOGY

127.0.0.1
AcceptSocket method of class
    TcpListener
Berkeley Sockets Interface
BinaryReader class
BinaryWriter class
Bind method of class **Socket**
binding a server to a port
block
block until connection received
client
client/server model
Close method of class **Socket**
Close method of class **TcpClient**
Connect method of class **TcpListener**
connection
connection attempt
connection between client and server terminates
connection port
connection to a server
connectionless service
connectionless transmission with datagrams
connection-oriented service
connection-oriented, streams-based transmission
datagram
datagram socket
echo a packet back to a client
Exit method of class **Environment**
ExitCode property of class **Environment**
file processing
GetStream method of class **Socket**
Internet Protocol Addresses (IP Address)
IP Address
IPAddress class
IPEndPoint class
Local Area Network (LAN)
localhost
loopback IP address
network address
networking as file I/O
NetworkStream class
OpenRead method of class **WebClient**
OpenWrite method of class **WebClient**
packet
pool of threads
port number
protocol
Read method of class **NetworkStream**
ReadByte method of class **NetworkStream**
reading a file on a Web server
ReadString method of class
    BinaryReader
receive a connection
receive data from a server

Chapter 22   Networking: Streams-Based Sockets and Datagrams   **1133**

`Receive` method of class `Socket`	streams-based transmission
`Receive` method of class `UdpClient`	system service
`ReceiveFrom` method of class `Socket`	`System.Net` namespace
send data to a server	`System.Net.Sockets` namespace
`Send` method of class `Socket`	TCP (Transmission Control Protocol)
`Send` method of class `UdpClient`	`TcpClient` class
`SendTo` method of class `Socket`	`TcpListener` class
server	`Thread` class
server Internet address	Transmission Control Protocol (TCP)
server port number	User Datagram Protocol (UDP)
socket	`UdpClient` class
socket-based communications	User Datagram Protocol
`Socket` class	User Datagram Protocol (UDP)
spawning	`Write` method of class `BinaryWriter`
`Start` method of class `TcpListener`	`Write` method of class `NetworkStream`
stream	`WriteByte` method of class `NetworkStream`
stream socket	

SELF-REVIEW EXERCISES

22.1 State whether each of the following is *true* or *false*. If *false*, explain why.
   a) UDP is a connection-oriented protocol.
   b) With stream sockets, a process establishes a connection to another process.
   c) Datagram-packet transmission over a network is reliable—packets are guaranteed to arrive in sequence.
   d) Most of the time TCP protocol is preferred over the UDP protocol.
   e) Each `TcpListener` can accept only one connection.
   f) A `TcpListener` can listen for connections at more than one port at a time.
   g) A `UdpClient` can send information only to one particular port.
   h) Packets sent via a UDP connection are sent only once.
   i) Clients need to know the port number at which the server is waiting for connections.

22.2 Fill in the blanks in each of the following statements:
   a) Many of Visual Basic's networking classes are contained in namespaces _____ and _____.
   b) Class _____ is used for unreliable datagram transmission.
   c) An object of class _____ represents an Internet Protocol (IP) address.
   d) The two types of sockets we discussed in this chapter are _____ sockets and _____ sockets.
   e) The acronym URL stands for _____.
   f) Class _____ listens for connections from clients.
   g) Class _____ connects to servers.
   h) Class _____ provides access to stream data on a network.

ANSWERS TO SELF-REVIEW EXERCISES

22.1 a) False. UDP is a connectionless protocol, and TCP is a connection-oriented protocol. b) True. c) False. Packets can be lost, arrive out of order or even be duplicated. d) True. e) False. `TcpListener AcceptSocket` may be called as often as necessary—each call will accept a new connection. f) False. A `TcpListener` can listen for connections at only one port at a time. g) False. A `UdpClient` can send information to any port represented by an `IPEndPoint`. h) False. Packets may be sent more than once, to make it more likely that at least one copy of each packet arrives. i) True.

22.2 a) `System.Net`, `System.Net.Sockets`. b) `UdpClient`. c) `IPAddress`. d) stream, datagram. e) Uniform Resource Locator. f) `TcpListener`. g) `TcpClient`. h) `NetworkStream`.

EXERCISES

22.3 Use a socket connection to allow a client to specify a file name and have the server send the contents of the file or indicate that the file does not exist. Allow the client to modify the file contents and to send the file back to the server for storage.

22.4 Multithreaded servers are quite popular today, especially because of the increasing use of multiprocessing servers (i.e., servers with more than one processor unit). Modify the simple server application presented in Section 22.4 to be a multithreaded server. Then, use several client applications and have each of them connect to the server simultaneously.

22.5 Create a client/server application for the game of Hangman, using socket connections. The server should randomly pick a word or phrase from a file or a database. After connecting, the client should be allowed to begin guessing. If a client guesses incorrectly five times, the game is over. Display the original phrase or word on the server. Display underscores (for letters that have not been guessed yet) and the letters that have been guessed in the word or phrase on the client.

22.6 Modify the previous exercise to be a connectionless game using datagrams.

22.7 *(Modifications to the Multithreaded Tic-Tac-Toe Program)* The programs of Fig. 22.5–Fig. 22.8 implement a multithreaded, client/server version of the game Tic-Tac-Toe. Our goal in developing this game was to demonstrate a multithreaded server that could process multiple connections from clients at the same time. The server in the example is really a mediator between the two clients—it makes sure that each move is valid and that each client moves in the proper order. The server does not determine who won or lost or whether there was a draw. Also, there is no capability to allow a new game to be played or to terminate an existing game.

The following is a list of suggested modifications to the multithreaded Tic-Tac-Toe application:
  a) Modify class `Server` to test for a win, loss or draw on each move in the game. When the game is over, send a message to each client that indicates the result of the game.
  b) Modify class `Client` to display a button that, when clicked, allows the client to play another game. The button should be enabled only when a game completes. Note that both class `Client` and class `Server` must be modified to reset the board and all state information. Also, the other `Client` should be notified of a new game, so that client can reset its board and state information.
  c) Modify class `Client` to provide a button that allows a client to terminate the program at any time. When the button is clicked, the server and the other client should be notified. The server should then wait for a connection from another client so that a new game can begin.
  d) Modify class `Client` and class `Server` so that the loser of a game can choose game piece X or O for the next game. Remember that X always goes first.

22.8 *(Networked Morse Code)* Perhaps the most famous of all coding schemes is the Morse code, developed by Samuel Morse in 1832 for use with the telegraph system. The Morse code assigns a series of dots and dashes to each letter of the alphabet, each digit, and a few special characters (such as period, comma, colon and semicolon). In sound-oriented systems, the dot represents a short sound and the dash represents a long sound. Other representations of dots and dashes are used with light-oriented systems and signal-flag systems.

Separation between words is indicated by a space, or, quite simply, the absence of a dot or dash. In a sound-oriented system, a space is indicated by a short period of time during which no sound is transmitted. The international version of the Morse code appears in Fig. 22.9.

Character	Code	Character	Code
A	•−	T	−
B	−•••	U	••−
C	−•−•	V	•••−
D	−••	W	•−−
E	•	X	−••−
F	••−•	Y	−•−−
G	−−•	Z	−−••
H	••••		
I	••	Digits	
J	•−−−	1	•−−−−
K	−•−	2	••−−−
L	•−••	3	•••−−
M	−−	4	••••−
N	−•	5	•••••
O	−−−	6	−••••
P	•−−•	7	−−•••
Q	−−•−	8	−−−••
R	•−•	9	−−−−•
S	•••	0	−−−−−

Fig. 22.9 English letters of the alphabet and decimal digits as expressed in international Morse code.

Write an application that reads an English-language phrase and encodes the phrase into Morse code. Also, write a program that reads a phrase in Morse code and converts the phrase into the English-language equivalent. Use one blank between each Morse-coded letter and three blanks between each Morse-coded word. Then, enable these two applications to send Morse Code messages to each other through a multithreaded-server application. Each application should allow the user to type normal characters into a **TextBox**. The application should then translate the characters into Morse Code and send the coded message through the server to the other client. When messages are received, they should be decoded and displayed as normal characters and as Morse Code. The application should have two **TextBox**es: One for displaying the other client's messages, and one for typing.

23

Data Structures and Collections

Objectives

- To be able to form linked data structures using references, self-referential classes and recursion.
- To be able to create and manipulate dynamic data structures, such as linked lists, queues, stacks and binary trees.
- To understand various applications of linked data structures.
- To understand how to create reusable data structures with classes, inheritance and composition.

Much that I bound, I could not free;
Much that I freed returned to me.
Lee Wilson Dodd

'Will you walk a little faster?' said a whiting to a snail,
'There's a porpoise close behind us, and he's treading on my tail.'
Lewis Carroll

There is always room at the top.
Daniel Webster

Push on—keep moving.
Thomas Morton

I think that I shall never see
A poem lovely as a tree.
Joyce Kilmer

Chapter 23

Outline

23.1 Introduction
23.2 Self-Referential Classes
23.3 Linked Lists
23.4 Stacks
23.5 Queues
23.6 Trees
    23.6.1 Binary Search Tree of Integer Values
    23.6.2 Binary Search Tree of **IComparable** Objects
23.7 Collection Classes
    23.7.1 Class **Array**
    23.7.2 Class **ArrayList**
    23.7.3 Class **Stack**
    23.7.4 Class **Hashtable**

Summary • Terminology • Self-Review Exercises • Answers to Self-Review Exercises • Exercises

23.1 Introduction

The *data structures* that we have studied thus far, such as single-subscripted and double-subscripted arrays, have been of fixed sizes. This chapter introduces *dynamic data structures*, which can grow and shrink at execution time. *Linked lists* are collections of data items "lined up in a row"—users can make insertions and deletions anywhere in a linked list. *Stacks* are important in compilers and operating systems; insertions and deletions are made only at the stack's *top*. *Queues* represent waiting lines; insertions are made only at the back (also referred to as the *tail*) of a queue, and deletions are made only from the front (also referred to as the *head*) of a queue. *Binary trees* facilitate high-speed searching and sorting of data, efficient elimination of duplicate data items, representation of file-system hierarchies and compilation of expressions into machine language. The various data structures we just mentioned have many other interesting applications, as well.

In this chapter, we discuss each of the major types of data structures and then implement programs that create and manipulate these data structures. We use classes, inheritance and composition to create and package the data structures in ways that enhance reusability and maintainability.

The chapter examples are practical programs that students will find useful in advanced courses and in industrial applications. The programs devote special attention to reference manipulation.

23.2 Self-Referential Classes

A *self-referential class* contains a reference member referring to a class object of the same class type. For example, the class definition in Fig. 23.1 defines type **CNode**. This type has two **Private** instance variables (lines 5–6)—**Integer mData** and **CNode** reference

mNextNode. Member **mNextNode** references an object of type **CNode**, the same type as the current class—hence the term, "self-referential class." Member **mNextNode** is referred to as a *link* (this means that **mNextNode** can be used to "tie" an object of type **CNode** to another object of the same type). Class **CNode** also has two properties: One for variable **mData**, named **Data** (lines 13–23), and another for variable **mNextNode**, named **NextNode** (lines 26–36).

Self-referential objects can be linked together to form useful data structures, such as lists, queues, stacks and trees. Figure 23.2 illustrates the linking of two self-referential objects to form a list. A backslash (representing a **Nothing** reference) is placed in the link member of the second self-referential object to indicate that the link does not refer to another object. A **Nothing** reference usually defines the end(s) of a data structure.

```vb
1   ' Fig. 23.01: Node.vb
2   ' Self-referential Node class.
3
4   Class CNode
5       Private mData As Integer
6       Private mNextNode As CNode
7
8       Public Sub New(ByVal dataValue As Integer)
9           ' constructor body
10      End Sub ' New
11
12      ' Property Data
13      Public Property Data() As Integer
14
15          Get
16              ' get body
17          End Get
18
19          Set(ByVal dataValue As Integer)
20              ' set body
21          End Set
22
23      End Property ' Data
24
25      ' Property NextNode
26      Public Property NextNode As CNode
27
28          Get
29              ' get next node
30          End Get
31
32          Set(ByVal nodeValue As CNode)
33              ' set next node
34          End Set
35
36      End Property ' NextNode
37
38  End Class 'CNode
```

Fig. 23.1 Self-referential **CNode** class definition.

Fig. 23.2 Self-referential class objects linked together.

Common Programming Error 23.1

Failure to set the link in the last node of a list (or other linear data structure) to **Nothing** *is a common logic error.*

Creating and maintaining dynamic data structures requires *dynamic memory allocation*—a program's ability to obtain additional memory (to hold new variables) and to release unneeded memory at execution time. Recall that, instead of releasing dynamically allocated memory explicitly, Visual Basic programs perform automatic garbage collection.

Dynamic memory allocation is limited by the amount of available physical memory in the computer (and the amount of available disk space in a virtual-memory system). In most cases, the limits for an individual program are much smaller—the computer's available memory must be shared among many applications.

Keyword **New** is essential to dynamic memory allocation. Keyword **New** takes the class name of an object as an operand. It then dynamically allocates the memory for a new object, calls the class constructor and returns a reference to the newly created object. For example, the statement:

```
Dim nodeToAdd As CNode = New CNode(10)
```

allocates the appropriate amount of memory to store a **CNode**, calls the **CNode** constructor with an argument of **10** (for the **CNode**'s **mData** member) and stores a reference to this object in **nodeToAdd**. If no memory is available, **New** throws an **OutOfMemoryException**.

The following sections discuss lists, stacks, queues and trees. These data structures are created and maintained with dynamic memory allocation and self-referential classes.

Good Programming Practice 23.1

When creating an object, it is a good idea to test for an **OutOfMemoryException**. *Perform appropriate error processing if the requested memory is not allocated.*

23.3 Linked Lists

A *linked list* is a linear collection (i.e., a sequence) of self-referential class objects, called *nodes*, that are connected by reference links—hence the term, "linked" list. A program accesses a linked list via a reference to the first node of the list. Each subsequent node is accessed via the current node's link-reference member. By convention, the link reference in the last node of a list is set to **Nothing**, marking the end of the list. Data is stored in a linked list dynamically—each node is created as necessary. A node can contain data of any type.

Although arrays also can store lists of data, linked lists provide several advantages over arrays. It is appropriate to use a linked list when the number of data elements to be represented in the data structure is unpredictable. Unlike a linked list, the size of a "conventional" Visual Basic array cannot be altered, because the array size is fixed when the array is created. Conventional arrays can become full, but linked lists become full only when the system has insufficient memory to satisfy dynamic storage allocation requests.

Performance Tip 23.1
An array can be declared to contain more elements than the expected number of items, but this would waste memory. Linked lists can provide better memory utilization in these situations. In general, the use of dynamic memory allocation (instead of arrays) for data structures that grow and shrink at execution time can save memory.

Programmers can maintain linked lists in sorted order simply by inserting each new element at the proper point in the list. Although locating the proper insertion point does take time, it is not necessary to move existing list elements.

Performance Tip 23.2
Insertion and deletion in a sorted array can consume time, because all elements following the inserted or deleted element must be shifted appropriately.

Performance Tip 23.3
The elements of an array are stored contiguously in memory to allow immediate access to any array element—the address of any element can be calculated directly as its offset from the beginning of the array. Linked lists do not afford such immediate access to their elements—an element can be accessed only by traversing the list from the front.

Normally, memory does not store linked-list nodes contiguously. Rather, the nodes are logically contiguous. Figure 23.3 illustrates a linked list containing several nodes.

The program of Fig. 23.4–Fig. 23.6 uses an object of class **CList** to manipulate a list of objects of type **Object**. Method **Main** of module **modListTest** (Fig. 23.7) creates a list of objects, inserts objects at the beginning of the list (using **CList** method **InsertAtFront**), inserts objects at the end of the list (using **CList** method **InsertAtBack**), deletes objects from the front of the list (using **CList** method **RemoveFromFront**) and deletes objects from the end of the list (using **CList** method **RemoveFromBack**). Each insertion or deletion operation invokes **CList** method **Print** to display the current list contents. A detailed discussion of the program follows. An **EmptyListException** occurs if an attempt is made to remove an item from an empty list.

The program consists of four classes—**CListNode** (Fig. 23.4), **CList** (Fig. 23.5), **EmptyListException** (Fig. 23.6) and module **modListTest** (Fig. 23.7). The classes in Fig. 23.4–Fig. 23.6 create a linked-list library. These classes belong to namespace **LinkedListLibrary** (i.e., we store them in the **LinkedListLibrary** class library), enabling us to reuse the classes throughout this chapter.

Encapsulated in each **CList** object is a linked list of **CListNode** objects. Class **CListNode** (Fig. 23.4) consists of two member variables—**mData** and **mNextNode**. Member **mData** can refer to any **Object**. Member **mNextNode** stores a reference to the next **CListNode** object in the linked list. A **CList** accesses the **CListNode** member variables via properties **Data** (lines 22–28) and **NextNode** (lines 31–41), respectively.

Class **CList** (Fig. 23.5) contains **Private** members **firstNode** (a reference to the first **CListNode** in a **CList**) and **lastNode** (a reference to the last **CListNode** in a **CList**). The constructors (lines 10–14 and 17–19) initialize both references to **Nothing**. Methods **InsertAtFront** (lines 22–36), **InsertAtBack** (lines 39–54),

RemoveFromFront (lines 57–81) and **RemoveFromBack** (lines 84–117) are the primary methods of class **CList**. Each method uses a **SyncLock** block to ensure that **CList** objects are *multithread safe* when used in a multithreaded program. This means that, if one thread is modifying the contents of a **CList** object, no other thread can modify the same **CList** object at the same time. Method **IsEmpty** (lines 120–132) is a *predicate method* that determines whether the list is empty (i.e., whether the reference to the first node of the list is **Nothing**). Predicate methods typically test a condition and do not modify the object on which they are called. If the list is empty, method **IsEmpty** returns **True**; otherwise, it returns **False**. Method **Print** (lines 135–159) displays the list's contents. Both method **IsEmpty** and method **Print** use **SyncLock** blocks, ensuring that the state of the list does not change while the methods are performing their tasks.

Class **EmptyListException** (Fig. 23.6) defines an exception class to handle illegal operations on an empty **CList**. For example, an **EmptyListException** occurs if the program attempts to remove a node from an empty **CList**.

Module **modListTest** (Fig. 23.7) uses the linked-list library to create and manipulate a linked list. Line 10 creates an instance of type **CList** named **list**. Then, lines 13–16 create data to add to the list. Lines 19–29 use **CList** insertion methods to insert these objects and use **CList** method **Print** to output the contents of **list** after each insertion. The code inside the **Try** block (lines 35–70) removes objects (using **CList** deletion methods), outputs the removed object and outputs **list** after every deletion. If there is an attempt to remove an object from an empty list, the **Catch** block (lines 66–68) catches the **EmptyListException**. Note that module **modListTest** uses namespace **LinkedListLibrary** (Fig. 23.4); thus, the project containing module **modListTest** must contain a reference to the **LinkedListLibrary** class library.

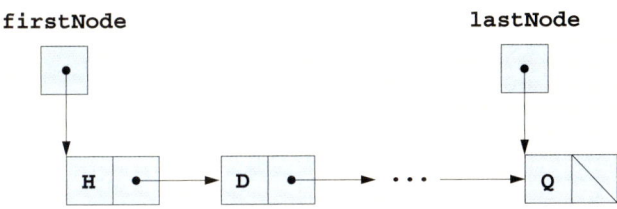

Fig. 23.3 Linked-list graphical representation.

```
1   ' Fig. 23.04: ListNodes.vb
2   ' Class to represent one node in a CList.
3
4   Public Class CListNode
5      Private mData As Object
6      Private mNextNode As CListNode
7
```

Fig. 23.4 Self-referential class **CListNode** (part 1 of 2).

```vbnet
 8        ' create CListNode with dataValue in list
 9        Public Sub New(ByVal dataValue As Object)
10           MyClass.New(dataValue, Nothing)
11        End Sub ' New
12
13        ' create CListNode with dataValue and nextNodeValue in list
14        Public Sub New(ByVal dataValue As Object, _
15           ByVal nextNodeValue As Object)
16
17           mData = dataValue
18           mNextNode = nextNodeValue
19        End Sub ' New
20
21        ' property Data
22        Public ReadOnly Property Data() As Object
23
24           Get
25              Return mData
26           End Get
27
28        End Property ' Data
29
30        ' property mNext
31        Public Property NextNode() As CListNode
32
33           Get
34              Return mNextNode
35           End Get
36
37           Set(ByVal value As CListNode)
38              mNextNode = value
39           End Set
40
41        End Property ' NextNode
42
43     End Class ' CListNode
```

Fig. 23.4 Self-referential class `CListNode` (part 2 of 2).

```vbnet
 1     ' Fig. 23.05: List.vb
 2     ' Class CList definition.
 3
 4     Public Class CList
 5        Private firstNode As CListNode
 6        Private lastNode As CListNode
 7        Private name As String
 8
 9        ' construct empty List with specified name
10        Public Sub New(ByVal listName As String)
11           name = listName
12           firstNode = Nothing
```

Fig. 23.5 Linked-list `CList` class (part 1 of 4).

```vbnet
13          lastNode = Nothing
14       End Sub ' New
15
16       ' construct empty List with "list" as its name
17       Public Sub New()
18          MyClass.New("list")
19       End Sub ' New
20
21       ' insert object at front of List
22       Public Sub InsertAtFront(ByVal insertItem As Object)
23
24          SyncLock (Me) ' ensure thread safe
25
26             ' if this list is empty, create node
27             If IsEmpty() Then
28                lastNode = New CListNode(insertItem)
29                firstNode = lastNode
30             Else ' create node and insert before first node
31                firstNode = New CListNode(insertItem, firstNode)
32             End If
33
34          End SyncLock
35
36       End Sub ' InsertAtFront
37
38       ' insert object at end of List
39       Public Sub InsertAtBack(ByVal insertItem As Object)
40
41          SyncLock (Me) ' ensure thread safety
42
43             ' if list is empty create node and set firstNode
44             If IsEmpty() Then
45                lastNode = New CListNode(insertItem)
46                firstNode = lastNode
47             Else ' create node and insert after last node
48                lastNode.NextNode = New CListNode(insertItem)
49                lastNode = lastNode.NextNode
50             End If
51
52          End SyncLock
53
54       End Sub ' InsertAtBack
55
56       ' remove first node from list
57       Public Function RemoveFromFront() As Object
58
59          SyncLock (Me) ' ensure thread safety
60             Dim removeItem As Object = Nothing
61
62             ' throw exception if removing node from empty list
63             If IsEmpty() Then
64                Throw New EmptyListException(name)
65             End If
```

Fig. 23.5 Linked-list **CList** class (part 2 of 4).

```vb
66
67            removeItem = firstNode.Data ' retrieve data
68
69            ' reset firstNode and lastNode references
70            If firstNode Is lastNode Then
71               firstNode = Nothing
72               lastNode = Nothing
73            Else
74               firstNode = firstNode.NextNode
75            End If
76
77            Return removeItem ' return removed item
78
79         End SyncLock
80
81      End Function ' RemoveFromFront
82
83      ' remove last node from CList
84      Public Function RemoveFromBack() As Object
85
86         SyncLock (Me) ' ensure thread safe
87            Dim removeItem As Object = Nothing
88
89            ' throw exception if removing node from empty list
90            If IsEmpty() Then
91               Throw New EmptyListException(name)
92            End If
93
94            removeItem = lastNode.Data ' retrieve data
95
96            ' reset firstNode and last node references
97            If firstNode Is lastNode Then
98               lastNode = Nothing
99               firstNode = lastNode
100           Else
101              Dim current As CListNode = firstNode
102
103              ' loop while current node is not lastNode
104              While (Not (current.NextNode Is lastNode))
105                 current = current.NextNode ' move to next node
106              End While
107
108              ' current is new lastNode
109              lastNode = current
110              current.NextNode = Nothing
111           End If
112
113           Return removeItem ' return removed data
114
115        End SyncLock
116
117     End Function ' RemoveFromBack
118
```

Fig. 23.5 Linked-list `CList` class (part 3 of 4).

```
119     ' return true if list is empty
120     Public Function IsEmpty() As Boolean
121
122        SyncLock (Me)
123
124           If firstNode Is Nothing Then
125              Return True
126           Else
127              Return False
128           End If
129
130        End SyncLock
131
132     End Function ' IsEmpty
133
134     ' output List contents
135     Public Overridable Sub Print()
136
137        SyncLock (Me)
138
139           If IsEmpty() Then
140              Console.WriteLine("Empty " & name)
141
142              Return
143           End If
144
145           Console.Write("The " & name & " is: ")
146
147           Dim current As CListNode = firstNode
148
149           ' output current node data while not at end of list
150           While Not current Is Nothing
151              Console.Write(current.Data & " ")
152              current = current.NextNode
153           End While
154
155           Console.WriteLine(vbCrLf)
156
157        End SyncLock
158
159     End Sub ' Print
160
161  End Class ' CList
```

Fig. 23.5 Linked-list **CList** class (part 4 of 4).

```
1   ' Fig. 23.06: EmptyListException.vb
2   ' Class EmptyListException definition.
3
4   Public Class EmptyListException
5      Inherits ApplicationException
6
```

Fig. 23.6 Exception thrown when removing node from empty linked list (part 1 of 2).

```vbnet
 7      Public Sub New(ByVal name As String)
 8         MyBase.New("The " & name & " is empty")
 9      End Sub ' New
10
11   End Class ' EmptyListException
```

Fig. 23.6 Exception thrown when removing node from empty linked list (part 2 of 2).

```vbnet
 1   ' Fig. 23.07: ListTest.vb
 2   ' Testing class CList.
 3
 4   ' Deitel namespaces
 5   Imports LinkedListLibrary
 6
 7   Module modListTest
 8
 9      Sub Main()
10         Dim list As CList = New CList() ' create CList container
11
12         ' create data to store in CList
13         Dim aBoolean As Boolean = True
14         Dim aCharacter As Char = "$"c
15         Dim anInteger As Integer = 34567
16         Dim aString As String = "hello"
17
18         ' use CList insert methods
19         list.InsertAtFront(aBoolean) ' insert Boolean at front
20         list.Print()
21
22         list.InsertAtFront(aCharacter) ' insert Char at front
23         list.Print()
24
25         list.InsertAtBack(anInteger) ' insert Integer at back
26         list.Print()
27
28         list.InsertAtBack(aString) ' insert String at back
29         list.Print()
30
31         ' use CList remove methods
32         Dim removedObject As Object
33
34         ' remove data from list and print after each removal
35         Try
36
37            ' remove object from front of list
38            removedObject = list.RemoveFromFront()
39            Console.WriteLine(Convert.ToString(removedObject) & _
40               " removed")
41
42            list.Print()
```

Fig. 23.7 Linked-list demonstration (part 1 of 2).

```vbnet
43
44              ' remove object from front of list
45              removedObject = list.RemoveFromFront()
46              Console.WriteLine(Convert.ToString(removedObject) & _
47                  " removed")
48
49              list.Print()
50
51              ' remove object from back of list
52              removedObject = list.RemoveFromBack()
53              Console.WriteLine(Convert.ToString(removedObject) & _
54                  " removed")
55
56              list.Print()
57
58              ' remove object from back of list
59              removedObject = list.RemoveFromBack()
60              Console.WriteLine(Convert.ToString(removedObject) & _
61                  " removed")
62
63              list.Print()
64
65          ' Catch exception if list is empty
66          Catch emptyListException As EmptyListException
67              Console.Error.WriteLine(vbCrLf & _
68                  Convert.ToString(emptyListException))
69
70          End Try
71
72      End Sub ' Main
73
74  End Module ' modListTest
```

```
The list is: True

The list is: $ True

The list is: $ True 34567

The list is: $ True 34567 hello

$ removed
The list is: True 34567 hello

True removed
The list is: 34567 hello

hello removed
The list is: 34567

34567 removed
Empty list
```

Fig. 23.7 Linked-list demonstration (part 2 of 2).

Over the next several pages, we discuss each of the methods of class **CList** in detail. Method **InsertAtFront** (Fig. 23.5, lines 22–36) places a new node at the front of the list. This method consists of three steps, which are outlined below:

1. Call **IsEmpty** to determine whether the list is empty (Fig. 23.5, line 27).

2. If the list is empty, set both **firstNode** and **lastNode** to refer to a new **CListNode** initialized with object **insertItem** (lines 28–29). The **CListNode** constructor in lines 9–11 (Fig. 23.4) calls the **CListNode** constructor on lines 14–19 (Fig. 23.4) to set instance variable **mData** to refer to the **Object** passed as the first argument and then sets the **mNextNode** reference to **Nothing**.

3. If the list is not empty, the new node is "threaded" (not to be confused with multithreading) into the list by setting **firstNode** to refer to a new **CListNode** object initialized with object **insertItem** and **firstNode** (line 30). When the **CListNode** constructor (lines 14–19 of Fig. 23.4) executes, it sets instance variable **mData** to refer to the **Object** passed as the first argument and performs the insertion by setting the **mNextNode** reference to the **CListNode** passed as the second argument.

Figure 23.8 illustrates method **InsertAtFront**. Part a) of the figure depicts the list and the new node during the **InsertAtFront** operation and before the threading of the new **ListNode** (containing value **12**) into the list. The dotted arrows in part b) illustrate step 3 of the **InsertAtFront** operation, which enables the **ListNode** to become the new list front.

Method **InsertAtBack** (Fig. 23.5, lines 39–54) places a new node at the back of the list. This method consists of three steps:

1. Call **IsEmpty** to determine whether the list is empty (Fig. 23.5, line 44).

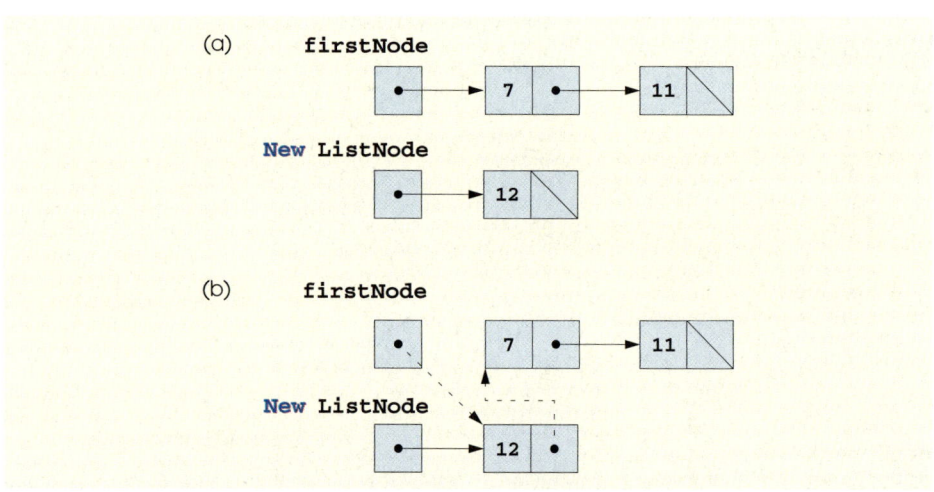

Fig. 23.8 **InsertAtFront** graphical representation.

2. If the list is empty, set both **firstNode** and **lastNode** to refer to a new **CListNode** initialized with object **insertItem** (lines 45–46). The **CListNode** constructor in lines 9–11 (Fig. 23.4) calls the **CListNode** constructor in lines 14–19 (Fig. 23.4) to set instance variable **mData** to refer to the **Object** passed as the first argument and then sets the **mNextNode** reference to **Nothing**.

3. If the list is not empty, thread the new node into the list by setting **lastNode** and **lastNode.NextNode** to refer to a new **CListNode** object initialized with object **insertItem** (Fig. 23.5, lines 48–49). When the **CListNode** constructor (lines 9–11 of Fig. 23.4) executes, it sets instance variable **mData** to refer to the **Object** passed as an argument and sets the **mNextNode** reference to **Nothing**.

Figure 23.9 illustrates method **InsertAtBack**. Part a) of the figure depicts the list and the new **ListNode** (containing value **5**) during the **InsertAtBack** operation and before the new node has been threaded into the list. The dotted arrows in part b) illustrate the steps of method **InsertAtBack** that enable a new **ListNode** to be added to the end of a list that is not empty.

Method **RemoveFromFront** (Fig. 23.5, lines 57–81) removes the front node of the list and returns a reference to the removed data. The method throws a **EmptyListException** (line 63) if the program tries to remove a node from an empty list. This method consists of four steps:

1. Assign **firstNode.Data** (the data being removed from the list) to reference **removeItem** (line 67).

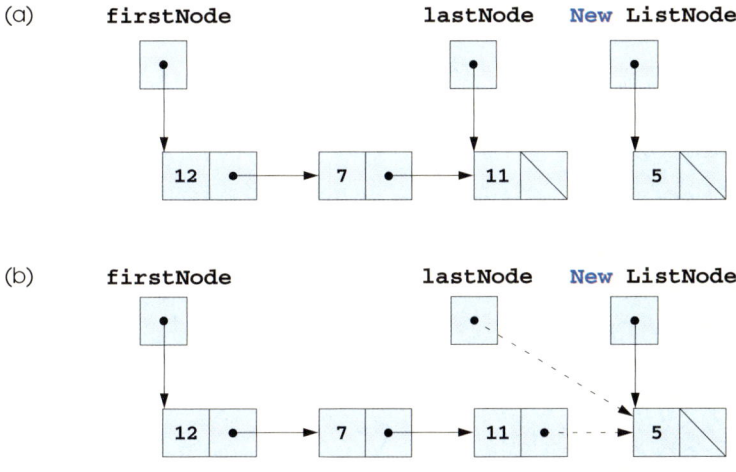

Fig. 23.9 **InsertAtBack** graphical representation.

2. If the objects to which **firstNode** and **lastNode** refer are the same object, this indicates that the list contains only one element prior to the removal attempt. In this case, the method sets **firstNode** and **lastNode** to **Nothing** (lines 71–72) to "dethread" (remove) the node from the list (leaving the list empty).

3. If the list contains more than one node prior to removal, then the method leaves reference **lastNode** as is and simply assigns **firstNode.NextNode** to reference **firstNode** (line 77). Thus, **firstNode** references the node that was the second node prior to the **RemoveFromFront** call.

4. Return the **removeItem** reference (line 77).

Figure 23.10 illustrates method **RemoveFromFront**. Part a) illustrates the list before the removal operation. Part b) portrays the actual reference manipulations.

Method **RemoveFromBack** (Fig. 23.5, lines 84–117) removes the last node of a list and returns a reference to the removed data. The method throws a **EmptyListException** (line 91) if the program attempts to remove a node from an empty list. This method consists of seven steps:

1. Assign **lastNode.Data** (the data being removed from the list) to reference **removeItem** (line 94).

2. If the objects to which **firstNode** and **lastNode** refer are the same object (line 97), this indicates that the list contains only one element prior to the removal attempt. In this case, the method sets **firstNode** and **lastNode** to **Nothing** (lines 98–99) to dethread (remove) that node from the list (leaving the list empty).

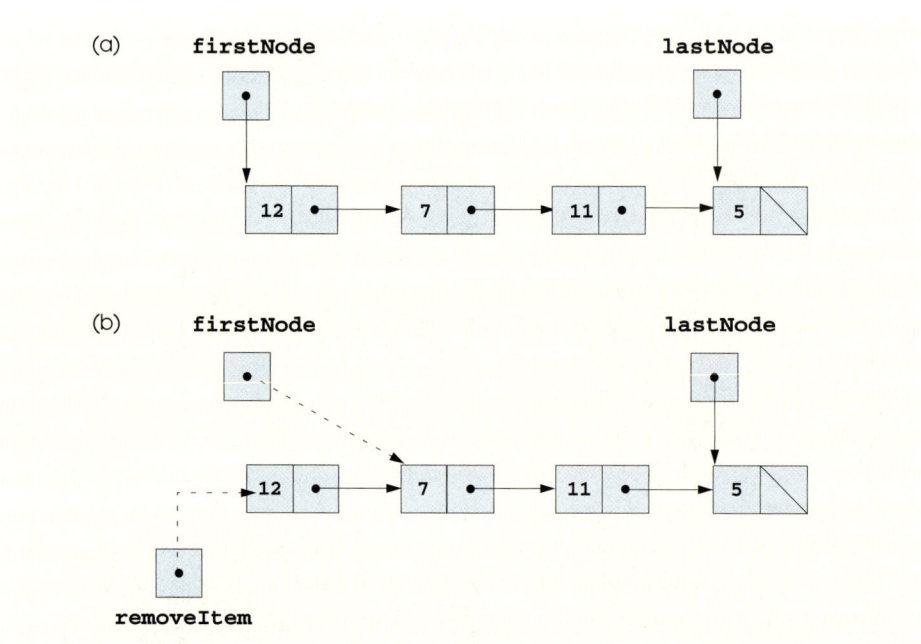

Fig. 23.10 RemoveFromFront graphical representation.

3. If the list contains more than one node prior to removal, create the **CListNode** reference **current** and assign it **firstNode** (line 101).

4. Use **current** to traverse the list until **current** references the node directly preceding the last node. The **While** loop (lines 104–106) assigns **current.NextNode** to reference **current** as long as **current.NextNode** is not equal to **lastNode**.

5. After locating the second-to-last node, assign **current** to **lastNode** (line 109) to dethread the last node from the list.

6. Set **current.NextNode** to **Nothing** (line 110) in the new last node of the list to ensure proper list termination.

7. Return the **removeItem** reference (line 113).

Figure 23.11 illustrates method **RemoveFromBack**. Part a) illustrates the list before the removal operation. Part b) portrays the actual reference manipulations.

Method **Print** (Fig. 23.5, lines 135–159) first determines whether the list is empty (line 139). If so, **Print** displays a **String** consisting of **"Empty "** and the list's **name** and then returns control to the calling method. Otherwise, **Print** outputs the data in the list. The method prints a **String** consisting of the string **"The "**, the **name** of the list and the string **" is: "**. Then, line 147 creates **CListNode** reference **current** and initializes it with **firstNode**. While **current** is not **Nothing**, there are more items in the list. Therefore, the method prints **current.Data** (line 151) then assigns **current.NextNode** to **current** (line 152) thus moving to the next node in the list. Note that, if the link in the last node of the list is not **Nothing**, the printing algorithm will erroneously attempt to print past the end of the list. The printing algorithm is identical for linked lists, stacks and queues.

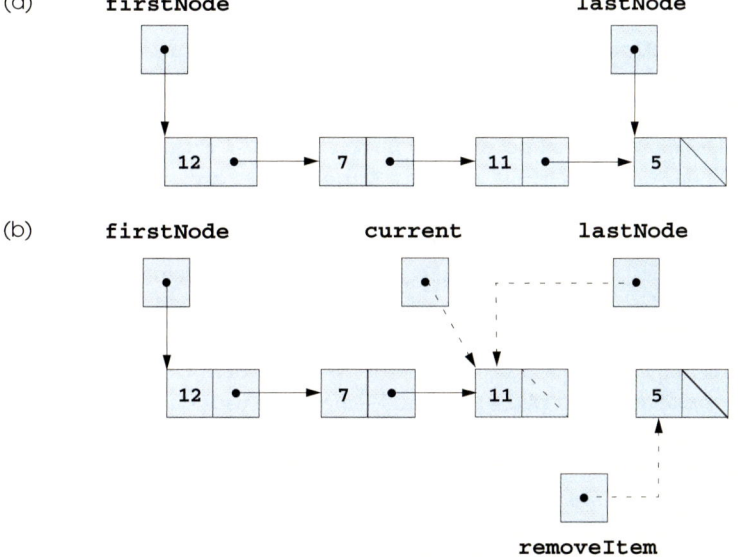

Fig. 23.11 RemoveFromBack graphical representation.

23.4 Stacks

A *stack* is a constrained version of a linked list—new nodes can be added to a stack and removed from a stack only at its top. For this reason, a stack is referred to as a *last-in, first-out* (*LIFO*) data structure. The link member in the bottom (i.e., last) node of the stack is set to **Nothing** to indicate the bottom of the stack.

The primary operations used to manipulate a stack are *push* and *pop*. Operation *push* adds a new node to the top of the stack. Operation *pop* removes a node from the top of the stack and returns the data from the popped node.

Stacks have many interesting applications. For example, when a program calls a method, the called method must know how to return to its caller, so the return address is pushed onto the *program execution stack*. If a series of method calls occurs, the successive return values are pushed onto the stack in last-in, first-out order so that each method can return to its caller. Stacks support recursive method calls in the same manner that they support conventional nonrecursive method calls.

The program execution stack contains the space created for local variables on each invocation of a method during a program's execution. When the method returns to its caller, the space for that method's local variables is popped off the stack, and those variables are no longer known to the program.

Compilers use stacks to evaluate arithmetic expressions and to generate machine-language code required to process the expressions. The **System.Collections** namespace contains class **Stack** for implementing and manipulating stacks that can grow and shrink during program execution. Section 23.7 discusses class **Stack**.

We take advantage of the close relationship between lists and stacks to implement out own stack class by reusing a list class. We demonstrate two different forms of reusability. First, we implement the stack class by inheriting from class **CList** of Fig. 23.5. Then, we implement an identically performing stack class through composition by including a **CList** object as a **Private** member of a stack class. This chapter implements list, stack and queue data structures to store **Object** references, which encourages further reusability—objects of any type can be stored in such a list, stack or queue.

The program of Fig. 23.12 and Fig. 23.13 creates a stack class by inheriting from class **CList** of Fig. 23.5. We want the stack to provide methods **Push**, **Pop**, **IsEmpty** and **Print**. Essentially, these are the methods **InsertAtFront**, **RemoveFromFront**, **IsEmpty** and **Print** of class **List**. Class **List** contains other methods, such as **InsertAtBack** and **RemoveFromBack**, which we would rather not make accessible through the **Public** interface of the stack. It is important to remember that all methods in the **Public** interface of class **CList** are also **Public** methods of the derived class **CStackInheritance** (Fig. 23.12).

When we implement the stack's methods, we have each **CStackInheritance** method call the appropriate **CList** method—method **Push** calls **InsertAtFront**, and method **Pop** calls **RemoveFromFront**. Class **CStackInheritance** does not define methods **IsEmpty** and **Print**, because **CStackInheritance** inherits these methods from class **CList** into **CStackInheritance**'s **Public** interface. The methods in class **CStackInheritance** do not use **SyncLock** statements. Each of the methods in this class calls a method from class **CList** that uses **SyncLock**. If two threads call **Push** on the same stack object, only one thread at a time will be able to call **CList** method **InsertAtFront**. Note that class **CStackInheritance** uses namespace **LinkedListLibrary** (Fig. 23.4); thus, the project that contains class **CStackInheritance** must contain a reference to the **LinkedListLibrary** class library.

Module **modStackInheritanceTest**'s **Main** method (Fig. 23.13) uses class **CStackInheritance** to instantiate a stack of **Object**s, called **stack**. Lines 15–18 define four objects that will be pushed onto the stack and popped off the stack. The program pushes onto the stack (lines 21, 24, 27 and 30) a **Boolean** with value **True**, a **Char** with value **$**, an **Integer** with value **34567** and a **String** with value **"hello"**. An infinite **While** loop (lines 40–44) pops the elements from the stack. When there are no objects left to pop, method **Pop** throws an **EmptyListException**, and the program displays the exception's stack trace, which depicts the program execution stack at the time the exception occurred. The program uses method **Print** (inherited from class **CList**) to output the contents of the stack after each operation. Note that module **modStackInheritanceTest** uses namespaces **LinkedListLibrary** (Fig. 23.4) and **CStackInheritanceLibrary** (Fig. 23.12); thus, the project containing module **modStackInheritanceTest** must contain references to both class libraries.

```vb
1   ' Fig: 23.12: StackInheritance.vb
2   ' Implementing a stack by inheriting from class CList.
3
4   ' Deitel namespaces
5   Imports LinkedListLibrary
6
7   ' class CStackInheritance inherits class CList
8   Public Class CStackInheritance
9      Inherits CList
10
11     ' pass name "stack" to CList constructor
12     Public Sub New()
13        MyBase.New("stack")
14     End Sub ' New
15
16     ' place dataValue at top of stack by inserting dataValue at
17     ' front of linked list
18     Public Sub Push(ByVal dataValue As Object)
19        MyBase.InsertAtFront(dataValue)
20     End Sub ' Push
21
22     ' remove item from top of stack by removing item at front of
23     ' linked list
24     Public Function Pop() As Object
25        Return MyBase.RemoveFromFront()
26     End Function ' Pop
27
28  End Class ' CStackInheritance
```

Fig. 23.12 Stack implementation by inheritance from class **CList**.

```vb
 1   ' Fig. 23.13: StackTest.vb
 2   ' Testing stack implementations.
 3
 4   ' Deitel namespaces
 5   Imports LinkedListLibrary
 6   Imports StackInheritanceLibrary
 7
 8   ' demonstrates functionality of stack implementations
 9   Module modStackInheritanceTest
10
11      Sub Main()
12         Dim stack As CStackInheritance = New CStackInheritance()
13
14         ' create objects to store in stack
15         Dim aBoolean As Boolean = True
16         Dim aCharacter As Char = Convert.ToChar("$")
17         Dim anInteger As Integer = 34567
18         Dim aString As String = "hello"
19
20         ' use method Push to add items to stack
21         stack.Push(aBoolean) ' add Boolean
22         stack.Print()
23
24         stack.Push(aCharacter) ' add Char
25         stack.Print()
26
27         stack.Push(anInteger) ' add Integer
28         stack.Print()
29
30         stack.Push(aString) ' add String
31         stack.Print()
32
33         ' use method Pop to remove items from stack
34         Dim removedObject As Object = Nothing
35
36         ' remove items from stack
37         Try
38
39            ' pop item and output removed item
40            While True
41               removedObject = stack.Pop()
42               Console.WriteLine(removedObject & " popped")
43               stack.Print()
44            End While
45
46            ' catch exception if Pop was called while stack empty
47         Catch emptyListException As EmptyListException
48            Console.Error.WriteLine(emptyListException.StackTrace)
49         End Try
50
51      End Sub ' Main
52
53   End Module ' modStackTest
```

Fig. 23.13 Stack-by-inheritance test (part 1 of 2).

```
The stack is: True

The stack is: $ True

The stack is: 34567 $ True

The stack is: hello 34567 $ True

hello popped
The stack is: 34567 $ True

34567 popped
The stack is: $ True

$ popped
The stack is: True

True popped
Empty stack
   at LinkedListLibrary.CList.RemoveFromFront() in
C:\books\2001\vbhtp2\ch23\Examples\Fig23_04\LinkedListLi-
brary\List.vb:line 64
   at StackInheritanceLibrary.CStackInheritance.Pop() in
C:\books\2001\vbhtp2\ch23\Examples\Fig23_12\StackInheritanceLi-
brary\StackInheritance.vb:line 25
   at StackInheritanceTest.modStackInheritance.Main() in
C:\books\2001\vbhtp2\ch23\Examples\Fig23_13\StackTest\Stack-
Test.vb:line 41
```

Fig. 23.13 Stack-by-inheritance test (part 2 of 2).

Another way to implement a stack class is by reusing a list class through composition. The class in Fig. 23.14 uses a **Private** object of class **CList** (line 9) in the definition of class **CStackComposition**. Composition enables us to hide the methods of class **CList** that should not appear in our stack's **Public** interface by providing **Public** interface methods only to the required **CList** methods. Class **CStackComposition** implements each stack method by delegating its work to an appropriate **CList** method. In particular, **CStackComposition** calls **CList** methods **InsertAtFront**, **RemoveFromFront**, **IsEmpty** and **Print**. We do not show module **modStackCompositionTest** for this example, because this class differs from that in Fig. 23.13 only is that we change the type of the stack from **CStackInheritance** to **CStackComposition** in line 12 (Fig. 23.13). If students execute the application from the code on the CD accompanying this book, they will see that the output for the two applications are identical.

```
1   ' Fig. 23.14: StackComposition.vb
2   ' StackComposition definition with composed CList object.
3
4   ' Deitel namespaces
5   Imports LinkedListLibrary
```

Fig. 23.14 Stack-by-composition test (part 1 of 2).

```
 6
 7      ' class CStackComposition encapsulates CList's capabilities
 8      Public Class CStackComposition
 9         Private stack As CList
10
11         ' construct empty stack
12         Public Sub New()
13            stack = New CList("stack")
14         End Sub ' New
15
16         ' add object to stack
17         Public Sub Push(ByVal dataValue As Object)
18            stack.InsertAtFront(dataValue)
19         End Sub ' Push
20
21         ' remove object from stack
22         Public Function Pop() As Object
23            Return stack.RemoveFromFront()
24         End Function ' Pop
25
26         ' determine whether stack is empty
27         Public Function IsEmpty() As Boolean
28            Return stack.IsEmpty()
29         End Function ' IsEmpty
30
31         ' output stack content
32         Public Sub Print()
33            stack.Print()
34         End Sub ' Print
35
36      End Class ' CStackComposition
```

Fig. 23.14 Stack-by-composition test (part 2 of 2).

23.5 Queues

Another common data structure is the *queue*. A queue is similar to a checkout line in a supermarket—the first person in line is served first, and other customers enter the line at the end and wait to be served. Queue nodes are removed only from the *head* of the queue and are inserted only at the *tail* of the queue. For this reason, a queue is a *first-in, first-out* (*FIFO*) data structure. The insert and remove operations are known as *enqueue* and *dequeue*.

Queues have many applications in computer systems. Most computers contain only a single processor, enabling them to provide service for at most one user at a time. Thus, entries for other users are placed in a queue. The entry at the front of the queue receives the first available service. Each entry gradually advances to the front of the queue as users receive service.

Information packets in computer networks wait in queues. Each time a packet arrives at a network node, the routing node must route it to the next node on the network, following the path to the packet's final destination. The routing node routes one packet at a time, so additional packets are enqueued until the router can route them.

Another example of queries is presented by the file server in a computer network, which handles file-access requests from many clients throughout the network. Servers have a limited capacity to service requests from clients. When client requests exceed that capacity, the requests wait in queues.

The program of Fig. 23.15 and Fig. 23.16 creates a queue class through inheritance from a list class. We want the **CQueueInheritance** class (Fig. 23.15) to include methods **Enqueue**, **Dequeue**, **IsEmpty** and **Print**. Note that these methods essentially are the **InsertAtBack**, **RemoveFromFront**, **IsEmpty** and **Print** methods of class **CList**. This class contains other methods, such as methods **InsertAtFront** and **RemoveFromBack**, which we would rather not make accessible through the **Public** interface to the queue class. Remember that all methods in the **Public** interface of the **CList** class are also **Public** methods of the derived class **CQueueInheritance**.

When we implement the queue's methods, we have each **CQueueInheritance** method call the appropriate **CList** method—method **Enqueue** calls **InsertAtBack**, and method **Dequeue** calls **RemoveFromFront**, whereas **IsEmpty** and **Print** calls invoke their base-class versions. Class **CQueueInheritance** does not define methods **IsEmpty** and **Print**, because **CQueueInheritance** inherits these methods from class **CList** into **CQueueInheritance**'s **Public** interface. The methods in class **CQueueInheritance** do not use **SyncLock** statements. Each method in this class calls a corresponding method from class **CList** that uses **Synclock**. Note that class **CQueueInheritance** uses namespace **LinkedListLibrary** (Fig. 23.4); thus, the project that contains class **CQueueInheritance** must include a reference to the **LinkedListLibrary** class library.

Module **modQueueInheritanceTest**'s **Main** method (Fig. 23.16) uses class **CQueueInheritance** to instantiate a queue of **Object**s, called **queue**. Lines 15–18 define four objects that will be pushed onto the stack and popped off the stack. The program enqueues (lines 21, 24, 27 and 30) a **Boolean** with value **True**, a **Char** with value **'$'**, an **Integer** with value **34567** and a **String** with value **"hello"**.

```
1   ' Fig. 23.15: QueueInheritance.vb
2   ' Implementing a queue by inheriting from class CList.
3
4   ' Deitel namespaces
5   Imports LinkedListLibrary
6
7   ' class CQueueInheritance inherits from class CList
8   Public Class CQueueInheritance
9      Inherits CList
10
11     ' pass name "queue" to CList constructor
12     Public Sub New()
13        MyBase.New("queue")
14     End Sub
15
16     ' place dataValue at end of queue by inserting dataValue at end
17     ' of linked list
18     Public Sub Enqueue(ByVal dataValue As Object)
19        MyBase.InsertAtBack(dataValue)
20     End Sub ' Enqueue
21
```

Fig. 23.15 Queue implemented by inheritance from class **CList** (part 1 of 2).

```
22          ' remove item from front of queue by removing item at front of
23          ' linked list
24          Public Function Dequeue() As Object
25              Return MyBase.RemoveFromFront()
26          End Function ' Dequeue
27
28      End Class ' CQueueInheritance
```

Fig. 23.15 Queue implemented by inheritance from class **CList** (part 2 of 2).

An infinite **While** loop (lines 40–44) dequeues the elements from the queue. When no objects are left to dequeue, method **Dequeue** throws an **EmptyListException**. At this point, the program displays the exception's stack trace, which shows the program execution stack at the time the exception occurred. The program uses method **Print** (inherited from class **CList**) to output the contents of the queue after each operation. Note that class **CQueueInheritance** uses namespaces **LinkedListLibrary** and **QueueInheritanceLibrary** (Fig. 23.15); thus, the project containing module **modQueueInheritanceTest** must include references to both class libraries.

```
1   ' Fig. 23.16: QueueTest.vb
2   ' Testing queue implementation.
3
4   ' Deitel namespaces
5   Imports LinkedListLibrary
6   Imports QueueInheritanceLibrary
7
8   ' demonstrate queue functionality
9   Module modQueueTest
10
11      Sub Main()
12          Dim queue As CQueueInheritance = New CQueueInheritance()
13
14          ' create data to store in queue
15          Dim aBoolean As Boolean = True
16          Dim aCharacter As Char = Convert.ToChar("$")
17          Dim anInteger As Integer = 34567
18          Dim aString As String = "hello"
19
20          ' use method Enqueue to add items to queue
21          queue.Enqueue(aBoolean) ' add Boolean
22          queue.Print()
23
24          queue.Enqueue(aCharacter) ' add Char
25          queue.Print()
26
27          queue.Enqueue(anInteger) ' add Integer
28          queue.Print()
29
30          queue.Enqueue(aString) ' add String
31          queue.Print()
```

Fig. 23.16 Queue-by-inheritance test (part 1 of 2).

```vbnet
32
33          ' use method Dequeue to remove items from queue
34          Dim removedObject As Object = Nothing
35
36          ' remove items from queue
37          Try
38
39             ' dequeue item and output removed item
40             While True
41                removedObject = queue.Dequeue()
42                Console.WriteLine(removedObject & " dequeue")
43                queue.Print()
44             End While
45
46          ' if exception occurs, print stack trace
47          Catch emptyListException As EmptyListException
48             Console.Error.WriteLine(emptyListException.StackTrace)
49          End Try
50
51       End Sub ' Main
52
53    End Module ' modQueueTest
```

```
The queue is: True

The queue is: True $

The queue is: True $ 34567

The queue is: True $ 34567 hello

True dequeue
The queue is: $ 34567 hello

$ dequeue
The queue is: 34567 hello

34567 dequeue
The queue is: hello

hello dequeue
Empty queue
   at LinkedListLibrary.CList.RemoveFromFront() in
C:\books\2001\vbhtp2\ch23\Examples\Fig23_04\LinkedListLi-
brary\List.vb:line 64
   at QueueInheritanceLibrary.CQueueInheritance.Dequeue() in
C:\books\2001\vbhtp2\ch23\Examples\Fig23_15\QueueInheritanceLi-
brary\QueueInheritance.vb:line 25
   at QueueTest.modQueueInheritanceTest.Main() in
C:\books\2001\vbhtp2\ch23\Examples\Fig23_16\QueueTest\QueueTest.vb:
line 41
```

Fig. 23.16 Queue-by-inheritance test (part 2 of 2).

23.6 Trees

Linked lists, stacks and queues are *linear data structures* (i.e., *sequences*). By contrast, *tree* is a nonlinear, two-dimensional data structure with special properties. Tree nodes contain two or more links. This section discusses *binary trees* (Fig. 23.17), or trees whose nodes each contain two links (none, one or both of which can be **Nothing**). The *root node* is the first node in a tree. Each link in the root node refers to a *child*. The *left child* is the first node in the *left subtree*, and the *right child* is the first node in the *right subtree*. The children of a specific node are called *siblings*. A node with no children is called a *leaf node*. Computer scientists normally draw trees as cascading down from the root node—exactly opposite to the way most trees grow in nature.

Common Programming Error 23.2
*Failure to set to **Nothing** the links in leaf nodes of a tree is a common logic error.*

Our binary-tree example creates a special binary tree called a *binary search tree*. A binary search tree (with no duplicate node values) has the characteristic that the values in any left subtree are less than the value in the subtree's parent node, and the values in any right subtree are greater than the value in the subtree's parent node. Figure 23.18 depicts a binary search tree containing 12 integers. Note that the shape of a binary search tree that corresponds to a set of data can vary depending on the order in which the values are inserted into the tree.

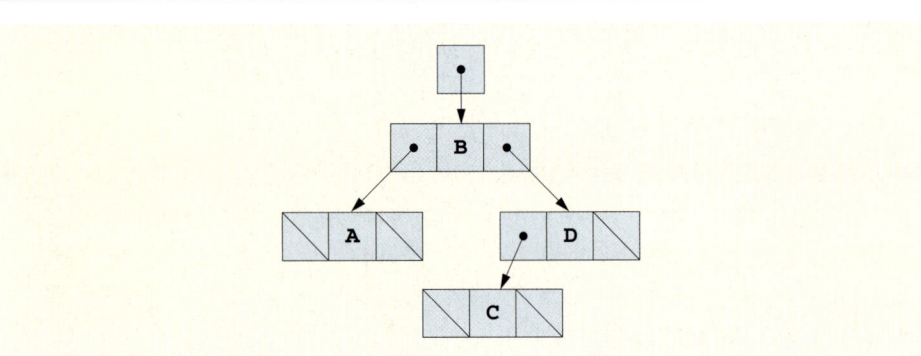

Fig. 23.17 Binary tree graphical representation.

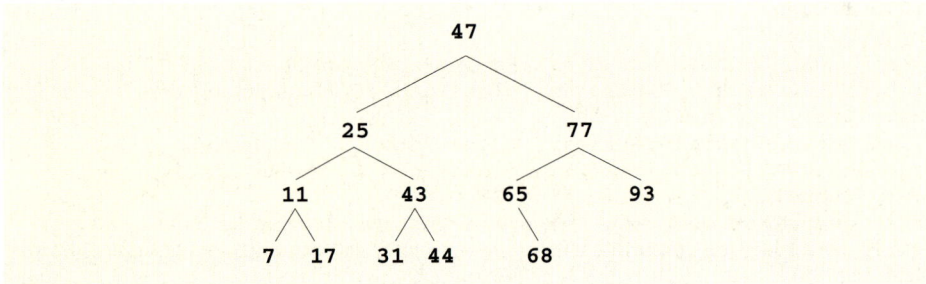

Fig. 23.18 Binary search tree containing 12 values.

23.6.1 Binary Search Tree of Integer Values

The application of Fig. 23.19, Fig. 23.20 and Fig. 23.21 creates a binary search tree of integers and then traverses it (i.e., walks through all its nodes) in three ways—using recursive *inorder, preorder* and *postorder traversals*. The program generates 10 random numbers and inserts each into the tree. Figure 23.20 defines class **CTree** in namespace **BinaryTreeLibrary** (for reuse purposes). Figure 23.21 defines module **modTreeTest**, which demonstrates class **CTree**'s functionality. Method **Main** of module **modTreeTest** instantiates an empty **CTree** object, randomly generates 10 integers and inserts each value in the binary tree using **CTree** method **InsertNode**. The program then performs preorder, inorder and postorder traversals of the tree. We will discuss these traversals shortly.

    Class **CTreeNode** (Fig. 23.19) is a self-referential class containing three **Private** data members—**mLeftNode** and **mRightNode** of type **CTreeNode** and **mData** of type **Integer** (lines 5–7). Initially, every **CTreeNode** is a leaf node, so the constructor (lines 10–14) initializes references **mLeftNode** and **mRightNode** to **Nothing**. Properties **LeftNode** (lines 17–27), **Data** (lines 30–40) and **RightNode** (lines 43–53) provide access to a **CTreeNode**'s **Private** data members. We discuss **CTreeNode** method **Insert** (lines 56–84) shortly.

    Class **CTree** (Fig. 23.20) manipulates objects of class **CTreeNode**. Class **CTree** contains a **Private root** node (line 5)—a reference to the root node of the tree. The class also contains **Public** method **InsertNode** (lines 13–26), which inserts a node in the tree, and **Public** methods **PreorderTraversal** (lines 29–35), **InorderTraversal** (lines 56–62) and **PostorderTraversal** (lines 83–89), which begin traversals of the tree. Each traversal method calls a separate recursive utility method to perform the traversal operations on the internal representation of the tree. The **CTree** constructor (lines 8–10) initializes **root** to **Nothing** to indicate that the tree initially is empty.

    The **CTree** class's method **InsertNode** first locks the **CTree** object (to ensure thread safety) and then determines whether the tree is empty. If so, line 19 instantiates a **CTreeNode** object, initializes the node with the integer being inserted in the tree and assigns the new node to **root**. If the tree is not empty, method **InsertNode** calls **CTreeNode** (Fig. 23.19) method **Insert** (lines 56–84), which recursively determines the location for the new node in the tree and inserts the node at that location. In a binary search tree, nodes can be inserted only as leaf nodes.

    The **CTreeNode** method **Insert** compares the value to insert with the **mData** value in the root node. If the insert value is less than the root-node data, the program determines whether the left subtree is empty (line 62). If so, line 63 instantiates a **CTreeNode** object, initializes it with the integer being inserted and assigns the new node to reference **mLeftNode**. Otherwise, line 67 recursively calls method **Insert** on the left subtree to insert the value into the left subtree. If the insert value is greater than the root node data, the program determines whether the right subtree is empty (line 74). If so, line 75 instantiates a **CTreeNode** object, initializes it with the integer being inserted and assigns the new node to reference **mRightNode**. Otherwise, line 79 recursively calls method **Insert** on the right subtree to insert the value in the right subtree.

    Methods **InorderTraversal**, **PreorderTraversal** and **PostorderTraversal** call helper methods **InorderHelper** (lines 65–80), **PreorderHelper** (lines 38–53) and **PostorderHelper** (lines 92–107), respectively, to traverse the tree and print the node values. The helper methods in class **CTree** allow the programmer to

```vb
1   ' Fig. 23.19: TreeNode.vb
2   ' Class CTreeNode represents a node in a CTree.
3
4   Public Class CTreeNode
5      Private mLeftNode As CTreeNode
6      Private mData As Integer
7      Private mRightNode As CTreeNode
8
9      ' initialize data and make that a leaf node
10     Public Sub New(ByVal nodeData As Integer)
11        mData = nodeData
12        mRightNode = Nothing ' node has no children
13        LeftNode = Nothing ' node has no children
14     End Sub ' New
15
16     ' property LeftNode
17     Public Property LeftNode() As CTreeNode
18
19        Get
20           Return mLeftNode
21        End Get
22
23        Set(ByVal value As CTreeNode)
24           mLeftNode = value
25        End Set
26
27     End Property ' LeftNode
28
29     ' property Data
30     Public Property Data() As Integer
31
32        Get
33           Return mData
34        End Get
35
36        Set(ByVal value As Integer)
37           mData = value
38        End Set
39
40     End Property ' Data
41
42     ' property RightNode
43     Public Property RightNode() As CTreeNode
44
45        Get
46           Return mRightNode
47        End Get
48
49        Set(ByVal value As CTreeNode)
50           mRightNode = value
51        End Set
52
53     End Property ' RightNode
```

Fig. 23.19 Tree-node data structure (part 1 of 2).

```vb
54
55      ' insert node into tree
56      Public Sub Insert(ByVal insertValue As Integer)
57
58         ' insert in left subtree
59         If insertValue < mData Then
60
61            ' insert new CTreeNode
62            If mLeftNode Is Nothing Then
63               LeftNode = New CTreeNode(insertValue)
64
65            ' continue traversing left subtree
66            Else
67               LeftNode.Insert(insertValue)
68            End If
69
70         ' insert in right subtree
71         ElseIf insertValue > mData Then
72
73            ' insert new CTreeNode
74            If RightNode Is Nothing Then
75               RightNode = New CTreeNode(insertValue)
76
77            ' continue traversing right subtree
78            Else
79               RightNode.Insert(insertValue)
80            End If
81
82         End If
83
84      End Sub ' Insert
85
86   End Class ' CTreeNode
```

Fig. 23.19 Tree-node data structure (part 2 of 2).

start a traversal without first obtaining a reference to the **root** node first and then calling the recursive method with that reference. Methods **InorderTraversal**, **PreorderTraversal** and **PostorderTraversal** simply take the **Private** reference **root** and pass it to the appropriate helper method to initiate a traversal of the tree. For the following discussion, we use the binary search tree shown in Fig. 23.22.

```vb
1   ' Fig. 23.20: Tree.vb
2   ' Class CTree is a tree containing CTreeNodes.
3
4   Public Class CTree
5      Private root As CTreeNode
6
```

Fig. 23.20 Tree data structure (part 1 of 3).

```vbnet
 7        ' construct an empty CTree of integers
 8        Public Sub New()
 9           root = Nothing
10        End Sub ' New
11
12        ' insert new node in binary search tree
13        Public Sub InsertNode(ByVal insertValue As Integer)
14
15           SyncLock (Me)
16
17              ' if node does not exist, create node
18              If root Is Nothing Then
19                 root = New CTreeNode(insertValue)
20              Else ' otherwise insert node into tree
21                 root.Insert(insertValue)
22              End If
23
24           End SyncLock
25
26        End Sub ' InsertNode
27
28        ' begin preorder traversal
29        Public Sub PreorderTraversal()
30
31           SyncLock (Me)
32              PreorderHelper(root)
33           End SyncLock
34
35        End Sub ' PreOrderTraversal
36
37        ' recursive method to perform preorder traversal
38        Private Sub PreorderHelper(ByVal node As CTreeNode)
39
40           If node Is Nothing Then
41              Return
42           End If
43
44           ' output node data
45           Console.Write(node.Data & " ")
46
47           ' traverse left subtree
48           PreorderHelper(node.LeftNode)
49
50           ' traverse right subtree
51           PreorderHelper(node.RightNode)
52
53        End Sub ' PreorderHelper
54
55        ' begin inorder traversal
56        Public Sub InorderTraversal()
57
58           SyncLock (Me)
59              InorderHelper(root)
```

Fig. 23.20 Tree data structure (part 2 of 3).

```vbnet
60          End SyncLock
61
62      End Sub ' InorderTraversal
63
64      ' recursive method to perform inorder traversal
65      Private Sub InorderHelper(ByVal node As CTreeNode)
66
67          If node Is Nothing Then
68              Return
69          End If
70
71          ' traverse left subtree
72          InorderHelper(node.LeftNode)
73
74          ' output node data
75          Console.Write(node.Data & " ")
76
77          ' traverse right subtree
78          InorderHelper(node.RightNode)
79
80      End Sub ' InorderHelper
81
82      ' begin postorder traversal
83      Public Sub PostorderTraversal()
84
85          SyncLock (Me)
86              PostorderHelper(root)
87          End SyncLock
88
89      End Sub ' PostorderTraversal
90
91      ' recursive method to perform postorder traversal
92      Private Sub PostorderHelper(ByVal node As CTreeNode)
93
94          If node Is Nothing Then
95              Return
96          End If
97
98          ' traverse left subtree
99          PostorderHelper(node.LeftNode)
100
101         ' traverse right subtree
102         PostorderHelper(node.RightNode)
103
104         ' output node data
105         Console.Write(node.Data & " ")
106
107     End Sub ' PostorderHelper
108
109 End Class ' CTree
```

Fig. 23.20 Tree data structure (part 3 of 3).

```vbnet
1   ' Fig. 23.21: TreeTest.vb
2   ' This program tests class CTree.
3
4   ' Deitel namespaces
5   Imports BinaryTreeLibrary
6
7   Module modTreeTest
8
9      ' test class CTree
10     Sub Main()
11        Dim tree As CTree = New CTree()
12        Dim insertValue As Integer
13        Dim i As Integer
14
15        Console.WriteLine("Inserting Values: ")
16        Dim randomNumber As Random = New Random()
17
18        ' insert 10 random integers from 0-99 in tree
19        For i = 1 To 10
20           insertValue = randomNumber.Next(100)
21           Console.Write(insertValue & " ")
22           tree.InsertNode(insertValue)
23        Next
24
25        ' perform preorder traversal of tree
26        Console.WriteLine(vbCrLf & vbCrLf & "Preorder Traversal")
27        tree.PreOrderTraversal()
28
29        ' perform inorder traversal of tree
30        Console.WriteLine(vbCrLf & vbCrLf & "Inorder Traversal")
31        tree.InOrderTraversal()
32
33        ' perform postorder traversal of tree
34        Console.WriteLine(vbCrLf & vbCrLf & "Postorder Traversal")
35        tree.PostOrderTraversal()
36
37        Console.WriteLine()
38     End Sub ' Main
39
40  End Module ' modTreeTest
```

```
Inserting Values:
83 13 83 96 81 26 25 13 10 89

Preorder Traversal
83 13 10 81 26 25 96 89

Inorder Traversal
10 13 25 26 81 83 89 96

Postorder Traversal
10 25 26 81 13 89 96 83
```

Fig. 23.21 Tree-traversal demonstration.

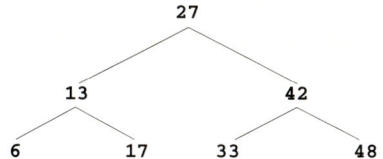

Fig. 23.22 A binary search tree.

Method **InorderHelper** (lines 65–80) defines the steps for an inorder traversal. Those steps are as follows:

1. If the argument is **Nothing**, return immediately.
2. Traverse the left subtree with a call to **InorderHelper** (line 72).
3. Process the value in the node (line 75).
4. Traverse the right subtree with a call to **InorderHelper** (line 78).

The inorder traversal does not process the value in a node until the values in that node's left subtree are processed. The inorder traversal of the tree in Fig. 23.22 is:

    6 13 17 27 33 42 48

Note that the inorder traversal of a binary search tree prints the node values in ascending order. The process of creating a binary search tree actually sorts the data; thus, this process is called the *binary tree sort*.

Method **PreorderHelper** (lines 38–53) defines the steps for a preorder traversal. Those steps are as follows:

1. If the argument is **Nothing**, return immediately.
2. Process the value in the node (line 45).
3. Traverse the left subtree with a call to **PreorderHelper** (line 48).
4. Traverse the right subtree with a call to **PreorderHelper** (line 51).

The preorder traversal processes the value in each node as the node is visited. After processing the value in a given node, the preorder traversal processes the values in the left subtree, then the values in the right subtree. The preorder traversal of the tree in Fig. 23.22 is:

    27 13 6 17 42 33 48

Method **PostorderHelper** (lines 92–107) defines the steps for a postorder traversal. Those steps are as follows:

1. If the argument is **Nothing**, return immediately.
2. Traverse the left subtree with a call to **PostorderHelper** (line 99).
3. Traverse the right subtree with a call to **PostorderHelper** (line 102).
4. Process the value in the node (line 105).

The postorder traversal processes the value in each node after the values of all that node's children are processed. The postorder traversal of the tree in Fig. 23.22 is:

```
6  17  13  33  48  42  27
```

The binary search tree facilitates *duplicate elimination*. During the construction of a binary search tree, the insertion operation recognizes attempts to insert a duplicate value, because a duplicate follows the same "go left" or "go right" decisions on each comparison as does the original value. Thus, the insertion operation eventually compares the duplicate with a node containing the same value. At this point, the insertion operation might discard the duplicate value.

Searching a binary tree for a value that matches a key value can be fast, especially in *tightly packed* binary trees. In a tightly packed binary tree, each level contains approximately twice as many elements as does the previous level. Figure 23.22 is a tightly packed binary tree. A binary search tree with n elements has a minimum of $\log_2 n$ levels. Thus, at least $\log_2 n$ comparisons could be required either to find a match or to determine that no match exists. For example, searching a (tightly packed) 1000-element binary search tree requires at most 10 comparisons, because $2^{10} > 1000$. Similarly, searching a (tightly packed) 1,000,000-element binary search tree requires at most 20 comparisons, because $2^{20} > 1,000,000$.

The chapter exercises present algorithms for other binary-tree operations, such as a *level-order traversal of a binary tree*. Such a traversal visits the nodes of the binary tree row by row, starting at the root-node level. On each level of the tree, a level-order traversal visits the nodes from left to right.

23.6.2 Binary Search Tree of **IComparable** Objects

The binary-tree example in Section 23.6.1 works nicely when all data is of type **Integer**. However, suppose that a programmer wants to manipulate a binary tree consisting of double values. The programmer could rewrite the **CTreeNode** and **CTree** classes with different names and customize the classes so that they manipulate double values. In fact, programmers could create similar customized versions of classes **CTreeNode** and **CTree** for each data type. This would result in a proliferation of code, which can become difficult to manage and maintain.

Ideally, we would like to define the binary-tree functionality once and reuse that functionality for many data types. Visual Basic provides polymorphic capabilities that enable all objects to be manipulated in a uniform manner. The use of these capabilities enables us to design a more flexible data structure.

In our next example, we take advantage of Visual Basic's polymorphic capabilities. We implement classes **CTreeNode** and **CTree**, which manipulate objects that implement interface **IComparable** (of namespace **System**). It is imperative that we be able to compare objects stored in a binary search tree so that we can determine the path to the insertion point of a new node. Classes that implement interface **IComparable** define method **CompareTo**, which compares the object that invokes the method with the object that the method receives as an argument. The method returns an **Integer** value less than zero if the calling object is less than the argument object, zero if the objects are equal or an **Integer** greater than zero if the calling object is greater than the argument object. Also, both the calling and argument objects must be of the same data type; otherwise, the method throws an **ArgumentException**.

Chapter 23 Data Structures and Collections

The program of Fig. 23.23 and Fig. 23.24 enhances the program from Section 23.6.1 to manipulate **IComparable** objects. One restriction on the new versions of classes **CTreeNode** and **CTree** (Fig. 23.23 and Fig. 23.24) is that each **CTree** object can contain objects of only one data type (e.g., all **String**s or all **Double**s). If a program attempts to insert multiple data types in the same **CTree** object, **ArgumentException**s will occur. We modified only seven lines of code in class **CTreeNode** (lines 6, 10, 30, 36, 56, 59 and 71) and one line of code in class **CTree** (line 13) to enable the processing of **IComparable** objects. With the exception of lines 59 and 71, all other changes simply replaced the type **Integer** with the type **IComparable**. Lines 59 and 71 previously used the **<** and **>** operators to compare the value being inserted with the value in a given node. These lines now compare **IComparable** objects using the interface's method **CompareTo**; the method's return value then is tested to determine whether it is less than zero (the calling object is less than the argument object), zero (the calling and argument objects are equal) or greater than zero (the calling object is greater than the argument object).

```vb
1   ' Fig. 23.23: TreeNode2.vb
2   ' Class CTreeNode uses IComparable objects for objects
3
4   Public Class CTreeNode
5      Private mLeftNode As CTreeNode
6      Private mData As IComparable
7      Private mRightNode As CTreeNode
8
9      ' initialize data and make this a leaf node
10     Public Sub New(ByVal nodeData As IComparable)
11        mData = nodeData
12        mRightNode = Nothing ' node has no children
13        LeftNode = Nothing ' node has no children
14     End Sub ' New
15
16     ' property LeftNode
17     Public Property LeftNode() As CTreeNode
18
19        Get
20           Return mLeftNode
21        End Get
22
23        Set(ByVal value As CTreeNode)
24           mLeftNode = value
25        End Set
26
27     End Property ' LeftNode
28
29     ' property Data
30     Public Property Data() As IComparable
31
32        Get
33           Return mData
34        End Get
```

Fig. 23.23 Tree node contains **IComparable**s as data (part 1 of 2).

```vbnet
35
36              Set(ByVal value As IComparable)
37                  mData = value
38              End Set
39
40          End Property ' Data
41
42          ' property RightNode
43          Public Property RightNode() As CTreeNode
44
45              Get
46                  Return mRightNode
47              End Get
48
49              Set(ByVal value As CTreeNode)
50                  mRightNode = value
51              End Set
52
53          End Property ' RightNode
54
55          ' insert node into tree
56          Public Sub Insert(ByVal insertValue As IComparable)
57
58              'insert in left subtree
59              If insertValue.CompareTo(mData) < 0 Then
60
61                  ' insert new TreeNode
62                  If mLeftNode Is Nothing Then
63                      LeftNode = New CTreeNode(insertValue)
64
65                  ' continue traversing left subtree
66                  Else
67                      LeftNode.Insert(insertValue)
68                  End If
69
70              ' insert in right subtree
71              ElseIf insertValue.CompareTo(mData) Then
72
73                  ' insert new TreeNode
74                  If RightNode Is Nothing Then
75                      RightNode = New CTreeNode(insertValue)
76
77                  ' continue traversing right subtree
78                  Else
79                      RightNode.Insert(insertValue)
80                  End If
81
82              End If
83
84          End Sub ' Insert
85
86      End Class ' CTreeNode
```

Fig. 23.23 Tree node contains **IComparable**s as data (part 2 of 2).

```vb
1    ' Fig. 23.24: Tree2.vb
2    ' Class CTree contains nodes with IComparable data
3
4    Public Class CTree
5       Private root As CTreeNode
6
7       ' construct an empty CTree of integers
8       Public Sub New()
9          root = Nothing
10      End Sub ' New
11
12      ' insert new node in binary search tree
13      Public Sub InsertNode(ByVal insertValue As IComparable)
14
15         SyncLock (Me)
16
17            ' if node does not exist, create one
18            If root Is Nothing Then
19               root = New CTreeNode(insertValue)
20            Else ' otherwise insert node in tree
21               root.Insert(insertValue)
22            End If
23
24         End SyncLock
25
26      End Sub ' InsertNode
27
28      ' begin preorder traversal
29      Public Sub PreorderTraversal()
30
31         SyncLock (Me)
32            PreorderHelper(root)
33         End SyncLock
34
35      End Sub ' PreorderTraversal
36
37      ' recursive method to perform preorder traversal
38      Private Sub PreorderHelper(ByVal node As CTreeNode)
39
40         If node Is Nothing Then
41            Return
42         End If
43
44         ' output node data
45         Console.Write(Convert.ToString(node.Data) & " ")
46
47         ' traverse left subtree
48         PreOrderHelper(node.LeftNode)
49
50         ' traverse right subtree
51         PreOrderHelper(node.RightNode)
52
53      End Sub ' PreOrderHelper
```

Fig. 23.24 Binary tree stores nodes with **IComparable** data (part 1 of 3).

```
54
55          ' begin inorder traversal
56          Public Sub InorderTraversal()
57
58              SyncLock (Me)
59                  InorderHelper(root)
60              End SyncLock
61
62          End Sub ' InorderTraversal
63
64          ' recursive method to perform inorder traversal
65          Private Sub InorderHelper(ByVal node As CTreeNode)
66
67              If node Is Nothing Then
68                  Return
69              End If
70
71              ' traverse left subtree
72              InorderHelper(node.LeftNode)
73
74              ' output node data
75              Console.Write(Convert.ToString(node.Data) & " ")
76
77              ' traverse right subtree
78              InorderHelper(node.RightNode)
79
80          End Sub ' InorderHelper
81
82          ' begin postorder traversal
83          Public Sub PostorderTraversal()
84
85              SyncLock (Me)
86                  PostOrderHelper(root)
87              End SyncLock
88
89          End Sub ' PostorderTraversal
90
91          ' recursive method to perform postorder traversal
92          Private Sub PostorderHelper(ByVal node As CTreeNode)
93
94              If node Is Nothing Then
95                  Return
96              End If
97
98              ' traverse left subtree
99              PostorderHelper(node.LeftNode)
100
101             ' traverse right subtree
102             PostorderHelper(node.RightNode)
103
```

Fig. 23.24 Binary tree stores nodes with **IComparable** data (part 2 of 3).

```
104             ' output node data
105             Console.Write(Convert.ToString(node.Data) & " ")
106
107      End Sub ' PostorderHelper
108
109 End Class ' CTree
```

Fig. 23.24 Binary tree stores nodes with **IComparable** data (part 3 of 3).

Module **modTreeTest2** (Fig. 23.25) creates three **CTree** objects to store **Integer**, **Double** and **String** values, all of which the .NET Framework defines as **IComparable** types. The program populates the trees from the values in arrays **integerArray** (line 11), **doubleArray** (lines 12–13) and **stringArray** (lines 15–16), respectively, and then calls method **TraverseTree** to output the preorder, inorder and postorder traversals of the three **CTree**s. Method **PopulateTree** (lines 36–47) receives as arguments an **Array** containing the initializer values for the **CTree**, a **CTree** into which the array elements will be placed and a **String** representing the **CTree** name. Method **PopulateType** then inserts each **Array** element in the **CTree**.

Note that the inorder traversal of each **CTree** outputs the data in sorted order, regardless of the data type stored in the **CTree**. Our polymorphic implementation of class **CTree** invokes the appropriate data type's **CompareTo** method, which uses standard binary search tree insertion rules to determine the path to each value's insertion point. In addition, notice that the **CTree** of **String**s is output in alphabetical order.

```
1  ' Fig. 23.25: TreeTest2.vb
2  ' This program tests class CTree.
3
4  ' Deitel namespaces
5  Imports BinaryTreeLibrary2
6
7  Module modTreeTest2
8
9     ' test class CTree.
10    Sub Main()
11       Dim integerArray As Integer() = {8, 2, 4, 3, 1, 7, 5, 6}
12       Dim doubleArray As Double() = _
13          {8.8, 2.2, 4.4, 3.3, 1.1, 7.7, 5.5, 6.6}
14
15       Dim stringArray As String() = {"eight", "two", "four", _
16          "three", "one", "seven", "five", "six"}
17
18       ' create Integer tree
19       Dim integerTree As CTree = New CTree()
20       PopulateTree(integerArray, integerTree, "integerTree")
21       TraverseTree(integerTree, "integerTree")
22
```

Fig. 23.25 IComparable binary-tree demonstration (part 1 of 3).

```vbnet
23         ' create Double tree
24         Dim doubleTree As CTree = New CTree()
25         populateTree(doubleArray, doubleTree, "doubleTree")
26         TraverseTree(doubleTree, "doubleTree")
27
28         ' create String tree
29         Dim stringTree As CTree = New CTree()
30         populateTree(stringArray, stringTree, "stringTree")
31         TraverseTree(stringTree, "stringTree")
32
33      End Sub ' Main
34
35      ' populate tree with array elements
36      Public Sub PopulateTree(ByVal array As Array, _
37         ByVal tree As CTree, ByVal name As String)
38
39         Dim data As IComparable
40         Console.WriteLine(vbCrLf & "Inserting into " & name & ":")
41
42         For Each data In array
43            Console.Write(Convert.ToString(data) & " ")
44            tree.InsertNode(data)
45         Next
46
47      End Sub ' PopulateTree
48
49      ' perform traversals
50      Public Sub TraverseTree(ByVal tree As CTree, _
51         ByVal treeType As String)
52
53         ' perform preorder traversal of tree
54         Console.WriteLine(vbCrLf & vbCrLf & _
55            "Preorder Traversal of " & treeType)
56
57         tree.PreorderTraversal()
58
59         ' perform inorder traversal of tree
60         Console.WriteLine(vbCrLf & vbCrLf & _
61            "Inorder Traversal of " & treeType)
62
63         tree.InorderTraversal()
64
65         ' perform postorder traversal of tree
66         Console.WriteLine(vbCrLf & vbCrLf & _
67            "Postorder Traversal of " & treeType)
68
69         tree.PostorderTraversal()
70
71         Console.WriteLine(vbCrLf)
72      End Sub ' TraverseTree
73
74   End Module ' CTreeTest2
```

Fig. 23.25 `IComparable` binary-tree demonstration (part 2 of 3).

```
Inserting into integerTree:
8 2 4 3 1 7 5 6

Preorder Traversal of integerTree
8 2 1 4 3 7 5 6

Inorder Traversal of integerTree
1 2 3 4 5 6 7 8

Postorder Traversal of integerTree
1 3 6 5 7 4 2 8


Inserting into doubleTree:
8.8 2.2 4.4 3.3 1.1 7.7 5.5 6.6

Preorder Traversal of doubleTree
8.8 2.2 1.1 4.4 3.3 7.7 5.5 6.6

Inorder Traversal of doubleTree
1.1 2.2 3.3 4.4 5.5 6.6 7.7 8.8

Postorder Traversal of doubleTree
1.1 3.3 6.6 5.5 7.7 4.4 2.2 8.8


Inserting into stringTree:
eight two four three one seven five six

Preorder Traversal of stringTree
eight two four five three one seven six

Inorder Traversal of stringTree
eight five four one seven six three two

Postorder Traversal of stringTree
five six seven one three four two eight
```

Fig. 23.25 `IComparable` binary-tree demonstration (part 3 of 3).

Common Programming Error 23.3

When comparing `IComparable` objects, the argument to method `CompareTo` must be of the same type as the object on which `CompareTo` is invoked; otherwise, an `ArgumentException` occurs.

23.7 Collection Classes

In the previous sections of this chapter, we discussed how to create and manipulate data structures. The discussion was "low level," in the sense that we painstakingly created each element of each data structure dynamically using keyword **New** and then modified the data structures by directly manipulating their elements and references to those elements. In this section, we consider the prepackaged data-structure classes provided by the .NET Framework. These classes are known as *collection classes*—they store collections of data. Each instance of one of these classes is known as a *collection*, which is a set of items.

With collection classes, instead of creating data structures, the programmer uses existing data structures without worrying about how the data structures are implemented. This methodology represents a marvelous example of code reuse. Programmers can code more quickly and can expect excellent performance, maximizing execution speed and minimizing memory consumption.

Examples of collections include the cards that players hold in a card game, a group of favorite songs stored in a computer and the real-estate records in the local registry of deeds (which map book numbers and page numbers to properties). The .NET Framework provides several collections. We demonstrate four collection classes—**Array**, **ArrayList**, **Stack** and **Hashtable**—and built-in array capabilities. Namespace **System.Collections** also provides several other data structures, including **BitArray** (a collection of **True**/**False** values), **Queue** and **SortedList** (a collection of key/value pairs that are sorted by key and can be accessed either by key or by index).

The .NET Framework provides ready-to-go, reusable components; programmers do not need to write their own collection classes. The collections are standardized so that applications can use them easily, without requiring knowledge of the implementation details. These collections are written for broad reuse. They are tuned for rapid execution, as well as for efficient use of memory. The .NET collections encourage further reusability—as new data structures and algorithms that fit this framework are developed, a large base of programmers already will be familiar with the interfaces and algorithms implemented by those data structures.

23.7.1 Class **Array**

Chapter 7 presented basic array-processing capabilities, and many subsequent chapters used the techniques that were demonstrated in that chapter. We mentioned that all arrays inherit from class **Array** (of namespace **System**), which defines property **Length** specifying the number of elements in an array. In addition, class **Array** provides **Shared** methods that define algorithms for processing arrays. These class **Array** methods are overloaded to provide multiple options for performing algorithms. For example, **Array** method **Reverse** can reverse the order of the elements in an entire array or can reverse the elements in a specified range of elements in an array. For a complete list of class **Array**'s **Shared** methods and their overloaded versions, see the online documentation for the class. Figure 23.26 demonstrates several **Shared** methods of class **Array**.

```vb
1   ' Fig. 23.26: UsingArray.vb
2   ' Using class Array to perform common array manipulations.
3
4   Imports System.Windows.Forms
5   Imports System.Collections
6
7   ' demonstrate algorithms of class Array
8   Public Class CUsingArray
9      Private integerValues As Integer() = {1, 2, 3, 4, 5, 6}
```

Fig. 23.26 **Array** class demonstration (part 1 of 3).

```vbnet
10      Private doubleValues As Double() = _
11         {8.4, 9.3, 0.2, 7.9, 3.4}
12
13      Private integerValuesCopy(6) As Integer
14      Private output As String
15
16      ' build and display program output
17      Public Sub Start()
18         Dim result As Integer
19
20         output = "Initial Array Values:" & vbCrLf
21         PrintArray() ' output initial array contents
22
23         ' sort doubleValues
24         Array.Sort(doubleValues)
25
26         ' copy integerValues into integerValuesCopy
27         Array.Copy(integerValues, integerValuesCopy, _
28            integerValues.Length)
29
30         output &= vbCrLf & vbCrLf & _
31            "Array values after Sort and Copy:" & vbCrLf
32
33         PrintArray() ' output array contents
34         output &= vbCrLf & vbCrLf
35
36         ' search for value 5 in integerValues
37         result = Array.BinarySearch(integerValues, 5)
38
39         If result >= 0 Then
40            output &= "5 found at element " & result & _
41               " in integerValues"
42         Else
43            output &= "5 not found" & " in integerValues"
44         End If
45
46         output &= vbCrLf
47
48         ' search for value 8763 in integerValues
49         result = Array.BinarySearch(integerValues, 8763)
50
51         If result >= 0 Then
52            output &= "8763 found at element " & _
53               result & " in integerValues"
54         Else
55            output &= "8763 was not found" & " in integerValues"
56         End If
57
58         MessageBox.Show(output, "Using Class Array", _
59            MessageBoxButtons.OK, MessageBoxIcon.Information)
60
61      End Sub ' Start
62
```

Fig. 23.26 `Array` class demonstration (part 2 of 3).

```vbnet
63          ' append array output to output string
64          Private Sub PrintArray()
65              Dim doubleElement As Double
66              Dim integerElement As Integer
67
68              output &= "doubleValues: "
69
70              ' output each element in array doubleValues
71              For Each doubleElement In doubleValues
72                  output &= doubleElement & " "
73              Next
74
75              output &= vbCrLf & " integerValues: "
76
77              ' output each element in array integerValues
78              For Each integerElement In integerValues
79                  output &= integerElement & " "
80              Next
81
82              output &= vbCrLf & " integerValuesCopy: "
83
84              ' output each element in array integerValuesCopy
85              For Each integerElement In integerValuesCopy
86                  output &= integerElement & " "
87              Next
88
89          End Sub ' PrintArray
90
91          ' main entry point for application
92          Shared Sub Main()
93              Dim application As CUsingArray = New CUsingArray()
94              application.Start()
95          End Sub ' Main
96
97      End Class ' CUsingArray
```

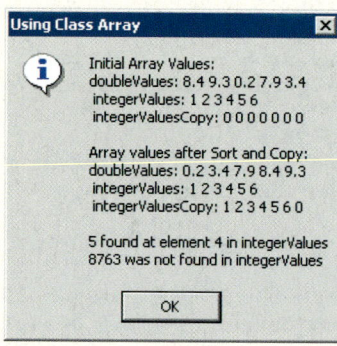

Fig. 23.26 **Array** class demonstration (part 3 of 3).

Line 24 uses **Shared Array** method **Sort** to sort an array of **Double** values. When this method returns, the array contains its original elements sorted in ascending order.

Lines 27–28 uses **Shared Array** method *Copy* to copy elements from array **integerArray** into array **integerArrayCopy**. The first argument is the array to copy (**integerValues**), the second argument is the destination array (**integerValuesCopy**) and the third argument is an integer representing the number of elements to copy (in this case, property **integerValues.Length** specifies "all elements").

Lines 37 and 49 invoke **Shared Array** method *BinarySearch* to perform binary searches on array **integerValues**. Method **BinarySearch** receives the *sorted* array in which to search and the key for which to search. The method returns the index in the array at which it finds the key, or if the key is not found, the method returns a negative number.

Other **Shared Array** methods include *Clear* (to set a range of elements to **0** or **Nothing**), *CreateInstance* (to create an array of a specified data type), *IndexOf* (to locate the first occurrence of a specific object in an array or portion of an array), *LastIndexOf* (to locate the last occurrence of a specific object in an array or portion of an array) and *Reverse* (to reverse the contents of an array or portion of an array).

23.7.2 Class `ArrayList`

In most programming languages, conventional arrays have a fixed size—they cannot be changed dynamically to an application's execution-time memory requirements. In some applications, this fixed-size limitation presents a problem for programmers. Such programmers must choose whether to use fixed-size arrays that are large enough to store the maximum number of elements the program might require, or to use dynamic data structures, which can grow or shrink at execution time to accommodate a program's memory needs.

Visual Basic's `ArrayList` collection (namespace `System.Collections`) mimics the functionality of conventional arrays and provides dynamic resizing capabilities. At any time, an `ArrayList` contains a certain number of elements, which is either less than or equal to its *capacity*—the number of elements currently reserved for the `ArrayList`. A program can manipulate the capacity with `ArrayList` property `Capacity`. If an `ArrayList` needs to grow, it by default doubles its current `Capacity`.

Performance Tip 23.4

As with linked lists, the insertion of additional elements into an `ArrayList` whose current size is less than its capacity is a fast operation.

Performance Tip 23.5

Inserting an element into an `ArrayList` that must grow larger to accommodate a new element is a slow operation.

Performance Tip 23.6

If storage is at a premium, use method `TrimToSize` of class `ArrayList` to trim an `ArrayList` to its exact size. This optimizes an `ArrayList`'s memory use. However be careful—if the program later needs to insert additional elements, the process will be slower, because the `ArrayList` must grow dynamically (trimming leaves no room for growth).

Performance Tip 23.7

The default capacity increment, which is a doubling of the `ArrayList`'s size might seem to waste storage, but doubling is an efficient way for an `ArrayList` to grow quickly to "about the right size." This is a much more efficient use of time than growing the `ArrayList` by one element at a time in response to insert operations.

ArrayLists store references to **Object**s. All classes derive from class **Object**, so an **ArrayList** can contain objects of any type. Figure 23.27 lists some useful methods of class **ArrayList**.

Figure 23.28 demonstrates class **ArrayList** and several of its methods. Users can type a **String** into the user interface's **TextBox** and then press a button representing an **ArrayList** method to see that method's functionality. A **TextBox** displays messages indicating each operation's results.

The **ArrayList** in this example stores **String**s that users input in the **TextBox**. Line 32 creates an **ArrayList** with an initial capacity of one element. This **ArrayList** will double in size each time the user fills the array and then attempts to add another element.

ArrayList method *Add* appends an element to the end of an **ArrayList**. When the user clicks **Add**, event handler **cmdAdd_Click** (lines 35–41) invokes method **Add** (line 38) to append the **String** in the **inputTextBox** to the **ArrayList**.

Method	Description
Add	Adds an **Object** to the **ArrayList**. Returns an **Integer** specifying the index at which the **Object** was added.
Clear	Removes all elements from the **ArrayList**.
Contains	Returns **True** if the specified **Object** is in the **ArrayList**; otherwise, returns **False**.
IndexOf	Returns the index of the first occurrence of the specified **Object** in the **ArrayList**.
Insert	Inserts an **Object** at the specified index.
Remove	Removes the first occurrence of the specified **Object**.
RemoveAt	Removes an object at the specified index.
RemoveRange	Removes a specified number of elements starting at a specified index in the **ArrayList**.
Sort	Sorts the **ArrayList**.
TrimToSize	Sets the **Capacity** of the **ArrayList** to the number of elements that the **ArrayList** currently contains.

Fig. 23.27 **ArrayList** methods (partial list).

```vb
1   ' Fig. 23.28: ArrayListTest.vb
2   ' Demonstrating class ArrayList functionality.
3
4   Imports System.Collections
5   Imports System.Text
6   Imports System.Windows.Forms
7
8   Public Class FrmArrayList
9       Inherits Form
10
```

Fig. 23.28 **ArrayList** class demonstration (part 1 of 5).

```vbnet
11         ' Buttons for invoking ArrayList functionality
12         Friend WithEvents cmdAdd As Button
13         Friend WithEvents cmdRemove As Button
14         Friend WithEvents cmdFirst As Button
15         Friend WithEvents cmdLast As Button
16         Friend WithEvents cmdIsEmpty As Button
17         Friend WithEvents cmdContains As Button
18         Friend WithEvents cmdLocation As Button
19         Friend WithEvents cmdTrim As Button
20         Friend WithEvents cmdStatistics As Button
21         Friend WithEvents cmdDisplay As Button
22
23         ' TextBox for user input
24         Friend WithEvents txtInput As TextBox
25         Friend WithEvents lblEnter As Label
26
27         Friend WithEvents txtConsole As TextBox ' TextBox for output
28
29         ' Visual Studio .NET generated code
30
31         ' ArrayList for manipulating Strings
32         Private arrayList As ArrayList = New ArrayList(1)
33
34         ' add item to end of arrayList
35         Private Sub cmdAdd_Click(ByVal sender As System.Object, _
36            ByVal e As System.EventArgs) Handles cmdAdd.Click
37
38            arrayList.Add(txtInput.Text)
39            txtConsole.Text = "Added to end: " & txtInput.Text
40            txtInput.Clear()
41         End Sub ' cmdAdd_Click
42
43         'remove specified item from arrayList
44         Private Sub cmdRemove_Click(ByVal sender As System.Object, _
45            ByVal e As System.EventArgs) Handles cmdRemove.Click
46
47            arrayList.Remove(txtInput.Text)
48            txtConsole.Text = "Removed: " & txtInput.Text
49            txtInput.Clear()
50         End Sub ' cmdRemove_Click
51
52         ' display first element
53         Private Sub cmdFirst_Click(ByVal sender As System.Object, _
54            ByVal e As System.EventArgs) Handles cmdFirst.Click
55
56            ' get first element
57            Try
58               txtConsole.Text = "First element: " & arrayList(0)
59
60            ' show exception if no elements in arrayList
61            Catch outOfRange As ArgumentOutOfRangeException
62               txtConsole.Text = outOfRange.ToString()
63            End Try
```

Fig. 23.28 `ArrayList` class demonstration (part 2 of 5).

```vbnet
64
65         End Sub ' cmdFirst_Click
66
67         ' display last element
68         Private Sub cmdLast_Click(ByVal sender As System.Object, _
69            ByVal e As System.EventArgs) Handles cmdLast.Click
70
71            ' get last element
72            Try
73               txtConsole.Text = "Last element: " & _
74                  arrayList(arrayList.Count - 1)
75
76            ' show exception if no elements in arrayList
77            Catch outOfRange As ArgumentOutOfRangeException
78               txtConsole.Text = outOfRange.ToString()
79            End Try
80
81         End Sub ' cmdLast_Click
82
83         ' determine whether arrayList is empty
84         Private Sub cmdIsEmpty_Click(ByVal sender As System.Object, _
85            ByVal e As System.EventArgs) Handles cmdIsEmpty.Click
86
87            If arrayList.Count = 0 Then
88               txtConsole.Text = "arrayList is empty"
89            Else
90               txtConsole.Text = "arrayList is not empty"
91            End If
92
93         End Sub ' cmdIsEmpty_Click
94
95         ' determine whether arrayList contains specified object
96         Private Sub cmdContains_Click(ByVal sender As System.Object, _
97            ByVal e As System.EventArgs) Handles cmdContains.Click
98
99            If arrayList.Contains(txtInput.Text) Then
100              txtConsole.Text = "arrayList contains " & _
101                 txtInput.Text()
102           Else
103              txtConsole.Text = txtInput.Text & " not found"
104           End If
105
106        End Sub ' cmdContains_Click
107
108        ' determine location of specified object
109        Private Sub cmdLocation_Click(ByVal sender As System.Object, _
110           ByVal e As System.EventArgs) Handles cmdLocation.Click
111
112           txtConsole.Text = "Element is at location " & _
113              arrayList.IndexOf(txtInput.Text)
114        End Sub ' cmdLocation_Click
115
```

Fig. 23.28 `ArrayList` class demonstration (part 3 of 5).

```
116      ' trim arrayList to current size
117      Private Sub cmdTrim_Click(ByVal sender As System.Object, _
118         ByVal e As System.EventArgs) Handles cmdTrim.Click
119
120         arrayList.TrimToSize()
121         txtConsole.Text = "Vector trimmed to size"
122      End Sub ' cmdTrim_Click
123
124      ' show arrayList current size and capacity
125      Private Sub cmdStatistics_Click(ByVal sender As System.Object, _
126         ByVal e As System.EventArgs) Handles cmdStatistics.Click
127
128         txtConsole.Text = "Size = " & arrayList.Count & _
129            "; capacity = " & arrayList.Capacity
130      End Sub ' cmdStatistics_Click
131
132      ' display contents of arrayList
133      Private Sub cmdDisplay_Click(ByVal sender As System.Object, _
134         ByVal e As System.EventArgs) Handles cmdDisplay.Click
135
136         Dim enumerator As IEnumerator = arrayList.GetEnumerator()
137         Dim buffer As StringBuilder = New StringBuilder()
138
139         While enumerator.MoveNext()
140            buffer.Append(enumerator.Current & " ")
141         End While
142
143         txtConsole.Text = buffer.ToString()
144      End Sub ' cmdDisplay_Click
145
146  End Class ' FrmArrayList
```

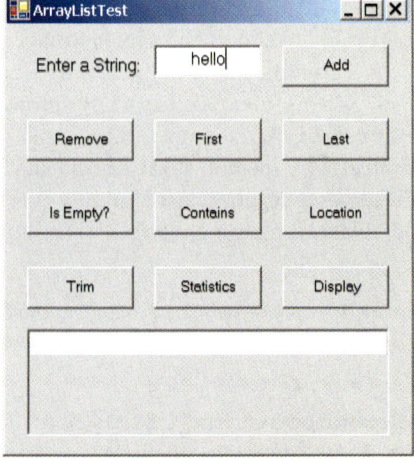
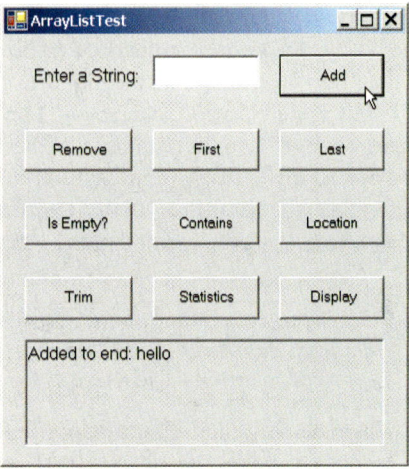

Fig. 23.28 `ArrayList` class demonstration (part 4 of 5).

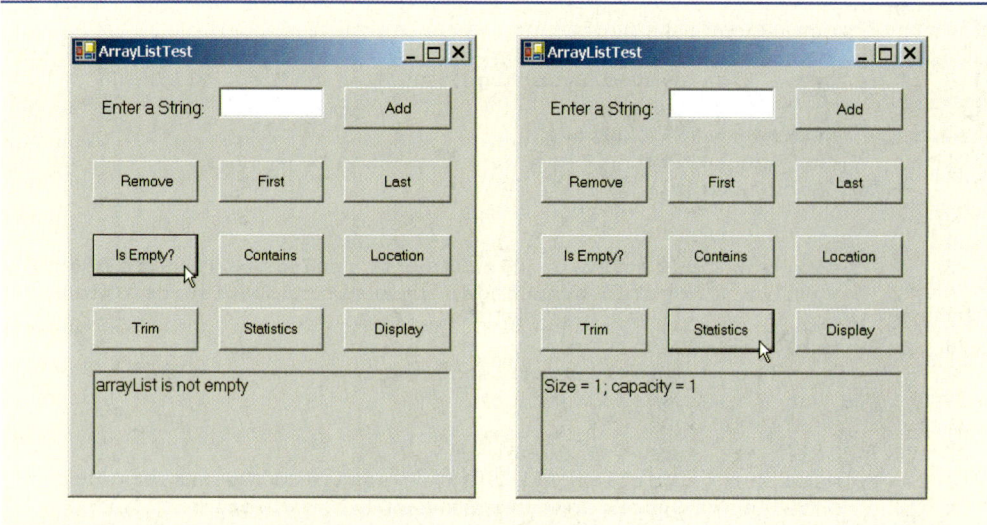

Fig. 23.28 `ArrayList` class demonstration (part 5 of 5).

`ArrayList` method `Remove` deletes a specified item from an `ArrayList`. When the user clicks **Remove**, event handler `cmdRemove_Click` (line 44–50) invokes `Remove` (line 47) to remove the `String` specified in the `inputTextBox` from the `ArrayList`. If the object passed to `Remove` is in the `ArrayList`, the first occurrence of that object is removed, and all subsequent elements shift toward the beginning of the `ArrayList` to fill the empty position.

A program can access `ArrayList` elements in the same way that conventional array elements are accessed: By following the `ArrayList` reference name with the array subscript operator (`()`) and the desired index of the element. Event handlers `cmdFirst_Click` (lines 53–65) and `cmdLast_Click` (lines 68–81) use the `ArrayList` subscript operator to retrieve the first element (line 58) and last element (line 74), respectively. An `ArgumentOutOfRangeException` occurs if the specified index is less than zero or greater than the number of elements currently stored in the `ArrayList`.

Event handler `cmdIsEmpty_Click` (lines 84–93) uses `ArrayList` property `Count` (line 87) to determine whether the `ArrayList` is empty. Event handler `cmdContains_Click` (lines 96–106) uses `ArrayList` method `Contains` (line 99) to determine whether the object that `Contains` receives as an argument currently is in the `ArrayList`. If so, the method returns `True`; otherwise, it returns `False`.

Performance Tip 23.8

`ArrayList` method `Contains` performs a linear search, which is a costly operation for large `ArrayList`s. If the `ArrayList` is sorted, use `ArrayList` method `BinarySearch` to perform a more efficient search.

When the user clicks **Location**, event handler `cmdLocation_Click` (lines 109–114) invokes `ArrayList` method `IndexOf` (line 113) to determine the index of a particular object in the `ArrayList`. `IndexOf` returns `-1` if the element is not found.

When the user clicks **Trim**, event handler `cmdTrim_Click` (lines 117–122) invokes method `TrimToSize` (line 120) to set the `Capacity` property so that it is equal to the

Count property. This reduces the storage capacity of the **ArrayList** to the exact number of elements currently in the **ArrayList**.

When users click **Statistics**, **cmdStatistics_Click** (lines 125–130) uses the **Count** and **Capacity** properties to display the current number of elements in the **ArrayList** and the maximum number of elements that can be stored without the allocation of more memory to the **ArrayList**.

When users click **Display**, **cmdDisplay_Click** (lines 133–144) outputs the contents of the **ArrayList**. This event handler uses an **IEnumerator** (sometimes called an *enumerator*, or an *iterator*) to traverse the elements of an **ArrayList** one element at a time. Interface **IEnumerator** defines methods *MoveNext* and *Reset* and property **Current**. *MoveNext* moves the enumerator to the next element in the **ArrayList**. The first call to *MoveNext* positions the enumerator at the first element of the **ArrayList**. *MoveNext* returns **True** if there is at least one more element in the **ArrayList**; otherwise, the method returns **False**. Method **Reset** positions the enumerator before the first element of the **ArrayList**. Methods **MoveNext** and **Reset** throw an **InvalidOperationException** if the contents of the collection are modified after the enumerator's creation. Property **Current** returns the object at the current location in the **ArrayList**.

Line 136 creates an **IEnumerator**, called **enumerator**, and assigns it the result of a call to **ArrayList** method *GetEnumerator*. Lines 139–141 use **enumerator** to iterate the **ArrayList** (as long as **MoveNext** returns **True**), retrieve the current item via property **Count** and append it to **StringBuilder buffer**. When the loop terminates, line 143 displays the contents of **buffer**.

23.7.3 Class `Stack`

The **Stack** class (namespace **System.Collections**) implements a stack data structure. This class provides much of the functionality that we defined in our implementation in Section 23.4. The application in Fig. 23.29 provides a GUI that enables the user to test many **Stack** methods. Line 31 of the **FrmStackTest** constructor creates a **Stack** with the default initial capacity (10 elements).

Class **Stack** provides methods **Push** and **Pop** to perform the basic stack operations. Method **Push** takes an **Object** as an argument and adds it to the top of the **Stack**. If the number of items on the **Stack** (the **Count** property) is equal to the capacity at the time of the **Push** operation, the **Stack** grows to accommodate more **Object**s. Event handler **cmdPush_Click** (lines 37–42) uses method **Push** to add a user-specified string to the stack (line 40).

```
1   ' Fig. 23.29: StackTest.vb
2   ' Demonstrates class Stack functionality.
3
4   Imports System.Collections
5   Imports System.Text
6   Imports System.Windows.Forms
7
8   Public Class FrmStackTest
9      Inherits Form
```

Fig. 23.29 `Stack` class demonstration (part 1 of 4).

```vbnet
10
11      ' Buttons invoking Stack functionality
12      Friend WithEvents cmdPush As Button
13      Friend WithEvents cmdPop As Button
14      Friend WithEvents cmdPeek As Button
15      Friend WithEvents cmdIsEmpty As Button
16      Friend WithEvents cmdSearch As Button
17      Friend WithEvents cmdDisplay As Button
18
19      ' TextBox receives input from user
20      Friend WithEvents txtInput As TextBox
21      Friend WithEvents lblStatus As Label
22      Friend WithEvents lblEnter As Label
23
24      Private stack As Stack
25
26      Public Sub New()
27         MyBase.New()
28
29         InitializeComponent()
30
31         stack = New Stack() ' create stack
32      End Sub ' New
33
34      ' Visual Studio .NET generated code
35
36      ' push element onto stack
37      Private Sub cmdPush_Click(ByVal sender As System.Object, _
38         ByVal e As System.EventArgs) Handles cmdPush.Click
39
40         Stack.Push(txtInput.Text)
41         lblStatus.Text = "Pushed: " & txtInput.Text
42      End Sub ' cmdPush_Click
43
44      ' pop element from stack
45      Private Sub cmdPop_Click(ByVal sender As System.Object, _
46         ByVal e As System.EventArgs) Handles cmdPop.Click
47
48         ' pop element
49         Try
50            lblStatus.Text = "Popped: " & stack.Pop()
51
52         ' print message if stack is empty
53         Catch invalidOperation As InvalidOperationException
54            lblStatus.Text = invalidOperation.ToString()
55         End Try
56
57      End Sub ' cmdPop_Click
58
59      ' peek at top element of stack
60      Private Sub cmdPeek_Click(ByVal sender As System.Object, _
61         ByVal e As System.EventArgs) Handles cmdPeek.Click
62
```

Fig. 23.29 **Stack** class demonstration (part 2 of 4).

```vbnet
63         ' view top element
64         Try
65            lblStatus.Text = "Top: " & stack.Peek()
66
67            ' print message if stack is empty
68         Catch invalidOperation As InvalidOperationException
69            lblStatus.Text = invalidOperation.ToString()
70         End Try
71
72      End Sub ' cmdPeek_Click
73
74      ' determine whether stack is empty
75      Private Sub cmdIsEmpty_Click(ByVal sender As System.Object, _
76         ByVal e As System.EventArgs) Handles cmdIsEmpty.Click
77
78         If stack.Count = 0 Then
79            lblStatus.Text = "Stack is empty"
80         Else
81            lblStatus.Text = "Stack is not empty"
82         End If
83
84      End Sub ' cmdIsEmpty_Click
85
86      ' determine whether specified element is on stack
87      Private Sub cmdSearch_Click(ByVal sender As System.Object, _
88         ByVal e As System.EventArgs) Handles cmdSearch.Click
89
90         If stack.Contains(txtInput.Text) Then
91            lblStatus.Text = txtInput.Text & " found"
92         Else
93            lblStatus.Text = txtInput.Text & " not found"
94         End If
95
96      End Sub ' cmdSearch_Click
97
98      ' display stack contents
99      Private Sub cmdDisplay_Click(ByVal sender As System.Object, _
100        ByVal e As System.EventArgs) Handles cmdDisplay.Click
101
102        Dim enumerator As IEnumerator = stack.GetEnumerator()
103        Dim buffer As StringBuilder = New StringBuilder()
104
105        While enumerator.MoveNext()
106           buffer.Append(enumerator.Current & " ")
107        End While
108
109        lblStatus.Text = buffer.ToString()
110     End Sub ' cmdDisplay_Click
111
112 End Class ' FrmStackTest
```

Fig. 23.29 `Stack` class demonstration (part 3 of 4).

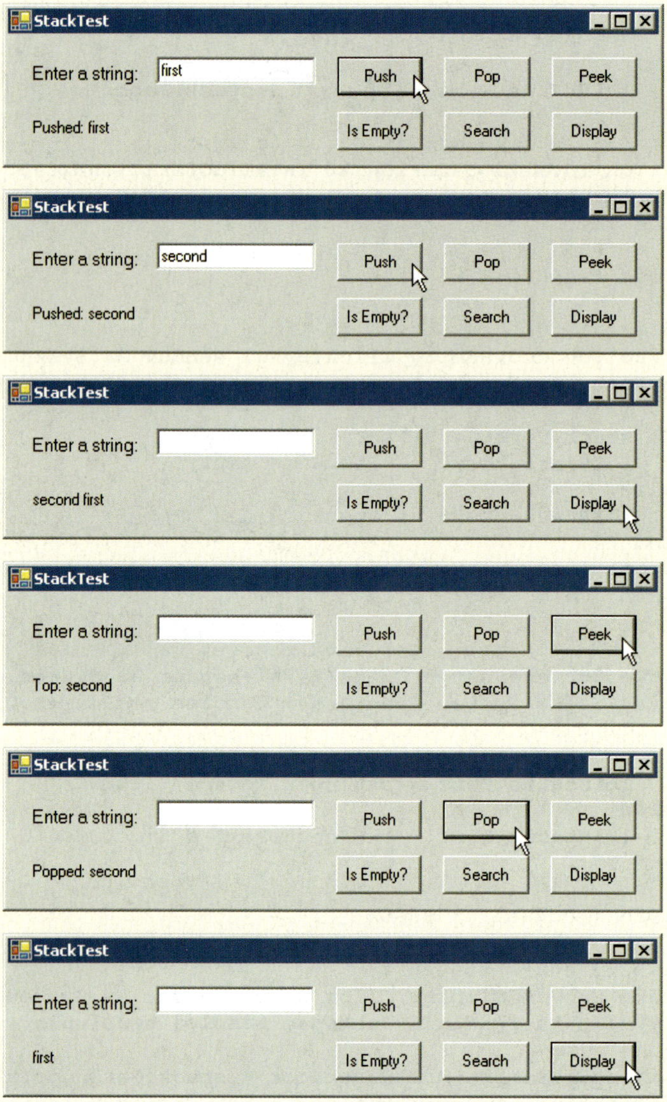

Fig. 23.29 `Stack` class demonstration (part 4 of 4).

Method **Pop** takes no arguments. This method removes and returns the object currently on top of the **Stack**. Event handler **cmdPop_Click** (lines 45–57) calls method **Pop** (line 50) to remove an object from the **Stack**. An **InvalidOperationException** occurs if the **Stack** is empty when the program calls **Pop**.

Method **Peek** returns the value of the top stack element, but does not remove the element from the **Stack**. We demonstrate **Peek** in line 65 of event handler **cmdPeek_Click** (lines 60–72) to view the object on top of the **Stack**. As with **Pop**, an **InvalidOperationException** occurs if the **Stack** is empty when the program calls **Peek**.

Common Programming Error 23.4

Attempting to **Peek** *or* **Pop** *an empty* **Stack** *(a* **Stack** *whose* **Count** *property equals zero) causes an* **InvalidOperationException**.

Event handler **cmdIsEmpty_Click** (lines 75–84) determines whether the **Stack** is empty by comparing the **Stack**'s **Count** property to zero. If it is zero, the **Stack** is empty; otherwise, it is not. Event handler **cmdSearch_Click** (lines 87–96) uses **Stack** method **Contains** (lines 90) to determine whether the **Stack** contains the object specified as its argument. **Contains** returns **True** if the **Stack** contains the specified object and **False** otherwise.

Event handler **cmdDisplay_Click** (lines 99–110) uses an **IEnumerator** to traverse the **Stack** and display its contents.

23.7.4 Class `Hashtable`

Object-oriented programming languages facilitate creating types. When a program creates objects of new or existing types, it then must manage those objects efficiently. This includes storing and retrieving objects. It is efficient to store and retrieve information in arrays if some aspect of the data directly matches the key values and if those keys are unique and tightly packed. If a company has 100 employees with nine-digit Social Security numbers and wants to store and retrieve employee data using Social Security numbers as keys, nominally would require an array with 999,999,999 elements, because there are 999,999,999 unique nine-digit numbers. This is impractical for virtually all applications that key on Social Security numbers. If it were possible to have an array that large, programmers could achieve very high performance storing and retrieving employee records by simply using the Social Security number as the array index.

Many applications have this problem—namely, either that the keys are of the wrong type (i.e., negative integers) or that they are of the right type, but they are spread sparsely over a large range.

The solution to this problem must involve a high-speed scheme for converting keys, such as Social Security numbers and inventory part numbers, to unique array subscripts. Then, when an application needs to store some value, the scheme could convert the application key rapidly to a subscript, and the record of information could be stored at that location in the array. Retrieval now occurs the same way. Once the application has a key for retrieving the data record, the application applies the same conversion to the key, producing the appropriate array subscript, and retrieves the data.

The scheme we describe here provides the basis for a technique called *hashing*. When we convert a key to an array subscript, we literally scramble the bits, forming a kind of "mishmash" number. The number has no real significance beyond its usefulness in storing and retrieving the particular data record.

Problems in the scheme arise when *collisions* occur [i.e., two different keys "hash into" the same cell (or element) in the array]. Because we cannot store two different data records into the same space, we need to find alternative homes for all records beyond the first that hash to a particular array subscript. Many schemes exist for doing this. One is to "hash again" (i.e., to reapply the hashing operation to the key to produce a next candidate cell in the array). Because the hashing process is designed to be random, we can assume that, with just a few hashes, an available cell will be found.

Another scheme uses one hash to locate the first candidate cell. If the cell is occupied, successive cells are searched linearly until an available cell is found. Retrieval works the same way—the key is hashed once, the resulting cell is checked to determine whether it contains the desired data. If it does, the search is complete. If it does not, successive cells are searched linearly until the desired data is found.

The most popular solution to hash-table collisions is to have each cell of the table be a hash "bucket," which typically is a linked list of all the key/value pairs that hash to that cell. This is the solution that Visual Basic's **Hashtable** class (namespace **System.Collections**) implements.

The *load factor* affects the performance of hashing schemes. The load factor is the ratio of the number of occupied cells in the hash table to the size of the hash table. The closer the ratio gets to 1.0, the greater the chance of collisions.

Performance Tip 23.9

The load factor in a hash table is a classic example of a space/time trade-off: By increasing the load factor, we achieve better memory utilization, but cause the program to be slowed by increased hashing collisions. By decreasing the load factor, we achieve better program speed due to a reduction in hashing collisions, but we get poorer memory utilization, because a larger portion of the hash table remains empty.

The proper programming of hash tables is too complex for most casual programmers. Computer science students study hashing schemes thoroughly in courses called "Data Structures" and "Algorithms." Recognizing the value of hashing, Visual Basic provides class **Hashtable** and some related features to enable programmers to take advantage of hashing without studying the complex details of the technique.

The preceding sentence is profoundly important in our study of object-oriented programming. Classes encapsulate and hide complexity (i.e., implementation details) while offering user-friendly interfaces. Crafting classes to do this properly is one of the most valued skills in the field of object-oriented programming.

A *hash function* performs a calculation that determines where to place data in the hashtable. The hash function is applied to the key in a key/value pair of objects. Class **Hashtable** can accept any object as a key. For this reason, class **Object** defines method **GetHashCode**, which is inherited by all Visual Basic objects. Most classes that can be used as keys in hash tables override this method to provide one that performs efficient hashcode calculations for the specific data type. For example, a **String** has a hashcode calculation that is based on the contents of the **String**. Figure 23.30 demonstrates several methods of class **Hashtable**.

```
1   ' Fig. 23.30: FrmHashTableTest.vb
2   ' Demonstrate class Hashtable functionality.
3
4   Imports System.Collections
5   Imports System.Text
6   Imports System.Windows.Forms
7
8   Public Class FrmHashTableTest
9      Inherits Form
```

Fig. 23.30 **Hashtable** class demonstration (part 1 of 5).

```vbnet
10
11       ' Buttons invoke Hashtable functionality
12       Friend WithEvents cmdAdd As Button
13       Friend WithEvents cmdGet As Button
14       Friend WithEvents cmdRemove As Button
15       Friend WithEvents cmdEmpty As Button
16       Friend WithEvents cmdContains As Button
17       Friend WithEvents cmdClear As Button
18       Friend WithEvents cmdListObjects As Button
19       Friend WithEvents cmdListKeys As Button
20
21       ' TextBoxes enable user to input hashtable data
22       Friend WithEvents txtFirst As TextBox
23       Friend WithEvents txtLast As TextBox
24       Friend WithEvents txtConsole As TextBox
25
26       Friend WithEvents lblFirst As Label
27       Friend WithEvents lblLast As Label
28       Friend WithEvents lblStatus As Label
29
30       Private table As Hashtable
31
32       Public Sub New()
33          MyBase.New()
34
35          'This call is required by the Windows Form Designer.
36          InitializeComponent()
37
38          table = New Hashtable() ' create Hashtable object
39       End Sub ' New
40
41       ' Visual Studio .NET generated code
42
43       ' add last name and CEmployee object to table
44       Private Sub cmdAdd_Click(ByVal sender As System.Object, _
45          ByVal e As System.EventArgs) Handles cmdAdd.Click
46
47          Dim employee As New CEmployee(txtFirst.Text, txtLast.Text)
48
49          ' add new key/value pair
50          Try
51             table.Add(txtLast.Text, employee)
52             lblStatus.Text = "Put: " & employee.ToString()
53
54          ' if key does not exist or is in table, throw exception
55          Catch argumentException As ArgumentException
56             lblStatus.Text = argumentException.ToString()
57          End Try
58
59       End Sub ' cmdAdd_Click
60
```

Fig. 23.30 `Hashtable` class demonstration (part 2 of 5).

```vbnet
61        ' get object for given key
62        Private Sub cmdGet_Click(ByVal sender As System.Object, _
63           ByVal e As System.EventArgs) Handles cmdGet.Click
64
65           Dim result As Object = table(txtLast.Text)
66
67           If Not result Is Nothing Then
68              lblStatus.Text = "Get: " & result.ToString()
69           Else
70              lblStatus.Text = "Get: " & txtLast.Text & " not in table"
71           End If
72
73        End Sub ' cmdGet_Click
74
75        ' remove key/value pair from table
76        Private Sub cmdRemove_Click(ByVal sender As System.Object, _
77           ByVal e As System.EventArgs) Handles cmdRemove.Click
78
79           table.Remove(txtLast.Text)
80           lblStatus.Text = "Object Removed"
81        End Sub ' cmdRemove_Click
82
83        ' determine whether table is empty
84        Private Sub cmdEmpty_Click(ByVal sender As System.Object, _
85           ByVal e As System.EventArgs) Handles cmdEmpty.Click
86
87           lblStatus.Text = "Table is "
88
89           If table.Count = 0 Then
90              lblStatus.Text &= "empty"
91           Else
92              lblStatus.Text &= "not empty"
93           End If
94
95        End Sub ' cmdEmpty_Click
96
97        ' determine whether table contains specified key
98        Private Sub cmdContains_Click(ByVal sender As System.Object, _
99           ByVal e As System.EventArgs) Handles cmdContains.Click
100
101          lblStatus.Text = "Contains key: " & _
102             table.ContainsKey(txtLast.Text)
103       End Sub ' cmdContains_Click
104
105       ' discard all table contents
106       Private Sub cmdClear_Click(ByVal sender As System.Object, _
107          ByVal e As System.EventArgs) Handles cmdClear.Click
108
109          table.Clear()
110          lblStatus.Text = "Clear: Table is now empty"
111       End Sub ' cmdClear_Click
112
```

Fig. 23.30 **Hashtable** class demonstration (part 3 of 5).

```vbnet
113         ' display list of all objects in table
114         Private Sub cmdListObjects_Click( _
115            ByVal sender As System.Object, ByVal e As System.EventArgs) _
116            Handles cmdListObjects.Click
117
118            Dim enumerator As IDictionaryEnumerator = _
119               table.GetEnumerator()
120
121            Dim buffer As StringBuilder = New StringBuilder()
122
123            While enumerator.MoveNext()
124               buffer.Append(Convert.ToString(enumerator.Value) & _
125                  vbCrLf)
126            End While
127
128            txtConsole.Text = buffer.ToString()
129         End Sub ' cmdListObjects_Click
130
131         ' display list of keys in table
132         Private Sub cmdListKeys_Click(ByVal sender As System.Object, _
133            ByVal e As System.EventArgs) Handles cmdListKeys.Click
134
135            Dim enumerator As IDictionaryEnumerator = _
136                  table.GetEnumerator()
137
138            Dim buffer As StringBuilder = New StringBuilder()
139
140            While enumerator.MoveNext()
141               buffer.Append(enumerator.Key & vbCrLf)
142            End While
143
144            txtConsole.Text = buffer.ToString()
145         End Sub ' cmdListKeys_Click
146
147      End Class ' FrmHashTableTest
```

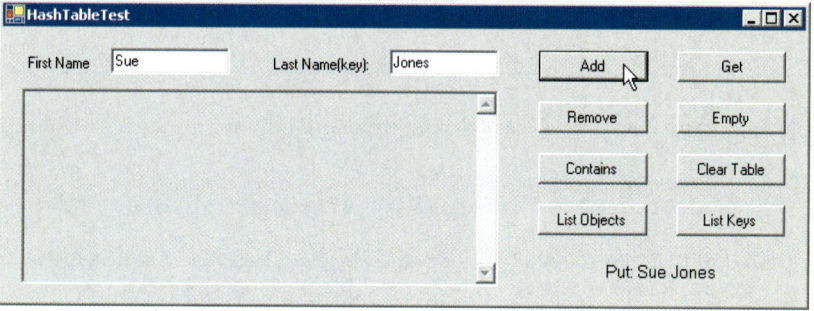

Fig. 23.30 Hashtable class demonstration (part 4 of 5).

1194 Data Structures and Collections   Chapter 23

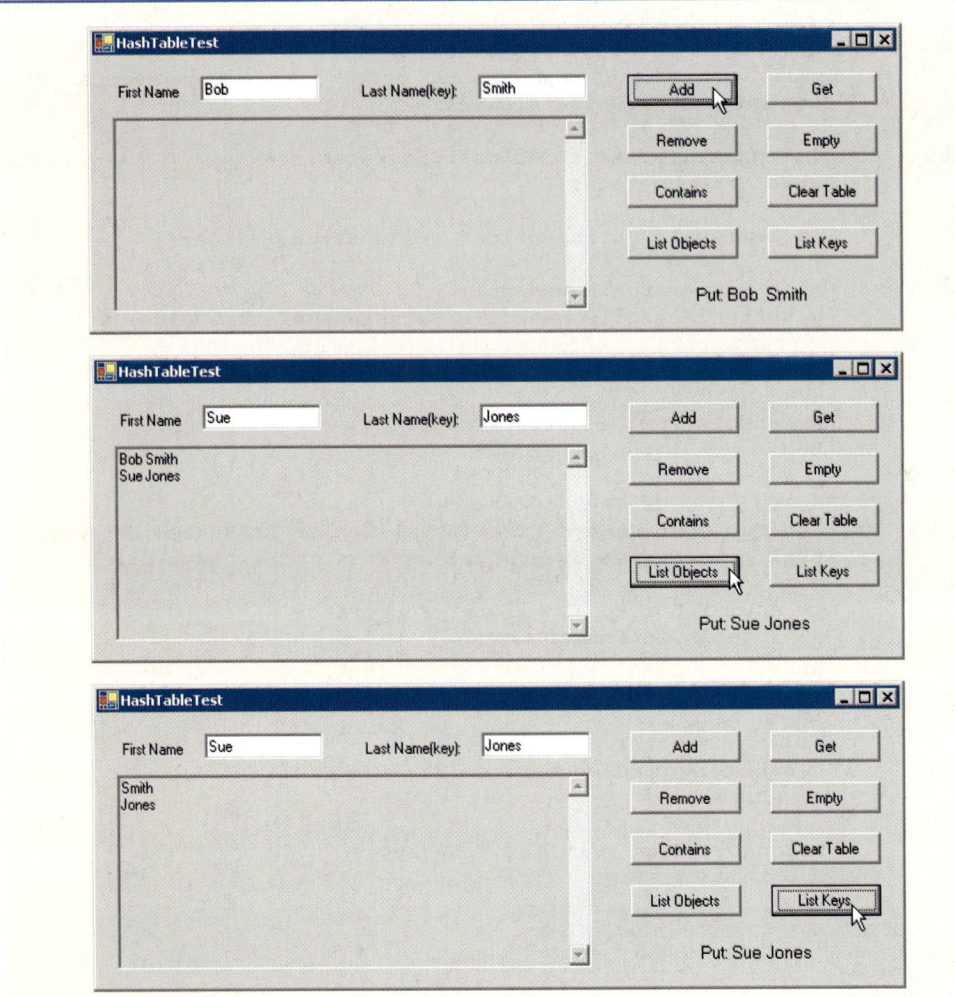

Fig. 23.30 `Hashtable` class demonstration (part 5 of 5).

```
1    ' Fig. 23.31: Employee.vb
2    ' Class CEmployee for use with HashTable.
3
4    Public Class CEmployee
5       Private firstName, lastName As String
6
7       Public Sub New(ByVal first As String, ByVal last As String)
8          firstName = first
9          lastName = last
10      End Sub ' New
11
```

Fig. 23.31 `CEmployee` class (part 1 of 2).

```
12        ' return Employee first and last names as String
13        Public Overrides Function ToString() As String
14           Return firstName & " " & lastName
15        End Function ' ToString
16
17    End Class ' CEmployee
```

Fig. 23.31 `CEmployee` class (part 2 of 2).

Event handler **cmdAdd_Click** (lines 44–59) reads the first name and last name of an employee from the user interface, creates an object of class **CEmployee** (Fig. 23.31) and adds that **CEmployee** to the **Hashtable** with method **Add** (line 51). This method receives two arguments—a key object and a value object. In this example, the key is the last name of the **CEmployee** (a **String**), and the value is the corresponding **CEmployee** object. An **ArgumentException** occurs if the **Hashtable** already contains the key or if the key is **Nothing**.

Event handler **cmdGet_Click** (lines 62–73) retrieves the object associated with a specific key using the **Hashtable**'s subscript operator (as shown on line 65). The expression in parentheses is the key for which the **Hashtable** should return the corresponding object. If the key is not found, the result is **Nothing**.

Event handler **cmdRemove_Click** (lines 76–81) invokes **Hashtable** method **Remove** to delete a key and its associated object from the **Hashtable**. If the key does not exist in the table, nothing happens.

Event handler **cmdEmpty_Click** (lines 84–95) uses **Hashtable** property **Count** to determine whether the **Hashtable** is empty (i.e., **Count** is **0**).

Event handler **cmdContainsKey_Click** (lines 98–103) invokes **Hashtable** method **ContainsKey** to determine whether the **Hashtable** contains the specified key. If so, the method returns **True**; otherwise, it returns **False**.

Event handler **cmdClear_Click** (lines 106–111) invokes **Hashtable** method **Clear** to delete all **Hashtable** entries.

Class **Hashtable** provides method **GetEnumerator**, which returns an enumerator of type **IDictionaryEnumerator**, which is derived from **IEnumerator**. Such enumerators provide properties **Key** and **Value** to access the information for a key/value pair. The event handler in lines 114–129 (**cmdListObjects_click**) uses property **Value** of the enumerator to output the objects in the **Hashtable**. The event handler in lines 132–145 (**cmdListKeys_click**) uses the **Key** property of the enumerator to output the keys in the **Hashtable**.

SUMMARY

- Dynamic data structures can grow and shrink at execution time.
- Creating and maintaining dynamic data structures requires dynamic memory allocation—the ability of a program to obtain more memory at execution time (to hold new nodes) and to release memory no longer needed.
- The limit for dynamic memory allocation can be as large as the available physical memory in the computer and the amount of available disk space in a virtual-memory system.

- Operator **New** takes as an operand the type of the object to allocate dynamically and returns a reference to a newly created object of that type. If no memory is available, **New** throws an **OutOfMemoryException**.
- A self-referential class contains a reference to an object of the same class type. Self-referential objects can be linked to form such data structures as lists, queues, stacks and trees.
- A linked list is a linear collection (i.e., a sequence) of self-referential class objects called nodes, which are connected by reference links.
- A node can contain data of any type, including objects of other classes.
- A linked list is accessed via a reference to the first node of the list. Each subsequent node is accessed via the link-reference member stored in the previous node.
- By convention, the link reference in the last node of a list is set to **Nothing**, marking the end of the list.
- A stack is a constrained version of a linked list—nodes can be added to a stack and removed from a stack only at its top. A stack is a last-in, first-out (LIFO) data structure.
- The primary stack operations are push and pop. Operation push adds a node to the top of the stack. Operation pop removes a node from the top of the stack and returns the data object from the popped node.
- Queues represent waiting lines. Insertions occur at the back (also referred to as the tail) of the queue, and deletions occur from the front (also referred to as the head) of the queue.
- A queue is similar to a checkout line in a supermarket—the first person in line is served first; other customers enter the end of the line and then wait to be served.
- Queue nodes are removed only from the head of the queue and are inserted only at the tail of the queue. For this reason, a queue is referred to as a first-in, first-out (FIFO) data structure.
- The insert and remove operations for a queue are known as enqueue and dequeue.
- Binary trees facilitate high-speed searching and sorting of data, efficient elimination of duplicate data items, representing of file-system hierarchies and compiling of expressions into machine language.
- Tree nodes contain two or more links.
- A binary tree is a tree whose nodes each contain two links. The root node is the first node in a tree.
- Each link in the root node of a binary tree refers to a child. The left child is the first node in the left subtree, and the right child is the first node in the right subtree.
- The children of a node of a binary tree are called siblings. A node with no children is a leaf node.
- In a binary search tree with no duplicate node values has the characteristic that the values in any left subtree are less than the values that subtree's parent node and the values in any right subtree are greater than the values in that subtree's parent node.
- In a binary search tree, nodes can be inserted only as a leaf node.
- An inorder traversal of a binary search tree processes the node values in ascending order.
- Creating a binary search tree actually sorts the data—hence the term, "binary tree sort."
- In an inorder traversal, the value in each node is processed after the node's left subtrees are processed, but before the node's right subtrees are processed.
- In a preorder traversal, the value in each node is processed as the node is visited. After the value in a given node is processed, the values in the left subtree are processed, then the values in the right subtree are processed.
- In a postorder traversal, the value in each node is processed after the node's left and right subtrees are processed.

- The binary search tree facilitates duplicate elimination. As the tree is created, attempts to insert a duplicate value are recognized, because a duplicate follows the same "go left" or "go right" decisions on each comparison as did the original value. Thus, the duplicate eventually is compared with a node containing the same value.
- Classes that implement interface **IComparable** define method **CompareTo**, which compares the object that invokes the method with the object that the method receives as an argument.
- Class **ArrayList** can be used as a dynamic array.
- **ArrayList** method **Add** adds an **Object** to the **ArrayList**.
- **ArrayList** method **Remove** removes the first occurrence of the specified **Object** from the **ArrayList**.
- The **ArrayList** subscript operator accesses elements of an **ArrayList** as if the **ArrayList** were an array.
- Class **Stack** is provided in the **System.Collections** namespace.
- **Stack** method **Push** performs the push operation on the **Stack**.
- **Stack** method **Pop** performs the pop operation on the **Stack**.
- Class **Hashtable** is provided in the **System.Collections** namespace.
- **Hashtable** method **Add** adds a key/value pair to the **Hashtable**.
- Programs can use an **IEnumerator** (also called an enumerator or an iterator) to traverse elements of an **ArrayList** one element at a time.
- Interface **IEnumerator** defines methods **MoveNext** and **Reset** and property **Current**. **MoveNext** moves the enumerator to the next element in the **ArrayList**. Method **Reset** positions the enumerator before the first element of the **ArrayList**. Property **Current** returns the object residing at the current location in the **ArrayList**.

TERMINOLOGY

Add method of ArrayList
ArgumentException
ArrayList class
binary tree
BinarySearch method of ArrayList
Capacity property of ArrayList
Clear method of ArrayList
Clear method of Hashtable
collection
Contains method of ArrayList
Contains method of Stack
ContainsKey method of Hashtable
Count property of ArrayList
Count property of Stack
Current property of IEnumerator
data structure
dynamic data structure
enumerator
GetEnumerator method of IEnumerable
GetHashCode method of Object
Hashtable class
IDictionaryEnumerator interface

IEnumerator interface
IndexOf method of ArrayList
InvalidOperationException
linked list
MoveNext method of IEnumerator
Peek method of Stack
Pop method of Stack
Push method of Stack
queue
Remove method of ArrayList
Remove method of Hashtable
RemoveAt method of ArrayList
RemoveRange method of ArrayList
Reset method of IEnumerator
searching
self-referential class
Sort method of ArrayList
sorting
stack
Stack class
System.Collections namespace
TrimToSize method of ArrayList

SELF-REVIEW EXERCISES

23.1 State whether each of the following is *true* or *false*. If *false*, explain why.
  a) In a queue, the first item to be added is the last item to be removed.
  b) Trees can have no more than two child nodes per node.
  c) A tree node with no children is called a leaf node.
  d) Class **Stack** belongs to namespace **System.Collections**.
  e) A class implementing interface **IEnumerator** must define only methods **MoveNext** and **Reset**.
  f) A hashtable stores key/value pairs.
  g) Linked-list nodes are stored contiguously in memory.
  h) The primary operations of the stack data structure are enqueue and dequeue.
  i) Lists, stacks and queues are linear data structures.

23.2 Fill in the blanks in each of the following statements:
  a) A _____ class is used to define nodes that reference nodes of the same type to form dynamic data structures, which can grow and shrink at execution time.
  b) Operator _____ allocates memory dynamically; this operator returns a reference to the allocated memory.
  c) A _____ is a constrained version of a linked list, in which nodes can be inserted and deleted only from the start of the list; this data structure returns node values in last-in, first-out (LIFO) order.
  d) A queue is a _____ data structure, because the first nodes inserted are the first nodes removed.
  e) A _____ is a constrained version of a linked list in which nodes can be inserted only at the end of the list and deleted only from the start of the list.
  f) A _____ is a nonlinear, two-dimensional data structure that contains nodes with two or more links.
  g) The nodes of a _____ tree contain two link members.
  h) **IEnumerator** method _____ advances the enumerator to the next item.
  i) The binary-tree-traversal algorithm that processes the root node, then all the nodes to its left and finally all the nodes to its right, is called the _____ traversal.

ANSWERS TO SELF-REVIEW EXERCISES

23.1 a) False. A queue is a first-in, first-out (FIFO) data structure—the first item added is the first item removed. b) False. In general, trees can have as many child nodes per node as is necessary. Only binary trees are restricted to no more than two child nodes per node. c) True. d) True. e) False. The class must also implement property **Current**. f) True. g) False. Linked-list nodes are logically contiguous, but they need not be stored in physically contiguous memory space. h) False. Those are the primary operations of a queue. The primary operations of a stack are push and pop. i) True.

23.2 a) self-referential. b) **New**. c) stack. d) first-in, first-out (FIFO). e) queue. f) tree. g) binary. h) **MoveNext**. i) preorder.

EXERCISES

23.3 Write a program that merges two ordered list objects of integers into a single ordered list object of integers. Method **Merge** of class **ListMerge** should receive references to each of the list objects to be merged and should return a reference to the merged list object.

23.4 Write a program that inputs a line of text and then uses a stack object to print the line reversed.

23.5 Write a program that uses a stack to determine whether a string is a palindrome (i.e., the string is spelled identically backward and forward). The program should ignore spaces, case sensitivity and punctuation (so, "**A man, a plan, a canal, Panama**" would be recognized as a palindrome).

23.6 Compilers use stacks to help in the process of evaluating expressions and generating machine-language code. In this and the next exercise, we investigate how compilers evaluate arithmetic expressions consisting only of constants, operators and parentheses.

Humans generally write expressions like **3 + 4** and **7 / 9**, in which the operator (**+** or **/** here) is written between its operands—this is called *infix notation*. Computers "prefer" *postfix notation*, in which the operator is written to the right of its two operands. The preceding infix expressions would appear in postfix notation as **3 4 +** and **7 9 /**, respectively.

To evaluate a complex infix expression, a compiler would first convert the expression to postfix notation, then evaluate the postfix version of the expression. Each of these algorithms requires only a single left-to-right pass of the expression. Each algorithm uses a stack object in support of its operation, and, in each algorithm, the stack is used for a different purpose.

In this exercise, you will write a Visual Basic version of the infix-to-postfix conversion algorithm. In the next exercise, you will write a Visual Basic version of the postfix expression-evaluation algorithm. In a later exercise, you will discover that code you write in this exercise can help you implement a complete working compiler.

Write class **InfixToPostfixConverter** to convert an ordinary infix arithmetic expression (assume a valid expression is entered) with single-digit integers, such as:

```
(6 + 2) * 5 - 8 / 4
```

to a postfix expression. The postfix version of the preceding infix expression (note that no parentheses are needed) is:

```
6 2 + 5 * 8 4 / -
```

The program should read the expression into **StringBuilder infix**. Use class **CStackComposition** (implemented in Fig. 23.14) to help create the postfix expression in **StringBuilder postfix**. The algorithm for creating a postfix expression is as follows:

a) Push a left parenthesis **'('** onto the stack.
b) Append a right parenthesis **')'** to the end of **infix**.
c) While the stack is not empty, read **infix** from left to right and do the following:
   If the current character in **infix** is a digit, append it to **postfix**.
   If the current character in **infix** is a left parenthesis, push it onto the stack.
   If the current character in **infix** is an operator:
       Pop operators (if there are any) at the top of the stack while they have equal
          or higher precedence than the current operator, and append the popped
          operators to **postfix**.
       Push the current character in **infix** onto the stack.
   If the current character in **infix** is a right parenthesis:
       Pop operators from the top of the stack and append them to **postfix** until
          a left parenthesis is at the top of the stack.
       Pop (and discard) the left parenthesis from the stack.

The arithmetic operations allowed in an expression are:
- **+** addition
- **-** subtraction
- ***** multiplication
- **/** division
- **^** exponentiation
- **%** modulus

Some of the methods you might want to provide in your program are as follows:
  a) Method **ConvertToPostfix**, which converts the infix expression to postfix notation.
  b) Method **IsOperator**, which determines whether a character is an operator.
  c) Method **Precedence**, which determines whether the precedence of **operator1** (from the infix expression) is less than, equal to or greater than the precedence of **operator2** (from the stack). The method returns **True** if **operator1** has lower precedence than **operator2**. Otherwise, **False** is returned.
  d) Add this method to the class definition for class **StackComposition**.

23.7 Write class **PostfixEvaluator**, which evaluates a postfix expression (assume it is valid) such as:

   6 2 + 5 * 8 4 / -

The program should read a postfix expression consisting of digits and operators into a **StringBuilder**. Using class **StackComposition** from Exercise 23.6, the program should scan the expression and evaluate it. The algorithm is as follows:
  a) Append a right parenthesis ('**)**') to the end of the postfix expression. When the right-parenthesis character is encountered, no further processing is necessary.
  b) When the right-parenthesis character has not been encountered, read the expression from left to right.
     If the current character is a digit, do the following:
        Push its integer value on the stack (the integer value of a digit character is its value in the computer's character set minus the value of '**0**' in Unicode).
     Otherwise, if the current character is an *operator*:
        Pop the two top elements of the stack into variables **x** and **y**.
        Calculate **y** *operator* **x**.
        Push the result of the calculation onto the stack.
  c) When the right parenthesis is encountered in the expression, pop the top value of the stack. This is the result of the postfix expression.

[*Note*: In b) above (based on the sample expression at the beginning of this exercise), if the operator is '**/**', the top of the stack is **2** and the next element in the stack is **8**, then pop **2** into **x**, pop **8** into **y**, evaluate **8 / 2** and push the result, **4**, back onto the stack. This note also applies to operator '**-**'.] The arithmetic operations allowed in an expression are:
  + addition
  - subtraction
  * multiplication
  / division
  ^ exponentiation
  % modulus

You might want to provide the following methods:
  a) Method **EvaluatePostfixExpression**, which evaluates the postfix expression.
  b) Method **Calculate**, which evaluates the expression **op1** *operator* **op2**.

23.8 (*Binary Tree Delete*) In this exercise, we discuss deleting items from binary search trees. The deletion algorithm is not as straightforward as the insertion algorithm. There are three cases that are encountered in the deleting of an item—the item is contained in a leaf node (i.e., it has no children), the item is contained in a node that has one child or the item is contained in a node that has two children.

If the item to be deleted is contained in a leaf node, the node is deleted, and the reference in the parent node is set to **Nothing**.

If the item to be deleted is contained in a node with one child, the reference in the parent node is set to reference the child node, and the node containing the data item is deleted. This causes the child node to take the place of the deleted node in the tree.

The last case is the most difficult. When a node with two children is deleted, another node in the tree must take its place. However, the reference in the parent node cannot simply be assigned to reference one of the children of the node to be deleted. In most cases, the resulting binary search tree would not adhere to the following characteristic of binary search trees (with no duplicate values): *The values in any left subtree are less than the value in the parent node, and the values in any right subtree are greater than the value in the parent node.*

Which node is used as a *replacement node* to maintain this characteristic? Either the node containing the largest value in the tree less than the value in the node being deleted, or the node containing the smallest value in the tree greater than the value in the node being deleted. Let us consider the node with the smaller value. In a binary search tree, the largest value less than a parent's value is located in the left subtree of the parent node and is guaranteed to be contained in the rightmost node of that subtree. This node is located by walking down the left subtree to the right until the reference to the right child of the current node is **Nothing**. We are now referencing the replacement node, which is either a leaf node or a node with one child to its left. If the replacement node is a leaf node, the steps to perform the deletion are as follows:

 a) Store the reference to the node to be deleted in a temporary reference variable.
 b) Set the reference in the parent of the node being deleted to reference the replacement node.
 c) Set the reference in the parent of the replacement node to **Nothing**.
 d) Set the reference to the right subtree in the replacement node to reference the right subtree of the node to be deleted.
 e) Set the reference to the left subtree in the replacement node to reference the left subtree of the node to be deleted.

The deletion steps for a replacement node with a left child are similar to those for a replacement node with no children, but the algorithm also must move the child into the replacement node's position in the tree. If the replacement node is a node with a left child, the steps to perform the deletion are as follows:

 a) Store the reference to the node to be deleted in a temporary reference variable.
 b) Set the reference in the parent of the node being deleted to reference the replacement node.
 c) Set the reference in the parent of the replacement node reference to the left child of the replacement node.
 d) Set the reference to the right subtree in the replacement node reference to the right subtree of the node to be deleted.
 e) Set the reference to the left subtree in the replacement node to reference the left subtree of the node to be deleted.

Write method **DeleteNode**, which takes as its argument the value to be deleted. Method **DeleteNode** should locate in the tree the node containing the value to be deleted and use the algorithms discussed here to delete the node. If the value is not found in the tree, the method should print a message that indicates whether the value is deleted. Modify the program of Fig. 23.20 to use this method. After deleting an item, call the methods **InorderTraversal**, **PreorderTraversal** and **PostorderTraversal** to confirm that the delete operation was performed correctly.

23.9 (*Level-Order Binary Tree Traversal*) The program of Fig. 23.20 illustrated three recursive methods of traversing a binary tree—inorder, preorder and postorder traversals. This exercise presents the *level-order traversal* of a binary tree, in which the node values are printed level by level, starting at the root-node level. The nodes on each level are printed from left to right. The level-order traversal is not a recursive algorithm. It uses a queue object to control the output of the nodes. The algorithm is as follows:

a) Insert the root node in the queue.
b) While there are nodes left in the queue, do the following:
   Get the next node in the queue.
   Print the node's value.
   If the reference to the left child of the node is not **Nothing**:
      Insert the left child node in the queue.
   If the reference to the right child of the node is not **Nothing**:
      Insert the right child node in the queue.

Write method **LevelOrder** to perform a level-order traversal of a binary tree object. Modify the program of Fig. 23.20 to use this method. [*Note*: You also will need to use the queue-processing methods of Fig. 23.16 in this program.]

24

Accessibility

Objectives

- To introduce the World Wide Web Consortium's Web Content Accessibility Guidelines 1.0 (WCAG 1.0).
- To understand how to use the **alt** attribute of the XHTML **<img>** tag to describe images to people with visual impairments, mobile-Web-device users and others unable to view the image.
- To understand how to make tables more accessible to page readers.
- To understand how to verify that XHTML tags are used properly and to ensure that Web pages can be viewed on any type of display or reader.
- To understand how VoiceXML™ and CallXML™ are changing the way in which people with disabilities access information on the Web.
- To introduce the various accessibility aids offered in Windows 2000.

'Tis the good reader that makes the good book...
Ralph Waldo Emerson

I once was lost, but now am found,
Was blind, but now I see.
John Newton

Outline

24.1 Introduction
24.2 Regulations and Resources
24.3 Web Accessibility Initiative
24.4 Providing Alternatives for Images
24.5 Maximizing Readability by Focusing on Structure
24.6 Accessibility in Visual Studio .NET
    24.6.1 Enlarging Toolbar Icons
    24.6.2 Enlarging the Text
    24.6.3 Modifying the Toolbox
    24.6.4 Modifying the Keyboard
    24.6.5 Rearranging Windows
24.7 Accessibility in Visual Basic
24.8 Accessibility in XHTML Tables
24.9 Accessibility in XHTML Frames
24.10 Accessibility in XML
24.11 Using Voice Synthesis and Recognition with VoiceXML™
24.12 CallXML™
24.13 JAWS® for Windows
24.14 Other Accessibility Tools
24.15 Accessibility in Microsoft® Windows® 2000
    24.15.1 Tools for People with Visual Impairments
    24.15.2 Tools for People with Hearing Impairments
    24.15.3 Tools for Users Who Have Difficulty Using the Keyboard
    24.15.4 Microsoft Narrator
    24.15.5 Microsoft On-Screen Keyboard
    24.15.6 Accessibility Features in Microsoft Internet Explorer 5.5
24.16 Internet and World Wide Web Resources

Summary • Terminology • Self-Review Exercises • Answers to Self-Review Exercises • Exercises

24.1 Introduction

Throughout this book, we discuss the creation of Visual Basic applications. Later chapters also introduce the development of Web-based content using Web Forms, ASP .NET, XHTML and XML. In this chapter, we explore the topic of accessibility, which refers to the level of usability that an application or Web site provides to people with various disabilities. Disabilities that might affect an individual's computer or Internet usage are common; they include visual impairments, hearing impairments, other physical injuries (such as the inability to use a keyboard) and learning disabilities. In today's computing environment, such impediments prevent many users from taking full advantage of applications and Web content.

The design of applications and sites to meet the needs of individuals with disabilities should be a priority for all software companies and e-businesses. People affected by disabilities represent a significant portion of the population, and legal ramifications could exist for companies that discriminate by failing to provide adequate and universal access to their resources. In this chapter, we explore the World Wide Web Consortium's *Web Accessibility Initiative* and its guidelines, and we review various laws regarding the availability of computing and Internet resources to people with disabilities. We also highlight companies that have developed systems, products and services that meet the needs of this demographic. As students use Visual Basic and its related technologies to design applications and Web sites, they should keep in mind the accessibility requirements and recommendations that we discuss in this chapter.

24.2 Regulations and Resources

Over the past several years, the United States has taken legislative steps to ensure that people with disabilities are given the tools they need to use computers and access the Web. A wide variety of legislation, including the *Americans With Disabilities Act* (ADA) of 1990, governs the provision of computer and Web accessibility (Fig. 24.1). These laws have inspired significant legal action. For example, according to the ADA, companies are required to offer equal access to an individual with visual problems. The National Federation for the Blind (NFB) cited this law in a 1999 suit against AOL, responding to the company's failure to make its services available to individuals with disabilities.

There are 54 million Americans with disabilities, and these individuals represent an estimated $1 trillion in annual purchasing power. **WeMedia.com**™ (Fig. 24.2) is a Web site that provides news, information, products and services to the millions of people with disabilities and to their families, friends and caregivers. *We Media* also provides online educational opportunities for people with disabilities.

Act	Purpose
Americans with Disabilities Act	The ADA prohibits discrimination on the basis of disability in employment, state and local government, public accommodations, commercial facilities, transportation and telecommunications.
Telecommunications Act of 1996	The Telecommunications Act of 1996 contains two amendments to Section 255 and Section 251(a)(2) of the Communications Act of 1934. These amendments require that communication devices, such as cell phones, telephones and pagers, be accessible to individuals with disabilities.

Fig. 24.1 Acts designed to ensure Internet access for people with disabilities (part 1 of 2).

Act	Purpose
Individuals with Disabilities Education Act of 1997	The Individuals with Disabilities Education Act stipulates that education materials in schools must be made accessible to children with disabilities.
Rehabilitation Act	Section 504 of the Rehabilitation Act states that college-sponsored activities receiving federal funding cannot discriminate against individuals with disabilities. Section 508 mandates that all government institutions receiving federal funding must design their Web sites so that they are accessible to individuals with disabilities. Businesses that sell services to the government also must abide by this act.

Fig. 24.1 Acts designed to ensure Internet access for people with disabilities (part 2 of 2).

Fig. 24.2 We Media's home page. (Courtesy of We Media Inc.)

The Internet enables individuals with disabilities to work in a vast array of new fields. This is partly because the Internet provides a medium through which disabled people can telecommute to jobs and interact easily with others without traveling. Such technologies as voice activation, visual enhancers and auditory aids create additional employment opportunities. For example, people with visual impairments can use computer monitors with enlarged text, and people with physical impairments can use head pointers with on-screen keyboards.

Federal regulations that are similar to the disability ramp mandate will be applied to the Internet to accommodate the needs of people with hearing, vision, speech and other impairments. In the following sections, we explore various products and services that provide Internet access to people with disabilities.

24.3 Web Accessibility Initiative

Currently, the majority of Web sites are considered to be either partially or totally inaccessible to people with visual, learning or mobility impairments. Total accessibility is difficult to achieve, because of the variety of disabilities that must be accommodated and because of problems resulting from language barriers and hardware and software inconsistencies. However, a high level of accessibility is attainable. As more people with disabilities use the Internet, it is imperative that Web-site designers increase the accessibility of their sites. Although recent legislation focuses on accessibility, standards organizations also see the need for industry recommendations. In an attempt to address issues of accessibility, the World Wide Web Consortium (W3C) launched the *Web Accessibility Initiative* (WAI™) in April 1997. To learn more about the WAI and to read its mission statement, visit **www.w3.org/WAI**.

This chapter explains various techniques used to develop accessible Web sites. In 1999, the WAI published the *Web Content Accessibility Guidelines* (*WCAG*) *1.0* to help businesses determine whether their Web sites are universally accessible. The WCAG 1.0 (available at **www.w3.org/TR/WCAG10**) uses checkpoints to list specific accessibility requirements. Each checkpoint also is accompanied by a corresponding priority rating that indicates its importance. *Priority-one checkpoints* are goals that must be met to ensure accessibility; we focus on these points in this chapter. *Priority-two checkpoints*, though not essential, are highly recommended. If these checkpoints are not satisfied, people with certain disabilities will experience difficulty accessing Web sites. *Priority-three checkpoints* slightly improve accessibility.

At the time of publication, the WAI was working on *WCAG 2.0*; a working draft of this publication can be found at **www.w3.org/TR/WCAG20**. A single checkpoint in the WCAG 2.0 Working Draft might encompass several checkpoints from WCAG 1.0. Once WCAG 2.0 has been reviewed and published by W3C, its checkpoints will supersede those of WCAG 1.0. Furthermore, the new version can be applied to a wider range of markup languages (e.g., XML and WML) and content types than can its predecessor.

The WAI also presents a supplemental checklist of *quick tips*, which reinforce ten important points relating to accessible Web-site design. More information on the WAI Quick Tips can be found at **www.w3.org/WAI/References/Quicktips**.

24.4 Providing Alternatives for Images

One important WAI requirement specifies that every image on a Web page should be accompanied by a textual description that clearly defines the purpose of the image. To accomplish this task, Web developers can use the **alt** attribute of the **img** and **input** tags to include a textual equivalent for each item.

Web developers who do not use the **alt** attribute to provide text equivalents increase the difficulties that people with visual impairments experience in navigating the Web. Specialized *user agent*s (or *accessibility aids*), such as *screen readers* (programs that allow users to hear all text and text descriptions displayed on their screens) and *braille displays* (devices that receive data from screen-reading software and then output the data as braille), enable people with visual impairments to access text-based information that normally is displayed on the screen. A user agent visually interprets Web-page source code and translates it into information that is accessible to people with impairments. Web browsers, such as Microsoft Internet Explorer and Netscape Communicator, and the screen readers mentioned throughout this chapter are examples of user agents.

Similarly, Web pages that do not provide text equivalents for video and audio clips are difficult for people with visual and hearing impairments to access. Screen readers cannot interpret images, movies and most other non-XHTML content from these Web pages. However, by providing multimedia-based information in a variety of ways (i.e., using the **alt** attribute or providing in-line descriptions of images), Web designers can help maximize the accessibility of their sites' content.

Web designers should provide useful and appropriate text equivalents in the **alt** attribute for use by nonvisual user agents. For example, if the **alt** attribute describes a sales growth chart, it should provide a brief summary of the data, but should not describe the data in the chart. Instead, a complete description of the chart's data should be included in the ***longdesc*** (long description) *attribute*, which is intended to augment the **alt** attribute's description. The **longdesc** attribute contains a link to a Web page describing the image or multimedia content. Currently, most Web browsers do not support the **longdesc** attribute. An alternative for the **longdesc** attribute is *D-link*, which provides descriptive text about graphs and charts. More information on D-links can be obtained at the *CORDA Technologies* Web site (**www.corda.com**).

The use of a screen reader to facilitate Web–site navigation can be time-consuming and frustrating, for screen readers cannot interpret pictures and other graphical content. The inclusion of a link at the top of each Web page that provides direct access to the page's content could allow disabled users to bypass long lists of navigation links or other irrelevant or inaccessible content. This jump can save time and eliminate frustration for individuals with visual impairments.

Emacspeak (**www.cs.cornell.edu/home/raman/emacspeak/emacspeak.html**) is a screen interface that improves the quality of Internet access for individuals with visual disabilities by translating text to voice data. The open-source product also implements auditory icons that play various sounds. Emacspeak can be customized with Linux operating systems and provides support for the IBM *ViaVoice* speech engine.

In March 2001, We Media introduced the *WeMedia Browser*, which allows people with vision impairments and cognitive disabilities (such as dyslexia) to use the Internet more conveniently. The WeMedia Browser enhances traditional browser capabilities by providing oversized buttons and keystroke commands that assist in navigation. The browser "reads" text that the user selects, allowing the user to control the speed and volume at which the browser reads the contents of the Web page. The WeMedia Browser free download is available at **www.wemedia.com**.

IBM Home Page Reader (HPR) is another browser that "reads" text selected by the user. The HPR uses IBM ViaVoice technology to synthesize an audible voice. A trial version of HPR is available at **www-3.ibm.com/able/hpr.html**.

24.5 Maximizing Readability by Focusing on Structure

Many Web sites use XHTML tags for aesthetic purposes, ignoring the tags' intended functions. For example, the **<h1>** heading tag often is used erroneously to make text large and bold rather than to indicate a major section head for content. This practice might create a desired visual effect, but it also causes problems for screen readers. When the screen–reader software encounters the **<h1>** tag, it might verbally inform the user that a new section has been reached. If this is not in fact the case, the **<h1>** tag might confuse users. Therefore, developers should use **h1** only in accordance with its XHTML specifications (e.g., to markup a heading that introduces an important section of a document). Instead of using **h1** to make text large and bold, developers can use CSS (Cascading Style Sheets) or XSL (eXtensible Stylesheet Language) to format and style the text. For further examples of this nature, refer to the WCAG 1.0 Web site at **www.w3.org/TR/WCAG10**. [*Note:* The **<strong>** tag also can be used to make text bold; however, screen readers emphasize bold text, which affects the inflection of what is spoken.]

Another accessibility issue is *readability*. When creating a Web page intended for the general public, it is important to consider the reading level (i.e., level of difficulty to read and understand) at which content is written. Web-site designers can make their sites easier to read by using shorter words. Furthermore, slang terms and other nontraditional language could be problematic for readers from other countries, and developers should limit the use of such words.

WCAG 1.0 suggests using a paragraph's first sentence to convey its subject. When a Web site states the point of a paragraph in its first sentence, it is easier both to find crucial information and to bypass unwanted material.

The *Gunning Fog Index*, a formula that produces a readability grade when applied to a text sample, can evaluate a Web site's readability. To obtain more information about the Gunning Fog Index, visit **www.trainingpost.org/3-2-inst.htm**.

24.6 Accessibility in Visual Studio .NET

Visual Studio .NET provides guidelines for the design of accessible software within its programming environment. For instance, one guideline recommends reserving the use of color for the enhancement or emphasis of information, instead of for aesthetic purposes. A second guideline recommends providing information about objects (e.g., desktop icons and open windows) to the accessibility aids (specialized software that renders applications to individuals with disabilities). Such information might include the name, location and size of a window. A third guideline recommends designing user interfaces so that they can accommodate user preferences. For example, people with visual disabilities should be able to modify the font size of a user interface. A fourth guideline recommends allowing users to adjust the time setting for applications that have time constraints. For example, users with mobility or speech disabilities might experience difficulty when using applications that require users to enter input within a predetermined period of time (such as 10 seconds). However, if such applications provide adjustable time settings, users can modify the settings to suit their needs.

In addition to suggesting guidelines that help developers create accessible applications, Visual Studio .NET also offers features that enable disabled individuals to use the development environment itself. For example, users can enlarge icons and text, customize the toolbox and keyboard and rearrange windows. The next subsections illustrate these capabilities.

24.6.1 Enlarging Toolbar Icons

To enlarge icons in Visual Studio .NET, select **Customize** from the **Tools** menu. In the **Customize** window's **Options** tab, select the **Large Icons** check box (Fig. 24.3). Then, select **Close**. Figure 24.4 depicts the enlarged icons on the Visual Studio development window.

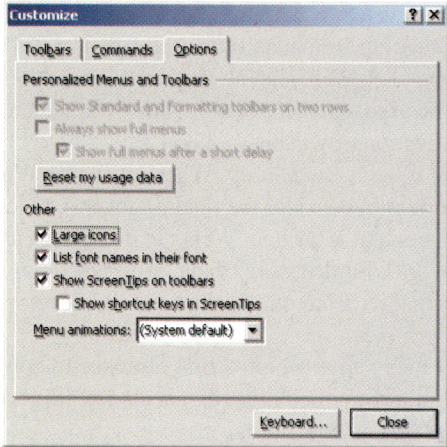

Fig. 24.3 Enlarging icons using the **Customize** feature.

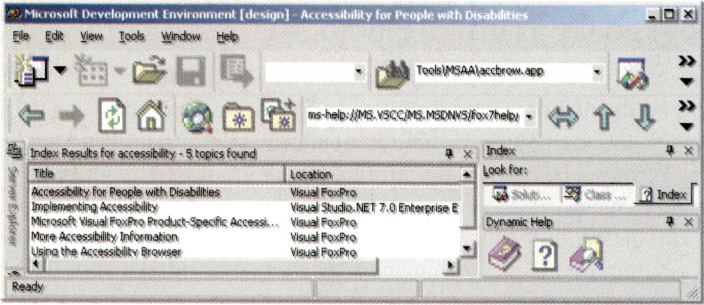

Fig. 24.4 Enlarged icons in the development window.

24.6.2 Enlarging the Text

Visual Studio uses the default operating-system font settings when displaying text. However, some individuals cannot read these default font settings, so the applications are inaccessible for them. To remedy this, Visual Studio allows users to modify the font size. Select **Options** from the **Tools** menu. In the **Options** window, open the **Environment** directory and choose **Fonts and Colors**. In the **Show settings for** drop-down box, select **Text Editor**. In the **Font** drop-down box, select a different style of font, and, in the **Size** drop-down box, select a different font size. Figure 24.5 depicts the **Text Editor** before we modified the font size, Fig. 24.6 shows the **Options** window with new font settings and Fig. 24.7 displays the **Text Editor** after the changes have been applied.

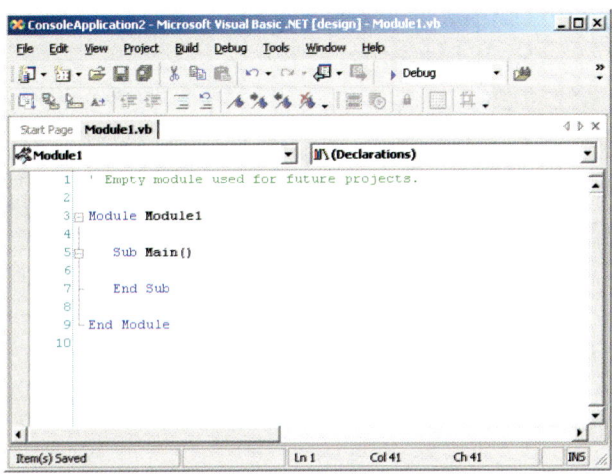

Fig. 24.5 **Text Editor** before modifying the font size.

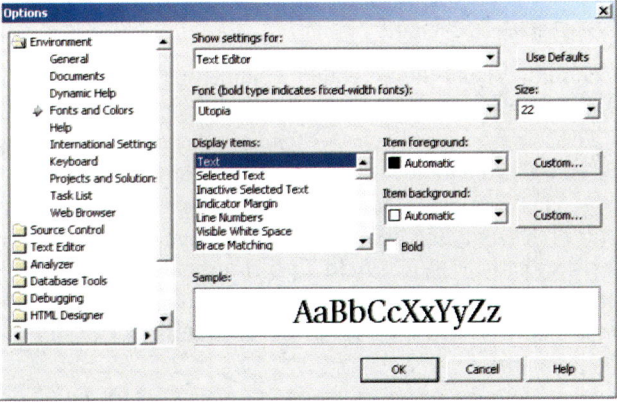

Fig. 24.6 Enlarging text in the **Options** window.

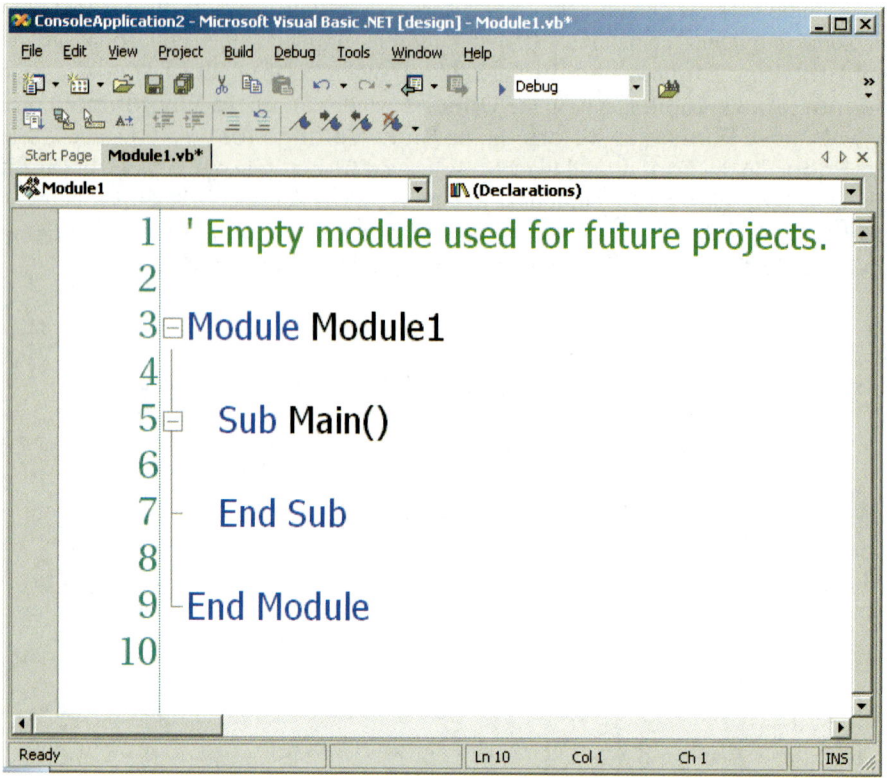

Fig. 24.7 **Text Editor** after the font size is modified.

24.6.3 Modifying the Toolbox

The **Toolbox** feature of Visual Studio contains numerous design elements that facilitate the creation of Web applications; however, some developers might use only a few of these design elements. To accommodate the needs of individual developers, Visual Studio allows programmers to customize the toolbox by creating new tabs and then inserting design elements into the tabs. This eliminates the need for users with disabilities to navigate among multiple tabs or scroll through long lists in search of design elements. To create a new tab, right-click any existing tab and select **Add Tab** from the context menu. In the text box, type an identifier for the tab (such as "Frequently Used") and click *Enter*. By default, the **Pointer** element is placed in all tabs (Fig. 24.8). The **Pointer** element simply allows the cursor to function normally.

To insert elements into the newly created tab, select **Customize Toolbox** from the **Tools** menu. In the **.NET Framework Components** tab, select the elements to include in the new tab, and click **OK**. The selected elements will now appear in the tab.

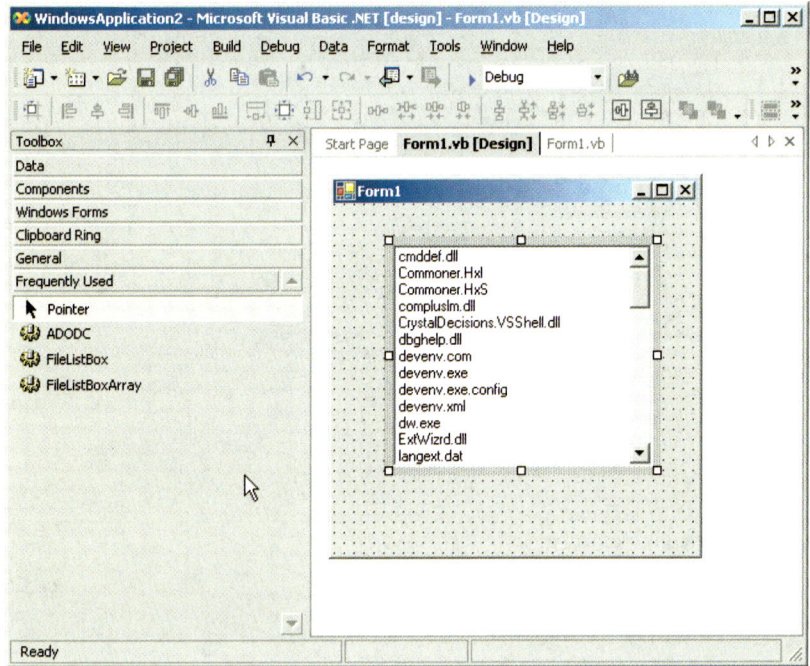

Fig. 24.8 Adding tabs to the **Toolbox**.

24.6.4 Modifying the Keyboard

Another accessibility feature in Visual Studio .NET allows individuals with disabilities to customize their keyboards by creating *shortcut keys* (i.e., combinations of keyboard keys that, when pressed together, perform frequent tasks; for example *Ctrl + V* causes text to be pasted from the clipboard). To create a shortcut key, begin by selecting **Options** from the **Tools** menu. In the **Options** window, select the **Keyboard** item from the **Environment** directory. From the **Keyboard mapping scheme** drop-down list, select a scheme, and click the **Save As** button. Then, assign a name to the scheme in the **Save Scheme** dialog box, and click **OK**. Enter the task of the shortcut key in the **Show commands containing** text box. For example, to create a shortcut key for the paste function, enter **Paste** in the text box—or, from the selection list directly below the text box, select the proper task. Then, in the **Use new shortcut** drop-down list, select the applications that will use the shortcut key. If the shortcut key will be used in all applications, select **Global**. Finally, in the **Press shortcut key(s)** text box, assign a shortcut key to the task in the form *non-text key + text key*. Valid non-text keys include *Ctrl*, *Shift* and *Alt*; valid text keys include A–Z, inclusive. [*Note*: To enter a non-text key, select the key itself—do not type the word *Ctrl*, *Shift* or *Alt*. It is possible to include more than one non-text key as part of a shortcut key. Do not enter the + symbol.] Thus, a valid shortcut key might be *Ctrl+Alt+D*. After assigning a shortcut key, select **Assign** and then **OK**. Figure 24.9 illustrates the process of creating a shortcut key for the `NewBreakpoint` function. The shortcut key (*Ctrl+Alt+D*) is valid only in the **Text Editor**.

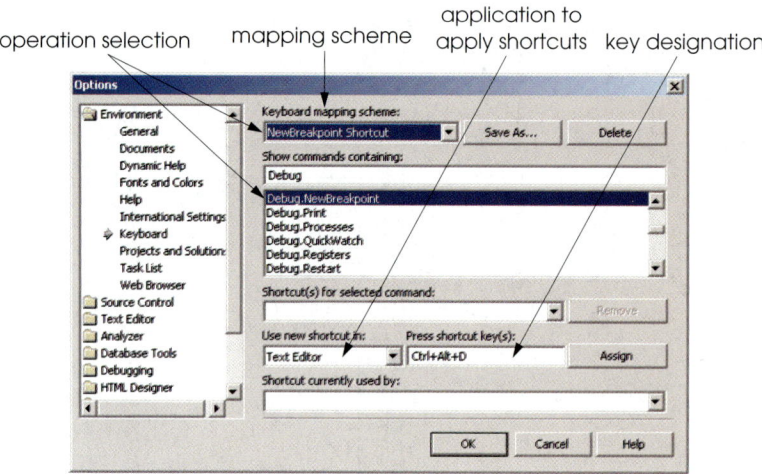

Fig. 24.9 Shortcut key creation.

24.6.5 Rearranging Windows

Some screen readers have difficulty interpreting user interfaces that include multiple tabs, because most screen readers can read information on only one screen. To accommodate such screen readers, Visual Studio allows developers to customize their user interfaces so that only the console window appears. To remove tabs, select **Options** from the **Tools** menu. Then, in the **Options** window, select the **General** item from the **Environment** directory. In the **Settings** section, select the **MDI environment** radio button, and click **OK**. Figure 24.10 depicts the **Options** window, and Fig. 24.11 illustrates a console window with and without tabs.

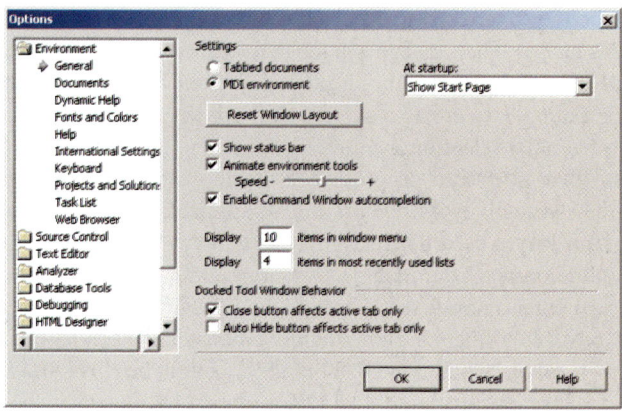

Fig. 24.10 Removing tabs from the Visual Studio environment.

Chapter 24 Accessibility 1215

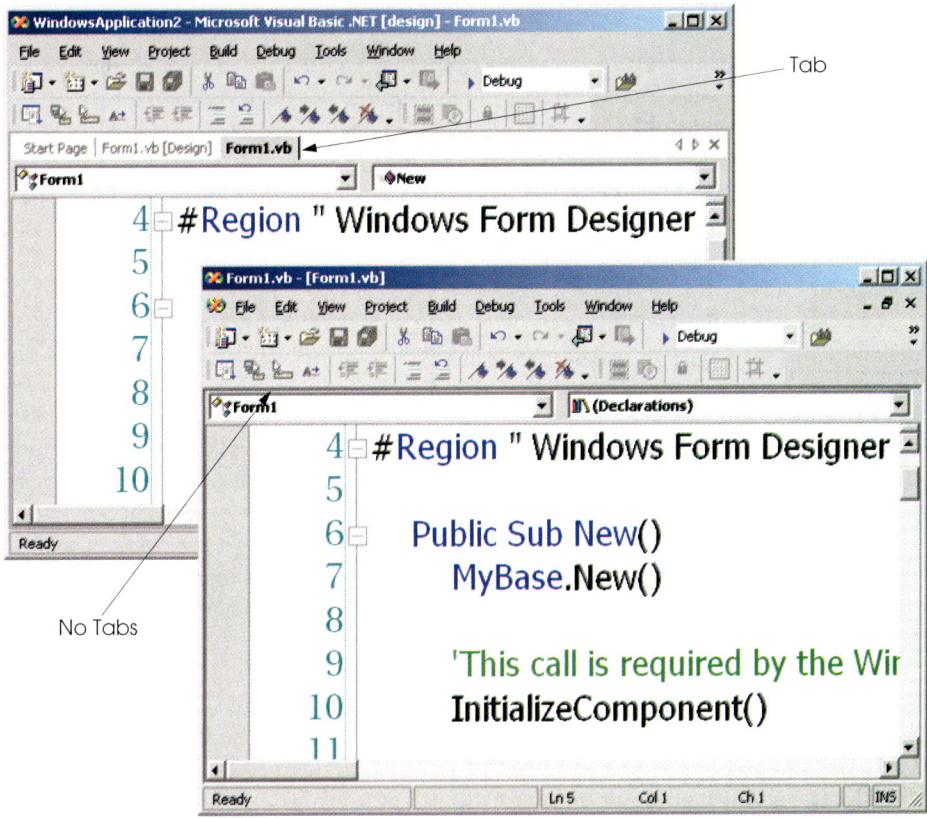

Fig. 24.11 Console windows with tabs and without tabs.

24.7 Accessibility in Visual Basic

We now discuss options that Visual Basic programmers have for designing applications to be more accessible to people with disabilities. It is important that applications be geared toward not only the average user—with some modifications, it is possible to reach a variety of users with disabilities. Some general guidelines for designing accessible applications follow.

1. Use larger-sized fonts—this aids people with visual impairments see the text.
2. Create flexible applications that provide keyboard shortcuts for all features within the application—this allows users to use the application without a mouse.
3. Allow information to be conveyed to the user both in a visual and in an audio manner.
4. Use graphics and images whenever helpful—visual cues may provide help to people who have trouble reading text on the screen.
5. Never signal information through sound only—someone accessing the information might not have speakers or might be hearing impaired.[1]

6. Test the application without using either a mouse or a keyboard. Accessing an application's functionality should not be limited to one input device.

For more information on these and other design guidelines for accessible applications, please refer to the Visual Studio .NET documentation under the **overview** subsection of the index topic **accessibility**. This section provides links to discussions of how to design more accessible Windows and ASP.NET applications.

One specific way programmers can make their applications more accessible is to use a *text-to-speech* control in their programs. A text-to-speech control can convert text into speech—a computerized voice speaks the words provided as text to the control. This helps people who cannot see the screen.

Another way to make applications more accessible is to use *tab stops*. Tab stops occur when the user presses the *Tab* key—this causes the focus to transfer to another control. The order in which the controls gain focus is called the *tab order*. This order is determined by the **TabIndex** value of the controls—controls gain focus in ascending order. Each control also has a **TabStop** property—if it is **True**, the control is included in the tab order, otherwise, it is not. By using the **TabIndex** and **TabStop** properties, it is easier to create more navigable applications. If these properties are set incorrectly, the logical ordering of the application may not be maintained. Consider an application that has **TextBox**es for inputting the first name, the last name and address of a user. The logical tab order would take the user from the **TextBox** to input the first name, to the one to input the last name and the address.

A third and important way for programmers to increase accessibility of their applications is to use the classes provided by .NET. Class **Control**, for example, has many properties designed for conveying information to accessibility applications. These applications can then, in turn, find the required information stored as properties. Figure 24.12 lists some properties of class **Control** that are designed to provide information to accessibility applications.

Property	Purpose
`AccessibleDescription`	Describes the control to an accessibility client application. For example, a **CheckBox** that says **"New User"** would not need more of a description, but a **CheckBox** with an image of a cat would have its **AccessibleDescription** property set to something like **"A CheckBox with an image of a cat on it"**.
`AccessibleName`	Contains a short name or identifier for the control.
`AccessibleRole`	Member of the **AccessibleRole** enumeration. Represents the role of this control in the application—this may help the accessibility-client application determine what actions it should take.

Fig. 24.12 Properties of class **Control** related to accessibility (part 1 of 2).

---

1. "Basic Principles of Accessible Design," *.NET Framework Developer's Guide*, Visual Studio .NET Online Help

Property	Purpose
`IsAccessible`	Contains a `Boolean` value specifying whether this control is visible to accessibility-client applications.

Fig. 24.12 Properties of class `Control` related to accessibility (part 2 of 2).

    The application in Fig. 24.13 uses the text-to-speech control, tab stops and accessibility-related properties. It consists of a **Form** with three **Label**s, three **TextBox**es and a **Button** to submit the information. Submitting the information simply terminates the application—the application is intended only to show the user of the text-to-speech control.

    The accessibility features in this program work as follows: When the mouse is over a **Label**, the text-to-speech control prompts the user to enter the appropriate information in the **TextBox** to the right. If the mouse is over a **TextBox**, the contents of the **TextBox** are spoken. Lastly, if the mouse is over the **Button**, the user is told that the button should be clicked to submit the information. The tab order is the following: the **TextBox**es where the user inputs the name, phone number and password, then the **Button**. The **Label**s and text-to-speech control are not included in the tab order because the user cannot interact with them and including them would serve no purpose. The accessibility properties are set so that accessibility-client applications will get the appropriate information about the controls. Please note that only the relevant code generated by Visual Studio .NET is included in Fig. 24.13. To use the text-to-speech control, first add it to the **Toolbox**. To do so, select **Customize Toolbox** from the **Tools** menu. The **Customize Toolbox** dialog pops up—check the box next to the **TextToSpeech Class** option. Click **OK** to dismiss the dialog box. The **VText** control is now in the **ToolBox** and can be dragged onto a form like any other control.

```vb
1   ' Fig. 24.13: TextToSpeech.vb
2   ' Voice user information on selected Label and TextBox
3   ' components.
4
5   Imports System.Windows.Forms
6
7   ' helps users navigate a form with aid of audio cues
8   Public Class FrmTextToSpeech
9      Inherits System.Windows.Forms.Form
10
11     ' name, phone number and password labels
12     Friend WithEvents lblName As Label
13     Friend WithEvents lblPhoneNumber As Label
14     Friend WithEvents lblPassword As Label
15
16     ' name, phone number and password textboxes
17     Friend WithEvents txtName As TextBox
18     Friend WithEvents txtPhoneNumber As TextBox
19     Friend WithEvents txtPassword As TextBox
20
```

Fig. 24.13 Application with accessibility features (part 1 of 4).

```vbnet
21      ' TextToSpeech engine
22      Friend WithEvents speaker As AxHTTSLib.AxTextToSpeech
23
24      ' submit button
25      Friend WithEvents cmdSubmit As System.Windows.Forms.Button
26
27      ' Visual Studio .NET generated code
28
29      ' inform user label name
30      Private Sub lblName_MouseHover(ByVal sender As Object, _
31         ByVal e As System.EventArgs) Handles lblName.MouseHover
32
33         ' voice label name
34         VoiceLabelName(sender)
35      End Sub ' lblName_MouseHover
36
37      ' inform user label name
38      Private Sub lblPhoneNumber_MouseHover( _
39         ByVal sender As Object, ByVal e As System.EventArgs) _
40         Handles lblPhoneNumber.MouseHover
41
42         ' voice label name
43         VoiceLabelName(sender)
44      End Sub ' lblPhoneNumber_MouseHover
45
46      ' inform user label name
47      Private Sub lblPassword_MouseHover( _
48         ByVal sender As Object, ByVal e As System.EventArgs) _
49         Handles lblPassword.MouseHover
50
51         ' voice label name
52         VoiceLabelName(sender)
53      End Sub ' lblPassword_MouseHover
54
55      ' inform user value input in textbox
56      Private Sub txtName_MouseHover( _
57         ByVal sender As Object, ByVal e As System.EventArgs) _
58         Handles txtName.MouseHover
59
60         ' speak textbox state
61         VoiceTextBoxValue(sender, "Name TextBox")
62      End Sub ' txtName_MouseHover
63
64      ' inform user value input in textbox
65      Private Sub txtPhoneNumber_MouseHover( _
66         ByVal sender As Object, ByVal e As System.EventArgs) _
67         Handles txtPhoneNumber.MouseHover
68
69         ' speak textbox state
70         VoiceTextBoxValue(sender, "Phone Number TextBox")
71      End Sub ' txtPhoneNumber_MouseHover
72
```

Fig. 24.13 Application with accessibility features (part 2 of 4).

```vbnet
73        ' inform user value input in textbox
74        Private Sub txtPassword_MouseHover( _
75           ByVal sender As Object, ByVal e As System.EventArgs) _
76           Handles txtPassword.MouseHover
77
78           ' speak textbox state
79           VoiceTextBoxValue(sender, "Password TextBox")
80        End Sub ' txtPassword_MouseHover
81
82        ' inform user to purpose of submit button
83        Private Sub cmdSubmit_MouseHover( _
84           ByVal sender As Object, ByVal e As System.EventArgs) _
85           Handles cmdSubmit.MouseHover
86
87           ' tell user to click button to submit information
88           speaker.Speak("Click on this button to submit your " & _
89              "information")
90        End Sub ' cmdSubmit_MouseHover
91
92        ' thank user for information submition
93        Private Sub cmdSubmit_Click(ByVal sender As Object, _
94           ByVal e As System.EventArgs) Handles cmdSubmit.Click
95
96           speaker.Speak("Thank you, your information has been " & _
97              "submitted.")
98
99           Application.Exit()
100       End Sub ' cmdSubmit_Click
101
102       ' voices textboxes' states
103       Private Sub VoiceTextBoxValue(ByVal sender As TextBox, _
104          ByVal sourceFieldName As String)
105          Dim inputValue As String
106
107          ' if textbox empty, voice "Nothing"
108          If sender.Text = "" Then
109             inputValue = "Nothing"
110          Else
111             inputValue = sender.Text
112          End If
113
114          ' voice textbox state
115          speaker.Speak("You have entered " & inputValue & _
116             " in the " & sourceFieldName)
117       End Sub ' VoiceTextBoxValue
118
119       ' voice label states
120       Private Sub VoiceLabelName(ByVal sender As Label)
121
122          ' if mouse over Label, tell user to enter information
123          speaker.Speak("Please enter your " & sender.Text & _
124             " in the textbox to the right")
125       End Sub ' VoiceLabelName
```

Fig. 24.13 Application with accessibility features (part 3 of 4).

```
126
127         ' set each control's IsAccessible property to true
128         Private Sub FrmTextToSpeech_Load(ByVal sender As System.Object, _
129             ByVal e As System.EventArgs) Handles MyBase.Load
130
131             Dim current As Control
132
133             For Each current In Me.Controls
134                 current.IsAccessible = True
135             Next
136
137         End Sub ' FrmTextToSpeech_Load
138
139     End Class ' FrmTextToSpeech
```

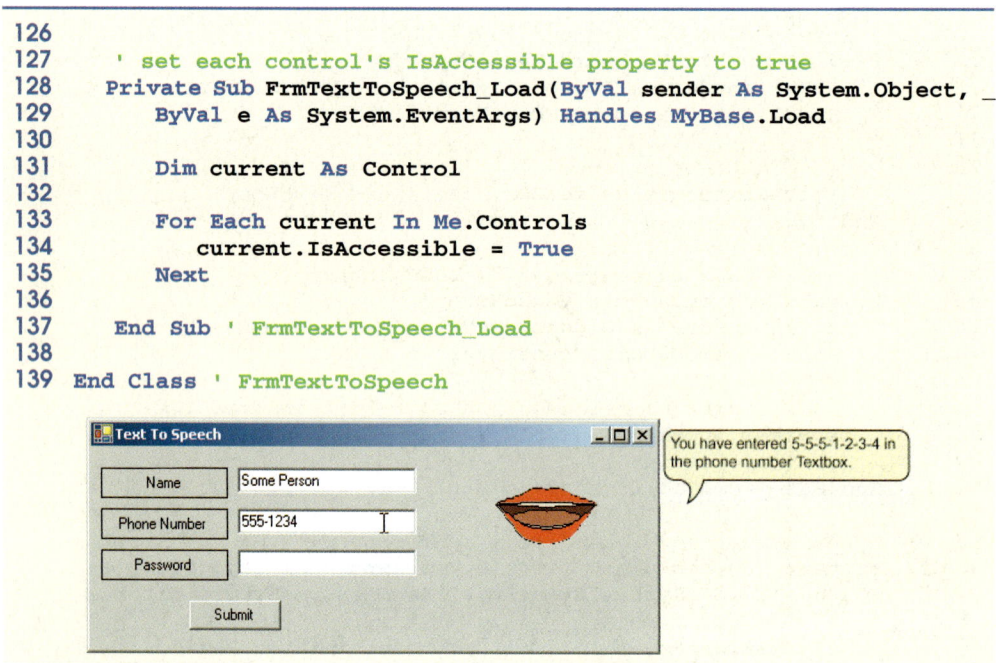

Fig. 24.13 Application with accessibility features (part 4 of 4).

The application has three **Label**s, to prompt for the user's name, phone number and password. There are three **TextBox**es to accept the user's input and a **Button** for the user to click when done. Line 22 declares a text-to-speech control named **speaker**. We want the user to hear audio descriptions of controls when the mouse is over them. Lines 30–53 define the **MouseHover** event handlers for the **Label**s, and lines 56–80 define the **MouseHover** event handlers for the **TextBox**es.

Event handlers **lblName_MouseHover**, **lblPhoneNumber_MouseHover**, and **lblPassword_MouseHover** call method **VoiceLabelName** (lines 120–125), which generates the appropriate audio for each **Label**. Method **VoiceLabelName** uses the **Label** name to construct a **String** that describes that the user should enter the corresponding information in the appropriate **TextBox** (lines 123–124). Lines 123–124 pass this **String** to **speaker**'s method **Speak**. Method **Speak** converts the **String** argument to speech. As is indicated in the output, the image is animated while the **String** argument is being spoken.

A similar process is performed to determine when the mouse hovers over a **TextBox**. The event handlers that handle these events are **txtName_MouseHover**, **txtPhoneNumber_MouseHover** and **txtPassword_MouseHover** in lines 56–80; they call method **VoiceTextBoxValue** (lines 103–117) to generate each **TextBox**'s appropriate audio. Method **VoiceTextBoxValue** constructs a **String** that describes the contents of a given **TextBox**. Lines 108–112 ensure that, if a **TextBox** is empty, the text that will be converted to speech will indicate that the value in the **TextBox** is pronounced as **"Nothing"** (as opposed to **""**). If the value of **TextBox** is not empty, the value input into the **TextBox** by the user will appear in the **String** that will be converted to speech. Lines 115–116 call **speaker**'s method **Speak** to convert the constructed **String** to speech.

Method **cmdSubmit_Click** (lines 93–100) executes when the user clicks **Button Submit**. Method **cmdSubmit_Click** calls **speaker**'s method **Speak**, providing as a **String** argument a thank-you message. Method **cmdSubmit_Click** then exits the application.

In the **Properties** window, we set the **Text** property of **cmdSubmit** to **"&Submit"**. This is an example of providing keyboard access to the functionality of the application. Recall that in Chapter 13 (Graphical User Interface Concepts: Part 2), we assigned shortcut keys by placing a **"&"** in front of the letter to be the shortcut key. Here, we do the same for **cmdSubmit**—pressing **Alt+S** on the keyboard is equivalent to clicking **Button Submit**.

The tab order in this application is established through the setting of the **TabIndex** and **TabStop** properties. The **TabIndex** properties of the controls are assigned through the **Properties** window. The **TextBox**es are assigned tab indices 1–3, in order of their appearance (vertically) on the form. The **Button** has the tab index 4, and the rest of the controls have the tab indices 5–8. We want the tab order to include only the **TextBox**es and the **Button**. The default setting for the **TabStop** property of **Label**s is **False**—thus, we do not need to change it; it will not be included in the tab order. The **TabStop** property of **TextBox**es and **Button**s is **True**—we do not need to change it in those controls, either. The **TabStop** property of **speaker**, however, is **True** by default. We set it to **False**, indicating we do not want it included in the tab order. In general, those controls that the user cannot directly interact with should have their **TabStop** property set to **False**.

The last accessibility feature of this application involves setting the accessibility properties of the controls to allow client-accessibility applications to access and properly process the controls. We set the **AccessibleDescription** property of all the controls (including the **Form**) through the **Properties** window. We do the same for the **AccessibleName** properties of all the controls (including the **Form**). The **IsAccessible** property is not visible in the **Properties** window during design time, so we must write code to set it to **True**. Lines 133–135 loop through each of the controls on the **Form** and set each of their **IsAccessible** properties to **True**. The **Form** and all its controls will now be visible to client-accessibility applications.

24.8 Accessibility in XHTML Tables

Complex Web pages often contain tables that format content and present data. However, many screen readers are incapable of translating tables correctly unless developers design the tables with screen-reader requirements in mind. For example, the *CAST eReader*, a screen reader developed by the Center for Applied Special Technology (**www.cast.org**), starts at the top-left-hand cell and reads columns from left to right, then top to bottom. This technique of reading data from a table is done in a *linearized* manner. Figure 24.14 creates a simple table listing the cost of various fruits; later, we provide this table to the CAST eReader to demonstrate its linear reading of the table. The CAST eReader reads the table in Fig. 24.14 as follows:

```
Price of Fruit Fruit Price Apple $0.25 Orange $0.50 Banana
$1.00 Pineapple $2.00
```

```
 1  <?xml version = "1.0"?>
 2  <!DOCTYPE html PUBLIC "-//W3C//DTD XHTML 1.0 Strict//EN"
 3     "http://www.w3.org/TR/xhtml1/DTD/xhtml1-strict.dtd">
 4
 5  <!-- Fig. 24.14: withoutheaders.html -->
 6  <!-- Table without headers            -->
 7
 8  <html xmlns = "http://www.w3.org/1999/xhtml">
 9     <head>
10        <title>XHTML Table Without Headers</title>
11
12        <style type = "text/css">
13           body { background-color: #ccffaa;
14                  text-align: center }
15        </style>
16     </head>
17
18     <body>
19
20        <p>Price of Fruit</p>
21
22        <table border = "1" width = "50%">
23
24           <tr>
25              <td>Fruit</td>
26              <td>Price</td>
27           </tr>
28
29           <tr>
30              <td>Apple</td>
31              <td>$0.25</td>
32           </tr>
33
34           <tr>
35              <td>Orange</td>
36              <td>$0.50</td>
37           </tr>
38
39           <tr>
40              <td>Banana</td>
41              <td>$1.00</td>
42           </tr>
43
44           <tr>
45              <td>Pineapple</td>
46              <td>$2.00</td>
47           </tr>
48
49        </table>
50
51     </body>
52  </html>
```

Fig. 24.14 XHTML table without accessibility modifications (part 1 of 2).

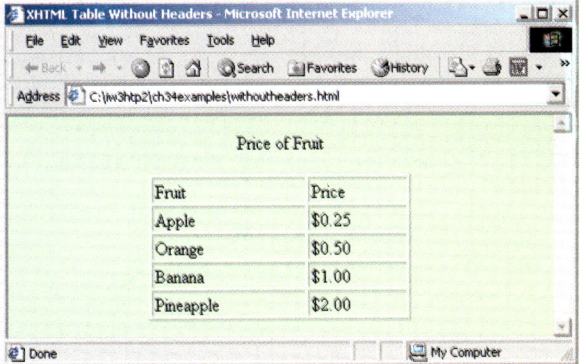

Fig. 24.14 XHTML table without accessibility modifications (part 2 of 2).

This reading does not present the content of the table adequately: The reading neither specifies caption and header information nor links data contained in cells to the column headers that describe them. WCAG 1.0 recommends using Cascading Style Sheets (CSS) instead of tables, unless the tables' content linearizes in an understandable manner.

If the table in Fig. 24.14 were large, the screen reader's linearized reading would be even more confusing to users. By modifying the **<td>** tag with the **headers** attribute and by modifying *header cells* (cells specified by the **<th>** tag) with the **id** attribute, a table will be read as intended. Figure 24.15 demonstrates how these modifications change the way in which a screen reader interprets a table.

```
1   <?xml version = "1.0"?>
2   <!DOCTYPE html PUBLIC "-//W3C//DTD XHTML 1.0 Strict//EN"
3      "http://www.w3.org/TR/xhtml1/DTD/xhtml1-strict.dtd">
4
5   <!-- Fig. 24.15: withheaders.html -->
6   <!-- Table with headers                -->
7
8   <html xmlns = "http://www.w3.org/1999/xhtml">
9      <head>
10        <title>XHTML Table With Headers</title>
11
12        <style type = "text/css">
13           body { background-color: #ccffaa;
14                  text-align: center }
15        </style>
16     </head>
17
18     <body>
19
20        <!-- This table uses the id and headers attributes to      -->
21        <!-- ensure readability by text-based browsers. It also    -->
22        <!-- uses a summary attribute, used by screen readers to   -->
23        <!-- describe the table.                                   -->
```

Fig. 24.15 Table optimized for screen reading using attribute **headers** (part 1 of 2).

```
24
25          <table width = "50%" border = "1"
26             summary = "This table uses th elements and id and
27             headers attributes to make the table readable
28             by screen readers">
29
30             <caption><strong>Price of Fruit</strong></caption>
31
32             <tr>
33                <th id = "fruit">Fruit</th>
34                <th id = "price">Price</th>
35             </tr>
36
37             <tr>
38                <td headers = "fruit">Apple</td>
39                <td headers = "price">$0.25</td>
40             </tr>
41
42             <tr>
43                <td headers = "fruit">Orange</td>
44                <td headers = "price">$0.50</td>
45             </tr>
46
47             <tr>
48                <td headers = "fruit">Banana</td>
49                <td headers = "price">$1.00</td>
50             </tr>
51
52             <tr>
53                <td headers = "fruit">Pineapple</td>
54                <td headers = "price">$2.00</td>
55             </tr>
56
57          </table>
58
59       </body>
60   </html>
```

Fig. 24.15 Table optimized for screen reading using attribute **headers** (part 2 of 2).

This table does not appear to be different from a standard XHTML table shown in Fig. 24.14. However, the formatting of this table allows a screen reader to read the contained data more intelligently. A screen reader vocalizes the data from the table in Fig. 24.15 as follows:

```
Caption: Price of Fruit
Summary: This table uses th elements and id and headers
attributes to make the table readable by screen readers
Fruit: Apple, Price: $0.25
Fruit: Orange, Price: $0.50
Fruit: Banana, Price: $1.00
Fruit: Pineapple, Price: $2.00
```

Every cell in the table is preceded by its corresponding header when read by the screen reader. This format helps the listener understand the table. The **headers** attribute is intended specifically for use in tables that hold large amounts of data. Most small tables linearize fairly well as long as the `<th>` tag is used properly. We also suggest using the **summary** attribute and **caption** element to enhance clarity. To view additional examples that demonstrate how to make tables accessible, visit **www.w3.org/TR/WCAG**.

24.9 Accessibility in XHTML Frames

Web designers often use frames to display more than one XHTML file in a single browser window. Frames are a convenient way to ensure that certain content always displays on the screen. Unfortunately, frames often lack proper descriptions, and this prevents users with text-based browsers and users listening via speech synthesizers from navigating the Web site.

A site that uses frames must provide a meaningful descriptions of each frame in the frame's `<title>` tag. Examples of good titles include, "*Navigation Frame*" and, "*Main Content Frame*." Users navigating via text-based browsers, such as Lynx, must choose which frame they want to open; descriptive titles make this choice simpler. However, the assignment of titles to frames does not solve all the navigation problems associated with frames. Web designers should use the `<noframes>` tag, which provides alternative content for browsers that do not support frames.

Look-and-Feel Observation 24.1
Always provide titles for frames to ensure that user agents that do not support frames have alternatives.

Look-and-Feel Observation 24.2
Include a title for each frame's contents with the **frame** *element; if possible, provide links to the individual pages within the frameset, so that users still can navigate through the Web pages. To provide alternate content to browsers that do not support frames, use the* `<noframes>` *tag. This also improves access for browsers that offer limited support for frames.*

WCAG 1.0 suggests using Cascading Style Sheets (CSS) as an alternative to frames, because CSS can provide similar functionality and is highly customizible. Unfortunately, the ability to display multiple XHTML documents in a single browser window requires the complete support of HTML 4, which is not widespread. However, the second generation of Cascading Style Sheets (CSS2) can display a single document as if it were several documents. CSS2 is not yet fully supported by many user agents.

24.10 Accessibility in XML

XML gives developers the freedom to create new markup languages. Although this feature provides many advantages, the new languages might not incorporate accessibility features. To prevent the proliferation of inaccessible languages, the WAI is developing guidelines—the *XML Guidelines (XML GL)*—to facilitate the creation of accessible XML documents. The XML Guidelines recommend including a text description, similar to XHTML's `<alt>` tag, for each non-text object on a page. To enhance accessibility further, element types should allow grouping and classification and should identify important content. Without an accessible user interface, other efforts to implement accessibility are less effective. Therefore, it is essential to create style sheets that can produce multiple outputs, including document outlines.

Many XML languages, including Synchronized Multimedia Integration Language (SMIL) and Scalable Vector Graphics (SVG), have implemented several of the WAI guidelines. The WAI XML Accessibility Guidelines can be found at **www.w3.org/WAI/PF/xmlgl.htm**.

24.11 Using Voice Synthesis and Recognition with VoiceXML™

A joint effort by AT&T®, IBM®, Lucent™ and Motorola® has created an XML vocabulary that marks up information for use by *speech synthesizers*—tools that enable computers to speak to users. This technology, called *VoiceXML*, can provide tremendous benefits to people with visual impairments and to people who are illiterate. VoiceXML-enabled applications read Web pages to the user and then employ *speech recognition* technology to understand words spoken into a microphone. An example of a speech-recognition tool is IBM's *ViaVoice* (**www-4.ibm.com/software/speech**). To learn more about speech recognition and synthesis, consult Chapter 16, Graphics and Multimedia.

The VoiceXML interpreter and the VoiceXML browser process VoiceXML. In the future, Web browsers might incorporate these interpreters. VoiceXML is derived from XML, so VoiceXML is platform independent. When a VoiceXML document is loaded, a *voice server* sends a message to the VoiceXML browser and begins a verbal conversation between the user and the computer.

The IBM *WebSphere Voice Server SDK 1.5* is a VoiceXML interpreter that can be used to test VoiceXML documents on the desktop. To download the VoiceServer SDK, visit **www.alphaworks.ibm.com/tech/voiceserversdk**. [*Note*: To run the VoiceXML program in Fig. 24.16, download *Java 2 Platform Standard Edition* (Java SDK) 1.3 from **www.java.sun.com/j2se/1.3**. Installation instructions for both the VoiceServerSDK and the Java SDK are located on the Deitel & Associates, Inc., Web site at **www.deitel.com**.]

Figure 24.16 and Fig. 24.17 depict examples of VoiceXML that could be included on a Web site. The computer speaks a document's text to the user, and the text embedded in the VoiceXML tags enables verbal interaction between the user and the browser. The output included in Fig. 24.17 demonstrates a conversation that might take place between a user and a computer after this document is loaded.

```
 1  <?xml version = "1.0"?>
 2  <vxml version = "1.0">
 3
 4  <!-- Fig. 24.16: main.vxml -->
 5  <!-- Voice page            -->
 6
 7  <link next = "#home">
 8     <grammar>home</grammar>
 9  </link>
10
11  <link next = "#end">
12     <grammar>exit</grammar>
13  </link>
14
15  <var name = "currentOption" expr = "'home'"/>
16
17  <form>
18     <block>
19        <emp>Welcome</emp> to the voice page of Deitel and
20        Associates. To exit any time say exit.
21        To go to the home page any time say home.
22     </block>
23
24     <subdialog src = "#home"/>
25  </form>
26
27  <menu id = "home">
28     <prompt count = "1" timeout = "10s">
29        You have just entered the Deitel home page.
30        Please make a selection by speaking one of the
31        following options:
32        <break msecs = "1000" />
33        <enumerate/>
34     </prompt>
35
36     <prompt count = "2">
37        Please say one of the following.
38        <break msecs = "1000" />
39        <enumerate/>
40     </prompt>
41
42     <choice next = "#about">About us</choice>
43     <choice next = "#directions">Driving directions</choice>
44     <choice next = "publications.vxml">Publications</choice>
45  </menu>
46
47  <form id = "about">
48     <block>
49        About Deitel and Associates, Inc.
50        Deitel and Associates, Inc. is an internationally
51        recognized corporate training and publishing
52        organization, specializing in programming languages,
53        Internet and World Wide Web technology and object
```

Fig. 24.16 Home page written in VoiceXML (part 1 of 2).

```
54          technology education. Deitel and Associates, Inc. is a
55          member of the World Wide Web Consortium. The company
56          provides courses on Java, C++, Visual Basic, C, Internet
57          and World Wide Web programming and Object Technology.
58          <assign name = "currentOption" expr = "'about'"/>
59          <goto next = "#repeat"/>
60       </block>
61    </form>
62
63    <form id = "directions">
64       <block>
65          Directions to Deitel and Associates, Inc.
66          We are located on Route 20 in Sudbury,
67          Massachusetts, equidistant from route
68          <sayas class = "digits">128</sayas> and route
69          <sayas class = "digits">495</sayas>.
70          <assign name = "currentOption" expr = "'directions'"/>
71          <goto next = "#repeat"/>
72       </block>
73    </form>
74
75    <form id = "repeat">
76       <field name = "confirm" type = "boolean">
77          <prompt>
78             To repeat say yes. To go back to home, say no.
79          </prompt>
80
81          <filled>
82             <if cond = "confirm == true">
83                <goto expr = "'#' + currentOption"/>
84             <else/>
85                <goto next = "#home"/>
86             </if>
87          </filled>
88
89       </field>
90    </form>
91
92    <form id = "end">
93       <block>
94          Thank you for visiting Deitel and Associates voice page.
95          Have a nice day.
96          <exit/>
97       </block>
98    </form>
99
100   </vxml>
```

Fig. 24.16 Home page written in VoiceXML (part 2 of 2).

A VoiceXML document contains a series of dialogs and subdialogs resulting in spoken interaction between the user and the computer. The **<form>** and **<menu>** tags implement the dialogs. A ***form*** element both presents information to the user and gathers data from the user. A **menu** element provides users with list options and then transfers control to another dialog to suit the user selection.

Lines 7–9 (of Fig. 24.16) use element **link** to create an active link to the home page. Attribute **next** specifies the URI navigated to when a user selects the link. Element **grammar** marks up the text that the user must speak to select the link. In the **link** element, we navigate to the element with **id home** when a user speaks the word **home**. Lines 11–13 use element **link** to create a link to **id end** when a user speaks the word **exit**.

Lines 17–25 create a form dialog using element **form**, which collects information from the user. Lines 18–22 present introductory text. Element **block**, which can exist only within a **form** element, groups together elements that perform an action or an event. Element **emp** indicates that a section of text should be spoken with emphasis. If the level of emphasis is not specified, then the default level—*moderate*—is used. Our example uses the default level. [*Note*: To specify an emphasis level, use the **level** attribute. This attribute accepts the following values: *strong*, *moderate*, *none* and *reduced*.]

The **menu** element in line 27 enables users to select the page to which they would like to link. The **choice** element, which always is part of either a **menu** or a **form**, presents the options. The **next** attribute indicates the page that is loaded when a user makes a selection. The user selects a **choice** element by speaking the text marked up between the tags into a microphone. In this example, the first and second **choice** elements in lines 42–43 transfer control to a *local dialog* (i.e., a location within the same document) when they are selected. The third **choice** element transfers the user to the document **publications.vxml**. Lines 28–34 use element **prompt** to instruct the user to make a selection. Attribute **count** maintains a record of the number of times that a prompt is spoken (i.e., each time the computer reads a prompt, **count** increments by one). The **count** attribute transfers control to another prompt once a certain limit has been reached. Attribute **timeout** specifies how long the program should wait after outputting the prompt for users to respond. In the event that the user does not respond before the timeout period expires, lines 36–40 provide a second, shorter prompt that reminds the user to make a selection.

When the user chooses the **publications** option, **publications.vxml** (Fig. 24.17) loads into the browser. Lines 107–113 define **link** elements that provide links to **main.vxml**. Lines 115–117 provide links to the **menu** element (lines 121–141), which asks users to select one of the following publications: Java, C or C++. The **form** elements in lines 143–217 describe books that correspond to these topics. Once the browser speaks the description, control transfers to the **form** element with an **id** attribute whose value equals **repeat** (lines 219–234).

Figure 24.18 provides a brief description of each VoiceXML tag that we used in the previous example (Fig. 24.17).

```
101   <?xml version = "1.0"?>
102   <vxml version = "1.0">
103
104   <!-- Fig. 24.17: publications.vxml         -->
105   <!-- Voice page for various publications  -->
```

Fig. 24.17 Publication page of Deitel and Associates' VoiceXML page (part 1 of 4).

```
106
107   <link next = "main.vxml#home">
108      <grammar>home</grammar>
109   </link>
110
111   <link next = "main.vxml#end">
112      <grammar>exit</grammar>
113   </link>
114
115   <link next = "#publication">
116      <grammar>menu</grammar>
117   </link>
118
119   <var name = "currentOption" expr = "'home'"/>
120
121   <menu id = "publication">
122
123      <prompt count = "1" timeout = "12s">
124         Following are some of our publications. For more
125         information visit our web page at www.deitel.com.
126         To repeat the following menu, say menu at any time.
127         Please select by saying one of the following books:
128         <break msecs = "1000" />
129         <enumerate/>
130      </prompt>
131
132      <prompt count = "2">
133         Please select from the following books.
134         <break msecs = "1000" />
135         <enumerate/>
136      </prompt>
137
138      <choice next = "#java">Java.</choice>
139      <choice next = "#c">C.</choice>
140      <choice next = "#cplus">C plus plus.</choice>
141   </menu>
142
143   <form id = "java">
144      <block>
145         Java How to program, third edition.
146         The complete, authoritative introduction to Java.
147         Java is revolutionizing software development with
148         multimedia-intensive, platform-independent,
149         object-oriented code for conventional, Internet,
150         Intranet and Extranet-based applets and applications.
151         This Third Edition of the world's most widely used
152         university-level Java textbook carefully explains
153         Java's extraordinary capabilities.
154         <assign name = "currentOption" expr = "'java'"/>
155         <goto next = "#repeat"/>
156      </block>
157   </form>
```

Fig. 24.17 Publication page of Deitel and Associates' VoiceXML page (part 2 of 4).

```
158
159  <form id = "c">
160     <block>
161        C How to Program, third edition.
162        This is the long-awaited, thorough revision to the
163        world's best-selling introductory C book! The book's
164        powerful "teach by example" approach is based on
165        more than 10,000 lines of live code, thoroughly
166        explained and illustrated with screen captures showing
167        detailed output.World-renowned corporate trainers and
168        best-selling authors Harvey and Paul Deitel offer the
169        most comprehensive, practical introduction to C ever
170        published with hundreds of hands-on exercises, more
171        than 250 complete programs written and documented for
172        easy learning, and exceptional insight into good
173        programming practices, maximizing performance, avoiding
174        errors, debugging, and testing. New features include
175        thorough introductions to C++, Java, and object-oriented
176        programming that build directly on the C skills taught
177        in this book; coverage of graphical user interface
178        development and C library functions; and many new,
179        substantial hands-on projects.For anyone who wants to
180        learn C, improve their existing C skills, and understand
181        how C serves as the foundation for C++, Java, and
182        object-oriented development.
183        <assign name = "currentOption" expr = "'c'"/>
184        <goto next = "#repeat"/>
185     </block>
186  </form>
187
188  <form id = "cplus">
189     <block>
190        The C++ how to program, second edition.
191        With nearly 250,000 sold, Harvey and Paul Deitel's C++
192        How to Program is the world's best-selling introduction
193        to C++ programming. Now, this classic has been thoroughly
194        updated! The new, full-color Third Edition has been
195        completely revised to reflect the ANSI C++ standard, add
196        powerful new coverage of object analysis and design with
197        UML, and give beginning C++ developers even better live
198        code examples and real-world projects. The Deitels' C++
199        How to Program is the most comprehensive, practical
200        introduction to C++ ever published with hundreds of
201        hands-on exercises, roughly 250 complete programs written
202        and documented for easy learning, and exceptional insight
203        into good programming practices, maximizing performance,
204        avoiding errors, debugging, and testing. This new Third
205        Edition covers every key concept and technique ANSI C++
206        developers need to master: control structures, functions,
207        arrays, pointers and strings, classes and data
```

Fig. 24.17 Publication page of Deitel and Associates' VoiceXML page (part 3 of 4).

```
208            abstraction, operator overloading, inheritance, virtual
209            functions, polymorphism, I/O, templates, exception
210            handling, file processing, data structures, and more. It
211            also includes a detailed introduction to Standard
212            Template Library containers, container adapters,
213            algorithms, and iterators.
214            <assign name = "currentOption" expr = "'cplus'"/>
215            <goto next = "#repeat"/>
216         </block>
217      </form>
218
219      <form id = "repeat">
220         <field name = "confirm" type = "boolean">
221
222            <prompt>
223               To repeat say yes. Say no, to go back to home.
224            </prompt>
225
226            <filled>
227               <if cond = "confirm == true">
228                  <goto expr = "'#' + currentOption"/>
229               <else/>
230                  <goto next = "#publication"/>
231               </if>
232            </filled>
233         </field>
234      </form>
235   </vxml>
```

> *Computer speaks:*
> **Welcome to the voice page of Deitel and Associates. To exit any time say exit. To go to the home page any time say home.**
>
> *User speaks:*
> **Home**
>
> *Computer speaks:*
> **You have just entered the Deitel home page. Please make a selection by speaking one of the following options: About us, Driving directions, Publications.**
>
> *User speaks:*
> **Driving directions**
>
> *Computer speaks:*
> **Directions to Deitel and Associates, Inc.**
> **We are located on Route 20 in Sudbury,**
> **Massachusetts, equidistant from route 128**
> **and route 495.**
> **To repeat say yes. To go back to home, say no.**

Fig. 24.17 Publication page of Deitel and Associates' VoiceXML page (part 4 of 4).

VoiceXML Tag	Description
`<assign>`	Assigns a value to a variable.
`<block>`	Presents information to users without any interaction between the user and the computer (i.e., the computer does not expect any input from the user).
`<break>`	Instructs the computer to pause its speech output for a specified period of time.
`<choice>`	Specifies an option in a `menu` element.
`<enumerate>`	Lists all the available options to the user.
`<exit>`	Exits the program.
`<filled>`	Contains elements that execute when the computer receives input for a `form` element from the user.
`<form>`	Gathers information from the user for a set of variables.
`<goto>`	Transfers control from one dialog to another.
`<grammar>`	Specifies grammar for the expected input from the user.
`<if>`, `<else>`, `<elseif>`	Indicates a control statement used for making logic decisions.
`<link>`	Performs a transfer of control similar to the `goto` statement, but a `link` can be executed at any time during the program's execution.
`<menu>`	Provides user options and transfers control to another dialog to suit the selected option.
`<prompt>`	Specifies text to be read to users when they must make a selection.
`<subdialog>`	Calls another dialog. After executing the subdialog, the calling dialog resumes control.
`<var>`	Declares a variable.
`<vxml>`	Top-level tag that specifies that the document should be processed by a VoiceXML interpreter.

Fig. 24.18 VoiceXML tags.

24.12 CallXML™

Another advancement benefiting people with visual impairments is *CallXML*, a voice technology created and supported by *Voxeo* (**www.voxeo.com**). CallXML creates phone-to-Web applications that control incoming and outgoing telephone calls. Examples of CallXML applications include voice mail, interactive voice response systems and Internet call waiting. Whereas VoiceXML allows computers to read Web pages to users with visual impairments, CallXML reads Web content to users via a telephone. CallXML has important implications for individuals who do not have a computer, but do have a telephone.

When users access CallXML applications, a *text-to-speech (TTS)* engine converts text to automated voice. The TTS engine then reads information contained within CallXML elements to the users. Web applications are tailored to respond to input from callers. [*Note*: Users must have a touch-tone phone to access CallXML applications.]

Some CallXML applications play prerecorded audio clips or text as output, requesting responses as input. An audio clip might contain a greeting that introduces callers to the applications or it might recite a menu of options, requesting that callers make a touch-tone entry. Certain applications, such as voice mail, might require both verbal and touch-tone input. Once the application receives the necessary input, it responds by invoking CallXML elements (such as **text**) that contain the information a TTS engine reads to users. If the application does not receive input within a designated time frame, it prompts the user to enter valid input.

When a user accesses a CallXML application, the incoming telephone call is referred to as a *session*. A CallXML application can support multiple sessions, which means that the application can process multiple telephone calls at once (e.g., a conferencing application). Each session is independent of the others and is assigned a unique *sessionID* for identification. A session terminates either when the user hangs up the telephone or when the CallXML application invokes the **hangup** element.

Our first CallXML application demonstrates the classic "Hello World" example (Fig. 24.19). Line 1 contains the optional *XML declaration*. Value **version** indicates the XML version to which the document conforms. The current XML recommendation is version **1.0**. Value **encoding** indicates the type of *Unicode* encoding that the application uses. For this example, we employ UTF-8, which requires eight bits to transfer and receive data. More information on Unicode can be found in Appendix F, Unicode®.

```
1   <?xml version = "1.0" encoding = "UTF-8"?>
2
3   <!-- Fig. 24.19: hello.xml            -->
4   <!-- The classic Hello World example  -->
5
6   <callxml>
7      <text>Hello World.</text>
8   </callxml>
```

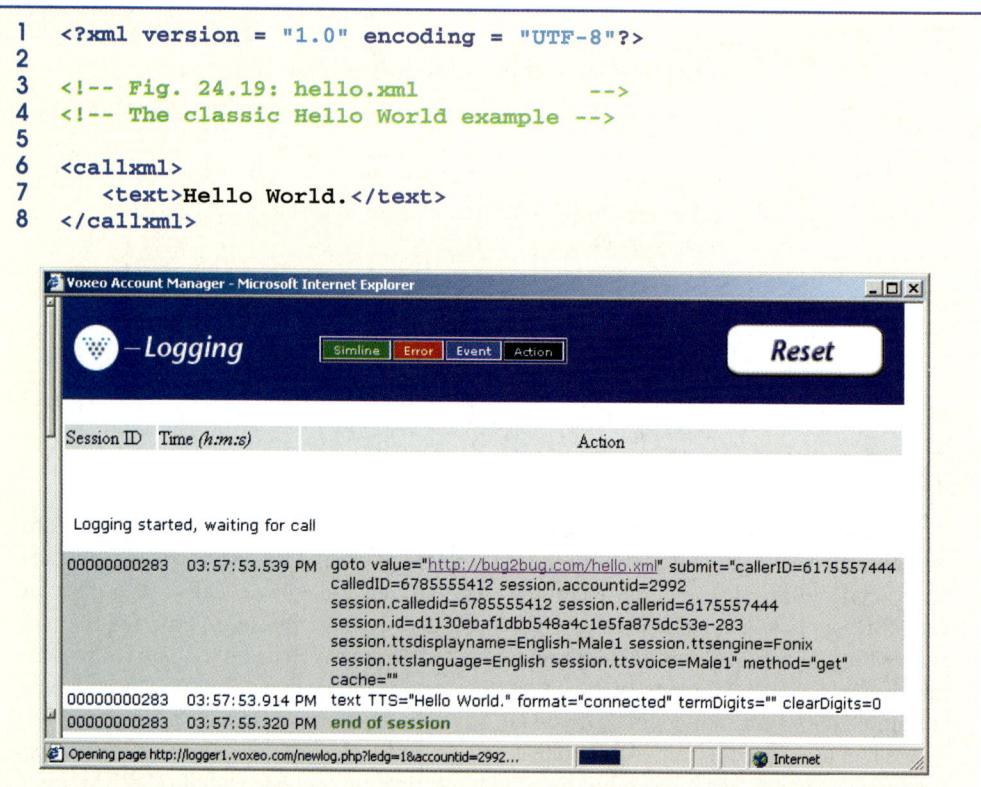

Fig. 24.19 Hello World CallXML example. (Courtesy of Voxeo, © Voxeo Corporation 2000–2001).

The `<callxml>` tag in line 6 declares that the content is a CallXML document. Line 7 contains the **Hello World text**. All text that is to be spoken by a text-to-speech (TTS) engine must be placed within `<text>` tags.

To deploy a CallXML or VoiceXML application, register with the *Voxeo* Community (`community.voxeo.com`), a Web resource that facilitates the creation, debugging and deployment of phone applications. For the most part, Voxeo resources are free. The company does charge fees when CallXML applications are deployed commercially. The Voxeo Community assigns a unique telephone number to a CallXML application, so that external users can access and interact with the application. [*Note*: Voxeo assigns telephone numbers only to applications that reside on the Internet. If you have access to a Web server (such as IIS, PWS or Apache), use it to post your CallXML application. Otherwise, open an Internet account through one of the many Internet-service companies (such as `www.geocities.com`, `www.angelfire.com`, `www.stormpages.com`, `www.freewebsites.com`, or `www.brinkster.com`). These companies allow individuals to post documents on the Internet through their Web servers.]

Figure 24.19 demonstrates the *logging* feature of the **Voxeo Account Manager**, which is accessible to registered members. The logging feature records and displays the "conversation" between the user and the application. The first row of the logging feature lists the URL of the CallXML application and the *global variables* associated with each session. When a session begins, the application creates and assigns values to global variables that the entire application can access and modify. The subsequent row(s) display the "conversation." This example demonstrates a one-way conversation (i.e., the application does not accept any input from the user) in which the TTS engine says **Hello World**. The last row displays the **end of session** message, which states that the phone call has terminated. The logging feature assists developers in the debugging of their applications. By observing a CallXML "conversation," a developer can determine the point at which the application terminates. If the application terminates abruptly ("crashes"), the logging feature displays information regarding the type and location of the error, pointing the developer toward the section of the application causing the problem.

The next example (Fig. 24.20) depicts a CallXML application that reads the ISBN numbers of are of three Deitel textbooks—*Internet and World Wide Web How to Program: Second Edition, XML How to Program* or *Java How to Program: Fourth Edition*—in response to a user's touch-tone input. [*Note*: The code has been formatted for presentation purposes.]

```
1   <?xml version = "1.0" encoding = "UTF-8"?>
2
3   <!-- Fig. 24.20: isbn.xml                              -->
4   <!-- Reads the ISBN value of three Deitel books        -->
5
6   <callxml>
7      <block>
8         <text>
9            Welcome. To obtain the ISBN of the Internet and World
10           Wide Web How to Program: Second Edition, please enter 1.
```

Fig. 24.20 CallXML example that reads three ISBN values (part 1 of 3). (Courtesy of Voxeo, © Voxeo Corporation 2000–2001.)

```xml
11              To obtain the ISBN of the XML How to Program,
12              please enter 2. To obtain the ISBN of the Java How
13              to Program: Fourth Edition, please enter 3. To exit the
14              application, please enter 4.
15          </text>
16
17          <!-- Obtains the numeric value entered by the user and -->
18          <!-- stores it in the variable ISBN. The user has 60   -->
19          <!-- seconds to enter one numeric value                -->
20          <getDigits var = "ISBN"
21              maxDigits = "1"
22              termDigits = "1234"
23              maxTime = "60s" />
24
25          <!-- Requests that the user enter a valid numeric -->
26          <!-- value after the elapsed time of 60 seconds   -->
27          <onMaxSilence>
28              <text>
29                  Please enter either 1, 2, 3 or 4.
30              </text>
31
32              <getDigits var = "ISBN"
33                  termDigits = "1234"
34                  maxDigits = "1"
35                  maxTime = "60s" />
36
37          </onMaxSilence>
38
39          <onTermDigit value = "1">
40              <text>
41                  The ISBN for the Internet book is 0130308978.
42                  Thank you for calling our CallXML application.
43                  Good-bye.
44              </text>
45          </onTermDigit>
46
47          <onTermDigit value = "2">
48              <text>
49                  The ISBN for the XML book is 0130284173.
50                  Thank you for calling our CallXML application.
51                  Good-bye.
52              </text>
53          </onTermDigit>
54
55          <onTermDigit value = "3">
56              <text>
57                  The ISBN for the Java book is 0130341517.
58                  Thank you for calling our CallXML application.
59                  Good-bye.
60              </text>
61          </onTermDigit>
62
```

Fig. 24.20 CallXML example that reads three ISBN values (part 2 of 3). (Courtesy of Voxeo, © Voxeo Corporation 2000–2001.)

```
63          <onTermDigit value = "4">
64             <text>
65                Thank you for calling our CallXML application.
66                Good-bye.
67             </text>
68          </onTermDigit>
69       </block>
70
71       <!-- Event handler that terminates the call -->
72       <onHangup />
73    </callxml>
```

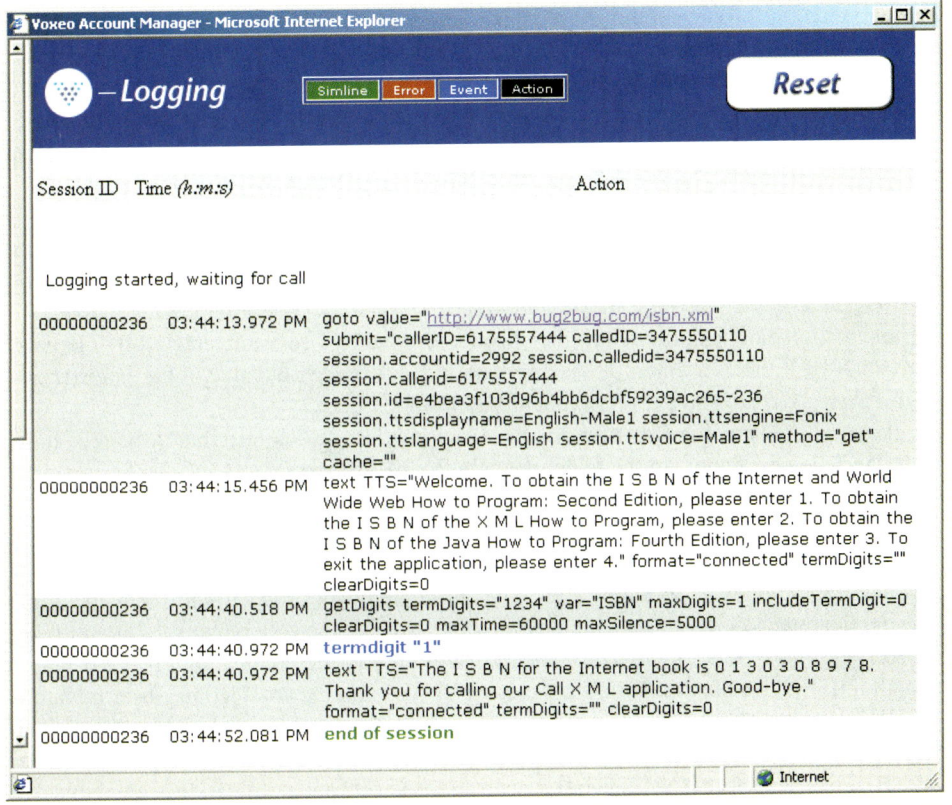

Fig. 24.20 CallXML example that reads three ISBN values (part 3 of 3). (Courtesy of Voxeo, © Voxeo Corporation 2000–2001.)

The **<block>** tag (line 7) encapsulates other CallXML tags. Usually, sets of CallXML tags that perform similar tasks are enclosed within **<block>**...**</block>**. The **block** element in this example encapsulates the **<text>**, **<getDigits>**, **<onMaxSilence>** and **<onTermDigit>** tags. A **block** element also can be nested in other **block** elements.

Lines 20–23 contain some attributes of the **<getDigits>** tag. The **getDigits** element obtains the user's touch-tone response and stores it in the variable declared by the **var** attribute (i.e., **ISBN**). The **maxDigits** attribute (line 21) indicates the maximum number of digits that the application can accept. This application accepts only one character. If no maximum is stated, then the application uses the default value, *nolimit*.

The **termDigits** attribute (line 22) contains the list of characters that terminate user input. When a user inputs a character from this list, the application is notified that it has received the last acceptable input; any character entered after this point is invalid. These characters do not terminate the call; they simply notify the application to proceed to the next instruction, because the necessary input has been received. In our example, the values for **termDigits** are **1**, **2**, **3** or **4**. The default value for **termDigits** is the null value (**""**).

The **maxTime** attribute (line 23) indicates the maximum amount of time that the application will wait for a user response. If the user fails to enter input within the given time frame, then the CallXML application invokes the event handler **onMaxSilence**. The default value for this attribute is 30 seconds.

The **onMaxSilence** element (lines 27–37) is an *event handler* that is invoked when attribute **maxTime** (or **maxSilence**) expires. The event handler specified notifies the application of the appropriate action to perform when a user fails to respond. In this case, the application asks the user to enter a value, because the **maxTime** has expired. After receiving input, **getDigits** (line 32) stores the entered value in the **ISBN** variable.

The **onTermDigit** element (lines 39–68) is an event handler that notifies the application of the appropriate action to perform when a user selects one of the **termDigits** characters. At least one **<onTermDigit>** tag must be associated with (appear after) the **getDigits** element, even if the default value (**""**) is used. We provide four actions that the application can perform to suit the specific **termDigits** value entered by the user. For example, if the user enters **1**, the application reads the ISBN value of the *Internet and World Wide Web How to Program: Second Edition* textbook.

Line 72 contains the **<onHangup/>** event handler, which terminates the telephone call when the user hangs up the telephone. Our **<onHangup>** event handler is an empty tag (i.e., no action is performed when this tag is invoked).

The logging feature (Fig. 24.20) displays the "conversation" between the application and the user. As in the previous example, the first row specifies the URL of the application and the global variables of the session. The subsequent rows display the "conversation": The application asks the caller which ISBN value to read, the caller enters **1** (*Internet and World Wide Web How to Program: Second Edition*) and the application reads the corresponding ISBN. The **end of session** message states that the application has terminated.

We provide brief descriptions of various logic and action CallXML elements in Fig. 24.21. *Logic elements* assign values to, and clear values from, the session variables; *action elements* perform specified tasks, such as answering and terminating a telephone call during the current session. A complete list of CallXML elements is available at

www.oasis-open.org/cover/callxmlv2.html

Elements	Description
assign	Assigns a **value** to a variable, **var**.
clear	Clears the contents of the **var** attribute.

Fig. 24.21 CallXML elements (part 1 of 2).

Elements	Description
`clearDigits`	Clears all digits that the user has entered.
`goto`	Navigates to another section of the current CallXML application or to a different CallXML application. The **value** attribute specifies the URL of the application. The **submit** attribute lists the variables that are passed to the invoked application. The **method** attribute states whether to use the HTTP *get* or *post* request type when sending and retrieving information. A *get* request retrieves data from a Web server without modifying the contents, whereas the *post* request receives modified data.
`run`	Starts a new CallXML session for each call. The **value** attribute specifies the CallXML application to retrieve. The **submit** attribute lists the variables that are passed to the invoked application. The **method** attribute states whether to use the HTTP *get* or *post* request type. The **var** attribute stores the identification number of the session.
`sendEvent`	Allows multiple sessions to exchange messages. The **value** attribute stores the message, and the **session** attribute specifies the identification number of the session that receives the message.
`answer`	Answers an incoming telephone call.
`call`	Calls the URL specified by the **value** attribute. The **callerID** attribute contains the phone number that is displayed on a CallerID device. The **maxTime** attribute specifies the length of time to wait for the call to be answered before disconnecting.
`conference`	Connects multiple sessions so that individuals can participate in a conference call. The **targetSessions** attribute specifies the identification numbers of the sessions, and the **termDigits** attribute indicates the touch-tone keys that terminate the call.
`wait`	Waits for user input. The **value** attribute specifies how long to wait. The **termDigits** attribute indicates the touch-tone keys that terminate the **wait** element.
`play`	Plays an audio file or pronounces a value that is stored as a number, date or amount of money and is indicated by the **format** attribute. The **value** attribute contains the information (location of the audio file, number, date or amount of money) that corresponds to the **format** attribute. The **clearDigits** attribute specifies whether to delete the previously entered input. The **termDigits** attribute indicates the touch-tone keys that terminate the audio file and more.
`recordAudio`	Records an audio file and stores it at the URL specified by **value**. The **format** attribute indicates the file extension of the audio clip. Other attributes include **termDigits**, **clearDigits**, **maxTime** and **maxSilence**.

Fig. 24.21 CallXML elements (part 2 of 2).

24.13 JAWS® for Windows

JAWS (Job Access with Sound) is one of the leading screen readers currently on the market. Henter-Joyce, a division of Freedom Scientific™, created this application to help people with visual impairments interact with technology.

To download a demonstration version of JAWS, visit **www.freedomscientific.com**. The JAWS demo is fully functional and includes an extensive, highly customized help system. Users can select the voice that "reads" Web content and the rate at which text is spoken. Users also can create keyboard shortcuts. Although the demo is in English, the full version of JAWS allows the user to choose one of several supported languages.

JAWS also includes special key commands for popular programs, such as Microsoft Internet Explorer and Microsoft Word. For example, when browsing in Internet Explorer, the capabilities of JAWS extend beyond the reading of content on the screen. If JAWS is enabled, pressing *Insert + F7* in Internet Explorer opens a **Links List** dialog, which displays all the links available on a Web page. For more information about JAWS and the other products offered by Henter-Joyce, visit **www.freedomscientific.com**.

24.14 Other Accessibility Tools

Many accessibility products are available to assist people with disabilities. One such technology, Microsoft's *Active Accessibility*®, establishes a protocol by which an accessibility aid can retrieve information about an application's user interface in a consistent manner. Accessibility aids require such information as the name, location and layout of particular GUI elements within an application, so that the accessibility aid can render the information properly to the intended audience. Active Accessibility also enables software developers and accessibility-aid developers to design programs and products that are compatible with each other. Moreover, Active Accessibility is packaged in two components, enabling both programmers and individuals who use accessibility aids to use the software. The *Software Development Kit (SDK)* component is intended for programmers: It includes testing tools, programmatic libraries and header files. The *Redistribution Kit (RDK)* component is intended for those who use accessibility aids: It installs a runtime component into the Microsoft operating system. Accessibility aids use the Active Accessibility runtime components to interact with and obtain information from any application software. For more information on Active Accessibility, visit

> **www.microsoft.com/enable/msaa/**

Another important accessibility tool for individuals with visual impairments is the *braille keyboard*. In addition to providing keys labeled with the letters they represent, a braille keyboard also has the equivalent braille symbol printed on each key. Most often, braille keyboards are combined with a speech synthesizer or a braille display, enabling users to interact with the computer to verify that their typing is correct.

Speech synthesis also provides benefits to people with disabilities. *Speech synthesizers* have been used for many years to aid people who are unable to communicate verbally. However, the growing popularity of the Web has prompted a surge of interest in the fields of speech synthesis and speech recognition. Now, these technologies are allowing individuals with disabilities to use computers more than ever before. The development of speech synthesizers is also making possible the improvement of other technologies, such as

VoiceXML and *AuralCSS* (**www.w3.org/TR/REC-CSS2/aural.html**). These tools allow people with visual impairments and illiterate people to access Web sites.

Despite the existence of adaptive software and hardware for people with visual impairments, the accessibility of computers and the Internet is still hampered by the high costs, rapid obsolescence and unnecessary complexity of current technology. Moreover, almost all software currently available requires installation by a person who can see. *Ocularis* is a project launched in the open-source community that aims to address these problems. Open-source software for people with visual impairments already exists; although it is often superior to its proprietary, closed-source counterparts, it has not yet reached its full potential. Ocularis ensures that the blind can access and use all aspects of the Linux operating system. Products that integrate with Ocularis include word processors, calculators, basic finance applications, Internet browsers and e-mail clients. A screen reader also will be included for use with programs that have a command-line interface. The official Ocularis Web site is located at **ocularis.sourceforge.net**.

People with visual impairments are not the only beneficiaries of efforts to improve markup languages. People with hearing impairments also have a number of tools to help them interpret auditory information delivered over the Web. One of these tools, *Synchronized Multimedia Integration Language* (SMIL™), is designed to add extra *tracks* (layers of content found within a single audio or video file) to multimedia content. The additional tracks can contain closed captioning.

Technologies are also being designed to help people with severe disabilities, such as quadriplegia, a form of paralysis that affects the body from the neck down. One such technology, *EagleEyes*, developed by researchers at Boston College (**www.bc.edu/eagleeyes**), is a system that translates eye movements into mouse movements. A user moves the mouse cursor by moving his or her eyes or head and is thereby able to control the computer.

The company CitXCorp is developing a new technology that translates Web information through the telephone. Information on a specific topic can be accessed by dialing the designated number. For more information on regulations governing the design of Web sites to accommodate people with disabilities, visit **www.access-board.gov**.

GW Micro, Henter-Joyce and Adobe Systems, Inc., are also working on software that assists people with disabilities. Adobe Acrobat 5.0 complies with Microsoft's application programming interface (API) to allow businesses to provide information to a wider audience. JetForm Corp is also accommodating the needs of people with disabilities by developing server-based XML software. The new software allows users to download information in a format that best meets their needs.

There are many services on the Web that assist e-businesses in designing Web sites to be accessible to individuals with disabilities. For additional information, the U.S. Department of Justice (**www.usdoj.gov**) provides extensive resources detailing legal and technical issues related to people with disabilities.

24.15 Accessibility in Microsoft® Windows® 2000

Beginning with Microsoft *Windows 95*, Microsoft has included accessibility features in its operating systems and many of its applications, including *Office 97*, *Office 2000* and *Netmeeting*. In Microsoft *Windows 2000*, Microsoft has significantly enhanced the operating system's accessibility features. All the accessibility options provided by Windows 2000 are available through the **Accessibility Wizard**, which guides users through Windows 2000 accessibility features and then configures their computers in accordance with the chosen specifications. This section uses the **Accessibility Wizard** to guide users through the configuration of their Windows 2000 accessibility options.

To access the **Accessibility Wizard**, users' computers must be equipped with Microsoft Windows 2000. Click the **Start** button, and select **Programs** followed by **Accessories**, **Accessibility** and **Accessibility Wizard**. When the wizard starts, the **Welcome** screen displays. Click **Next**. The next dialog (Fig. 24.22) asks the user to select a font size. Modify the font size, if necessary, and then click **Next**.

Figure 24.23 depicts the **Display Settings** dialog. This dialog allows the user to activate the font-size settings chosen in the previous window, change the screen resolution, enable the *Microsoft Magnifier* (a program that displays an enlarged section of the screen in a separate window) and disable personalized menus. Personalized menus hide rarely used programs from the start menu and can be a hindrance to users with disabilities. Make selections, and click **Next**.

The **Set Wizard Options** dialog (Fig. 24.24) asks questions about the user's disabilities; the answers to these questions allow the **Accessibility Wizard** to customize Windows to better suit the user's needs. For demonstration purposes, we selected every type of disability included in the dialogue. Click **Next** to continue.

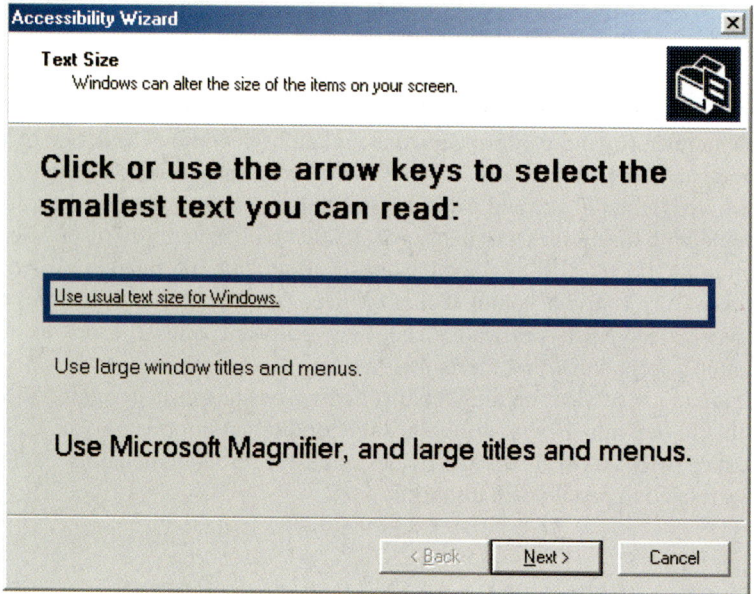

Fig. 24.22 Text Size dialog.

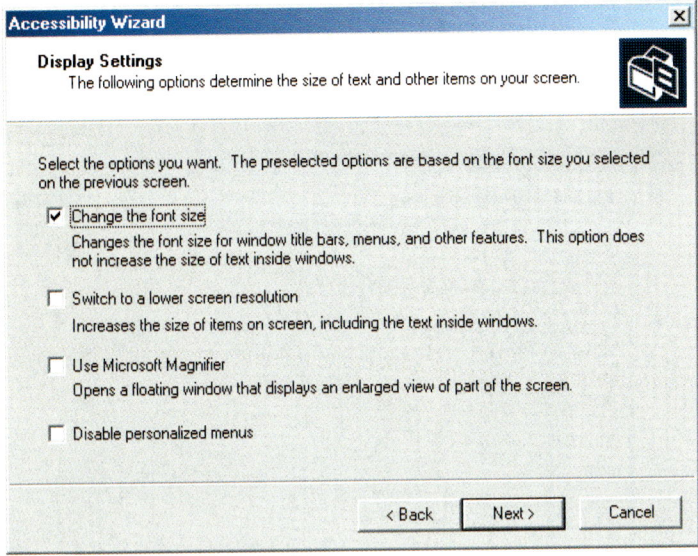

Fig. 24.23 Display Settings dialog.

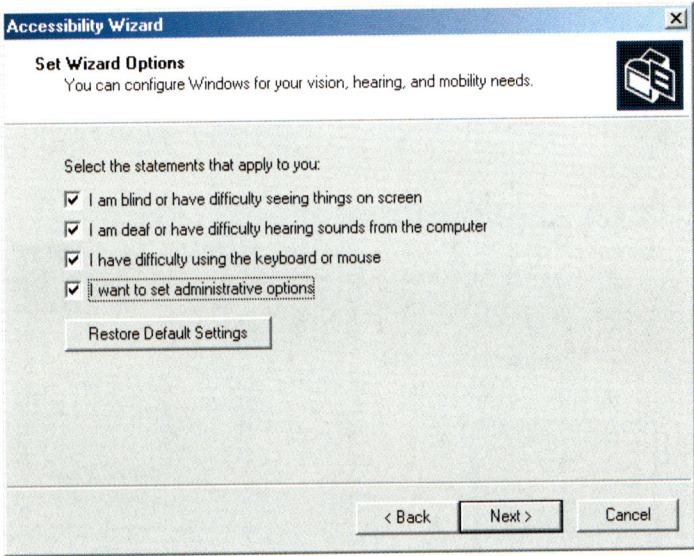

Fig. 24.24 Accessibility Wizard initialization options.

24.15.1 Tools for People with Visual Impairments

After we have checked options in Fig. 24.24, the wizard begins to configure Windows so that it is accessible to people with visual impairments. The dialog box shown in Fig. 24.25 allows the user to resize the scroll bars and window borders to increase their visibility. Click **Next** to proceed to the next dialog.

Figure 24.26 contains a dialog that allows the user to resize icons. Users with poor vision and users who are illiterate or have trouble reading benefit from large icons.

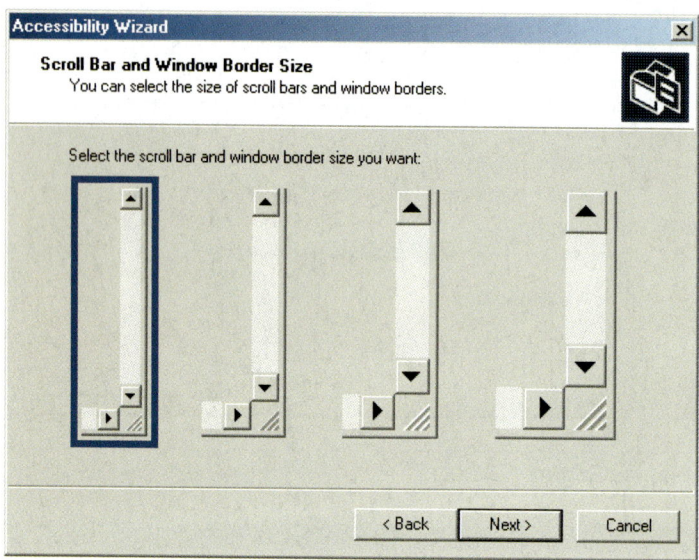

Fig. 24.25 **Scroll Bar and Window Border Size** dialog.

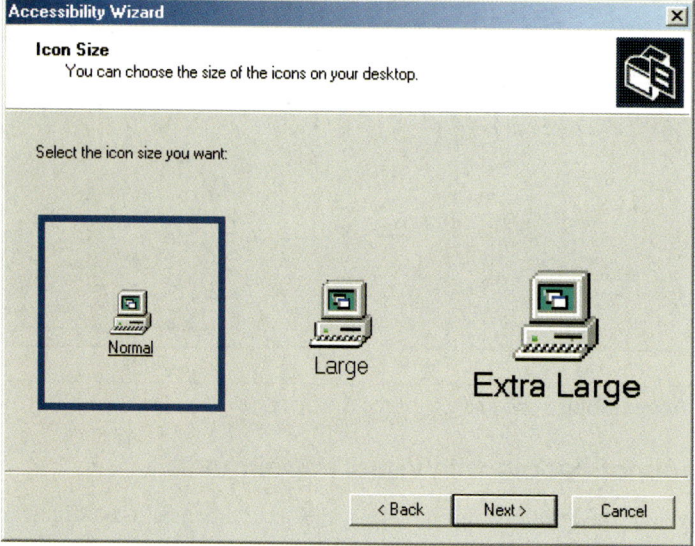

Fig. 24.26 Adjusting up window element sizes.

Clicking **Next** displays the **Display Color Settings** dialog (Fig. 24.27). These settings enable the user to change the Windows color scheme and resize various screen elements.

Click **Next** to view the dialog (Fig. 24.28) that enables customization of the mouse cursor. Anyone who has ever used a laptop computer knows how difficult it can be to see the mouse cursor. This is even more problematic for people with visual impairments. To address this problem, the wizard offers users the options of larger cursors, black cursors and cursors that invert the colors of objects underneath them. Click **Next**.

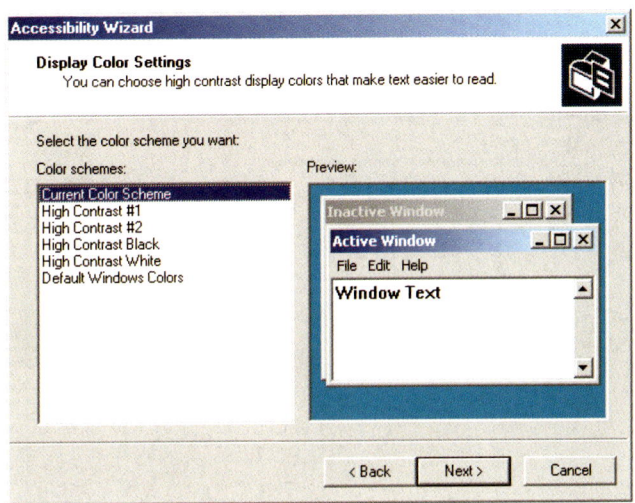

Fig. 24.27 Display Color Settings options.

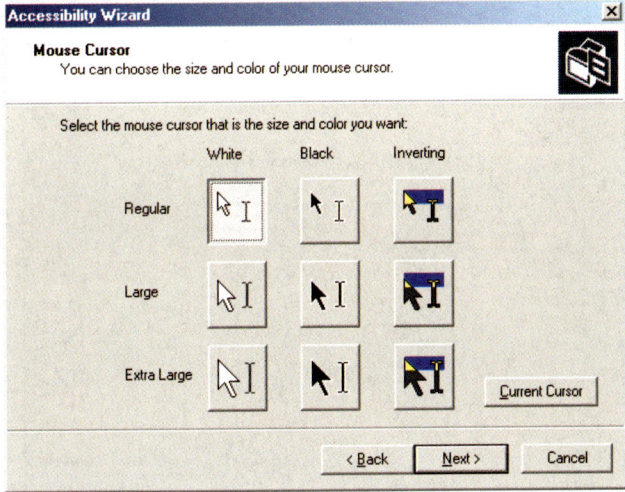

Fig. 24.28 Accessibility Wizard mouse cursor adjustment tool.

24.15.2 Tools for People with Hearing Impairments

This section, which focuses on accessibility for people with hearing impairments, begins with the **SoundSentry** window (Fig. 24.29). **SoundSentry** is a tool that creates visual signals to notify users of system events. For example, people with hearing impairments are unable to hear the beeps that normally indicate warnings, so **SoundSentry** flashes the screen when a beep occurs. To continue on to the next dialog, click **Next**.

The next window is the **ShowSounds** window (Fig. 24.30). **ShowSounds** adds captions to spoken text and other sounds produced by today's multimedia-rich software. Note that, for **ShowSounds** to work in a specific application, developers must provide the captions and spoken text specifically within their software. Make selections, and click **Next**.

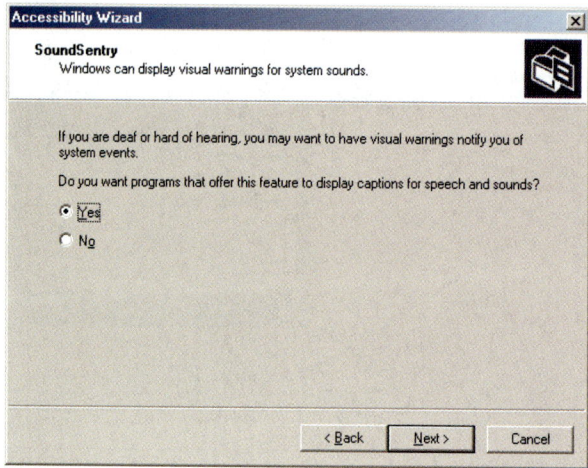

Fig. 24.29 SoundSentry dialog.

Fig. 24.30 ShowSounds dialog.

24.15.3 Tools for Users Who Have Difficulty Using the Keyboard

The next dialog describes **StickyKeys** (Fig. 24.31). **StickyKeys** is a program that helps users who have difficulty pressing multiple keys at the same time. Many important computer commands can be invoked only by pressing specific key combinations. For example, the reboot command requires the user to press *Ctrl+Alt+Delete* simultaneously. **StickyKeys** enables the user to press key combinations in sequence, rather than at the same time. Click **Next** to continue to the **BounceKeys** dialog (Fig. 24.32).

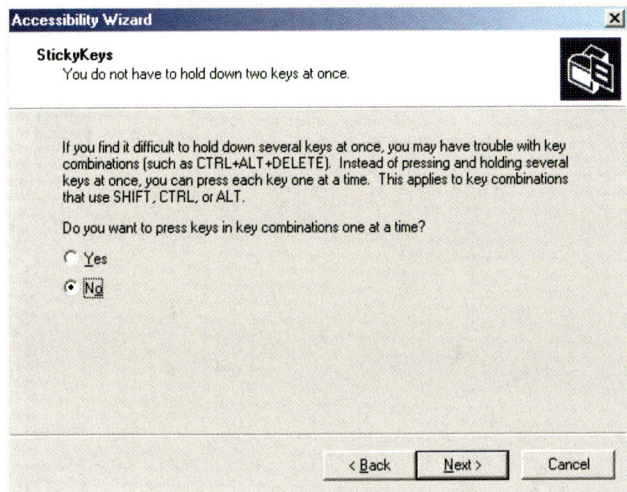

Fig. 24.31 StickyKeys window.

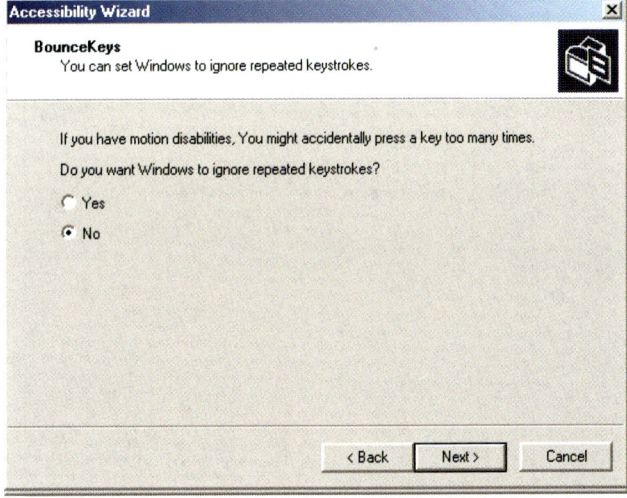

Fig. 24.32 BounceKeys dialog.

A common problem that affects certain users with disabilities is the accidental pressing of the same key multiple times. This problem typically is caused by holding a key down too long. **BounceKeys** forces the computer to ignore repeated keystrokes. Click **Next**.

ToggleKeys (Fig. 24.33) alerts users that they pressed one of the lock keys (i.e., *Caps Lock*, *Num Lock* or *Scroll Lock*) by sounding an audible beep. Make selections and click **Next**.

Next, the **Extra Keyboard Help** dialog (Fig. 24.34) is displayed. This dialogue can activate a tool that displays such information as keyboard shortcuts and tool tips when such information is available. Like **ShowSounds**, this tool requires that software developers provide the content to be displayed.

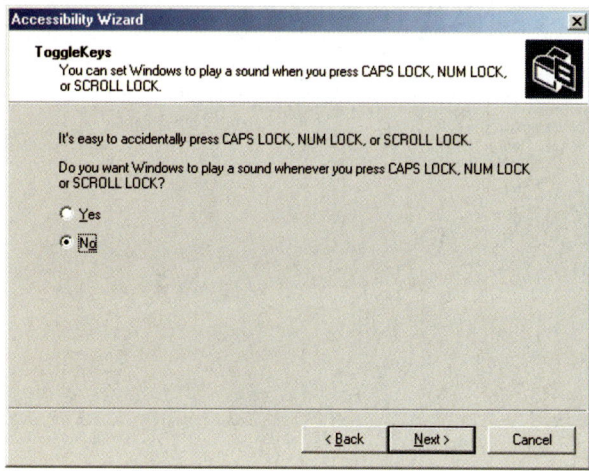

Fig. 24.33 ToggleKeys window.

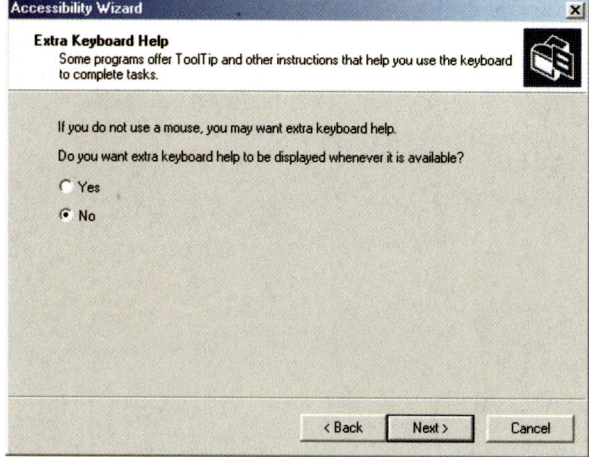

Fig. 24.34 Extra Keyboard Help dialog.

Clicking **Next** will load the **MouseKeys** (Fig. 24.35) customization window. **MouseKeys** is a tool that uses the keyboard to imitate mouse movements. The arrow keys direct the mouse, and the *5* key indicates a single click. To double click, the user must press the *+* key; to simulate the holding down of the mouse button, the user must press the *Ins* (Insert) key. To release the mouse button, the user must press the *Del* (Delete) key. Choose whether to enable **MouseKeys**, and then click **Next**.

Today's computer tools, including most mice, are almost exclusively for right-handed users. Microsoft recognized this problem and added the **Mouse Button Settings** window (Fig. 24.36) to the **Accessibility Wizard**. This tool allows the user to create a virtual left-handed mouse by swapping the button functions. Click **Next**.

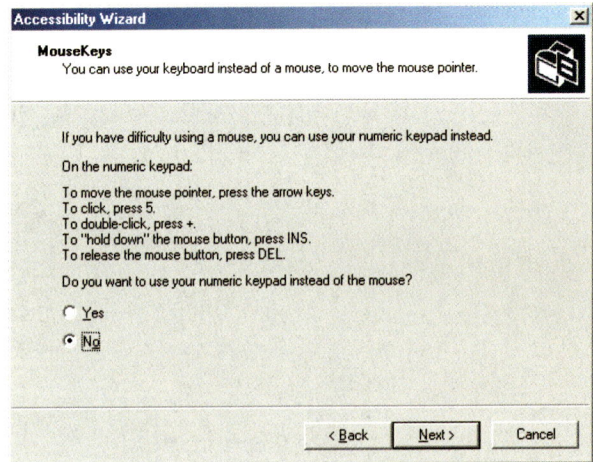

Fig. 24.35 MouseKeys window.

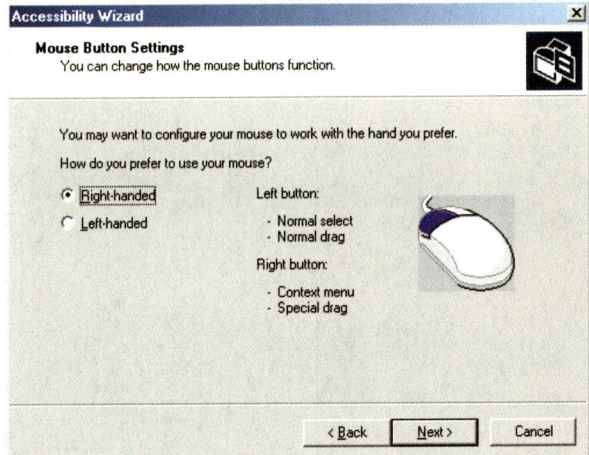

Fig. 24.36 Mouse Button Settings window.

User can adjust mouse speed via the **MouseSpeed** (Fig. 24.37) section of the **Accessibility Wizard**. Dragging the scroll bar changes the speed. Clicking the **Next** button sets the speed and displays the wizard's **Set Automatic Timeouts** window (Fig. 24.38). Although accessibility tools are important to users with disabilities, they can be a hindrance to users who do not need them. In situations where varying accessibility needs exist, it is important that the user be able to turn the accessibility tools on and off as necessary. The **Set Automatic Timeouts** window specifies a *timeout* period for enabling or disabling accessibility tools. A timeout either enables or disables a certain action after the computer has idled for a specified amount of time. A screen saver is a common example of a program with a timeout period. Here, a timeout is set to toggle the accessibility tools.

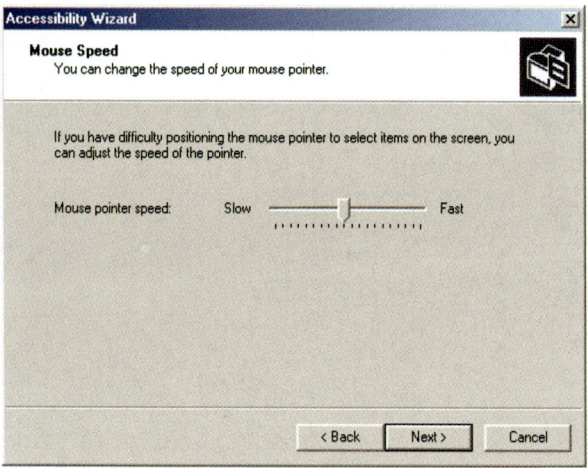

Fig. 24.37 Mouse Speed dialog.

Fig. 24.38 Set Automatic Timeouts dialog.

After the user clicks **Next**, the **Save Settings to File** dialog appears (Fig. 24.39). This dialog determines whether the accessibility settings should be used as the *default settings*, which are loaded when the computer is rebooted or after a timeout. Set the accessibility settings as the default if the majority of users needs them. Users also can save multiple accessibility settings. The user can create a `.acw` file, which, when chosen, activates the saved accessibility settings on any Windows 2000 computer.

24.15.4 Microsoft Narrator

Microsoft Narrator is a text-to-speech program designed for people with visual impairments. It reads text, describes the current desktop environment and alerts the user when certain Windows events occur. **Narrator** is intended to aid in the configuration of Microsoft Windows. It is a screen reader that works with Internet Explorer, Wordpad, Notepad and most programs in the **Control Panel**. Although its capabilities are limited outside these applications, **Narrator** is excellent at navigating the Windows environment.

To explore **Narrator**'s functionality, we explain how to use the program in conjunction with several Windows applications. Click the **Start** button, and select **Programs**, followed by **Accessories**, **Accessibility** and **Narrator**. Once **Narrator** is open, it describes the current foreground window. It then reads the text inside the window aloud to the user. When the user clicks **OK**, the dialog in Fig. 24.40 displays.

Checking the first option instructs **Narrator** to describe menus and new windows when they are opened. The second option instructs **Narrator** to speak characters as they are typed. The third option moves the mouse cursor to the region currently being read by **Narrator**. Clicking the **Voice...** button enables the user to change the pitch, volume and speed of the narrator voice (Fig. 24.41).

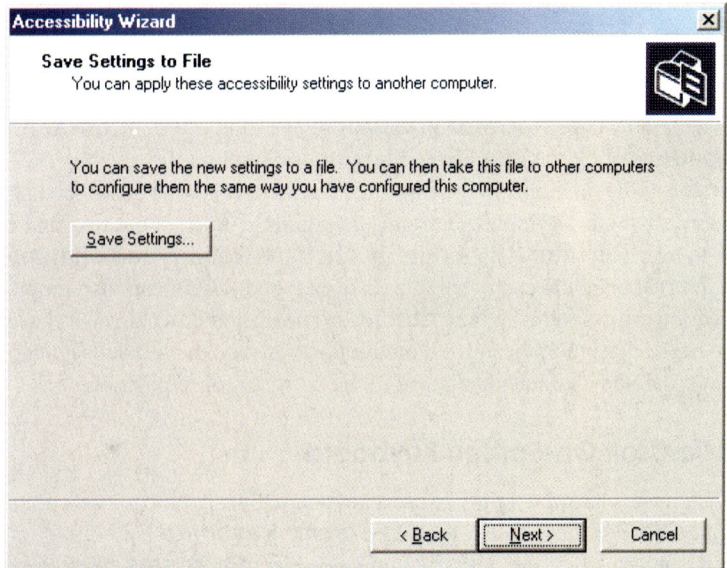

Fig. 24.39 Saving new accessibility settings.

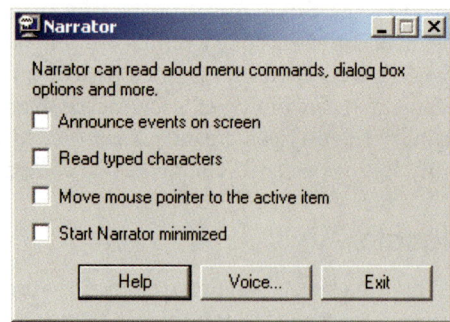

Fig. 24.40 Narrator window.

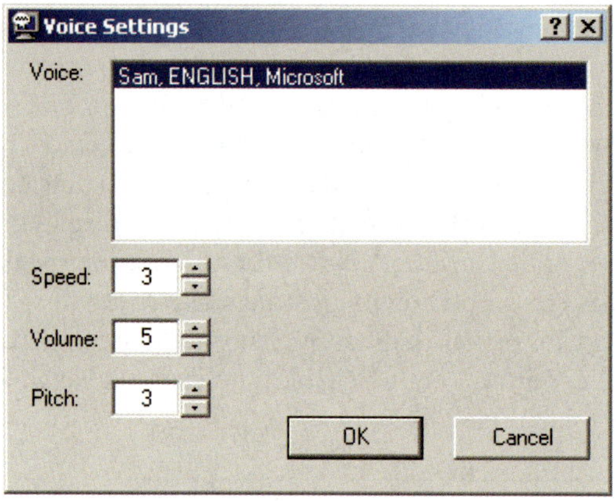

Fig. 24.41 Voice Settings window.

Now, we demonstrate **Narrator** in various applications. When **Narrator** is running, open **Notepad** and click the **File** menu. **Narrator** announces the opening of the program and begins to describe the items in the **File** menu. As a user scrolls down the list, **Narrator** reads the item to which the mouse currently is pointing. Type some text and press *Ctrl–Shift–Enter* to hear **Narrator** read it (Fig. 24.42). If the **Read typed characters** option is checked, **Narrator** reads each character as it is typed. Users can also employ the keyboard's direction arrows to make **Narrator** read. The up and down arrows cause **Narrator** to speak the lines adjacent to the current mouse position, and the left and right arrows cause **Narrator** to speak the characters adjacent to the current mouse position.

24.15.5 Microsoft On-Screen Keyboard

Some computer users lack the ability to use a keyboard, but are able to use a pointing device (such as a mouse). For these users, the ***On-Screen Keyboard*** is helpful. To access the On-Screen Keyboard, click the **Start** button, and select **Programs** followed by **Accessories**, **Accessibility** and **On-Screen Keyboard**. Figure 24.43 depicts the layout of the Microsoft On-Screen Keyboard.

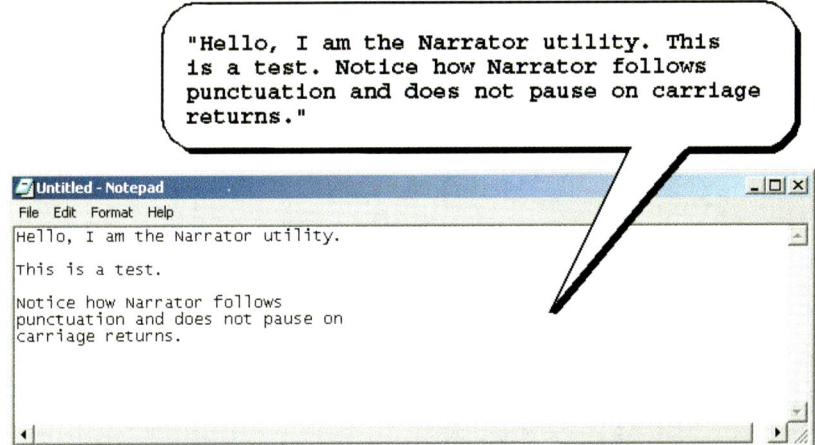

Fig. 24.42 Narrator reading **Notepad** text.

Fig. 24.43 Microsoft **On-Screen Keyboard**.

Users who have difficulty using the On-Screen Keyboard can purchase more sophisticated products, such as *Clicker 4*™ by *Inclusive Technology*. Clicker 4 is an aid designed for people who cannot use a keyboard effectively. Its best feature is that it can be customized. Keys can have letters, numbers, entire words or even pictures on them. For more information regarding Clicker 4, visit **www.inclusive.co.uk/catalog/clicker.htm**.

24.15.6 Accessibility Features in Microsoft Internet Explorer 5.5

Internet Explorer 5.5 offers a variety of options that can improve usability. To access IE5.5's accessibility features, launch the program, click the **Tools** menu and select **Internet Options....** Then, from the **Internet Options** menu, press the button labeled **Accessibility...** to open the accessibility options (Fig. 24.44).

The accessibility options in IE5.5 are designed to improve the Web-browsing experiences of users with disabilities. Users are able to ignore Web colors, Web fonts and font-size tags. This eliminates accessibility problems arising from poor Web-page design and allows users to customize their Web browsing. Users can even specify a *style sheet,* which formats every Web site that users visit according to their personal preferences.

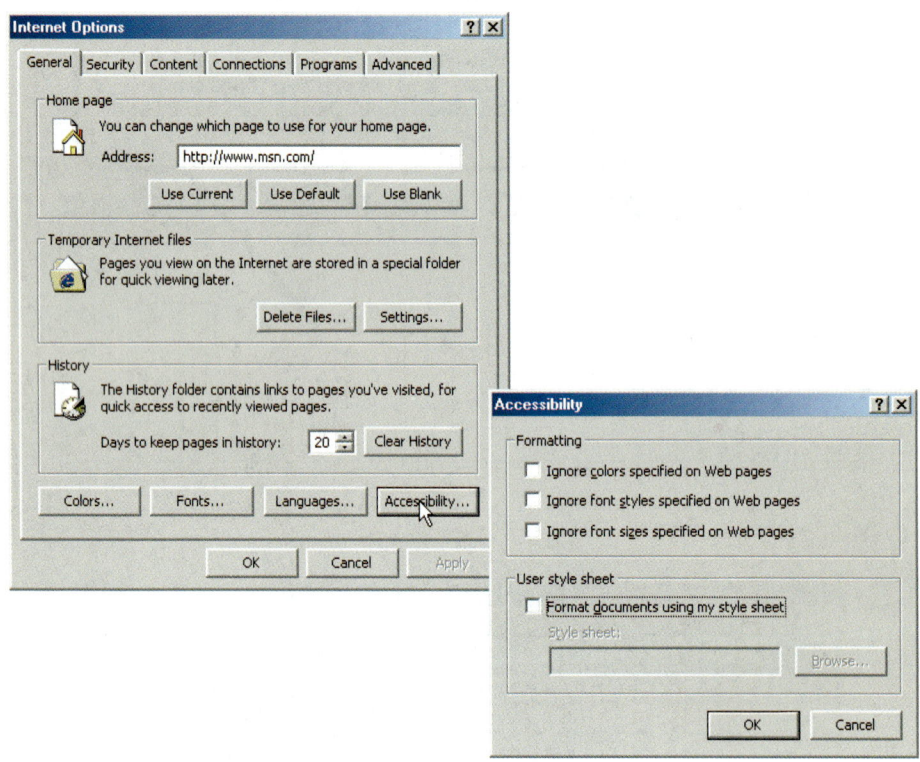

Fig. 24.44 Microsoft Internet Explorer 5.5's accessibility options.

In the **Internet Options** dialog, click the **Advanced** tab. This opens the dialog depicted in Fig. 24.45. The first available option is labeled **Always expand ALT text for images**. By default, IE5.5 hides some of the `<alt>` text if the size of the text exceeds that of the image it describes. This option forces IE5.5 to show all the text. The second option reads **Move system caret with focus/selection changes**. This option is intended to make screen reading more effective. Some screen readers use the *system caret* (the blinking vertical bar associated with editing text) to determine what to read. If this option is not activated, screen readers might not read Web pages correctly.

Web designers often forget to take accessibility into account when creating Web sites; in an attempt to provide large amounts of content, they use fonts that are too small. Many user agents have addressed this problem by allowing the user to adjust the text size. Click the **View** menu, and select **Text Size** to change the font size in pages rendered by IE5.5. By default, the text size is set to **Medium**.

In this chapter, we presented a wide variety of technologies that help people with various disabilities use computers. We hope that all our readers will join us in emphasizing the importance of these capabilities in their schools and workplaces.

Well, that's it for now. We sincerely hope that you have enjoyed learning with *Visual Basic How To Program*. As this book went to the presses, we were already at work on *Advanced Visual Basic How To Program*, a book appropriate for professional developers writing enterprise applications and for advanced college courses in software development.

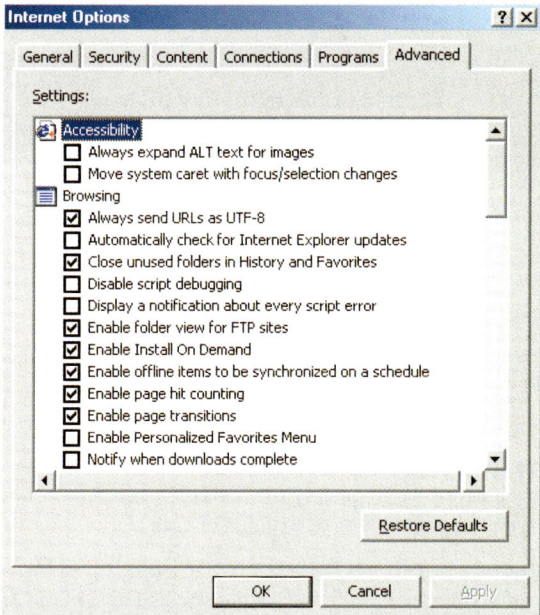

Fig. 24.45 Advanced accessibility settings in Microsoft Internet Explorer 5.5.

24.16 Internet and World Wide Web Resources

There are many accessibility resources available on the Internet and World Wide Web; this section lists a variety of these resources.

General Information, Guidelines and Definitions

`www.w3.org/WAI`
The World Wide Web Consortium's *Web Accessibility Initiative (WAI)* site promotes the design of universally accessible Web sites. This site contains the current guidelines and forthcoming standards for Web accessibility.

`www.w3.org/TR/xhtml1`
The *XHTML 1.0 Recommendation* contains XHTML 1.0 general information, compatibility issues, document type definition information, definitions, terminology and much more.

`www.abledata.com/text2/icg_hear.htm`
This page contains a consumer guide that discusses technologies designed for people with hearing impairments.

`www.washington.edu/doit`
The University of Washington's DO-IT (Disabilities, Opportunities, Internetworking and Technology) site provides information and Web-development resources for the creation of universally accessible Web sites.

`www.webable.com`
The *WebABLE* site contains links to many disability-related Internet resources; the site is geared towards those developing technologies for people with disabilities.

www.webaim.org
The *WebAIM* site provides a number of tutorials, articles, simulations and other useful resources that demonstrate how to design accessible Web sites. The site provides a screen-reader simulation.

deafness.about.com/health/deafness/msubvib.htm
This site provides information on vibrotactile devices, which allow individuals with hearing impairments to experience audio in the form of vibrations.

Developing Accessible Applications with Existing Technologies

wdvl.com/Authoring/Languages/XML/XHTML
The Web Developers Virtual Library provides an introduction to XHTML. This site also contains articles, examples and links to other technologies.

www.w3.org/TR/1999/xhtml-modularization-19990406/DTD/doc
The XHTML 1.0 DTD documentation site provides links to DTD documentation for the strict, transitional and frameset document type definitions.

www.webreference.com/xml/reference/xhtml.html
This Web page contains a list of the frequently used XHTML tags, such as header tags, table tags, frame tags and form tags. It also provides a description of each tag.

www.w3.org/TR/REC-CSS2/aural.html
This site discusses Aural Style Sheets, outlining the purpose and uses of this new technology.

www.islandnet.com
Lynxit is a development tool that allows users to view any Web site as if they were using a text-only browser. The site's form allows you to enter a URL and returns the Web site in text-only format.

www.trill-home.com/lynx/public_lynx.html
This site allows users to browse the Web with a Lynx browser. Users can view how Web pages appear to users who are not using the most current technologies.

java.sun.com/products/java-media/speech/forDevelopers/JSML
This site outlines the specifications for JSML, Sun Microsystem's Java Speech Markup Language. This language, like VoiceXML, helps improve accessibility for people with visual impairments.

ocfo.ed.gov/coninfo/clibrary/software.htm
This is the U.S. Department of Education's Web site that outlines software accessibility requirements. The site helps developers produce accessible products.

www.speech.cs.cmu.edu/comp.speech/SpeechLinks.html
The *Speech Technology Hyperlinks* page has over 500 links to sites related to computer-based speech and speech-recognition tools.

www.islandnet.com/~tslemko
The *Micro Consulting Limited* site contains shareware speech-synthesis software.

www.chantinc.com/technology
This page is the *Chant* Web site, which discusses speech technology and how it works. Chant also provides speech–synthesis and speech-recognition software.

searchmiddleware.techtarget.com/sdefinition/ 0,,sid26_gci518993,00.html
This site provides definitions and information about several topics, including CallXML. Its thorough definition of CallXML differentiates CallXML from VoiceXML, another technology developed by Voxeo. The site also contains links to other published articles that discuss CallXML.

www.oasis-open.org/cover/callxmlv2.html
This site provides a comprehensive list of the CallXML tags, complete with a description of each tag. The site also provides short examples on how to apply the tags in various applications.

web.ukonline.co.uk/ddmc/software.html
This site provides links to software designed for people with disabilities.

www.freedomscientific.com
Henter-Joyce is a division of Freedom Scientific that provides software for people with visual impairments. It is the homepage of JAWS (Job Access with Sound).

www-3.ibm.com/able/
This is the homepage of IBM's accessibility site. It provides information on IBM products and their accessibility and discusses hardware, software and Web accessibility.

www.w3.org/TR/voice-tts-reqs
This page explains the speech-synthesis markup requirements for voice markup languages.

www.cast.org
CAST (Center for Applied Special Technology) offers software, including a valuable accessibility checker, that can help individuals with disabilities use computers. The accessibility checker is a Web-based program that validates the accessibility of Web sites.

Information on Disabilities

deafness.about.com/health/deafness/msubmenu6.htm
This is the home page of **deafness.about.com**. It provides a wealth of information on the history of hearing loss, the current state of medical developments and other resources related to these topics.

www.trainingpost.org/3-2-inst.htm
This site presents a tutorial on the Gunning Fog Index. The Gunning Fog Index is a method of grading text according to its readability.

laurence.canlearn.ca/English/learn/accessibility2001/neads/index.shtml
INDIE stands for "Integrated Network of Disability Information and Education." This site is home to a search engine that helps users find information on disabilities.

www.wgbh.org/wgbh/pages/ncam/accesslinks.html
This page provides links to other accessibility pages across the Web.

SUMMARY

- Enabling a Web site to meet the needs of individuals with disabilities is an important issue.
- Enabling a Web site to meet the needs of individuals with disabilities is an issue relevant to all business owners.
- Technologies such as voice activation, visual enhancers and auditory aids enable individuals with disabilities to have access to the Web and to software applications.
- In 1997, the World Wide Web Consortium (W3C) launched the Web Accessibility Initiative (WAI). The WAI is an attempt to make the Web more accessible; its mission is described at **www.w3.org/WAI**.
- Accessibility refers to the level of usability of an application or Web site for people with disabilities. Total accessibility is difficult to achieve because there are many different disabilities, language barriers, and hardware and software inconsistencies.
- The majority of Web sites are considered to be either partially or totally inaccessible to people with visual, learning or mobility impairments.

- The WAI published the Web Content Accessibility Guidelines 1.0, which assign accessibility priorities to a three-tier structure of checkpoints. The WAI currently is working on a draft of the Web Content Accessibility Guidelines 2.0.
- One important WAI requirement is to ensure that every image, movie and sound on a Web site is accompanied by a description that clearly defines the item's purpose; the description is called an **<alt>** tag.
- Specialized user agents, such as screen readers (programs that allow users to hear what is being displayed on their screen) and braille displays (devices that receive data from screen-reading software and output the data as braille), allow people with visual impairments to access text-based information that normally is displayed on the screen.
- Using a screen reader to navigate a Web site can be time consuming and frustrating, because screen readers are unable to interpret pictures and other graphical content that do not have alternative text.
- Including links at the top of each Web page provides easy access to the page's main content.
- Web pages with large amounts of multimedia content are difficult for user agents to interpret unless they are designed properly. Images, movies and most non-XHTML objects cannot be read by screen readers.
- Misused heading tags (**<h1>**) also present challenges to some Web users—particularly those who cannot use a mouse.
- Web designers should avoid misuse of the **alt** attribute; it is intended to provide a short description of an XHTML object that might load improperly on some user agents.
- The value of the **longdesc** attribute is a text-based URL, linked to a Web page, that describes the image associated with the attribute.
- When creating a Web page for the general public, it is important to consider the reading level at which it is written. Web site designers can make their sites more readable through the use of shorter words; some users may have difficulty understanding slang and other nontraditional language.
- Web designers often use frames to display more than one XHTML file at a time. Unfortunately, frames often lack proper descriptions, which prevents users with text-based browsers and users with visual impairments from navigating the Web site.
- The **<noframes>** tag allows the designer to offer alternative content to users whose browsers do not support frames.
- VoiceXML has tremendous implications for people with visual impairments and for illiterate people. VoiceXML, a speech recognition and synthesis technology, reads Web pages to users and understands words spoken into a microphone.
- A VoiceXML document is composed of a series of dialogs and subdialogs, which result in spoken interaction between the user and the computer. VoiceXML is a voice-recognition technology.
- CallXML, a language created and supported by Voxeo, creates phone-to-Web applications. These applications tailor themselves to the user's input.
- When a user accesses a CallXML application, the incoming telephone call is referred to as a session. A CallXML application can support multiple sessions that enable the application to receive multiple telephone calls at any given time.
- A session terminates either when the user hangs up the telephone or when the CallXML application invokes the **hangup** element.
- The contents of a CallXML application are inserted within the **<callxml>** tag.
- CallXML tags that perform similar tasks should be enclosed within the **<block>** and **</block>** tags.

- To deploy a CallXML application, register with the Voxeo Community, which assigns a telephone number to the application so that other users may access it.
- Voxeo's logging feature enables developers to debug their telephone application by observing the "conversation" between the user and the application.
- Braille keyboards are similar to standard keyboards, except that, in addition to having each key labeled with the letter it represents, braille keyboards have the equivalent braille symbol printed on the key. Most often, braille keyboards are combined with a speech synthesizer or a braille display, so users are able to interact with the computer to verify that their typing is correct.
- People with visual impairments are not the only beneficiaries of the effort being made to improve markup languages. Individuals with hearing impairments also have a great number of tools to help them interpret auditory information delivered over the Web.
- Speech synthesis is another area in which research is being done to help people with disabilities.
- Open-source software for people with visual impairments already exists and is often superior to most of its proprietary, closed-source counterparts. However, it still does not use the Linux OS to its fullest extent.
- People with hearing impairments will soon benefit from what is called Synchronized Multimedia Integration Language (SMIL). This markup language is designed to add extra tracks—layers of content found within a single audio or video file. The additional tracks can contain data such as closed captioning.
- EagleEyes, developed by researchers at Boston College (**www.bc.edu/eagleeyes**), is a system that translates eye movements into mouse movements. Users move the mouse cursor by moving their eyes or head and are thereby able to control the computer.
- All of the accessibility options provided by Windows 2000 are available through the **Accessibility Wizard**. The **Accessibility Wizard** takes users step-by-step through all of the Windows accessibility features and configures their computers according to the chosen specifications.
- Microsoft Magnifier enlarges the section of your screen surrounding the mouse cursor.
- To solve problems with seeing the mouse cursor, Microsoft offers the ability to use larger cursors, black cursors and cursors that invert objects underneath them.
- **SoundSentry** is a tool that creates visual signals when system events occur.
- **ShowSounds** adds captions to spoken text and other sounds produced by today's multimedia-rich software.
- **StickyKeys** is a program that helps users who have difficulty in pressing multiple keys at the same time.
- **BounceKeys** forces the computer to ignore repeated keystrokes, solving the problem of accidentally pressing the same key more than once.
- **ToggleKeys** causes an audible beep to alert users that they have pressed one of the lock keys (i.e., *Caps Lock*, *Num Lock*, or *Scroll Lock*).
- **MouseKeys** is a tool that uses the keyboard to emulate mouse movements.
- The **Mouse Button Settings** tool allows you to create a virtual left-handed mouse by swapping the button functions.
- A timeout either enables or disables a certain action after the computer has idled for a specified amount of time. A common example of a timeout is a screen saver.
- Default settings are loaded when the computer is rebooted.
- You can create a **.acw** file, which, when chosen, will automatically activate the saved accessibility settings on any Windows 2000 computer.

- Microsoft **Narrator** is a text-to-speech program for people with visual impairments. It reads text, describes the current desktop environment and alerts the user when certain Windows events occur.

TERMINOLOGY

accessibility
accessibility aids in Visual Studio .NET
Accessibility Wizard
Accessibility Wizard initialization option
Accessibility Wizard mouse-cursor
 adjustment tool
`AccessibilityDescription` property of
 class `Control`
`AccessibilityName` property of
 class `Control`
`AccessibleDescription` property of
 class `Control`
`AccessibleName` property of
 class `Control`
`AccessibleRole` enumeration
`AccessibleRole` property of
 class `Control`
action element
Active Accessibility
Acts designed to ensure Internet access
 for people with disabilities
`.acw`
ADA (Americans with Disabilities Act)
advanced accessibility settings in Microsoft
 Internet Explorer 5.5
`alt` attribute
`<alt>` tag
Americans with Disabilities Act (ADA)
`answer` element
`assign` element
`<assign>` tag (`<assign>`…`</assign>`)
Aural Style Sheet
AuralCSS
`block` element
`<block>` tag (`<block>`…`</block>`)
BounceKeys
braille display
braille keyboard
`<break>` tag (`<break>`…`</break>`)
`call` element
`callerID` attribute
CallXML
`callxml` element
CallXML elements
CallXML `hangup` element
`caption` element

Cascading Style Sheets (CSS)
CAST eReader
Center for Applied Special Technology
`choice` element of `form` tag
`choice` element of `menu` tag
`<choice>` tag (`<choice>`…`</choice>`)
`clear` element
`clearDigits` element
Clicker 4
`conference` element
CORDA Technologies
`count` attribute if `prompt` element
CSS (Cascading Style Sheets)
CSS2
default setting
Display Color Settings
Display Settings
D-link
EagleEyes
Emacspeak
`encoding` declaration
end of session message
`<enumerate>` tag (`<enumerate>`…
 `</enumerate>`)
event handler
`hello.xml`
`isbn.xml`
`main.vxml`
`publications.vxml`
`withheaders.html`
`withoutheaders.html`
`<exit>` tag (`<exit>`…`</exit>`)
Extra Keyboard Help
`<filled>` tag (`<filled>`…`</filled>`)
Font Size dialog
`<form>` tag (`<form>`…`</form>`)
`format` attribute
frame
Freedom Scientific
get request type
`getDigits` element
global variable
`goto` element
`<goto>` tag (`<goto>`…`</goto>`)
`<grammar>` tag (`<grammar>`…
 `</grammar>`)

Gunning Fog Index
`headers` attribute
Henter-Joyce
Home Page Reader (HPR)
HPR (Home Page Reader)
HTTP (HyperText Transfer Protocol)
`<if>` tag (`<if>`…`</if>`)
`img` element
Inclusive Technology
`<input>`
`IsAccessible` property of class `Control`
Java Development Kit (Java SDK 1.3)
JAWS (Job Access with Sound)
JSML
linearized
`link` element in VoiceXML
`<link>` tag (`<link>`…`</link>`)
local dialog
logging feature
logic element
`longdesc` attribute
Lynx
`maxDigits` attribute
`maxTime` attribute
`<menu>` tag (`<menu>`…`</menu>`)
`method` attribute
Microsoft Internet Explorer accessibility options
Microsoft **Magnifier**
Microsoft Narrator
Microsoft **Narrator**
Microsoft **On-Screen Keyboard**
Mouse Button Settings
mouse cursor
Mouse Speed dialog
`MouseHover` event
MouseKeys
Narrator reading **Notepad** text
`next` attribute of `choice` element
`object`
Ocularis
`onHangup` element
`onMaxSilence` element
On-Screen Keyboard
`onTermDigit` element
`play` element
post request type
`prompt` element in VoiceXML
`<prompt>` tag (`<prompt>`…`</prompt>`)
RDK (Redistribution Kit)
readability

`recordAudio` element
Redistribution Kit (RDK)
`run` element
screen reader
scroll bar and window border size dialog
SDK (Software Development Kit)
`sendEvent` element
session
`session` attribute
sessionID
Set Automatic Timeouts
setting up window element size
shortcut key
ShowSounds
SMIL (Synchronized Multimedia
   Integration Language)
Software Development Kit (SDK)
SoundSentry
speech recognition
speech synthesis
speech synthesizer
StickyKeys
style sheet
`<subdialog>` tag (`<subdialog>`…
   `</subdialog>`)
`submit` attribute
`summary` attribute
Synchronized Multimedia Integration
   Language (SMIL)
system caret
tab order
tab stop
`TabIndex` property of class `Control`
table
`TabStop` property of class `Control`
`targetSessions` attribute
`termDigits` attribute
`text` element
text to speech (TTS)
`th` element
timeout
`timeout` attribute of `prompt` element
`title` tag (`<title>`…`</title>`)
ToggleKeys
track
TTS (text-to-speech) engine
`Type` class
user agent
`value` attribute
`var` attribute

`<var>` tag (`<var>`...`</var>`)
version declaration
ViaVoice
Visual Studio accessibility guidelines
Voice Server SDK 1.0
voice synthesis
voice technology
VoiceXML
VoiceXML tags
Voxeo (`www.voxeo.com`)
Voxeo Account Manager
`<vxml>` tag (`<vxml>`...`</vxml>`)
WAI (Web Accessibility Initiative)
WAI Quick Tip
wait element
Web Accessibility Initiative (WAI)
Web Content Accessibility Guidelines 1.0
Web Content Accessibility Guidelines 2.0 (Working Draft)
World Wide Web Consortium (W3C)
`www.voxeo.com` (Voxeo)
XHTML Recommendation
XML GL (XML Guidelines)
XML Guidelines (XML GL) 1930

SELF-REVIEW EXERCISES

24.1 Expand the following acronyms:
  a) W3C.
  b) WAI.
  c) JAWS.
  d) SMIL.
  e) CSS.

24.2 Fill in the blanks in each of the following statements.
  a) The highest priority of the Web Accessibility Initiative is to ensure that _____, _____ and _____ are accompanied by descriptions that clearly define their purposes.
  b) Technologies such as _____, _____ and _____ enable individuals with disabilities to work in a large number of positions.
  c) Although they are a great layout tool for presenting data, _____ are difficult for screen readers to interpret and convey clearly to a user.
  d) To make a frame accessible to individuals with disabilities, it is important to include _____ tags on the page.
  e) Blind people using computers often are assisted by _____ and _____.
  f) CallXML is used to create _____ applications that allow individuals to receive and send telephone calls.
  g) A _____ tag must be associated with the `<getDigits>` tag.

24.3 State whether each of the following is *true* or *false*. If *false*, explain why.
  a) Screen readers have no problem reading and translating images.
  b) When writing Web pages for the general public, it is important to consider the reading level of the context.
  c) The `<alt>` tag helps screen readers describe the images on a Web page.
  d) Blind people have been helped by the improvements made in speech-recognition technology more than any other group of people.
  e) VoiceXML lets users interact with Web content using speech recognition and speech synthesis technologies.
  f) Elements such as `onMaxSilence`, `onTermDigit` and `onMaxTime` are event handlers because they perform specified tasks when invoked.
  g) The debugging feature of the **Voxeo Account Manager** assists developers in debugging their CallXML applications.

ANSWERS TO SELF-REVIEW EXERCISES

24.1 a) World Wide Web Consortium. b) Web Accessibility Initiative. c) Job Access with Sound. d) Synchronized Multimedia Integration Language. e) Cascading Style Sheets.

24.2 a) image, movie, sound. b) voice activation, visual enhancers and auditory aids. c) tables. d) `<noframes>`. e) braille displays, braille keyboards. f) phone-to-Web. g) `<onTermDigit>`.

24.3 a) False. Screen readers cannot directly interpret images. If the programmer includes an `alt` attribute inside the `<img>` tag, the screen reader reads this description to the user. b) True. c) True. d) False. Although speech-recognition technology has had a large impact on blind people, speech-recognition technology has had also a large impact on people who have trouble typing. e) True. f) True. g) False. The logging feature assists developers in debugging their CallXML application.

EXERCISES

24.4 Insert XHTML markup into each segment to make the segment accessible to someone with disabilities. The contents of images and frames should be apparent from the context and filenames.

a) ```<img src = "dogs.jpg" width = "300" height = "250" />```

b) ```
<table width = "75%">
    <tr><th>Language</th><th>Version</th></tr>
    <tr><td>XHTML</td><td>1.0</td></tr>
    <tr><td>Perl</td><td>5.6.0</td></tr>
    <tr><td>Java</td><td>1.3</td></tr>
</table>
```

c) ```
<map name = "links">
    <area href = "index.html" shape = "rect"
       coords = "50, 120, 80, 150" />
    <area href = "catalog.html" shape = "circle"
       coords = "220, 30" />
</map>
<img src = "antlinks.gif" width = "300" height = "200"
    usemap = "#links" />
```

24.5 Define the following terms:
  a) Action element.
  b) Gunning Fog Index.
  c) Screen reader.
  d) Session.
  e) Web Accessibility Initiative (WAI).

24.6 Describe the three-tier structure of checkpoints (priority one, priority two and priority three) set forth by the WAI.

24.7 Why do misused `<h1>` heading tags create problems for screen readers?

24.8 Use CallXML to create a voice-mail system that plays a voice-mail greeting and records a message. Have friends and classmates call your application and leave a message.

Operator Precedence Chart

Operators are shown in decreasing order of precedence from top to bottom with each level of precedence separated by a horizontal line. Visual Basic operators associate from left to right.

Operator	Type
^	exponentiation
+	unary plus
-	unary minus
*	multiplication
/	division
\	integer division
Mod	modulus
+	addition
-	subtraction
&	concatenation
=	relational is equal to
<>	relational is not equal to
<	relational less than
<=	relational less than or equal to
>	relational greater than
>=	relational greater than or equal to
Like	pattern matching
Is	reference comparison
TypeOf	type comparison

Fig. A.1 Operator precedence chart (part 1 of 2).

Appendix A

Operator	Type
`Not`	logical negation
`And`	logical AND without short-circuit evaluation
`AndAlso`	logical AND with short-circuit evaluation
`Or`	logical inclusive OR without short-circuit evaluation
`OrElse`	logical inclusive OR with short-circuit evaluation
`Xor`	logical exclusive OR

Fig. A.1 Operator precedence chart (part 2 of 2).

Number Systems (on CD)

Objectives

- To understand basic number system concepts such as base, positional value and symbol value.
- To understand how to work with numbers represented in the binary, octal and hexadecimal number systems
- To be able to abbreviate binary numbers as octal numbers or hexadecimal numbers.
- To be able to convert octal numbers and hexadecimal numbers to binary numbers.
- To be able to covert back and forth between decimal numbers and their binary, octal and hexadecimal equivalents.
- To understand binary arithmetic and how negative binary numbers are represented using two's complement notation.

Appendix B is included on the CD that accompanies this book in printable Adobe® Acrobat® PDF format. The appendix includes pages 1266–1279.

Career Opportunities (on CD)

Objectives

- To explore the various online career services.
- To examine the advantages and disadvantages of posting and finding jobs online.
- To review the major online career services Web sites available to job seekers.
- To explore the various online services available to employers seeking to build their workforces.

Appendix C is included on the CD that accompanies this book in printable Adobe® Acrobat® PDF format. The appendix includes pages 1280–1301.

Visual Studio .NET Debugger

Objectives

- To understand syntax and logic errors.
- To become familiar with the Visual Studio .NET debugging tools.
- To understand the use of breakpoints to suspend program execution.
- To be able to examine data using expressions in the debugging windows.
- To be able to debug procedures and objects.

And often times excusing of a fault
Doth make the fault the worse by the excuse.
William Shakespeare

To err is human, to forgive divine.
Alexander Pope, *An Essay on Criticism*

Outline

D.1	Introduction
D.2	Breakpoints
D.3	Examining Data
D.4	Program Control
D.5	Additional Procedure Debugging Capabilities
D.6	Additional Class Debugging Capabilities

Summary

D.1 Introduction

Syntax errors (or compilation errors) occur when program statements violate the grammatical rules of a programming language, such as forgetting to end a module with **End Module** (Fig. D.1). Syntax errors are caught by the compiler. In Visual Studio .NET, syntax errors appear in the *Task List* window along with a description, line number and the file name. For additional information on a specific syntax error, select it in the **Task List** and press *F1* to open a help window. Programs that contain syntax errors cannot be executed.

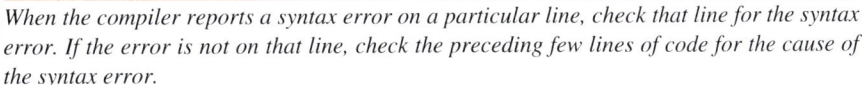

When the compiler reports a syntax error on a particular line, check that line for the syntax error. If the error is not on that line, check the preceding few lines of code for the cause of the syntax error.

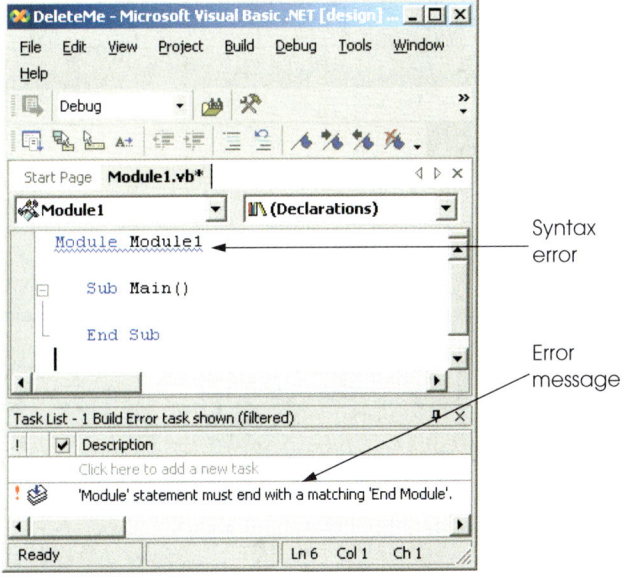

Fig. D.1   Syntax error.

Testing and Debugging Tip D.2

After fixing one error, recompile your program. You may observe that the number of overall errors perceived by the compiler is significantly reduced.

Debugging is the process of finding and correcting *logic errors* in applications. Logic errors are more subtle than syntax errors because the program compiles successfully, but does not run as expected. Logic errors are often difficult to debug because the programmer cannot see the code as it is executing. Some programmers attempt to debug programs using message boxes or `Console.WriteLine` statements. For example, the programmer might print the value of a variable when the variable's value changes to determine if it is being set correctly. This method is cumbersome, because programmers must write a line of code wherever they suspect may be a problem. Once the program has been debugged, the programmer must remove these printing statements.

Debuggers provide a set of tools that allow the programmer to analyze a program while it is running. These tools allow the programmer to suspend program execution, examine and set variables, call procedures without having to modify the program and much more. In this appendix, we introduce the Visual Studio .NET debugger and several of its debugging tools. [*Note*: A program must successfully compile before it can be used in the debugger.]

D.2 Breakpoints

Breakpoints are a simple but powerful debugging tool. A breakpoint is a marker that can be set at any executable line of code. When a program reaches a breakpoint, execution pauses, allowing the programmer to examine the state of the program and ensure that everything is working properly. We use the following program (Fig. D.2) to demonstrate debugging a loop using the features of the Visual Studio .NET debugger. This program is designed to output the value of ten factorial (10!), but contains two logic errors—the first iteration of the loop multiplies **x** by **10** instead of **9**, and the result of the factorial calculation **0**.

```vb
1   ' Fig. D.2: DebugExample.vb
2   ' Sample program to debug.
3
4   Module modDebug
5
6      Sub Main()
7         Dim x As Integer = 10
8         Dim i As Integer
9
10        Console.Write("The value of " & x & " factorial is: ")
11
12        ' loop to determine x factorial, contains logic error
13        For i = x To 0 Step -1
14           x *= i
15        Next
16
17        Console.WriteLine(x)
18     End Sub ' Main
19
20  End Module ' modDebug
```

Fig. D.2 Debug sample program (part 1 of 2).

```
The value of 10 factorial is: 0
```

Fig. D.2 Debug sample program (part 2 of 2).

To enable the debugger, compile the program using the debug configuration (Fig. D.3). Select **Debug** from the configuration toolbar item if it is not already selected. Alternatively, select **Build > Configuration Manager** and change the **Active Solution Configuration** to **Debug**.

To set breakpoints in Visual Studio, click the gray area to the left of any line of code (Fig. D.4) or right-click a line of code and select **Insert Breakpoint**. A solid red circle appears, indicating that the breakpoint has been set. When the program executes, it suspends when it reaches the line containing the breakpoint.

Selecting **Debug > Start** begins the debugging process. When debugging a console application, the console window appears (Fig. D.5), allowing program interaction (input and output). When the breakpoint (line 14) is reached, program execution is suspended, and the IDE becomes the active window. Programmers may need to switch between the IDE and the console window while debugging programs.

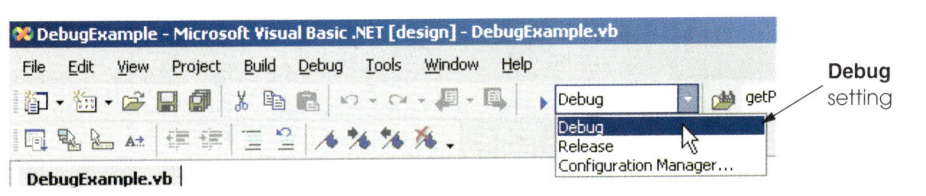

Fig. D.3 Debug configuration setting.

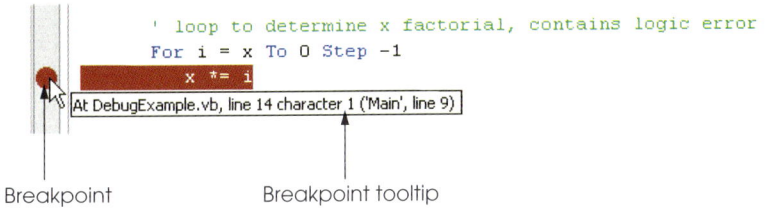

Fig. D.4 Setting a breakpoint.

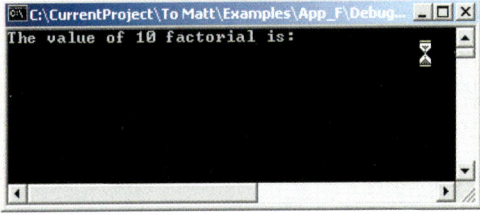

Fig. D.5 Console application suspended for debugging.

Figure D.6 shows the IDE with program execution suspended at a breakpoint. The *yellow arrow* to the left of the statement

```
x *= i
```

indicates that execution is suspended at this line and that this line contains the next statement to execute. Note that the title bar of the IDE displays **[break]**—this indicates that the IDE is in *break mode* (i.e., the debugger is being used). Once the program has reached the breakpoint, you may "hover" with the mouse on a variable (in this case **x** or **i**) in the source code to see the value of that variable.

Testing and Debugging Tip D.3

*Loops that iterate many times can be executed in full (without stopping every time through the loop) by placing a breakpoint after the loop and selecting **Start** from the **Debug** menu.*

D.3 Examining Data

Visual Studio .NET includes several debugging windows, all accessible from the **Debug > Windows** submenu. Some windows are listed only when the IDE is in break mode (also called *debug mode*). The **Watch** window (Fig. D.7), which is available only in break mode, allows the programmer to examine variable values and expressions. Visual Studio provides a total of four windows that allow programmers to organize and view variables and expressions.

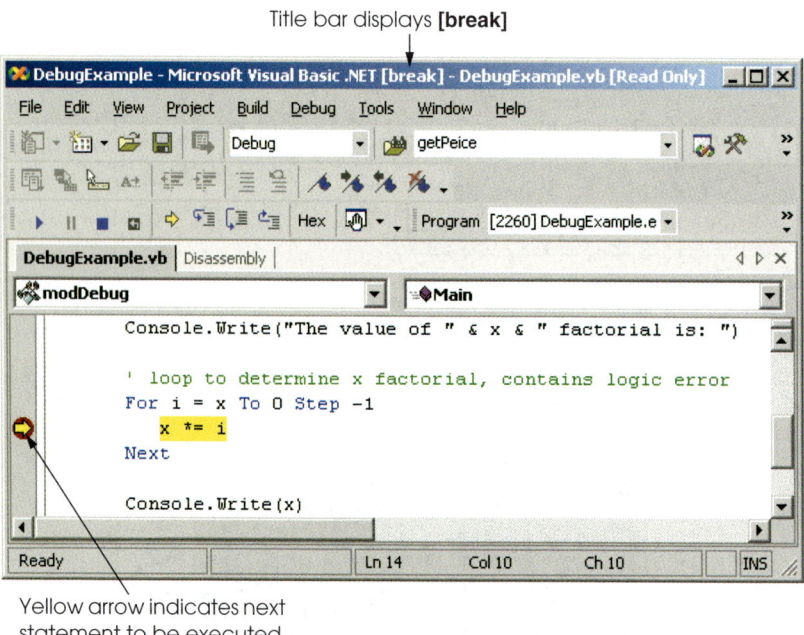

Fig. D.6 Execution suspended at a breakpoint.

The **Watch** window is initially empty. To examine data, type an expression into the **Name** field. Most valid Visual Basic expressions can be entered in the **Name** field, including expressions that contain procedure calls. Consult the documentation under "debugger, expressions" for a full description of valid expressions.

Once an expression has been entered, its type and value appear in the **Value** and **Type** fields. The first expression in Fig. D.7 is the variable `i`—it is **10** because the **For** loop (line 13) assigns the value of `x` (**10**) to `i`. The **Watch** window also can evaluate more complex arithmetic expressions (e.g., **(i + 3) * 5**). Note that expressions containing the **=** symbol are treated as **Boolean** expressions instead of assignment statements. For example, the expression **i = 3** evaluates to **False**. The value of `i` is not altered.

To debug the program in Fig. D.2, we might enter the expression **i * x** in the **Watch** window. When we reach the breakpoint for the first time, this expression has a value **100**, which indicates a logic error in our program (our calculation contains an extra factor of 10). To fix the error, we could subtract **1** from the initial value of the **For** loop (i.e., change **10** to **9**).

If a **Name** field in the **Watch** window contains a variable name, the variable's value can be modified for debugging purposes. To modify a variable's value, click its value in the **Value** field and enter a new value. Any modified value appears in red.

If an expression is invalid, an error appears in the **Value** field. For example, the fourth expression in Fig. D.7 is an invalid expression because **VariableThatDoesNotExist** is not an identifier used in the program. Visual Studio .NET issues an error message and displays its contents in the **Value** field. To remove an expression, select it and press *Delete*.

Testing and Debugging Tip D.4

*When a procedure is called from a **Watch** window, the program does not stop at breakpoints inside the procedure. Do not call procedures that may have errors from the **Watch** window.*

The **Locals** and **Autos** windows are similar to the **Watch** window, except the programmer does not specify their contents. The **Locals** window displays the name and current value for all the local variables or objects in the current scope. The **Autos** window displays the variables and objects used in the previous statement and the current statement (indicated by the yellow arrow). Variables can be changed in either window by clicking the appropriate **Value** field and entering a new value. When executing an object's procedure, the **Me** window displays data for that object. If the program is inside a procedure that does not belong to an object (such as **Main**), the **Me** window is empty.

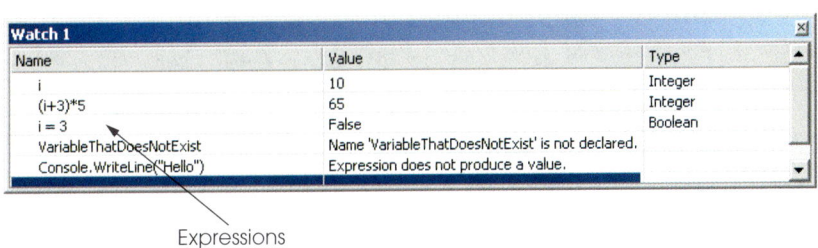

Fig. D.7 **Watch** window.

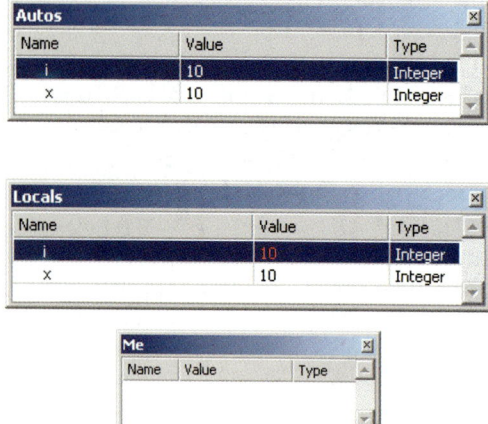

Fig. D.8 **Autos** and **Locals** windows.

The ***Immediate*** window provides a convenient way to execute statements (Fig. D.9). To execute a statement, type it into the window and press *Enter*. Procedure calls can be executed as well. For example, typing `Console.WriteLine(i)` then pressing *Enter* outputs the value of **i** in the console window. Notice that the **=** symbol can be used to perform assignments in the **Immediate** window. Notice that the values for **i** and **x** in the **Locals** window contain these updated values.

Testing and Debugging Tip D.5

Use the **Immediate** *window to call a procedure exactly once. Placing a procedure call inside the* **Watch** *window calls it every time the program breaks.*

D.4 Program Control

The **Debug** toolbar (Fig. D.10) contains buttons for controlling the debugging process. These buttons provide convenient access to actions in the **Debug** menu. To display the **Debug** toolbar, select **View > Toolbars > Debug**.

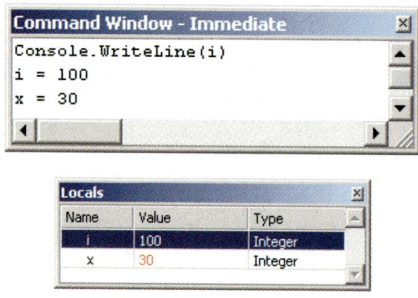

Fig. D.9 **Immediate** window.

Appendix D   Visual Studio .NET Debugger   1309

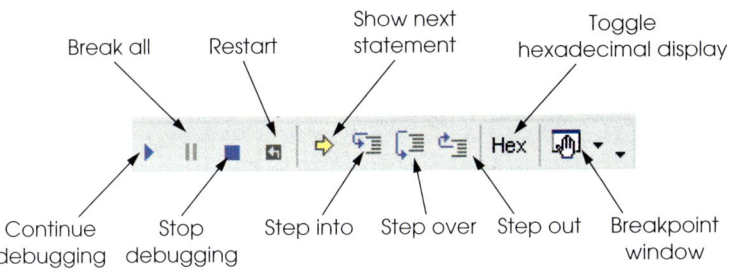

Fig. D.10 Debug toolbar icons.

The **Restart** button restarts the application, pausing at the beginning of the program to allow the programmer to set breakpoints before the program executes. The **Continue** button resumes execution of a suspended program. The **Stop Debugging** button ends the debugging session. The **Break All** button allows the user to suspend an executing program directly (i.e., without explicitly setting breakpoints). After execution is suspended, the yellow arrow appears indicating the next statement to be executed.

Testing and Debugging Tip D.6

When a program is executing, problems such as infinite loops usually can be interrupted by selecting **Debug > Break All** *or by clicking the corresponding button on the toolbar.*

Clicking the **Show Next Statement** button places the cursor on the same line as the yellow arrow that indicates the next statement to execute. This command is useful when returning to the current execution point after setting breakpoints in a program that contains a large number of lines of code.

The **Step Over** button executes the next executable line of code and advances the yellow arrow to the next line. If the next line of code contains a procedure call, the procedure is executed in its entirety as one step. This button allows the user to execute the program one line at a time without seeing the details of every procedure that is called. We discuss the **Step Into** and **Step Out** buttons in the next section.

The **Hex** button toggles the display format of data. If enabled, **Hex** displays data in hexadecimal (base 16) form, rather than decimal (base 10) form. Experienced programmers often prefer to read values in hexadecimal format—especially large numbers. For more information about the hexadecimal and decimal number formats, see Appendix B, Number Systems.

The **Breakpoints** window displays all the breakpoints currently set for the program (Fig. D.11). A checkbox appears next to each breakpoint, indicating whether the breakpoint is *active* (checked) or *disabled* (unchecked). Lines with disabled breakpoints contain an unfilled red circle rather than a solid one (Fig. D.12). The debugger does not pause execution at disabled breakpoints.

The **Condition** field displays the condition a that must be satisfied to suspend program execution at that breakpoint. The **Hit Count** field displays the number of times the debugger has stopped at each breakpoint. Double-clicking an item in the **Breakpoints** window moves the cursor to the line containing that breakpoint. The down-arrow immediately to the right of the **Breakpoints** button provides access to the various debugging windows. [*Note*: Choosing another debugging window from the list changes the icon displayed.]

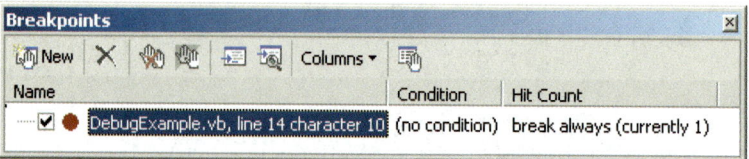

Fig. D.11 Breakpoints window.

```
' loop to determine x factorial, contains logic error
For i = x To 0 Step -1
    x *= i
Next
```

Disabled breakpoint

Fig. D.12 Disabled breakpoint.

> **Testing and Debugging Tip D.7**
>
> *Disabled breakpoints allow the programmer to maintain breakpoints in key locations in the program so they can be used again when needed. Disabled breakpoints are always visible.*

Breakpoints can be added using the **Breakpoints** window by clicking the **New** button, which displays the **New Breakpoint** dialog (Fig. D.13). The **Function**, **File**, **Address** and **Data** tabs allow the programmer to cause execution to suspends at a procedure, a line in a particular file, an instruction in memory or when the value of a variable changes. The **Hit Count...** button (Fig. D.14) can be used to specify when the breakpoint should suspend the program (the default is to always break). A breakpoint can be set to suspend the program when the hit count reaches a specific number, is a multiple of a number or is greater than or equal to a specific number.

The Visual Studio debugger also allows execution to suspend at a breakpoint depending upon the value of an expression. Clicking the **Condition...** button opens the **Breakpoint Condition** dialog (Fig. D.15). The **Condition** checkbox indicates whether breakpoint conditions are enabled. The radio buttons determine how the expression in the text box is evaluated. The **is true** radio button pauses execution at the breakpoint whenever the expression is true. The **has changed** radio button causes program execution to suspend when it first encounters the breakpoint and again time the expression differs from its previous value when the breakpoint is encountered.

For example, suppose we set `x * i <> 0` as the condition for the breakpoint in our loop with the **has changed** option enabled. (We might choose to do this because the program produces an incorrect output of `0`). Program execution suspends when it first reaches the breakpoint and records that the expression has a value of `True`, because `x * i` is `100` (or `10` if we fixed the earlier logic error). We continue, and the loop decrements `i`. While `i` is between `10` and `1`, the condition's value never changes, and execution is not suspended at that breakpoint. When `i` is `0`, the expression `x * i <> 0` is `False`, and execution is suspended. This leads to the identification of the second logic error in our program—that the final iteration of the **For** loop multiplies the result by **0**. When finished debugging, click the **Stop Debugging** button on the **Debug** toolbar. The IDE returns to design mode.

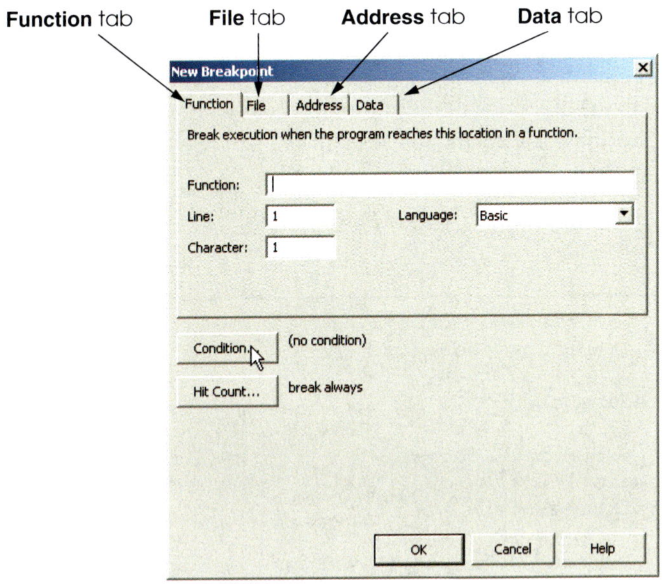

Fig. D.13 New Breakpoint dialog.

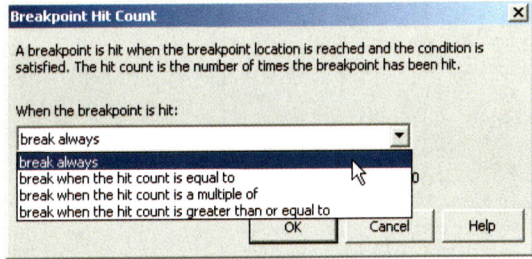

Fig. D.14 Breakpoint Hit Count dialog.

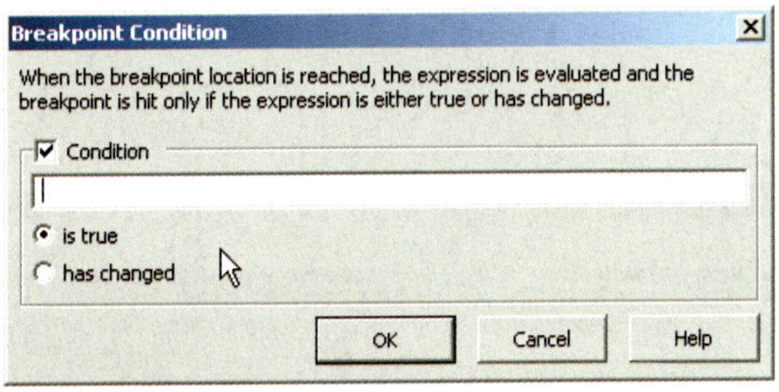

Fig. D.15 Breakpoint Condition dialog.

D.5 Additional Procedure Debugging Capabilities

The Visual Studio debugger includes tools for analyzing procedures and procedure calls. We demonstrate some procedure-debugging tools with the following example (Fig. D.16).

The **Call Stack** window contains the program's *procedure call stack*, which allows the programmer to determine the exact sequence of calls that led to the current procedure and to examine calling procedures on the stack. This window helps the programmer see the flow of control that led to the execution of the current procedure. For example, if we place a breakpoint in **MyProcedure**, we get the call stack in Fig. D.17. The program called procedure **Main** first, followed by **MyProcedure**.

```vb
 1  ' Fig. D.16: ProcedureDebugExample.vb
 2  ' Demonstrates debugging procedures.
 3
 4  Module modProcedureDebug
 5
 6     ' entry point for application
 7     Public Sub Main()
 8        Dim i As Integer
 9
10        ' display MyProcedure return values
11        For i = 0 To 10
12           Console.WriteLine(MyProcedure(i))
13        Next
14     End Sub ' Main
15
16     ' perform calculation
17     Public Function MyProcedure(ByVal x As Integer) As Integer
18        Return (x * x) - (3 * x) + 7
19     End Function ' MyProcedure
20
21     ' method with logic error
22     Public Function BadProcedure(ByVal x As Integer) As Integer
23        Return MyProcedure(x) \ x
24     End Function ' BadProcedure
25
26  End Module ' modProcedureDebug
```

Fig. D.16 Demonstrates procedure debugging.

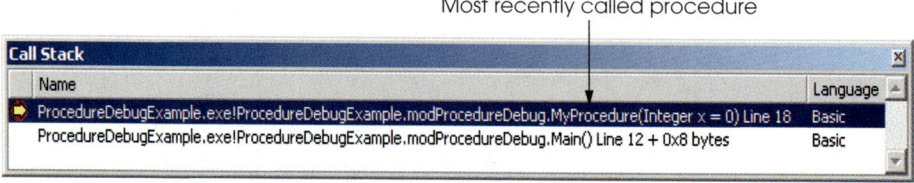

Fig. D.17 **Call Stack** window.

Appendix D   Visual Studio .NET Debugger   1313

Double-clicking any line in the **Call Stack** window displays the last executed line in that procedure. Visual Studio .NET highlights the line in green and displays the tooltip shown in Fig. D.18. A green triangle also is displayed to the left of the line to emphasize the line further.

Visual Studio .NET also provides additional program control buttons for debugging-procedures. The **Step Over** button executes one statement in a procedure, then pauses program execution again. As previously mentioned, if a statement contains a procedure call, the called procedure executes in its entirety. The next statement that will be executed is the statement that follows the procedure call. In contrast, the **Step Into** button executes program statements, one per click, including statements in the procedures that are called. **Step Into** transfers control to the procedure, which allows programmers to confirm the procedure's execution, line-by-line. The **Step Out** finishes executing the procedure and returns control to the line that called the procedure.

> **Testing and Debugging Tip D.8**
>
> *Use **Step Out** to finish a procedure that was stepped into accidentally.*

Figure D.19 lists each program-control debug feature, its shortcut key and a description. Experienced programmers often use these shortcut keys in preference to accessing the menu commnads.

```
        ' display MyProcedure return values
        For i = 0 To 10
            Console.WriteLine(MyProcedure(i))
[This code has called into another function. When that function is finished, this is the next statement that will be executed.]
        End Sub ' Main

        ' perform calculation
        Public Function MyProcedure(ByVal x As Integer) As Integer
            Return (x * x) - (3 * x) + 7
        End Function   ' MyProcedure
```

Fig. D.18 IDE displaying a procedures calling point.

Control Button	Shortcut Key	Description
Continue	F5	Continue running program. Execution continues until either a breakpoint is encountered or the program ends (through normal execution).
Stop Debugging	Shift + F5	Stop debugging and return to Visual Studio design mode.
Step Over	F10	Step to next command, do not step into procedure calls.
Step Into	F11	Execute next statement. If the statement contains a procedure call, control transfers to the procedure for line-by-line debugging. If the statement does not contain a procedure call, **Step Into** behaves like **Step Over**.
Step Out	Shift + F11	Finishes executing the current procedure and suspends program execution in the calling procedure.

Fig. D.19 Debug program control features.

The **Immediate** window (Fig. D.20) discussed in Section D.3 is useful for testing arguments passed to a procedure. This helps determine if a procedure is functioning properly without the programmer modifying code.

D.6 Additional Class Debugging Capabilities

Visual Studio includes class debugging features which allow the programmer to determine the current state of objects used in a program. We demonstrate some class debugging features using the code presented in Fig. D.21. We place a breakpoint at the location shown in Fig. D.22. [*Note*: A Visual Basic file may contain multiple classes, as is the case with this example.]

```
Command Window - Immediate
Console.WriteLine(MyProcedure(0))
Console.WriteLine(BadProcedure(0))
Run-time exception thrown : System.DivideByZeroException - Attempted to divide by zero.
```

Fig. D.20 Using the **Immediate** window to debug procedures.

```vb
1   ' Fig. D.21: DebugClass.vb
2   ' Console application to demonstrate debugging objects.
3
4   Public Class CDebugEntry
5      Private mSomeInteger As Integer = 123
6      Private mIntegerArray As Integer() = {74, 101, 102, 102}
7      Private mDebugClass As CDebugClass
8      Private mRandomObject As Random
9      Private mList As Object() = New Object(2) {}
10
11     Public Sub New()
12        mRandomObject = New Random()
13        mDebugClass = New CDebugClass("Hello World", _
14           New Object())
15
16        mList(0) = mIntegerArray
17        mList(1) = mDebugClass
18        mList(2) = mRandomObject
19     End Sub ' New
20
21     Public Sub DisplayValues()
22        Console.WriteLine(mRandomObject.Next())
23        Console.WriteLine(mDebugClass.SomeString)
24        Console.WriteLine(mIntegerArray(0))
25     End Sub ' DisplayValues
26
27     ' main entry point for application
28     Public Shared Sub Main()
29
```

Fig. D.21 Debugging a class (part 1 of 2).

```vbnet
30         Dim entry As CDebugEntry = New CDebugEntry()
31         entry.DisplayValues()
32      End Sub ' Main
33
34   End Class ' DebugEntry
35
36   ' demonstrates class debugging
37   Public Class CDebugClass
38
39      ' declarations
40      Private mSomeString As String
41      Private mPrivateRef As Object
42
43      Public Sub New(ByVal stringData As String, _
44         ByVal objectData As Object)
45
46         mSomeString = stringData
47         mPrivateRef = objectData
48
49      End Sub ' New
50
51      Public Property SomeString() As String
52
53         Get
54            Return SomeString
55         End Get
56
57         Set(ByVal Value As String)
58
59            SomeString = Value
60         End Set
61
62      End Property ' SomeString
63
64   End Class ' CDebugClass
```

Fig. D.21 Debugging a class (part 2 of 2).

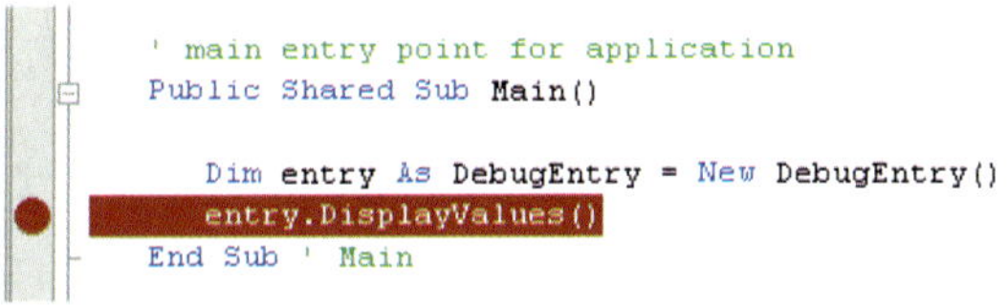

Fig. D.22 Breakpoint location for class debugging.

To assist class debugging, Visual Studio .NET allows the programmer to expand and view all data members and properties of a class, including **Private** members. In any of the four windows (i.e., **Watch**, **Locals**, **Autos** and **Me**), a class that has data members is displayed with a plus (**+**) next to it (Fig. D.23). Clicking the plus box displays all of the object's data members and their values. If a member references an object, the object's data members also can be listed by clicking the object's plus box.

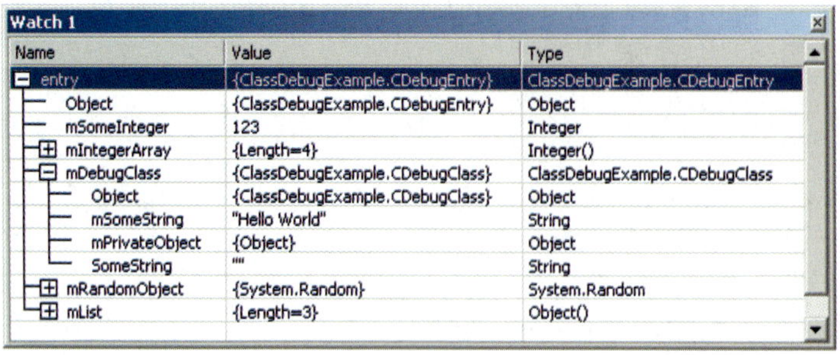

Fig. D.23 Expanded class in **Watch** window.

One of the most valuable features of the debugger is the ability to display all the values in an array. Figure D.24 displays the contents of the `mList` array. At index `0` is `mIntegerArray`, which is expanded to show its contents. Index `1` contains a `DebugClass` object—expanded to show the object's `Private` data members, as well as a `Public` property. Index `2` contains a `Random` object, defined in the Framework Class Library (FCL).

The Visual Studio debugger contains several other debugging windows, including **Threads**, **Modules**, **Memory**, **Disassembly** and **Registers**. These windows are used by experienced programmers to debug large, complex projects—consult the Visual Studio .NET documentation for more details on these features.

In this appendix we demonstrated several techniques for debugging programs, procedures and classes. The Visual Studio .NET debugger is a powerful tool, which allows programmers to build more robust fault tolerant programs.

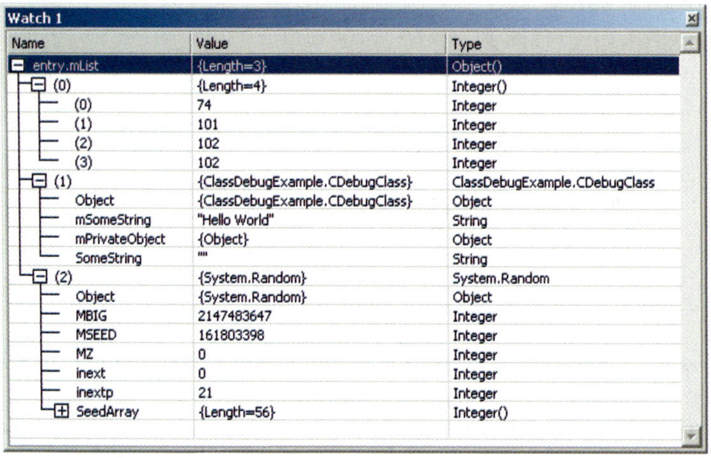

Fig. D.24 Expanded array in **Watch** window.

SUMMARY

- Debugging is the process of finding logic errors in applications.
- Syntax errors (or compilation errors) occur when program statements violate the grammatical rules of a programming language. These errors are caught by the compiler.
- Logic errors are more subtle than syntax errors. They occur when a program compiles successfully, but does not run as expected.
- Debuggers can suspend a program at any point, which allows programmers to examine and set variables and call procedures.
- A breakpoint is a marker set at a line of code. When a program reaches a breakpoint, execution is suspended. The programmer then can examine the state of the program and ensure that the program is working properly.
- To enable the debugging features, the program must be compiled using the debug configuration.
- To set breakpoints, click the gray area to the left of any line of code. Alternatively, right-click a line of code and select **Insert Breakpoint**.
- The **Watch** window allows the programmer to examine variable values and expressions. To examine data, type a valid Visual Basic expression, such as a variable name, into the **Name** field. Once the expression has been entered, its type and value appear in the **Type** and **Value** fields.
- Variables in the **Watch** window can be modified by the user for testing purposes. To modify a variable's value, click the **Value** field and enter a new value.
- The **Locals** window displays the name and current value for all the local variables or objects in the current scope.
- The **Autos** window displays the variables and objects used in the previous statement and the current statement (indicated by the yellow arrow).
- To evaluate an expression in the **Immediate** window, simply type the expression into the window and press *Enter*.
- The **Continue** button resumes execution of a suspended program.
- The **Stop Debugging** button ends the debugging session.
- The **Break All** button allows the programmer to place an executing program in break mode.
- The **Show Next Statement** button places the cursor on the same line as the yellow arrow that indicates the next statement to execute.
- The **Step Over** button executes the next executable line of code and advances the yellow arrow to the following executable line in the program. If the line of code contains a procedure call, the procedure is executed in its entirety as one step.
- The **Hex** button toggles the display format of data. If enabled, **Hex** displays data in a hexadecimal (base 16) form, rather than decimal (base 10) form.
- The **Breakpoints** window displays all the breakpoints currently set for a program.
- Disabled breakpoints allow the programmer to maintain breakpoints in key locations in the program so they can be used again when needed.
- The **Call Stack** window contains the program's procedure call stack, which allows the programmer to determine the exact sequence of calls that led to the current procedure and to examine calling procedures on the stack.
- The **Step Over** button executes one statement in a procedure, then pauses program execution.
- The **Step Into** button executes next statement. If the statement contains a procedure call, control transfers to the procedure for line-by-line debugging. If the statement does not contain a procedure call, **Step Into** behaves like **Step Over**.

- The **Step Out** finishes executing the procedure and returns control to the line that called the procedure.
- The **Immediate** window is useful for testing arguments passed to a procedure. This helps determine if a procedure is functioning properly.
- Visual Studio .NET includes class debugging features which allow the programmer to determine the current state of any objects used in a program.
- To assist class debugging, Visual Studio .NET allows the programmer to expand and view all data members variables and properties of an object, including those declared `Private`.

ASCII Character Set

	0	1	2	3	4	5	6	7	8	9
0	nul	soh	stx	etx	eot	enq	ack	bel	bs	ht
1	nl	vt	ff	cr	so	si	dle	dc1	dc2	dc3
2	dc4	nak	syn	etb	can	em	sub	esc	fs	gs
3	rs	us	sp	!	"	#	$	%	&	`
4	(	)	*	+	,	-	.	/	0	1
5	2	3	4	5	6	7	8	9	:	;
6	<	=	>	?	@	A	B	C	D	E
7	F	G	H	I	J	K	L	M	N	O
8	P	Q	R	S	T	U	V	W	X	Y
9	Z	[	\	]	^	_	'	a	b	c
10	d	e	f	g	h	i	j	k	l	m
11	n	o	p	q	r	s	t	u	v	w
12	x	y	z	{	|	}	~	del		

Fig. E.1 ASCII character set.

The digits at the left of the table are the left digits of the decimal equivalent (0–127) of the character code, and the digits at the top of the table are the right digits of the character code. For example, the character code for "F" is 70, and the character code for "&" is 38.

Most users of this book are interested in the ASCII character set used to represent English characters on many computers. The ASCII character set is a subset of the Unicode character set used by Visual Basic to represent characters from most of the world's languages. For more information on the Unicode character set, see Appendix F.

F

Unicode® (on CD)

Objectives

- To become familiar with Unicode.
- To discuss the mission of the Unicode Consortium.
- To discuss the design basis of Unicode.
- To understand the three Unicode encoding forms: UTF-8, UTF-16 and UTF-32.
- To introduce characters and glyphs.
- To discuss the advantages and disadvantages of using Unicode.
- To provide a brief tour of the Unicode Consortium's Web site.

Appendix F is included on the CD that accompanies this book in printable Adobe® Acrobat® PDF format. The appendix includes pages 1320–1331.

G

COM Integration (on CD)

Appendix G is included on the CD that accompanies this book in printable Adobe® Acrobat® PDF format. The appendix includes pages 1332–1343.

Introduction to HyperText Markup Language 4: Part 1 (on CD)

Objectives

- To understand the key components of an HTML document.
- To be able to use basic HTML elements to create World Wide Web pages.
- To be able to add images to your Web pages.
- To understand how to create and use hyperlinks to traverse Web pages.
- To be able to create lists of information.

Appendix H is included on the CD that accompanies this book in printable Adobe® Acrobat® PDF format. The appendix includes pages 1344–1366.

9

Introduction to HyperText Markup Language 4: Part 2 (on CD)

Objectives

- To be able to create tables with rows and columns of data.
- To be able to control the display and formatting of tables.
- To be able to create and use forms.
- To be able to create and use image maps to aid hyperlinking.
- To be able to make Web pages accessible to search engines.
- To be able to use the **frameset** element to create more interesting Web pages.

Appendix I is included on the CD that accompanies this book in printable Adobe® Acrobat® PDF format. The appendix includes pages 1367–1399.

J

Introduction to XHTML: Part 1 (on CD)

Objectives

- To understand important components of XHTML documents.
- To use XHTML to create World Wide Web pages.
- To be able to add images to Web pages.
- To understand how to create and use hyperlinks to navigate Web pages.
- To be able to mark up lists of information.

Appendix J is included on the CD that accompanies this book in printable Adobe® Acrobat® PDF format. The appendix includes pages 1400–1425.

Introduction to XHTML: Part 2 (on CD)

Objectives

- To be able to create tables with rows and columns of data.
- To be able to control table formatting.
- To be able to create and use forms.
- To be able to create and use image maps to aid in Web-page navigation.
- To be able to make Web pages accessible to search engines through `<meta>` tags.
- To be able to use the `frameset` element to display multiple Web pages in a single browser window.

Appendix K is included on the CD that accompanies this book in printable Adobe® Acrobat® PDF format. The appendix includes pages 1426–1460.

HTML/XHTML Special Characters

The table of Fig. L.1 shows many commonly used HTML/XHTML special characters—called *character entity references* by the World Wide Web Consortium. For a complete list of character entity references, see the site

    `www.w3.org/TR/REC-html40/sgml/entities.html`

Character	HTML/XHTML encoding	Character	HTML/XHTML encoding
non-breaking space	` `	ê	`&#234;`
§	`&#167;`	ì	`&#236;`
©	`&#169;`	í	`&#237;`
®	`&#174;`	î	`&#238;`
π	`&#188;`	ñ	`&#241;`
∫	`&#189;`	ò	`&#242;`
Ω	`&#190;`	ó	`&#243;`
à	`&#224;`	ô	`&#244;`
á	`&#225;`	õ	`&#245;`
â	`&#226;`	÷	`&#247;`
ã	`&#227;`	ù	`&#249;`
å	`&#229;`	ú	`&#250;`
ç	`&#231;`	û	`&#251;`
è	`&#232;`	•	`&#8226;`
é	`&#233;`	™	`&#8482;`

Fig. L.1   XHTML special characters.

HTML/XHTML Colors

Colors may be specified by using a standard name (such as **aqua**) or a hexadecimal RGB value (such as **#00FFFF** for **aqua**). Of the six hexadecimal digits in an RGB value, the first two represent the amount of red in the color, the middle two represent the amount of green in the color, and the last two represent the amount of blue in the color. For example, **black** is the absence of color and is defined by **#000000**, whereas **white** is the maximum amount of red, green and blue and is defined by **#FFFFFF**. Pure **red** is **#FF0000**, pure green (which is called **lime**) is **#00FF00** and pure **blue** is **#0000FF**. Note that **green** in the standard is defined as **#008000**. Figure M.1 contains the HTML/XHTML standard color set. Figure M.2 contains the HTML/XHTML extended color set.

Color name	Value	Color name	Value
aqua	#00FFFF	navy	#000080
black	#000000	olive	#808000
blue	#0000FF	purple	#800080
fuchsia	#FF00FF	red	#FF0000
gray	#808080	silver	#C0C0C0
green	#008000	teal	#008080
lime	#00FF00	yellow	#FFFF00
maroon	#800000	white	#FFFFFF

Fig. M.1 HTML/XHTML standard colors and hexadecimal RGB values.

Color name	Value	Color name	Value
aliceblue	#F0F8FF	deeppink	#FF1493
antiquewhite	#FAEBD7	deepskyblue	#00BFFF
aquamarine	#7FFFD4	dimgray	#696969
azure	#F0FFFF	dodgerblue	#1E90FF
beige	#F5F5DC	firebrick	#B22222
bisque	#FFE4C4	floralwhite	#FFFAF0
blanchedalmond	#FFEBCD	forestgreen	#228B22
blueviolet	#8A2BE2	gainsboro	#DCDCDC
brown	#A52A2A	ghostwhite	#F8F8FF
burlywood	#DEB887	gold	#FFD700
cadetblue	#5F9EA0	goldenrod	#DAA520
chartreuse	#7FFF00	greenyellow	#ADFF2F
chocolate	#D2691E	honeydew	#F0FFF0
coral	#FF7F50	hotpink	#FF69B4
cornflowerblue	#6495ED	indianred	#CD5C5C
cornsilk	#FFF8DC	indigo	#4B0082
crimson	#DC1436	ivory	#FFFFF0
cyan	#00FFFF	khaki	#F0E68C
darkblue	#00008B	lavender	#E6E6FA
darkcyan	#008B8B	lavenderblush	#FFF0F5
darkgoldenrod	#B8860B	lawngreen	#7CFC00
darkgray	#A9A9A9	lemonchiffon	#FFFACD
darkgreen	#006400	lightblue	#ADD8E6
darkkhaki	#BDB76B	lightcoral	#F08080
darkmagenta	#8B008B	lightcyan	#E0FFFF
darkolivegreen	#556B2F	lightgoldenrodyellow	#FAFAD2
darkorange	#FF8C00	lightgreen	#90EE90
darkorchid	#9932CC	lightgrey	#D3D3D3
darkred	#8B0000	lightpink	#FFB6C1
darksalmon	#E9967A	lightsalmon	#FFA07A
darkseagreen	#8FBC8F	lightseagreen	#20B2AA
darkslateblue	#483D8B	lightskyblue	#87CEFA
darkslategray	#2F4F4F	lightslategray	#778899
darkturquoise	#00CED1	lightsteelblue	#B0C4DE
darkviolet	#9400D3	lightyellow	#FFFFE0

Fig. M.2 XHTML extended colors and hexadecimal RGB values (part 1 of 2).

Appendix M

Color name	Value	Color name	Value
limegreen	#32CD32	mediumblue	#0000CD
mediumpurple	#9370DB	mediumorchid	#BA55D3
mediumseagreen	#3CB371	plum	#DDA0DD
mediumslateblue	#7B68EE	powderblue	#B0E0E6
mediumspringgreen	#00FA9A	rosybrown	#BC8F8F
mediumturquoise	#48D1CC	royalblue	#4169E1
mediumvioletred	#C71585	saddlebrown	#8B4513
midnightblue	#191970	salmon	#FA8072
mintcream	#F5FFFA	sandybrown	#F4A460
mistyrose	#FFE4E1	seagreen	#2E8B57
moccasin	#FFE4B5	seashell	#FFF5EE
navajowhite	#FFDEAD	sienna	#A0522D
oldlace	#FDF5E6	skyblue	#87CEEB
olivedrab	#6B8E23	slateblue	#6A5ACD
orange	#FFA500	slategray	#708090
orangered	#FF4500	snow	#FFFAFA
orchid	#DA70D6	springgreen	#00FF7F
palegoldenrod	#EEE8AA	steelblue	#4682B4
palegreen	#98FB98	tan	#D2B48C
paleturquoise	#AFEEEE	thistle	#D8BFD8
palevioletred	#DB7093	tomato	#FF6347
papayawhip	#FFEFD5	turquoise	#40E0D0
peachpuff	#FFDAB9	violet	#EE82EE
peru	#CD853F	wheat	#F5DEB3
pink	#FFC0CB	whitesmoke	#F5F5F5
mediumaquamarine	#66CDAA	yellowgreen	#9ACD32

Fig. M.2 XHTML extended colors and hexadecimal RGB values (part 2 of 2).

Crystal Reports® for Visual Studio .NET

N.1 Introduction

All industries collect and maintain data relevant to their businesses. For example, manufacturing companies maintain information about inventories and production, retail shops record sales, health care organizations maintain patient records and publishers track book sales and inventories. However, just storing data is not enough: Managers must use these data to make informed business decisions. Information must be properly organized, easily accessible and shared among various individuals, departments and affiliates. This facilitates data analysis that can reveal business-critical information, such as sales trends or potential inventory shortages. To make this possible, developers have created reporting software—a key tool enabling the presentation of stored data sources.

Crystal Reports was first released in 1992 as a Windows-based report writer, and Microsoft adopted the reporting software as the standard for Visual Basic in 1993.[1] Visual Studio .NET now integrates a special edition of Crystal Reports, further tying Crystal Reports to Windows and Web development. This appendix presents the resources that *Crystal Decisions*, the company that produces Crystal Reports, offers on its Web site, and overviews Crystal Report's unique functionality and features in Visual Studio .NET.

N.2 Crystal Reports Web Site Resources

Crystal Decisions offers resources to developers working in Visual Studio .NET at their Web site, `www.crystaldecisions.com/net`. The site updates the changes in Visual Studio .NET versions in English, Simplified Chinese, Traditional Chinese, French, German, Italian, Japanese, Korean and Spanish. Crystal Decisions also provides e-mail-based technical support for Crystal Reports Visual Basic .NET developers. The site offers walk-

---

1. "Company History," `<www.crystaldecisions.com/about/ourcompany/history.asp>`.

throughs, an online newsletter, a multimedia product demo, discussion groups, a developer's zone and an overview of Crystal Reports in Visual Studio .NET.

N.3 Crystal Reports and Visual Studio .NET

Developers working in Visual Studio .NET's integrated development environment (IDE) can create and integrate reports in their applications using Crystal Reports software. The Visual Studio .NET edition of the software provides powerful capabilities to developers. Features in the Visual Studio .NET Crystal Reports include an API (application programming interface) that allows developers to control how reports are cached on servers—setting timeouts, restrictions, etc. Developers can create reports in multiple languages, because Crystal Reports now fully supports Unicode data types. The reports that are created can be viewed in many file formats. A user can convert a report to Microsoft Word, Adobe's Portable Document Format (PDF), Hypertext Markup Language (HTML) and others so that report information can be distributed easily and used in a wide variety of documentation. Any Crystal Report created in Visual Studio .NET can become an embedded resource for use in Windows and Web applications and Web services. This section overviews the initial stages of creating reports as well as some more advanced capabilities.

To aid Visual Studio .NET developers design reports, Crystal Reports provides a *Report Expert*. Experts are similar to "templates" and "wizards"—they guide users through the creation of a variety of reports while handling the details of how the report is created, so the user need not be concerned with them. The available Experts create several types of reports, including standard, form-letter, form, cross-tab, subreport, mail label and drill-down reports (Fig. N.1). Figure N.2 illustrates the **Standard Report Expert** interface.

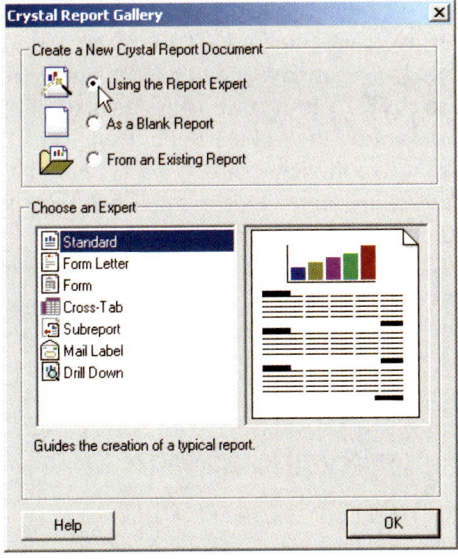

Fig. N.1 Report expert choices. (Courtesy Crystal Decisions)

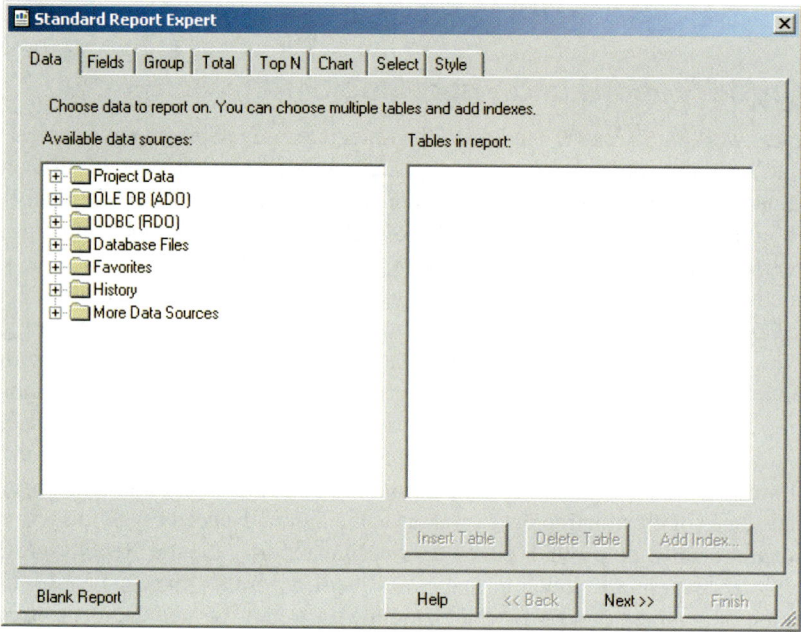

Fig. N.2 Expert formatting menu choices. (Courtesy of Crystal Decisions)

The Crystal Reports software for Visual Studio .NET is comprised of several components. Once a report is set up, either manually or by using an Expert, developers use the Crystal Reports Designer in Visual Studio .NET to modify, add and format objects and fields, as well as to format the report layout and manipulate the report design (Fig. N.3). The Designer then generates RPT files (`.rpt` is the file extension for a Crystal Report). These RPT files are processed by the Crystal Reports engine, which delivers the report output to one of two Crystal Report viewers—a Windows Forms viewer control or a Web Forms viewer control, depending on the type of application the developer specifies. The viewers then present the formatted information to the user.

Walkthroughs illustrating the new functionality are available on the Crystal Decisions Web site at **www.crystaldecisions.com/x-jump/scr_net/default.asp**. The walkthroughs include integrating and viewing Web reports through Windows applications, creating interactive reports in Web applications, exposing Crystal Reports through Web services and reporting from ActiveX Data Objects (ADO) .NET data.[2] (For a detailed discussion of ADO .NET and other database tools, see Chapter 19, Database, SQL and ADO .NET.) This section overviews the functionality of some of the Web applications and Web services walkthroughs.

---

2. The walkthroughs on the Crystal Decisions Web site were tested using C# in Visual Studio .NET, but a developer should be able to use the walkthroughs with any language supported by Visual Studio .NET.

Appendix N Crystal Reports® for Visual Studio .NET

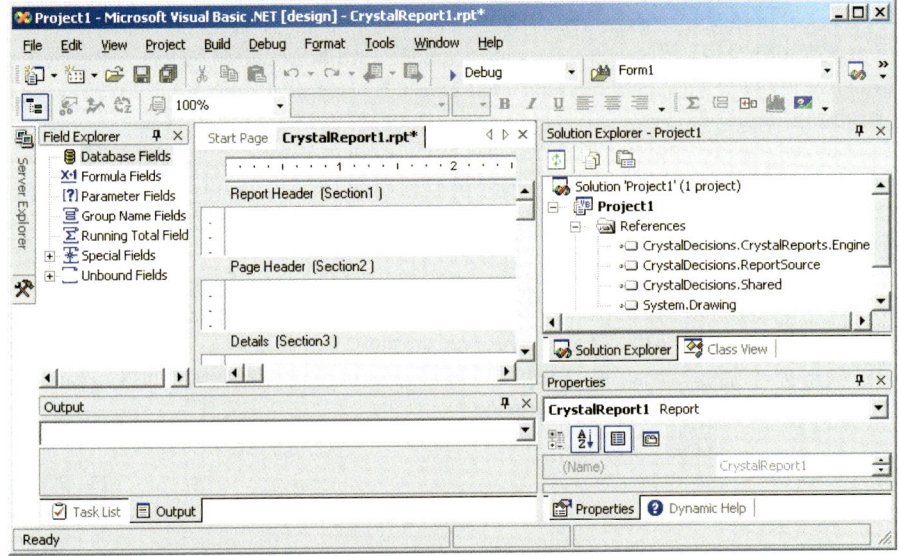

Fig. N.3 Crystal Reports designer interface. (Courtesy of Crystal Decisions)

N.3.1 Crystal Reports in Web Applications

Using Visual Studio .NET, a developer can integrate a Crystal Report in a static Web page, or can use a variety of technologies available in Visual Studio .NET to create interactive and dynamic reports in Web applications. ASP .NET technology integrated into Visual Studio .NET enables interactivity by producing cross-platform, dynamic Web applications. We discuss these technologies in detail in Chapter 20, ASP .NET, Web Forms and Web Controls.

Web Forms consist of HTML files with embedded Web Controls and code-behind files that contain event-handling logic. Crystal Reports provides a Web Forms Report Viewer, which is a Web Form that hosts the report. When a client accesses such a Web form, the event handler can update and format information in a Crystal Report and send the updated report to the user.[3]

A walkthrough on the Crystal Decision's Web site instructs a programmer how to enable Web page interactivity and how to use ASP .NET and its controls. In the walk-through, the user accesses information about countries by first entering a country name in the text box. When the user submits the information, the country name is passed to the Web forms viewer control and the report is updated—the Web forms page updates the report in HTML and sends it to the client browser.

N.3.2 Crystal Reports and Web Services

Any Crystal Report created in Visual Basic .NET can be published as a part of a Web application or a Web service. A Web service provides methods that are accessible over the

---

3. "Interactivity and Reports in Web Applications," *Crystal Reports for Visual Studio .NET*. `<www.crystaldecisions.com>`.

Internet to any application, independent of programming language or platform. A report Web service would be an excellent vehicle with which business partners could access specific report information. Crystal Decisions provides a walkthrough to overview the steps to familiarize the user with implementing a report as a Web service. (We discuss Web services in detail in Chapter 21, ASP .NET and Web Services.)

When a Crystal report is published as a Web service, Visual Studio .NET generates a DLL file that contains the report, and an XML file. Both files are published to a Web server so that a client can access the report. The XML-based Simple Object Access Protocol (SOAP) message passes the data to and from the Web service.

When a developer uses Visual Studio .NET to create and publish the Web service, the developer can bind the service either to a Windows or to a Web application to display the data returned from the Web service. The walkthrough details how to create and generate the Web service, bind the service to either a Windows or Web viewer and how to build the client application that will view the service.[4]

---

4. "Exposing Reports as Web Services," *Crystal Reports for Visual Studio .NET.* `<www.crystal-decidecisions.com>`.

Bibliography

Anderson, R., A. Homer, R. Howard and D. Sussman. *A Preview of Active Server Pages+*. Birmingham, UK: Wrox Press, 2001.

Appleman, D. *Moving to VB .NET: Strategies, Concepts, and Code*. Berkeley, CA: Apress Publishing, 2001.

Archer, T. *Inside C#*. Redmond, WA: Microsoft Press, 2001.

Barwell, F., R. Blair, R. Case, J. Crossland, B. Forgey, W. Hankison, B. S. Hollis, R. Lhotka, T. McCarthy, J. D. Narkiewicz, J. Pinnock, R. Ramachandran, M. Reynolds, J. Roth, B. Sempf, B. Sheldon and S. Short. *Professional VB .NET*. Birmingham, UK: Wrox Press, 2001.

Blaha, M. R., W. J. Premerlani and J. E. Rumbaugh. "Relational Database Design Using an Object-Oriented Methodology." *Communications of the ACM*, Vol. 31, No. 4, April 1988, 414–427.

Carr, D. "Hitting a High Note." *Internet World*. March 2001, 71.

Carr, D. "Slippery SOAP." *Internet World*. March 2001, 72–74.

Carr, D. F. "Dave Winer: The President of Userland and Soap Co-Creator Surveys the Changing Scene." *Internet World*. March 2001, 53–58.

Chappel, D. "Coming Soon: The Biggest Platform Ever." *Application Development Trends Magazine*, May 2001,15.

Chappel, D. "A Standard for Web Services: SOAP vs. ebXML." *Application Development Trends*, February 2001, 17.

Codd, E. F. "A Relational Model of Data for Large Shared Data Banks." *Communications of the ACM*, June 1970.

Codd, E. F. "Further Normalization of the Data Base Relational Model." *Courant Computer Science Symposia*, Vol. 6, *Data Base Systems*. Upper Saddle River, N.J.: Prentice Hall, 1972.

Codd, E. F. "Fatal Flaws in SQL." *Datamation*, Vol. 34, No. 16, August 15, 1988, 45–48.

Conard, J., P. Dengler, B. Francis, J. Glynn, B. Harvey, B. Hollis, R. Ramachandran, J. Schenken, S. Short and C. Ullman. *Introducing .NET*. Birmingham, UK: Wrox Press, 2000.

Correia, E. J. "Visual Studio .NET to Speak in Tongues." *Software Development Times*, April 2001, 12.

Cornell, G. and J. Morrison. *Moving to VB .NET: Strategies, Concepts, and Code.* Berkeley, CA: Apress Publishing, 2001.

Cornes, O., C. Goode, J. T. Llibre, C. Ullman, R. Birdwell, J. Kauffman, A. Krishnamoorthy, C. L. Miller, N. Raybould and D. Sussman. *Beginning ASP .NET Using VB .NET.* Birmingham, UK: Wrox Press, 2001.

Date, C. J. *An Introduction to Database Systems, Seventh Edition.* Reading, MA: Addison-Wesley Publishing, 2000.

Davydov, M. "The Road to the Future of Web Services." *Intelligent Enterprise.* May 2001, 50–52.

Deitel, H. M. and Deitel, P. J. *Java How To Program, Fourth Edition.* Upper Saddle River, NJ: Prentice Hall, 2001

Deitel, H. M., Deitel, P. J. and T. R. Nieto. *Visual Basic 6 How To Program.* Upper Saddle River, NJ: Prentice Hall, 1999.

Deitel, H. M., P. J. Deitel, T. R. Nieto, T. M. Lin and P. Sadhu. *XML How To Program.* Upper Saddle River, NJ: Prentice Hall, 2001

Deitel, H. M. *Operating Systems, Second Edition.* Reading, MA: Addison Wesley Publishing, 1990.

Dejong, J. "Raising the Bar." *Software Development Times,* March 2001, 29–30.

Dejong, J. "Microsoft's Clout Drives Web Services." *Software Development Times,* March 2001, 29, 31.

Dejong, J. "One-Stop Shopping: A Favored Method." *Software Development Times,* February 2001, 20.

Erlanger. L. ".NET Services." *Internet World,* March 2001, 47.

Erlanger. L. "Dissecting .NET." *Internet World,* March 2001, 30–36.

Esposito, D. "Data Grid In-Place Editing." *MSDN Magazine,* June 2001, 37–45.

Esposito, D. "Server-Side ASP .NET Data Binding: Part 2: Customizing the Data Grid Control." *MSDN Magazine,* April 2001, 33–45.

Finlay, D. "UDDI Works on Classification, Taxonomy Issues." *Software Development Times,* March 2001, 3.

Finlay, D. "New York Prepares for .NET Conference." *Software Development Times,* June 2001, 23.

Finlay, D. "GoXML Native Database Clusters Data, Reduces Seek Time." *Software Development Times,* March 2001, 5.

Fontana, J. "What You Get in .NET." *Network World,* April 2001, 75.

Galli, P. and R. Holland. ".NET Taking Shape, but Developers Still Wary." *eWeek,* June 2001, pages 9, 13.

Gillen, A. "Sun's Answer to .NET." *EntMag,* March 2001, 38.

Gillen, A. "What a Year It's Been." *EntMag,* December 2000, 54.

Gladwin, L. C. "Microsoft, eBay Strike Web Services Deal." *Computer World,* March 2001, 22.

Grimes, R. "Make COM Programming a Breeze with New Feature in Visual Studio .NET." *MSDN Magazine,* April 2001, 48–62.

Harvey, B., S. Robinson, J. Templeman and K. Watson. *C# Programming With the Public Beta.* Birmingham, UK: Wrox Press, 2000.

Holland, R. "Microsoft Scales Back VB Changes." *eWeek*, April 2001, 16.

Holland, R. "Tools Case Transition to .NET Platform." *eWeek*, March 2001, 21.

Hollis, B. S. and R Lhotka. *VB .NET Programming With the Public Beta.* Birmingham, UK: Wrox Press, 2001.

Hulme, G, V. "XML Specification May Ease PKI Integration." *Information Week*, December 2000, 38.

Hutchinson, J. "Can't Fit Another Byte." *Network Computing*, March 2001, 14.

Jepson, B. "Applying .NET to Web Services." *Web Techniques*, May 2001, 49–54.

Karney. J. ".NET Devices." *Internet World*, March 2001, 49–50.

Kiely, D. "Doing .NET In Internet Time." *Information Week*, December 2000, 137–138, 142–144, 148.

Kirtland, M. "The Programmable Web: Web Services Provides Building Blocks for the Microsoft .NET Framework." *MSDN Magazine*, September 2000 `<msdn.microsoft.com/msdnmag/issues/0900/WebPlatform/WebPlatform.asp>`.

Levitt, J. "Plug-And-Play Redefined." *Information Week*, April 2001, 63–68.

McCright, J. S. and D. Callaghan. "Lotus Pushes Domino Services." *eWeek*, June 2001, 14.

"Microsoft Chimes in with New C Sharp Programming Language." Xephon Web site. June 30, 2000 `<www.xephon.com/news/00063019.html>`.

Microsoft Developer Network Documentation. Visual Studio .NET CD-ROM, 2001.

Microsoft Developer Network Library. .NET Framework SDK. Microsoft Web site `<msdn.microsoft.com/library/default.asp>`.

Moran, B. "Questions, Answers, and Tips." *SQL Server Magazine*, April 2001, 19–20.

MySQL Manual. MySQL Web site `<www.mysql.com/doc/>`.

Oracle Technology Network Documentation. Oracle Web site. `<otn.oracle.com/docs/content.html>`.

Otey, M. "Me Too .NET." *SQL Server Magazine*. April 2001, 7.

Papa, J. "Revisiting the Ad-Hoc Data Display Web Application." *MSDN Magazine*, June 2001, 27–33.

Pratschner, S. "Simplifying Deployment and Solving DLL Hell with the .NET Framework." *MSDN Library*, September 2000 `<msdn.microsoft.com/library/techart/dplywithnet.htm>`.

Prosise, J. "Wicked Code." *MSDN Magazine*, April 2001, 121–127.

Relational Technology, *INGRES Overview*. Alameda, CA: Relational Technology, 1988.

Ricadela, A. and P. McDougall. "eBay Deal Helps Microsoft Sell .NET Strategy." *Information Week*, March 2001, 33.

Ricadela, A. "IBM Readies XML Middleware." *Information Week*, December 2000, 155.

Richter, J. "An Introduction to Delegates." *MSDN Magazine*, April 2001, 107–111.

Richter, J. "Delegates, Part 2." *MSDN Magazine*, June 2001, 133–139.

Rizzo, T. "Let's Talk Web Services." *Internet World*, April 2001, 4–5.

Rizzo, T. "Moving to Square One." *Internet World*, March 2001, 4–5.

Robinson, S., O. Cornes, J. Glynn, B. Harvey, C. McQueen, J. Moemeka, C. Nagel, M. Skinner and K. Watson. *Professional C#*. Birmingham, UK: Wrox Press, 2001.

Rollman, R. "XML Q & A." *SQL Server Magazine*, April 2001, 57–58.

Rubinstein, D. "Suit Settled, Acrimony Remains." *Software Development Times*, February 2001, pages 1, 8.

Rubinstein, D. "Play It Again, XML." *Software Development Times*, March 2001, 12.

Scott, G. "Adjusting to Adversity." *EntMag*, March 2001, 38.

Scott, G. "Putting on the Breaks." *EntMag*, December 2000, 54.

Sells, C. "Managed Extensions Bring .NET CLR Support to C++." *MSDN Magazine*. July 2001, 115–122.

Seltzer, L. "Standards and .NET." *Internet World*, March 2001, 75–76.

Shohoud, Y. "Tracing, Logging, and Threading Made Easy with .NET." *MSDN Magazine*, July 2001, 60–72.

Sliwa, C. "Microsoft Backs Off Changes to VB .NET." *Computer World*, April 2001, 14.

Songini, Marc. "Despite Tough Times, Novell Users Remain Upbeat." *Computer World*, March 2001, 22.

Spencer, K. "Cleaning House." *SQL Server Magazine*, April 2001, 61–62.

Spencer, K. "Windows Forms in Visual Basic .NET." *MSDN Magazine*, April 2001, 25–45.

Stonebraker, M. "Operating System Support for Database Management." *Communications of the ACM*, Vol. 24, No. 7, July 1981, 412–418.

Surveyor. J. ".NET Framework." *Internet World*, March 2001, 43–44.

Tapang, C. C. "New Definition Languages Expose Your COM Objects to SOAP Clients." *MSDN Magazine*, April 2001, 85–89.

Utley, C. *A Programmer's Introduction to Visual Basic .NET*. Indianapolis, IN: Sams Publishing, 2001.

Visual Studio .NET ADO .NET Overview. Microsoft Developers Network Web site <`msdn.microsoft.com/vstudio/nextgen/technology/adoplusdefault.asp`>.

Ward, K. "Microsoft Attempts to Demystify .NET." *EntMag*, December 2000, 1.

Waymire, R. "Answers from Microsoft." *SQL Server Magazine*, April 2001, 71–72.

Winston, A. "A Distributed Database Primer." *UNIX World*, April 1988, 54–63.

Whitney, R. "XML for Analysis." *SQL Server Magazine*, April 2001, 63–66.

Zeichick, A. "Microsoft Serious About Web Services." *Software Development Times*, March 2001, 3.

Index

Symbols
- minus operator 77
" double quotation 64
"" 839
& (menu access shortcut) 526
& operator 648
&= string concatenation assignment operator 111
& 1357
© 1357
¼ 1416
&H*yyyy*; notation 1325
< 1415, 1416
( ) parentheses 76
* multiplication operator 74, 77, 874
*= multiplication assignment operator 111
+ addition operator 77
+ sign 77
+= addition assignment operator 110, 111
. (dot operator) 64, 192, 193, 306, 327, 354, 370
/ 835
/ division (float) operator 75, 77
/= division assignment operator 111
< less than operator 79
<!--...--> tags 835, 1347
<= less than or equal to operator 79, 164
<> "is not equal to" 164

<> angle brackets 835
<> inequality operator 79, 80
<? and ?> delimiters 870
= assignment operator 71, 110
= comparison operator 639
= equality operator 79
-= subtraction assignment operator 111
> greater than operator 79
>= greater than or equal to 79
? regular expression metacharacter 762
\ integer division operator 75
\ separator character 757
\= integer division assignment operator 111
^ exponentiation operator 75
^= exponentiation assignment operator 111
_ line-continuation character 83
_ underscore 63

A
A binary search tree 1167
a element 1351, 1355, 1409, 1414
A portion of a **Shape** class hierarchy 354
A property of structure **Color** 688
abbreviating an assignment expression 110
Abbreviations for controls introduced in chapter 517

Abort method of class **Thread** 596
AbortRetryIgnore constant 152
AboutBox method of class **AxMediaPlayer** 731
Abs method of class **Math** 194
absolute positioning 955
absolute value 194
abstract base class 398
abstract class 398, 409
Abstract **CShape** base class 400
abstract data type (ADT) 22, 298
Abstract data type representing time in 24-hour format 299
abstract derived class 409
abstract method 398, 409
abstraction 351
AcceptButton property 479
AcceptSocket method of class **TcpListener** 1099
AcceptsReturn property 492
access method 301
access shared data 609
access shortcut 525
accessibility 1208, 1240, 1241, 1250, 1251, 1253, 1254, 1255
accessibility aids in Visual Studio .NET 1208, 1209
Accessibility Wizard 1242, 1245, 1250

Accessibility Wizard
  initialization option 1243
Accessibility Wizard mouse
  cursor adjustment tool 1245
`AccessibilityDescription` property of class
  `Control` 1221
`AccessibilityName`
  property of class `Control`
  1221
`AccessibleDescription`
  property of class `Control`
  1216
`AccessibleName` property of
  class `Control` 1216
`AccessibleRole` enumeration
  1216
`AccessibleRole` property of
  class `Control` 1216
accessing shared memory without
  synchronization 604
action 64, 334
`action` attribute 1435
action element 1238
action oriented 298
action symbol 99
action/decision model of
  programming 103
`Activation` property of class
  `ListView` 555, 556
Active Accessibility 1240
Active Server Pages (ASP) .NET
  17, 26
active tab 37
active window 479
`ActiveLinkColor` property of
  class `LinkLabel` 534
`ActiveMdiChild` property of
  class `Form` 568, 569
ActiveX 1333
ActiveX COM control integration
  in Visual Basic .NET 1335
ActiveX control 28, 1334
ActiveX DLL 28
Acts designed to ensure Internet
  access for people with
  disabilities 1205
`.acw` 1251
`Ad` attribute 967
Ada programming language 11,
  593
add a reference 85
add custom control to a form 584
Add member of enumeration
  `MenuMerge` 570
Add method 867

Add method of class `ArrayList`
  716, 1057, 1180
Add method of class `Hashtable`
  982, 1081
Add method of class `TreeNode-`
  `Collection` 551
Add method of `Columns`
  collection 1004
Add method of `Hashtable`
  1195
Add Reference dialog 86
Add Reference dialog DLL
  Selection 1338
Add Tab menu item 563
Add User Control... option in
  Visual Studio .NET 582
Add Web Reference dialog
  1046
Add Windows Form... option
  in Visual Studio .NET 567
adding a Web service reference to
  a project 1045
adding **Web References** in
  Visual Studio 1045
addition assignment operator (`+=`)
  110, 111
Addition program to add two
  values entered by the user 70
`Addition.vb` 1339
`AddLine` method of class
  `GraphicsPath` 712
`AddressOf` keyword 433, 438
Adjusting up window element size
  1244
"administrative" section of the
  computer 4
ADO .NET 26, 38, 889, 912
Adobe® Photoshop™ Elements
  51
`AdRotator` class 964, 965
`AdRotatorInforma-`
  `tion.xml` 967
ADT (abstract data type) 22, 298
advanced accessibility settings in
  Microsoft Internet Explorer
  5.5 1255
Advanced Research Projects
  Agency (ARPA) 14
Advantage Hiring, Inc. 1288
`AdvertisementFile`
  property of class
  `AdRotator` 965
advertisment 979
`AfterSelect` event of class
  `TreeView` 551
aggregation 306

Airline Reservation Web service
  1066
algebraic notation 75
algorithm 21, 98, 112, 123, 224
algorithm for traversing a maze
  295
`Alignment` property 50
allocating an array with `New` 255
allocating arrays 249
`AllowPaging` property of a
  `DataGrid` control 1018
`AllowSorting` property of
  `DataGrid` control 1019
Alphabetic icon 42
alphabetizing 639
`alt` attribute 27, 1208, 1353,
  1412
Alt key 513
Alt key shortcut 525
`Alt` property 516
`<alt>` tag 1254
ALU (arthimetic and logic unit) 4
America's Job Bank 1286
American Society for Female
  Entrepreneurs 1288
American Standard Code for
  Information Interchange
  (ASCII) 28
ampersand (`&`) 1357
Analytical Engine mechanical
  computing device 11
ancestor node 842
anchor 1350, 1355
anchor control 489
`Anchor` property 490
anchoring a control 488
Anchoring demonstration 489
`AND` 910, 911
`And` (logical AND without short-
  circuit evaluation) 164, 166,
  170
`AndAlso` (logical AND with
  short-circuit evaluation)
  164, 165, 166
angle bracket (`<>`) 835, 1345
animated character 25
animation 686
`answer` element 1239
Apache 1375
API (application programming
  interface) 684
APL progamming language 19
`Append` method of class
  `StringBuilder` 655
`AppendFormat` method of class
  `StringBuilder` 656, 657

Index

AppendText method of class **File** 757
Apple computer 5
Apple Computer, Inc. 1322
Application class 533
application programming interface (API) 684
application service provider (ASP) 1288
application tracing 1019
Application.Exit method 533, 542
ApplicationException class 450
ApplicationException derived class thrown when a program performs illegal operations on negative numbers 465
Applying rule 3 of Fig. 5.25 to the simplest flowchart 174
Aquent.com 1291
Arc 702
arc angle 702
arc method 702
AREA element 1386
area element 1447
ARGB values 687
argument 64, 189
ArgumentOutOfRangeException 637, 648, 658, 1184
arithmetic and logic unit (ALU) 4
arithmetic calculation 74
arithmetic mean (average) 77
arithmetic operator 74
arithmetic overflow 442, 445
ARPA (Advanced Research Projects Agency) 14
ARPAnet 14
ArrangeIcons value in **LayoutMdi** enumeration 571
array 22, 246
array allocated with **New** 255
array bounds 249, 255
Array class 1176, 1178
Array class demonstration 1176
Array consisting of 12 elements 247
array declaration 248
array elements passed call-by-value 261
array indexer (**()**) 247
array initialized to zero 255
array of arrays 280
array of primitive data types 249
array passed call-by-reference 261
array subscript operator, **()** 1184
ArrayList class 716, 1056, 1057, 1176, 1179, 1180
ArrayList methods (partial list) 1180
ArrayReferenceTest.vb 265
arrays are Visual Basic objects 297
arrays as object 264
article.xml 834
article.xml displayed by Internet Explorer 837
ASC 901, 903
ASC (ascending order) 901
ascending order (ASC) 874, 901
ascent 697
ASCII (American Standard Code for Information Interchange) 28, 1322
ASCII character set Appendix 1319
ASCII character, test for 514
ASCX code for the header 1007
ASCX file 1006
ASMX file 1033
ASMX file rendered in Internet Explorer 1033
ASMX page 1036
ASP (Active Server Pages) .NET 17
ASP .NET comment 947
ASP .NET server controls 942
ASP .NET Web service 1036
ASP.NET Web service project type 1043
ASP.NET_SessionId cookie 988
ASPX file 942
.aspx file extension 942
ASPX file that allows a user to select an author from a drop-down list 1013
ASPX file that takes ticket information 1069
ASPX listing for the guestbook page 999
ASPX page that displays the Web server's time 946
ASPX page with tracing turned off 1020
assembler 7
assembly 84, 339
assembly language 6
AssemblyTest.vb 339

<assign> tag (**<assign>...</assign>**) 1233
assign element 1238
assign value to a variable 71
assignment operator (**=**) 71, 72, 110
Assignment operators 111
assignment statement 71
associativity of operators 76
asterisk (*****) 897, 1450
asterisk (*****) indicating multiplication 74
asterisk (*****) occurence indicator 861
asynchronous event 445
Attempting to access restricted class members results in a syntax error 307
ATTLIST element 862
attribute 128, 838, 1351
attribute of an element 1403
audio clip 593
audio-video interleave (AVI) 729
Aural Style Sheet 1256
AuralCSS 1241
authorISBN table of **books** database 890, 891, 892
authorization 1012
authors table of **books** database 890
auto hide 39
auto hide, disable 39
AutoEventWireup attribute of ASP.NET page 947
automatic duration 203
automatic garbage collection 452, 594
automatic variable 203
Autos window 1307
AutoScroll property 495
average 77
average calculation 112, 114
Average1.vb 112
AVI (audio-video interleave) 729
AxAgent class 743
AxAgent control 744
AxMediaPlayer class 731

B

B property of structure **Color** 688
B2B 1033
Babbage, Charles 11
BackColor property 48, 487
background color 48, 522

BackgroundImage property 487
Ballmer, Steve 20
bandwidth 14, 714
bar chart 256, 257
base case(s) 218, 222, 224
base class 128, 350, 351, 353
base-class constructor 355
base-class constructor call syntax 370
base-class default constructor 355
base-class destructor 386
base-class method is overridden in a derived class 382
base-class **Private** member 354
base-class reference 394, 395
baseline 1432
BASIC (Beginner's All-Purpose Symbolic Instruction Code) 7
batch 5
batch processing 5
BCPL programming language 9
Beginner's All-Purpose Symbolic Instruction Code (BASIC) 7
behavior 128, 297
Berkeley System Distribution (BSD) 19
Berners-Lee, Tim 15
BilingualJobs.com 1288
binary 180
binary digit 753
binary operator 71, 74, 167
binary search 272, 275, 294
Binary search of a sorted array 276
binary search tree 1160
Binary search tree containing 12 values 1160
binary tree 1137, 1160, 1167
Binary tree graphical representation 1160
binary tree sort 1167
Binary tree stores nodes with **IComparable** data 1171
BinaryFormatter class 756, 777
BinaryReader class 806, 807, 1108
BinarySearch method of class **Array** 1179
BinarySearch method of class **ArrayList** 1184
BinarySearchTest.vb 276
BinaryWriter class 1108
Bind method of class **Socket** 1098

binding a server to a port 1098
bit 753
bit (size of unit) 1322
bit manipulation 754
BitArray class 1176
Bitmap class 711
bitwise operators 500
bitwise Xor operator 534
BizTalk 26, 839
BizTalk Framework 877
BizTalk Schema Library 877
BizTalk Server (BTS) 877
BizTalk Terminologies 877
Black Shared property of structure **Color** 688
blackjack 27, 1053
Blackjack game that uses **Blackjack** Web service 1057
Blackjack Web service 1054
Blackjack.vb 1057
BlackjackService.asmx.vb 1054
Blackvoices.com 1287
blank line 64
block 187, 1099
block element 1237
block for input/output 597
block scope 203, 204, 306
<block> tag (**<block>**...**</block>**) 1233
block until connection received 1108
blocked state 596
Blue Shared property of structure **Color** 688
Bluetooth 1290
BMP (Windows bitmap) 51
body element **<body>**...**</body>** 1348
body element 1006, 1403, 1404
body of a class definition 300
body of a loop 149
body of the **If/Then** structure 78
body of the procedure definition 64
body of the **While** 106
body section 1403
Bohm, C. 99, 173
Bold member of enumeration **FontStyle** 695
Bold property of class **Font** 694
book.xdr 866
book.xml 865
books database 890
books database table relationships 896

Boolean values 169
BORDER = "0" 1370
border attribute 1370, 1429
bottom tier 945
BounceKeys 1247, 1248
boundary of control 581
bounding rectangle 701, 702
bounding rectangle for an oval 702
br (line break) element 1356, 1415
braces (**{** and **}**) 249
braille display 1208, 1240
braille keyboard 1240
Brassringcampus.com 1293
Break All button 1309
break program 1309
<break> tag (**<break>**...**</break>**) 1233
breakpoint 1304
breakpoint condition 1310
breakpoint hit count 1309
breakpoint, active 1309
breakpoint, disabled 1309
breakpoint, set 1305
Breakpoints window 1309
bricks-and-mortar store 979
Browse... button 46
browser request 1375, 1432
Brush class 684, 689, 699, 701
BSD (Berkeley System Distribution) 19
(BTS) BizTalk Server 877
bubble sort 268
Bubble sort using delegates 433
Bubble-sort **Form** application 435
BubbleSort procedure in mod-**BubbleSort** 268
BubbleSort.vb 268
BubbleSortTest.vb 269
buffer 603
buffer empty 603
BufferedStream class 756
buffering 25
bug.png 51
Build menu 38
building block 97
building-block approach 12
built-in array capabilities 1176
built-in data type 70, 334
Business letter DTD 861
business logic 946
business rule 946
Business-two-Business (B2B) 1033
button 34, 84, 87, 477
Button class 214, 492

Index

button label 492
Button properties and events 493
Buttons for message dialogs 151
ByRef keyword 200
ByRefTest.vb 201
byte 754
byte offset 790
ByVal and **ByRef** used to pass value-type arguments 201
ByVal keyword 200

C

C formatting code 154
C programming language 9, 298, 1346, 1401
c type character 199
C# How to Program 3
C# programming language 10, 19, 839
C++ programming language 9, 839, 1346
cache 912
calculation 4
call-by-reference 200
call-by-value 200
call element 1239
Call Stack 1312
call stack 459
callerID attribute 1239
CallXML 27, 1233
callxml element 1235
CallXML **hangup** element 1234
CampusCareerCenter.com 1293
CancelButton property 479
Candidate Recommendation 15
capacity of a collection 1179
Capacity property of class **ArrayList** 1179, 1184
Capacity property of class **StringBuilder** 652
<CAPTION>...</CAPTION> 1370
caption element 1225, 1429
card games 663
Career.com 1286
CareerPath.com 1286
CareerWeb 1286
carriage return/linefeed 121
carry bit 1275
Cascade value in **LayoutMdi** enumeration 571
Cascading Style Sheets (CSS) 15, 16, 27

Case Else keywords 158
Case keyword 155
case sensitive 64, 1345
CAST eReader 1221
cast operation 394
catch all exception types 445
Catch block (or handler) 445, 449
Catch handler 449
catch-related errors 451
Categorized icon 42
CBoss class inherits from class **CEmployee** 411
CCard class 663
CCircle class contains an *x-y* coordinate and a radius 358
CCircle class that inherits from class **CPoint** 391
CCircle2 class that inherits from class **CPoint** 362
CCircle2 class that inherits from class **CPoint2** 403
CCircle3 class that inherits from class **CPoint2** 365
CCircle3 class that inherits from class **CPoint3** 427
CCircle4 class that inherits from class **CPoint** but does not use **Protected** data 369
CCircle5 class inherits from class **CPoint3** and overrides a finalizer method 379
CCylinder class inherits from class **CCircle4** and **Overrides** method **Area** 373
CCylinder2 class inherits from class **CCircle2** 404
CCylinder3 class inherits class **CCircle3** 429
CDATA flag 862
CDay class encapsulates day, month and year information 321
CD-ROM 3
Ceil method of class **Math** 194
CEmployee class encapsulates employee name, birthday and hire date 323
CEmployee2 class objects share **Shared** variable 328

CEmployee3 class object modifies **Shared** variable when created and destroyed 336
CEmployee3 class to store in class library 336
Center for Applied Special Technology 1221, 1257
central processing unit (CPU) 4
CERN (the European Organization for Nuclear Research) 15
CGI (Common Gateway Interface) 1375
CGI script 1375, 1435
chance 206
changes in server-side data 1375
Changing a property in the code view 132
Changing a property in the code view editor 132
Changing a property value at runtime 134
Char array 636
Char structure 634, 661
Char.IsDigit method 662
Char.IsLetter method 663
Char.IsLetterOrDigit method 663
Char.IsLower method 663
Char.IsPunctuation method 663
Char.IsSymbol method 663
Char.IsUpper method 663
Char.IsWhiteSpace method 663
Char.ToLower method 663
Char.ToUpper method 663
character 754, 1323
character class 668
character constant 634
character entity reference 29
character set 754, 1322
character string 64
Characters property of class **AxAgent** 744
Chars property of class **String** 637
checkbox 477, 492, 498, 1436
CheckBox class 497
checkbox label 498
CheckBox properties and events 498
checkboxes 1376
CheckBoxes property of class **ListView** 556

CheckBoxes property of class
    TreeView 550
checked attribute 1379, 1439
checked context 468, 472
Checked property 498, 501
Checked property of class
    MenuItem 528
Checked property of class
    TreeNode 551
CheckedChanged event 498,
    502
CheckedIndices property of
    class **CheckedListBox**
    543
CheckedItems property of
    class **CheckedListBox**
    543
CheckedListBox 524
CheckedListBox and a
    ListBox used in a program
    to display a user selection
    544
CheckedListBox class 538,
    542
CheckedListBox properties
    and events 543
CheckState property 498
CheckStateChanged event
    498
Chemical Markup Language
    (CML) 26
ChessGame.vb 720
ChessPiece.vb 718
ChiefMonster™ 1292
child 1160
child element 836, 838
child node 550, 842
child window maximized 570
child window minimized 570
choice element of **form** tag
    1229
choice element of **menu** tag
    1229
<choice> tag (**<choice>**...
    </choice>) 1233
CHourlyWorker class inherits
    from class **CEmployee** 416
circle 1420
"circle" attribute value 1420
circular buffer 618, 628
circular hotspot 1388, 1448
circumference 94
CityWeather.vb 1076
clarity 2
class 12, 22, 298
class definition 299

class hierarchy 389, 398
Class keyword 128
class library 13, 335, 351, 383
class scope 203, 306
Class that stores equation
    information 1082
Class that stores weather
    information about a city
    1076
Class using **Me** reference 325
Class-average program with
    counter-controlled repetition
    112
Class-average program with
    sentinel-controlled
    repetition 117
ClassAverage2.vb 117
classes to implement abstract data
    types 335
class-scope variable hidden by
    method-scope variable 306
class-wide information 327
clear element 1238
Clear method of class **Array**
    1179
Clear method of class **ArrayList** 1180
Clear method of class **TreeNodeCollection** 551
Clear method of **DataSet** 922
Clear method of **Hashtable**
    1195
clearDigits element 1239
click a button 492
Click event of class **MenuItem**
    526, 528
Clicker 4 1253
clicking 34
client 6, 334
Client interacting with server and
    Web server. Step 1
    The **GET** request, **GET /
    books/down-
    loads.htm HTTP/1.0**
    944
Client interacting with server and
    Web server. Step 2
    The HTTP response, **HTTP/
    1.0 200 OK** 944
Client portion of a client/server
    stream socket connection
    1104
Client portion of connectionless
    client/server computing
    1112

Client side of client/server Tic-
    Tac-Toe program 1122
client tier 946
Client.vb 1077
client/server chat 1101
client/server computing 6
ClipRectangle property of
    class **PaintEventArgs**
    580, 581
clock 580
close a file 783
close button 54
Close button icon 54
Close method of class **Form** 479
Close method of class **Socket**
    1099, 1109
Close method of class **StreamReader** 789
Close method of class **TcpClient** 1100, 1101
closed polygon 705
CloseFigure method of class
    GraphicsPath 712
closing a project 38
CLR (Common Language
    Runtime) 19, 452, 465
CLS (Common Language
    Specification) 18
CML (Chemical Markup
    Language) 26
CNN.com 979
COBOL (COmmon Business
    Oriented Language) 10,
    1401
COBOL progamming language 19
Code generated by the IDE for
    lblWelcome 130
code reuse 1176
code value 1323
code-behind file 942, 1006, 1007
Code-behind file for a page that
    updates the time every
    minute 948
Code-behind file for page
    demonstrating the
    AdRotator class 965
Code-behind file for the guest
    book application 1001
Code-behind file for the log in
    page for authors application
    1007
Code-behind file for the page that
    allows a user to choose an
    author 1014
Code-behind file for the
    reservation page 1070

Code-behind file for the word generator page 972
code-behind file in Web services 1033
coercion of arguments 195
coin tossing 207, 243
`col` element 1373, 1430
colgroup element `<COL-GROUP>...</COLGROUP>` 1372, 1373
`colgroup` element 1430
collapse code 129
`Collapse` method of class `TreeNode` 552
collapse node 550
collapsing a tree 40
`Collect` method in `System.GC` 330
`Collect` method of `GC` 381
collection 1176
collection class 1176
`Collegegrads.com` 1293
collision detection 718
color constant 687
color manipulation 686
`Color` methods and properties 688
`Color` property of class `ColorDialog` 692
`Color` structure 684, 687, 688
`ColorDialog` class 692
`cols` attribute 1378, 1391, 1435, 1450
`colspan` attribute 1430
`colspan` attributes 1373
column 279, 889, 890, 1368
column heading 1370
column number 898
`Columns` collection 1004
COM (Component Object Model) 28, 1332, 1334
COM component 28, 1333
COM limitation 1333
combo box 477
`ComboBox` 524
`ComboBox` class 545
`ComboBox` demonstration 546
`ComboBox` properties and events 546
`ComboBox` used to draw a selected shape 547
comma (`,`) 157
comma-separated list of arguments 72
comma-separated list of variable names 71

command-and-control system 593
command prompt 62, 88
command window 62, 69, 605, 616, 617
`Commands` property of interface 744
comment 62, 81, 1347, 1402
comments in HTML 1347
commercial application 753
`CommissionWorker` class inherits from class `CEmployee` 412
COmmon Business Oriented Language (COBOL) 10
Common Gateway Interface (CGI) 1375, 1433
Common Language Runtime (CLR) 19, 452, 465
Common Language Specification (CLS) 18
Common Programming Error 13
Common Runtime Library proxy 1334
`CompareTo` method of `IComparable` 1168
`CompareTo` method of structure `Char` 663
`Comparison.vb` 80
compilation error 1303
compile-time error 68
compile, debug setting 1305
compiled classes 84
compiler 7
Compiler error messages generated from overloaded procedures 228
compiling 1137
complete representation of a program 115, 120
complex curve 712
complexity theory 224
component 9, 478
Component Object Model (COM) 28, 1332, 1334
Component Pascal progamming language 19
component selection 43
composition 22, 306, 321, 351, 353
Composition demonstration 324
comprehensive job sites 1281
computation 3
computational complexity 272
computer 3
computer program 3
computer programmer 3

Computing the sum of the elements of an array 252
`Concat` method of class `String` 648
`Concat Shared` method 648
concrete class 398
concurrency 593
concurrent producer and consumer threads 609
concurrent programming 593
concurrent threads 609
condition 78
condition variable 616
conditional expression 302
`conference` element 1239
`Connect` method of class `TcpListener` 1100
connect to a database 913
connected lines 705
connection 1098
connection attempt 1100
connection between client and server terminates 1101
connection to a server 1100, 1130
Connection`Connection` property of `OleDbCommand` 920
connectionless service 1098
connectionless transmission with datagrams 1110, 1131
connection-oriented, streams-based transmission 1110, 1131
connector symbol 99
consistent state 302, 305, 314
console application 62
`Console` class 756
console window 62
`Console.Write` method 69
`Console.WriteLine` method 64, 105
`Const` and `ReadOnly` class members 333
`Const` keyword 23, 214, 331
`ConstAndReadOnly.vb` 333
constant 75, 121, 331
constant identifier 214
Constants used in class `CCircleConstants` Examples
Constants used in class `CCircleConstants` 332
constituent controls 580
constrained version of a linked list 1152
constructor 302, 308, 381

consume method 603
consumer 616
Consumer reads **Integer**s from synchronized shared buffer 612
Consumer reads **Integer**s from synchronized, circular buffer 624
Consumer reads **Integer**s from unsynchronized shared buffer 606
consumer thread 603
consuming a Web service 1037
contact.html 1351, 1356, 1410, 1415
container 477, 479
container elements 836
Contains method of class **ArrayList** 1180, 1184
Contains method of class **Stack** 1189
ContainsKey method of **Hashtable** 1195
content 866
content attribute of a **meta** tag 1448
content attribute of **meta** element 948
CONTENT frame 1390
CONTENT of a **META** tag 1389
Contents command 44
context-sensitive help 45
contiguous memory location 246
control 21, 41, 476, 478
control boundary 581
Control class 487, 580
Control key 513
control layout 38
control layout and properties 487
Control property 516
control structure 99, 100, 145, 175
control variable 145, 147
control variable final value 145
control variable inital value 145
control variable name 145, 149
controlling expression 155
control-structure nesting 101
control-structure stacking 100, 172
ControlToValidate property of class **RegularExpressionValidator** 971
converge on a base case 218
Convert class 197

Converting a binary number to decimal 1272
Converting a hexadecimal number to decimal 1273
Converting an octal number to decimal 1272
cookie 979, 980, 987, 988
  deletion 980
  domain 989
  expiration 980
  expiration date 980
  Expires property 980
  header 980
CookieContainer class 1056, 1065
Cookies getting created in an ASP .NET Web application 983
Cookies property of **Request** class 987
Cookies recieved in an ASP .NET Web application 987
Cooljobs.com 1294
coordinate system 685, 686
coordinates (0, 0) 685
coords element 1388, 1447
Copy method of class **Array** 1179
Copy method of class **File** 757
copy of an argument 200
copyright 28
CopyTo method of class **String** 637
CORDA Technologies 1208
corporate culture 1284, 1287
Cos method of class **Math** 194
cosine 194
count attribute if **prompt** element 1229
Count property of class **ArrayList** 1184
Count property of **Hashtable** 1195
counter 112, 113, 115
counter-controlled loop 120, 162
counter-controlled repetition 112, 118, 112, 124, 125, 145, 146, 147
Counter-controlled repetition with the **For/Next** structure 146
Counter-controlled repetition with the **While** structure 146
Counts property of **HttpSessionState** class 995
CPieceWorker class inherits from class **CEmployee** 414

CPlayer class represents a Tic-Tac-Toe player 1119
CPoint class represents an *x-y* coordinate pair 355, 390
CPoint2 class inherits from **MustInherit** class **CShape** 401
CPoint2 class represents an *x-y* coordinate pair as **Protected** data 364
CPoint3 base class contains constructors and finalizer 378
CPoint3 class implements interface **IShape** 426
CProcess class 535
CPU (Central Processing Unit) 4
CRandomAccessRecord class represents a record for random-access file-processing applications 791
Craps game using class **Random** 214
create custom control 580
Create method of class **File** 757
create new classes from existing class definitions 299
CreateArray.vb 250
CreateDirectory method of class **Directory** 758
CreateInstance method of class **Array** 1179
CreateText method of class **File** 757
creating a child form to be added to an MDI form 567
creating data types 335
Creating variable-length parameter lists 287
CRecord class represents a record for sequential-access file-processing applications 770
Crystal Decisions 1466
Crystal Reports 1466
Crystal Reports Designer 1468
CSquare class represents a square on the Tic-Tac-Toe board 1128
CSS (Cascading Style Sheets) 15, 16, 27, 1225
CSS2 1225
CTest class tests the **CEmployee** class hierarchy 417

Index

`CTest2` demonstrates polymorphism in Point-Circle-Cylinder hierarchy 406
`CTest3` uses interfaces to demonstrate polymorphism in Point-Circle-Cylinder hierarchy 431
`CTransaction` class handles record transactions for the transaction-processor case study 808
`CubeTest.vb` 238
`Current` property of `IEnumerator` 1185
current scope, variable in 1307
current statement, variable in 1307
current time 582
`CurrentPageIndex` property of a `DataGrid` control 1019
`CurrentThread Shared Thread` property 599
`CurrentValue` event of class `CheckedListBox` 543
Curriculum progamming language 19
cursor 64, 69
curve 712
custom control 580, 581
Custom control added to a `Form` 584
Custom control added to the `ToolBox` 584
Custom control creation 581, 583
custom controls 580
Custom palette 48
Custom tab 48
customization 980
customize a form 41
Customize Toolbox 1334
Customize Toolbox dialog selecting an ActiveX control 1334
Customize Toolbox... option in Visual Studio .NET 583
customize Visual Studio .NET IDE 35, 38
customizing the **Toolbox** 729
`CustomValidator` class 1007, 1011
cut 38
`Cyan Shared` property of structure `Color` 688
cylinder 404

D

D formatting code 154
`DarkBlue Shared` property of structure `Color` 695
`DarkGray Shared` property of structure `Color` 688
`Dash` member of enumeration `DashStyle` 712
`DashCap` enumeration 711
`DashCap` property of class `Pen` 711
`DashStyle` enumeration 711
`DashStyle` property of class `Pen` 711
data 3
data abstraction 334
data entry 87
data hierarchy 754, 755
data in support of actions 334
data independence 16
data manipulation 714
data member 298
Data menu 38
data representation of an abstract data type 334
data structure 22, 27, 246, 301, 1137
data tier 945
database 38, 888, 1345, 1401
Database access and information display 913
database management system (DBMS) 755, 888
Database modification demonstration 923
database table 889
datagram 1110
`DataGrid` class 913, 920
`DataGrid` control 1004, 1018, 1019
   `AllowPaging` property 1018
   `CurrentPageIndex` property 1019
   `DataSource` property 1004
   `PageIndexChange` event 1018
   `PagerStyle` property 1018
   `PageSize` property 1018
`DataSet` class 912, 932
`DataSource` property of a `DataGrid` control 1004
`DataTable` class 1004
`data-type` attribute 874

`DataView`
   `Sort` property 1018
date and time 582
`DateTime` structure 582
DBCS (double byte character set) 1324
DBMS (database management system) 755
DB2 888
Dead thread state 596
deadlock 602, 603
debug configuration setting 1305
Debug menu 38, 1306, 1308
Debug sample program 1304
Debug toolbar 1308
`DebugClass.vb` 1314
`DebugExample.vb` 1304
debugger 1304
debugging 1019, 1303, 1347, 1402
Debugging a class. 1314
debugging, begin 1305
debugging, call stack 1312
debugging, step into 1313
debugging, step out 1313
debugging, step over 1309
decendant node 842
`Decimal` data type 152, 154
decimal digit 754
decision 78
decision symbol 100, 103
declaration 70
declaration and initialization of an array 249
declaration space 203
declare each variable on a separate line 71
declaring an array 249
decreasing order 268
decrement of loop 145
default constructor 355
default font 695
default namespace 841
Default namespaces demonstration 841
default package 303
default properties 129
default setting 1251
default sorting order is ascending 901
default values for `Optional` arguments 229
`defaultnamespace.xml` **841**, 841
Defining `NotInheritable` class `CHourlyWorker` 416

definite repetition 112
degree 702
deitel@deitel.com 3
del element 1416
delegate 432, 480
Delegate class 433
DELETE FROM 897, 911
Delete method of class **Directory** 758
Delete method of class **File** 757
DELETE statement 911
DeleteCommand property of **OleDbAdapter** 920
deletion 1140
delimit 835
Demonstrates function debugging. 1312
Demonstrating keyboard events 514
Demonstrating logical operators 168
Demonstrating order in which constructors and finalizers are called 381
Demonstrating the **While** repetition structure 107
Demonstrating XML namespaces 839
deny 1012
dequeue operation of queue 335, 1156
derived class 128, 350, 351, 353
DESC 901, 902
Description property of a **WebMethod** attribute 1038
Description property of a **WebService** attribute 1037
deselected state 501
Deserialize method of class **BinaryFormatter** 777
design mode 53, 54
design units 695
Design view 36
designing form 54
diacritic 1323
dialog 36, 82, 84
dialog displaying a run-time error 72
diameter 94
diamond symbol 100, 103, 107, 149, 159
dice game 213
dice-rolling program 257
Dice.com 1290

DiceModule.vb 231
DiceModuleTest.vb 232
direct-access files 790
direct base class 350
directive in ASP.NET page 947
Directory class methods (partial list) 758
DirectoryInfo class 561, 757
disabled scroll arrow 41
disc 1417, 1420
"disc" attribute value 1420
DISCO (Discovery file) 1048
.disco file extension 1045
disconnected 912
discovery (DISCO) files 1048
disk 3, 13
disk I/O completion 445
disk space 1139
dismiss (hide) a dialog 84
display 64
Display Color Settings 1245
Display member of enumeration **GraphicsUnit** 695
display output 82
Display Settings 1243
displaying a phrase 64
displaying data on the screen 88
Displaying multiple lines in a dialog 83
displaying numeric data graphically 256
DisplayLogo.vb 714
distributed computing 6, 1032
diversity 1288
divide-and-conquer approach 183
divide by zero 446
DivideByZeroException class 446, 449
division (float) operator, **/** 75
division assignment operator (**/=**) 111
division by zero 116
division by zero is undefined 335
D-link 1208
DLL (Dynamic Link Library) 22, 1332, 1334, 1338, 1339
.dll file 1338
"DLL hell" 1332
DNS (domain name server) 943
DNS lookup 943
Do Until/Loop repetition structure 100
Do Until/Loop repetition structure demonstration 109

Do Until/Loop repetition structure flowchart 110
Do Until/Loop structure 160, 174
Do While/Loop repetition structure 100, 108
Do While/Loop repetition structure demonstration 108
Do While/Loop repetition structure flowchart 109
Do While/Loop structure 174
Do/Loop Until repetition structure 100
Do/Loop Until repetition structure flowchart 161
Do/Loop Until structure 160, 161, 171, 174
Do/Loop While repetition structure 100, 159
Do/Loop While repetition structure flowchart 160
Do/Loop While structure 159, 171, 174
do/while structure 21
Dock property 490
docking demonstration 490
DockPadding property 490
Document member of enumeration **GraphicsUnit** 695
Document Object Model (DOM) 842
Document Style and Semantics Specification Language (DSSSL) 16
document type 947, 1346
Document Type Definition (DTD) 860, 861, 862
Dogfriendly.com 1294
DOM (Document Object Model) 842
DOM parser 842
DOM structure of an XML document illustrated by a class 846
domain name server (DNS) 943
Domain property of **HttpCookie** class 989
dot operator (**.**) 64, 192, 193, 306, 327, 354, 370
Double 83
double-byte character set (DBCS) 1324
Double class 465
double-clicking 34
double quotes (**""**) 64, 839

Index

double-selection structure 100, 173
double-subscripted array 279
double-precision floating-point number 114
double-selection structure 172
`DoUntil.vb` 109
`DoWhile.vb` 108, 159
down-arrow button 48
Downloads page 35
drag and drop 480
draw on control 581
draw shapes 684
`DrawArc` method of class `Graphics` 703
`DrawArcs.vb` 703
`DrawEllipse` method of class `Graphics` 549, 700, 701
drawing a line 699
drawing a rectangle 699
drawing an oval 699
`DrawLine` method of class `Graphics` 699
`DrawLines` method of class `Graphics` 705
`DrawPie` method of class `Graphics` 549, 703
`DrawPolygon` method of class `Graphics` 705
`DrawPolygons.vb` 705
`DrawRectangle` method of class `Graphics` 549, 700, 701
`DrawShapes.vb` 709
`DrawStars.vb` 712
`DrawString` method of Class `Graphics` 691
`DrawString` method of class `Graphics` 695
drop-down list 477, 545
`DropDown` style for `ComboBox` 547
`DropDownList` class 1007
`DropDownList` style for `ComboBox` 547
`DropDownStyle` property of class `ComboBox` 546, 547
DSSSL (Document Style and Semantics Specification Language) 16
DTD (Document Type Definition) 860, 862
`.dtd` file extension 862
DTD for a business letter 861
DTD repository 866
dummy value 114

duplicate elimination 1168
duplicate of datagram 1110
duration 202
dynamic content 10
dynamic data structures 1137
dynamic help 44
Dynamic Help window 44
dynamic link library 339
dynamic link library (`.dll`) 84
Dynamic Link Library (DLL) 22, 1332, 1334, 1338, 1339
dynamic memory allocation 1139, 1140

E

`E` formatting code 154
EagleEyes 1241
EBNF (Extended Backus-Naur Form) grammar 861
echo a packet back to a client 1110
ECMA (European Computer Manufacturer's Association) 18
ECMAScript 969
Edit menu 38
Edit menu in Internet Explorer 87
editable list 547
efficient (Unicode design basis) 1322
Eiffel progamming language 19
eights position 1268
eLance.com 1291
electronic devices with two stable states 753
electronic mail (e-mail) 14
element 247, 1345
`!ELEMENT` element 861
element of chance 206
element type declaration 861
elements 835
`ElementType` 866
eliminate resource leak 453
ellipsis button 50
`Else` keyword 104
`ElseIf` keyword 106
`eltOnly` attribute 867
emacs text editor 1346, 1401
Emacspeak 1208
e-mail (electronic mail) 14, 1099, 1411
e-mail anchor 1352, 1411
embedded parentheses 76
employee 396
empty element 839, 1413, 1415
`EMPTY` keyword 862

`Enabled` property 487
`EnableSession` property of a `WebMethod` attribute 1056
`EnableSessionState` attribute 947
`EnableViewState` attribute 947, 978
encapsulate 297
encoding 1321
`encoding` declaration 1234
encoding scheme 28
encrypt 1012
end of data entry 114
end-of-file marker 755
end of session message 1235, 1238
`End Select` statement 157
`End Sub` 64
end tag 835, 1403
`EndsWith` method of class `String` 641
enqueue operation of queue 335, 1156
`EnsureCapacity` method of class `StringBuilder` 653
Enter (or *Return*) key 46, 65, 70
`Enter` method of class `Monitor` 602, 609, 616, 617, 619
entity
& 862
< 862
entity reference 862, 1415
entry point 304
entry point of a control structure 172
entry point of a program 64
entry point of control structure 100
entry-level position 1281
`Enum` keyword 214
`<enumerate>` tag (`<enumerate>`… `</enumerate>`) 1233
enumeration 214
enumerator 1185
envelope (SOAP) 16
environment variable 1375
equal likelihood 207
Equality and relational operators 79
equality operator (`=`) 78
`Equals` method of class `String` 639, 641
`Equation.vb` 1082
`Error` constant 151
error-processing code 443

Error property of class **Console** 755
ErrorMessage property 971
ErrorMessage property in a Web Form 1012
escape character 910
European Computer Manufacturer's Association (ECMA) 18
event 24, 191, 480
event argument 485
event driven 480
event-driven process 687
event-driven programming 2
event handler 191, 192, 217, 222, 480, 1238
event handler, create 485
event handler, documentation 485
event handling model 480
event multicasting 485
event procedure 184
events at an interval 581
eWork® Exchange 1291
examination-results problem 122
Examples 837
   A binary seach tree 1167
   A picture with links anchored to an image map 1386
   A portion of a **Shape** class hierarchy 354
   Abstract **CShape** base class 400
   Abstract data type representing time in 24-hour format 299
   ActiveX COM control integration in Visual Basic .NET 1335
   Add Reference dialog 86
   Adding a reference to an assembly in the Visual Studio .NET IDE 86
   Adding a Web service reference to a project 1045
   Addition program that adds two numbers entered by the user 70
   Addition.vb 1339
   AdRotatorInformation.xml 967
   Airline Reservation Web service 1066
   Anchoring demonstration 489
   Animation of a series of images 717

Append methods of class **StringBuilder** 655
Applying rule 3 of Fig. 5.25 to the simplest flowchart 174
Arc Method demonstration 703
Arithmetic operators 75
Array class demonstration 1176
ArrayReferenceTest.vb 265
ASCX code for the header 1007
ASMX file rendered in Internet Explorer 1033
ASPX file that allows a user to select an author from a drop-down list 1013
ASPX file that takes ticket information 1069
ASPX listing for the guestbook page 999
ASPX page that displays the Web server's time 946
ASPX page with tracing turned off 1020
AssemblyTest.vb 339
Assignment operators 111
Attempting to access restricted class members results in a syntax error 307
Average1.vb 112
Binary search of a sorted array 276
Binary search tree containing 12 values 1160
Binary tree graphical representation 1160
Binary tree stores nodes with **IComparable** data 1171
BinarySearchTest.vb 276
BizTalk terminologies 877
Blackjack game that uses **Blackjack** Web service 1057
Blackjack Web service 1054
Blackjack.vb 1057
BlackjackService.asmx.vb 1054
Bubble sort using delegates 433
Bubble-sort **Form** application 435

BubbleSort procedure in **modBubbleSort** 268
BubbleSort.vb 268
BubbleSortTest.vb 269
Business letter DTD 861
Buttons for message dialogs 151
ByRefTest.vb 201
CallXML example that reads three ISBN values 1235
CBoss class inherits from class **CEmployee** 411
CCard class 663
CCircle class contains an x-y coordinate and a radius 358
CCircle2 class that inherits from class **CPoint** 362
CCircle2 class that inherits from class **CPoint2** 403
CCircle3 class that inherits from class **CPoint2** 365
CCircle3 class that inherits from class **CPoint3** 427
CCircle4 class that inherits from class **CPoint** but does not use **Protected** data 369
CCircle5 class inherits from class **CPoint3** and overrides a finalizer method 379
CCommissionWorker class inherits from class **CEmployee** 412
CCylinder2 class inherits from class **CCircle2** 404
CCylinder3 class inherits class **CCircle3** 429
CDay class encapsulates day, month and year information 321
CEmployee class encapsulates employee name, birthday and hire date 323
CEmployee2 class objects share **Shared** variable 328
CEmployee3 class object modifies **Shared** variable when created and destroyed 336
CEmployee3 class to store in class library 336
Changing a property in the code view 132
Changing a property in the code view editor 132

Index

Changing a property value at runtime 134
CheckedListBox and a **ListBox** used in a program to display a user selection 544
Chess-game code 720
ChessGame.vb 720
ChessPiece.vb 718
CHourlyWorker class inherits from class **CEmployee** 416
CityWeather.vb 1076
Class that stores equation information 1082
Class that stores weather information about a city 1076
Class using **Me** reference 325
Class-average program with counter-controlled repetition 112
Class-average program with sentinel-controlled repetition 117
ClassAverage2.vb 117
Client portion of a client/server stream socket connection 1104
Client portion of connectionless client/server computing 1112
Client side of client/server Tic-Tac-Toe program 1122
Client.vb 1077
Code generated by the IDE for **lblWelcome** 130
Code-behind file for a page that updates the time every minute 948
Code-behind file for page demonstrating the **AdRotator** class 965
Code-behind file for the guest book application 1001
Code-behind file for the log in page for authors application 1007
Code-behind file for the page that allows a user to choose an author 1014
Code-behind file for the reservation page 1070
Code-behind file for the word generator page 972
Color value and alpha demonstration 689

ColorDialog used to change background and text color 692
COM DLL component in Visual Basic.NET 1339
ComboBox used to draw a selected shape 547
Comparison.vb 80
Complex XHTML table 1430
Composition demonstration 324
Computing the sum of the elements of an array 252
Concat Shared method 648
Const and **ReadOnly** class members 333
ConstAndReadOnly.vb 333
Consumer reads **Integer**s from synchronized shared buffer 612
Consumer reads **Integer**s from unsynchronized shared buffer 606
Consumer reads **Integer**s in synchronized, circular buffer 624
contact.html 1351, 1356, 1410, 1415
Container class for chess pieces 718
Cookies getting created in an ASP .NET Web application 983
Cookies recieved in an ASP .NET Web application 987
Counter-controlled repetition with the **For/Next** structure 146
Counter-controlled repetition with the **While** structure 146
CPieceWorker class inherits from class **CEmployee** 414
CPlayer class represents a Tic-Tac-Toe player 1119
CPoint class represents an *x-y* coordinate pair 355, 390
CPoint2 class inherits from **MustInherit** class **CShape** 401
CPoint2 class represents an *x-y* coordinate pair as **Protected** data 364

CPoint3 base class contains constructors and finalizer 378
CPoint3 class implements interface **IShape** 426
CRandomAccessRecord class represents a record for random-access file-processing applications 791
CreateArray.vb 250
Creating a **Console Application** with the **New Project** dialog 65
Creating an array 250
Creating variable-length parameter lists 287
CRecord class represents a record for sequential-access file-processing applications 770
CTest class tests the **CEmployee** class hierarchy 417
CTest2 demonstrates polymorphism in Point-Circle-Cylinder hierarchy 406
CTest3 uses interfaces to demonstrate polymorphism in Point-Circle-Cylinder hierarchy 431
CTransaction class handles record transactions for the transaction-processor case study 808
Cylinder class inherits from class **CCircle4** and **Overrides** method **Area** 373
Database access and information display 913
Database modification demonstration 923
Debug sample program 1304
DebugClass.vb 1314
DebugExample.vb 1304
Debugging a class. 1314
Default namespaces demonstration 841
Demonstrates function debugging. 1312
Demonstrating keyboard events 514
Demonstrating logical operators 168
Demonstrating order in which constructors and finalizers are called 381

Demonstrating the **While** repetition structure 107
Demonstrating XML namespaces 839
Demonstration of methods that draw lines, rectangles and elipses 700
Dialog displayed by calling **MessageBox.Show** 85
DiceModule.vb 231
DiceModuleTest.vb 232
Displaying text in a dialog 83
DisplayLogo.vb 714
Do Until/Loop repetition structure demonstration 109
Do Until/Loop repetition structure flowchart 110
Do While/Loop repetition structure demonstration 108
Do While/Loop repetition structure flowchart 109
Do/Loop Until repetition structure flowchart 161
Do/Loop While repetition structure 159
Do/Loop While repetition structure flowchart 160
DOM structure of an XML document illustrated by a class 846
DoUntil.vb 109
DoWhile.vb 108, 159
DrawArcs.vb 703
DrawPolygons.vb 705
DrawShapes.vb 709
DrawStars.vb 712
DTD for a business letter 861
Equality and relational operators 79
Equation.vb 1082
Exception handlers for **FormatException** and **DivideByZeroException** 447
Exception properties and demonstrating stack unwinding 462
Exception thrown when removing node from empty linked list 1145
Executing the program of Fig. 3.1 68, 85
Exit keyword in repetition structures 162
ExitTest.vb 162

Exponentiation using an assignment operator 111
Factorial.vb 220
Fibonacci.vb 222
Finally statements always execute, despite whether an exception occurs 454
First program in Visual Basic 63
Flowcharting a double-selection **If/Then/Else** structure 105
Flowcharting a single-selection **If/Then** structure 103
Font and **FontStyles** 695
FontFamily class used to obtain font metric information 697
For/Next repetition structure 148
For/Next repetition structure flowchart 149
For/Next structure used for summation 150
For/Next structure used to calculate compound interest 152
ForCounter.vb 146
ForEach.vb 288
Form including radio buttons and drop-down lists 1439
Form including textareas, password boxes and checkboxes 1376
form.html 1433
form2.html 1436
form3.html 1439
Formatting codes for **String**s 154
Framed Web site with a nested frameset 1393, 1455
FrmBankUI class is the base class for GUIs in our file-processing applications 767
FrmCreateRandomAccessFile class create files for random-access file-processing applications 794
FrmCreateSequentialAccessFile class creates and writes to sequential-access files 772
FrmCreditInquiry class is a program that displays credit inquiries 783

FrmDeleteDialog class enables users to remove records from files in transaction-processor case study 825
FrmFileSearch class uses regular expressions to determine file types 762
FrmFileTest class tests classes **File** and **Directory** 759
FrmHashTableTest.vb 1190
FrmNewDialog class enables users to create records in transaction-processor case study 816
FrmReadRandomAccessFile class reads records from random-access files sequentially 802
FrmReadSequentialAccessFile class reads sequential-access file 779
FrmSquareRoot class throws an exception if an error occurs when calculating the square root 466
FrmStartDialog class enables users to access dialog boxes associated with various transactions 813
FrmTransactionProcessor class runs the transaction-processor application 812
FrmUpdateDialog class enables users to update records in transaction-processor case study 819
FrmWriteRandomAccessFile class writes records to random-access files 798
Function procedure for squaring an integer 188
FunctionDebugExample.vb 1312
Generator.asmx.vb 1085
Generator.aspx 970
GetHashCode method demonstration 643
Graphical user interface for class **CTime3** 318

Index

Header elements `h1` through `h6` 1349, 1407
`header.html` 1349, 1407
`hello.xml` 1234
Hierarchical boss method/worker method relationship 185
`Histogram.vb` 256
`HugeInteger` Web service 1038
`HugeInteger.asmx.vb` 1038
IDE showing program code for a simple program 129
IDE with an open console application 66
`If/Then` single-selection structure flowchart 103
`If/Then/Else` double-selection structure flowchart 105
Image resizing 714
Image with links anchored to an image map 1446
Important methods of class `HttpCookie` 989
`index.html` 1450
`index2.html` 1455
Inheritance examples 352
Inheritance hierarchy for university `CCommunityMembers` 353
`InitArray.vb` 251
Initializing array elements two different ways 251
Initializing element arrays three different ways 251
Initializing multidimensional arrays 281
`InsertAtBack` graphical representation 1149
`InsertAtFront` graphical representation 1148
Inserting special characters into HTML 1356
Inserting special characters into XHTML 1415
IntelliSense feature of the Visual Studio .NET IDE 68
`Interest.vb` 152
Internet Explorer window with GUI components 87
Invoking the **Object Browser** from the development environment 342
`isbn.xml` 1235

`IShape` interface provides methods `Area` and `Volume` and property `Name` 426
`JaggedArray.vb` 283
Keywords in Visual Basic 101
`LabelScrollBar.vb` 1335
`letter.xml` 837
`LinearSearch.vb` 272
`LinearSearchTest.vb` 272, 273
`LinesRectangles-Ovals.vb` 700
Linked-list `CList` class 1142
Linked-list demonstration 1146
Linked-list graphical representation 1141
Linking to an e-mail address 1410
Linking to an email address 1351
Linking to other Web pages 1350, 1408
`LinkLabels` used to link to a folder, a Web page and an application 536
`links.html` 1350, 1358, 1408, 1443
`list.html` 1359, 1418
`List.vb` 1142
`ListBox` on an ASPX page 986
`ListBox` used in a program to add, remove and clear items 540
Listing for `namespace.xml` 839
`ListNodes.vb` 1141
`ListTest.vb` 1146
`ListView` displaying files and folders 557
Literals with type characters 199
Log in Web Form 1005
Logical operator truth tables 168
`LogicalOperator.vb` 168
`LogoAnimator.vb` 717
`LoopUntil.vb` 160
`main.html` 1347, 1402, 1448
`main.vxml` 1227
Manipulating the size of a `StringBuilder` 653

Math tutor application 1087
`Maximum.vb` 190
MDI child `FrmChild` 575
MDI parent window class 572
`Me` reference demonstration 326
Memory location showing name and value of variable `number1` 74
Menus used to change text font and color 528
Message dialog button constants 151
Message dialog icon constants 151
Method `FrmASimple-Program_Load` 133
Method that determines the largest of three numbers 190
`MethodOverload.vb` 226
`MethodOverload2.vb` 228
MMiscellaneous `String` methods 649
`modCircleTest` demonstrates class `CCircle` functionality 360
`modCircleTest3` demonstrates class `CCircle3` functionality 367
`modCircleTest4` demonstrates class `CCircle4` functionality 371
`modPointTest` demonstrates class `CPoint` functionality 357
Module used to define a group of related procedures 231
`Multidimensional Arrays.vb` 281
`MustInherit` class `CEmployee` definition 410
`nav.html` 1354, 1413, 1453
Nested and ordered lists in HTML 1359
Nested and ordered lists in XHTML 1418
Nested control structures used to calculate examination results 122
Nested repetition structures used to print a square of `*`s 126

New **Text** property value reflected in design mode 132
News article formatted with XML 834
Object Browser when user selects **Object** from development environment 343
Obtaining documentation for a class using the **Index** dialog 85
Optional argument demonstration with method **Power** 229
Options supplied on an ASPX page 981, 989
Order in which a second-degree polynomial is evaluated 79
OverflowException cannot occur if user disables integer-overflow checking 468
Overloaded methods 226
Overloaded-constructor demonstration 312
Overloading constructors 309
ParamArrayTest.vb 287
Parameter Info and Parameter List windows 68
PassArray.vb 261
Passing an array reference using **ByVal** and **ByRef** with an array 265
Passing arrays and individual array elements to procedures 261
Paths used to draw stars on a form 712
Payment.vb 185
Performing comparisons with equality and relational operators 80
Picture with links anchored to an image map 1386
picture.html 1352, 1411, 1446
Placing images in HTML files 1352
Placing images in XHTML files 1411
Polygon drawing demonstration 705
Power.vb 229
Precedence and associativity chart 169

Precedence and associativity of operators introduced in this chapter 82
Precedence of arithmetic operators 76
PrintSquare.vb 126
Procedures for performing a linear search 272
Producer and consumer threads accessing a circular buffer 625
Producer and consumer threads accessing a shared object with syncronization 613
Producer and consumer threads accessing a shared object without syncronization 608
Producer places **Integer**s in synchronized shared buffer 612
Producer places **Integer**s in synchronized, circular buffer 623
Producer places **Integer**s in unsynchronized shared buffer 605
Program that prints histograms 256
Program to display hidden text in a password box 493
Properties in a class 314
Properties window used to set a property value 131
Publication page of Deitel's VoiceXML page 1229
publications.vxml 1229
Quantifiers used in regular expressions 670
Queue implemented by inheritance from class **CList** 1157
Queue-by-inheritance test 1158
QueueInheritance.vb 1157
QueueTest.vb 1158
Random class used to simulate rolling 12 six-sided dice 211
RandomInt.vb 208
Recursive calls to method **Fibonacci** 224

Recursive evaluation of 5! 219
Recursive factorial program 220
Recursively generating Fibonacci numbers 222
Regex methods **Replace** and **Split** 675
Regular expressions checking birthdays 668
RemoveFromBack graphical representation 1151
RemoveFromFront graphical representation 1150
Renaming the program file in the **Properties** window 66
Repeatedly applying rule 2 of Fig. 5.25 to the simplest flowchart 173
Replacing text with class **StringBuilder** 659
Reservation.asmx.vb 1066
RollDie.vb 209, 257
RollDie2.vb 211
Scoping rules in a class 204
Searching for characters and substrings in **String**s 644
Second refinement of the pseudocode 126
Select Case multiple-selection structure flowchart 158
Select Case structure used to count grades 155
SelectTest.vb 155
Self-referential class **CListNode** 1141
Self-referential class objects linked together 1139
Self-referential **CNode** class definition 1138
Sequence structure flowchart 100
Server portion of a client/server stream socket connection 1101
Server side of client/server Tic-Tac-Toe program 1116
Server-side portion of connectionless client/server computing 1110
Service description for a Web service 1034

Session information displayed in a `ListBox` 995
Sessions created for each user in an ASP .NET Web application 991
Shapes drawn on a form 709
`Shared` class member demonstration 330
`Shared` method `Concat` 648
`ShowColors.vb` 689
`ShowColorsComplex.vb` 692
Simple Class Library project 338
Simple form with hidden fields and a text box 1433
Simple student-poll analysis program 254
Simple Visual Basic program 63
Simplest flowchart 173
SOAP request message for the `HugeInteger` Web service 1036
Sorting an array with bubble sort 269
SQL statements executed on a database 921
`SquareInteger.vb` 188
`Stack` class demonstration 1185
Stack implementation by inheritance from class `CList` 1153
Stack-by-composition test 1155
Stack-by-inheritance test 1154
`StackComposition.vb` 1155
Stacked, nested and overlapped building blocks 175
`StackInheritance.vb` 1153
`StackTest.vb` 1185
`String` 635
`String Length` property, the `CopyTo` method and `StrReverse` function 637
`String` methods `Replace`, `ToLower`, `ToUpper` and `Trim` 649
`String` testing for equality 639

`StringBuilder` class constructor 651
`StringBuilder` size manipulation 653
`StringBuilder` text replacement 659
`StringBuilder`'s `AppendFormat` method 656
Structured programming rules 172
`StudentPoll.vb` 254
`Sub` procedure for printing payment information 185
Substrings generated from `String`s 647
`Sum.vb` 150
`SumArray.vb` 252
Synchronized shared circular buffer 620
Synchronized shared `Integer` buffer 610
Syntax error generated from overloaded methods 228
`TabControl` used to display various font settings 564
Table optimized for screen reading using attribute headers 1223
`table1.html` 1427
`table2.html` 1430
`TemperatureServer.asmx.vb` 1073
Testing class `CCylinder` 375
Testing the `modDice` procedures 232
Thread life cycle 595
Threads sleeping and printing 600
`ThreadStart` delegate `Print` displays message and sleeps for arbitrary duration of time 598
`TicketReservation.aspx` 1069
`TicketReservation.aspx.vb` 1070
Tree data structure 1163
Tree node contains `IComparables` as data 1169
Tree structure for Fig. 18.1 842
`Tree.vb` 1163
`Tree2.vb` 1171
Tree-node data structure. 1162

`TreeNode.vb` 1162
`TreeNode2.vb` 1169
`TreeTest.vb` 1166
`TreeTest2.vb` 1173
Tree-traversal demonstration. 1166
`TreeView` used to display directories 553
Truth table for the `AndAlso` operator 165
Truth table for the `OrElse` operator 166
Truth table for the `Xor` (logical exclusive OR) operator 167
`Tutor.vb` 1087
Unordered lists in HTML 1358
Unordered lists in XHTML 1417
Unstructured flowchart 175
Unsynchronized shared `Integer` buffer 604
`UserControl` defined clock 581
Using `<META>` and `<DOCTYPE>` 1388
Using a `PictureBox` to display images 508
Using an abstract data type 303
Using arrays to eliminate a `Select Case` structure 257
Using `CheckBox`es to change font styles 498
Using default namespaces 841
Using `For Each/Next` with an `array` 288
Using `GroupBox`es and `Panel`s to arrange `Button`s 496
Using images as link anchors 1354, 1413
Using internal hyperlinks to make your pages more navigable 1383, 1443
Using jagged two-dimensional arrays 283
Using `meta` to provide keywords and a description 1448
Using overloaded constructors 312
Using `RadioButton`s to set message-window options 502

Using temperature and weather data 1077
Using the `HugeInteger` Web service 1049
`UsingArray.vb` 1176
`UsingFontMetrics.vb` 697
`UsingFonts.vb` 695
`UsingHugeInteger-Service.vb` 1049
Validating user information using regular expressions 670
Viewing the tracing information for a project 1021
Visual Basic console application 66
Visual Basic's single-entry/single-exit repetition structures 171
Visual Basic's single-entry/single-exit sequence and selection structures 170
Web service that generates random equations 1085
Web site using two frames: navigational and content 1390, 1450
`WebTime.aspx.vb` 948
`While` repetition structure flowchart 107
`While` repetition structure used to print powers of two 107
`While.vb` 107
`WhileCounter.vb` 146
Windows Form Designer generated code expanded 130
Windows Form Designer generated code reflecting new property values 132
`withheaders.html` 1223
`withoutheaders.html` 1222
XHTML document displayed in the left frame of Fig. 5.9. 1453
XHTML table 1427
XHTML table without accessibility modifications 1222
XML document containing book information 871
XML document that describes various sports 859
XML document using Unicode encoding 1326

XML file containing `AdRotator` information 967
XML namespaces demonstration 839
XML representation of a `DataSet` written to a file 932
XML to mark up a business letter 837
XML used to mark up an article 834
XML Validator displaying an error message 865
XML Validator used to validate an XML document 864
`XmlNodeReader` used to iterate through an XML document 843
`XPathNavigator` class used to navigate selected nodes 852
XSL document that transforms `sorting.xml` into XHTML. 872
XSL style sheet applied to an XML document 875
exception 23, 256, 442
`Exception` class 445, 450, 458, 459
exception for invalid array indexing 256
exception handler 442, 445, 451
Exception handlers for `FormatException` and `DivideByZeroException` 447
`Exception` library class 23
`Exception` properties and demonstrating stack unwinding 462
Exception thrown when removing node from empty linked list 1145
exception thrown within a `SyncBlock` 619
`Exclamation` constant 151
exclusive OR operator (`Xor`) 164, 167
`.exe` file 67
`ExecuteNonQuery` property of `OleDbCommand` 932
Execution of the `Welcome1` program 68, 72, 85
execution stack 1152
exhaust free memory 594

exhausting memory 221
`Exists` method of class `Directory` 758
`Exit Do` 162
`Exit For` 162
`Exit` keyword 21, 162
`Exit` method of class `Application` 533, 542
`Exit` method of class `Environment` 1109
`Exit` method of class `Monitor` 602, 609, 616, 617, 619
exit point of control structure 100, 172
`Exit Sub` statement 187, 188
`<exit>` tag (`<exit>`…`</exit>`) 1233
`Exit While` 162
`ExitTest.vb` 162
`Exp` method of class `Math` 194
`Expand` method of class `TreeNode` 552
expand node 550
expand tree 40
`ExpandAll` method of class `TreeNode` 552
expanded code 129
`Experience.com` 1293
`Expires` property of `HttpCookie` class 980, 989
explicit conversion 197
explicit relationships between data 835
exponential "explosion" of calls 225
exponential method 194
exponentiation 194
exponentiation assignment operator (`^=`) 111
Exponentiation using an assignment operator 111
exposing a Web service method 1032
expression 1307
Extended Backus-Naur Form (EBNF) grammar 861, 865
extensibility 16
Extensible HyperText Markup Language (XHTML) 15, 26, 29, 870, 1401
extensible language 303
Extensible Linking Language (XLink) 16
Extensible Markup Language (XML) 15, 1033

Extensible Stylesheet Language (XSL) 16, 839, 870
Extensible Stylesheet Language Transformation (XSLT) 26
external DTD 862
external help 45
External Help option 45
Extra Keyboard Help 1248

F

`F` formatting code 154
F1 help key 45, 1303
factorial 180, 218, 219
`Factorial.vb` 220
`fail.xml` 869
falsity 78
fatal logic error 103
fault-tolerant program 442
FCL (Framework Class Library) 18, 20, 27, 82
Fibonacci series 221, 224
`Fibonacci.vb` 222
field 754, 889, 890
FIFO (first-in, first-out) 335
file 754
file as a collection of bytes 754
`File` class methods (partial list) 757
File menu 38
File menu in Internet Explorer 87
File Name property 65
file opening in Windows 535
file-position 783
file-position pointer 783
file processing 753
file synchronization 18
`FileAccess` enumeration 777
`FileName` property of class `Ax-MediaPlayer` 731
file-processing programs 756
files 753
`FileStream` class 756, 777, 783
`Fill` method of class `Graphics` 713
`Fill` method of `OleDbAdapter` 920
`<filled>` tag (`<filled>`… `</filled>`) 1233
`FillEllipse` method of class `Graphics` 549, 700, 701
`FillPie` method of class `Graphics` 549, 703
`FillPolygon` method of class `Graphics` 705

`FillRectange` method of class `Graphics` 549
`FillRectangle` method of class `Graphics` 691, 701
`FillRectangles` method of class `Graphics` 700
filter 84
final value of control variable 145, 146, 148, 149, 161
finalizer 326
`Finally` block 445, 453
`Finally` statements always execute, regardless of whether an exception occurs 454
find 38
firewall 1036
First program in Visual Basic 63
first refinement 120, 124
first-in, first-out (FIFO) 335, 1156
`FirstNode` property of class `TreeNode` 551
five-pointed star 712
fixed-length records 790
flag value 114
`FlipDog.com` 1282
floating-point number 119
floating-point data type 198
floating-point number 118
`Floor` method of class `Math` 194
flow of control 88, 107, 118, 161
flowchart 21, 99, 103
flowchart of `For/Next` structure 149
flowchart reducible to the simplest flowchart 173
`FlowLayout` 955
flowline 99, 103
`Focus` method 488
`Focused` property 488
font 685, 694
`Font` class 684, 695
font control 694
font descent 697
Font dialog 50
font height 697
font leading 697
font manipulation 686
font metrics 697
font name 695
`Font` property 50, 488, 499
font size 50, 695
Font Size dialog 1242
font style 50, 498, 695
Font window 51
`FontFamily` class 685, 697

`FontFamily` property of class `Font` 694
`FontStyle` enumeration 695
`For Each/Next` repetition structure 100
`For Each/Next` structure 174, 288
`For/Next` header 148
`For/Next` header components 148
`For/Next` repetition structure 100
`For/Next` repetition structure flowchart 149
`For/Next` structure 21, 146, 147, 148, 149, 153, 171, 174
`For/Next` structure used for summation 150
`For/Next` structure used to calculate compound interest 152
`ForCounter.vb` 146
`For-Each` logic 407
`ForEach.vb` 288
`ForeColor` property 488
foreign key 896
`</FORM>` 1376
`<form>` tag (`<form>`… `</form>`) 1228
`<form>` tag (`<form>`… `</form>`) 1233
form 37, 478, 1368, 1373, 1427, 1432
`Form` array 975
form background color 48
`Form` class 128, 479
`Form Close` method 479
`form` element 1375, 1433
Form including textareas, password boxes and checkboxes 1376
form input 1383
`Form` properties, methods and events 479
`Form` property `IsMdi_Container` 567
form title bar 46
`Form1.vb` 54
format 73
`format` attribute 1239
format control string 302
Format menu 38
`Format` method of `String` 302
format string 657
`FormatException` class 446, 449

formation of structured programs 172
formatting code 153
Formatting codes for **Strings** 154
forms 1012
forms authentication 1012
FormsAuthentication class 1012
FORmula TRANslator (Fortran) 10
Fortran 1401
Fortran (FORmula TRANslator) 10
Fortran progamming language 19
forward slash character (**/**) 835, 1413
ForwardDiagonal member of enumeration **LinearGradientMode** 709
frame 1225, 1390, 1449
frame element 1392, 1453
Framed Web site with a nested frameset 1393, 1455
frameset document type 1450
frameset element 1391, 1392
Framework Class Library (FCL) 18, 20, 27, 82
FreeBSD operating system 18
Freedom Scientific 1240
Friend member access 354
FrmBankUI class is the base class for GUIs in our file-processing applications 767
FrmCreateRandomAccessFile class create files for random-access file-processing applications 794
FrmCreateSequentialAccessFile class creates and writes to sequential-access files 772
FrmCreditInquiry class is a program that displays credit inquiries 783
FrmDeleteDialog class enables users to remove records from files in transaction-processor case study 825
FrmDiceModuleTest 232
FrmDiceStatistics 211
FrmFibonacci 222
FrmFileSearch class uses regular expressions to determine file types 762

FrmFileTest class tests classes **File** and **Directory** 759
FrmHashTableTest.vb 1190
FrmNewDialog class enables users to create records in transaction-processor case study 816
FrmOverload 226
FrmRandomDice 209
FrmReadRandomAccessFile class reads records from random-access files sequentially 802
FrmReadSequentialAccessFile class reads sequential-access file 779
FrmSquareRoot class throws an exception if an error occurs when calculating the square root 466
FrmStartDialog class enables users to access dialog boxes associated with various transactions 813
FrmTransactionProcessor class runs the transaction-processor application 812
FrmUpdateDialog class enables users to update records in transaction-processor case study 819
FrmWriteRandomAccessFile class writes records to random-access files 798
FROM 897, 901, 902, 903, 904
FromArgb method of structure **Color** 688
FromImage method of class **Graphics** 711
FromName method 688
FullName property 561
FullPath property of class **TreeNode** 551
fully qualified name 905
Function procedure 184, 188
Function procedure for squaring an integer 188
functionalization 3
FunctionDebugExample.vb 1312
Futurestep.com 1288

G

G formatting code 154

G property of structure **Color** 688
gallery.yahoo.com 1411
game playing 206
game-playing program 206
games.xml 859, 859
garbage collection 326, 452, 594
garbage collector 326, 377, 636
garbage-collector thread 594
Gates, Bill 8
GC namespace of **System** 330
GDI+ (Graphics Device Interface+) 25, 684
general path 712
Generator.asmx.vb 1085
Generator.aspx 970
Genie **Microsoft Agent** character 731
Get accessor 307
Get method of **Property** 318
get request type 1239, 1434
Get Started page 34
GetCellAscent method of class **FontFamily** 697
GetCellDescent method of class **FontFamily** 697
GetCreationTime method of class **Directory** 758
GetCreationTime method of class **File** 757
GetCurrentDirectory method 208, 510
getDigits element 1237, 1238
GetDirectories method of class **Directory** 553, 758
GetDirectories method of class **DirectoryInfo** 561
GetEmHeight method of class **FontFamily** 697
GetEnumerator method of **ArrayList** 1185
GetEnumerator method of **Hashtable** 1195
GetFiles method of class **Directory** 758
GetFiles method of class **DirectoryInfo** 561
GetHashCode method demonstration 643
GetHashCode method of class **Object** 1190
GetHashCode of class **String** 643

Index

`GetItemChecked` method of class `CheckedListBox` 543
`GetLastAccessTime` method of class `Directory` 758
`GetLastAccessTime` method of class `File` 757
`GetLastWriteTime` method of class `Directory` 758
`GetLastWriteTime` method of class `File` 757
`GetLineSpacing` method of class `FontFamily` 697
`GetNodeCount` method of class `TreeNode` 552
`GetSelected` method of class `ListBox` 539
`GetStream` method of class `Socket` 1100
`GetUpperBound` method of class `System.Array` 248
`GetXml` method of `DataSet` 932
GIF (Graphic Interchange Format) 51
global variable 327, 1235
Globally Unique Identifier (GUID) 1337
glyph 1323
golden mean 221
golden ratio 221
Goldfarb, Charles 880
Good Programming Practice 12
Gosling, James 9
`goto` element 1239
`GoTo` elimination 99
`GoTo`-less programming 99
`GoTo` statement 99
`<goto>` tag (`<goto>`... `</goto>`) 1233
`<grammar>` tag (`<grammar>`... `</grammar>`) 1233
graph information 257
Graphic Interchange Format (GIF) 51
graphical representation of an algorithm 99
Graphical User Interface (GUI) 24, 37, 87, 476
Graphical User Interface for class `CTime3` 318
graphics 684
`Graphics` class 549, 684, 686, 695, 699, 711, 712, 713
graphics context 686

Graphics Device Interface+ (GDI+) 25, 684
Graphics Interchange Format (GIF) 1411
`Graphics` property of class `PaintEventArgs` 581
`GraphicsPath` class 712
`GraphicsUnit` structure 695
`Gray Shared` property of structure `Color` 688
greedy quantifier 670
Green project 9
`Green Shared` property of structure `Color` 688
grid 54
`GridLayout` 955
GROUP BY 897
group of related fields 754
`GroupBox` 494
`GroupBox` class 214
`GroupBox Controls` property 495
`GroupBox` properties and events 495
guest book 998
GUI (Graphical User Interface) 24, 37, 87
GUI component 87, 476
GUI component, basic examples 477
GUID (Globally Unique Identifier) 1337
Gunning Fog Index 1209, 1257

H

`h1` header element 1349, 1350, 1406
`h6` header element 1349, 1406
HailStorm Web services 18
hardware 3
"has-a" relationship 351
hash code 643
hash table 643
`Hashtable` class 982, 1081, 1176, 1190
Haskell progamming language 19
`HatchBrush` class 689, 709
`HatchStyle` enumeration 689
head 1403
`head` element 947, 1348, 1403
head of a queue 1137, 1156
head section 1403
header 1349, 1406
header cell 1370, 1429
header element 1406

`header.html` 1349, 1407
`headers` element 27, 1223, 1225
Headhunter.net 1289
Headlines page 35
`height` attribute 1353, 1411, 1412
`Height` property of class `Font` 694
Hejlsberg, Anders 10
Help menu 38, 44
help, context-sensitive 45
help, dynamic 44
help, external 45
help, internal 45
helper method 301, 1163
`HelpLink` property of `Exception` 460
Henter-Joyce 1240, 1257
hex code 1357
hexadecimal (base16) number system 180
hexadecimal value 1416
`hidden`
    element 979
    field 979
hidden form element 979
hidden input elements 1375
hide an internal data representation 335
`Hide` method 488
`Hide` of class `Form` 480
hiding implementation details 184, 305, 334
Hierarchical boss method/worker method relationship 184, 185
hierarchy 835
hierarchy diagram 352
hierarchy of shapes 396
`Highest ThreadPriority` enumeration member 596
high-level language 6, 7
Hire.com 1288
HireAbility.com 1290
Hirediversity.com 1287
histogram 256, 257
`Histogram.vb` 256
hit count 1309
Hoare, C. A. R. 601
home page 1346
Home Page Reader (HPR) 1209
horizontal coordinate 685
horizontal rule 28, 1417
host 943
hostname 943
hot key 525

HotDispatch.com 1290
HotJobs.com 1285, 1289
hotspot 1386, 1446
hotwired.lycos.com/
    webmonkey/00/50/
    index2a.html 1421
HPR (Home Page Reader) 1209
`<hr>` tag (horizontal rule) 1358,
    1417
hr element 1358, 1417
HREF 1386
href attribute 1351, 1355, 1409,
    1445
.htm (html file extension) 1346
.html (html file name extension)
    1346
.html (XHTML file name
    extension) 1401
`<html>…</html>` 1345
HTML (Hyper Text Markup
    Language) 15, 25, 26, 28,
    942, 943, 1345, 1401
    form 980, 998
    HTML element 1006
HTML comment 1347
HTML document 28
html element 947, 1403
HTML frame 28
HTML-Kit 1346
HTML list 28
HTML recommendation 1346
HTML source code 1346
HTML table 28
HTML tag 943, 1345
HTTP (HyperText Transfer
    Protocol) 16, 20, 943, 979,
    1239
HTTP being used with firewalls
    1036
HTTP GET request 1034
HTTP header 945
HTTP method 944
HTTP POST request 1034
HTTP transaction 944
HttpCookie class 986, 988, 989
    Domain property 989
    Expires property 989
    Name property 988, 989
    Path property 989
    Secure property 989
    Value property 988, 989
HttpCookieCollection 987
HttpSession class 995
    SessionID property 995
HttpSessionState 995
    Timeout property 995

HttpSessionState class 989,
    991, 994, 995, 998, 1026
    Counts property 995
    IsNewSession property
        995
    IsReadOnly property 995
    Keys property 995, 998
    SessionID property 995
    Timeout property 995
HugeInteger Web service
    1038
HugeInteger.asmx.vb 1038
hyperlink 943, 1350, 1355, 1408
hypertext 943
HyperText Markup Language
    (HTML) 15, 25, 26, 942,
    943, 1401
HyperText Transfer Protocol
    (HTTP) 16, 20, 943, 979
HyTime 16

I

I/O completion 597
IAgentCtlCharacter
    interface 743, 744
IAgentCtlUserInput
    interface 745
IBM (International Business
    Machines) 5
IBM Corporation 1322
IBM Personal Computer 6
IComparable interface 1168
IComponent interface 478
icon 38
IDE (Integrated Development
    Environment) 8, 21, 24, 34
IDE showing program code for a
    simple program 129
IDE's toolbox and **La-**
    belScrollbar properties
    1335
identifier 63
identifier's duration 202
IDictionaryEnumerator
    interface 1195
IE (Internet Explorer) 836
IEEE 754 floating-point 199
IEnumerator interface 1185,
    1195
`<if>` tag (`<if>…</if>`) 1233
If/Then selection structure 21,
    78, 81, 100, 102, 104, 117,
    155, 170, 173, 175
If/Then single-selection
    structure flowchart 103

If/Then/Else double-selection
    structure flowchart 105
If/Then/Else selection
    structure 100, 104, 155, 170,
    173
ignoring array element zero 255
IIS (Internet Information Services)
    943
image anchor 1383
Image Collection Editor 555
image hyperlink 1355, 1414
image map 28, 1386, 1388, 1447
Image property 51, 52, 508
ImageIndex property of class
    ListViewItem 555
ImageIndex property of class
    TreeNode 551
ImageList class 555
ImageList collection 551
ImageList property of class
    TabControl 564
ImageList property of class
    TreeView 551
images in Web pages 1352, 1411
ImageUrl attribute 967
img element 27, 1208, 1355,
    1388, 1411, 1412, 1414
Immediate window 1308
immutable **String** 636
implement an interface 425
implementation 298, 305
implementation of a class hidden
    from its clients 305
implementation-dependent code
    305
Implements keyword 421, 425
implicit conversion 72
implicitly **NotOverridable**
    method 408
#IMPLIED flag 862
Important methods of class
    HttpCookie 989
Imports directive 86
Imports keyword 82
Imports statement 87
Impressions attribute 967
In property of class **Console**
    755
Inch member of enumeration
    GraphicsUnit 695
Inclusive Technology 1253
increasing order 268
increment of a **For/Next**
    structure 147
increment of control variable 146,
    148, 149

Index

increment of loop 145
indefinite postponement 597
indefinite repetition 114
indentation convention 102, 104
indentation in **If/Then**
    statements 82
indentation techniques 64, 88
Indenting each level of a nested
    list in code 1361
index 256, 279
Index command 44
Index event of class
    CheckedListBox 544
index of an array 247
Index property of class **Menu-**
    Item 528
index.html 1346
indexer for class **Hashtable**
    1081
IndexOf method of class **Array**
    1179
IndexOf method of class
    ArrayList 1180, 1184
IndexOf method of class
    String 644
IndexOfAny method of class
    String 644
IndexOutOfRange-
    Exception class 256, 451
indirect base class 352
infinite loop 108, 159, 161, 221,
    1115
infinite recursion 221
infinity symbol 895
Information constant 151
information hiding 297, 298, 334
information parameter 835
information tier 945
Informix 888
inherit from class **Control** 581
inherit from Windows Form
    control 581
inherit implementation 440
inherit interface 398, 440
inheritance 22, 298, 299, 306, 350,
    353, 382, 389, 425
Inheritance examples 352
inheritance hierarchy 352, 399
Inheritance hierarchy for
    university **CCommunity-**
    Members 353
inheritance with exceptions 451
inheriting interface versus
    inheriting implementation
    440

Inherits attribute of ASP.NET
    page 947
Inherits keyword 128
Init event 950
InitArray.vb 251
initial set of classes 298
initial value of control variable
    145, 148, 149
initialization phase 117
initialize implicitly to default
    values 308
initialize instance variables 305
initializer 308
initializer list 249, 280
Initializing array elements two
    different ways 251
initializing arrays 249
Initializing element arrays three
    different ways 251
Initializing multidimensional
    arrays 281
initializing two-dimensional
    arrays in declarations 281
inner block 204
inner **For** structure 257, 282
INNER JOIN 897, 904
inner loop 125
InnerException property of
    Exception 460, 461
innermost pair of parentheses 76
innermost set of parentheses 255
inorder traversal of a binary tree
    1161
<input> 1208
input 37
input 979
input data from the keyboard 477
input device 4
input element 1375, 1376, 1435
INPUT TYPE = "reset" 1376
INPUT TYPE = "submit"
    1376
input unit 4
input/output 756
input/output blocking 597
input/output operation 99
input/output request 596
inputting data from the keyboard
    88
INRIA (Institut National de
    Recherche en Informatique
    et Automatique) 15
insert an item into a container
    object 301
INSERT INTO 897, 909

Insert method of class **Array-**
    List 1180
Insert Separator option 526
INSERT statement 909
InsertAtBack graphical
    representation 1149
InsertAtFront graphical
    representation 1148
InsertCommand property of
    OleDbAdapter 920
inserting separators in a menu 526
insertion 1140
insertion point 1140
instance of a built-in type 298
instance of a user-defined type 298
instance variable 301, 314, 324,
    355, 358
"instant-access" application 789
instantiate (or create) objects 298
Institut National de Recherche en
    Informatique et
    Automatique (INRIA) 15
Int32 structure 197
Int32.MaxValue constant 206
integer division assignment
    operator (**\=**) 111
integer division operator (****) 75
integer mathematics 334
Integer primitive data type 70,
    114
integer value 70
integral data type 198, 468
Integrated development
    environment (IDE) 34
integrated development
    environment (IDE) 8, 21
intelligent agent 1282
IntelliSense 67, 68
IntelliSense feature of the Visual
    Studio .NET IDE 193
interactions among objects 334
interactive animated character 25,
    731
Interest.vb 152
interface 307, 419, 420, 421, 425,
    889
Interface keyword 419, 425
internal data representation 335
internal help 45
Internal Help option 45
internal hyperlinks 1386, 1445
internal linking 28, 1383, 1443
internal Web browser 36
International Business Machines
    (IBM) 5
Internet 14, 15

Internet Explorer (IE)
  IE (Internet Explorer) 476, 535, 836, 1401, 1412
Internet Information Services (IIS) 943
Internet Protocol (IP) 14
Internet Protocol Addresses (IP Address) 1098
Internet Service Provider (ISP) 1375, 1435
Internshipprograms.com 1293
interpreter 7
Interrupt method of class **Thread** 596
Interval property of class **Timer** 581
InterviewSmart™ 1294
intranet 11, 13
Invalidate method of class **Control** 687
InvalidCastException 394, 395
InvalidOperationException 1189
Invoke 1035
invoking a method 194
Invoking a method of a Web service from a Web browser 1035
Invoking the **Object Browser** from the development environment 342
IP (Internet Protocol) 14
IP Address 943, 1098
IPAddress class 1100
IPEndPoint class 1100
"is-a" relationship 351, 394, 397
Is keyword 158
is-a relationship 425
IsAccessible property of class **Control** 1217, 1221
isbn attribute 874
IsDigit method of class **Char** 662
IsFull method 301
IShape interface provides methods **Area** and **Volume** and property **Name** 426
IsLetter method of class **Char** 663
IsLetterOrDigit method of class **Char** 663
IsLower method of class **Char** 663

IsMdiChild property of class **Form** 569
IsMdiContainer property of class **Form** 567, 569
IsNewSession property of **HttpSessionState** class 995
ISP (Internet Service Provider) 1375, 1435
IsPostBack property of class **Page** 975
IsPunctuation method of class **Char** 663
IsReadOnly property of **HttpSessionState** class 995
IsSymbol method of class **Char** 663
IsUpper method of class **Char** 663
IsValid property of **ServerValidateEventArgs** class 1011, 1012
IsWhiteSpace method of class **Char** 663
Italic member of enumeration **FontStyle** 695
Italic property of class **Font** 694
ItemActivate event of class **ListView** 556
ItemCheck event of class **CheckedListBox** 543
ItemCheckEventArgs event of class **CheckedListBox** 543
Items property of class **ComboBox** 546
Items property of class **ListBox** 538
Items property of class **ListView** 556
ItemSize property of class **TabControl** 564
iteration 125
iteration of a **For** loop 255
iteration of a loop 145
iterative 221
iterative binary search 275
iterator 400, 1185
iterator class 400

J

J# progamming language 19
Jacopini, G. 99, 173

jagged array 279, 280, 281
JaggedArray.vb 283
Jasc® Paint Shop Pro™ 51
Java Development Kit (Java SDK 1.3) 1226
JAWS (Job Access with Sound) 1240, 1257
job 5
jobfind.com 1285
Jobs.com 1286
JobsOnline.com 1289
Join method of class **Thread** 596, 629
joining tables 896
Joint Photographic Experts Group (JPEG) 51, 1411
JPEG (Joint Photographic Experts Group) 51
JScript scripting language 20
JSML 1256
JustCJobs.com 1290
JustComputerJobs.com 1290
JustJavaJobs.com 1281, 1290

K

Keio University 15
Kemeny, John 7
key code 516
key data 516
key event 513
key value 272, 516, 1168
key-value pairs 982
key, modifier 513
keyboard 3, 5, 476
KeyDown event 513
KeyEventArgs properties 513
KeyPress event 513
KeyPressEventArgs properties 513
Keys property of **HttpSessionState** class 995, 998
KeyUp event 513
keyword 63, 100, 101
Keywords in Visual Basic 101
Koenig, Andrew 442
Kurtz, Thomas 7

L

label 49, 50, 87, 476, 477, 491
Label class 214, 491
LabelScrollBar.vb 1335
LAN (local area network) 6

language attribute 947
language independence 19
language interoperability 8, 19, 20
LargeImageList property of class ListView 556
LastChild property of XmlNode 851
last-in, first-out (LIFO) data structure 1152
LastIndexOf method of class Array 1179
LastIndexOf method of class String 644, 646
LastIndexOfAny method of class String 644
last-in-first-out (LIFO) 334
LastNode property of class TreeNode 551
Latin World 1288
layout control 38, 487
layout window 38
LayoutMdi enumeration 571, 572
LayoutMdi method of class Form 569, 571
LayoutMdi.ArrangeIcons 571
LayoutMdi.Cascade 571
LayoutMdi.TileHorizontal 571
LayoutMdi.TileVertical 571
lazy quantifier 670
leaf node 1160
leaf node in a binary search tree 1161
left child 1160
left subtree 1160, 1161, 1201
left-to-right evaluation 78
length of an array 248
Length property of class 248
Length property of class String 637, 638
Length property of class StringBuilder 652
letter 754
letter.dtd 861, 861
letter.xml 837
levels of nesting 125, 172, 1361
level of refinement 115, 117
level-order binary tree traversal 1168
llexicographical comparison 641
<li> (list item) tag 1359, 1417
lifetime of an identifier 202
LIFO (last-in, first-out) 334

LIKE 899, 900, 903
likelihood 207
line 684
linear collection 1139
linear data structure 1160
linear search 272, 275, 294
LinearGradientBrush class 689, 709
LinearGradientMode enumeration 709
linearized 1221
LinearSearch.vb 272
LinearSearchTest.vb 272, 273
line-continuation character _ 83
LinesRectanglesOvals.vb 700
link 1139, 1160
link element in VoiceXML 1229
link for a self-referential class 1138
link one Web page to another 1383
<link> tag (<link>… </link>) 1233
LinkArea property of class LinkLabel 534
LinkBehavior property of class LinkLabel 535
LinkButton 1019
LinkClicked event of class LinkLabel 534, 535
LinkColor property of class LinkLabel 535
linked document 1350
linked list 27, 301, 400, 1137, 1139
Linked-list CList class 1142
Linked-list demonstration 1146
Linked-list graphical representation 1141
linked list in sorted order 1140
LinkLabel class 524, 534
LinkLabel properties and events 534
LinkLabels used to link to a folder, a Web page and an application 536
Links property of class LinkLabel 535
links.html 1350, 1358, 1408
links2.html 1417
LinkVisited property of class LinkLabel 535
Linux operating system 5, 6
list 477
list, editable 547

list.html 1359, 1418
List.vb 1142
ListBox class 524, 538
ListBox of namespace System.Web.UI.WebControls 971
ListBox on an ASPX page 986
ListBox properties, methods and events 538
ListBox used in a program to add, remove and clear items 540
ListBox Web control 995
Listing for namespace.xml 839
ListNodes.vb 1141
ListTest.vb 1146
ListView class 555
ListView displaying files and folders 557
ListView properties and events 556
literal 199
literal String objects 635
Literals with type characters 199
live-code™ approach 3
Load event 480
Load method in XslTransform 875
Load method of XMLDocument 843
local area network (LAN) 6
local dialog 1229
local variable 203, 204
local variable "goes out of scope" 753
local variable is destroyed 263
local variables of a method 306, 324
localhost 1109
localization 1321
Locals window 1307
local-variable declaration space 204
location in the computer's memory 73
Location property 490
lock 616, 617
locking objects 601
Log in Web Form 1005
Log method of class Math 194
logarithm 194
logarithmic calculation 22
logging feature 1235
logic element 1238
logic error 103, 115, 116, 1304

logical AND with short-circuit evaluation (`AndAlso`) 164, 165, 166
logical AND without short-circuit evaluation (`And`) 164, 166, 170
logical decision 3
logical exclusive OR operator (`Xor`) 164, 167
logical inclusive OR with short-circuit evaluation (`OrElse`) 164, 165, 166
logical inclusive OR without short-circuit evaluation (`Or`) 164, 166
logical NOT operator (`Not`) 164, 167
logical operator 21, 164, 167
Logical operator truth tables 168
logical unit 4
`LogicalOperator.vb` 168
`loginUrl` 1012
`LogoAnimator.vb` 717
long-term retention of data 753
`longdesc` attribute 1208
Look-and-Feel Observation 13
loop 114
loop body 159
loop counter 145
loopback IP address 1109
loop-continuation condition 146, 147, 148, 159, 161
loop-continuation test 109
looping process 120
`LoopUntil.vb` 160
Lovelace, Ada 11
lowercase 64
`Lowest ThreadPriority` enumeration member 596
lvalue ("left value") 110, 247
Lynx 1225

M

m-by-*n* array 279
machine dependent 6
machine language 6
MacOS operating system 6
`Magenta Shared` property of structure `Color` 688
magnetic disk 753
magnetic tape 753
`mailto:` URL 1352, 1409
`Main` method 147, 583
`Main` method of class `CTest` 415
`Main` procedure 64, 68, 81

`Main` thread of execution 598
`main.html` 1347, 1402
`MainMenu` 525
`MainMenu` class 525
`MainMenu` control 59
`MainMenu` properties 527
`MainMenu` properties and events 527
maintenance of software 12
making decisions 88
Manipulating the size of a `StringBuilder` 653
"manufacturing" section of the computer 4
many-to-many relationship 896
`map` element `<map>…</map>` 1386
`map` element 1447
marked for garbage collection 328
markup 943
markup language 28, 1345, 1401
Massachusetts Institute of Technology (MIT) 15
`match` 874
`Match` class 668, 675
match the selection criteria 898
`MatchCollection` class 668
matching left and right braces 73
`Math` class 22, 83, 1087
`Math` class methods 190, 194
Math tutor application 1087
`Math.Abs` method 194
`Math.Ceiling` method 194
`Math.Cos` method 194
`Math.E` constant 194
`Math.Exp` method 194
`Math.Floor` method 194
`Math.Log` method 194
`Math.Max` method 194
`Math.Min` method 194
`Math.PI` constant 194
`Math.Pow` method 194
`Math.Sin` method 194
`Math.Sqrt` method 83, 195
`Math.Tan` method 195
mathematical formula 834
Mathematical Markup Language (MathML) 26
MathML (Mathematical Markup Language) 26
`Max` method of class `Math` 194
`maxDigits` attribute 1237
`MaxDropDownItems` property of class `ComboBox` 545, 546
`Maximum.vb` 190

`MaximumSize` property 491
`maxlength` attribute 1376, 1435
`maxOccurs` attribute 867
`maxTime` attribute 1238, 1239
`MaxValue` constant of `Int32` 469
maze traversal 295
`MBAFreeAgent.com` 1291
MBCS (multi-byte character set) 1324
MDI (multiple document interface) 24, 567
MDI child `FrmChild` 575
MDI form 569
MDI parent and MDI child events and properties 569
MDI parent window class 572
MDI title bar 569
`MdiChildActivate` event of class `Form` 569
`MdiChildren` property of class `Form` 568, 569
`MdiList` property of class `MenuItem` 570
`MdiParent` property of class `Form` 567, 569
`Me` keyword 324, 328
`Me` reference demonstration 326
mean (average) 77
member access modifier `Private` 301
member access modifier `Public` 301
member access modifiers 301
member access operator 354, 370
memory 3, 4, 13
memory consumption 1176
memory leak 326, 452, 594
memory location 255
memory unit 4
`MemoryStream` class 756
menu 37, 87, 476, 524
menu access shortcut 525
menu access shortcut, create 526
menu bar 87, 476
menu bar in Visual Studio .NET IDE 37
Menu Designer in VS .NET 525
menu item 37, 525
menu separator 526
`<menu>` tag (`<menu>`… `</menu>`) 1228, 1233
menu, ellipsis convention 527
menu, expanded and checked 525
`MenuItem` 525

Index 1501

MenuItem class 526
MenuItem properties 528
MenuItem properties and events 527
MenuItem property MdiList example 571
MenuItems property of class MainMenu 527
MenuItems property of class MenuItem 528
MenuMerge enumeration 570
MenuMerge.Add 570
MenuMerge.MergeItems 570
MenuMerge.Remove 570
MenuMerge.Replace 570
Menus used to change text font and color 528
Mercury programming language 20
Merge records from Tables 903
MergeItems member of enumeration MenuMerge 570
MergeOrder property of class MenuItem 569
MergeType property of class MenuItem 569
Merlin Microsoft Agent character 731
message box 21, 1304
message dialog 151, 191
message dialog button 151
Message dialog button constants 151
message dialog icon 151
Message dialog icon constants 151
Message property of Exception 450, 454, 459
MessageBox class 82, 84, 257
MessageBoxButtons class 151
MessageBox-Buttons.AbortRetry-Ignore 152
MessageBoxButtons.OK 151
MessageBoxButtons.OK-Cancel 151
MessageBoxButtons.RetryCancel 151
MessageBoxButtons.Yes-No 151
MessageBoxButtons.Yes-NoCancel 151
MessageBoxIcon class 151
MessageBoxIcon.Error 151

MessageBoxIcon.Exclamation 151
MessageBoxIcon.Information 151
MessageBoxIcon.Question 151
meta element 947, 1390, 1448, 1449
META tag 1388
method 175
method = "get" 1375, 1434
method = "post" 1375, 1434
method attribute 1239, 1375, 1433
method call stack 459
method definition 64
Method FrmASimple-Program_Load 133
method overloading 226
Method that determines the largest of three numbers 190
MethodOverload.vb 226
MethodOverload2.vb 228
MFC (Microsoft Foundation Classes) 12
microprocessor chip technology 13
Microsoft 1322
Microsoft Agent 25
Microsoft Agent 731, 743
Microsoft Agent Character Editor 732
Microsoft Agent Control 2.0 743
Microsoft Intermediate Language (MSIL) 19, 67
Microsoft Internet Explorer accessibility options 1254
Microsoft Linguistic Sound Editing Tool 732
Microsoft Magnifier 1242
Microsoft Narrator 1251
Microsoft Narrator 1251, 1253
Microsoft .NET 17
Microsoft **On-Screen Keyboard** 1252, 1253
Microsoft Paint 51
Microsoft SansSerif font 695
Microsoft Serif font 695
Microsoft SQL Server 888
Microsoft Windows 95/98 62
Microsoft Windows NT/2000 62
middle array element 275
middle tier 946
MIDI (Musical Instrument Digital Interface) 729

Millimeter member of enumeration Graphics-Unit 695
MIME (Multipurpose Internet Mail Extensions) 945, 980
Min method of class Math 194
minimized and maximized child window 570
MinimumSize property 491
minOccurs attribute 867
minus box 40
minus sign (-) 836
Miscellaneous String methods 649
MIT (Massachusetts Institute of Technology) 15
MIT's Project Mac 14
Mod (modulus operator) 74, 75, 77
Mod keyword 74
modal dialog 777
modCircleTest demonstrates class CCircle functionality 360
modCircleTest3 demonstrates class CCircle3 functionality 367
modCircleTest4 demonstrates class CCircle4 functionality 371
mode attribute 1012
model attribute 867
modifier key 513
modify a variable at run time 1307
modPointTest demonstrates class CPoint functionality 357
module scope 203
Module used to define a group of related procedures 231
modulus 75
modulus operator (Mod) 74, 75
Monitor class 595, 596, 597, 601, 609, 616, 617
monolithic excecutable 1332
Monster.com 1281, 1285, 1289, 1291
MonthCalendar control 60
Moore's Law 13
More Windows... option in Visual Studio .NET 570
Morse code 1134, 1135
Motion Pictures Experts Group (MPEG) 729
mouse 3, 476

Mouse Button Settings 1249
mouse click 510
mouse cursor 84, 1245
mouse event 510
mouse move 510
mouse pointer 39, 41, 84
mouse press 510
Mouse Speed dialog 1250
MouseDown event 510
MouseEventArgs class 510
MouseEventArgs properties 511
MouseHover event 510
MouseKeys 1249
MouseLeave event 510
MouseMove event 511
MouseUp event 511
Move method of class Directory 758
Move method of class File 757
MoveNext of IEnumerator 1185
MoveTo method of interface IAgentCtlCharacter 745
MPEG format 729
MS-DOS prompt 62
MSDN documentation 151
msdn.microsoft.com/downloads/samples/Internet/xml/xml_validator/sample.asp 863
MSIL (Microsoft intermediate language) 19, 67
MSN.com 979
msxml parser 836
mulit-byte character set (MBCS) 1324
multi-tier application 945
multicast delegate 433
multicast event 480, 485
MulticastDelegate class 433, 480
MultiColumn property of class ListBox 539
multidimensional array 246, 279
Multidimensional Arrays.vb 281
MultiExtended value of SelectionMode 539
multilevel priority queue 597
MultiLine property of class TabControl 492, 564
multimedia 729

Multiple Document Interface (MDI) 24
multiple document interface (MDI) 567
multiple inheritance 350
multiple selection logic 159
multiple-subscripted array 279
multiple-selection structure 100, 155, 173
multiplication assignment operator (*=) 111
multiprogramming 5
Multipurpose Internet Mail Extensions (MIME) 945, 980
MultiSelect property of class ListView 555, 556
MultiSimple value of SelectionMode 539
multitasking 11
multithread safe 1141
multithreading 11, 24, 593
Musical Instrument Digital Interface (MIDI) 729
MustInherit 398, 399, 408, 409
MustInherit class 409, 431
MustInherit class CEmployee definition 410
MustInherit keyword 756
MustOverride method 399, 409
mutual exclusion 501
mutually exclusive options 501
My Documents folder 36
My Profile page 35, 45
MyBase reference 382
MySQL 888

N

N formatting code 154
n-tier application 945
name 1375
name = "keywords" 1389
name attribute 1435
name attribute of meta element 948
name node-set function 874
name of a control variable 145
name of a variable 73
name of an attribute 1403
(Name) property 492
Name property of class Font 694
Name property of HttpCookie class 988, 989

Name property of structure Color 691
namespace 82, 208, 299, 303, 839
namespace prefix 839, 841
Namespace property of a WebService attribute 1037
namespace scope 203
namespace.xml 839, 839
NamespaceURI 851
naming collision 336, 839
NaN constant of class Double 465
Narrator reading Notepad text 1253
narrowing conversion 195
natural logarithm 194
nav.html 1354, 1413
NavigateUrl attribute 967
navigation bar 1006
navigational frame 1390, 1450
negative arc angles 702
negative infinity 447
nested tags 1392
nested building block 175
nested control structure 119, 125, 159, 172
Nested control structures used to calculate examination results 122
nested element 835, 1404
nested For loop 257, 281, 283, 286
nested frameset element 1394, 1454, 1456
nested If/Then/Else structure 104
nested list 1359, 1361, 1418
nested loop 125
nested parentheses 76
nested repetition structure 125
Nested repetition structures used to print a square of *s 126
nested within a loop 121
nesting 119, 175
nesting rule 172
.NET initiative 17
.NET-compliant language 19
.NET component 1333
.NET Framework 18
.NET Framework Class Library (FCL) 27, 183, 193, 234, 593
.NET Languages 19
Netscape Communicator 1401
network address 1098
network message arrival 445
networking 27, 753

Index

NetworkStream class 1100
New keyword 249, 1139, 1175
New Project dialog 37, 46
new project in Visual Studio .NET IDE 38
New **Text** property value reflected in design mode 132
newline 102
News article formatted with XML 834
newsgroup 34
NewValue event of class **CheckedListBox** 544
next attribute of **choice** element 1229
Next keyword 147
Next method of class **Random** 206, 1087
NextNode property of class **TreeNode** 551
node 550
node, child 550
node, expand and collapse 550
node, parent 550
node, root 550
Nodes property of class **TreeNode** 551
Nodes property of class **TreeView** 551
node-set function 874
noframes element 1392, 1393, 1453
nondestructive read from memory 74
None value of **SelectionMode** 539
nonfatal logic error 103
nonrecursive method call 225
nonvalidating XML parser 860
Not (logical NOT) 164, 167
not-selected state 501
Notepad 535, 1401
Notepad text editor 1346
Nothing keyword 217, 249, 1138
NotInheritable class 408, 409
NotOverridable method 409
noun 12
Now property of structure **DateTime** 582
n-tier application 6
NullReferenceException 451
Number systems Appendix 1266

O

Oberon programming language 19
object 9, 12, 297, 298
object-based programming 2
Object Browser when user selects **Object** from development environment 343
Object class 299, 407, 643
object of a derived class 389
object of a derived class is instantiated 376
object orientation 297
object oriented 298
object-oriented programming (OOP) 2, 9
object passed by reference 298
"object speak" 297
"object think" 297
object-based programming (OBP) 298
object-oriented language 12
object-oriented programming (OOP) 2, 9, 298, 350, 389, 839
objects constructed "inside out" 381
OBP (object-based programming) 298
occurence indicator 861
octal (base8) 180
Ocularis 1241
.OCX file 1333, 1334
off-by-one error 147, 248
OK button on a dialog 84
OK constant 151
OKCancel constant 151
ol (ordered list) tag **<ol>**... **</ol>** 1362
OleDbCommand class 912
OleDbConnection class 912
OleDbDataAdapter class 912
OleDbDataReader 1011
one comparison in the binary search algorithm 275
one-dimensional array 279
one-to-many relationship 895
One value of **SelectionMode** 539
one's complement 1274
ones position 1268
onHangup element 1238
Online Community 34
online contracting service 1291
online guest book 998

online recruiting 1283
onMaxSilence element 1237, 1238
OnPaint method of class **Control** 580, 686
On-Screen Keyboard 1252
onTermDigit element 1237, 1238
OOP (object-oriented programming) 2, 9, 298, 350, 389, 839
Open method of class **File** 757
open-source software 5
open technology 834
opened 756
OpenFileDialog class 778, 789
opening a file in Windows 535
opening a project 38
OpenRead method of class **File** 757
OpenRead method of class **WebClient** 1076
OpenText method of class **File** 757
OpenWrite method of class **File** 757
operand 71
operating system 5
operations of an abstract data type 335
operator precedence 76
operator precedence chart 27
Operator precedence chart Appendix 1264
optical disk 753
optional argument 226
Optional argument demonstration with method **Power** 229
Optional keyword 228, 236
Options supplied on an ASPX page 981, 989
Or (logical inclusive OR without short-circuit evaluation) 164, 166
Oracle Corporation 888, 1322
Orange Shared property of structure **Color** 688
order attribute 874
ORDER BY 897, 901, 902, 903
ordered 889
ordered list 1418, 1420
ordered list element 1362
ordering of records 897

OrElse (logical inclusive OR with short-circuit evaluation) 164, 165, 166
out-of-range array subscript 445, 451
Out property of class **Console** 755
outer block 204
outer **For** structure 286
outer set of parentheses 255
OutOfMemoryException Exception 1139
output 37
output cursor 64, 69
output device 4
output directory 583
output file 583
output unit 4
oval symbol 99
overflow 445, 468
OverflowException cannot occur if user disables integer-overflow checking 468
OverflowException class 468, 472
overhead of recursion 225
overlapped building block 175
overload resolution 227
overloaded constructor 308
overloaded method 226, 309
Overloaded-constructor demonstration 312
overloading 371
Overloading constructors 309
Overridable keyword 425
Overridable method 408
overridden 351
override method **ToString** 371
Overrides keyword 399
Oz programming language 19

P

p (paragraph) element 1348, 1404
P format code (percent) 210
packet 1098
Page class 949, 975, 991
    Session property 991
    Trace property 1019
page content 1348
page layout software 634
page tracing 1019
Page_Unload method 950
PageIndexChange event for a **DataGrid** control 1018

pageLayout property of ASP.NET page 955
PagerStyle property of a **DataGrid** control 1018
PageSize property of a **DataGrid** control 1018
Paint 557
Paint Shop Pro 1411
PaintEventArgs class 580, 686
PaintEventArgs properties 581
palette 48
palindrome 293
Palo Alto Research Center (PARC) 9
panel 477
Panel class 494, 685
Panel Controls property 495
Panel properties and events 495
panel with scrollbars 495
paper 4
parallelogram 351
ParamArray keyword 287
ParamArrayTest.vb 287
parameter 186, 189
Parameter Info feature of the Visual Studio .NET IDE 193
parameter list 187
parameter variable 186
parameterized constructor 308
parameterless **Catch** block 445
PARC (Palo Alto Research Center) 9
parent element 836
parent menu 525
parent node 550, 842, 1160, 1200
parentheses **()** 76
parsed character data 862
parser 836, 840
partition 294
partitioning step 294, 295
Pascal programming language 10, 11, 19
Pascal, Blaise 11
pass-by-reference 200
pass-by-value 200
pass of a sorting algorithm 268
PassArray.vb 261
passing an array element to a procedure 261
Passing an array reference using **ByVal** and **ByRef** with an array 265
passing an array to a procedure 260, 261

Passing arrays and individual array elements to procedures 261
password box 1376, 1436
password textbox 491
PasswordChar property 492
PasswordChar property of **TextBox** class 491
paste 38
Path property of **HttpCookie** class 989
path to a resource 943
PathGradientBrush class 709
pattern matching 899
pattern of **1**s and **0**s 754
Payment.vb 185
payroll system 396, 754
#PCDATA flag 862
PDA (personal digital assistant) 8
Peedy the Parrot Microsoft Agent character 731
Peek method of class **Stack** 1188
Pen class 684, 688, 699, 701
Performance Tip 13
performing a calculation 88
Perl progamming language 19
permission setting 557
persistent data 753
persistent information 979
personal computer 3
personal computing 5
personal digital assistant (PDA) 8
personalization 979
PhotoShop Elements 1411
PhysicalApplication-Path property of **Request** class 1001
picture box 51, 508
picture.html 1352, 1411
PictureBox class 214, 508, 571
PictureBox properties and events 508
Pig Latin 682
pin a window 39
pin icon 39
Pink Shared property of structure **Color** 688
pixel 1411
Pixel member of enumeration **GraphicsUnit** 695
platform independence 17, 19
play element 1239

Index 1505

Play method of interface
  IAgentCtlCharacter
  744
playback, choppy 594
player thread 594
plus box 40
plus sign (+) 836
plus sign (+) occurence indicator
  861
PNG (Portable Networks Graphic)
  51
point-of-sale system 789
Point structure 686
poker 681
polymorphic programming 396,
  400
polymorphic screen manager 397
polymorphism 23, 159, 298, 383,
  389, 394, 397, 399, 409
polymorphism as an alternative to
  Select Caselogic 440
polynomial 78, 79
pool of threads 1100
Pop method of class **Stack**
  1185, 1188
pop stack operation 1152
popping off a stack 334
port number 1098, 1099
portability 19, 1324
Portability Tip 13
portable 834
Portable Networks Graphic (PNG)
  51
porting 19
position number 247
positional notation 1268
Positional value 1269
Positional values in the decimal
  number system 1269
positive and negative arc angles
  702
positive infinity 447
post request type 1239, 1434
postback 975
postorder traversal 1161
postorder traversal of a binary tree
  1161
Pow method 1087
Pow method of class **Math** 194
power 194
Power.vb 229
Precedence and associativity chart
  169
precedence chart Appendix 1264
precedence of arithmetic operators
  76

precedence rule 76
predicate method 301, 1141
premature program termination
  255
preorder traversal of a binary tree
  1161
prepackaged data structures 1175
preprocessor directives 519
presentation logic 946
presentation of a document 1345,
  1401
previous statement, variable in
  1307
PrevNode property of class
  TreeNode 551
primary interop assembly 1337
primary key 889, 895
primary memory 4
primitive (or built-in) data-type
  198
primitive data type 70
Princeton Review 1293
principle of least privilege 203
print 64
printing a project 38
PrintSquare.vb 126
Priority property of class
  Thread 597
priority scheduling 597
privacy invasion 979
privacy protection 979
Private keyword 301, 306, 307,
  314, 408
Private members of a base
  class 353
probability 206
procedural programming language
  12, 298
procedure 63, 64
procedure body 187
procedure definition 186
procedure for solving a problem
  97
procedure header 187
procedure overloading 288
procedure-name 187
Procedures for performing a linear
  search 272
processing instruction 870
processing instruction target 871
processing instruction value 871
processing phase 117
processing unit 3
produce method 603
producer 616

producer and consumer threads
  accessing a circular buffer
  625
producer and consumer threads
  accessing a shared object
  with syncronization 613
producer and consumer threads
  accessing a shared object
  without syncronization 608
Producer places **Integer**s in
  synchronized shared buffer
  612
Producer places **Integer**s in
  synchronized, circular buffer
  623
Producer places **Integer**s in
  unsynchronized shared
  buffer 605
producer thread 603
producer/consumer relationship
  603
productivity 13
program 3, 62
program construction principles
  145
program control 98
program development 62
program development process 334
program development tool 127
program execution stack 1152
program in the general 440
program termination 255
Program that prints histograms
  256
Program to display hidden text in a
  password box 493
program, break execution 1309
program, suspend 1304
programmer 3
programmer-defined exception
  class 464, 465
programmer-defined type 298
project 34, 36
Project Location dialog 46
Project Mac 14
Project menu 38
project properties dialog 583
project, Windows control library
  582
promotion 979
prompt 71
prompt element in VoiceXML
  1229
<prompt> tag (**<prompt>**...
  </prompt>) 1233
Properties in a class 314

Properties window 41, 42, 43, 46, 50, 129, 955
Properties window on a Web Page 1019
Properties window used to set a property value 131
property 41
property for a form or control 41
property of an object 12, 21
Proposed Recommendation 15
Protected 354
protection 1012
proxy 1334
proxy class for Web services 1037, 1044, 1045
pseudocode 21, 98, 102, 106, 112, 115, 122, 123
pseudocode algorithm 116
pseudocode **If/Else** structure 104
pseudocode representation of the top 124
pseudocode statement 106
pseudo-random number 206
Public interface 302
Public keyword 301, 302, 411
Public member of a derived class 353
public operations encapsulated in an object 305
Public service 302
Public Shared members 327
publishers table of **books** database 890, 891
publishing a Web service 1037
Pulse method of class **Monitor** 596, 602, 609, 616, 617
PulseAll method of class **Monitor** 596, 602
Push method of class **Stack** 1185
push stack operation 1152
pushing into a stack 334
PWS (Personal Web Server) 1375
Pythagorean Triples 180
Python progamming language 19

Q

quantifier 670
Quantifiers used in regular expressions 670
quantum 596
quantum expiration 595
query 888, 889
query a database 913

Question constant 151
question mark (**?**) occurence indicator 861
queue 27, 301, 335, 1137, 1156
Queue class 1176
Queue implemented by inheritance from class **CList** 1157
Queue-by-inheritance test 1158
QueueInheritance.vb 1157
QueueTest.vb 1158
quicksort 294

R

R property of structure **Color** 688
RAD (rapid application development) 8, 24
RAD (rapid applications development) 335
radian 194
radio 1379, 1439
radio button 492, 501
radio button group 501
radio buttons, using with **TabPage** 567
RadioButton class 497, 501
RadioButton properties and events 501
RadioCheck property of class **MenuItem** 528, 533
raise event 480
RAM (Random Access Memory) 4
random-access file 753, 790, 802
random access memory (RAM) 4
Random class 206, 235, 1087
Random class used to simulate rolling 12 six-sided dice 211
random number generation 663, 682
random-access file 25
Random-access file with fixed-length records 790
RandomInt.vb 208
rapid applications development (RAD) 8, 24, 335
RCW (Runtime Callable Wrapper) 1338
RDBMS (relational database management system) 945
RDK (Redistribution Kit) 1240
Read method 869
Read method of class **Console** 756

Read method of class **NetworkStream** 1100
read-only text 491
readability 62, 64, 125, 1209, 1257, 1402
ReadByte method of class **NetworkStream** 1100
ReadLine method 71
ReadLine method of class **Console** 756
ReadOnly keyword 23, 331
ReadOnly property 493
ReadString method of class **BinaryReader** 1109
ReadXml method of **DataSet** 932
Ready thread state 595
receive a connection 1108
receive data from a server 1109
Receive method of class **Socket** 1099
Receive method of class **UdpClient** 1110, 1115
ReceiveFrom method of class **Socket** 1099
receiving an array through a procedure call 261
"receiving" section of the computer 4
recent project 34
reclaim memory 330
reclaiming dynamically allocated memory 594
recognizing clients 979
record 754, 889, 895
record key 754, 790
record set 889
record size 790
recordAudio element 1239
Recruitsoft.com 1288
rectangle 684, 700
Rectangle structure 686, 709
rectangle symbol 99, 103, 107, 149, 159, 172
rectangular array 279, 280
rectangular hotspot 1388, 1447, 1448
recursion 218, 555
recursion overhead 225
recursion step 218, 222
recursion vs. iteration 225
recursive call 218, 222, 224
Recursive calls to method **Fibonacci** 224
Recursive evaluation of 5! 219
Recursive factorial program 220

Index 1507

recursive method 22, 218, 221
recursive method **Factorial** 219
recursive program 224
recursive searching 294
recursive step 294
recursive version of the binary search 272
recursive version of the linear search 272
Recursively generating Fibonacci numbers 222
red circle, solid 1305, 1309
Red Shared property of structure **Color** 688
Redistribution Kit (RDK) 1240
redundant parentheses 78
reference 198, 249
reference manipulation 1137
reference to a new object 303
reference type 198
reference variable 249
referring to a base-class object with a base-class reference 395
referring to a base-class object with a derived-class reference 396
referring to a derived-class object with a base-class reference 396
referring to a derived-class object with a derived-class reference 395
refinement process 115
Regex class 634, 668, 669
Regex methods **Replace** and **Split** 675
regional invalidation 718
<%@Register...%> directive 1006
Registering an ActiveX control 1333
RegSvr32 utility 1333, 1337
regular expression 761
Regular expressions checking birthdays 668
Regular member of enumeration **FontStyle** 695
relational database 888
relational database management system (RDBMS) 945
relational database model 889
relational database table 889
relational operator 161

relative positioning 955
release a lock 616, 617
release resource 453
release the lock 619
remainder 75
remote machine 1032
Remote Procedure Call (RPC) 16, 1032
Remove member of enumeration **MenuMerge** 570
Remove method of class **ArrayList** 1180, 1184
Remove method of class **StringBuilder** 658
Remove method of class **TreeNodeCollection** 551
Remove method of **Hashtable** 1195
RemoveAt method of class **ArrayList** 1180
RemoveFromBack graphical representation 1151
RemoveFromFront graphical representation 1150
RemoveRange method of class **ArrayList** 1180
Removing tabs from Visual Studio environment 1214
renders 945
Repeatedly applying rule 2 of Fig. 5.25 to the simplest flowchart 173
repetition 171, 173, 174
repetition control structure 99, 100, 106, 116
repetition structure 21
Replace member of enumeration**MenuMerge** 570
Replace method of class **Regex** 675, 677
Replace method of class **String** 649, 650
Replace method of class **StringBuilder** 659
Replacing text with class **StringBuilder** 659
Report Expert 1467
Request class 1001
    Cookies property 987
    PhysicalApplicationPath property 1001
request for proposal 1291
Request object 975, 987
RequiredFieldValidator class 971

Reservation.asmx.vb 1066
"reset" input 1435
Reset of **IEnumerator** 1185
resolution 685
resource leak 326, 444, 452
Response.Write 1019
responses to a survey 253, 255
Restart button 1309
result of an uncaught exception 445
result set 889, 898
result tree 870
Results of invoking a Web service method from a Web browser 1035
resume 1282, 1287
Resume method of class **Thread** 596
resume-filtering software 1287
resumption model of exception handling 445
rethrow an exception 458
RetryCancel constant 151
Return keyword 187, 188, 190, 218
Return statement 189
reusability 1137
reusable component 351
reusable software component 12, 13
Reverse method of class **Array** 1179
RGB values 687, 688
Richards, B. Martin 9
RichTextBox control 59, 60
right child 1160
right subtree 1160, 1161
RightToLeft property of class **MainMenu** 528
rise-and-shine algorithm 98
Ritchie, Dennis 9
Robby the Robot Microsoft Agent character 731
robust 71
robust application 442
RollDie.vb 209, 257
RollDie2.vb 211
root element 835, 862
root node 550, 842, 1160
root node, create 552
RotateTransform method of class **Graphics** 713
Round member of enumeration **DashCap** 711
round-robin 597
rounding 75

rounding error 195
rounds 194
row 279, 889
rows attribute (**textarea**) 1378, 1435
rows to be retrieved 897
rowspan attribute (**tr**) 1373, 1430
RPC (Remote Procedure Call) 16, 1032
RPG progamming language 19
Rule of Entity Integrity 895
Rule of Referential Integrity 896
rules of operator precedence 76
Run command in Windows 535
run element 1239
run mode 53
run-time exception 451
Runnable thread state 595
running an application 535
Running thread state 595, 599
Runtime Callable Wrapper (RCW) 1338
run-time error 71

S

Salary.com 1293
Sample data for the program of Fig. 17.8 779
SaveFileDialog class 776
scaling factor 207
scheduling 596
Schema 860, 865, 866
schema repository 866
Schemas property of **XmlSchema-Collection** 867
Scheme progamming language 19
scope 202, 203, 306
Scoping 204
Scoping rules in a class 204
screen 3, 4, 5
screen-manager program 397
screen reader 1208, 1221, 1240, 1251, 1254
script 1327, 1403
scroll arrow 41
scroll bar and window border size dialog 1244
scrollbar 476, 477
scrollbar in panel 495
SDI (single document interface) 567
SDK (Software Development Kit) 1240

Search command 44
search engine 1348, 1388, 1404, 1448
search key 272
Search Online page 35
searching 272, 1137
Searching for characters and substrings in **String**s 644
searching technique 246
second-degree polynomial 78
second refinement 121, 125
Second refinement of the pseudocode 126
secondary storage 4, 13
secondary storage device 753
sector 703
Secure property of **HttpCookie** class 989
secure protocol 989
SeekOrigin enumeration 802
SeekOrigin.Begin constant 802
SELECT 889, 897, 898, 900, 901, 902, 903, 904
select 889, 897
select all fields from a table 898
Select Case logic 396
Select Case multiple-selection structure flowchart 158
Select Case selection structure 100
Select Case structure 21, 155, 157, 159, 170, 173
Select Case structure used to count grades 155
SelectCommand property of **OleDbAdapter** 920
selected attribute 1443
selected state 501
SelectedImageIndex property of class **TreeNode** 551
SelectedIndex property of class **ComboBox** 546
SelectedIndex property of class **ListBox** 539
SelectedIndex property of class **TabControl** 564
SelectedIndexChanged event of class **ComboBox** 546
SelectedIndexChanged event of class **ListBox** 539
SelectedIndexChanged event of class **TabControl** 564

SelectedIndices property of class **ListBox** 539
SelectedItem property of class **ComboBox** 546
SelectedItem property of class **ListBox** 539
SelectedItems property of class **ListBox** 539
SelectedItems property of class **ListView** 556
SelectedNode property of class **TreeView** 551
SelectedTab property of class **TabControl** 564
selecting 34
selecting data from a table 890
selection 170, 172, 173
selection control structure 99, 100
selection criteria 898
selection structure 21
SelectionMode enumeration 539
SelectionMode property of class **CheckedListBox** 543
SelectionMode property of class **ListBox** 539
SelectionMode.MultiExtended 539
SelectionMode.MultiSimple 539
SelectionMode.None 539
SelectionMode.One 539
SelectTest.vb 155
self-documenting 71
self-referential class 1137, 1139
Self-referential class **CListNode** 1141
Self-referential class objects linked together 1139
Self-referential **CNode** class definition 1138
Self-referential object 1138
send data to a server 1109
Send method of class **Socket** 1099
Send method of class **UdpClient** 1110, 1115
sendEvent element 1239
SendTo method of class **Socket** 1099
sentinel-controlled repetition 114, 116, 119
sentinel value 114, 115, 119, 162
sentinel-controlled loop 162
separator bar 526

separator, menu 526
sequence 170, 173, 175, 1160
sequence control structure 99, 100, 115
sequence of items 1139
sequence structure 21
Sequence structure flowchart 100
sequence type 1420
sequential-access file 25, 753, 755, 771, 789
sequential execution 98
Serializable attribute 771
SerializationException 783
Serialize method of class **BinaryFormatter** 777
serialized object 771
server 6
server Internet address 1109
server port number 1109
Server portion of a client/server stream socket connection 1101
Server side of client/server Tic-Tac-Toe program 1116
Server-side portion of connectionless client/server computing 1110
ServerValidate event 1007, 1011
ServerValidate event of **CustomValidator** class 1011
ServerValidate-EventArgs class 1011
service 306
Service description for a Web service 1033, 1034
session 979, 1234
   tracking 979
session attribute 1239
Session information displayed in a **ListBox** 995
session item 991
Session property of **Page** class 991
session tracking 979
session tracking in Web services 1032
sessionID 1234
SessionID property of **HttpSession** class 995
SessionID property of **Ht-tpSessionState** class 995

Sessions created for each user in an ASP .NET Web application 991
session-tracking 980
SET 910
Set accessor 307
Set accessor of a property 318
Set Automatic Timeouts 1250
SET keyword 910
setAttribute method of interface **HttpSession** 994
SetAuthCookie method of **FormAuthenication** class 1012
SetDataBinding method of **DataGrid** 920
SGML (Standard Generalized Markup Language) 15
SHAPE = "circle" 1388
shape class hierarchy 353, 354, 387
Shared attribute 203
shared buffer 603, 616, 617
Shared class member demonstration 330
Shared class variable 327
Shared class variables have class scope 327
Shared class variables save storage 327
Shared keyword 327
shared library 1332
shared memory 603
Shared method cannot access non-**Shared** class members 328
Shared method **Concat** 648
Shift key 513
Shift property 516
Shifted random integers 207
"shipping" section of the computer 4
short-circuit evaluation 166
shortcut key 525, 1213
Shortcut key creation 1214
Shortcut property of class **MenuItem** 528
shortcuts with the **&** symbol 526
show all files icon 41
Show method 488
Show method of class **Form** 567, 576
Show method of class **Message-Box** 84, 151, 176

Show method of interface **IAgentCtlCharacter** 744
Show Next Statement button 1309
Show of class **Form** 480
ShowColors.vb 689
ShowColorsComplex.vb 692
ShowDialog method of class **OpenFileDialog** 778, 789
ShowDialog method of class **SaveFileDialog** 777
ShowShortcut property of class **MenuItem** 528
ShowSounds 1246, 1248
sibling 1160
sibling node 550, 842
side effect 166
signal value 114
signature 227, 309, 371
silicon chip 3
simple condition 164
Simple Object Access Protocol (SOAP) 8, 16, 20, 1031, 1032
Simple student-poll analysis program 254
Simple style for **ComboBox** 547
Simple-Class-Library project 338
simplest flowchart 172, 173, 174
Simula 67 programming language 9
simulate coin tossing 243
simulation 206
Sin method of class **Math** 194
sine 194
Single data type 114
singlecast delegate 433
single-clicking with left mouse button 34
single document interface (SDI) 567
single-entry/single-exit control structure 100, 103, 172
single-entry/single-exit sequence, selection, and repetition structures 170, 171
single inheritance 350
single-line comment 73
single-precision floating-point number 114
single-quote character (**'**) 62, 839, 900
single selection 173
single-selection structure 100

single-subscripted array 279
sinking sort 268
SixFigureJobs 1292
Size attribute (**input**) 1376, 1435
size of a variable 73
size of an array 249
Size property 490
Size property of class **Font** 694
SizeInPoints property of class **Font** 694
SizeMode property 52, 508
sizing handle 47
sizing handle, disabled 47
sizing handle, enabled 47
Sleep method of class **Thread** 596, 598, 599, 605, 606, 607
sleeping thread 597
small circle symbol 99, 159
SmallImageList property of class **ListView** 556
Smalltalk programming language 9, 19
SMIL (Synchronized Multimedia Integration Language) 26, 1241
"sneakernet" 6
SOAP (Simple Object Access Protocol) 8, 16, 20, 1031, 1032, 1034
SOAP encoding rule 16
SOAP envelope 1036, 1037
SOAP message 1036
SOAP request 1037
SOAP request message for the **HugeInteger** Web service 1036
socket 1097
Socket class 1108
software 3
software component 17
Software Development Kit (SDK) 1240
Software Engineering Observation 12
software reusability 350
software reuse 12, 306, 335, 336
Solaris operating system 6
solid arc 703
solid polygon 705
solid rectangle 700
SolidBrush class 691, 695, 701
solution 36
Solution Explorer 1337

Solution Explorer after adding a Web reference to a project 1047
Solution Explorer in Visual Studio .NET 576
Solution Explorer in Visual Studio .NET IDE 40
Solution Explorer window 40
solution, debug setting 1305
Sort method of class **Array** 1178
Sort method of class **ArrayList** 1180
Sort property in **DataView** class 1018
sorted array 1140
Sorted property of class **ComboBox** 546
Sorted property of class **ListBox** 539
SortedList class 1176
sorting 268, 1137
sorting a large array 272
Sorting an array with bubble sort 269
sorting schemes 268
sorting technique 246
sorting.xml 871
SoundSentry 1246
source-code form 1401
Source property of **Exception** 460
source tree 870
source-code form 1346
space character 64
spacing convention 64
span attribute 948, 1430
spawning 1099
special character 635, 1357, 1375, 1415, 1416
special symbol 754
speech device 1429
speech recognition 25, 1240, 1256
speech recognition engine 731
speech synthesis 25, 1240, 1256, 1257
speech synthesizer 1240, 1412
spiral 221
Split method of class **Regex** 675, 677
SQL (Structured Query Language) 888, 889, 896
SQL keywords 897
SQL statement 889
SQL statements executed on a database 921

Sqrt method of class **Math** 195, 465
square 351, 1420
"square" attribute value 1420
square brackets in a query 897
square root 195
SquareInteger.vb 188
src attribute 1411, 1414
src attribute (**img**) 1355
Src file 1007
stack 27, 243, 301, 334, 1152
Stack class 1176, 1185
Stack class demonstration 1185
Stack implementation by inheritance from class **CList** 1153
stack unwinding 446, 460
Stack-by-composition test 1155
Stack-by-inheritance test 1154
StackComosition.vb 1155
Stacked, nested and overlapped building blocks 175
stacking 175
stacking rule 172
StackInheritance.vb 1153
StackTest.vb 1185
StackTrace property of **Exception** 459, 460, 461
standard character 1375
standard error 756
Standard Generalized Markup Language (SGML) 15
standard input 756
Standard ML language 19
standard number format 119
standard output 756
standard reusable component 351
standard time format 303
Start method of class **Process** 535
Start method of class **TcpListener** 1099
Start method of class **Thread** 595, 599
Start Page 34, 37
start tag 835, 838, 1403
Started thread state 595, 616, 617
starting angle 702
StartsWith method of class **String** 641
startup project 40
starvation 597
state button 497
stateless protocol 979
statement 64
static entities 246

Step Into button 1313
Step keyword 147
Step Out button 1313
Step Over button 1309
stepwise refinement 123
StickyKeys 1247
Stop Debugging button 1309, 1311
Stopped thread state 596, 629
straight line 712
straight-line form 75
stream 1098
Stream class 756
stream input/output 753
stream of bytes 755
stream socket 1116
StreamReader class 756
streams-based transmission 1110, 1131
StreamWriter class 756
StretchImage value 52
Strikeout member of enumeration **FontStyle** 695
Strikeout property of class **Font** 694
string 24, 64
String class 302, 411, 412, 414, 634
String Collection Editor in Visual Studio .NET 540
string concatenation assignment operator (**&=**) 111
string concatenation operator (**&**) 84
string constant 635
String constructors 635
String Length property, the **CopyTo** method and **StrReverse** method 637
string literal 64, 635
string of characters 64
String testing for equality 639
String type 70
StringBuilder class 634, 651
StringBuilder class constructor 651
StringBuilder size manipulation 653
StringBuilder text replacement 659
StringBuilder's **AppendFormat** method 656
strong element 1408
strong typing 198
Stroustrup, Bjarne 9, 442

Structure 660
structure 660
structured programming 2, 10, 11, 21, 88, 99, 145, 164, 175, 334
Structured programming rules 172
Structured Query Language (SQL) 888, 889, 890, 896
structured systems analysis and design 11
StudentPoll.vb 254
style sheet 836, 1253, 1403
sub element 1357, 1416
sub-initializer list 280
Sub keyword 64
Sub procedure 184, 185, 188
Sub procedure for printing payment information 185
subarray 275
subclass 128
<subdialog> tag (**<subdialog>…</subdialog>**) 1233
submenu 525
submit attribute 1239
submit data to a server 1376
"submit" input 1435
submit input 1376
subscript 1357, 1416
subscription-based software 18
Substring method of class **String** 647
Substrings generated from **String**s 647
subtraction assignment operator (**-=**) 111
Success property of **Match** 674
sum function 875
Sum.vb 150
SumArray.vb 252
summarizing responses to a survey 253
summary attribute 1225, 1429
Sun Microsystems, Inc. 1322
sup element 1416
superclass 128
supercomputer 3
superscript 1357, 1416
suspend a program 1304
Suspend method of class **Thread** 596
Suspended thread state 596
swapping elements in an array 268
sweep 702
Sybase, Inc. 888, 1322
symbol 1321

SyncBlock 602, 616
synchronization 601, 603, 609
synchronize 1141
Synchronized Multimedia Integration Language (SMIL) 1241
Synchronized shared circular buffer 620
Synchronized shared **Integer** buffer 610
synchronous error 445
SyncLock block 619, 620
SyncLock keyword 602, 619, 1141, 1152
syntax error 68, 103
syntax error in HTML 1346
syntax error underlining 69
syntax-color highlighting 65
system caret 1254
SYSTEM flag 862
System namespace 299, 634
system service 1099
System.Collections namespace 1152, 1176
System.Data namespace 26, 912
System.Data.OleDb namespace 912
System.Data.Sqlclient namespace 912
System.dll 87
System.Drawing namespace 684, 686, 709
System.Drawing.Drawing2D namespace 684, 711, 712
System.IO namespace 756
System.Net 1065
System.Runtime.Serialization.Formatters.Binary namespace 778
System.Text namespace 634
System.Text.RegularExpressions namespace 634, 668
System.Web namespace 949
System.Web.Security namespace 1012
System.Web.UI namespace 949
System.Web.UI.WebControls namespace 950
System.Windows.Forms namespace 82, 85, 87, 128, 214, 479

System.Win-
    dows.Forms.dll 84,
    150
System.
    Windows.
    Forms.dll assembly 87
System.Xml namespace 842
System.Xml.Xsl namespace
    875
SystemException class 450,
    451, 465

T

tab 102
tab character 64
tab order 1216
tab stop 1216
Tabbed pages in Visual Studio
    .NET 562
tabbed window 37
TabControl class 562
TabControl used to display
    various font settings 564
TabControl with TabPages
    example 563
TabControl, adding a
    TabPage 563
TabCount property of class
    TabControl 564
TabIndex property 488
TabIndex property of class
    Control 1221
table 889, 1221, 1223, 1345, 1368,
    1401
table body 1429
table column 889
table data 1429
table element 279
table element 1429
table head element 1429
table in which record will be
    updated 910, 911
table of values 279
table row 889, 1429
table tag <table>…
    </table> 1369
tableName.fieldName 905
TabPage class 562
TabPage, add to TabControl
    563
TabPage, using radio buttons
    567
TabPages added to a Tab-
    Control 563

TabPages property of class
    TabControl 564
TabStop property 488
TabStop property of class
    Control 1221
tabular format 250, 251
tag 943, 1345
    name 1006
    prefix 948
tail of a queue 1156
Tan method of class Math 195
tangent 195
target = "_blank" 1454
target = "_self" 1454
target = "_top" 1454
target="_blank" 1392
target="_parent" 1392
target="_self" 1392
target="_top" 1392
targetSessions attribute
    1239
TargetSite property of
    Exception 460
task 5
Task List window 68, 1303
tbody (table body) element
    1370, 1429
TCP (Transmission Control
    Protocol) 1098
TCP/IP (Transmission Control
    Protocol/Internet Protocol)
    14
TcpClient class 1100
TcpListener class 1098, 1099
td element 1429
TEI (Text Encoding Initiative) 16
telephone system 1110
TemperatureServer Web
    service 1073
TemperatureServ-
    er.asmx.vb 1073
temporary data storage 753
termDigits attribute 1238,
    1239
terminal 5
termination 255
termination housekeeping 326
termination model of exception
    handling 445
termination phase 117
Testing and Debugging Tip 13
Testing class CCylinder 375
Testing the modDice procedures
    232
text 731
text-based browser 1412

text box 87, 1435
text editor 65, 634, 1346, 1401
text element 1234, 1235, 1237
Text Encoding Initiative (TEI) 16
text file 842
"text" input 1435
Text property 50, 488, 494
Text property of class Link-
    Label 535
Text property of class Menu-
    Item 528
Text property of class Tree-
    Node 551
text-to-speech (TTS) 1216, 1235,
    1251
TextAlign property 488
textarea 1376
textarea element 1378, 1435,
    1436
text-based browser 1354
text-based browsers 1370
TextBox class 273, 476, 477,
    491, 492
TextChanged event 493
TextReader class 756
text-to-speech engine 731
TextureBrush class 689, 709,
    711
TextWriter class 756
tfoot (table foot) element 1430
th (table header column) element
    1429
th element 1223
The Diversity Directory 1288
The National Business and
    Disability Council (NBDC)
    1288
thead (table head) tag
    <thead>…</thead>
    1370
thead element 1429
Then keyword 82
Thompson, Ken 9
Thread class 595, 1108
thread life cycle 595
thread of execution 593
thread-priority scheduling 597
thread scheduling 607
thread state 595
thread state *Dead* 596
thread state *Ready* 595
thread state *Runnable* 595
thread state *Running* 595, 599
thread state *Started* 595
thread state *Stopped* 596, 629
thread state *Suspended* 596

thread state *Unstarted* 595
thread state *WaitSleepJoin* 596, 599, 602, 603
thread synchronization 601
ThreadAbortException 596
ThreadPriority enumeration 596, 597
threads sleeping and printing 600
ThreadStart delegate 595, 599, 600
three-dimensional application 714
throughput 5
throw an exception 445, 449
throw point 445, 459
Throw statement 454
Tick event of class **Timer** 581, 717
TicketReservation.aspx 1069
TicketReservation.aspx.vb 1070
Tic-Tac-Toe 1116
tightly packed binary tree 1168
tightly packed tree 1168
TileHorizontal value in **LayoutMdi** enumeration 571
TileVertical value in **LayoutMdi** enumeration 571
time and date 582
Time class 22
timeout 1250
timeout attribute of **prompt** element 1229
Timeout property of **HttpSessionState** class 995
timer 581
Timer class 716
timesharing 5, 11
timeslicing 596
`<title>...</title>` 1348
title tag (`<title>...</title>`) 1225
title bar 46, 1404
title bar, MDI parent and child 569
title element 874, 1348, 1404
title HTML element 943
title of a document 1403
titles table of **books** database 890, 892, 893
.tlb file 1338
To keyword 147, 157
ToggleKeys 1248

ToLongTimeString method of structure **ToLongTimeString** 582
ToLower method of class **Char** 663
ToLower method of class **String** 649, 650
tool tip 39
toolbar 38
toolbar icon 38
Toolbox 21, 41, 955
Tools menu 38
tooltip 967
top 115, 120, 124
top 1373
top-down, stepwise refinement 3, 115, 117, 119, 123, 124
top tier 946
top-down, stepwise refinement 21
ToString method of class **Decimal** 419
ToString method of class **String** 651
ToString method of class **StringBuilder** 652, 655
ToString method of class **Exception** 461
ToString method of **Object** 356
total 113
ToUpper method of class **Char** 663
ToUpper method of class **String** 649, 650
Towers of Hanoi 243
tr (table row) element 1370, 1429
Trace class 1019
  Warn method 1019
  Write property 1019
Trace element in a **Web.config** file 1020
Trace property 26
Trace property of **Page** class 1019
trace.axd file 1021
TraceContext class 1019
tracing 1019
track 1241
tracking customers 979
trademark symbol 28
trailing white-space character 650
transaction-processing system 789
transfer of control 99
Transform method in **XslTransform** 875

TranslateTransform method of class **Graphics** 712
translation step 6
translator program 7
Transmission Control Protocol/Internet Protocol (TCP/IP) 14
trapezoid 351
traverse a tree 1161
tree 27, 550, 1160
Tree data structure 1163
Tree node contains **IComparables** as data 1169
tree structure 836
Tree structure for **article.xml** 842
Tree structure for Fig. 18.1 842
Tree.vb 1163
Tree2.vb 1171
TreeNode class 551
Tree-node data structure. 1162
TreeNode Editor in VS .NET 552
TreeNode properties and methods 551
TreeNode.vb 1162
TreeNode2.vb 1169
TreeTest.vb 1166
TreeTest2.vb 1173
Tree-traversal demonstration. 1166
TreeView class 524, 550
TreeView displaying a sample tree 550
TreeView properties and events 550
TreeView used to display directories 553
trigger an event 477
trigonometric calculation 22
trigonometric cosine 194
trigonometric sine 194, 195
trigonometric tangent 195
trillion-instruction-per-second computers 3
Trim method of class **String** 649
Trim method of **String** 860
TrimToSize method of class **ArrayList** 1180, 1184
truncate 75
truth 78
Truth table for operator **Not** (logical NOT) 167

Truth table for the **AndAlso** operator 165
Truth table for the **OrElse** operator 166
Truth table for the **Xor** (logical exclusive OR) operator 167
Try block 445, 449
Try block expires 445
TTS (text-to-speech) engine 1234, 1235
Tutor.vb 1087
two-dimensional array 279
Two-dimensional array with three rows and four columns 280
two-dimensional data structure 1160
two-dimensional shape 684
twos position 1268
two's complement 1275
type = "hidden" 1375
type = "password" 1379
type = "radio" 1379
type = "reset" 1376
type = "submit" 1376
type = "text" 1376
type attribute 1375, 1420, 1435
type of a variable 73
typesetting system 634

U

U+*yyyy* (Unicode notational convention) 1323
UDDI (Universal Description, Discovery and Integration) 1048
UDP (User Datagram Protocol) 1098
UdpClient class 1110
ul element 1417
unambiguous (Unicode design basis) 1322
unary negative (-) 76
unary operator 74, 167
unary plus (+) 76
UnauthorizedAccess- Exception class 553
unchecked context 468, 472
Underline member of enumeration **FontStyle** 695
Underline property of class **Font** 694
underscore (_) 63
undo 38
uneditable text or icons 477

Unicode 198, 199
Unicode character 754
Unicode character set 634
Unicode Consortium 1322
Unicode Standard 28, 1321
Unicode Standard design basis 1322
uniform (Unicode design basis) 1322
Uniform Resource Identifier (URI) 840
Uniform Resource Locator (URL) 840, 943
Univac 1108 14
universal (Unicode design principle) 1322
universal data access 18
Universal Description, Discovery and Integration (UDDI) 1048
Universal Resource Locator (URL) 840
universal-time format 300, 302, 303
UNIX operating system 5, 6, 9
Unload event 950
unmanaged resource 950
unnecessary parentheses 78
unordered list 1358, 1359, 1417
unordered list element (**ul**) 1358, 1417
Unstarted thread state 595
unstructured flowchart 173, 175
Unsynchronized shared **Integer** buffer 604
UPDATE 897, 910
UPDATE query 1068
UpdateCommand property of **OleDbAdapter** 920
updating a database 1375
upper-left corner of a GUI component 685
URI (Uniform Resource Identifier) 840
URL (Uniform Resource Locator) 840, 943
  rewriting 979
USEMAP 1388
usemap attribute 1448
UseMnemonic property of class **LinkLabel** 535
user agent 1208, 1254
user control 1006
User Datagram Protocol (UDP) 1098
user-defined control 580

user-defined type 298
user interface 946
UserControl class 580
UserControl defined clock 581
userInput of class **_AgentEvents_Comman dEvent** 745
Using **<META>** and **<DOCTYPE>** 1388
Using a **PictureBox** to display images 508
Using an abstract data type 303
Using arrays to eliminate a **Se- lect Case** structure 257
Using **CheckBox**es to change font styles 498
Using default namespaces 841
Using elements of an array as counters 257
Using **For Each/Next** with an array 288
Using **GroupBox**es and **Panel**s to arrange **Button**s 496
Using internal hyperlinks to make pages more navigable 1383, 1443
Using jagged two-dimensional arrays 283
Using **meta** to provide keywords and a description 1448
Using overloaded constructors 312
using parentheses to force the order of evaluation 76
Using **RadioButton**s to set message-window options 502
Using **String** indexer, **Length** property and **CopyTo** method 637
Using temperature and weather data 1077
Using the **HugeInteger** Web service 1049
UsingArray.vb 1176
UsingFontMetrics.vb 697
UsingFonts.vb 695
UsingHugeInteger- Service.vb 1049
UTF-8 1322
UTF-16 1322
UTF-32 1322
utility method 301

Index

V

valid 860
valid identifier 63
Validating user information using regular expressions 670
validating XML parser 860
validation service 1405
ValidationExpression property of class **RegularExpressionValidator** 971
validator 969
validator.w3.org 1346, 1405, 1421
validator.w3.org/file-upload.html 1405
validity 861
validity checking 314
valign = "middle" 1373
valign attribute (**th**) 1373, 1432
value attribute 1238, 1239, 1375, 1376, 1435
value of a variable 73
value of an attribute 1403
Value property of **HttpCookie** class 989
Value property of **HttpCookie** class 988
Value property of **ServerValidateEventArgs** class 1011
value type 198
VALUES 909
ValueType class 661
<var> tag (**<var>**...**</var>**) 1233
var attribute 1237, 1238
variable 70, 73, 298
variable name 73
variable number of arguments 287
variable size 73
variable type 73
variable value 73
variable, in current scope 1307
variable, in previous statement 1307
variable, modify at run time 1307
Vault.com 1284
.vb file name extension 40
vbCrLf constant 121
vbTab constant 121
version 871
version declaration 1234
version in **xml** declaration 835

vertex 1448
vertical alignment formatting 1373
vertical coordinate 685
vertical spacing 102
vi text editor 1346, 1401
ViaVoice 1208, 1226
video clip 593
View menu 38, 39
View menu in Internet Explorer 87
View property of class **ListView** 556
Viewing the tracing information for a project 1021
__VIEWSTATE hidden input 978
virtual directory 943
virtual key code 516
virtual memory operating system 11
Visible property 488
VisitedLinkColor property of class **LinkLabel** 535
Visual Basic 396, 397
Visual Basic .NET 20
Visual Basic primitive data types 198
Visual Basic Projects folder 36, 46
Visual Basic's single-entry/single-exit repetition structures 171
Visual Basic's single-entry/single-exit sequence and selection structures 170
Visual Basic's view of a file of *n* bytes 756
Visual Basic's view of an *n*-byte file 756
Visual C++ .NET 20
visual programming 21, 34, 479
Visual Studio .NET 21, 34
Visual Studio .NET Debugger 28
Visual Studio .NET-generated console application 65
Visual Studio accessibility guidelines 1209
Visual Studio Projects folder 36
vocabulary 16, 839
Voice Server SDK 1.0 1226
Voice settings window 1252
voice synthesis 1226
VoiceXML 26, 27, 1226, 1228, 1241, 1256
VoiceXML tags 1233

volatile memory 4
Voxeo (**www.voxeo.com**) 1233, 1235
Voxeo Account Manager 1235
.vsdisco file extension 1045
<vxml> tag (**<vxml>**... **</vxml>**) 1233

W

W3C (World Wide Web Consortium) 15, 27, 880, 1420
W3C host 15
W3C member 15
W3C Recommendation 15, 1401
W3C XML Schema 864
WAI (Web Accessibility Initiative) 27
WAI (Web Accessiblity Initiative) 1208
WAI Quick Tip 1207
wait element 1239
Wait method of class **Monitor** 596, 602, 609, 616, 617, 634
waiting line 1137
waiting thread 616, 617
WaitSleepJoin thread state 596, 599, 602, 603
"walk" past end of an array 255
"warehouse" section of the computer 4
Warn method of **Trace** class 1019
WAV file format 729
Web 28
Web Accessibility Initiative (WAI) 27, 1255
Web-based application development 942
Web Content Accessibility Guidelines 1.0 1207, 1209, 1223, 1225
Web Content Accessibility Guidelines 2.0 (Working Draft) 1207
Web control 26, 942
Web Form 26, 942, 980, 994, 1019
Properties window 1019
Web Form page 942
Web Hosting page 35
Web reference 1045
Web server 1099, 1375, 1402, 1432
Web servers 943
Web service 8, 17, 26, 35, 1032

Web Service Description
    Language (WSDL) 1033
Web-service method 1032
Web service that generates
    random equations 1085
Web site 3
Web site using two frames:
    navigational and content
    1390, 1450
Web user control 1006
Web.config namespace 1012,
    1020
WebClient class 1076
WebControl class 950
WebHire 1285
WebMethod attribute 1032,
    1034, 1038
WebService attribute 1037
WebService class 1038
WebTime.aspx.vb 948
well-formed document 860
What's New page 34
WHERE 897, 898, 899, 900, 903,
    910, 911
While repetition structure 21,
    100, 106, 117, 118, 146, 171,
    174, 175
While repetition structure
    flowchart 107
While repetition structure used to
    print powers of two 107
While.vb 107
WhileCounter.vb 146
White Shared property of
    structure **Color** 688
white-space character 102
whitespace 64
whitespace character 64, 650, 668
widening conversion 195, 196
widget 476
width attribute 1353, 1411,
    1412, 1429
width of text input 1376
width-to-height ratio 1412, 1353
Wiltamuth, Scott 10
Win32 API (Windows 32-bit
    Application Programming
    Interface) 8
window auto hide 39
window gadget 476
window layout 38
window tab 37
Windows 2000 6, 27, 36
Windows 32-bit Application
    Programming Interface
    (Win32 API) 8

Windows 95/98 62
Windows application 36
Windows bitmap (BMP) 51
Windows control library 582
Windows Control Library
    project 769
Windows Explorer 535
Windows Form 24
Windows form 478
Windows Form Designer
    generated code expanded
    130
Windows Form Designer
    generated code reflecting
    new property values 132
Windows Forms proxy 1334
Windows Media Player 729
Windows menu 38
Windows NT/2000/XP 62
Windows Registry 1333
Windows wave file format (WAV)
    729
Windows XP 6, 36
WinForms 478
wire format 1034
wire protocol 1034
wireless application protocol
    (WAP) 1290
Wireless Markup Language
    (WML) 26
WirelessResumes.com 1290
Wirth, Nicklaus 10
WML (Wireless Markup
    Language) 26
word character 668
word processor 634, 644
Wordpad 1401
Working Draft 15
WorkingSolo.com 1291
workstation 6
World Wide Web (WWW) 3, 15,
    27, 476, 593
World Wide Web Consortium
    (W3C) 15, 27, 834, 880,
    1255
World Wide Web site 87
Write method of class **Binary-**
    Writer 1109
Write method of class **Console**
    756
Write method of class
    NetworkStream 1100
Write property of **Trace** class
    1019
WriteByte method of class
    NetworkStream 1100

WriteLine method 119, 1304
WriteLine method of class
    Console 756
WriteXml method of **DataSet**
    932
WSDL (Web Service Description
    Language) 1033
WWW (World Wide Web) 3, 15,
    27
www.adobe.com 51
www.advantagehir-
    ing.com 1288
www.advisorteam.net/
    AT/User/kcs.asp 1288
www.biztalk.com 879
www.careerpower.com 1293
www.chami.com/html-kit
    1346
www.chiefmonster.com
    1292
www.deitel.com 3, 29, 45,
    1346, 1409
www.elsop.com/wrc/
    h_comput.htm 29
www.etest.net 1288
www.ework.com 1291
www.execunet.com 1292
www.InformIT.com/dei-
    tel 3
www.jasc.com 51, 1411
www.jobfind.com 1286
www.jobtrak.com 1289
www.microsoft.com 29
www.microsoft.com/net
    18
www.mindexchange.com
    1288
www.msdn.microsoft.com
    /vstudio 55
www.nationjob.com 1292
www.netvalley.com/
    intval.html 29
www.prenhall.com/
    deitel 3, 29
www.recruitsoft.com/
    process 1288
www.review.com 1293
www.sixfigurejobs.com
    1292
www.softlord.com/comp
    29
www.unicode.org 1324
www.vbi.org 55
www.voxeo.com (Voxeo)
    1233, 1235
www.w3.org 15, 29

Index

www.w3.org/
    History.html 29
www.w3.org/markup 1401
www.w3.org/TR/xhtml1
    1421
www.w3.org/XML/
    Schema.html 863
www.w3schools.com/
    xhtml/default.asp
    1421
www.webhire.com 1285
www.worldofdotnet.net
    55
www.xhtml.org 1421
www.yahoo.com 1351

X

x-axis 685
x-coordinate 685
X formatting code 154
Xalan XSLT processor 870
XBRL (Extensible Business
    Reporting Language) 26
Xerces parser 836
XHTML (Extensible HyperText
    Markup Language) 15, 26,
    27, 870, 1401
XHTML comment 1402
XHTML form 1432
XHTML Recommendation 1255,
    1421
XLink (Extensible Linking
    Language) 16
XML (Extensible Markup
    Language) 15, 20, 25, 834,
    1033
XML declaration 835
XML document containing book
    information 871
XML document that conforms to a
    Microsoft Schema document
    865
XML document that describes
    various sports 859
XML file containing **AdRotator**
    information 967
.xml file extension 836
XML GL (XML Guidelines) 1226
XML Guidelines (XML GL) 1226
xml namespace 839
XML namespaces demonstration
    839
XML node 836, 842
XML parser 836

XML representation of a
    DataSet written to a file
    932
XML root 836
XML Schema 26, 839, 865
XML serialization 1082
XML tag 835
XML to mark up a business letter
    837
XML used to mark up an article
    834
XML Validator 863
XML Validator displaying an
    error message 865
XML Validator used to validate an
    XML document 864
XML Web services 1031
XML Web Services page 35
XML.org 880
XML4J parser 836
XmlNodeReader class 842
XmlNodeReader used to iterate
    through an XML document
    843
xmlns attribute 840, 841
XmlReader class 842
XmlValidatingReader class
    867
Xor (logical exclusive OR) 164,
    167
Xor bitwise operator 534
XPath expression 852, 860, 882
XPathNavigator class used to
    navigate selected nodes 852
XPathNodeIterator Class
    860
xsl
    template 874
XSL (Extensible Stylesheet
    Language) 16, 839, 870
XSL document that transforms
    sorting.xml into
    XHTML 872
XSL specification 880
XSL style sheet applied to an
    XML document 875
XSL variable 875
XSLT (Extensible Stylesheet
    Language Transformation)
    26
XSLT processor 870
XsltArgumentList class 875
XslTransform class 875
xy-coordinate 1448
x-y coordinate 1388

Y

y-axis 685
y-coordinate 685
Yahoo! 1286
yellow 687
yellow arrow 1306
Yellow Shared property of
    structure **Color** 688
YesNo constant 151
YesNoCancel constant 151

Z

zero-based counting 251
zeroth element 247

Prentice Hall License Agreement and Limited Warranty

READ THE FOLLOWING TERMS AND CONDITIONS CAREFULLY BEFORE OPENING THIS SOFTWARE PACKAGE. THIS LEGAL DOCUMENT IS AN AGREEMENT BETWEEN YOU AND PRENTICE-HALL, INC. (THE "COMPANY"). BY OPENING THIS SEALED SOFTWARE PACKAGE, YOU ARE AGREEING TO BE BOUND BY THESE TERMS AND CONDITIONS. IF YOU DO NOT AGREE WITH THESE TERMS AND CONDITIONS, DO NOT OPEN THE SOFTWARE PACKAGE. PROMPTLY RETURN THE UNOPENED SOFTWARE PACKAGE AND ALL ACCOMPANYING ITEMS TO THE PLACE YOU OBTAINED THEM FOR A FULL REFUND OF ANY SUMS YOU HAVE PAID.

1. GRANT OF LICENSE: In consideration of your purchase of this book, and your agreement to abide by the terms and conditions of this Agreement, the Company grants to you a nonexclusive right to use and display the copy of the enclosed software program (hereinafter the "SOFTWARE") on a single computer (i.e., with a single CPU) at a single location so long as you comply with the terms of this Agreement. The Company reserves all rights not expressly granted to you under this Agreement.

2. OWNERSHIP OF SOFTWARE: You own only the magnetic or physical media (the enclosed media) on which the SOFTWARE is recorded or fixed, but the Company and the software developers retain all the rights, title, and ownership to the SOFTWARE recorded on the original media copy(ies) and all subsequent copies of the SOFTWARE, regardless of the form or media on which the original or other copies may exist. This license is not a sale of the original SOFTWARE or any copy to you.

3. COPY RESTRICTIONS: This SOFTWARE and the accompanying printed materials and user manual (the "Documentation") are the subject of copyright. The individual programs on the media are copyrighted by the authors of each program. Some of the programs on the media include separate licensing agreements. If you intend to use one of these programs, you must read and follow its accompanying license agreement. You may not copy the Documentation or the SOFTWARE, except that you may make a single copy of the SOFTWARE for backup or archival purposes only. You may be held legally responsible for any copying or copyright infringement which is caused or encouraged by your failure to abide by the terms of this restriction.

4. USE RESTRICTIONS: You may not network the SOFTWARE or otherwise use it on more than one computer or computer terminal at the same time. You may physically transfer the SOFTWARE from one computer to another provided that the SOFTWARE is used on only one computer at a time. You may not distribute copies of the SOFTWARE or Documentation to others. You may not reverse engineer, disassemble, decompile, modify, adapt, translate, or create derivative works based on the SOFTWARE or the Documentation without the prior written consent of the Company.

5. TRANSFER RESTRICTIONS: The enclosed SOFTWARE is licensed only to you and may not be transferred to any one else without the prior written consent of the Company. Any unauthorized transfer of the

Prentice Hall License Agreement and Limited Warranty EULA-2

SOFTWARE shall result in the immediate termination of this Agreement.

6. TERMINATION: This license is effective until terminated. This license will terminate automatically without notice from the Company and become null and void if you fail to comply with any provisions or limitations of this license. Upon termination, you shall destroy the Documentation and all copies of the SOFTWARE. All provisions of this Agreement as to warranties, limitation of liability, remedies or damages, and our ownership rights shall survive termination.

7. MISCELLANEOUS: This Agreement shall be construed in accordance with the laws of the United States of America and the State of New York and shall benefit the Company, its affiliates, and assignees.

8. LIMITED WARRANTY AND DISCLAIMER OF WARRANTY: The Company warrants that the SOFTWARE, when properly used in accordance with the Documentation, will operate in substantial conformity with the description of the SOFTWARE set forth in the Documentation. The Company does not warrant that the SOFTWARE will meet your requirements or that the operation of the SOFTWARE will be uninterrupted or error-free. The Company warrants that the media on which the SOFTWARE is delivered shall be free from defects in materials and workmanship under normal use for a period of thirty (30) days from the date of your purchase. Your only remedy and the Company's only obligation under these limited warranties is, at the Company's option, return of the warranted item for a refund of any amounts paid by you or replacement of the item. Any replacement of SOFTWARE or media under the warranties shall not extend the original warranty period. The limited warranty set forth above shall not apply to any SOFTWARE which the Company determines in good faith has been subject to misuse, neglect, improper installation, repair, alteration, or damage by you. EXCEPT FOR THE EXPRESSED WARRANTIES SET FORTH ABOVE, THE COMPANY DISCLAIMS ALL WARRANTIES, EXPRESS OR IMPLIED, INCLUDING WITHOUT LIMITATION, THE IMPLIED WARRANTIES OF MERCHANTABILITY AND FITNESS FOR A PARTICULAR PURPOSE. EXCEPT FOR THE EXPRESS WARRANTY SET FORTH ABOVE, THE COMPANY DOES NOT WARRANT, GUARANTEE, OR MAKE ANY REPRESENTATION REGARDING THE USE OR THE RESULTS OF THE USE OF THE SOFTWARE IN TERMS OF ITS CORRECTNESS, ACCURACY, RELIABILITY, CURRENTNESS, OR OTHERWISE.

IN NO EVENT, SHALL THE COMPANY OR ITS EMPLOYEES, AGENTS, SUPPLIERS, OR CONTRACTORS BE LIABLE FOR ANY INCIDENTAL, INDIRECT, SPECIAL, OR CONSEQUENTIAL DAMAGES ARISING OUT OF OR IN CONNECTION WITH THE LICENSE GRANTED UNDER THIS AGREEMENT, OR FOR LOSS OF USE, LOSS OF DATA, LOSS OF INCOME OR PROFIT, OR OTHER LOSSES, SUSTAINED AS A RESULT OF INJURY TO ANY PERSON, OR LOSS OF OR DAMAGE TO PROPERTY, OR CLAIMS OF THIRD PARTIES, EVEN IF THE COMPANY OR AN AUTHORIZED REPRESENTATIVE OF THE COMPANY HAS BEEN ADVISED OF THE POSSIBILITY OF SUCH DAMAGES. IN NO EVENT SHALL LIABILITY OF THE COMPANY FOR DAMAGES WITH RESPECT TO THE SOFTWARE EXCEED THE AMOUNTS ACTUALLY PAID BY YOU, IF ANY, FOR THE SOFTWARE.

SOME JURISDICTIONS DO NOT ALLOW THE LIMITATION OF IMPLIED WARRANTIES OR LIABILITY FOR INCIDENTAL, INDIRECT, SPECIAL, OR CONSEQUENTIAL DAMAGES, SO THE ABOVE LIMITATIONS MAY NOT ALWAYS APPLY. THE WARRANTIES IN THIS AGREEMENT GIVE YOU SPECIFIC LEGAL RIGHTS AND YOU MAY ALSO HAVE OTHER RIGHTS WHICH VARY IN ACCORDANCE WITH LOCAL LAW.

ACKNOWLEDGMENT

YOU ACKNOWLEDGE THAT YOU HAVE READ THIS AGREEMENT, UNDERSTAND IT, AND AGREE TO BE BOUND BY ITS TERMS AND CONDITIONS. YOU ALSO AGREE THAT THIS AGREEMENT IS THE COMPLETE AND EXCLUSIVE STATEMENT OF THE AGREEMENT BETWEEN YOU AND THE COMPANY AND SUPERSEDES ALL PROPOSALS OR PRIOR AGREEMENTS, ORAL, OR WRITTEN, AND ANY OTHER COMMUNICATIONS BETWEEN YOU AND THE COMPANY OR ANY REPRESENTATIVE OF THE COMPANY RELATING TO THE SUBJECT MATTER OF THIS AGREEMENT.

Should you have any questions concerning this Agreement or if you wish to contact the Company for any reason, please contact in writing at the address below.

Robin Short
Prentice Hall PTR
One Lake Street
Upper Saddle River, New Jersey 07458

The DEITEL™ Suite of Products...

HOW TO PROGRAM BOOKS

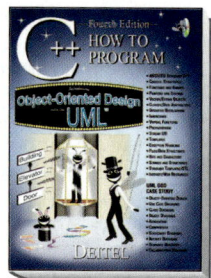

C++ How to Program Fourth Edition

BOOK / CD-ROM

©2003, 1400 pp., paper
(0-13-038474-7)

The world's best selling C++ book is now even better! Designed for beginning through intermediate courses, this comprehensive, practical introduction to C++ includes hundreds of hands-on exercises, plus roughly 250 complete programs written and documented for easy learning. It also features exceptional insight into good programming practices, maximizing performance, avoiding errors, debugging and testing. The Fourth Edition features a new code-highlighting style that uses an alternate background color to focus the reader on new code elements in a program. The OOD/UML case study is upgraded to the latest UML standard, and includes significant improvements to the exception handling and operator overloading chapters. It features enhanced treatment of strings and arrays as objects using standard C++ classes, string and vector. It also retains every key concept and technique ANSI C++ developers need to master, including control structures, functions, arrays, pointers and strings, classes and data abstraction, operator overloading, inheritance, virtual functions, polymorphism, I/O, templates, exception handling, file processing, data structures and more. *C++ How to Program Fourth Edition* includes a detailed introduction to Standard Template Library (STL) containers, container adapters, algorithms and iterators.

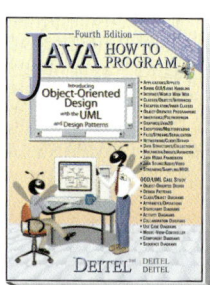

Java™ How to Program Fourth Edition

BOOK / CD-ROM

©2002, 1546 pp., paper
(0-13-034151-7)

The world's best-selling Java text is now even better! The Fourth Edition of *Java How to Program* includes a new focus on object-oriented design with the UML, design patterns, full-color program listings and figures and the most up-to-date Java coverage available.

Readers will discover key topics in Java programming, such as graphical user interface components, exception handling, multithreading, multimedia, files and streams, networking, data structures and more. In addition, a new chapter on design patterns explains frequently recurring architectural patterns—information that can help save designers considerable time when building large systems.

The highly detailed optional case study focuses on object-oriented design with the UML and presents fully implemented working Java code.

Updated throughout, the text includes new and revised discussions on topics such as Swing, graphics and socket- and packet-based networking. Three introductory chapters heavily emphasize problem solving and programming skills. The chapters on RMI, JDBC™, servlets and JavaBeans have been moved to *Advanced Java 2 Platform How to Program*, where they are now covered in much greater depth. (See *Advanced Java 2 Platform How to Program* below.)

Advanced Java™ 2 Platform How to Program

BOOK / CD-ROM

©2002, 1811 pp., paper
(0-13-089560-1)

Expanding on the world's best-selling Java textbook—*Java How to Program—Advanced Java 2 Platform How To Program* presents advanced Java topics for developing sophisticated, user-friendly GUIs; significant, scalable enterprise applications; wireless applications and distributed systems. Primarily based on Java 2 Enterprise Edition (J2EE), this textbook integrates technologies such as XML, JavaBeans, security, Java Database Connectivity (JDBC), JavaServer Pages (JSP), servlets, Remote Method Invocation (RMI), Enterprise JavaBeans™ (EJB) and design patterns into a production-quality system that allows developers to benefit from the leverage and platform independence Java 2 Enterprise Edition provides. The book also features the development

Sign up now for the new DEITEL™ Buzz Online newsletter at:

of a complete, end-to-end e-business solution using advanced Java technologies. Additional topics include Swing, Java 2D and 3D, XML, design patterns, CORBA, Jini™, JavaSpaces™, Jiro™, Java Management Extensions (JMX) and Peer-to-Peer networking with an introduction to JXTA. This textbook also introduces the Java 2 Micro Edition (J2ME™) for building applications for handheld and wireless devices using MIDP and MIDlets. Wireless technologies covered include WAP, WML and i-mode.

C# How to Program
BOOK / CD-ROM

©2002, 1568 pp., paper
(0-13-062221-4)

An exciting new addition to the How to Program series, *C# How to Program* provides a comprehensive introduction to Microsoft's new object-oriented language. C# builds on the skills already mastered by countless C++ and Java programmers, enabling them to create powerful Web applications and components—ranging from XML-based Web services on Microsoft's .NET platform to middle-tier business objects and system-level applications. *C# How to Program* begins with a strong foundation in the introductory and intermediate programming principles students will need in industry. It then explores such essential topics as object-oriented programming and exception handling. Graphical user interfaces are extensively covered, giving readers the tools to build compelling and fully interactive programs. Internet technologies such as XML, ADO .NET and Web services are also covered as well as topics including regular expressions, multithreading, networking, databases, files and data structures.

Also coming soon in the Deitels' .NET Series:
- Visual C++ .NET How to Program

Visual Basic .NET How to Program Second Edition
BOOK / CD-ROM

©2002, 1400 pp., paper
(0-13-029363-6)

Teach Visual Basic .NET programming from the ground up! This introduction of Microsoft's .NET Framework marks the beginning of major revisions to all of Microsoft's programming languages. This book provides a comprehensive introduction to the next version of Visual Basic—Visual Basic .NET—featuring extensive updates and increased functionality. *Visual Basic .NET How to Program, Second Edition* covers introductory programming techniques as well as more advanced topics, featuring enhanced treatment of developing Web-based applications. Other topics discussed include an extensive treatment of XML and wireless applications, databases, SQL and ADO .NET, Web forms, Web services and ASP .NET.

Also coming soon in the Deitels' .NET Series:
- Visual C++ .NET How to Program

C How to Program Third Edition
BOOK / CD-ROM

©2001, 1253 pp., paper
(0-13-089572-5)

Highly practical in approach, the Third Edition of the world's best-selling C text introduces the fundamentals of structured programming and software engineering and gets up to speed quickly. This comprehensive book not only covers the full C language, but also reviews library functions and introduces object-based and object-oriented programming in C++ and Java. The Third Edition includes a new 346-page introduction to Java 2 and the basics of GUIs, and the 298-page introduction to C++ has been updated to be consistent with the most current ANSI/ISO C++ standards. Plus, icons throughout the book point out valuable programming tips such as Common Programming Errors, Portability Tips and Testing and Debugging Tips.

Getting Started with Microsoft® Visual C++™ 6 with an Introduction to MFC
BOOK / CD-ROM

©2000, 163 pp., paper (0-13-016147-0)

Internet & World Wide Web How to Program, Second Edition
BOOK / CD-ROM

©2002, 1428 pp., paper
(0-13-030897-8)

The revision of this groundbreaking book in the Deitels' *How to Program Series* offers a thorough treatment of

www.deitel.com/newsletter/subscribe.html

programming concepts that yield visible or audible results in Web pages and Web-based applications. This book discusses effective Web-based design, server- and client-side scripting, multitier Web-based applications development, ActiveX® controls and electronic commerce essentials. This book offers an alternative to traditional programming courses using markup languages (such as XHTML, Dynamic HTML and XML) and scripting languages (such as JavaScript, VBScript, Perl/CGI, Python and PHP) to teach the fundamentals of programming "wrapped in the metaphor of the Web."

Updated material on www.deitel.com and www.prenhall.com/deitel provides additional resources for instructors who want to cover Microsoft® or non-Microsoft technologies. The Web site includes an extensive treatment of Netscape® 6 and alternate versions of the code from the Dynamic HTML chapters that will work with non-Microsoft environments as well.

Wireless Internet & Mobile Business How to Program

©2002, 1292 pp., paper
(0-13-062226-5)

While the rapid expansion of wireless technologies, such as cell phones, pagers and personal digital assistants (PDAs), offers many new opportunities for businesses and programmers, it also presents numerous challenges related to issues such as security and standardization. This book offers a thorough treatment of both the management and technical aspects of this growing area, including coverage of current practices and future trends. The first half explores the business issues surrounding wireless technology and mobile business, including an overview of existing and developing communication technologies and the application of business principles to wireless devices. It also discusses location-based services and location-identifying technologies, a topic that is revisited throughout the book. Wireless payment, security, legal and social issues, international communications and more are also discussed. The book then turns to programming for the wireless Internet, exploring topics such as WAP (including 2.0), WML, WMLScript, XML, XHTML™, wireless Java programming (J2ME)™, Web Clipping and more. Other topics covered include career resources, wireless marketing, accessibility, Palm™, PocketPC, Windows CE, i-mode, Bluetooth, MIDP, MIDlets,

ASP, Microsoft .NET Mobile Framework, BREW™, multimedia, Flash™ and VBScript.

Python How to Program

BOOK / CD-ROM

©2002, 1376 pp., paper
(0-13-092361-3)

This exciting new book provides a comprehensive introduction to Python— a powerful object-oriented programming language with clear syntax and the ability to bring together various technologies quickly and easily. This book covers introductory-programming techniques and more advanced topics such as graphical user interfaces, databases, wireless Internet programming, networking, security, process management, multithreading, XHTML, CSS, PSP and multimedia. Readers will learn principles that are applicable to both systems development and Web programming. The book features the consistent and applied pedagogy that the *How to Program Series* is known for, including the Deitels' signature LIVE-CODE™ Approach, with thousands of lines of code in hundreds of working programs; hundreds of valuable programming tips identified with icons throughout the text; an extensive set of exercises, projects and case studies; two-color four-way syntax coloring and much more.

e-Business & e-Commerce for Managers

©2001, 794 pp., cloth
(0-13-032364-0)

This comprehensive overview of building and managing e-businesses explores topics such as the decision to bring a business online, choosing a business model, accepting payments, marketing strategies and security, as well as many other important issues (such as career resources). The book features Web resources and online demonstrations that supplement the text and direct readers to additional materials. The book also includes an appendix that develops a complete Web-based shopping-cart application using HTML, JavaScript, VBScript, Active Server Pages, ADO, SQL, HTTP, XML and XSL. Plus, company-specific sections provide "real-world" examples of the concepts presented in the book.

Sign up now for the new DEITEL™ *Buzz Online* newsletter at:

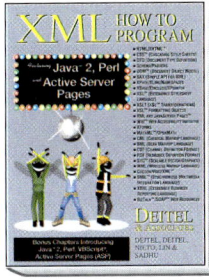

XML How to Program

BOOK / CD-ROM

©2001, 934 pp., paper (0-13-028417-3)

This book is a comprehensive guide to programming in XML. It teaches how to use XML to create customized tags and includes chapters that address standard custom-markup languages for science and technology, multimedia, commerce and many other fields. Concise introductions to Java, JavaServer Pages, VBScript, Active Server Pages and Perl/CGI provide readers with the essentials of these programming languages and server-side development technologies to enable them to work effectively with XML. The book also covers cutting-edge topics such as XSL, DOM™ and SAX, plus a real-world e-commerce case study and a complete chapter on Web accessibility that addresses Voice XML. It includes tips such as Common Programming Errors, Software Engineering Observations, Portability Tips and Debugging Hints. Other topics covered include XHTML, CSS, DTD, schema, parsers, XPath, XLink, namespaces, XBase, XInclude, XPointer, XSLT, XSL Formatting Objects, JavaServer Pages, XForms, topic maps, X3D, MathML, OpenMath, CML, BML, CDF, RDF, SVG, Cocoon, WML, XBRL and BizTalk™ and SOAP™ Web resources.

Perl How to Program

BOOK / CD-ROM

©2001, 1057 pp., paper (0-13-028418-1)

This comprehensive guide to Perl programming emphasizes the use of the Common Gateway Interface (CGI) with Perl to create powerful, dynamic multi-tier Web-based client/server applications. The book begins with a clear and careful introduction to programming concepts at a level suitable for beginners, and proceeds through advanced topics such as references and complex data structures. Key Perl topics such as regular expressions and string manipulation are covered in detail. The authors address important and topical issues such as object-oriented programming, the Perl database interface (DBI), graphics and security. Also included is a treatment of XML, a bonus chapter introducing the Python programming language, supplemental material on career resources and a complete chapter on Web accessibility. The text includes tips such as Common Programming Errors, Software Engineering Observations, Portability Tips and Debugging Hints.

e-Business & e-Commerce How to Program

BOOK / CD-ROM

©2001, 1254 pp., paper (0-13-028419-X)

This innovative book explores programming technologies for developing Web-based e-business and e-commerce solutions, and covers e-business and e-commerce models and business issues. Readers learn a full range of options, from "build-your-own" to turnkey solutions. The book examines scores of the top e-businesses (examples include Amazon, eBay, Priceline, Travelocity, etc.), explaining the technical details of building successful e-business and e-commerce sites and their underlying business premises. Learn how to implement the dominant e-commerce models—shopping carts, auctions, name-your-own-price, comparison shopping and bots/ intelligent agents—by using markup languages (HTML, Dynamic HTML and XML), scripting languages (JavaScript, VBScript and Perl), server-side technologies (Active Server Pages and Perl/CGI) and database (SQL and ADO), security and online payment technologies. Updates are regularly posted to www.deitel.com and the book includes a CD-ROM with software tools, source code and live links.

ORDER INFORMATION

SINGLE COPY SALES:
Visa, Master Card, American Express, Checks, or Money Orders only
Toll-Free: 800-643-5506; Fax: 800-835-5327

GOVERNMENT AGENCIES:
Prentice Hall Customer Service (#GS-02F-8023A)
Phone: 201-767-5994; Fax: 800-445-6991

COLLEGE PROFESSORS:
For desk or review copies, please visit us on the World Wide Web at www.prenhall.com

CORPORATE ACCOUNTS:
Quantity, Bulk Orders totaling 10 or more books. Purchase orders only — No credit cards.
Tel: 201-236-7156; Fax: 201-236-7141
Toll-Free: 800-382-3419

CANADA:
Pearson Technology Group Canada
10 Alcorn Avenue, suite #300
Toronto, Ontario, Canada M4V 3B2
Tel.: 416-925-2249; Fax: 416-925-0068
E-mail: phcinfo.pubcanada@pearsoned.com

UK/IRELAND:
Pearson Education
Edinburgh Gate
Harlow, Essex CM20 2JE UK
Tel: 01279 623928; Fax: 01279 414130
E-mail: enq.orders@pearsoned-ema.com

EUROPE, MIDDLE EAST & AFRICA:
Pearson Education
P.O. Box 75598
1070 AN Amsterdam, The Netherlands
Tel: 31 20 5755 800; Fax: 31 20 664 5334
E-mail: amsterdam@pearsoned-ema.com

ASIA:
Pearson Education Asia
317 Alexandra Road #04-01
IKEA Building
Singapore 159965
Tel: 65 476 4688; Fax: 65 378 0370

JAPAN:
Pearson Education
Nishi-Shinjuku, KF Building 101
8-14-24 Nishi-Shinjuku, Shinjuku-ku
Tokyo, Japan 160-0023
Tel: 81 3 3365 9001; Fax: 81 3 3365 9009

INDIA:
Pearson Education Indian Liaison Office
90 New Raidhani Enclave, Ground Floor
Delhi 110 092, India
Tel: 91 11 2059850 & 2059851
Fax: 91 11 2059852

AUSTRALIA:
Pearson Education Australia
Unit 4, Level 2
14 Aquatic Drive
Frenchs Forest, NSW 2086, Australia
Tel: 61 2 9454 2200; Fax: 61 2 9453 0089
E-mail: marketing@pearsoned.com.au

NEW ZEALAND/FIJI:
Pearson Education
46 Hillside Road
Auckland 10, New Zealand
Tel: 649 444 4968; Fax: 649 444 4957
E-mail: sales@pearsoned.co.nz

SOUTH AFRICA:
Pearson Education
P.O. Box 12122
Mill Street
Cape Town 8010 South Africa
Tel: 27 21 686 6356; Fax: 27 21 686 4590

LATIN AMERICA:
Pearson Education Latinoamerica
815 NW 57th Street Suite 484
Miami, FL 33158

www.deitel.com/newsletter/subscribe.html

BOOK/MULTIMEDIA PACKAGES

Complete Training Courses

Each complete package includes the corresponding *How to Program Series* book and interactive multimedia CD-ROM Cyber Classroom. *Complete Training Courses* are perfect for anyone interested Web and e-commerce programming. They are affordable resources for college students and professionals learning programming for the first time or reinforcing their knowledge.

Each *Complete Training Course* is compatible with Windows 95, Windows 98, Windows NT and Windows 2000 and includes the following features:

Intuitive Browser-Based Interface

You'll love the *Complete Training Courses'* new browser-based interface, designed to be easy and accessible to anyone who's ever used a Web browser. Every *Complete Training Course* features the full text, illustrations and program listings of its corresponding *How to Program* book—all in full color—with full-text searching and hyperlinking.

Further Enhancements to the Deitels' Signature LIVE-CODE™ Approach

Every code sample from the main text can be found in the interactive, multimedia, CD-ROM-based *Cyber Classrooms* included in the *Complete Training Courses*. Syntax coloring of code is included for the *How to Program* books that are published in full color. Even the recent two-color and one-color books use effective multi-way syntax shading. The *Cyber Classroom* products always are in full color.

Audio Annotations
Hours of detailed, expert audio descriptions of thousands of lines of code help reinforce concepts.

Easily Executable Code
With one click of the mouse, you can execute the code or save it to your hard drive to manipulate using the programming environment of your choice. With selected *Complete Training Courses*, you can also load all of the code into a development environment such as Microsoft® Visual C++™, enabling you to modify and execute the programs with ease.

Abundant Self-Assessment Material
Practice exams test your understanding with hundreds of test questions and answers in addition to those found in the main text. Hundreds of self-review questions, all with answers, are drawn from the text; as are hundreds of programming exercises, half with answers.

www.phptr.com/phptrinteractive

Sign up now for the new DEITEL™ *Buzz Online* newsletter at:

BOOK/MULTIMEDIA PACKAGES

The Complete C++ Training Course, Fourth Edition
(0-13-100252-X)

You can run the hundreds of C++ programs with the click of a mouse and automatically load them into Microsoft® Visual C++™, allowing you to modify and execute the programs with ease.

The Complete C# Training Course
(0-13-064584-2)

The Complete e-Business & e-Commerce Programming Training Course
(0-13-089549-0)

The Complete Internet & World Wide Web Programming Training Course, Second Edition
(0-13-089550-4)

The Complete Java™ 2 Training Course, Fourth Edition
(0-13-064931-7)

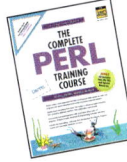

The Complete Perl Training Course
(0-13-089552-0)

The Complete Python Training Course
(0-13-067374-9)

The Complete Visual Basic 6 Training Course
(0-13-082929-3)

You can run the hundreds of Visual Basic programs with the click of a mouse and automatically load them into Microsoft®'s Visual Basic® 6 Working Model edition software, allowing you to modify and execute the programs with ease.

The Complete Visual Basic .NET Training Course, Second Edition
(0-13-042530-3)

The Complete Wireless Internet & Mobile Business Programming Training Course
(0-13-062335-0)

The Complete XML Programming Training Course
(0-13-089557-1)

All of these ISBNs are retail ISBNs. College and university instructors should contact your local Prentice Hall representative or write to cs@prenhall.com for the corresponding student edition ISBNs.

If you would like to purchase the Cyber Classrooms separately...

Prentice Hall offers Multimedia Cyber Classroom CD-ROMs to accompany the *How to Program* series texts for the topics listed at right. If you have already purchased one of these books and would like to purchase a stand-alone copy of the corresponding *Multimedia Cyber Classroom*, you can make your purchase at the following Web site:

www.informit.com/cyberclassrooms

For **C++ Multimedia Cyber Classroom, 4/E**, ask for product number 0-13-100253-8

For **C# Multimedia Cyber Classroom**, ask for product number 0-13-064587-7

For **e-Business & e-Commerce Cyber Classroom**, ask for product number 0-13-089540-7

For **Internet & World Wide Web Cyber Classroom, 2/E**, ask for product number 0-13-089559-8

For **Java Multimedia Cyber Classroom, 4/E**, ask for product number 0-13-064935-X

For **Perl Multimedia Cyber Classroom**, ask for product number 0-13-089553-9

For **Python Multimedia Cyber Classroom**, ask for product number 0-13-067375-7

For **Visual Basic 6 Multimedia Cyber Classroom**, ask for product number 0-13-083116-6

For **Visual Basic .NET Multimedia Cyber Classroom, 2/E**, ask for product number 0-13-065193-1

For **XML Multimedia Cyber Classroom**, ask for product number 0-13-089555-5

For **Wireless Internet & m-Business Programming Multimedia Cyber Classroom**, ask for product number 0-13-062337-7

www.deitel.com/newsletter/subscribe.html

e-LEARNING • www.InformIT.com/deitel

Deitel & Associates, Inc. has partnered with Prentice Hall's parent company, Pearson PLC, and its information technology Web site, **InformIT.com**, to launch the Deitel InformIT kiosk at **www.InformIT.com/deitel**. The Deitel InformIT kiosk contains information on the continuum of Deitel products, including:

- Free informational articles
- Deitel e-Matter
- Books and e-Books
- Web-based training
- Instructor-led training by Deitel & Associates
- Complete Training Courses/Cyber Classrooms

Deitel & Associates is also contributing to two separate weekly InformIT e-mail newsletters.

The first is the InformIT promotional newsletter, which features weekly specials and discounts on Pearson publications. Each week a new Deitel™ product is featured along with information about our corporate instructor-led training courses and the opportunity to read about upcoming issues of our own e-mail newsletter, the DEITEL™ BUZZ ONLINE.

The second newsletter is the InformIT editorial newsletter, which contains approximately 50 new articles per week on various IT topics, including programming, advanced computing, networking, security, databases, creative media, business, Web development, software engineering, operating systems and more. Deitel & Associates contributes 2-3 articles per week pulled from our extensive existing content base or material being created during our research and development process.

Both of these publications are sent to over 750,000 registered users worldwide (for opt-in registration, visit **www.InformIT.com**).

e-LEARNING • from Deitel & Associates, Inc.

Cyber Classrooms, Web-Based Training and Course Management Systems

DEITEL is committed to continuous research and development in e-Learning.

We are pleased to announce that we have incorporated examples of Web-based training, including a five-way Macromedia® Flash™ animation of a `for` loop in Java™, into the *Java 2 Multimedia Cyber Classroom, 4/e* (which is included in *The Complete Java 2 Training Course, 4/e*). Our instructional designers and Flash animation team are developing additional simulations that demonstrate key programming concepts.

We are enhancing the Multimedia Cyber Classroom products to include more audio, pre- and post-assessment questions and Web-based labs with solutions for the benefit of professors and students alike. In addition, our Multimedia Cyber Classroom products, currently available in CD-ROM format, are being ported to Pearson's CourseCompass course-management system—*a powerful e-platform for teaching and learning*. Many Deitel materials are available in WebCT, Blackboard and CourseCompass formats for colleges, and will soon be available for various corporate learning management systems.

Sign up now for the new DEITEL™ Buzz Online newsletter at:

WHAT'S COMING FROM THE DEITELS

Future Publications

Here are some new titles we are considering for 2002/2003 release:

Computer Science Series: *Operating Systems 3/e, Data Structures in C++, Data Structures in Java, Theory and Principles of Database Systems.*

Database Series: *Oracle, SQL Server, MySQL.*

Internet and Web Programming Series: *Open Source Software Development: Apache, Linux, MySQL and PHP.*

Programming Series: *Flash™.*

.NET Programming Series: *ADO .NET with Visual Basic .NET, ASP .NET with Visual Basic .NET, ADO .NET with C#, ASP .NET with C#.*

Object Technology Series: *OOAD with the UML, Design Patterns, Java™ and XML.*

Advanced Java™ Series: *JDBC, Java 2 Enterprise Edition, Java Media Framework (JMF), Java Security and Java Cryptography (JCE), Java Servlets, Java2D and Java3D, JavaServer Pages™ (JSP), JINI and Java 2 Micro Edition™ (J2ME).*

DEITEL™ BUZZ ONLINE Newsletter

The Deitel and Associates, Inc. free opt-in newsletter includes:

- Updates and commentary on industry trends and developments
- Resources and links to articles from our published books and upcoming publications.
- Information on the Deitel publishing plans, including future publications and product-release schedules
- Support for instructors
- Resources for students
- Information on Deitel Corporate Training

To sign up for the Deitel™ Buzz Online newsletter, visit `www.deitel.com/newsletter/subscribe.html`.

E-Books

We are committed to providing our content in traditional print formats and in emerging electronic formats, such as e-books, to fulfill our customers' needs. Our R&D teams are currently exploring many leading-edge solutions.

Visit `www.deitel.com` and read the DEITEL™ BUZZ ONLINE for periodic updates.

Turn the page to find out more about Deitel & Associates!

`www.deitel.com/newsletter/subscribe.html`

CORPORATE TRAINING FROM THE WORLD'S BEST-SELLING

The Deitels are the authors of best-selling Java™, C++, C#, C, Visual Basic® and Internet and World Wide Web Books and Multimedia Packages

Corporate Training Delivered Worldwide

Deitel & Associates, Inc. provides intensive, lecture-and-laboratory courses to organizations worldwide. The programming courses use our signature LIVE-CODE™ approach, presenting complete working programs.

Deitel & Associates, Inc. has trained hundreds of thousands of students and professionals worldwide through corporate training courses, public seminars, university teaching, *How to Program Series* books, *Deitel™ Developer Series* books, *Cyber Classroom Series* multimedia packages, *Complete Training Course Series* book and multimedia packages, broadcast-satellite courses and Web-based training.

Educational Consulting

Deitel & Associates, Inc. offers complete educational consulting services for corporate training programs and professional schools including:

- Curriculum design and development
- Preparation of Instructor Guides
- Customized courses and course materials
- Design and implementation of professional training certificate programs
- Instructor certification
- Train-the-trainers programs
- Delivery of software-related corporate training programs

Visit our Web site for more information on our corporate training curriculum and to purchase our training products.

www.deitel.com

Would you like to review upcoming publications?

If you are a professor or senior industry professional interested in being a reviewer of our forthcoming publications, please contact us by email at **deitel@deitel.com**. Insert "Content Reviewer" in the Subject heading.

Are you interested in a career in computer education, publishing, and training?

We are growing rapidly and have a limited number of full-time competitive opportunities available for college graduates in computer science, information systems, information technology, management information systems, English and communications, marketing, multimedia technology and other areas. Please contact us by email at **deitel@deitel.com**. Insert "Full-time Job" in the subject heading.

Are you a Boston-area college student looking for an internship?

We have a limited number of competitive summer positions and 20-hr./week school-year opportunities for computer science, English and business majors. Students work at our worldwide headquarters about 35 minutes west of Boston. We also offer full-time internships for students taking a semester off from school. This is an excellent opportunity for students looking to gain industry experience or for students who want to earn money to pay for school. Please contact us by email at **deitel@deitel.com**. Insert "Internship" in the Subject heading.

Would you like to explore contract training opportunities with us?

Deitel & Associates, Inc. is growing rapidly and is looking for contract instructors to teach software-related topics at our clients' sites in the United States and worldwide. Applicants should be experienced professional trainers or college professors. For more information, please visit **www.deitel.com** and send your resume to Abbey Deitel, President at **abbey.deitel@deitel.com**

Are you a training company in need of quality course materials?

Corporate training companies worldwide use our *Complete Training Course Series* book and multimedia packages, and our *Web-Based Training Series* courses in their classes. We have extensive ancillary instructor materials for each of our products. For more details, please visit **www.deitel.com** or contact Abbey Deitel, President at **abbey.deitel@deitel.com**

Sign up now for the new DEITEL™ Buzz Online newsletter at:

PROGRAMMING LANGUAGE TEXTBOOK AUTHORS

Check out our Corporate On-site Seminars...

Java
- Java for Nonprogrammers
- Java for VB/COBOL Programmers
- Java for C/C++ Programmers

Advanced Java
- Java™ Web Services
- J2ME™
- Graphics (2D & 3D)
- JavaServer Pages (JSP)
- Servlets
- Enterprise JavaBeans (EJB™)
- Jiro™
- Jini
- Advanced Swing GUI
- RMI
- Web Services
- JDBC
- Messaging with JMS
- CORBA
- JavaBeans™

Internet & World Wide Web Programming
- Client-Side Internet & World Wide Web Programming
- Server-Side Internet & World Wide Web Programming
- JavaScript™
- VBScript®
- XHTML
- Dynamic HTML
- Active Server Pages (ASP)
- XML, XSLT™
- Perl/CGI, Python, PHP

C/C++
- C and C++ Programming: Part 1 (for Nonprogrammers)
- C and C++ Programming: Part 2 (for Non-C Programmers)
- C++ and Object-Oriented Programming
- Advanced C++ and Object-Oriented Programming

XML
- XML Programming for programmers with Java, Web or other programming experience

.NET Programming
- C# Programming
- Advanced C# Programming
- Visual Basic .NET Programming
- Advanced Visual Basic .NET Programming
- Visual C++ .NET Programming
- Advanced Visual C++ .NET Programming

Wireless Programming
- Wireless Programming
- WAP/WML/WMLScript
- J2ME
- i-mode and cHTML
- XHTML Basic

Other Topics
- Object-Oriented Analysis and Design with the UML
- SQL Server

For Detailed Course Descriptions, Visit Our Web Site: www.deitel.com

Through our worldwide network of trainers, we would be happy to attempt to arrange corporate on-site seminars for you in virtually any software-related field.

For Additional Information about Our Corporate On-Site and Public Seminars, contact:

Abbey Deitel, President
Email: **abbey.deitel@deitel.com**
Phone: (978) 461-5880/Fax: (978) 461-5884

Deitel & Associates has delivered training for the following organizations:

3Com
Argonne National Laboratories
Art Technology
Arthur Andersen
Avid Technology
Bank of America
BEA Systems
Boeing
Bristol-Myers Squibb
Cambridge Technology Partners
Cap Gemini
Compaq
Concord Communications
Dell
Dunn & Bradstreet
Eastman Kodak
EMC²
Federal Reserve Bank of Chicago
Fidelity
GE
General Dynamics Electric Boat Corporation
Gillette
GTE
Hitachi
IBM
JPL Laboratories
Lockheed Martin
Lucent
Motorola
NASA's Kennedy Space Center
NASDAQ
National Oceanographic and Atmospheric Administration
Nortel Networks
Omnipoint
One Wave
Open Market
Oracle
Progress Software
Rogue Wave Software
Schlumberger
Stratus
Sun Microsystems
Symmetrix
The Foxboro Company
Thompson Technology
Tivoli Systems
Toys "R" Us
U.S. Army at Ft. Leavenworth
Visa International
Washington Post Newsweek Interactive
White Sands Missile Range
and many others...

www.deitel.com/newsletter/subscribe.html

Announcing the _new_ DEITEL™ DEVELOPER SERIES!

Deitel & Associates is recognized worldwide for its best-selling _How to Program_ series of books for college and university students and its signature LIVE-CODE™ approach to teaching programming languages. Now, for the first time, Deitel & Associates brings its proven teaching methods to a new series of books specifically designed for professionals.

THREE TYPES OF BOOKS FOR THREE DISTINCT AUDIENCES:

A Technical Introduction — **A Technical Introduction** books provide programmers, technical managers, project managers and other technical professionals with introductions to broad new technology areas.

A Programmer's Introduction — **A Programmer's Introduction** books offer focused treatments of programming fundamentals for practicing programmers. These books are also appropriate for novices.

For Experienced Programmers — **For Experienced Programmers** books are for experienced programmers who want a detailed treatment of a programming language or technology. These books contain condensed introductions to programming language fundamentals and provide extensive intermediate level coverage of high-end topics.

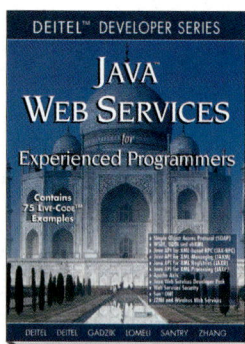

Java™ Web Services for Experienced Programmers

© 2003, 700 pp., paper (0-13-046134-2)

Java™ Web Services for Experienced Programmers from the DEITEL™ Developer Series provides the experienced Java programmer with 103 LIVE-CODE™ examples and covers industry standards including XML, SOAP, WSDL and UDDI. Learn how to build and integrate Web services using the Java API for XML RPC, the Java API for XML Messaging, Apache Axis and the Java Web Services Developer Pack. Develop and deploy Web services on several major Web services platforms. Register and discover Web services through public registries and the Java API for XML Registries. Build Web Services clients for several platforms, including J2ME. Significant Web Services case studies also are included.

Sign up now for the new _DEITEL™ Buzz Online_ newsletter at:

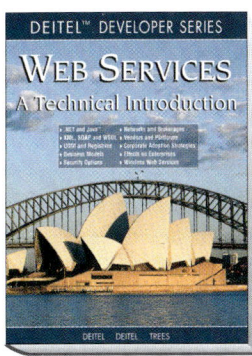

Web Services:
A Technical Introduction

© 2003, 400 pp., paper (0-13-046135-0)

Web Services: A Technical Introduction from the DEITEL™ Developer Series familiarizes programmers, technical managers and project managers with key Web services concepts, including what Web services are and why they are revolutionary. The book covers the business case for Web services—the underlying technologies, ways in which Web services can provide competitive advantages and opportunities for Web services-related lines of business. Readers learn the latest Web-services standards, including XML, SOAP, WSDL and UDDI; learn about Web services implementations in .NET and Java; benefit from an extensive comparison of Web services products and vendors; and read about Web services security options. Although this is not a programming book, the appendices show .NET and Java code examples to demonstrate the structure of Web services applications and documents. In addition, the book includes numerous case studies describing ways in which organizations are implementing Web services to increase efficiency, simplify business processes, create new revenue streams and interact better with partners and customers.

Visual C++ .NET
for Experienced Programmers:
A Managed Code Approach

© 2003, 1500 pp., paper (0-13-045821-X)

Visual C++ .NET for Experienced Programmers: A Managed Code Approach from the DEITEL™ Developer Series teaches programmers with C++ programming experience how to develop Visual C++ applications for Microsoft's new .NET Framework. The book begins with a condensed introduction to Visual C++ programming fundamentals, then covers more sophisticated .NET application-development topics in detail. Key topics include: creating reusable software components with assemblies, modules and dynamic link libraries; using classes from the Framework Class Library (FCL); building graphical user interfaces (GUIs) with the FCL; implementing multithreaded applications; building networked applications; manipulating databases with ADO .NET and creating XML Web services. In addition, the book provides several chapters on unmanaged code in Visual C++ .NET. These chapters demonstrate how to use "attributed programming" to simplify common tasks (such as connecting to a database) and improve code readability; how to integrate managed- and unmanaged-code software components; and how to use ATL Server to create Web-based applications and Web services with unmanaged code. The book features detailed LIVE-CODE™ examples that highlight crucial .NET-programming concepts and demonstrate Web services at work. A substantial introduction to XML also is included.

www.deitel.com/newsletter/subscribe.html

Ordering Visual Studio .NET

Visual Studio.NET can be ordered directly from Microsoft.

Please go to the following link for more details and to order:

    http://msdn.microsoft.com/vstudio/default.asp

If you are a member of the Microsoft Developer Network then please use the following link:

    http://msdn.microsoft.com/default.asp